Management

MAN 2021

AF854523

Hillsborough Community College

Connect Access Included

McGraw Hill create®

create.mheducation.com

McGraw Hill create®

ISBN-13: 9781307567588

ISBN-10: 1307567584

Contents

dedication

To Joyce Kinicki, the love of my life, best friend, and the wind beneath my wings.

—Angelo

about the author

Courtesy of Angelo Kinicki

Angelo Kinicki is an emeritus professor of management and held the Weatherup/Overby Chair in Leadership from 2005 to 2015 at the W.P. Carey School of Business at Arizona State University. He joined the faculty in 1982, the year he received his doctorate in business administration from Kent State University. He was inducted into the W.P. Carey Faculty Hall of Fame in 2016. Angelo currently is the Dean's Scholar in Residence at Kent State University. He is teaching in the MBA program and serves on the Dean's National Advisory Board.

Angelo is the recipient of six teaching awards from Arizona State University, where he taught in its nationally ranked MBA and PhD programs. He also received several research awards and was selected to serve on the editorial review boards for four scholarly journals. His current research interests focus on the dynamic relationships among leadership; organizational culture; organizational change; and individual, group, and organizational performance. Angelo has published over 95 articles in a variety of academic journals and proceedings and is co-author of eight textbooks (32 including revisions) that are used by hundreds of universities around the world. Several of his books have been translated into multiple languages, and two of his books were awarded revisions of the year by McGraw-Hill. Angelo was identified as being among the top 100 most influential (top .6%) Organizational Behavioral authors in 2018 out of a total of 16,289 academics.

Angelo is a busy international consultant and is a principal at Kinicki and Associates, Inc., a management consulting firm that works with top management teams to create organizational change aimed at increasing organizational effectiveness and profitability. He has worked with many Fortune 500 firms as well as numerous entrepreneurial organizations in diverse industries. His expertise includes facilitating strategic/operational planning sessions, diagnosing the causes of organizational and work-unit problems, conducting organizational culture interventions, implementing performance management systems, designing and implementing performance appraisal systems, developing and administering surveys to assess employee attitudes, and leading management/executive education programs. He developed a 360° leadership feedback instrument called the Performance Management Leadership Survey (PMLS) that is used by companies throughout the world.

Angelo and his wife of 37 years, Joyce, have enjoyed living in the beautiful Arizona desert for 36 years. They are both natives of Cleveland, Ohio. They enjoy traveling, hiking, and spending time in the White Mountains with Gracie, their adorable golden retriever. Angelo also has a passion for golfing.

new to the ninth edition

We are pleased to share these exciting updates and new additions!

Two major changes were implemented in the ninth edition. The first involved a new strategic career readiness theme throughout the product to address employers' concerns about students graduating without being career ready. The second was to extend our emphasis on the practical application of management. Below is a review of these substantive changes.

Career Readiness Theme Promotes Employable Skills

Global surveys of CEOs and recruiters reveal that college graduates do not possess the knowledge, skills, and attributes desired by employers, resulting in a lack of career readiness. We want to promote the development of your students' career readiness competencies so that they are more employable. Therefore, we've introduced a new strategic theme of career readiness to create a link between the principles of management and the objective of providing students with the tools they need to flourish on their chosen employment path. This integration takes five forms:

- The career readiness theme is thoroughly introduced in Chapter 1. We introduce a major section, 1.7, entitled **"Building Your Career Readiness,"** and present a model of career readiness along with a table of competencies desired by employers.
- Over 40 of the product's 66 **Self-Assessments** pertain directly to a career readiness competency. Feedback from these self-assessment can be used to assist students in creating a development plan focused on being career ready.
- Each chapter concludes with a new section entitled **"Career Corner: Managing Your Career Readiness."** This section serves two purposes. First, it assists students in linking chapter content with the competencies of career readiness, which provides a powerful association between the principles of management and the skills desired by employers. Second, this material provides students with practical tips for developing targeted career readiness competencies. We believe students can become more career ready by following the advice in these Career Corner sections.
- We developed a **targeted set of exercises in Connect,** our online teaching and learning platform, that give students hands-on experience working with the career readiness competencies desired by employers.
- We created a set of experiential exercises for each chapter in our **unique Teaching Resource Manual** that are targeted to develop students' career readiness competencies.

Extending the Practical Application of Management Concepts

Practical application has always been a major feature of this product. We want students to understand how to use what they are learning in both their personal and professional lives. We extend our emphasis on practicality by:

- Every chapter begins with a new feature entitled "**Manage U**." It replaces the Manager's Toolbox and provides students with actionable tips for applying the material in each chapter.
- Each chapter includes two new boxes that provide testimonials from millennials about their experiences with effective and ineffective management. **"I wish I . . ." boxes** illustrate real-world examples in which students recall an instance when they or their boss could have better applied certain management concepts. **"I'm glad I . . ." boxes** discuss positive applications of management concepts.
- To promote mastery of management concepts, we developed a **continuing case on Uber** for each chapter. Application learning can be assessed in Connect.
- To promote critical thinking and problem solving, a key career readiness competency, we revamped our **Management in Action Cases.** They now focus on higher levels of

learning by asking students to solve real organizational problems using relevant management concepts.

Fully revised Teaching Resource Manual (TRM) provides complete guidance for instructors

The TRM was new to the eighth edition and was developed to provide instructors with a turnkey solution to fostering a discussion-based and experiential learning experience. It amounts to a traditional instructor's manual on steroids by providing suggestions for creatively teaching topics, suggested videos outside of the McGraw Hill arsenal (e.g., YouTube, *The Wall Street Journal,* etc.), group exercises, lecture enhancers, and supplemental exercises that correspond with cases and Self-Assessments. The TRM has been praised by instructors around the world for its depth, navigation, and experiential-based content. We improved this resource based on feedback from faculty.

Our first change acknowledges that many of us teach online or in larger, in-person classes (sometimes both!). The ninth edition TRM not only includes revised activities for the traditional classroom, but also includes new online and large, in-person class activities for every chapter.

The next set of changes involve providing follow-up activities for the new career readiness-based exercises in Connect because we believe students need these developmental activities to increase their career readiness. We also provide in-depth teaching notes for new Manager's Hot Seat videos and Application-Based Activities in the form of simulations.

Finally, we provide new web video links for each chapter. These free, short videos allow instructors to illustrate the practical applications of management principles. We also include new current online article links instructors can use to discuss material that supplements the text.

> “*The TRM is top of the line.*”
>
> **—Todd Korol,**
> *Monroe Community College*

> “*The TRM is by far the most comprehensive and useful on the market. It is very user friendly for both faculty and students.*”
>
> **—Gerald Schoenfeld,**
> *Florida Gulf Coast University*

Completely revamped, revised, and updated chapters

In each chapter, we refreshed examples, research, figures, tables, statistics, and photos, as well as modified the design to accommodate new changes to this ninth edition. We have also largely replaced topics in such popular features as Example boxes, Practical Action boxes, Management in Action cases, and Legal/Ethical Challenges cases.

While the following list does not encompass all the updates and revisions, it does highlight some of the more notable changes.

CHAPTER 1

- New Manage U feature: Using Management Skills for College Success.
- Section 1.1—New Example box on efficiency versus effectiveness discusses how Delta Airlines handled an emergency at Atlanta's Hartsfield-Jackson Airport. Updated CEO pay and labor statistics. New example of museum curator in discussion of rewards of management.
- Section 1.2—New boxed feature "I wish my manager was more of a leader than a manager."
- Section 1.3—This section was moved to section 1.7 and section 1.4 was moved here. Introduces new key term "nonmanagerial employees." Updated salary information for first-line managers. New examples for "for-profit" and "nonprofit" organizations. New data in "Managers for Three Types of Organizations."
- Section 1.4—Section 1.6 became section 1.4, "Roles Managers Must Play Successfully." New example of Mary Bara, CEO of GM, to illustrate managerial work activities. New Practical Action box on mindfulness. New example of Google CEO Sundar Pichai in discussion of informational roles.

- Section 1.5—New running example of Mary Bara used to explain the skills needed to manage. New boxed interview feature "I'm glad I have conceptual skills." New Practical Action box on developing soft skills.
- Section 1.6—Updated Example box about Airbnb. Introduces new key terms "information technology application skills" and "meaningfulness." New discussion of the Fourth Industrial Revolution. Updated statistics regarding workforce diversity. New discussion of Volkswagen and ethical standards. Updated Practical Action box on cheating. New reference to sexual harassment in discussion of ethical standards. New suggestions for building meaning into your life.
- Section 1.7—Entire new section on building career readiness. Introduces new key terms "attitude," "career readiness," "proactive learning orientation," and "resilience." Includes Figure 1.3 regarding gaps in college graduates and employers' assessment of students' career readiness; Table 1.2 description of KSAOs needed for career readiness; Figure 1.4, Model of Career Readiness; and discussion of developing career readiness. New Self-Assessment 1.2, To What Extent Do You Accept Responsibility for Your Actions?
- Section 1.8—New section titled "Career Corner: Managing Your Career Readiness." Includes Figure 1.5, Process for Managing Career Readiness, and review of its application.
- New Management in Action case: Did Major League Baseball Value Money over Bob Bowman's Behavior?
- New continuing case on Uber.

CHAPTER 2

- New Manage U feature: What Type of Work Do I Prefer?
- Section 2.1—New Example box explores the successes and failures of Zappos' management experiment called "holacracy."
- Section 2.2—New coverage of Charles Clinton Spaulding's role in administrative management.
- Section 2.3—New Example boxes including the new boxed feature "I'm glad I work in an organization with a Theory Y culture" and an update to the Example box studying open-plan offices as an application of the behavioral science approach.
- Section 2.4—New Example box discussing operations management at Intel.
- Section 2.5—New Example box applying systems thinking.
- Section 2.6—New Example box applying the contingency viewpoint with manufacturers "pitching" jobs to parents of college students hoping they'll influence their children to consider open positions after high school graduation. A new Practical Action box exploring Big Data.
- Section 2.7—New boxed feature "I wish my manager believed in a quality-management viewpoint," as well as expanded content to include a deeper discussion of Six Sigma and ISO 9000, including definitions of both as well as practical examples of companies using each approach.
- Section 2.8—Expanded and updated in-content examples to showcase the three parts of a learning organization as well as expanded content examples on the three roles managers play in building learning organizations. Updated company examples for learning organizations, including a discussion of Google Buzz, American Express, and Apple.
- New Career Corner feature on Managing Your Career Readiness.
- New Management in Action case: The Decline of Sears.
- New continuing case on Uber.

CHAPTER 3

- New Manage U feature: Increase Ethical Behavior by Fostering an Ethical Climate.
- Section 3.1—Updated content regarding Millennials and their search for meaning.
- Section 3.2—Updated content and company applications for internal stakeholders at SAS and the board of directors at Facebook.
- Section 3.3—New Example box discussing United Airlines and its responsibilities to its stakeholders versus customers. New boxed feature "I wish I kept a closer eye on trends affecting our suppliers." Updated statistics regarding unions. New Example box discussing Amazon's new headquarters and whether it will benefit the city chosen. New boxed feature "I'm glad I kept current on my industry's general environment." Updated Example discussing the Internet of Things. Introduces new key term "LGBTQ." New figure showcasing the states in which marijuana is legal. Various content updates, including company examples for the task environment (including an updated list of "America's Most Hated Companies") and special interest groups with a discussion of the #MeToo movement and international forces such as Brexit. Updated examples for sociocultural forces to include seismic changes. Updated statistics for demographic forces of change.
- Section 3.4—New Example box featuring Volkswagen and ethics. Introduces new key term "abusive supervision." Updated statistics on workplace cheating. New Example box discussing "whistleblowing" photographer Simon Edelman's photos of the Trump administration and the fallout. Updated content examples for recent Sarbox cases and the most common ethics violations at work.
- Section 3.5—New content example of Tom's Shoes as a company showcasing social responsibility. New example of the benefits to Coca-Cola for going green and new table showing how being ethical and socially responsible pays off.
- Section 3.6—New Example box discussing HD Supply Holdings and Fox News and the good and bad of corporate governance.
- New Career Corner feature on Managing Your Career Readiness.
- New Management in Action case: Who's to Blame for College Basketball's Dark Underbelly?

- Updated Legal/Ethical Challenge: Should You Apply to Have Your Student Loans Forgiven?
- New continuing case on Uber.

CHAPTER 4

- New Manage U feature: Working Successfully Abroad: Developing Cultural Awareness.
- Section 4.1—Updated section opener with new statistics regarding United States imports in 2016. Updated Table 4.1 and corresponding content with competitiveness rankings for 2016–2017. New Example box featuring international e-commerce company Alibaba. Updated content on the positive and negative effects of globalization. New content examples featuring recent megamergers including CVS/Dignity Health, Amazon/Wholefoods.
- Section 4.2—New Example box discussing how to get an edge in the global job market. Introduces new key term "cross-cultural awareness." The career readiness competency of cross-cultural awareness is defined and leads into the corresponding Practical Action box. Features an updated discussion of U.S. brands that are foreign owned. New boxed feature "I wish I considered the impact of ethnocentrism."
- Section 4.3—Updated discussion on the foreign manufacturing of Apple products. An updated discussion of why companies expand internationally, including Netflix, Amazon, and Ford Motor Company and expanded discussion of foreign subsidiaries. Updated examples for how companies expand internationally, including Under Armour. Updated examples of global outsourced jobs, including an updated Table 4.2 with top exporting countries through 2016. Updated list of U.S. companies opening franchises overseas, including Chick-fil-A and Cold Stone.
- Section 4.4—Updated Table 4.3 with the U.S.'s top ten trading partners. Updated content regarding tariffs with a discussion of the Trump administration as well as updated content pertaining to import quotas, dumping, and embargoes and sanctions. New table featuring organizations promoting international trade. Updated discussion on NAFTA, the EU, and other trading blocs complete with a new Example box discussing Brexit's impact on Britain and the EU. Updated Example box to showcase the exchange rates on various common products like rent, Starbucks, and designer jeans. Updated statistics for major economies, including China, India and Brazil.
- Section 4.5—Changed the section title to "The Value of Understanding International Differences" and expanded the opening with a discussion on international differences. An updated discussion on language and personal space with a discussion on learning foreign language online and through apps and a new Example box discussing the differences in personal space in various countries. Updated content on differences in communication. New Practical Action box discussing how to run an international meeting. New Figure 4.2 discussing current followers of world religions. Current examples of expropriation, corruption, and labor abuses. An updated discussion on expatriates and why U.S. managers often fail. New boxed feature "I'm glad I understood the GLOBE Project's cultural dimensions."
- New Career Corner feature: Managing Your Career Readiness: Working Overseas. New key term "context."
- New Management in Action case: The Growth and Stall of Didi Chuxing.
- New Legal/Ethical Challenge: Should Qatar Be Hosting the 2022 World Cup?
- New continuing case on Uber.

CHAPTER 5

- New Manage U feature: Making an Effective Plan for Starting Your Career.
- Section 5.1—New Example box on how to write a business plan. The previous discussion of VRIO was moved from this section to Chapter 6. New research on the benefits of planning.
- Section 5.2—Opens with a new Table 5.1 discussing and summarizing mission, vision, and values statements. New example box on Coca-Cola includes the company's mission, vision, and values statements. A new Example box discusses Coca-Cola's six long-term strategies. New boxed feature "I wish my manager put more effort into operational planning."
- Section 5.3—New boxed feature "I'm glad I developed an action plan." Updated Example box pertaining to long and short-term goals at Southwest Airlines.
- Section 5.4—New Example box on setting clear goals at Snapchat. Included new research on goal setting programs. Revised the three types of goals used in MBO: performance-based, behavioral-based, and learning-based. New Self-Assessment determining whether students have a proactive learning orientation. Added Tornier as an example of an Action Plan. New Practical Action box for small businesses and goal setting.
- Section 5.5—New Example box applying the planning/control cycle through Tesla's Model 3.
- New Career Corner feature: Managing Your Career Readiness.
- New Management in Action case: Fender Rebrands to Stay in Tune with the Times.
- New Legal/Ethical Challenge: Is Pfizer Putting Profits above Alzheimer's Patients?
- New continuing case on Uber.

New Learning Module: Entrepreneurship

- New Manage U feature: So You Want to Start a Business?
- Section LM 1.1—Introduces entrepreneurship and its foundation, including a discussion of Elon Musk. Introduces

the concept of intrapreneurship, leading to a new Example box discussing Intel's Genevieve Bell. Discusses how entrepreneurship is different from self-employment. A new figure LM 1.1 lists the characteristics of entrepreneurs. New Self-Assessment to determine if students have an "entrepreneurial spirit." A discussion of entrepreneurship across the globe. New Table LM 1.1 with facts about small business.

- Section LM 1.2—Begins by discussing how entrepreneurs come up with ideas to start a business. Discusses how to write a business plan. Reviews the options for creating a legal structure for a business and how to obtain financing. The importance of creating the right organizational culture and design is explored. New Example box featuring the start and growth of a small business.

CHAPTER 6

- New Manage U feature: Building Your Personal Brand.
- Section 6.1—New coverage regarding levels of strategy. New Figure 6.1 shows three levels of strategy. Introduces the new key term "functional level strategy." Updated research on strategic planning at small and large firms. New Example box illustrates strategic planning at Evernote and Groove HQ.
- Section 6.2—The five steps of the strategic management process were changed to reflect current thinking. New boxed feature "I wish my company would have evaluated its current reality before opening the doors for business." New Self-Assessment on strategic thinking.
- Section 6.3—Begins with new key term "sustainable competitive advantage." Updated Example box of SWOT analysis for Toyota; VRIO discussion from Chapter 5 now featured in this section with updated content and a new Figure 6.3. New Example box on developing competitive advantage in the Internet economy. Updated Example box with contingency planning in the wake of Hurricane Harvey with a discussion on CVS, Walgreens, and Fed Ex.
- Section 6.4—Renamed "Establishing Corporate Level Strategy." Section now opens with Three Overall Types of Corporate Strategy and includes a new table showcasing how a company can implement overall corporate level strategies. New discussion of the BCG Matrix and different diversification strategies. Introduces new key term "unrelated diversification." Discussion on Porter's five competitive forces and four competitive strategies moved to Section 6.5.
- Section 6.5—Renamed "Establishing Business Level Strategy." The discussion on Porter's competitive forces and strategies moved to this section. New examples used to illustrate these concepts.
- Section 6.6—Renamed "Executing and Controlling Strategy." New boxed feature "I'm glad my company adjusts its strategy as we go."
- New Career Corner feature: Managing Your Career Readiness.
- New Management in Action case: General Electric's Evolving Strategy.
- New Legal/Ethical Challenge: Is Your School Selling Your Bank Accounts?
- New continuing case on Uber.

CHAPTER 7

- New Manage U feature: How to Make Good Decisions.
- Section 7.1—Updated Example box on Starbucks. Expanded content on intuition with a new Example box on the power of intuition and a new Practical Action box on how to improve intuition.
- Section 7.2—Section opens with updated examples on business ethics including medication profiteering, the #MeToo movement, CEOs being punished for unethical behavior, and as a contrast to bad behavior, philanthropists Bill and Melinda Gates. New boxed feature "I'm glad I found an employer who cares about ethics more than just making money."
- Section 7.3—Begins with an updated discussion of ethics at Google. New examples of companies using evidenced-based decision making. Updated Example box on using analytics in sports. Use of Big Data at companies such as Target, JetBlue, HP Labs, and the Obama administration is discussed. New Example box on data and hacking, featuring the Equifax breech.
- Section 7.4—New examples of various decision-making styles of CEOs, including Elon Musk, Jeff Bezos, Ginni Rometty, and Madeline Bell.
- Section 7.5—Renamed "Decision-Making Biases and the Use of Artificial Intelligence." Section opens with a discussion on heuristics and leads into updated content and discussion illustrating overconfidence bias with BP oil and the government's spy plane for the escalation of commitment bias. Introduces a new section on AI, reviewing its pros and cons. The use of AI at various companies is highlighted, including Google and Microsoft.
- Section 7.6—New boxed feature "I wish my workplace didn't have a toxic group decision-making environment." New discussion on the Delphi technique and devil's advocacy, along with a figure illustrating their implementation. Section concludes with an introduction to the concept of project post-mortems with practical examples from Disney and Pixar.
- New Career Corner feature: Managing Your Career Readiness.
- New Management in Action case: New York Subway System.
- New Legal/Ethical Challenge: It's All about a Peacock (featuring a discussion on emotional support animals).
- New continuing case on Uber.

CHAPTER 8

- New Manage U feature: How to Get Noticed in a New Job: Fitting into an Organization's Culture in the First 60 Days.
- Section 8.1—New boxed feature "I wish my company had integrated its corporate strategy and organizational culture." New Table 8.1 reviews the drivers of organizational culture. Updated Example box on how strategy affects culture at Cleveland Clinic.
- Section 8.2—New examples illustrate the three levels of organizational culture. New examples used to explain the four types of culture within the competing values framework. New examples used to explain how employees learn culture. Updated research on person-organization fit.
- Section 8.3—New boxed feature "I'm glad management embraced an empowering culture during a merger." New examples used to illustrate the 12 methods organizations use to change culture.
- Section 8.5—New Practical Action box on how to effectively delegate.
- Section 8.6—Opens with an updated discussion on Google and its culture of innovation. An updated Example box on Whole Foods is used to explain horizontal designs.
- Section 8.7—Section is introduced with a new key term: "contingency approach to organizational design." New example of Etsy is used to frame discussion of mechanistic and organic organizations.
- New Career Corner feature: Managing Your Career Readiness.
- New Management in Action case: Wells Fargo's Sales Culture Fails the Company.
- Updated Legal/Ethical Challenge: Should Socializing Outside Work Hours Be Mandatory?
- New continuing case on Uber.

CHAPTER 9

- New Manage U feature: How to Prepare for a Job Interview.
- Section 9.1—New examples from *Fortune's* 10 best work places for Millennials, including Ultimate Software, SAS, Quicken Loans, Salesforce, and Encompass Home Health and Hospice. Updated research on the effectiveness of HR practices. New information on company rewards. New examples to illustrate human and social capital including New Brunswick Power and Inter-American Development Bank.
- Section 9.2—New statistics on recruiting trends and examples for internal and external recruiting, including Visto and Glassdoor. New boxed feature "I'm glad my company is serious about its recruiting and selection processes." Updated Example box discussing the changing job market, Millennials, and the gig economy. New research regarding the lies job applicants tell. New boxed feature "I wish my company used a structured interview process." A new Practical Action box discussing what employers are looking for in a job interview. Updated information on the legality of employment tests. New Example box listing the pros and cons of personality tests and updated information on personality tests including Myers-Briggs. Section closes with a discussion on AI and how it is changing the recruitment and selection process.
- Section 9.3—Updated statistics on benefits, including a new discussion regarding gender-based preferences.
- Section 9.4—Renamed "Orientation and Learning and Development." Opens with a new example of onboarding with Facebook's new employee boot camp. New content on learning and development including Millennials, SAS, and Estee Lauder. Updated research on L&D programs. New Example box on Keller Williams and its learning and development program.
- Section 9.5—New Example box on performance management at Edward Jones. Updated research on performance management and performance appraisal, and new performance management examples pertaining to Deloitte, Accenture, Cigna, Microsoft, and Adobe. Discussion of how forced ranking is losing favor. New discussion of how to give effective performance feedback.
- Section 9.6—Updated Practical Action box on the right way to handle a dismissal.
- Section 9.7—Updated statistics and information regarding workplace discrimination and bullying. New Example box discussing sexual harassment at work.
- Section 9.8—Opens with updated statistics on labor unions. Updated Figure 9.4 showing right-to-work states.
- New Career Corner feature: Managing Your Career Readiness.
- New Management in Action case: Difficulties Attracting and Retaining Human Capital in the Nursing Profession.
- New Legal/Ethical Challenge: Should Noncompete Agreements Be Legal?
- New continuing case on Uber.

CHAPTER 10

- New Manage U feature: How Can I Be More Creative at Work?
- Section 10.1—New Example box discussing the decline of Toys R Us. New examples of companies experiencing change. Updated Example box on BP and the oil spill in the Gulf of Mexico. New examples to explain the forces for change. Updated Example box on ridesharing and self-driving cars.
- Section 10.2—New examples to illustrate three kinds of change. New boxed feature "I'm glad my company unfroze employees before implementing organizational change." Added a new section on applying the systems model of change featuring Stora Enso.

- Section 10.3—Updated statistics regarding the effectiveness of organizational development.
- Section 10.4—This section was completely rewritten, restructured, and renamed "Organizational Innovation." Introduces the new key term "innovation." New Figure 10.5 shows the various approaches to innovation. A new figure illustrates the supporting forces for innovation. A new table lists the most innovative companies. A new Self-Assessment measures organizational climate for innovation. New boxed feature "I wish my company considered the components of an innovation system." Introduces new key term "crowdsourcing." New Example box discussing IDEO's approach to innovation. Recent research is used to support our discussion of innovation.
- Section 10.5—Updated research regarding resistance to change.
- New Career Corner feature: Managing Your Career Readiness. New key terms "self-affirmations" and "self-compassion."
- New Management in Action case: Chipotle Needs to Change.
- New Legal/Ethical Challenge: Did L'Oreal Go Too Far in Firing Its Patent Lawyer?
- New continuing case on Uber.

CHAPTER 11

- New Manage U feature: How to Make a Positive First Impression at Work.
- Section 11.1—Opens with updated information and statistics for employment and personality testing and the Big Five personality dimensions. Updated research regarding personality and individual behavior and work attitudes. Introduced the new key term "generalized self-efficacy" with a discussion on the topic and its tie to career readiness with a new Self-Assessment measuring levels of generalized self-efficacy. A new Practical Action box discussing how technology can be used to develop Emotional Intelligence.
- Section 11.2—New Self-Assessment to measure the career readiness competency of having a positive approach to work. New Practical Action box on using cognitive reframing to reduce cognitive dissonance.
- Section 11.3—Updated research regarding stereotypes and implicit bias. Updated discussion on distortions in perception, including gender stereotypes. New Example box discussing the halo effect and how body weight affects careers. New Example box on the Pygmalion effect.
- Section 11.4—Opens with entirely new content on employee engagement with a new table showing the predictors of engagement. Updated research on job satisfaction, organizational commitment, and important workplace behaviors like performance, organizational citizenship, and counterproductive behavior. Updated the Example box on toxic workplaces.
- Section 11.5—Updated examples and statistics regarding trends in workplace diversity, including age, gender pay gap, race, and sexual orientation. New example discussing Google's internal memo regarding women in tech and how it showcases a barrier to diversity. Updated research pertaining to barriers to diversity. New boxed feature "I'm glad my manager embraced diversity and fostered inclusiveness." New Example box showcasing Ultimate Software.
- Section 11.6—Updated research on stress and its consequences. Introduces new key term "work–life conflict." New Table 11.4 discusses the negative consequences of conflict, including work, family, and other life demands. A new boxed feature "I wish my manager alleviated my work-related stress." Reworked the content regarding workplace stress and its consequences. New coverage of resilience and its role in career readiness. A new Self-Assessment assesses levels of resilience. Updated content on holistic wellness and a new Example box showcasing Google's corporate wellness program.
- New Career Corner feature: Managing Your Career Readiness.
- New Management in Action case: Does the Financial Services Industry Lack Diversity?
- New Legal/Ethical Challenge: Should Airlines Accommodate Oversized People?
- New continuing case on Uber.

CHAPTER 12

- New Manage U feature: Managing for Motivation: Building your Own Motivation.
- Section 12.1—New company examples and statistics on extrinsic and intrinsic rewards, including Uber, McDonald's, Outback Steakhouse, and MARS. A new section provides an overview of all motivation theories discussed in the chapter.
- Section 12.2—Added a quick summation of the motivation theories discussed in the section. Updated Example box on hotel company Joie de Vivre. Updated research on need theories. New boxed feature "I'm glad I fostered employees' sense of competence." Updated research regarding the application of Herzberg's two factor theory.
- Section 12.3—Updated research on process theories of motivation. Updated statistics on CEO pay. New examples to illustrate the application of equity theory. New Example box showcasing transparency at Buffer. New examples of Tesla and Kronos to demonstrate the application of expectancy theory. New coverage of stretch goals and two types of goal orientations—learning goal orientation and performance goal orientation.
- Section 12.4—Updated research on job design. New Example box on how job characteristics matter in the modern workforce.

- Section 12.5—Updated research on rewards. New examples to illustrate the four types of reinforcement. New boxed feature "I wish my manager used positive reinforcement rather than punishment."
- Section 12.6—Updated research on compensation, nonmonetary incentives, and other rewards. Updated statistics on money as a motivator. Updated content on incentive plans. Updated the example box on successful workspaces. New Practical Action box on how managers can encourage gratitude.
- New Career Corner feature: Managing Your Career Readiness.
- New Management in Action case: Motivation Challenges in the Fast-Food World.
- New Legal/Ethical Challenge: Are Workplace Wellness Programs Using Proper Motivational Tools?
- New continuing case on Uber.

CHAPTER 13

- New Manage U feature: Effectively Managing Team Conflict.
- Section 13.1—Updated research on teams. Updated Example box on informal groups and informal learning. Updated content regarding self-managed and virtual teams. Updated Practical Action box regarding best practices for virtual teams.
- Section 13.2—Updated content on punctuated equilibrium and its tie to Brexit.
- Section 13.3—Updated research regarding building high-performance teams. Updated discussion on collaboration, including new a new study of the relationship between listening to happy music, mood, and collaboration. New boxed feature "I'm glad my manager fosters collaboration." New Example box focuses on building trust. New Practical Action box on building effective team norms. Added new material regarding effective team processes and their role in building high-performance teams. Introduces the new key terms "team processes," "team charter," "team reflexivity," and "team voice."
- Section 13.4—Updated research on conflict. New examples of dysfunctional and functional conflict. New boxed feature "I wish I was able to manage interpersonal conflict more effectively." Updated the discussions on kinds of conflict. Updated discussion on ways intergroup conflicts are expressed, including an example for ambiguous jurisdictions with a racial-profiling incident at Starbucks. New Example box on playing the devil's advocate as a way to resolve conflict. Section closes with a new figure on five conflict handling styles.
- New Career Corner feature: Managing Your Career Readiness.
- New Management in Action case: IBM Wants Its Employees Back in the Office.
- New Legal/Ethical Challenge: When Employees Smoke Marijuana Socially: A Manager's Quandary.
- New continuing case on Uber.

CHAPTER 14

- New Manage U feature: Improving Your Leadership Skills.
- Section 14.1—Introduces key term "leadership coaching" and the difference between leading and managing, including a new Table 14.1 showing the characteristics of managers and leaders. Introduces new key term "managerial leadership." New coverage of managerial leadership and coping with complexity versus coping with change. Updated Table 14.2 on influence tactics with new example of exchange and legitimizing tactics. Developed a new integrated model of leadership (Figure 14.1) to foreshadow the theories covered in the chapter.
- Section 14.2—Opens with an example of Phebe Novakovic, CEO of General Dynamics, as someone who embodies the trait approach to leadership. Table 14.3 updated to show how the Big Five personality traits, which were introduced in Chapter 11, represent positive, task-oriented traits. Expanded the discussion on narcissism and gender and leadership. Updated the Example box discussing great worldwide leaders. Renamed "strategic skills" in Table 14.4 to "conceptual skills." New for theories drawn from trait theory, including Martha Stewart as a micromanager. New company examples for organizations using trait assessments, including Citigroup, ExxonMobil, Ford Motor, Procter & Gamble, Hewlett-Packard, and JPMorgan. Replaced the discussion on "cross-cultural competency" with a "global mind-set" and illustrated its tie to career readiness. Updated research on leadership traits.
- Section 14.3—New examples of initiating structure leadership, including Meg Whitman and David Miliband. New examples for transactional and empowering leadership, including Nick Saban and Sheryl Sandberg. New Example box showcasing Lauren Bush Lauren's values-driven leadership. Introduces key term "passive leadership." Updated research on behavioral approaches.
- Section 14.4—Updated research on contingency leadership.
- Section 14.5—New Example box discussing Pepsi's Indra Nooyi and her transactional and transformational leadership. New examples of John Hennessy, Dr. Donald Hopkins, Meg Whitman, and John Mackey used to illustrate the four key behaviors of transformational leaders. New boxed feature "I'm glad I understood the value of using individualized consideration." Section closes with an updated summary on what we know about transformational leadership. Updated research on transformational leadership.

- Section 14.6—Expanded the discussion on the usefulness of the LMX model. New boxed feature "I wish I had known about the impact of a poor LMX: I do now!" Updated research on LMX and humility.
- New Career Corner feature: Managing Your Career Readiness. New key term "Dunning-Kruger effect."
- New Management in Action case: VA Turnaround: A Waiting Game.
- New Legal/Ethical Challenge: Should Starbucks Have a Corporate Loitering Policy?
- New continuing case on Uber.

CHAPTER 15

- New Manage U feature: Improving Your Use of Empathy.
- Section 15.1—Kicks off with new research on communication effectiveness. New boxed feature "I'm glad my manager was an effective communicator." New example of noise. Updated the Example box on "Secrecy and Silence" to include Volkswagen and Theranos. Updated research on media richness and selecting the best medium.
- Section 15.2—Updated discussion and research on the grapevine. Updated Practical Action box on how to streamline meetings.
- Section 15.3—Updated discussion on the physical barriers of communication, including open office plans. Updated discussion and statistics for personal barriers to communication and nonverbal communication. New Example box discussing personal and cross-cultural barriers to communication and how they adversely affect organizations. New Practical Action box on improving communications between men and women.
- Section 15.4—Updated Figure 15.3 showing the use of social media across various age groups. Updated research on social media and managerial and organizational effectiveness. New Practical Action box on building your own social media brand. New examples for crowdsourcing. New Example box on TD Bank and its use of social media. New content pertaining to the downsides of social media, including new key term "FOMO" and a discussion of microaggressions and recent threats to cybersecurity, including attacks at Target, Equifax, and Verizon. New boxed feature "I wish I didn't have FOMO." Updated Table 15.8 to show elements of an effective social media policy. New Example box illustrating samples of social media policies at IBM, Best Buy, McDonald's, Walmart, *Washington Post*, and Intel.
- Section 15.5—New statistics on the cost of poor communication. Expanded the discussion of empathy. Updated and expanded Table 15.11, which discusses rules for business writing. Updated research on nondefensive communication, empathy, and listening.
- New Career Corner feature: Managing Your Career Readiness.
- New Management in Action case: Fyre and Fury.
- Updated Legal/Ethical Challenge: Was ESPN Fair in Firing Curt Schilling for His Social Media Post?
- New continuing case on Uber.

CHAPTER 16

- New Manage U feature: Using a Mentor to Exercise Control in Your Career.
- Section 16.1—New examples on why control is needed and new company examples for control, including Takata, FedEx, UPS, *The New York Times*, and Uber. New boxed feature "I'm glad my company made employees feel valued and engaged by regularly monitoring performance." Introduces the new key term "control charts" with a discussion on the topic, including an example and new figure. New example of feedforward control at Southwest Airlines.
- Section 16.2—New Example box regarding fair labor practices at Adidas. New examples on levels of control and the supply chain at KFC in the UK.
- Section 16.3—New examples of the balanced scorecard, including an internal business perspective at National Marrow Donor Program and an innovation and learning perspective at Tolko Industries LTD. New example of cascading a strategy map.
- Section 16.4—New examples for internal audits, including Citigroup.
- Section 16.5—Opens with updates to the winner of the Baldrige Award, Bristol Tennessee Essential Services (BTES). New boxed feature "I wish my company were focused on continuously improving work processes." New examples to illustrate Deming's PDCA framework. New Example box discussing Hyundai and its challenge to the luxury car market. Kia Motors is introduced as a new example of improvement orientation. Updated Example box on Kaizen principles. New Example box on service excellence with a discussion including Nordstrom's and Trader Joes. Updated statistics on outsourcing. Updated discussion on ISO 9000 standards.
- Section 16.6—New discussion on managing micromanagers.
- Section 16.7—Updated Table 16.2 with statistics for GDP through 2018. Updated statistics on productivity growth. New content on processes used to increase productivity, including new key terms "benchmarking" and "best practices." Updated content on managing individual productivity.
- New Career Corner feature: Managing Your Career Readiness.
- New Management in Action case: Is Tesla Out of Control?
- New Legal/Ethical Challenge: Should Companies use GPS to Track Employees?
- New continuing case on Uber.

Walkthrough Preface of 9e

Kinicki/Williams, *Management: A Practical Introduction*, 9e empowers students to develop the management career skills necessary in everyday life through the practical and relevant application of theory. Developed to help students learn management with a purpose, K/W 9e takes a student-centered approach. **The revision introduces a new strategic career readiness theme throughout to address employers' concerns about students graduating without being career ready and extends our emphasis on practicality.** The hallmark strengths that have made it the market best-seller have been maintained and include:

- A student-centered approach to learning.
- Imaginative writing for readability and reinforcement.
- Emphasis on practicality.
- Resources that work.

Our product covers the principles that most management instructors have come to expect in an introductory text—planning, organizing, leading, and controlling—plus current issues that students need to be to be aware of to succeed: customer focus, globalism, diversity, ethics, social media, entrepreneurship, teams, innovation, artificial intelligence, Big Data, and empowerment.

> “*It (the book) is well written and provides relevant examples in the text with great online support. The TRM (Teaching Resource Manual) is very useful and important in teaching the course. I have found the product to be one of the best I have ever used.*”
>
> **—Jerry D. Stevens,**
> *Texas Tech University*

Based on a wealth of instructor feedback and blending Angelo's scholarship, teaching, publishing, and management-consulting with Brian's writing and publishing background, we have worked tirelessly to create a research-based yet highly readable, practical, and motivational product for the introductory principles of management course. Our goal to make a difference in the lives of you and your students.

Focus on Career Readiness

Global research shows that employers are finding it hard to find college graduates who possess the skills needed to be successful. These employers also think that colleges and universities need to do a better job making students career ready. Our goal in 9e is to contribute to overcoming this problem with new content and a variety of developmental techniques.

Building Your Career Readiness

Chapter 1 contains a section devoted to explaining the need, value, and process for becoming career ready. It includes a model of career readiness along with a table of competencies desired by employers.

1.7 Building Your Career Readiness

THE BIG PICTURE

Companies want to hire *career-ready* college graduates. In this section we describe a model of career readiness and offer tips for building your readiness.

LO 1-7

Define the knowledge, soft skills, attitudes, and other characteristics needed for career readiness and discuss how they can be developed.

About 80,000 undergraduate students from over 350 universities across the United States rated 2017's most attractive employers. The top 10 were: (1) Google, (2) Walt Disney Company, (3) Apple, (4) Nike, (5) Amazon, (6) J.P. Morgan, (7), Goldman Sachs, (8) Ernst & Young, (9) Deloitte, and (10) FBI.[115] Would you like to work at these companies or another like them? If so, you need to be career ready.

Career readiness represents the extent to which you possess the knowledge, skills, and attributes desired by employers. How ready do you believe you are? Recent surveys of college graduates and recruiters reveal a big gap in the degree of readiness each group perceives in students. Figure 1.3 shows the results of a study of 400 employers and 613 college students. The majority of students rated themselves as career-ready on 11 of 17 skills, while the majority of employers did not perceive students to be well-prepared on any of the skills.[116] The three largest gaps were in critical/analytical thinking, written communication, and locating, organizing, and evaluating information, skills that are very important to employers.[117] Other studies have similarly demonstrated that employers see a major skills gap in college students' interpersonal skills.[118]

You'll want to close these gaps for three reasons:

1. **To get a job and earn more money.** Today's jobs require greater interpersonal or soft skills, and employers are willing to pay higher salaries to those possessing them.[119]
2. **To impress employers with your self-awareness.** Companies prefer to hire people with realistic perceptions of their own strengths and weaknesses. This underscores the need to obtain information about your strengths and weaknesses throughout your career.
3. **To create your own motivation to learn.** Studies of human behavior reveal that people won't spend time on personal development unless they feel the need. Overinflated perceptions of career readiness will not motivate you to develop the attributes that enhance that readiness. You need to motivate yourself to learn and develop.

TABLE 1.2 Description of KSAO Skills Needed for Career Readiness

KSAO	COMPETENCY	DESCRIPTION
Knowledge	Task-Based/Functional	Demonstrated ability to apply academic and practical knowledge in pursuit of organizational and individual goals/assignments.
	Information Technology Application	Effective use of IT and learning new applications as needed.
	Cross-Cultural Competency	Awareness of cross-cultural differences; respect for diverse cultures, races, ages, genders, and religions; and demonstrated openness, inclusiveness, and ability to interact with diverse people.
	Computational Thinking	Ability to use numbers to distill abstract concepts and conduct data-based reasoning. Ability to work with and interpret Big Data.
	Understanding the Business	Understanding of the company's business and strategies and the needs of stakeholders, and ability to see how your work fits into the larger organizational puzzle.
	New Media Literacy	Ability to develop, evaluate, and use new media forms, and to apply these media for persuasive communication. Ability to stay up-to-date with the latest media trends and leverage them in the interest of the organization.
Soft Skills	Critical Thinking/Problem Solving	Sound reasoning to analyze situations, make decisions, and solve problems. Ability to obtain, interpret, and analyze both qualitative and quantitative information while creatively solving problems.
	Oral/Written Communication	Ability to effectively express your thoughts, ideas, and messages to diverse people in oral and written form. Public speaking skills and ability to write/edit emails, letters, and technical reports.
	Teamwork/Collaboration	Ability to work effectively with and build collaborative relationships with diverse people, work within a team structure, and manage interpersonal conflict.
	Leadership	Skill at influencing a group of people to achieve common goals. Ability to motivate, coach, and develop others.
	Decision Making	Ability to collect, process, and analyze information in order to identify and choose from alternative solutions that lead to optimal outcomes.

Self-Assessments

Over 66 Self- Assessments allow students to assess the extent to which they possess aspects of the career readiness competencies desired by employers.

SELF-ASSESSMENT 3.1 CAREER READINESS

Assessing My Perspective on Ethics

This survey is designed to assess your views about ethics. It provides feedback about your status on the Career Readiness "other characteristic" of *professionalism/work ethic.*

Please be prepared to answer these questions if your instructor has assigned Self-Assessment 3.1 in Connect.

1. Are your views more idealistic or more relativistic?
2. What do you think about students cheating on homework assignments in school? What about cheating on exams?
3. Are your answers consistent with your score? Explain.
4. What can you say during an interview to demonstrate an ethical orientation?

Career Corner

Each chapter concludes with a new section entitled "Career Corner: Managing Your Career Readiness." This material provides students with practical tips for developing targeted career readiness competencies.

2.9 Career Corner: Managing Your Career Readiness

LO 2-9

Describe how to develop the career readiness competency of *understanding the business.*

Figure 2.5 shows the model of career readiness we discussed in Chapter 1. What does a chapter on management history have to do with your career readiness? How about its application to the **Knowledge** competency of *understanding the business?* This competency was defined in Table 1.2 as the extent to which you understand a company's business and strategies and the needs of its stakeholders. It comes into play whenever you interview for a job.

Recruiters expect you to do some research, just as you would for a class assignment. They want you to act like Sherlock Holmes and do some snooping. That's good for both you and a potential employer in that it helps identify the likely level of fit between the two of you. Good fit, in turn, is associated with more positive work attitudes and task performance, lower intentions to quit, and less job-related stress.[65] Moreover, doing your homework on a company makes you a more attractive job candidate. It shows interest on your part, and recruiters are impressed by the fact that you took the time to learn about the business.[66] It also prepares you to ask smart questions, a behavior recruiters want to see. Remember, sometimes it's the small things like this that land a job.

Concept Mastery

New exercises in Connect allow students to demonstrate lower levels of learning regarding career readiness. The Teaching Resource Manual provides opportunities for higher levels of learning for career readiness competencies.

McGraw Hill Education connect®

Student-Centered Approach to Learning

Our writing style and product design is based on neuroscience research. Greater learning occurs when information is "chunked" to keep student attention. We break down topics into easily digestible portions with purposeful pedagogy to make theories and concepts easier to learn and apply. This accounts for the use of purposeful color, an extensive photo program, bulleted lists, and headings to appeal to the visual sensibilities, time constraints, and diverse learning styles of today's students.

Chapter Openers

Each chapter begins with a list of key learning objectives that appeal to students concern about "what's in it for me?" and to help them read with purpose.

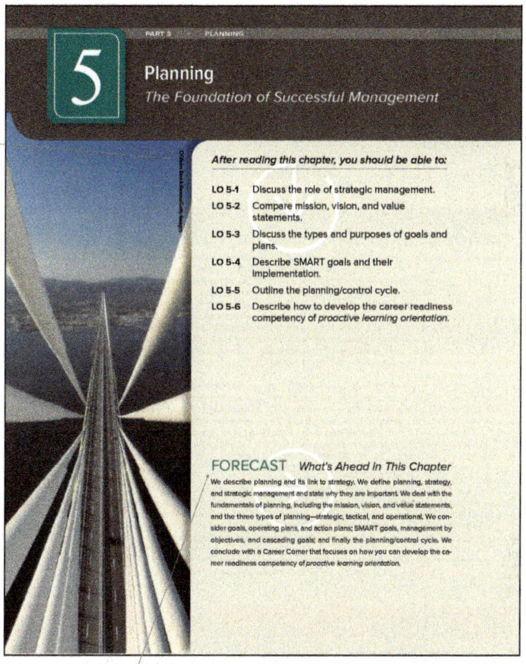

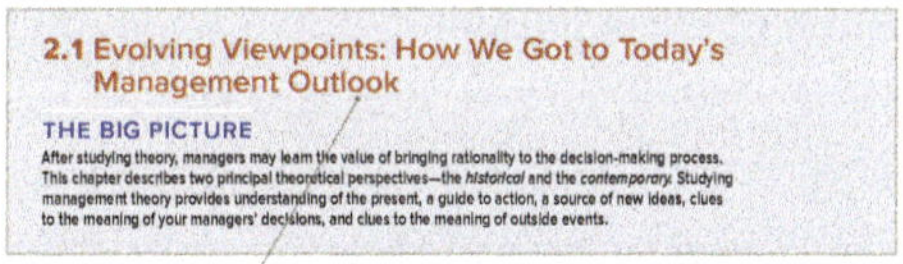

2.1 Evolving Viewpoints: How We Got to Today's Management Outlook

THE BIG PICTURE

After studying theory, managers may learn the value of bringing rationality to the decision-making process. This chapter describes two principal theoretical perspectives—the *historical* and the *contemporary*. Studying management theory provides understanding of the present, a guide to action, a source of new ideas, clues to the meaning of your managers' decisions, and clues to the meaning of outside events.

Chapter Sections

Within each chapter, sections are organized according to the major learning objectives. Generous use of headings and bulleted lists provide students with bite-sized chunks of information to facilitate retention. Each section begins with a recap of the **Learning Objective** and includes **The Big Picture**, which presents an overview of how the section addresses the stated objective.

Forecast

Shown below the learning objectives, the forecast provides a high-level of summary of what is covered in the chapter.

> *Many management texts are simply dense and a slog to read. Kinicki is far more approachable in its pedagogy. It is well organized—the topics are arranged very logically in each chapter. The approach speaks directly to the student. This personalized, conversational approach engages my students. It has a new career theme that is critical to help our students demonstrate employable skills. The Teaching Resource Manual is also the best in its class.*
>
> —**Todd Korol,**
> *Monroe Community College*

> *Layout, highlighted captions, use of boxes, bolding, pictures, and color are all great. It's easier for students to read than other textbooks I have used. The key points summaries at end of chapters are useful and it's overall very user-friendly and engaging.*
>
> —**Linsey Willis,**
> *Florida Atlantic University*

Extended Emphasis on Practicality

We want this ninth edition to be a cherished resource that students keep as they move into future courses and their future careers. We give students a great deal of practical advice in addition to covering the fundamental concepts of management.

Manage U

This new feature provides a pedagogical device that gives students practical, actionable tips for applying the material in each chapter. Students will find it interesting and valuable to their future careers.

MANAGE U

Making an Effective Plan for Starting Your Career

The thought of starting a career (or switching to a new one) can be either intimidating or exciting. What's the difference? Having goals and a plan.

Setting Goals and Making a Plan

Here are some steps in the career-management process for you to consider as you set about building your career.[1]

1. Identify your options. Use the career readiness skill of self-awareness to write down areas and ideas that interest and are important to you and the functional, cross-cultural, computational, interpersonal, and other skills you can offer an employer. Then make a written list of the opportunities available to you through your networking, earlier work and volunteer experience, and other resources (don't forget the alumni and placement offices at your school). Now match up the two lists to discover where you should focus your career-building efforts.

2. Explore conditions in your target field. The career readiness skill of understanding the business will guide you to identify important factors like the demand for new hires in your chosen field or fields, the competencies expected of incoming employees, the likely salary range and opportunities for advancement, and any geographic limitations or requirements in the industry to be aware of. If your field or industry is concentrated in one or two parts of the country, for instance, be ready to move.

3. Create your action plan. Using what you learned from steps 1 and 2, write a list of actions you can take to achieve your goal of breaking into a new career. You are more likely to achieve your goals if they are "SMART"—specific, measurable against clear criteria to show progress, attainable with a chance of 50% or higher, relevant to you, and time bound with target dates for completion. We discuss the process of writing SMART goals in Section 5.4. Try to keep your steps or goals to a manageable number; somewhere between three and five is recommended. Prioritize and schedule them to create your plan, and if it helps you to give each one a name, by all means do so.

4. Track your progress. You'll see as you study this chapter that monitoring or controlling progress toward goals is an inherent part of the planning process. Each time you get a result from one of your efforts, whether it's positive or negative, that result constitutes feedback on how well you've selected your goals and how effective your plan is. If one step doesn't work out as planned, don't give up. Rely on your positive attitude and ability to adapt (more career readiness skills) and realize you have other opportunities to succeed. Try broadening your search, and begin again.

Staying Resilient during the Process

Here are a few ideas about what else you can do to keep your hopes—and your finances—afloat during the career-building process.

1. Know that it takes time to find a job, especially one that's a good fit for both you and the company that hires you. College graduates spend about six months, on average, landing their first job after graduation.[2] If you are already working, even part-time, stay in the job while you pursue a new one. It's always easier to find a job if you have one. If you are not working, consider taking a part-time or short-term job to generate some income, since you'll want to avoid running up credit card debt.

2. Create a budget to be sure your income will cover your day-to-day expenses. This is a lifelong habit that will serve you well.

3. Avoid making any major financial commitments until you've actually landed your target job. You won't know how much you can afford to pay for a car until you know your salary, for instance, and you may not want to be encumbered by a new lease if your dream job requires you to relocate. As long as you have an appropriate interview outfit, even splurging on a professional wardrobe can wait until you know the dress code at your new employer.

For Discussion What fields or industries are interesting or appealing to you as places to work? What news and information about these areas can you start tracking now, and how will you will do that? Is there anyone in your network who can help you increase your understanding of the way this industry works? If not, how could you find someone?

Practical Action boxes

Practical Action boxes offer students practical and interesting advice on issues they will face in the workplace.

PRACTICAL ACTION Developing Your Soft Skills

Are you persistent, creative, curious? How do you deal with frustration or anxiety? Do you see yourself as part of a larger whole that gives your work purpose? How do you perceive problems—as temporary and solvable, or as a personal burden you are doomed to bear? Are you a good listener? Your answers will give you an idea about how well developed some of your soft skills are.

More than 90 percent of respondents to a recent Global Human Capital Trends survey by the consulting firm Deloitte identified soft skills like communication, emotional understanding, and problem solving as a critical priority.[59] Many employers say these skills are hard to find in college graduates, who often value hard skills more highly.[60] Companies are eagerly looking for soft skills as well, however; Google, for example, now prioritizes persistence and curiosity in its hiring process.[61] The good news is that soft skills can be taught. Employers are finding it worth investing money to develop these abilities in their employees. A new study shows that training employees in soft skills doesn't just marginally improve individual performance and employee retention; it actually betters these metrics enough to provide a 250% return on the financial investment a company makes in training programs.[62]

For firms that can spare their employees for three days, the American Management Association (AMA) offers a soft-skills seminar for managers at all levels including front-line supervisors.[63] Among the skills they can gain are the ability to give direction without generating conflict, to lead and motivate groups and teams, to influence others including "difficult" people, to offer effective feedback, and to get things done in an atmosphere of trust and respect. The seminar topics are a comprehensive list of essential soft skills employers look for in college graduates and new hires—and say they seldom find: communication proficiency, which includes verbal, nonverbal, and listening skills; self-understanding, lack of defensiveness, and emotional understanding and responsiveness; the ability to productively manage conflict; and an understanding of team development and the role of a team player in getting work done.

For those who want to learn online and at their own pace, many inexpensive online classes are available.[64] These short interactive programs are geared for everyone from CEOs to entry-level employees. They cover everything from self-confidence to emotional intelligence, coaching teams, building healthy work relationships, handling business etiquette, resolving conflicts, decision making, reading body language, negotiating, dealing with angry customers to becoming a successful leader.

YOUR CALL

Look back at the first paragraph in this Practical Action box. Which of the soft skills listed there would you like to improve by the time you graduate, in order to make yourself a more attractive candidate to prospective employers?

Self-Assessments

Self-Assessment evaluations help students relate what they are learning to their own experiences and promote self-reflection, engagement, and development of their career readiness. Of the 66 total Self-Assessments included, nearly 40 of them pertain to a career readiness competency. For each of these, students are asked to consider how they might display the competency in an employment interview.

SELF-ASSESSMENT 3.1 CAREER READINESS

Assessing My Perspective on Ethics

This survey is designed to assess your views about ethics. It provides feedback about your status on the Career Readiness "other characteristic" of *professionalism/work ethic*.

Please be prepared to answer these questions if your instructor has assigned Self-Assessment 3.1 in Connect.

1. Are your views more idealistic or more relativistic?
2. What do you think about students cheating on homework assignments in school? What about cheating on exams?
3. Are your answers consistent with your score? Explain.
4. What can you say during an interview to demonstrate an ethical orientation?

Testimonials from Millennials

Each chapter includes two new boxed features that provide testimonials from millennials about their experiences with effective and ineffective management. **"I wish I . . ."** boxes illustrate real-world examples in which students recall an instance when they or their boss could have better applied certain management concepts. **"I'm glad I . . ."** boxes discuss positive applications of management concepts.

I Wish I...

...considered the impact of ethnocentrism.

Jordin Hansen Courtesy Jordin Hansen

Jordin Hansen is a senior director of strategic operations for a global information technology company. She experienced a clashing of cultures ... develop... part of... strategy... An e... United... togethe... busines... business within a larger company. Part o... deciding on company vocabulary. "When... nization, having consistent nomenclature... things is extremely important, especially... customers," said Jordin.

The approach that was used to de... nomenclature was a very top-down ap... team claimed they were listening to outs... moved forward with what they thought w...

What was not taken into consideration was that English was not the main language for a majority of the company's global stakeholders. One of the terms chosen to be part of the company nomenclature was "solution." As Jordin explained, this word means very different things to people of different cultures.

I'm glad I...

...work in an organization with a Theory Y culture.

Cameron Monkellen works in the banking industry as a team leader. He believes his company does a great job of making employees at all levels feel **included** and **empowered**.

Cameron Monkellen Courtesy Cameron Monkellen

Cameron works for a large company with a popular name and a lot of power, but, as Cameron puts it, "It really has its head on its shoulders. They give a lot of tools and capabilities to everybody—not just supervisors and managers, but all the way down to the bottom level."

Cameron feels interconnected with all aspects of his job because of the documentation and networking his company has worked many years to build. "There isn't a guessing game where you have to figure out who you need to talk to or where you need to go to get information. That's something that a lot of my other jobs didn't have: a database and network of people and documents that point you in the right direction in any given situation," said Cameron.

Another way that the company works to make its employees feel included is to have monthly meetings where employees can interact with people other than their direct supervisors. This helps employees to feel like upper management is listening to their concerns and ideas, and that they can really make a difference within the organization.

Cameron also feels safe to take risks and make mistakes rather than fearing the consequences of doing so. "I have personally taken several risks because I have enough confidence in my performance and belief in my team that I can go out on a limb for them and for myself," said Cameron. But ultimately, Cameron believes his direct supervisor cultivates an environment where employees feel safe to take risks and make mistakes. "My supervisor does a really good job about not coming down on us when something goes wrong. Instead she asks, 'How can we improve this going forward?'"

Cameron takes this lesson from his supervisor and works to make sure his own employees feel safe taking risks. "The first time one of my employees had a setback was almost two years into his role. He felt like it was such a personal defeat on his part. I had to have a discussion with him where I said, 'Having a failure does not mean that you are a failure. It means that there is still room for growth, room for learning, and room for improvement.'"

Cameron's company has taken additional steps to create an environment of empowerment by changing some of the job titles. "Instead of being a manager or a supervisor, you get the title of 'leader' because it instills the idea that instead of being in charge of your employees, you are leading them."

Courtesy of Cameron Monkellen

Management in Action cases

Rather than using stories about companies, the new Management in Action cases now focus on higher levels of learning by asking students to solve real organizational problems using relevant management concepts.

Management in Action

Who's to Blame for College Basketball's "Dark Underbelly"?

The National Collegiate Athletic Association (NCAA) is "a member-led organization dedicated to the well-being and lifelong success of college athletes."[188] Founded in 1906, the NCAA "functions as a general legislative and administrative authority for men's and women's intercollegiate athletics" and "formulates and enforces the rules of play for various sports and the eligibility criteria for athletes."[189]

One of the "bedrock principles" of the NCAA is maintaining the spirit of amateur competition. Students are not allowed to be professional athletes, education holds top priority, and all athletes receive a fair chance to compete.[190] The NCAA outlines specific rules athletes must follow to maintain amateur status and, thus, eligibility to continue playing collegiate sports. Student athletes are, among other things, prohibited from publicly endorsing companies[191] and from receiving a salary for athletic participation or benefits from prospective agents.[192]

Although NCAA guidelines prohibit corporate sponsorships at the individual-athlete level, college teams have benefited from such alliances since 1977, when shoe-company executive Sonny Vaccaro "signed several coaches he knew . . . to contracts with Nike." According to Vaccaro, "'the world changed' in 1987, when Nike signed its first all-school deal" to sponsor all of the University of Miami's athletic teams. With these deals, said Vaccaro, "you own everything in that school. That shoe company is now your business partner."[193]

A BLURRY LINE BETWEEN AMATEURISM AND PROFESSIONALISM

Benefits aside, strategic relationships between apparel companies and universities blur the line between amateurism and professionalism for two reasons. The first is money flowing to universities. Companies such as Nike, Under Armour, and Adidas "pay tens of millions of dollars a year to equip (and, from a marketing standpoint, align themselves) with major university programs."[194] These alliances benefit universities due to increased revenues generated by the sponsorships, and they earn sports apparel companies not only exclusive rights to partner with large academic institutions, but also insider access to the country's top athletic talent.

The second reason is money for college athletes. A particular challenge in NCAA basketball is the reality that some athletes don't intend to graduate from college. Due in large part to the NBA's "one-and-done" rule prohibiting athletes from playing professionally before their 19th birthday, elite players often attend classes for a year until they age into the NBA draft.[195] Apparel sponsors are often overly eager to secure exclusive deals with elite athletes who may earn coveted spots in the NBA because these arrangements generate lots of money for the sponsors.

ASSISTANT COACHES AND FEDERAL INDICTMENTS

Assistant coaches serve as the primary recruiters of top high-school talent and are expected to act as salespersons for their universities and build strong relationships with prize recruits.[196] They are expected to follow NCAA guidelines, and they do not always do so.

In November 2017, four assistant college basketball coaches were among 10 individuals indicted by a federal grand jury. *Fortune* described the lead-up to the indictments as "a detailed and clandestine FBI investigation that exposed alleged under-the-table payments to agents, coaches, and parents to influence talented athletes to choose particular colleges to play

Legal/Ethical Challenge cases

Legal/Ethical Challenge cases ask students to resolve real ethical challenges faced by managers and organizations. They help develop students critical thinking and problem-solving skills around ethical issues.

Legal/Ethical Challenge

Should You Apply to Have Your Student Loans Forgiven?

Student loan debt nearly tripled in the last decade, thanks to increased attendance at for-profit colleges along with rising college tuition and living expenses.[220] For hundreds of thousands buried in student loan debt, a little known 1994 program called "Borrower Defense" or "Defense to Repayment" sponsored by the Education Department offers a lifeline.

The program is available for those students who obtained loans from the government's Direct Loan program. "The law says students are entitled to forgiveness of any existing debt—and, possibly, reimbursement of any repaid loans—if they can show that their school violated state law in getting them to take out the debt.

Uber Continuing cases

These new cases ask students to synthesize and apply what they've learned across the course to Uber. Based on reviewer feedback, we've introduced these at the chapter level.

Uber Continuing Case connect

Learn how Uber's corporate strategies have changed from those pursued by founder and CEO Travis Kalanick to those identified by current CEO Dara Khosrowshahi. Assess your ability to apply concepts discussed in this chapter to the case by going to Connect.

Imaginative Writing for Readability and Reinforcement

Research shows that products written in an imaginative, story-telling style significantly improve students' ability to retain information. We employ numerous journalistic devices to make the material engaging and relevant to students lives.

Example boxes

We utilize numerous Example boxes to emphasize the practical applications of business. These mini cases use snapshots of real-world companies to explain text concepts. **Your Call** questions stimulate class discussions and help students develop their critical thinking skills. Suggestions for how to use the Example boxes are found in the Teaching Resource Manual (TRM).

EXAMPLE **Informal Groups and Informal Learning: Sharing Knowledge in the Lunchroom and on Social Media**

As a manager, what would you think if you saw employees making brief conversation near the lunchroom coffeepot? Are they talking about the season finale of their favorite show, or is something more productive taking place? Office kitchens have been hidden out of sight for generations, an unloved necessity kept stark to make sure workers didn't linger, says the *Los Angeles Times*. Companies are now seeing office kitchens in a new light. Kitchens are being turned into showplaces intended to boost morale, encourage collaboration, and create a learning environment.[11] Why the change of heart?

Workplace Learning: Mostly Informal Research has found that 70 percent of workplace learning is informal.[12] Organizations are taking notice of this phenomenon. For example, Siemens managers have placed overhead projectors and empty pads of paper in the lunchroom to facilitate the exchange of information.[13] The highest-performing Google employees teach and support those employees looking to improve. Google certainly has the resources to afford fancy training programs. The company instead opts for peer-to-peer training in order to foster a culture of learning that values continuous development and the sharing of knowledge and expertise.[14]

Talking it out. Ever worked in a job in which you got a lot of informal training through conversations over coffee? Could this be done with social networking? ©Jacobs Stock Photography/Photodisc/Getty Images

Online Peer-to-Peer Networks What about when employees are in far-flung places? "Sales reps are out in the field and they're kind of on islands," pointed out an Indianapolis software-firm executive. "It's a challenge to keep everyone connected."[15] So when the 75 reps started overwhelming the sales-support staff with questions about product details and client information, the company created a website on which the reps could post and answer questions in an informal peer-to-peer learning setting.[16] These types of portals can also be used for employees in distant locations to tell each other personal and professional stories to share experiences. Research has shown that when people talk informally, 65 percent of the time they are telling stories. So providing an online venue for storytelling can be quite effective.[17]

YOUR CALL

Can games (such as the online multiplayer game *Second Life*) or other social media (Facebook, Twitter, Instagram, etc.) be used to foster informal workplace collaboration? How about allowing employees to BYOD—"bring your own device" to work, such as their own smartphone or tablet?[18]

> *"Readability is very good for the undergraduate audience. Updates are frequent and provide current examples."*
>
> **—Justin Davis,**
> *University of West Florida*

> *"The order and quality of information within the textbook (is great). Logical for faculty, plenty of examples for students; Kinicki provides better detail and examples, and good supplemental materials."*
>
> **—Alex Williams,**
> *Texas A&M Commerce*

Resources That Work

No matter how you teach your course: face-to-face, hybrid, or online—you're in the driver's seat. We offer the most robust set of resources to enhance your Principles of Management course. In addition to our unique Teaching Resource Manual, packed with additional activities and supplemental teaching tools; PowerPoint presentations; and Test Bank questions, we have a wealth of assignable resources available in Connect®.

Connect®

The ninth edition continues to build on the power of Connect and furthers our quest to help students move from comprehension to application. McGraw-Hill Connect® is a personalized teaching and learning tool powered by adaptive technologies so your students learn more efficiently, retain more, and achieve better outcomes. We used this platform to create exercises that are auto-graded in order to assist students in developing their career readiness. Here you will find a wide variety of learning resources that develop students' higher-order thinking skills, including:

- **SmartBook®–**As part of Connect, students have access to SmartBook®, fueled by LearnSmart, an adaptive learning and reading tool. SmartBook prompts students with questions based on the material they are studying. By assessing individual answers, SmartBook learns what each student knows and identifies which topics they need to practice. This adaptive technology gives each student a personalized learning experience and path to success. SmartBook provides students with a seamless combination of practice, assessment, and remediation.
- **Click & Drag exercises–**These activities help make the connection between theory and application through matching, ranking, or grouping. Every Career Corner has an exercise to help you assess students understanding about how to improve targeted career readiness competencies.
- **iSeeIt animated videos–**These brief, contemporary videos offer dynamic student-centered introductions, illustrations, and animations to guide students through challenging concepts. Ideal for before class as an introduction, during class to launch or clarify a topic, or after class for formative assessment.
- **Self-Assessments–**Designed to promote student self-awareness and self-reflection, these research-based activities also provide personal and professional development. For this edition, five new assessments were created to measure different career readiness competencies. In addition, new structured feedback explains how students should interpret their scores.
- **Case Analyses and Video Cases–**Our assortment of written and video cases challenge students to analyze concepts as they manifest in scenarios related to a real-life product or company, fostering students' ability to think critically in lecture and beyond. Thought-provoking questions check the students' application of the course material and develop their workplace readiness skills.
- **Manager's Hot Seat videos–**These actor-portrayed videos depict real-life situations where a manager is faced with a dilemma that needs to be analyzed based on management concepts. The videos have been a hit throughout the years because they put students at the center of controversial situations and contribute to their use of critical thinking to solve problems. Eleven new Manager's Hot Seats have been added to Connect for concepts such as motivation, decision making, organizational structure, and more. Each Hot Seat includes follow-up multiple-choice questions that are assignable and auto-gradable.
- **Uber Continuing Case–**Students understand the application of and relationship between different concepts by applying them to the same company throughout the semester. We conducted an extensive revision to the case based on current events and the need to offer a more flexible method for using it. Instructors now have a continuing case on Uber that can be used for every chapter or as a summary case for each part. Each chapter case includes multiple-choice questions that are assignable and auto-gradable, as well essay-based questions.
- **Application-Based Activities–**These activities provide students valuable practice using problem-solving skills to apply their knowledge to realistic scenarios. Students progress from understanding basic concepts to using their knowledge to analyze complex scenarios and solve real-life problems. Along the way, students see the implications of their decisions and are provided with feedback on how management theory should be informing their actions. They also receive detailed feedback at the conclusion of the activity. The simulations are assignable and auto-gradable. Ten new application-based activities have been added to Connect for concepts such as ethics, organizational culture, change management, and more.

> *"It is the best Management textbook on the market. Most importantly, and the key competitive advantage, is the Connect material. LearnSmart/SmartBook is above and beyond anything else out there."*
>
> **—Gerald Schoenfeld,**
> *Florida Gulf Coast University*

acknowledgments

I have the pleasure of working with one of the best teams in the business. Their dedication and effort significantly contribute to the quality of this revision. It all begins with the captain of the team, Michael Ablassmier. As my editorial director he provides the internal support to launch and manage the revision process. He also spends much time traveling in support of my products. Thanks for your continuing support over the last 10 years! To Anne Ehrenworth, product developer, thank you for paying attention to the details, keeping us all focused on the schedule, and coordinating all the moving pieces.

To Debbie Claire, executive marketing manager, you are the energizer bunny who works tirelessly in support of this product. Your creativity, passion, and effort make you the absolute best at your job, and you push me more than anyone to raise my "marketing" game. Thank you! To Harvey Yep, your knowledge and experience with the production process keep us on schedule and responsive to all the change requests.

To Patrick Soleymani, your support as my digital faculty consultant is invaluable. Your work on the Teaching Resource Manual and writing cases were instrumental in creating essential teaching materials. To Denise Breaux Soignet, your efforts in writing cases and developing digital activities to assess student learning greatly enhanced the product.

To Sarah Thomas, market development manager, Keri Johnson, content project manager; and Jessica Cuevas, designer, thanks for all you do to in support of the product. I would also like to thank Elisa Adams for her editorial assistance; Lindy Archambeau, Barbara Larson, Grace McLaughlin, and Jennifer Muryn for their work on the Teaching Resource Manual; Shelly Arneson for the PowerPoint slides; and to Ken Carson for his work on the Self-Assessments for Connect.

To McGraw-Hill company, it is a world-class publisher and I am grateful to be a member of the family.

Warmest thanks and appreciation go to the individuals who provided valuable input during the developmental stages of this edition, as follows:

Dr. M. Ruhul Amin,
Bloomsburg University of Pennsylvania

Joel Andexler,
Cuyahoga Community College

Lindy Archambeau,
Warrington College of Business, University of Florida

Joseph Aranyosi,
University of Phoenix

Shelly Arneson,
Colorado State University

Lisa Augustyniak,
Lake Michigan College

Tanya Balcom,
Macomb Community College

Amy S. Banta,
Ohio University

Valerie Barnett,
Kansas State University

Lynn Becker,
Univeristy of Central Florida

William Belcher,
Troy University

Jessie Bellflowers,
Fayetteville Technical Community College

Michael Bento,
Owens Community College

George Bernard,
Seminole State College of Florida

Stephen Betts,
William Patterson University

Jim Bishop,
New Mexico State University

Alison Bolton,
Solano Community College

Anne Brantley,
Central Piedmont Community College

Reginald Bruce,
University of Louisville

Regina Cannon,
Tarrant County College

Tara Carr,
University of Wisconsin–Green Bay

Shari Carpenter,
Eastern Oregon University

Anastasia Cortes,
Virginia Tech

Justin L. Davis,
University of West Florida

Carrie L. Devone,
Mott Community College

Jennifer Egrie,
Keiser University

Bennie Felts,
North Carolina Wesleyan College

Charla Fraley,
Columbus State Community College

Dana Frederick,
Missouri State University

Patricia Galitz,
Southeast Community College

Barbara Garrell,
Delaware County Community College

Terry Girdon,
Pennsylvania College of Technology

Lacey Gonzalez-Horan,
Lehigh Carbon Community College

Jan Grimes,
Georgia Southern University

William Habacivch,
Central Penn College

Gordon Haley,
Palm Beach State College

R. Hall,
Tarleton State University

Lisa M. Harris,
Southeast Community College

Joanne Hartsell,
East Carolina University

Ahmad Hassan,
Morehead State University

Karen H. Hawkins,
Miami Dade College–Kendall Campus

Cathy Henderson,
Stephen F. Austin State University

Nhung Hendy,
Towson University

Lara Hobson,
Western Michigan University

Anne Hoel,
University of Wisconsin–Stout

Gregory A. Hoffeditz,
Southern Illinois University–Carbondale

James Hopkins,
University of Georgia

Tammy Hunt,
University of North Carolina–Wilmington

Perwaiz Ismaili,
Metropolitan State University

Jacquelyn Jacobs,
University of Tennessee

Paul D. Johnson,
University of Mississippi

Sue Joiner,
Tarleton State University

John Kirn,
University of Kentucky

Bobbie Knoblauch,
Wichita State University

Todd Korol,
Monroe Community College

Zahir Latheef,
University of Houston Downtown

Dave Lanzilla,
College of Central Florida

Barbara Larson,
Northeastern University

Zahir Latheef,
University of Houston–Downtown

Blaine Lawlor,
University of West Florida

Benjamin Lipschutz,
Central Penn College

Charles Lyons,
University of Georgia

Professor Cheryl Macon,
Butler County Community College

Zengie Mangaliso,
University of Massachusetts–Amherst

Christine Marchese,
Nassau Community College

D. Kim McKinnon,
Arizona State University

Ben McLarty,
Mississippi State Univerisity

Erin McLaughlin,
University of Alabama–Huntsville

Christine Miller,
Tennessee Tech University

Lorianne Mitchell,
East Tennessee State University

Debra L. Moody,
Virginia Commonwealth University

Vivianne Moore,
Davenport University

Byron Morgan,
Texas State University

Jennifer Muryn,
Robert Morris University

Troy Nielson,
Brigham Young University

Paul O'Brien,
Keiser University

Nathan Oliver,
University of Alabama at Birmingham

Rhonda Palladi,
Georgia State University

Thomas Philippe,
St. Petersburg College

Michael Pirson,
Fordham University

Beth Polin,
Eastern Kentucky University

Elizabeth Prejean,
Northwestern State University

Kenneth Rasheed,
Chattahoochee Technical College

Chelsea Hood Reese,
Southeast Community College

Martha Robinson,
University of Memphis

David Ruderman,
University of Colorado–Denver

Jerry Schoenfeld,
Florida Gulf Coast University

Marina Sebastijanovic,
University of Houston

Sarah Shike,
Western Illinois University

Raj K. Singh,
University of California–Riverside

Paula Kirch Smith,
Cincinnati State

Dustin Smith, PhD.,
Webster University

George E. Stevens,
Kent State University

Jerry Stevens,
Texas Tech University

C. Justice Tillman,
Baruch College, City University of New York

Jim Turner,
Davenport University

Brandi Ulrich,
Anne Arundel Community College

George Valcho,
Bossier Parish Community College

Tim Waid,
University of Missouri

Wendy Walker,
University of North Georgia

Charlene Walters,
Strayer University

Rick Webb,
Johnson County Community College

Joette Wisnieski,
Indiana University of Pennsylvania

Anthony Weinberg,
Daymar College

David Wernick,
Florida International University

Wallace Alexander Williams Jr.,
Texas A&M University–Commerce

Dr. Linsey Willis,
Florida Atlantic University

M. Susan Wurtz,
University of Northern Iowa

Jan Zantinga,
University of Georgia

I would also like to thank the following colleagues who served as manuscript reviewers during the development of previous editions:

Steven W. Abram,
Kirkwood Community College

G. Stoney Alder,
University of Nevada–Las Vegas

Phyllis C. Alderdice,
Jefferson Community and Technical College

Laura L. Alderson,
University of Memphis

Danielle Beu Ammeter,
University of Mississippi

William Scott Anchors,
University of Maine at Orono

Jeffrey L. Anderson,
Ohio University

Darlene Andert,
Florida Gulf Coast University

John Anstey,
University of Nebraska at Omaha

Maria Aria,
Camden County College

Mona Bahl,
Illinois State University

Pamela Ball,
Clark State Community College

Valerie Barnet,
Kansas State University

James D. Bell,
Texas State University–San Marcos

Jessie Bellflowers,
Fayetteville Technical Community College

Victor Berardi,
Kent State University

Patricia Bernson,
County College of Morris

David Bess,
University of Hawaii

Stephen Betts,
William Paterson University

Randy Blass,
Florida State University

Larry Bohleber,
University of Southern Indiana

Melanie Bookout,
Greenville Technical College

Robert S. Boothe,
University of Southern Mississippi

Carol Bormann Young,
Metropolitan State University

Susan M. Bosco,
Roger Williams University

David Allen Brown,
Ferris State University

Roger Brown,
Northwestern Oklahoma State University

Marit Brunsell,
Madison Area Technical College

Jon Bryan,
Bridgewater State University

Becky Bryant,
Texas Woman's University

Paul Buffa,
Jefferson College, Missouri Baptist University

Mark David Burdsall,
University of Pittsburgh

Neil Burton,
Clemson University

Barbara A. Carlin,
University of Houston

Pamela Carstens,
Coe College

Julie J. Carwile,
John Tyler Community College

Daniel A. Cernas Ortiz,
University of North Texas

Glen Chapuis,
St. Charles Community College

Rod Christian,
Mesa Community College

Mike Cicero,
Highline College

Jack Cichy,
Davenport University

Anthony Cioffi,
Lorain County Community College

Deborah Clark,
Santa Fe Community College

J. Dana Clark,
Appalachian State University

Dean Cleavenger,
University of Central Florida

Sharon Clinebell,
University of Northern Colorado

Loretta Fergus Cochran,
Arkansas Tech University

Glenda Coleman,
South University

Ron Cooley,
South Suburban College

Melissa M. Cooper,
School of Management, Texas Woman's University

Gary Corona,
Florida State College

Keith Credo,
University of Louisiana–Lafayette

Derek E. Crews,
Texas Woman's University

Daniel J. Curtin,
Lakeland Community College

Ajay Das,
Baruch College

Tom Deckelman,
Owens Community College

Linda I. DeLong,
University of La Verne

Margaret Deck,
Virginia Tech

Kate Demarest,
University of Baltimore

E. Gordon DeMeritt,
Shepherd University

Kathleen DeNisco,
Erie Community College

Anant R. Deshpande,
SUNY Empire State College

John DeSpagna,
Nassau Community College

Pamela A. Dobies,
University of Missouri–Kansas City

David Dore,
Pima Community College

Lon Doty,
San Jose State University

Ron Dougherty,
Ivy Tech Community College/ Columbus Campus

Scott Droege,
Western Kentucky University

Ken Dunegan,
Cleveland State University

Steven Dunphy,
Indiana University Northwest

Linda Durkin,
Delaware County Community College

Subhash Durlabhji,
Northwestern State University of Louisiana

Jack Dustman,
Northern Arizona University

Ray Eldridge,
Lipscomb University

Bob Eliason,
James Madison University

Valerie Evans,
Kansas State University

W. Randy Evans,
University of Tennessee at Chattanooga

Paul A. Fadil,
University of North Florida

Crystal Saric Fashant,
Metropolitan State University

Jud Faurer,
Metropolitan State University of Denver

Judy Fitch,
Augusta State University

Carla Flores,
Ball State University

Christopher Flynn,
University of North Florida

David Foote,
Middle Tennessee State University

Lucy R. Ford,
Saint Joseph's University

Charla Fraley,
Columbus State Community College

Gail E. Fraser,
Kean University

Dana Frederick,
Missouri State University

Tony Frontera,
Binghamton University

Dane Galden,
Columbus State Community College

Michael Garcia,
Liberty University

Evgeniy Gentchev,
Northwood University

Lydia Gilmore,
Columbus State Community College

James Glasgow,
Villanova University

Ronnie Godshalk,
Penn State University

Connie Golden,
Lakeland Community College

Deborah Cain Good,
University of Pittsburgh

Kris Gossett,
Mercyhurst University

Marie Gould,
Horizons University

Tita Gray,
Maryland University of Integrative Health

Ryan Greenbaum,
Oklahoma State University–Stillwater

Kevin S. Groves,
Pepperdine University

Joyce Guillory,
Austin Community College

Reggie Hall,
Tarleton State University

Stephen F. Hallam,
The University of Akron

Marie DK. Halvorsen-Ganepola,
University of Notre Dame

Charles T. Harrington,
Pasadena City College

Santhi Harvey,
Central State University

Karen H. Hawkins,
Miami Dade College, Kendall Campus

Samuel Hazen,
Tarleton State University

Jack Heinsius,
Modesto Junior College

Duane Helleloid,
University of North Dakota

Evelyn Hendrix,
Lindenwood University

Kim Hester,
Arkansas State University

Anne Kelly Hoel,
University of Wisconsin–Stout

Mary Hogue,
Kent State University

David Hollomon,
Victor Valley College

Tammy Hunt,
University of North Carolina–Wilmington

Aviad Israeli,
Kent State University

Edward Johnson,
University of North Florida

Nancy M. Johnson,
Madison Area Technical College

Kathleen Jones,
University of North Dakota

Rusty Juban,
Southeastern Louisiana University

Dmitriy Kalyagin,
Chabot College

Heesam Kang,
Trident University International

Marvin Karlins,
University of South Florida

Marcella Kelly,
Santa Monica College

Richard Kimbrough,
University of Nebraska–Lincoln

Renee N. King,
Eastern Illinois University

Shaun C. Knight,
Penn State University

Bobbie Knoblauch,
Wichita State University

Todd Korol,
Monroe Community College

Leo C. Kotrodimos,
NC Wesleyan College

Sal Kukalis,
California State University–Long Beach

Chalmer E. Labig Jr.,
Oklahoma State University

Wendy Lam,
Hawaii Pacific University

Robert L. Laud,
William Paterson University

Rebecca Legleiter,
Tulsa Community College

David Leonard,
Chabot College

Chris Levan,
University of Tennessee–Chattanooga

David Levy,
United States Air Force Academy

Chi Lo Lim,
Northwest Missouri State University

Natasha Lindsey,
University of North Alabama

Beverly Little,
Western Carolina University

Guy Lochiatto,
MassBay Community College

Mary Lou Lockerby,
College of DuPage

Michael Dane Loflin,
York Technical College

Jessica Lofton,
University of Mount Olive

Paul Londrigan,
Charles Stewart Mott Community College

Tom Loughman,
Columbus State University

Ivan Lowe,
York Technical College

Gregory Luce,
Bucks County Community College

Margaret Lucero,
Texas A & M–Corpus Christi

James Manicki,
Northwestern College

Christine I. Mark,
University of Southern Mississippi

Marcia A. Marriott,
Monroe Community College

Dr. David Matthews,
SUNY Adirondack

Brenda McAleer,
University of Maine at Augusta

Daniel W. McAllister,
University of Nevada–Las Vegas

David McArthur,
Utah Valley University

Tom McFarland,
Mount San Antonio College

Joe McKenna,
Howard Community College

Zack McNeil,
Metropolitan Community College

Jeanne McNett,
Assumption College

Spencer Mehl,
Coastal Carolina Community College

Mary Meredith,
University of Louisiana

Lori Merlak,
Kirkwood Community College

Douglas Micklich,
Illinois State University

Christine Miller,
Tennessee Tech University

Val Miskin,
Washington State University

Kelly Mollica,
University of Memphis

Gregory Moore,
Middle Tennessee State University

Rob Moorman,
Elon University

Jaideep Motwani,
Grand Valley State University

Troy Mumford,
Colorado State University

Robert Myers,
University of Louisville

Christopher P. Neck,
Arizona State University

Patrick J. Nedry,
Monroe County Community College

Francine Newth,
Providence College

Margie Nicholson,
Columbia College, Chicago

Thomas J. Norman,
California State University–Dominguez Hills

Joanne Orabone,
Community College of Rhode Island

John Orife,
Indiana University of Pennsylvania

Eren Ozgen,
Florida State University–Panama City

Fernando Pargas,
James Madison University

Jack Partlow,
Northern Virginia Community College

Don A. Paxton,
Pasadena City College

John Paxton,
Wayne State College

John Pepper,
The University of Kansas

Clifford R. Perry,
Florida International University

Sheila Petcavage,
Cuyahoga Community College–Western Campus

Barbara Petzall,
Maryville University

Shaun Pichler,
Mihaylo College of Business, California State University, Fullerton

Anthony Plunkett,
Harrison College

Tracy H. Porter,
Cleveland State University

Paula Potter,
Western Kentucky University

Cynthia Preston,
University of Northwestern Ohio

Ronald E. Purser,
San Francisco State University

Gregory R. Quinet,
Kennesaw State University

George Redmond,
Franklin University

Deborah Reed,
Benedictine College

Rosemarie Reynolds,
Embry Riddle Aeronautical University

H. Lynn Richards,
Johnson County Community College

Leah Ritchie,
Salem State College

Gary B. Roberts,
Kennesaw State University

Sean E. Rogers,
University of Rhode Island

Katherine Rosenbusch,
George Mason University

Barbara Rosenthal,
Miami Dade Community College/ Wolfson Campus

Gary Ross,
Cardinal Stritch University

Catherine Ruggieri,
St. John's University–Staten Island

Storm Russo,
Valencia Community College

Cindy Ruszkowski,
Illinois State University

William Salyer,
Illinois State University

Diane R. Scott,
Wichita State University

Alex J. Scrimpshire,
Xavier University

Marianne Sebok,
College of Southern Nevada

Thomas J. Shaughnessy,
Illinois Central College

Joanna Shaw,
Tarleton State University

Randi Sims,
Nova Southeastern University

Frederick J. Slack,
Indiana University of Pennsylvania

Erika E. Small,
Coastal Carolina University

Jim Smas,
Kent State University

Gerald F. Smith,
University of Northern Iowa

Mark Smith,
University of Southwest Louisiana

Shane Spiller,
Western Kentucky University

Jeff Stauffer,
Ventura College

George E. Stevens,
Kent State University

Martin St. John,
Westmoreland County Community College

Raymond Stoudt,
DeSales University

Barb Stuart,
Daniels College of Business

Robert Scott Taylor,
Moberly Area Community College

Virginia Anne Taylor,
William Patterson University

Wynn Teasley,
University of West Florida

Marguerite Teubner,
Nassau Community College

Jerry Thomas,
Arapahoe Community College

C. Justice Tillman,
Baruch College–City University of New York

Jody Tolan,
University of Southern California, Marshall School of Business

Joseph Tomkiewicz,
East Carolina University

Robert Trumble,
Virginia Commonwealth University

Joy Turnheim Smith,
Elizabeth City State University

Isaiah Ugboro,
North Carolina Agricultural & Technical State University

Brandi Ulrich,
Anne Arundel Community College

Anthony Uremovic,
Joliet Junior College

Barry Van Hook,
Arizona State University

Scot W. Vaver,
University of Wisconsin–Stout

Susan Verhulst,
Grand View University

Annie Viets,
Prince Mohammad Bin Fahd University

Tom Voigt Jr.,
Judson University

Carolyn Waits,
Cincinnati State

Bruce C. Walker,
University of Louisiana at Monroe

Tekle O. Wanorie,
Northwest Missouri State University

Charles Warren,
Salem State College

Kerry Webb,
Texas Woman's University

Brian D. Webster,
Ball State University

Velvet Weems-Landingham,
Kent State University–Geauga

Allen Weimer,
University of Tampa

David A. Wernick,
Florida International University

James Whelan,
Manhattan College

John Whitelock,
Community College of Baltimore/ Catonsville Campus

Eric S. Williams,
University of Alabama– Tuscaloosa

Joette Wisnieski,
Indiana University of Pennsylvania

Colette Wolfson,
Ivy Tech Community College

Wendy V. Wysocki,
Monroe County Community College

Carol Bormann Young,
Metropolitan State University, Minnesota

Ned D. Young,
Sinclair Community College

Jan T. Zantinga,
University of Georgia

Mary E. Zellmer-Bruhn,
University of Minnesota

Mark Zorn,
Butler County Community College

Finally, I would like to thank my wife, Joyce, for being understanding, patient, and encouraging throughout the process of writing this edition. Your love and support helped me endure the trials of completing this text.

I hope you enjoy reading and applying the book. Best wishes for success in your career.

Angelo Kinicki

Introduction

PART 1 • INTRODUCTION

1 The Exceptional Manager

What You Do, How You Do It

©Olivier Renck/Aurora/Getty Images

After reading this chapter, you should be able to:

LO 1-1 Identify the rewards of being an exceptional manager.

LO 1-2 List the four principal functions of a manager.

LO 1-3 Describe the levels and areas of management.

LO 1-4 Identify the roles an effective manager must play.

LO 1-5 Discuss the skills of an outstanding manager.

LO 1-6 Identify the seven challenges faced by most managers.

LO 1-7 Define the knowledge, soft skills, attitudes, and other characteristics needed for career readiness and discuss how they can be developed.

LO 1-8 Describe the process for managing your career readiness.

FORECAST *What's Ahead in This Chapter*

We describe the rewards, benefits, and privileges managers might expect. We also describe the four principal functions of management—planning, organizing, leading, and controlling. We consider levels and areas of management and describe the three roles managers must play. We describe the three skills required of a manager and the three roles managers play and discuss seven challenges to managers in today's world. We then focus on a model of career readiness and offer tips for building your career readiness. The chapter concludes with a Career Corner that presents a process that can be used to develop your career readiness.

MANAGE U

Using Management Skills for College Success

Our goal is *to make this book as practical as possible for you.* One place we do this is in the Manager's Toolbox, like this one, which appears at the beginning of every chapter and offers practical advice for applying the topic of the chapter to your personal life and career. Here, for instance, we show you how to make teamwork one of your job strengths, starting now. This is an important skill that recruiters look for when hiring college graduates.[1]

Functions of Management

In the chapter you will read about the four functions of management—planning, organizing, leading, and controlling. They represent essential activities that all managers undertake in the course of doing their jobs. Although they may sound a little abstract right now, you can use them today to work more successfully on team projects assigned by your professors.

Applying the Functions of Management to School Projects

Consider the students in a Princeton University summer business program. Working in teams, they had 10 weeks to prepare a pitch for a start-up idea and ask for funding. One of the teams ran a four-week pilot after-school program for five Trenton, NJ girls and asked for $324,000 to scale the program up to include 40 girls on a year-round basis. Their pitch was that the program would help more young women graduate from high school and have a positive effect on the entire community. The students planned their pilot program, its budget, and its schedule and curriculum; they organized the four weeks of activities for the girls they recruited; they led the girls through each day's events; and they used before and after surveys to control (that is, measure) the effects of their efforts. In other words, they relied on the four functions of management to ensure that they worked together to achieve their goals.[2]

Think about how you might make better use of planning and controlling in a team assignment for a course. You might draw up a detailed schedule of tasks and assign them to team members (planning), and then identify checkpoint dates on which you measure progress toward your deadline (controlling). You could set up a way to best use the resources at your disposal, such as time, library materials, personal expertise, and outside experts (organizing), and then use the progress checkpoints to motivate your fellow team members to continue putting forth their best effort (leading). The experience you can gain by using these essential management skills now will serve you well in your studies and throughout your career.

Applying the Functions of Management in your Personal Life

Consider how you might use the functions of management to lose 10 pounds. Your plan would include dates and times to exercise on your Google or Outlook calendar along with ideas for how you will change your eating habits. You then would make sure you have the resources (time, clothing, support network, dietary plan) to assist you along your weight loss journey (organizing). You also may find it valuable to have an exercise buddy during some of your workouts (leading). Alternatively, some people find it motivational to have someone hold them accountable via weekly weigh-ins (controlling).

For Discussion Why would employers seek to hire people with good management skills? How can you strive to improve your managerial skills while working on class projects?

1.1 Management: What It Is, What Its Benefits Are

THE BIG PICTURE

Management is defined as the pursuit of organizational goals efficiently and effectively. Organizations, or people who work together to achieve a specific purpose, value managers because of the multiplier effect: Good managers have an influence on the organization far beyond the results that can be achieved by one person acting alone. Managers are well paid, with the chief executive officers (CEOs) and presidents of even small and midsize businesses earning good salaries and many benefits.

LO 1-1

Identify the rewards of being an exceptional manager.

When chief executive officer Mary Barra took the reins of Detroit-based General Motors (GM) in January 2014, she became the first female CEO of a global automaker anywhere in the world. She also became only the 22nd woman at the helm of a Fortune 500 company, one of those 500 largest U.S. companies that appear on the prestigious annual list compiled by *Fortune* magazine. (Other female CEOs of major companies are IBM's Virginia "Ginni" Rometty, Hewlett-Packard's Meg Whitman, Lynne Doughtie of KPMG, Sofra Katz of Oracle, Marillyn Hewson of Lockheed Martin, and Mondelez International's Irene Rosenfeld.)

What kind of a person is Barra, a 30-year GM veteran? She has been called "nearly impossible to dislike" and is credited with bringing a much-needed "calm stability" to GM. Among her many people skills is the ability to engage and motivate others, including top executives who may have vied for her job but who have been persuaded to stay and work with her.[3] Are these qualities—which many people have—enough to propel someone to the top of a great organization?

The Rise of the Die Maker's Daughter

The daughter of a die maker, Barra grew up in suburban Detroit, joined GM at age 18 as an intern on the factory floor, graduated from General Motors Institute (now Kettering University) with a degree in electrical engineering, and then became a plant engineer in GM's Pontiac Division. Spotting her talent, GM gave her a scholarship to Stanford University, where she earned a graduate degree in business. She then began moving up the GM ladder, first as the executive assistant to the CEO and then as the company's head of human resources—formerly often as high as female executives ever got in the auto industry and many others. In 2011, Barra's big break came when she was promoted to lead GM's $15 billion vehicle-development operations, a high-profile role that became the stepping-stone to the CEO spot. In 2016, she was also made chairwoman of the board.[4]

The driving force. One quality that stands out about General Motors CEO Mary Barra is her obvious enthusiasm for cars. She is said to be given to talking excitedly about whatever car she is currently driving and what it demonstrates about GM's product line. Do you think passion about one's work is a necessary quality for managerial success?
©Mark Lennihan/AP Images

Key to Career Growth: "Doing Things I've Never Done Before"

Did it help that Barra has such deep experience in the auto industry and at GM in particular? No doubt it did. But there is another key to career growth—the ability to take risks. Jeff Bezos, the founder of Amazon.com, was holding down a lucrative job as a Wall Street hedge fund manager in the 1990s when he read that the Internet had recently grown 2,300% in a single year. Even though it meant leaving a stable job with a big bonus on the way, Bezos made the risky leap to the start-up he called Amazon, working out of a garage. "I knew that I might sincerely regret not having participated in this thing called the Internet that I thought was going to be a revolutionizing event," he says. "When I thought about it that way . . . it was incredibly easy to make the decision."[5] Bezos built his company into the largest e-commerce hub in the world and now operates several other businesses and charities as well. He is one of the two or three richest people in the world.

The Art of Management Defined

Is being an exceptional manager a gift, like a musician having perfect pitch? Not exactly. But in good part it may be an art.[6] Fortunately, it is one that is teachable.

Management, said one pioneer of management ideas, is "the art of getting things done through people."[7]

Getting things done. Through people. Thus, managers are task oriented, achievement oriented, and people oriented. And they operate within an **organization**—a group of people who work together to achieve some specific purpose.

More formally, **management** is defined as (1) the pursuit of organizational goals efficiently and effectively by (2) integrating the work of people through (3) planning, organizing, leading, and controlling the organization's resources.

Note the words *efficiently* and *effectively,* which basically mean "doing things right."

- ***Efficiency—the means.*** Efficiency is the means of attaining the organization's goals. To be **efficient** means to use resources—people, money, raw materials, and the like—wisely and cost-effectively.
- ***Effectiveness—the ends.*** Effectiveness regards the organization's ends, the goals. To be **effective** means to achieve results, to make the right decisions, and to successfully carry them out so that they achieve the organization's goals.

Good managers are concerned with trying to achieve both qualities. Often, however, organizations will erroneously strive for efficiency without being effective. Retired U.S. Army general Stanley McChrystal, former commander of all American and coalition forces in Afghanistan, suggests that effectiveness is a more important outcome in today's organizations.[8]

EXAMPLE Efficiency versus Effectiveness: How Did Delta Airlines Deal with the Emergency at Atlanta's Hartsfield-Jackson Airport?

Atlanta's Hartsfield-Jackson Airport is the busiest in the world, serving a quarter million passengers daily. So when an electrical fire blacked out the airport one Sunday afternoon before Christmas 2017, the potential for chaos was high. Over a long night without power, tens of thousands of passengers were stranded with no light, heat, or communications, and thousands of flights were canceled or diverted across the United States, disrupting travel for several days.

The blackout halted computer systems, escalators, baggage carousels, inter-terminal transportation, and even the automatic soap dispensers and toilets in the airport's restrooms. Passengers slept in the darkened airport overnight, unable to check social media, use travel apps, or recharge their phones, while employees gave out blankets, bottled water, and paper towels.

Passengers scrambling for help during the power outage at Hartsfield-Jackson Airport in Atlanta. Do you think more effective management might have prevented this accident? ©Jessica McGowan/Getty Images

Efficiency. Three-quarters of the airport's traffic consists of Delta flights to and from more than 200 cities around the world.[9] Atlanta is Delta's hub and the location of its Operations and Customer Center, where 300 employees monitor local and global weather and air traffic. The Center had power during the blackout, and emergency staff arrived to help rebook passengers and cope with 400 additional flight cancelations made on Monday because the needed planes had not been able to land the day before. Delta's staff also had to get its pilots and crews from Atlanta to the cities where they were needed next, but without unlawfully lengthening their shifts.

Delta distributed donated food at the terminal and reimbursed passengers for Atlanta hotel stays on Sunday night. Those who rebooked flights were given waivers to make the change. On Monday Delta was reporting progress. Gil West, Senior Executive Vice President and COO, said, "At the airport, Delta people . . . have been serving customers—from passing out refreshments to assisting customers with wheelchair support. Thanks to everyone's hard work, we're nearly back to normal at our biggest hub." By Tuesday the airline was reporting a nearly 90 percent on-time arrival rate at Atlanta, all passengers had been rebooked, and a dedicated phone line had opened to help reunite passengers with their luggage, most of which had already been delivered.[10]

Effectiveness. Passengers on one Delta flight spent six hours on the runway, consuming the plane's stores of food and drinks until they could disembark. "Under the circumstances it was well-managed," said one passenger, who praised Delta employees for doing their best to keep everyone calm and comfortable.[11]

Still, many who spent hours at the darkened airport wondering what happened felt Delta could have done more. Said one, "There was no one who could help us. There wasn't a single Delta employee who knew what was going on. They could have at least used a megaphone to say, 'This is what's happening.'"[12] Many others echoed these comments and said that despite a repeated recorded announcement that an emergency had occurred, no further information ever came.

YOUR CALL

The fire that caused the blackout was apparently an accident, partly attributed to aging equipment, a factor over which Delta may have little control though it is the airport's major lessee. Some, including a former U.S. Secretary of Transportation who was stranded, saw "no excuse" for the failure of the airport's backup power system.[13] Delta believes the outage and ripple effects may have cost it $25 to $50 million and said it would seek reimbursement. "I don't know whose responsibility it is between the airport and Georgia Power," said Delta's CEO Ed Bastian, "but we're going to have conversations with both of them."[14] Do you think Delta handled the airport emergency efficiently? Could the airline have been more effective from a passenger's point of view? How?

Why Organizations Value Managers: The Multiplier Effect

Some great achievements of history, such as scientific discoveries or works of art, were accomplished by individuals working quietly by themselves. But so much more has been achieved by people who were able to leverage their talents and abilities by being managers. For instance, of the top 10 great architectural wonders of the world named by the American Institute of Architects, none was built by just one person. All were triumphs of management, although some reflected the vision of an individual. (The wonders are the Great Wall of China, the Great Pyramid, Machu Picchu, the Acropolis, the Coliseum, the Taj Mahal, the Eiffel Tower, the Brooklyn Bridge, the Empire State Building, and Frank Lloyd Wright's Falling Water house in Pennsylvania.)

Good managers create value. The reason is that in being a manager you have a *multiplier effect:* Your influence on the organization is multiplied far beyond the results that can be achieved by just one person acting alone. Thus, while a solo operator such as a salesperson might accomplish many things and incidentally make a very good living, his or her boss could accomplish a great deal more—and could well earn two to seven times the income. And the manager will undoubtedly have a lot more influence.

The Financial Rewards of Being an Exceptional Manager

How well compensated are managers? According to the U.S. Bureau of Labor Statistics, the median weekly wage for full-time U.S. workers is $859, or $44,688 a year.[15] Education pays: The median 2017 yearly income for full-time workers with at least a bachelor's degree was $66,092, compared to $37,128 for high-school graduates. People employed full-time in management, professional, and related occupations had the highest median incomes, $73,372 for men and $55,016 for women.[16]

The business press frequently reports on the astronomical earnings of top chief executive officers. The top earner in 2016 was Thomas Rutledge, CEO of Charter Communications, whose total compensation topped $98 million.[17] Average compensation for CEOs at the 350 largest companies was $15.6 million in 2016, or 271 times the salary of the average worker, based on a survey by *Fortune*.[18] The more usual median wage for CEOs in 2015 was $737,613, according to Salary.com, and for general and operations managers $102,750, according to the Bureau of Labor Statistics.[19]

Managers farther down in the organization usually don't make this much, of course; nevertheless, they do fairly well compared with most workers. At the lower rungs, managers may make between $35,000 and $60,000 a year; in the middle levels, between $50,000 and $135,000. (For examples of managerial salaries, go to *www.bls.gov/ooh/management/home.html.*)

There are also all kinds of fringe benefits and status rewards that go with being a manager, ranging from health insurance to stock options to large offices. And the higher you ascend in the management hierarchy, the more privileges may come your way: personal parking space, better furniture, and—for those on the top rung of big companies—company car and driver, corporate jet, company-paid resort-area villa, and even executive sabbaticals (months of paid time off to pursue alternative projects).

Best paid. Thomas Rutledge, CEO of Charter Communications, earned $98 million in 2016 making him the highest-paid manager in the United States that year. That's far greater than the largest salary paid to any NBA player in that period ($25 million to Kobe Bryant of the Los Angeles Lakers). What do you think your chances are of making even $100 million in your entire lifetime?
©Michael Nagle/Bloomberg/Getty Images

What Are the Rewards of Studying and Practicing Management?

Are you studying management but have no plans to be a manager? Or are you trying to learn techniques and concepts that will help you be an exceptional management practitioner? Either way, you will use what you learn. Mike Dikison, for instance, is the curator of natural history at the Whanganui Regional Museum in New Zealand. As his recent "A Day in the Life . . ." blog post reveals, Dikison uses the skills of a manager every day, whether he is planning the loan of some rare mounted specimens to another organization, valuing the collection for insurance purposes, answering visitors' questions, arranging publicity on social media for a guest lecturer who will speak about poisons in the environment, organizing a donated collection of bone specimens for display in the museum's galleries, meeting with a community conservation group, or exploring the possibility of collaborative research with the Department of Conservation.[20] Time management, people skills, mastery of interpersonal and e-communication, and the capacity to organize and plan are some of the management abilities that serve him well in his busy days.

The Rewards of Studying Management

Students sign up for an introductory management course for all kinds of reasons. Many, of course, are planning business careers, but others are taking it to fulfill a requirement or an elective. Some students are in technical or nonprofit fields—computer science, education, health, and the like—and never expect to have to supervise people.

Here are just a few of the payoffs of studying management as a discipline:

- **You will have an insider's understanding of how to deal with organizations from the outside.** Since we all are in constant interaction with all kinds of organizations, it helps to understand how they work and how the people in them make decisions. Such knowledge may give you skills that you can use in dealing with organizations from the outside, as a customer or investor, for example.

- **You will know from experience how to relate to your supervisors.** Since most of us work in organizations and most of us have bosses, studying management will enable you to understand the pressures managers deal with and how they will best respond to you.
- **You will better interact with co-workers.** The kinds of management policies in place can affect how your co-workers behave. Studying management can give you the understanding of teams and teamwork, cultural differences, conflict and stress, and negotiation and communication skills that will help you get along with fellow employees.
- **You will be able to manage yourself and your career.** Management courses in general, and this book in particular, give you the opportunity to realize insights about yourself—your personality, emotions, values, perceptions, needs, and goals. We help you build your skills in areas such as self-management, listening, handling change, managing stress, avoiding groupthink, and coping with organizational politics.

The Rewards of Practicing Management Many young people want not only to make money but also to make a difference. As Swarthmore psychology professor Barry Schwartz, author of *Why We Work,* suggests, "We care about more than money. We want work that is challenging and engaging, that enables us to exercise some discretion and control over what we do, and that provides us with opportunities to learn and grow."[21] Becoming a management practitioner offers many rewards apart from money and status, as follows:

- **You and your employees can experience a sense of accomplishment.** Every successful goal accomplished provides you not only with personal satisfaction but also with the satisfaction of all those employees you directed who helped you accomplish it.
- **You can stretch your abilities and magnify your range.** Every promotion up the hierarchy of an organization stretches your abilities, challenges your talents and skills, and magnifies the range of your accomplishments.
- **You can build a catalog of successful products or services.** Every product or service you provide—the personal Eiffel Tower or Empire State Building you build, as it were—becomes a monument to your accomplishments. Indeed, studying management may well help you in running your own business.
- **You can become a mentor and help others.** According to one survey, 84% of workers who had a **mentor**—an experienced person who provided guidance to someone new to the work world—said the mentor helped them advance their careers.[22] ●

These three machinists are using several managerial skills to produce better products. One involves mentoring from the man in the middle.
©stockbroker/123RF

1.2 What Managers Do: The Four Principal Functions

THE BIG PICTURE

Management has four functions: *planning, organizing, leading,* and *controlling.*

LO 1-2

List the four principal functions of a manager.

What do you as a manager do to get things done—that is, to achieve the stated goals of the organization you work for? You perform what is known as the management process, also called the **four management functions:** planning, organizing, leading, and controlling. (The abbreviation "POLC" may help you to remember them.) As the diagram illustrates, all these functions affect one another, are ongoing, and are performed simultaneously. *(See Figure 1.1.)*

FIGURE 1.1

The management process

What you as a manager do to get things done—to achieve the stated goals of your organization.

Although the process of management can be quite varied, these four functions represent its essential principles. Indeed, as a glance at our text's table of contents shows, they form four of the part divisions of the book. Let's consider what the four functions are, using the management (or "administration," as it is called in nonprofit organizations) of your college to illustrate them.

Planning: Discussed in Part 3 of This Book

Planning is defined as setting goals and deciding how to achieve them. Your college was established for the purpose of educating students, and its present managers, or administrators, now must decide the best way to accomplish this. Which of several possible degree programs should be offered? Should the college be a residential or a commuter campus? What sort of students should be recruited and admitted? What kind of faculty should be hired? What kind of buildings and equipment are needed?

Organizing: Discussed in Part 4 of This Book

Organizing is defined as arranging tasks, people, and other resources to accomplish the work. College administrators must determine the tasks to be done, by whom, and what the reporting hierarchy is to be. Should the institution be organized into schools with departments, with department chairpersons reporting to deans who in return report to vice presidents? Should the college hire more full-time instructors than part-time instructors? Should English professors teach just English literature or also composition, developmental English, and "first-year experience" courses?

Leading: Discussed in Part 5 of This Book

Leading is defined as motivating, directing, and otherwise influencing people to work hard to achieve the organization's goals. At your college, leadership begins, of course, with the president (who would be the chief executive officer, or CEO, in a for-profit organization). He or she is the one who must inspire faculty, staff, students, alumni, wealthy donors, and residents of the surrounding community to help realize the college's goals. As you might imagine, these groups often have different needs and wants, so an essential part of leadership is resolving conflicts.

Controlling: Discussed in Part 6 of This Book

Controlling is defined as monitoring performance, comparing it with goals, and taking corrective action as needed. Is the college discovering that fewer students are majoring in nursing than they did five years previously? Is the fault with a change in the job market? With the quality of instruction? With the kinds of courses offered? Are the nursing department's student recruitment efforts not going well? Should the department's budget be reduced? Under the management function of controlling, college administrators must deal with these kinds of matters. ●

I Wish My Manager...

...was more of a leader than a manager.

Tom Haley loves to ride. He also wishes his manager was more of a leader than a manager. Courtesy Tom Haley

Tom Haley works in the motorcycle retail industry. "My boss is a great numbers guy," said Tom, "But he is a manager and not a leader."

Tom's manager strives at **planning** by setting achievable goals for each month, like prioritizing the sale of wheels over handlebars. And his manager strives at **organizing** by delegating the right tasks to the right people. "We pool together and talk about everyone's individual strengths. We have one employee who is very computer savvy, so he takes care of the online orders. We have another employee who manages the work orders because he's really good at itemizing and breaking the orders down properly. And we have other employees out on the floor because they are talented in sales," said Tom.

While Tom's boss is successful at the planning and organizing steps of management, he is less successful at **leading** and **controlling**. Tom believes this is because his boss lacks **human skills** and doesn't interact well with other people. "He has even said he doesn't like to deal with people. He likes being back in the warehouse. He mostly stays behind the scenes," said Tom.

While Tom's manager struggles with leading and controlling, there is another employee that Tom works with who functions as the team leader, even though he isn't the manager. "Instead of just taking care of customers by himself and sending them on their way, he makes sure that the team sees what he does and why he does it so that if he's ever not there, we're able to give the customers the same kind of service."

"I remember the first time I witnessed his incredible talent on the floor," said Tom. "We had a gentleman come in who had visited five other dealerships and was really frustrated. He drove three hours to get to our store, and he was just tired and fed up. He said, 'I'm trying to buy a bike and I want to make this happen, can you guys do it?' And my co-worker, without missing a beat, said, 'Whatever you want to do, I'll make it happen.'"

The customer came into the shop with a $3,000 budget. An hour and a half later, the customer's total came out to $12,500 on top of the price of his motorcycle, but he was more than happy to pay extra. All because Tom's co-worker made the customer excited to build his dream bike and worked with him to make it happen.

"Truthfully, our motivation comes from sales commissions. But come winter time when things slow down, the motivation drags a little bit. But this leader's personality keeps you intrigued and happy to keep coming into work every day."

1.3 Pyramid Power: Levels and Areas of Management

THE BIG PICTURE

Within an organization, there are four levels of managers: *top, middle,* and *first-line managers* as well as *team leaders*. Managers may also be *general managers*, or they may be *functional managers*, responsible for just one organizational activity, such as Research & Development, Marketing, Finance, Production, or Human Resources. Managers may work for for-profit, nonprofit, or mutual-benefit organizations.

LO 1-3

Describe the levels and areas of management.

The workplace of the future may resemble a symphony orchestra, famed management theorist Peter Drucker said.[23] Employees, especially so-called knowledge workers—those who have a great deal of technical skills—can be compared to concert musicians. Their managers can be seen as conductors.

In Drucker's analogy, musicians are used for some pieces of music—that is, work projects—and not others, and they are divided into different sections (teams) based on their instruments. The conductor's role is not to play each instrument better than the musicians but to lead them all through the most effective performance of a particular work.

This model differs from the traditional pyramid-like organizational model, where one leader sits at the top, with layers of managers beneath, each of whom must report to and justify his or her work to the manager above (what's called *accountability,* as we discuss in Chapter 8). We therefore need to take a look at the traditional arrangement first.

The Traditional Management Pyramid: Levels and Areas

A new Silicon Valley technology start-up company staffed by young people in sandals and shorts may be so small and so loosely organized that only one or two members may be said to be a manager. General Motors or the U.S. Army, in contrast, has thousands of managers doing thousands of different things. Is there a picture we can draw that applies to all the different kinds of organizations and describes them in ways that make sense? Yes: by levels and by areas, as the pyramid shows. *(See Figure 1.2.)*

Three Levels of Management

Not everyone who works in an organization is a manager, of course, but those who are may be classified into three levels—top, middle, and first-line managers. Nonmanagerial employees represent the foundation of an organizational pyramid.

Top Managers: Determining Overall Direction

Their offices may be equipped with expensive leather chairs and have lofty views. Or, as with one Internet company, they may have plastic lawn chairs in the CEO's office and beat-up furniture in the lobby. Whatever their decor, an organization's top managers tend to have titles such as chief executive officer (CEO), chief operating officer (COO), president, and senior vice president.

Some may be the stars in their fields, the men and women whose pictures appear on the covers of business magazines, people such as Nike CEO Mark Parker or IBM CEO Virginia Rommety or Lucasfilm president Kathleen Kennedy or Apple CEO Tim Cook, all of whom have appeared on the front of *Fortune.*

Top managers make long-term decisions about the overall direction of the organization and establish the objectives, policies, and strategies for it. They need to pay a lot of

FIGURE 1.2

The levels and areas of management

Top managers make long-term decisions, middle managers implement those decisions, and first-line managers make short-term decisions. Team leaders facilitate team activities toward achieving a goal.

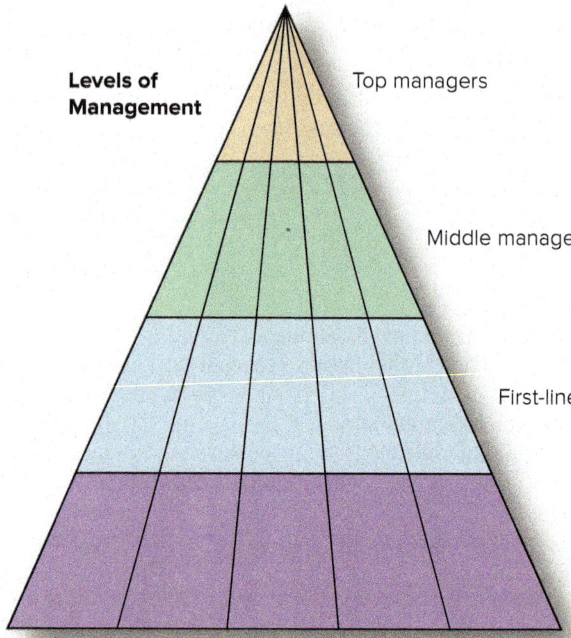

Successful top manager. India-born Satya Nadella, who joined Microsoft in 1992, became CEO of the technology company in early 2014 and has helped transition it to cloud computing. His net worth in 2018 was over $126 million. Do you see yourself joining a company and staying with it for life, as Nadella has (after an earlier job at Sun Microsystems), or is that even possible anymore? ©Justin Sullivan/Getty Images

attention to the environment outside the organization, being alert for long-run opportunities and problems and devising strategies for dealing with them. Thus, executives at this level must be future oriented, strategic, and able to deal with uncertain, highly competitive conditions.

These people stand at the summit of the management pyramid. But the nature of a pyramid is that the farther you climb, the less space remains at the top. Thus, most pyramid climbers never get to the apex. However, that doesn't mean that you shouldn't try. Indeed, you might end up atop a much smaller pyramid of some other organization than the one you started out in–and happier with the result.

Middle Managers: Implementing Policies and Plans

Middle managers implement the policies and plans of the top managers above them and supervise and coordinate the activities of the first-line managers below them. Titles might include plant manager, district manager, and regional manager, among others. In the nonprofit world, middle managers may have titles such as clinic director, dean of student services, and the like.

Middle managers are critical for organizational success because they implement the strategic plans created by CEOs and top managers. (Strategic planning is discussed in Chapter 6.) In other words, these managers have the type of "high-touch" jobs–dealing with people rather than computer screens or voice-response systems–that can directly affect employees, customers, and suppliers.

First-Line Managers: Directing Daily Tasks

The job titles at the bottom of the managerial pyramid tend to be on the order of department head, foreman or forewoman, or supervisor–clerical supervisor, production supervisor, research supervisor, and so on. Indeed, *supervisor* is the name often given to first-line managers as a whole. Their salaries may run from $43,000 to $74,000 a year.[24]

Following the plans of middle and top managers, **first-line managers make short-term operating decisions, directing the daily tasks of nonmanagerial personnel,** who are, of course, all those people who work directly at their jobs but don't oversee the work of others.

No doubt the job of first-line manager will be the place where you would start your managerial career. This can be a valuable experience because it will be the training and testing ground for your management ideas.

Nonmanagerial Employees

Nonmanagerial employees either work alone on tasks or with others on a variety of teams. They do not formally supervise or manage other people, and they are the bulk of a company's workforce.

Areas of Management: Functional Managers versus General Managers

We can represent the levels of management by slicing the organizational pyramid horizontally. We can also slice the pyramid vertically to represent the organization's departments or functional areas, as we did in Figure 1.2.

In a for-profit technology company, these might be Research & Development, Marketing, Finance, Production, and Human Resources. In a nonprofit college, these might be Faculty, Student Support Staff, Finance, Maintenance, and Administration. Whatever the names of the departments, the organization is run by two types of managers—functional and general. (These are line managers, with authority to direct employees. Staff managers mainly assist line managers.)

Functional Managers: Responsible for One Activity

If your title is Vice President of Production, Director of Finance, or Administrator for Human Resources, you are a functional manager. **A functional manager is responsible for just one organizational activity.** Google is particularly noteworthy for its unusual functional management job titles, such as Fitness Program Manager, Green Team Lead, and Vice President of Search Products & User Experience. Yahoo! also has unusual functional titles, such as VP of Talent Acquisition, VP Consumer Platforms, and VP of Research for Europe & LatAm.

General Managers: Responsible for Several Activities

If you are working in a small organization of, say, 100 people and your title is Executive Vice President, you are probably a general manager over several departments, such as Production and Finance and Human Resources. **A general manager is responsible for several organizational activities.**

At the top of the pyramid, general managers are those who seem to be the subject of news stories in magazines such as *Bloomberg Businessweek, Fortune, Forbes,* and *Inc.* Examples are big-company CEOs Denise Morrison of Campbell Soup and Jeff Bezos of Amazon.com, as well as small-company CEOs such as Gayle Martz, founder/CEO of GMinc who heads New York-based Sherpa's Pet Trading Co., which sells travel bags. But not all general managers are in for-profit organizations.

Nonprofit general manager. As CEO of the nonprofit New York Stem Cell Foundation, Susan L. Solomon does a lot of fundraising, along with directing the activities of the foundation's research scientists, plus keeping up with the latest scientific research. "As a lawyer, you learn how to learn about a new field instantly," she says. In addition, she learned how to read quickly—and "I'm really comfortable asking dumb questions." Do you think managerial skills are different for nonprofit and for-profit organizations? ©D Dipasupil/Getty Images

Susan L. Solomon is the chief executive officer of the nonprofit New York Stem Cell Foundation. As the parent of a 10-year-old boy diagnosed with Type 1 diabetes, Solomon began reading widely about the disease and came to think that stem cells might transform the understanding and treatment of diabetes, which led her to co-found NYSCF as a research foundation out of her apartment in 2005. As CEO, Solomon has helped to raise $150 million, which makes NYSCF one of the biggest nonprofits dedicated to stem-cell research, employing 45 full-time scientists and funding 75 others around the world. Earlier she started out in law, then went into business and finance, worked for the online auction house Sothebys.com, then formed her own consulting business.[25]

Managers for Three Types of Organizations: For-Profit, Nonprofit, Mutual-Benefit

There are three types of organizations classified according to the three purposes for which they are formed—*for-profit, nonprofit,* and *mutual-benefit.*

1. **For-Profit Organizations: For Making Money** For-profit, or business, organizations are formed to make money, or profits, by offering products or services. When most people think of "management," they think of business organizations, ranging from Allstate to Zynga, from Amway to Zagat. There are 3,766 public companies in the United States today, more than 1,000 fewer than 40 years ago. A mere 30 of these firms accounted for half the total profit U.S. public firms made in 2015.[26]
2. **Nonprofit Organizations: For Offering Services** Managers in nonprofit organizations are often known as administrators. Nonprofit organizations may be either in the public sector, such as the University of California, or in the private sector, such as Stanford University. Either way, their purpose is to offer services to some clients, not to make a profit. Examples of such organizations are hospitals, colleges, and social-welfare agencies (the Salvation Army, the Red Cross). According to the National Center for Charitable Statistics (NCCS), more than 1.5 million nonprofit organizations are registered in the United States. This number includes public charities, private foundations, and other types of nonprofit organizations, including chambers of commerce, fraternal organizations and civic leagues.[27]

   One particular type of nonprofit organization is called the *commonweal organization.* Unlike nonprofit service organizations, which offer services to *some* clients, commonweal organizations offer services to *all* clients within their jurisdictions. Examples are the military services, the U.S. Postal Service, and your local fire and police departments.
3. **Mutual-Benefit Organizations: For Aiding Members** Mutual-benefit organizations are voluntary collections of members—political parties, farm cooperatives, labor unions, trade associations, and clubs—whose purpose is to advance members' interests. There are nearly 10,000 such organizations.[28]

Different Organizations, Different Management?

If you became a manager, would you be doing the same types of things regardless of the type of organization? Generally you would be; that is, you would be performing the four management functions—planning, organizing, leading, and controlling—that we described in Section 1.2.

The single biggest difference, however, is that in a for-profit organization, the measure of its success is how much profit (or loss) it generates. In the other two types of organizations, although income and expenditures are very important concerns, the measure of success is usually the effectiveness of the services delivered—how many students were graduated, if you're a college administrator, or how many crimes were prevented or solved, if you're a police chief. ●

1.4 Roles Managers Must Play Successfully

THE BIG PICTURE

Managers tend to work long hours at an intense pace; their work is characterized by fragmentation, brevity, and variety; and they rely more on verbal than on written communication. According to management scholar Henry Mintzberg, managers play three roles—*interpersonal, informational,* and *decisional*. Interpersonal roles include figurehead, leader, and liaison activities. Informational roles are monitor, disseminator, and spokesperson. Decisional roles are entrepreneur, disturbance handler, resource allocator, and negotiator.

LO 1-4

Identify the roles an effective manager must play.

Clearly, being a successful manager requires playing several different roles and exercising several different skills. We discuss managerial roles in this section and key managerial skills in the next.

The Manager's Roles: Mintzberg's Useful Findings

Maybe, you think, it might be interesting to follow some managers around to see what it is they actually do. That's exactly what management scholar **Henry Mintzberg** did when, in the late 1960s, he shadowed five chief executives for a week and recorded their working lives.[29] And what he found is valuable to know, since it applies not only to top managers but also to managers on all levels.

Consider this portrait of a manager's workweek: "There was no break in the pace of activity during office hours," reported Mintzberg about his subjects. "The mail (average of 36 pieces per day), telephone calls (average of five per day), and meetings (average of eight) accounted for almost every minute from the moment these executives entered their offices in the morning until they departed in the evening."[30]

Multitasking. Multiple activities are characteristic of a manager—which is why so many managers use their smartphones to keep track of their schedules. Interestingly, although many of us multitask, research shows that very few people are good it. In general, multitasking reduces your productivity. Why do you think this happens? ©Olivier Lantzendörffer/Getty Images

Only five phone calls per day? And, of course, this was back in an era before e-mail, texting, and Twitter, which nowadays can shower some executives with 100, even 300, messages a day. Indeed, says Ed Reilly, who heads the American Management Association, all the e-mail, cell-phone calls, text messaging, and so on can lead people to end up "concentrating on the urgent rather than the important."[31]

Obviously, the top manager's life is extraordinarily busy. Here are three of Mintzberg's findings, important for any prospective manager:

1. A Manager Relies More on Verbal Than on Written Communication

Writing letters, memos, and reports takes time. Most managers in Mintzberg's research tended to get and transmit information through telephone conversations and meetings. No doubt this is still true, although the technologies of e-mail, texting, and Twitter now make it possible to communicate almost as rapidly in writing as with the spoken word.

2. A Manager Works Long Hours at an Intense Pace

"A true break seldom occurred," wrote Mintzberg about his subjects. "Coffee was taken during meetings, and lunchtime was almost always devoted to formal or informal meetings."

Long hours at work are standard, he found, with 50 hours being typical and up to 90 hours not unheard of. More recently, decades following the Mintzberg research, another study found that many professionals worked a whopping 72 hours a week, including weekend work.[32] In highly competitive industries such as finance and technology, where employees are often considered to be on call even when they're not in the office, it's not uncommon for many employees to work more than 60 hours a week.[33]

3. A Manager's Work Is Characterized by Fragmentation, Brevity, and Variety

Only about one-tenth of the managerial activities observed by Mintzberg took more than an hour; about half were completed in under 9 minutes. Phone calls averaged 6 minutes, informal meetings 10 minutes, and desk-work sessions 15 minutes. "When free time appeared," wrote Mintzberg, "ever-present subordinates quickly usurped it."

No wonder the executive's work time has been characterized as "the interrupt-driven day" and that many managers—such as GM's Mary Barra—are often in their offices by 6 a.m., so that they will have a quiet period in which to work undisturbed. No wonder that finding balance between work and family lives—work-life balance, as we consider in Chapter 12—is an ongoing concern. No wonder, in fact, that the division between work and nonwork hours is considered almost obsolete in newer industries such as information technology, where people seem to use their smartphones 24/7 to stay linked to their jobs.[34]

It is clear from Mintzberg's work that it is easy for managers to get distracted and lose focus and attention during the workday. The practice of mindfulness can help overcome these tendencies (see the Practical Action box, "Mindfulness: How Good Are You at Focusing Your Thoughts, Controlling Your Impulses, and Avoiding Distractions?").

PRACTICAL ACTION — Mindfulness: How Good Are You at Focusing Your Thoughts, Controlling Your Impulses, and Avoiding Distractions?

How many other things are you trying to do right now, besides read this chapter? If you are a fan of multitasking, you may want to challenge yourself to try its more effective opposite: practicing mindfulness. If you've never done it before, consider this challenge a practical test of your curiosity, it is an important soft skill.

So what is mindfulness?

Snake River at Grand Teton ©SeanXu/Getty Images

Mindfulness is "the awareness that emerges through paying attention on purpose, in the present moment, and nonjudgmentally to the unfolding of experience moment by moment."[35] In case you are thinking this sounds like an impractical trait for a busy manager to cultivate, consider that learning how to focus just on the task or conversation at hand is actually an invaluable way to get *more* done. By focusing on one thing at a time, you can complete it fully, put it behind you, and be ready to move on unencumbered by distracting thoughts. Multitasking, on the other hand, divides the mind's attention and actually slows work down.[36]

One of the most effective strategies for increasing your ability to be mindful is meditation, which has also been shown to relieve anxiety and depression and improve sleep.[37] Meditation can literally recharge your brain as well as strengthen your ability to break out of destructive thought patterns that have become habitual.[38] There is even some evidence that meditation can improve your memory.[39] All these are mental traits that will serve anyone well.

Companies that now offer their employees mindfulness training include American Express, Ford, LinkedIn, General Mills, Intel, Goldman Sachs, Apple, Nike, and Target.[40] A study at General Mills showed that after its 7-week program, 80% of participating managers were making better decisions and nearly 90% felt they had become better listeners.[41] Many businesses now believe that mindfulness leads to greater self-awareness, and that this, in turn, makes for stronger leaders who can better manage their own emotions as well as respond more effectively to the concerns of others.[42]

YOUR CALL

Meditation is called a practice because it's a skill that you improve over time. If you're new to it, try repeating this simple method for five minutes a day: Sit still in a quiet place, inhale while counting to seven, hold your breath for seven counts, and exhale for seven counts.[43] Clear your mind, thinking of nothing but your breathing, and if you find other thoughts intruding, don't be discouraged. Put them gently aside and try again. If you find it helpful, place a neutral object in front of you on which to focus, like a candle or a small object that has religious or spiritual meaning for you, or close your eyes.

Three Types of Managerial Roles: Interpersonal, Informational, and Decisional

From his observations and other research, Mintzberg concluded that managers play three broad types of roles or organized sets of behavior: *interpersonal, informational,* and *decisional.*

1. Interpersonal Roles—Figurehead, Leader, and Liaison

In their **interpersonal roles**, **managers interact with people inside and outside their work units.** The three interpersonal roles include *figurehead, leader,* and *liaison activities.*

2. Informational Roles—Monitor, Disseminator, and Spokesperson

The most important part of a manager's job, Mintzberg believed, is information handling, because accurate information is vital for making intelligent decisions. In their three **informational roles**—**as monitor, disseminator, and spokesperson—managers receive and communicate information with other people inside and outside the organization.**

At Google, CEO Sundar Pichai scheduled a company-wide "town hall" meeting that was abruptly canceled when some employees revealed they were being harassed online because their names and concerns had been leaked to outside websites. Pichai's memo announcing the cancelation needed to communicate clearly and calmly in a tense situation. In it he explained the employees' concerns for their safety and promised to set up several smaller forums "where people can feel comfortable to speak freely." Pichai also acknowledged the many personal meetings and e-mails in which he had heard employees' views and their concerns about being able to speak out. He closed by reminding Googlers that their "desire to build great products" is what unites them and communicated his own excitement about carrying that goal onward.[44]

3. Decisional Roles—Entrepreneur, Disturbance Handler, Resource Allocator, and Negotiator

In their **decisional roles**, **managers use information to make decisions to solve problems or take advantage of opportunities. The four decision-making roles are entrepreneur, disturbance handler, resource allocator, and negotiator.**

These roles are summarized in Table 1.1.

Did anyone say a manager's job is easy? Certainly it's not for people who want to sit on the sidelines of life. Above all else, managers are *doers.* •

TABLE 1.1 Three Types of Managerial Roles: Interpersonal, Informational, and Decisional

BROAD MANAGERIAL ROLES	TYPES OF ROLES	DESCRIPTION
Interpersonal	Figurehead role	In your *figurehead* role, you show visitors around your company, attend employee birthday parties, and present ethical guidelines to your subordinates. In other words, you perform symbolic tasks that represent your organization.
	Leadership role	In your role of *leader,* you are responsible for the actions of your subordinates, as their successes and failures reflect on you. Your leadership is expressed in your decisions about training, motivating, and disciplining people.
	Liaison role	In your *liaison* role, you must act like a politician, working with other people outside your work unit and organization to develop alliances that will help you achieve your organization's goals.
Informational	Monitor role	As a *monitor,* you should be constantly alert for useful information, whether gathered from newspaper stories about the competition or gathered from snippets of conversation with subordinates you meet in the hallway.
	Disseminator role	Workers complain they never know what's going on? That probably means their supervisor failed in the role of *disseminator.* Managers need to constantly disseminate important information to employees, as via e-mail and meetings.
	Spokesperson role	You are expected, of course, to be a diplomat, to put the best face on the activities of your work unit or organization to people outside it. This is the informational role of *spokesperson.*
Decisional	Entrepreneur role	A good manager is expected to be an *entrepreneur,* to initiate and encourage change and innovation.
	Disturbance handler role	Unforeseen problems—from product defects to international currency crises—require you be a *disturbance handler,* fixing problems.
	Resource allocator role	Because you'll never have enough time, money, and so on, you'll need to be a resource *allocator,* setting priorities about use of resources.
	Negotiator role	To be a manager is to be a continual *negotiator,* working with others inside and outside the organization to accomplish your goals.

1.5 The Skills Exceptional Managers Need

THE BIG PICTURE

Good managers need to work on developing three principal skills. The first is *technical,* the ability to perform a specific job. The second is *conceptual,* the ability to think analytically. The third is *human*, the ability to interact well with people.

LO 1-5

Discuss the skills of an outstanding manager.

Lower- and middle-level managers are a varied lot, but what do top managers have in common? A supportive spouse or partner, suggests one study.[45] Regardless of gender, reaching the top demands a person's all-out commitment to work and career, and someone needs to be there to help with children and laundry. Thus, in 2017, the majority of the 54 Fortune 1000 female CEOs were married and told the Korn Ferry Institute that they had supportive spouses: "Being a CEO, they acknowledge, is not a one-person job; a CEO's partner has to 'lean in' too. The partners of the women CEOs often took primary responsibility on the home front."[46]

General Motors CEO Mary Barra, who is married and is the mother of two grown children, has been assisted in her rise by her husband, Tony Barra, a technology consultant. Although female managers with supportive partners are becoming more common, society is still struggling with what it means for men and women to be peers and whether one's career should come first or both should be developed simultaneously.

Whether or not they have support at home, aspiring managers also need to have other kinds of the "right stuff." In the mid-1970s, researcher **Robert Katz** (in this book we **boldface** important scholar names to help you remember key contributors to the field of management) found that through education and experience managers acquire three principal skills—*technical, conceptual,* and *human.*[47]

1. Technical Skills—The Ability to Perform a Specific Job

Technical skills consist of the job-specific knowledge needed to perform well in a specialized field. Having the requisite technical skills seems to be most important at the lower levels of management—that is, among employees in their first professional job and first-line managers.

Mary Barra has a bachelor's degree in electrical engineering and a master's in business administration and a well-rounded resume that includes important experience as executive assistant to the CEO, being head of midsize car engineering, managing GM's Detroit-Hamtramck plant, and leading the company's human resources division. Then in 2011 she was made head of GM's huge worldwide product development, where she "brought order to chaos," according to one account, "mostly by flattening its bureaucracy . . . reducing the number of expensive, global vehicle platforms, and bringing new models to market faster and at lower cost."[48]

Said by her predecessor to be "one of the most gifted executives" he had met in his career, she displays an engineer's enthusiasm for cars, a quality not found among other car-company CEOs promoted from finance operations.[49] Indeed, says one account, "Ms. Barra can often be found on the company's test track putting vehicles through their paces at high speeds."[50]

Triple threat. Mary Barra unveils the new-model Chevrolet Volt hybrid electric car in Las Vegas in January 2016. Barra seems to have the three skills—technical, conceptual, and human—necessary to be a terrific manager in the complex organization that is General Motors. Which skill do you think you need to work on the most? (Human skills are the most difficult to master.) ©Tony Ding/AP Images

2. Conceptual Skills—The Ability to Think Analytically

Conceptual skills consist of the ability to think analytically, to visualize an organization as a whole and understand how the parts work together. Conceptual skills are more important as you move up the management ladder, particularly for top managers, who must deal with problems that are ambiguous but that could have far-reaching consequences. Today a top car executive must deal with several radical trends—autonomous (self-driving) cars, electric-powered vehicles, and new business models of start-ups like Uber and Lyft.

Said a GM executive about Barra, "When you put her in a position that's completely new to her, she does an amazing job of getting grounded, understanding what's important and what's not, and executing very well."[51] Or, as Barra said about her management approach, "Problems don't go away when you ignore them—they get bigger. In my experience, it is much better to get the right people together, to make a plan, and to address every challenge head on."[52]

At every stop along the way in rising through GM, Barra analyzed the situation and simplified things. For example, in her product-development job, she streamlined designs by using the same parts in many different models. She also assigned engineers to work in car dealerships to learn more about what customers want in their vehicles.[53] When promoted to CEO, she stepped into the middle of a safety crisis in which GM had to admit to misleading regulators and consumers about a defective ignition switch and agree to pay a $900 million penalty.[54]

Now she is dealing with bigger issues and trying to make GM a more nimble and forward-thinking company. "We know our industry is being disrupted," Barra says. The century-old company is leading the industry in connected-car technology, new electric and hybrid vehicles, and investing in the ride-share service Lyft to prepare for a future in which city residents use self-driving cars to get around.[55]

I'm Glad I...

...have conceptual skills.

Spencer McGuffey works in construction management. Because the employees in his industry are naturally self-motivated by pay and time off needs, he does not have to put as much energy into the leading and controlling steps of the management process. Instead, Spencer spends the majority of his time planning and organizing.

"I am a site manager for a residential building, so I'm busy making schedules and making sure everyone is here on time. I would say 75% of my day is planning tomorrow as well as the coming weeks, and making sure that everyone is able to not only make the schedule, but also perform the quality work that I expect in a timely manner," said Spencer.

When it comes to planning out the schedule, Spencer converses with his employees before doing anything else. "I typically call my employees before I even start plugging in dates and getting everything situated. I ask if there is anything special about this particular unit or house that we're going to be building that would require them to take more time than normal," said Spencer. "After that, I go into our computer system that allows us to process the schedule and send it to the employees as quickly as possible so they have a copy."

Spencer understands that, once the schedule is in place, he still has to remain flexible with emergencies and last-second changes. "I carry around a hard copy of the schedule so that if someone doesn't show up one day, I can quickly and easily track who didn't show up, and it also allows me to correct the schedule for everyone else later. That also goes for people who are working slower than we expected," said Spencer. He has to be able to adjust constantly, visualizing the project as a whole from start to finish.

While human skills do come into play occasionally for Spencer and his team, Spencer's **conceptual skills** are what help to keep his team organized and running smoothly.

"I have found that it works best if you invite all of the supervisors from across the organization to lunch and have a real heart-to-heart meeting with them to figure out who needs to be where and when so that no one is stepping on anyone else's toes," said Spencer. "This helps me a lot. I started doing this after my first month or two on the job, and it helped me to realize that the employees weren't in the best order prior to our discussion over lunch."

This personal touch provides Spencer with an opportunity for occasional face-to-face communication with his employees. The skill that keeps his team running smoothly on a day-to-day basis, however, is his ability to think analytically and visualize a project from start to finish with all its moving parts.

Courtesy of Spencer McGuffey

3. Human Skills—"Soft Skills," the Ability to Interact Well with People

This may well be the most difficult set of skills to master. **Human skills** consist of the ability to work well in cooperation with other people to get things done—especially with people in teams, an important part of today's organizations (as we discuss in Chapter 13).

Often these are thought of as "soft skills." **Soft skills are interpersonal "people" skills needed for success at all levels.** As discussed in Section 1.7, developing your soft skills is an ongoing, lifelong effort.

During her more than three decades at GM, Barra has demonstrated exceptionally strong soft skills. She has "an ability with people," says her previous boss, that is critical to GM's team-first approach.[56] "She is known inside GM as a consensus builder who calls her staff together on a moment's notice to brainstorm on pressing issues," says another report.[57] "She's fiercely intelligent yet humble and approachable," says a third account. "She's collaborative but is often the person who takes charge. And she's not afraid to make changes."[58]

Among her most significant changes: hiring people with "diverse views, diverse backgrounds, diverse experiences," she says, to try to reshape the company's notoriously insular corporate culture and to bring GM into the age of Apple and Google.

The Most Valued Traits in Managers

Clearly, Barra embodies the qualities sought in star managers, especially top managers. "The style for running a company is different from what it used to be," says a top executive recruiter of CEOs. "Companies don't want dictators, kings, or emperors."[65] Instead of someone who gives orders, they want executives who ask probing questions and invite people to participate in decision making and power sharing.

Among the chief skills companies seek in top managers are the following:

- The ability to motivate and engage others.
- The ability to communicate.
- Work experience outside the United States.
- High energy levels to meet the demands of global travel and a 24/7 world.[66]

PRACTICAL ACTION — Developing Your Soft Skills

Are you persistent, creative, curious? How do you deal with frustration or anxiety? Do you see yourself as part of a larger whole that gives your work purpose? How do you perceive problems—as temporary and solvable, or as a personal burden you are doomed to bear? Are you a good listener? Your answers will give you an idea about how well developed some of your soft skills are.

More than 90 percent of respondents to a recent Global Human Capital Trends survey by the consulting firm Deloitte identified soft skills like communication, emotional understanding, and problem solving as a critical priority.[59] Many employers say these skills are hard to find in college graduates, who often value hard skills more highly.[60] Companies are eagerly looking for soft skills as well, however; Google, for example, now prioritizes persistence and curiosity in its hiring process.[61] The good news is that soft skills can be taught. Employers are finding it worth investing money to develop these abilities in their employees. A new study shows that training employees in soft skills doesn't just marginally improve individual performance and employee retention; it actually betters these metrics enough to provide a 250% return on the financial investment a company makes in training programs.[62]

For firms that can spare their employees for three days, the American Management Association (AMA) offers a soft-skills seminar for managers at all levels including front-line supervisors.[63] Among the skills they can gain are the ability to give direction without generating conflict, to lead and motivate groups and teams, to influence others including "difficult" people, to offer effective feedback, and to get things done in an atmosphere of trust and respect. The seminar topics are a comprehensive list of essential soft skills employers look for in college graduates and new hires—and say they seldom find: communication proficiency, which includes verbal, nonverbal, and listening skills; self-understanding, lack of defensiveness, and emotional understanding and responsiveness; the ability to productively manage conflict; and an understanding of team development and the role of a team player in getting work done.

For those who want to learn online and at their own pace, many inexpensive online classes are available.[64] These short interactive programs are geared for everyone from CEOs to entry-level employees. They cover everything from self-confidence to emotional intelligence, coaching teams, building healthy work relationships, handling business etiquette, resolving conflicts, decision making, reading body language, negotiating, dealing with angry customers to becoming a successful leader.

YOUR CALL

Look back at the first paragraph in this Practical Action box. Which of the soft skills listed there would you like to improve by the time you graduate, in order to make yourself a more attractive candidate to prospective employers?

1.6 Seven Challenges to Being an Exceptional Manager

THE BIG PICTURE

Seven challenges face any manager: You need to manage for competitive advantage—to stay ahead of rivals. You need to manage for the effects of globalization and of information technology. You need to manage for diversity in race, ethnicity, gender, and so on, because the future won't resemble the past. You always need to manage to maintain ethical standards. You need to manage for sustainability—to practice sound environmental policies. Finally, you need to manage for the achievement of your own happiness and life goals.

LO 1-6

Identify the seven challenges faced by most managers.

Would you agree that the ideal state many people seek is an emotional zone somewhere between boredom and anxiety? That's the view of psychologist Mihaly Csikszentmihalyi (pronounced Me-*high* Chick-sent-me-*high*-ee), founder of the Quality of Life Research Center at Claremont Graduate University.[67]

Boredom, he says, may arise because skills and challenges are mismatched: You are exercising your high level of skill in a job with a low level of challenge, such as licking envelopes. Anxiety arises when someone has low levels of skill but a high level of challenge, such as (for many people) suddenly being called upon to give a rousing speech to strangers.

As a manager, could you achieve a balance between these two states—between boredom and anxiety, or between action and serenity? Certainly managers have enough challenges to keep their lives more than mildly interesting. Let's see what they are.

EXAMPLE

The Struggle for Competitive Advantage: Airbnb Shakes Up the Hotel Business

In San Francisco a few years ago, jobless industrial designers Brian Chesky and Joe Gebbia, wondering how to make the rent, realized that a major design conference was about to be held in the city and that hotel rooms would be scarce. Gebbia had three air mattresses and suggested turning their apartment into an "air bed and breakfast." Within three days they had a quicky website up and had booked three guests, each paying about $70 for several nights.[68]

Thus Airbnb was born, which today appeals to everyone from tourists to business travelers with $18 shared downtown living rooms but can even offer Beyoncé, in northern California for a halftime appearance at the 2016 Super Bowl, a $10,000-a-night estate in Los Altos Hills. Offering more than a million rooms in homes, apartments, even treehouses or barns—indeed, even European castles—in 34,000 cities in 190 countries ranging from Cuba to Israel's West Bank, the company is valued at $30 billion.[69]

The Rise of the New Sharing Economy. Airbnb represents an example of the *sharing economy,* also known as collaborative or peer-to-peer marketplaces, a technological variation on past behavior. "Peer-to-peer lodging has been around for quite a while," points out one writer. "For hundreds of years, family-owned boardinghouses were the lodging alternative for frugal travelers; homeowners listed their spare rooms in newspapers; . . . and European families often purchased second homes together."[70]

What is different about today's sharing economy is that ordinary people can now take advantage of the Internet and widespread use of credit cards to effectively turn their homes into hotel rooms.

Trouble for the Hotel Industry. Airbnb has had a major impact on the hotel industry, offering more places to sleep than Hilton, Hyatt, or Wyndham combined. In the beginning there were few complaints from traditional hotels, although there is evidence that the greater room supply created by Airbnb helped restrain traditional hotel prices.[71] Some small hotels even started joining the service themselves, such as the Box House Hotel in Brooklyn, New York.

Before long, however, hotels began to feel the upstart's effects and now are fighting back.[72] Large hotel chains have launched new chains (such as Tru by Hilton) aimed at Airbnb's core market of Millennials looking for a lodging experience suited to their tastes and budget. They also started creating "micro-hotels," such as Pod, Yotel, and citizenM, hotels with tiny rooms (think 50 square feet) but big public spaces that appeal to social travelers.

Some hotels now offer "pillow menus," allowing guests to choose from a range of pillow firmnesses and shapes to suit different sleep habits. Some remade their rooms with flexible tables, laptop trays, and abundant electrical outlets to accommodate different work styles. Roughly 40 hotels worldwide joined in creating LobbyFriend, a temporary social network that enables users to get information on nearby events, as well as send messages to other guests.

The hotel industry also funded research that suggests some Airbnb operators are running "illegal" hotels.[73] And it has lobbied for laws that will stop or slow Airbnb's growth by restricting the apartments and homes that can be listed on the service.

Airbnb is upping the stakes again, however. Its Niido project is a venture into several co-branded apartment buildings to appeal to tenants as well as tourists. The first apartment complex will open in Kissimmee, FL, in early 2018 with about 325 units. Renters can list their apartments on Airbnb for any part of the year. They also enjoy perks like a concierge-type service to look after guests on their behalf.[74]

YOUR CALL

Airbnb is an example of *disruptive innovation,* a process in which a product or service first takes root in simple applications at the bottom of the market (Chesky and Gebbia's air mattresses on the floor) and then relentlessly moves up market, eventually displacing established competitors. The notion of "disruptive innovation" by computer technology is a far-reaching development in the ongoing struggle of organizations to stay ahead of rivals by maintaining competitive advantage, and we describe the concept further in Chapter 10.

Which sector, Airbnb or hotels, do you think will prevail in the lodging industry? Why?

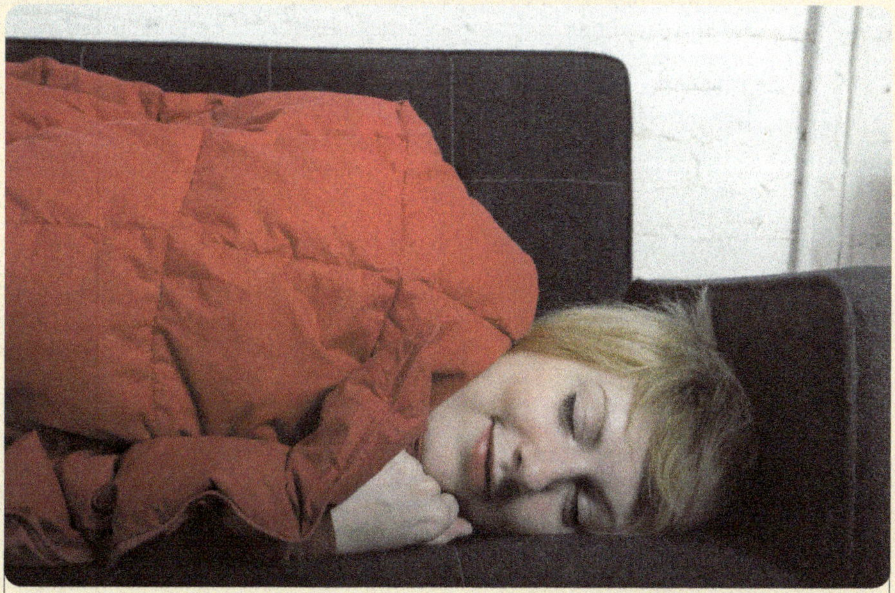

Competitive advantage? Do you think traditional hotels will still exist 10 years from now? ©Antenna/Getty Images

Challenge #1: Managing for Competitive Advantage—Staying Ahead of Rivals

Competitive advantage is the ability of an organization to produce goods or services more effectively than competitors do, thereby outperforming them. This means an organization must stay ahead in four areas: (1) being responsive to customers, (2) innovation, (3) quality, and (4) efficiency.

1. Being Responsive to Customers The first law of business is *Take care of the customer.* Without customers—buyers, clients, consumers, shoppers, users, patrons, guests, investors, or whatever they're called—sooner or later there will be no organization. Nonprofit organizations are well advised to be responsive to their "customers," too, whether they're called citizens, members, students, patients, voters, rate-payers, or whatever, since they are the justification for the organizations' existence.

2. Innovation Finding ways to deliver new or better goods or services is called **innovation**. No organization, for-profit or nonprofit, can allow itself to become complacent—especially when rivals are coming up with creative ideas. "Innovate or die" is an important adage for any manager. We discuss innovation in Chapter 10.

3. Quality If your organization is the only one of its kind, customers may put up with products or services that are less than stellar (as they have with some airlines that have a near monopoly on flights out of certain cities), but only because they have no choice. But if another organization comes along and offers a better-quality travel experience, TV program, cut of meat, computer software, or whatever, you may find your company falling behind. Making improvements in quality has become an important management idea in recent times, as we shall discuss.

4. Efficiency A generation ago, organizations rewarded employees for their length of service. Today, however, the emphasis is on efficiency: Companies strive to produce goods or services as quickly as possible using as few employees (and raw materials) as possible. Although a strategy that downgrades the value of employees might ultimately backfire—resulting in the loss of essential experience and skills and even customers—an organization that is overstaffed may not be able to compete with leaner, meaner rivals. This is the reason why, for instance, today many companies rely so much on temp (temporary) workers.

Challenge #2: Managing for Information Technology—Dealing with the "New Normal"

The challenge of managing for information technology, not to mention other technologies affecting your business, will require your unflagging attention. Some observers even see a Fourth Industrial Revolution evolving from the Third, which was notable for introducing electronics and information technology as means to automate the production of physical goods. (The First Revolution relied on steam and water power and the Second on electric power.) Justifying the idea that a fourth revolution is on the horizon are the unprecedented speed, scope, and impact of technological breakthroughs in every industry, including AI, robotics, self-driving cars, 3D printers, the Internet of Things, and many more innovations.[75] Julio Portalatin, president and CEO of Mercer Consulting, is very concerned about this issue. He told *The Wall Street Journal* "that high on his priority list is guarding against unforeseen, nimble rivals that could harness automation and artificial intelligence to poach customers in niche markets."[76]

U.S. consumers spent more than $395 billion online in 2016, nearly 12% of overall retail spending, and are expected to spend as much as $603 billion in 2021.[77] **E-commerce**, or electronic commerce—the buying and selling of goods or services over computer networks—has reshaped entire industries and revamped the very notion of what a company is. More important than e-commerce, information technology has led to the growth of **e-business**, using the Internet to facilitate every aspect of running a business. Because the Internet so dramatically lowers the cost of communication, it can radically alter any activity that depends heavily on the flow of information. The result is that disruption has become the "new normal," according to Forrester Research.[78]

Some of the implications of information technology that we will discuss throughout the book are as follows:

- **Far-ranging electronic management: e-communication all the time.** Using mobile devices such as smartphones and tablets, 21st-century managers will be masters of electronic communication, able to create powerful messages to motivate and lead teams of specialists all over the world. The next section notes that employers are looking to hire college graduates with information technology application skills. **Information technology application skills** reflect the extent to which you can effectively use information technology and learn new applications on an ongoing basis. You will clearly want to excel at e-communication.

- **Ever more data: a challenge to decision making.** The digital universe is expected to at least double in size every two years, and by 2020, it will be 50 times as large as it was in 2010.[79] Ninety percent of generated data from now on, says one source, "will be unstructured and this includes tweets, photos, customer purchase history, and even customer service call logs."[80] The Internet, then, not only speeds everything up; through **cloud computing**—the storing of software and data on gigantic collections of computers located away from a company's principal site ("in the cloud")—and huge, interconnected **databases**—computerized collections of interrelated files—it can also assemble astonishing quantities of information and make them available to us instantaneously. This has led to the phenomenon known as **Big Data**, stores of data so vast that conventional database management systems cannot handle them, so very sophisticated analysis software and supercomputers are required. The challenge: How do we deal with this massive amount of data to make useful decisions without violating people's right to privacy? We discuss Big Data in Chapter 7.
- **The rise of artificial intelligence: more automation in the workforce.** **Artificial intelligence (AI)** is the discipline concerned with creating computer systems that simulate human reasoning and sensation, as represented by robots, natural language processing, pattern recognition, and similar technologies. Some people fear that increasingly sophisticated robots powered by AI technology will be able to take over even complex jobs that have been thought safe from automation, such as the work of surgeons, writers, lawyers, and airline pilots.[81] They point out that most workers will need expensive retraining to fill the jobs that remain. But others are more optimistic and argue for focusing on what technology has created rather than on what might be lost. For instance, a report by McKinsey & Co. points out that 33% of the jobs created in the United States in the last 25 years are in careers that did not even exist when today's college students were born.[82] Work will be transformed, these observers say, rather than eliminated, and the change will be slow enough for employers, and employees, to adapt.[83] What will be the implications of these events for you as a manager for staffing and training employees and for your own professional development?
- **Organizational changes: shifts in structure, jobs, goals, and management.** With computers and telecommunications technology, organizations and teams become "virtual"; they are no longer as bound by time zones and locations. Employees, for instance, may **telecommute**, or work from home or remote locations using a variety of information technologies. Telecommuting was found to enhance employee satisfaction and performance.[84] Meetings may be conducted via **videoconferencing**, using video and audio links along with computers to let people in different locations see, hear, and talk with one another. Goal setting and feedback will be conducted via web-based software programs such as eWorkbench, which enables managers to create and track employee goals. Such managers will also rely on **project management software**, programs for planning and scheduling the people, costs, and resources to complete a project on time.
- **Knowledge management and collaborative computing.** The forms of interaction just described will require managers and employees to be more flexible, and there will be an increased emphasis on **knowledge management**—the implementing of systems and practices to increase the sharing of knowledge and information throughout an organization. In addition, **collaborative computing**, using state-of-the-art computer software and hardware, will help people work better together. Many hospitals, for example, now knit various functions together—patient histories, doctors' orders, lab results, prescription information, billing—in a single information system, parts of which patients can access themselves to schedule appointments, question doctors, and request prescription refills.

Challenge #3: Managing for Diversity— The Future Won't Resemble the Past

In 2015, more than 43 million people in the United States were foreign born, representing 13.4% of the population.[85] In 2020, there will be nearly 48 million foreign born, representing 14.3% of the population, and by 2060 they are projected to be 18.8%.[86]

But greater changes are yet to come. By mid-century, the mix of American racial or ethnic groups will change considerably, with the United States becoming half (54%) racial or ethnic minority. Non-Hispanic whites are projected to decrease from 62% of the population in 2014 to 43% in 2060. African Americans will increase from 13% to 14%, Asians from 5% to 9%, and Hispanics (who may be of any race) from 17% to 29%.[87]

In addition, in the coming years there will be a different mix of women, immigrants, and older people in the general population, as well as in the workforce. For instance, in 2030, nearly one in five U.S. residents is expected to be 65 and older. This age group is projected to increase to 98.1 million in 2060, more than doubling the number in 2014 (40.1 million).[88]

Some scholars think that diversity and variety in staffing produce organizational strength, as we in discuss in Chapter 11. Clearly, however, the challenge to the manager of the near future is to maximize the contributions of employees diverse in gender, age, race, ethnicity, and sexual orientation.

Challenge #4: Managing for Globalization— The Expanding Management Universe

When you ask some Russians "How are you?" the response may not be a simple "Fine" but rather the complete truth as to how they really feel—"a blunt pronouncement of dissatisfaction punctuated by, say, the details of any recent digestive troubles," as one American world traveler explained it.[89] And when you meet Cambodians or Burmese and are asked "Have you eaten yet?" you should not mistake this as an invitation to lunch—all it means is "Hello."[90]

The point is this: Verbal expressions and gestures don't mean the same thing to everyone around the world. Failure to understand such differences can affect organizations' ability to manage globally.

U.S. firms have been going out into the world in a major way, even as the world has also been coming to them. This increasingly interconnected nature of business around the word, called globalization, has had economic downsides for workers in some industries, such as

Cross-border burger business. The manager of this Johnny Rockets hamburger store, which opened in Lagos, Nigeria, in 2012, found that to achieve an authentic, U.S.-style taste he needed to fly in the toppings—onions, mushrooms, and iceberg lettuce—which meant that he had to start prices at $14 for a single-patty burger. ©Sunday Alamba/AP Images clothing, shoe, and toy manufacturing, which have largely moved out of the United States to countries where labor is less expensive. Some critics have therefore pushed back against the idea that globalization is always a good idea, but the fact is that it is likely here to stay.[91] "We know from experience that international cooperation works—from reconstruction after World War II more than 70 years ago to fighting Ebola just a few years back," says Christine Lagarde, the International Monetary Fund's Managing Director.[92] Managing for globalization will be a complex, ongoing challenge, as we discuss at length in Chapter 4.[93]

Challenge #5: Managing for Ethical Standards

Under pressure to meet sales, production, and other targets, managers can find themselves confronting ethical dilemmas. What would you do if, as an employee, you discovered that your company was deliberately falsifying data about its product? In 2015, Volkswagen was found to have installed, in some 11 million cars sold in the United States, software that deactivated required emissions controls while on the road, releasing many times more emissions than allowed by law, because the controls reduced the cars' advertised fuel economy and drivers might complain. When the vehicles were being tested for compliance with EPA standards, however, their computer systems sensed the test in progress and turned the emissions controls back on, concealing the cars' real environmental cost. Fines and other costs resulting from the scandal are expected to cost VW more than $15 billion.[94] Some executives were forced to resign and at least one was sentenced to jail time.[95] How far would you go to satisfy demanding customers in a highly competitive international market? In an era of climate change, with increasingly severe storms and rising sea levels, what is your responsibility to "act green"—to avoid company policies that are damaging to the environment?

Ethical behavior is not just a nicety; it is an essential principle to follow in every industry, and one that is even more compelling when you are in a position of power. This was certainly made clear in late 2017, when several women raised accusations of sexual misconduct against Hollywood mogul Harvey Weinstein in a story published in the *New York Times*.[96] This opening in a longstanding wall of silence about mistreatment of women and men by men in power was followed in rapid succession by similar charges against such prominent figures as actor Kevin Spacey, former senator Al Franken (among several other members of Congress), Def Jam Recordings co-founder Russell Simons, "Today" show host Matt Lauer, celebrity chef Mario Batali, federal court judge Alex Kozinski, actor and comedian Louis C. K., opera conductor James Levine, and longtime newscaster Charlie Rose, to name only a few. All have retired, been fired, or resigned.[97]

How would you treat others if you were in a position of power? Would you offer to boost someone's career in return for sexual favors, or ruin someone who refused you? These incidents, and many similar ones that continue to be revealed, show the enormous repercussions when people fail to realize that ethical standards must be followed in every area of life. Clearly ethical lapses have the potential to do great harm, and not only financial harm.

We consider ethics in Chapter 3 and throughout the book.

Harvey Weinstein, cofounder of Miramax, has been accused by dozens of women of committing sexual assault and sexual abuse. The allegations span 30 years. Weinstein has denied engaging in nonconsensual sex. The courts will ultimately decide. ©Paul Zimmerman/WireImage/Getty Images

PRACTICAL ACTION — Preparing Yourself to Behave Right When You're Tempted to Cheat

All kinds of pressures influence people to cheat. Some people may cheat more in the afternoon than in the morning, perhaps because mental fatigue sets in as the day wears on.[98] They may cheat more when technology makes it easy. (Access to copy/paste tools was associated with a higher rate of cheating.)[99] One recent study of 300 college students found that 9 in 10 admitted to cheating, and some believed their instructors did as well.[100]

Of course, just because you may feel okay about cheating doesn't mean it's right, or, from a hard-headed business point of view, even effective—either for you or for the organization you work for.[101] Did you know, for instance, that you can be fired for lying on a job application or resume?

Learning to Be Ethical. Concerned about transgressions in the managerial world, some of the top U.S. researchers in business ethics recently introduced a new website, EthicalSystems.org (*www.ethicalsystems.org*). One of its purposes is to examine the problem that, as one article describes it, "how we think we're going to act when faced with a moral decision and how we really do act are often vastly different."[102] Originally business ethics grew out of philosophy that ethical behavior was the right thing to do. Now research is uncovering the underlying reasons people act the way they do, to develop a more psychologically realistic approach and learn what tools will nudge people toward right behavior. We include a "Legal/Ethical Challenge" case at the end of every chapter to assist you in developing an ethical orientation.

Doing Right versus Being Liked. When people predict how they're going to act in a given situation, "the 'should' self dominates—we should be fair, we should be generous, we should assert our values," says business ethics professor Ann E. Tenbrunsel. "But when the time for action comes, the 'want' self dominates—I don't want to look like a fool, I don't want to be punished."[103] Thus, you may see some wrong occur (such as an act of cheating) and actually mean to do something about it, but can't quite figure how—and then the moment passes and you let it go and tell yourself that what you did was okay.

YOUR CALL

How can you learn to be ethical? First, recognize the reasons you are tempted to overlook wrongdoing—reluctance to disappoint your friends, worry about what others will think of you, or fear that you'll get in trouble if you speak up. Then realize that the discomfort you're experiencing is a signal that you need to be courageous and act. What will you tell yourself the next time you're tempted to cheat or see someone cheating?

Challenge #6: Managing for Sustainability—The Business of Green

An apparently changing climate, bringing increased damage from hurricanes, floods, and fires throughout the United States and the world, has brought the issue of "being green" to increased prominence. Following *The World Is Flat,* Thomas Friedman wrote *Hot, Flat, and Crowded,* urging a strategy of "Geo-Greenism" in addressing the crises of destabilizing climate change and rising competition for energy.[104] Earlier former U.S. Vice President Al Gore's documentary film *An Inconvenient Truth,* along with his book by the same name, further popularized the concepts of global climate change and the idea of sustainability as a business model.[105]

Our economic system has brought prosperity, but it has also led to unsustainable business practices because it has assumed that natural resources are limitless, which they are not. **Sustainability** **is defined as economic development that meets the needs of the present without compromising the ability of future generations to meet their own needs.**[106] A number of companies–from PepsiCo to Walmart to REI–have recognized that corporations have a responsibility to address the causes of climate change.[107] Engineering and consulting firm CH2M is a good example. Chairman and CEO Jacqueline Hinman told *Fortune* "as engineers and project managers, we have an inherent opportunity and responsibility to make a positive difference in the world, so our entire business is predicated on that purpose. We lead in delivering sustainable solutions for growth and a better quality of life, ultimately to achieve greater social, environmental, and economic outcomes–with intentional emphasis on the 'and.'"[108]

Challenge #7: Managing for Happiness and Meaningfulness

Which would you rather have, a happy life or a meaningful life? We recommend both!

One study found that "Happiness was linked to being a taker rather than a giver, whereas meaningfulness went with being a giver rather than a taker," as a study author put it.[109] Happiness is getting what you want, having your desires fulfilled. **Meaningfulness** **is the sense of "belonging to and serving something that you believe is bigger than the self."**[110] In our case, for example, we derive meaning from writing this book because we believe it can enrich your life and help you manage others more effectively. Research clearly shows that a sense of meaningfulness in your life is associated with better health, work and life satisfaction, and performance.[111]

We have three suggestions for building meaning into your life.

1. **Identify activities you love doing.** Try to do more of these activities or find ways to build them into your work role. Employees at St. Jude Children's Research Hospital embody this suggestion. They truly enjoy participating in the St. Jude Marathon weekend because it raises money for the children being treated at the hospital. One employee, a cancer survivor, commented, "Each year it provides me with another opportunity to give back so that we can help countless other children have anniversaries of their own."[112]
2. **Find a way to build your natural strengths into your personal and work life.** Doing this requires that you assess yourself along a host of competencies desired by employers. The next section identifies these competencies and discusses how you might evaluate your strengths and development opportunities.
3. **Go out and help someone.** Research shows that people derive a sense of meaningfulness from helping others.[113] Salesforce, ranked as the eighth best place to work by *Fortune,* follows this suggestion. The company donates "subscriptions for its technology to nonprofits and educators, it grants employees seven days off to volunteer each year and has given away more than $137 million."[114]

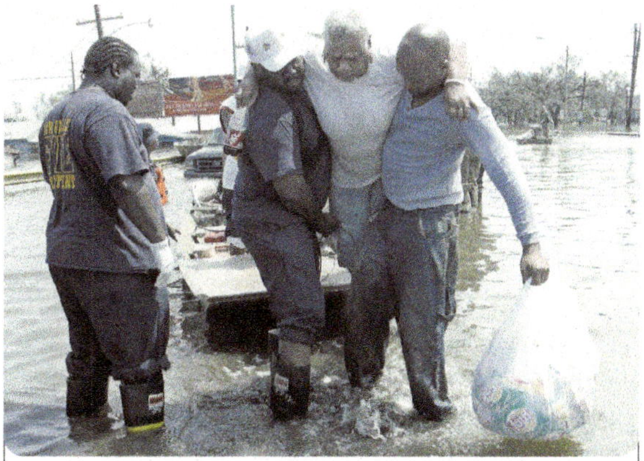

Hurricane Katrina left many people in need of help. The three men here rescued the women in the middle from flood waters caused by the breakdown of levees in New Orleans, Louisiana. These good samaritans likely felt a great deal of meaningfulness from helping others. ©JAMES NIELSEN/AFP/Getty Images

How Strong Is Your Motivation to Be a Manager? The First Self-Assessment

As we stated at the beginning of this chapter, it is our desire to make this book *as practical as possible* for you. As an important means of advancing this goal, we developed 65 **self-assessments**—two to four per chapter—that allow you to gauge how you feel about the material you are reading and how you can make use of it.

Go to the self-assessment website at *connect.mheducation.com,* complete the assessment, then answer the self-assessment questions in the book. (Note: These assessments are available only if your instructor uses *Connect* and assigns them to you.) Taking them is a valuable way to develop your self-awareness and interpersonal skills. The first one assesses your motivation to lead. Do you desire to hold leadership positions? Find out by taking the self-assessment. ●

SELF-ASSESSMENT 1.1 CAREER READINESS

How Strong Is My Motivation to Lead?

Please be prepared to answer these questions if your instructor has assigned Self-Assessment 1.1 in *Connect.*

Are you motivated to lead others? Go to connect.mheducation.com and take the self-assessment. When you're done, answer the following questions:

1. Do results match your desire to assume leadership roles at school, work, and home? Explain.
2. Which of the three dimensions do you think is most likely to affect your future success as a leader? Discuss.
3. What things would you say during an interview to demonstrate that you possess the career readiness competency of leadership?

1.7 Building Your Career Readiness

THE BIG PICTURE

Companies want to hire *career-ready* college graduates. In this section we describe a model of career readiness and offer tips for building your readiness.

LO 1-7

Define the knowledge, soft skills, attitudes, and other characteristics needed for career readiness and discuss how they can be developed.

About 80,000 undergraduate students from over 350 universities across the United States rated 2017's most attractive employers. The top 10 were: (1) Google, (2) Walt Disney Company, (3) Apple, (4) Nike, (5) Amazon, (6) J.P. Morgan, (7), Goldman Sachs, (8) Ernst & Young, (9) Deloitte, and (10) FBI.[115] Would you like to work at these companies or another like them? If so, you need to be career ready.

Career readiness represents the extent to which you possess the knowledge, skills, and attributes desired by employers. How ready do you believe you are? Recent surveys of college graduates and recruiters reveal a big gap in the degree of readiness each group perceives in students. Figure 1.3 shows the results of a study of 400 employers and 613 college students. The majority of students rated themselves as career-ready on 11 of 17 skills, while the majority of employers did not perceive students to be well-prepared on any of the skills.[116] The three largest gaps were in critical/analytical thinking, written communication, and locating, organizing, and evaluating information, skills that are very important to employers.[117] Other studies have similarly demonstrated that employers see a major skills gap in college students' interpersonal skills.[118]

You'll want to close these gaps for three reasons:

1. **To get a job and earn more money.** Today's jobs require greater interpersonal or soft skills, and employers are willing to pay higher salaries to those possessing them.[119]
2. **To impress employers with your self-awareness.** Companies prefer to hire people with realistic perceptions of their own strengths and weaknesses. This underscores the need to obtain information about your strengths and weaknesses throughout your career.
3. **To create your own motivation to learn.** Studies of human behavior reveal that people won't spend time on personal development unless they feel the need. Overinflated perceptions of career readiness will not motivate you to develop the attributes that enhance that readiness. You need to motivate yourself to learn and develop.

Moreover, these gaps are critical to employers too. Kate Davidson, a reporter for *The Wall Street Journal*, concluded that a lack of soft skills "is limiting organizational productivity," and "it is becoming increasingly difficult to find applicants who can communicate clearly, take initiative, problem-solve and get along with co-workers."[120] Knowing this, we want reading our textbook to help you become career-ready. The process starts with focusing on the ideas and suggestions in this section.

A Model of Career Readiness

Being career-ready is a lifelong process requiring you to continually learn and develop in response to changes in organizational needs and skill requirements. It is not a one-time event that stops after graduation. Consider what René Steiner, President/CEO of Büler North America, had to say about career readiness. "Realize that learning is not complete when you graduate. Today, more so than in the past, there is the opportunity to continue to develop, through education, learning company culture, and exploring different areas of business. And, you need to adapt to future needs."[121] Authors of the *Future Work Skills 2020* report similarly concluded that individuals "will increasingly be

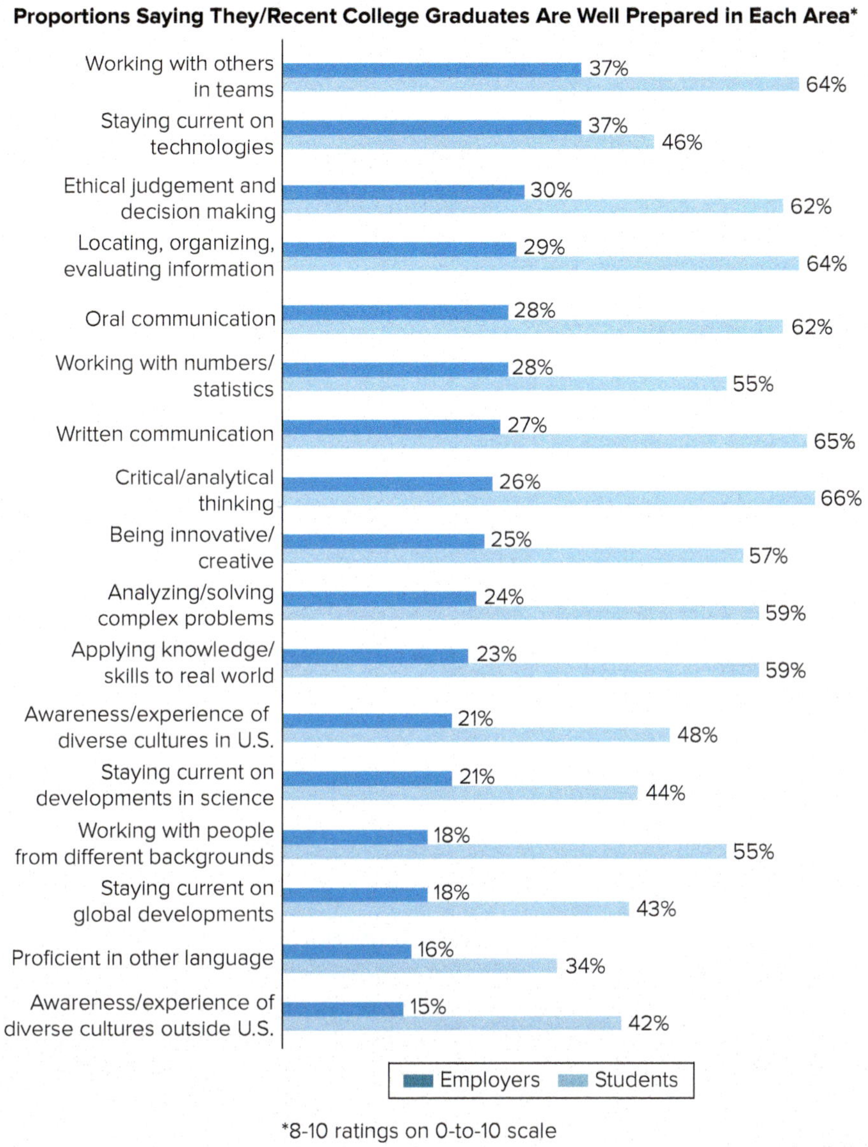

FIGURE 1.3

Employers and college graduates disagree about levels of career readiness

Hart Research Associates, "Employers Give College Graduates Low Scores for Preparedness Across Learning Outcomes; Students Think They are Better Prepared" *Falling Short? College Learning and Career Success,* 2015, 12.

called upon to continually reassess the skills they need, and quickly put together the right resources to develop and update these. Workers in the future need to be adaptable lifelong learners."[122]

Being career ready is more encompassing than you might think. Four key categories of competency fuel career readiness: knowledge, soft skills, attitudes, and other characteristics (KSAOs for short; see Figure 1.4). Let's look at each.

Knowledge (K) Skills in the knowledge category, generally referred to as "hard skills," encompass the basic knowledge employers expect you to possess. They develop from your ability to apply academic and practical knowledge while performing the job. Your grade point average is one way to assess your current level of this type of knowledge.[123] Other types of knowledge desired by employers include information technology application, cross-cultural awareness, computational thinking, understanding the business, and new media literacy (see Table 1.2).

FIGURE 1.4

Model of career readiness

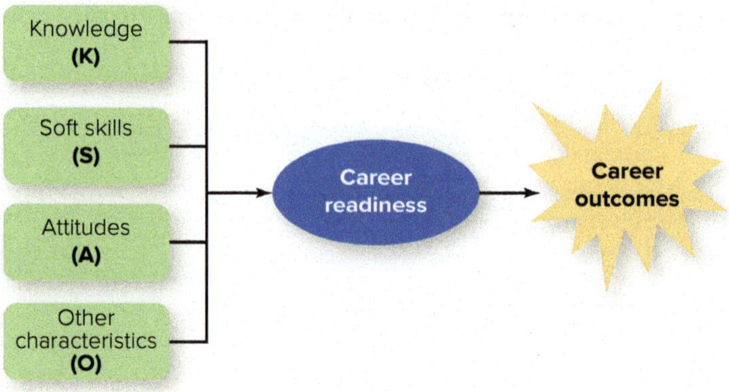

TABLE 1.2 **Description of KSAO Skills Needed for Career Readiness**

KSAO	COMPETENCY	DESCRIPTION
Knowledge	**Task-Based/Functional**	Demonstrated ability to apply academic and practical knowledge in pursuit of organizational and individual goals/assignments.
	Information Technology Application	Effective use of IT and learning new applications as needed.
	Cross-Cultural Competency	Awareness of cross-cultural differences; respect for diverse cultures, races, ages, genders, and religions; and demonstrated openness, inclusiveness, and ability to interact with diverse people.
	Computational Thinking	Ability to use numbers to distill abstract concepts and conduct data-based reasoning. Ability to work with and interpret Big Data.
	Understanding the Business	Understanding of the company's business and strategies and the needs of stakeholders, and ability to see how your work fits into the larger organizational puzzle.
	New Media Literacy	Ability to develop, evaluate, and use new media forms, and to apply these media for persuasive communication. Ability to stay up-to-date with the latest media trends and leverage them in the interest of the organization.
Soft Skills	**Critical Thinking/Problem Solving**	Sound reasoning to analyze situations, make decisions, and solve problems. Ability to obtain, interpret, and analyze both qualitative and quantitative information while creatively solving problems.
	Oral/Written Communication	Ability to effectively express your thoughts, ideas, and messages to diverse people in oral and written form. Public speaking skills and ability to write/edit emails, letters, and technical reports.
	Teamwork/Collaboration	Ability to work effectively with and build collaborative relationships with diverse people, work within a team structure, and manage interpersonal conflict.
	Leadership	Skill at influencing a group of people to achieve common goals. Ability to motivate, coach, and develop others.
	Decision Making	Ability to collect, process, and analyze information in order to identify and choose from alternative solutions that lead to optimal outcomes.

TABLE 1.2 **Description of KSAO Skills Needed for Career Readiness (*Continued*)**

KSAO	COMPETENCY	DESCRIPTION
	Social Intelligence	Ability to connect with others in a meaningful way, to recognize and understand another person's feelings and thoughts, and to use this information to stimulate positive relationships and beneficial interactions.
	Networking	Ability to build and maintain a strong, broad professional network of relationships.
	Emotional Intelligence	Ability to monitor your emotions and those of others, to discriminate among them, and to use this information to guide your thinking and behavior.
Attitudes	**Ownership/Accepting Responsibility**	Willingness to accept responsibility for your actions.
	Self-Motivation	Ability to work productively without constant direction, instruction, and praise. Ability to establish and maintain good work habits and consistent focus on organizational goals and personal development.
	Proactive Learning Orientation	Desire to learn and improve your knowledge, soft skills, and other characteristics in pursuit of personal development.
	Showing Commitment	Willingness to support others and positively work toward achieving individual and company goals.
	Positive Approach	Willingness to accept developmental feedback, to try and suggest new ideas, and to maintain a positive attitude at work.
	Career Management	Ability to proactively manage your career and identify opportunities for professional development.
Other Characteristics	**Professionalism/Work Ethic**	Accountability and positive work habits such as punctuality, time management, appropriate dress and appearance, and willingness to go beyond a job description or ask for help when needed. Demonstrated integrity, ethical behavior, and concern for the greater good.
	Resilience	Ability to bounce back from adversity and to remain motivated when confronted with challenges.
	Personal Adaptability	Ability and willingness to adapt to changing situations.
	Self-Awareness	A realistic view of your strengths and weaknesses relative to a specific job and context, and the ability to create and implement a personal development plan.
	Service/Others Orientation	Willingness to put the needs of others over self-interests.
	Openness to Change	Flexibility when confronted with change, ability to see change as a challenge, and willingness to apply new ideas, processes, or directives.
	Generalized Self-Efficacy	Confidence in your ability to perform across a variety of situations.

Source: Based on material in NACE Staff, "Employers Rate Career Competencies, New Hire Proficiency," December 11, 2017, www.naceweb.org; Matthew Tarpey, "The Skills You Need for the Jobs of the Future," February 16, 2017, www.careerbuilder.com; Alex Gray, "The 10 Skills You Need to Thrive in the Fourth Industrial Revolution," January 19, 2016, https://www.weforum.org; and Kevin Lowden, Stuart Hall. Dely Elliot, and Jon Lewin, "Employers' Perceptions of the Employability Skills of New Graduates," 2011, www.gla.ac.uk.

Soft Skills (S) We defined *soft skills* above as interpersonal or "people" skills needed for success at work. These are not knowledge or technical skills. Soft skills are becoming increasingly important as companies outsource and automate routine tasks. For example, a *Wall Street Journal* survey reported that 92% of executives believed "soft skills were equally important or more important than technical skills." Further, 89% said they had "a very or somewhat difficult time finding people with the requisite attributes." These gaps were found across all age groups and experience levels.[124] You can increase your career readiness by focusing on the eight soft skills described in Table 1.2. You will learn more about each one as we progress through this book.

Attitudes (A) Attitudes are beliefs and feelings directed toward *specific* objects, people, or events. More formally, an **attitude is defined as a learned predisposition toward a given object.** Attitudes are thoroughly discussed in Chapter 11.

Table 1.2 indicates that recruiters prefer to find six attitudes in college graduates they hire. All have a positive and proactive focus. People perceive our attitudes by observing what we do and say. For example, taking ownership or responsibility is a key attitude preferred by recruiters. It reflects the extent to which a person accepts responsibility for his or her actions. We suspect recruiters desire this attitude because it is positively associated with employees' commitment, job satisfaction, and engagement. Feelings of ownership also reduce employees' desire to quit.[125] All told, you can create more favorable impressions during interviews if you demonstrate this attitude. Find out where you stand on this attitude by taking self-assessment 1.2. It was designed to enhance your self-awareness about the extent you accept responsibility for your actions.

SELF-ASSESSMENT 1.2 CAREER READINESS

Please be prepared to answer these questions if your instructor has assigned Self-Assessment 1.2 in *Connect*.

To What Extent Do You Accept Responsibility for Your Actions?

Building Your Career Readiness

People are more likely to diligently work toward accomplishing their goals and accept performance feedback when they accept responsibility for their actions. They also are less likely to blame others for their mistakes or poor performance. This self-assessment allows you to determine your status regarding this important attitude. The survey feedback will help you to maintain or improve your attitude about taking ownership/responsibility for your actions.

Go to connect.mheducation.com and take the self-assessment. When you're done, answer the following questions:

1. Do you have a strong attitude about accepting responsibility for your actions? Do you agree with these results? Explain your thinking.
2. What can you do to increase the strength of this attitude?
3. What things would you say during an interview to demonstrate that you possess the career readiness competency of ownership/accepting responsibility?

Other Characteristics (O) This category contains a host of personal characteristics that prompt positive impressions among others and help you effectively adapt to personal and work-related changes. Consider professionalism/work ethic and resilience. Aaron Michel, cofounder and CEO at PathSource, a career navigation and education software company, believes professionalism/work ethic "cannot be overvalued in the job market." He concluded that "just being on time and behaving responsibly can leave a strong impression."[126]

Resilience is the ability to bounce back from adversity and to sustain yourself when faced with a challenge. Research shows that it is a key trait of successful people [127] The Arizona State women's golf team displayed resiliency in 2017. After finishing sixth in the Pac-12 Women's Golf Championship, they came back and won the 2017 NCAA National Championship. Head coach Missy Farr-Kaye said the team "dug a little deeper, practiced a little harder and showed what they were made of." She told the team

Missy Farr-Kay, at the far left, is head coach of the Arizona State University women's golf team since 2015. She led her team to a NCAA national championship in 2017. It is a nation leading 8th time that the women's golf team at ASU has won a national championship truly creating a golf dynasty at the collegiate level. Farr-Kaye notes that her team was highly resilient, never giving up even in the face of adversity. How do you think Farr-Kay and her coaches develop a resilient mindset within the players? ©Steve Woltmann/NCAA Photos/Getty Images

that its poor showing in the conference championship wasn't a bad thing but rather an opportunity.[128] This type of cognitive reframing is key to becoming resilient.[129] Can you see why employers want to hire people who are professional and resilient?

Developing Career Readiness

We classify the many ways to develop career readiness into six categories: (1) *build self-awareness,* (2) *learn from educational activities,* (3) *model others possessing the desired competencies,* (4) *learn from on-the-job-activities,* (5) *seek experience from student groups and organizations,* and (6) *experiment.*

1. **Build Self-Awareness.** There are two ways to gather the data or information you need to make an accurate evaluation of your strengths and developmental opportunities.
   - Ask for honest, targeted feedback from fellow students, co-workers, managers, teachers, and family. Find people you trust.
   - Take validated self-assessment surveys. This textbook provides 66 assessments for this purpose. Each provides developmental feedback, enabling you to devise a path toward improvement of a particular skill.
2. **Learn from Educational Activities.** To continue the lifelong process of learning, you need a proactive learning orientation. As defined in Table 1.2, a **proactive learning orientation** **is the desire to learn and improve your knowledge, soft skills, and other characteristics in pursuit of personal development.** This orientation allows you to improve your chances of learning new skills by means of the following:
   - Taking courses at your university or attending training seminars that focus on the competencies you need, such as time management or communication.
   - Watching training videos and documentaries.

- Reading books, magazines, and research articles in pursuit of developmental ideas.[130] This textbook is a good source. You can also consult the references cited in this book to find more detailed information about a variety of topics.
- Search the Internet or Amazon for relevant source materials from reputable sources.

3. **Model others possessing the targeted competencies.** To learn from others around you, you can:
   - Identify role models or mentors who possess the skills or traits you need and then interview them. Try to learn how they execute their competencies.
   - Observe people who possess the targeted competency and learn from their behavior.
   - Try out new behaviors and then discuss your results with a mentor, coach, or colleague.
4. **Learn from on-the-job activities.** Steps you can take include:
   - Seeking new assignments that require you to use one of your targeted competencies.
   - Representing a member of management at a meeting or business function.
   - Serving as a coach to another employee.
   - Asking to serve as a team leader or project manager.
   - Making presentations and facilitating meetings.
   - Volunteering for special projects or committees.
   - Transferring to another job to obtain new skills and experience.
5. **Seek Experience from Student Groups and Organizations.** The following activities are useful:
   - Join student groups and seek leadership positions.
   - Join and network at student organizations such as Toastmasters.
   - Volunteer at organizations where you can practice your developing skills.
   - Enroll in internships, research projects, service learning opportunities, or co-ops. Internships generally last one semester or summer and can be paid or unpaid. Co-ops are paid full-time jobs that typically last 3 to 12 months.[131]
   - Make presentations to professional or civic organizations.
   - Volunteer in religious, civic, or community organizations.
6. **Experiment.** Developing soft skills requires you to put new knowledge or information to use. Try these ideas:
   - Identify new behaviors you want to master and then practice them. For example, if you want to increase your leadership skills, volunteer to facilitate your next team meeting at school or work. Practice using the influence skills we'll discuss in Chapter 14.
   - Keep a career journal. Record the details of your developmental efforts and learn from both success and missteps. Collect stories about your strengths and improvements you've made and then use them during job interviews.

Let Us Help

Our two overriding goals for writing this book are to (1) assist you in leading a happy and meaningful life and (2) help you become career ready by learning about the principles of management. Thus we have created a feature for each chapter titled "Career Corner: Managing Your Career Readiness." The purpose of this feature is to help you integrate what you learn in a chapter into the process of building your career readiness. The next section is our first installment. ●

1.8 Career Corner: Managing Your Career Readiness

LO 1-8

Describe the process for managing your career readiness.

The goal of this section is to help you apply what you learn to building your career readiness. Let's begin with three keys to success:

1. It's your responsibility to manage your career. Don't count on others.
2. Personal reflection, motivation, commitment, and experimentation are essential.
3. Success is achieved by following a process. **A process is defined as a series of actions or steps followed to bring about a desired result.**

Figure 1.5 illustrates a process to guide the pursuit of managing your career readiness.

The first step entails examining the list of knowledge, skills, attitudes, and other characteristics (KSAOs) in Table 1.2 and picking two or three that impact your current performance at school, work, or extracurricular activities. You then need to assess your skill level for these competencies. This textbook contains 65 self-assessments you can take for this purpose. The first one was presented on page 29.

The second step requires you to consider how you can use the material covered in a chapter to develop your targeted competencies. For example, do your targeted KSAOs at this point relate to any of the four functions of management: planning, organizing, leading, or control? If yes, reflect on what you learned while reading material regarding the functions of management and consider how you can apply ideas, concepts, or suggestions that were discussed.

The third step involves experimenting with small steps aimed at developing your targeted KSAOs. The final step is to evaluate what happened during your small-step experiments. This entails reflecting on what went right and wrong. Remember, you can learn as much from failure as success.

Figure 1.5 shows that *willingness* is at the center of developing your career readiness. This reinforces the point that it's up to you to shape and direct your future. We are confident that you can develop your career readiness by following this process and using the guidance provided at the end of every chapter.[132]

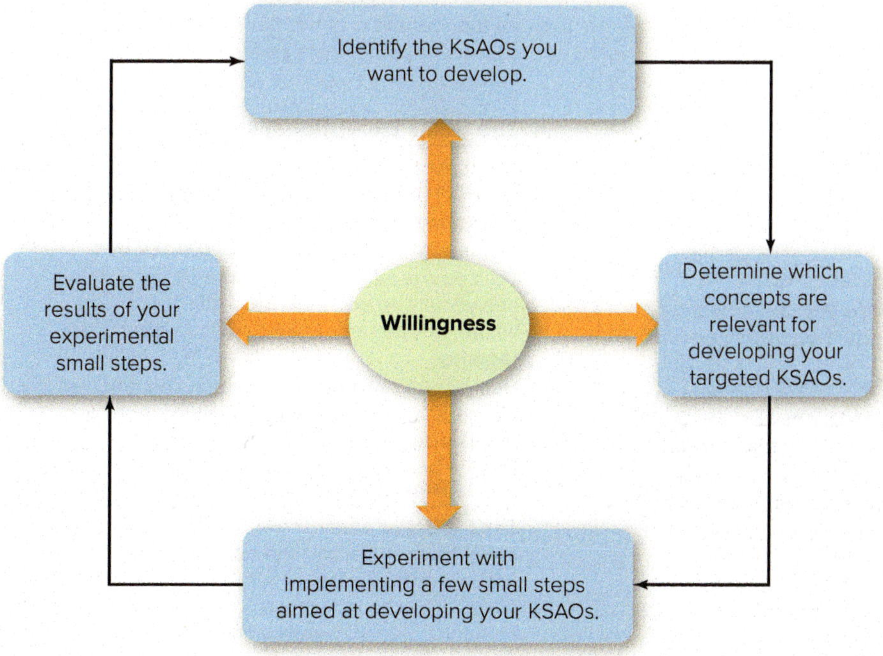

FIGURE 1.5

Process for managing career readiness

Key Terms Used in This Chapter

artificial intelligence (AI) 25
attitude 34
Big Data 25
career readiness 30
cloud computing 25
collaborative computing 25
competitive advantage 23
conceptual skills 19
controlling 10
databases 25
decisional roles 17
e-business 24
e-commerce 24
effective 5
efficient 5
first-line managers 12
four management functions 9
functional manager 13
general manager 13
human skills 20
information technology application skills 24
informational roles 17
innovation 24
interpersonal roles 17
knowledge management 25
leading 10
management 5
meaningfulness 28
mentor 8
middle managers 12
mindfulness 16
nonmanagerial employees 13
organization 5
organizing 9
planning 9
proactive learning orientation 35
process 37
project management software 25
resilience 34
soft skills 21
sustainability 28
technical skills 19
telecommute 25
top managers 11
videoconferencing 25

Key Points

1.1 Management: What It Is, What Its Benefits Are

- Management is defined as the pursuit of organizational goals *efficiently*, meaning to use resources wisely and cost-effectively, and *effectively* by integrating the work of people through planning, organizing, leading, and controlling the organization's resources.

1.2 What Managers Do: The Four Principal Functions

- The management process consists of four functions.
- *Planning* is setting goals and deciding how to achieve them.
- *Organizing* is arranging tasks, people, and other resources to accomplish the work.
- *Leading* is motivating, directing, and otherwise influencing people to work hard to achieve the organization's goals.
- *Controlling* is monitoring performance, comparing it with goals, and taking corrective action as needed.

1.3 Pyramid Power: Levels and Areas of Management

- Within an organization, there are managers at three levels.
- *Top managers* make long-term decisions about the overall direction of the organization and establish the objectives, policies, and strategies for it.
- *Middle managers* implement the policies and plans of their superiors and supervise and coordinate the activities of the managers below them.
- *First-line managers* make short-term operating decisions, directing the daily tasks of nonmanagerial personnel.
- There are three types of organizations—for-profit, nonprofit, and mutual benefit.
- *For-profit* organizations are formed to make money by offering products or services.
- *Nonprofit* organizations offer services to some, but not to make a profit.
- *Mutual-benefit* organizations are voluntary collections of members created to advance members' interests.

1.4 The Skills Exceptional Managers Need

- The three skills that exceptional managers cultivate are technical, conceptual, and human.
- *Technical* skills consist of job-specific knowledge needed to perform well in a specialized field.
- *Conceptual* skills consist of the ability to think analytically, to visualize an organization as a whole, and to understand how the parts work together.
- *Human* skills consist of the ability to work well in cooperation with other people in order to get things done.

1.5 Roles Managers Must Play Successfully

- The Mintzberg study shows that, first, a manager relies more on verbal than on written communication; second, managers work long hours at an intense pace; and, third, a manager's work is characterized by fragmentation, brevity, and variety.

- Mintzberg concluded that managers play three broad roles: (1) *interpersonal*—figurehead, leader, and liaison; (2) *informational*—monitor, disseminator, and spokesperson; and (3) *decisional*—entrepreneur, disturbance handler, resource allocator, and negotiator.

1.6 Seven Challenges to Being an Exceptional Manager

- Managing for competitive advantage, which means an organization must stay ahead in four areas—being responsive to customers, innovating new products or services offering better quality, being more efficient.
- Managing for diversity among different genders, ages, races, and ethnicities.
- Managing for globalization, the expanding universe.
- Managing for computers and telecommunications—information technology.
- Managing for right and wrong, or ethical standards.
- Managing for sustainability.
- Managing for your own happiness and meaningful life goals.

1.7 Building Your Career Readiness

- Career readiness reflects the extent to which you possess the knowledge, skills, attitudes and other characteristics (KSAOs) desired by employers.
- Research uncovered 27 KSAOs preferred by employers (see Table 1.2).
- Six actions develop career readiness: Build self-awareness, learn from educational activities, model others possessing the targeted competencies, learn from on-the-job activities, seek experience from student groups and organizations, and experiment.

1.8 Career Corner: Managing Your Career Readiness

- A four-step process is recommended for managing your career readiness: Identify the KSAOs you want to develop, determine which concepts are relevant for developing your targeted KSAOs, experiment with implementing a few small steps aimed at developing your KSAOs, and evaluate the results of your experimental small steps.
- It takes willingness on your part to manage career readiness.

Understanding the Chapter: What Do I Know?

1. What is the difference between being efficient and being effective?
2. What is the formal, three-part definition of management?
3. How would I define the four functions of management?
4. What are the differences among the four levels of managers in the organizational pyramid?
5. Mintzberg's study in the 1960s came up with three important findings about a manager's routine. What are they, and are they probably still the same today?
6. Mintzberg also found that managers play three important roles. What are they, and what examples can I think of?
7. What are the three skills that exceptional managers need to cultivate, and which one do I probably have to work on most?
8. What are the seven challenges of being a manager, and which one is the one I will probably most have to worry about during my lifetime?
9. What does it mean to be career ready, and what are the attributes that define it?
10. How can I build my level of career readiness?

Management in Action

Did Major League Baseball Value Money Over Bob Bowman's Behavior?

Major League Baseball (MLB) is the oldest major professional sports league in the United States. It is composed of 30 teams in two leagues, the National League and the American League, each containing 15 teams. The two leagues merged into a single organization in 2000 and are led by the Commissioner of Baseball.[133]

The Commissioner oversees the hiring and management of umpiring crews and negotiates all contracts controlling marketing, labor, and television rights. MLB Advanced Media (MLBAM) is the multimedia arm of MLB. It was formed in 2000 by then Commissioner Bud Selig: Selig was Commissioner from 1998 to 2015. MLBAM "operates the official website for the league and the 30 Major League Baseball club websites via MLB.com, which draws four million hits per day. The site offers news, standings, statistics, and schedules, and subscribers have access to live audio and video broadcasts of most games. The company also employs reporters, with one assigned to each team for the season and others serving more general beats. MLB Advanced Media also owns and operates Baseball-Channel.tv and MLB Radio."[134]

BOWMAN AND HIS SUCCESS AT MLBAM

Bob Bowman was hired to run MLBAM in 2000. Prior to that he worked as treasurer of the state of Michigan from 1983 to 1990 and then for ITT Corp. He ultimately became ITT's president and chief operating officer.[135]

Bowman was given great latitude and autonomy by Commissioner Selig. He thus decided to locate MLBAM's headquarters two miles away from the league office on Park Avenue and ran his operation like a fiefdom, according to *The Wall Street Journal.* A reporter from the *New York Times* concluded that the physical distance between the two corporate offices and Bowman's "ability to deliver enormous profits for the league and its team owners, apparently enabled Bowman to operate with little scrutiny from league officials."[136]

MLBAM prospered under Bowman. The *New York Times* reported that MLBAM "became the crown jewel of Major League Baseball, the envy of every sports league and one of the most important companies as the broadcast world transitioned to digital streaming. It generates hundreds of millions of dollars in revenue annually, and 75 percent of a spinoff company, Bam-Tech, has been sold for $2.58 billion."[137] Current MLB Commissioner Rob Manfred said "Bob's vision made our game even more accessible and enjoyable to millions of fans."[138]

Bowman's success led one reporter to conclude that he "was once considered one of the two or three most powerful figures in all of professional sports."[139] It was even suggested that Bowman should have been selected over Rob Manfred as Commissioner, and as a possible successor to replace Bob Iger as CEO of The Walt Disney Company.[140]

ALLEGATIONS PERSIST ABOUT BOWMAN'S BEHAVIOR

Reporters from *The Wall Street Journal* concluded that Bowman was forced to resign "after years of troubling workplace behavior that former baseball executives were said to be made aware of at least a decade ago." The reporters noted evidence suggesting that Bowman "engaged in a pattern of behavior that included propositioning female colleagues, allegedly having consensual relationships with subordinate co-workers and cultivating a culture of partying and heavy drinking with employees outside the office." These concerns were raised at least 10 years ago with Bob DuPuy, MLB's president and chief operating officer, who in turn informed Commissioner Selig.[141]

Bowman was considered brilliant yet hard on others. *The Wall Street Journal* reported that he "would just talk down to people," often yelling. "Just disrespectful."[142]

More recently, Bowman was accused of "pushing an executive for the Fenway Sports Management, the Red Sox parent company, and verbally abusing an employee in October" [2017]. It also was alleged that Bowman hired women to entertain people at the 2016 All-Star Game. These women were believed to be escorts and "some of them were heard encouraging attendees to leave to have sex quickly so that they could return to solicit another attendee," according to *The Wall Street Journal.*[143]

A former high-ranking baseball official told *Wall Street Journal* reporters that what Bowman "gave in heartburn was always overshadowed by what he gave in money." This individual also stated that Bud Selig "had no interest in dealing with it."[144]

NOW WHAT?

Current MLB Commissioner Rob Manfred said he was unaware of Bowman's historically bad behavior. He did, however, believe that the latest incidents necessitated a conversation with Bowman. This conversation resulted in a joint decision that it was time for Bowman to leave.[145]

Bowman provided a statement to *The Wall Street Journal.* He acknowledged that MLBAM's culture was hardworking and driven, and that his behavior was inappropriate. He took full responsibility for his actions. He also apologized to those he offended or hurt.

Following Bowman's departure, Commissioner Manfred made it mandatory for all full and part-time staff to participate in a 45-minute online training course that focused on discrimination and harassment. Manfred wants employees to have practical tools they can use in combatting disruptive employee behavior, according to *The Wall Street Journal.*[146]

Manfred also is addressing the culture gap between MLB and MLBAM. His solution is to combine the two offices in one location in the summer of 2019.

FOR DISCUSSION

Problem Solving Perspective

1. What is the underlying problem in this case from Commissioner Rob Manfred's perspective?
2. Why do you think Bowman's behavior was ignored for over 10 years?
3. What would you have done if you were Commissioner Manfred?

Application of Chapter Content

1. Did Commissioner Bud Selig operate more from a principle of efficiency or effectiveness? Explain your rationale.
2. Which of the seven challenges to being an exceptional manager did Commissioner Manfred face in dealing with Bowman? How did he handle them?
3. Which of the three skills exceptional managers need did Bowman most lack? Which ones does Commissioner Manfred most need? Explain your answers.
4. Which of the KSAOs needed for career readiness did Bowman lack? Which ones did he display?
5. Given the facts of this case, do you believe Bud Selig should have been inducted into the Baseball Hall of Fame in 2016? Why or why not?

Legal/Ethical Challenge

To Delay or Not to Delay?

You have been hired by a vice president of a national company to create an employee attitude survey, to administer it to all employees, and to interpret the results. You have known this vice president for more than 10 years and have worked for her on several occasions. She trusts and likes you, and you trust and like her. You have completed your work and now are ready to present the findings and your interpretations to the vice president's management team. The vice president has told you that she wants your honest interpretation of the results, because she is planning to make changes based on the results. Based on this discussion, your report clearly identifies several strengths and weaknesses that need to be addressed. For example, employees feel that they are working too hard and that management does not care about providing good customer service. At the meeting you will be presenting the results and your interpretations to a group of 15 managers. You also have known most of these managers for at least five years.

You arrive for the presentation armed with slides, handouts, and specific recommendations. Your slides are loaded on the computer, and most of the participants have arrived. They are drinking coffee and telling you how enthused they are about hearing your presentation. You also are excited to share your insights. Ten minutes before the presentation is set to begin, however, the vice president takes you out of the meeting room and says she wants to talk with you about your presentation. The two of you go to another office, and she closes the door. She then tells you that her boss's boss decided to come to the presentation unannounced. She thinks that he is coming to the presentation to look solely for negative information in your report. He does not like the vice president and wants to replace her with one of his friends. If you present your results as planned, it will provide this individual with the information he needs to create serious problems for the vice president. Knowing this, the vice president asks you to find some way to postpone your presentation. You have 10 minutes to decide what to do.

SOLVING THE CHALLENGE

What would you do?

1. Deliver the presentation as planned.
2. Give the presentation but skip over the negative results.
3. Go back to the meeting room and announce that your spouse has had an accident at home and you must leave immediately. You tell the group that you just received this message and that you will contact the vice president to schedule a new meeting.
4. Invent other options. Discuss.

Uber Continuing Case

Learn about Uber's history, starting from its beginning to the company's current challenges. Assess your ability to apply concepts discussed in this chapter to the case by going to Connect.

2 Management Theory

Essential Background for the Successful Manager

©Olivier Renck/Aurora/Getty Images

After reading this chapter, you should be able to:

LO 2-1 Describe the development of current perspectives on management.

LO 2-2 Discuss the insights of the classical view of management.

LO 2-3 Describe the principles of the behavioral view of management.

LO 2-4 Discuss the two quantitative approaches to solving problems.

LO 2-5 Identify takeaways from the systems view of management.

LO 2-6 Explain why there is no one best way to manage in all situations.

LO 2-7 Discuss the contributions of the quality-management view.

LO 2-8 Define how managers foster a learning organization.

LO 2-9 Describe how to develop the career readiness competency of understanding the business.

FORECAST *What's Ahead in This Chapter*

This chapter gives you a short overview of the three principal *historical* perspectives or viewpoints on management—*classical, behavioral,* and *quantitative*. It then describes the three principal *contemporary* viewpoints—*systems, contingency,* and *quality-management*. We also consider the concept of *learning organizations*. We conclude with a Career Corner that focuses on how you can demonstrate the career readiness competency of *understanding the business.*

MANAGE U

What Type of Work Environment Do I Prefer?

You'll see a bit later in this chapter that a view of the organization that considers employees to be capable, creative, responsible, and motivated to work and learn is called Theory Y. It contrasts sharply with Theory X, which suggests that workers are resistant and unwilling and need to be monitored and controlled in order to achieve anything. Theory Y is obviously a more benevolent and optimistic view of workers, and it has lately given rise to a real-world phenomenon known as the *people-focused organization*.

What Does It Mean for You?

People-focused organizations are guided by the Theory Y view that people are essentially good, trustworthy, and productive, and that they flourish when they are empowered to act independently in an atmosphere that respects their diversity and values their well-being. Efforts to improve the work experience in people-focused organizations might become the responsibility of managers in such newly created jobs as Diversity Director, Director of Inclusion, and People Success Manager. Some consulting companies even focus on helping their clients nurture younger workers by designating a Millennial Generation Expert. As *Forbes* magazine notes, "companies have started to figure out that they can stay competitive with customers and in the war for talent if they become more people-focused."[1] The key is for managers to see the company's positive internal culture as a competitive advantage.

For young and entry-level workers, the rise of this new focus on people means there may be more choices about the kind of environment in which you can work. *Self-awareness* is one of the career readiness competencies employers desire in new college graduates. Are you aware of the type of work environment you prefer? While you may not find yourself in an organization with four-day workweeks and almost no managers—two innovations the e-learning company Treehouse briefly experimented with[2]—you might be given some responsibility for deciding how to accomplish your work with less direct oversight and fewer rules than you are used to. Of course, to succeed in this kind of culture, you need to be self-directed, motivated, and able to quickly identify the questions you need to ask, all competencies associated with career readiness.

How Can You Get a Job in a People-Focused Organization?

Nearly 70% of U.S. college students work while in school, many of them full time.[3] If you are one of these students, or if you are thinking ahead to getting an entry-level job after graduation, you may want to consider how well you would fit into a people-focused organization that takes the optimistic Theory Y view of its employees. For instance, do you like to work independently? That calls for you to set your own goals and figure out how to achieve them on time and on budget. You'll need to develop and demonstrate good organizational and time-management skills, a willingness to contribute to the organization's larger purpose, and the ability to do so without a manager's heavy hand.

REI, the maker of outdoor and camping gear, is a good example of a people-focused organization. In describing how to get hired there, the company says, "We're looking for passionate and knowledgeable employees who want to work with purpose and a shared belief that a life outdoors is a life well lived. We hire people who intentionally direct their skills and experience toward a greater good. People who are already living by our values—authenticity, integrity, quality, respect, balance and service."[4]

For Discussion Would you like to work for a company that follows a people-focused, Theory Y view of its employees? What about Theory X? What questions might you ask a recruiter to determine whether a company believes in a Theory Y or Theory X view of its employees?

2.1 Evolving Viewpoints: How We Got to Today's Management Outlook

THE BIG PICTURE

After studying theory, managers may learn the value of bringing rationality to the decision-making process. This chapter describes two principal theoretical perspectives—the *historical* and the *contemporary.* Studying management theory provides understanding of the present, a guide to action, a source of new ideas, clues to the meaning of your managers' decisions, and clues to the meaning of outside events.

LO 2-1

Describe the development of current perspectives on management.

"The best way to predict the future is to create it," Peter Drucker said.

The purpose of this book is, to the extent possible, to *give you the tools to create your own future* in your career and as a manager.

Creating Modern Management: The Handbook of Peter Drucker

Who is **Peter Drucker**? "He was the creator and inventor of modern management," says management guru Tom Peters (author of *In Search of Excellence*). "In the early 1950s, nobody had a tool kit to manage these incredibly complex organizations that had gone out of control. Drucker was the first person to give us a handbook for that."[5]

An Austrian trained in economics and international law, Drucker came to the United States in 1937, where he worked as a correspondent for British newspapers and later became a college professor. In 1954, he published his famous text *The Practice of Management,* in which he proposed the important idea that *management was one of the major social innovations of the 20th century and should be treated as a profession,* like medicine or law.

In this and other books, he introduced several ideas that now underlie the organization and practice of management—namely:

- That workers should be treated as assets.
- That the corporation could be considered a human community.
- That there is "no business without a customer."
- That institutionalized management practices are preferable to charismatic cult leaders.

True learner. In his 70-year career, Peter Drucker published over 35 books and numerous other publications, received the Presidential Medal of Freedom, and achieved near rockstar status for his management ideas, which influenced organizations from General Electric to the Girl Scouts. A true learner who constantly expanded his knowledge, he understood that new experiences are key to nurturing new ideas and new ventures. Do you have this kind of curiosity? ©Jonathan Alcorn/ZUMAPRESS/Newscom

Many ideas that you will encounter in this book—decentralization, management by objectives, knowledge workers—are directly traceable to Drucker's pen. "Without his analysis," says one writer, "it's almost impossible to imagine the rise of dispersed, globe-spanning corporations."[6] In our time, Drucker's rational approach has culminated in *evidence-based management,* as we describe in Section 2.6 in this chapter.

Six Practical Reasons for Studying This Chapter

"Theory," say business professors Clayton Christensen and Michael Raynor, "often gets a bum rap among managers because it's associated with the word 'theoretical,' which connotes 'impractical.' But it shouldn't."[7]

After all, what could be more practical than studying different approaches to see which work best?

Indeed, there are six good reasons for studying theoretical perspectives:

1. **Understanding of the present.** "Sound theories help us interpret the present, to understand what is happening and why," say Christensen and Raynor.[8] Or as

scholars Scott Montgomery and Daniel Chirot argue, ideas "do not merely matter, they matter immensely, as they have been the source for decisions and actions that have structured the modern world."[9] Understanding history will help you understand why some practices are still favored, whether for right or wrong reasons.

2. **Guide to action.** Good theories help you make predictions and enable you to develop a set of principles that will guide your actions. For example, the theory of supply and demand tells us that prices go up when demand is high and supply is low. This is the situation with respect to the cost of labor in 2018. Firms are having to pay more for workers due to the shortage of qualified employees looking for work.
3. **Source of new ideas.** It can also provide new ideas that may be useful to you when you come up against new situations. For example, theories of employee engagement, which are discussed in Chapter 11, offer managers new ideas for how to best engage their workers. Contrary to the notion that compensation drives employee performance, these theories reveal that employees become engaged when an organization has the kind of cuture that promotes employee development, recognition, and trust between management and employees.
4. **Clues to meaning of your managers' decisions.** It can help you understand your firm's focus, where the top managers are "coming from."
5. **Clues to meaning of outside events.** It may allow you to understand events outside the organization that could affect it or you.
6. **Producing positive results.** It can help you understand why certain management practices–such as setting goals that stretch you to the limit (stretch goals), basing compensation and promotion on performance, and monitoring results–have been so successful for many firms.

EXAMPLE Zappos' Holacracy: A Success or a Failure?

©Jonathan Weiss/Alamy Stock Photo

A few years ago Zappos, the innovative online clothing and shoe retailer, undertook a radical management experiment called holacracy. The company eliminated job titles and organizational hierarchy, replacing them with democratic assemblies called "circles" in which its 1,500 employees proposed their own job descriptions, ratified the roles of others, and decided what projects the group should undertake.[10] Holacracy, says CEO Tony Hsieh (pronounced *shay*), "enables employees to act more like entrepreneurs and self-direct their work instead of reporting to a manager who tells them what to do."[11]

In its early days, Zappos was so successful at creating a vibrant culture based on fun, "a little weirdness," and open relationships that it started a separate business unit to help other companies learn from its example. But a few years into its experiment with holacracy, employees seemed shaken and confused by the pace of change and resulting uncertainty. For the first time in eight years, the company had fallen off *Fortune's* list of Best Companies to Work. Turnover increased, partly because some managers were given buyouts and some people felt the wrong leaders had left. Meanwhile a new self-management initiative called "teal" is being implemented. "The one thing I'm absolutely sure of," Hsieh says, "is that the future is about self-management."[12] If he could do it all over again, he says, he would introduce it even sooner.[13]

The basic reason Hsieh introduced holacracy was to avoid cutting off innovation with an increasingly stifling bureaucracy. Although holacracy itself requires several different kinds of meetings and its own versions of rules, structure, and discipline, it offers everyone in the organization the opportunity to make big decisions, including about their own roles. As one employee says, "My worst day at Zappos is still better than my best day anywhere else. I can't imagine going back to traditional hierarchy anymore."[14] Flattened hierarchies in some form also work for other large organizations, such as W.L. Gore, maker of Gore-Tex fabric, which employs 10,000 people.

YOUR CALL

Why do you think, then, that many organizations resist using flat structures? Do you think studying management theory could help you answer this question? Why or why not?

Two Overarching Perspectives about Management: Historical and Contemporary

In this chapter, we describe two overarching perspectives about management. *(See Figure 2.1.)*

- The **historical perspective** (1911–1950s) includes three viewpoints—*classical, behavioral,* and *quantitative.*
- The **contemporary perspective** (1960s–present) also includes three viewpoints—*systems, contingency,* and *quality-management.*

FIGURE 2.1

The two overarching perspectives—historical and contemporary

The Historical Perspective (1911–1950s)

Classical Viewpoint
1911–1947
Emphasis on ways to manage work more efficiently

Behavioral Viewpoint
1913–1950s
Emphasis on importance of understanding human behavior and motivating and encouraging employees toward achievement

Quantitative Viewpoint
1940s–1950s
Applies quantitative techniques to management

The Contemporary Perspective (1960s–Present)

The Systems Viewpoint
Regards the organization as systems of interrelated parts that operate together to achieve a common purpose

The Contingency Viewpoint
Emphasizes that a manager's approach should vary according to—i.e., be contingent on—the individual and environmental situation

The Quality-Management Viewpoint
Three approaches

2.2 Classical Viewpoint: Scientific and Administrative Management

THE BIG PICTURE

The *three historical management viewpoints* we will describe are (1) the classical, described in this section; (2) the behavioral; and (3) the quantitative. The classical viewpoint, which emphasized ways to manage work more efficiently, had two approaches: (a) scientific management and (b) administrative management. *Scientific management,* pioneered by Frederick W. Taylor and Frank and Lillian Gilbreth, emphasized the scientific study of work methods to improve the productivity of individual workers. *Administrative management,* pioneered by Charles Spaulding, Henri Fayol, and Max Weber, was concerned with managing the total organization.

LO 2-2

Discuss the insights of the classical view of management.

Have you ever heard of a *therblig? Therblig* is a made-up word coined by Frank Gilbreth and is, in fact, "Gilbreth" spelled backward, with the "t" and the "h" reversed. It refers to 1 of 17 basic motions workers can perform. By identifying the therbligs in a job, such as that of a bricklayer (which he had once been), Gilbreth and his wife, Lillian Gilbreth, were able to help workers eliminate unnecessary motions and reduce their fatigue.

The Gilbreths were industrial engineers and pioneers in one of the classical approaches to management, part of the *historical perspective (1911–1950s).* As we mentioned, there are *three historical management viewpoints* or approaches.[15] *(See Figure 2.2, next page.)*

- Classical viewpoint (1911–1947)
- Behavioral viewpoint (1913–1950s)
- Quantitative viewpoint (1940s–1950s)

In this section, we describe the classical perspective of management, which originated during the early 1900s. The **classical viewpoint, which emphasized finding ways to manage work more efficiently, assumed that people are rational. It had two branches—*scientific* and *administrative***—each of which is identified with particular pioneering theorists. Let's compare the two approaches.

Scientific Management: Pioneered by Taylor and the Gilbreths

The problem for which scientific management emerged as a solution was this: In the expansive economy of the early 20th century, labor was in such short supply that managers looked for ways to raise the productivity of workers. **Scientific management applied the scientific study of work methods to improving the productivity of individual workers.** Two of its chief proponents were Frederick W. Taylor and the team of Frank and Lillian Gilbreth.

Frederick Taylor and the Four Principles of Scientific Management

Known as "the father of scientific management," Taylor was an engineer from Philadelphia who believed managers could improve workers' productivity by applying four principles of science:[16]

1. Evaluate a task by scientifically studying each part of it (not by using old rule-of-thumb methods). This leads to the establishment of realistic performance goals for a job.
2. Carefully select workers with the right abilities for the task.

FIGURE 2.2

The historical perspective: three viewpoints—classical, behavioral, and quantitative

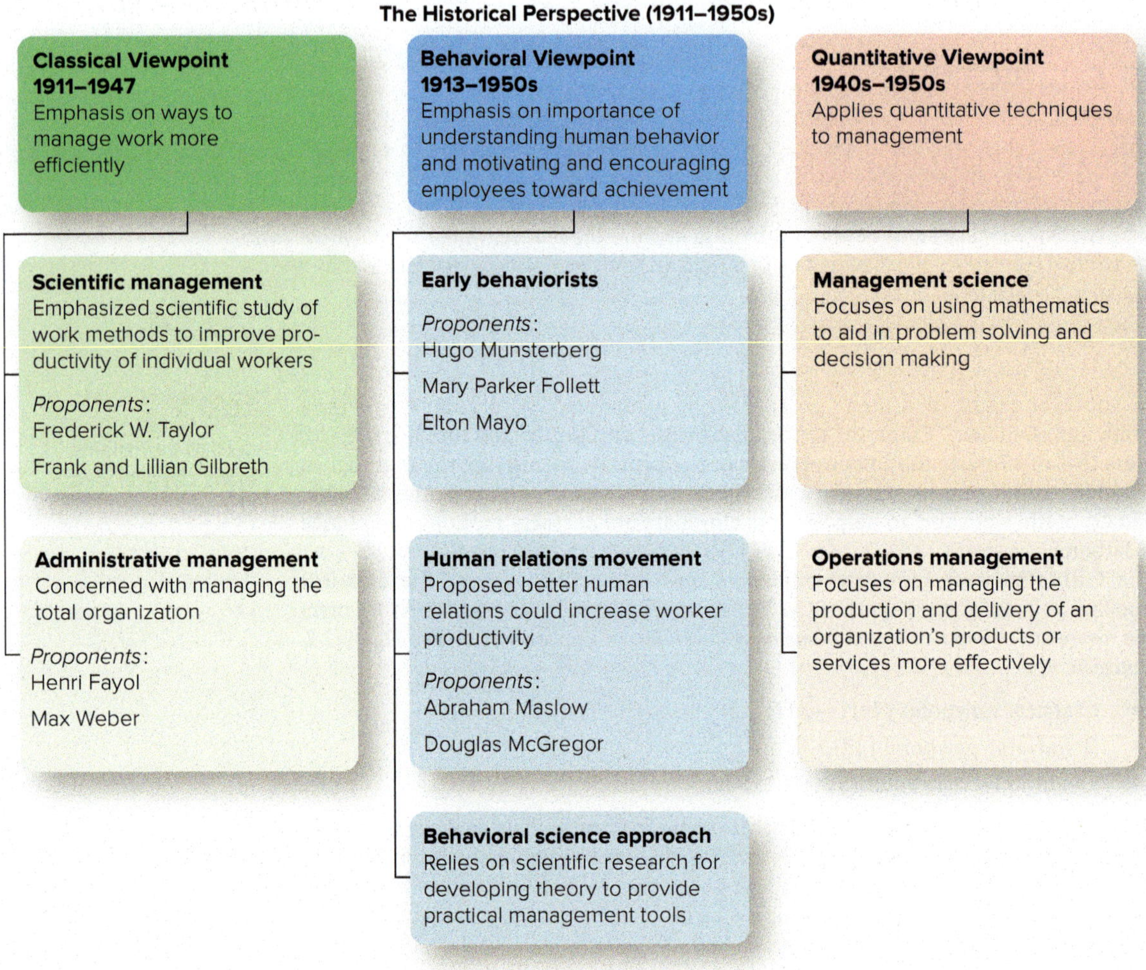

Frederick W. Taylor. Called the father of scientific management, Taylor published *The Principles of Scientific Management* in 1911. ©Bettmann/Getty Images

3. Give workers the training and incentives to do the task with the proper work methods.
4. Use scientific principles to plan the work methods and ease the way for workers to do their jobs.

Taylor based his system on *motion studies,* in which he broke down each worker's job–moving pig iron at a steel company, say–into basic physical motions and then trained workers to use the methods of their best-performing co-workers. He suggested employers institute a *differential rate system,* in which more efficient workers earned higher rates of pay.

Why Taylor Is Important: "Taylorism" met considerable resistance from workers, who feared it would lead to lost jobs except for the highly productive few. In fact, Taylor believed that increasing production would benefit both labor and management by increasing profits to the point where they no longer had to quarrel over them. If used correctly, the principles of scientific management can enhance productivity, and innovations like motion studies and differential pay are still used today.

Lillian and Frank Gilbreth with 11 of their dozen children. As industrial engineers, the Gilbreths pioneered time and motion studies. If you're an athlete, you can appreciate how small changes can make you more efficient. ©Bettmann/Getty Images

Frank and Lillian Gilbreth and Industrial Engineering Frank and Lillian Gilbreth's experiences raising 12 children—to which they applied some of their ideas about improving efficiency—were later popularized in a book, two movies, and a TV sitcom, *Cheaper by the Dozen*. The Gilbreths expanded on Taylor's motion studies—for instance, by using movie cameras to film workers in order to isolate the parts of a job.

Lillian Gilbreth, who received a PhD in psychology, was the first woman to be a major contributor to management science.

Administrative Management: Pioneered by Spaulding, Fayol, and Weber

Scientific management is concerned with the jobs of individuals. **Administrative management is concerned with managing the total organization.** Among the pioneering theorists were Charles Clinton Spaulding, Henri Fayol, and Max Weber.

Charles Clinton Spaulding and the "Fundamental Necessities" of Management Spaulding was the son of a farmer and had 13 siblings. He proposed eight "necessities" of management based on his experiences working at his father's fields as a boy and later leading the North Carolina Mutual Life Insurance Company. He is recognized as the "Father of African-American Management" and published his classic article in the *Pittsburgh Courier* in 1927.[17]

Why Spaulding Is Important: Spaulding's "necessities" went beyond the task-orientation of scientific management, thereby broadening the view of what it takes to effectively manage people and organizations. He suggested that considerations such as the need for authority, division of labor, adequate capital, proper budgeting, and cooperation and teamwork were essential for smooth organizational operations. He also was one of the first management practitioners to highlight the need to enrich "the lives of his organizational and community family" while simultaneously focusing on making a profit.[18]

Henri Fayol and the Functions of Management Fayol was not the first to investigate management behavior, but he was the first to systematize it. A French engineer and industrialist, he became known to American business when his most important work, *General and Industrial Management,* was translated into English in 1930.

Why Fayol Is Important: Fayol was the first to identify the major functions of management—planning, organizing, leading, and controlling, as well as coordinating—the first four of which you'll recognize as the functions providing the framework for this and most other management books.[19]

Max Weber and the Rationality of Bureaucracy In our time, the word *bureaucracy* has come to have negative associations: impersonality, inflexibility, red tape, a molasses-like response to problems. But to German sociologist Max Weber, a *bureaucracy* was a rational, efficient, ideal organization based on principles of logic. After all, in Weber's Germany in the late 19th century, many people were in positions of authority (particularly in the government) not because of their abilities but because of their social status. The result, Weber wrote, was that they didn't perform effectively.

A better-performing organization, he felt, should have five positive bureaucratic features:

1. A well-defined hierarchy of authority.
2. Formal rules and procedures.
3. A clear division of labor, with parts of a complex job being handled by specialists.
4. Impersonality, without reference or connection to a particular person.
5. Careers based on merit.

Why Weber Is Important: Weber's work was not translated into English until 1947, but it came to have an important influence on the structure of large corporations, such as the Coca-Cola Company.

The Problem with the Classical Viewpoint: Too Mechanistic

A flaw in the classical viewpoint is that it is mechanistic: It tends to view humans as cogs within a machine, not taking into account the importance of human needs. Behavioral theory addressed this problem, as we explain next.

Why the Classical Viewpoint Is Important: The essence of the classical viewpoint was that work activity was amenable to a rational approach, that through the application of scientific methods, time and motion studies, and job specialization it was possible to boost productivity. Indeed, these concepts are still in use today, the results visible to you every time you visit McDonald's or Pizza Hut. The classical viewpoint also led to such innovations as management by objectives and goal setting. ●

Scientific management. Carmakers have broken down automobile manufacturing into its constituent tasks, as shown here for an assembly plant. This reflects the contributions of the school of scientific management. Is there anything wrong with this approach? How could it be improved? ©RainerPlendl/Getty Images

2.3 Behavioral Viewpoint: Behaviorism, Human Relations, and Behavioral Science

THE BIG PICTURE

The second of the three historical management perspectives was the *behavioral* viewpoint, which emphasized the importance of understanding human behavior and of motivating employees toward achievement. The behavioral viewpoint developed over three phases: (1) *Early behaviorism* was pioneered by Hugo Munsterberg, Mary Parker Follett, and Elton Mayo. (2) The *human relations movement* was pioneered by Abraham Maslow (who proposed a hierarchy of needs) and Douglas McGregor (who proposed a Theory X and Theory Y view to explain managers' attitudes toward workers). (3) The *behavioral science approach* relied on scientific research for developing theories about behavior useful to managers.

LO 2-3

Describe the principles of the behavioral view of management.

The **behavioral viewpoint emphasized the importance of understanding human behavior and of motivating employees toward achievement.** The behavioral viewpoint developed over three phases: (1) early behaviorism, (2) the human relations movement, and (3) behavioral science.

Early Behaviorism: Pioneered by Munsterberg, Follett, and Mayo

The three people who pioneered behavioral theory were Hugo Munsterberg, Mary Parker Follett, and Elton Mayo.

Hugo Munsterberg and the First Application of Psychology to Industry

Called "the father of industrial psychology," German-born Hugo Munsterberg had a PhD in psychology and a medical degree and joined the faculty at Harvard University in 1892. Munsterberg suggested that psychologists could contribute to industry in three ways. They could:

1. Study jobs and determine which people are best suited to specific jobs.
2. Identify the psychological conditions under which employees do their best work.
3. Devise management strategies to influence employees to follow management's interests.

Why Munsterberg Is Important: His ideas led to the field of *industrial psychology*, the study of human behavior in workplaces, which is still taught in colleges today.

Mary Parker Follett and Power Sharing among Employees and Managers

A Massachusetts social worker and social philosopher, Mary Parker Follett was lauded on her death in 1933 as "one of the most important women America has yet produced in the fields of civics and sociology." Instead of following the usual hierarchical arrangement of managers as order givers and employees as order takers, Follett thought organizations should become more democratic, with managers and employees working cooperatively.

The following ideas were among her most important:

1. Organizations should be operated as "communities," with managers and subordinates working together in harmony.
2. Conflicts should be resolved by having managers and workers talk over differences and find solutions that would satisfy both parties—a process she called *integration*.

3. The work process should be under the control of workers with the relevant knowledge, rather than of managers, who should act as facilitators.

Why Follett Is Important: With these and other ideas, Follett anticipated some of today's concepts of "self-managed teams," "worker empowerment," and "interdepartmental teams"—that is, members of different departments working together on joint projects.

Elton Mayo and the Supposed "Hawthorne Effect"

Do you think workers would be more productive if they thought they were receiving special attention? This was the conclusion drawn by a Harvard research group in the late 1920s.

Conducted by Elton Mayo and his associates at Western Electric's Hawthorne (Chicago) plant, what came to be called the *Hawthorne studies* began with an investigation into whether workplace lighting level affected worker productivity. (This was the type of study that Taylor or the Gilbreths might have done.) In later experiments, other variables were altered, such as wage levels, rest periods, and length of workday. Worker performance varied but tended to increase over time, leading Mayo and his colleagues to hypothesize what came to be known as the **Hawthorne effect**—**namely, that employees worked harder if they received added attention, if they thought that managers cared about their welfare and that supervisors paid special attention to them.**

Elton Mayo. In the 1920s, Elton Mayo (shown with long cigarette holder) and his team conducted studies of Western Electric's Hawthorne plant. Do you think you'd perform better in a robotlike job if you thought your supervisor cared about you and paid more attention to you?
©AP Images

However, later investigators found flaws in the studies, such as variations in ventilation and lighting or inadequate follow-through, that were overlooked by the original researchers. Critics also point out that it's doubtful that workers improved their productivity merely on the basis of receiving more attention rather than because of a particular instructional method or social innovation.[20]

Why the Hawthorne Studies Are Important: Ultimately, the Hawthorne studies were faulted for being poorly designed and not having enough empirical data to support the conclusions. Nevertheless, they succeeded in drawing attention to the importance of "social man" (social beings) and how managers using good human relations could improve worker productivity. This in turn led to the so-called human relations movement in the 1950s and 1960s.

The Human Relations Movement: Pioneered by Maslow and McGregor

The two theorists who contributed most to the **human relations movement**—**which proposed that better human relations could increase worker productivity**—were Abraham Maslow and Douglas McGregor.

Abraham Maslow and the Hierarchy of Needs

What motivates you to perform: Food? Security? Love? Recognition? Self-fulfillment? Probably all of these, Abraham Maslow would say, although some needs must be satisfied before others. The chairman of the psychology department at Brandeis University and one of the earliest researchers to study motivation, in 1943 Maslow proposed his famous *hierarchy of human needs:* physiological, safety, love, esteem, and self-actualization.[21]

We discuss this hierarchy in detail in Chapter 12, where we explain why Maslow is important.

Douglas McGregor and Theory X versus Theory Y Having been a college president for a time (at Antioch College in Ohio), Douglas McGregor came to realize that it was not enough for managers to try to be liked; they also needed to be aware of their attitudes toward employees.[22] Basically, McGregor suggested in a 1960 book, these attitudes could be thought of either "X" or "Y," which we introduced in the chapter opener about people-focused organizations.

Theory X represents a pessimistic, negative view of workers. In this view, workers are considered to be irresponsible, to be resistant to change, to lack ambition, to hate work, and to want to be led rather than to lead.

Theory Y represents a human relations outlook–an optimistic, positive view of workers as capable of accepting responsibility, having self-direction and self-control, and being imaginative and creative.

Why Theory X/Theory Y Is Important: The principal contribution offered by the Theory X/Theory Y perspective is that it helps managers understand how their beliefs affect their behavior. For example, Theory X managers are more likely to micromanage, which leads to employee dissatisfaction, because they believe employees are inherently lazy.

I'm glad I...
...work in an organization with a Theory Y culture.

Cameron Monkelien works in the banking industry as a team leader. He believes his company does a great job of making employees at all levels feel **included** and **empowered**.

Cameron Monkelien Courtesy Cameron Monkelien

Cameron works for a large company with a popular name and a lot of power, but, as Cameron puts it, "It really has its head on its shoulders. They give a lot of tools and capabilities to everybody—not just supervisors and managers, but all the way down to the bottom level."

Cameron feels interconnected with all aspects of his job because of the documentation and networking his company has worked many years to build. "There isn't a guessing game where you have to figure out who you need to talk to or where you need to go to get information. That's something that a lot of my other jobs didn't have: a database and network of people and documents that point you in the right direction in any given situation," said Cameron.

Another way that the company works to make its employees feel included is to have monthly meetings where employees can interact with people other than their direct supervisors. This helps employees to feel like upper management is listening to their concerns and ideas, and that they can really make a difference within the organization.

Cameron also feels safe to take risks and make mistakes rather than fearing the consequences of doing so. "I have personally taken several risks because I have enough confidence in my performance and belief in my team that I can go out on a limb for them and for myself," said Cameron. But ultimately, Cameron believes his direct supervisor cultivates an environment where employees feel safe to take risks and make mistakes. "My supervisor does a really good job about not coming down on us when something goes wrong. Instead she asks, 'How can we improve this going forward?'"

Cameron takes this lesson from his supervisor and works to make sure his own employees feel safe taking risks. "The first time one of my employees had a setback was almost two years into his role. He felt like it was such a personal defeat on his part. I had to have a discussion with him where I said, 'Having a failure does not mean that you are a failure. It means that there is still room for growth, room for learning, and room for improvement.'"

Cameron's company has taken additional steps to create an environment of empowerment by changing some of the job titles. "Instead of being a manager or a supervisor, you get the title of 'leader' because it instills the idea that instead of being in charge of your employees, you are leading them."

Courtesy of Cameron Monkelien

Underlying both Maslow's and McGregor's theories is the notion that more job satisfaction leads to greater worker performance–an idea that is somewhat controversial, as we'll discuss in Chapter 11.

What is your basic view of human nature? Your attitude could be key to your career success. To see the general direction of your outlook, try the following self-assessment if your instructor assigns it to you.

SELF-ASSESSMENT 2.1

What Is Your Orientation: Toward Theory X/Theory Y?

This self-assessment is designed to reveal your orientation as a manager—whether it tends toward Theory X or Theory Y.

Please be prepared to answer these questions if your instructor has assigned Self-Assessment 2.1 in Connect.

1. To what extent do you think your results are an accurate reflection of your beliefs about others? Are you surprised by the results?
2. As a leader of a student or work-related project team, how might your results affect your approach toward leading others? Explain.
3. If an employee doesn't seem to show ambition, can that be changed? Discuss.

The Behavioral Science Approach

The human relations movement was a necessary correction to the sterile approach used within scientific management, but its optimism came to be considered too simplistic for practical use. More recently, the human relations view has been superseded by the behavioral science approach to management. **Behavioral science approach relies on scientific research for developing theories about human behavior that can be used to provide practical tools for managers.** The disciplines of behavioral science include psychology, sociology, anthropology, and economics. •

EXAMPLE Application of Behavioral Science Approach: The Open-Plan Office—Productivity Enhancer or Productivity Killer?

Today as many as 80% of U.S. office spaces have an open floor plan,[23] mixing managers and workers in completely open offices, often using shared tables and desks.[24]

When the concept originated in the 1950s, its purpose was to "facilitate communication and idea flow," according to one report.[25] Other goals were to save money (because such spaces are cheap to build[26]) and to increase productivity. The idea was not only that open spaces encourage collaboration but also that workers are discouraged from wasting time if everyone can see them. But do open-plan offices work? The latest results suggest they are a mixed blessing at best.

Noise is one of the biggest distractions of open work spaces. When people are actively collaborating or socializing in a large room without walls, the sound of their conversation is hard to ignore and can even be amplified by the open space. The same goes for the sound of phones ringing and desktop alerts going off, or even worse, the sound of someone eating lunch or having a personal phone conversation. Some workers respond to the stress that can result from such constant distractions and over-stimulation by emotionally isolating themselves, using rooms intended for private meetings as their personal offices, or even repeatedly calling in sick or working from home. Headphones are one of the most common ways not only to block out noise distractions but to send the message, "Please don't interrupt me now." All this evidence tends to weigh against the idea that working without walls will encourage people to work together more often, more productively, or more creatively.

"Visual noise" is a distraction too. As a *Wall Street Journal* article[27] reports, "Visual noise, the activity or movement around the edges of an employee's field of vision, can erode concentration and disrupt analytical thinking or creativity." It's almost impossible, for instance, to see a group of co-workers gathering nearby and not wonder what they are talking about, or to keep your focus when co-workers are visibly and chronically late.

©Kelvin Murray/Taxi/Getty Images

One study[28] of more than 40,000 U.S. workers in 300 different office buildings concluded that the expected benefits of open-plan offices showed were outweighed by the noise and lack of privacy. Some research suggests that even employee relationships are better when everyone has an office than when they are all in the same room.[29] Apple is moving 12,000 employees to a new 175-acre campus in Cupertino, CA, where many of them are reportedly going to be working at long tables rather than in cubicles or offices. *Business Inside* reports that one Apple team has requested a different location for its workspace, and a blogger who follows the company says some employees have threatened to quit over their unhappiness with the new floor plan.[30]

A team of researchers studied seating arrangements from over 2,000 employees of a large technology company. Results showed that 10% of a person's performance spills over to those nearby. If you want to improve your performance, try to get a desk near a high performer. The researchers estimated that "a strategic seating chart" could bring in $1 million in annual profit from greater productivity for an organization of 2,000 workers.[31]

YOUR CALL

If so many U.S. employees now work in open offices, yet behavioral science studies largely show they are not a productive or beneficial arrangement, why do you suppose they continue to be so prevalent? What kind of office arrangements do you think would work best and why?

2.4 Quantitative Viewpoints: Management Science and Operations Management

THE BIG PICTURE

The third and last category under historical perspectives consists of *quantitative viewpoints,* which emphasize the application to management of quantitative techniques, such as statistics and computer simulations. Two approaches of quantitative management are *management science* and *operations management.*

LO 2-4

Discuss the two quantitative approaches to solving problems.

During the air war known as the Battle of Britain in World War II, a relative few of England's Royal Air Force fighter pilots and planes were able to successfully resist the overwhelming might of the German military machine. How did they do it? Military planners drew on mathematics and statistics to determine how to most effectively allocate use of their limited aircraft.

When the Americans entered the war in 1941, they used the British model to form *operations research (OR)* teams to determine how to deploy troops, submarines, and other military personnel and equipment most effectively. For example, OR techniques were used to establish the optimum pattern that search planes should fly to try to locate enemy ships.

American engineer Jack Kilby invented the first integrated circuit, also known as a silicon chip by using quantitative methods. He was awarded the Nobel Prize in Physics in 2000. Chips like this have brought tremendous changes in our lives including computers, smartphones, and GPS. ©WidStock/Alamy Stock Photo

After the war, businesses also began using these techniques. One group of former officers, who came to be called the Whiz Kids, used statistical techniques at Ford Motor Co. to make better management decisions. Later Whiz Kid Robert McNamara, who had become Ford's president, was appointed Secretary of Defense and introduced similar statistical techniques and cost-benefit analyses throughout the Department of Defense. Since then, OR techniques have evolved into **quantitative management, the application to management of quantitative techniques, such as statistics and computer simulations. Two branches of quantitative management are *management science* and *operations management.***

Management Science: Using Mathematics to Solve Management Problems

How would you go about deciding how to assign utility repair crews during a blackout? Or how many package sorters you needed and at which times for an overnight delivery service such as FedEx or UPS? You would probably use the tools of management science.

Management science is not the same as Taylor's scientific management. **Management science focuses on using mathematics to aid in problem solving and decision making.** Sometimes management science is called *operations research.*

Why Management Science Is Important: Management science stresses the use of rational, science-based techniques and mathematical models to improve decision making and strategic planning. Management science is a forerunner to analytics and Big Data, as we will discuss in Chapter 7.

FedEx. FedEX uses a variety of management science tools to schedule employees and aircraft to deal with wide variations in package volume—such as December 23 versus December 26.
©Jim Weber/The Commercial Appeal/ZUMAPRESS.com/Alamy Stock Photo

Operations Management: Being More Effective

Operations management focuses on managing the production and delivery of an organization's products or services more effectively. In the day-to-day running of the company, it consists of all the job functions and activities in which managers schedule and delegate work and job training, plan production to meet customer needs, design services customers want and how to deliver them, locate and design company facilities, and choose optimal levels of product inventory to keep costs down and reduce backorders. It governs managers' decisions about how to increase productivity and efficiency, as well as how to achieve the highest possible quality of both goods and services. Another major function of operations management is managing the supply chain, which is the process of creating the product, starting with designing and obtaining raw materials for physical goods or technology for services and going all the way through delivery to customers' hands, and sometimes even beyond to responsible disposal or recycling.

Why Operations Management Is Important: Through the rational management of resources and distribution of goods and services, operations management helps ensure that business operations are efficient and effective. •

EXAMPLE Operations Management at Intel

Intel is a leading global maker of semiconductors for computers and other electronic devices. It retains that status by functioning as a highly efficient operation, thanks to its well-oiled operations management functions. For instance, operations management helps keep the design process efficient by focusing it on keeping costs down and using resources sustainably. Intel gathers market research about its products from customers and distributors to feed into its quality control processes and even to help shape the company's overall strategies for future growth, based on what customers may need in the future. Managers develop different kinds of schedules for different kinds of processes, such as short-term manufacturing schedules for products made in batches like microprocessors, or ongoing schedules for tasks done on a continuous basis like equipment maintenance. Inventory is managed by the proven "first in, first out" or FIFO method. The sustainability of the supply chain is constantly monitored via computer systems and databases that can head off potential problems in the flow of manufacturing components in or finished products out.[32]

YOUR CALL

In Chapter 1, we described the problem of "efficiency versus effectiveness." Does it seem that Intel has chosen efficiency over effectiveness, or does it demonstrate both?

2.5 Systems Viewpoint

THE BIG PICTURE

Three contemporary management perspectives are (1) the *systems,* (2) the *contingency,* and (3) the *quality-management* viewpoints. The *systems viewpoint* sees organizations as a system, either open or closed, with inputs, outputs, transformation processes, and feedback. The systems viewpoint has led to the development of complexity theory, the study of how order and pattern arise from very complicated, apparently chaotic systems. The *contingency viewpoint* emphasizes that a manager's approach should vary according to the individual and environmental situation. It is a forerunner to evidence-based management. The *quality-management viewpoint* has two traditional approaches: *quality control,* the strategy for minimizing errors by managing each stage of production, and *quality assurance,* which focuses on the performance of workers, urging employees to strive for zero defects. A third quality approach is the movement of *total quality management (TQM),* a comprehensive approach dedicated to continuous quality improvement, training, and customer satisfaction.

LO 2-5

Identify takeaways from the systems view of management.

Being of a presumably practical turn of mind, could you run an organization or a department according to the theories you've just learned? Probably not. The reason: People are complicated. To be an exceptional manager, you need to learn to deal with individual differences in a variety of settings.

Thus, to the historical perspective on management (classical, behavioral, and quantitative viewpoints), let us now add the *contemporary perspective,* which consists of three viewpoints. *(See Figure 2.3.)*

- Systems
- Contingency
- Quality-management

In this section, we discuss the systems viewpoint.

FIGURE 2.3

The contemporary perspective: three viewpoints—systems, contingency, and quality-management

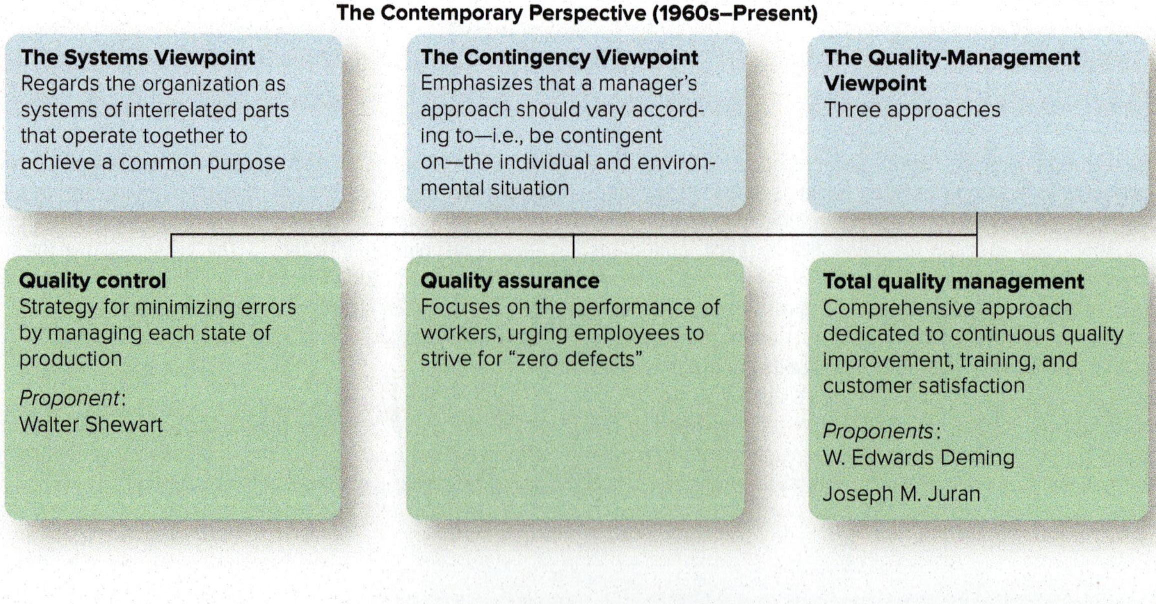

The Systems Viewpoint

The 27 bones in the hand. The monarchy of Great Britain. A weather storm front. Each of these is a system. **A system is a set of interrelated parts that operate together to achieve a common purpose.** Even though a system may not work very well—as in the inefficient way the Italian government collects taxes, for example—it is nevertheless still a system.

The systems viewpoint regards the organization as a system of interrelated parts. By adopting this point of view, you can look at your organization both as (1) a collection of **subsystems—parts making up the whole system**—and (2) a part of the larger environment. A college, for example, is made up of a collection of academic departments, support staffs, students, and the like. But it also exists as a system within the environment of education, having to be responsive to parents, alumni, legislators, nearby townspeople, and so on.

The Four Parts of a System

The vocabulary of the systems perspective is useful because it gives you a way of understanding many different kinds of organizations. The four parts of a system are defined as follows:

1. **Inputs are the people, money, information, equipment, and materials required to produce an organization's goods or services.** Whatever goes into a system is an input.
2. **Transformational processes are the organization's capabilities in management, internal processes, and technology that are applied to converting inputs into outputs.** The main activity of the organization is to transform inputs into outputs.
3. **Outputs are the products, services, profits, losses, employee satisfaction or discontent, and the like that are produced by the organization.** Whatever comes out of the system is an output.
4. **Feedback is information about the reaction of the environment to the outputs that affects the inputs.** Are the customers buying or not buying the product? That information is feedback.

The four parts of a system are illustrated in *Figure 2.4*.

FIGURE 2.4

The four parts of a system

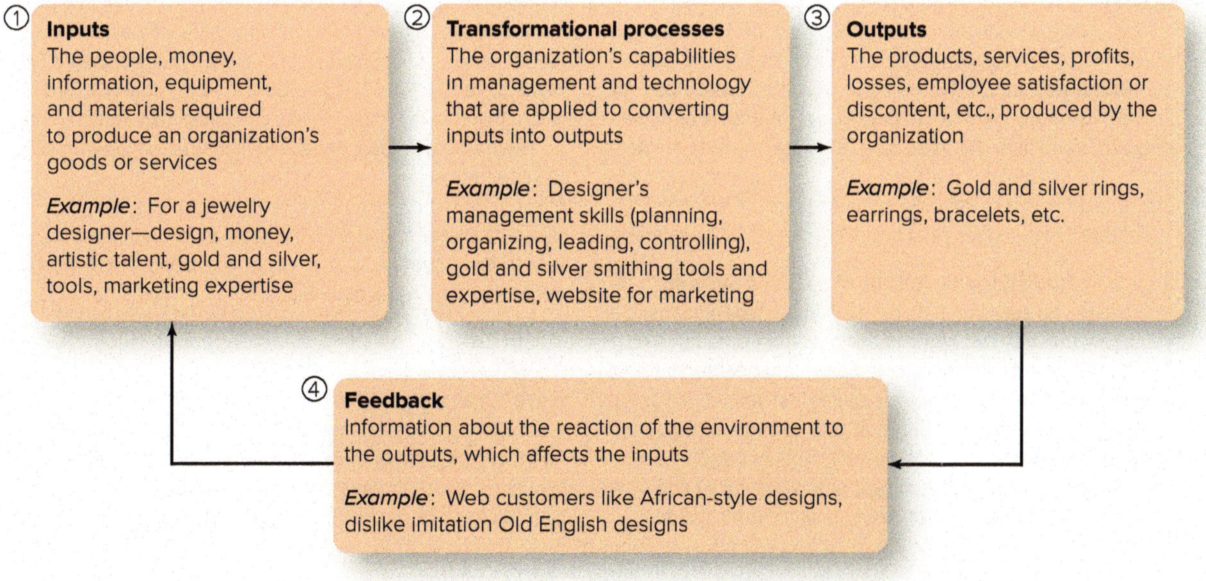

Closed Systems, Open Systems, and the Concept of Synergy A **closed system has little interaction with its environment**; that is, it receives very little feedback from the outside. The classical management viewpoint often considered an organization a closed system. So does the management science perspective, which simplifies organizations for purposes of analysis. However, any organization that ignores feedback from the environment opens itself up to possibly spectacular failures.

An **open system continually interacts with its environment.** Today nearly all organizations are, at least to some degree, open systems rather than closed. Open systems have the potential of producing synergy. **Synergy (pronounced "*sin*-ur-jee") is the idea that two or more forces combined create an effect that is greater than the sum of their individual effects,** as when a guitarist, drummer, and bassist combine to play a better version of a song than any of them would playing alone. Or a copywriter, art director, and photographer combine to create a magazine ad, each representing various influences from the environment.

Complexity Theory: The Ultimate Open System The systems viewpoint has led to the development of **complexity theory, the study of how order and pattern arise from very complicated, apparently chaotic systems.** Complexity theory recognizes that all complex systems are networks of many interdependent parts that interact with each other according to certain simple rules. Used in strategic management and organizational studies, the discipline seeks to understand how organizations, considered as relatively simple and partly connected structures, adapt to their environments.

Why the Systems Viewpoint—Particularly the Concept of Open Systems—Is Important: History is full of accounts of products that failed (such as the 1959 Ford Edsel) because they were developed in closed systems and didn't have sufficient feedback. Open systems stress multiple feedback from both inside and outside the organization, resulting in a continuous learning process to try to correct old mistakes and avoid new ones. ●

EXAMPLE Do Nudges Achieve Results? Using the Systems Viewpoint to Find Out

What does it take to change your mind? Can a small nudge or incentive motivate you to make a big decision?

Richard H. Thaler thinks so. Thaler is a professor at the University of Chicago who has long championed the field of behavioral economics. He recently won the Nobel Prize for Economics for his many years of work on the effects of human bias and irrationality. His work built "a bridge between the economic and psychological analyses of individual decision making," according to the Royal Swedish Academy of Sciences.[33]

Let's see how nudges work in the real world of student loans.

Repaying Student Loans: Results of a Closed System. If after college you are struggling to repay your student loans, did you know that you can apply to the government to have your monthly payments reduced to a more manageable share of your income? The government mandates that you are obligated to repay your debt, but in this alternate arrangement you are allowed to do so more slowly. However, lots of borrowers who are new to repayment are unaware of this possibility and miss their first payments. This is an example of a closed system.

Repaying Student Loans: Results of an Open System. The problem, observes economist Justin Wolfers, is that few people are aware of this possibility of making reduced payments over a longer period of time, and so few apply. "That's a shame," says Wolfers, "because the federal government actually knows who is struggling to repay their loans and could help them directly."

How would things be different under an open system? Researchers sent e-mails to student loan borrowers who had missed their first payments reminding them that they had missed a payment and directed them to information about different repayment plans. The result was a four-fold increase in applications for repayment plans.[34]

YOUR CALL

Using "small nudges" like this to create open feedback systems and testing their results to see what works has proven successful in reducing use of printing paper, increasing retirement contributions, spurring health care enrollment, and other matters. Can you think of an idea in which you'd like to try small nudges?

2.6 Contingency Viewpoint

THE BIG PICTURE

The second viewpoint in the contemporary perspective, the contingency viewpoint, emphasizes that a manager's approach should vary according to the individual and environmental situation.

LO 2-6

Explain why there is no one best way to manage in all situations.

The classical viewpoints advanced by Taylor, Spaulding, and Fayol assumed that their approaches had universal applications—that they were "the one best way" to manage organizations. The contingency viewpoint began to develop when managers discovered that under some circumstances better results could be achieved by breaking the one-best-way rule. **The contingency viewpoint emphasizes that a manager's approach should vary according to—that is, be contingent on—the individual and the environmental situation.**

A manager subscribing to the Gilbreth approach might try to get workers to be more productive by simplifying the steps. A manager of the Theory X/Theory Y persuasion might try to use motivational techniques. But the manager following the contingency viewpoint would simply ask, "What method is the best to use under these particular circumstances?"

EXAMPLE The Contingency Viewpoint: Manufacturers Pitch Parents to Recruit Their Kids

Parents around the country are increasingly worried about paying for their children to attend college. Young college graduates are worried about succeeding in a tough job market. And U.S. manufacturers are worried about how they're going to fill approximately 400,000 open positions, the highest number reported by the Bureau of Labor Statistics since 2001. What's wrong with this picture?

Some U.S. manufacturers are taking creative steps to recruit workers for critical and well-paid jobs, including reaching out to the parents of young people they hope to hire. "Parents are the missing part of this," said one economic development manager in Colorado.

One engine parts maker in Colorado recently hosted a "Parents' Night" at its plant for about 200 people with high-school age children. As the company's vice president of operations (and lifelong employee) explained, "We're really trying to get after the parents—the parents are influential with their kids. Our message was 'there's another option'" to a four-year college degree. Recruiters from Michelin pitched parents at a recent parents' night hosted by the Greenville SC Chamber of Commerce, offering to hire their children part-time while paying their tuition for a two-year technical program at a local college. Graduates of the program can be hired into full-time jobs at Michelin with starting pay of around $53,000 and generous benefits.[35]

Said one parent who is reconsidering his teenage son's options, "Well, you know, not everyone is an accountant."

YOUR CALL

U.S. manufacturers are trying a novel contingency plan for meeting the challenge of recruiting young people for profitable careers that don't necessarily require a four-year degree. Are there any downsides to their appeal to parents? What other contingency approaches can you suggest to help solve their recruiting problem?

Gary Hamel: Management Ideas Are Not Fixed, They're a Process

Discussion of the contingency viewpoint leads us naturally to the thoughts of **Gary Hamel,** co-founder of the Management Innovation Lab and ranked by *The Wall Street Journal* in 2008 as the most influential business thinker.[36] "Over time," he says, "every great invention, management included, travels a road that leads from birth to maturity, and occasionally to senescence."[37] Hamel holds that much of management theory is dated and doesn't fit the current realities of organizational life and that management innovation is essential to future organizational success. Indeed, he suggests, what we need to do is look at management as a *process,* and then make improvements and innovation ongoing and systematic. After all, if managers now innovate by creating new products or new business strategies, why can't they be equally innovative in how they manage their companies?

How do forward-looking managers get the ball rolling in management innovation, particularly in a traditional, conventional company? Hamel believes that the answer can be found by identifying *core beliefs that people have about the organization,* especially those that detract from the pursuit of management innovation. He suggests that these beliefs can be rooted out by repeatedly asking the right questions—namely, the following:

1. **Is this a belief worth challenging?** Is it debilitating? Does it get in the way of an important organizational attribute that we'd like to strengthen?
2. **Is this belief universally valid?** Are there counterexamples? If so, what do we learn from those cases?
3. **How does this belief serve the interests of its adherents?** Are there people who draw reassurance or comfort from this belief?
4. **Have our choices and assumptions conspired to make this belief self-fulfilling?** Is this belief true simply because we have made it true—and, if so, can we imagine alternatives?[38]

Why the Contingency Viewpoint Is Important: The contingency viewpoint would seem to be the most practical of the viewpoints discussed so far because it addresses problems on a case-by-case basis and varies the solution accordingly.

Evidence-Based Management: Facing Hard Facts, Rejecting Nonsense

Evidence-based management is very much in the spirit of the contingency viewpoint's practical approach to management. **Evidence-based management means translating principles based on best evidence into organizational practice, bringing rationality to the decision-making process.**

As its two principal proponents, Stanford business scholars **Jeffrey Pfeffer** and **Robert Sutton,** put it, evidence-based management is based on the belief that "facing the hard facts about what works and what doesn't, understanding the dangerous half-truths that constitute so much conventional wisdom about management, and rejecting the total nonsense that too often passes for sound advice will help organizations perform better."[39]

Learning to make managerial decisions based on evidence is the approach we hope you will learn to take after studying many other approaches—the perspectives we covered in this chapter. We will consider evidence-based management further, along with analytics and Big Data, in Chapter 7. •

PRACTICAL ACTION Evidence-Based Management: Big Data

Big Data, as the name implies, refers to sets of data so vast and complex that new methods have been developed to analyze them. Businesses and governments will find many applications for the information Big Data can yield. Amazon, Spotify, and Delta Airlines are just a handful of the companies already doing so; about three-quarters of U.S. companies say their competitors are as well.[40]

Drug manufacturers, for instance, can analyze insurance claims, research results, and clinical trial data to accurately demonstrate the benefits of their products, helping them support value-based prices.[41] The Weather Channel combines consumer information with climate data to tailor its sponsors' ads with pinpoint accuracy.[42] Hotels can use Big Data to anticipate the needs of even first-time guests; the hotel-search company Trivago is already capitalizing on Big Data's capabilities to match users with their preferred lodging.[43] Transportation safety, emergency preparedness and response, and climate research are just a few of the government applications of Big Data.[44]

Privacy is an issue users of Big Data must confront. As one writer says, "Transparency and ethical use of data is vital . . . . Companies should do what they can where they can to be transparent and help consumers understand what data they are collecting and for what purpose. The Big Data ecosystem is becoming increasingly complex . . . . Companies who are forthright and build trust will be increasingly important to their customers."[45]

YOUR CALL

Do you think the application of Big Data could stifle managers' creativity?

2.7 Quality-Management Viewpoint

THE BIG PICTURE

The quality-management viewpoint, the third category under contemporary perspectives, consists of *quality control, quality assurance,* and especially the movement of *total quality management (TQM),* dedicated to continuous quality improvement, training, and customer satisfaction.

LO 2-7

Discuss the contributions of the quality-management view.

Although not a "theory" as such, the **quality-management viewpoint**, which includes quality control, quality assurance, and total quality management, deserves to be considered because of its impact on contemporary management perspectives.

Quality Control and Quality Assurance

Quality refers to the total ability of a product or service to meet customer needs. Quality is seen as one of the most important ways of adding value to products and services, thereby distinguishing them from those of competitors. Two traditional strategies for ensuring quality are quality control and quality assurance.

Quality Control

Quality control is defined as the strategy for minimizing errors by managing each stage of production. Quality control techniques were developed in the 1930s at Bell Telephone Labs by **Walter Shewart,** who used statistical sampling to locate errors by testing just some (rather than all) of the items in a particular production run.

Quality Assurance

Developed in the 1960s, **quality assurance** focuses on the performance of workers, urging employees to strive for "zero defects." Quality assurance has been less successful because often employees have no control over the design of the work process.

Total Quality Management: Creating an Organization Dedicated to Continuous Improvement

In the years after World War II, the imprint "Made in Japan" on a product almost guaranteed that it was cheap and flimsy. That began to change with the arrival in Japan of two Americans, **W. Edwards Deming** and **Joseph M. Juran.**

W. Edwards Deming

Desperate to rebuild its war-devastated economy, Japan eagerly received mathematician W. Edwards Deming's lectures on "good management." Deming believed that quality stemmed from "constancy of purpose"—steady focus on an organization's mission—along with statistical measurement and reduction of variations in production processes. He also thought that managers should stress teamwork, be helpful rather than simply give orders, and make employees feel comfortable about asking questions.

Joseph M. Juran

Another pioneer with Deming in Japan's quality revolution was Joseph M. Juran, who defined quality as "fitness for use." By this he meant that a product or service should satisfy a customer's real needs. Thus, the best way to focus a company's efforts, Juran suggested, was to concentrate on the real needs of customers.

TQM: What It Is

From the work of Deming and Juran has come the strategic commitment to quality known as total quality management. **Total quality management** (TQM) is a comprehensive approach—led by top management and supported throughout the organization—dedicated to continuous quality improvement, training, and customer satisfaction.

The four components of TQM are as follows:

1. **Make continuous improvement a priority.** TQM companies are never satisfied. They make small, incremental improvements an everyday priority in all areas of the organization. By improving everything a little bit of the time all the time, the company can achieve long-term quality, efficiency, and customer satisfaction.
2. **Get every employee involved.** To build teamwork, trust, and mutual respect, TQM companies see that every employee is involved in the continuous improvement process. This requires that workers must be trained and empowered to find and solve problems.
3. **Listen to and learn from customers and employees.** TQM companies pay attention to their customers, the people who use their products or services. In addition, employees within the companies listen and learn from other employees, those outside their own work areas.
4. **Use accurate standards to identify and eliminate problems.** TQM organizations are always alert to how competitors do things better, then try to improve on them—a process known as benchmarking. Using these standards, they apply statistical measurements to their own processes to identify problems.

Why Total Quality Management Is Important: The total quality management viewpoint emphasizes infusing concepts of quality throughout the total organization in a way that will deliver quality products and services to customers. The "I Wish My Manager ..." box provides a great illustration. The adoption of TQM helped American companies deal with global competition.

I Wish My Manager...

...believed in a quality-management viewpoint.

Ashley Rippentrop Courtesy Ashley Rippentrop

Ashley Rippentrop works in the home health care industry. When she first began her job as a medical records manager, her company was in the early stages of implementing a computer charting system.

The system was new for both Ashley and the company, and there were a lot of kinks to work out. "The year before I got there, they had just started using the computer charting system. It was intense to jump into because the company was learning the system, and I was learning as I went because I took care of all of the medical records. I filed all of the patient information, and I printed and sent all of the documentation to the doctors' offices and received signed copies back," said Ashley. "But the company hated the new system. They wanted to use the old paper system instead."

While they were working through the kinks of the new process, Ashley started to notice some significant errors. "Something we had a problem with, which was difficult to explain to my manager, was that we were missing orders," said Ashley. "For example, when you call a doctor and ask to prescribe a certain medication to a patient and the doctor says yes, the nurse has to document this and send it in to the doctor to sign for permission and send it back to us. We were missing some of these orders. And there were duplicates of other orders, too."

"It was easy for me to see these errors because I was working with this system every day, but it was hard to describe to my manager because these errors could get the company in trouble legally," said Ashley. If the company did not have a signed order from a doctor giving permission for a patient to use a certain medication, and that patient began to experience negative side effects, the company could be in serious trouble if someone were to inquire about the missing order.

Ashley brought these errors to her manager's attention, but Ashley's ideas were not well-received. "They didn't want to change how they were documenting. They weren't receptive to the information I was trying to give them. Ultimately, they weren't happy with me when I was trying to get them to fix the issue," said Ashley. This began to affect how the company was communicating with the doctors they worked with—some doctors even refused to work with the company due to these issues. There were other legal issues that came about when insurance companies audited them and their paperwork was not in order.

Eventually, Ashley's managers fixed most of the errors, but not without suffering some setbacks due to their **resistance to new ideas and change.**

Courtesy of Ashley Rippentrop

Want to find out how committed to TQM the organizations are that you are most familiar with? Even the most sophisticated organizations, you may be surprised to learn in Self-Assessment 2.2, may not measure up very well when it comes to the quality of their products.

TQM pioneer. W. Edwards Deming in 1961. Deming proposed his so-called 85–15 rule—namely, when things go wrong, there is an 85% chance that the system is at fault, only a 15% chance that the individual worker is at fault. Most of the time, he thought, managers erroneously blamed individuals rather than the system.

Six Sigma and ISO 9000

Two other noteworthy quality management initiatives are Six Sigma and ISO 9000. Six Sigma, as we'll see in Chapter 16, is a rigorous statistical-analysis process that measures and reduces defects in and improves manufacturing and service-related processes. Its name is a reference to the statistical methods behind its goal, which is to have no more than 3.4 defects per million products or procedures.[46]

Six Sigma relies on two processes. The first is **DMAIC, or the series of steps called Define, Measure, Analyze, Improve, and Control, which is intended to improve existing processes.** The second is **DFSS (Design for Six Sigma), which managers can employ to create new products or processes.** Lean Six Sigma is a variation on the original approach that focuses on problem solving and process improvement, combining speed with excellence.

One successful adopter of Lean Six Sigma is the Akron-Canton Regional Foodbank in Ohio, where donated food is now sorted, inspected, packed, and delivered to those in need within 39 days instead of the 92 days it used to take.[47] Staples, the office-supply giant, has deployed Lean Six Sigma to cut four weeks off the time it needs to open a new store, shorten its product-ordering cycle, redesign its loading docks, and make dozens of other changes worth tens of millions of dollars saved.[48]

ISO 9000, also discussed in Chapter 16, is a series of quality-control standards set by the International Organization for Standardization (ISO) to reduce manufacturing flaws and improve productivity. Companies must adopt a set of processes covering business functions like purchasing, manufacturing, inventory, and shipping; carefully document their use of these processes; and train their employees to use them, all of which takes time and financial investment. If they pass an audit by the ISO organization, they become ISO certified, a credential that has been credited with improving a company's marketability and reputation, reducing its costs, improving customer service and customer satisfaction, and even making it more attractive to investors. Of course, quality improvement is the first and foremost goal.[49] More than 1 million companies in 170 countries around the world have adopted ISO standards.[50] •

SELF-ASSESSMENT 2.2

To What Extent Is Your Organization Committed to Total Quality Management?

This self-assessment is designed to gauge the extent to which the organization you have in mind is committed to total quality management (TQM).

Please be prepared to answer these questions if your instructor has assigned Self-Assessment 2.2 in Connect.

1. Which of the five dimensions is most and least important to the organization? Are you surprised by this conclusion? Explain.
2. Based on the three lowest-rated items in the survey, what advice would you give to senior leaders in the company?
3. Considering all of the questions in the survey, which three do you think are most important in terms of fostering TQM in a company? Why?

2.8 The Learning Organization in an Era of Accelerated Change

THE BIG PICTURE

Learning organizations actively create, acquire, and transfer knowledge within themselves and are able to modify their behavior to reflect new knowledge. There are three ways you as a manager can help build a learning organization.

LO 2-8

Define how managers foster a learning organization.

Ultimately, the lesson we need to take from the theories, perspectives, and viewpoints we have described is this: We need to keep on learning. Organizations are the same way: Like people, they must continually learn new things in order to improve and innovate.[51] A key challenge for managers, therefore, is to establish a culture of shared knowledge and values that will enhance their employees' ability to learn—to build so-called learning organizations. An offsetting advantage for tomorrow's managers is that Millennials, now the largest generation ever, don't just appreciate but actively *expect* to have learning opportunities at work.[52]

Learning organizations, says Massachusetts Institute of Technology professor **Peter Senge,** who coined the term, are places "where people continually expand their capacity to create the results they truly desire, where new and expansive patterns of thinking are nurtured, where collective aspiration is set free, and where people are continually learning how to learn together."[53]

The Learning Organization: Handling Knowledge and Modifying Behavior

More formally, a **learning organization** **is an organization that actively creates, acquires, and transfers knowledge within itself and is able to modify its behavior to reflect new knowledge.**[54] Note the three parts:

1. **Creating and acquiring knowledge.** In learning organizations, managers try to actively infuse their organizations with new ideas and information, which are the prerequisites for learning. They acquire such knowledge by constantly scanning their external environments, by hiring new talent and expertise when needed, and by devoting significant resources to training and developing their employees. Another helpful strategy is to maintain a learning culture within the organization, which encourages people to ask questions without negative consequences (such as being made to feel ignorant) and recognizes that differences of opinion, when handled with respect, can often lead to new and better ideas. Also critical to acquiring new knowledge is learning from failure, as Google did when its Google Buzz project fizzled.[55]

A learning organization is like a lightbulb. It must be turned on before it creates value. How do you think organizations promote the value of continually learning? ©Photodisc/Getty Images

The learning organization. In rigid organizations, employees often keep information to themselves. In learning organizations, workers are encouraged to share information with each other—both inside and outside their department. ©Sam Edwards/Getty Images

2. **Transferring knowledge.** American Express and Apple are not only standouts in their business sectors, says management studies professor Robert Grossman, they "nurture top-to-bottom learning cultures."[56] Companies can also institute formal training and career-development programs for their employees; AT&T and Pixar call theirs "universities."[57] Individual managers should actively work at transferring knowledge throughout the organization, reducing barriers to sharing information and ideas among employees. One consultant suggests three strategies for managers: share your personal success story and challenges overcome, be ready to learn any and everything from peers and employees, and align your learning goals for the company with its business goals.[58] Managers should not be afraid to try new technologies to help employees learn; Walmart is using virtual reality to train employees in management and customer service skills and will soon expand its program to all the 150,000 employees who receive training each year.[59]
3. **Modifying behavior.** Learning organizations are nothing if not results oriented. First, managers should make sure the learning or training opportunity meets a real employee or organizational need. Does it solve a specific problem, and how? The link between learning and performance improvement, and the way the improvement will be measured, should be clear to the employee as well.[60] Next, both formal and informal learning experiences should be followed up with surveys or other measures to see whether the employee is applying the new skills or information or needs more coaching or encouragement.[61]

How to Build a Learning Organization: Three Roles Managers Play

To create a learning organization, managers must perform three key functions or roles: (1) *build a commitment to learning,* (2) *work to generate ideas with impact,* and (3) *work to generalize ideas with impact.*[62]

1. **You can build a commitment to learning.** To instill in your employees an intellectual and emotional commitment to the idea of learning, you as a manager need to lead the way by investing in it, publicly promoting it, creating rewards

and symbols of it, and performing similar activities. For example, the CEO of a hospitality company in the Asia Pacific region, curious about why a group of people had gathered in the office on a Saturday morning, decided to investigate. On finding an orientation program for new employees under way, he found himself a chair and stayed for most of the day, listening and contributing along with the others.[63]

2. **You can work to generate ideas with impact.** As a manager, you need to try to generate ideas with impact—that is, ideas that add value for customers, employees, and shareholders—by increasing employee competence through training, experimenting with new ideas, and engaging in other leadership activities. Xerox, for example, hired researchers called "innovation managers" to hunt for inventions and products from start-ups in India that could be adapted for the North American market. Hewlett-Packard used its research lab in India to see how it could adapt mobile phone web-interface applications in Asia and Africa to markets in developed countries.[64]
3. **You can work to generalize ideas with impact.** Besides generating ideas with impact, you can also generalize them—that is, reduce the barriers to learning among employees and within your organization. You can create a climate that reduces conflict, increases communication, promotes teamwork, rewards risk taking, reduces the fear of failure, and increases cooperation. In other words, you can create a psychologically safe and comforting environment that increases the sharing of successes, failures, and best practices.

Based on the given discussion, do you wonder about the specific behaviors that people exhibit in a learning organization? It would be interesting to determine if you have ever worked for such an organization. The following self-assessment was created to evaluate whether an organization you now work for or formerly worked for could be considered a serious learning organization. The survey items provide a good indication of what it takes to become a learning organization. •

SELF-ASSESSMENT 2.3

Are You Working for a Learning Organization?

This self-assessment provides a measure of the extent to which an organization of your choice is a learning organization. Please be prepared to answer these questions if your instructor has assigned Self-Assessment 2.3 in Connect.

1. What are the strengths and weaknesses of this company in terms of being a learning organization?
2. If you were CEO of this organization, what changes would you make based on your survey results? Explain.
3. What suggestions would you make for how this organization might (1) build a commitment to learning, (2) work to generate ideas with impact, and (3) work to generalize ideas with impact? Discuss.
4. How does the learning score for the organization probably compare with the scores of other organizations you are familiar with?

2.9 Career Corner: Managing Your Career Readiness

LO 2-9

Describe how to develop the career readiness competency of *understanding the business.*

Figure 2.5 shows the model of career readiness we discussed in Chapter 1. What does a chapter on management history have to do with your career readiness? How about its application to the **Knowledge** competency of *understanding the business?* This competency was defined in Table 1.2 as the extent to which you understand a company's business and strategies and the needs of its stakeholders. It comes into play whenever you interview for a job.

Recruiters expect you to do some research, just as you would for a class assignment. They want you to act like Sherlock Holmes and do some snooping. That's good for both you and a potential employer in that it helps identify the likely level of fit between the two of you. Good fit, in turn, is associated with more positive work attitudes and task performance, lower intentions to quit, and less job-related stress.[65] Moreover, doing your homework on a company makes you a more attractive job candidate. It shows interest on your part, and recruiters are impressed by the fact that you took the time to learn about the business.[66] It also prepares you to ask smart questions, a behavior recruiters want to see. Remember, sometimes it's the small things like this that land a job.

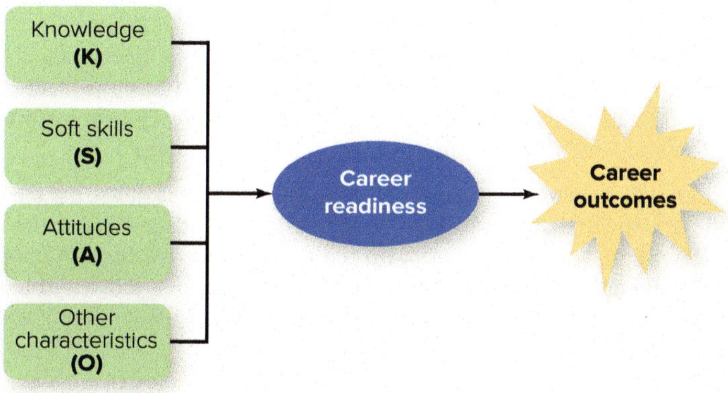

FIGURE 2.5
Model of Career Readiness

So, what does it take to demonstrate that you understand a business? We recommend that you learn the following seven things about a company before showing up at a job interview:[67]

1. **The company's mission and vision statements.** These statements tell you why the company exists and what it wants to become or achieve over time. The question to answer is whether you support these pursuits and would like to be part of the journey. If you do, you will be a better fit for the company. This is important because employees are more likely to be productive and stay at a company when they fit in. For example, if you like outdoor activities, you will most likely be a better fit at Recreational Equipment, Inc. (REI), which sells sporting goods, camping gear, and outdoor clothing, than Whole Foods. You can find this information on the company's website.
2. **The company's core values and culture.** The values an organization endorses represent the foundation of its culture. You can find clues about this by studying a company's website. Try to find a list of company values. What do these

values tell you about the company? Next, look for statements that inform you about how the company treats its employees. For example, does the company support empowerment and employee development? Look at any photos posted online and consider what they tell you. If you see pictures only of products and not of people, for instance, it suggests the company really cares about products. What type of goals is the company pursuing? Does the company care about the environment, quality, or customers' opinions?

3. **The history of the company?** When was the company founded? What were the values and background of the founder? Try to find out how the company evolved, grew, or changed over the years.
4. **Key organizational players.** It's important to demonstrate this knowledge during a job interview. Who holds important positions in the company? What are their backgrounds? You can find this out by reading the employer's "About" page and top employees' bios. You might check them out on LinkedIn or read what they say on Twitter.

You must do research to understand a business. This takes time and attention. At what point in the interview process should you investigate a potential employer? ©Kraska/Shutterstock

5. **The company's products, services, and clients.** What are people saying about the company's products and services? You can explore this by locating reviews or comments about the company's products and services. It would also be useful to try the company's products and services. This would enable you to speak directly from experience.
6. **Current events and accomplishments.** Look for current news stories about the company and examine its website for a list of accomplishments. Note what this information reveals about the company and decide whether it matches what you learned about the company's mission, vision, stated values, and organizational culture. Inconsistencies are a red flag.
7. **Comments from current or previous employees.** Talk to anyone you know at the company. Ask their opinion about working there and how they feel about management and corporate policies. Search websites like Glassdoor to find inside information such as salary ranges and company reviews.

These activities will increase your career readiness and chances of getting a desired job. They also demonstrate that you care or have passion about working at the company. This will differentiate you from others who did not do their research. Remember, it is important to stand out from other applicants when looking for a job. More importantly, understanding the business will help you determine if you are a good fit for an employer. Go get 'em! ●

Key Terms Used in This Chapter

administrative management 49
behavioral science approach 54
behavioral viewpoint 51
classical viewpoint 47
closed system 60
complexity theory 60
contemporary perspective 46
contingency viewpoint 61
DFSS (design for six sigma) 65
DMAIC 65
evidence-based management 62
feedback 59
Hawthorne effect 52
historical perspective 46
human relations movement 52
inputs 59
learning organization 66
management science 56
open system 60
operations management 57
outputs 59
quality 63
quality assurance 63
quality control 63
quality-management viewpoint 63
quantitative management 56
scientific management 47
subsystems 59
synergy 60
system 59
systems viewpoint 59
total quality management (TQM) 63
transformational processes 59

Key Points

2.1 Evolving Viewpoints: How We Got to Today's Management Outlook

- The two overarching perspectives on management are (1) the historical perspective, which includes three viewpoints—classical, behavioral, and quantitative; and (2) the contemporary perspective, which includes three other viewpoints—systems, contingency, and quality-management.
- Six practical reasons for studying theoretical perspectives are that they provide (1) understanding of the present, (2) a guide to action, (3) a source of new ideas, (4) clues to the meaning of your managers' decisions, (5) clues to the meaning of outside ideas, and (6) understanding as to why certain management practices produce positive outcomes.

2.2 Classical Viewpoint: Scientific and Administrative Management

- The first of the historical perspectives was the classical viewpoint, which emphasized finding ways to manage work more efficiently. It had two branches, scientific management and administrative management.
- Scientific management emphasized the scientific study of work methods to improve productivity by individual workers. It was pioneered by Frederick W. Taylor, who offered four principles of science that could be applied to management, and by Frank and Lillian Gilbreth, who refined motion studies that broke job tasks into physical motions.
- Administrative management was concerned with managing the total organization. Among its pioneers were Charles Clinton Spaulding, the "Father of African-American Management"; Henri Fayol, who identified the major functions of management (planning, organizing, leading, controlling); and Max Weber, who identified five positive bureaucratic features in a well-performing organization.
- The classical viewpoint showed that work activity was amenable to a rational approach, but it has been criticized as being too mechanistic, viewing humans as cogs in a machine.

2.3 Behavioral Viewpoint: Behaviorism, Human Relations, and Behavioral Science

- The second of the historical perspectives, the behavioral viewpoint emphasized the importance of understanding human behavior and of motivating employees toward achievement. It developed over three phases: (1) early behaviorism, (2) the human relations movement, and (3) the behavioral science approach.
- Early behaviorism had three pioneers: (a) Hugo Munsterberg suggested that psychologists could contribute to industry by studying jobs, identifying the psychological conditions for employees to do their best work; (b) Mary Parker Follett thought organizations should be democratic, with employees and managers working together; (c) Elton Mayo hypothesized a so-called Hawthorne effect, suggesting that employees worked harder if they received added attention from managers.
- The human relations movement suggested that better human relations could increase worker productivity. Among its pioneers were (a) Abraham Maslow, who proposed a hierarchy of human needs, and (b) Douglas McGregor, who proposed a Theory X (managers have pessimistic view of workers) and Theory Y (managers have positive view of workers).
- The behavioral science approach relied on scientific research for developing theories about human behavior that can be used to provide practical tools for managers.

2.4 Quantitative Viewpoints: Management Science and Operations Management

- The third of the historical perspectives, quantitative viewpoints emphasized the application to management of quantitative techniques.
- Two approaches are (1) management science, which focuses on using mathematics to aid in problem solving and decision making; and (2) operations management, which focuses on managing the production and delivery of an organization's products or services more effectively.

2.5 Systems Viewpoint

- Following the historical perspective, the contemporary perspective includes three viewpoints: (1) systems, (2) contingency, and (3) quality-management.
- The systems viewpoint regards the organization as a system of interrelated parts or collection of subsystems that operate together to achieve a common purpose. A system has four parts: inputs, outputs, transformational processes, and feedback.
- A system can be closed, having little interaction with the environment, or open, continually interacting with it.
- Open systems have the potential of producing synergy, the idea that two or more forces combined create an effect that is greater than the sum of their individual efforts.
- The systems viewpoint has led to the development of complexity theory, the study of how order and pattern arise from very complicated, apparently chaotic systems.

2.6 Contingency Viewpoint

- The second viewpoint in the contemporary perspective, the contingency viewpoint emphasizes that a manager's approach should vary according to the individual and the environmental situation.
- In the spirit of the contingency viewpoint is evidence-based management, which means translating principles based on best evidence into organizational practice, bringing rationality to the decision-making process.

2.7 Quality-Management Viewpoint

- The third category in the contemporary perspective, the quality-management viewpoint is concerned with quality, the total ability of a product or service to meet customer needs.
- Quality management has three aspects: (1) quality control is the strategy for minimizing errors by managing each stage of production; (2) quality assurance focuses on the performance of workers, urging employees to strive for "zero defects"; (3) total quality management (TQM) is a comprehensive approach dedicated to continuous quality improvement, training, and customer satisfaction.
- TQM has four components: (a) make continuous improvement a priority; (b) get every employee involved; (c) listen to and learn from customers and employees; and (d) use accurate standards to identify and eliminate problems.

2.8 The Learning Organization in an Era of Accelerated Change

- A learning organization is one that actively creates, acquires, and transfers knowledge within itself and is able to modify its behavior to reflect new knowledge.
- Three roles that managers must perform to build a learning organization are to (1) build a commitment to learning, (2) work to generate ideas with impact, and (3) work to generalize ideas with impact.

2.9 Career Corner: Managing Your Career Readiness

- You can increase the competency of *understanding the business* by engaging in seven activities. They are: (1) learn the company's mission and vision, (2) identify the company's core values and culture, (3) learn the history of the company, (4) identify the key organizational players, (5) learn about the company's products, services, and clients, (6) study current events and accomplishments about the company, and (7) talk to current or former employees.

Understanding the Chapter: What Do I Know?

1. What are the two overarching perspectives about management, and what are the three viewpoints that each one covers?
2. What are six practical reasons for studying theoretical perspectives?
3. What are the contributions of scientific management?
4. How would I summarize the behavioral viewpoint, and what are its contributions?
5. What is the difference between management science and operations management?
6. What would be an example of the application of the four parts of a system?
7. What would be an example of the application of the contingency viewpoint?
8. Where have I seen an organization employ evidence-based management?
9. Why should I adopt a total quality management viewpoint?
10. What are three roles I could play as a manager in a learning organization?

Management in Action

The Decline of Sears

Sears, Roebuck and Company, commonly called Sears, was founded in 1892 to sell one product–watches. By 1989 the company had grown into the largest retailer in the United States. Sears initially focused on selling its products via a mail-order business that relied on a catalog.[68] "When the catalog first appeared on doorsteps in the 1890s, it fundamentally changed how Americans shopped. Back then, much of the population lived in rural areas, and they bought almost everything from little shops at rural junctions. These general stores had limited selection and charged exorbitant prices. They were the only game in town."[69] Sears' mail-order business was a disruptor.

Over the years Sears evolved along with changing consumer tastes. When people moved from rural areas to cities, for example, the company opened hundreds of standalone urban stores to meet consumers' desire to shop in attractive department stores rather than via catalog. Sears was also one of the first retailers to offer a credit card in the 1980s–the Discover card–that earned cash rewards for customers based on their purchases. This innovation brought in a consistent source of revenue for many years. The next change was to accommodate consumer preferences for shopping at malls. Sears responded by anchoring its stores in malls across the country.

The retail environment started to change in the 1990s, and Sears began to fall behind as discount shopping at Walmart and Kmart took off. These companies were nimbler, changing prices and inventory to meet customer preferences. Sears was more bureaucratic and was stuck with higher overhead costs and catalog prices that had been set months earlier. Not surprisingly, Walmart's revenue grew while Sears' did not. Enter online shopping.

The combination of convenience, selection, speed, and low prices available through online shopping has been a disruptive force for all retailers. Like its competitors, Sears has struggled against online sellers such as Amazon.[70] According to a writer from *USA Today*, however, the venerable retailer faces even deeper challenges: Sears "has also suffered in the wake of its management's decisions, including the sale of its more than $30 billion credit card portfolio to Citibank in 2003, and a merger with Kmart."[71]

THE MERGER OF SEARS AND KMART

In 2004, Sears was acquired by Kmart, a company that was then coming out of bankruptcy. The new firm was christened Sears Holdings and led by Edward Lampert. He had a background in investments but no retail experience at that time.[72]

Some business writers suggest Lambert purchased Sears for the land on which hundreds of its stores stood. According to one writer, "Lampert saw real estate value as the key, and he has managed the two chains as a value play ever since, ignoring the fundamentals of running a retail business. Under Lampert, the company chronically underinvested in store maintenance, spending as little as one-fifth of what its rivals spent to keep stores clean and up to date. The result has been a customer exodus, as no one likes shopping in dilapidated stores."[73]

Another writer described Sears Holdings as having "all the charm of a dollar store without the prices, nor even the service, and with even more disengaged employees. Bright fluorescent lights highlight the drab floors, peeling paint and sad displays of merchandising that are reminiscent of department stores in the communist Soviet Union. Some employees carry iPads, others do not: Lampert's affections for technology led to a policy of employees required to use tablets on the shop floor, even though most clerks said they were unnecessary."[74]

WHAT LED TO SEARS' DECLINE?

Forbes reported that "the popular opinion is that poor management has led to the demise of both companies" (Sears and Kmart). The magazine suggested that Lampert pursued the wrong strategies, assuming the goal was to improve Sears' profitability and long-term survival.[75] Consider the organizational structure Lampert installed at Sears Holdings.

Following a structural model used in the finance industry in which different teams compete for scarce company resources, Lampert segmented the company into 30 autonomous business units such as men's wear, shoes, and home furnishings. Each had its own executive staff and board of directors. Rather than fostering collaboration, this structural arrangement led to "cutthroat competition and sabotage. Incentives were tied to the success of the individual business divisions, which often came at the expense of other parts of the company."[76] A former executive told the *New York Times* that "managers would tell their sales staff not to help customers in adjacent sections, even if someone asked for help. Mr. Lampert would praise polices like these, said the executive."[77]

Another aspect of Lampert's strategy was to spend on technology rather than on stores. Lampert thought Sears was competing against Amazon. He thus "plowed investment, new talent and marketing into Sears' website and a customer loyalty program called Shop Your Way. The program allows customers to earn points, for purchases not only at Sears but at partnering businesses including Burger King, Under Armour, and Uber, that can be redeemed for Sears merchandise."[78] Store appearance languished under this strategy.

WHAT'S THE LATEST?

Sears closed more than 350 stores in 2017 and plans to sell an additional 100 in spring 2018. The company generated much-needed cash by selling off some of its key brands such as Craftsman for about $900 million.[79] It also established new sources of revenue by making a deal to sell "its DieHard-branded products—such as car batteries, jump starters, and tires—on Amazon's website. The retailer also started selling its Kenmore-branded appliances on Amazon" in 2017.[80]

Despite these efforts, Sears is "hemorrhaging money" according to *Business Insider.* "Sales are down 45% since early 2013, its debt load has spiked to $4 billion, and the company is losing well over $1 billion annually."[81]

Making matters worse, "Sears said in a filing with the Securities and Exchange Commission [in 2017] that it had 'substantial doubt' about its ability to stay in business unless it can borrow more and tap cash from assets."[82] The company is definitely pursuing this strategy according to *CNNMoney.* This source reported in 2018 that the company announced it will "cut another $200 million a year (beyond the stores it already planned to close). And it's looking to increase the amount of money it is able to borrow."[83]

According to the *New York Times,* Lampert believes the company can turn things around. He told a reporter that "while there is still work to do, we are determined to do what is necessary to remain a competitive retailer in a challenging environment."[84] Others doubt this conclusion because Lampert is too disengaged from the running of Sears' operations. Former executives say he managed the company from his home in Miami, setting foot in the company headquarters only for its annual meeting.[85]

FOR DISCUSSION

Problem Solving Perspective

1. What is the underlying problem in this case from Edward Lampert's perspective?
2. What are the key causes of Sears' decline?
3. Do you think Lampert can turn the company around? Why or why not?

Application of Chapter Content

1. What does the Human Relations Movement suggest went wrong at Sears?
2. Use the four parts of a system to diagnose the company's decline. Provide support for your conclusions.
3. To what extent did Sears use a total quality management perspective in running its business? Explain.
4. What key lessons from this chapter could Lampert have used to improve Sears' performance following the merger with Kmart? Explain.

Legal/Ethical Challenge

What Should You Do about an Insubordinate Employee?

You are a vice president for a company in the insurance industry, and you supervise five managers. These managers in turn supervise a host of employees working in their departments. Your company is having trouble achieving its sales growth goals and your boss, the president of a division, called a meeting with you and your peers to create a plan of action.

The meeting was a bit volatile because layoffs were proposed and it was agreed that all vice presidents had to decrease their budgets. This means that you and your peers were not allowed to hire consultants or send employees to training. You also have to reduce your labor costs by $300,000. This means that you must lay off employees. You informed the managers that report to you about these decisions and asked them to come up with a list of potential people to lay off. You suggested that performance should be the key criterion for deciding layoffs.

Two weeks later one of your reporting managers walked into your office with a worried look. He told you that Jim, one of your other reporting managers, had just hired a consultant to lead a teambuilding session with his group in another state. Not only did this require significant travel expenses, but the consultant's fees were well outside of your budgeted expenses. Further, your other employees were expressing feelings of unfairness because Jim was taking his team on a teambuilding trip and they were being forced to cut costs. It also was a bit inconsistent to spend money on teambuilding when impending layoffs were just around the corner.

In terms of layoffs, all your reporting managers submitted a list of potential employees to let go except for Jim. You have no idea why he avoided this task.

Jim's behavior clearly violates the agreement that was made about cost cutting, and you are upset that he has not submitted his list of employees to lay off. You have not yet spoken to him about this insubordination, and now you are wondering what to do.

SOLVING THE CHALLENGE

What would you do?

1. Meet with Jim to review his behavior. Tell him that any more acts of insubordination will result in termination. Don't make a big deal about these events and don't include documentation in his personnel file.

2. Put Jim on the list of people to be laid off. Although the company will have to pay him a severance check, it reduces the chance of any lawsuit.
3. Call your human resource representative and discuss the legality of firing Jim. Jim was insubordinate in hiring a consultant and irresponsible for not submitting his list of potential employees to be laid off. If human resources agrees, I would fire Jim.
4. Reprimand Jim by putting him on a Performance Improvement Plan (PIP). This plan outlines specific changes Jim needs to make going forward, and it gives him a chance to make up for his poor decisions.
5. Invent other options. Discuss.

Uber Continuing Case connect

Learn more about Uber's history by considering events that occured under Uber's first CEO, Travis Kalanick, and his replacement, Dara Khsrowshahi. Assess your ability to apply concepts discussed in this chapter to the case by going to Connect.

The Environment of Management

PART 2 • THE ENVIRONMENT OF MANAGEMENT

3 The Manager's Changing Work Environment and Ethical Responsibilities

Doing the Right Thing

After reading this chapter, you should be able to:

LO 3-1 Describe the triple bottom line of people, planet, and profit.

LO 3-2 Identify important stakeholders inside the organization.

LO 3-3 Identify important stakeholders outside the organization.

LO 3-4 Explain the importance of ethics and values in effective management.

LO 3-5 Describe the concept of social responsibility and its role in today's organizations.

LO 3-6 Discuss the role of corporate governance in assessing management performance.

LO 3-7 Describe how to develop the career readiness competency of professionalism/work ethic.

FORECAST *What's Ahead in This Chapter*

The triple bottom line of people, planet, and profit represents new standards of success for businesses. This helps define the new world in which managers must operate and their responsibilities, including the community of stakeholders, both internal and external, they must deal with. The chapter also considers a manager's ethical and social responsibilities, as well as the importance of corporate governance. We conclude with a Career Corner that focuses on how you can develop the career readiness competency of professionalism/work ethic.

MANAGE U

Increase Ethical Behavior by Fostering an Ethical Climate

Just as a car needs gasoline or electric power to run, employees need the right environment to flourish. The term "right environment" refers to what academics call organizational climate. This chapter is concerned with one type of climate, namely an ethical one. An **ethical climate represents employees' perceptions about the extent to which work environments support ethical behavior.** It is important for managers to foster ethical climates because they significantly affect the frequency of ethical behavior, which in turn impacts employee performance and a firm's profitability.[1] Let's consider whether Wells Fargo has an ethical climate.

Ethics at Wells Fargo

It's not often that 5,300 people are fired from a single company—and all for the same reason. At Wells Fargo Bank, however, that's what happened in 2016 when it was discovered that employees throughout the organization had secretly created 3.5 million unauthorized new accounts in order to generate profitable fees from unsuspecting depositors. Under pressure to achieve ambitious sales goals, these employees may have decided it was worth it to cheat in order to meet the company's high (and perhaps unrealistic) expectations. They may have reasoned that the harm to each customer was small compared to the gains to themselves of posting stellar performances. And repetition may have made each transgression easier to rationalize than the last one.[2]

The scandal had lingering effects on Wells Fargo's financial position and led some to think the company would not survive.[3] Could it have been prevented? Whistle-blowing—alerting authorities to illegal or unethical behavior you witness in an organization—is an ethical action we consider later in the chapter. Here, we'll focus on how to work ethically, demonstrating the career readiness competency of *professionalism* and *work ethic* when others around you are being rewarded for dishonesty.

Showing Integrity and Ethics in an Unethical Climate

You first must decide the kind of person you want to be. Integrity and ethical character are difficult to demonstrate if you have a record of cheating, even if you feel you can justify your efforts because "I had no choice" or "Everybody's doing it." If the goal you're trying to achieve is unrealistic, as was probably true at Wells Fargo, ask yourself how you can influence the outcome. Can you negotiate a more achievable goal or deadline? Can you find allies who will help you pursue this option? Together you might even be able to work for the greater good of your fellow students or employees (honing another career readiness skill).

If you work in a company like Wells Fargo where people are doing unethical things, it takes courage to confront the culprits. As you will learn later when we discuss whistle-blowing, there can be career risks when you expose unethical actions. Deciding what to do in this case takes us right back to considering what type of person you want to be.

As a manager you'll want to be sure you model ethical behavior yourself, since an organization's ethical climate is shaped by managerial actions.[4] Make sure you are rewarding the right behaviors—perhaps good stewardship of customers' finances is a better goal for bank employees, for instance, than the number of new accounts opened. Finally, be sure you're aware of the family and cultural values that create your ethics, be open about what they are, and be willing to act on them.[5]

For Discussion To what extent did Wells Fargo have an ethical climate? Why do you think employees failed to challenge the unethical organizational practices? How can you model ethical behavior to others at school?

3.1 The Triple Bottom Line: People, Planet, and Profit

THE BIG PICTURE

Many businesses, small and large, are beginning to subscribe to a new standard of success—the triple bottom line, representing people, planet, and profit. This outlook has found favor with many young adults (Millennials) who are more concerned with finding meaning than material success.

LO 3-1

Describe the triple bottom line of people, planet, and profit.

"Profit is a tool," says Judy Wicks, who founded the White Dog Café in Philadelphia 30 years ago. "The major purpose of business is to serve."[6]

In Wicks's view, making money should be only one goal of business. The others are to foster social and environmental consciousness—the two other elements of what's known as the "triple bottom line." **The triple bottom line—representing people, planet, and profit (the 3 Ps)—measures an organization's social, environmental, and financial performance.** In this view of corporate performance, an organization has a responsibility to its employees and to the wider community (people); is committed to sustainable (green) environmental practices (planet); and includes the costs of pollution, worker displacement, and other factors in its financial calculations (profit), matters high in the minds of many of today's consumers.[7] Success in these areas can be measured through **a social audit, a systematic assessment of a company's performance in implementing socially responsible programs, often based on predefined goals.**

The White Dog Café (now in three locations), for instance, is known for such social and environmental activities as buying wind-powered electricity, organic produce, and humanely raised meat and poultry, as well as sharing ideas with competitors and opening up its premises for educational forums and speakers. But the triple bottom line isn't just to be practiced by small businesses. As a co-author of *Everybody's Business: The Unlikely Story of How Big Business Can Fix the World* observes, "big businesses can . . . be really powerful, positive engines for social change."[8] For instance, Ben & Jerry's ice cream, according to its director of social mission, now has a bigger impact since being taken over by Unilever.[9] The file-storage company Box offers its products free to certain nonprofits.[10] The online bookseller Better World Books donates one book for every book it sells.[11]

The Millennials' Search for Meaning

The "Millennial" generation, generally defined as people born between 1977 and 2000, care about the triple bottom line.[12] Millennials now make up more than 25% of the U.S. workforce and could be as much as 50% in just a few years.[13]

In Chapter 1, we mentioned that one of the great challenges for a manager is in trying to achieve personal success, whether in striving for a happy life or a meaningful life—or, if possible, both.[14] Millennials are no different, and they expect more from the organizations they work for and do business with. "More than any other previous generation," reports *Forbes,* "millennials are concerned about business ethics, motives and methods. According to a Deloitte study of millennials, 58% of respondents indicated they believed corporations, in general, are moving in a more ethical direction, yet 64% still believed companies operate according to their own agenda first and society's needs second. Slightly over half believed the average company has 'no ambition' beyond turning a profit."[15] Another study finds that Millennials who came of age during the 2007–2009 Great Recession reported more concern for others and less interest in material goods.[16] They also want work/life balance.[17]

In this chapter, we discuss two factors in achieving a meaningful life:

- Understanding the environment in which a manager operates—the community of stakeholders inside and outside the organization.
- The ethical and social responsibilities of being a manager. •

3.2 The Community of Stakeholders inside the Organization

THE BIG PICTURE

Managers operate in two organizational environments—internal and external—both made up of stakeholders, the people whose interests are affected by the organization. The first, or internal, environment consists of employees, owners, and the board of directors.

LO 3-2

Identify important stakeholders inside the organization.

Is a company principally responsible only to its stockholders and executives? Or are other groups equal in significance?

Perhaps we need a broader term than "stockholders" to indicate all those with a stake in an organization. That term, appropriately, is **stakeholders**—the people whose interests are affected by an organization's activities.

Internal and External Stakeholders

Managers operate in two organizational environments, both made up of various stakeholders. *(See Figure 3.1.)* As we describe in the rest of this section, the two environments are these:

- Internal stakeholders.
- External stakeholders.

Internal Stakeholders

Whether small or large, the organization to which you belong has people in it who have an important stake in how it performs. These **internal stakeholders** consist of employees, owners, and the board of directors, if any. Let us consider each in turn.

Employees

As a manager, could you run your part of the organization if you and your employees were constantly in conflict? Labor history, of course, is full of accounts of just that. But such conflict may lower the performance of the organization, thereby hurting everyone's stake. In many of today's forward-looking organizations, employees are considered "the talent"—the most important resource.

"My chief assets drive out the gate every day," says Jim Goodnight, CEO of North Carolina-based SAS Institute. "My job is to make sure they come back."[18] SAS is the world's largest privately held software business and was ranked No. 15 on *Fortune*'s 2017 list of "100 Best Companies to Work For."[19] In the recent past, it has been in the magazine's top spot in attracting and holding on to the best talent (it ranked 1, 1, 3, and 2, respectively, in the years 2010–2014), but that prize now belongs to Google.

Even so, SAS treats its employees exceptionally well, resulting in a turnover rate of only 4%, compared with a software industry average of 22%.

As we saw in Chapter 1 (manager's challenge 3), the U.S. workforce of the future will consist of employees diverse in gender, age, race, ethnicity, and sexual orientation from what we've been accustomed to. We consider this further in Chapter 11.

Owners

The **owners** of an organization consist of all those who can claim it as their legal property, such as Walmart's stockholders. There are five principal types of ownership.

- **Sole proprietorship:** In the for-profit world, if you're running a one-person graphic design firm, the owner is just you—you're what is known as a sole proprietorship.

FIGURE 3.1

The organization's environment

The two main groups are internal and external stakeholders.

Source: From Diverse Teams at Work *by Lee Gardenswartz. Published by the Society for Human Resource Management.*

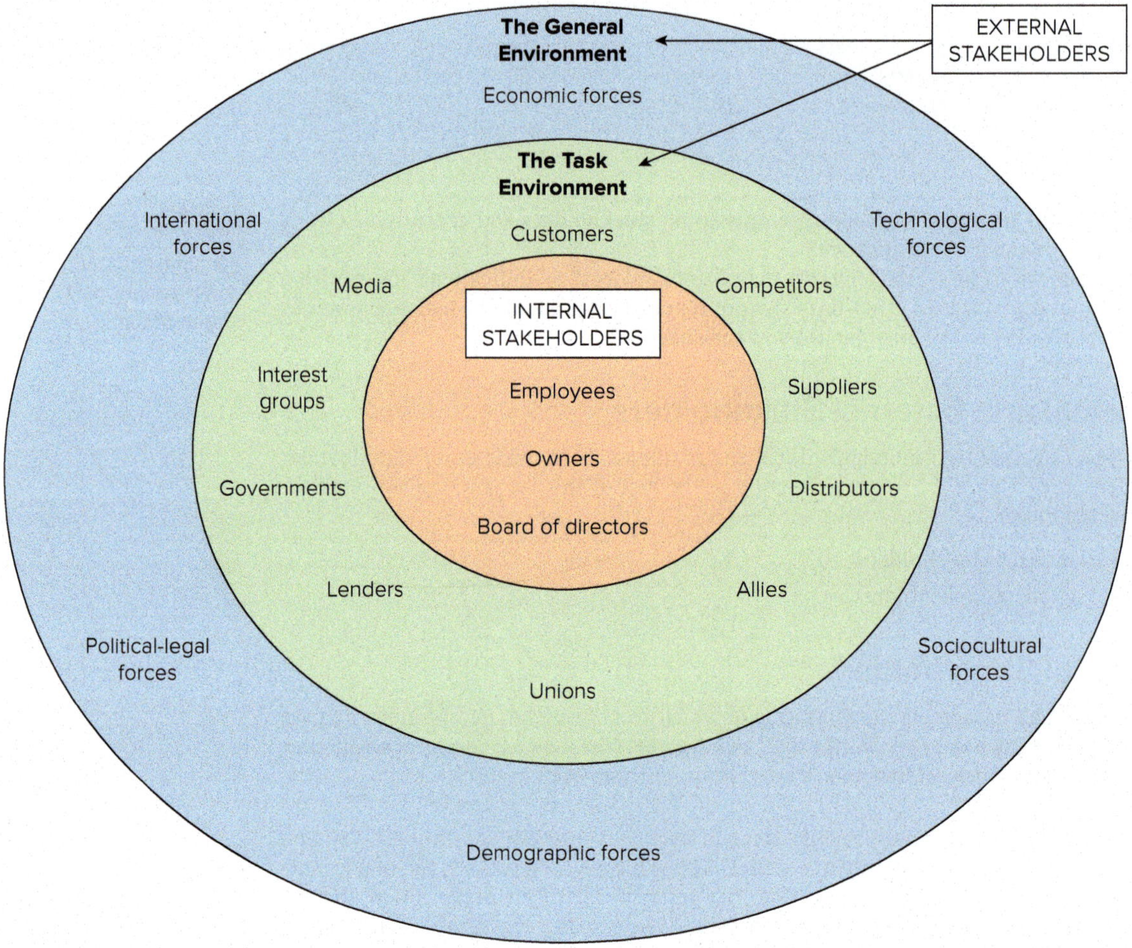

- **Partnership:** If you're in an Internet start-up with your brother-in-law, you're both owners—you're a partnership.
- **Private investors:** If you're a member of a family running a car dealership, you're all owners—you're investors in a privately owned company.
- **Employee owners:** If you work for a company that is more than half owned by its employees (such as W. L. Gore & Associates, maker of Gore-Tex fabric and No. 52 on *Fortune*'s 2017 "Best Companies to Work For" list, or Lakeland, Florida's Publix Super Markets, No. 21), you are one of the joint owners—you're part of an Employee Stock Ownership Plan (ESOP).[20]
- **Stockholders:** And if you've bought a few shares of stock in a company whose shares are listed for sale on the New York Stock Exchange, such as General Motors, you're one of thousands of owners—you're a stockholder.

In all these examples, of course, the stated goal of the owners is to make a profit.

These Naples, Florida Publix grocery store employees are focused on helping customers. Their motivation may be enhanced by the fact that Publix is an employee-owned American supermarket. Why would employee ownership fuel employee motivation? ©Education & Exploration 3/Alamy Stock Photo

Board of Directors Who hires the chief executive of a for-profit or nonprofit organization? In a corporation, it is the *board of directors*, whose members are elected by the stockholders to see that the company is being run according to their interests. In nonprofit organizations, such as universities or hospitals, the board may be called the *board of trustees* or *board of regents*. Board members are very important in setting the organization's overall strategic goals and in approving the major decisions and salaries of top management.

A large corporation might have eight or so members on its board of directors. Some of these directors (inside directors) may be top executives of the firm. The rest (outside directors) are elected from outside the firm. The board of directors at Facebook, for instance, includes not only insiders CEO Mark Zuckerberg and chief operating officer (COO) Sheryl Sandberg but also executives from outside firms including Netflix, BDT Capital Partners, the Bill and Melinda Gates Foundation, Palantir Technologies, Andreesen Horowitz, and a member of the board of WhatsApp (owned by Facebook).[21]

Boards of directors can play an important role in setting corporate strategy and executive compensation. Research shows that companies with good boards "did not pay CEOs high bonuses for luck." Conscientious boards also prevented self-serving CEOs from skimming corporate profits.[22] Some experts further speculate that balanced gender representation on boards was an important characteristic of a "good" board.

Interest in the gender composition of boards grew partly in response to a study by Catalyst. Catalyst claimed "the *Fortune* 500 companies that had the greatest representation of women board directors had . . . a 66% higher return on investment than the companies with fewer women on their boards." Unfortunately, this finding suffered from two statistical problems. *Forbes* reviewed these problems and concluded that "women aren't miracle workers for an organization. But that's okay, because neither are men. Women should be provided the same opportunities to sit on boards as their male counterparts, because it is the fair thing to do."[23] We clearly have room for improvement, given that women account for only 21.2% of board seats in S&P companies.[24]

We consider directors further in Section 3.6, "Corporate Governance." •

3.3 The Community of Stakeholders outside the Organization

THE BIG PICTURE

The external environment of stakeholders consists of the task environment and the general environment. The task environment consists of customers, competitors, suppliers, distributors, strategic allies, employee associations, local communities, financial institutions, government regulators, and special-interest groups. The general environment consists of economic, technological, sociocultural, demographic, political–legal, and international forces.

LO 3-3

Identify important stakeholders outside the organization.

In the first section, we described the environment inside the organization. Here let's consider the environment outside it, which consists of **external stakeholders**—**people or groups in the organization's external environment that are affected by it.** This environment consists of:

- The task environment.
- The general environment.

The Task Environment

We all are customers in one way or another on a daily basis. Do you feel that most companies really care about our attitudes toward their levels of service? ©Ingram Publishing

The **task environment** consists of 11 groups that present you with daily tasks to handle: customers, competitors, suppliers, distributors, strategic allies, employee organizations, local communities, financial institutions, government regulators, and special-interest groups.

1. Customers The first law of business (and even nonprofits), we've said, is *take care of the customer*. **Customers are those who pay to use an organization's goods or services.** Many customers are generally frustrated by poor customer relations at airlines, banks, cable and satellite service providers, and some big retailers, in part because many of these companies have few competitors and so don't have to worry about making customers happy. Among "America's most hated companies," by one account: Comcast, Bank of America, Mylan (which dramatically raised the price of its EpiPen, the emergency treatment for allergic reaction), McDonald's, Wells Fargo Bank, Facebook, Spirit Airlines, DISH Network, Sears, Walmart, and Charter Communications. The most frequent reason is poor customer service; Facebook also suffers because of its massive data collection and lax privacy policies.[25]

EXAMPLE **Did United Sacrifice a Customer's Well-Being to Its Own Needs?**

A writer for *Forbes* says, "Just as chess players sacrifice pawns to meet the needs of other pieces, companies routinely sacrifice customers' interests and well-being to feed their own needs of well-being and prosperity." The problem, says this writer, occurs when employees who abuse customers are following practices they believe have been demonstrated by management.[26]

A recent example drew shocked attention around the world after a video of it went viral. In April 2017, Dr. David Dao, a passenger on a United Airlines flight who had refused to give up his seat on an overbooked flight, was eventually forcibly dragged shouting and bloodied from the plane, sparking a public relations nightmare, accusations of racism, a threatened consumer boycott, and calls for an investigation. United apologized and promised to review its policies, but its response was late and its message inconsistent. The damage had been done.[27] "The back-against-the-wall, through-gritted-teeth apology isn't generally a winning strategy," said one public relations executive.[28] The airline's stock price dropped, and the Senate Commerce Committee called on the Chicago Department of Aviation for a full accounting of Dr. Dao's experience.[29]

United explained the overbooking of Dr. Dao's Chicago-to-Louisville flight as caused by the airline's need to transport several crew members to Kentucky to avoid canceling a scheduled flight from Louisville the next day. When there are not enough volunteers willing to give up their seats, the airline says it implements a "written policy on boarding priority" (which it would not share with the media) to deny some passengers their seats. "We recognize that our response . . . did not reflect the gravity of the situation," said a United spokesperson. "And for that we also apologize. Our focus now is looking ahead and making this right."[30]

YOUR CALL

"Despite all the posturing and loud advertising . . . the dominant reality still is that 'the company matters more than the customer.'"[31] Do you agree that this is how businesses view their customers? Does an airline's need to staff or cancel a flight supersede paying passengers' needs to travel to their destination? What if the airline makes a poor choice, as in Dr. Dao's case, that affects its external stakeholders by jeopardizing its stock price?

2. Competitors Is there any line of work you could enter in which there would *not* be **competitors—people or organizations that compete for customers or resources,** such as talented employees or raw materials? We mentioned that some of the most hated companies in America have little competition—but every organization has to be on the lookout for *possible* competitors, even if not yet in sight.

E-commerce companies such as Amazon already represent huge threats to such retailers as Walmart, Sears, Macy's, Kohl's, and Pier 1, for example.[32] In addition, studies seem to show that experiences, not objects, bring the most happiness, and, points out one writer, "the Internet is bursting with 'Buy Experiences, Not Things' type of stories that can give retailing executives nightmares."[33]

3. Suppliers **A supplier,** or vendor, **is a person or an organization that provides supplies—that is, raw materials, services, equipment, labor, or energy—to other organizations.** Suppliers in turn have their own suppliers. For instance, Werner Paddles makes handcrafted kayak paddles from carbon fiber reinforced plastic. When the company wanted to improve the appearance of its product, not usually a priority for components made of carbon fiber, it went to its supplier, KASO Plastics, for help. KASO, in turn, searched out a recycled material made by RTP Company, which was working in partnership with aircraft maker Boeing to reclaim manufacturing scrap from Boeing's 787 Dreamliner. The result was a paddle blade that met Werner's aesthetic criteria at no increase in cost, with the bonus of including recycled content that would appeal to its environmentally conscious customers.[34]

The "I Wish I..." box provides a great example of what can happen when U.S. companies fail to pay attention to economic conditions faced by international suppliers.

I Wish I...

...kept a closer eye on trends affecting our suppliers.

Yuvraj Singh works in the manufacturing industry as a commodity manager. Recently, his company experienced financial setbacks due to an unanticipated change in the external environment.

The company that Yuvraj works for purchases electrical components for their machinery from a supplier in China. Recently, the company ran into issues with the dollar exchange rate against China.

"We got a lot of pushback from our suppliers in China on the price increase. We have a contract in place with this supplier that covers inflation and depreciation, but there is something that we did not cover in our contract: the labor costs," said Yuvraj. "Our suppliers are claiming that labor rates are increasing in their area. This gives them double the pressure—they are not just dealing with the depreciation of the dollar, but the increase in labor rates, as well."

Yuvraj Singh Courtesy Yuvraj Singh

As a result, the supplier received fewer dollars from Yuvraj's company, and they also had to pay a premium to cover the increased labor costs. This increased pressure threatened the long-term relationship between the companies. It seemed that the supplier would not be able to recover from such a significant loss despite attempts to negotiate.

The company Yuvraj works for receives parts from suppliers, puts them into assembly, and ships them to customers. They do not store the parts for long periods of time, and they are very dependent on the suppliers. If they cannot receive the parts from one of their suppliers for an extended period of time, it can result in delays in manufacturing and meeting customer requirements.

"Within China, you have different provinces. There are different labor rates in each province. You have to keep an eye on where your suppliers are and whether their rates are fluctuating," said Yuvraj. "This was one thing that we didn't consider to put in the contract. In the end we couldn't push back and we had to accept the price increase." By accepting the price increase, Yuvraj was able to maintain a long-term relationship with his supplier and meet customer requirements on time.

Learning from this mistake, Yuvraj says that his company can work to get income statements from both public and private companies that they do business with. "For public companies in China, you can get all of their balance sheets and income statements. From now on, we will put in the contract that all private companies will have to share their numbers with us going forward, as well."

Yuvraj hopes that planning ahead and developing a mitigation strategy will help prevent unseen roadblocks like this in the future.

Courtesy of Yuvraj Chibber

4. Distributors A **distributor**, sometimes called a middle man, **is a person or an organization that helps another organization sell its goods and services to customers.** Publishers of magazines, for instance, don't sell directly to newsstands; rather, they go through a distributor, or wholesaler. Tickets to Maroon Five, Phish, or other artists' performances might be sold to you directly by the concert hall, but they are also sold through such distributors as TicketMaster, LiveNation, and StubHub.

Distributors can be quite important because in some industries (such as movie theaters and magazines), there is not a lot of competition, and the distributor has a lot of power over the ultimate price of the product. However, the popularity of the Internet has allowed manufacturers of cell phones, for example, to cut out the "middleman"—the distributor—and to sell to customers directly.

5. Strategic Allies Companies, and even nonprofit organizations, frequently link up with other organizations (even competing ones) in order to realize strategic advantages. The term **strategic allies describes the relationship of two organizations who join forces to achieve advantages neither can perform as well alone.**

With their worldwide reservation systems and slick marketing, big companies—Hilton, Hyatt, Marriott, Starwood, and so on—dominate the high-end business-center hotels. But in many cities, there are still independents—such as The Rittenhouse in Philadelphia; The Hay-Adams in Washington, DC; and The Adolphus in Dallas—that compete with the chains by promoting their prestigious locations, grand architecture, rich history, and personalized service. In recent years, however, some high-end independents have become affiliated with chains as strategic allies because chains can buy supplies for less and they have more far-reaching sales channels. The 105-year-old U.S. Grant in downtown San Diego, for example, became part of Starwood's Luxury Collection to get better worldwide exposure.

6. Employee Organizations: Unions and Associations As a rule of thumb, labor unions (such as the United Auto Workers or the Teamsters Union) tend to represent hourly workers; professional associations (such as the National Education Association or The Newspaper Guild) tend to represent salaried workers. Nevertheless, during a labor dispute, salary-earning teachers in the American Federation of Teachers might well act in sympathy with the wage-earning janitors in the Service Employees International Union.

In recent years, the percentage of the labor force represented by unions has steadily declined (from 35% in the 1950s to 10.7% in 2017).[35] Indeed, more than five times as many union members are now public-sector workers than private-sector workers, whose unionizing has sharply fallen off, mainly because of job losses in manufacturing and construction. The unionization rates remain highest in protective service occupations (34.7%) and in education, training, and library occupations (33.5%).[36] Men have maintained a slightly higher union membership rate (11.4%) than women (10.0)%), while among the states, New York has the highest membership rate (23.8%) compared to South Carolina (2.6%).[37]

7. Local Communities Local communities are obviously important stakeholders, as becomes evident not only when a big organization arrives but also when it leaves, sending government officials scrambling to find new industry to replace it. Schools and municipal governments rely on the organization for their tax base. Families and merchants depend on its employee payroll for their livelihoods. In addition, everyone from the United Way to the Little League may rely on it for some financial support.

If a community gives a company tax breaks in return for the promise of new jobs and the firm fails to deliver, does the community have the right to institute **clawbacks—rescinding the tax breaks when firms don't deliver promised jobs?** But what is a town to do if a company goes bankrupt, as did Hoku Materials, manufacturer of materials for solar panels, after the struggling town of Pocatello, Idaho, gave it numerous concessions?[38]

EXAMPLE — Local Communities as Stakeholders: Does Amazon Really Need the Tax Break?

The Amazon Spheres at its urban campus in the Belltown neighborhood.
©Paul Christian Gordon/Alamy Stock Photo

Amazon recently announced it would be opening a second U.S. headquarters, dubbed HQ2 and meant to be "fully equal" to its Seattle campus. The company then issued a set of criteria it would seek in the new location, inviting cities and communities around the country to bid.[39] Its requirements focused on population size, ease of transportation, presence of a local university, and plenty of tech talent. Cities and towns jumped on the opportunity, just as many have done in the past when NFL teams have come in search of a new home. In this case, a truly glittering prize of as many as 50,000 well-paid jobs and as much as $5 billion worth of local investment will go to the winner.[40]

From a list of more than 230 possibilities, a team of Amazon executives including founder and CEO Jeff Bezos sat down in early 2018 and selected 20 finalists for its shortlist. These included Atlanta, Austin, Denver, Nashville, Raleigh, New York, and Washington DC. Toronto was the only finalist outside the United States.[41]

While some contestants kept their financial incentives confidential, several cities were known to have offered tax breaks worth $1 billion to $7 billion. And Amazon is hinting that nearly everyone could be a winner at some level. "All the proposals showed tremendous enthusiasm and creativity," said the company's head of economic development. "Through this process we learned about many new communities across North American that we will consider as locations for future infrastructure investment and job creation."[42]

But even given the payoff in jobs and infusions of capital, will the future home of HQ2 really be getting a good deal? Some economists have raised doubts about this kind of auction-like process, warning that giving huge tax breaks to incoming businesses does little more than rob cities of resources needed by arguably more important entities like their school, housing, and transportation systems. All these systems could also need expensive upgrades and improvements to accommodate a hugely increased workforce after Amazon moves in, and existing businesses and individual taxpayers would end up footing the bill.[43]

One small-business owner, who already struggles to compete with Amazon, said of Jeff Bezos, "Why should the richest man in the history of the world get money to open his business?"[44]

YOUR CALL

How would you advise local public officials to handle the matter of tax incentives for business—especially if they are across the table from the shrewd negotiators representing a huge company such as Amazon? What obligations should a community expect of the companies located there?

8. Financial Institutions Want to launch a small company? Although normally reluctant to make loans to start-ups, financial institutions–banks, savings and loans, and credit unions–may do so if you have a good credit history or can secure the loan with property such as a house. You might also receive help from venture capitalists. **Venture capital** is money provided by investors to start-up firms and small businesses with high risk but perceived long-term growth potential, in return for an ownership stake.

During the Great Recession, when even good customers found loans hard to get, a new kind of financing emerged called **crowdfunding**, raising money for a project or venture by obtaining many small amounts of money from many people ("the crowd"), using websites such as Kickstarter. We discuss crowdfunding further in Chapter 10.

Established companies also often need loans to tide them over when revenues are down or to finance expansion, but they rely for assistance on lenders such as commercial banks, investment banks, and insurance companies.

9. Government Regulators The preceding groups are external stakeholders in your organization since they are clearly affected by its activities. But why would **government regulators**—regulatory agencies that establish ground rules under which organizations may operate—be considered stakeholders?

We are talking here about an alphabet soup of agencies, boards, and commissions that have the legal authority to prescribe or proscribe the conditions under which you may conduct business. To these may be added local and state regulators on the one hand and foreign governments and international agencies (such as the World Trade Organization, which oversees international trade and standardization efforts) on the other.

Such government regulators can be said to be stakeholders because not only do they affect the activities of your organization, they are in turn affected by it. The Federal Aviation Agency (FAA), for example, specifies how far planes must stay apart to prevent midair collisions. But when the airlines want to add more flights on certain routes, the FAA may have to add more flight controllers and radar equipment because those are the agency's responsibility. Recently, the FAA has had to take on the heavy responsibility of regulating the use of drones, which could number well over a million by 2021.[45]

10. Special-Interest Groups In recent times, efforts to ban horse-drawn carriages that serve tourists wanting to take in urban sights have spread across the country, from Salt Lake City to Atlanta. In New York City, the 1,200 operators of horse-drawn carriage rides

Oprah Winfrey accepts the 2018 Cecil B. DeMille Award during the 75th Annual Golden Globe Awards. ©Paul Drinkwater/Handout/NBCUniversal/Getty Images

were being pressured by opponents who insisted the horses weren't equipped to handle city noise and traffic, as well as intense summer heat. Spurred by some highly publicized deaths and injuries to horses, many of the complaints came from animal-rights groups, such as People for the Ethical Treatment of Animals (PETA). In New York, however, two-thirds of city voters said they didn't want the bans. Some visitors also said they liked "the clip-clop of the horse's feet."[46]

Special-interest groups are groups whose members try to influence specific issues, some of which may affect your organization. Examples are People for the Ethical Treatment of Animals, Mothers Against Drunk Driving, the National Organization for Women, and the National Rifle Association.

Special-interest groups may try to exert political influence, as in contributing funds to lawmakers' election campaigns or in launching letter-writing efforts to officials. Or they may organize picketing and *boycotts*—holding back their patronage—of certain companies. Other groups have made striking visual statements, such as the many women attending the 2018 Golden Globe awards who wore black dresses in support of the #MeToo movement, which has exposed widespread sexual harassment of women in the entertainment industry.[47]

The General Environment

Beyond the task environment is the **general environment, or macroenvironment, which includes six forces: economic, technological, sociocultural, demographic, political–legal, and international.**

You may be able to control some forces in the task environment, but you can't control those in the general environment. Nevertheless, they can profoundly affect your organization's task environment without your knowing it, springing nasty surprises on you. Clearly, then, as a manager you need to keep your eye on the far horizon because these forces of the general environment can affect long-term plans and decisions. The "I'm Glad I . . . box provides a great illustration of how a brand manager at a mobile tire installation company stays ahead of competition by paying attention to the general environment.

I'm glad I...

...kept current on my industry's general environment.

Katie Lord works as a brand manager at a mobile tire installation start-up company. Customers are able to schedule appointments via the company's phone line or website to have their tires replaced—in their own driveways! Rather than taking your vehicle to an automotive tire store to have your tires replaced and rotated, you can have an installer come directly to you.

Since the company Katie works for is one of the first of its kind, it is extremely important for management to keep an eye on the external environment while the company grows and takes shape.

"One of the things we keep a close eye on is the state legislature," said Katie. "Our state does not have state inspections for vehicles, whereas the majority of other states do. That is one thing that is hurting us now. If someone has tires that are really worn down, there is no law in place that says you have to replace them." However, as the company grows and moves into other states, this is something that could actually benefit other locations because drivers will have to replace their tires if an inspection deems them unsafe for driving.

Katie Lord Courtesy Katie Lord

Aside from laws and policies already in place, Katie keeps an eye on legislature that might pass in the future. "They are looking to put laws in place in our state where you are unable to sell used tires or tires worn below a certain percentage," said Katie. "This is important because, in certain areas of our state, there are a ton of used tire shops. So that hurts us a little right now—we have a lot of people calling and looking for used tires. But once that legislation passes, that will certainly help us to gain more customers and capture more sales."

Katie also stays up-to-date on cultural trends. "Our target group is millennials, and we've done a lot of research on this group to be able to reach them. The millennial group is all about convenience and the experience versus the price or the actual product," said Katie. The company markets to this target group through social media, and emphasizes a unique experience in an industry that has been around for a long time.

It is also important for the start-up company to stay current with technology trends. "Our company is totally disrupting the automotive industry by using technology and coming to your doorstep. It's like ordering from Amazon or Walmart.com instead of going to the physical store," said Katie. The mobile tire installation company is able to leverage technology trends to compete with traditional automotive tire stores.

Courtesy of Katie Lord

1. Economic Forces **Economic forces consist of the general economic conditions and trends—unemployment, inflation, interest rates, economic growth—that may affect an organization's performance.** These are forces in your nation and region and even the world over which you and your organization probably have no control, as happened in the Great Recession and its aftermath. The "I Wish I..." box on page 83 shows an example of what can happen when U.S. managers fail to pay attention to economic forces that impact suppliers from China.

Are banks' interest rates going up in the United States? Then it will cost you more to borrow money to open new stores or build new plants. Is your region's unemployment rate rising? Then maybe you'll have more job applicants to hire from, yet you'll also have fewer customers with money to spend. (Currently, 43.1 million people in the United States are considered poor, according to the Census Bureau's 2016 estimates; the poverty rate has fallen only to 14% from 19% in two generations.)[48] Are natural resources getting scarce in an important area of supply? Then your company will need to pay more for them or switch to alternative sources.

One indicator that managers often pay attention to is productivity growth. Rising productivity leads to rising profits, lower inflation, and higher stock prices. In recent times, companies have been using information technology to cut costs, resulting in productivity in the nonfarm business sector growing at an annual rate of 2.6% from 2000 to 2007. From 2007 to 2016, a period that included the recession of 2008 and 2009 and the start of the recovery, productivity growth averaged a low 1.2%.[49] In 2016, productivity declined slightly. Economists disagree on the reasons. They could signal reduced capital investment by businesses, a slowdown in the rate of innovation, business failure to take full advantage of the innovations that have occurred such as the Internet of Things, or simply a measurement problem that fails to accurately account for the business and consumer benefits of free products like social media and Internet search engines.[50] Falling productivity affects a company's costs, which in turn, of course, affects its profits.

2. Technological Forces **Technological forces are new developments in methods for transforming resources into goods or services.** The true age of technological innovation, suggests science writer Michael Hanlon, ran from about 1945 to 1971. "Just about everything that defines the modern world either came about or had its seeds sown during that time," he writes. "The pill. Electronics. Computers and the birth of the Internet. Nuclear power. Television. Antibiotics. Space travel."[51] (Social sciences professor Robert Gordon has his own list: Electricity. The telephone. The combustion engine. Mass production. Indoor plumbing. The conquest of infectious diseases. The computer. Everything else—including the Internet and the smartphone—is simply a variation on these themes, in his view.)[52]

Hanlon thinks we have fewer truly significant technological innovations in the present. "Today, progress is defined almost entirely by consumer-driven, often banal improvements in information technology," he says. "That's not the same as being able to fly across the Atlantic in eight hours or eliminating smallpox."[53] Some, however, might disagree, as suggested by the examples.

EXAMPLE Technology Changes Everything

The key fact about computer technology is its capacity for *disruption*—disruption of service industries, certainly, such as communication, music, and travel, but also disruption in the world's access to knowledge, in health care, in energy sources, and in many other areas.

The Internet of Things. The Internet of Things (IoT) is a set of everyday devices like cars, refrigerators, medical devices, thermostats, and even toys that are connected to each other through the Internet, enabling them to collect and share data. It's expected that soon blockchain, the encrypted digital ledger system, will also form a part of the Internet of Things.[54] How does the IoT work? Your IoT refrigerator, for example, could recognize that you are getting low on hot sauce, order it from the supermarket, and tell your bank to pay for it. One report suggests there will be 20 billion such "smart devices," or nearly four for every person on Earth, by the time you read this.[55] Security and privacy are big consumer concerns, however.[56] Even toys can be hacked.[57] Business leaders believe IoT is the most important new technology, and 9 in 10 (of 502 surveyed around the world) say it will play a major role in the future of their company.[58]

Driverless Cars. Self-driving cars being developed by companies such as Google and Tesla promise many benefits, including fewer traffic accidents and the freedom to complete other tasks (or even sleep) while commuting. By improving both safety and productivity, autonomous cars may even make it possible for more local governments to use congestion pricing (charging tolls in heavily trafficked areas or during peak driving times) to raise revenue for maintaining roads.[59] A recent study showed that only about a quarter of U.S. adults say they trust self-driving cars, but Google's Waymo project has logged 2 million miles with only one accident in which the autonomous car was at fault. Why are most accidents with self-driving cars caused by human drivers of other cars? Some say the reason is that self-driving cars are better at following the rules of the road, taking human drivers by surprise.[60]

YOUR CALL

Which technological change do you think is apt to affect you personally during the next decade? What kind of strategies for change will managers have to adopt? What issues should be most important to them?

3. Sociocultural Forces

Sociocultural forces are influences and trends originating in a country's, a society's, or a culture's human relationships and values that may affect an organization or industry. "With more access to social media," says one account, "young people are driving less than they used to and evincing a lack of interest in cars (causing deep worry in the automotive industry)."[61] Piano stores are closing as fewer children take up the instrument, the Associated Press reports; "people are interested in things that don't take much effort," a piano consultant believes.[62] Gambling casinos are "bringing in tattoo studios, mixed martial arts competitions, and other offbeat attractions" to attract Millennial-age patrons, reports another AP story.[63] These are three examples of industries affected by sociocultural forces.

Seismic changes are occurring in people's views about sociocultural issues. A recent survey conducted by the Harris Poll, for example, showed that U.S. adults are less accepting of LGBTQ people for the first time since 2014. The term **LGBTQ is a widely recognized acronym to represent lesbian, gay, bisexual, trangender, and questioning or queer.**[64] Diversity is discussed in detail in Chapter 11. Smoking marijuana is another sociocultural change. It is now legal for medical reasons in 29 states, and for recreational use in 9 *(see Figure 3.2)*, reflecting the fact that about two-thirds of U.S. adults now support legalization. At the same time, however, federal laws that banned the sale and use of marijuana 80 years ago are still in effect.[65]

Entire industries have been rocked when the culture underwent a lifestyle change, most notably changes in approaches to health. Diet sodas, for instance, have gone through a nearly decade-long decline, causing major concerns for Coca-Cola and PepsiCo, because more Americans worry that artificial sweeteners are unhealthy, despite numerous studies that find them safe.[66] Some killer diseases, such as measles, whooping cough, and meningitis, are creeping back because of an anti-vaccine movement based on philosophical and religious exemptions.[67] With roughly 36.5% of U.S. adults being obese, health professionals and organizations are concerned about the

FIGURE 3.2

States where marijuana is legal

Source: M. Robinson, "States Where Marijuana is Legal," Business Insider, June 28, 2018.

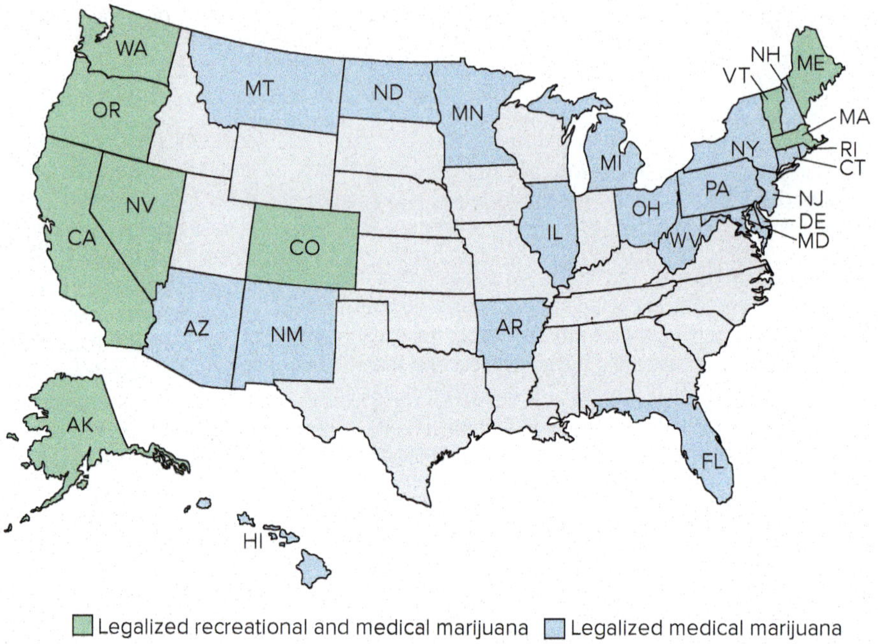

rising medical costs associated with treatment. Estimates suggest that medical costs for "people who have obesity were $1,429 higher than [for] those of normal weight."[68] (Obesity can also alter one's personal fortunes. People who are overweight are viewed as being less competent than normal-weight people in a workplace setting, and so it is harder for the overweight to get ahead.)[69]

These trends are affecting the fast-food industry, with a changing customer base calling for more food with ingredients free of additives and antibiotics, that focuses on regional flavors, that is influenced by fine-dining chefs, and that reflects principles of "mindful dining"—sustainability, reduction of food waste, and humane treatment of animals.[70]

4. Demographic Forces *Demographics* derives from the ancient Greek word for "people"—*demos*—and deals with statistics relating to human populations. Age, gender, race, sexual orientation, occupation, income, family size, and the like are known as demographic characteristics when they are used to express measurements of certain groups. **Demographic forces are influences on an organization arising from changes in the characteristics of a population, such as age, gender, or ethnic origin.**

We mentioned in Chapter 1 several instances of major shifts to come in racial and ethnic diversity. Among other recent changes: Marriage rates are down, more couples are marrying later, black-white and same-sex marriages are increasing, one-person households are growing, the decline in fertility rates is leveling off, divorce rates are down, secularism (being nonreligious) is up, more households are multigenerational, and the percentage of people living in rural areas is the lowest ever.[71] By 2060, it's predicted, the U.S. population will soar to 417 million (from about 319 million today), and minorities are expected to reach 64.4% of the population by 2060.[72] We consider demographic and diversity matters in more detail in Chapter 9.

5. Political–Legal Forces **Political–legal forces are changes in the way politics shape laws and laws shape the opportunities for and threats to an organization.** In the United States, the currently dominant political view may be reflected in the way the government addresses environmental and sustainability issues, such as those we described in Chapter 1. For instance, should the government pursue an agenda of nationalism and isolation?[73] Should coal mining be allowed on public lands?[74] How should public money be spent on dealing with climate change and ocean warming?[75]

As for legal forces, some countries have more fully developed legal systems than others. And some countries have more lawyers per capita. (The United States reportedly has one lawyer for every 300 people versus one for every 1,400 people in France.)[76] U.S. companies may be more willing to use the legal system to advance their interests, as in suing competitors to gain competitive advantage. But they must also watch that others don't do the same to them.

6. International Forces

International forces are changes in the economic, political, legal, and technological global system that may affect an organization.

This category represents a huge variety of influences. How does the economic integration of the European Union create threats and opportunities for U.S. companies? What does the UK's impending exit from the EU (nicknamed Brexit) mean for the rest of the EU and the world? Does it represent the start of a widespread rejection of globalization, and if so what effect will that have on multinational businesses, their employees, and their customers?[77]

U.S. companies that do significant business in Europe are subject to regulation by the European Union. For instance, in one antitrust case, several companies in Europe were able to get Google to change the way it displays its search results after they complained that, as one consumer rights advocacy group stated, Google could "stack its search results as suits itself."[78] Google is blocking certain of these results[79] but is now preparing to fight the EU's "right to be forgotten."[80]

Uber is just one of the other U.S. companies to face difficulties overseas; it recently lost its license to operate on London's streets after irregularities were found in its business and operating methods, to the relief of London's cab drivers and other competitors. The company will continue operating while it appeals the British court's decision.[81]

Meanwhile, for several reasons—including a strong U.S. dollar and strict visa requirements—foreign tourism to the United States has been declining for four or five years, alarming the domestic travel industry.[82] The number of international students at U.S. universities has also dropped, due in part to the recent rise of nationalist sentiment in the United States and the lure of other countries. Nearly $40 billion of revenue from these students is at stake.[83]

How well U.S. businesspeople can handle international forces depends a lot on their training. Unfortunately, only 18% report speaking a language other than English, whereas 53% of Europeans, for example, can converse in a second language.[84] Almost all U.S. high schools offer foreign languages, but fewer than 1% of U.S. adults are proficient in a foreign language they studied in a U.S. classroom.[85]

Another factor to keep in mind is the need for flexibility when dealing with other countries and cultures. Behaviors as habitual to U.S. employees as asking questions and expressing your unsolicited opinion might need to be tailored to fit new circumstances abroad, where they may seem overbearing. At the same time, behaviors like bribery and gift-giving can carry different meanings in different cultures, proving that there is no substitute for learning as much as possible about the countries with which you are dealing.[86] ●

3.4 The Ethical Responsibilities Required of You as a Manager

THE BIG PICTURE

Managers need to be aware of what constitutes ethics, values, the four approaches to ethical dilemmas, and how organizations can promote ethics.

LO 3-4

Explain the importance of ethics and values in effective management.

Would you take supplies from the office supply closet on leaving a job? (Twenty-six percent of workers said they would, 74% said they wouldn't, in one survey.)[87] That may be an easy decision. But how would you handle a choice between paying a client money under the table in order to land a big contract, for example, and losing your job if you didn't? That's a much harder matter.

One of a manager's major challenges, as we stated in Chapter 1, is managing for ethical standards. In business, most ethical conflicts are about choosing between *economic performance* and *social performance*.[88] This is known as an **ethical dilemma, a situation in which you have to decide whether to pursue a course of action that may benefit you or your organization but that is unethical or even illegal.** Volkswagen managers, for instance, allowed software to be installed on diesel-powered cars that would cheat on emissions tests (so that the vehicles seemed more fuel efficient—perceived as an *economic* benefit) and spew more oxides into the air (adding more greenhouse gases and contributing to climate change—working against the intended *social benefit*).[89]

EXAMPLE Volkswagen Fails the Test

Following up a tip from puzzled researchers, the Environmental Protection Agency (EPA) discovered in 2014 that Volkswagen had deliberately installed cheating software in more than 500,000 diesel passenger cars sold in the United States. The software allowed the cars' computers to sense when the vehicles were being tested for harmful emissions and to switch, undetected, to a driving mode that artificially reduced nitrogen oxide or NOx (linked to smog and lung cancer) so the cars could pass the test. Once back on the road, the computers adjusted the driving mode again, permitting drivers to experience the power and mileage the company was touting while allowing some cars to emit as much as 40 times the volume of pollutants permitted by law. Volkswagen had done the same in more than 10 million other cars sold around the world.[90]

The U.S. government's case against VW resulted in a settlement of almost $15 billion and included massive repair and buy-back programs. Another $4.3 billion in civil and criminal penalties was levied against the company, some of which is to fund projects to reduce NOx in the air; eight high-ranking executives were charged with crimes, and two received prison sentences. The company lost more than a quarter of its market value as its stock price plummeted.[91]

How did a venerable and successful company come to commit what one business publication called "a truly brazen act of business malfeasance"[92] in the first place? More stringent controls on NOx took effect in 1999, and of the two possible ways it could meet them, VW chose the one that did not require a costly reengineering of the interior of its cars. This might have seemed like the right business decision to make, but as a side effect, VW's new NOx controls dramatically reduced the degree of fuel economy the company was advertising. It was apparently at this point that the decision to rig the cars to falsify emissions tests was made.[93]

Volkswagen's financial performance has returned to prescandal levels even as the possibility remains that more huge fines will be levied, this time by European investigators.[94] In early 2018, another scandal broke when the company was forced to apologize for exposing monkeys to engine fumes to research the effects of diesel exhaust. "We're convinced the scientific methods chosen then were wrong," said a company statement. "It would have been better to do without such a study in the first place."[95]

YOUR CALL

What is the fundamental ethical dilemma faced by Volkswagen's managers? How well do you think Volkswagen is managing the balance between its economic and its social performance? What could it be doing better?

Solving ethical dilemmas is an important skill, according to a recent study. An investigation of 400 senior executives and 455 college students revealed that 62% of the students believed that they were well prepared to deal with ethical judgments whereas only 30% of executives see students as prepared.[96] To help you develop this skill, we ask you to solve an ethical/legal dilemma at the end of each chapter.

Defining Ethics and Values

A report from the Ethics Resource Center revealed that 41 percent of workers in the U.S. are likely to have witnessed some form of ethical misconduct at work. Sadly, most of this unethical behavior was committed by someone with managerial authority.[97] Most of us assume we know what "ethics" and "values" mean, but do we? Let's consider them.

Ethics

Ethics are the standards of right and wrong that influence behavior. These standards may vary among countries and among cultures. **Ethical behavior** is behavior that is accepted as "right" as opposed to "wrong" according to those standards.

Sometimes it's hard to know whether something like a tip, a gratuity, or a gift is a token of appreciation or a bribe. For example, pharmaceutical companies have provided doctors with small gifts—pads with logos, tickets to sports events, free drug samples—to promote their drugs. However, in recent years, points out one editorial, "those trinkets have evolved into big money for doctors to speak to other doctors about new drugs," as in presentations at dinner lectures.[98] Do these behaviors represent marketing gifts or unethical attempts to influence the sales of drugs? Sometimes it is hard to tell the difference.

The Ethics Resource Center tried to clarify this issue by identifying the five most common unethical behaviors at work: They are:[99]

- **Misusing company time.** Covering for others, taking long breaks, lying about being sick, altering time sheets, and doing personal business on company time all represent instances of this behavior. Electronic monitoring is one way to curtail such behaviors, and the practice is growing. According to Lewis Maltby, president of the National Workrights Insititute, "virtually every company conducts electronic monitoring."[100] Beware the next time you conduct personal business on company time.
- **Abusive behavior.** An expert defined **abusive supervision** as "subordinates' perceptions of the extent to which supervisors engage in the sustained display of hostile verbal and nonverbal behaviors, excluding physical contact."[101] Examples include bullying, gossiping, backstabbing, and repeatedly calling people names like "loser," "stupid," or "worthless." This type of behavior erodes employees' self-esteem, engagement, job satisfaction, and performance.[102]
- **Employee theft.** Estimates suggest that 75% of employees have stolen from an employer at least once, and such theft costs U.S. businesses about $50 billion annually.[103] Although there are many reasons for stealing, often it is a form of retaliation for abusive supervision.[104]
- **Workplace cheating.** Have you ever lied, scammed, or deceived someone to advance your self-interests? **Workplace cheating** is defined as "unethical acts that are intended to create an unfair advantage or help attain benefits that an employee would not otherwise be entitled to receive."[105] Workplace cheating is far too common among college students. A poll of 30,000 students revealed that about 61% admitted to cheating, and 16.5% don't regret it.[106] These behaviors occur because it has "become easier and more widely tolerated, and both schools and parents have failed to give students strong, repetitive messages

about what is allowed and what is prohibited," according to *The New York Times.*[107] They also occur in response to performance pressures to deliver results or face negative consequences.[108]

- **Violating corporate Internet policies.** Are you a cyberslacker or cyberloafer? These terms describe people who surf the Web for personal reasons during work hours. It is both rampant and costly in terms of lost productivity. A survey by Salary.com revealed that roughly 64 percent of U.S. employees are cyberslackers.[109] We discuss this issue in more detail in Chapter 15.

Values Ethical dilemmas often take place because of an organization's **value system, the pattern of values within an organization. Values are the relatively permanent and deeply held underlying beliefs and attitudes that help determine a person's behavior**, such as the belief that "fairness means hiring according to ability, not family background." Values and value systems are the underpinnings for ethics and ethical behavior.

Organizations may have two important value systems that can conflict: (1) the value system stressing financial performance versus (2) the value system stressing cohesion and solidarity in employee relationships.[110]

Example: A car dealership may hire an accounting firm to send an accountant to audit its books, and she works alongside employees of the car dealer for several weeks, establishing cohesion and solidarity. But when a task that she estimated would take 10 hours actually takes 15, the dealership's employees might say, "You charged us more hours than you said you would," and so she might report just 10 hours to her superiors at the accounting firm. This action makes the subordinate look good, and keeps the client happy, thereby improving social cohesion. But, of course, the accounting firm unknowingly takes a loss on financial performance.[111] This kind of value system conflict happens all the time.

Many people surf the internet for personal reasons during work hours. Is there anything wrong with this? Do you think this woman surfing at work is experiencing a value conflict? ©McGraw-Hill Education

Four Approaches to Resolving Ethical Dilemmas

How do alternative values guide people's decisions about ethical behavior? Here are four approaches, which may be taken as guidelines:

1. The Utilitarian Approach: For the Greatest Good

Ethical behavior in the **utilitarian approach** **is guided by what will result in the greatest good for the greatest number of people.** Managers often take the utilitarian approach, using financial performance—such as efficiency and profit—as the best definition of what constitutes "the greatest good for the greatest number."[112]

Thus, a utilitarian "cost-benefit" analysis might show that in the short run the firing of thousands of employees may improve a company's bottom line and provide immediate benefits for the stockholders. The drawback of this approach, however, is that it may result in damage to workforce morale and the loss of employees with experience and skills—actions not so readily measurable in dollars.

2. The Individual Approach: For Your Greatest Self-Interest Long Term, which Will Help Others

Ethical behavior in the **individual approach** **is guided by what will result in the individual's best *long-term* interests, which ultimately are in everyone's self-interest.** The assumption here is that you will act ethically in the short run to avoid others harming you in the long run.

The flaw here, however, is that one person's short-term self-gain may *not,* in fact, be good for everyone in the long term. After all, the manager of an agribusiness that puts chemical fertilizers on the crops every year will always benefit, but the fishing industries downstream could ultimately suffer if chemical runoff reduces the number of fish. Indeed, this is one reason why Puget Sound Chinook, or king salmon, has been threatened with extinction in the Pacific Northwest.[113]

3. The Moral-Rights Approach: Respecting Fundamental Rights Shared by Everyone

Ethical behavior in the **moral-rights approach** **is guided by respect for the fundamental rights of human beings,** such as those expressed in the U.S. Constitution's Bill of Rights. We would all tend to agree that denying people the right to life, liberty, privacy, health and safety, and due process is unethical. Thus, most of us would have no difficulty condemning the situation of immigrants illegally brought into the United States and then effectively enslaved—as when made to work seven days a week as maids.

The difficulty, however, is when rights are in conflict, such as employer and employee rights. Should employees on the job have a guarantee of privacy? Actually, it is legal for employers to listen to business phone calls and monitor all nonspoken personal communications.[114]

4. The Justice Approach: Respecting Impartial Standards of Fairness

Ethical behavior in the **justice approach** **is guided by respect for impartial standards of fairness and equity.** One consideration here is whether an organization's policies—such as those governing promotions or sexual harassment cases—are administered impartially and fairly regardless of gender, age, sexual orientation, and the like.

Fairness can often be a hot issue. For instance, many employees are loudly resentful when a corporation's CEO is paid a salary and bonuses worth hundreds of times more than what they receive—even when the company performs poorly—and when fired is then given a "golden parachute," or extravagant package of separation pay and benefits.

White-Collar Crime, SarbOx, and Ethical Training

At the beginning of the 21st century, U.S. business erupted in an array of scandals represented in such names as Enron, WorldCom, Tyco, and Adelphia, and their chief executives went to prison on various fraud convictions. Executives' deceits generated a great deal of public outrage, as a result of which Congress passed the Sarbanes-Oxley Act, as we'll describe. Did that stop the raft of business scandals? Not quite.

Next to hit the headlines were cases of **insider trading, the illegal trading of a company's stock by people using confidential company information.** The federal government launched a six-year crackdown on insider trading on Wall Street that resulted in 87 convictions (14 of which were dismissed or lost on appeal; one trial ended in acquittal).[115] Among many other well-publicized cases, in 2016 three Chinese hackers used information they had stolen from top New York law firms to conduct insider trading deals and were extradited to the United States to face charges.[116]

Most recently, Martin Shkreli created a huge public outcry by acquiring and then unapologetically increasing the price of the life-saving drug Daraprim by 5,000% when he was head of Turing Pharmaceuticals. But what actually got Shkreli into legal trouble were acts of securities and wire fraud he committed while running two hedge funds he managed, MSMB Capital and MSMB Healthcare. He was convicted and sentenced for these offenses in 2017, at the age of 34.[117]

The Sarbanes–Oxley Reform Act The **Sarbanes–Oxley Act of 2002, often shortened to *SarbOx*, or *SOX*, established requirements for proper financial record keeping for public companies and penalties of as much as 25 years in prison for noncompliance.**[118] Administered by the Securities and Exchange Commission (SEC), SarbOx requires a company's chief executive officer (CEO) and chief financial officer (CFO) to personally certify the organization's financial reports, prohibits them from taking personal loans or lines of credit, and makes them reimburse the organization for bonuses and stock options when required by restatement of corporate profits. It also requires the company to have established procedures and guidelines for audit committees.[119] Recently, the agribusiness giant Monsanto paid the government $80 million in penalties under SarbOx for misstating earnings associated with a sales program for the herbicide Roundup.[120]

How Do People Learn Ethics? Kohlberg's Theories U.S. business history is permeated with occasional malfeasance, from railroad tycoons trying to corner the gold market (the 1872 Crédit Mobilier scandal) to 25-year-old bank customer service representatives swindling elderly customers out of their finances. Legislation such as SarbOx can't head off all such behavior. No wonder that now many colleges and universities have required more education in ethics.

Martin Shkreli speaks to the press after the verdict in his court case. He was found guilty on three of eight counts of securities fraud and conspiracy to commit securities and wire fraud. Do you see any remorse in his facial expression? ©Drew Angerer/Getty Images

"Schools bear some responsibility for the behavior of executives," says Fred J. Evans, dean of the College of Business and Economics at California State University at Northridge. "If you're making systematic errors in the [business] world, you have to go back to the schools and ask, 'What are you teaching?'"[121]

The good news is that more graduate business schools are changing their curriculums to teach ethics, although there is some question as to their effectiveness.[122] The bad news, as discussed earlier, is that students across educational levels are still cheating.

Cheating extends to corporations. Goldman Sachs fired 20 analysts for cheating on internal training exams, while JPMorgan Chase fired 10 employees for similar lapses in judgment.[123]

Of course, most students' levels of moral development are established by personalities and upbringing long before they get to college, with some being more advanced than others. One psychologist, **Laurence Kohlberg,** has proposed three levels of personal moral development–preconventional, conventional, and postconventional.[124]

- **Level 1, preconventional–follows rules.** People who have achieved this level tend to follow rules and to obey authority to avoid unpleasant consequences. Managers of the Level 1 sort tend to be autocratic or coercive, expecting employees to be obedient for obedience's sake.
- **Level 2, conventional–follows expectations of others.** People whose moral development has reached this level are conformist but not slavish, generally adhering to the expectations of others in their lives. Level 2 managers lead by encouragement and cooperation and are more group and team oriented. Most managers are at this level.
- **Level 3, postconventional–guided by internal values.** The farthest along in moral development, Level 3 managers are independent souls who follow their own values and standards, focusing on the needs of their employees and trying to lead by empowering those working for them. Only about a fifth of American managers are said to reach this level.

What level of development do you think you've reached?

How Organizations Can Promote Ethics

Ethics needs to be an everyday affair, not a one-time thing. This is why many large U.S. companies now have a *chief ethics officer*, whose job is to make ethical conduct a priority issue.

There are several ways an organization may promote high ethical standards on the job, as follows.[125]

1. Creating a Strong Ethical Climate The first step is to foster an ethical climate, as discussed in the chapter-opening Manager's toolbox. Managers can promote ethical climates through the policies, procedures, and practices that are used on a daily basis.

2. Screening Prospective Employees Companies try to screen out dishonest, irresponsible employees by checking applicants' resumes and references. Some firms, for example, run employee applications through E-Verify, a federal program that allows employers to check for illegal immigrants. Some also use personality tests and integrity testing to identify potentially dishonest people.

3. Instituting Ethics Codes and Training Programs **A code of ethics consists of a formal written set of ethical standards guiding an organization's actions.** Most codes offer guidance on how to treat customers, suppliers, competitors, and other stakeholders. The purpose is to clearly state top management's expectations for all employees. As you might expect, most codes prohibit bribes, kickbacks, misappropriation of corporate assets, conflicts of interest, and "cooking the books"—making false accounting statements and other records. Other areas frequently covered in ethics codes are political contributions, workforce diversity, and confidentiality of corporate information.

In addition, according to the Society for Human Resource Management, 81 percent of U.S. companies are providing ethics training, and 66 percent include ethical behavior as a measure of employee evaluations.[126] The approaches vary, but one way is to use a case approach to present employees with ethical dilemmas. By clarifying expectations, this kind of training may reduce unethical behavior.[127]

4. Rewarding Ethical Behavior: Protecting Whistle-Blowers It's not enough to simply punish bad behavior; managers must also reward good ethical behavior, as in encouraging (or at least not discouraging) whistle-blowers.

A whistle-blower is an employee, or even an outside consultant, who reports organizational misconduct to the public, such as health and safety matters, waste, corruption, or overcharging of customers.[128] Photographer Simon Edelman is a good example (see Example box). Edelman's case reinforces the point that whistle-blowers sometimes risk their jobs by coming forward and thus need to be protected. For instance, the law that created the Occupational Safety and Health Administration (OSHA) gives "employees and their representatives the right to file a complaint and request an OSHA inspection of their workplace if they believe there is a serious hazard or their employer is not following OSHA standards. Workers do not have to know whether a specific OSHA standard has been violated in order to file a complaint."[129] In some cases, whistle-blowers may receive a reward; the Internal Revenue Service (IRS), for instance, is authorized to pay tipsters rewards as high as 30% in cases involving large amounts of money.[130]

Whistle-blowing has been on the rise since the Great Recession, and the number of whistle-blower tips received by the Securities and Exchange Commission, for example, is now nearly 4,000 a year.[131] True whistle-blowing involves acts that are against the law. However, the principal kinds of misconduct reported in one study—misuse of company time, abusive behavior, and lying to employees—aren't necessarily illegal, although they may create an offensive work environment, the leading reason people leave their jobs.[132] Retaliation against whistle-blowers is also on the rise, ranging from giving them the cold shoulder to passing them over for promotion.

EXAMPLE The Whistle-Blowing Photographer

In early 2017, Department of Energy (DOE) photographer Simon Edelman, on routine assignment, took a photo of then-new Department Secretary Rick Perry in a bear hug with Robert E. Murray, an energy company executive who had been a major donor to the Trump campaign and to Perry's own failed presidential bid. Another photo Edelman took that day showed the cover page of a confidential document Murray presented to Perry during their meeting, outlining a plan that would guide the DOE to make drastic staff reductions and restore policies favorable to the coal industry. In releasing the photos to a magazine a few months later, Edelman says he hoped to make the public aware of the close relationship between the two men and the ease with which industry was exerting influence over a government department charged with regulating it. Less than a year after the meeting, *The New York Times* reported, nearly all the points in Murray's plan had been achieved or were on track to completion.[133]

THE REPERCUSSIONS

"It seemed like that was the right thing to do—exercising my First Amendment rights to get the information out there," Edelman said of his decision. But a day after the photos were published, Edelman found himself placed on administrative leave and escorted out of the DOE building, forced to leave his personal laptop and expensive camera equipment behind. He was subsequently told his contract with the department would not be renewed as promised—essentially he was fired—and he has filed a federal lawsuit seeking whistle-blower protection, reinstatement, and an ethics investigation into Perry and Murray for "public corruption."[134] Retaliation against whistle-blowers is against federal law; the DOE is calling Edelman's accusations "ridiculous."[135]

Whistlebloweraid.org is a nonprofit law firm that assists government whistle-blowers like Edelman with confidential free legal advice, especially if they witness lawbreaking when the evidence is classified and don't know where to turn.[136] Though he is working with the group, Edelman insists his photos are in the public domain. "I'm definitely proud of what I did," he says. "I know that I did the right thing. I just hope that more people take this as inspiration that they can also speak up and blow the whistle because it's an important part of democracy."[137]

FOR DISCUSSION

What are some of the reasons someone might become a whistleblower? Why would someone choose *not* to be? Is that position defensible given the value of job attitudes like professional and ethical standards? Why or why not? What would you have done in Edelman's position?

In exposing unethical behavior, then, it's important to be clear why you're doing it (trying to help the company or just get someone in trouble), not report something for the wrong reason (discuss your concerns with someone who has similar values), and follow proper channels (like addressing the supervisor of the supposed culprit). Don't try to report externally (lashing out on Facebook, for instance) without speaking to those who might resolve the problem.[138]

Some people view ethics in ideal terms, which means that ethical principles or standards apply universally across situations and time. Others, however, take a relativistic view and believe that what is ethical depends on the situation. These differences can create conflict among managers trying to make decisions.

Consider the situation faced by a group of executives working with Angelo to make a decision about opening a new office overseas. Angelo was consulting with a global company that was dealing with the issue of whether or not it should pay local officials for helping establish a new office overseas. Some executives in the meeting concluded that the company should pay these officials because it was a normal cost of doing business in this country. Others viewed the situation quite differently. They thought the payments amounted to bribes and were totally against the idea. The company ultimately decided that it would not make the payments, which resulted in their inability to open the new office.

All told, it is important for you to learn more about your ethical tendencies. This will help you to behave in ways that are consistent with your values and beliefs. •

SELF-ASSESSMENT 3.1 CAREER READINESS

Assessing My Perspective on Ethics

This survey is designed to assess your views about ethics. It provides feedback about your status on the Career Readiness "other characteristic" of *professionalism/work ethic*.

Please be prepared to answer these questions if your instructor has assigned Self-Assessment 3.1 in Connect.

1. Are your views more idealistic or more relativistic?
2. What do you think about students cheating on homework assignments in school? What about cheating on exams?
3. Are your answers consistent with your score? Explain.
4. What can you say during an interview to demonstrate an ethical orientation?

3.5 The Social Responsibilities Required of You as a Manager

THE BIG PICTURE

Managers need to be aware of the viewpoints supporting and opposing social responsibility and whether being and doing good pays off financially for the organization.

LO 3-5

Describe the concept of social responsibility and its role in today's organizations.

Is money the be-all and end-all in business? This is the concern behind the triple bottom line discussed earlier. For TOMS Shoes, profit must be balanced with the higher purpose of helping children in developing countries who lack belongings as simple as a pair of shoes. Founded more than 10 years ago with the simple idea to donate one pair of shoes to a child in need for every pair purchased by a consumer, the company has established a "one for one" model other companies have since adopted. For founder Blake Mycoski, who recently stepped down as CEO to focus on promoting the company as it expands into bags and eyewear, TOMS Shoes was always "mission with a company" rather than a company with a mission. "I think it's incredibly sustainable," he says of the firm. "Built into our cost structure is the intention to provide great benefit to our customers because they feel like they're getting to be part of something more than just a transaction."[139]

If ethical responsibility is about being a good individual citizen, social responsibility is about being a good *organizational citizen.* More formally, **social responsibility** **is a manager's duty to take actions that will benefit the interests of society as well as of the organization.** When generalized beyond the individual to the organization, social responsibility is called **corporate social responsibility (CSR), the notion that corporations are expected to go above and beyond following the law and making a profit.** Areas of CSR include the environment, philanthropy, and ethical labor practices.[140]

Corporate Social Responsibility: The Top of the Pyramid

According to University of Georgia business scholar **Archie B. Carroll,** corporate social responsibility rests at the top of a pyramid of a corporation's obligations, right up there with economic, legal, and ethical obligations. Some people might hold that a company's first and only duty is to make a profit. However, Carroll suggests the responsibilities of an organization in the global economy should take the following priorities, with profit being the most fundamental (base of the pyramid) and corporate citizenship at the top:[141]

- *Be a good global corporate citizen,* as defined by the host country's expectations.
- *Be ethical in its practices,* taking host-country and global standards into consideration.
- *Obey the law* of host countries as well as international law.
- *Make a profit* consistent with expectations for international business.

These priorities are illustrated in the pyramid opposite. *(See Figure 3.3.)*

Is Social Responsibility Worthwhile? Opposing and Supporting Viewpoints

In the old days of cutthroat capitalism, social responsibility was hardly thought of. A company's most important goal was to make money pretty much any way it could, and the consequences be damned. Today, for-profit enterprises in the United States

FIGURE 3.3

Carroll's global corporate social responsibility pyramid

Source: A. Carroll, "Managing Ethically and Global Stakeholders: A Present and Future Challenge," Academy of Management Executive, *May 2004, p. 116.*

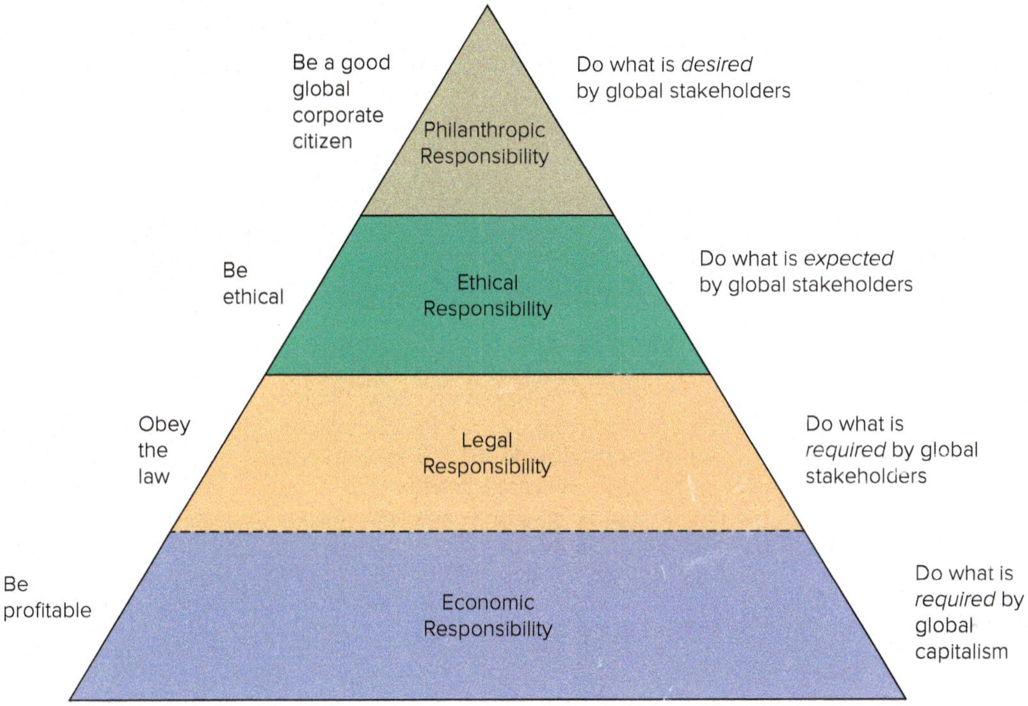

and Europe—but, increasingly, multinational firms from developing nations as well—generally make a point of "putting something back" into society as well as taking something out.[142]

Not everyone, however, agrees with these new priorities. Let's consider the two viewpoints.

Against Social Responsibility "Few trends could so thoroughly undermine the very foundations of our free society," argued the late free-market economist Milton Friedman, "as the acceptance by corporate officials of social responsibility other than to make as much money for their stockholders as possible."[143]

Do you think social responsibility should be equally shared by companies and governments around the world?
©EyeEm/Getty Images

Friedman represents the view that, as he said, "The social responsibility of business is to make profits." That is, unless a company focuses on maximizing profits, it will become distracted and fail to provide goods and services, benefit the stockholders, create jobs, and expand economic growth—the real social justification for the firm's existence.

This view would presumably support the efforts of companies to set up headquarters in name only in offshore Caribbean tax havens (while keeping their actual headquarters in the United States) in order to minimize their tax burden.

Marc Benioff speaks at the Salesforce keynote during Dreamforce 2015 at Moscone Center on September 16, 2015 in San Francisco, California.

For Social Responsibility "A large corporation these days not only may engage in social responsibility," said famed economist Paul Samuelson, who passed away in 2009, "it had damned well better to try to do so."[144] That is, a company must be concerned for society's welfare as well as for corporate profits.

Beyond the fact of ethical obligation, the rationale for this view is based on the belief that it is good for business, morally appropriate, or important to employees. That is, CEOs support CSR because they think it promotes sales, provides a favorable public image that can help head off government regulation, or increases employees' attachment to the firm.[145]

EXAMPLE Corporate Social Responsibility: Salesforce.com Wants to Change the Way the World Works

There are all kinds of ways by which corporate social responsibility is expressed. Marc Benioff, founder and CEO of Salesforce.com, a San Francisco business software company, says, "Companies can do more than just make money, they can serve others. The business of business is improving the state of the world."[146] Here are some of the ways in which Salesforce.com does that.[147]

Operating with Integrity. Salesforce.com has adopted Business Conduct Principles and a Code of Conduct that, among other things, support ethical business practices, anti-corruption, antidiscrimination, and rejection of forced or involuntary labor.

"1/1/1" Charitable Giving. When founder and CEO Marc Benioff set up Salesforce.com in 1999, he also created a foundation with a powerful but simple vision: Donate 1% of Salesforce.com resources, 1% of employees' time, and 1% of the firm's technology to improving communities around the world. For instance, since 1999, the company has donated $65 million and 175,00 employee volunteer hours to education in San Francisco and Oakland's school districts. In San Francisco, the company has helped increased enrollment of girls in computer science courses by 2,000 percent.[148]

Journey toward Sustainability. Although Salesforce.com does no manufacturing or mining, it still strives to reduce carbon emissions in the operation of its data centers and office buildings, as well as in employee travel.

Fostering Employee Success. At Salesforce.com, says the company, "our goal is to deliver a dream job experience for our employees. We are intense, passionate people on a mission to change the way the world works." Employees are so heavily compensated with stock options that the company hasn't posted an actual profit for five years.[149]

YOUR CALL

Do you believe corporate social responsibility really has benefits? Can you think of any highly profitable and legal businesses that *do not* practice any kind of social responsibility?

One Type of Social Responsibility: Climate Change, Sustainability, and Natural Capital

Nearly everyone is aware of the growing threat of climate change and global warming, and the vast majority (64%) of U.S. adults in a 2016 poll said they were worried about global warming. Sixty-five percent put most of the blame on human activity, and 59% believe the impacts are already being felt.[150] (Scientists say global warming is "unequivocal" and that it is extremely likely that humans are the primary contributors to it.)[151] **Climate change** refers to major changes in temperature, precipitation, wind patterns, and similar matters occurring over several decades. **Global warming**, one aspect of climate change, refers to the rise in global average temperature near the Earth's surface, caused mostly by increasing concentrations in the atmosphere of greenhouse gases, such as carbon emissions from fossil fuels.[152] *Sustainability*, as we said in Chapter 1, is economic development that meets the needs of the present without compromising the ability of future generations to meet their own needs. (For more about the social, political, and cultural responses to climate change, including dissenters, see *Why We Disagree about Climate Change* by Mike Hume.)[153]

The Benefits of Being Green

"Coca-Cola has always been more focused on its economic bottom line than on global warming," writes reporter Coral Davenport. But "as global droughts dried up the water needed to produce its soda," its profits took some serious hits. Now the company "has embraced the idea of climate change as an economically disruptive force," she writes, and is focused on water-conservation technologies, along with other sustainability measures.[154] Beyond water conversation, the Coca-Cola Company established 2020 sustainability goals in the following aspects of its business: agriculture, climate protection, giving back, human and workplace rights, packaging and recycling, and women's economic empowerment.[155]

Today, going green has entered the business mainstream, where sustainability programs are producing not only environmental benefits, but also cost savings, revenue growth, and competitive advantages.[156] Carmaker Subaru of Indiana Automotive, for example, has proved that adopting environmentally friendly processes does not add to the cost of doing business but actually makes it more efficient (reducing water use by 50%, electricity by 14%, and so on).[157] Dow Chemical, collaborating with the Nature Conservancy, an environmental group, is exploring coastal marsh and dune restoration (and paying nearby homeowners to replace lawns with native plants) to shield its Freeport, Texas, chemical complex from storm surges coming off the Gulf of Mexico.[158]

The Value of Earth's Resources: Natural Capital

Indeed, planet (of the triple bottom line people, planet, and profit) is now identified by the name *natural capital* (or *natural capital accounting*), which many scholars think should figure seriously in economic decision making. **Natural capital** is the value of natural resources, such as topsoil, air, water, and genetic diversity, which humans depend on. "We're driving natural capital to its lowest levels ever in human history," says Stanford University ecologist Gretchen Daily.[159]

According to this view, we are approaching the planet's limitations, with human activity threatening to exceed the earth's capacity to generate resources and absorb wastes. For example, the mountain of electrical waste disposed of annually worldwide—cell phones, laptops, appliances, anything with a battery or a cord—was projected to be nearly 50 million tons in 2018 and to grow by 5% a year.[160] Nearly all such waste can be recycled, but worldwide only about 15 to 20% is.[161] One United Nations report suggests climate change poses a risk to world food supplies, with output dropping perhaps 2% each decade, as rising temperatures make it harder for crops to thrive.[162] The report

Marine pollution occurs when chemicals, particles, residential waste, industrial and agricultural waste enter the oceans or seas. This example comes from the sea in Spain. The majority of marine pollution comes from land. ©Perry van Munster/Alamy Stock Photo

also warns that waiting to cut carbon emissions could even outstrip technology's ability to preserve the planet.[163] Alarming predictions indeed.

Another Type of Social Responsibility: Undertaking Philanthropy, "Not Dying Rich"

"He who dies rich dies thus disgraced," 19th-century steel magnate Andrew Carnegie is supposed to have said, after he turned his interests from making money to **philanthropy**, **making charitable donations to benefit humankind.** Carnegie became well known as a supporter of free libraries.

When Bill Gates of Microsoft, one of the richest people in the world (with 2017 net worth of $92.9 billion) stepped down from day-to-day oversight of Microsoft, the company he co-founded, he turned his attention to the Bill and Melinda Gates Foundation, through which he and his wife have pledged to spend billions on health, education, and overcoming poverty.[164] The Gateses have been joined by 169 other billionaires from 22 countries, including Facebook founder Mark Zuckerberg and his wife, oil and gas financier T. Boone Pickens, Berkshire Hathaway chairman Warren Buffett, Chobani yogurt founder Handi Ulukaya, and others—in taking the Giving Pledge, a commitment to dedicate a majority of their wealth to philanthropy.[165]

Does Being Good Pay Off?

We answered this question by reviewing relevant research. Our conclusion is that indeed it pays to be ethical or socially responsible. Supportive findings are shown in Table 3.1.

TABLE 3.1 **Being Ethical and Socially Responsible Pays Off**

OUTCOMES	RESEARCH FINDINGS
Employees	• Millennials more likely to stay with a company when management is committed to helping society. • Millennials report higher job satisfaction when a company treats its employees and society in an ethical manner.[166]
Interpersonal relationships	• Employees feel confident in doing the right thing when faced with an ethical situation when the organization has an effective ethics and compliance culture. • Employees are less likely to retaliate against one another when the company has an effective ethics and compliance culture.[167]
Customers	• Believe it's important to purchase from socially responsible companies. • Made past purchases and plan to spend more with socially responsible companies in the future.[168]
Revenue	• Investing in responsible companies topped $8.7 trillion in 2017 and accounts for a fifth of professionally managed investments.[169] • Quality service and ethical behavior are essential for long-term revenue growth.[170]
Stock price	• Equifax stock price dropped nearly 18% after inappropriately handling a major security breach that affected nearly 143 million people in the U.S.[171] • Wynn Resorts lost $3 billion in market value in 2018 following Steve Wynn's alleged sexual misconduct.[172]
Profits	• Companies ranked as "America's Best Corporate Citizens" by *Forbes*, outperform their competition by 1 to 4 percentage points. • Generate 3.5% higher 5-year return on invested capital.[173]

SELF-ASSESSMENT 3.2 CAREER READINESS

Assessing Your Attitudes toward Corporate Responsibility

This self-assessment assesses your attitudes toward corporate responsibility. It partially overlaps with the Career Readiness "other characteristic" of *professional/work ethic.* Please be prepared to answer these questions if your instructor has assigned Self-Assessment 3.2 in Connect.

1. Where do you stand on corporate social responsibility?
2. What life events have influenced your attitudes toward corporate social responsibility? Discuss.
3. Based on the three lowest-rated items in the survey, how might you foster a more positive attitude toward social responsibility? Explain.
4. What can you say during an interview to demonstrate a positive attitude toward corporate responsibility?

3.6 Corporate Governance

THE BIG PICTURE

Corporate governance is the system of governing a company so that the interests of corporate owners and other stakeholders are protected. Company directors should be clearly separated in their authority from the CEO by insisting on strong financial reporting systems and more accountability.

LO 3-6

Discuss the role of corporate governance in assessing management performance.

What, you might ask, were the company boards of directors doing prior to 2001-2002 when Enron, WorldCom, Tyco, and Adelphia filed for bankruptcy amid allegations their CEOs were committing fraud—for which they later went to prison? Aren't directors elected by the stockholders to see that a company is run according to their interests? Indeed, after the Enron and other scandals there was renewed interest in what is known as **corporate governance**, **the system of governing a company so that the interests of corporate owners and other stakeholders are protected.**

Ethics and Corporate Governance

Is there any connection between ethics and corporate governance? Certainly, says scholar Henrik Syse. Corporate governance is about such matters as long-term strategies, sustainable finances, accurate reporting, and positive work environment. All are obviously ethical because they are concerned with how a firm relates to stakeholders inside and out.[174]

How can members of the board of directors be chosen to act ethically? As mentioned earlier, inside directors may be members of the firm, but outside directors are supposed to be elected from outside the firm. However, in some companies, the outside directors have been handpicked by the CEO—because they are friends, because they have a business relationship with the firm, or because they supposedly "know the industry." In such instances, how tough do you think the board of directors is going to be on its CEO when he or she asks for leeway to pursue certain policies?

Now, more attention is being paid to strengthening corporate governance so that directors are clearly separated in their authority from the CEO. While, of course, directors are not supposed to get involved with day-to-day management issues, they are now feeling more pressure from stockholders and others to have stronger financial reporting systems and more accountability.[175]

The Need for Trust

In the end, suggests Fordham professor Robert Hurley, "We do not have a crisis of ethics in business today. We have a crisis of trust."[178] Customers or employees may well think that certain people or companies are ethical—that is, moral, honest, and fair—but that does not mean they should trust them. Trust, says Hurley, "comes from delivering every day on what you promise—as a manager, an employee, and a company. It involves constant teamwork, communication, and collaboration."

Trust comes from asking how likely the people you're dealing with are to serve your interests, how much they have demonstrated concern for others, how well they delivered on their promises, how much they try to keep their word—and how effectively they communicate these skills.

Would you agree? •

EXAMPLE Corporate Governance, Good and Bad: HD Supply Holdings, Fox News

The news has been filled with cases of sexual harassment. Sexual harassment consists of unwanted sexual attention that creates an adverse work environment. Why do you think the type of behavior depicted here continues to happen at work? ©Kaspars Grinvalds/Shutterstock

HD Supply. The report of a 2017 hacking attack at the credit-reporting firm Equifax, exposing untold amounts of personal data to cybercriminals, caused alarm and chaos among consumers and businesses alike. Though their company was not directly affected, the board of directors at HD Supply Holdings Inc., a large industrial distributor, knew immediately what they had to do. "Equifax triggered a reactive review of the thoroughness of our oversight and compliance and of our gaps," recalls board member Betsy Atkins, "and we acted." Working with the company's management team, the board addressed its lack of formal procedures for dealing with hacking or ransom attacks. HD Supply's new response plan included the opening of a bitcoin account with which to pay hackers ransom money if needed.[176]

Fox News. Cable television is used to scandal, but when Fox's celebrity news commentator Bill O'Reilly was accused in April 2017 of having paid several women sums totaling millions of dollars to quiet allegations of sexual harassment, advertisers fled his show, *The O'Reilly Factor*. Before the month was over, O'Reilly had been forced to resign. Could anything have looked worse for the company? Possibly the revelation, shortly after O'Reilly's departure, that when they renewed his $25 million contract in February, top executives at the network's parent company were already well aware of the payouts and, in particular, one made in January for $32 million.[177] Neither O'Reilly nor Fox have admitted any wrongdoing to date.

YOUR CALL

How would you compare the ethical values and standards that appear to be in place in each of these two companies?

3.7 Career Corner: Managing Your Career Readiness

LO 3-7

Describe how to develop the career readiness competency of professionalism/work ethic.

Figure 3.4 shows the model of career readiness we discussed in Chapter 1. We see one clear link between the content of this chapter and this model. It's the Career Readiness competency of *professionalism/work ethic.* The relevant aspect of this competency for this chapter is "demonstrated integrity, ethical behavior, and concern for the greater good" (look back at Table 1.2).

FIGURE 3.4

Model of career readiness

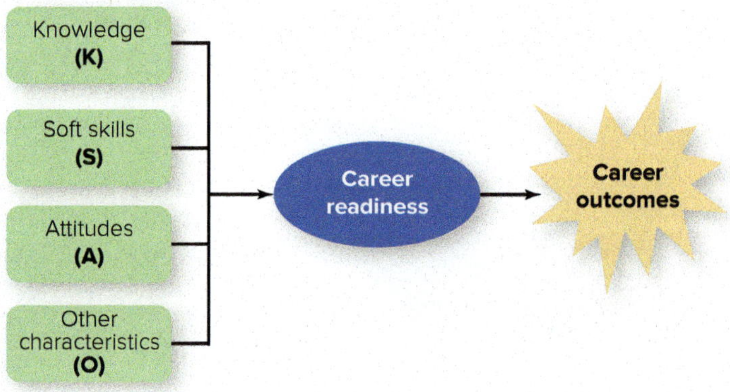

Can you really develop integrity and ethical behavior? We think you can, even though this competency is partly based on stable characteristics like values, moral perspective, and religious beliefs that are all resistant to change. Our goal is not to suggest modifying these fundamental aspects of your life. Rather, we believe this competency is best developed by engaging in activities that facilitate a habit of showing integrity, ethicality, and concern for the greater good. Doing so will give you behavioral examples of your *professionalism/work ethic* to discuss during job interviews.

Focus on the Greater Good and on Being More Ethical

Experiment with implementing some of the following:

1. **Reduce your carbon footprint.** Activities include walking or using public transportation more frequently, turning off lights when you leave a room, unplugging devices that are not in use, purchasing a reusable water bottle, reducing your use of air conditioning, reusing glass jars, and annually servicing your air-conditioning/heating units.[179]
2. **Foster positive emotions in yourself and others.** Positivity and helping others beget positivity and helping behavior, thereby enhancing the greater good. Psychologist Barbara Fredrickson said it best, "Beyond the dance of positivity between you and the person you helped, those who witness your good deed may well feel inspired, their hearts uplifted and elevated."[180] This self-reinforcing and perpetuating aspect of positive emotion, and of positivity

more generally, is what leads to upward spirals of positivity, in which your positive behaviors and attitudes generate the same in others in an ongoing process. Focus on displaying the positive emotions of joy, gratitude, hope, pride, inspiration, and love. Start by thinking every day of one thing you are thankful for.

3. **Spend time in nature.** Research shows that people are more helpful, trusting, and generous when they have recently experienced natural beauty. This occurs because positive emotions are associated with time spent in nature.[181] Get outside and see for yourself.
4. **Get the proper amount of sleep.** Research shows that people are more likely to succumb to temptation to engage in unethical behavior when they are sleep-deprived.[182] For better sleep, try going to bed at the same time each night and avoiding looking at electronic screens (phone, tablet, TV) for at least half an hour before.
5. **Increase your level of exercise.** Besides providing obvious health benefits, exercise can increase your feelings of virtuousness and pride.[183] Pride enhances self-esteem, but it also provides a greater sense of responsibility, a key attitude associated with career readiness. Don't like gyms? Go for a long walk a few times a week.
6. **Expand your awareness of social realities.** Watching documentaries such as *Inequality for All*, available on Netflix, and reading books by reputable commentators can increase your understanding of social issues that affect the greater good.[184]
7. **Fulfill your promises and keep appointments.** Failing to meet promises and commitments undermines your integrity. Use your phone to send yourself reminders of appointments and don't allow yourself to shrug them off.
8. **Avoid people who lack integrity.** People make judgments about you based on those you choose to associate with. Socializing or working with individuals known to be unethical will detract from a positive personal image.[185]

Become an Ethical Consumer

Try these suggestions:

1. **Purchase Fair Trade items.** Purchasing Fair Trade products increases the chances that your money will help provide a decent wage for the people who made them. Low prices often result from the producers' paying low wages to their workers. Take a look at "Fair Trade USA" (*https://www.fairtradecertified.org/*) to discover where you might find clothing, alcohol, and home goods from producers who treat workers ethically.[186]
2. **Bring your own grocery bags.** You can lower your carbon footprint and reduce the price of goods sold by bringing your own reusable cloth or natural fiber bags when purchasing groceries.
3. **Don't purchase items that aren't ethically made or sourced.** Research where and how a company makes its products. You may pay more for your purchases, but passing on low prices to support more ethical companies supports the greater good.[187]
4. **Don't buy knockoffs.** Cheap counterfeit and illegal merchandise are often made in sweatshop conditions. Although forgoing the low prices on such items may hurt your pocketbook, it's another way you can help the greater good. ●

Key Terms Used in This Chapter

abusive supervision 93
clawbacks 85
climate change 103
code of ethics 97
competitors 83
corporate governance 106
corporate social responsibility (CSR) 100
crowdfunding 86
customers 82
demographic forces 90
distributor 84
economic forces 88
ethical behavior 93
ethical climate 77
ethical dilemma 92
ethics 93
external stakeholders 82
general environment 87
global warming 103
government regulators 86
individual approach 95
insider trading 96
internal stakeholders 79
international forces 91
justice approach 95
LGBTQ 89
macroenvironment 87
moral-rights approach 95
natural capital 103
owners 79
philanthropy 104
political–legal forces 90
Sarbanes–Oxley Act of 2002 96
social audit 78
social responsibility 100
sociocultural forces 89
special-interest groups 87
stakeholders 79
strategic allies 84
supplier 83
task environment 82
technological forces 88
triple bottom line 78
utilitarian approach 95
value system 94
values 94
venture capital 86
whistle-blower 98
workplace cheating 93

Key Points

3.1 The Triple Bottom Line: People, Planet, and Profit

- Many businesses subscribe to a new standard of success—the triple bottom line, representing people, planet, and profit. It measures an organization's social, environmental, and financial performance.
- Success in these areas can be measured through a social audit, a systematic assessment of a company's performance in implementing socially responsible programs, often based on predefined goals.
- The triple bottom line has particular appeal to many young adults (Millennials) who are less concerned with finding financial success than with making a difference and achieving a meaningful life.

3.2 The Community of Stakeholders inside the Organization

- Managers operate in two organizational environments—internal and external—both made up of stakeholders, the people whose interests are affected by the organization's activities.
- The first, or internal, environment includes employees, owners, and the board of directors.

3.3 The Community of Stakeholders outside the Organization

- The external environment of stakeholders consists of the task environment and the general environment.
- The task environment consists of 10 groups that present the manager with daily tasks to deal with. (1) Customers pay to use an organization's goods and services. (2) Competitors compete for customers or resources. (3) Suppliers provide supplies—raw materials, services, equipment, labor, or energy—to other organizations. (4) Distributors help another organization sell its goods and services to customers. (5) Strategic allies join forces to achieve advantages neither organization can perform as well alone. (6) Employee organizations are labor unions and employee associations. (7) Local communities are residents, companies, governments, and nonprofit entities that depend on the organization's taxes, payroll, and charitable contributions. (8) Financial institutions are commercial banks, investment banks, and insurance companies that deal with the organization. (9) Government regulators are regulatory agencies that establish the ground rules under which the organization operates. (10) Special-interest groups are groups whose members try to influence specific issues that may affect the organization.
- The general environment consists of six forces. (1) Economic forces consist of general economic conditions and trends—unemployment, inflation, interest rates, economic growth—that may affect an organization's performance. (2) Technological forces are new developments in methods for transforming

resources into goods and services. (3) Sociocultural forces are influences and trends originating in a country, society, or culture's human relationships and values that may affect an organization. (4) Demographic forces are influences on an organization arising from changes in the characteristics of a population, such as age, gender, and ethnic origin. (5) Political–legal forces are changes in the way politics shapes laws and laws shape the opportunities for and threats to an organization. (6) International forces are changes in the economic, political, legal, and technological global system that may affect an organization.

3.4 The Ethical Responsibilities Required of You as a Manager

- Ethics are the standards of right and wrong that influence behavior. Ethical behavior is behavior that is accepted as "right" as opposed to "wrong" according to those standards.
- Ethical dilemmas often take place because of an organization's value system. Values are the relatively permanent and deeply held underlying beliefs and attitudes that help determine a person's behavior.
- Managers should strive for ethical leadership, defined as leadership that is directed by respect for ethical beliefs and values for the dignity and rights of others.
- There are four approaches to deciding ethical dilemmas. (1) Utilitarian—ethical behavior is guided by what will result in the greatest good for the greatest number of people. (2) Individual—ethical behavior is guided by what will result in the individual's best long-term interests, which ultimately is in everyone's self-interest. (3) Moral-rights—ethical behavior is guided by respect for the fundamental rights of human beings, such as those expressed in the U.S. Constitution's Bill of Rights. (4) Justice—ethical behavior is guided by respect for the impartial standards of fairness and equity.
- Public outrage over white-collar crime (Enron, Tyco) led to the creation of the Sarbanes–Oxley Act of 2002 (SarbOx), which established requirements for proper financial record keeping for public companies and penalties for noncompliance.
- Laurence Kohlberg proposed three levels of personal moral development: (1) preconventional level of moral development—people tend to follow rules and to obey authority; (2) conventional level—people are conformist, generally adhering to the expectations of others; and (3) postconventional level—people are guided by internal values.
- There are three ways an organization may foster high ethical standards. (1) Top managers must support a strong ethical climate. (2) The organization may have a code of ethics, which consists of a formal written set of ethical standards. (3) An organization must reward ethical behavior, as in not discouraging whistle-blowers, employees who report organizational misconduct to the public.

3.5 The Social Responsibilities Required of You as a Manager

- Social responsibility is a manager's duty to take actions that will benefit the interests of society as well as of the organization.
- The idea of social responsibility has opposing and supporting viewpoints. The opposing viewpoint is that the social responsibility of business is to make profits. The supporting viewpoint is that since business creates some problems (such as pollution), it should help solve them.
- One scholar, Archie Carroll, suggests the responsibilities of an organization in the global economy should have the following priorities: (1) Be a good global corporate citizen, (2) be ethical in its practices, (3) obey the law, and (4) make a profit.
- One type of social responsibility is sustainability, "going green," or meeting humanity's needs without harming future generations. A major threat is climate change, which refers to major changes in temperature, precipitation, wind patterns, and similar matters over several decades. Global warming, one aspect of climate change, refers to the rise in global average temperature near the Earth's surface, caused mostly by increasing concentrations in the atmosphere of greenhouse gases, such as carbon emissions from fossil fuels.
- The component of the triple bottom line called planet is now identified by the name *natural capital*, which is the value of natural resources, such as topsoil, air, water, and genetic diversity, which many scholars think should figure seriously in economic decision making.
- Another type of social responsibility is philanthropy, making charitable donations to benefit humankind.
- Positive ethical behavior and social responsibility can pay off in the form of customer goodwill, more efficient and loyal employees, better quality of job applicants and retained employees, enhanced sales growth, less employee misconduct and fraud, better stock price, and enhanced profits.

3.6 Corporate Governance

- Corporate governance is the system of governing a company so that the interests of corporate owners and other stakeholders are protected.
- One way to further corporate governance is to be sure directors are clearly separated in their authority from the CEO by insisting on stronger financial reporting systems and more accountability.

3.7 Career Corner: Managing Your Career Readiness

- You can develop the competency of *professionalism/work ethic* by engaging in activities that facilitate a habit of showing integrity, ethical behavior, and concern for the greater good.

Understanding the Chapter: What Do I Know?

1. How would you explain the difference between internal and external stakeholders?
2. Among external stakeholders, what's the difference between the task environment and the general environment?
3. Of the 11 groups in the task environment, which five do you consider most important, and why?
4. Of the six groups in the general environment, which one do you think has the least importance, and why?
5. Distinguish among the four approaches to deciding ethical dilemmas.
6. What's the difference between insider trading and a Ponzi scheme?
7. How would you summarize Kohlberg's levels of personal moral development?
8. What are four ways that organizations can promote ethics?
9. Describe the levels in Carroll's corporate social responsibility pyramid. Where does trying to achieve sustainability fit in?
10. How would you explain the concept of corporate governance?

Management in Action

Who's to Blame for College Basketball's "Dark Underbelly"?

The National Collegiate Athletic Association (NCAA) is "a member-led organization dedicated to the well-being and lifelong success of college athletes."[188] Founded in 1906, the NCAA "functions as a general legislative and administrative authority for men's and women's intercollegiate athletics" and "formulates and enforces the rules of play for various sports and the eligibility criteria for athletes."[189]

One of the "bedrock principles" of the NCAA is maintaining the spirit of amateur competition. Students are not allowed to be professional athletes, education holds top priority, and all athletes receive a fair chance to compete.[190] The NCAA outlines specific rules athletes must follow to maintain amateur status and, thus, eligibility to continue playing collegiate sports. Student athletes are, among other things, prohibited from publicly endorsing companies[191] and from receiving a salary for athletic participation or benefits from prospective agents.[192]

Although NCAA guidelines prohibit corporate sponsorships at the individual-athlete level, college teams have benefited from such alliances since 1977, when shoe-company executive Sonny Vaccaro "signed several coaches he knew . . . to contracts with Nike." According to Vaccaro, "'the world changed' in 1987, when Nike signed its first all-school deal" to sponsor all of the University of Miami's athletic teams. With these deals, said Vaccaro, "you own everything in that school. That shoe company is now your business partner."[193]

A BLURRY LINE BETWEEN AMATEURISM AND PROFESSIONALISM

Benefits aside, strategic relationships between apparel companies and universities blur the line between amateurism and professionalism for two reasons. The first is money flowing to universities. Companies such as Nike, Under Armour, and Adidas "pay tens of millions of dollars a year to equip (and, from a marketing standpoint, align themselves) with major university programs."[194] These alliances benefit universities due to increased revenues generated by the sponsorships, and they earn sports apparel companies not only exclusive rights to partner with large academic institutions, but also insider access to the country's top athletic talent.

The second reason is money for college athletes. A particular challenge in NCAA basketball is the reality that some athletes don't intend to graduate from college. Due in large part to the NBA's "one-and-done" rule prohibiting athletes from playing professionally before their 19th birthday, elite players often attend classes for a year until they age into the NBA draft.[195] Apparel sponsors are often overly eager to secure exclusive deals with elite athletes who may earn coveted spots in the NBA because these arrangements generate lots of money for the sponsors.

ASSISTANT COACHES AND FEDERAL INDICTMENTS

Assistant coaches serve as the primary recruiters of top high-school talent and are expected to act as salespersons for their universities and build strong relationships with prize recruits.[196] They are expected to follow NCAA guidelines, and they do not always do so.

In November 2017, four assistant college basketball coaches were among 10 individuals indicted by a federal grand jury. *Fortune* described the lead-up to the indictments as "a detailed and clandestine FBI investigation that exposed alleged under-the-table payments to agents, coaches, and parents to influence talented athletes to choose particular colleges to play basketball."[197] Joon Kim, then the acting U.S. attorney for the Southern District of New York, portrayed "a two-part scheme: One involving bribes from managers to coaches for their assistance in securing future clients, and the other in which the sportswear firm and advisors would make 'coach-requested' payments to players and their families."[198]

According to sports journalist Mark Titus, "dirty recruiting tactics were the worst-kept secret in college sports. Even the most naïve fan knew that a day of reckoning was coming, when the house of cards built by apparel companies, agents, financial advisers, shady coaches, and handlers of big-time recruits would all come crashing down."[199] Some go so far as to characterize assistant college basketball coaches as downright unscrupulous. *The New York Times* reported that "the weeds of college basketball have long been filled with snakes, and assistant coaches have sometimes proved the most reptilian. The widely held presumption is that many successful head coaches are backed by a little-known assistant or two willing to do the dirty work–to bend the rules of recruitment, to tiptoe through the minefield of N.C.A.A. regulations."[200]

According to *Inside Higher Ed*, "assistant coaches have historically been likeliest to do the dirty work that gets NCAA sports programs in trouble, even though critics often believe that the aides are acting with the implicit support of–if not under outright pressure from–their bosses, the head coaches."[201] Not a single head coach was charged in the 2017 federal indictments.

Also indicted in the scandal was Jim Gatto, director of global marketing for Adidas for basketball, who helped "facilitate six-figure payments to the families of high school basketball recruits in exchange for the recruits' commitment to play at college basketball programs sponsored by Adidas."[202] Gatto worked through assistant coaches to reach and incentivize high school recruits, and assistants accepted bribes from Gatto to funnel "significant cash payments" between Adidas and recruits.[203] In exchange for the payments, recruits were expected to sign on with the Adidas-sponsored university and, eventually, to choose Adidas as their exclusive apparel sponsor once they made it to the NBA.

PRESSURE TO PERFORM

While many attribute these scandals to assistant coaches' moral shortcomings, other evidence speaks to at least three sources of intense pressure in the NCAA basketball environment worth noting.

First, assistant coaches are under extreme pressure to recruit top talent. In discussing whether hiring more ethical coaches could curtail the problem, University of Kansas head basketball coach Bill Self said, "You could say, 'well, if everybody's squeaky clean, then we wouldn't have these problems.' No no no, that's not true either. There would still be pressure to sign guys, there would still be coaches losing jobs, there would still be assistant coaches not having opportunities to move on to get better paying positions. There's a lot of things going on that is dictated by how well you recruit."[204]

Head basketball coaches represent a second source of pressure. Some suggest head coaches were aware of the schemes all along but were emboldened by an environment that provided them free rein to enable ethically questionable behavior with little fear of permanent consequences. While none were explicitly named in the indictments, several head coaches lost their jobs because they were held accountable for the actions of their assistants. One was Louisville's Rick Pitino, who was fired by the University of Louisville Athletics Association after the scandal came to light.[205] Although Pitino said the allegations "come as a complete shock to me,"[206] FBI phone records indicate Pitino made three phone calls to Jim Gatto prior to an unnamed recruit's commitment to Louisville.[207]

Finally, consider pressures from the university and alumni community. According to *ESPN*, "division I football and basketball are multibillion-dollar industries, paying coaches and administrators multimillion-dollar salaries while generating billions from media-rights deals and hundreds of millions from apparel deals with Adidas, Nike and Under Armour."[208] University of Kansas men's coach Bill Self described "pressure from the alumni that expects certain things and have given a lot of money, and in order to make the bills meet you jack up ticket prices ridiculous, so now there's pressure on coaches even from alums that say, 'You're not giving us the product we're paying for.'"[209]

WHAT ABOUT THE NCAA?

The NCAA exists to protect college athletes and the spirit of amateurism. So why didn't it initiate an investigation before the federal government did? Some believe the NCAA knew about the behaviors and remained quiet because of pressure from apparel companies. According to *Fortune*, "while the NCAA enforcement staff has investigated coaches and recruiting violations for years, it has not been successful in rooting out this type of corruption, nor has it really tried because of the danger of cutting off the money. Previous punishments have been light, ineffective, and often slanted to protect high-profile coaches and players as much as possible."[210] Further, "in simple terms, NCAA Division I men's basketball is too big to fail and too important financially to the NCAA membership . . . it is the ultimate Catch-22. Coaches are solely judged on winning and losing, universities oftentimes value their high-profile intercollegiate athletic programs more than academic primacy and candidly, fans do not seem to care whether the athletes are students or being paid under the table. They just want to see the games. Thus, the reward far outweighs any risk, and the chances that the NCAA would address and attempt to stop a lucrative black market of player peddling the highest bidder stretches the limits of credibility. It can be hard to bite the hand that feeds you."[211]

NOW WHAT?

Justice Joon Kim described those indicted as "assistant coaches of major Division I schools with top-tier programs" who have "been in and around the game for a long time. All of them had the trust of players they recruited. Young men who looked up to them and believed their coaches had their best interests at heart."[212] Kim described a scenario of coaches "taking cash bribes, managers and advisers circling blue-chip prospects like coyotes, and employees of a global sportswear company funneling cash to families of high school recruits."[213] Kim added, "Month after month, the defendants exploited the hoop dreams of athletes around the country, allegedly treating them as little more than opportunities to enrich themselves through bribery and fraud schemes . . . The defendants' alleged conduct not only sullied the spirit of amateur athletics, but it showed contempt for the thousands of players and coaches who follow the rules and play the game the right way."[214]

As a result of the investigation and subsequent indictments, "the NCAA has established a Commission on College basketball" with members including "former Secretary of State Condoleezza Rice, former Chairman of the Joint Chiefs of Staff Gen. Martin Dempsey, and former NBA stars David Robinson and Grant Hill."[215] Further, the federal courts have stated that these indictments are the first in a series of many that will come to light in the coming months. The FBI has set up a tip line where those with knowledge regarding these schemes can call and share information.[216] Sources believe the ongoing probe will likely implicate additional college programs, sports apparel companies, and agents.[217]

There is hope that these indictments will send a strong message that these behaviors will not be tolerated and will be punished to the fullest extent of the law. "With the federal government's threat of serious punishment, coaches are more likely to operate within NCAA rules. At the very least, they will think twice, knowing that indictments, potential jail time and huge legal fees are on the table."[218]

William Sweeney Jr., the Assistant Director-in-Charge of the FBI's New York office, said the "arrests serve as a warning to others choosing to conduct business this way in the world of college athletics: We have your playbook."[219]

FOR DISCUSSION

Problem Solving Perspective

1. What is the underlying problem in this case from the federal government's perspective?
2. Why do you think assistant coaches play such a significant role in these scandals?
3. How do you think the NCAA and the Commission on College basketball should move forward to prevent illegal behavior from occurring in the future?

Application of Chapter Content

1. How do you think the basketball teams' task environment, particularly competitors, allies, customers, regulators, and media, played into the corruption in the NCAA?
2. Are the high school recruits who accepted bribes from apparel companies and coaches purely victims in this situation, or should their behavior also be considered unethical? Explain your answer using one of the four approaches to deciding ethical dilemmas.
3. What might the NCAA do to promote higher ethical standards among its schools, coaches, players, and allies?
4. How do you think the scandal has and will continue to affect customers, players' attitudes on the court, and NCAA sales?

Legal/Ethical Challenge

Should You Apply to Have Your Student Loans Forgiven?

Student loan debt nearly tripled in the last decade, thanks to increased attendance at for-profit colleges along with rising college tuition and living expenses.[220] For hundreds of thousands buried in student loan debt, a little known 1994 program called "Borrower Defense" or "Defense to Repayment" sponsored by the Education Department offers a lifeline.

The program is available for those students who obtained loans from the government's Direct Loan program. "The law says students are entitled to forgiveness of any existing debt—and, possibly, reimbursement of any repaid loans—if they can show that their school violated state law in getting them to take out the debt.

(An example might be if a school lied in its advertisements about how many of its graduates landed jobs.) However, it's not clear what documentation the borrower needs to prove fraud."[221]

Thousands have applied to have their loans expunged under the program. In the first seven months of 2017, nearly 15,000 former students had applied to have student loans expunged.[222] The U.S. Education Department has already agreed to cancel nearly $28 million in debt and indicated many more will likely get forgiveness.[223]

Assume that you recently graduated from a state university. You took the required courses for your bachelor's degree and excelled in your studies. You made the Dean's List each semester of your last two years and interned for a social services organization in your community. You hoped you'd be able to work in your chosen field of psychology and be able to pay off the debt a few years after graduation.

Like many students, you paid for the majority of your education with student loans. Three years after graduation, your career has not turned out as expected. Instead of working in your chosen field of psychology, you have a low-paying job at a retail chain and wait tables on weekends to make ends meet. You weren't aware that psychology positions required a graduate degree. Your student loan debt remains unpaid, and you recently heard about the borrower defense program.

You are considering whether or not to apply for the Borrower Defense program.

SOLVING THE CHALLENGE

What would you do?

1. Apply for loan forgiveness and hope that the broad language of the law will make an exception for your state college education and loan. Besides, what's wrong with asking?
2. Apply for loan forgiveness. After all, you aren't benefiting from your education, someone should have told you that you needed a graduate degree in psychology to get a good job, and there is no clear definition of fraud.
3. Don't apply. You were never promised a job and you made the decision to major in psychology. You could have chosen a field with more job opportunities.
4. Invent other options. Discuss.

Uber Continuing Case connect

Learn about the manner in which Uber interacts with its internal and external stakeholders. Assess your ability to apply concepts discussed in this chapter to the case by going to Connect.

4 Global Management

Managing across Borders

©Olivier Renck/Aurora/Getty Images

After reading this chapter, you should be able to:

LO 4-1 Identify three influential effects of globalization.

LO 4-2 Describe the characteristics of a successful international manager.

LO 4-3 Outline the ways in which companies can expand internationally.

LO 4-4 Discuss barriers to free trade and ways companies try to overcome them.

LO 4-5 Explain the value to managers of understanding cultural differences.

LO 4-6 Describe how to develop your cross-cultural competency.

FORECAST *What's Ahead in This Chapter*

This chapter covers the impact of globalization—the rise of the global village, of one big market, of both worldwide megafirms and minifirms. We also describe the characteristics of the successful international manager and why and how companies expand internationally. We describe the barriers to free trade and the major organizations promoting trade and the major competitors. We discuss some of the cultural differences you may encounter if you become an international manager, and conclude with a Career Corner that focuses on how you can develop the career readiness competency of cross-cultural awareness.

MANAGE U

Working Successfully Abroad: Developing Cultural Awareness

Whether you travel abroad on your own or on a work assignment for your company, there are many ways to develop cultural awareness, a career readiness competency that can help ensure your international experience enhances your career success.[1] The general idea is to be global in your focus but think in terms of your local environment.

Do Your Research

Don't wait until you arrive to start the process of familiarizing yourself with the culture of your new environment; start reading books and articles and watching videos well in advance. Study the geography and the transportation systems ahead of time. Talk to people who have been there, and before you leave, begin seeking out and contacting people from the local area who can help you now or in the future. A few general rules always apply when you are the outsider: Learn by listening more than you speak; follow the example of others; and be moderate, open-minded, and humble.

Check Your Attitude

In a recent interview with *Business Insider*, Karoli Hinricks, CEO of Jobbatical, the international tech marketplace, offered some good advice about leaving biased attitudes at home. "Don't move abroad if you're looking to find things to be exactly like they were back home," she says. "Only when you open your mind to the experience and grasp all the quirks that your new home has in store for you, will the journey boost your creativity and become positive." Be ready to embrace the opportunity, and don't let minor problems or the novelty of your experience throw you. Maintain a positive, can-do attitude and overcome the small stuff.

There are important cross-cultural differences between Americans and people from the Middle East. ©Image Source/Getty Images

Learn the Appropriate Behavior

Before you go, spend some time learning about patterns of interpersonal communication and interaction. A quick online search can clue you in about expectations in the particular country or areas where you'll be living or working. Pay attention to social customs about such everyday behaviors as making introductions, being introduced, order of speaking in a meeting or group, use and nonuse of humor, dining etiquette, and the norms for personal space, which can be very different from what you're used to.

Become at Least Minimally Skilled in the Language

Whatever foreign country you're in, at the very least you should learn a few key phrases—such as "hello," "please," and "thank you"—in your host country's language. The effort you make to do this will go a long way to enhancing your relationships with others, even if your grammar and accent aren't perfect.

Pack Wisely

Packing wisely means more than just bringing the right clothes for the climate, although you should do that, too. But also inform yourself about the attire that's appropriate for the places you'll visit and the events you'll attend. More conservative clothing is often the norm abroad, and you'll want to be sensitive to your cultural surroundings. Consider, too, that living spaces are often smaller in other countries. Pack light, bring outfits that are versatile and easy to care for, and don't anticipate a walk-in closet.

Finally, Be Prepared

Get a head start on making sure all your paperwork is in order—a valid passport (with an expiration date at least several months in the future), a visa and work permit if needed, debit and credit cards that are accepted in your host country, and health insurance that covers you outside the United States. Know your rights, too; working abroad is not the same as being a tourist. Be prepared for emergencies, such as running out of cash unexpectedly (though you should always have some in reserve), and have a plan that will help you stay calm and focused while you resolve the issue.

For Discussion One fashion photography intern working in London found herself spending the first month doing the very unglamorous work of painting and cleaning the studio, which had recently moved. Disappointed at first, she soon realized she was actually learning a great deal, including "how a photo studio is built from the ground up, how to support oneself, and make connections and contacts."[2] How would you manage your own attitudes and keep learning if your job overseas was not everything you thought it would be?

4.1 Globalization: The Collapse of Time and Distance

THE BIG PICTURE

Globalization, the trend of the world economy toward becoming a more interdependent system, is reflected in three developments: the rise of the "global village" and e-commerce, the trend of the world's becoming one big market, and the rise of both megafirms and Internet-enabled minifirms worldwide.

LO 4-1

Identify three influential effects of globalization.

Is everything for sale in the United States now made abroad? What does that mean for U.S. consumers and the economy? Although it is the third-largest exporter in the world, the United States imports more than it exports. In 2016, the nation imported \$2.2 trillion in goods and \$502 billion in services. Only the European Union imports more. Consumer goods account for almost \$600 billion of U.S. imports, mostly consisting of cell phones, TVs, clothing, shoes, and drugs. Imported services include travel, transportation, and computer services, valued at just over \$500 billion.[3] Three in four U.S. consumers would like to buy products made at home if they could, but when forced to choose between a domestic product and a cheaper imported one, two-thirds say they would choose the cheaper option.[4]

TABLE 4.1

Country Rankings for Competitiveness, 2016–2017

1. Switzerland
2. United States
3. Singapore
4. Netherlands
5. Germany
6. Hong Kong SAR
7. Sweden
8. United Kingdom
9. Japan
10. Finland
11. Norway
12. Denmark
13. New Zealand
14. Canada
15. Taiwan, China

Source: "The Global Competitiveness Report, 2016-2017," World Economic Forum, *September 28, 2016, https://www.weforum.org/reports/the-global-competitiveness-report-2016-2017-1.*

Competition and Globalization: Who Will Be No. 1 Tomorrow?

It goes without saying that the world is a competitive place. Where does the United States stand in it? What's our report card?

The United States remained the world's largest economy in 2017,[5] but was it the most competitive? Actually, the World Economic Forum ranks the United States as No. 2, behind Switzerland. *(See Table 4.1.)*

Is the United States the richest nation? In terms of gross domestic product per capita (the total value of all goods and services produced in the country divided by the population), the International Monetary Fund's annual ranking for 2017 puts the United States at No. 12 in the world, behind San Marino, Hong Kong, Switzerland, United Arab Emirates, Kuwait, Norway, Ireland, Brunei, Singapore, Luxembourg, and in first place, Qatar.[6]

How about "most free"? Here Hong Kong, part of the People's Republic of China, is No. 1. The United States is No. 17, according to criteria embraced by the 2017 Index of Economic Freedom (produced by the Heritage Foundation). Hong Kong is considered "free" by this standard; both Canada, at No. 7, and the United States are considered "mostly free."[7]

There are many reasons the winners on these lists achieved their status, but one thing is clear: They didn't do it all by themselves; other countries were involved. We are living in a world being rapidly changed by **globalization**—**the trend of the world economy toward becoming a more interdependent system.** Time and distance, which have been under assault for 150 years, have now virtually collapsed, as reflected in three important developments we shall discuss:[8]

1. The rise of the "global village" and electronic commerce.
2. The world's becoming one market instead of many national ones.
3. The rise of both megafirms and Internet-enabled minifirms worldwide.

The Rise of the "Global Village" and Electronic Commerce

The hallmark of great civilizations has been their great systems of communications. In the beginning, communication was based on transportation: The Roman Empire had its network of roads, as did other ancient civilizations, such as the Incas. Later, the great European powers had their far-flung navies. In the 19th century, the United States and Canada unified North America by building transcontinental railroads. Later the airplane reduced travel time between continents.

From Transportation to Communication Transportation began to yield to the electronic exchange of information. Beginning in 1844, the telegraph ended the short existence of the Pony Express and, beginning in 1876, found itself in competition with the telephone. The amplifying vacuum tube, invented in 1906, led to commercial radio. Television came into being in England in 1925. During the 1950s and 1960s, as television exploded throughout the world, communications philosopher Marshall McLuhan posed the notion of a "global village," where we all share our hopes, dreams, and fears in a "worldpool" of information. **The global village refers to the "shrinking" of time and space as air travel and the electronic media have made it easier for the people around the globe to communicate with one another.**

Then the world became even faster and smaller. When AT&T launched the first cellular communications system in 1983, it predicted there would be fewer than a million users by 2000. And by 2019, there will be almost 250 million smartphone users in the United States.[9]

The Net, the Web, and the World Then came the Internet, the worldwide computer-linked "network of networks." Today, of the 7.5 billion people in the world, 52% are Internet users.[10] The arrival of the web quickly led to the introduction of **e-commerce, or electronic commerce, the buying and selling of products and services through computer networks.** U.S. online sales of goods surpassed $409 billion in 2017, or 9% of that year's total retail sales, and are projected to top $630 billion by 2022.[11]

EXAMPLE E-Commerce: Alibaba

The biggest U.S. e-commerce site is Amazon.com, which was started in 1994 by Jeffrey Bezos as an online bookstore and now offers an unimaginable stream of products and services that accounts for 50 cents of every dollar spent online in the United States.[12] If there are any Amazon challengers left in online retail, they may be coming from overseas. Consider Alibaba, the Amazon of China. By some measures, it is already the world's largest e-commerce company and, likely, the fastest growing.

Alibaba was founded about 20 years ago to serve as a hub for small businesses to sell online and has grown into a leading global wholesale and retail marketplace and provider of cloud competing, digital media, and entertainment services. In a country with more than 600 million Internet users, the company sees itself as "the future infrastructure of commerce" and intends to last "at least 102 years" in order to span three centuries.[13] Hundreds of millions of users frequent its three separate websites, participating in transactions worth about $248 billion a year, more than eBay and Amazon recently earned together.[14] In addition to its e-commerce sites, Alibaba offers a payment app called Alipay, through which users can pay cab drivers or invest in a money-market fund worth $87 billion. And it is planning to set up shop in the real world as well, with gigantic vending machines from which select customers can obtain a car for a three-day test drive and then either purchase it or try another one. The company plans to follow its two initial outlets with "dozens" more.[15]

The leader of Alibaba's founding group of 18, Jack Ma, is a former English teacher and now the richest man in China. Ma recently stepped down as CEO, but not before promising employees that Alibaba would always put customers before shareholders. "Most companies, when they're doing good, they enjoy today's wonderful life," says Ma. "They don't worry about five years later—but I worry about five years later."

YOUR CALL

Alibaba has a few data centers in the United States but so far has not done more than engage in exploratory talks with U.S. firms about joining its growing network of retailers.[16] Do you think it makes sense for Alibaba to remain focused on its home market of China, and why or why not?

One Big World Market: The Global Economy

"We are seeing the results of things started in 1988 and 1989," said Rosabeth Moss Kantor of the Harvard Business School, referring to three historic global changes.[17] The first was in the late 1980s when the Berlin Wall came down, signaling the beginning of the end of communism in Eastern Europe. The second was when Asian countries began to open their economies to foreign investors. The third was the worldwide trend of governments deregulating their economies. These three events set up conditions by which goods, people, and money could move more freely throughout the world—a global economy. **The global economy refers to the increasing tendency of the economies of the world to interact with one another as one market instead of many national markets.**

It's no secret the economies of the world are increasingly tied together, connected by information arriving instantaneously through currency traders' screens, CNN news reports, Twitter feeds, text messages, and other technology. Money, represented by digital blips, changes hands globally in a matter of keystrokes.

Positive Effects Is a global economy really good for the United States? "Most people see speedy travel, mass communications, and quick dissemination of information through the Internet as benefits of globalization," says University College London historian Michael Collins.

Other positives are that there is now a worldwide market for companies and consumers who have access to products of different countries, and there is more influx of information between two countries, more cultural intermingling, and often more openness and tolerance toward other people.[18] Faster technological improvements can result from increased communication and information sharing, and as we've seen, many products and services can be produced more cheaply.[19]

In addition, in some industries foreign firms are building plants in the United States, revitalizing some industrial areas. Thirteen foreign automakers have manufacturing operations in the United States that produce more than 60 models of trucks and cars for domestic sale and export; they employ a total of 130,000 people.[20] Employment in the auto industry is inching downward, however, thanks to falling sales and automakers' desire to avoid building up expensive inventory.[21]

But will worldwide economic growth create "rising prosperity and higher living standards," as some have predicted?[22]

Globalization. Coke and Pepsi already dominate India's beverage market of 1.3 billion people, and now both companies are going after the fruit-juice market among India's increasingly health-conscious consumers. Do you see any negative effects to this? ©Taylor Ross/SIPA/Newscom

Negative Effects The large-scale effects of the rise of global economy have included much-publicized job losses across the United States. Despite an apparent rise in protectionist sentiment in some of the world's largest economies, some of those jobs will not return. Other negative effects of globalization are more closely tied to individual managers' day-to-day challenges. These include potential threats to information security because data must be shared, possible loss of control over quality and standards because products or components are made hundreds or thousands of miles away, and the risk of hidden or unanticipated costs, especially transportation costs, that can offset some of the savings expected from moving manufacturing to countries with lower labor costs.[23] The company's work culture can be affected too, as employees adjust to changes in their workflow and responsibilities or watch co-workers being reassigned or laid off. And communication and cultural differences are a challenge managers can count on.[24]

Cross-Border Business: The Rise of Both Megamergers and Minifirms Worldwide

The global market driven by electronic information "forces things to get bigger and smaller at the same time," suggests technology philosopher Nicholas Negroponte. "There will be an increasing absence of things that aren't either very local or very global."[25]

If Negroponte is correct, this means we will see more and more of two opposite kinds of businesses: mergers of huge companies into even larger companies, and small, fast-moving, start-up companies.

Megamergers Operating Worldwide

The last 20 years have seen a surge in mergers.[26] More than 50,000 mergers and acquisitions were announced in the global economy in 2017, hitting a high for the third year in a row.[27] Certain industries—automobiles, airlines, telecommunications, health care, and pharmaceuticals, for instance—aren't suited to being midsize, let alone small and local, so companies in these industries are trying to become bigger and cross-border. The way to do this is to merge with other big companies. CVS Health, the retail pharmacy, has announced a merger with health insurer Aetna, for instance. While some in the health industry have discovered that size is not always an advantage, other mergers include Advocate Health Care and Aurora Health Care, UnitedHealth Group and DaVita Medical Group, and Catholic Health Initiatives and Dignity Health, all of which will create huge organizations serving millions of patients and bringing in revenues in the billions of dollars.[28]

Even companies that are already large are looking at mergers and acquisitions that can open doors into new markets. Amazon purchased the grocer Whole Foods, while Walmart, which already sells groceries online, bought the flexible-pricing e-commerce company Jet.com.[29] Dell merged with EMC in 2016, as did Microsoft and LinkedIn the same year. Intel reached overseas to purchase MobileEye, an Israeli start-up.[30]

Walmart says its purchase of Jet.com will speed its growth, better serve existing customers, help attract new ones, add people with vision to its management team, and "win the future of retail." Not all observers think big mergers are a good idea, however. "The presence of a few dominant companies in an industry," said one editorial, "makes it harder for entrepreneurs to start new businesses in that sector."[31] For instance, two giant beer makers—Anheuser-Busch InBev (Budweiser, Corona, Beck's) and SABMiller (Miller, Coors)—consolidated distributors as a way of thwarting the advance of craft breweries, which now account for 11% of the beer market.[32]

Craft beers. At Costco, craft beers account for 30% of the company's beer sales. What kind of threat do you think the merger of giant breweries Anheuser-Busch InBev (makers of Budweiser, Corona, Beck's) and SABMiller (Miller, Coors) represents to craft breweries?
©David Caudery/Future Publishing/Getty Images

Minifirms Operating Worldwide

The Internet and the World Wide Web allow almost anyone to be global, with two important results:

1. **Small companies can get started more easily.** Because anyone can put goods or services on a website and sell worldwide, this wipes out the former competitive advantages of distribution and scope that large companies used to have.
2. **Small companies can maneuver faster.** Little companies can change direction faster, which gives them an advantage in terms of time and distance over large companies. ●

4.2 You and International Management

THE BIG PICTURE

Studying international management prepares you to work with foreign customers or suppliers, for a foreign firm in the United States, or for a U.S. firm overseas. Successful international managers aren't ethnocentric or polycentric but geocentric.

LO 4-2

Describe the characteristics of a successful international manager.

Can you see yourself working overseas? It can definitely be an advantage to your career. "There are fewer borders," says Paul McDonald, executive director of recruitment firm Robert Half Management Resources. "Anyone with international experience will have a leg up, higher salary, and be more marketable."[33] The recent brutal U.S. job market has also spurred more U.S. workers to hunt for jobs overseas. The following Example box explores how you might pursue a job overseas.

EXAMPLE Managing Your Career: Getting the Edge in the Global Job Market

According to one writer, "There's an uptick in desire among millennial workers to move abroad for work. It's no surprise either, as many millennials are perfectly positioned to pick up their life and start fresh in a new city or country." A recent survey found that 70% of Millennials cite their desire to travel as the primary reason they work in the first place,[34] and more than 4 in 10 want to live abroad. If you are someone who wants to work abroad, how can you increase your chances of landing the job?

1. Brush up your cultural awareness, and your foreign language skills (see the discussion later in this chapter). Being able to converse freely in an overseas environment makes you valuable to employers of all kinds.
2. Demonstrate your flexibility, one of the most important skills you will take abroad with you. A corporate communications intern who worked in Brussels had this to say about the need for flexibility: "I was on a team with people from all over Europe and Asia, so in addition to a slight language barrier, our ethics, ideas, and methods almost never matched, which made for some challenges in communication. Working abroad taught me how to be flexible, bend what I know about my field, and adapt it to fit any environment or client's needs."[35]
3. If you are already employed, find out whether your current company has positions overseas, and research the responsibilities and requirements of these jobs. See whether your boss will support you, or find a mentor in the company who will (this might be someone who currently holds or has recently returned from such an assignment).
4. Build your network of people who work for companies with overseas opportunities, and tell them what you're looking for and what you can offer.
5. Look into jobs with entry requirements you may already meet, such as tutoring or teaching English abroad. These may not be the highest-paying openings, but once in a foreign country, you can more easily make local connections to expand your opportunities and use your experience to move up.

YOUR CALL

What are the key challenges in pursuing an international job after graduation?

Foreign experience demonstrates independence, resourcefulness, and entrepreneurship, according to management recruiters. "You are interested in that person who can move quickly and is nimble and has an inquiring mind," says one. People who have worked and supported themselves overseas, she says, tend to be adaptive and inquisitive–valuable skills in today's workplace.[36] This outlook represents the career readiness competency of **cross-cultural awareness**, **defined as the ability to operate in different cultural settings.** This competency is expected to become more important over the next decade in response to our globally connected world. According to the Institute for the Future, "In a truly globally connected world, a worker's skill set could see them posted in any number of locations . . . This demands specific content, such as linguistic skills, but also adaptability to changing circumstances and an ability to sense and respond to new contexts."[37] The Practical Action box (on page 146) provides insight into building true cross-cultural awareness.

Why Learn about International Management?

International management is management that oversees the conduct of operations in or with organizations in foreign countries, whether it's through a multinational corporation or a multinational organization.

Multinational Corporations A **multinational corporation, or multinational enterprise, is a business firm with operations in several countries.** Our publisher, McGraw-Hill Education, is owned by Apollo Global Management, one such multinational. In terms of sales revenue, the largest American multinational corporations in 2015 were Wal-Mart Stores, ExxonMobil, Chevron, Berkshire Hathaway, Apple, McKesson, General Motors, Phillips 66, General Electric, and Ford Motor. The largest foreign firms were the oil companies SinoPec Group, Royal Dutch Shell (Netherlands), PetroChina, ExxonMobil (USA), and BP (Britain), followed by State Grid (utilities, China), Volkswagen (Germany), and Toyota Motor (Japan).[38]

Multinational Organizations A **multinational organization is a nonprofit organization with operations in several countries.** Examples are the World Health Organization, the International Red Cross, and the Church of Latter Day Saints.

Even if in the coming years you never travel to the wider world outside North America—an unlikely proposition, we think—the world will assuredly come to you. That, in a nutshell, is why you need to learn about international management.

More specifically, consider yourself in the following situations:

You May Deal with Foreign Customers or Partners While working for a U.S. company you may have to deal with foreign customers. Or you may have to work with a foreign company in some sort of joint venture. The people you're dealing with may be outside the United States or visitors to it. Either way you would hate to blow a deal—and maybe all future deals—because you were ignorant of some cultural aspects you could have known about.

You May Deal with Foreign Employees or Suppliers You may have to purchase important components, raw materials, or services for your U.S. employer from a foreign supplier. And you never know where foreign practices may diverge from what you're accustomed to. Many software developer jobs, for instance, have been moved outside the United States—to places such as India, New Zealand, and Eastern Europe. Among the U.S. tech companies with overseas subsidiaries (and plenty of cash there as well) are Apple, Microsoft, Cisco, Oracle, Alphabet, and Intel.[39]

You May Work for a Foreign Firm in the United States You may sometime take a job with a foreign firm doing business in the United States, such as an electronics, pharmaceutical, or car company. And you'll have to deal with managers above and below you whose outlook is different from yours. For instance, Japanese companies, with their emphasis on correctness and face saving, operate in significantly different ways from U.S. companies.

Sometimes it is even hard to know that an ostensibly U.S. company actually has foreign ownership. For example, among some classic U.S. brands that are now foreign owned are Anheuser-Busch, sold to InBev of Belgium in 2008; Ben & Jerry's, owned by multinational giant Unilever; Burger King, purchased by Restaurant Brands International of Canada; Trader Joe's, a subsidiary of German supermarket chain Aldi Nord;

Working for a foreign firm. If you think you might work for a foreign firm, either at home or overseas, what should you be doing now to prepare for it? ©CKDJ/Corbis/VCG/Getty Images

General Electric, owned by China's Haier, the largest appliance company in the world; American Apparel, bought by Gildan Activewear, a Canadian clothier; and 7-Eleven, owned by the Japanese retail group Seven & i Holdings.[40]

You May Work for a U.S. Firm outside the United States—or for a Foreign One

You might easily find yourself working abroad in the foreign operation of a U.S. company. Most big U.S. corporations have overseas subsidiaries or divisions. On the other hand, you might also work for a foreign firm in a foreign country, such as a big Indian company in Bangalore or Mumbai.

The Successful International Manager: Geocentric, Not Ethnocentric or Polycentric

Maybe you don't really care that you don't have much understanding of the foreign culture you're dealing with. "What's the point?" you may think. "The main thing is to get the job done." Certainly there are international firms with managers who have this perspective. They are called *ethnocentric*, one of three primary attitudes among international managers, the other two being *polycentric* and *geocentric*.[41]

Ethnocentric Managers—"We Know Best" What do foreign executives fluent in English think when they hear Americans using an endless array of baseball, basketball, and football phrases (such as "out of left field" or "Hail Mary pass"). **Ethnocentric managers** believe that their native country, culture, language, and behavior are superior to all others. Ethnocentric managers tend to believe that they can export the managers and practices of their home countries to anywhere in the world and that they will be more capable and reliable. Often, the ethnocentric viewpoint is less attributable to prejudice than it is to ignorance because such managers obviously know more about their home environment than the foreign environment. Ethnocentrism might also be called **parochialism**—that is, a narrow view in which people see things solely through their own perspective.

I Wish I...
...considered the impact of ethnocentrism.

Jordin Hansen Courtesy Jordin Hansen

Jordin Hansen is a senior director of strategic operations for a global information technology company. She experienced a clashing of cultures when her company developed nomenclature as part of a global business strategy.

An executive team in the United States was put together to develop a global business strategy for a new business within a larger company. Part of the strategy involved deciding on company vocabulary. "When you run a global organization, having consistent nomenclature in how you talk about things is extremely important, especially when you have global customers," said Jordin.

The approach that was used to decide on the company nomenclature was a very top-down approach. The strategy team claimed they were listening to outside opinions but really moved forward with what they thought was the best decision.

What was not taken into consideration was that English was not the main language for a majority of the company's global stakeholders. One of the terms chosen to be part of the company nomenclature was "solution." As Jordin explained, this word means very different things to people of different cultures.

"The word 'solution' in our industry in the United States can mean a piece of a larger solution; whereas in Europe when you talk about solutions it usually means the full end-to-end supply chain or product," said Jordin.

There may have been short-term benefits to quickly announcing and implementing company vocabulary, but the long-term effects were negative. The team had to rethink the strategy several times, and the buy-in from stakeholders was minimal. "We took two steps forward just to take fourteen steps back," said Jordin.

Perhaps the most negative impact of presenting company vocabulary that was not culturally sensitive was a loss of credibility and trust among stakeholders. "This overstepped the opinions and the input of the global stakeholders. It ruined credibility for anything later down the road that we wanted to implement," said Jordin. "In a world where relationships are everything, this is incredibly important."

Courtesy of Jordin Hansen

Ethnocentric views also affect our purchasing decisions. Some people believe that we should only purchase products made in our home country.[42] What are your views about being an ethnocentric consumer? You can find out by taking Self-Assessment 4.1.

SELF-ASSESSMENT 4.1

Assessing Your Consumer Ethnocentrism

This survey is designed to assess your consumer ethnocentrism. Please be prepared to answer these questions if your instructor has assigned Self-Assessment 4.1 in Connect.

1. Are you surprised by the results? What do they suggest about your purchasing decisions? What are the pros and cons of being an ethnocentric consumer?
2. How do American companies, associations, and unions encourage us to be ethnocentric consumers?

Polycentric Managers—"They Know Best"

Polycentric managers **take the view that native managers in the foreign offices best understand native personnel and practices, and so the home office should leave them alone.** Thus, the attitude of polycentric managers is nearly the opposite of that of ethnocentric managers.

Geocentric Managers—"What's Best Is What's Effective, Regardless of Origin"

Geocentric managers **accept that there are differences and similarities between home and foreign personnel and practices and that they should use whatever techniques are most effective.** Clearly, being an ethno- or polycentric manager takes less work. But the payoff for being a geocentric manager can be far greater. •

4.3 Why and How Companies Expand Internationally

THE BIG PICTURE

Multinationals expand to take advantage of availability of supplies, new markets, lower labor costs, access to finance capital, or avoidance of tariffs and import quotas. Five ways they do so are by global outsourcing; importing, exporting, and countertrading; licensing and franchising; joint ventures; and wholly owned subsidiaries.

LO 4-3

Outline the ways in which companies can expand internationally.

Who makes Apple's iPhone? The iPhone 6s is a good example of the complexity of Apple's supply chain. The modem, battery, and wifi module come from three different Chinese suppliers; the radio frequency transceiver is made by Qualcomm, also of China; rare minerals for the circuitry, speakers, and screen colors come from California and China; and the processor's parts come from South Korea and Taiwan. The RAM device is made by Samsung in South Korea, and the display and camera came from two different suppliers in Japan. The chassis or body comes from China.[43]

Where is Netflix going for new business as its U.S. growth slows? Now that it is streaming content in at least 130 countries around the world and in 20 different languages, the company has more international than U.S. subscribers.[44]

There are many reasons U.S. companies are going global. Let us consider why and how they are expanding beyond U.S. borders.

The Gross Domestic Product of Dubai has grown from 82 billion in U.S. dollars in 2008 to 382 billion in 2017. This tremendous economic growth has resulted in the development of the beautiful skyscrapers at the Dubai Marina in the United Arab Emirates. ©Boule/Shutterstock

Why Companies Expand Internationally

Many a company has made the deliberate decision to restrict selling its product or service to just its own country. Is anything wrong with that?

The answer is: It depends. It would probably have been a serious mistake for NEC, Sony, or Hitachi to have limited their markets solely to Japan during the 1990s, a time when the country was in an economic slump and Japanese consumers weren't consuming. During that same period, however, some American banks might have been better off not making loans abroad, when the U.S. economy was booming but foreign economies were not. Going international or not going international—it can be risky either way.

Why, then, do companies expand internationally? There are at least five reasons, all of which have to do with making or saving money.

1. Availability of Supplies Mining companies, banana growers, sellers of hard woods—all have to go where their basic supplies or raw materials are located. For years oil companies, for example, expanded their activities outside the United States in seeking cheaper or more plentiful sources of oil.

2. New Markets Sometimes a company will find, as cigarette makers have, that demand for their product has declined domestically but they can still make money overseas. Or sometimes a company will launch a concerted effort to expand into foreign markets, as Coca-Cola did under the leadership of legendary CEO Robert Goizueta. Apple expanded efforts to sell more iPhones and other products in India, as sales to China slowed.[45] Swedish retailer IKEA did likewise, thinking India's blossoming middle class was a good bet to buy "flat-pack dining tables, cotton dish towels, and Scandinavian-sounding sofas."[46] Amazon is expanding to a new market, Australia.[47]

3. Lower Labor Costs The decline in manufacturing jobs in the United States is partly attributable to the fact that U.S. companies have found it cheaper to manufacture outside the States. For example, the rationale for using **maquiladoras**—**foreign-owned manufacturing plants allowed to operate in Mexico with special privileges in return for employing Mexican citizens**—is that they provide less expensive labor for assembling everything from appliances to cars. As another example, Ford Motor Company plans to move production of its Focus passenger car from the United States to China. Not only is China a key new market for the car, but starting in 2019 the Focus will be more spacious and stylish, and better equipped, but with a higher price tag. Ford hopes lower labor costs will help offset the cost of revamping the design and shipping cars back to the United States.[48]

Even professional or service kinds of jobs, such as computer programming, may be shipped overseas.

4. Access to Finance Capital Companies may be enticed into going abroad by the prospects of capital put up by foreign companies or subsidies from foreign governments. A sovereign wealth fund is a government-owned investment fund that often invests in foreign assets. China's sovereign wealth fund, China Investment Company (CIC), hopes to increase its investments abroad, for instance, and especially in the United States, through investments in infrastructure projects, though it may face resistance from increasing nationalist and protectionist sentiment.[49] "As CIC and China make more foreign investments, we're seeing the rise of protectionism in some countries and regions, be it the U.S. or Europe. They're making some protectionist moves, some specifically targeting China," said the fund's president.[50]

5. Avoidance of Tariffs and Import Quotas Countries place tariffs (fees) on imported goods or impose import quotas—limitations on the numbers of products allowed in—for the purpose of protecting their own domestic industries. For example, Japan imposes tariffs on agricultural products, such as rice, imported from the United States. To avoid these penalties, a company might create a subsidiary to produce the product in the foreign country. General Electric and Whirlpool, for example, have foreign subsidiaries to produce appliances overseas.

How Companies Expand Internationally

Most companies don't start out to be multinationals. Generally, they edge their way into international business, at first making minimal investments and taking minimal risks, as shown in the drawing. *(See Figure 4.1.)*

Let's consider the five ways of expanding internationally shown in the figure.

FIGURE 4.1

Five ways of expanding internationally

These range from lowest risk and investment *(left)* to highest risk and investment *(right)*.

1. Global Outsourcing

A common practice of many companies, **outsourcing** is defined as using suppliers outside the company to provide goods and services. For example, airlines farm out a lot of aircraft maintenance to other companies. Management philosopher Peter Drucker believed that in the near future organizations might be outsourcing all work that is "support"–such as information systems–rather than revenue producing.

Global outsourcing extends this technique outside the United States. **Global outsourcing**, or **offshoring**, is defined as using suppliers outside the United States to provide labor, goods, or services. The reason may be that the foreign supplier has resources not available in the United States, such as Italian marble. Or the supplier may have special expertise, as do Pakistani weavers. Or–more likely these days–the supplier's labor is cheaper than American labor. As a manager, your first business trip outside the United States might be to inspect the production lines of one of your outsourcing suppliers. The Example box below discusses jobs that are prone to outsourcing.

However, in a countertrend called "reshoring," some companies are moving production back home in order to respond faster and more flexibly to consumer trends. For example, the fashion industry, one of the first to undertake outsourcing for its lower costs, has brought more than 17,000 jobs back to the United States since 2010, and more could follow. In South Baltimore, athletic wear maker Under Armour has acted on its "local for local" initiative to create a kind of incubator facility that puts engineers and product developers under the same roof. The goal is to speed innovation, support small-batch manufacturing and lower inventories, and shorten the supply chain. One result is that the interval between design and production has shrunk from 18 months[51] to 4; another is the addition of potentially thousands of jobs. "We're going to bring scale that allows us to bring manufacturing back," said Under Armour's president of product and innovation.[52]

2. Importing, Exporting, and Countertrading

When **importing**, a company buys goods outside the country and resells them domestically. Nothing might seem to be more American than Caterpillar tractors, but they are made not only in the United States but also in Mexico, from which they are imported and made available for sale in the United States.[53] Many of the products we use are imported, ranging from Heineken beer (Netherlands) to Texaco gasoline (Saudi Arabia) to Honda snowblowers (Japan).

EXAMPLE Global Outsourcing: Which Jobs Have Fallen Victim?

Workers in the United States are rightly concerned about the changing jobs picture, brought about in part by offshoring of work to low-wage countries such as China, India, and the Philippines. Companies look to reduce their production costs and, thereby, the prices they must charge their customers. Few of the approximately 14 million jobs that have been lost will be replaced, and according to the U.S. Bureau of Labor Statistics, just 8% of U.S. workers are employed in manufacturing today.[54] In a recent survey of working adults, more than half said it would be "essential for them to get training and develop new skills throughout their work life in order to keep up with changes in the workplace," and nearly half had taken a class to improve their work skills during the last year.[55]

More recently, the same trend—global outsourcing—has been siphoning off white-collar jobs. Among the top careers that reportedly lost jobs to outsourcing in the last few years were those of computer programmers, accountants, lawyers, insurance sales agents, real estate agents, chemists, and physicists.[56]

Which Jobs Will Likely Remain in the United States? It is difficult to predict which jobs will remain in the United States because even the Bureau of Labor Statistics often can't make accurate predictions. However, jobs that endure may share certain traits regardless of the industry they serve:[57]

- **Face-to-face.** Some jobs consist of *face-to-face contact*, such as being a salesperson with a specific territory or an emergency room doctor.
- **Physical contact.** Other jobs require *physical contact*, such as those of dentists, nurses, massage therapists, gardeners, and nursing-home aides.

- **High-end products.** *High-end products* that require intensive research, precision assembly, and complex technology need skilled workers and are good candidates for remaining in the U.S. labor market.
- **Complex patterns.** Other jobs rely on the human ability to *recognize complex patterns*, which is hard to automate, such as a physician's ability to diagnose an unusual disease (even if the X-rays are read by a radiologist in India). This characteristic also predominates in such jobs as teaching first grade or selling a mansion to a millionaire, and in jobs that demand an intimate knowledge of the United States, such as marketing to U.S. teenagers or lobbying members of Congress.

What Does the Future Look Like? Wage differences across countries are beginning to shrink, thanks in part to the United States' slow recovery from the 2008 recession, and in part to the rising standard of living in many developing countries with educated, English-speaking workers who hold those outsourced jobs.[58] This means some service jobs, such as for call-center workers, may come back to the United States if the savings from outsourcing are eliminated. It is too early to tell whether many U.S. companies will take advantage of lower corporate tax rates and other possible incentives to bring jobs back to the United States, or whether foreign companies will follow the lead of Japanese and German automakers to open production plants on U.S. shores. In the meantime, some workers may face a bigger threat from the increasing sophistication of robots in the domestic workplace than from cheap labor oversees.

One fact remains clear, however: The more education you have, the more likely you are to keep your footing during times of economic change. LinkedIn recently analyzed member data about salary and education and found that those who complete four years of college earn an average median salary of almost $80,000 a year, compared to less than $52,000 for those who complete only high school.[59] College graduates can expect to earn, on average, $1 million more over the course of their lifetimes than those without a degree.[60]

YOUR CALL

What kind of job or jobs are you interested in that would seem to provide you with some hope of prevailing in a fast-changing world?

When **exporting**, a company produces goods domestically and sells them outside the country. The United States was ranked the number 1 exporter in the world in 2015, up from number 3 two years earlier. *(See Table 4.2.)* One of the greatest U.S. exports is pop culture, in the form of movies, music, and fashion. The United States is also a leader in exporting computers and other information technology.

Sometimes other countries may wish to import U.S. goods but lack the currency to pay for them. In that case, the exporting U.S. company may resort to **countertrading**—that is, bartering goods for goods. When the Russian ruble plunged in value in 1998, some goods became a better medium of exchange than currency.

TABLE 4.2 Top 10 Exporting Countries, 1999 and 2016

RANK IN 1999	RANK IN 2016
1. United States	China
2. Germany	United States
3. Japan	Germany
4. France	Japan
5. Britain	Netherlands
6. Canada	Hong Kong
7. Italy	France
8. Netherlands	South Korea
9. China	Italy
10. Belgium	United Kingdom

Sources: "World Trade Statistical Review, 2016," World Trade Organization, *accessed February 19, 2018, https://www.wto.org/english/res_e/statis_e/wts2016_e/wts2016_e.pdf; and "Top Ten Highest Exporting Countries in the World,"* Wevio, *March 6, 2015, www.wevio.com/general/top-10-highest-exporting-countries-in-the-world (accessed March 10, 2016).*

3. Licensing and Franchising

Licensing and franchising are two aspects of the same thing, although licensing is used by manufacturing companies and franchising is used more frequently by service companies.

In **licensing**, a company allows a foreign company to pay it a fee to make or distribute the first company's product or service. For example, the Du Pont chemical company might license a company in Brazil to make Teflon, the nonstick substance that is found on some frying pans. Thus, Du Pont, the licensor, can make money without having to invest large sums to conduct business directly in a foreign company. Moreover, the Brazilian firm, the licensee, knows the local market better than Du Pont probably would.

Franchising is a form of licensing in which a company allows a foreign company to pay it a fee and a share of the profit in return for using the first company's brand name

and a package of materials and services. For example, Burger King, Hertz, and Hilton Hotels, which are all well-known brands, might provide the use of their names plus their operating know-how (facility design, equipment, recipes, management systems) to companies in the Philippines in return for an up-front fee plus a percentage of the profits.

By now so-called U.S. stores are opening everywhere, and many franchise chains are experiencing the bulk of their growth overseas. Sonic Drive-In and Chick Fil-A are said to be considering opening restaurants abroad, joining other U.S. brands, including Cold Stone Creamery, with 50 outlets in Japan; Dale Carnegie Training, which has 120 locations in Africa, Asia, Europe, and Latin America; and Massage Envy, with six stores in Australia and plans for dozens more.[61]

Volvo. Who owns what car brand these days? Formerly British brands Jaguar and Land Rover now belong to Tata of India. Volkswagen owns the formerly British Bentley and Italian Lamborghini. Volvo, whose cars and trucks are still made in Sweden, is owned by Chinese automaker Geely. Do you think the American companies General Motors and Ford could ever wind up under foreign ownership, as Chrysler has (owned by Fiat)? ©Gerlach Delissen/Corbis Sport/Getty Images

4. Joint Ventures

Strategic allies (described in Chapter 3) are two organizations that have joined forces to realize strategic advantages that neither would have if operating alone. A U.S. firm may form a **joint venture, also known as a *strategic alliance*, with a foreign company to share the risks and rewards of starting a new enterprise together in a foreign country.** For instance, General Motors operates a joint venture with Shanghai Automotive Industry Group to build Buicks in China (which are now being imported into the United States).[62] Ford also has a joint venture in China with Changan Ford.[63]

Sometimes a joint venture is the only way a U.S. company can have a presence in a certain country, whose laws may forbid foreigners from ownership. Indeed, in China, this is the only way foreign cars may be sold in that country.

5. Wholly Owned Subsidiaries

A wholly owned subsidiary is a foreign subsidiary that is totally owned and controlled by an organization. The foreign subsidiary may be an existing company that is purchased outright. **A greenfield venture is a foreign subsidiary that the owning organization has built from scratch.**

General Motors owns majority stakes in Adam Opel AG in Germany and Vauxhall Motor Cars Ltd. in the United Kingdom. •

4.4 The World of Free Trade: Regional Economic Cooperation and Competition

THE BIG PICTURE

Barriers to free trade are tariffs, import quotas, and embargoes. Organizations promoting international trade are the World Trade Organization, the World Bank, and the International Monetary Fund. We discuss two major trading blocs, NAFTA and the EU, as well as the still to-be-approved Trans-Pacific Partnership. Major competitors with the United States are the "BRICS" countries—Brazil, Russia, India, China, and South Africa.

LO 4-4

Discuss barriers to free trade and ways companies try to overcome them.

If you live in the United States, you see foreign products on a daily basis–cars, appliances, clothes, foods, beers, wines, and so on. Based on what you see every day, which countries would you think are our most important trading partners? China? Japan? Germany? United Kingdom? South Korea?

These five countries do indeed appear among the top leading U.S. trading partners. Interestingly, however, our foremost trading partners are our immediate neighbors–Canada and Mexico–whose products may not be quite so visible. *(See Table 4.3.)*

Let's begin to consider **free trade**, **the movement of goods and services among nations without political or economic obstruction.**

TABLE 4.3 **Top 10 U.S. Trading Partners in Goods, January 2016**

TOP 10 NATIONS THE U.S. EXPORTS TO	TOP 10 NATIONS THE U.S. IMPORTS FROM
1. Canada	China
2. Mexico	Mexico
3. China	Canada
4. Japan	Japan
5. United Kingdom	Germany
6. Germany	South Korea
7. South Korea	United Kingdom
8. Netherlands	India
9. Hong Kong	Italy
10. Brazil	France

Source: "Top Trading Partners, January 2018," United States Census Bureau, *https://www.census.gov/foreign-trade/statistics/highlights/toppartners.html.*

Barriers to International Trade

Countries often use **trade protectionism**—**the use of government regulations to limit the import of goods and services**—to protect their domestic industries against foreign competition. The justification they often use is that this saves jobs. Actually, protectionism is not considered beneficial, mainly because of what it does to the overall trading atmosphere.

The devices by which countries try to exert protectionism consist of *tariffs*, *import quotas*, and *trade embargoes* and *sanctions*.

1. Tariffs

A **tariff** **is a trade barrier in the form of a customs duty, or tax, levied mainly on imports.** At one time, for instance, to protect the American shoe industry, the United States imposed a tariff on Italian shoes. Actually, there are two types of tariffs: One, called a *revenue tariff*, is designed simply to raise money for the government, such as a tax on all oil imported into the United States. The other, which concerns us more, is a *protective tariff*, which is intended to raise the price of imported goods to make the prices of domestic products more competitive.

In early 2018, the Trump administration imposed new tariffs and other trade restrictions on solar panels and washing machines from China and was considering additional barriers on imported steel and aluminum. Observers were split about whether the tariffs on solar panels in particular would protect U.S. jobs or harm the domestic solar industry and cost it jobs by raising the price of clean energy.[64]

2. Import Quotas

An **import quota** **is a trade barrier in the form of a limit on the numbers of a product that can be imported.** Like a tariff, its intent is to protect domestic

The U.S. used import quotas against cars made in South Korea in the 1980s. Although these quotas are long gone, today the U.S. has import quotas on many products including steel, beef, and dairy. Do you think the use of import quotas is good over the longterm? ©Monty Rakusen/Getty Images

industry by restricting the availability of foreign products. Consumers in countries using tariffs and import quotas are likely to find price increases due to the reduction of imported products.[65] In late 2017, China issued import quotas on crude oil to three independent refineries.

Quotas are designed to prevent **dumping, the practice of a foreign company's exporting products abroad at a lower price than the price in the home market—or even below the costs of production—in order to drive down the price of the domestic product.** The U.S. Commerce Department recently began an antidumping investigation into imports of aluminum sheet from China. The Department said the investigation was "based on information indicating that the United States price of common alloy sheet from China may be less than the normal value of such or similar merchandise and that imports of common alloy sheet from China may be benefitting from countervailable subsidies."[66]

3. Embargoes and Sanctions

For more than 50 years, a Cold War embargo prohibited anyone from importing Cuban cigars and sugar into the United States and prevented U.S. companies from doing business in Cuba. Then in 2014, President Barack Obama ordered the restoration of full diplomatic relations with Cuba, and in March 2016, he paid a visit to the island nation, the first U.S. president to do so in nearly 90 years.[67] In 2017, however, the Trump administration began restoring prohibitions and restrictions on travel and trade with Cuba, "to channel economic activity away from the Cuban military and to encourage the government to move toward greater political and economic freedom for the Cuban people."[68]

An embargo is a complete ban or prohibition of trade of one country with another so that no goods or services can be imported or exported from or to the embargoed nation. The key word here is *complete*, as in "complete ban." In response to North Korea's ramped-up testing of intercontinental ballistic missiles, for example, the Trump administration has pressured China to completely cut off its sales of oil and oil products to North Korea.[69] China is North Korea's chief trading partner.[70]

An embargo is different from a sanction. **A sanction is the trade prohibition on certain types of products, services, or technology to another country for specific reasons,** including nuclear nonproliferation and humanitarian purposes. The key words here are *certain types*. Sanctions may be considered "partial embargoes," since they restrict trade in certain areas. For instance, the United States has trade sanctions with North Korea that prohibit the export of any material that would help North Korea in its nuclear program.[71] In 2017, the U.S. Congress passed a nearly unanimous resolution to impose new economic sanctions on Russia in response to its suspected interference in the 2016 presidential election. The Trump administration has so far not imposed these measures.[72]

Organizations Promoting International Trade

In the 1920s, the institution of tariff barriers did not so much protect jobs as depress the demand for goods and services, thereby leading to the loss of jobs anyway—and the massive unemployment of the Great Depression of the 1930s.[73] As a result of this lesson, after World War II the advanced nations of the world began to realize that if all countries could freely exchange the products that each could produce most efficiently, this would lead to lower prices all around. Thus began the removal of barriers to free trade.

The three principal organizations designed to facilitate international trade are the *World Trade Organization*, the *World Bank*, and the *International Monetary Fund*. Table 4.4 summarizes the background on each organization.

TABLE 4.4

Organizations Promoting International Trade

ORGANIZATIONS PROMOTING INTERNATIONAL TRADE				
PRINCIPAL ORGANIZATIONS	**PURPOSE**	**ESTABLISHED**	**MEMBER COUNTRIES**	**IN THE NEWS**
World Trade Organization (WTO)	To monitor and enforce trade agreements	1995 in Geneva to replace the General Agreement on Tariffs and Trade	164	In 2017, the EU contributed EUR 1 million to improve the trading capacity of developing countries and to help them play a more active role in trade.*
World Bank	To provide low-interest loans to developing nations for improving transportation, education, health, and telecommunications	After WWII to help European countries rebuild	189	January 2018, World Bank's Chief Economist Paul Romer stepped down after the World Bank came under fire when Chilean officials claimed it deliberately skewed the country's economic data in its annual "Doing Business Report," indicating massive deceleration in spite of a robust and booming economy.**
International Monetary Fund (IMF)	Designed to assist in smoothing the flow of money between nations	1945	189	In 2017, Morocco implemented a more flexible foreign exchange system recommended by the IMF that protects its economy from external forces and safeguards its reserves. The recommendations make the country more attractive to investors, and better able to service Africa with financial services. ***

Source: "EU Gives EUR 1 Million to Enhance Trading Skills of Developing Countries," World Trade Organization, accessed on February 19, 2018, https://www.wto.org/english/news_e/pres17_e/pr814_e.htm.

***Source: "UPDATE 1-Chile Slams World Bank for Bias in Competitiveness Rankings," CNBC, accessed February 19, 2018, https://www.cnbc.com/2018/01/13/reuters-america-update-1-chile-slams-world-bank-for-bias-in-competitiveness-rankings.html.*

****Source: U. Laessing, "UPDATE 1-Morocco's Currency Move a Step in Right Direction – IMF," CNBC, January 29, 2018, https://www.cnbc.com/2018/01/29/reuters-america-update-1-moroccos-currency-move-a-step-in-right-direction--imf.html.*

Major Trading Blocs: NAFTA and the EU

A trading bloc, also known as an *economic community*, is a group of nations within a geographical region that have agreed to remove trade barriers with one another. The two major trading blocs we will consider are the *NAFTA nations* and the *European Union.*

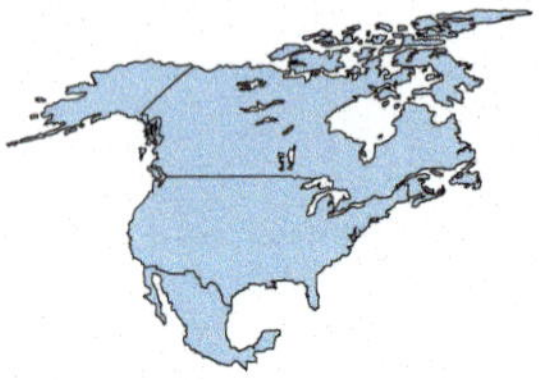

1. NAFTA—The Three Countries of the North American Free Trade Agreement

Formed in 1994, the **North American Free Trade Agreement (NAFTA) is a trading bloc consisting of the United States, Canada, and Mexico,** encompassing 444 million people. The agreement is supposed to eliminate 99% of the tariffs and quotas among these countries, allowing for freer flow of goods, services, and capital in North America. While many predicted the pact would cost the United States thousands of jobs, it seems to have both lost and created employment, while some of the benefits that Mexico would have enjoyed, as the NAFTA partner with the lowest labor costs, went to China instead when that country's low-wage economy began to boom. It is difficult to isolate all the real effects of the trade agreement, given the many other factors in each country's economy, but overall, the United States appears to have lost low-skilled manufacturing jobs and gained employment in autos and aerospace, according to the Economic Policy Institute.[74]

EXAMPLE What Will Brexit Mean for Britain and the EU?

Brexit is the planned British exit from the European Union, announced in 2016 following a bitterly contested public vote. Scheduled to occur in March 2019, the break will have profound effects not only on Great Britain, but also on the EU's remaining 27 countries. Some are already being felt. Almost immediately after the decision was announced, for example, industries and companies started making business decisions based on a future in which old trade, travel, and other barriers between the UK and the continent will once again be in place. The financial industry's decisions will have major impacts.

Citigroup and Morgan Stanley are among several global U.S. banks that have announced they will move their EU headquarters from London, which had been the EU's financial capital, to Frankfurt. Other banks are leaving London for Paris; still others, like Bank of America and Goldman Sachs, have not yet named their new hubs. Among the short-term effects of these departures: London could lose up to a quarter million financial-industry jobs, and related business losses might rise to almost $250 billion a year, representing well over 10% of the British economy.[75] Britain has said it will ease some regulations on banks' remaining London operations to avoid taking a drastic hit to one of its largest industries; the financial sector brings in $93 billion a year in tax revenues for the British government.[76]

Despite dire predictions by opponents of Brexit, the UK economy has so far continued to grow, though slowly (as are the economies of other industrialized nations). How life in the UK and Europe will change remains to be seen; the EU will remain a single market (if somewhat shaken by Britain's departure and rising nationalist sentiment in member countries), but Britain and its citizens will become outsiders to it. The British government is in the process of deciding which EU laws will remain in effect for its population after Brexit and whether its exit will be "hard," meaning it rejects compromise with the EU on issues like open travel and trade between Britain and EU countries, or "soft," meaning some portion of the EU's intercountry cooperation and openness would remain.[77]

Thousands of Pro-Europe protesters march in central London in opposition to Brexit, the planned British exit from the European Union. What are the pros and cons of Brexit for the people of the U.K? ©JUSTIN TALLIS/AFP/Getty Images

YOUR CALL

The EU is more than a common market. It not only eliminates tariffs and quotas on goods that members trade with each other (as a common market would do); it also has a common currency (the euro) and its own parliament, and it allows services and money to flow and people to work and travel freely throughout the union, as if it were a single country. EU supporters have championed these economic and personal freedoms, while critics have pointed to the proliferation of rules, which they believe reduce each country's independence, and to the unimpeded flow into wealthier countries of people from poorer ones. Do you think the advantages of a single market like the EU outweigh the disadvantages for member countries? Why or why not?

The terms of the agreement are now the subject of ongoing negotiations among the three member countries that may last until 2019. The Trump administration has threatened to pull the United States out of NAFTA but has so far not taken that step.[78]

2. The EU—The 28 Countries of the European Union Formed in 1957, the **European Union (EU) consists of 28 trading partners in Europe**, covering nearly 500 million consumers. In 2016, the United Kingdom narrowly decided to remove itself from the EU, a process that will likely take several years to complete (see Example box).

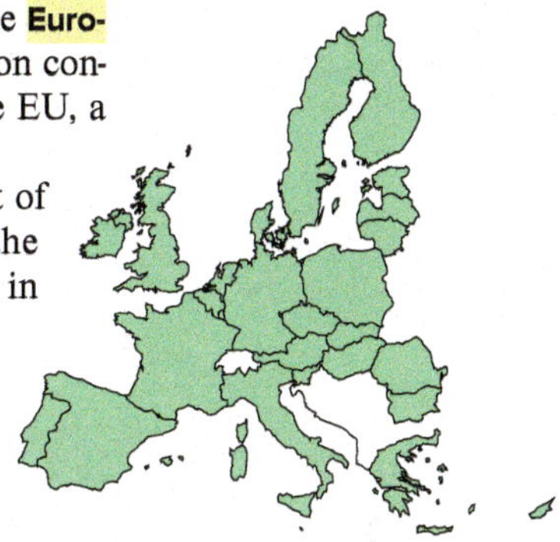

Nearly all internal trade barriers have been eliminated (including movement of labor between countries), making the EU a union of borderless neighbors and the world's largest free market, with a gross domestic product of $16.487 trillion in 2016, compared to $18.625 trillion for the United States.[79]

Recently, the influx of thousands of refugees pouring out of war-torn and poverty-stricken nations in the Middle East and Africa, including many middle-class Syrians, has put more pressure on the European Union, including calls to either reduce or severely limit free movement across Europe's borders. The EU also faces challenges to its founding principles from the apparent increase in populist and nationalist sentiments in some member countries. "We are seeing nationalism, populism and in a lot of countries a polarized atmosphere," said Germany's leader Angela Merkel in early 2018. "We believe that isolation won't help us. We believe we need to cooperate, that protectionism is not the answer."[80]

Four other trading blocs–APEC, ASEAN, Mercosur, and CAFTA–are described below. *(See Table 4.5.)*

TRADING BLOC	COUNTRIES	PURPOSES
Asia-Pacific Economic Cooperation (APEC)	21 Pacific Rim countries, most with a Pacific coastline, including the U.S., Canada, and China	To improve economic and political ties and to reduce tariffs and other trade barriers across the Asia-Pacific region
Association of Southeast Asian Nations (ASEAN)	10 countries in Asia, comprising a market of 610 million people: Brunei, Cambodia, Indonesia, Laos, Malaysia, Myanmar (Burma), the Philippines, Singapore, Thailand, and Vietnam	To reduce trade barriers among member countries. A China-ASEAN Free Trade Area was established in 2010, the largest free trade area in the world in terms of population.
Mercosur	Largest trade bloc in Latin America, with 5 core members—Argentina, Brazil, Paraguay, Uruguay, and Venezuela (currently suspended) —and 7 associate members: Bolivia, Chile, Colombia, Ecuador, Guyana, Peru, and Suriname	To reduce tariffs by 75% and achieve full economic integration. The alliance is also negotiating trade agreements with NAFTA, the EU, and Japan.
Central America Free Trade Agreement (CAFTA-DR)	Costa Rica, the Dominican Republic, El Salvador, Guatemala, Honduras, Nicaragua, and the U.S.	To reduce tariffs and other barriers to free trade

TABLE 4.5
Four Other Important Trading Blocs
Source: Brian Williams.

The Trans-Pacific Partnership—11 Pacific Rim Countries Negotiated over seven years, the **Trans-Pacific Partnership (TPP) is a trade agreement among 11 Pacific Rim countries.** It was signed on February 4, 2016. The United States, originally a party to the agreement, withdrew from the pact under the Trump administration; remaining members are Australia, Brunei, Canada, Chile, Japan, Malaysia, Mexico, New Zealand, Peru, Singapore, and Vietnam. The United States could rejoin the agreement in the future but is not currently expected to do so.[81]

Over time, the TPP will remove several further barriers to trade, including most tariffs, and set commercial rules for everything from labor and environmental standards to drug patents. A World Bank study found that Japan, Vietnam, and Malaysia would get a big economic boost (from increasing their exports) from the TPP, while the three North American countries would see much smaller gains.[82]

Currency from around the world. It's important to understand exchange rates when traveling internationally. ©Paul Maguire/Shutterstock

Most Favored Nation Trading Status

Besides joining together in trade blocs, countries will also extend special, "most favored nation" trading privileges to one another. **Most favored nation trading status describes a condition in which a country grants other countries favorable trading treatment such as the reduction of import duties.** The purpose is to promote stronger and more stable ties between companies in the two countries.

Exchange Rates

The exchange rate is the rate at which the currency of one area or country can be exchanged for the currency of another's. Americans deal in dollars with each other, but beyond the U.S. border we have to deal with pounds in England, euros in Europe, pesos in Mexico, and yuan in China. Because of changing economic conditions, the values of currencies fluctuate in relation to each other, so that sometimes a U.S. dollar, for example, will buy more goods and sometimes it will buy less.

Get out much? The number of U.S. passports issued per year has grown steadily over the last several years, reaching more than 21.3 million for 2017 according to the Department of State. How does travel figure in your career plans? ©Ulrich Baumgarten/Getty Images

EXAMPLE Dealing with Currency Exchange—How Much *Are* Those Jeans, Really?

Assume that $1 trades equal to 1 British pound, symbolized by £1. Thus, an item that costs 3 pounds (£3) can be bought for $3. If the exchange rate changes so that $1 buys £1.5, then an item that costs £3 can be bought for $2 (the dollar is said to be "stronger" against the pound). If the rate changes so that $1 buys only £0.5, an item that costs £6 can be purchased for $9 (the dollar is "weaker").[83] In early 2018, the dollar was stronger, buying £.72, whereas back in 2014, it was weaker, averaging £.59. (Stated another way, £1 bought $1.68 in April 2014 and $1.40 in February 2018.)

How the Exchange Rate Matters. As this is written, the dollar is strong and the pound is weak, so that $1 will buy £.72. Thus, staying in London became less expensive for U.S. travelers. A hotel room that rents for £100 cost a U.S. visitor $168 in 2014, but only $140 in 2016. Indeed, if during those years, 2014 to 2018, you were living in England working for a U.S. company and were paid in dollars, your standard of living went up.

The Varying Cost of Living for Different Cities. Prices also vary among countries and cities throughout the world, with the standard of living of London, say, being 29% more than that of Chicago.[84] Table 4.6 provides a sense of what a U.S. visitor's purchasing power is worth in London when $1 equals £72 (or £1 equals $1.40)—the exchange rate in February 2018—consider these prices for various goods in Chicago versus London (estimated in U.S. dollars, computed on *www.expatistan.com*):

TABLE 4.6 Comparison of Prices in Chicago and London

AVERAGE COSTS FOR:	CHICAGO*	LONDON**
2-liter Coke	$2.24	$2.53
Combo meal (Big Mac or similar)	$8.00	$8.00
Monthly rent, furnished studio (expensive area)	$1458.00	$3235.00
Monthly Rent, furnished studio (average area)	$957.00	$2499.00
Pair of designer jeans	$53.00	$102.00
Nike or similar sports shoes	$90.00	$100.00
Monthly Internet 8mbps	$44.00	$31.00
Starbucks latte	$5.08	$4.59***

**Source: "Cost of Living in Chicago, Illinois, United States," Expatistan, accessed February 19, 2018, https://www.expatistan.com/cost-of-living/chicago.*

***Source: "Cost of Living in London, United Kingdom,"* Expatistan, *accessed February 19, 2018, https://www.expatistan.com/cost-of-living/london?currency=USD.*

****Source: B. Pemberton, "How Much Would YOU Pay for a Caffeine Fix on Holiday? The Price of a Starbucks Latte in 30 Countries Revealed (and You'll Need Deep Pockets if You're Off to Zurich),"* Daily Mail, *March 3, 2016, http://www.dailymail.co.uk/travel/travel_news/article-3473320/How-pay-caffeine-fix-holiday-price-Starbucks-latte-30-countries-revealed-ll-need-deep-pockets-Zurich.html.*

With this example, you can see why it's important to understand how exchange rates work and what value your U.S. dollars actually have.

YOUR CALL

Planning to visit Mexico, Canada, or any EU countries (Germany, France) that use the euro? Go online to *www.x-rates.com* and figure out the exchange rate of the U.S. dollar and that country's currency. Then go to *www.expatistan.com* and figure out what things cost in that country's principal city versus a U.S. city near you. Could you afford to go?

The BRICS Countries: Important International Competitors Coined by a financial analyst who saw the countries as promising markets for finance capital in the 21st century, the term *BRICS* stands for the five major emerging economies of Brazil, Russia, India, China, and South Africa.[85] *(See Table 4.7.)*

TABLE 4.7 BRICS Countries, 2015

	POPULATION	ECONOMY (GDP) (IN U.S. $)	GDP PER CAPITA (IN U.S. $)	GROWTH RATE
China	1.36 billion	$19,510 billion	$8,154	6.8%
India	1.25 billion	$8,027 billion	$1,808	7.3%
Brazil	204 million	$3,208 billion	$9,312	-3.0%
Russia	146 million	$3,474 billion	$8,184	-3.8%
South Africa	50 million	$724 billion	$5,902	1.4%
For comparison, U.S.	321 million	$17,968 billion	$56,421	2.6%

Sources: Internet World Stats, *www.internetworldstats.com /stats8.htm;* Knoema, and IMF World Economic Outlook, *October 15, 2015, http://knoema.com/nwnfkne/world-gdp-ranking- 2015-data-and-charts;* Statistics Times, and IMF World Economic Outlook, *April 18, 2015, http://statisticstimes.com/economy/countries-by-projected-gdp-capita.php (all accessed March 12, 2016).*

Though not a trading bloc as such, the BRICS are important because they hold 40% of the world's population, represent about 20% of the world's economic activity, and have established their own $100 billion reserve fund to rival the International Monetary Fund.[86] By 2050, economists predict, they will join the United States in the exclusive club of the six largest economies in the world.[87] Let's consider the largest of these countries in the order of their population size: China, India, and Brazil.

China China's economy is now the second-largest in the world after that of the United States, and it may soon be the largest. Its share of the world's middle class and its share of global manufacturing output skyrocketed from almost nothing in the 1990s to 16 percent and 25 percent by 2015, respectively. The World Bank, however, warns that nearly 8 in 10 jobs in China could be vulnerable to automation.[88]

India If China is well known for its manufacturing advantages, India's have been its large English-speaking population, its technological and scientific expertise, and its reputation in services, such as "back office" accounting systems and software engineering. Services, and especially IT, make up almost two-thirds of India's GDP; its middle class now accounts for 8 percent of the world's total, up from 1 percent in the 1990s.[89] Whereas China's working-age population began a steep decline in 2015, India's working-age population is not expected to peak until about 2050.

Brazil With the eighth-largest economy in the world,[90] benefiting from agriculture, mining, manufacturing, and services, Brazil experienced a decade of economic and social progress from 2003 to 2014, lifting 29 million people out of poverty.[91] In 2016, however, the country suffered a recession, the worst economic slump in 25 years, brought about by worldwide declines in commodity prices, a domestic political crisis, and rising inflation.[92] Its economic growth rate has been negative for the last few years.[93] •

4.5 The Value of Understanding Cultural Differences

THE BIG PICTURE

Managers trying to understand other cultures need to understand the importance of national culture and cultural dimensions and basic cultural perceptions embodied in language, interpersonal space, communication, time orientation, religion, and law and political stability.

LO 4-5

Explain the value to managers of understanding cultural differences.

Whether you are abroad or at home, you are likely to find yourself working with people whose cultural norms and traditions are very different from your own. What time you arrive for a business meeting, where you sit in the room, how you introduce yourself or introduce people to each other, whether you tip in a restaurant and how much, and even what you eat and whether you share it with others at the table are just a few behaviors influenced by culture. Your author, Angelo Kinicki, encountered several of these scenarios during several recent business trips to the United Arab Emirates. He was surprised to see men, who were very familiar with each other, touch noses when saying hello. He also realized that Arabs have a much different orientation toward time. It's much more fluid and flexible than in the United States. Angelo also had to adjust his style of introducing himself to women; no shaking hands unless a woman offered her hand. The start of business meetings is quite different than in the United States. Arabs like to spend more time engaging in pleasantries before getting down to business.

Tipping point. The culture of tipping in restaurants varies from country to country. Some restaurants in the United States and Canada are eliminating tipping or adding an 18% "auto-gratuity" to the bill, but in most places, the customer is expected to add 15%–20% to the total bill as a standard tip (10% is considered insulting). However, in Japan and China, tips are not expected and are even considered inappropriate. In Hong Kong, it's up to the diner's discretion (a 10% service charge is already added to the bill). In Europe, hotels and restaurants add a 10% charge and tipping is expected only for exceptional service. In Latin America, a tip of 10% is customary in most restaurants, and you're expected to hand it to the person directly, not just leave it on the table. All clear?
©AAGAMIA/The Image Bank/Getty Images

Cultural differences affect businesses in many ways. As one example, Western manufacturers of personal care products have faced an uphill battle to introduce deodorant products in China and other Asian countries, in part because people do not perceive sweating as embarrassing. Rather, it is seen as a normal aspect of human metabolism. "The traditional thinking [in China] is that sweating is good because it helps people detox," said Unilever's assistant manager for skin care. "There is a marketing barrier that is really hard to overcome." Unilever's cowboy- and boxer-themed ads also missed the mark for cultural reasons. "The series of advertisements we designed relied on the Western sense of humor," said the company's creative director. "Not many Chinese would understand this."[94]

The Importance of National Culture

A nation's **culture** **is the shared set of beliefs, values, knowledge, and patterns of behavior common to a group of people.** We begin learning our culture starting at an early age through everyday interaction with people around us. This is why, from the outside looking in, a nation's culture can seem so intangible and perplexing. As cultural anthropologist Edward T. Hall puts it, "Since much of culture operates outside our awareness, frequently we don't even know what we know. . . . We unconsciously learn what to notice and what not to notice, how to divide time and space, how to walk and talk and use our bodies, how to behave as men or women, how to relate to other people, how to handle responsibility. . . ."[95] Indeed, says Hall, what we think of as "mind" is really internalized culture.

And because a culture is made up of so many nuances, this is why visitors to another culture may experience feelings of discomfort and disorientation associated with being in an unfamiliar culture. These feelings are generally associated with "not understanding the verbal and non-verbal communication of the host culture" and the adaptability needed to accommodate "differences in lifestyles, living conditions and business practices in another cultural setting."[96]

Cultural Dimensions: The Hofstede and GLOBE Project Models

Misunderstandings and miscommunications often arise in international business relationships because people don't understand the expectations of the other side. A person from North America, Great Britain, Scandinavia, Germany, or Switzerland, for example, comes from a **low-context culture, in which shared meanings are primarily derived from written and spoken words.** Someone from China, Korea, Japan, Vietnam, Mexico, or many Arab cultures, on the other hand, comes from a **high-context culture, in which people rely heavily on situational cues for meaning when communicating with others,** relying on nonverbal cues as to another person's official position, status, or family connections.

One way to avoid cultural collisions is to have an understanding of various cultural dimensions, as expressed in the Hofstede model and the GLOBE project.[97]

Hofstede's Model of Four Cultural Dimensions

Thirty years ago, Dutch researcher and IBM psychologist **Geert Hofstede** collected data from 116,000 IBM employees in 53 countries and proposed his **Hofstede model of four cultural dimensions, which identified four dimensions along which national cultures can be placed: (1) individualism/collectivism, (2) power distance, (3) uncertainty avoidance, and (4) masculinity/femininity.**[98]

Individualism/collectivism indicates how much people prefer a loosely knit social framework in which people are expected to take care of themselves (as in the United States and Canada) or a tightly knit social framework in which people and organizations are expected to look after each other (as in Mexico and China). *Power distance* refers to the degree to which people accept inequality in social situations (high in Mexico and India, low in Sweden and Australia). *Uncertainty avoidance* expresses people's intolerance for uncertainty and risk (high in Japan, low in the United States). *Masculinity/femininity* expresses how much people value performance-oriented traits (masculinity: high in Mexico) or how much they embrace relationship-oriented traits (femininity: high in Norway). In general, the United States ranked very high on individualism, relatively low on power distance, low on uncertainty avoidance, and moderately high on masculinity.

The GLOBE Project's Nine Cultural Dimensions Started in 1993 by University of Pennsylvania professor **Robert J. House,** the **GLOBE project is a massive and ongoing cross-cultural investigation of nine cultural dimensions involved in leadership and organizational processes.**[99] (GLOBE stands for Global Leadership and Organizational Behavior Effectiveness.) GLOBE extends Hofstede's theory and results and evolved into a network of more than 150 scholars from 62 societies. Most of these researchers are native to the particular cultures being studied. The nine cultural dimensions are as follows:

- **Power distance—how much unequal distribution of power should there be in organizations and society?** *Power distance* expresses the degree to which a society's members expect power to be unequally shared.
- **Uncertainty avoidance—how much should people rely on social norms and rules to avoid uncertainty?** *Uncertainty avoidance* expresses the extent to which a society relies on social norms and procedures to alleviate the unpredictability of future events.
- **Institutional collectivism—how much should leaders encourage and reward loyalty to the social unit?** *Institutional collectivism* expresses the extent to which individuals are encouraged and rewarded for loyalty to the group as opposed to pursuing individual goals.
- **In-group collectivism—how much pride and loyalty should people have for their family or organization?** In contrast to individualism, *in-group collectivism* expresses the extent to which people should take pride in being members of their family, circle of close friends, and their work organization.[100]
- **Gender egalitarianism—how much should society maximize gender role differences?** *Gender egalitarianism* expresses the extent to which a society should minimize gender discrimination and role inequalities.
- **Assertiveness—how confrontational and dominant should individuals be in social relationships?** *Assertiveness* represents the extent to which a society expects people to be confrontational and competitive as opposed to tender and modest.
- **Future orientation—how much should people delay gratification by planning and saving for the future?** *Future orientation* expresses the extent to which a society encourages investment in the future, as by planning and saving.
- **Performance orientation—how much should individuals be rewarded for improvement and excellence?** *Performance orientation* expresses the extent to which society encourages and rewards its members for performance improvement and excellence.
- **Humane orientation—how much should society encourage and reward people for being kind, fair, friendly, and generous?** *Humane orientation* represents the degree to which individuals are encouraged to be altruistic, caring, kind, generous, and fair.

Awareness of these dimensions helped Wenjing Yang while working with people from different national cultures (see the "I'm glad I ..." feature).

I'm glad I...
...understood the GLOBE Project's cultural dimensions.

Wenjing Yang Courtesy Wenjing Yang

Wenjing Yang works as a senior sourcing analyst in the procurement department for a health care organization. Her company implements several measures to ensure its employees are rooted in the company's core values.

"We have a company value proposition, and it is being constantly communicated to us that the company expects everyone to exemplify values such as integrity, excellence, caring, and inspiration," said Wenjing. "These values are the foundation of every award within the company. Every employee has to complete annual mandated business conduct and integrity training that stresses these values and teaches us how to practice them in day-to-day work."

While the values stressed by Wenjing's company might be universal across cultures, it is important for Wenjing to understand various cultural dimensions that might impact her work relationships.

Wenjing is a Chinese citizen working for an American-based health care company. There are many areas in which Chinese culture and American culture differ, and it is important for Wenjing to understand this when dealing with her co-workers.

"Growing up in a **high-power distance** culture in China, I guess I may be more tolerant and obedient to authority and power compared to my American peers," said Wenjing. "For example, my manager once gave the team an aggressive project deadline, and I worked extremely hard and spent overtime to meet the deadline while some of my colleagues argued that the timeline was unattainable and that they needed more time."

Another cultural dimension Wenjing must consider when working with co-workers from another culture is the concept of **assertiveness**. "Chinese culture promotes modesty, humbleness, and harmonious social relationships. It discourages confrontational or aggressive communication styles. In the United States, modesty is often considered as weakness, and humbleness can be interpreted as incapability. U.S. culture encourages people to be confident and assertive when communicating themselves," said Wenjing.

Wenjing must understand how her modest or humble behavior might be interpreted by her American colleagues, and her American colleagues must understand the same thing about how Wenjing might interpret their aggressive or assertive behavior. Without taking these cultural dimensions into account, Wenjing's work relationships can be negatively affected by misconceptions and misunderstandings.

Data from 18,000 managers yielded the GLOBE country profiles shown below. *(See Table 4.8.)*

TABLE 4.8 Countries Ranking Highest and Lowest on the GLOBE Cultural Dimensions

DIMENSION	HIGHEST	LOWEST
Power distance	Morocco, Argentina, Thailand, Spain, Russia	Denmark, Netherlands, South Africa (black sample), Israel, Costa Rica
Uncertainty avoidance	Switzerland, Sweden, Germany (former West), Denmark, Austria	Russia, Hungary, Bolivia, Greece, Venezuela
Institutional collectivism	Sweden, South Korea, Japan, Singapore, Denmark	Greece, Hungary, Germany (former East), Argentina, Italy
In-group collectivism	Iran, India, Morocco, China, Egypt	Denmark, Sweden, New Zealand, Netherlands, Finland
Gender egalitarianism	Hungary, Poland, Slovenia, Denmark, Sweden	South Korea, Egypt, Morocco, India, China

TABLE 4.8 **Countries Ranking Highest and Lowest on the GLOBE Cultural Dimensions (*Continued*)**

DIMENSION	HIGHEST	LOWEST
Assertiveness	Germany (former East), Austria, Greece, United States, Spain	Sweden, New Zealand, Switzerland, Japan, Kuwait
Future orientation	Singapore, Switzerland, Netherlands, Canada (English speaking), Denmark	Russia, Argentina, Poland, Italy, Kuwait
Performance orientation	Singapore, Hong Kong, New Zealand, Taiwan, United States	Russia, Argentina, Greece, Venezuela, Italy
Humane orientation	Philippines, Ireland, Malaysia, Egypt, Indonesia	Germany (former West), Spain, France, Singapore, Brazil

Source: "How Cultures Collide," Psychology Today, *July 1976, p. 69.*

Have you thought about how you stand in relation to various norms—in both your society and others? Would your views affect your success in taking an international job? The following self-assessment was created to provide feedback regarding these questions and to aid your awareness about your views of the GLOBE dimensions.

SELF-ASSESSMENT 4.2 CAREER READINESS

Assessing Your Standing on the GLOBE Dimensions

This survey is designed to assess your values in terms of the GLOBE dimensions. Please be prepared to answer these questions if your instructor has assigned Self-Assessment 4.2 in Connect.

1. What are your three highest and lowest rated dimensions? How might these beliefs affect your ability to work with people from Europe, Asia, and South America?
2. How do your dimensional scores compare to the norms for Americans shown in Table 4.8?
3. What can you say during an interview to demonstrate that you possess the career readiness competency of cross-cultural awareness?

Recognizing Cultural Tendencies to Gain Competitive Advantage The GLOBE dimensions show a great deal of cultural diversity around the world, but they also show how cultural patterns vary. For example, the U.S. managerial sample scored high on assertiveness and performance orientation—which is why Americans are widely perceived as being pushy and hardworking. Switzerland's high scores on uncertainty avoidance and future orientation help explain its centuries of political neutrality and world-renowned banking industry. Singapore is known as a great place to do business because it is clean and safe and its people are well educated and hardworking—no surprise, considering the country's high scores on social collectivism, future orientation, and performance orientation. By contrast, Russia's low scores on future orientation and performance orientation could foreshadow a slower-than-hoped-for transition from a centrally planned economy to free-enterprise capitalism. The practical lesson to draw from all this: *Knowing the cultural tendencies of foreign business partners and competitors increases your career readiness and can give you a strategic competitive advantage.*[101]

GLOBE researchers also set out to find which, if any, attributes of leadership were universally liked or disliked. Throughout the world, visionary and inspirational leaders who are good team builders generally do the best; self-centered leaders who are seen as loners or face-savers receive a poor reception.[102]

Other Cultural Variations: Language, Interpersonal Space, Communication, Time Orientation, Religion, and Law and Political Stability

How do you go about bridging cross-cultural gaps? It begins with understanding. Let's consider variations in six basic culture areas: (1) *language,* (2) *interpersonal space,* (3) *communication,* (4) *time orientation,* (5) *religion,* and (6) *law and political stability.*

Note, however, that such cultural differences are to be viewed as *tendencies* rather than absolutes. We all need to be aware that the *individuals* we are dealing with may be exceptions to the cultural rules. After all, there *are* talkative and aggressive Japanese, just as there are quiet and deferential people in the United States, stereotypes notwithstanding.

1. Language More than 7,000 different languages are spoken throughout the world, and it's indeed true that global business speaks English,[103] although Chinese and Spanish are spoken by more people globally.[104]

In communicating across cultures you have four options: (a) You can speak your own language. (b) You can use a translator. (Try to get one who will be loyal to you rather than to your overseas host.) (c) You can use a translation app, such as Google Translate, that turns a smartphone into an interpreter. (d) You can learn the local language—by far the best option.

It's possible to gain some language proficiency online. Several free apps, like Duolingo and Memrise, can provide instruction and practice in many widely spoken languages, including Spanish, Chinese, Russian, French, Italian, Arabic, German, and more. Most of these apps are easy to use and customizable; you can choose the level at which you want to begin (so you can brush up on the language you studied in high school, for instance, or start a brand-new one), and you can test yourself with quizzes, flashcards, memory games, and more.[105]

2. Interpersonal Space It is common for men to hold hands in friendship in the Middle East, and it does not carry any sexual connotation.

People of different cultures have different ideas about what is acceptable interpersonal space—that is, how close or far away one should be when communicating with another person. A global study of almost 9,000 people from 42 countries revealed some interesting patterns. (*See Figure 4.2.*) For instance, the people of North America and northern Europe tend to conduct business conversations at a range of 3.1 to 3.4 feet. For people in Asia, the range is about 3.6 to 4.2 feet. The average interpersonal space for social distance, personal distance, and intimate distance across the 42 countries was 4.43 feet, 3 feet, and 1 foot, respectively.[106]

3. Communication There is no question that awareness of cross-cultural communication is important when interacting with people from other countries. For small companies doing business abroad, "the important thing to remember is that you don't know what you don't know," says the head of a U.S. firm that advises clients on cross-cultural matters.[107] Angelo has tried to deal with this issue by reading books targeted for specific countries. For example, Angelo read "Doing Business in the Middle East" to prepare him for a consulting project in the United Arab Emirates (UAE).[108] While he learned much from the book, a big takeaway was not to take everything at face value. For instance, it was suggested that females would not actively participate in classroom

FIGURE 4.2

Comfortable interpersonal space for different countries

United States
Social distance 3.1 feet
Personal distance 2.3 feet
Intimate distance 1.6 feet

Canada
Social distance 3.4 feet
Personal distance 2.8 feet
Intimate distance 2.5 feet

Mexico
Social distance 3.3 feet
Personal distance 2.7 feet
Intimate distance 2.2 feet

Germany
Social distance 3.2 feet
Personal distance 2.3 feet
Intimate distance 1.4 feet

United Kingdom
Social distance 3.3 feet
Personal distance 2.7 feet
Intimate distance 1.8 feet

Russia
Social distance 3.4 feet
Personal distance 2.4 feet
Intimate distance 1.5 feet

Saudi Arabia
Social distance 4.2 feet
Personal distance 3.5 feet
Intimate distance 3.2 feet

India
Social distance 3.6 feet
Personal distance 2.9 feet
Intimate distance 1.9 feet

China
Social distance 3.8 feet
Personal distance 2.8 feet
Intimate distance 1.9 feet

Source: Data taken from A. Sorokowska, P. Sorokowski, P. Hilpert, K. Cantarero, T. Frackowiak, K. Ahmadi, et al, "Preferred Interpersonal Distances: A Global Comparison," Journal of Cross-Cultural Psychology, *March 2017, pp. 577–592.*

discussions and presenters should not try to encourage group discussion by randomly calling on people. He found that both of these recommendations did not fit for his managerial audience in Abu Dhabi.

We consider communication matters in more detail in Chapter 15.

4. Time Orientation Time orientation is different in many cultures. For example, Americans are accustomed to calling ahead for appointments, but South Koreans believe in spontaneity. Thus, when Seoul erupted in protests over tainted American beef, Korean legislators simply hopped on a plane to the United States, saying they would negotiate with the U.S. government. "But since they failed to inform the Americans ahead of time," says one report, "they were unable to meet with anyone of importance."[109]

Anthropologist Hall makes a useful distinction between *monochronic* time and *polychronic* time:

- **Monochronic time.** This kind of time is standard American business practice—at least until recently. That is, **monochronic time is a preference for doing one thing at a time.** In this perception, time is viewed as being limited, precisely segmented, and schedule driven. This perception of time prevails, for example, when you schedule a meeting with someone and then give the visitor your undivided attention during the allotted time.[110]

  Indeed, you probably practice monochronic time when you're in a job interview. You work hard at listening to what the interviewer says. You may well take careful notes. You certainly don't answer your cell phone or gaze repeatedly out the window.

- **Polychronic time.** This outlook on time is the kind that prevails in Mediterranean, Latin American, and especially Arab cultures. **Polychronic time is a preference for doing more than one thing at a time.** Here time is viewed as being flexible and multidimensional. This orientation can lead to work stress as people try to accomplish multiple things at once.[111]

  This perception of time prevails when you visit a Latin American client, find yourself sitting in the waiting room for 45 minutes, and then learn in the meeting that the client is dealing with three other people at the same time.

PRACTICAL ACTION How to Run an International Meeting[112]

Meetings are a fact of life in most workplaces, and whether you are at home holding a virtual meeting or working abroad and dealing with people face to face, you'll want to employ your cultural awareness skills, along with your time management and people skills, to run effective gatherings. The standard meeting rules in U.S. culture, which advise having a clear goal, distributing an agenda, starting and ending on time, encouraging everyone to speak, and summing up to be sure everyone knows what follow-up actions are expected, may not apply everywhere or all the time. What will be different in an international setting, and how can you handle it successfully?

1. As in any setting where you will be speaking or making a presentation, know your audience. You can find out most of what you need to know by simply asking questions ahead of time. Does everyone have the background information they need to participate effectively in your meeting? Does anyone have a particular goal for the meeting or an item to add to the agenda? Are the participants decision makers, or will they need to defer to others and get back to you? What time differences do you need to consider when scheduling the meeting, especially if it's virtual, so everyone can attend?
2. Be aware of participants' cultural norms for personal interactions. In some cultures, people bow when introduced; in others they shake hands. In Japan and China, they exchange business cards, handling the cards with both hands and reading them carefully. Some cultures use first names on short acquaintance, while in others it's considered disrespectful. Seating arrangements should consider cultural differences as well; some groups highly value status markers like a person's position at the table.
3. Respect cultural differences in the perception of time in particular. In Sweden for instance, setting deadlines is acceptable and being on time is a sign of respect. In India time is measured in terms of what needs to be done, not in hours and minutes. In some Latin cultures, time is fluid and being late is not considered a problem. The same is true in parts of the Middle East.
4. Be ready to adapt. Some participants may arrive late or even early, some may bring guests, some may not consider it appropriate to speak up in front of others, or before others of higher rank have spoken, while others may interrupt. In some cultures, it's considered rude to get right down to business, as U.S. employees are trained to do, so participants may expect to socialize for a time before beginning. Some cultures may prefer not to have refreshments, while others may expect them and feel free to judge their quality.
5. Consider differences in decision-making styles. The British may sound like they're still open to discussion, but they are actually announcing their decision. The Chinese prefer long-term decisions to short-term choices. Business managers in Sweden prefer compromise to debate, and decisions can be long in the making in India because it's considered important to get everyone's input so the decision will last.

YOUR CALL

If you were holding a virtual meeting so you and your colleagues in the UK could present a sales proposal to a potential client in India, what questions would you want to ask participants ahead of time?

5. Religion Trying to get wealthy Muslim investors in Dubai to buy some of your bank's financial products? Are you a Protestant doing business in a predominantly Catholic country? Or a Muslim in a Buddhist country? What are the most popular world religions, and how does religion influence the work-related values of the people we're dealing with? *(See Figure 4.3.)*

About 7 in 10 U.S. adults identify as Christians, but almost 23% say they have no religion,[113] up from 18% in 2011. Slightly more than a quarter of them are atheists and agnostics; the others say they have no religion, though they may or may not believe in God. They tend to be predominantly male and white or Asian. Twenty-five percent of U.S. whites are without a religious affiliation, as are more than one in three Asian Americans.[114]

6. Law and Political Stability Every firm contemplating establishing itself abroad must deal with other countries' laws and business practices, which frequently involves making calculations about political risk that might cause loss of a company's assets or impair its foreign operations. Among the risks an organization might anticipate abroad are *instability, expropriation, corruption,* and *labor abuses.*

- **Instability.** Even in a developed country a company may be victimized by political instability, such as riots or civil disorders, as happened in 2014 among Russian-speaking populations in Ukraine. In some developed nations, their very existence is threatened by separatist movements, with large sections clamoring

FIGURE 4.3

Current followers of the major world religions

All population counts are estimated.

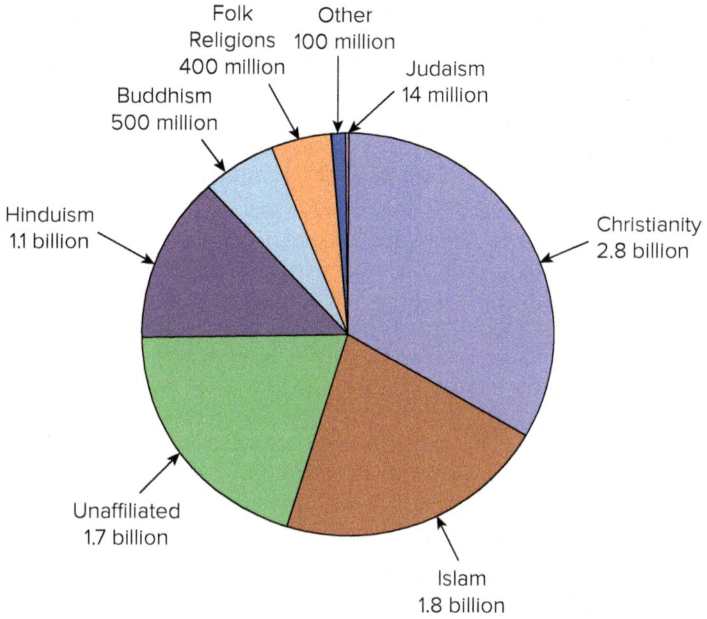

Sources: See "Major World Religions Populations Pie Chart Statistics List," http://www.age-of-the-sage.org/mysticism/world_religions_populations.htm, accessed June 8, 2018; https://www.israelnationalnews.com/News/News.aspx/221859; http://www.pewresearch.org/fact-tank/2017/04/07/why-people-with-no-religion-are-projected-to-decline-as-a-share-of-the-worlds-population/.

to split off and become independent states–Quebec from Canada, Scotland from the United Kingdom, and Catalonia from Spain, for example–which could result in changes to the currency in use.

- **Expropriation.** **Expropriation is defined as a government's seizure of a domestic or foreign company's assets.** In recent years the Venezuelan government has stepped up a campaign to seize land and businesses, such as a rice plant owned by Cargill, one of the United States's largest privately owned companies. In a single recent week, Venezuela won three lawsuits brought by companies claiming losses from the government's seizure of their property without compensating them. The companies were a U.S. oil driller from which Venezuela had seized 11 drilling rigs several years ago, two Spanish investors claiming Venezuela had violated their rights by illegally expropriating their food distribution business, and a bank based in Curacao seeking compensation for $350 million worth of seized properties. In the latter case, the International Centre for Settlement of Investment Disputes not only sided with Venezuela but ordered the plaintiffs to pay that nation court costs of $1.7 million, with interest. Said one international lawyer, "It was a good week for Venezuela but a bad week for investors who have had their property stolen. . . . it is time to further update the expropriation rules."[115]
- **Corruption.** Whether it's called *mordida* (Mexico), *huilu* (China), or *vzyatka* (Russia), it means the same thing: a bribe. Although the United States is relatively free of such

Prayer. The term "Muslim culture" covers many diverse groups—Middle Eastern, African, Asian Muslim, and European and American Muslims—each with its own customs. Muslims strive to pray five times a day, prostrating themselves on a prayer mat. The mat is supposed to face Mecca, the holy city of Islam. ©Purestock/Getty Images corruption, it is an acceptable practice in other countries. Among the countries where bribery is most common are Cambodia, Yemen, Kyrgyzstan, DR Congo, Ukraine, South Sudan, Bangladesh, Afghanistan, Myanmar, and Iraq.[116]

U.S. businesspeople are prevented from participating in overseas bribes under the 1978 **Foreign Corrupt Practices Act**, **which makes it illegal for employees of U.S. companies to make "questionable" or "dubious" contributions to political decision makers in foreign nations.** While this creates a competitive disadvantage for those working in foreign countries in which government bribery may be the only way to obtain business, the United Nations Global Compact is attempting to level the playing field by promoting anti-corruption standards for business.

- **Labor abuses.** Overseas suppliers may offer low prices, but working conditions can be harsh, as has been the case for garment makers in Bangladesh, Cambodia, the Dominican Republic, Haiti, Mexico, Pakistan, and Vietnam. Despite widely publicized fatalities in some countries where substandard and dangerous working conditions exist, human rights groups say little tangible progress has been made. Fire exits and access to drinking water may be lacking, women can be discriminated against, sexually harassed, and underpaid, and workers who protest may be fired, beaten, or even killed. Western consumers' desire for low-priced goods and "fast fashion" fuel some of the abuses because manufacturers can pressure suppliers in the developing world to keep production up and costs down.[117] At least 20 million people across the world are said to be forced to work with no pay.[118]

U.S. Managers on Foreign Assignments: Why Do They Fail?

The U.S. State Department estimated in 2016 that about 9 million U.S. citizens live abroad.[119] These individuals are called **expatriates**—**people living or working in a foreign country.** Many of them, perhaps 300,000, are managers, and supporting them and their families overseas is not cheap. A partner at one human resources consulting firm estimates that it costs twice an executive's $300,000 salary to send him or her from the United States to Shanghai for a year.[120] Are the employers getting their money's worth? Not necessarily.

Early turnover is a common problem with expatriates. It can partially be reduced, however, when the hiring company provides tangible sources of support. These might include offering seminars on cross-cultural differences, facilitating the establishment of social contacts, and other socialization activities.[121] Unfortunately, problems continue when expatriates return home. "Studies suggest between 8% to 25% of managers may leave a company after returning to the U.S.," says one report.[122] Another study found that a failure to effectively manage the return of expatriates reduced a company's return on investment. These studies underscore the importance of managing the repatriation process.[123]

Do you think you have what it takes to be an effective global manager? The following self-assessment can provide input to answering this question. It assesses your potential to be a successful global manager. •

SELF-ASSESSMENT 4.3 CAREER READINESS

Assessing Your Global Manager Potential

This survey is designed to assess how well suited you are to becoming a global manager. Please be prepared to answer these questions if your instructor has assigned Self-Assessment 4.3 in Connect.

1. What is your reaction to the results?
2. Based on considering your five lowest-rated survey items, what can you do to improve your global manager potential?
3. How might you let a recruiter know that you are interested in working overseas and managing people from a different culture?

4.6 Career Corner: Managing Your Career Readiness

LO 4-6

Describe how to develop your cross-cultural competency.

You may think that this chapter does not offer much when it comes to career readiness if you have no plans to work overseas. Don't make this assumption! We all live in a "hyper-connected world, where cultural borders have become blurred with the adoption of technology and the increase in diversity in the workplaces," notes a business writer.[124] Whether you work in the United States or abroad, workplace changes require us to understand, embrace, and use cultural awareness to enhance our personal and professional relationships.

Figure 4.4 shows the model of career readiness we discussed in Chapter 1. This chapter links with three of the KSAOs contained in this model. The most important is the knowledge factor, *cross-cultural competency*. The remaining two are the "other characteristics," *personal adaptability* and *self-awareness*. Personal adaptability is important because it helps when interacting with diverse people and when living or working in another country. Self-awareness is essential for becoming more culturally aware.

FIGURE 4.4

Model for career readiness

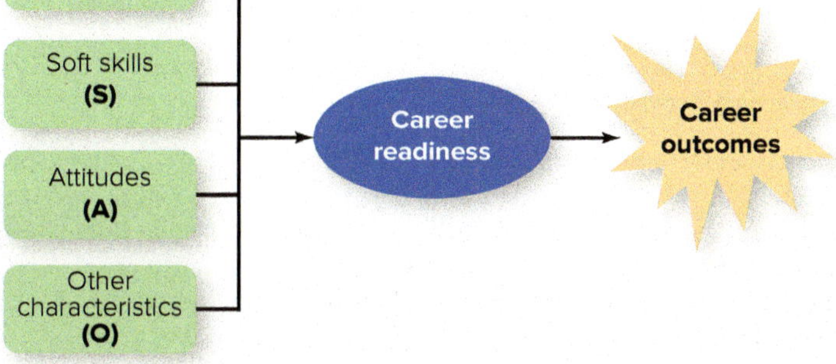

It may take a bit of effort to improve these competencies because they are firmly rooted in our experience and belief systems. A writer for *Fast Company* concluded that "our cultural influences are so deeply embedded in who we are that it is difficult for most of us to recognize them in our own behavior. As a result, we don't think much about the cultural information expressed in many of the things we do or the fact that the vast majority of our behavior is shaped by our cultural surroundings. We just think of what we do as being natural."[125]

We recommend the following activities to enhance the career readiness knowledge of cross-cultural competency:

1. Listen and Observe

Try to take the perspective of a native when interacting with others in a new cultural context. Listening and observing are the foundations of this kind of perspective taking. If a behavior or statement seems odd or confusing to you, look for the cultural logic or set of values that may explain it. For example, Angelo's international students rarely challenged him in the classroom. He felt they were not adequately contributing to classroom discussion due to a lack of confidence or inability to speak English. This assumption was wrong! Their behavior was caused by cultural values that grant tremendous respect and esteem to the role of professor. By understanding this cross-cultural perspective, Angelo was able to encourage his international students to take a more critical and participative perspective during classroom activities. Remember, it is generally good practice to check your understanding by first asking questions of someone familiar with the context at hand.

2. Become Aware of the Context

Context refers to the situational or environmental characteristics that influence our behavior.[126] Understanding context gives you insights that let you correctly interpret the "what" and "why" of someone's behavior. This in turn enables you to more effectively communicate with and influence others. You can develop awareness of context by "learning to read and adapt to the existing structure, rules, customs, and leaders in an unfamiliar situation," according to Bruce Tulgan, an expert on developing soft skills. Tulgan recommends answering four questions about structure, rules, customs, and leadership to increase your contextual awareness:

- "What do you know?
- What don't you know or understand?
- What do you need to know or understand better?
- How can you learn? What resources and support do you need?"[127]

Answering these questions increases your insights into the contextual effects of culture and enhances your ability to fit comfortably in a particular context.

3. Choose Something Basic

English is the generally accepted language of business. If you are a native speaker, it is still advisable to try and learn another language if you plan to work overseas or in a context where many people speak another language. Even a small effort shows respect and promotes cultural sensitivity.

A host of other activities can enhance your cross-cultural competency. Make it a goal to select several of them from the following list:[128]

- Study the principles or values of another religion.
- Participate in a sporting event related to a different culture (croquet, karate, rugby, bocce, pétanque).
- Learn about traditions and celebratory days from other countries.
- Watch international films.
- Try the cuisine of other countries.
- Learn the history of dance forms in other countries.
- Strive to interact with a wider set of culturally diverse students or employees.[129]
- Attend seminars or speeches by culturally diverse speakers.
- Donate to global relief funds.
- Organize a diversity celebration.
- Follow world news on a regular basis.
- Take courses in black history, women's studies, Asian American studies, Chicano studies, and Native American studies.
- Take an anthropology class. ●

Key Terms Used in This Chapter

context 150
countertrading 129
cross-cultural awareness 122
culture 140
dumping 132
e-commerce 119
embargo 132
ethnocentric managers 124
European Union (EU) 135
exchange rate 136
expatriates 148
exporting 129
expropriation 147
Foreign Corrupt Practices Act 148
franchising 129
free trade 131
geocentric managers 125
global economy 120
globalization 118
global outsourcing 128
global village 119
GLOBE project 141
greenfield venture 130
high-context culture 140
Hofstede model of four cultural dimensions 140
import quota 131
importing 128
joint venture 130
licensing 129
low-context culture 140
maquiladoras 127
monochronic time 145
most favored nation 136
multinational corporation 123
multinational organization 123
North American Free Trade Agreement (NAFTA) 134
offshoring 128
outsourcing 128
parochialism 124
polycentric managers 125
polychronic time 145
sanction 133
tariff 131
trade protectionism 131
trading bloc 134
Trans-Pacific Partnership (TPP) 135
wholly owned subsidiary 130

Key Points

4.1 Globalization: The Collapse of Time and Distance

- Globalization is the trend of the world economy toward becoming more interdependent. Globalization is reflected in three developments: (1) the rise of the global village and e-commerce, (2) the trend of the world's becoming one big market, and (3) the rise of both megafirms and Internet-enabled minifirms.
- The rise of the "global village" refers to the "shrinking" of time and space as air travel and the electronic media have made global communication easier. The Internet and the web have led to e-commerce, the buying and selling of products through computer networks.
- The global economy is the increasing tendency of the economies of nations to interact with one another as one market.
- The rise of cross-border business has led to megamergers, as giant firms have joined forces, and minifirms, small companies in which managers can use the Internet and other technologies to get enterprises started more easily and to maneuver faster.

4.2 You and International Management

- Studying international management prepares you to work with foreign customers or partners, with foreign suppliers, for a foreign firm in the United States, or for a U.S. firm overseas. International management is management that oversees the conduct of operations in or with organizations in foreign countries.
- The successful international manager is not ethnocentric or polycentric but geocentric. Ethnocentric managers believe that their native country, culture, language, and behavior are superior to all others. Polycentric managers take the view that native managers in the foreign offices best understand native personnel and practices. Geocentric managers accept that there are differences and similarities between home and foreign personnel and practices, and they should use whatever techniques are most effective.

4.3 Why and How Companies Expand Internationally

- Companies expand internationally for at least five reasons. They seek (1) cheaper or more plentiful supplies, (2) new markets, (3) lower labor costs, (4) access to finance capital, and (5) avoidance of tariffs on imported goods or import quotas.
- There are five ways in which companies expand internationally. (1) They engage in global outsourcing, using suppliers outside the company and the United States to provide goods and services. (2) They engage in importing, exporting, and countertrading (bartering for goods). (3) They engage in licensing (allow a foreign company to pay a fee to make or distribute the company's product) and franchising (allow a foreign company to pay a fee and a share of the profit in return for using the first company's brand name). (4) They engage in joint ventures, a strategic alliance to share the risks and rewards of starting a

new enterprise together in a foreign country. (5) They become wholly owned subsidiaries, or foreign subsidiaries that are totally owned and controlled by an organization.

4.4 The World of Free Trade: Regional Economic Cooperation and Competition

- Free trade is the movement of goods and services among nations without political or economic obstructions.
- Countries often use trade protectionism—the use of government regulations to limit the import of goods and services—to protect their domestic industries against foreign competition. Three barriers to free trade are tariffs, import quotas, and embargoes and sanctions. (1) A tariff is a trade barrier in the form of a customs duty, or tax, levied mainly on imports. (2) An import quota is a trade barrier in the form of a limit on the numbers of a product that can be imported. (3) An embargo is a complete ban on the import or export of certain products. A sanction is the trade prohibition on certain types of products, services, or technology to another country for specific reasons, including nuclear nonproliferation and humanitarian purposes.
- Three principal organizations exist that are designed to facilitate international trade. (1) The World Trade Organization is designed to monitor and enforce trade agreements. (2) The World Bank is designed to provide low-interest loans to developing nations for improving transportation, education, health, and telecommunications. (3) The International Monetary Fund is designed to assist in smoothing the flow of money between nations.
- A trading bloc is a group of nations within a geographical region that have agreed to remove trade barriers. We considered two major trading blocs: (1) the North American Free Trade Agreement (NAFTA: United States, Canada, and Mexico), and (2) the European Union (EU: 28 trading partners in Europe). Others are the Association of Southeast Asian Nations, Asia-Pacific Economic Cooperation, Mercosur, and the Central America Free Trade Agreement. Negotiated over seven years, the Trans-Pacific Partnership (TPP) is a proposed trade agreement among 12 Pacific Rim countries that can't take effect until it is approved by the U.S. Congress and other parliaments in the bloc. Besides joining together in trade blocs, countries also extend special, "most favored nation" trading privileges—that is, grant other countries favorable trading treatment such as the reduction of import duties.
- When doing overseas trading, managers must consider exchange rates, the rate at which the currency of one area or country can be exchanged for the currency of another's, such as American dollars in relation to Mexican pesos or European euros.
- The term BRICS stands for the five major emerging economies of Brazil, Russia, India, China, and South Africa—five countries that make up 40% of the world's population, represent about 20% of the world's economic activity, and have established their own $100 billion reserve fund. The largest of these countries in the order of their population size are China, India, and Brazil.

4.5 The Value of Understanding Cultural Differences

- Misunderstandings and miscommunications often arise because one person doesn't understand the expectations of a person from another culture. In low-context cultures, shared meanings are primarily derived from written and spoken words. In high-context cultures, people rely heavily on situational cues for meaning when communicating with others.
- Geert Hofstede proposed the Hofstede model of four cultural dimensions, which identified four dimensions along which national cultures can be placed: (1) individualism/collectivism, (2) power distance, (3) uncertainty avoidance, and (4) masculinity/femininity.
- Robert House and others created the GLOBE (for Global Leadership and Organizational Behavior Effectiveness) Project, a massive and ongoing cross-cultural investigation of nine cultural dimensions involved in leadership and organizational processes: (1) power distance, (2) uncertainty avoidance, (3) institutional collectivism, (4) in-group collectivism, (5) gender egalitarianism, (6) assertiveness, (7) future orientation, (8) performance orientation, and (9) humane orientation.
- A nation's culture is the shared set of beliefs, values, knowledge, and patterns of behavior common to a group of people. Visitors to another culture may experience culture shock—feelings of discomfort and disorientation. Managers trying to understand other cultures need to understand six basic cultural perceptions embodied in (1) language, (2) interpersonal space, (3) communication, (4) time orientation, (5) religion, and (6) law and political stability.
- Regarding language, when you are trying to communicate across cultures you have three options: Speak your own language (if others can understand you), use a translator, or learn the local language.
- Interpersonal space involves how close or far away one should be when communicating with another person, with Americans being comfortable at 3–4 feet but people in other countries often wanting to be closer.
- Communication involves not only differences in understanding about words and sounds and their meanings but also in expectations about relationships and business concepts.
- Time orientation of a culture may be either monochronic (preference for doing one thing at a time) or polychronic (preference for doing more than one thing at a time).

- Managers need to consider the effect of religious differences. In order of size (population), the major world religions are Christianity, Islam, Hinduism, Buddhism, Chinese traditional religions, primal-indigenous, and African traditional and diasporic religions.
- Every company must deal with other countries' laws and business practices, which means weighing the risks of political instability; expropriation, or government seizure of a domestic or foreign company's assets; political corruption, including bribery; and labor abuses.

4.6 Career Corner: Managing Your Career Readiness

- You can develop your cross-cultural competency by engaging in three activities: (1) listen and observe, (2) become aware of the context, and (3) choose something basic.

Understanding the Chapter: What Do I Know?

1. What are three important developments in globalization?
2. What are some positives and negatives of globalization?
3. What are the principal reasons for learning about international management?
4. How do ethnocentric, polycentric, and geocentric managers differ?
5. What are five reasons companies expand internationally, and what are five ways they go about doing this expansion?
6. What are some barriers to international trade?
7. Name the three principal organizations designed to facilitate international trade and describe what they do.
8. What are the principal major trading blocs, and what are the BRICS countries?
9. Define what's meant by "culture" and describe some of the cultural dimensions studied by the Hofstede model and the GLOBE project.
10. Describe the six important cultural areas that international managers have to deal with in doing cross-border business.

Management in Action

The Growth and Stall of Didi Chuxing

Chinese ridesharing company Didi Chuxing was formed from the 2015 merger of rival firms Didi Dache and Kuaidi Dache. The company currently provides transportation services for more than 450 million users across 400 cities in China, and it was valued at US $28 billion in 2016. Didi employs more than 7,000 people, of whom 40 percent are female. Its mission is to provide "services including taxi hailing, private car hailing, Hitch (social ride-sharing), DiDi Chauffeur, DiDi Bus, DiDi Test Drive, DiDi Car Rental, DiDi Enterprise Solutions, DiDi Minibus, DiDi Luxe and bike-sharing to users in China via a smartphone application."[130]

Didi Chuxing outmaneuvered Uber in China, finally purchasing Uber's Chinese business in 2016. Didi is now the dominant player in China, but the market is saturated and the company's growth has slowed. Cheng Wei, CEO of Didi Chuxing since the 2015 merger, is implementing a new strategy aimed at increasing growth. A company spokesperson described this strategy to *Forbes* as one in which "we will put more energy and resources in the international market to explore the frontier technology, innovate new models of business, and seek like-minded partners."[131] The question is whether the company can achieve its strategy by expanding outside mainland China into territory dominated by its rival Uber.

DIDI'S EXPANSION OUTSIDE CHINA

Things have not been going well for Uber, the world's most valuable start-up (valued at $70 billion). Its controversial founder, Travis Kalanick, was sacked after a series of scandals. The company suffered from the leak of 57 million rider and driver records, was accused of spying on competitors, and has been enmeshed in costly litigation in several different countries.[132] Didi is capitalizing on Uber's setbacks while implementing its own growth strategies.

Didi's growth strategy focuses on expanding across multiple continents at the same time. This is risky because of the cost and risk associated with expanding overseas, especially when you have entrenched competitors like Uber in North America, South America, and Europe. According to an analyst with *Bloomberg News*, Didi should start its overseas expansion in Southeast Asian markets like Vietnam and Malaysia, which don't have as much entrenched competition.[133] However, the company seems to want to make a bigger splash by expanding across multiple continents at once via different expansion models.

The expansion outside China is starting with a partnership in the island neighbor of Taiwan. Didi is planning to start operations there with the help of a Taiwanese partner named LEDI Technology, which will be Didi's authorized franchisee in the country. Taiwan is a tricky market to enter because its lawmakers and its taxi industry have been successful in forcing organizations to conform to its transportation rules. Fines for illegally transporting passengers can be as high as $834,000 per infraction, and Uber reportedly racked up more than $30 million in fines in one month alone, causing the company to briefly suspend service across the country. Didi is trying to avoid making the same mistake. The company states that LEDI "is conducting market research and exploring extensive community partnerships in Taiwan" in addition to support for recruiting drivers.[134]

Didi is using another model of expansion in South America by purchasing existing companies. As *Fortune* reports, in 2018 Didi acquired Uber's largest Brazilian rival, 99, "potentially creating a formidable rival to Uber in Latin America's largest economy." Cheng Wei stated that "globalization is a top strategic priority for Didi."[135] Globalization is not easy in the ridesharing industry because of competition from Uber. An analyst told *The Wall Street Journal* that "It's a fight for brand," and Didi doesn't "have a global brand name that probably has a same recognition level as Uber."[136]

Didi has not been shy about expanding north of Brazil, even without significant brand recognition in the Americas. As *Reuters* reports, the company hopes to enter the Mexican market next year without the assistance of a Mexican partner. This would be the first overseas operation outside China without local partner management or the purchase of an existing organization. It would also allow Didi to utilize its own smartphone app and recruit local drivers to its platform.[137] This is especially significant in Mexico City, one of Uber's busiest markets in the world.[138] And the move would mark Didi's debut in North America, which puts it right on the United States's doorstep. Trying to enter an Uber-dominated market that also includes Cabify (a Spanish rideshare company) without local partner support could be quite costly and risky. Consider what happened to Uber when it challenged Didi in China: It lost billions of dollars subsidizing drivers to keep its prices low, and in the end it still had to bow out.[139] Is Didi ready for another price war in order to gain market share?

FOR DISCUSSION

Problem-Solving Perspective

1. What is the underlying problem in this case from CEO Cheng Wei's perspective?
2. What obstacles remain for Didi as it challenges Uber's control of the ride-sharing industry?

Application of Chapter Content

1. Didi's CEO Cheng Wei stated that globalization is a top strategic priority for the organization. Explain how Didi is utilizing major developments in globalization to its advantage.
2. If you were leading Didi's expansion into the Americas, what type of international manager would you want to be—ethnocentric, polycentric, or geocentric? Explain your decision.
3. Based on Figure 4.1, which ways of expanding internationally has Didi employed? Provide specific examples.
4. Didi is based in China and looking to expand to Brazil; China and Brazil are BRICS nations. Why is this significant?
5. Assume Didi is planning on entering the U.S. ride-sharing market. Based on GLOBE cultural dimensions, the United States scores lower than China on power distance, in-group collectivism, and uncertainty avoidance. With this in mind, how would you advise Didi, a Chinese company, to modify its practices if it plans on entering the U.S. market?

Legal/Ethical Challenge

Should Qatar Be Hosting the 2022 World Cup?

In May 2015, seven Fédération Internationale de Football Association (FIFA) officials were arrested at the Hotel Baur au Lac in Zurich as they were preparing to attend the 65th FIFA Congress. The arrests were tied to a multiyear investigation by the United States into collusion between FIFA officials and international marketing firms. The alleged collusion included the payment of at least $150 million in bribes by the firms in exchange for lucrative broadcasting and hosting rights for prestigious soccer tournaments. More than 40 other officials, executives, and corporations around the world have since been charged. Many pleaded guilty and agreed to testify against others to secure leniency.[140]

This scandal has cast a spotlight on Qatar, the host of the 2022 soccer World Cup. Qatar's selection to host the world's most prestigious tournament has been tainted for a number of years by suspicions about the individuals who supported the bid of a rich nation that lacked facilities to host the event. The *Chicago Tribune* reported on an Argentine marketing executive who paid bribes for media rights and then made a deal with prosecutors to testify during the first trial of FIFA executives in a U.S. courthouse. The Argentinian did not provide bribes for the Qatari World Cup bid, but he was told of the Qatari bribes by FIFA members. This executive noted that one of the FIFA members sold his vote for Qatar for a paltry $1.5 million and then complained that another voting member got tens of millions more. Some voting members of FIFA have been charged as part of the corruption scandal but have yet to be extradited to the United States for trial. Another Argentine witness testified that a ledger of bribes, including payments of $750,000 and $500,000 to South American soccer federation presidents, was found. Though these presidents did not have World Cup hosting votes, the payments were labeled "Q2022."[141]

Qataris' alleged bribing of FIFA officials could be cultural. Bribery in the Middle East continues to be more acceptable than in North America and Europe. Ernst & Young conducted a survey of 66 Middle East-based senior managers and directors to ascertain their thoughts on bribery and corruption. The results were that 20% of respondents believed it was impossible to conduct business competitively in the Middle East without committing fraud. Furthermore, 66% of those interviewed believed corruption was a major problem in the region.[142]

FIFA claims it has been unable to uncover evidence that would lead it to prevent Qatar from hosting the World Cup. Qatar also continues to deny it acted improperly or bought its right to host the tournament.

SOLVING THE CHALLENGE

What option would you choose if you were running FIFA?

1. Qatar should be stripped of its right to host the 2022 World Cup. There is obviously evidence of bribery and such an important tournament should not be tainted.
2. So far, prosecutors have not uncovered anything directly tying the Qataris to the corruption scandal. Stripping Qatar of its hosting privileges while it is building the infrastructure to host the tournament will lead to millions, or possibly billions, of dollars in losses and a significant number of lost jobs. Do nothing.
3. FIFA should have a third party open its own investigation of the events leading up to Qatar's being granted hosting privileges. The conclusion of this investigation should dictate what happens to the 2022 bid.
4. Suggest other options.

Uber Continuing Case connect

Learn about the strategies Uber used to globalize its business. The company learned that some of its practices were not well received in other countries. Assess your ability to apply concepts discussed in this chapter to the case by going to Connect.

Planning

5 Planning

The Foundation of Successful Management

©Olivier Renck/Aurora/Getty Images

After reading this chapter, you should be able to:

LO 5-1 Discuss the role of strategic management.

LO 5-2 Compare mission, vision, and value statements.

LO 5-3 Discuss the types and purposes of goals and plans.

LO 5-4 Describe SMART goals and their implementation.

LO 5-5 Outline the planning/control cycle.

LO 5-6 Describe how to develop the career readiness competency of *proactive learning orientation.*

FORECAST *What's Ahead in This Chapter*

We describe planning and its link to strategy. We define planning, strategy, and strategic management and state why they are important. We deal with the fundamentals of planning, including the mission, vision, and value statements, and the three types of planning—strategic, tactical, and operational. We consider goals, operating plans, and action plans; SMART goals, management by objectives, and cascading goals; and finally the planning/control cycle. We conclude with a Career Corner that focuses on how you can develop the career readiness competency of *proactive learning orientation.*

MANAGE U

Making an Effective Plan for Starting Your Career

The thought of starting a career (or switching to a new one) can be either intimidating or exciting. What's the difference? Having goals and a plan.

Setting Goals and Making a Plan

Here are some steps in the career-management process for you to consider as you set about building your career.[1]

1. Identify your options. Use the career readiness skill of self-awareness to write down areas and ideas that interest and are important to you and the functional, cross-cultural, computational, interpersonal, and other skills you can offer an employer. Then make a written list of the opportunities available to you through your networking, earlier work and volunteer experience, and other resources (don't forget the alumni and placement offices at your school). Now match up the two lists to discover where you should focus your career-building efforts.

2. Explore conditions in your target field. The career readiness skill of understanding the business will guide you to identify important factors like the demand for new hires in your chosen field or fields, the competencies expected of incoming employees, the likely salary range and opportunities for advancement, and any geographic limitations or requirements in the industry to be aware of. If your field or industry is concentrated in one or two parts of the country, for instance, be ready to move.

3. Create your action plan. Using what you learned from steps 1 and 2, write a list of actions you can take to achieve your goal of breaking into a new career. You are more likely to achieve your goals if they are "SMART"—specific, measurable against clear criteria to show progress, attainable with a chance of 50% or higher, relevant to you, and time bound with target dates for completion. We discuss the process of writing SMART goals in Section 5.4. Try to keep your steps or goals to a manageable number; somewhere between three and five is recommended. Prioritize and schedule them to create your plan, and if it helps you to give each one a name, by all means do so.

4. Track your progress. You'll see as you study this chapter that monitoring or controlling progress toward goals is an inherent part of the planning process. Each time you get a result from one of your efforts, whether it's positive or negative, that result constitutes feedback on how well you've selected your goals and how effective your plan is. If one step doesn't work out as planned, don't give up. Rely on your positive attitude and ability to adapt (more career readiness skills) and realize you have other opportunities to succeed. Try broadening your search, and begin again.

Staying Resilient during the Process

Here are a few ideas about what else you can do to keep your hopes—and your finances—afloat during the career-building process.

1. Know that it takes time to find a job, especially one that's a good fit for both you and the company that hires you. College graduates spend about six months, on average, landing their first job after graduation.[2] If you are already working, even part-time, stay in the job while you pursue a new one. It's always easier to find a job if you have one. If you are not working, consider taking a part-time or short-term job to generate some income. since you'll want to avoid running up credit card debt.

2. Create a budget to be sure your income will cover your day-to-day expenses. This is a lifelong habit that will serve you well.

3. Avoid making any major financial commitments until you've actually landed your target job. You won't know how much you can afford to pay for a car until you know your salary, for instance, and you may not want to be encumbered by a new lease if your dream job requires you to relocate. As long as you have an appropriate interview outfit, even splurging on a professional wardrobe can wait until you know the dress code at your new employer.

For Discussion What fields or industries are interesting or appealing to you as places to work? What news and information about these areas can you start tracking now, and how will you will do that? Is there anyone in your network who can help you increase your understanding of the way this industry works? If not, how could you find someone?

5.1 Planning and Strategy?

THE BIG PICTURE

The first of four functions in the management process is planning, which involves setting goals and deciding how to achieve them and which is linked to strategy. We define planning, strategy, and strategic management. We then describe three reasons strategic management and strategic planning are important.

LO 5-1

Discuss the role of strategic management.

The *management process,* as you'll recall (from Chapter 1), involves the four management functions of *planning, organizing, leading,* and *controlling,* which form four of the part divisions of this book. In this and the next two chapters, we discuss *planning* and *strategy.*

Planning, Strategy, and Strategic Management

"Move fast and break things."

Is that a plan or strategy? No, it's a slogan. In fact, it used to be Facebook's mantra to its software developers, suggesting that "moving quickly is so important that we were even willing to tolerate a few bugs in order to do it," as Facebook CEO Mark Zuckerberg explained.[3] (Then, he says, the company realized "that it wasn't helping us to move faster because we had to slow down to fix these bugs.")

Planning, which we discuss in this chapter, is used in conjunction with *strategy* and *strategic management,* as we describe in Chapter 6. Let's consider some definitions.

Planning: Coping with Uncertainty As we've said (Chapter 1), **planning is defined as setting goals and deciding how to achieve them.** Another definition: planning is coping with uncertainty by formulating future courses of action to achieve specified results.[4] A **plan is a document that outlines how goals are going to be met.** When you make a plan, you make a blueprint for action that describes what you need to do to realize your goals.

Example: One important type of plan is a **business plan, a document that outlines a proposed firm's goals, the strategy for achieving them, and the standards for measuring success.** Here you would describe the basic idea behind your business—the **business model, which outlines the need the firm will fill, the operations of the business, its components and functions, as well as the expected revenues and expenses.** It also describes the industry you're entering, how your product will be different, how you'll market to customers, how you're qualified to run the business, and how you will finance your business.

EXAMPLE Why Write a Business Plan?

More than 5 in 10 Millennials say that if they had the resources they need, they'd start their own business in the next year. Most are attracted to the idea of being their own boss and making a lot of money by opening a business of their own if they could.[5] But planning and management control are critical to the success of small businesses as only 33 percent of them survive 10 years or more according to the Bureau of Labor Statistics.[6]

It was by planning, not by accident, that popular singer Rihanna recently launched a cosmetics business that got off to a spectacular start and was immediately named one of the "best inventions of 2017" by *Time* magazine. Her company, Fenty Beauty (a brand of the luxury label LVMH), boasts a jaw-dropping 40 different shades of foundation in order to cater to women of every color and every skin type. In its first month in business alone, Fenty far outsold a rival celebrity line, Kylie Cosmetics, which has earned hundreds of millions of dollars in its first two years. In its second month, Fenty sales were already up 34% and showing no signs of slowing.

Rihanna experimented with beauty products for years before finally deciding the void in the market—for products designed for hard-to-match skin tones—was hers to fill. Among the many business factors for which she had to plan in starting her company were the target market, women who are underserved by existing beauty lines but who spend generously on makeup (averaging almost $500 a year); her promotional plan, which included outreach to her 60 million Instagram followers; and her financial plan, which relies on the backing of LVMH. To her knowledge of existing makeup lines, Rihanna added close scrutiny of her chosen competitors, Kylie and KKW Beauty (Kim Kardashian West's brand). And she explored her distribution options, choosing online sales and in-store distribution by Sephora. As *Time* reported, Fenty has become the brand to beat, as even established companies like L'Oreal begin launching marketing campaigns aimed at its long-neglected market.[7]

YOUR CALL

Got an idea for a business? Think about your pre-launch planning process. What questions about your product or service, your target market, your promotional plans, and your distribution method would you need to answer before you made the leap?

Strategy: Setting Long-Term Direction **A strategy, or strategic plan, sets the long-term goals and direction for an organization.** It represents an "educated guess" about what long-term goals or direction to pursue for the survival or prosperity of the organization. We hear the word expressed in terms like "Apple's ultimate strategy . . ." or "Visa's overseas strategy . . ." or financial strategy, marketing strategy, and human resource strategy.

An example of a strategy is "Grow the business organically," which means "Increase revenue from existing and new customers rather than from acquiring other companies." However, strategy is not something that can be decided on just once. It generally is reconsidered every year because of ever-changing business conditions.

Strategic Management: Involving All Managers in Strategy In the late 1940s, most large U.S. companies were organized around a single idea or product line. By the 1970s, *Fortune* 500 companies were operating in more than one industry and had expanded overseas. It became apparent that to stay focused and efficient, companies had to begin taking a strategic-management approach.

Strategic management is a process that involves managers from all parts of the organization in the formulation and the implementation of strategies and strategic goals. This definition doesn't mean that managers at the top dictate ideas to be followed by people lower down. Indeed, precisely because middle managers in particular are the ones who will be asked to understand and implement the strategies, they should also help to formulate them.

As we will see, strategic management is a process that involves managers from all parts of the organization—top managers, middle managers, and first-line managers—in the formulation, implementation, and execution of strategies and strategic goals to advance the purposes of the organization. Thus, planning covers not only strategic planning (done by top managers), but also tactical planning (done by middle managers) and operational planning (done by first-line managers).

Planning and strategic management derive from an organization's mission and vision about itself, as we describe in the next section. *(See Figure 5.1.)*

Why Planning and Strategic Management Are Important

An organization should adopt planning and strategic management for three reasons: They can (1) *provide direction and momentum,* (2) *encourage new ideas,* and above all (3) *develop a sustainable competitive advantage.*[8] Let's consider these three matters.

FIGURE 5.1

Planning and strategic management

The details of planning and strategic management are explained in Chapters 5 and 6.

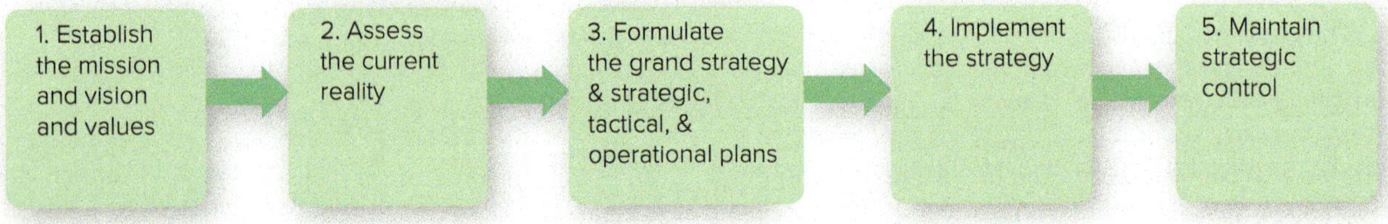

1. Providing Direction and Momentum Some executives are unable even to articulate what their strategy is.[9] Others are so preoccupied with day-to-day pressures that their organizations can lose momentum. But planning and strategic management can help people focus on the most critical problems, choices, and opportunities.

If a broad group of employees is involved in the process, that can foster teamwork, promote learning, and build commitment across the organization. Indeed, as we describe in Chapter 8, strategy can determine the very structure of the organization—for example, a top-down hierarchy with lots of management levels, as might be appropriate for an electricity-and-gas power utility, versus a flat organization with few management levels and flexible roles, as might suit a fast-moving social media start-up.

Unless a plan is in place, managers may well focus on just whatever is in front of them, putting out fires—until they get an unpleasant jolt when a competitor moves out in front because it has been able to take a long-range view of things and act more quickly. In recent times, this surprise has been happening over and over as companies have been confronted by some digital or Internet trend that emerged as a threat—as Amazon.com was to Borders bookstores; as Uber has been to taxi cabs; as Google News, blogs, and citizen media were to newspapers.

Of course, a poor plan can send an organization in the wrong direction. Bad planning usually results from faulty assumptions about the future, poor assessment of an

New Barbies. Mattel, maker of the famous Barbie doll, whose sales have been cut by rival brands, is adding tall, petite, and curvy dolls to its product line, trying to better connect with young girls. Parents and interested grassroots organizations have long been campaigning to make children's toys less stereotypical, but social media have amplified their voices and forced companies to listen. Mattel and other companies are also bringing out inexpensive (under $400) 3-D printers that allow children to create their own plastic toys, including doll-like ones (monsters). Do you think Mattel should plan for the gradual elimination of Barbie? ©Mattel/Splash News/Newscom organization's capabilities, ineffective group dynamics, and failure to use management control as a feedback mechanism.[10] And it needs to be said that while a detailed plan may be comforting, it's not necessarily a strategy.[11]

2. Encouraging New Ideas Some people object that planning can foster rigidity, that it creates blinders that block out peripheral vision and reduces creative thinking and action. "Setting oneself on a predetermined course in unknown waters," says one critic, "is the perfect way to sail straight into an iceberg."[12]

Actually, far from being a straitjacket for new ideas, strategic planning can help encourage them by stressing the importance of innovation in achieving long-range success. Management scholar Gary Hamel says that companies such as Apple have been successful because they have been able to unleash the spirit of "strategy innovation." Strategy innovation, he says, is the ability to reinvent the basis of competition within existing industries–"bold new business models that put incumbents on the defensive."[13]

Some successful innovators are companies creating new wealth in the food and restaurant industries, where Starbucks Coffee, Trader Joe's, ConAgra, and Walmart, for example, developed entirely new grocery product categories and retailing concepts. Starbucks, when entering the Chinese market, decided not to threaten China's tea-drinking culture and, instead, introduced drinks with green tea along with a chic restaurant interior that made young Chinese feel "cool and trendy."[14] GrubHub Seamless, an online takeout and delivery company, serves customers armed with cell phones and delivery apps, delivering pizzas and other foods anywhere they want–at the gym, in the park, on the playground.[15] Vending machines are now serving everything from salads to smoothies to caviar, and supermarkets are experimenting with personalized pricing, using complex shopping data to ascertain the unique needs of individual customers.[16]

3. Developing a Sustainable Competitive Advantage Strategic management can provide a sustainable *competitive advantage*, which, you'll recall (from Chapter 1), is the ability of an organization to produce goods or services more effectively than its competitors do, thereby outperforming them. We discuss the manner in which companies create competitive advantage more thoroughly in Chapter 6. You will learn that companies must have products or services that are valuable, rare, and non-imitable, and an organization poised to exploit its strengths. In today's global marketplace, competitive advantage can vary across countries. Uber is a good example.

Uber definitely had, and still has, competitive advantage when it comes to ride sharing in the U.S. It's a different story when it comes to Africa. A start-up called Taxify created its own competitive advantage by being the first company to offer motorbike-hailing. Motorbikes, which are called boda bodas, were a hit because they were more nimble when traveling through congested streets and communities. Taxify's success is clearly linked to its ability to localize it product offerings more quickly than larger firms like Uber. It also gained competitive advantage by paying drivers with mobile money, "a technology popular in Uganda and other emerging economies because it allows people to receive and immediately store funds using a mobile phone."[17] ●

5.2 Fundamentals of Planning

THE BIG PICTURE

Planning consists of translating an organization's mission and vision into objectives. The organization's purpose is expressed as a mission statement, and what it becomes is expressed as a vision statement; both should represent the organization's values, expressed in a values statement. From these are derived strategic planning, then tactical planning, then operational planning.

LO 5-2

Compare mission, vision, and value statements.

Are you hopeful? That's a good thing. Students who have more hope reportedly have higher grades and are more apt to finish college.

"Hope is the belief that the future will be better than the present," says columnist Elizabeth Bernstein, "and that you have some power to make it so." People who are hopeful "don't just have a goal or a wish, they have a strategy to achieve it and the motivation to implement their plan."[18]

First, however, you must determine your "goal or wish"—that is, your purpose. An organization must determine its purpose, too—what's known as its *mission*. And managers must have an idea of where they want the organization to go—the *vision*. Both mission and vision should express the organization's *values*. The approach to planning can be summarized in the diagram below, which shows how an organization's mission becomes translated into action plans. *(See Figure 5.2.)*

FIGURE 5.2

Making plans

An organization's reason for being is expressed in a *mission statement*. What the organization wishes to become is expressed in a *vision statement*. The values the organization wishes to emphasize are expressed in a *values statement*. From these are derived *strategic planning*, then *tactical planning*, and finally *operational planning*. The purpose of each kind of planning is to specify *goals* and *action plans* that ultimately pave the way toward achieving an organization's vision.

Mission, Vision, and Values Statements

The planning process begins with three attributes: a mission statement (which answers the question "What is our reason for being?"), a vision statement (which answers the question "What do we want to become?"), and a values statement (which answers the question "What values do we want to emphasize?"). *(See Table 5.1.)*

TABLE 5.1 **Mission, Vision, and Values Statements**

MISSION STATEMENTS: DOES YOUR COMPANY'S MISSION STATEMENT ANSWER THESE QUESTIONS?
1. Who are our customers? 2. What are our major products or services? 3. In what geographical areas do we compete? 4. What is our basic technology? 5. What is our commitment to economic objectives? 6. What are our basic beliefs, values, aspirations, and philosophical priorities? 7. What are our major strengths and competitive advantages? 8. What are our public responsibilities, and what image do we wish to project? 9. What is our attitude toward our employees?
VISION STATEMENTS: DOES YOUR COMPANY'S VISION STATEMENT ANSWER "YES" TO THESE QUESTIONS?
1. Is it appropriate for the organization and for the times? 2. Does it set standards of excellence and reflect high ideals? 3. Does it clarify purpose and direction? 4. Does it inspire enthusiasm and encourage commitment? 5. Is it well articulated and easily understood? 6. Does it reflect the uniqueness of the organization, its distinctive competence, what it stands for, what it's able to achieve? 7. Is it ambitious?
VALUES STATEMENTS: DOES YOUR COMPANY'S VALUES STATEMENT ANSWER "YES" TO THESE QUESTIONS?
1. Does it express the company's distinctiveness, its view of the world? 2. Is it intended to guide all the organization's actions, including how you treat employees, customers, etc.? 3. Is it tough, serving as the foundation on which difficult company decisions can be made? 4. Will it be unchanging, as valid 100 years from now as it is today? 5. Does it reflect the beliefs of those who truly care about the organization—the founders, CEO, and top executives—rather than represent a consensus of all employees? 6. Are the values expressed in the statement limited (five or so) and easy to remember, so that employees will have them top-of-mind when making decisions? 7. Would you want the organization to continue to hold these values, even if at some point they become a competitive disadvantage?

Sources: B. Nanus, Visionary Leadership: Creating a Compelling Sense of Direction for Your Organization *(San Francisco: Jossey-Bass, 1992), pp. 28–29; "How to Write a Vision Statement,"* Cleverism, *March 2, 2017, https://www.cleverism.com/write-vision-statement; P. M. Lencioni, "Make Your Values Mean Something,"* Harvard Business Review, *July 2002, pp. 113–117; and A Loehr, "6 Steps to Defining Your Organizational Values,"* Rework, *March 7, 2016, https://www.cornerstoneondemand.com/rework/6-steps-defining-your-organizational-values.*

The Mission Statement—"What Is Our Reason for Being?"

An organization's mission is its purpose or reason for being. Determining the mission is the responsibility of top management and the board of directors. It is up to them to formulate a **mission statement, which expresses the purpose of the organization.**

"Only a clear definition of the mission and purpose of the organization makes possible clear and realistic . . . objectives," said Peter Drucker.[19] Whether the organization is for-profit or nonprofit, the mission statement identifies the goods or services the organization provides and will provide. Sometimes it also gives the reasons for providing them (to make a profit or to achieve humanitarian goals, for example).

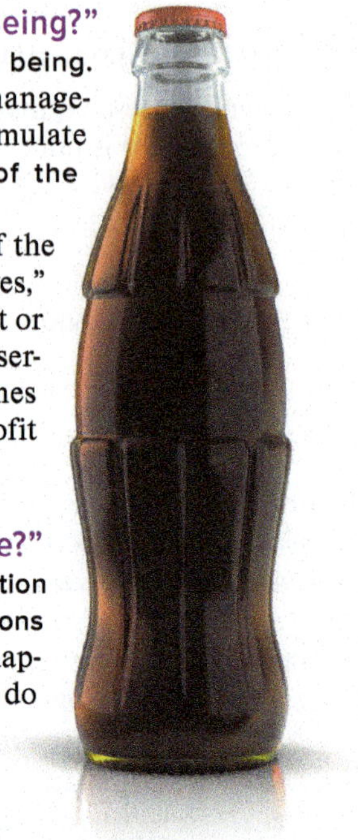

©heromen30/Shutterstock

The Vision Statement—"What Do We Want to Become?"

A vision is a long-term goal describing "what" an organization wants to become. It is a clear sense of the future and the actions needed to get there. "[A] vision should describe what's happening to the world you compete in and what you want to do about it," says one *Fortune* article. "It should guide decisions."[20]

After formulating a mission statement, top managers need to develop a **vision statement, which expresses what the organization should become, where it wants to go strategically.**

EXAMPLE Mission, Vision, and Values at Coca-Cola

With 500 brands, 21 of which are worth more than $1 billion dollars each, Coca-Cola is the world's largest beverage company. Consumers in nearly every country in the world consume a Coca-Cola–branded beverage every day, for a total of almost 2 billion servings. Headquartered in Atlanta, the company is more than 130 years old. It employs about 700,000 people worldwide and has received a 100% rating on the Human Rights Campaign's corporate equality index for 11 years in a row. Some of its best-known brands are Coke, Coke Zero, Powerade, Schweppes, Dasani, Minute Maid, Fanta, Sprite, Vitamin Water, and Smart Water. Many of its beverages are available in low-calorie or no-calorie versions.[21]

The company's website lists its mission, vision, and values, which comprise its "Roadmap for winning," as follows.

Our Mission[22]

Our Roadmap starts with our mission, which is enduring. It declares our purpose as a company and serves as the standard against which we weigh our actions and decisions.

- To refresh the world . . .
- To inspire moments of optimism and happiness . . .
- To create value and make a difference.

Our Vision

Our vision serves as the framework for our Roadmap and guides every aspect of our business by describing what we need to accomplish in order to continue achieving sustainable, quality growth.

- **People:** Be a great place to work where people are inspired to be the best they can be.
- **Portfolio:** Bring to the world a portfolio of quality beverage brands that anticipate and satisfy people's desires and needs.
- **Partners:** Nurture a winning network of customers and suppliers, together we create mutual, enduring value.
- **Planet:** Be a responsible citizen that makes a difference by helping build and support sustainable communities.
- **Profit:** Maximize long-term return to shareowners while being mindful of our overall responsibilities.
- **Productivity:** Be a highly effective, lean and fast-moving organization.

Live Our Values

Our values serve as a compass for our actions and describe how we behave in the world.

- **Leadership:** The courage to shape a better future
- **Collaboration:** Leverage collective genius
- **Integrity:** Be real
- **Accountability:** If it is to be, it's up to me
- **Passion:** Committed in heart and mind
- **Diversity:** As inclusive as our brands
- **Quality:** What we do, we do well

YOUR CALL

What do you think of Coca-Cola's mission, vision, and values? Are they explicit enough to guide employee behavior and company actions? Why or why not? Could any of them apply equally well to other businesses? Why or why not?

The concept of a vision statement also is important for individuals. Harvard professor Clayton Christensen believes that creating a personal life vision statement is akin to developing a strategy for your life. He finds that people are happier and lead more meaningful lives when they are directed by personal vision statements.[23] Do you have a vision for your future career? Is it vague or specific? The following self-assessment was created to help you evaluate the quality of your career vision and plan.

SELF-ASSESSMENT 5.1 CAREER READINESS

Assessing Career Behaviors and Future Career Identity

This self-assessment is designed to help you reflect on the vision of your career identity. Please be prepared to answer these questions if your instructor has assigned Self-Assessment 5.1 in Connect.

1. What did you learn about your future career identity? Are you surprised by the results?
2. Write a personal mission and vision statement using ideas discussed in this section. Share it with a friend for feedback.
3. Based on your results, what might you do to enhance your future career identity? Explain.
4. What things can you say during an interview to demonstrate that you possess the career-readiness competency of *Career Management*.

The Values Statement—"What Values Do We Want to Emphasize?"

Values, we said in Chapter 3, are the relatively permanent and deeply held underlying beliefs and attitudes that help determine a person's behavior: integrity, dedication, teamwork, excellence, compassion, or whatever. Values reflect the qualities that represent an organization's deeply held beliefs, highest priorities, and core guiding principles.

After formulating a vision statement, then, top managers need to develop a **values statement**, also called a ***core values statement***, **which expresses what the company stands for, its core priorities, the values its employees embody, and what its products contribute to the world.**[24] Values statements "become the deeply ingrained principle and fabric that guide employee behavior and company decisions and actions–the behaviors the company and employees expect of themselves," says former executive Eric Jacobsen. "Without a statement, the company will lack soul."[25]

Are you a gamer? Have you played "World of Warcraft"? If yes, then you will appreciate the values that guide Blizzard Entertainment's operations. Headquartered in Irvine, California, the company is a top developer and publisher of wildly popular entertainment software, including the *Warcraft*, *StarCraft*, and *Diablo* series and the online-gaming service Battle.net. Its eight core values, described on the company website, are: Gameplay first, commit to quality, be nice—play fair, embrace your inner geek, every voice matters, think globally, lead responsibly, and learn and grow. These are unique values and they define what matters most to the company. Would you like to work at Blizzard?

Three Types of Planning for Three Levels of Management: Strategic, Tactical, and Operational

Inspiring, clearly stated mission statements and vision statements provide the focal point of the entire planning process. Then three things happen:

- ***Strategic planning by top management.*** Using their mission and vision statements, top managers do **strategic planning**—**they determine what the organization's long-term goals should be for the next one to five years with the resources they expect to have available.** "Strategic planning requires visionary and directional thinking," says one authority.[26] It should communicate not only general goals about growth and profits, but also ways to achieve them. Today, because of the frequency with which world competition and information technology alter marketplace conditions, a company's strategic planning may have to be done closer to every one or two years than every five. Still, at a big company like Boeing or Ford or Amazon, top executives cannot lose sight of long-range, multiyear planning.

A lighthouse is a great metaphor for strategic planning. A lighthouse provides a navigational aid and it warns boats about dangerous or hazardous areas. A strategic plan similarly provide direction to both employees and shareholders. It defines what an organization is trying to achieve and signifies what markets or opportunities are not going to be pursued. ©George Diebold/Blend Images LLC

EXAMPLE Coca-Cola's Five-Plus Strategies

Coca-Cola recently announced progress made on five strategic actions it has taken to revamp its business:[27]

1. **Focused on driving revenue and profit growth.** In emerging markets, the focus was on increasing volume with affordable products, and in developed markets that meant improving profitability with more small and premium packages.
2. **Invested in our brands and business.** More and better marketing was the goal of this strategy, which meant a boost of more than $250 million in the company's media ad budget.
3. **Became more efficient.** "Zero-based work" assumes that organizational budgets begin at zero and must be justified every year. One result of adopting this budgeting strategy was realizing "more than $600 million in productivity improvements in 2015," some of which was reinvested in the company and some of which went to shareholders.
4. **Simplified our company.** Coca-Cola eliminated one layer of management, streamlined some internal business processes, and connected its regional operations more closely to headquarters.
5. **Refocused on our core business model.** Among the company's more than 500 brands are 20 that generate more than a billion dollars a year. To retain focus on these core products, the company has begun franchising out the 18% of its bottling operations that it still handled itself, aiming to reduce that amount to 3%.

A year later, in 2017, the company added a sixth strategy for "our way forward":[28]

6. **Keep people at the heart of our company.** This means rethinking package sizes in all the company's markets and more heavily promoting low- and no-sugar drinks in order to reduce sugar intake and help the global fight against obesity.

YOUR CALL

Does it surprise you that a large company like Coca-Cola would frequently revisit and revise its strategic plans? Why or why not? Which of the first five goals listed here do you think best support(s) goal 6?

- ***Tactical planning by middle management.*** The strategic priorities and policies are then passed down to middle managers, who must do **tactical planning—that is, they determine what contributions their departments or similar work units can make with their given resources during the next 6–24 months.**
- ***Operational planning by first-line management.*** Middle managers then pass these plans along to first-line managers to do **operational planning—that is, they determine how to accomplish specific tasks with available resources within the next 1–52 weeks.**

I Wish My Manager...

...and I put more effort into operational planning.

Courtesy Josephine Schulte

Josephine Schulte works as a procurement manager for a telecommunications company. The company had to change its process for onboarding vendors after acquiring another company. The company hit a lot of road bumps because of poor **operational planning** while rolling out the new process.

"There has been a lot of change management around what the process is to get vendors on board and bring them onsite," said Josephine, "I wish we would have planned better up front in terms of the process of getting the correct information in front of the people who needed it so they could understand what needed to happen and the timeline involved with getting a vendor on board."

The new process for onboarding vendors involves making sure the vendors have contracts in place if they need one and routing those contracts for signatures and internal approval. What the company did to implement the training of this new process was to schedule a few training sessions with managers from each business unit.

"We rolled the process out to a group of people with the intent that they would push it down through their business units, but it is hard to get that to happen," said Josephine. Each business unit had its own unique questions as to how the process would work for its specific groups. This made it difficult to present the same training to one group of representatives to relay back to each business unit.

"We are very decentralized, so it was hard to figure out who to talk to about rolling the process out. We originally spoke to the facilities directors, but there wasn't a good way for them to send the information out to the business units in their regions. Essentially, we presented this to about 12 people in a company of 100,000 employees—and of course, not every person needs to know about this process, but there are quite a few that do, and they are all in different business units in different locations throughout the country," said Josephine.

One of the biggest hurdles the company had was making sure that all necessary employees were caught in the initial training so they did not have to go back later and train some employees on an individual basis. This would save time and money.

In hindsight, Josephine had several suggestions for what the company could have done better when rolling this process out to the employees. "I would have sent a step-by-step slide deck out to the employees right away," said Josephine. "I would have gotten as many people as possible across the business units and company to attend those virtual trainings. A recorded webinar would have been the best move up front because we were saying the same thing in every training session and it would have saved a lot of time to record one session."

Josephine admits that the process could have been much smoother if only more planning had gone into the training and implementation of the new system before rolling it out.

Courtesy of Josephine Schulte

The three kinds of managers are described further in the following figure. *(See Figure 5.3.)* •

FIGURE 5.3

Three levels of management, three types of planning

Each type of planning has different time horizons, although the times overlap because the plans are somewhat elastic.

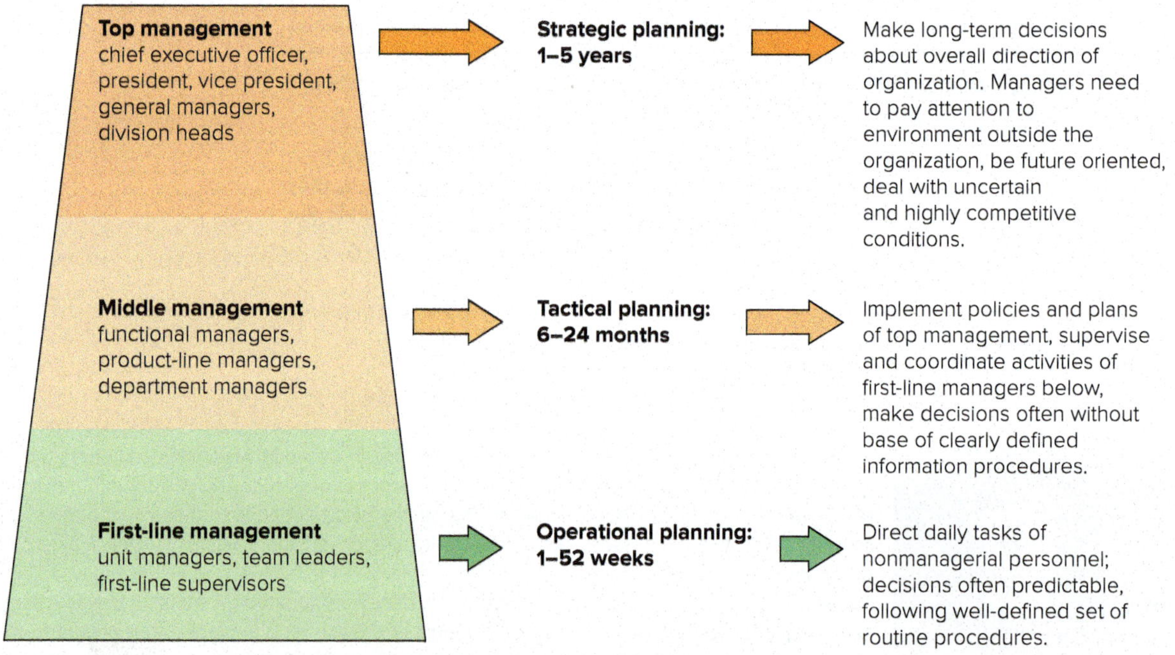

5.3 Goals and Plans

THE BIG PICTURE

The purpose of planning is to set a goal and then an action plan. There are two types of goals, short-term and long-term, and they are connected by a means-end chain. Types of plans include standing and single-use plans.

Whatever its type—long term or short term—the purpose of planning is to set a *goal* and then to formulate an *action plan.*

LO 5-3

Discuss the types and purposes of goals and plans.

Long-Term and Short-Term Goals

A **goal**, also known as an **objective**, **is a specific commitment to achieve a measurable result within a stated period of time.** Goals may be long-term or short-term.

Long-term goals **are generally referred to as** **strategic goals**. **They tend to span one to five years and focus on achieving the strategies identified in a company's strategic plan.** An example is to increase revenue from new customers by 10% over the next 12 months.

Short-term goals **are sometimes referred to as** ***tactical*** **or** ***operational goals***, **or just plain *goals*. They generally span 12 months and are connected to strategic goals in a hierarchy known as a means-end chain.**

A **means-end chain** **shows how goals are connected or linked across an organization.** For example, a low-level goal such as responding to customer inquiries in less than 24 hours is the means to accomplishing a higher-level goal of achieving 90% customer satisfaction.

As we will see later in Section 5.4, goals should be SMART—specific, measurable, attainable, results-oriented, and with target dates.

The Operating Plan and Action Plan

Larry Bossidy, former CEO of both Honeywell International and Allied Signal, and global consultant Ram Charan define an **operating plan** **as a plan that "breaks long-term output into short-term targets" or goals.**[29] In other words, operating plans turn strategic plans into actionable short-term goals and action plans.

An **action plan** **defines the course of action needed to achieve a stated goal.** Whether the goal is long-term or short-term, action plans outline the tactics that will be used to achieve a goal. Each tactic also contains a projected date for completing the desired activities (read about Amanda Lawrence's experience in the I'm Glad . . . feature).

I'm Glad I...

...developed an action plan.

Amanda Lawrence served as the president of a nonprofit organization for women in business. She was in charge of planning a first annual fundraising event for her organization, and the action plan that she developed resulted in a successful event that has been running for almost 10 years.

Amanda began by looking at the big picture to get a better idea of the long-term goal of the project. Once she had long-term goals in place, she was able to develop action plans and begin delegating tasks to others based on their skillsets.

"Planning was integral for an event that had never been done before. I had to start with the big picture of what the goals and objectives of the event were, and then figure out how to reach those goals and determine who was going to take care of each area of the event," said Amanda.

Courtesy Amanda Lawrence

There were several things that Amanda had to think about when organizing the event, from venue and keynote speakers to alternate weather plans.

"We had to find a venue based on how many people we expected would attend an event like this. We had to determine how much we wanted to charge for the tickets—did we want this to be a $20 per ticket event with a cash bar, or did we want this to be a $200 per chair black tie event? We determined we wanted to be somewhere in the middle of the road, about $50 per ticket with a good meal and a keynote speaker who would provide value to the event," said Amanda.

"We also had a rainy day plan. We were in Phoenix, Arizona, so we planned to host the event in April so it would be warm but not too warm, but we still had to consider the possibility of rain. We planned an outdoor, covered dinner with an outdoor, uncovered cocktail hour. We planned for people to have umbrellas to walk the guests from their cars to the venue if it rained," said Amanda. "We talked through all of our contingency plans ahead of time."

Once plans were in place, Amanda began to delegate a person to each area of the event. "I took on the venue and the catering, and then we discussed what each board member's individual strengths were and what they felt they could help the most with," said Amanda. "One of our board members had some experience with selling tickets for another event, so she took on the research to determine what the best way for us to sell tickets would be. We had someone else who felt comfortable approaching some corporate females in the area to build our guest list. We had another person who was a marketer by day, so she handled the marketing calendar."

The event sold out and raised $5,000 for Amanda's organization in the first year alone, and it has been running strong for almost 10 years. The event's success can be attributed to Amanda's strong planning skills.

Courtesy of Amanda Lawrence

EXAMPLE Long-Term and Short-Term Goals at Southwest Airlines

Ranking No. 8 among *Fortune*'s 2018 Most Admired Companies, a list on which it has appeared for 24 years in a row, Dallas-based Southwest Airlines has continually achieved its strategic goals and as of 2018 had been profitable for 45 consecutive years.[30]

Long-Term Strategic Goals. Employee engagement, customer satisfaction, and profitability have been key strategic goals for Southwest since its inception. Employee engagement is created through the company's corporate culture, which focuses on employee satisfaction and well-being. The page of the company website announcing its vision and mission includes this central statement about its employees: "We are committed to provide our Employees a stable work environment with equal opportunity for learning and personal growth. Creativity and innovation are encouraged for improving the effectiveness of Southwest Airlines. Above all, Employees will be provided the same concern, respect, and caring attitude within the organization that they are expected to share externally with every Southwest Customer."[31] Employees were awarded a total of $543 million in profit sharing in 2017, amounting to more than 5 weeks' pay per person.[32]

Lookalikes. One key to the success of Southwest Airlines is that all the planes in its fleet have been the same type, Boeing 737s, which saves on maintenance and training costs. ©Charles Rex Arbogast/AP Images

The goal of Southwest's top managers is to ensure that the airline is highly profitable, and for years it has followed the general strategy of (a) keeping costs and fares down, to appeal to budget rather than business travelers, (b) offering a superior on-time arrival record and squeezing more flights per day from every plane, and (c) keeping passengers happy with its cheerful cabin crew and staff. One of the most important strategic decisions Southwest made was to fly just one type of airplane—Boeing 737s, 692 of them—to hold down training, maintenance, and operating expenses.[33] Competing head to head with legacy carriers, Southwest now flies to key airports of major cities—and even on international routes, principally to Latin America and the Caribbean.

Short-Term Goals. Cutting costs and keeping fares low have traditionally been key operational goals for Southwest. To achieve its second operational goal, a superior on-time arrival record, the company did away with guaranteed seat reservations before ticketing so that no-shows wouldn't complicate (and therefore delay) the boarding process. To attract business travelers, Southwest changed the reservations policy slightly to ensure that passengers paying extra for "business select" fares would be placed at the front of the line. It also rewards "high-level" business travelers with what is called the "A-List" designation. These individuals get automatic check-in and are guaranteed to board with the A-group or immediately before the B-group starts boarding. In addition, the airline tries to turn planes around in exactly 20 minutes so that on-time departures are more apt to produce on-time arrivals.

The company plans to improve pre-tax revenue by about $200 million thanks to a new reservation system and to continue reducing operating costs. It recently announced plans to add Hawaii to its many destinations.[34] Said CEO Gary C. Kelly, "Overall, our strong financial performance, solid outlook, healthy balance sheet, and significantly lower federal income taxes, provide the cash flow to continue to reward our Employees, keep our costs and fares low for our Customers, reinvest in our business, return value to our Shareholders, and support our communities."[35]

YOUR CALL

Do you think the company will continue to achieve its strategic goals? Why or why not?

Types of Plans: Standing Plans and Single-Use Plans

Plans are of two types—*standing plans* and *single-use plans. (See Table 5.2.)* Standing plans cover activities that are repeated or occur frequently over time. A standing plan, for example, might direct the way employees in a retail store should handle returns. L.L.Bean recently changed its standing plan on returned items and will now accept them for only one year from purchase rather than indefinitely as it once did. Forever 21, which used to accept returns only for exchange or credit, now has a standing plan that offers refunds[36] for returned items.

A single-use plan directs activity, such as a project, that is unlikely to be repeated. The successful 2018 launch of the Falcon Heavy, the rocket built by entrepreneur Elon Musk's space exploration company SpaceX, was a program consisting of a number of activities[37] and directed by a single-use plan. ●

TABLE 5.2 Standing Plans and Single-Use Plans

There are three types of standing plans and two types of single-use plans.

PLAN	DESCRIPTION
• **Standing plan**	For activities that occur repeatedly over a period of time
• **Policy**	Outlines general response to a designated problem or situation
• **Procedure**	Outlines response to particular problems or circumstances
• **Rule**	Designates specific required action
• **Single-use plan**	For activities not likely to be repeated in the future
• **Program**	Encompasses a range of projects or activities
• **Project**	Has less scope and complexity than a program

5.4 Promoting Consistencies in Goals: SMART Goals, Management by Objectives, and Goal Cascading

THE BIG PICTURE

This section discusses SMART goals—goals that are specific, measurable, attainable, results-oriented, and have target dates. It also briefly discusses a technique for setting goals, management by objectives (MBO), a four-step process for motivating employees. Finally, it introduces the concept of goal cascading, which attempts to ensure that higher-level goals are communicated and aligned with the goals at the next levels down in the organizational hierarchy.

LO 5-4

Describe SMART goals and their implementation.

Anyone can define goals. But as we mentioned earlier, the five characteristics of a good goal are represented by the acronym SMART.

SMART Goals

A SMART goal is one that is specific, measurable, attainable, results-oriented, and has target dates.

Specific Goals should be stated in *specific* rather than vague terms. The goal "As many planes as possible should arrive on time" is too general. The goal that "Ninety percent of planes should arrive within 15 minutes of the scheduled arrival time" is specific.

Measurable Whenever possible, goals should be *measurable*, or quantifiable (as in "90% of planes should arrive within 15 minutes"). That is, there should be some way to measure the degree to which a goal has been reached.

Of course, some goals—such as those concerned with improving quality—are not precisely quantifiable. In that case, something on the order of "Improve the quality of customer relations by instituting 10 follow-up telephone calls every week" will do. You can certainly quantify how many follow-up phone calls were made.

FIGURE 5.4

Relationship between goal difficulty and performance

Source: Adapted from E. A. Locke and G. P. Latham, A Theory of Goal Setting and Task Performance *(Englewood Cliffs, NJ: Prentice Hall, 1990).*

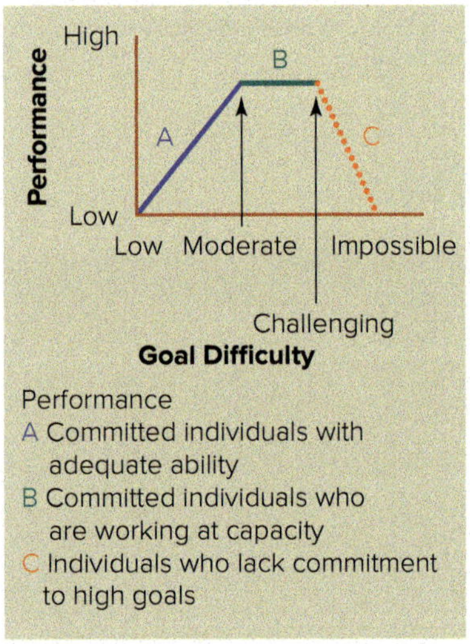

Attainable Goals should be challenging, of course, but above all, they should be realistic and *attainable.* It may be best to set goals that are quite ambitious so as to challenge people to meet high standards. Always, however, the goals should be achievable within the scope of the time, equipment, and financial support available. *(See Figure 5.4.)*

If too easy (as in "half the flights should arrive on time"), goals won't impel people to make much effort. If impossible ("all flights must arrive on time, regardless of weather"), employees won't even bother trying. Or they will try and continually fail, which will end up hurting morale. Or they will cheat. (An example was the unrealistic goal of cutting wait times for appointments by more than half at Veterans Affairs hospitals, as revealed in ongoing scandals in which VA administrators were found to have falsified figures.)[38]

Results-Oriented Only a few goals should be chosen—say, five for any work unit. And they should be *results-oriented*—they should support the organization's vision.

In writing out the goals, start with the word "To" and follow it with action-oriented verbs—"complete," "acquire," "increase" ("to decrease by 10% the time to get passengers settled in their seats before departure").

Some verbs should not be used in your goal statement because they imply activities—the ways used to accomplish goals (such as having baggage handlers waiting). For example, you should not use "to develop," "to conduct," "to implement."

Target Dates Goals should specify the *target dates* or deadline dates when they are to be attained. For example, it's unrealistic to expect an airline to improve its on-time arrivals by 10% overnight. However, you could set a target date—three to six months away, say—by which this goal is to be achieved. That allows enough time for lower-level managers and employees to revamp their systems and work habits and gives them a clear time frame in which they know what they are expected to do.

EXAMPLE — Setting Goals: Are Snapchat's Goals Clear?[39]

Snapchat's user base grew slowly following its first public offering of stock in early 2017, and investors became concerned that profits might dip. In response, Snapchat's parent company, Snap Inc., announced that the app would be redesigned in order to make it easier for a wider audience to use, with the stated goal of increasing its user base in 2018. The announcement represented a change in the company's main goal, which had been to provide an inviting home for chat and video for people looking for real connections, not to build a platform for billions of users such as Facebook and YouTube have become.

Some observers were doubtful that Snapchat could achieve its new goal with the specific design changes it announced. The plan to essentially lump messages and videos from friends together in a single hub, separate from content produced by publishers, didn't convince everyone that the app would now be easier for new users. CEO Evan Spiegel's explanation seemed off-target to some commentators, too. Spiegel spoke of the dangers of getting news and information from online sources that select from a narrow set of sources. Separating "the social from the media," as the company described it, isn't necessary a bad idea, given the proliferation of fake news in social media, but how would it enlarge the app's user base? Snapchat didn't say.

By the fall of 2017, the company's revenues were still running below expectations, and costs and losses were higher than expected. Snap's stock price seemed stuck at a point below its initial offering price of $17 a share. Five million new users had been added, but analysts had expected 8 million. Investors were thus still unclear what the company's goal was—and how and even whether it would achieve it. When the updated Snapchat was rolled out in February 2018, initial reactions from users were largely negative, especially among younger fans who called the new version "twisted" and "super confusing."[40]

YOUR CALL

Do you think Snapchat's goal was attainable? Was it communicated clearly? What could the company have done better?

Management by Objectives: The Four-Step Process for Motivating Employees

First suggested by **Peter Drucker** in 1954, *management by objectives* has spread largely because of the appeal of its emphasis on converting general objectives into specific ones for all members of an organization.[41]

Management by objectives (MBO) is a four-step process in which (1) managers and employees jointly set objectives for the employee, (2) managers develop action plans, (3) managers and employees periodically review the employee's performance, and (4) the manager makes a performance appraisal and rewards the employee according to results. The purpose of MBO is to *motivate* rather than to control subordinates.

Before we begin discussing these four steps, you may want to consider the quality of the goal-setting process in a current or former employer. Management by objectives and goal cascading will not work without an effective goal setting process. The following self-assessment was developed to provide insight into the quality of goal setting within an organization.

SELF-ASSESSMENT 5.2

What Is the Quality of Goal Setting within a Current or Past Employer?

This self-assessment is designed to assess the quality of goal setting in a company. Please be prepared to answer these questions if your instructor has assigned Self-Assessment 5.2 in Connect.

1. What are the strengths and weaknesses of goal setting in the company you selected?
2. Based on your results, what recommendations would you provide to senior management about improving the goal-setting process in this company? Explain.
3. What actions could you take to improve the goal-setting process in this company? Be specific.

1. Jointly Set Objectives You sit down with your manager and the two of you jointly set objectives for you to attain. Research shows that an assigned goal from your boss is just as effective as setting goals participatively. Moreover, people tend to set their own personal goals in response to receiving an assigned goal. A team of goal-setting experts noted that "the assignment of a goal encourages individuals to also set a personal performance goal, which in turn contributes to their performance."[42] It is important to remember what we learned about SMART goals. Managers garner greater acceptance to goal setting when employees believe the goal is attainable and they possess the skills and resources to achieve it.[43] Managers tend to set three types of objectives, shown in the following table. *(See Table 5.3.)*

Jointly setting objectives. An important part of MBO is joint manager/subordinate participation in setting objectives. Have you ever held a job that featured this kind of process? ©Chris Ryan/age fotostock

TABLE 5.3 **Three Types of Objectives Used in MBO: Performance, Behavioral, and Learning**

PERFORMANCE OBJECTIVES
Focus Express the objective as an outcome or end-result. **Examples** "Increase sport utility sales by 10%." "Reduce food spoilage by 15%."
BEHAVIORAL OBJECTIVES
Focus Express the objective as the behaviors needed to achieve an outcome. **Examples** "Greet all potential automobile customers with a smile and offer to assist." "Ensure food is stored in seal-proof containers." "Attend five days of leadership training." "Learn basics of Microsoft Office software by June 1."
LEARNING OBJECTIVES
Focus Express the objective in terms of acquiring knowledge or competencies. **Examples** "Attend sales training class." "Learn how the features in our sports utility vehicles compare to competitors."

Source: These descriptions were based on G. Latham, G. Seijts, and J. Slocum, "The Goal Setting and Goal Orientation Labyrinth: Effective Ways for Increasing Employee Performance," Organizational Dynamics, *October–December 2016, pp. 271–277.*

We want to briefly focus on the career readiness competency of *proactive learning orientation* because it fuels the achievement of learning objectives. Proactive learning orientation represents a desire to learn and improve one's knowledge, soft skills, and other characteristics in pursuit of personal development. Employers value this attitude because it helps drive the creativity and innovation needed in today's global economy. They also desire this competency because the "fast-paced business environment requires employees to refine and enhance their skills sets throughout their careers."[44] So where do you stand on this competency? Find out by taking the proactive learning orientation self-assessment.

SELF-ASSESSMENT 5.3 CAREER READINESS

Do I Have a Proactive Learning Orientation?

This self-assessment is designed to assess the extent to which you possess a proactive learning orientation. Please be prepared to answer these questions if your instructor has assigned Self-Assessment 5.3 in Connect.

1. What is your level of learning orientation? How might it affect a recruiter's perception of your employability?
2. Based on your results, what might you do to increase the career readiness competency of *proactive learning orientation*? Explain.
3. What things might you say during an interview to demonstrate that you possess this career readiness competency?

2. Develop Action Plan Once objectives are set, employees are encouraged to prepare an action plan for attaining them. Action plans may be prepared for both individuals and work units, such as departments. For example, teams of employees at Tornier, a medical device manufacturer in Amsterdam, meet every 45, 60, and 90 days to create action plans for completing their goals. Implementation of the plans can take between six and 18 months depending on the complexity of the goal.[45] Setting and using action plans also reduces procrastination. If this is sometimes a problem for you, break your goals into smaller and more specific subgoals.[46] This will get you going.

3. Periodically Review Performance You and your manager should meet reasonably often—either informally as needed or formally every three months—to review progress, as should you and your subordinates. Indeed, frequent communication is necessary so that everyone will know how well he or she is doing in meeting the objectives.

During each meeting, managers should give employees feedback, and objectives should be updated or revised as necessary to reflect new realities. Feedback is essential for improving performance.[47] If you were managing a painting or landscaping business, for example, changes in the weather, loss of key employees, or a financial downturn affecting customer spending could force you to reconsider your objectives.

4. Give Performance Appraisal and Rewards, If Any At the end of 6 or 12 months, you and your subordinate should meet to discuss results, comparing performance with initial objectives. *Deal with results*, not personalities, emotional issues, or excuses.

Because the purpose of MBO is to *motivate* employees, performance that meets the objectives should be rewarded—with compliments, raises, bonuses, promotions, or other suitable benefits. Failure can be addressed by redefining the objectives for the next 6- or 12-month period, or even by taking stronger measures, such as demotion. Basically, however, MBO is viewed as being a learning process. After step 4, the MBO cycle begins anew.

A good performance appraisal is like kicking a field goal. It feels good, is rewarding, and fosters continued motivation. Have you had good and bad reviews? What makes a performance review effective versus ineffective?
©Steven Puetzer/Getty Images

Cascading Goals: Making Lower-Level Goals Align with Top Goals

For goal setting to be successful, the following three things have to happen.

1. Top Management and Middle Management Must Be Committed "When top-management commitment [to MBO] was high," said one review, "the average gain in productivity was 56%. When commitment was low, the average gain in productivity was only 6%."[48]

2. The Goals Must Be Applied Organizationwide The goal-setting program has to be put in place throughout the entire organization. That is, it cannot be applied in just some divisions and departments; it has to be done in all of them.

3. Goals Must "Cascade"—Be Linked Consistently Down through the Organization **Cascading goals is the process of ensuring that the strategic goals set at the top level align, or "cascade," downward with more specific short-term goals at lower levels within an organization, including employees' objectives and activities.** Top managers set *strategic goals*, which are translated into *divisional goals*, which are translated into *departmental goals*, which are translated into *individual goals*. The cascading process ends when all individuals have a set of goals that support the overall strategic goals. This process helps employees understand how their work contributes to overall corporate success.

Example: The Vice President of the Claims Division of an automobile insurance company, which pays off requests (or claims) by customers seeking insurance payments to repair damage to their cars, may set the major goal (and SMART goal) of "increase customer satisfaction in Claims Division by 10%." In the cascading goals process, the same goal would be embraced by the Assistant Vice President of Claims and the Recovery Director beneath him or her. Further down the hierarchy, the Recovery Unit Manager would reword the goal to be more specific: "Decrease the number of customer complaints about claims by 10% over last year's average." For the individual Recovery Analyst at the lowest level, the goal could become: "Return all customer phone calls about claims within 24 hours."[49] Thus, all the subgoals in the organization are in alignment with the major goal of top management.

The Importance of Deadlines

There's no question that college is a pressure cooker for many students. The reason, of course, is the seemingly never-ending deadlines. But consider: Would you do all the course work you're doing—and realize the education you're getting—if you *didn't* have deadlines?

As we saw under the "T" (for "has target dates") in SMART goals, deadlines are as essential to goal setting in business as they are to your college career. Because the whole purpose of planning and goals is to deliver to a client specified results within a specified period of time, deadlines become a great motivator, both for you and for the people working for you.

It's possible, of course, to let deadlines mislead you into focusing too much on immediate results and thereby ignoring overall planning—just as students will focus too much on preparing for a test in one course while neglecting others. In general, however, deadlines can help you keep your eye on the "big picture" while simultaneously paying attention to the details that will help you realize the big picture. Deadlines can help concentrate the mind, so that you make quick decisions rather than put them off. Deadlines help you ignore extraneous matters (such as cleaning up a messy desk) in favor of focusing on what's important—realizing the goals on time and on budget. Deadlines provide a mechanism for giving ourselves feedback. •

PRACTICAL ACTION Setting Goals for a Small Business

Goal setting can seem like an intimidating process, but it's both a necessary and a helpful one for the millions of small businesses in the United States. These firms, officially defined as having 500 or fewer employees, produce almost half of U.S. non-farm GDP and two-thirds of the nation's new private-sector jobs.[50] What are some typical goal-setting steps for a small business?[51]

1. Break large goals down into smaller ones.
   Anita-Maria Quillen is the owner and manager of Diversified Engineering & Plastics (DER), a profitable auto parts manufacturer with 78 employees in Jackson, MI. She hopes to keep her small business profitable despite a recent drop in U.S. auto sales that will eventually affect sales of her company's mirror brackets, pistons, and window frames as car makers seek to cut their costs. Quillen is firmly focused on her bottom line; one of her business practices is to break her annual profit goal into monthly sales goals.
2. Track progress toward goals.
   DER tracks sales monthly sales and recently posted its most profitable month in several years.
3. Keep the goal in sight.
   One of Quillen's goals is to increase her personal contacts in the industry in order to drive orders to the firm. "I need to be out meeting people, establishing those relationships, getting those potential work opportunities in the door," she said. She recently attended a business fair in Dearborn in order to meet buyers from potential customer firms like Fiat Chrysler and Toyota.
4. Accept that setbacks will come.
   Quillen sometimes meets with potential customers over the phone to pitch her company's products. One recent phone meeting was a disappointment; DER had presented a prototype of a new product, but the customer said her company would have to bid the order out to other suppliers before making a purchase. Because DER had invested money in developing its product, Quillen feared her price would be undercut in the bidding process.
5. Celebrate success.
   On learning her company had posted its most profitable month in several years, Quillen celebrated with a toast shared with company executives. Then it was back to work.

YOUR CALL

What major goal of your own have you broken into smaller parts? If you have never done this, for what future goal do you think it would be an effective strategy for you?

5.5 The Planning/Control Cycle

THE BIG PICTURE

The four-step planning/control cycle helps you keep in control, to make sure you're headed in the right direction.

LO 5-5

Outline the planning/control cycle.

Once you've made plans, how do you stay in control to make sure you're headed in the right direction? Actually, there is a continuous feedback loop known as the planning/control cycle. (The "organizing" and "leading" steps within the Planning–Organizing–Leading–Controlling sequence are implied here.) **The planning/control cycle has two planning steps (1 and 2) and two control steps (3 and 4), as follows: (1) Make the plan. (2) Carry out the plan. (3) Control the direction by comparing results with the plan. (4) Control the direction by taking corrective action in two ways—namely, by (a) correcting deviations in the plan being carried out or (b) improving future plans.** *(See Figure 5.5.)* (We will see this model echoed later in Chapter 16 in the discussion of the Plan-Do-Check-Act cycle.)

The planning/control cycle loop exists for each level of planning—strategic, tactical, and operational. The corrective action in step 4 of the cycle (a) can get a project back on track before it's too late or (b) if it's too late, can provide data for improving future plans. ●

FIGURE 5.5

The planning/control cycle

This describes a constant feedback loop designed to ensure plans stay headed in the right direction.

Source: Robert Kreitner, Management, *8th edition.*

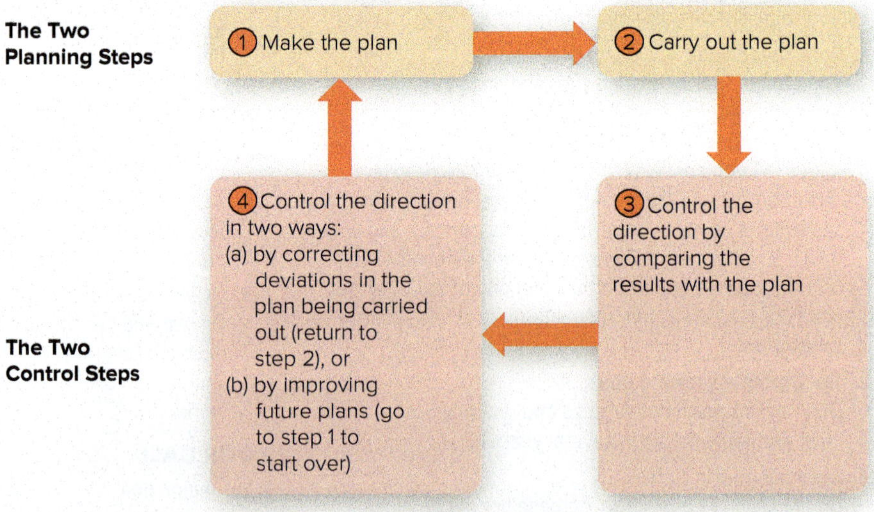

EXAMPLE The Planning/Control Cycle: Tesla's Long-Awaited Model 3

By early 2018, Tesla's Model 3, the electric-car company's long anticipated, more affordable new vehicle (whose price begins at $35,000) had missed its announced production goals at least twice. In the summer of 2017, the company had promised to make 20,000 Model 3 vehicles by December, but it actually made fewer than 300 during that year's third quarter, and orders placed at that time were not expected to be filled until the middle of 2018, a projection that was later pushed back to "late 2018 or early 2019." The date by which the company would achieve its forecasted production run of 5,000 cars a week was also moved, from the end of 2017 to the end of the second quarter of 2018, with the expectation that in the first quarter only 2,500 cars a week would come off the assembly line. According to Tesla, the change to a slower ramp-up was meant "to focus on quality and efficiency rather than simply pushing for the highest possible volume in the shortest period of time."[52]

The Tesla model 3 has experienced tremendous production and logistics problems. One cause is that the company does not have the ability to custom-build the cars in a timely fashion to meet customer demand. This demand is partly driven by the car's features and a competitive price of roughly $49,000. CEO Elon Musk has totally immersed himself in the production process in order to improve the planning/control process. ©Salwan Georges/The Washington Post/Getty Images

"Production bottlenecks" were blamed for these disappointing results, along with the fact that some production systems were not running as quickly as the company had planned. The assembly line was less fully automated than Tesla had wanted, for example, with human workers filling the gaps. The company plans to make production as fully automated as possible but hasn't yet achieved that goal. Battery production has also been slower than hoped, after Tesla was forced to bring it back in house when outside suppliers failed to deliver. The company addressed that problem by creating automatic assembly lines for its batteries. But these lines were built in Germany, so they needed to be disassembled and shipped to the United States to be put back together again, which apparently had still not happened by early 2018. "We view the 2,500 target in March, in particular, as extremely aggressive due to management's acknowledgment of needing to get the robotic equipment in Germany disassembled, shipped to the US, and then reassembled and programmed in order to hit roughly 2,000 to 2,500 units per week,"[53] said one market analyst.

Tesla's CEO Elon Musk said he was confident that the difference between projections and reality was "getting smaller with each passing week." But in the fourth quarter of 2017, only 2,425 units were made, and only 1,550 were delivered to customers (leaving almost 300,000 people still waiting for their cars).[54] But almost 800 of those fourth-quarter cars had rolled off the line in a mere seven days, leading some to hope that Tesla had begun producing faster than its newly conservative projections suggested. One possible reason was the company's decision to pull workers off the production of two of the company's other cars and assign them to the Model 3. "The whole team is on it, we've got it covered, it's just going to take us a few months longer than expected," Musk said.[55]

YOUR CALL

Some analysts believe Tesla would have been better off announcing less ambitious production plans for the Model 3 in the first place. Are they right? Do you think the company is doing a good job of making and controlling its paces for the Model 3? Why or why not?

5.6 Career Corner: Managing Your Career Readiness

LO 5-6

Describe how to develop the career readiness competency of *proactive learning orientation*.

Planning is not one of the career readiness competencies associated with the model shown below. *(See Figure 5.6.)* The reason is not that employers don't value planning skills. Rather, it's the fact that other Career Readiness competencies are foundational to good planning. The soft skill of critical thinking/problem solving is a prime example.

The competency of *critical thinking/problem solving* is defined as sound reasoning to analyze situations, make decisions, and solve problems. These are all critical activities associated with planning and require the ability to obtain, interpret, and analyze both qualitative and quantitative information. In turn, this competency is driven by another career readiness competency: *proactive learning orientation*. Let's consider the link between planning, critical thinking, and proactive learning in more detail.

Critical thinkers don't make quick or rash decisions during the planning process. Instead, they consider alternative solutions to problems and remain open-minded. They remain open-minded by obtaining and considering a wide range of information before making a judgment. This is precisely what happens when someone has a proactive learning orientation. Proactive learners seek information and knowledge so that they expand their knowledge base, which makes them more effective planners. The point is that good planning requires critical thinking, which in turn requires a proactive learning orientation. This process ultimately results in expanding the career readiness competency of *task-based/functional* knowledge.

Effective planning requires you to be a proactive learner in areas beyond the technicalities of your profession. It also applies to two additional career readiness competencies: *understanding the business* and *networking*. Organizations want all of us to stay abreast of what is happening in the industries and markets in which we work. Doing so enables us to consider a wider bandwidth of information when planning. For example, staying current about trends in higher education enables us as authors to do a better job in planning the revisions of this product. We also find that many people fail to keep their social and professional networks up to date over time. This is a mistake! Failing to proactively maintain such networks means that we are losing contacts and valuable information that can aid the planning process and our career progression. As authors, for instance, we rely on our social networks to get feedback about what students and educational institutions are looking for in a textbook. As you can see, effective planning is grounded in information that comes from staying current about events within the industry in which we work and with people in our social networks.

FIGURE 5.6

Model of Career Readiness

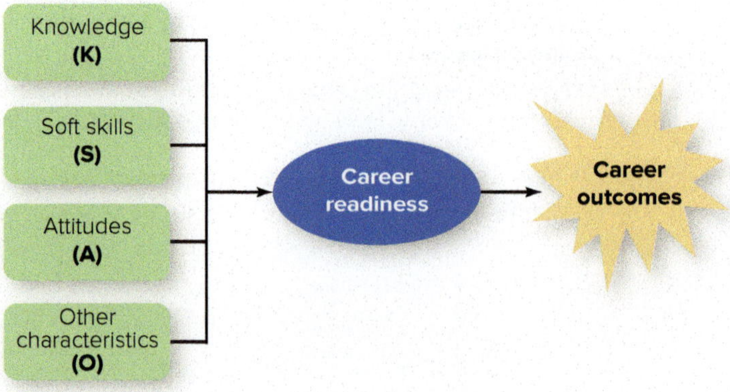

Becoming More Proactive

Being "intentionally proactive" is the first step to becoming a proactive learner. "Being proactive means relying on your own choices instead of luck and circumstances. It's about controlling the situation rather than simply waiting for the outcomes," said one business writer.[56] Lina Tinsley, a brand manager at MARS, put this recommendation into practice. "I give my 100 percent every day and I'm committed to be intentional in all I do. For me, work is an opportunity to live my purpose and bring my best, to deliver consistent results, and to positively influence the people around me," she said.[57] You can put Lina's beliefs into practice by following four key recommendations:[58]

1. Focus on solutions rather than problems.
2. Take initiative and rely on yourself.
3. Set realistic goals and don't overpromise.
4. Participate and contribute to personal and professional conversations.

Keeping an Open Mind and Suspending Judgment

Keeping an open mind and suspending judgment are essential for developing a proactive learning orientation. This exercise was designed to assist you in this pursuit. Focus on your school work or a current job to practice the technique. You can repeat this process in the future whenever you desire to be open-minded.[59]

- **Step 1** Make a list of your current tasks, projects, or commitments at school or work.
- **Step 2** For each task listed in step one, identify the key moments it would be important to be open-minded and suspend judgment.
- **Step 3** For each of these moments, think of how you might apply the four key skills of being open minded:[60]

1. Question your beliefs. Many of us make decisions based on false beliefs and assumptions. You can check yourself by asking: What specific evidence supports my view? Is my knowledge based on facts or my experience? Why am I arguing with others who have more experience and knowledge? Am I offering an opinion or being opinionated? Based on answers to these questions, you can either proceed in the discussion or take a step back and allow your mind to take in new information.
2. Pause and seek feedback. Observe how others respond to your opinions and recommendations. Don't be married to a perspective. If the goal of a discussion is to conduct better planning and make better decisions, then it does not matter whether people agree or disagree with your views. Your goal is to arrive at better decisions and help people to grow.
3. Watch for communication blocks. Be aware of words, concepts, or communication styles that elicit emotional responses from you and others. Emotionality leads to defensiveness and the blocking of listening. Be aware of your emotions when talking with others.
4. Check the accuracy of your past judgments and predictions. If your judgments and predictions have been wrong, consider the reasons and adjust in the future. ●

Key Terms Used in This Chapter

action plan 169
business model 158
business plan 158
cascading goals 176
goal 169
long-term goals 169
management by objectives (MBO) 173
means-end chain 169
mission 164
mission statement 164
objective 169
operating plan 169
operational goals 169
operational planning 167
plan 158
planning 158
planning/control cycle 178
policy 171
procedure 171
program 171
project 171
rule 171
short-term goals 169
single-use plans 171
SMART goal 172
standing plans 171
strategic goals 169
strategic management 159
strategic planning 166
strategy 159
tactical goals 169
tactical planning 167
values statement 165
vision 164
vision statement 164

Key Points

5.1 Planning and Strategy

- Planning is defined as setting goals and deciding how to achieve them. It is also defined as coping with uncertainty by formulating future courses of action to achieve specified results.
- A plan is a document that outlines how goals are going to be met. One important type of plan is a business plan, a document that outlines a proposed firm's goals, the strategy for achieving them, and the standards for measuring success. The business plan describes the business model, which outlines the need the firm will fill, the operations of the business, its components and functions, as well as the expected revenues and expenses.
- A strategy, or strategic plan, sets the long-term goals and direction for an organization.
- Strategic management is a process that involves managers from all parts of the organization in the formulation and implementation of strategies and strategic goals.
- An organization should adopt planning and strategic management for three reasons: They can (1) provide direction and momentum, (2) encourage new ideas, and above all (3) develop a sustainable competitive advantage.

5.2 Fundamentals of Planning

- An organization's reason for being is expressed in a mission statement.
- A vision is a long-term goal describing "what" an organization wants to become. It is a clear sense of the future and the actions needed to get there. A vision statement expresses what the organization should become, where it wants to go strategically.
- Both mission and vision should express the organization's values. A values statement, or core values statement, expresses what the company stands for, its core priorities, the values its employees embody, and what its products contribute to the world.
- From these are derived strategic planning, then tactical planning, then operational planning. In strategic planning, managers determine what the organization's long-term goals should be for the next 1–5 years with the resources they expect to have available. In tactical planning, managers determine what contributions their work units can make with their given resources during the next 6–24 months. In operational planning, they determine how to accomplish specific tasks with available resources within the next 1–52 weeks.

5.3 Goals and Plans

- Whatever its type, the purpose of planning is to set a goal and then formulate an action plan.
- Goals are of two types: long-term and short-term.
- Long-term goals are generally referred to as strategic goals. They tend to span one to five years and focus on achieving the strategies identified in a company's strategic plan.
- Short-term goals are sometimes referred to as tactical goals, operational goals, or just plain goals. They generally span 12 months and are connected to strategic goals in a hierarchy known as a means-end chain.
- A means-end chain shows how goals are connected or linked across an organization. The accomplishment of low-level goals is the means leading to the accomplishment of high-level goals or ends.
- Strategic goals are set by and for top management and focus on objectives for the organization as a whole. Tactical goals are set by and for middle managers and focus on the actions needed to achieve strategic goals. Operational goals are

set by first-line managers and are concerned with short-term matters associated with realizing tactical goals.

- An operating plan is a plan that breaks long-term output into short-term targets or goals. Operational plans turn strategic plans into actionable short-term goals and action plans.
- An action plan defines the course of action needed to achieve the stated goal. Whether the goal is long-term or short-term, action plans outline the tactics that will be used to achieve the goal. Each tactic also contains a projected date for completing the desired activities.
- The goal should be followed by an action plan, which defines the course of action needed to achieve the stated goal. The operating plan, which is typically designed for a one-year period, defines how you will conduct your business based on the action plan; it identifies clear targets such as revenues, cash flow, and market share.
- Plans may be either standing plans, developed for activities that occur repeatedly over a period of time, or single-use plans, developed for activities that are not likely to be repeated in the future.
- There are three types of standing plans: (1) A policy is a standing plan that outlines the general response to a designated problem or situation. (2) A procedure outlines the response to particular problems or circumstances. (3) A rule designates specific required action.
- There are two types of single-use plans: (1) A program encompasses a range of projects or activities. (2) A project is a single-use plan of less scope and complexity.

5.4 Promoting Consistencies in Goals: SMART Goals, Management by Objectives, and Goal Cascading

- The five characteristics of a good goal are represented by the acronym SMART. A SMART goal is one that is specific, measurable, attainable, results-oriented, and has target dates.
- Management by objectives (MBO) is a four-step process in which (1) managers and employees jointly set objectives for the employee, (2) managers develop action plans, (3) managers and employees periodically review the employee's performance, and (4) the manager makes a performance appraisal and rewards the employee according to results. The purpose of MBO is to motivate rather than to control subordinates.
- For MBO to be successful three things have to happen. (1) The commitment of top management is essential. (2) The goals must be applied organizationwide. (3) Goals must cascade—be linked consistently down through the organization. Cascading goals is the process of ensuring that the strategic goals set at the top level align, or "cascade," downward with more specific short-term goals at lower levels within an organization, including employees' objectives and activities.
- Deadlines are essential to planning because they become great motivators both for the manager and for subordinates.

5.5 The Planning/Control Cycle

- Once plans are made, managers must stay in control using the planning/control cycle, which has two planning steps (1 and 2) and two control steps (3 and 4), as follows: (1) Make the plan. (2) Carry out the plan. (3) Control the direction by comparing results with the plan. (4) Control the direction by taking corrective action in two ways—namely, by (a) correcting deviations in the plan being carried out or (b) improving future plans.

5.6 Career Corner: Managing Your Career Readiness

- Planning requires the use of multiple career readiness competencies, including *critical thinking/problem solving, proactive learning orientation, task-based/functional knowledge, understanding the business, and networking.*
- You can increase the competency of *proactive learning orientation* by becoming more proactive and keeping an open mind and suspending judgement.

Understanding the Chapter: What Do I Know?

1. What are planning, strategy, and strategic management?
2. Why are they important?
3. What is the difference between a mission and a vision, a mission statement and a vision statement?
4. What are three types of planning?
5. What are two types of goals?
6. What are different kinds of plans?
7. What are SMART goals?
8. What is management by objectives?
9. What three things have to happen for MBO to be successful?
10. Explain the planning/control cycle.

Management in Action

Fender Rebrands to Stay in Tune with the Times

Fender Musical Instruments Corporation produces some of the most recognized electric and bass guitars in the world. The organization was one of the first to mass produce guitars and has an illustrious history dating back to the late 1940s. Fender's guitars revolutionized popular music by allowing smaller groups of musicians to play together.[61]

Today, these small groups include megastar customers like Eric Clapton, Sheryl Crow, and U2. With stars of this caliber using Fender guitars on stage, you might imagine business is booming. Sadly, it is not. *Fortune* reports that Fender "spent the better part of the past decade struggling with debt and a lack of growth, and in 2012 abandoned an IPO, citing unfavorable market conditions."[62] Andy Mooney was hired as CEO in 2015 to turn around the company. Let's consider his plan.

A NEW PLAN FOR AN UNRELIABLE CONSUMER

Fender began its transformation by coming to terms with the high quit-rate of beginning guitar players. According to Mooney, "Almost everyone who picks up a guitar, about 90 percent, abandons it within the first year."[63] There are two main contributors to this dire statistic—the method of learning the instrument and the cost associated with doing so.

Fender's plan focused on how amateur players preferred to learn. Ethan Kaplan, Fender's general manager of digital, noted that "The way that I learned piano when I was a kid is no longer the way most people learn. They sit at a computer. They sit on an iPhone. They do things in little bites versus sitting through hour-long lessons."[64] Mooney and Kaplan's assessment of Fender's current reality provided crucial insight into the cost of lessons. According to *Fortune*, " . . . new players spend four times as much on lessons as they do on the instrument."[65]

The company's plan to overcome these challenges was based on experimenting with different apps. The plan strives to ensure that beginning guitar players can easily use digitized materials to quickly learn how to play guitar at a reasonable cost.

Fender's first app was Fender Play. This subscription-based app can be used on a mobile device as a way to assist a "do-it-yourself" society learn how to quickly play the guitar. The app uses bite-sized, multi-angle video lessons focused on helping new players learn popular songs. A professional guitarist provides step-by-step lessons in the videos, and players can track their progress in the app. Beginners quickly learn how to play a familiar song from bands such as the Rolling Stones, Foo Fighters, Tim McGraw, and Coldplay. They will be less likely to quit once they achieve this milestone and more likely to buy more Fender guitars in the future.[66] Players will also be spending much less than they would have with private lessons, since the subscription costs only $20 a month.

The software may not be for everybody, though. As *Business Insider* reports, "No program of instruction will be perfect, and Fender Play isn't going to work for everyone . . . And for those who don't like it, there are many free options on the web, and you can always hire a real, live teacher!"[67] Obviously, Fender cannot rely on a one-product-fits-all plan.

The company has developed additional apps to speed up the learning process. For example, Fender developed Fender Tune to teach players how to tune a guitar without having any level of proficiency. "When the kid plugs [the guitar] in for the first time, it doesn't sound like a screaming cat when it comes out of an amp," according to Mooney.[68]

Fender is also looking to release a practice-room app that can assist someone in playing any song in its music library. This provides an opportunity for amateur players to practice and develop their skills.

Another app lets an amp emulate the sounds of famous guitarists. The company's newest amp model will be able to connect to this app wirelessly, through Bluetooth, so players can alter and share sound effects.[69]

IMPACT ON THE BOTTOM LINE

Although Fender has built guitars for Eric Clapton, Stevie Ray Vaughn, and Jimi Hendrix, its growth plan is based on the needs of amateur musicians. According to Kaplan, "We never really concentrated on those 45% of players who buy a guitar for the first time every year." Even a slight improvement in that 90% abandonment statistic would be significant for the company. If Fender can get a 10% increase in the number of beginners who stick with their guitar, it could double the size of its instrument business.[70]

Fender also plans on tapping into an important evolution process with its digital products. If it can get players hooked on cheap starter guitars, then have them upgrade to fancier guitars as they become more committed to playing, it may be able to turn players into collectors. The company would be able to realize more revenue by following the lifecycle of its customers.[71]

Fender's sales strategy goes beyond digital. The company does almost all its business through traditional retailers, with online sales from its website making up less than 2% of North American sales. However, the National Retail Federation says that online sales hit a record $108.2 billion during the 2017 holiday season (a 14.7% increase from the year before).[72] These statistics suggest that Fender's strategy of using traditional retailers may be outdated. Mooney doesn't seem to be worried. "Players need to touch, feel, and play a guitar before they buy one," he says. Fender, he says, prefers to use the Internet as a learning tool, rather than a sales mechanism.[73]

Some factors seem to be out of the company's control. As *Bloomberg* reports, "Detractors have predicted the death of the electric guitar for years, pointing to the rise of rap and electronic music on pop charts." Fender doesn't seem overly concerned about this either. "More women are playing guitar these days," says Mooney, a trend he credits to singer Taylor Swift. The company is also quick to point to rising guitar sales over the past decade. "The pendulum swings back and forth," Mooney says.

Can Fender's new digital strategy swing the pendulum in its direction?

FOR DISCUSSION

Problem-Solving Perspective

1. What is the underlying problem in this case from Fender CEO Andy Mooney's perspective?
2. What are some of the causes of this problem?
3. Do you believe Fender's strategy and plans will turn around the company? Explain.

Application of Chapter Content

1. Using the steps in Figure 5.1, describe how Fender is transforming into a digital company.
2. Define one specific strategic, tactical, and operational plan that Fender can utilize for its transformation.
3. Develop a simple strategic goal, operational goal, and action plan for Fender Play: The goals need to be SMART. Then utilize a means-end chain to illustrate the relationship among the three.
4. Assume 8% of Fender's current customers are women. Would it be wise for the company to set a strategic goal of increasing this number to 40% in the next 12 months? Why or why not? Explain your response using Figure 5.4.
5. Based on CEO Mooney's standard for success in making sure beginners stick with their guitars, develop a planning/control cycle to make sure Fender is headed in the right direction.

Legal/Ethical Challenge

Is Pfizer Putting Profits above Alzheimer's Patients?

Planning and strategy go together, and they flow from a company's mission and vision. Decisions made in the pursuit of corporate strategy are challenging because they ultimately involve choices about how to spend valuable resources. U.S. pharmaceutical giant Pfizer is a good illustration.

Pfizer decided in January 2018 to no longer pursue new research and development (R&D) in treatments for Alzheimer's disease, resulting in the loss of hundreds of jobs. Worse yet, the approximately 5.5 million U.S. adults with this neurological disease no longer have one of the biggest pharmaceutical companies in their corner.[74] Pfizer made this challenging decision because of either low profitability or limited capacity.

With respect to profitability, Alzheimer's research has proven to be costlier than most other R&D pursuits. A neuroscientist at Edinburgh University told *BBC Radio* that "More than 99% of trials for Alzheimer's drugs have failed in past 15 years."[75] Investors thus are pressuring pharmaceutical companies to spend less on this research when they can pursue more profitable projects, such as treatments for anxiety disorders and erectile dysfunction.

Capacity becomes an issue in pharmaceutical research and development because it's difficult to run multiple large-scale R&D programs at the same time. This has led pharmaceutical companies to focus only on specific drugs. A former head of research and development at Pfizer told the *Financial Times* that "You can't run several programmes of that size, even with a budget like Pfizer's. . . . How many times can these companies take another shot when other parts of science like gene therapy are exploding, and when there's a desperate need for new drugs to replace opioids? There are many more areas where you can see the goal lines."[76] Pfizer's management team apparently agrees with this conclusion. The organization said in a statement that not pursuing Alzheimer's research "was an exercise to reallocate [spending] across our portfolio, to focus on those areas where our pipeline, and our scientific expertise, is strongest."[77]

Though Pfizer may be changing its strategy and its resource allocations, the company has kept its mission statement the same: "To be the premier, innovative biopharmaceutical company." Its values include "customer focus" and "integrity."[78] However, its latest decision is seen by some as contradictory to its mission and values. Alzheimer's Research UK says that companies should be encouraged to invest in research into neuroscience. For its part, the Alzheimer's Society called Pfizer's decision "disappointing" and a "heavy blow" to those living with dementia.[79]

Other big drug makers are not letting profit and limited capacity get in their way. A top scientist at Eli Lilly, one of Pfizer's competitors, told *Financial Times* that "Taking care of Alzheimer's patients is a huge economic cost to society and now is not the time to give up." Eli Lilly's most advanced Alzheimer's drug failed in a large trial in 2016, but the company has vowed to continue Alzheimer's treatment R&D.[80] Another U.S. competitor, AstraZeneca, also remains committed to fighting the disease.

SOLVING THE CHALLENGE

What would you do if you were Pfizer's CEO?

1. Move on to other projects. Pfizer has an obligation to its shareholders not to throw money at projects that prove to be unsuccessful.
2. Continue funding Alzheimer's R&D. As a global leader in the pharmaceutical industry, Pfizer has an obligation to society to find treatments for diseases affecting millions of people. This would also be in line with its mission statement and values.
3. Contribute to agencies such as the National Institutes of Health so they can continue their studies of Alzheimer's.
4. Suggest other options.

Uber Continuing Case connect

Learn how Uber's corporate strategies have changed from those pursued by founder and CEO Travis Kalanick to those identified by current CEO Dara Khosrowshahi. Assess your ability to apply concepts discussed in this chapter to the case by going to Connect.

6 Strategic Management

How Exceptional Managers Realize a Grand Design

©Olivier Renck/Aurora/Getty Images

After reading this chapter, you should be able to:

LO 6-1 Identify the three principles underlying strategic positioning.

LO 6-2 Outline the five steps in the strategic-management process.

LO 6-3 Explain how an organization assesses the competitive landscape.

LO 6-4 Explain the three methods of corporate-level strategy.

LO 6-5 Discuss Porter's five competitive forces and the four techniques for formulating strategy.

LO 6-6 Describe the role of effective execution in strategic management.

LO 6-7 Describe how to enhance your strategic thinking.

FORECAST *What's Ahead in This Chapter*

We describe strategic positioning and three levels of strategy, and then consider the five steps in the strategic-management process. In assessing current reality, we describe the tools of SWOT analysis, VRIO, forecasting, and benchmarking. When discussing corporate-level strategy, we review three types of overall strategies, the BCG matrix, and diversification. In describing business-level strategy, we discuss Porter's five competitive forces and Porter's four competitive strategies. Under execution and strategic control, we discuss the importance of execution. We conclude with a Career Corner that focuses on how to develop your strategic thinking.

MANAGE U

Building Your Personal Brand

As part of their overall competitive strategy, organizations create and build memorable brands for their products and services. Among the world's most valuable brands are Apple, Google, Microsoft, Coca-Cola, and Amazon, but brands don't have to be global to have value. For her blog about getting kids to eat vegetables, London mom Mandy Mazliah created a brand name, Sneaky Veg, and asked an artist to design a logo and distinctive graphics to help her creation stand out from the crowd.[1] Do you have your own personal brand? Do you need one? The answer is yes if you are pursuing a strategy to gain employment upon graduation.

Why You Need a Personal Brand

Ceejay Dawkins, a tax manager at Deloitte, advises new college graduates thus:

> Build your brand. Be known for something. Whether it's being the first person at work in the morning or being the person that always asks intelligent questions—be known for something. Building that brand, building that solid reputation, will follow you through your career. People will notice that and will want you on their assignments.[2]

Quite simply, branding sells. Personal branding goes beyond having a résumé or a Twitter, LinkedIn, or Instagram profile.[3] A strong personal brand lets potential employers learn about who you are, your passions, your areas of expertise, your relevant experience, and your aspirations. That's why it's a good idea for you to take control of the message you want to send employers about your career readiness, and the information you want them to see on social media.

How to Create Your Brand

Your personal brand should have two components. The first reflects your unique identity and strengths, while the second conveys the fact that you are career ready. Developing this type of brand increases your chances of obtaining a desired job and a rewarding career.

Create and promote your personal brand with these steps:

1. Identify the core message of your brand. Consider any special training, education, talents, skills, family background, and special challenges overcome. Where do you see yourself in five years? Ten?

2. Write a personal branding statement. Your personal branding statement is a short paragraph describing who you are, what you stand for, and what you like to do. It emphasizes your unique knowledge and expertise.[4]

3. Develop a social media strategy.[5] Choose the most appropriate platform for your message (Twitter and LinkedIn have very different audiences and purposes); polish your writing style; and make sure everything you share, whether in posts, comments, or a blog, is a good and truthful representation of your brand. Remember, everything an employer sees or reads about you tells a story about your brand. Consider registering your own domain name and creating a personal website for a professional-looking personal brand.

4. Start networking. Don't wait until graduation to network; start now! Join groups and attend meetings for people in your field of interest. Meeting others in your industry, whether online or in person, can lead to great collaborative opportunities that will home your teamwork skills.

For Discussion Do you have a personal brand? If not, why are you waiting to create one? Using the preceding steps, how would you shift your social media presence to make it more appealing to potential employers?

6.1 Strategic Positioning and Levels of Strategy

THE BIG PICTURE

Strategic positioning attempts to achieve sustainable competitive advantage by preserving what is distinctive about a company. It is based on the principles that strategy is the creation of a unique and valuable position, requires trade-offs in competing, and involves creating a "fit" among activities. There are three levels of strategy: corporate, business level, and functional.

LO 6-1

Identify the three principles underlying strategic positioning.

Harvard Business School professor **Michael Porter** is recognized as one of the most influential business school professors. *Fortune* writer Geoffrey Colvin described him "as the all-time greatest strategy guru."[6]

Is this high praise deserved? Certainly Porter's status as a leading authority on competitive strategy is unchallenged. The Strategic Management Society, for instance, voted Porter the most influential living strategist. We refer to him repeatedly in this chapter.

Strategic Positioning and Its Principles

According to Porter, **strategic positioning attempts to achieve sustainable competitive advantage by preserving what is distinctive about a company.** "It means," he says, "performing *different* activities from rivals, or performing *similar* activities in different ways."[7]

Three key principles underlie strategic positioning.[8]

1. Strategy Is the Creation of a Unique and Valuable Position

Strategic position emerges from three sources:

- **Few needs, many customers.** Strategic position can be derived from serving the few needs of many customers. Example: Jiffy Lube provides only lubricants, but it provides them to all kinds of people with all kinds of motor vehicles.
- **Broad needs, few customers.** A strategic position may be based on serving the broad needs of just a few customers. Example: Wealth management and investment advisory firm Bessemer Trust focuses exclusively on high-net worth clients.
- **Broad needs, many customers.** Strategy may be oriented toward serving the broad needs of many customers. Example: National movie theater operator Carmike Cinemas operates only in cities with populations of fewer than 200,000 people.

Strategy guru. Harvard Business School professor Michael Porter suggests that every company is subject to five forces: its current competitors, possible new competitors, the threat of substitutes for its products or services, the bargaining power of its suppliers, and the bargaining power of its customers. Operating within that five-forces framework, a company must choose the right strategy—or be beaten by competitors. Do you think there are other forces that are equally important in forming strategy? ©Adam Rountree/Bloomberg/Getty Images

2. Strategy Requires Trade-Offs in Competing As a glance at the preceding choices shows, some strategies are incompatible. Thus, a company has to choose not only what strategy to follow but what strategy *not* to follow. Example: Neutrogena soap, points out Porter, is positioned more as a medicinal product than as a cleansing agent. In achieving this narrow positioning, the company gives up sales based on deodorizing; gives up large volume; and, accordingly, gives up some manufacturing efficiencies.

3. Strategy Involves Creating a "Fit" among Activities "Fit" has to do with the ways a company's activities interact and reinforce one another. Example: A mutual fund such as Vanguard Group follows a low-cost strategy and aligns all its activities accordingly, distributing funds directly to consumers and minimizing portfolio turnover. However, when the short-lived (1993–1995) Continental Lite airline tried to match some, but not all, of Southwest Airlines's activities, it was not successful because it didn't apply Southwest's entire interlocking system.

Levels of Strategy

Strategic management takes places at three levels, each supporting the other, as shown in Figure 6.1.

Level 1: Corporate-Level Strategy **Corporate-level strategy focuses on the organization as a whole.** Executives at the most senior levels, generally referred to as the "C-Suite," typically conduct this type of strategic planning. This analysis answers questions such as "what business are we in?" and "what products and services shall we offer?" Strategic decisions at this level can involve acquisitions, such as Amazon's acquisition of Whole Foods, joint ventures like the one between Volvo and Autoliv to develop software for driverless vehicles, and significant investments in plant and equipment.[9]

Level 2: Business-Level Strategy **Business-level strategy focuses on individual business units or product/service lines.** Senior-level managers below the C-Suite typically are responsible for this level of strategy. Issues under consideration flow from decisions made at the corporate level and involve considerations such as how much to spend on marketing, new-product development, product expansion or contraction, facilities

FIGURE 6.1
Three levels of strategy

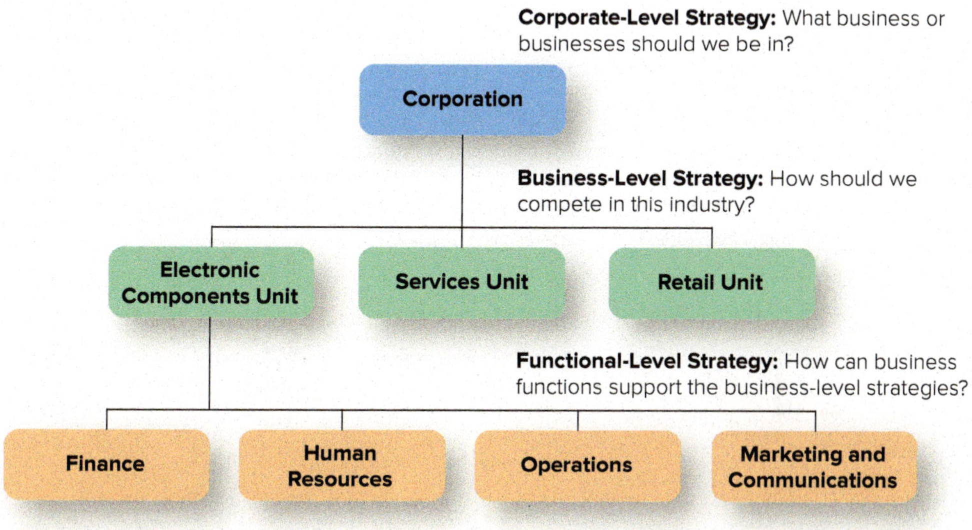

expansion or reduction, equipment, pricing, and employee development. For example, the *Education* business unit of McGraw-Hill Education, the publisher of this product, and iFlipd, a weekly textbook rental platform, teamed up allow students to rent select McGraw-Hill titles in both digital and print versions. This strategy is aimed at growing revenue.[10]

Level 3: Functional-Level Strategy **Functional-level strategy applies to the key functional departments or units within the business units.** Functional managers lead planning discussions at this level, and the focus is on more tactical issues that support business-level strategies. For example, McGraw-Hill's decision to go into the textbook leasing business would require marketing managers to decide how to market the program, royalty managers to determine the formula for paying author royalties, and production managers to decide the best way to integrate digital and print versions of a product.

Does Strategic Management Work for Small as Well as Large Firms?

Evidence reveals that the use of strategic management techniques and processes are associated with increased small business performance.[11] Surprisingly, however, many small business owners do not engage in strategic planning.[12] We suspect the cause is a short-term rather than long-term focus. Strategic planning requires a long-term orientation. ●

EXAMPLE Evernote and Groove HQ Get Started with Strategic Planning

Evernote is a California-based company of about 325 people that makes apps and other products to help people collect and manage the information they need in their jobs and daily lives. The company recently found that it had been putting so much time and energy into creating a wide array of new features for its products that it risked losing sight of its core purpose. While most customers were happy with the small percentage of Evernote products they chose, it seemed that no one used the same products or had the same experience with the company. So, perhaps by falling prey to the tech industry's pressure to innovate and constantly release new products, Evernote was expending a lot of its resources supporting features that each had only a very small user base. The goal of new CEO Chris O'Neill is to better align Evernote's strategy with its core product by paring back some of its many other offerings.[13]

Another firm that hopes to refocus on its core strategy is using a slightly different path to get there. Groove HQ, which develops help desk and online customer support software for small businesses, has fewer than 50 employees, all of whom work remotely. When the company decided to refocus its far-flung staff on core goals like trouble-shooting its long-term plans, finding new customers, and delivering growth for investors, CEO Alex Turnbull decided to hire a business strategy coach. The results of the Groove team's three-day huddle with its coach were promising in boosting their shared sense of accountability for achieving what they had planned and showing them formal business processes for getting there. The session was so productive that now Turnbull plans to get the team together more often for in-person leadership meetings and retreats.[14]

YOUR CALL

Why do you think Evernote and Groove temporarily lost sight of their strategic goals? Do you agree with their CEOs about their plans for refocusing their respective companies? Why or why not?

6.2 The Strategic-Management Process

THE BIG PICTURE

The strategic-management process has five steps: Establish the mission, vision, and values statements. Assess the current reality. Formulate corporate, business, and functional strategies. Execute strategy. Maintain strategic control. All steps may be affected by feedback that enables the taking of constructive action.

LO 6-2

Outline the five steps in the strategic-management process.

When is a good time to begin the strategic-management process? Often it's touched off by some crisis.

As we'll see later in the chapter, in 2009 and 2010 Toyota Motor encountered severe quality problems involving what seemed to be uncontrollable acceleration in its automobiles. President Akio Toyoda concluded that these problems were partly due to the company's "excessive focus on market share and profits," requiring that the company reorient its strategy toward quality and innovation.[15]

The Five Steps of the Strategic-Management Process

The strategic-management process has five steps, plus a feedback loop, as shown below. *(See Figure 6.2.)* Let's consider these five steps, and, along the way, we'll see how Macy's has recently implemented each in its efforts to stave off "the retail apocalypse."

Step 1: Establish the Mission, Vision, and Values Statements We discussed mission, vision, and values statements in Chapter 5. The *mission statement*, you'll recall, expresses the organization's purpose or reason for being. The *vision statement* states what the organization wants to become, where it wants to go strategically. The *values statement* describes what the organization stands for, its core priorities, the values its employees embody, and what its products contribute to the world. Macy's has identified a number of core values, including abiding by ethical practices in every facet of business, protecting the interests of shareholders, practicing "open and honest communications" with all stakeholders, providing customers with quality and value, treating others "as we want them to treat us," and being good corporate citizens.[16]

Step 2: Assess the Current Reality The second step is to do a **current reality assessment**, or ***organizational assessment***, **to look at where the organization stands and see what is working and what could be different so as to maximize efficiency and effectiveness in achieving the organization's mission.** Among the tools for assessing the current reality are SWOT analysis, VRIO analysis, forecasting, and benchmarking, all of which we discuss in Section 6.3. Macy's is a good example of a firm whose current reality has radically changed.

FIGURE 6.2

The strategic-management process

The process has five steps.

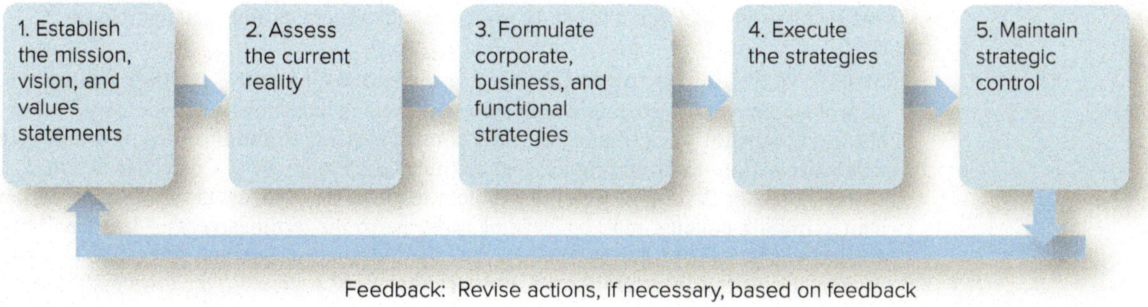

The company was among several big retailers that reported lower 2016 sales despite a 4 percent increase in total retail spending during the holiday shopping season. The "retail apocalypse" predicted by some industry analysts appeared to have begun as customers increasingly preferred the convenience of online shopping to driving to a mall or store. As one writer put it, "growth is in the clicks not the bricks when it comes to retailing." Like other retailers, Macy's had fallen back on heavy discounting, which reduced revenues and led it to announce the planned closing, over the next few years, of 100 stores.[17]

Step 3: Formulate Corporate, Business, and Functional Strategies

The next step is to translate the broad mission and vision statements into a corporate strategy, which, after the assessment of the current reality, explains how the organization's mission is to be accomplished. Three common grand strategies are growth, stability, and defensive, as we'll describe. Macy's knew it had to "reset our business model to thrive in a future . . . driven by rapid evolution in consumer preferences and shopping habits."[18] This resetting included streamlining management decision making to enable faster responses to market changes, adding more exclusive merchandise to help differentiate the Macy's shopping experience and bring in 40 percent of sales rather than the previous 29 percent, tracking sales data better in order to improve price-cutting for unsold items, and finding ways to bring customers back to the physical store.[19]

Macy's store in Manhattan, New York, USA. ©Kord.com/age fotostock/Getty Images

Strategy formulation is the process of choosing among different strategies and altering them to best fit the organization's needs. Formulating strategy is a time-consuming process both because it is important and because the strategy must be translated into more specific *strategic plans*, which determine what the organization's long-term goals should be for the next one to five years.

In Sections 6.4 and 6.5 we discuss the process by which managers create corporate-level strategy and business-level strategy, respectively.

Step 4: Execute the Strategy

Putting strategic plans into effect is strategy implementation. Strategic planning isn't effective, of course, unless it can be translated into lower-level plans. This means that top managers need to check on possible roadblocks within the organization's structure and culture and see if the right people and control systems are available to execute the plans.[20] Strategic implementation is essential for success and is considered to elicit the greatest challenge for managers.[21] "You have to create more reasons for consumers to come into our store," Macy's outgoing CEO advised his successor. To achieve that, Macy's set out to enhance the customer's store experience, opening boutiques for brands like Apple and Best Buy and even making Etsy offerings available in some locations. Among other changes, customers can now check store inventory on a mobile app before they travel to the store, and they can order online and pick up at the store, which usually generates additional purchases.[22]

Step 5: Maintain Strategic Control: The Feedback Loop

Strategic control consists of monitoring the execution of strategy and making adjustments, if necessary. To keep strategic plans on track, managers need control systems to monitor progress and take corrective action—early and rapidly—when things start to go awry. Corrective action constitutes a feedback loop in which a problem requires that managers return to an earlier step to rethink policies, redo budgets, or revise personnel arrangements. Macy's had better-than-expected sales during the 2017 holiday shopping season and saved $300 million in annual expenses by closing some stores, capital it will reinvest in the business. The new

CEO says the company is "focused on continuous improvement and will take the necessary steps to move faster, execute more effectively and allocate resources to invest in growth."[23,24]

We describe strategic implementation and strategic control in Section 6.6.

We discuss the details of the steps in the strategic-management process in the rest of this chapter. You can get a good sense of this process by reading Maria Kato's description of the process at her employer (see I Wish... feature).

I Wish...

...my company would have assessed its current reality before opening the doors for business.

Maria Kato works as a marketing manager for a local meal kit delivery company. This small start-up company began with an opportunity to compete with larger meal kit delivery companies but struggled to maintain strategic control due to a lack of strategy formulation and execution.

Maria knew what her company's mission was: "To provide customers with a convenient and healthy way to eat dinner." However, this mission was not clearly communicated to the company's employees.

"This was something that we didn't tell our employees explicitly. With each new hire, we threw them into the culture and expected them to understand that this is how we deal with customers. There was no protocol in place for managing customer concerns," said Maria. "Looking back, I would have liked to create a guide to help the customer service representatives deal with customers. Also, upon hiring, it would have been nice to have an orientation where we established our company mission and what our overall goals were."

Maria Kato Courtesy Maria Kato

One of the start-up company's biggest opportunities was to address the pain points that customers had with other meal kit delivery companies. "Some customers said they don't like chopping or doing all of the prep work involved with cooking. Despite our competitors not being able to address these customer pain points, the market was still growing. People were still looking for a convenient way to eat at home," said Maria.

"Instead of sending a customer an entire head of cabbage, we would give them the perfect amount of cabbage chopped up already. If a customer were to make a slaw for dinner one night, we would have the vinaigrette made for them and the cabbage chopped up so that all he had to do was mix it in a bowl. We changed our product constantly to meet customer demands," said Maria.

Unfortunately, the company's weaknesses and threats overcame their strengths and opportunities because they did not have a strategy in place to achieve their mission. "We just kind of threw our goals out there and didn't hold anyone accountable for them," said Maria. "We had a 'pie in the sky' goal, but we had no idea how to get there."

After suffering financially and experiencing significant employee layoffs, the start-up company was eventually bought out by a larger company that had the resources to execute on the plans and strategies that never came to fruition for the start-up. Today, the start-up's employees are part of the larger company, learning from their missteps and using it to form sustainable strategies.

Courtesy of Maria Kato.

SELF-ASSESSMENT 6.1

Assessing Strategic Thinking

This survey is designed to assess an organization's level of strategic thinking. Please be prepared to answer these questions if your instructor has assigned Self-Assessment 6.1 in Connect.

1. What is the level of strategic thinking? Are you surprised by the results?
2. If you were meeting with an executive from the company you evaluated, what advice would you provide based on the survey results and what you learned about assessing current reality?

6.3 Assessing the Current Reality

THE BIG PICTURE

To develop a grand strategy, you need to gather data and make projections, using tools such as SWOT analysis, VRIO analysis, forecasting, and benchmarking.

LO 6-3

Explain how an organization assesses the competitive landscape.

Figure 6.2 (and Chapter 5) demonstrate that the first step in the strategic-management process is to establish the organization's mission, vision, and values statements. The second step in the strategic-management process, *assess the current reality*, looks at where the organization stands internally and externally—to determine what's working and what's not, to see what can be changed to create sustainable competitive advantage: **Sustainable competitive advantage exists when other companies cannot duplicate the value delivered to customers.** An assessment helps to create an objective view of everything the organization does: its sources of revenue or funding, its work-flow processes, its organizational structure, client satisfaction, employee turnover, and other matters.

Among the tools for assessing the current reality are *SWOT analysis*, *VRIO analysis*, *forecasting*, and *benchmarking*.

SWOT Analysis

SWOT analysis is a good first step at gaining insight into whether or not a company has competitive advantage. **SWOT analysis is a situational analysis in which a company assesses its strengths, weaknesses, opportunities, and threats.** Results from a SWOT analysis provide you with a realistic understanding of your organization in relation to its internal and external environments so you can better formulate strategy in pursuit of its mission. *(See Figure 6.3.)*

FIGURE 6.3

SWOT analysis

SWOT stands for strengths, weaknesses, opportunities, and threats.

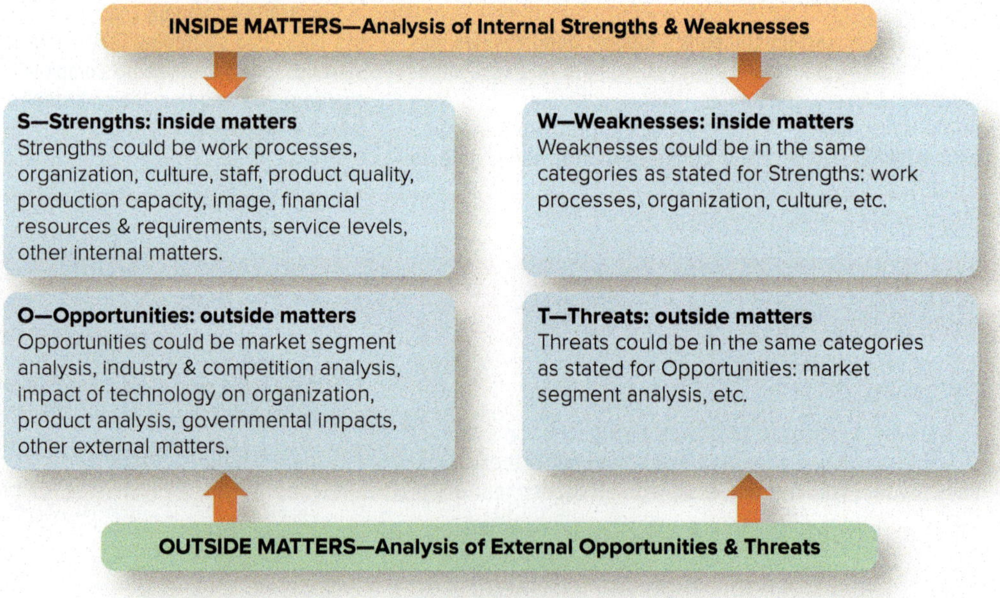

The SWOT analysis is divided into two parts: inside matters and outside matters—that is, an analysis of *internal strengths and weaknesses* and an analysis of *external opportunities and threats*. The following table gives examples of SWOT characteristics that might apply to a college. *(See Table 6.1.)*

TABLE 6.1
SWOT Characteristics That Might Apply to a College

S—STRENGTHS (INTERNAL STRENGTHS)	**W—WEAKNESSES (INTERNAL WEAKNESSES)**
• Faculty teaching and research abilities • High-ability students • Loyal alumni • Strong interdisciplinary programs	• Limited programs in business • High teaching loads • Insufficient racial diversity • Lack of high-technology infrastructure
O—OPPORTUNITIES (EXTERNAL OPPORTUNITIES)	**T—THREATS (EXTERNAL THREATS)**
• Growth in many local skilled jobs • Many firms give equipment to college • Local minority population increasing • High school students take college classes	• Depressed state and national economy • High school enrollments in decline • Increased competition from other colleges • Funding from all sources at risk

Inside Matters: Analysis of Internal Strengths and Weaknesses

Does your organization have a skilled workforce? a superior reputation? strong financing? These are examples of **organizational strengths—the skills and capabilities that give the organization special competencies and competitive advantages in executing strategies in pursuit of its vision.**

Or does your organization have obsolete technology? outdated facilities? a shaky marketing operation? These are examples of **organizational weaknesses—the drawbacks that hinder an organization in executing strategies in pursuit of its vision.**

Outside Matters: Analysis of External Opportunities and Threats

Is your organization fortunate to have weak rivals? emerging markets? a booming economy? These are instances of **organizational opportunities—environmental factors that the organization may exploit for competitive advantage.**

Alternatively, is your organization having to deal with new regulations? a shortage of resources? substitute products? These are some possible **organizational threats—environmental factors that hinder an organization's achieving a competitive advantage.**

EXAMPLE SWOT Analysis: How Would You Analyze Toyota?

The world's leading automaker and most valuable auto brand, Toyota has been making cars since 1937 and sells them in more than 170 countries. North America is one of its top two markets; the other is Japan, its headquarters. Along with the luxury Lexus brand, Toyota markets the Scion, Corolla, Camry, Avalon, Sienna, Rav-4, Highlander, 4Runner, and Prius, among other models. While the company plans big investments in automated driving and artificial intelligence and posted 2017 operating profits of $17.54 billion, it has been struggling, particularly in North America, due to heavy competition and discounting. Executive Vice President Osamu Nagata says of the North American market, "We still have a lot of work to do there."[25]

If you were a top Toyota manager, what strengths, weaknesses, opportunities, and threats would you identify in a SWOT analysis?

Internal Strengths The original "Toyota Way" stressed the values of continuous improvement and eliminating waste, from assembly line to boardroom. This innovative and much-copied philosophy helped Toyota develop a culture focused on planning, identifying rather than hiding problems, and prizing teamwork. The company's continued focus on quality and reliability, called the Toyota Production System, has enhanced its image as a strong brand.[26] Toyota models regularly make J.D. Power's rankings for dependability; in 2017, the Avalon, Camry, Corolla, and Yaris were all among Most Dependable Sedans.[27]

Toyota is also known for its strong research and development, with 17 R&D facilities in eight countries and a research budget of nearly $10 billion. The company is outspent in R&D only by Volkswagen.[28] Toyota's research has led to innovations like its best-selling hybrid car, the Prius. The company also has solid cash reserves,[29] and the enormous value of its brand is another strength.

Internal Weaknesses Beginning in 2000, Toyota suffered some widely publicized recalls, due to sticking accelerators (causing a U.S. criminal probe and $1.2 billion penalty) and an array of potential hazards including unstable steering columns and faulty airbags. Things didn't improve in 2016, when worldwide the company recalled millions more cars, including nearly 6 million for problems with Takata-branded airbags.[30] In 2017, the airbag recall continued, and thousands of Tacoma, Lexus, and Prius models were also recalled for various problems. In early 2018, certain Sequoia, Tundra, Camry, Lexus, and Prius models were recalled as well.[31] While recalls (including for faulty Takata airbags) are not unique to Toyota, they weakened its image in passenger safety and helped reduce sales.

A Toyota Yaris hybrid. ©Michele Eve Sandberg/Corbis Historical/Getty Images

Toyota currently sells more than half its cars in Japan and North America and earns almost two-thirds of its revenue from these two markets.[32] In China, however, the largest car market in the world, Toyota has only 4.5% share, trailing competitors like General Motors and Volkswagen, which also offer many more brands than Toyota's four.

External Opportunities It's anticipated that demand for hybrid vehicles will only increase, which will help Toyota profit from the investment it has made in such autos. At the same time, companies all over the world are exploring autonomous cars as the next big opportunity, in a market that could be worth $45 billion within 10 years. Even Google has joined Ford, Tesla, and others in developing the required technology.[33] Toyota will need to be in this market as well.

The release of new models, with exciting designs and innovative features, represents a constant opportunity in all Toyota's markets. The company is also moving aggressively in India, the world's fifth-largest car market. Its initial forays there, with no-frills models, were unsuccessful, but the company has changed its strategy, targeting an expanding middle class with high-end vehicles like SUVs. "We are now a little successful in India, but it is not enough," says Akito Tachibana, managing director of Toyota Kirloskar Motor.[34]

External Threats Fluctuations in currency exchange rates regularly threaten every global company, and Toyota is no exception. Its assembly lines in Japan have been halted more than once when parts suppliers were hampered by earthquake damage, which, along with flooding, remains an ever-present risk. The company could face U.S. tariffs on cars it makes in Mexico, raising prices in North America, if the Trump administration seeks changes in the North American Free Trade Agreement (NAFTA).[35] And competitors have had time to catch up with Toyota on quality and safety. Finally, given the number of companies pushing ahead with electric and self-driving cars, and the possibility that the U.S. car market is reaching peak size, Toyota faces a continuing threat from competitors[36] and even the possibility of a saturated market.

YOUR CALL

Which internal strengths could Toyota make better use of in the future? Which internal weaknesses are most important for it to address? Is Toyota situated to take advantage of all its current external opportunities? Which external threats should it prioritize, and why?

Using VRIO to Assess Competitive Potential: Value, Rarity, Imitability, and Organization

Say you have an idea for a product or service, such as "Let's develop a ride service for kids, similar to Uber and Lyft for adults." Nick Allen started such a business in San Francisco in 2014 and called it Shuddle.[37] How does someone determine whether a new idea like Shuddle might work? A VRIO analysis can help.

VRIO (pronounced by its letters, "V-R-I-O") is a framework for analyzing a resource or capability to determine its competitive strategic potential by answering four questions about its value, rarity, imitability, and organization.[38] The questions are shown in Figure 6.4.

VRIO is a way to analyze a firm's competitive potential by asking four questions about value, rarity, imitability, and organization. A yes answer to each question means the resource or capability—that is, the business idea—has a competitive advantage (see Figure 6.4).

FIGURE 6.4

Is the resource or capability . . .

Source: Adapted from F. T. Rothaermel, Strategic Management: Concepts and Cases *(New York: McGraw-Hill Education, 2012), p. 91.*

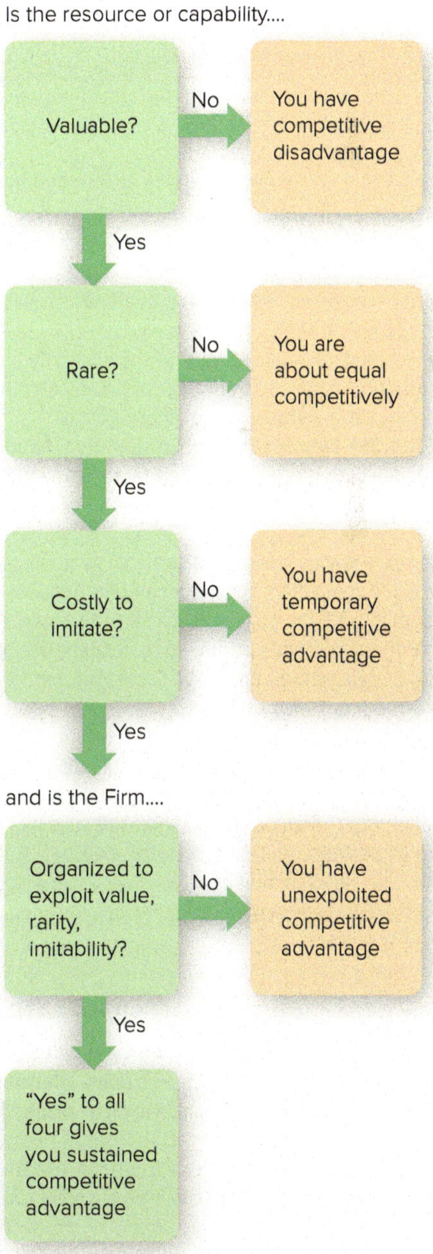

Value: Is the Resource or Capability Valuable?

Valuable means "Does the resource or capability allow your firm to exploit an opportunity or neutralize a threat?" If the answer is yes, the resource puts you in a competitive position. If no, then you're at a competitive disadvantage.

Example: The idea of an on-demand ride service for unaccompanied children provided by drivers in their personal cars exploits an opportunity—because some parents say they really need such a service.

Rarity: Is the Resource or Capability Currently Controlled by Only a Few Firms or No Other Firms?

If the answer is yes, that status gives your firm at least some temporary competitive advantage. If the answer is no (several competing firms exist), you're at least at equal competitive advantage, because you're no worse than the competition.

Example: No other firms in your area are yet offering on-demand children's ride services, but Uber and Lyft would love to drive the kids around town. This is not a competitive advantage.

Imitability: Is the Resource or Capability Costly for Other Firms to Imitate?

If the answer is yes, that gives you a definite competitive advantage. If no—because other firms can get into the market without much expense—that gives you only a temporary competitive advantage.

Example: Offering a children's ride service with drivers using their own personal cars is probably not so costly that other firms might not try to imitate you. As we already said, Uber and Lyft can offer this service. Here you have no competitive advantage.

Organization: Is the Firm Organized to Exploit the Resource or Capability?

If the answer is yes—that is, the firm has the necessary structure, culture, control systems, employee policies, and particularly financing—then, assuming yes answers on Value, Rarity, and Imitability, it would seem the firm has the competitive potential to go forward. If no, it may only have a temporary competitive advantage.

Example: San Francisco's Shuddle began operating in fall 2014 with 350 independent-contractor drivers and soon grew to serve about 2,600 customers booking 7,000 rides a month. But the service was more expensive than Uber and Lyft (owing to higher expenses for more-extensive background checks and additional insurance for Shuddle drivers), with trips averaging $24 each. Unfortunately, Shuddle suffered from having not only too few riders but also too few drivers to reach an ideal balance between supply and demand. It also was unable to raise additional venture capital money. Clearly, then, it did not have everything needed to answer yes to the question of "organization." All told, Shuddle did not have competitive advantage, and it went out of business in April 2016.[39]

EXAMPLE Developing Competitive Advantage: Who Dominates the Internet Economy and Who's Losing?

Who are now the lords of tech? Which giant companies control our digital life?

It's generally agreed that the "frightful five" companies that dominate the Internet economy are Amazon, Apple, Facebook, Google, and Microsoft.[40] These are the companies that power the virtual technology infrastructure that delivers "online search, messaging, advertising, applications, computing, and storage on demand," says one report. "They own the digital equivalent of railroad lines just as the Web enters a new phase of growth," rapidly expanding in cloud computing, mobile devices, social networks, and other services.[41]

The Big Five Platforms: Competitive Advantages The basic building blocks dominated by these five companies on which every other business depends are called *platforms*, points out technology writer Farhad Manjoo.[42] Each platform also represents a company's competitive advantage. Amazon has cloud computing, on which many start-ups run, as well as a shopping and shipping infrastructure.[43] Apple controls one form of mobile phone operating system and the apps that run on it; Google controls another. Google (now part of parent company Alphabet) also rules web search and has its own cloud infrastructure. Google and Facebook dominate the Internet advertising business, and Facebook "keeps amassing greater power in that most fundamental of platforms: human social relationships," Manjoo writes. Microsoft still has Windows, the king of desktop operating systems, and has moved aggressively into cloud computing.

Who's Up, Who's Down? In the struggle for competitive advantage, the state of play is constantly shifting. "Not long ago people thought IBM, Cisco Systems, Intel, and Oracle were unbeatable in tech," Manjoo observes. "They're all still large companies, but they're far less influential than they were once."[44] Meanwhile, Yahoo!, once a huge success story, may be running out of time. Its ad revenues are slipping far behind those of its rivals, and its decline is being hastened by the rise of mobile devices and social media.[45]

The Stack Fallacy. Why do some companies lose their competitive advantage? Venture capitalist Anshu Sharma suggests one possibility. Although a company may have the resources and brainpower to build "the next big thing," it may subscribe to the *stack fallacy*—"the mistaken belief that it is trivial to build the layer above yours" in the stack that is the layer cake of technology.[46] The reason, argues Sharma: the companies don't have firsthand understanding of what customers of the product one level above theirs in the stack actually want. Thus, Oracle, which is a database company, can't seem to beat Salesforce in building database management software for customer relations because Oracle doesn't truly understand how this kind of customer relations works.

YOUR CALL

If you can visualize a "frightful 5" Internet company losing its competitive advantage, how do you think it would come about?

Forecasting: Predicting the Future

Once they've analyzed their organization's Strengths, Weaknesses, Opportunities, and Threats, planners need to do forecasting for making long-term strategy. **A forecast is a vision or projection of the future.**

Lots of people make predictions, of course—and often they are wrong.[47] In the 1950s, the head of IBM, Thomas J. Watson, estimated that the demand for computers would never exceed more than five for the entire world. In the late 1990s, many computer experts predicted power outages, water problems, transportation disruptions, bank shutdowns, and far worse because of computer glitches (the "Y2K bug") associated with the change from year 1999 to 2000.

Of course, the farther into the future one makes a prediction, the more difficult it is to be accurate, especially in matters of technology. Yet forecasting is a necessary part of planning.

Trend Analysis

A trend analysis is a hypothetical extension of a past series of events into the future. The basic assumption is that the picture of the present can be projected into the future. This is not a bad assumption, if you have enough historical data, but it is always subject to surprises. And if your data are unreliable, they will produce erroneous trend projections.

An example of trend analysis is a time-series forecast, which predicts future data based on patterns of historical data. Time-series forecasts are used to predict long-term trends, cyclic patterns (as in the up-and-down nature of the business cycle), and seasonal variations (as in Christmas sales versus summer sales).

The days of crystal balls are gone. Modern forecasting techniques rely on sophisticated mathematical simulation models analyzed on computers.
©Eric Audras/Getty Images

Contingency Planning: Predicting Alternative Futures

Contingency planning—also known *as scenario planning* and scenario analysis—is the creation of alternative hypothetical but equally likely future conditions. For example, scenarios may be created with spreadsheet software such as Microsoft Excel to present alternative combinations of different factors—different economic pictures, different strategies by competitors, different budgets, and so on. The Example box illustrates contingency planning for firms affected by Hurricane Harvey.

EXAMPLE Contingency Planning: How CVS, Walgreens, and FedEx Coped with Hurricane Harvey

Traffic on flooded roads in Houston, Texas.
©IrinaK/Shutterstock

Severe weather events like Hurricane Harvey, which flooded Houston and parts of Louisiana in 2017, demonstrate the critical need for organizations of all kinds to have contingency plans. Especially for maintaining their supply chains, for example, companies must have plans in place that direct employees to get parts, supplies, and other needs from other than their usual warehouse or distribution center. If the emergencies can be anticipated, as extreme storms often are, companies that are well prepared with contingency plans are able to move more quickly than their competitors and avoid both shortages and price increases.[48] They can also protect employees' safety if conditions call for a temporary shutdown.

Although CVS had to close almost a quarter of its stores in areas battered by Harvey, the drugstore chain's contingency plan went into action. The company prepared its mobile pharmacy to move in as soon as it was deemed safe, and in the meantime, it was able to offer emergency prescriptions refills to customers who were not able to receive mail orders of their medications due to the temporary suspension of UPS, FedEx, and even postal service in the aftermath of the storm.[49]

FedEx had a contingency plan as well. After Harvey forced the closure of local airports and flooded many major roads, the package delivery company faced delays and disruptions in its service. It released a statement saying, "Our priority is always the safety of our team members and providing service to our customers. FedEx has implemented contingency plans to lessen the effect of Hurricane Harvey on operations and mitigate potential service delays."[50] The company stepped in to offer support to relief organizations like the American Red Cross and Heart to Heart, which were working to get supplies to storm-ravaged communities.[51]

CVS's competitor Walgreens was well prepared too and went into action before the storm arrived. "We began working on delivery alternatives before Hurricane Harvey hit," its CEO said in a statement. "We have called all patients in the affected areas and shipped medicines in advance to alleviate many issues ahead of time. The pharmacy also worked with select Walgreens stores in 'safe areas' to serve as depot locations to dispense medicines for those who are unable to get their medicine deliveries."[52]

YOUR CALL

How much do you think companies like FedEx and UPS can do to prepare in advance for a major weather event like a devastating hurricane? What other contingency plans could companies like CVS and Walgreens put in place?

Because the scenarios try to peer far into the future—perhaps five or more years—they are necessarily written in rather general terms. Nevertheless, the great value of contingency planning is that it not only equips an organization to prepare for emergencies and uncertainty, it also gets managers thinking strategically.

Benchmarking: Comparing with the Best

Benchmarking is a process by which a company compares its performance with that of high-performing organizations.[53] Consulting firm Bain & Company notes that "the objective of benchmarking is to find examples of superior performance and understand the processes and practices driving that performance. Companies then improve their performance by tailoring and incorporating these best practices into their own operations—not by imitating, but by innovating."[54] Airlines, investment firms, and cities regularly use benchmarking. For example, Southwest might compare its on-time departures and lost bag statistics against key competitors and the industry as a whole. Cities similarly benchmark quality of life measures against other cities in the region, country, or world.[55] ●

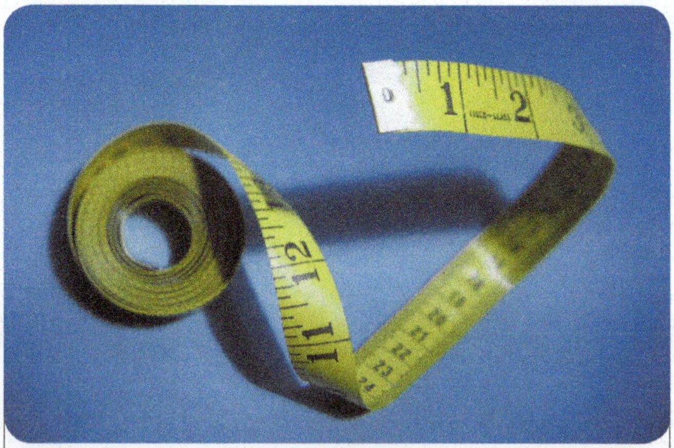

Benchmarking entails measuring and comparing performance across companies. Its effectiveness depends on comparing multiple companies on strategically relevant outcomes such as efficiency, customer service, or safety. Do you think companies would be reluctant to share their performance data with competitors? ©Ingram Publishing

6.4 Establishing Corporate-Level Strategy

THE BIG PICTURE

Common corporate-level strategies are growth, stability, or defensive strategies. The Boston Consulting Group (BCG) matrix and diversification considerations are used to formulate corporate strategy.

LO 6-4

Explain the three methods of corporate-level strategy.

After assessing the current reality (Step 2 in the strategic-management process) it's time to focus on corporate-level strategies. Three methods to understand corporate-level strategies are common grand strategies, the Boston Consulting Group (BCG) matrix, and diversification.

Three Overall Types of Corporate Strategy

The three fundamental types of corporate strategies are *growth*, *stability*, and *defensive*.

1. The Growth Strategy

A growth strategy is a grand strategy that involves expansion—as in sales revenues, market share, number of employees, or number of customers or (for nonprofits) clients served.

Often a growth strategy takes the form of an **innovation strategy, growing market share or profits by innovating improvements in products or services** (as in using an e-business approach in calculatedly disseminating information). We consider innovation further in Chapter 10.

Example: Etsy, a company based in Brooklyn, New York, runs an online marketplace for handmade and vintage goods–jewelry, housewares, T-shirts–for which it charges fees to sellers for use of its platform. Profits and revenues have grown multiple times over the last six years,[56] and third-quarter revenues for 2017 were more than $106 million, 21.5 percent higher than the year before and higher than had been estimated for the quarter.[57] What's behind the surge? In part it was an increase in the number of buyers and sellers using the platform, including internationally.[58] Another factor was the creation of a separate online enterprise called Etsy Manufacturing, a service that matches sellers with small manufacturers, many of which had been devastated by the shift of U.S. production generally to low-wage countries.[59] The innovation allowed Molly Goodall, for instance, to evolve from sewing her quirky animal coats one at a time at her dining room table to using small manufacturers near her Texas home.

2. The Stability Strategy

A stability strategy is a grand strategy that involves little or no significant change. Example: Without much changing their product, the makers of Timex watches decided to stress the theme of authenticity ("Wear it well") over durability (the old slogan was "It takes a licking and keeps on ticking"). In an age of smartphones and other gadgets, when people don't need a watch to tell the time, the new theme of authenticity makes sense, according to *The New York Times,* "as consumers watching what they spend seek out products with longevity whose ability to stand the test of time implies they are worth buying."[60] Most recently, the company has brought out a line of fashion watches with the theme "Share Your Style, #Take Time."[61]

3. The Defensive Strategy

A defensive strategy, or a *retrenchment strategy,* is a grand strategy that involves reduction in the organization's efforts. Example: The "big sales numbers that have sustained the recorded music business for years are way down, and it is hard to see how they could ever return to where they were even a decade ago," says one analysis. "The result is that the music industry finds itself fighting over pennies while waving goodbye to dollars."[62] Principal sources of revenue are now largely the

TABLE 6.2 **How Companies Implement Overall Corporate-Level Strategies**

GROWTH STRATEGY
• It can improve an existing product or service to attract more buyers. • It can increase its promotion and marketing efforts to try to expand its market share. • It can expand its operations, as in taking over distribution or manufacturing previously handled by someone else. • It can expand into new products or services. • It can acquire similar or complementary businesses. • It can merge with another company to form a larger company.
STABILITY STRATEGY
• It can go for a no-change strategy (if, for example, it has found that too-fast growth leads to foul-ups with orders and customer complaints). • It can go for a little-change strategy (if, for example, the company has been growing at breakneck speed and feels it needs a period of consolidation).
DEFENSIVE STRATEGY
• It can reduce costs, as by freezing hiring or tightening expenses. • It can sell off (liquidate) assets—land, buildings, inventories, and the like. • It can gradually phase out product lines or services. • It can divest part of its business, as in selling off entire divisions or subsidiaries. • It can declare bankruptcy. • It can attempt a turnaround—do some retrenching, with a view toward restoring profitability.

result of a 45% increase in streaming revenue, rather than from sales of CDs. There is also a growing but still specialized market for vinyl records.[63]

Variations of the three strategies are shown below. *(See Table 6.2.)*

The BCG Matrix

Developed by the Boston Consulting Group, the **BCG matrix** **is a management strategy by which companies evaluate their strategic business units on the basis of (1) their business growth rates and (2) their share of the market.** Business growth rate describes how quickly the entire industry is growing. Market share is the business unit's share of the market in relation to competitors. The purpose of evaluating each business unit in the company's portfolio is to identify the most effective way to direct the company's financial resources. In general, the BCG matrix suggests that an organization will do better in fast-growing markets in which it has high market share rather than in slow-growing markets in which it has low market share. These concepts are illustrated below. *(See Figure 6.5.)*[64]

A company should usually operate by investing profits from one or more successful but slow-growing units, called *cash cows*, into new products or services called *stars* that have demonstrated strong potential in growing markets and should be appropriately funded. Likewise, the BCG matrix will identify risky units with potential that may or may not produce revenue in the future and should be closely monitored. These are *question marks*. The final category, *dogs*, consists of units that are no longer succeeding and should be shut down or sold.

According to an analysis of Dell by the Boston Consulting Group, the PC continues to be a cash cow for the computer marker, despite slowing growth in the PC

FIGURE 6.5

The BCG matrix

Market growth is divided into two categories, low and high. Market share is also divided into low and high. Thus, in this matrix, "stars" are business units that are highly desirable (high growth, high market share), compared to "dogs," which are not so desirable (low growth, low market share).

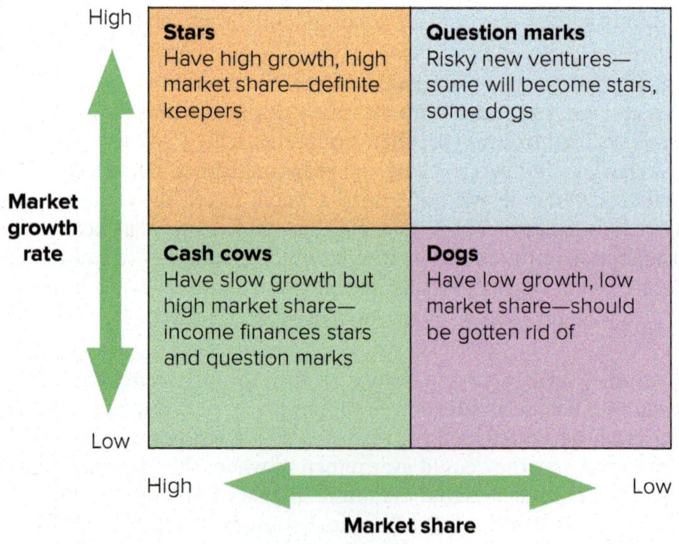

market. Dell has substantial market share here, which means it is still earning profits from its personal computer unit that it can invest in its other products, particularly stars. Dell's innovative ultrathin monitors have undergone some design changes, which is expected to allow them to develop into stars with strong growth and high market share in a market that is still growing. In the BCG matrix view, they may then eventually become cash cows. The company's entry into cloud computing is seen as a question mark because it is a new venture in a market that is quickly filling up. Dell smart phones, on the other hand, were unable to compete against such titans as Apple; one analyst said the product did not meet customer needs and preferences. High investment combined with low return made this Dell product a dog.[65]

One drawback of the BCG matrix is that in practice it is fairly easy for managers to mischaracterize their business units, thereby erroneously drawing investment away from cash cows that still need it or writing off as dogs units or product lines that can yet flourish.

Now that you have learned about the tools companies use to create their grand strategies, what type of skills do you think managers need to use these tools? Do you think you possess those skills?

Diversification Strategy

The strategy of moving into new lines of business, such as Amazon purchasing Whole Foods or CVS buying Aetna, is called diversification. Other examples include JAB Holdings, a European investment firm, acquiring bakery-café chain Panera Bread. This merger establishes a "formidable food-focused portfolio that includes Keurig Green Mountain, Krispy Kreme Doughnuts, Peet's Coffee & Tea, and Caribou Coffee Company." In addition to fitting in with JAB Holdings' other business units, Panera was a good purchase because it has demonstrated steady sales growth during a period in which other chains were hurting.[66]

Companies generally diversify to either grow revenue or reduce risk. They grow revenue because the company now has new products and services to sell. **When a company purchases a new business that is related to the company's existing business portfolio, the organization is implementing related diversification.** Examples are Disney's purchase of 21st Century Fox and the combination of United Technologies and Rockwell Collins in the aviation industry. Companies sometimes attempt to reduce risk by using an unrelated diversification strategy. **Unrelated diversification occurs when a company acquires another company in a completely unrelated business.** This strategy reduces risk because losses in one business or industry can be offset by profits from other companies in the corporate portfolio. Amazon's purchase of Whole Foods is a good example, The deal provides Amazon with access to hundreds of physical stores and provides a solid entry into the food industry.[67]

Organizations can also pursue a diversification strategy through vertical integration. In **vertical integration, a firm expands into businesses that provide the supplies it needs to make its products or that distribute and sell its products.** For many years, Hollywood movie studios followed this model, not only producing movies, but also distributing them and even owning their own theaters.[68] Today, Netflix follows the same path by producing and distributing its own entertainment programming. Starbucks has long followed a plan of vertical integration by buying and roasting all its own coffee and then selling it through Starbucks stores.[69] ●

6.5 Establishing Business-Level Strategy

THE BIG PICTURE

Business-level strategy begins with an assessment of Porter's five competitive forces. Companies then are advised to select from one of four competitive strategies.

LO 6-5

Discuss Porter's five competitive forces and the four techniques for formulating strategy.

The creation of business-level strategy flows from the details contained in corporate strategies. The overall objective of strategy formulation at this level is to answer the question of how the company wants to compete in industries represented by the business units. Harvard professor Michael Porter is credited with devising the models and processes for establishing business-level strategies. We start by focusing on his analysis of his five competitive forces and then delve into a discussion of his four key competitive strategies.

Porter's Five Competitive Forces

What determines competitiveness within a particular industry? After studying several kinds of businesses, strategic-management expert Michael Porter suggested, in his **Porter's model for industry analysis, that business-level strategies originate in five primary competitive forces in the firm's environment: (1) threats of new entrants, (2) bargaining power of suppliers, (3) bargaining power of buyers, (4) threats of substitute products or services, and (5) rivalry among competitors.**[70]

1. Threats of New Entrants New competitors can affect an industry almost overnight, taking away customers from existing organizations. For example, since Starbucks found success by transforming expensive coffee drinks into an affordable necessity, other food chains like McDonald's and Dunkin Donuts, which once focused on hamburgers and donuts, respectively, have stepped up promotion of their own coffee. They now regularly introduce new products to compete with Starbucks' core offering. Dunkin Donuts is even considering dropping the word "Donuts" from its name to highlight its new focus on coffee.[71]

2. Bargaining Power of Suppliers Some companies are readily able to switch suppliers in order to get components or services, but others are not. Starbucks has actively diversified the supply chain for all the inputs it uses, from food and beverage ingredients to signage, packaging, and energy. In this way, the company limits the influence of any one supplier on its ability to continue operations. It has also established a supplier diversity program; among other qualifications, "suppliers interested in doing business through Starbucks U.S./Canadian Supplier Diversity Program must be a U.S. or Canadian citizen or legal resident and 51% owned and operated by a women, minority, veteran, person with disability, LGBTQ, or a socio-economically disadvantaged small business."[72]

3. Bargaining Power of Buyers Informed customers become better negotiators. For example, use of the Internet enabled one of your authors to get a higher trade-in on his current vehicle and a lower sales price on a new car. Starbucks' loyalty program lets customers earn "star" points that can be redeemed for discounts in their stores as well as at other locations. The company sweetened the program by starting a "gold level" program that comes with perks like free refills on coffee and tea and free food and drinks. It takes 30 stars over a 12-month period to earn this benefit.[73]

4. Threats of Substitute Products or Services Like all retailers, Starbucks must ensure that customers continue to prefer its products to the many options available, not only other brands of coffee (purchased in store, online, or in the supermarket), but also other kinds of drinks, which may be less expensive or have lower sugar content. Even the company's innovative "third place" business model, which offers customers an alternative to office and home as a place to linger over an uninterrupted cup of coffee, is no longer unique, so customers can now make other choices for socializing with family friends as well.[74]

5. Rivalry among Competitors The preceding four forces influence the fifth force, rivalry among competitors. Think of the wild competition among food retailers and the enormous number of places you can get a cup of coffee, including at home. Once again, the Internet has intensified rivalries among all kinds of organizations.

An organization should do a good SWOT analysis that examines these five competitive forces, Porter felt. Then it was in a position to formulate effective strategy, using what he identified as four competitive strategies, as we discuss in the next section.

To what extent do you think that a current or past employer was good at strategic thinking? Based on past research, firms that are better at strategic thinking should outperform those that are not.

Porter's Four Competitive Strategies

Porter's four competitive strategies (also called *four generic strategies*) are (1) cost-leadership, (2) differentiation, (3) cost-focus, and (4) focused-differentiation. The first two strategies focus on *wide* markets, the last two on *narrow* markets. Time Warner, which produces lots of media and publications, serves wide markets around the world. Your neighborhood video store (if one still exists) serves a narrow market of just local customers.

Let's look at these four strategies.

1. Cost-Leadership Strategy: Keeping Costs and Prices Low for a Wide Market **The cost-leadership strategy is to keep the costs, and hence prices, of a product or service below those of competitors and to target a wide market.**

This puts the pressure on R&D managers to develop products or services that can be created cheaply, production managers to reduce production costs, and marketing managers to reach a wide variety of customers as inexpensively as possible.

Firms implementing the cost-leadership strategy include Timex, IKEA, computer maker Acer, retailers Walmart and Home Depot, and pen maker Bic.

2. Differentiation Strategy: Offering Unique and Superior Value for a Wide Market **The differentiation strategy is to offer products or services that are of unique and superior value compared with those of competitors but to target a wide market.**

Because products are expensive, managers may have to spend more on R&D, marketing, and customer service. This is the strategy followed by Ritz-Carlton hotels and the makers of Lexus automobiles.

The strategy is also pursued by companies trying to create *brands* to differentiate themselves from competitors. Bottled water brands like Dasani and Poland Spring invest in differentiation strategies based on packaging, convenience, health benefits, and even appeals to status, though their products are essentially all the same.[75]

Focused differentiation. Ford Motor Co. is building 250 high-performance GT supercars a year costing $450,000 each. The cars are so exclusive that buyers have to convince the company, through writing and supporting videos and social media posts, of their enthusiasm for driving it. "We really want to find those customers who will use this car and drive this car and be true ambassadors for Ford," says Henry Ford II, great-great grandson of the founder. The company clearly does not want the GT to become an object of the super wealthy to be stored away.

3. Cost-Focus Strategy: Keeping Costs and Prices Low for a Narrow Market

The cost-focus strategy is to keep the costs, and hence prices, of a product or service below those of competitors and to target a narrow market.

This is a strategy often executed with low-end products sold in discount stores, such as low-cost beer or cigarettes, or with regional gas stations, such as the Terrible Herbst, Rotten Robbie, and Maverik chains in parts of the West. Red Box, originally a kiosk-based video rental company, has added an on-demand streaming service with low costs. But, says one analyst, "The upside is similarly limited, since the appeal will mainly be to its existing kiosk customers."[76]

Needless to say, the pressure on managers to keep costs down is even more intense than it is with those in cost-leadership companies.

4. Focused-Differentiation Strategy: Offering Unique and Superior Value for a Narrow Market

The focused-differentiation strategy is to offer products or services that are of unique and superior value compared to those of competitors and to target a narrow market.

Lush Ltd. is a UK-based brand of natural soaps and bath products for women who appreciate the company's respect for social and corporate responsibility and enjoy the unique in-store experience it offers. The company's products are handmade and never tested on animals. Lush has almost 4 million followers on Instagram and took in $530 million in North American sales in 2017. Says its director of brand communications for North America, "Lush's customer experience is what sets us apart . . . In this age when digital sales are soaring, we truly believe nothing compares to the in-store experience where customers can touch, feel and play with our innovative products and engage with our knowledgeable and passionate staff."[77] ●

SELF-ASSESSMENT 6.2 CAREER READINESS

Core Skills Required for Strategic Planning

This survey is designed to assess the skills needed in strategic planning. Please be prepared to answer these questions if your instructor has assigned Self-Assessment 6.2 in Connect.

1. Do you have what it takes? Are you surprised by the results?
2. Based on the results, what are your top two strengths and deficiencies when it comes to strategic planning?
3. What would you say during an interview to demonstrate that you possess the career readiness competencies associated with strategic thinking? Consider guidance found in the Career Corner.

6.6 Executing and Controlling Strategy

THE BIG PICTURE

Strategic implementation is closely aligned with strategic control. Execution is a process that helps align these two phases of the strategic-management process.

LO 6-6

Describe the role of effective execution in strategic management.

Stage 1 of the strategic-management process was establishing the mission and the vision. Stage 2 was assessing the current reality. Stage 3 was formulate corporate, business, and functional strategies. Now we come to the last two stages—4, strategic execution, and 5, strategic control.

Executing the Strategy

Executing strategies entails putting strategic plans into effect. As we said, this means dealing with roadblocks within the organization's structure and culture and seeing if the right people and control systems are available to execute the plans.

Often implementation means overcoming resistance by people who feel the plans threaten their influence or livelihood. This is particularly the case when the plans must be implemented rapidly because delay is the easiest kind of resistance there is (all kinds of excuses are usually available to justify delays). Thus, top managers can't just announce the plans; they have to actively sell them to middle and supervisory managers.

Occupying a sprawling campus in Cary, North Carolina, software maker SAS has always been ranked in the top positions on *Fortune*'s lists of "100 Best Companies to Work For" (No. 1 in 2010 and 2011, No. 2 in 2013 and 2014, No. 3 in 2012, and No. 4 in 2015). Its ability to execute effectively has also made it highly profitable and the world's largest privately owned software company. Courtesy of SAS

Maintaining Strategic Control

Strategic control consists of monitoring the execution of strategy and taking corrective action, if necessary. To keep a strategic plan on track, suggests Bryan Barry, you need to do the following:[78]

- **Engage people.** You need to actively engage people in clarifying what your group hopes to accomplish and how you will accomplish it.
- **Keep it simple.** Keep your planning simple, unless there's a good reason to make it more complex.
- **Stay focused.** Stay focused on the important things.
- **Keep moving.** Keep moving toward your vision of the future, adjusting your plans as you learn what works.

Execution: Getting Things Done

In implementing strategy and maintaining strategic control, what we are talking about is effective *execution.* **Larry Bossidy**, former CEO of AlliedSignal (later Honeywell), and **Ram Charan**, a business adviser to senior executives, are authors of *Execution: The Discipline of Getting Things Done.*[79] **Execution**, they say, is not simply tactics; it is a central part of any company's strategy. It consists of using questioning, analysis, and

follow-through to mesh strategy with reality, align people with goals, and achieve results promised.

How important is execution to organizational success in today's global economy? A survey of 769 global CEOs from 40 countries revealed that "excellence in execution" was their most important concern—more important than "profit growth," "customer loyalty," "stimulating innovation," and "finding qualified employees."[80] In 2017, Ford's CEO Mark Fields left the company after the board of directors said it had lost confidence in his leadership and ability to implement the company's strategy. The company made about $9 billion in profits in 2017, but during Field's not quite three-year tenure as CEO it had lost market share and seen its share price drop 40 percent. In announcing Fields' successor, Ford said it did not plan any immediate changes in its strategy.[81]

Bossidy and Charan outline how organizations and managers can improve the ability to execute. Effective execution requires managers to build a foundation for execution within three core processes found in any business: people, strategy, and operations.[82] Consider how JJ Fairbanks' company is executing on a strategic goal of increasing revenue growth.

I'm Glad...

...my company adjusts its strategy as we go.

JJ Fairbanks Courtesy JJ Fairbanks

JJ Fairbanks is a senior consultant for a consulting firm's supply chain service group. As a consultant, he is able to see things from his company's perspective and the customer's perspective since he is constantly working with clients.

"One of the things my company has done well is to always look at how we can provide more services to the clients we already have," said JJ. "It's hard to find new clients; it's easier to find new ways to serve our existing clients. This is a growing shift in our strategy: finding new ways to sell products to the same customers."

JJ's company has recently adjusted its strategy to take advantage of this opportunity. Rather than continue with the same business model of finding new clients, they are leveraging their existing strengths and clients to rethink their strategy. While many companies need to adjust their strategy when things go wrong, JJ's company is adjusting their strategy to further its strategic control and continue to grow.

"One of the ways we are changing our business model is to include more groups within the company to service the clients. If more people are involved—different technology groups, different functional groups, different strategy groups—it's easier to find new projects and also deliver more value to the client," said JJ.

Company leadership communicated this business model change to the rest of the company via a team phone call. "We had an 'All Hands Call' for everyone in the supply chain service line—which is several hundreds of employees. Everyone was included in this two-hour call to introduce the improvement to our own operating model to create more working areas," said JJ.

It was also communicated that the goal of this new strategy is top line growth as well as profit margin growth based on year under year improvement, which JJ feels is a challenging but attainable goal that will help to keep employees focused, although not all employees can directly impact revenue growth.

"I think this is the right move for the company. It is also incorporating technology in every aspect of our service offerings. We cannot continue our supply chain work without the incorporation of technology. Instead of having technology as a separate group, we're working arm-in-arm more than we used to," said JJ.

So far, the company has been successful in the implementation of the new strategy and hopes to continue monitoring it so they can make further adjustments as needed in the future.

Courtesy of JJ Fairbanks

The Three Core Processes of Business: People, Strategy, and Operations

A company's overall ability to execute is a function of effectively executing according to three processes: *people*, *strategy*, and *operations*. Because all work ultimately entails some human interaction, effort, or involvement, Bossidy and Charan believe that the *people* process is the most important.

The First Core Process—People: "You Need to Consider Who Will Benefit You in the Future" "If you don't get the people process right," say Bossidy and Charan, "you will never fulfill the potential of your business." But today, most organizations focus on evaluating the jobs people are doing at present, rather than considering which individuals can handle the jobs of the future. An effective leader tries to evaluate talent by linking people to particular strategic milestones, developing future leaders, dealing with nonperformers, and transforming the mission and operations of the human resource department. Costco Wholesale is No. 12 on *Inc.* magazine's list of 50 best places to work.[83] Unlike some of its competitors in the discount retail market, it offers employees generous salaries and benefits, including for part-time workers.[84]

The Second Core Process—Strategy: "You Need to Consider How Success Will Be Accomplished" In most organizations, the strategies developed fail to consider the "how" of execution. According to the authors, a good strategic plan addresses nine questions. *(See Table 6.3.)* In considering whether the organization can execute the strategy, a leader must take a realistic and critical view of its capabilities and competencies. If it does not have the talent in finance, sales, and manufacturing to accomplish the vision, the chances of success are drastically reduced. One of Costco's most successful strategies is to promise–and deliver–the best deal on the brand-name and store-brand products it offers. It also makes shopping a fun experience by offering plenty of product samples and strategically placing merchandise to encourage customers to shop the whole store.[85]

TABLE 6.3 **Necessary Answers: What Questions Should a Strong Strategic Plan Address?**

1. What is the assessment of the external environment?
2. How well do you understand the existing customers and markets?
3. What is the best way to grow the business profitably, and what are the obstacles to growth?
4. Who is the competition?
5. Can the business execute the strategy?
6. Are the short term and long term balanced?
7. What are the important milestones for executing the plan?
8. What are the critical issues facing the business?
9. How will the business make money on a sustainable basis?

Source: From Execution *by Larry Bossidy and Ram Charan, Crown Business, a division of Random House, Inc., 2002.*

The Third Core Process—Operations: "You Need to Consider What Path Will Be Followed" The strategy process defines where an organization wants to go, and the people process defines who's going to get it done. The third core process, operations, or the operating plan, provides the path for people to follow. The operating plan, as we described in Chapter 5, should address all the major activities in which the company will engage—marketing, production, sales, revenue, and so on—and then define short-term objectives for these activities to provide targets for people to aim at. Costco's membership model (in which customers pay a nominal annual fee for admission to the store), its unique shopping experience, and its carefully selected array of high-quality products at wholesale prices have allowed it to remain competitive even in an increasingly online retail world.[86] We also discuss operations management in Chapter 16.

How Execution Helps Implement and Control Strategy

Many executives appear to have an aversion to execution, which they associate with boring tactics–with the tedium of doing, as opposed to the excitement of visioning–and which they hand off to subordinates. Further, there are many organizational obstacles to effective execution, and many of these are associated with organizational culture. Organizational culture is a system of shared beliefs and values within an organization that guides the behavior of its members. In this context, effective execution will not occur unless the culture supports an emphasis on getting quality work done in a timely manner. Chapter 8 presents 12 ways managers can attempt to create an execution-oriented culture.[87]

PRACTICAL ACTION

Building a Foundation of Execution

The foundation of execution is based on leadership (as we discuss in Chapter 14) and organizational culture (discussed in Chapter 8). The *Harvard Business Review* (HBR) surveyed senior managers about the importance of various abilities, and execution ranked first among 16.[88] Bossidy and Charan suggest that there are seven essential types of leader behaviors that are needed to fuel the engine of execution. Managers are advised to engage in seven kinds of behaviors, as follows.

Know Your People and Your Business: "Engage Intensely with Your Employees" In companies that don't execute, leaders are usually out of touch with the day-to-day realities. Now that you are becoming familiar with the career readiness skills we've been describing in this book, including knowing the business, you won't be surprised that Bossidy and Charan insist leaders must engage intensely and personally with their organization's people and its businesses. They cannot rely on secondhand knowledge through other people's observations, assessments, and recommendations.

Insist on Realism: "Don't Let Others Avoid Reality" Many people want to avoid or shade reality, hiding mistakes or avoiding confrontations. Making realism a priority begins with the leaders being realistic themselves, and making sure realism is the goal of all dialogues in the organization. Being "clear and methodical" was one of the stand-out behaviors that improved execution in HBR's survey of thousands of performance reviews.[89]

Set Clear Priorities: "Focus on a Few Rather Than Many Goals" Leaders who execute focus on a very few clear priorities that everyone can grasp. It's also helpful for goals and plans to be simple; they should not have an overwhelming number of steps, nor be vague and lack appropriate details.[90]

Follow Through: "Establish Accountability and Check on Results" Failing to follow through is a major cause of poor execution. "How many meetings have you attended where people left without firm conclusions about who would do what and when?" Bossidy and Charan ask. Accountability and follow-up are important and reflect mastery of the career readiness skill of integrity.

Reward the Doers: "Show Top Performers That They Matter" If people are to produce specific results, they must be rewarded accordingly, making sure that top performers are rewarded far better than ordinary performers. To advocate for these team members, you'll rely on your career readiness skills of decision making and leadership.

Expand People's Capabilities: "Develop the Talent" Coaching is an important part of the executive's job, providing useful and specific feedback that can improve performance. HBR's survey of performance reviews found that "leaders who are great executors are skilled at giving feedback," especially positive feedback.[91]

Know Yourself: "Do the Hard Work of Understanding Who You Are" Leaders must develop "emotional fortitude" based on honest self-assessments. Four core qualities are authenticity, self-awareness, self-mastery, and humility. Self-awareness is another of the career readiness skills we discuss in this book, along with self-efficacy and openness to change.

YOUR CALL

Which behavior is probably the most difficult for you to adopt personally?

Do you think your current or a past employer is or was good at execution? What obstacles may have impaired the company's ability to execute?

SELF-ASSESSMENT 6.3

Assessing the Obstacles to Strategic Execution

This survey is designed to assess the obstacles to strategic execution that may be impacting an organization's ability to execute. Please be prepared to answer these questions if your instructor has assigned Self-Assessment 6.3 in Connect.

1. How does the company stand with respect to execution?
2. Based on the results, what are the company's strengths and weaknesses when it comes to execution?
3. What advice would you give to senior management about improving the company's ability to execute based on the results? Be specific.

In conclusion, by linking people, strategy, and operating plans, execution allows executives to direct and control the three core processes that will advance their strategic vision. ●

6.7 Career Corner: Managing Your Career Readiness

Strategic thinking is not one of the competencies in the career readiness model shown below. The reason is not that employers don't want you to have this skill. Rather, it's because other more specific competencies drive your ability to think strategically. Strategic thinking is defined as "envisioning what might happen in the future and then applying that to our current circumstances."[92] There are four career readiness competencies that drive your ability to think strategically: Understanding the business, task-based functional knowledge, critical thinking/problem solving, and decision making.

LO 6-7

Describe how to enhance your strategic thinking.

Why Is Strategic Thinking Important to New Graduates?

Although you are unlikely to be hired as a strategic planner after graduation, don't be fooled into thinking that this skill is not important. A writer for the *Harvard Business Review* noted that strategic thinking "can, and must, happen at every level of the organization; it's one of those unwritten parts of all job descriptions. Ignore this fact and you risk getting passed over for a promotion."[93] Employers still value this skill in new graduates for four reasons.

1. Thinking strategically requires you to be forward-looking, and employers want people who are prepared to solve future problems that are difficult to predict.
2. The ability to see the big-picture helps people connect the dots about what needs to get done in order to complete today's tasks and projects that support strategic goals.
3. Strategic thinkers pay attention to what is happening in business and society at large. This skill essentially makes you a more informed employee, and employers truly value such people.
4. Strategic thinkers are more likely to have a worldly perspective, an orientation that fits today's global economy.[94]

Developing Strategic Thinking

There are four key activities for developing your ability to think more strategically: understand the business, broaden your task and functional knowledge, set aside time to reflect, and engage in lateral thinking.

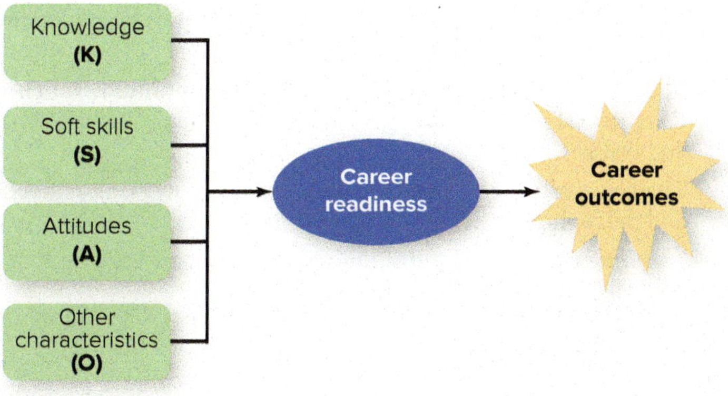

FIGURE 6.6

Model of career readiness

©2018 Kinicki and Associates, Inc.

Understand the Business This career readiness competency reflects the extent to which you understand a potential or current employer's business and strategies. This can be learned by studying a company's web page and annual report. You can look for any published SWOT analyses on a company or conduct one on your own. Once you are hired, you can also extend your knowledge by networking with current employees, proactively seeking mentoring from experienced employees, attempting to participate in a job rotation program, and attending as many cross-functional or business meetings as possible. You also might consider joining industry groups or other professional associations affiliated with the type of work you are doing.[95]

Broaden Your Task and Functional Knowledge Strategic thinking requires making connections between concepts, ideas, people, and events. The more ideas and experiences you have, the greater the ability to make connections. For example, international travel has enhanced our understanding about the nuances of cross-cultural behavior, which in turn has helped in writing about cross-cultural management. Make it a goal to try new things, visit new places, meet new people, and read about new topics. All of these activities will stimulate your mind and expand your base of knowledge. Some experts suggest that strategic thinkers have a knowledge base that represents a "T." The top of the "T" reflects your breadth of knowledge and the stem reflects the depth of understanding about your primary area of expertise.[96] So in addition to trying and reading about new things, it would help to learn about the finer aspects of your employer's industry. Here again, it would be useful to attend industry or functional conferences. The goal of doing this is twofold: learn about the industry or work function and network.

Set Aside Time to Reflect Strategic thinking involves connecting dots between things that others overlook. This takes time and reflection, which requires you to make a commitment to slow down and reserve time in your schedule for this activity. We recommend that you set aside time every week to engage in thinking. You might do it while going for a walk or sitting in a quiet environment. The key is to allocate the time and then use it to think rather than for planning how to get more things done on your task list.

Engage in Lateral Thinking The concept of lateral thinking was developed by Dr. Edward De Bono to encourage creativity and insight. It relies on what De Bono called the Six Thinking Hats. Individuals and teams are encouraged to mentally wear and switch "hats" during meetings. The six hats consist of the following:[97]

- The *White Hat* calls for gathering the facts known or needed.
- The *Yellow Hat* focuses on positivity and optimism. Here you explore and probe for the value of whatever you are discussing.
- The *Black Hat* entails judgment. When wearing this hat, you explore the reasons "why something may not work." Look for the dangers or difficulties associated with the issue at hand. This can be formalized by using a devil's advocate. This individual is given the role of providing a counterargument to what is being proposed.
- The *Red Hat* concentrates on feelings and intuition, which is discussed in Chapter 7. Try on this hat by discussing emotions, feelings, fears, hunch, likes, and dislikes.
- The *Green Hat* focuses on creativity. Explore new ideas, concepts, alternatives, and perceptions.
- The *Blue Hat* is the control function. It is used to ensure that all six hats are being used. ●

Key Terms Used in This Chapter

BCG matrix 204
benchmarking 202
business-level strategy 191
contingency planning 201
corporate-level strategy 191
cost-focus strategy 207
cost-leadership strategy 207
current reality assessment 193
defensive strategy 203
differentiation strategy 207
diversification 205
execution 209
focused-differentiation strategy 208
forecast 200
functional-level strategy 192
growth strategy 203
innovation strategy 203
organizational opportunities 197
organizational strengths 197
organizational threats 197
organizational weaknesses 197
Porter's four competitive strategies 207
Porter's model for industry analysis 206
related diversification 205
scenario analysis 201
stability strategy 203
strategic control 194
strategic positioning 190
strategy formulation 194
strategy implementation 194
sustainable competitive advantage 196
SWOT analysis 196
trend analysis 201
unrelated diversification 205
vertical integration 205
VRIO 199

Key Points

6.1 Strategic Positioning and Levels of Strategy

- Strategic positioning attempts to achieve sustainable competitive advantage by preserving what is distinctive about a company.
- Strategic positioning is based on the principles that strategy is the creation of a unique and valuable position, requires trade-offs in competing, and involves creating a "fit" among activities so that they interact and reinforce each other.
- The three levels of strategy are corporate, business, and functional.
- Strategic management works for both large and small firms.

6.2 The Strategic-Management Process

- The strategic-management process has five steps plus a feedback loop.
- Step 1 is to establish the mission, vision, and values statements. The mission statement expresses the organization's purpose or reason for being. The vision statement states what the organization wants to become and where it wants to go strategically. The values statement describes what the organization stands for, its core priorities, the values its employees embody, and what its products contribute to the world.
- Step 2 is to do a current reality assessment, to look at where the organization stands and see what is working and what could be different so as to maximize efficiency and effectiveness in achieving the organization's mission. Among the tools for assessing the current reality are SWOT analysis, VRIO analysis, forecasting, and benchmarking.
- Step 3 is to formulate corporate, business, and functional strategies. This means translating the company's broad mission and vision statements into a corporate strategy, which, after the assessment of the current reality, explains how the organization's mission is to be accomplished. Three common grand strategies are growth, stability, and defensive.
- Step 4 is strategy execution—putting strategic plans into effect.
- Step 5 is strategic control, monitoring the execution of strategy and making adjustments.
- Corrective action constitutes a feedback loop in which a problem requires that managers return to an earlier step to rethink policies, budgets, or personnel arrangements.

6.3 Assessing the Current Reality

- Step 2 in the strategic-management process, assess the current reality, looks at where the organization stands internally and externally—to determine what's working and what's not, to see what can be changed so as to increase efficiency and effectiveness in achieving the organization's vision.
- An assessment helps to create an objective view of everything the organization does: its sources of revenue or funding, its work-flow processes, its organizational structure, client satisfaction, employee turnover, and other matters.
- Among the tools for assessing the current reality are *SWOT analysis, VRIO analysis, forecasting*, and *benchmarking*.
- Organizational strengths are the skills and capabilities that give the organization special competencies and competitive advantages. Organizational weaknesses are the drawbacks that hinder an organization in executing strategies. Organizational opportunities are environmental factors that the organization may exploit for competitive advantage. Organizational threats are

environmental factors that hinder an organization's achieving a competitive advantage.

- SWOT is a tool for assessing current reality. It entails an evaluation of an organization's internal and external environments to detect early signs of opportunities and threats that may influence the firm's plans.
- VRIO is a framework for analyzing a resource or capability to determine its competitive strategic potential by answering four questions about its value, rarity, imitability, and organization.
- Forecating is another tool for assessing current reality. Two types of forecasting are (1) trend analysis, a hypothetical extension of a past series of events into the future, and (2) contingency planning, the creation of alternative hypothetical but equally likely future conditions.
- Benchmarking is a process by which a company compares its performance with that of high-performing organizations.

6.4 Establishing Corporate-Level Strategy

- Three common corporate-level strategies are (1) a growth strategy involving expansion—as in sales revenues or market share—and one form of growth strategy is an innovation strategy, growing market share or profits by innovating improvements in products or services; (2) a stability strategy, which involves little or no significant change; and (3) a defensive strategy, which involves reduction in the organization's efforts.
- The BCG matrix is a means of evaluating strategic business units on the basis of (1) their business growth rates and (2) their share of the market. In general, organizations do better in fast-growing markets in which they have a high market share rather than slow-growing markets in which they have low market shares.
- A diversification strategy pertains to deciding whether to expand or grow into other businesses. There are two types of diversification strategies: related and unrelated diversification.

6.5 Establishing Business-Level Strategy

- Formulating the business-level strategy makes use of Porter's five competitive forces and his four competitive strategies.
- Porter's model for industry analysis suggests that business-level strategies originate in five primary competitive forces in the firm's environment: (1) threats of new entrants, (2) bargaining power of suppliers, (3) bargaining power of buyers, (4) threats of substitute products or services, and (5) rivalry among competitors.
- Porter's four competitive strategies are as follows: (1) The cost-leadership strategy is to keep the costs, and hence the prices, of a product or service below those of competitors and to target a wide market. (2) The differentiation strategy is to offer products or services that are of unique and superior value compared with those of competitors but to target a wide market. (3) The cost-focus strategy is to keep the costs and hence prices of a product or service below those of competitors and to target a narrow market. (4) The focused-differentiation strategy is to offer products or services that are of unique and superior value compared with those of competitors and to target a narrow market.

6.6 Executing and Controlling Strategy

- The last two steps of the strategic-management process are strategy execution and strategic control.
- Strategy execution is putting strategic plans into effect, dealing with roadblocks within the organization's structure and culture, and seeing if the right people and control systems are available to execute the plans.
- Strategic control consists of monitoring the execution of strategy and taking corrective action, if necessary. To keep a strategic plan on track, you should engage people, keep your planning simple, stay focused, and keep moving.
- Execution is not simply tactics; it is a central part of any company's strategy; it consists of using questioning, analysis, and follow-through to mesh strategy with reality, align people with goals, and achieve results promised.
- Three core processes of execution are people, strategy, and operations. (1) You have to evaluate talent by linking people to particular strategic milestones, developing future leaders, dealing with nonperformers, and transforming the mission and operations of the human resource department. (2) In considering whether the organization can execute the strategy, a leader must take a realistic and critical view of its capabilities and competencies. (3) The third core process, operations, or the operating plan, provides the path for people to follow. The operating plan should address all the major activities in which the company will engage and then define short-term objectives for these activities, to provide targets for people to aim at. By linking people, strategy, and operating plans, execution allows executives to direct and control the three core processes that will advance their strategic vision.

6.7 Career Corner: Managing Your Career Readiness

- Four career readiness competencies—*understanding the business, task-based functional knowledge, critical thinking/problem solving, and decision making*—drive your ability to think strategically.
- There are four key activities for developing the ability to think more strategically: understand the business, broaden your task and functional knowledge, set aside time to reflect, and engage in lateral thinking.

Understanding the Chapter: What Do I Know?

1. What is strategic positioning, and what are the three principles that underlie it?
2. What are the five steps in the strategic management process?
3. What are the tools that can help you assess a company's current reality?
4. Based on the SWOT of Toyota contained in this chapter, what advice would you give to CEO Akio Toyoda?
5. How is VRIO different from a SWOT analysis?
6. What are the three overall types of corporate strategy?
7. Describe how the BCG matrix and diversification are used to establish corporate-level strategy.
8. What are Porter's five competitive forces?
9. Explain Porter's four competitive strategies.
10. In execution, what are the three core processes of business?

Management in Action

General Electric's Evolving Strategy

General Electric (GE) is one of the largest companies in the world. It has almost 300,000 employees and operates in more than 170 countries.[98] The multinational conglomerate traces its roots to the 19th century and is responsible for technology that has revolutionized daily life. GE has invented or commercialized a wide variety of products, starting with light bulbs in 1892 and transitioning to radio, television, and even jet engines. The organization also ventured into financial services and oil and gas.

GE was led by CEO Jack Welch from 1981 to 2001. The company's market value increased by 4,000 percent during Welch's tenure.[99] It had a value of over $396 billion in 2002 when Welch retired and Jeffrey Immelt took over as CEO.[100] Sadly, the financially successful firm Immelt inherited did not last.

GE's market value dropped to $261 billion by 2015.[101] The organization lost another 46 percent of its value between 2017 and 2018. This $120 billion loss occurred while the stock market was up 41 percent. Poor financial performance caused the company to cut its dividend in half in late 2017, which led analysts to lower their estimates of GE's earnings.[102] An analyst at Deutsche Bank told *CNBC* he believed GE could be removed from the Dow Jones Industrial average, even though it was an original member of the 30-company index over 120 years ago.[103] Let's examine the corporate strategies underlying GE's decline.

GE'S STRATEGY UNDER JEFF IMMELT

Immelt's grand strategy was to acquire or develop high-growth businesses instead of relying on GE's traditional businesses like lighting and plastics. He started by purchasing Amersham, a British medical company, for $10 billion in 2003. Amersham specialized in making contrast agents that were injected into the body before medical scanning. GE Medical Systems was already the leading maker of imaging machines,[104] and Immelt's plan was to double down on what he believed was a growing industry by manufacturing both medical equipment and its supporting products.

Immelt simultaneously started to sell off low-growth divisions. For example, he sold GE's life and mortgage insurance business in 2005 and then sold GE Plastics to a Saudi Arabian chemical company for $11.6 billion in 2007.[105] This sale was quite controversial because GE Plastics had been a reliable source of revenue for the organization since the 1970s. Immelt wanted to invest funds from these sales into high-growth markets such as software.

Immelt established GE Digital in 2011. The hope was that this division would develop a software language that could handle information transfer between next-generation industrial machines. *Bloomberg* reported that Immelt wanted to make GE a "top 10 software company."[106] GE invested $4 billion in this effort but faced technical problems and delays with its software platform. These issues hurt GE's reputation in a fast-moving digital market.[107]

GE then purchased French gas company Alstom for over $10 billion in 2015. At the time of the purchase Immelt said, "The completion of the Alstom power and grid acquisition is another significant step in GE's transformation."[108] This investment in a natural gas company occurred at the same time renewable energy was lifting off and oil and gas prices were dropping. The result was a $3 billion reduction in GE's cash flow.[109]

Immelt's strategies may have been misguided in that they focused on investing in products and services that were not market-leading themselves but supported market-leading products. For example, GE had experienced tremendous success as a world-leading producer of commercial jet engines since the 1970s.[110] On the other hand, it had not seen great success in the leasing, financing, and servicing of these engines, which is a support function. A *Forbes* analyst commented on GE's strategies by noting that GE should be "investing in the very few things in which [it] must be either best-in-class or world class and decisively simplifying or outsourcing the things that need be only good enough." This analyst was suggesting that one of GE's strategic errors was that many of its businesses had individual strategies, but the conglomerate did not have an overarching one. He believed this level of complexity underscored the need to split up the company.[111]

Part of GE's poor performance also stemmed from leadership and organizational culture, according to *The Wall Street Journal.* The *Journal* reported that Immelt seemed to ignore the company's performance and presented a positive view, stating, "This is a strong, very strong company," in May 2017. The newspaper further reported that "this culture of confidence trickled down the ranks and even affected how those gunning to succeed Mr. Immelt ran their business units, some of these people said, with consequences that included unreachable financial targets, mistimed bets on markets and sometimes poor decisions on how to deploy cash."[112]

Welch, Immelt's predecessor, had an overarching strategy. It was to keep things simple. Welch reduced employees and closed businesses that were underperforming so they would not be a drag on profitable businesses. Growth had to be profitable. GE's vision under Welch's leadership was "Fix it, close it, or sell it."[113] Welch has taken notice of Immelt's strategy and GE's performance. *Fox Business* reports that he blames GE's poor performance on "Immelt's...inability to grow businesses while keeping costs down."[114]

A NEW CEO, A NEW STRATEGY

In 2017, GE replaced Immelt with John Flannery. Flannery came from GE Capital and is known as a "fix-it" man. His first move was to stop large-scale acquisitions such as the one with Alstom in 2015. He also announced that GE Digital would be scaled back and have a basic strategy. The subsidiary will now sell limited software to existing GE customers only. "Complexity hurts us...complexity has hurt us," says Flannery.[115]

Some investment analysts believe that complex conglomerates like GE are a 20th-century entity that has outlived its expiration date. One analyst told *Forbes* that "only closely integrated, focused companies can thrive."[116] GE seems to be heeding this advice. Flannery's strategy is to focus on fewer businesses doing fewer things. He wants to sell divisions that make up a significant part of the company's assets but are not growing profits. These include large operations in locomotive building and industrial light manufacturing.[117] The company instead plans to focus on streamlined manufacturing of jet engines and medical equipment. "If all goes well, GE will become a more mundane brand," according to a *Bloomberg* report. "It will be less about spreading the gospel of innovation, managerial excellence, or digital disruption and more about...selling as many units as possible..."[118]

Critics say that Flannery's strategy is too short term and misses the big picture. GE is a symbol of U.S. innovation and dominance. Instead of downsizing, it should find operational synergies across multiple industries. 3D printing is one way that GE can achieve this. It recently spent $200 million on creating a "brilliant factory" in India that can make products for multiple divisions. Flexible 3D printers allow the factory to quickly switch lines. If industrial lighting is not selling but air travel is in demand, the plant can switch production lines to jet engines. GE Digital can support this by interconnecting suppliers and manufacturers via software. Another *Forbes* analyst says, "Now is exactly the wrong time for GE to break up." This analyst believes a longer-term perspective, based on streamlining instead of downsizing, will prove successful.[119]

Will Flannery's strategy help GE rebound?

FOR DISCUSSION

Problem-Solving Perspective

1. What is the underlying problem in this case from CEO John Flannery's perspective?
2. What are some of the causes of this problem?
3. Can GE survive as one organization? Explain why or why not.

Application of Chapter Content

1. Explain how GE is creating a "fit" among its activities at its factory in India.
2. Using the steps in Figure 6.2, describe how GE should be transforming the way it does business.
3. Develop a SWOT analysis for GE.
4. Is CEO Flannery employing a growth, stability, or defensive strategy? Is this different than Immelt's strategy? Explain.
5. Which of Michael Porter's four competitive strategies is GE trying to follow? Explain.

Legal/Ethical Challenge

Is Your School Selling You Bank Accounts?

Colleges and universities typically earn revenue from tuition, state taxes, and donations. The contribution from state taxes has been decreasing, creating a funding problem for many colleges and universities. This challenge focuses on a new source of revenue for campuses around the United States: the selling of bank accounts to students. Wells Fargo, U.S. Bank, and other financial institutions have signed a number of deals with schools in order to promote their banking services. The strategy is for banks to come to campus and pitch their services to students, with schools receiving royalties from the banks based on the number of new accounts students open. These royalties can sometimes be as high as hundreds of thousands of dollars annually, according to *The Wall Street Journal*.[120] Do you think the schools are working on behalf of their students or the banks?

Banks may be eager to pay royalties to schools because they represent a lucrative target market–young adults often strapped for cash. Students may not have enough in their accounts to cover nonacademic expenses like trips and off-campus meals. Banks often provide overdraft protection when student accounts are a bit short. This protection actually works like a high-cost loan, and banks can raise substantial revenue from the interest and fees they charge. In fact, the Consumer Financial Protection Bureau estimates that consumers pay $17 billion in bank fees annually.[121] Students at community colleges and regional public universities tend to pay the highest average fees, with some forking over more than $70 a year.[122]

Students are receiving benefits for these fees. Many schools allow then to conveniently link their campus identification cards to banking services. Others actually allow a contracted bank to open a location on campus.

These strategic relationships also allow the banks to offer special accounts for students. For example, a U.S. Bank spokesperson said the bank wants to build long-term relationships with students "by providing them with the best student banking account in the marketplace."[123] The bank does offer a student checking account with no monthly fees, but students still incur overdraft charges and non-U.S. Bank ATM fees after the first four transactions.[124]

Banks claim that schools benefit from the arrangement just as their students do. "Schools are looking for funding," says the head of PNC's university banking program. Schools receive that funding in return for allowing banks to set up tables at campus events, advertise their products in mailings to students, and be known as the school's preferred banking option. *The Wall Street Journal* found that 112 U.S. colleges received nearly $18.7 million in 2017 for these types of activities. Much of it was in the form of royalties, but some schools even receive a cut of the banks' fees.[125]

Consumer watchdogs are concerned about schools receiving any sort of incentive from banks in return for promoting them. This concern is magnified by the troubled history of banks and universities. In the early 2000s, some financial aid offices were steering students toward loan packages that provided kickbacks to administrators. Other schools were suspected of pitching credit cards with deceptive offers or illegal incentives.[126] New laws were passed to address this bad behavior, but most do not extend to checking or debit accounts.[127]

SOLVING THE CHALLENGE

What would you do if you were a university president and a bank approached you?

1. Sign a contract that provides the university with an incentive for each account opened. Both the university and bank are providing students with special benefits. So it is all right if the school is compensated based on volume.
2. Sign a flat-fee contract only. Schools should not receive an incentive for each account opened, but they should be compensated for allowing the bank to have an increased presence on campus.
3. Refuse to sign a contract. Schools should be neutral parties and not be promoting banks.
4. Invent other options.

Uber Continuing Case connect

Learn about the process Uber uses to implement strategies and an assessment of its current reality in this case. Assess your ability to apply concepts discussed in this chapter to the case by going to Connect.

LEARNING MODULE 1

Entrepreneurship

After reading this chapter, you should be able to:

LM 1-1 Define *entrepreneurship* and discuss its importance across the world.

LM 1-2 Identify how entrepreneurs get started.

MANAGE U

So You Want to Start a Business?

We would not be surprised if you answered yes, given the data shown in Figure LM 1.1. You can see that the number of start-ups has been growing since 2000, particularly in the last few years. An exit occurs when an establishment goes from having one employee to having none, and the business remains closed for one year. All told, the growth of small businesses continues to add net new jobs to the U.S. economy.

Speaking from experience, we can tell you that owning your own business can be highly rewarding, but it's no picnic. As one *Forbes* writer noted, "Entrepreneurship is more than dreaming and innovating, it's a way of life. It's enduring long hours and late nights and the uncertainty over making ends meet. It's risk taking, mistake-making and change embracing."[1] Still interested in starting your own business?

Below are five issues to consider if you desire to start your own business:

1. Identify your motives. Are you running away from something or running toward a goal? Either is okay, but it's important to understand your motives. If you are moving toward a goal, be specific about what you want and stay open to change. For example, when your author Angelo Kinicki began his consulting activities, he started with the goal of running a sole proprietorship, and he kept his job at the university. This goal changed, as did the business decisions, when he and his wife Joyce decided to incorporate. Joyce quit her job and served as president, running the company, and Angelo took a leave of absence from his university job. After growing the business to about nine employees and traveling around the world, they realized they were unhappy and needed a change. After discharging all but one employee, Angelo went back to the university and

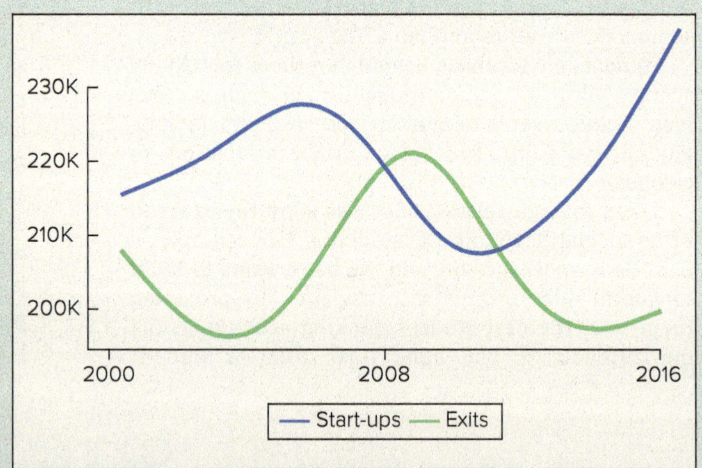

FIGURE LM 1.1 **Business start-ups and exits in the United States**

Source: "Small Business Profile," U.S. Small Business Administration Office of Advocacy, 2017, https://www.sba.gov/sites/default/files/advocacy/United_States_1.pdf.

Joyce continued to run the business with only one additional employee. The business has continued to operate this way for many years, and everybody is happy.

2. Build clients. If you are currently working and have a business idea, we encourage you to find a market or clients before quitting your job. After all, your business idea won't work if you can't find people who want your product or service. Consider providing it free until you build up market interest.[2] A friend of Angelo's is doing this as she attempts to market a new app. Her plan is to give it away, create demand, and then charge a nominal amount.

3. Practice humility. Don't assume you have all the answers. Seek input from others who have started businesses, regardless of the industry. You also might consider contacting the Small Business Association for advice and coaching. It's the mission of this organization to help small businesses to start and grow.

4. Surround yourself with the right people. Consider what Steve Jobs, cofounder of Apple, had to say about hiring the right people. "When you're in a start-up, the first ten people will determine whether the company succeeds or not. Each is ten percent of the company. So why wouldn't you take as much time as necessary to find all A-players?"[3] We couldn't agree more. Hire people who complement your skills and abilities by providing value differently than you do. Don't make the mistake of hiring only friends and family. They may be cheap and share your vision, but the company won't grow if they can't add value beyond your skill set.[4]

5. Learn the basics of accounting. All owners need to understand financial statements. These tools are discussed in Chapter 16. For now, recognize the need to understand how to create and adhere to a budget and how to read a balance sheet and income statement. We also encourage you to hire a good accountant.[5] And yes, those Introduction to Accounting courses are important!

For Discussion Have you ever thought about starting your own business? What excites you about the opportunity of starting a business, and what fears get in the way of your doing so? Explain.

FORECAST

What's Ahead in This Learning Module

This learning module considers entrepreneurship. We begin by exploring the foundation and importance of entrepreneurship, with emphasis on the personal characteristics of entrepreneurs and explaining its importance around the world. We then explore the process of starting a business. We review the basics of writing a business plan, choosing an appropriate legal structure, obtaining financing, and creating the "right" type of organizational culture and design.

1.1 Entrepreneurship: Its Foundation and Importance

THE BIG PICTURE

Entrepreneurship, a necessary attribute of business, means the taking of risks to create a new enterprise. It can increase the standard of living around the world.

LM 1-1

Define *entrepreneurship* and discuss its importance across the world.

Entrepreneurs drive innovation and growth around the world. According to *Inc.*, the 11 most famous entrepreneurs of all time include Oprah Winfrey, Walt Disney, J. K. Rowling, Steve Jobs, Andrew Carnegie, Benjamin Franklin, and Bill Gates.[6] These individuals started with an idea or passion and turned it into great wealth via hard work and entrepreneurial thinking. Elon Musk is a great example.

Multiple entrepreneur. South African–born Elon Musk was a cofounder of PayPal, which provides payment processing for online vendors. He went on to shake up the auto business with Tesla Motors, which builds electric cars; develop SpaceX, a space exploration company; and retool the energy sector with SolarCity, a residential solar energy provider. He was said to be worth $20.1 billion in 2017.[7] Musk reached an agreement with the Securities and Exchange Commission to step down as Chairman of Tesla after abandoning his effort to take Tesla private in 2018. © Chen Boyuan/Imaginechina/AP Images

Musk, born in South Africa in 1971, taught himself computer programming when he was 12. After receiving degrees in economics and physics, he pursued a doctoral degree in applied physics and material sciences at Stanford. He dropped out and started his foray into entrepreneurship. It began with cofounding Zip2, a software company acquired by Compaq for $340 million. He then founded X.co, an online payment company that merged with Confinity, which turned into PayPal, which was purchased by eBay for $1.5 billion in 2002. Great start, but it was just the beginning.

Musk used his income from these transactions to found or cofound five more companies: SpaceX, Tesla Inc., Open AI, Neuralink, and Boring Co. Like many entrepreneurs, he has a grand vision and goals. He has said that "the goals of SpaceX, Tesla, and SolarCity revolve around his vision to change the world and humanity. His goals include reducing global warming through sustainable energy production and consumption, and reducing the 'risk of human extinction' by establishing a human colony on Mars."[8] Whether you agree with or admire Musk's ambitions, he exemplifies the characteristics of an entrepreneur.

This section defines entrepreneurship and explains how it is different from self-employment. We then examine the research on characteristics of entrepreneurs and conclude by exploring why entrepreneurship is important around the world.

Entrepreneurship: It's Not the Same as Self-Employment

Most small businesses originate with entrepreneurs, the people with the idea, the risk takers. The most successful entrepreneurs become wealthy and make the covers of business magazines: Oprah Winfrey (Harpo Productions); Fred Smith (Federal Express); Larry Page and Sergey Brin (Google). Failed entrepreneurs may benefit from the experience to return and fight another day—as did Henry Ford, twice bankrupt before achieving success with Ford Motor Co.

What Is Entrepreneurship?

Although many definitions have been proposed, experts acknowledge three components of entrepreneurship. **Entrepreneurship** is a process of (a) recognizing opportunities for new venture creation or new value creation, (b) deciding to exploit these opportunities, and (c) "exploiting the opportunities by the way of new venture creation or new value creation . . . for realization of some desired value."[9] There are two types of entrepreneurs:

- An **entrepreneur** is someone who "organizes and operates a business or businesses, taking on greater than normal financial risks in order to do so."[10] Entrepreneurs start new businesses because they perceive an opportunity to introduce, change, or transform a product or service potentially desired by the market place. Steve Jobs, for example, invented the iPod and iPhone before there was any market demand.
- An **intrapreneur** is someone working inside an existing organization who sees an opportunity for a product or service and mobilizes the organization's resources to realize the idea. This person might be a researcher or a scientist but could also be a manager who sees an opportunity to create a new venture that might be profitable.

EXAMPLE An Intrapreneur: Intel's Anthropologist Genevieve Bell

If being an intrapreneur sounds more attractive than being a manager, consider this: Managers are vital to supporting the intrapreneur's efforts. Microsoft's in-house researchers, for instance, have brought forth many truly cutting-edge ideas, often beating out Apple and Google. The problem, says one analysis, is that such intrapreneurs were "not getting the buy-in from management to turn their discoveries into products," a difficulty that Microsoft's new CEO, Satya Nadella, has been urged to address.[11]

Backing In-House Risk Taking. Richard Branson, CEO of the Virgin Group, who says his 200 companies (including music and airline businesses) were built on the efforts of "a steady stream of intrapreneurs who looked for and developed opportunities," understands the importance of management support. In his view, CEO should stand for "chief enabling officer," to nurture in-house experimentation.[12]

Intel's Dr. Bell. Intel Corporation, best known for its computer chips but now anxious to move in other directions, certainly appreciates the infusion of new ideas. Indeed, it has hired anthropologist Genevieve Bell as its "director of user experience research" at Intel Labs, where she leads some 100 social scientists and designers who explore how people use technology in their homes and in public. "The team's findings help inform the company's product development process," says one report, "and are also often shared with the laptop makers, automakers, and other companies that embed Intel processors in their goods."[13]

For example, to find out how people shift back and forth between the built-in technologies in their cars and the personal mobile devices they carry, Bell and a fellow anthropologist have traveled around the world examining, photographing, and describing the contents of people's cars. They learned that, despite the fact that automakers have installed voice-command systems and other technology in their vehicles for the purpose of reducing distracted driving, drivers in traffic—especially when bored—often picked up their handheld personal devices anyway. This has led Intel to join with Jaguar Land Rover to find ways for consumers to better synchronize their personal devices with their cars.

YOUR CALL

Do you think most companies truly support intrapreneurship? Why would they not?

How Is Entrepreneurship Different from Self-Employment? Entrepreneurs and self-employed individuals share the commonality of owning a business, but they execute this role in very different ways. Let's explore these similarities and differences, starting with a definition of self-employment.

Self-employment **is a way of working for yourself "as a freelancer or the owner of a business rather than for an employer."**[14] As textbook writers, we are self-employed. We work for ourselves and hire contractors to help get things done. The same is true for many doctors, dentists, accountants, insurance agents, electricians, and general contractors. Self-employed people are frequently experts in their fields and recognized members of their communities. In contrast, recall that entrepreneurs are motivated to introduce, change, or transform a product or service potentially desired by the market place. They are more interested in innovation and business growth than self-employed individuals. Let's consider five points of comparison:

1. Self-employed people work for themselves and sometimes hire others to assist in getting things done. The success of the business lies on the shoulders of the owner. When the owner retires or quits, the business generally closes. In contrast, entrepreneurs have people who *work with them*. Employees work together as a team to accomplish the entrepreneur's vision. Success at electric car company Tesla, for example, is dependent on everyone, not just Elon Musk. This is why a company outlives the participation or ownership of an entrepreneur. Tesla will continue with or without Musk at the helm.[15]
2. Self-employed people tend to stay in one geographic area, work virtually, and prefer to avoid taking risks. Entrepreneurs, on the other hand, are global thinkers who understand the need to take and manage risk. They won't grow the business without taking calculated risks.[16] Entrepreneurs are not afraid

Launch preparation for the SpaceX Falcon Heavy rocket. © NASA/SpaceX

of failure or challenges. Musk's SpaceX program experienced quite a few failures and setbacks in its pursuit of launching the Falcon Heavy, "the fourth-highest capacity rocket ever built . . . and the most powerful rocket in operation as of 2018. The inaugural mission carried a Tesla Roadster belonging to Musk as a dummy payload."[17]

3. Self-employed owners and entrepreneurs have different mindsets. Self-employed people tend to do much of the work themselves, partly because they are experts and want to save costs to maximize profits. Your authors certainly fall into that camp. Entrepreneurs like Elon Musk, however, realize "that they can't do everything so they delegate responsibilities to people they trust, who are smarter and more experienced than them in those areas, but still keep people accountable for their actions."[18]
4. There are a number of operational differences. Although both entrepreneurs and self-employed individuals are required to create a legally recognized organization, there are a number of differences. Self-employed can incorporate or file as sole proprietors. Entrepreneurs, in contrast, have a broader set of legal requirements and insurance and tax considerations.[19]
5. The final point of comparison involves scope of interests and influence. Entrepreneurs have broader aspirations aimed at influencing industries, markets, and greater numbers of people. Elon Musk, for example, wants to change the world. Self-employed individuals are more focused on operating a business in a specific geographic area and market. Their aspirations, interests, and scope of influence are much smaller.

Characteristics of Entrepreneurs

Being an entrepreneur is what it takes to *start* a business; being a manager is what it takes to *grow or maintain* a business. As an entrepreneur or intrapreneur, you initiate new goods or services; as a manager you coordinate the resources to produce the goods or services– including, as we mentioned, the efforts of the intrapreneurs. Some of the examples of success we mentioned earlier–Oprah Winfrey (Harpo Productions) and Larry Page (Google)–are actually *both* entrepreneurs and effective managers. Other people, however, find they like the start-up part but dislike the management part. For example, Stephen Wozniak, entrepreneurial cofounder with Steve Jobs of Apple Computer, abandoned the computer industry completely and went back to college. Jobs, in contrast, went on to launch and manage another business, Pixar, which among other things, became the animation factory that made the movies *Toy Story* and *Finding Nemo*.

Do you think being an entrepreneur and being a manager require different skills? Researchers interested in this question typically compare personal characteristics of entrepreneurs with those of managers, and their answer is yes, the jobs require different skills. Although a long list of potential characteristics of entrepreneurs exists, nine are believed to be most important.[20] They are shown in Figure LM 1.2.

- **Risk propensity.** Risk taking is foundational to entrepreneurship. Managers must believe in themselves and be willing to make decisions; however, this statement applies even more to entrepreneurs. Precisely because they are willing to take risks in the pursuit of new opportunities–indeed, even to risk

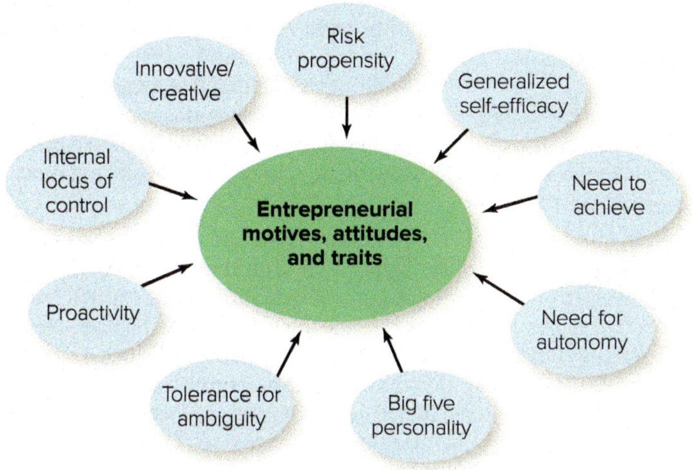

FIGURE LM 1.2
Research-based characteristics of entrepreneurs

personal financial failure—entrepreneurs need the confidence to act decisively. They prefer moderate levels of risk.

- **Generalized self-efficacy**. Generalized self-efficacy is a person's level of confidence about succeeding in different demanding situations. While managers and entrepreneurs both perform better when they have high self-efficacy, this characteristic is particularly important for entrepreneurs. They need confidence to achieve goals in a broader set of activities such as attracting customers, handling technical problems, obtaining financial funding, and adhering to governmental rules and regulations.
- **Need to achieve.** Both entrepreneurs and managers have a high need for achievement. However, entrepreneurs certainly seem to be motivated to pursue moderately difficult goals through their own efforts in order to realize their ideas and, they hope, financial rewards. Managers, by contrast, are more motivated by promotions and organizational rewards of power and perks.
- **Need for autonomy.** Although many of us prefer the freedom to act as opposed to being told what to do, entrepreneurs have a higher need for autonomy. They prefer to work for themselves, or with those they respect and admire, and they have a strong preference for shaping their own destiny. They are willing to forgo the security and comfort of working for an organization that provides stable salary and benefits. All told, entrepreneurs possess a greater need for autonomy than managers.
- **Big Five personality dimensions.** The Big Five are characteristics that psychologists have concluded define the core of our personality: they are discussed in detail in Chapter 11. The Big Five are *extroversion* (the quality of being outgoing, talkative, and sociable), *agreeableness* (being good-natured and cooperative), *conscientiousness* (being dependable, responsible, and persistent), *emotional stability* (being relaxed, secure, and even-keeled), and *openness to experience* (being imaginative, curious, and broadminded). Entrepreneurs tend to be more extroverted, conscientious, emotionally stable, and open to experiences than managers. They also are less agreeable than managers.
- **Tolerance for ambiguity.** Every manager needs to be able to make decisions based on ambiguous—that is, unclear or incomplete—information. However, entrepreneurs must have more tolerance for ambiguity because they are trying to do things that haven't been done before.

- **Proactivity**. Proactivity is a forward-looking perspective in which an individual is looking for opportunities to provide value beyond what others expect. This characteristic is desired by all organizations, but it is critical for entrepreneurs. You can't be entrepreneurial without being proactive. One academic concluded that entrepreneurial proactivity consists of "introducing new products and services ahead of the competition and acting in anticipation of future demand to create change and shape environment, thereby creating a first move advantage *vis-a-vis competitors*."[21]
- **Internal locus of control**. If you believe "I am the captain of my fate, the master of my soul," you have what is known as an internal locus of control, the belief that you control your own destiny and that external forces will have little influence. (*External locus of control* means the reverse—you believe you don't control your destiny but that external forces do.) Although both entrepreneurs and managers like to think they have personal control over their lives, entrepreneurs were found to have higher levels of internal locus than managers.[22]
- **Innovative/creative ability.** *Innovation* leads to the creation of something new that makes money, while *creativity* produces new ideas about products, services, processes, and procedures. These definitions highlight that both innovation and creativity are fundamental to entrepreneurship. Entrepreneurs are generally more innovative and creative than others.[23]

So where do you stand? Do you think you would like to be an entrepreneur? The following self-assessment was created to provide you with feedback about your entrepreneurial orientation, should your instructor assign it to you.

SELF-ASSESSMENT LM1.1 CAREER READINESS

To What Extent Do You Possess an Entrepreneurial Spirit?

Please be prepared to answer these questions if your instructor has assigned Self-Assessment LM1.1 in Connect.

How motivated are you to be an entrepreneur, to start your own company? Do you have the aptitudes and attitudes possessed by entrepreneurs? This self-assessment allows you to compare your motivations, aptitudes, and attitudes with those found in a sample of entrepreneurs from a variety of industries. Go to connect.mheducation.com and take the self-assessment. When you're done, answer the following questions:

1. To what extent are your motives, aptitudes, and attitudes similar to those of entrepreneurs? Explain.
2. Based on your results, where are you most different from entrepreneurs in individual motives, aptitudes, and attitudes?
3. What do these gaps suggest about your entrepreneurial spirit? Discuss.
4. What things might you say during a job interview to demonstrate that you possess entrepreneurial characteristics? Explain.

Entrepreneurship Matters across the Globe

Entrepreneurship continues to be an economic generator across industries and countries around the world. The United States was recently ranked the best environment for cultivating entrepreneurship across 138 countries, according to the Global Entrepreneurship and Development Index.[24] In this section, we discuss the importance of entrepreneurship from the perspective of start-ups, innovation, job creation, and global experience.

Start-Ups Generate Wealth and Economic Development Most of the get-rich stories we hear these days are about technology start-ups, such as Facebook, Yelp, Foursquare, and Uber. A **start-up** is a newly created company designed to grow fast.[25] But all kinds of new endeavors are constantly being launched. Not all rely on technology, and not all are intended to quickly become big. What all new start-ups do have in common is that they are driven by an individual or group that relies on entrepreneurial thinking.

Here are some of the best new start-ups from 2017.[26] Essential, founded by Andy Rubin (who created Android), was started to compete with Apple's iPhone and Samsung's Galaxy. Brandless, headquartered in San Francisco, is an e-commerce company selling consumer packaged goods under its own label for a single price of $3. The company is betting that people care more about price than about brand names. Nomadic VR is creating virtual reality arcades. Based in San Rafael, California, the founders believe VR will become a big draw for consumers' entertainment spending. DeepMap, founded by a group of ex-Googlers, is building maps for self-driving vehicles. VoiceOps, founded by Nate Becker, Daria Evdikimova, and Ethan Barhydt, "designed a machine learning-powered system that monitors calls made by enterprise sales teams."[27] It enables managers to engage in customized sales coaching.

Apple world headquarters in Cupertino, California. © Valeriya Zankovych/Alamy Stock Photo

While these businesses have so far remained small, others have experienced rapid growth. *Business Insider* identified 15 start-ups that began operating after 2011 and are now valued at over $1 billion each. They include Udacity's nanodegree programs, Vox Media, the Internet of Things company Uptake, fantasy sports site DraftKings, Amazon wannabe Jet, and health insurance company Oscar. Skilled entrepreneurship is driving the success of each firm.[28]

Entrepreneurship Drives Innovation Innovation is the fuel for economic development, and it represents the foundation of entrepreneurial activities. Entrepreneurs and entrepreneurial firms propose and create new products and services sold around the world. **Patents**, licenses with which the government authorizes a person or company to exclude others from making using or selling an invention for a time, protect innovations. Small businesses, defined by the U.S. Small Business Administration (SBA) as those having fewer than 500 employees, are the form of business with which most entrepreneurs enter a market.[29] Small firms in turn are the primary source of patent creation in the United States. They generated 16.5 times as many patents as large firms in 2007, according to the SBA.[30] This is probably one reason for the increased sales and profitability growth of U.S. small businesses in both 2016 and 2017.[31] Table LM1.1 reveals some interesting facts about small businesses in the United States.

Entrepreneurship Drives Job Creation How often do we hear politicians run on a platform promising job creation? It's standard these days because job creation is good for citizens, communities, states, and countries. Historical figures show that small businesses employ about 50 percent of all private-sector employees, and they created 63.3 percent of net new jobs from 1992 to 2013.[32] This data confirms the importance of entrepreneurial firms.

TABLE LM 1.1
Factoids about Small Businesses

• 36.3% of small businesses are owned by women.
• 19.3% of small businesses are family owned.
• 50% of small businesses are home-based.
• 80% of entrepreneurs use their own money to start their business.
• 39.2% of small business owners have at least a bachelor's degree.
• 19% of small business owners work at least 60+ hours per week.
• 64% think it is their duty to have a positive social and economic impact.
• 62% of the U.S.'s 585 billionaries are self-made.
• 23 million small businesses in the U.S. have no employees.
• 99.9% of all firms in the U.S. are small businesses.
• 66% of firms survive two years; 50% survive five years; and 33% survive 10 years.
• 30% of all new small businesses are started by immigrants.

Source: Data taken from "U.S. Small Business Administration: Office of Advocacy," Frequently Asked Questions, *June 2016; H. Kanapi, "15 Entrepreneurship Statistics That You Should Know,"* Fit Small Business, *July 30, 2017, https://fitsmallbusiness.com/entrepreneurship-statistics/; G. Schmid, "17 Statistics Every Business Owner Needs to Be Aware Of,"* Fundera Leger, *July 19, 2017, https://www.fundera.com/blog/small-business-statistics; and A Furnham, "Why Immigrants Make Such Good Entrepreneurs,"* The Wall Street Journal, *November 27, 2017, p. R4.*

Entrepreneurship Improves the World's Standard of Living The **standard of living is the level of "necessaries, comforts and luxuries which a person is accustomed to enjoy."**[33] Clearly, entrepreneurial job creation improves standards of living around the world by transferring profits from the business to employees (in the form of pay) and thus to communities as employees are better able to make purchases that maintain or improve their material life. So what is the status of entrepreneurial activity around the globe? The annual Global Entrepreneurship Monitor (GEM) has been studying global entrepreneurship for 18 consecutive years. Its 2017 report is a summary of more than 200,000 interviews with people from 54 countries. The good news is that entrepreneurial activity is positively perceived and actively pursued around the world. About 70 percent of respondents to the survey report that entrepreneurs are well regarded and enjoy high status in their countries. Most people also believe that starting a business is a good career choice. These two statistics suggest that people around the world are interested in starting a business. In support of this conclusion, the report shows that roughly 13.5 percent of adults have started or have been running a business in the last 3.5 years.[34]

1.2 Starting a Business

THE BIG PICTURE

Businesses start with an idea for a new product or service. Entrepreneurs then undertake a series of activities to build the foundation for getting the business off the ground. These activities include writing a business plan, choosing the company's legal structure, and arranging for financing. Once this foundation has been built, the job of building an organizational culture and design further helps the business take off.

LM 1-2

Identify how entrepreneurs get started.

Have you ever had an idea for a product that did not exist? Many of us do in the course of life as we encounter situations in which some device would help us accomplish a task or make us happy. Lowell Wood is a good example. He became the most prolific inventor in U.S. history when he received his 1,085th patent from the U.S. Patent and Trademark Office in 2015.

Wood is an astrophysicist, a self-taught paleontologist, and a computer scientist. He works hard at being creative. He told *Bloomberg Businessweek* that he "often failed or received the lowest score on the first exam given in a particular course and improved his marks through repetition and intense effort." He credits his ability to come up with new ideas and find creative solutions to problems to the amount of reading he does. He religiously reads three dozen academic journals from varying fields of study, a habit he learned from chemist and author Linus Pauling. Wood asked Pauling how he comes up with all his great ideas. Pauling said, "There's really nothing to it all. You just read, and you remember what you read."[35] Wood is currently working on developing a one-time universal vaccine. He hopes such a vaccine would enable us "to grab a newborn—literally right out of the uterus—pinch its thigh and push the stuff in, and all their pediatric vaccinations are done."[36]

Lowell Wood © Alex Wong/Getty Images News//Getty Images

Businesses Start with an Idea

Some people might not be as creative as Lowell Wood, but we all have the potential to come up with a viable business idea. The following actions can assist any aspiring entrepreneur to uncover a business idea.

1. **Identify your passions, skills, and talents.** Your author Angelo Kinicki and his wife Joyce started a consulting business that built on their passions, skills, and experience. The idea was conceived from their love of teaching and helping others to learn and develop. Joyce had extensive experience and skills in human resource management, and Angelo was a proven academic who could easily explain complicated concepts to managers. They put their skills together to offer services targeted at assisting companies in developing and achieving strategic plans. They also engage in leadership development programs for aspiring managers. The company has operated for more than 30 years. The takeaway is that your past experience and in-depth knowledge about an industry are great sources of new business ideas.[37]
2. **Identify a problem or frustration.** Chris Tidmarsh started Green Bridge Growers, "a commercial greenhouse in north central Indiana that provides herbs, lettuces and nasturtiums to local restaurants, and sunflowers and cosmos to florists," with his mother and cofounder Jan Pilarski. Tidmarsh has three college degrees from Hope College: chemistry, environmental studies, and French. He was diagnosed with autism during preschool and struggled to find meaningful employment after college. He started the company because his job as an environmental researcher ended due to his difficulty communicating with others, and he wanted to use his passion and knowledge about agriculture. The

problem was finding an employer and work role that benefited from his background and interpersonal style. To make it work, Tidmarsh's mom does the administrative activities like accounting, marketing, and sales. "He perfects the spacing between rows of kale and spinach, and keeps close tabs on water chemistry and soil acidity. He spends hours researching natural and effective pesticides to deal with aphids. The solution: 4,500 ladybugs." The company is doing well, with revenue of $80,000 and profit of $30,000 in fiscal year 2018. Tidmarsh plans to expand so he can reach his goal of $220,000 in sales by 2020.[38]

3. **Identify an opportunity or need**. Do you see any opportunities associated with the $1.2 billion people spend online? Brothers Patrick and John Collison did. They started Stripe Inc. in 2010 to help companies process their online transactions. The brothers built "software that businesses could plug into websites and apps to instantly connect with credit card and banking systems and receive payments. The product was a hit with Silicon Valley start-ups. Businesses such as Lyft, Facebook, DoorDash, and thousands that aspired to be like them turned Stripe into the financial backbone of their operations," according to *Bloomberg Businessweek*.[39] The company processes close to 50 billion online transactions annually, charging a small fee for each one. Patrick (28) and John (26) are among the youngest billionaires in the world.

Finding opportunities takes time, focus, and motivation. You first have to be looking for them. Jeff Bezos, who was a stock market researcher and hedge fund manager, followed Internet usage as part of his job. He decided to start Amazon when he realized that the surge in Internet usage provided an opportunity for online retailing. You can also find opportunities by considering markets that are not being served. Pay attention to current events and societal trends.[40] For instance, the development of mobile devices triggered an opportunity for Uber's founders Garret Camp and Travis Kalanick. While searching for a cab in Paris, they realized the need to create an app that would hail a vehicle. The rest is history.

Are you a glass half full or half empty kind of person? Entrepreneurs are more likely to see opportunity when others see challenges. ©Elenathewise/Getty Images

4. **Study customer complaints.** Customer complaints are a warning sign that something is wrong with a product or service. Thus they represent an opportunity to improve the offering. Consider Apple's response to the way iPhone batteries degraded as the product aged. To prolong the devices' lives, Apple used software controls to slow them down. Users were furious! The company decided to replace batteries in older phones for a reduced price instead and to provide more information about battery life within iOS.[41] We suspect this problem has also made its way to the design engineers working on the issue of battery life. Perhaps it will lead to a breakthrough idea.

Writing the Business Plan

A business plan is much more than a funding plan. It also answers critical questions such as, "What business are we in?" "What is our vision and where are we going?" and "What will we do to achieve our goals?" *Harvard Business Review* noted that "A plan helps detail how the opportunity is to be seized, what success looks like, and what resources are required, and it can be key to the investment decisions of angel investors, banks, and venture capitalists."[42] A good plan also attracts high-quality talent.[43]

There are two camps regarding the value of creating a business plan. The first believes that entrepreneurs "learn by doing" and that planning is a waste of time because it takes effort away from doing, improvising, and pivoting. The idea is that the future is ever changing and unknown, and planning doesn't lead to more control. The other camp, in contrast, believes structured planning provides the foundation entrepreneurs need to launch a business, organize resources, hire employees, and achieve results.[44] Which perspective sounds more reasonable to you?

Researchers have addressed this question. A recent six-year study of 1,000 would-be U.S. entrepreneurs compared planning practices and firm performance across one group that wrote formal plans and a second group that did not. The groups were balanced so that they were "statistical twins." Findings showed that entrepreneurs who planned were 16 percent more likely to survive than their identical non-planning cohorts. Entrepreneurs tended to plan when the company was a high-growth-oriented start-up and when they were seeking funding.[45] All told, it pays to plan.

The components of a business plan vary, and people disagree about the level of detail to be included. Some suggest a one-page plan,[46] but the general sentiment is that a longer plan is needed to cover the following areas:[47]

- **Executive summary.** This section is like a two-minute elevator speech about the business. It provides conclusions and wraps up everything else in the plan. People generally write this section last so it can include important information from other sections.
- **Business description.** The business description helps people connect with your vision by outlining the business, its mission, vision, product or service, and the reason you started it. You should also conduct an analysis of your strengths, weaknesses, opportunities, and threats (SWOT analysis, discussed in Chapter 6). It's also recommended that you identify the principals in the business and the legal structure you will use.
- **Market analysis.** The market analysis reviews information about the market you are trying to enter, your competitors, where you fit in the market, how your product or service is unique, and the level of market share you expect to obtain. You should also analyze trends in your market area and industry and discuss profiles of "ideal" customers and any additional market research that supports the validity of your idea.
- **Organization and management.** It's time to show off the talent of the management team and any special employees, such as a well-known technical expert, in the section on organization and management. Investors want to understand the talents of key team members and their previous successes. It's also useful to discuss the type of organizational culture and structure you think best positions the business for success.
- **Sales strategies.** The section on sales strategies reviews your ideas for marketing or promoting the product or service, your pricing strategy, your strategies for using the web and social media, and other activities for building brand awareness.
- **Funding requirements.** Now it's time to ask for the money you need to get this business running or to expand. Be realistic when you outline your funding requirements, and set a range if you are unsure about exact future costs. Provide a timeline that links funding to expansion activities. You want to provide investors with realistic expectations.
- **Financial projections.** Finally, develop revenue projections and conduct a cash flow statement. It's critical to identify your current financial needs and those expected in the future. Your revenue growth should be based on other information contained in the plan such as market trends, sales strategies, and human resource needs.

Choosing a Legal Structure

Your choice of a legal structure is one of the most important you will make as an entrepreneur. The reason is that this decision affects everything from the taxes you'll pay to your legal liability and control over the company. As we review the options, keep in mind that your choice depends on your personal and financial goals. Let's consider the four basic business entities: sole proprietorship, partnership, corporation, and limited liability (LLC).[48]

Sole Proprietorship The Internal Revenue Service defines a **sole proprietor** as "someone who owns an unincorporated business by himself or herself."[49] It's the simplest form of business structure. The sole proprietor gets to make all the decisions and has total control over the business. The key drawback, however, is that the owner has unlimited liability. If someone sues, the owner's personal and business assets are put at risk. Angelo Kinicki uncovered one key downside to this structure. It was hard to get financial backing for his consulting business when it operated as a sole proprietorship. Banks did not like the liability risk and would not lend them money to grow the business.

Partnership The Internal Revenue Service defines a **partnership** as a relationship "between two or more persons who join to carry on a trade or business. Each person contributes money, labor or skill, and expects to share in the profits and losses of the business."[50] Partnerships generally begin with a common interest or experience. François Pelen is a good example. He left his position as a VP at Pfizer to start Groupe Point Vision with Patrice Pouts and Raphael Schnitzer, two fellow MBA students at HEC Paris. *Forbes* reported that these three "built the business plan for Groupe Point Vision within the HAC incubator, and now have 25 centers, over a million patients, and annual revenue of more than $60 million."[51]

A partnership is an unincorporated business and there are two types: general and limited. In a *general partnership*, the partners equally share all profits and losses. In *limited partnerships*, "only one partner has control of its operation, while the other person or persons simply contribute to and receive only part of the profit."[52] This structure works well when you want to start a business with a family member or a friend. The drawbacks are the unlimited liability of the partners and the risk of disagreements between them. Income and losses are "passed through" to the partners' individual taxable incomes.

Corporation A **corporation** is an entity that is separate from its owners, meaning "it has its own legal rights, independent of its owners—it can sue, be sued, own and sell property, and sell the rights of ownership in the form of stocks."[53] There are two key types of corporations: C corporations and S corporations.

- C corporations are owned by shareholders and are taxed as separate entities. The Internal Revenue Service (IRS) states that this type of corporation "realizes net income or loss, pays taxes and distributes profits to shareholders. The profit of a corporation is taxed to the corporation when earned, and is taxed to the shareholders when distributed as dividends. This creates a double tax."[54] The benefit to the entrepreneur is that the legal entity and thus any liability exist separately from any individual owner of the business.
- S corporations "are corporations that elect to pass corporate income, losses, deductions, and credits through to their shareholders for federal tax purposes. Shareholders of S corporations report the flow-through of income and losses on their personal tax returns and are assessed at their individual income tax rates. This allows S corporations to avoid double taxation on the corporate income."[55] The benefit of an S corporation is that owners have limited

liability and don't incur corporate tax. S-corps were the legal structure most frequently used by entrepreneurs in 2017, according to the National Small Business Association.[56]

Limited Liability Company (LLC) A **limited liability company (LLC)** is a hybrid structure that combines elements of sole proprietor, partnership, and corporation. Each state may have different regulations regarding an LLC. "Limited liability means that its owners, also called members, are usually not personally responsible for the LLC's debts and lawsuits. . . . In the eyes of the IRS, LLC taxes usually resemble a sole proprietorship or partnership. The LLC does not pay income taxes itself: instead, the owners list business profits and losses on their personal tax returns."[57] Benefits of LLCs include fewer recordkeeping and reporting requirements than for corporations. LLCs were the second most frequently employed legal structure in 2017.[58]

Conclusions You should not make a decision about the legal structure of a new business by yourself. The preceding information does not provide enough details for you to decide on your own. You want to obtain professional advice. The Kinickis, for instance, relied on the combined advice of their accountant and their attorney when deciding to transition their consulting company from a sole proprietorship to an S corporation. Our discussion here is not intended to provide all the information you need to start a business. We want to provide enough detail to enable you to ask good questions should you consider entrepreneurship.

Obtaining Financing

Whether they need equipment to start a small landscape business or a large investment to drive growth for a financial software firm like the Collison brothers' Stripe Inc., all entrepreneurs must eventually obtain financing. The amount depends on the nature of the business. An estimate by the Wells Fargo Business index, for example, put average start-up cost at $10,000, whereas the Kauffman Firm Survey suggests that $80,000 is a more accurate assessment.[59]

The availability of financing to start or grow a business can make the difference between pursuing an entrepreneurial dream and giving up. The National Association of Small Businesses (NBSA), for example, found that 28% of businesses surveyed in 2017 were not able to receive adequate financing to run.[60] The lack of funding adversely affected 47% of these businesses.[61]

Below is a summary of financing options for start-ups:[62]

- **Personal funding.** A large percentage of entrepreneurs use their own savings or credit cards to initially fund a business. Banks like to see entrepreneurs invest in their own firms before they ask for a loan.
- **Family and friends (aka "love money").** Friends, parents, and other relatives are another common source of funding. You should expect to repay these loans as the business grows. Be careful when borrowing from or going into business with family and friends because people often have a hard time separating personal and business relationships.
- **Bank loans.** Bank loans were the most frequently used source of financing in 2017, according to the NBSA, used by 64 percent of surveyed entrepreneurs. Banks generally want to see a good business plan and personal guarantees before they will lend. Entrepreneurs frequently use their homes as collateral for bank loans. The Small Business Association is another good source of loan financing. The mission of the SBA is to help "Americans start, build and grow businesses. Through an extensive network of field offices and partnerships with public and private organizations, SBA delivers its services to people

How much money do you think it takes to start a business? Census data show that 40% of new businesses were started with under $5,000.
©Palto/Shutterstock

throughout the United States, Puerto Rico, the U.S. Virgin Islands and Guam."[63] The SBA provides loans, "loan guarantees, contracts, counseling sessions and other forms of assistance to small businesses." It provides "an array of financing from the smallest needs in microlending–to substantial debt and equity investment capital (venture capital)."[64]

- **Venture capital.** **Venture capitalists (VCs) exchange funds for an ownership share in the company.** They generally look for high-growth potential in industries like information technology, biotechnology, and communication and desire a high return on their investment. VCs essentially invest money for a share in controlling the company. This can include "the right to supervise the company's management practices" and "often involves a seat on the board of directors and assurance of transparency."[65]

Making a pitch to VCs is critical for those entrepreneurs needing a larger investment. The process begins with a business plan and a formal presentation. Lakshmi Balachandra worked at two VC firms and observed a number of these entrepreneurial presentations. She wondered why some proposals looked so good on paper and then turned into nonstarters based on presentations. She spent 10 years studying these dynamics.

Dr. Balachandra is now a professor at Babson College and is publishing insights from her research. They include the following:

1. Entrepreneurs are more successful getting financing when they laugh during pitches.
2. Entrepreneurs are more likely to get financing when they have friends or acquaintances in common with the VCs.
3. Judges prefer a calmer demeanor then over-the-top passion and excitement. People apparently equate calmness with effective leadership.
4. Interest in a start-up was due more to the entrepreneur's character and trustworthiness than to perceptions of competence.
5. Gender stereotypes play a role in investment decisions. People displaying stereotypically female behaviors such as warmth, sensitivity, and expressiveness were less likely than others to get funded.[66]

- **Angels.** **Angel investors are wealthy individuals or retired executives who invest in small firms.** "They are often leaders in their own field who do not only contribute their experience and network of contacts but also their technical and/or management knowledge. Angels tend to finance the early stages of the business with investments in the order of $25,000 to $100,000."[67] They like to mentor would-be entrepreneurs and thus prefer those who are responsive to feedback.[68]
- **Crowd investing.** **Crowd investing allows a group of people—the crowd—to invest in an entrepreneur or business online.** The investors can take either an equity position in which they exchange money for stock or ownership in the company, or they can engage in debt investing by making a loan to the business.[69]

Creating the "Right" Organizational Culture and Design

At this stage in starting a business, the entrepreneur has a viable idea for a new or improved product and service, an established legal structure, a physical location in which to operate, and some level of financing. It's now time to decide on the type of organizational culture and design to adopt. These are important decisions because they affect employee behavior and performance across the individual, group, and organizational levels.

All entrepreneurs learn that they can't complete all tasks alone. They need people. At the early stages of a business, entrepreneurs tend to hire people they trust or who have values similar to their own. This group frequently includes family, friends, or experts in the industry. People generally get along and the excitement and interest in the new business drives motivation and performance. As the business grows, however, the founder or founders need to hire people with different skills, who may bring with them values and beliefs a little different from those of the current workforce. This is where organizational culture and design start to exert their influence on the business's success.

Organizational culture, discussed in detail in Chapter 8, helps the business articulate its own values and beliefs, which generally flow from the founder's. There are different types of organizational culture, and the entrepreneur needs to identify the type that best fits the organization's vision and strategies, and his or her leadership style.[70] The business's evolving culture matters because it will influence employees' work attitudes and performance outcomes such as level of customer satisfaction, market share, operational efficiency, product/service quality, innovation, and financial performance.[71]

Organizational design, discussed in Chapter 8, is the process of designing the optimal structure of accountability and responsibility an organization will use to execute its strategies. In many small firms, the structure tends to form haphazardly and is rather simple. People pick up tasks as needed and there are no clear reporting relationships. This is feasible at first, but it quickly becomes dysfunctional as the business grows.

Growth brings the need for better organization and decision making. Like its culture, an organization's structure needs to fit the vision and strategies the business is pursuing. Chapter 8 discussed eight different organizational designs entrepreneurs might choose to organize the business. In the end, this decision can be difficult for entrepreneurs because they now must contend with sharing power, control, and decision making.

The Example box reviews the process Amanda Johnson used when transitioning from being an hourly employee to starting her own business. It illustrates many of the decisions entrepreneurs make as they start and grow a business.

EXAMPLE Amanda Johnson Starts and Grows a Business

My dream was to be a big-time writer, so I majored in journalism at Arizona State University. In preparation for my writing career, I had a part-time job and freelanced whenever possible. Then life happened.

I got married during my last semester at school, purchased a home, and thought I'd settle into freelancing as the thing I'd be doing for the rest of my life. Then my husband was laid off and we found we were expecting our first child. I felt the weight of growing bills and lack of health care. Did I want to give up freelancing and my flexible schedule to try to find something more stable, only to have to take maternity leave? Would I be able to work *and* afford day care? Did I really want to go into a full-time career while my daughter was little? Should I give up on my dream of being independent?

Courtesy Amanda Johnson

I'd always been creative and used those skills while working in a flower shop during college. I now found myself wondering whether I could turn back to flowers and somehow turn that passion into a viable source of income. We certainly needed the money.

Local shops were hiring but wanted only "designers" with years of experience. One shop admitted it was cautious about bringing me on since I'd be having a baby in the spring and might not be able to work on Valentine's Day! I started thinking about opening my own flower shop.

I knew what I loved about the flower shop I'd worked in during college: weddings, proms, and events. I loved the creative challenge and fun designs. I knew, too, what I didn't love: working holidays such as Valentine's Day and Mother's Day. Customers can be grouchy, and flowers have been getting more expensive. I also knew starting a flower shop required a lot of overhead—renting a space, hiring employees—and I didn't have a lot of money to spend.

Frustrated after trying to find work in a shop and weighing the pros and cons of being away from home while caring for our daughter, I decided to start my business. Strategically, I decided to focus only on wedding and event design. I kept the operation small by working with couples having small weddings so that I could easily design in the kitchen of my home. I invested in a small floral cooler. I named my company Butterfly Petals.

I'd always loved butterflies and, after an exhaustive search of available business names, I found "Petals" was the only floral-related word left! I started as a sole proprietorship. I didn't know the ins and outs of the business side at the time, and this was the fastest way to get up and running. I registered my business name and contacted floral suppliers to set up wholesale accounts. I knew from planning my own wedding that there were local bridal-focused magazines and websites. I started with free wedding websites and basic profiles. I purchased flowers and created fun, desert-inspired bouquets. I took my own photos and put together a very basic website. Then I hustled. I brought arrangements to venues, dropped my cards in bridal salons.

There was a lot on the line since I was using my personal income to finance this new venture. I met clients at my dining room table or drove to various coffee shops to meet them during their lunch breaks. It took time and a few trusting clients, but I had my first bookings shortly after my daughter was born.

I realized I needed help managing taxes and other business issues, so I hired a professional bookkeeper. One of the recommendations was to switch from a sole proprietorship to an LLC in order to protect myself personally from the company's debts. The company grew over the next few years. I started creating events for clients with large wedding parties and higher table counts. The flowers and supplies took over, and I could no longer keep the work in my home. I had to decide whether I wanted the overhead of a studio space and employees to help with the demand. I was worried that my little company could not support me and the additional costs.

On the other hand, I thought revenue would grow if I brought on extra team members because we could take on multiple weddings and events on the same weekend. I also believed moving the company out of my house would lead wedding and event professionals to take me more seriously, creating a bigger pipeline of customers. I thus decided to rent my first studio, purchase additional inventory, and hire part-time employees. By this time, the business was able to support the costs and still provide me with income. After two years, it was time to look for *another, larger* space!

This will be our 13th year. I'm operating out of my third and largest studio space. I have a massive rental inventory of vases, containers, and candle holders. We design multiple events every weekend and have corporate clients and standing orders throughout the week. I learned to delegate and share my design knowledge with key members of my team so we can take on larger-scale work and more events to keep the company afloat during the off-season. It's been an incredible ride. I never thought my little idea to bring in some extra income would become this successful business.

Courtesy of Amanda Johnson

Key Terms Used in This Learning Module

Key Points

LM1.1 Entrepreneurship: Its Foundation and Importance

- Entrepreneurship, a necessary attribute of business, is the process of recognizing and exploiting opportunities.
- Two types of entrepreneurship are entrepreneurs and intrapreneurs.
- Entrepreneurship is different from self-employment.
- Nine research-based characteristics of entrepreneurs are risk propensity, generalized self-efficacy, need to achieve, need for autonomy, Big Five personality, tolerance for ambiguity, proactivity, internal locus of control, and innovative/creative ability.
- Entrepreneurship matters around the globe because it (1) generates wealth and economic development, (2) drives innovation, (3) drives job creation, and (4) improves the world's standard of living.

LM1.2 Starting a Business

- All businesses start with an idea. Ideas come from four sources: (1) the entrepreneur's passions, skills, and talents; (2) a problem or frustration; (3) an opportunity or need; and (4) customer complaints.
- Business plans help set the direction of a new business. They answer questions such as "What business are we in?" "What is our vision and where are we going?" and "What will we do to achieve our goals?"
- A business plan is used in the process of obtaining funding.
- There are four fundamental legal structures entrepreneurs can use when starting a business: sole proprietorship, partnership, corporation, and limited liability company (LLC).
- There are a variety of funding sources entrepreneurs use to start and grow their new business. They include personal funding, loans from family and friends, bank loans, venture capital, angel investors, and crowd investing.
- Entrepreneurs need to establish an organizational culture and design that fit the vision and strategies being pursued by the new business.

7 Individual and Group Decision Making

How Managers Make Things Happen

After reading this chapter, you should be able to:

LO 7-1 Compare rational and nonrational decision making.

LO 7-2 Explain how managers can make decisions that are both legal and ethical.

LO 7-3 Describe how evidence-based management and business analytics contribute to decision making.

LO 7-4 Compare four decision-making styles.

LO 7-5 Identify barriers to rational decision making and ways to overcome them.

LO 7-6 Outline the basics of group decision making.

LO 7-7 Describe how to develop the career readiness competencies of *critical thinking/problem solving and decision making.*

FORECAST *What's Ahead in This Chapter*

We begin by distinguishing between rational and nonrational decision making, and we describe two nonrational models. We next discuss ethical decision making. We then consider evidence-based decision making and the use of analytics. Next we describe general decision-making styles. We follow by considering how individuals respond to decision situations and nine common decision-making biases. We then shift gears by examining group decision making and group problem-solving techniques. We conclude with a Career Corner that focuses on how you can develop the career readiness competencies of *critical thinking/problem solving* and *decision making.*

MANAGE U

How to Make Good Decisions

"If we're not making mistakes, we're not trying hard enough." Those are the words with which Coca-Cola's new CEO, James Quincey, recently addressed his rank-and-file managers.[1] Making mistakes is always a possibility, but that can't stop you from making decisions. And you can learn from the result, which will help you hone your career readiness competencies of critical thinking/problem solving and decision making. So how do you make good decisions? This chapter will discuss several kinds of decisions and different models for decision making. But here are a few general guidelines that apply to any formal or informal decision process.

Keep Your Mind Open

If you make prejudgments about a situation rather than keeping an open mind, you risk acting on your biases rather than on the facts. As one business writer says about decision making, "Without maintaining an open mind any formal process that you use will amplify the old adage, 'garbage in, garbage out.' "[2] In other words, to make good decisions you need to be ready to take in all valid information, even if it contradicts or questions your own beliefs and experience. (Just because you don't agree with something, that doesn't make it wrong.) The same writer also counsels avoiding the logical flaw called "information bias," in which you consider only information that supports assumptions you've already made.

Use your communication skills to become a good and patient listener and, with your proactive learning orientation, load up on new facts and information. Don't decide the outcome ahead of time, either. It's sometimes easy to assume a decision will not turn out well, or a problem will remain unsolved. Taking a positive approach instead can only improve your decision making.[3]

Prioritize Your Decisions

Sometimes you may have to make multiple decisions, and all within a limited time. Some may be large and some small. How do you effectively manage this task? Here are four steps to help you prioritize decisions and get to the important ones first.[4]

1. List the decisions you need to make over the relevant time period. Perhaps over the next six months you need to decide where and how to begin your job search, whether to buy a new car, and what to do with the belongings you left at home when you moved to your dorm or apartment. Make sure your list is complete and that you've identified the information you need to make each decision, such as the size of your budget for buying a car and the average price for the model you want.

2. Characterize each decision according to its complexity and magnitude. Who or what is affected by each, and how much do you need in terms of tools and information to make your choice? The more ramifications and the more information needed, the larger and more complex the decision.

3. Organize your decisions into three categories: *Strategic decisions,* like deciding how to frame your job search, will require the most time and attention, can affect the largest number of people, and probably also require you to gather the most information. *Significant decisions* demand less energy and information but are still important. Whether to buy a new car might fit into this category. Finally, *quick decisions* are the least complex you face, require the least input, and can often be resolved if you apply a simple rule. Deciding what old belongings to keep, throw out, or give away falls into this category.

4. Note the timing for each decision. If you've done the first three steps, this one should be easy. For instance, you may need to complete (not just start) your job search before you can buy a car or even know whether you need one.

Move on from Your Mistakes

If a decision doesn't turn out as well as you'd hoped, start by forgiving yourself. Solving problems and making decisions are skills everyone can practice and get better at. Next, review the steps you took to arrive at your decision, and if it's not already clear what went wrong, try to identify the weak spot in your process. Did you get too little information, or fail to consider opposing viewpoints? Did you spend too much time on quick decisions and not enough on strategic or significant ones? If the problem is one you can remedy, congratulations. You've just learned something, and you've improved your career readiness skills too. Now move on!

For Discussion Are you able to make the tough decisions effective managers have to make? What other kinds of decision-making tools do you think would be helpful to you? Can you describe an instance in which you were badly mistaken about something or someone? What did you do?

7.1 Two Kinds of Decision Making: Rational and Nonrational

THE BIG PICTURE

Decision making, the process of identifying and choosing alternative courses of action, may be rational, but often it is nonrational. Four steps in making a rational decision are (1) identify the problem or opportunity, (2) think up alternative solutions, (3) evaluate alternatives and select a solution, and (4) implement and evaluate the solution chosen. Two examples of nonrational models of decision making are (1) satisficing and (2) intuition.

LO 7-1

Compare rational and nonrational decision making.

The subject of decisions and decision making is a fascinating one that is at the heart of what managers and leaders do. A writer for *Forbes* noted that "you cannot separate leadership from decisioning . . . the outcome of a leader's choices and decisions can, and usually will, make or break them."[5] And this is why decision making is one of the KSAOs you will need to be career-ready.

A decision is a choice made from among available alternatives. Decision making is the process of identifying and choosing alternative courses of action.

If your company's product is in first place in its market and making a lot of money, is that a sign of great decision making? Consider the decisions that framed success at Starbucks.

EXAMPLE — Crisis Leading to the Strategic-Management Process: Starbucks Reclaims Its Soul

Among the many things that Starbucks has going for it is this: It survived a near-death experience.[6]

Starbucks' executive CEO, Howard Schultz, joined the Seattle-based company as marketing director in 1982, when it was a small chain selling coffee equipment. Over nearly two decades, he gained control of the firm and, inspired by the coffee houses of Europe, transformed it into a comfortable "third place" between home and work, a place with a neighborhood feel selling fresh-brewed by-the-cup lattes and cappuccinos. By 2000, Starbucks (named for the first mate of the whaling ship in Herman Melville's *Moby Dick*) had become the world's largest specialty coffee retailer, with 3,501 stores, 78 percent of them in the United States.[7]

Starbucks in India The world's biggest coffee chain launched its first Indian outlet in October 2012 in an upscale part of Mumbai. ©Punit Paranjpe/AFP/Getty Images

Shultz Steps Down the First Time Schultz stepped down as CEO in 2000 (remaining the board's chair), and for a while the business continued to thrive. Then two things happened that provoked a crisis. First, the company "lost a certain soul," says Schultz, as management became more concerned with profits than with store atmosphere and company values and extended existing product lines rather than creating new ones. Second, during the recession that began in 2007, tight-fisted consumers abandoned specialty coffees, causing the stock price to nosedive. In January 2008, after an eight-year absence, Schultz returned as CEO.

The Reinvention Begins "I didn't come back to save the company—I hate that description," Schultz told an interviewer. "I came back to rekindle the emotion that built it."[8]

Among the risks he took to restore the company's luster, he closed 800 U.S. stores, laid off 4,000 employees, and let go most top executives. As a morale booster, he flew 10,000 store managers to New Orleans, recently destroyed by hurricane Katrina. Along with attending strategy sessions, they bonded in community-service activities, contributing thousands of volunteer hours to helping to restore parts of the city. "We wanted to give back to that community post-Katrina," says Schultz, "and remind and rekindle the organization with the values and guiding principles of our company before we did a stitch of business."

The Payoff After a couple of years, the company turned around, the result of better operations, modernized technology, a reinvigorated staff, and several innovations: It offered new coffee products, switched to a cold-brew process for iced coffee instead of simply brewing hot coffee and then chilling it, acquired (and then later closed) the La Boulange bakery chain, opened (and then closed) Teavana "tea bars," enabled customers to pay for coffee via a mobile-payment app, and even launched alcohol sales.[9] By early 2016, it had 23,921 stores in 64 countries, and its revenues had risen 146 percent over the last decade, while earnings grew more than fivefold.[10] Starbucks' 2017 revenues reached $21.3 billion, built on serving 90 million customers a day, and the company planned to achieve $35 billion by 2021 while opening 12,000 new stores, most of which were to be in China.[11]

Schultz Steps Down Again In 2017, Schultz stepped down once again, this time to become executive CEO. The company's prospects are considered bright as it adds to its product line, adds to the utility of its mobile app, and remains a popular customer choice, particularly in the coveted youth market.[12]

YOUR CALL

Starbucks' premium-priced coffee drinks are often called an "affordable luxury." If we can't afford a McMansion or a Lexus, says one observer, we may be "willing to make that $5 splurge at Starbucks simply because it makes us feel a bit better about ourselves."[13] Assuming this is true, do you think another economic downturn could alter Starbucks' fortunes in spite of its product innovations, attempts to rekindle the cozy neighborhood café, and emphasis on positive social values,? Why or why not?

Decision Making in the Real World

Sometimes we are able to make thoughtful decisions, making rational choices among well-defined alternatives. But that is not always the way it works in the real world.

Two Systems of Decision Making

In *Thinking, Fast and Slow*, psychologist Daniel Kahneman, winner of the 2002 Nobel Prize in economics, describes two kinds of thinking, which he labels System 1 and System 2:[14]

- **System 1—intuitive and largely unconscious:** System 1 operates automatically and quickly; it is our fast, automatic, intuitive, and largely unconscious mode, as when we detect hostility in a voice or detect that one object is more distant than another.
- **System 2—analytical and conscious:** System 2 is our slow, deliberate, analytical, and consciously effortful mode of reasoning, which swings into action when we have to fill out a tax form or park a car in a narrow space.

"System 1 uses association and metaphor to produce a quick and dirty draft of reality," says one explanation, "which System 2 draws on to arrive at explicit beliefs and reasoned choices."[15]

Why don't we use the more deliberate and rational System 2 more often? Because our brain can be lazy and tires easily, so instead of slowing things down and analyzing them, it is content to accept the easy but unreliable story that System 1 feeds it.

The "Curse of Knowledge"

Why do some engineers design electronic products (such as DVD remote controls) with so many buttons, devices ultimately useful only to other engineers? Why are some professional investors and bankers prone to taking excess risks?[16] Why are some employees so reluctant to adopt new processes? The answer may be what's known as *the curse of knowledge*. As one writer put it about engineers, for example, "People who design products are experts cursed by their knowledge, and they can't imagine what it's like to be as ignorant as the rest of us."[17] Specialization improves efficiency, suggests another writer, but it also leads to tunnel vision and blind spots.[18] In other words, as our knowledge and expertise grow, we may be less and less able to see things from an outsider's perspective—hence, we are often apt to make irrational decisions.

Let us look at the two approaches managers may take to making decisions: They may follow a *rational model* or various kinds of *nonrational models*.

Rational Decision Making: Managers Should Make Logical and Optimal Decisions

The **rational model of decision making**, also called the *classical model*, **explains how managers** ***should*** **make decisions; it assumes managers will make logical decisions that are the optimal means of furthering the organization's best interests.**

Typically there are four stages associated with rational decision making. *(See Figure 7.1.)* These are also the steps in the standard model of problem solving. As step 1 in the figure shows, for example, a decision is often an opportunity to solve a problem, which is a gap between an actual and a desired state.

FIGURE 7.1 The four steps in rational decision making

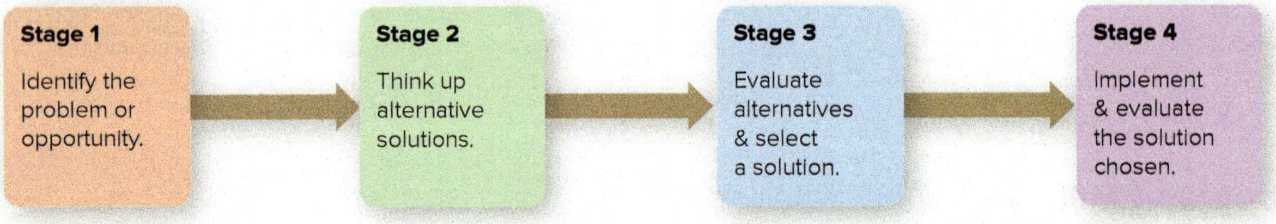

Stage 1: Identify the Problem or Opportunity—Determining the Actual versus the Desirable

As a manager, you'll probably find no shortage of **problems, or difficulties that inhibit the achievement of goals:** customer complaints, supplier breakdowns, staff turnover, sales shortfalls, competitor innovations, low employee motivation, and poor quality.

However, you'll also often find **opportunities—situations that present possibilities for exceeding existing goals.** It's the farsighted manager, however, who can look past the steady stream of daily problems and seize the moment to actually do *better* than the goals he or she is expected to achieve. When a competitor's top salesperson unexpectedly quits, that creates an opportunity for your company to hire that person away to promote your product more vigorously in that sales territory.

Whether you're confronted with a problem or an opportunity, the decision you're called on to make is how to make *improvements*–how to change conditions from the present to the desirable. This is a matter of **diagnosis—analyzing the underlying causes.**

Stage 2: Think Up Alternative Solutions—Both the Obvious and the Creative

Employees burning with bright ideas are an employer's greatest competitive resource. "Creativity precedes innovation, which is its physical expression," says *Fortune* magazine writer Alan Farnham. "It's the source of all intellectual property."[19]

After you've identified the problem or opportunity and diagnosed its causes, you need to come up with alternative solutions.

Stage 3: Evaluate Alternatives and Select a Solution—Ethics, Feasibility, and Effectiveness

In this stage, you need to evaluate each alternative not only according to cost and quality but also according to the following questions: (1) Is it *ethical*? (If it isn't, don't give it a second look.) (2) Is it *feasible*? (If time is short, costs are high, technology unavailable, or customers resistant, for example, it is not.) (3) Is it ultimately *effective*? (If the decision is merely "good enough" but not optimal in the long run, you might reconsider.)

Stage 4: Implement and Evaluate the Solution Chosen

With some decisions, implementation is usually straightforward (though not necessarily easy—firing employees who steal may be an obvious decision, but it can still be emotionally draining). With other decisions, implementation can be quite difficult; when one company acquires another, for instance, it may take months to consolidate the departments, accounting systems, inventories, and so on.

Successful Implementation

For implementation to be successful, you need to do two things:

- **Plan carefully.** Especially if reversing an action will be difficult, you need to make careful plans for implementation. Some decisions may require written plans.
- **Be sensitive to those affected.** You need to consider how the people affected may feel about the change—inconvenienced, insecure, even fearful, all of which can trigger resistance. This is why it helps to give employees and customers latitude during a changeover in business practices or working arrangements.

Now that you understand the four stages of the rational model, to what extent do you think you use them when making decisions? Would you like to improve the career readiness competency of decision making? If yes, then you will find the following self-assessment valuable. It assesses your problem-solving skills.

SELF-ASSESSMENT 7.1 CAREER READINESS

Assessing Your Problem-Solving Potential

This survey is designed to assess your approach to problem solving. Please be prepared to answer these questions if your instructor has assigned Self-Assessment 7.1 in Connect.

1. What is the status of your problem-solving skills? Are you surprised by the results?
2. Based on identifying the four lowest scored items on the assessment, what can you do to improve your problem-solving skills? Explain.
3. What things would you say during an interview to demonstrate that you possess this career readiness competency?

Evaluation

One "law" in economics is the Law of Unintended Consequences—things happen that weren't foreseen. For this reason, you need to follow up and evaluate the results of any decision.

What should you do if the action is not working? Some possibilities:

- **Give it more time.** You need to make sure employees, customers, and so on have had enough time to get used to the new action.
- **Change it slightly.** Maybe the action was correct, but it just needs "tweaking"—a small change of some sort.
- **Try another alternative.** If Plan A doesn't seem to be working, maybe you want to scrap it for another alternative.
- **Start over.** If no alternative seems workable, you need to go back to the drawing board—to stage 1 of the decision-making process.

What's Wrong with the Rational Model?

The rational model is *prescriptive*, describing how managers ought to make decisions. It doesn't describe how managers *actually* make decisions. Indeed, the rational model makes some highly desirable assumptions—that managers have complete information, are able to make an unemotional analysis, and are able to make the best decision for the organization. *(See Table 7.1.)* We all know that these assumptions are unrealistic.

TABLE 7.1
Assumptions of the Rational Model

- **Complete information, no uncertainty:** You should obtain complete, error-free information about all alternative courses of action and the consequences that would follow from each choice.
- **Logical, unemotional analysis:** Having no prejudices or emotional blind spots, you are able to logically evaluate the alternatives, ranking them from best to worst according to your personal preferences.
- **Best decision for the organization:** Confident of the best future course of action, you coolly choose the alternative that you believe will most benefit the organization.

Nonrational Decision Making: Managers Find It Difficult to Make Optimal Decisions

Nonrational models of decision making explain how managers make decisions; they assume that decision making is nearly always uncertain and risky, making it difficult for managers to make optimal decisions. The nonrational models are *descriptive* rather than prescriptive: They describe how managers *actually* make decisions rather than how they should. Two nonrational models are (1) *satisficing* and (2) *intuition*.

1. Bounded Rationality and the Satisficing Model: "Satisfactory Is Good Enough"

During the 1950s, economist **Herbert Simon**—who later received the Nobel Prize—began to study how managers actually make decisions. From his research he proposed that managers could not act truly logically because their rationality was bounded by so many restrictions.[20] Called **bounded rationality**, the concept suggests that the ability of decision makers to be rational is limited by numerous constraints, such as complexity, time and money, and their cognitive capacity, values, skills, habits, and unconscious reflexes. *(See Figure 7.2.)*

FIGURE 7.2 Some hindrances to perfectly rational decision making

- **Complexity:** The problems that need solving are often exceedingly complex, beyond understanding.
- **Time and money constraints:** There is not enough time or money to gather all relevant information.
- **Different cognitive capacity, values, skills, habits, and unconscious reflexes:** Managers aren't all built the same way, of course, and all have personal limitations and biases that affect their judgment.
- **Imperfect information:** Managers have imperfect, fragmentary information about the alternatives and their consequences.
- **Information overload:** There is too much information for one person to process.
- **Different priorities:** Some data are considered more important, so certain facts are ignored.
- **Conflicting goals:** Other managers, including colleagues, have conflicting goals.

Because of such constraints, managers don't make an exhaustive search for the best alternative. Instead, they follow what Simon calls the **satisficing model**—that is, managers seek alternatives until they find one that is satisfactory, not optimal. While "satisficing" might seem to be a weakness, it may well outweigh any advantages gained from delaying making a decision until all information is in and all alternatives weighed.

However, making snap decisions can also backfire. Example: In the fall of 2014, Amazon.com was about to release its new voice-controlled smart speaker (what came to be called the Echo), but there was one lingering uncertainty: the choice of "wake word" that, when spoken, would cue the device to take voice commands. (Because of technical limitations, a wake word cannot be just any sound.) One possibility was "Echo." Another was "Alexa." Amazon CEO Jeff Bezos thought the best word was "Amazon." However, the difficulty with Bezos's choice, according to Amazon's engineers, as reported in *Bloomberg Businessweek*, was that "the speakers would wake upon hearing Amazon ads on television and, because it connects to a Wi-Fi network, could start buying stuff from the Internet."[22] In the end Bezos agreed with his engineers that the wake word would be "Alexa"—a satisfactory, if not optimal, solution for him.

Nonrational decision making? When gasoline prices fall, Americans do two things:[21] They buy more gas but they also buy higher-octane gas. Thus, instead of saving money by buying their previous gallons and grades, they opt to go fancy on their fill-ups. Why do you suppose this is? How do you deal with this kind of nonrational decision?
©NithidPhoto/Getty Images

2. The Intuition Model: "It Just Feels Right" Small entrepreneurs often can't afford in-depth marketing research and so they make decisions based on hunches—their subconscious, visceral feelings. For instance, Ben Hugh, 32, decided to buy *I Can Has Cheezburger?*—a blog devoted to silly cat pictures paired with viewer-submitted quirky captions—when it linked to his own pet blog and caused it to crash from a wave of new visitors. Putting up $10,000 of his own money and acquiring additional investor financing, he bought the site for $2 million from the Hawaiian bloggers who started it. "It was a white-knuckle decision," he said later. But he expanded the Cheezburger blog into an empire that now includes 53 sites.[23]

"Going with your gut," or **intuition**, **is making a choice without the use of conscious thought or logical inference.**[24] Intuition that stems from *expertise*—a person's explicit and tacit knowledge about a person, a situation, an object, or a decision opportunity—is known as a *holistic hunch*. Intuition based on feelings—the involuntary emotional response to those same matters—is known as *automated experience*. It is important to try to develop your intuitive skills because they are as important as rational analysis in many decisions.[25] The Example box illustrates how Tesla CEO Elon Musk uses intuition.

EXAMPLE The Power of Intuition

You might be wishing that you could make all difficult decisions not after a long consideration of data and consequences, but in an "aha!" moment in which you spontaneously recognize the answer to the problem. This recognition is called an *epiphany*—that instant when something clicks in the brain, a mental light bulb goes on, and the road ahead becomes crystal-clear. Epiphanies are unfortunately rare, but the intuition that often leads to them can be carefully honed.

Elon Musk, the entrepreneurial founder of Tesla Motors, PayPal, and Space X, makes many decisions by relying on a form of the scientific method,[26] which consists of careful observation and information gathering, formulation of a hypothesis, prediction based on the hypothesis, and experimenting to test the hypothesis. But Musk is also known for acting on his intuition, as when he envisioned commercial space flight and reusable rockets, and when he started work on an electric car. When he recently came up with a way to increase efficiency on a production line, Musk called it "the biggest epiphany that I've had this year."[27] And after the successful launch of SpaceX's innovative Falcon Heavy Rocket in 2018, Musk marveled at the out-of-the-box thinking behind it: "Crazy things can come true," he said.[28] Musk's method for thinking intuitively (yes, there is a method) relies on breaking a problem down into its most basic components and questions in order to give his thinking a completely fresh start; see the Practical Action box for more.

Musk is not alone in harnessing the power of intuitive ideas. A well-known story about the origins of Amazon credits founder Jeff Bezos's intuitive recognition that if, as he'd just read, the Internet was growing at 2,300 percent a year, it was worth quitting his job on Wall Street and starting an online bookstore to take advantage of that opportunity.[29] Stephen Jobs, the late founder of Apple, believed "intuition is a very powerful thing, more powerful than intellect."[30] He also said, in a speech he made at Stanford University, "You have to trust in something, your gut, destiny, life, karma, whatever. This approach has never let me down, and it has made all the difference in my life."[31] And yet another genius, the physicist Albert Einstein, once said, "All great achievements of science must start from intuitive knowledge. At times I feel certain I am right while not knowing the reason."[32]

YOUR CALL

Have you ever relied on your intuition to make an important decision or solve a big problem? How did your solution come to you, and how pleased were you with the result?

As a model for making decisions, intuition has at least two benefits. It can speed up decision making, useful when deadlines are tight.[33] It also helps managers when resources are limited. A drawback, however, is that it can be difficult to convince others that your hunch makes sense. In addition, intuition is subject to the same biases as those that affect rational decision making, as we discuss in Section 7.5.[34] Finally, says one senior executive, intuition is fine for start-ups but "often deceives CEOs as their businesses become more complex."[35] Still, we believe that intuition and rationality are complementary and that managers should develop the courage to use intuition when making decisions.[36] Some suggestions for improving your intuitive skills are presented in the following Practical Action box. ●

PRACTICAL ACTION How to Improve Your Intuition

How can you improve your intuition and encourage "aha" moments of the kind Tesla and SpaceX founder Elon Musk has (see the preceding Example box)? Here are some steps that draw on Musks's own experience.[37]

1. **Immerse yourself in data and facts.** Intuition does not thrive in an information vacuum. Read, ask questions, study, and discuss. The more you know, the more likely that two or three pieces of related information you've acquired will surface in an insight that leads you to "aha."
2. **Practice "first principles thinking."** As Musk explains, to adopt this pattern of thinking you need to "boil things down to their fundamental truths and reason up from there, as opposed to reasoning by analogy."[38] Reasoning by analogy builds on existing assumptions; first principles thinking, however, questions all those assumptions and starts over from scratch. Try identifying all your assumptions first and putting them aside; then state your problem in its most basic terms. Instead of assuming, "We can't help it if our product is expensive," for instance, think about what is in the product and where or how you could get the components more cheaply. That's first principles thinking.
3. **Be mindful and open to insights.** Try meditating, even informally, and spend quiet time thinking about the problem in need of solving. Try to visualize a solution, and activate your insight by letting your thoughts freely flow for a time.
4. **Test your intuition.** It's useful to adopt a rational decision-making step here and test or challenge your intuitive solution. Consider your own track record with intuitive decisions you've made in the past. Ask others what they think about your current idea, and challenge your own thoughts with counterarguments. Test the counterarguments.
5. **Reward your intuitions.** Finally, when you have a flash of intuition or an epiphany, honor the process and reward yourself, to encourage and reinforce the kind of thinking that got you there.[39]

YOUR CALL

How can you use these five tips to improve your performance at school? Do you see any drawbacks to being more intuitive? Discuss.

Would you like to increase your level of intuition? It can be done, but first you need to know where you stand with respect to using intuition. Find out by taking Self-Assessment 7.2.

SELF-ASSESSMENT 7.2 CAREER READINESS

Assessing Your Level of Intuition

This survey is designed to assess the extent you use intuition in your current job. Please be prepared to answer these questions if your instructor has assigned Self-Assessment 7.2 in Connect.

1. Are you intuitive at work? Did the results surprise you?
2. What can you do to increase the amount of intuition you use at work? Describe.
3. What things might you say during a job interview to demonstrate that you possess the career readiness competency of critical thinking/problem solving?

7.2 Making Ethical Decisions

THE BIG PICTURE

A graph known as a decision tree can help one make ethical decisions.

LO 7-2

Explain how managers can make decisions that are both legal and ethical.

The ethical behavior of businesspeople, as we discussed at length in Chapter 3, has become of increasing concern in recent years, brought about by a number of events.

The Dismal Record of Business Ethics

Banks and others in the financial world furnished some of the worst recent examples of poor behavior by top management, such as profiting from mortgage loans made to unqualified buyers. These "subprime" loans led to a wave of housing foreclosures and helped push the country into a recession. Those ethical scandals were followed by corporate Ponzi schemes, insider trading, and safety violations that led to fatal accidents in U.S. workplaces and sweatshop-style factories abroad. Excessive profiteering made the news when a pharmaceutical company raised the price of one medication from $13.50 a pill to an astonishing $750.[40]

The #MeToo movement brought down prominent men in a wide range of industries over allegations of sexual misconduct, beginning with Harvey Weinstein, founder of a successful Hollywood film studio that bore his name, and going on to envelope dozens of politicians, business executives, sports figures, and popular and classical artists. The founder of Uber was forced to step down after revelations of a sexually charged work environment, allegations of theft of trade secrets, *and* a criminal probe into the company's use of software designed to avoid the law.[41] Public lying did not go unpunished; a legislative aide to one of Florida's state representatives was quickly fired for falsely claiming that students who protested lax gun laws after 17 of their peers and teachers were killed in a high school shooting were paid actors.[42]

Some unethical behaviors like sexual harassment have morphed into their own logo. ©Ing. Andrej Kaprinay/Shutterstock

A recent survey reports that CEOs are more likely than ever before to be ousted for ethical violations and that such cases are accounting for an increasing share of corporate successions at some of the largest publicly owned companies in the world, especially in the United States and Canada. The *Harvard Business Review* suggests five reasons for this trend: (1) the public is "less forgiving" of poor behavior by executives, (2) regulations are more stringent, (3) companies are expanding operations into developing countries where ethical risks may be higher and laws less protective, (4) digital communications increase exposure to risk from both hackers and whistleblowers, and (5) "the 24/7 news cycle and the proliferation of media in the 21st century publicizes and amplifies negative information in real time."[43]

Recent research sheds additional light on why unethical behavior occurs. One study demonstrated that unethical behavior is more apt to be tolerated when it comes from a high rather than a low performer.[44] Sadly, it seems that some organizations prefer performance over ethics. Other studies show that individual differences play a role in unethical behavior. For example, compassionate people were found to engage in prosocial lying, such as to prevent others from feeling hurt or embarrassed or to help others financially. Prosocial lying helps others rather than yourself.[45]

On the other side of the ledger, about 170 of the world's billionaires have pledged, along with Microsoft founder Bill Gates, his wife Melinda, and mega-investor Warren Buffet, to give away more than half their money to charitable causes like "poverty alleviation, refugee aid, disaster relief, global health, education, women and girls' empowerment, medical research, arts and culture, criminal justice reform and environmental sustainability."[46] The Giving Pledge has been signed by billionaires from 22 countries in every age cohort from 30 to 90.[47]

Ethical concerns have forced the subject of right-minded decision making to the top of the agenda in many organizations. Indeed, many companies now have an **ethics officer**, **someone trained about matters of ethics in the workplace, particularly about resolving ethical dilemmas.** More and more companies are also creating values statements to guide employees as to what constitutes desirable business behavior.[48] As a result of this raised consciousness, managers now must try to make sure their decisions are not just lawful but also ethical.[49]

I'm Glad I...

...found an employer who cares about ethics more than just making money.

Danielle Williams Courtesy Danielle Williams

Danielle Williams is a marketing director in the technology industry. It is very important for her to filter new clients to look for the ones who are searching for a partnership rather than a contract. The motivation behind these decisions must be ethical rather than financial.

"The company I work for develops custom software. We work with some really large companies, and we work directly with their IT management department. One of the things we do to filter our clients before we decide to partner with them is determine whether that business is willing to do a partnership with us rather than have a contract relationship," said Danielle.

Danielle explains that each type of relationship is completely different. "If you *partner* with someone, you're able to innovate on their behalf and they are willing to listen to your suggestions. Whereas, with a contract, you're getting lined items: they tell us what they want, we execute and hand it over to them."

While there might be opportunities for Danielle's company to gain recognition by signing contracts with some of these larger companies, she understands that doing so could disrupt company culture. "We've had to make that **ethical decision**, to not disrupt our organizational culture, and say no to some really big contracts that would help our revenue growth dramatically," said Danielle.

The positive financial impact of signing contracts with these large companies is outweighed by the negative effects these working relationships can have on employees. "It really takes away employee freedom to work with these companies. They would have a lot of outlined tasks which become monotonous. When we're looking to hire the top talent in the industry, that really deters people from wanting to work with us if they're not really getting to think outside the box and stretch what they can do," said Danielle. "The way we like to do business is to be able to truly innovate and find the best solutions for our clients."

Danielle and her team have to constantly weigh financial benefits and reputation against the practical implications of securing talent and maintaining company culture. For Danielle, employee well-being and culture are far more important than marketing prestige.

Courtesy of Danielle Williams

Road Map to Ethical Decision Making: A Decision Tree

Undoubtedly, the greatest pressure on top executives is to maximize shareholder value, to deliver the greatest return on investment to the owners of their company. But is a decision that is beneficial to shareholders yet harmful to employees—such as forcing them to contribute more to their health benefits, as IBM has done—unethical? Harvard Business School professor Constance Bagley suggests that what is needed is a decision tree to help with ethical decisions.[51] A **decision tree** **is a graph of decisions and their possible consequences; it is used to create a plan to reach a goal.** Decision trees are used to aid in making decisions. Bagley's ethical decision tree is shown in Figure 7.3.

When confronted with any proposed action for which a decision is required, a manager works through the decision tree by asking the following questions.

FIGURE 7.3 The ethical decision tree: What's the right thing to do?

Source: Data from "The Ethical Leader's Decision Tree," by C. E. Bagley, February 2003, Harvard Business School Publishing Corporation.

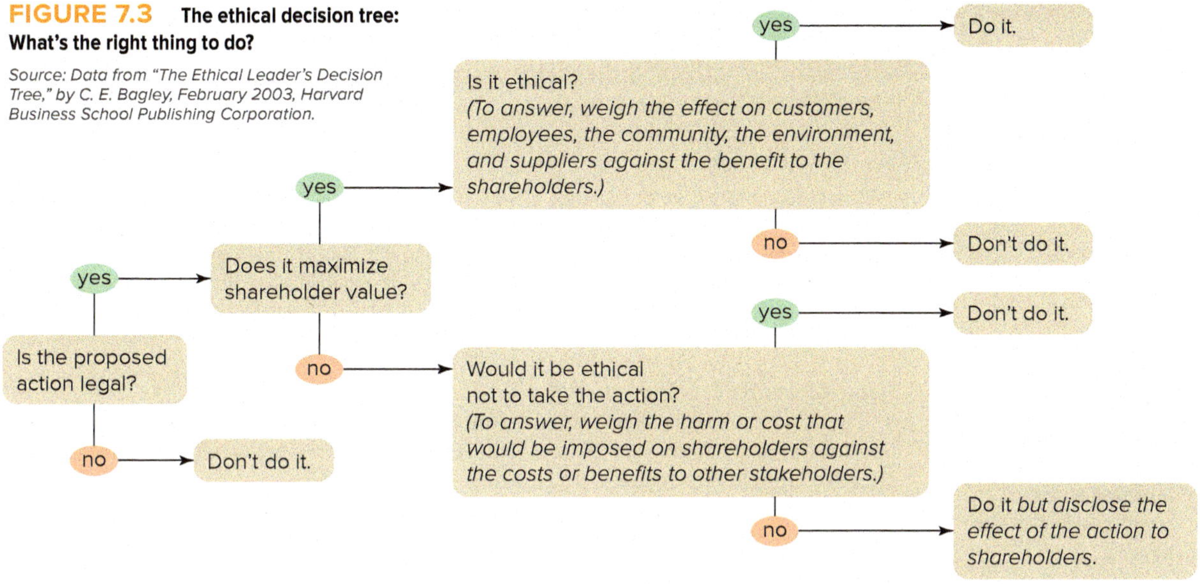

1. Is the Proposed Action Legal? This may seem an obvious question. But, Bagley observes, "corporate shenanigans suggest that some managers need to be reminded: If the action isn't legal, don't do it."

2. If "Yes," Does the Proposed Action Maximize Shareholder Value? If the action is legal, one must next ask whether it will profit the shareholders. If the answer is "yes," should you do it? Not necessarily.

3. If "Yes," Is the Proposed Action Ethical? As Bagley points out, though directors and top managers may believe they are bound by corporate law to always maximize shareholder value, the courts and many state legislatures have held they are not. Rather, their main obligation is to manage "for the best interests of the corporation," which includes the interests of the larger community.

Thus, says Bagley, building a profitable-but-polluting plant in a country overseas may benefit the shareholders but be bad for that country—and for the corporation's relations with that nation. Ethically, then, managers should add pollution-control equipment.

4. If "No," Would It Be Ethical *Not* to Take the Proposed Action? If the action would not directly benefit shareholders, might it still be ethical to go ahead with it?

Not building the overseas plant might be harmful to other stakeholders, such as employees or customers. Thus, the ethical conclusion might be to build the plant with pollution-control equipment but to disclose the effects of the decision to shareholders.

As a basic guideline to making good ethical decisions on behalf of a corporation, Bagley suggests that directors, managers, and employees need to follow their own individual ideas about right and wrong.[52] There is a lesson, she suggests, in the response of the pension fund manager who, when asked whether she would invest in a company doing business in a country that permits slavery, responded, "Do you mean me, personally, or as a fund manager?" When people feel entitled or compelled to compromise their own personal ethics to advance the interests of a business, "it is an invitation to mischief."[53]

To learn more about your own ethics, morality, and/or values (while contributing to scientific research), go to *www.yourmorals.org*.[54] ●

Buy a pair, give a pair. Warby Parker (named after two characters in a journal by 1950s Beat Generation writer Jack Kerouac) was established in 2010 by four former Wharton School students. The company operates on two premises: (a) Designer glasses can be sold at a fraction of the price of the hugely marked-up luxury alternatives. (b) For every pair of glasses sold, a pair could be distributed among the hundreds of thousands of people in need. "Glasses are one of the most effective poverty-alleviation tools in the world," says one of the founders. "They increase one's income by 20%, which is equivalent to adding a full extra day of work a week."[50] Are you more inclined to buy from companies like Warby Parker or shoe seller TOMS (which gives away a pair of shoes to a needy person for every pair sold) that tie sales of their products to helping impoverished people around the world? ©Astrid Stawiarz/WireImage/Getty Images

7.3 Evidence-Based Decision Making and Analytics

THE BIG PICTURE

Evidence-based decision making, which depends on an "attitude of wisdom," rests on three truths. This section describes seven principles for implementing evidence-based management. We also describe why it is hard to bring this approach to bear on one's decision making. Finally, we describe analytics and its three key attributes.

LO 7-3

Describe how evidence-based management and business analytics contribute to decision making.

"How do you build better bosses?"

That's what Google Inc. wanted to know when it embarked on a plan code-named Project Oxygen. After a year of work, statisticians produced eight rules for becoming an effective Google manager, as shown below. *(See Table 7.2.)*

TABLE 7.2 What the Evidence Shows: Google's Eight Rules for Being a Better Manager
Rules are listed in order of importance.

1. Be a good coach.
2. Empower your team, don't micromanage.
3. Express interest in team members' success and personal well-being.
4. Be productive and results oriented.
5. Be a good communicator and listen to your team.
6. Help your employees with career development.
7. Have a clear vision and strategy for the team.
8. Have key technical skills so you can help advise the team.

Source: J.C. Spender and B. A. Strong, Strategic Conversations: Creating and Directing the Entrepreneurial Workforce *(Cambridge, MA: Cambridge University Press, 2014), p. 141.*

A few years later, in 2018, Google revisited the list, slightly modifying items 3 and 6 and adding two completely new items:

9. Collaborate across Google.
10. Be a strong decision maker.[55]

Some of these directives may seem obvious. What's important here, however, is how Google arrived at changes in its list of eight rules. The company analyzed and interpreted information from performance reviews, employee surveys, nominations for top-manager awards, and other sources. Said one report of the original project, "The result was more than 10,000 observations of manager behaviors. The research team complimented the quantitative data with qualitative information from interviews."[56] And in 2018, the company revisited the list, wrote new survey questions based on internal research and feedback, and did more testing. Its new analysis showed that, "The two new behaviors were highly correlated with manager effectiveness and the updated list of ten Oxygen behaviors was even more predictive of team outcomes like turnover, satisfaction, and performance than our original list of eight."[57] In other words, Google looked at the *evidence.*

Evidence-Based Decision Making

"Too many companies and too many leaders are more interested in just copying others, doing what they've always done, and making decisions based on beliefs in what ought to work rather than what actually works," say Stanford professors **Jeffrey Pfeffer** and **Robert Sutton.** "They fail to face the hard facts and use the best evidence to help navigate the competitive environment."[58] Companies that use *evidence-based management*—the translation of principles based on best evidence into organizational practice, bringing rationality to the decision-making process, as we defined it in Chapter 2—routinely trump the competition, Pfeffer and Sutton suggest.[59]

Seven Implementation Principles

Pfeffer and Sutton identify seven implementation principles to help companies that are committed to doing what it takes to profit from evidence-based management:[60]

- **Treat your organization as an unfinished prototype.** Leaders need to think and act as if their organization were an unfinished prototype that won't be ruined by dangerous new ideas or impossible to change because of employee or management resistance. Example: Some Internet start-ups that find their original plan not working have learned to master "the art of the pivot," to fail gracefully by cutting their losses and choosing a new direction—as did the founders of Fabulus, a review site and social network that attracted no users, so they launched a high-end e-commerce site called Fab.com.[61] (Unfortunately, Fab CEO Jason Goldberg was inclined to pivot the business rather than solve basic problems. "You can change a business once or twice," says one former employee, "but after that you're drowning."[62] After creating and losing 500 jobs and creating and losing $850 million, Fab ended and was bought for a fraction of its value by another company.)
- **No brag, just facts.** This slogan is an antidote for over-the-top assertions about forthcoming products, such as "the deafening levels of managed hype across much of Silicon Valley," as one reporter characterized it.[63] Other companies, such as DaVita, which operates dialysis centers, take pains to evaluate data before making decisions. So does SAS Institute, the privately owned software company that ranks as No. 2 on *Fortune*'s 2017 "Best Places to Work For Millennials" list.[64] As we've seen, Google has used data to find out what makes a better boss.[65]
- **See yourself and your organization as outsiders do.** Most managers are afflicted with "rampant optimism," with inflated views of their own talents and prospects for success, which causes them to downplay risks and continue on a path despite evidence that things are not working. "Having a blunt friend, mentor, or counselor," Pfeffer and Sutton suggest, "can help you see and act on better evidence."

Evidence-based decisions. Google used evidence-based analysis to find out what makes a better boss. Like this photo, the company found that what employees value most are even-keeled bosses who take an interest in employees' lives and careers, who make time for one-on-one meetings, and who help people work through problems by asking questions instead of dictating answers. Would you expect a "just-the-facts" approach to be normal in high-tech businesses or unusual? ©Cole Burston/Bloomberg/Getty Images

- **Evidence-based management is not just for senior executives.** The best organizations are those in which everyone, not just the top managers, is guided by the responsibility to gather and act on quantitative and qualitative data and share results with others.
- **Like everything else, you still need to sell it.** "Unfortunately, new and exciting ideas grab attention even when they are vastly inferior to old ideas," the Stanford authors say. "Vivid, juicy stories and case studies sell better than detailed, rigorous, and admittedly dull data—no matter how wrong the stories or how right the data." To sell an evidence-based approach, you may have to identify a preferred practice based on solid if unexciting evidence, then use vivid stories to grab management attention.
- **If all else fails, slow the spread of bad practice.** Because many managers and employees face pressures to do things that are known to be ineffective, it may be necessary for you to practice "evidence-based misbehavior"—that is, ignore orders you know to be wrong or delay their implementation.
- **The best diagnostic question: What happens when people fail?** "Failure hurts, it is embarrassing, and we would rather live without it," the authors write. "Yet there is no learning without failure. . . . If you look at how the most effective systems in the world are managed, a hallmark is that when something goes wrong, people face the hard facts, learn what happened and why, and keep using those facts to make the system better."[66] From the U.S. civil aviation system, which rigorously examines airplane accidents, near misses, and equipment problems, to mall owners who look for new uses for space, like apartments and medical offices, as malls fall from favor and anchor stores like Sears and Macy's depart, evidence-based management makes the point that failure is a great teacher.[67] This means, however, that the organization must "forgive and remember" people who make mistakes, not be trapped by preconceived notions, and confront the best evidence and hard facts.

What Makes It Hard to Be Evidence Based Despite your best intentions, it's hard to bring the best evidence to bear on your decisions. Among the reasons:[68] (1) There's too much evidence. (2) There's not enough *good* evidence. (3) The evidence doesn't quite apply. (4) People are trying to mislead you. (5) *You* are trying to mislead yourself. (6) The side effects outweigh the cure. (Example: Despite the belief that social promotion in school is a bad idea—that is, that schools shouldn't advance children to the next grade when they haven't mastered the material—the side effect is skyrocketing costs because it crowds schools with older, angrier students who demand more resources.) (7) Stories are more persuasive, anyway.

In Praise of Analytics

Perhaps the purest application of evidence-based management is the use of **analytics**, or ***business analytics***, **the term used for sophisticated forms of business data analysis.** One example of analytics is portfolio analysis, in which an investment adviser evaluates the risks of various stocks. Another example is the time-series forecast, which predicts future data based on patterns of historical data.

Some leaders and firms have become exceptional practitioners of analytics. Gary Loveman, CEO of the Harrah's gambling empire, wrote a famous paper, "Diamonds in the Data Mine," in which he explained how data-mining software was used to analyze vast amounts of casino customer data to target profitable patrons.[69] Marriott International, through its Total Hotel Optimization program, has used quantitative data to establish the optimal price for hotel rooms, evaluate use of conference facilities and catering, and develop systems to optimize offerings to frequent customers.[70] To aid in recruitment, Microsoft studies correlations between its successful workers and the schools and companies they arrived from.[71]

EXAMPLE Analytics in Athletics: The Personal "Moneyball" Takeover of Sports

After her first set during a recent Bank of the West Classic at Stanford, California, pro tennis player Angelique Kerber called her coach over for a 90-second conference. Referring to his data-laden iPad, as well as his courtside observations, the coach told Kerber that her opponent was serving to her backhand nearly every time. With this knowledge Kerber went on to defeat her competitor, and then another opponent, to win the tournament and her fourth title of the year.[72]

Better Indicators of Player Success The obsession with analytics in professional sports is the logical result of the *Moneyball* phenomenon. The Brad Pitt film of that name was adapted from a book by Michael Lewis called *Moneyball: The Art of Winning an Unfair Game*. The book described how the Oakland Athletics, then one of the poorest teams in Major League Baseball (with a payroll about a third the size of the New York Yankees), managed to go to the playoffs five times in seven years against better-financed contenders. The Athletics accomplished this by avoiding the use of traditional baseball statistics and finding better indicators of player success in data such as on-base percentage, slugging percentage, and the like. For a time, this creative use of analytics enabled the managers of the California club to concentrate their limited payroll resources on draft picks who were primarily talented college players rather than veteran professionals.[73] The team continues to rely on analytics to improve its odds, and the Houston Astros have taken the strategy to another level, hiring a NASA engineer to help them with data analysis.[74]

Analytics in Pro Sports Since then, analytic measures have been used to find better ways to value players and strategies in all major sports. In basketball, the application of data and analytics reached its zenith with the Golden State Warriors, the National Basketball Association's defending champion. A group of data-loving Silicon Valley investors bought the floundering team a few years ago for $450 million (it's now worth $2 billion) and proceeded to fix it by asking the question "What would happen if you built a basketball team by ignoring every orthodoxy of building a basketball team?" One unusual idea: Focus less on recruiting big men who could stuff the basket and more on players who could make three-point shots.[75]

Delving into the statistics, the executives began to rebuild the team around star three-point shooters Stephen Curry and Klay Thompson and other players, which helped the Warriors make a higher percentage of three-pointers than any other team in the league. "We're lightyears ahead of probably every other team in structure, in planning, in how we're going to go about things," says Golden State majority owner Joe Lacob. "We're going to be a handful for the rest of the NBA to deal with for a long time."[76] The Warriors won the NBA championship in 2015 and again in 2017.

Four time NBA All-Star Klay Thompson from the Golden State Warriors driving to the basket against the Portland Trail Blazers. ©David Blair/ZUMA Press, Inc./Alamy Stock Photo

Data drives the NFL as well. Among the most enthusiastic teams are the Atlanta Falcons, whose website calls modern analytics "a priority." "We've become more and more intellectual as far as how we're looking at things and presenting things to [coach] Dan [Quinn] and how we sit down and talk a lot about the players we're looking at," says general manager Thomas Dimitroff. "[We're] using the comparatives, which are big for our process. We're a big comparative team when we start looking at our own players, how they stack against the players that are potentially in the draft."[77] The team even monitors its players' sleep habits and patterns, using an outside firm to collect data about how much sleep they get and find ways for them to get more restorative rest.[78]

In hockey, the Chicago Blackhawks credit their use of statistics with helping find hockey players "whose skill sets and style of play mesh well with the players who are already here and our style of play." Says their general manager Stan Bowman, "That's where I think the value of analytics comes in." The team has won three Stanley Cups in the last seven seasons.[79]

YOUR CALL

Executives and human resource professionals often make decisions as the old sports traditionalists did, relying on résumé, degree, years of experience, and even looks in evaluating job applicants. What other, more quantifiable measures might be used instead when hiring new college graduates?

Thomas H. Davenport and others at Babson College's Working Knowledge Research Center studied 32 organizations that made a commitment to quantitative, fact-based analysis and found three key attributes among analytics competitors: *use of modeling*, *multiple applications*, and *support from top management*.[80]

1. Use of Modeling: Going beyond Simple Descriptive Statistics Companies such as Capital One look well beyond basic statistics, using data mining and predictive modeling to identify potential and most profitable customers. **Predictive modeling** is a data-mining technique used to predict future behavior and anticipate the consequences of change. Thus, Capital One conducts more than 30,000 experiments a year, with different interest rates, incentives, direct-mail packaging, and other variables to evaluate which customers are most apt to sign up for credit cards and will pay back their debt.

2. Multiple Applications, Not Just One UPS (formerly United Parcel Service) applies analytics not only to tracking the movement of packages, but also to examining usage patterns to try to identify potential customer defections so that salespeople can make contact and solve problems. More recently, as e-commerce has required UPS to make lots of single-package deliveries throughout neighborhoods, it has invested in a same-day delivery startup called Deliv Inc., hoping to prevail in the so-called last-mile delivery, considered the priciest part of an order's journey.[81] The company is also exploring the use of drones to deliver life-saving medicines.[82] Analytics competitors "don't gain advantage from one killer app [application], but rather from multiple applications supporting many parts of the business," says Davenport.

3. Support from the Top "A companywide embrace of analytics impels changes in culture, processes, behavior, and skills for many employees," says Davenport. "And so, like any major transition, it requires leadership from executives at the very top who have a passion for the quantitative approach."[83]

Big Data: What It Is, How It's Used

A recent study says the store of the world's information will reach 163 zettabytes in size by 2025, 60 percent of which will be generated and managed by businesses.[84] (Just 1 zettabyte is equal to the contents of 20 million four-drawer file cabinets—multiplied by a million.[85]) This has led to a phenomenon known as *Big Data*, stores of data so vast that conventional database management systems cannot handle them and so very sophisticated analysis software and supercomputing-level hardware are required.[86] **Big Data** includes not only data in corporate databases, but also web-browsing data trails, social network communications, sensor data, and surveillance data.[87]

"One of the most extraordinary features of Big Data is that it signals the end of the reign of statistics," suggests technology writer Michael Malone. "For 400 years, we've been forced to sample complex systems and extrapolate. Now, with Big Data, *it is possible to measure everything*, from the movement of billions of stars to every beat of the human heart [our emphasis added]."[88] The concept of Big Data has been dubbed "the next frontier for innovation, competition, and productivity."[89] In a 2018 survey of nearly 60 large firms in the financial, pharmaceutical, and other industries, 97% of respondents said they are currently investing in Big Data and artificial intelligence (AI) projects, and 73% said they have already seen measurable results from these efforts.[90] **Big Data analytics** is the process of examining large amounts of data of a variety of types to uncover hidden patterns, unknown correlations, and other useful information. Among some of the uses of Big Data analytics are the following:[91]

- **Analyzing consumer behavior and spurring sales.** Online behavior can be analyzed "to create ads, products, or experiences that are most appealing to consumers—and thus most lucrative to companies," says one technology journalist. "There's also great potential to more accurately predict market fluctuations or react faster to shifts in consumer sentiment or supply chain issues."[92] Target used big data analytics to more accurately market product offers to a specific category of shopper by linking its Guest ID program with its baby shower registry. In this way the retailer was able to identify other items often purchased by expectant moms in addition to gifts they registered for.[93]

- **Improving hiring and human resource management.** JetBlue applies people analytics to hiring for all the airline's positions, which helps the company sort through the 125,000 job applications it receives each year.[94] One surprising conclusion the airline drew from this practice was that hiring flight attendants based on their helpfulness was more important than hiring them because they were "nice."[95] Some firms are using Big Data to figure out which employees might get sick, based on "the prescription drugs workers use, how they shop, and even whether they vote," in an effort to contain health costs, according to one description.[96]
- **Tracking movie, music, TV, and reading data.** HP Labs researchers have used Twitter data to accurately predict box-office revenues of Hollywood movies.[97] Record collectors and the music industry use Discogs.com to keep track of records and their various releases and to identify sources of royalties where copyrighted songs are played.[98] Television networks use new ways of pinpointing audience data to pitch live programs to advertisers.[99] Jellybooks, a reading analytics company based in London, hopes to use data about people's reading habits to reshape the way publishers acquire, edit, and market books.[100]
- **Advancing health and medicine.** Data for Health, a project of Bloomberg Philanthropies, strives to help countries make better health policy decisions for their citizens by improving the collection and recording of birth and death data. The project team notes that nearly 30 million deaths each year are not recorded, leaving governments without critical basic information.[101] Britain's

Down on the farm. This server farm, or data center, contains thousands of computers storing terabytes of information on everyone and everything—"Big Data" that can be subjected to data analytics to work on large-scale projects. With data centers like this, you can see why everything you enter online, whether via e-mail, Facebook, texting, or twittering, no matter how innocuous, can be stored and used later to try to sell you things. Are you okay with this?
©Ben Torres/Bloomberg/Getty Images

National Health Service collected data about treatments and drugs from 53 million patients and saved $784 million by comparing cost and effectiveness, a savings expected to nearly double by the end of 2018.[102] New internal and external monitoring devices are helping medical researchers gather enormous quantities of health data, helping us to understand, for instance, the effects of external influences on autism, what changes in lifestyle (social media usage, diminishing movement) can produce depression, or what procedures are more apt to lead to malpractice claims.[103]

- **Aiding public policy.** Two-thirds of the 11 million people detained in local U.S. jails are suffering from mental illness. The Data-Driven Justice Initiative was launched by the Obama administration to use data "to identify and proactively break the cycle of incarceration" and to "use data-driven, validated, pre-trial risk assessment tools to inform pre-trial release decisions." Another goal of the bipartisan group of more than 60 city, county, and state governments is to help provide law enforcement officers and first responders with tools to help people in mental health crises get help instead of getting arrested.[104] Boston mayor Marty Walsh relies on dozens of data charts and graphs to indicate whether the city is fulfilling its goals, such as achieving quicker ambulance response times. Analytics can tackle large-scale public-sector problems such as traffic congestion, train passenger commute patterns, and handling of federal funds in child welfare.[105] •

EXAMPLE Data, Hacking, and Privacy: Who's Stealing My Data?!

Big Data and analytics clearly have enormous benefits. But half the people in a Pew Research Center survey said they felt they had little or no control over their personal data. Indeed, two-thirds of adults said they were not confident that online video sites, search engine providers such as Google, or social media sites such as Facebook protected their information.[106] Are they right to be concerned?

In September 2017, the credit rating company Equifax admitted that its data had been breached by hackers that summer and that a huge online data store of 143 million customers' names, addresses, birthdates, and Social Security numbers had been hacked on its site. A few months later, the company revealed that even more information than it first reported, such as tax IDs and the state and issue date of driver's licenses, may also have been compromised by the hackers. Senator Elizabeth Warren echoed the sentiments of many customers when she reacted to the news: "As your company continues to issue incomplete, confusing and contradictory statements and hide information from Congress and the public, it is clear that five months after the breach was publicly announced, Equifax has yet to answer this simple question in full: What was the precise extent of the breach?"[107]

Equifax had experienced problems safeguarding customers' information for several years before the 2017 hack, fending off class-action suits that accused it of deliberately ignoring "known weaknesses in its data security, including prior hacks." Some of these known weaknesses included outdated software for running the site and the use of customer passwords that were too easy to crack.[108]

Equifax came under widespread public criticism after the 2017 attack, not only for failing to report it until six weeks afterward, but also for making itself vulnerable to hacking in the first place. The company had neglected to apply a corrective patch to its software that was available months before and that might have prevented the problem. "This vulnerability was disclosed back in March," said the maker of the software program Equifax used. "The fact that Equifax was subsequently attacked in May means that Equifax did not follow that advice [to install the manufacturer's update]. Had they done so this breach would not have occurred."[109]

The company was also attacked for its poor response to the crisis. Its efforts to assist customers by letting them temporarily "freeze" their credit reports on the site were difficult to access, hard to use, and unreliable. As customers struggled to assess their risk of identity theft and fraud as a result of the hack, government investigations of the breach were begun but then slowed,[110] while the Social Security Administration continued to rely on a user-verification system devised by the discredited firm.[111]

YOUR CALL

Some say Big Data is overrated and that "our gut will always be part of decision making."[112] Do you agree? Do you think risks to data, like those exposed by the Equifax breach, are worth the potential gains from the widespread use of Big Data? Why or why not?

7.4 Four General Decision-Making Styles

THE BIG PICTURE

Your decision-making style reflects how you perceive and respond to information. It could be directive, analytical, conceptual, or behavioral.

LO 7-4

Compare four decision-making styles.

A decision-making style reflects the combination of how an individual perceives and responds to information. A team of researchers developed a model of decision-making styles based on the idea that styles vary along two different dimensions: value orientation and tolerance for ambiguity.[113]

Value Orientation and Tolerance for Ambiguity

Value orientation reflects the extent to which a person focuses on either task and technical concerns or people and social concerns when making decisions. Some people, for instance, are very task focused at work and do not pay much attention to people issues, whereas others are just the opposite.

The second dimension pertains to a person's *tolerance for ambiguity*. This individual difference indicates the extent to which a person has a high need for structure or control in his or her life. Some people desire a lot of structure in their lives (a low tolerance for ambiguity) and find ambiguous situations stressful and psychologically uncomfortable. In contrast, others do not have a high need for structure and can thrive in uncertain situations (a high tolerance for ambiguity). Ambiguous situations can energize people with a high tolerance for ambiguity.

When the dimensions of value orientation and tolerance for ambiguity are combined, they form four styles of decision making: *directive*, *analytical*, *conceptual*, and *behavioral. (See Figure 7.4.)*

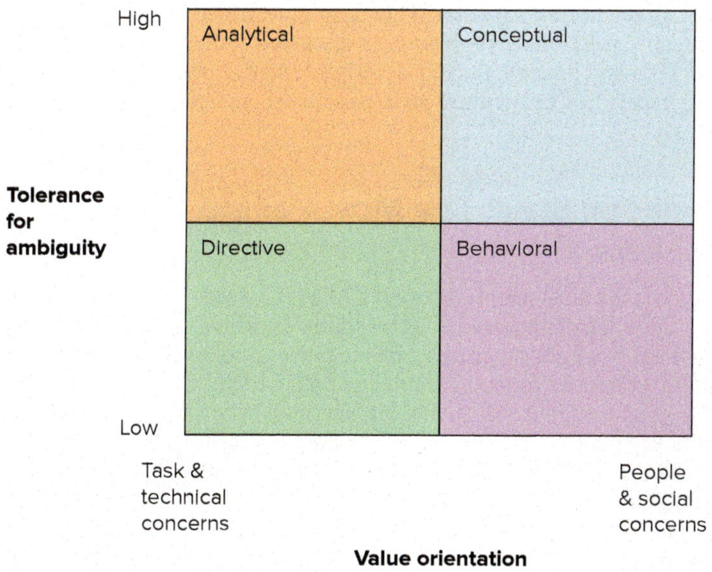

FIGURE 7.4

Decision-making styles

1. The Directive Style: Action-Oriented Decision Makers Who Focus on Facts

People with a directive style have a low tolerance for ambiguity and are oriented toward task and technical concerns in making decisions. They are efficient, logical, practical, and systematic in their approach to solving problems, and they are action oriented and decisive and like to focus on facts. Jeff Bezos fits this pattern. In a recent letter to Amazon shareholders, he said, "Most decisions should probably be made with somewhere around 70% of the information you wish you had. If you wait for 90%, in most cases, you're probably being slow."[114] In their pursuit of speed and results, however, these individuals can tend to be autocratic, to exercise power and control, and to focus on the short run.

Ginny Rometty is chairman, president, and CEO of IBM. She is the first woman to head the company. ©Ethan Miller/Getty Images

2. The Analytical Style: Careful Decision Makers Who Like Lots of Information and Alternative Choices

Managers with an analytical style have a much higher tolerance for ambiguity and respond well to new or uncertain situations. Ginni Rometty, CEO of IBM (and holder of a bachelor's degree in engineering), seems to have this style. Her decision to refocus the company on cloud-based technology and artificial intelligence puts it squarely in uncharted territory where it faces a great deal of uncertainty, especially given that revenue has declined for several years and success is not assured.[115] Analytical managers like to consider more information and alternatives than those adopting the directive style. They are careful decision makers who take longer to make decisions, but they may also tend to overanalyze a situation.

3. The Conceptual Style: Decision Makers Who Rely on Intuition and Have a Long-Term Perspective

People with a conceptual style have a high tolerance for ambiguity and tend to focus on the people or social aspects of a work situation. They take a broad perspective to problem solving and like to consider many options and future possibilities.

Conceptual types adopt a long-term perspective and rely on intuition and discussions with others to acquire information. They also are willing to take risks and are good at finding creative solutions to problems. As discussed earlier in this chapter, Elon Musk, founder of Tesla and SpaceX, fits this description well. However (although this is not true in Musk's case), a conceptual style can foster an indecisive approach to decision making.

4. The Behavioral Style: The Most People-Oriented Decision Makers

The behavioral style is the most people-oriented of the four styles. People with this style work well with others and enjoy social interactions in which opinions are openly exchanged. Behavioral types are supportive, are receptive to suggestions, show warmth, and prefer verbal to written information. Madeline Bell, CEO of Children's Hospital in Philadelphia, is a good example. "With any big decision," she says, "I create a stakeholder map of the key people who need to be on board. I identify the detractors and their concerns, and then I think about how I can take the energy that they might put into resistance and channel it into something positive. I make it clear to people that they're important to the process and they'll be part of a win."[116] Although they like to hold meetings, some people with this style have a tendency to avoid conflict and to be concerned about others. This can lead them to adopt a wishy-washy approach to decision making and to have a hard time saying no.

Which Style Do You Have?

Research shows that very few people have only one dominant decision-making style. Rather, most managers have characteristics that fall into two or three styles, and there is not a best decision-making style that applies to all situations. Studies also reveal that decision-making styles affect our purchasing decisions and leadership style.[117]

You can use knowledge of decision-making styles to increase your career readiness competencies in the following three ways.

Know Thyself Knowledge of styles helps you to understand yourself. Awareness of your style assists you in identifying your strengths and weaknesses as a decision maker and facilitates the potential for self-improvement.

Influence Others You can increase your ability to influence others by being aware of styles. For example, if you are dealing with an analytical person, you should provide as much information as possible to support your ideas.

Deal with Conflict Knowledge of styles gives you an awareness of how people can take the same information yet arrive at different decisions by using a variety of decision-making strategies. Different decision-making styles are one likely source of interpersonal conflict at work.

What style of decision making do you prefer? Would you like to learn how to use all of the styles more effectively? The following self-assessment can help. ●

SELF-ASSESSMENT 7.3 CAREER READINESS

What Is Your Decision-Making Style?

This survey is designed to assess your decision-making style. Please be prepared to answer these questions if your instructor has assigned Self-Assessment 7.3 in Connect.

1. What is your dominant decision-making style?
2. What are the pros and cons of your style?
3. What might you say to a recruiter during a job interview to demonstrate your awareness regarding your decision-making style?

7.5 Decision-Making Biases and the Use of Artificial Intelligence

THE BIG PICTURE

Managers should be aware of nine common decision-making biases. They will also face issues raised by the growing application of artificial intelligence.

LO 7-5

Identify barriers to rational decision making and ways to overcome them.

If someone asked you to explain the basis on which you make decisions, could you even say? Perhaps, after some thought, you might come up with some "rules of thumb." Scholars call them **heuristics** (pronounced "hyur-*ris*-tiks")—**strategies that simplify the process of making decisions.** This section reviews these heuristics and discusses the growing application of artificial intelligence (AI). You will learn about the pros and cons of AI.

Nine Common Decision-Making Biases: Rules of Thumb, or "Heuristics"

Despite the fact that people use rules of thumb all the time when making decisions, that doesn't mean they're reliable. Indeed, some are real barriers to high-quality decision making. Among those that tend to bias how decision makers process information are (1) *availability*, (2) *representativeness*, (3) *confirmation*, (4) *sunk cost*, (5) *anchoring and adjustment,* (6) *overconfidence*, (7) *hindsight*, (8) *framing*, and (9) *escalation of commitment.*[118]

1. The Availability Bias: Using Only the Information Available

If you had a perfect on-time work attendance record for nine months but were late for work four days during the last two months because of traffic, shouldn't your boss take into account your entire attendance history when considering you for a raise? Yet managers tend to give more weight to more recent behavior. The reason is the **availability bias**—**the use of information readily available from memory to make judgments.**

The bias, of course, is that readily available information may not present a complete picture of a situation. The availability bias may be stoked by the news media, which tend to favor news that is unusual or dramatic. Thus, for example, because of the efforts of interest groups or celebrities, more news coverage may be given to AIDS or to breast cancer than to heart disease, leading people to think the former are the bigger killers, when in fact the latter is.

2. The Representativeness Bias: Faulty Generalizing from a Small Sample or a Single Event

As a form of financial planning, playing state lotteries leaves something to be desired. When, for instance, in 2018 the U.S. Powerball jackpot stood at $570 million, the fifth largest in the game's history, the odds of winning it were put at 1 in 292.2 million. (A person would have a far greater chance of being struck by an asteroid, with odds of 1 in only 1.9 million.)[119] Nevertheless, millions of people buy lottery tickets because they read or hear about a handful of fellow citizens who have been the fortunate recipients of enormous winnings. This is an example of the **representativeness bias**, **the tendency to generalize from a small sample or a single event.**

The bias here is that just because something happens once, that doesn't mean it is representative—that it will happen again or will happen to you. For example, the fact that you hired an extraordinary sales representative from a particular university doesn't mean the same university will provide an equally qualified candidate next time. Yet managers make this kind of biased hiring decision all the time.

3. The Confirmation Bias: Seeking Information to Support Your Point of View

The **confirmation bias** occurs when people seek information to support their point of view and discount data that do not support it. Though this bias is so obvious you may think it should be easy to avoid, we practice it all the time, listening to the information we want to hear and ignoring the rest. "We typically focus on anything that agrees with the outcome we want," suggests economist Noreena Hertz. "We need to be aware of our natural born optimism. . . . We need to acknowledge our tendency to incorrectly process challenging news and actively push ourselves to hear the bad as well as the good."[120]

4. The Sunk-Cost Bias: Money Already Spent Seems to Justify Continuing

The **sunk-cost bias**, or ***sunk-cost fallacy***, occurs when managers add up all the money already spent on a project and conclude it is too costly to simply abandon it.

Most people have an aversion to "wasting" money. Especially if large sums have already been spent, they may continue to push on with an iffy-looking project to justify the money already sunk into it. The sunk-cost bias is sometimes called the "Concorde" effect, referring to the fact that the French and British governments continued to invest in the Concorde supersonic jetliner even when it was evident there was no economic justification for the aircraft.

5. The Anchoring and Adjustment Bias: Being Influenced by an Initial Figure

Managers will often give their employees a standard percentage raise in salary, basing the decision on whatever the workers made the preceding year. They may do this even though the raise is completely out of alignment with what other companies are paying for the same skills. This is an instance of the **anchoring and adjustment bias**, the tendency to make decisions based on an initial figure.

The bias is that the initial figure may be irrelevant to market realities. This phenomenon is sometimes seen in real estate sales. Before the 2008 crash in real estate markets, many homeowners might have been inclined at first to list their houses at an extremely high (but perhaps randomly chosen) selling price. These sellers were then unwilling to come down in price to match buying offers that reflected what the marketplace thought the house was really worth.

6. The Overconfidence Bias: Blind to Our Own Blindness

The **overconfidence bias** is the bias in which people's subjective confidence in their decision making is greater than their objective accuracy. Overconfidence, it's suggested, may be behind the reasons for the BP Deepwater Horizon drilling rig explosion and disaster in 2010 that flooded the Gulf of Mexico with 200 million gallons of oil. Because technology often works flawlessly, BP ignored warning signs that included a dead battery, a leaky cement job, and loose hydraulic fittings.[121]

"Overconfidence arises because people are often blind to their own blindness," says behavioral psychologist Daniel Kahneman. For instance, with experienced investment advisors whose financial outcomes simply depended on luck, he found "the illusion of skill is not only an individual aberration; it is deeply ingrained in the culture of the industry."[122] In general, he advises, we should not take assertive and confident people at their own evaluation unless we have independent reasons to believe they know what they're talking about.

7. The Hindsight Bias: The I-Knew-It-All-Along Effect

The **hindsight bias** is the tendency of people to view events as more predictable than they really are, as when at the end of watching a game we decide the outcome was obvious and predictable, even though in fact it was not. Sometimes called the "I-knew-it-all-along" effect, this occurs when we look back on a decision and try to reconstruct why we decided to do something.

8. The Framing Bias: Shaping the Way a Problem Is Presented

The **framing bias** is the tendency of decision makers to be influenced by the way a situation or problem is presented to them. For instance, customers have been found to prefer meat that is framed as "85% lean meat" instead of "15% fat," although they are the same thing.[123] In general, people view choices more favorably when they are framed in terms of gains rather than losses.[124] You would be more likely to invest in a product that had a 60 percent chance of success rather than a 40 percent chance of failure. Try framing your decision questions in alternate ways to avoid this bias.

9. The Escalation of Commitment Bias: Feeling Overly Invested in a Decision

If you really hate to admit you're wrong, you need to be aware of the **escalation of commitment bias**, **whereby decision makers increase their commitment to a project despite negative information about it.**

Would you invest more money in an old or broken car? The Drug Enforcement Administration and the Pentagon continued to spend on a spy plane for use in Afghanistan that was supposed to be completed in 2012 at a cost of $22 million, even though the project had missed every projected delivery date. As of early 2018, it was "not yet complete and is no longer intended to fly in Afghanistan," according to a review by the Justice Department. Total payouts had reached $86 million.[125]

To reduce the escalation of commitment, researchers recommend that decision makers set minimum targets for performance and then compare their performance results with their targets. Managers should also be rotated in key positions during a project, and decision makers should be encouraged to become less ego-involved with the work. Finally, decision makers should be made aware of the costs of persistence.[126]

The Decision-Making Potential of Artificial Intelligence

It certainly seems possible that, thanks to the power of artificial intelligence (AI), we will soon have robots, drones, driverless cars, and even home appliances and other devices that can make their own decisions and act independently of human oversight and direction. This clearly would reduce the use of decision-making biases. There is no question that one of the most promising applications of AI is in aiding human decision making. How far has AI come in this direction, what applications may be most promising, and what potential drawbacks should managers be aware of?

You still have at least one big advantage over artificial intelligence: AI "can't read a textbook and understand the questions in the back of the book," says Oren Etzioni, who runs Microsoft's Allen Institute for Artificial Intelligence. "It is devoid of common sense." Paul Allen, cofounder of Microsoft, agrees. He is doubling the Allen Institute's budget over the next three years to try to change that situation, primarily by closing the gap between humans' and machines' understanding of the world. It may take a while, however. A project called Cyc, working in collaboration with several big tech firms and the U.S. government, has been trying for some time to develop a "common sense engine" that can grasp such simple truths as the impossibility of being in two places at the same time. Thirty years and hundreds of millions of dollars later, the goal remains elusive.[127]

But that doesn't mean AI doesn't have valuable applications in aiding human decision making, often by drilling through data that is itself generated by human decisions. When it comes to building and evaluating models and simulations to make predictions, machines guided by AI are more powerful than humans and much, much faster. PricewaterhouseCooper (PwC), the global professional services company, uses a model of financial and purchasing decisions based on data drawn from multiple sources, including the U.S. Census, that describes characteristics of 320 million U.S. consumers. By creating realistic pictures of "someone like you" and "your future self," the model can evaluate common consumer behaviors like using credit cards, taking out loans, and buying insurance, thus predicting for its clients the way consumer choices and buying decisions might change over time and under different kinds of assumptions about both the larger economy and the individual (though hypothetical) consumer.[128]

Today's cars are already using AI applications. Though well short of being self-driving, AI-equipped cars are becoming increasingly safe and convenient. Sensors that alert drivers to potential accidents, accessory video cameras that do the same, and even adaptive cruise controls that automatically slow a car as it approaches a slower vehicle are among the applications already available. On a larger scale, commercial AI systems are churning through vast amounts of information culled from decisions by consumers, manufacturers, and taxi and ride-share operators to predict future conditions in the automotive and transportation industries. The models these systems develop can allow business managers to better choose marketing and pricing strategies and even the most profitable business models to adopt.[129]

Medicine is no stranger to AI. Google's parent company, Alphabet, says its DeepMind Health initiative, based in London, is helping save lives. The program uses AI to monitor hospital patients closely enough to alert doctors about those at risk of death two days earlier than can currently be done by other means. Doctors get a 48-hour head start on choosing treatments to stabilize and save these patients.[130]

Notice, however, that it's still business managers choosing their strategies and doctors deciding what their patients need. According to *Harvard Business Review*, advances in AI's decision-making capabilities will not reduce our reliance on human decision making but rather will enhance it.[131] "Economic theory suggests that AI will substantially raise the value of human judgment. People who display good judgment will become more valuable, not less," says a recent article. The reason is that while artificial intelligence is helpful in rapidly analyzing vast stores of data to make predictions, it does not have the capability to assess the costs and benefits of decisions and weigh the trade-offs. That's where human judgment steps in. Google already learned the value of human judgment the hard way, when it had to correct its photo recognition capability after the program tagged black people as gorillas.[132]

Another potential limitation from AI's lack of ability to make judgments or apply common sense is the possibility for it to make mistakes. Many people working in AI acknowledge that it remains difficult to program machine learning systems—essentially AI applications that can learn from experience by receiving virtual rewards—to act in ways that are desired and predictable. Sometimes, for instance, what machine learning systems learn from experience is how to cheat. Coding the rewards for even simple tasks is already immensely difficult and not yet perfected. One AI system that was supposed to learn to play a boat racing game called CoastRunners "learned" that the easiest way to score points was to drive around in circles rather than playing the course set out in the game.[133] The challenges in developing machine learning systems remain great.

And yet, says Anand Rao, of PwC Data & Analytics, "There's an immense opportunity to use AI in all kinds of decision making."[134] Most experts see three distinct areas in which AI can be applied to decision making. The most basic, *assisted intelligence*, simply automates basic tasks, making it faster and cheaper for humans to accomplish them. Next is *augmented intelligence*, which describes most of the applications discussed above. Here, in a kind of "symmetry," according to Rao, an augmented intelligence system learns from human inputs in order to assist humans in making better decisions. The third type of AI application to decision making includes self-driving cars. In this use of *autonomous intelligence*, humans have given operational control to the machine.[135]

Pros and Cons of Artificial Intelligence

A recent report by the consulting firm Accenture calls artificial intelligence "a new factor of production," alongside the traditional factors of labor, capital, entrepreneurship, and natural resources, and predicts that by 2035 its increasing use will boost labor productivity by up to 40% and double economic growth. The changed nature of work, if these predictions are accurate, will "enable people to make more efficient use of their time."[136] Although he admits to some worries about "superintelligence,"[137] Bill Gates, Microsoft's cofounder, says that with AI, "certainly we can look forward to the idea that vacations will be longer at some point. The purpose of humanity is not just to sit behind a counter and sell things. More free time is not a terrible thing."[138]

On the plus side, humans could be relieved of some of the drudgery of work—and even some of the time commitment today's jobs often require—as more tasks could be safely assigned to AI applications or machine learning systems. The struggle to find work-life balance or to accommodate the conflicting needs of boss and family could become a thing of the past. AI-assisted traffic lights that adjust to congested roads, bad weather, and accidents could make commuting in your self-driving car a breeze.

This AI drone is being used in Champagne, France to monitor vineyards. Drone likes this help growers to get a better idea of what is happening in the vineyard. They can provide information regarding water saturation and pest damage, and ultimately help improve the quality of grapes produced.
©freeprod/123RF

Consumers' privacy and personal data could be better safeguarded as AI systems monitor–and deflect–the activities of hackers. Companies could build more personal approaches to their customers by using AI to learn what they really want and then recommending products to suit.[139] San Francisco's Museum of Modern Art, for example, can text art lovers an image of one of its 35,000 works by using AI to match keywords texted with the request, "Send me." The service is free.[140]

Many business and personal tasks could become cheaper, allowing money to be put to other uses. And, by integrating AI into human resource strategies, managers might even be able to use AI to identify and eliminate human bias from hiring and promotion decisions, performance evaluation, benefits administration, and disciplinary or corrective actions. "We can be freed up to do what we should be doing," says Ashley Wilczek of Justice AV Solutions, "improving our people and their experiences at our company."[141]

But AI is not without its critics. Among some of the most outspoken are giants of the tech industry, such as Elon Musk of Tesla and SpaceX. The eminent physicist Stephen Hawking, who passed away in 2018, also warned of the dangers of weaponized artificial intelligence and the possibility that "AI could be the worst event in the history of our civilization."[142] In addition to the risk of errors noted above and the practical challenges that remain in making AI practical and reliable, these and other observers worry that AI can be put to malicious uses.

For instance, an airborne AI drone has already been cobbled together, inexpensively and from easily available parts, that can actually stalk someone. Meant to be simply entertaining, it could conceivably become something much worse. A *New York Times* writer called it an "automated bloodhound."[143] More worrying, perhaps, a recent report by a group of U.S. and British AI researchers warns AI developers against widely sharing their work.[144] "Less attention has historically been paid to the ways in which artificial intelligence can be used maliciously," the report says. Among those ways: AI can make it faster and easier to hack other systems, rather than protect them, and to do so more effectively. The report also cautions against the possibility that autonomous weapons could be developed and deployed, and that AI systems could undermine "truthful public debates," the hallmark of democracies, by expanding surveillance in authoritarian ways. Finally, according to the report, AI systems also learn in ways we do not yet understand, and it is already possible to use them to generate convincing–but false–images and sounds. As the *New York Times* reports, "deepfake" AI technology makes it possible to splice any face onto a random body in a video (most often pornography to date) or to show someone–such as a government official–saying things he or she never said.[145]

Elon Musk says AI presents "vastly more risk than North Korea" and believes "people should be really concerned about it," calling it "a fundamental risk to the existence of human civilization."[146] OpenAI, a nonprofit lab for which he provides some funding, has teamed up with Google's AI unit called DeepMind to address ways to enhance the safety of AI applications. One way the two organizations are exploring to prevent AI from going the way of HAL, the misbehaving computer of *2001*, is to perfect a machine learning system that takes its cues from humans rather than inventing its own unexpected solutions.[147]

The common denominator identified by AI critics is that the technology has the capacity to exceed human capabilities, a risk for which, in their view, society is not sufficiently prepared. But Steve Wozniak, who once counted himself among those concerned about an AI-assisted future, has changed his mind because AI lacks the simple ability of a two-year-old child to, say, recognize what a dog is after one viewing. Says Apple's cofounder now, "Artificial intelligence doesn't scare me at all."[148] ●

7.6 Group Decision Making: How to Work with Others

THE BIG PICTURE

Group decision making has five potential advantages and four potential disadvantages. The disadvantage of groupthink merits focus because it leads to terrible decisions. It is also important to consider the characteristics of group decision making before allowing a group to make a decision. Finally, knowledge about group problem-solving techniques can enhance group decision-making effectiveness.

LO 7-6

Outline the basics of group decision making.

The movies celebrate the lone heroes who, like Bruce Willis or Mark Wahlberg, make their own moves, call their own shots. Most managers, however, work with groups and teams (as we discuss in Chapter 13). Although groups don't make as high-quality decisions as the best individual acting alone, research suggests that groups make better decisions than *most* individuals acting alone.[149] Thus, to be an effective manager, you need to learn about decision making in groups.

Advantages and Disadvantages of Group Decision Making

Because you may often have a choice as to whether to make a decision by yourself or to consult with others, you need to understand the advantages and disadvantages of group-aided decision making.

Advantages

Using a group to make a decision offers five possible advantages.[150] For these benefits to happen, however, the group must be made up of diverse participants, not just people who all think the same way.

- **Greater pool of knowledge.** When several people are making the decision, there is a greater pool of information from which to draw. If one person doesn't have the pertinent knowledge and experience, someone else might.
- **Different perspectives.** Because different people have different perspectives—marketing, production, legal, and so on—they see the problem from different angles.
- **Intellectual stimulation.** A group of people can brainstorm or otherwise bring greater intellectual stimulation and creativity to the decision-making process than is usually possible with one person acting alone.
- **Better understanding of decision rationale.** If you participate in making a decision, you are more apt to understand the reasoning behind the decision, including the pros and cons leading up to the final step.
- **Deeper commitment to the decision.** If you've been part of the group that has bought into the final decision, you're more apt to be committed to seeing that the course of action is successfully implemented.

Disadvantages

The disadvantages of group-aided decision making spring from problems in how members interact.[151]

- **A few people dominate or intimidate.** Sometimes a handful of people will talk the longest and the loudest, and the rest of the group will simply give in. Or one individual, such as a strong leader, will exert disproportionate influence, sometimes by intimidation. This reduces creativity.
- **Groupthink.** **Groupthink** occurs when group members strive to agree for the sake of unanimity and thus avoid accurately assessing the decision situation.

Here the positive team spirit of the group actually works against sound judgment.[152] Groupthink is explored more thoroughly in the next section.

- **Satisficing.** Because most people would just as soon cut short a meeting, the tendency is to seek a decision that is "good enough" rather than to push on in pursuit of other possible solutions. Satisficing can occur because groups have limited time, lack the right kind of information, or are unable to handle large amounts of information.[153]
- **Goal displacement.** Although the primary task of the meeting may be to solve a particular problem, other considerations may rise to the fore, such as rivals trying to win an argument. **Goal displacement** occurs when the primary goal is subsumed by a secondary goal.

Different perspectives or groupthink? A diversified team can offer differing points of view, as well as a greater pool of knowledge and intellectual stimulation. Or it can offer groupthink and satisficing. What has been your experience as to the value of decision making in the groups you've been in?
©Sam Edwards/age fotostock

Groupthink

Cohesiveness isn't always good. When it results in groupthink, group or team members are friendly and tight-knit but unable to think "outside the box." Their "strivings for unanimity override their motivation to realistically appraise alternative courses of action," says Irwin Janis, author of *Groupthink*.[154]

The results of groupthink can include failure to consider new information and a loss of new ideas. For instance, some blame the 2015 ouster of Ellen Kullman, DuPont's high-performing CEO, who had 27 years with the company, on a case of groupthink by the firm's insulated board of directors, who never asked Kullman to meet with them to defend her actions.[155] Investors in Silicon Valley also often show a herd mentality in their desire to be part of "the next big thing," according to one writer.[156]

Symptoms of Groupthink

How do you know that you're in a group or team that is suffering from groupthink? Some symptoms include the following:[157]

- **Sense of invulnerability.** Group members have the illusion that nothing can go wrong, breeding excessive optimism and risk taking. They may also be so assured of the rightness of their actions that they ignore the ethical implications.
- **Rationalization.** Rationalizing protects the pet assumptions underlying the group's decisions from critical questions.
- **Illusion of unanimity and peer pressure.** The illusion of unanimity is another way of saying that a member's silence is interpreted as consent. If people do disagree, peer pressure leads other members to question the dissenters' loyalty.
- **"The wisdom of crowds."** Groupthink's pressure to conform often leads members with different ideas to censor themselves—the opposite of collective wisdom, says James Surowiecki, in which "each person in the group is offering his or her best independent forecast. It's not at all about compromise or consensus."[158]

No doubt you've felt yourself pulled into a "groupthink opinion" at some point. Probably we all have. Self-Assessment 7.4 provides you with a way to evaluate the extent to which groupthink is affecting a team. Results provide insight into reducing this counterproductive group dynamic.

SELF-ASSESSMENT 7.4

Assessing Groupthink

The following survey was designed to assess groupthink. Please be prepared to answer these questions if your instructor has assigned Self-Assessment 7.4 in Connect.

1. Where does the team stand on the three aspects of groupthink?
2. Based on your survey scores, what would you do differently to reduce groupthink in the group you evaluated? Be specific.

Preventing Groupthink: Making Criticism and Other Perspectives Permissible

Janis believes it is easier to prevent groupthink than to cure it. As preventive measures, he and other writers suggest the following:[159]

- **Allow criticism.** Each member of a team or group should be told to be a critical evaluator, able to actively voice objections and doubts. Subgroups within the group should be allowed to discuss and debate ideas. Once a consensus has been reached, everyone should be encouraged to rethink his or her position to check for flaws. It is sometimes helpful for the group leader to withhold his or her opinion at first, to encourage others to speak up.
- **Allow other perspectives.** Outside experts should be used to introduce fresh perspectives. Different groups with different leaders should explore the same policy questions. Top-level executives should not use policy committees to rubber-stamp decisions that have already been made. When major alternatives are discussed, someone should be made devil's advocate to try to uncover all negative factors.

Characteristics of Group Decision Making

If you're a manager deliberating whether to call a meeting for group input, there are four characteristics of groups to be aware of.

1. They Are Less Efficient Groups take longer to make decisions. Thus, if time is of the essence, you may want to make the decision by yourself. Faced with time pressures or the serious effect of a decision, groups use less information and fewer communication channels, which increases the probability of a bad decision.[160]

2. Their Size Affects Decision Quality The larger the group, the lower the quality of the decision.[161] Some research says that seven people is the optimal size.[162] Others suggest five is best.[163] (An odd number is also considered best, when the group uses majority rules.)

3. They May Be Too Confident Groups are more confident about their judgments and choices than individuals are. This, of course, can be a liability because it can lead to groupthink.

4. Knowledge Counts Decision-making accuracy is higher when group members know a good deal about the relevant issues. It is also higher when a group leader has the ability to weight members' opinions.[164] Depending on whether group members know or don't know one another, the kind of knowledge also counts. For example, people who are familiar with one another tend to make better decisions when members have a lot of unique information. However, people who aren't familiar with one another tend to make better decisions when the members have common knowledge.[165]

Remember that individual decisions are not *necessarily* better than group decisions. As we said, although groups don't make as high-quality decisions as the *best* individual acting alone, groups generally make better decisions than *most* individuals acting alone. Some guidelines to using groups are presented in Table 7.3.

Toward consensus. Working to achieve cooperation in a group can tell you a lot about yourself. How well do you handle the negotiation process? What do you do when you're disappointed in a result achieved by consensus?
©Xavier Arnau/Getty Images

TABLE 7.3 When a Group Can Help in Decision Making: Three Practical Guidelines

These guidelines may help you as a manager decide whether to include people in a decision-making process and, if so, which people.

1. **When it can increase quality:** If additional information would increase the quality of the decision, managers should involve those people who can provide the needed information. Thus, if a type of decision occurs frequently, such as deciding on promotions or who qualifies for a loan, groups should be used because they tend to produce more consistent decisions than individuals do.
2. **When it can increase acceptance:** If acceptance within the organization is important, managers need to involve those individuals whose acceptance and commitment are important.
3. **When it can increase development:** If people can be developed through their participation, managers may want to involve those whose development is most important.

Source: Derived from George P. Huber, Managerial Decision Making *(Glenview, IL: Scott, Foresman, 1980), p. 149.*

In general, group decision making is more effective when members feel that they can freely and safely disagree with each other. This belief is referred to as **minority dissent**, **dissent that occurs when a minority in a group publicly opposes the beliefs, attitudes, ideas, procedures, or policies assumed by the majority of the group.**[166] Minority dissent is associated with increased innovation within groups.[167] Do your teams at school or work allow minority dissent? If not, what can be done to increase its existence? Self-Assessment 7.5 can help answer these questions.

SELF-ASSESSMENT 7.5

Assessing Participation in Group Decision Making

The following survey measures minority dissent, participation in group decision making, and satisfaction with a group. Please be prepared to answer these questions if your instructor has assigned Self-Assessment 7.5 in Connect.

1. What is the level of minority dissent in the group, and to what extent are you satisfied with being a member of this group?
2. Use the three lowest items that measure minority dissent to answer the following question: What can you do to increase the level of minority dissent in this group? Be specific.
3. Why do you think many groups muzzle the level of minority dissent?

Claye Smith described how a lack of minority dissent affected his work environment in the "I Wish ..." feature.

I Wish...

...my workplace didn't have a toxic group decision-making environment.

Claye Smith works in the banking industry as a financial analyst. His managers have created a toxic decision-making environment where employees do not feel safe expressing opinions, and new ideas are rarely encouraged.

According to Claye, a lot of the executives have been with the company and the industry for a long time. While they have a wealth of knowledge, they are far removed from the day-to-day happenings in the banking centers.

"You can tell, on some of our phone calls, that these managers are on a different page," said Claye. "If you try to explain something to them, they don't take well to that. It's not that they feel you are talking down to them, but they think, 'This is how we've done it, and this is how it's supposed to go.'" Claye believes that if management were more welcoming of new ideas from all employees, it would go a long way to creating a better decision-making environment.

"Obviously, a lot of younger employees are not going to know everything that the managers know. At the same time, executive management might have an overview of how the banking centers work, but a lot of managers don't go out and see how the centers actually function. They did back when they were in our positions, but so much has changed since then," said Claye.

In addition to being removed from certain processes and procedures, the managers are also removed from the environment and atmosphere of the banking centers. "Our corporate work environment is very dry and quiet. They work hard and get things done without a lot of chatter," said Claye. "The banking centers are almost the complete opposite. They are really upbeat, and you have customers coming in and out all the time."

Clay Smith Courtesy Claye Smith

Managers from the corporate office have a harder time adjusting to the banking center atmosphere when they visit.

Action has been taken by Claye's company to alleviate this issue. "We've hired a new position right under our director that will be spending a lot more time in the banking centers and bringing feedback to the corporate office," said Claye.

He hopes that this will result in a better connection between the managers and the employees who work directly with customers. With a stronger connection, managers might be more receptive to hearing new ideas. If employees feel like they can participate in the decision-making process, they are likely to be more satisfied and committed to the company's goals.

Courtesy of Claye Smith

Group Problem-Solving Techniques: Reaching for Consensus

Using groups to make decisions generally requires that they reach a **consensus**, **which occurs when members are able to express their opinions and reach agreement to support the final decision.** More specifically, consensus is reached "when all members can say they either agree with the decision or have had their 'day in court' and were unable to convince the others of their viewpoint," says one expert in decision making. "In the final analysis, everyone agrees to support the outcome."[168] This does not mean, however, that group members agree with the decision, only that they are willing to work toward its success.

One management expert offers the following dos and don'ts for achieving consensus.[169]

- **Do's:** Use active listening skills. Involve as many members as possible. Seek out the reasons behind arguments. Dig for the facts.
- **Don'ts:** Avoid log rolling and horse trading ("I'll support your pet project if you'll support mine"). Avoid making an agreement simply to keep relations amicable and not rock the boat. Finally, don't try to achieve consensus by putting questions to a vote; this will only split the group into winners and losers, perhaps creating bad feelings among the latter.

More Group Problem-Solving Techniques

Decision-making experts have developed several group problem-solving techniques to aid in problem solving. Four we will discuss here are (1) *brainstorming*, (2) *devil's advocacy*, (3) the *dialectic method*, and (4) *post-mortems*.

1. Brainstorming: For Increasing Creativity

Brainstorming is a technique used to help groups generate multiple ideas and alternatives for solving problems.[170] Developed by advertising executive A. F. Osborn, the technique consists of having members of a group meet and review a problem to be solved. Individual members are then asked to silently generate ideas or solutions, which are then collected (preferably without identifying their contributors) and written on a board or flip chart. A second session is then used to critique and evaluate the alternatives. (Incidentally, taking a brief stroll, even around the office, can significantly increase creativity.)[171]

A modern-day variation is **electronic brainstorming, sometimes called *brainwriting*, in which members of a group come together over a computer network to generate ideas and alternatives.**[172] Technology has also turned the smartphone into a device that uses various apps to spur the thinking process and unblock creative juices.[173]

Some rules for brainstorming suggested by IDEO, a product design company, are shown below in Table 7.4.

TABLE 7.4
Six Rules for Brainstorming

1. **Defer judgment.** Don't criticize during the initial stage of idea generation. Phrases such as "we've never done it that way," "it won't work," "it's too expensive," and "our manager will never agree" should not be used.
2. **Build on the ideas of others.** Encourage participants to extend others' ideas by avoiding "buts" and using "ands."
3. **Encourage wild ideas.** Encourage out-of-the-box thinking. The wilder and more outrageous the ideas, the better.
4. **Go for quantity over quality.** Participants should try to generate and write down as many new ideas as possible. Focusing on quantity encourages people to think beyond their favorite ideas.
5. **Be visual.** Use different-colored pens (for example, red, purple, blue) to write on big sheets of flip-chart paper, whiteboards, or poster boards that are put on the wall.
6. **One conversation at a time.** The ground rules are that no one interrupts another person, no dismissing of someone's ideas, no disrespect, and no rudeness.

Source: These recommendations and descriptions were derived from B. Nussbaum, "The Power of Design," BusinessWeek, *May 17, 2004, pp. 86–94.*

Brainstorming is an effective technique for generating new ideas/alternatives, and research reveals that people can be trained to improve their brainstorming skills.[174]

2. Devil's Advocacy Devil's advocacy gets its name from a traditional practice of the Roman Catholic Church. When someone's name comes before the College of Cardinals for elevation to sainthood, it is absolutely essential to ensure that the person had a spotless record. Consequently, one individual is assigned the role of *devil's advocate* to uncover and air all possible objections to the person's canonization. In today's organizations **devil's advocacy assigns someone the role of critic.** Figure 7.5 shows the steps in this approach. Note how devil's advocacy alters the usual decision-making process in steps 2 and 3 on the left-hand side of the figure.

3. The Dialectic Method Like devil's advocacy, the dialectic method is a time-honored practice, going all the way back to ancient Greece. Plato and his followers attempted to identify a truth, called *thesis*, by exploring opposite positions, called *antithesis.* Court systems in the United States and elsewhere today rely on hearing directly opposing points of view to establish guilt or innocence. Accordingly, the *dialectic method* calls for managers to foster a structured dialogue or debate of opposing viewpoints prior to making a decision.[175] Steps 3 and 4 in the right-hand side of Figure 7.5 set the dialectic approach apart from common decision-making processes.

4. Project Post-Mortems Said to have originated as a debriefing strategy used by the military, a **project post-mortem** is, as the name suggests, **a review of recent decisions in order to identify possible future improvements.** The idea is to carefully evaluate project results after the fact, noting what could be done differently and better, and then to record those insights to inform future decisions.[176] The post mortem usually takes place during a meeting of the project team and should begin with a thorough look at how the reality of the project differed from plans and expectations. For instance, did the upgrade

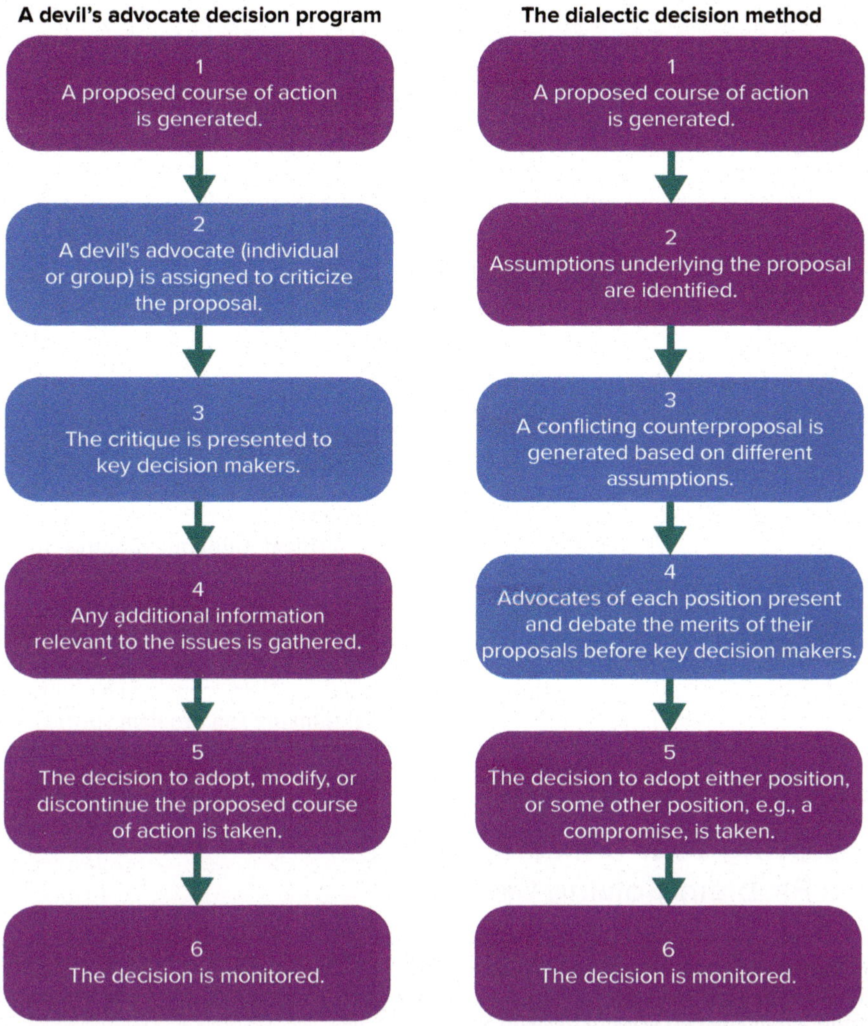

FIGURE 7.5

Techniques for stimulating functional conflict: Devil's advocacy and the dialectic method

Source: From R.A. Castler and R.C. Schwenk, "Agreement and Thinking Alike: Ingredients for Poor Decisions," Academy of Management Executive, *February 1990, pp. 72–73.*

of the company's computer system take more time or cost more money than budgeted? Were any steps in the process changed or eliminated as the project went along? How were unplanned contingencies handled? What went wrong, and what went right?

The purpose of this step is not to fix blame for anything that might have gone wrong, but rather to prepare the way for the next step: identifying ways in which recent experiences can help make future projects go more smoothly. For instance, if a project like upgrading a computer system took more time than anticipated, was the reason that the software vendor delivered late, that it took longer to train staff in the new program than planned, or that unanticipated compatibility problems delayed the cutover date? Only by identifying the reason can managers work on avoiding delays in similar projects in the future. The final step is to prepare a written report, which should be circulated to the team, to document the post mortem process and encourage the application of any lessons learned.

The length of the meeting, the number of participants, the degree of formality in its structure, and even the amount of time that has passed since project completion all can vary with the complexity of the project. A few basic strategies for any successful post mortem, however, are not to wait too long to schedule one, to prepare an agenda, and to encourage honest feedback from all participants, which should also include any customer comments and feedback received. At the very least, Ed Catmull of Pixar and Disney Animation, where project post mortems are popular, recommends doing at least this much after every project: Write down five things you would do again and five you wouldn't.[177] ●

7.7 Career Corner: Managing Your Career Readiness

LO 7-7

Describe how to develop the career readiness competencies of *critical thinking/problem solving* and *decision making.*

The career readiness soft skills of critical thinking/problem solving and decision making are highly desired competencies within our model of career readiness shown below. They also go hand in hand. Consider the definition of critical thinking/problem solving shown in Table 1.2. This competency entails the ability to use sound reasoning to analyze situations, make decisions, and solve problems. It also requires skills at obtaining, interpreting, and analyzing both qualitative and quantitative information while creatively solving problems.

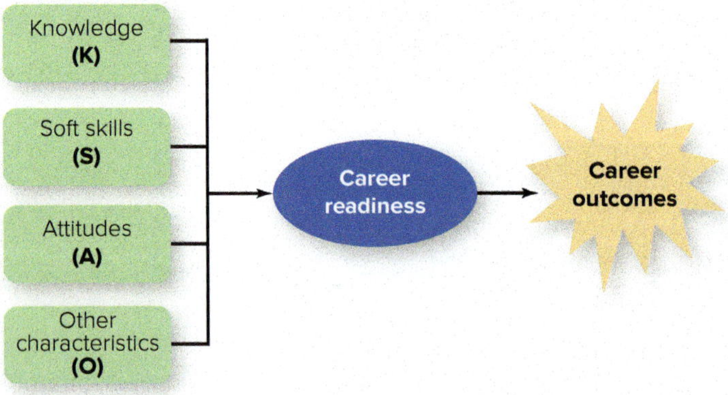

FIGURE 7.6
Model of career readiness

Critical thinking is much different from the moment-to-moment thinking that guides our everyday activities. Moment-to-moment thinking is automatic and highly susceptible to the biases discussed in this chapter. In contrast, critical thinking requires more deliberate mental processes. We need to stop and consciously process information when trying to critically think about a problem.

This section provides suggestions for improving your decision making by engaging in critical thinking and problem solving. We then discuss how you can demonstrate these skills during an employment interview.

Improving Your Critical Thinking and Problem-Solving Skills

Good decision-making ability amounts to being able to understand the relationship between causes and outcomes. In other words, good decision makers can predict what will occur in a given situation. Reflecting on your past experiences and using a decision methodology are two ways to develop this skill.

Reflect on Past Decisions

Most problems you will encounter at work after graduation will not be new, but they may be unfamiliar to you.[178] This means there are ready-made solutions you can use. One expert defined ready-made solutions as "best practices that have been captured and turned into standard operating procedures so that employees are better prepared to address regularly recurring problems."[179] By learning and applying these ready-made solutions, you can develop a larger set of options for solving problems, thereby improving your decision-making skills. This improvement will in turn assist you in resolving unanticipated problems. Use the following steps to increase your awareness of ready-made solutions.[180]

1. Think of a time in which you faced a problem either at work or in your personal life and you successfully resolved it. Now write down answers to the following questions:
   - What was the problem? Where did it occur and who was involved?
   - What was the solution?
   - Why did you select this solution?
   - What lessons can you derive from this experience that you can use when faced with similar problems?

2. Now think of a time you unsuccessfully solved a problem in your work or personal life. Write answers to the same questions listed above.
3. Think of someone you know who is very good at solving problems. Now focus on a specific problem you observed this person solving and write answers to the following questions:
   - What was the problem? Where did it occur and who was involved?
   - What was the solution?
   - What steps did the person follow in solving the problem?
   - What lessons can you learn from this and apply when faced with similar problems?

Establish a Decision Methodology

There is no single "right" way to solve problems. As you learned in this chapter, people have different decision-making styles. The key is to establish a process or method that works for you. Consider using or modifying the following steps:[181]

1. Analyze the situation. Why does a decision need to be made? What would happen if you delayed making a decision? Who will be affected by the decision? What information, data, analytics, or research do you need to consider in order to understand the causes and possible solutions? Are there political issues you need to take into account?
2. Consider what others would think about the solutions under consideration. Would you be proud of your decision if someone tweeted it out or printed it on the front page of the newspaper?
3. Seek advice or feedback from others before making a decision.
4. Conduct a cost-benefit analysis of different solutions. Do the benefits of any exceed the costs? Is it okay to incur higher short-term costs for a better long-term solution?
5. Is the decision consistent with your values and principles? Are you willing to co-opt your values or principles? Consider the cost of doing so.
6. Make the decision and observe the consequences. Then do a post-mortem.

Demonstrating These Competencies During a Job Interview

Being career ready means possessing the desired knowledge, skills, attitudes, and other characteristics (KSAOs) and being able to demonstrate them during a job interview. Assuming you possess some of these skills, now it's time to make a plan for making a positive impression. We recommend that you start by preparing answers to the following behaviorally based questions:[182]

- Describe the process you use to make decisions. Provide a specific example in which this process resulted in a positive outcome.
- Tell me about a time in which you had to make a quick decision. How did you approach the situation and what obstacles did you face? How did you make this decision without having all the necessary information?
- Describe a time in which you used intuition to make a decision rather than relying on data or hard facts. What was the outcome of your decision, and what did you learn from the experience? ●

Key Terms Used in This Chapter

analytics 252
anchoring and adjustment bias 261
availability bias 260
Big Data 254
Big Data analytics 254
bounded rationality 244
brainstorming 269
confirmation bias 261
consensus 269
decision 240
decision making 240
decision-making style 257
decision tree 248
devil's advocacy 270
diagnosis 242
electronic brainstorming 270
escalation of commitment bias 262
ethics officer 248
framing bias 261
goal displacement 266
groupthink 265
heuristics 260
hindsight bias 261
intuition 245
minority dissent 268
nonrational models of decision making 244
opportunities 242
overconfidence bias 261
predictive modeling 254
problems 242
project post-mortem 270
rational model of decision making 242
representativeness bias 260
satisficing model 244
sunk-cost bias 261

Key Points

7.1 Two Kinds of Decision Making: Rational and Nonrational

- A decision is a choice made from among available alternatives. Decision making is the process of identifying and choosing alternative courses of action. Two models managers follow in making decisions are rational and nonrational.
- In the rational model, there are four steps in making a decision: Step 1 is identifying the problem or opportunity. A problem is a difficulty that inhibits the achievement of goals. An opportunity is a situation that presents possibilities for exceeding existing goals. This is a matter of diagnosis—analyzing the underlying causes. Step 2 is thinking up alternative solutions. Step 3 is evaluating the alternatives and selecting a solution. Alternatives should be evaluated according to cost, quality, ethics, feasibility, and effectiveness. Step 4 is implementing and evaluating the solution chosen. The rational model of decision making assumes managers will make logical decisions that will be the optimum in furthering the organization's best interests. The rational model is prescriptive, describing how managers ought to make decisions.
- Nonrational models of decision making assume that decision making is nearly always uncertain and risky, making it difficult for managers to make optimum decisions. Two nonrational models are satisficing and intuition. (1) Satisficing falls under the concept of bounded rationality—that is, that the ability of decision makers to be rational is limited by enormous constraints, such as time and money. These constraints force managers to make decisions according to the satisficing model—that is, managers seek alternatives until they find one that is satisfactory, not optimal. (2) Intuition is making choices without the use of conscious thought or logical inference. The sources of intuition are expertise and feelings.

7.2 Making Ethical Decisions

- Corporate corruption has made ethics in decision making once again important. Many companies have an ethics officer to resolve ethical dilemmas, and more companies are creating values statements to guide employees as to desirable business behavior.
- To help make ethical decisions, a decision tree—a graph of decisions and their possible consequences—may be helpful. Managers should ask whether a proposed action is legal and, if it is intended to maximize shareholder value, whether it is ethical—and whether it would be ethical *not* to take the proposed action.

7.3 Evidence-Based Decision Making and Analytics

- Evidence-based management means translating principles based on best evidence into organizational practice. It is intended to bring rationality to the decision-making process.
- Scholars Jeffrey Pfeffer and Robert Sutton identify seven implementation principles to help companies that are committed to doing what it takes to profit from evidence-based management: (1) Treat your organization as an unfinished prototype; (2) "no brag, just facts"; (3) see yourself and your organization as outsiders do; (4) have everyone, not just top executives, be guided by the responsibility to gather and act on quantitative and qualitative data; (5) you may need to use vivid stories to sell unexciting evidence to others in the company; (6) at the very least, you should slow the spread of bad practices; and (7) you should learn from failure by using the facts to make things better.
- Applying the best evidence to your decisions is difficult, for seven reasons: (1) There's too much evidence. (2) There's not enough *good* evidence. (3) The evidence doesn't quite apply. (4) People are trying to mislead you. (5) *You* are trying to mislead

you. (6) The side effects outweigh the cure. (7) Stories are more persuasive, anyway.

- Perhaps the purest application of evidence-based management is the use of analytics, or business analytics, sophisticated forms of business data analysis. Analytics competitors have three key attributes: (1) They go beyond simple descriptive statistics and use data mining and predictive modeling to identify potential and most profitable customers. (2) They don't have just one principal application but rather use analytics in multiple applications. (3) The use of analytics is supported by top executives.
- A new concept is that of Big Data, which requires handling by very sophisticated analysis software and supercomputing-level hardware. Big Data includes not only data in corporate databases, but also web-browsing data trails, social network communications, sensor data, and surveillance data.
- Big Data analytics is the process of examining large amounts of data of a variety of types to uncover hidden patterns, unknown correlations, and other useful information.

7.4 Four General Decision-Making Styles

- A decision-making style reflects the combination of how an individual perceives and responds to information.
- Decision-making styles may tend to have a value orientation, which reflects the extent to which a person focuses on either task or technical concerns versus people and social concerns when making decisions.
- Decision-making styles may also reflect a person's tolerance for ambiguity, the extent to which a person has a high or low need for structure or control in his or her life.
- When the dimensions of value orientation and tolerance for ambiguity are combined, they form four styles of decision making: directive (action-oriented decision makers who focus on facts), analytical (careful decision makers who like lots of information and alternative choices), conceptual (decision makers who rely on intuition and have a long-term perspective), and behavioral (the most people-oriented decision makers).

7.5 Decision-Making Biases and the Use of Artificial Intelligence

- Nine common decision-making biases present real barriers to high-quality decision making. They are (1) availability, (2) representativeness, (3) confirmation, (4) sunk cost, (5) anchoring and adjustment, (6) overconfidence, (7) hindsight, (8) framing, and (9) escalation of commitment.
- Artificial intelligence (AI) presents vast potential to assist human decision making, with applications already under way in manufacturing, transportation (driverless cars), medicine, and other fields. Advantages include reduced costs, the potential to eliminate bias in decision making, and human freedom from drudgery. AI might also be able to better protect secure data stores and systems from hacks that endanger functionality, safety, and consumer privacy. On the other hand, critics warn of the potential for AI to be used to deceive and for runaway programs to make their own decisions, such as to hack the systems they are supposed to protect.

7.6 Group Decision Making: How to Work with Others

- Groups make better decisions than most individuals acting alone, though not as good as the best individual acting alone.
- Using a group to make a decision offers five possible advantages: (1) a greater pool of knowledge, (2) different perspectives, (3) intellectual stimulation, (4) better understanding of the reasoning behind the decision, and (5) deeper commitment to the decision.
- It also has four disadvantages: (1) a few people may dominate or intimidate; (2) it will produce groupthink, when group members strive for agreement among themselves for the sake of unanimity and so avoid accurately assessing the decision situation; (3) satisficing; and (4) goal displacement, when the primary goal is subsumed to a secondary goal.
- Some characteristics of groups to be aware of are (1) groups are less efficient, (2) their size affects decision quality, (3) they may be too confident, and (4) knowledge counts—decision-making accuracy is higher when group members know a lot about the issues.
- Using groups to make decisions generally requires that they reach a consensus, which occurs when members are able to express their opinions and reach agreement to support the final decision. Minority dissent should be allowed, so members can safely disagree with each other.
- Four techniques aid in problem solving. (1) Brainstorming helps groups generate multiple ideas and alternatives for solving problems. A variant is electronic brainstorming, in which group members use a computer network to generate ideas. 2. Devil's advocacy assigns someone the role of critic. Figure 7.5 shows the steps in this approach. 3. The dialectic method calls for managers to foster a structured dialogue or debate of opposing viewpoints prior to making a decision. Steps 3 and 4 on the right-hand side of Figure 7.5 set the dialectic approach apart from common decision-making processes. (4) A project post mortem is a review of recent decisions in order to identify possible future improvements. The idea is not to assign blame but to carefully evaluate project results after the fact, noting what could be done differently and better.

7.7 Career Corner: Managing Your Career Readiness

- The career readiness competencies of *critical thinking/problem solving* and *decision making* go hand in hand.
- Reflecting on your past experiences and using a decision methodology are two ways to improve critical thinking and problem solving.

Understanding the Chapter: What Do I Know?

1. What are the steps in rational decision making?
2. What are two models of nonrational decision making?
3. What are four ethical questions a manager should ask when evaluating a proposed action to make a decision?
4. Competitors using analytics have what three key attributes?
5. What is Big Data?
6. Describe the four general decision-making styles.
7. How does artificial intelligence support human decision making?
8. Can you name the nine common decision-making biases?
9. What are the advantages and disadvantages of group decision making?
10. What are four group problem-solving techniques?

Management in Action

New York's Subway System Is Crumbling

With 472 stations, the New York City subway system is the largest in the world, with a long and rich history. The system was first established in 1904 in the borough of Manhattan, before expanding to Brooklyn, Queens, and the Bronx by 1915. The Metropolitan Transportation Authority (MTA) oversees its 27 subway lines.[183]

Subway ridership had grown to 5.7 million daily passengers in 2017, double the number two decades earlier. The level of service and quality, however, has not kept up. Tunnels and track routes are crumbling. Signal problems and equipment failures have doubled between 2007 and 2017, and the system has the worst on-time performance of any major rapid transit system in the world. These problems are not due to acts of nature like a flood. Rather, decades of poor decision making seems to be a key cause, according to *The New York Times*.[184] Let's take a closer look at what's been plaguing the Empire State's transit system.

THE BIG APPLE'S TRANSIT PROBLEM

The derelict state of the New York City subway system is partly due to poor decision making by the MTA and other state-level government officials. Some decisions were made for political reasons or based on decision-making biases, and sometimes officials simply refused to make a decision at all. This type of governmental dysfunction is not out of the ordinary, but it is surprising given the number of people who rely on the subway daily to get around.

Politics was the first problem with the city's decision making. The MTA decided in 2008 to renovate stations by installing glass domes and mirrors. These cosmetic improvements were to be made in the home district of New York's then Assembly speaker. The *Times* reported that the Assembly speaker demanded the project be completed; otherwise, MTA's budget would be vetoed. The project cost $1.4 billion (more than the annual budget of the entire Chicago rapid transit system).[185] Not a penny was spent on signals or tracks, which are vital to keep the trains running safely and on time. The executive director of TransitCenter told *amNewYork* that there "has been sort of the lack of accountability in Albany and the continual depletion of resources from the MTA and misprioritization on cosmetics instead of the nuts and bolts of actually running the system reliably."[186]

The MTA tried to minimize future political decision making by assembling an independent Transportation Reinvention Commission in 2014 to study the city's deteriorating system. The Commission was made up of successful transportation leaders from all over the world. It provided seven strategies to rehabilitate the subway system, including capacity expansion, a dedicated transportation fund, and congestion pricing.[187]

You might imagine that the Commission's findings then provided a starting point for the MTA's future decisions. This was not the case. For example, the Commission diagnosed capacity expansion, not cosmetic remodeling, as a major problem for the subway system. Capacity expansion would allow the subway to continue to handle increased ridership in a safe, sustainable way.[188] Instead of investing in capacity expansion, however, as *NBC New York* reported, the agency decided years after the Commission's report to again invest in cosmetically remodeling dozens of stations, this time to the tune of $1 billion.[189]

The MTA's choice to make cosmetic repairs wasn't the only example of poor decision making. State leadership contributed to the problem as well. For example, the MTA owed Albany for expenses related to the subway system that the state had incurred. The agency could have been allowed to keep the money and invest in its crumbling infrastructure, but state leaders instead ordered the MTA to bail out state-run ski resorts. *The New York Daily News* reported that in 2013 around $5 million was sent to the Olympic Regional Development Authority, which operates the state ski resorts.

Lawmakers and transportation advocates questioned the decision to bail out ski resorts when the subway system urgently needed attention. A state senator told the *Daily News*, "The MTA needs more money, not less. It's having enough trouble funding its own needs. I don't see why we'd be sending MTA resources to ski slopes." The MTA does not oversee state-run ski resorts, but it sent the money anyway.[190] The agency's board hired a law firm to investigate the decision. It was found to be legal, but the board still labeled it as inappropriate.[191]

IT'S IN THE DATA!

Why all these poor decisions? One reason is that leaders may not have been utilizing data to support their actions. For example, the MTA's sloppy data collection prevented it from adopting congestion pricing, a strategy of increasing fares during times of peak ridership (similar to Uber's "surge pricing"). Supporters of congestion pricing told *CBS News* that this scheme would address gridlock and raise money for mass transit. Skeptics of congestion pricing included Bill de Blasio, New York City's mayor. De Blasio believed congestion pricing in general was a burden on middle class and low-income commuters.[192] These conflicting views, coupled with a lack of evidence to support an ideal solution, may have led to indecision on fare price increases.

All these issues have made the subway situation so bad that New York's governor declared a "state of emergency" for the system in 2017.[193] Riders also made declarations of their own. A group of them rallied at the State Capitol in Albany in 2018. The protestors, representing subway riders, told *amNewYork* they were "desperate for change" and that state legislators could not leave Albany without approving new funding for the system.[194] New Yorkers' patience had reached its end.

A NEW DECISION MAKER ENTERS THE PICTURE

Andy Byford became head of the New York City Transit Authority (NYCTA) in January 2018. The NYCTA is the division of the MTA that oversees the New York City subway and bus systems. Byford came from the Toronto transit system, where he executed a five-year modernization plan. The plan significantly improved the subway system, and Toronto earned "outstanding public transit system of the year" in 2017. A Toronto transit activist told the *Guardian* that upon his arrival in Canada, Byford had been "looking for, in the short term, quick wins." Byford understood that a reputation for indecisiveness doesn't bode well for a new leader. "That's the basic thing any new manager does: they come in and want to be seen as doing something . . . " said the activist.[195] The question is whether Byford can duplicate Toronto's success with the New York City's subway system, which is four times bigger than Toronto's.[196]

Byford doesn't just make decisions for the sake of expediency in pursuit of quick wins. He first wants to study the New York subway system by riding it to work every day. He believes this experience will garner useful feedback from commuters and MTA employees. Byford cultivated this hands-on style in Toronto, where he once spent hours navigating the subway in a wheelchair with a member of the system's accessibility forum. This experience provided him useful insights about the challenges faced by those who have a mobility impairment. Gathering first-hand information meant he could make more informed decisions to their benefit.[197]

The new NYCTA chief's style seems to be making an impact at the MTA as well. His influence stems from serving on the 2014 MTA Transportation Reinvention Commission. In that role, Byford was able to help convince the agency to halt the $1 billion modernization project it had slated for summer 2018 because it did not address urgent needs. Not everyone is in agreement with halting the project, though, including the MTA chairman. He argues that fresh paint, better lighting, and working MetroCard machines are more about safety, not luxury.[198]

Byford doesn't seem to be a fan of cosmetic makeovers. He told *The Wall Street Journal* that, "We've got to get the basics right, day in, day out." These basics include service reliability. Byford plans to shake up the agency's workforce, processes, and infrastructure in a new plan to be released in late 2018. The plan will not be centered solely on his views though. Byford wants to engage city board members in the process as well. This way, even if they don't agree with his plans in the end, they won't feel shut out of the process.[199]

Byford must effectively balance time and discussion if he wants to get past the indecisiveness of his predecessors. The *Journal* reports that it could take up to 40 years to modernize the subway's signal system. Byford wants to speed the process up, but not at any cost. For example, an MTA spokesman mentioned in 2018 that wireless technology might speed up modernization efforts. Byford was cautious though. "I would need to be convinced that an alternative is viable because we don't have the time to waste going down a blind alley," he says.[200]

Will Byford's decision-making style put the subway system back on track?

FOR DISCUSSION

Problem-Solving Perspective

1. What is the underlying problem in this case from NYCTA President Andy Byford's perspective?
2. What do you think about Byford's approach for solving the problem? Explain.

Application of Chapter Content

1. What are some barriers to Byford's ability to utilize rational decision making? Explain.
2. Which nonrational decision making model does Byford employ? How?
3. Is the MTA's practice of bailing out state-run ski resorts with subway funds ethical? Use Figure 7.3 in your response.
4. How can the MTA use evidence-based decision making? Explain.
5. What decision making style does Byford utilize? Provide examples to support your assertion.
6. What barriers to decision making were prevalent before Byford's arrival? Explain.

Legal/Ethical Challenge

It's All about a Peacock

Emotional support pets help people suffering from anxiety and other psychological disorders during airline travel. Airlines have responsively recognized this issue within the structure of federal guidelines. According to *ABC News*, federal regulations allow an emotional support animal such as a dog, a cat, or even a pot-bellied pig to travel on airplanes in the cabin with the owner. The animal can be outside a carrier and flies for free if the owner has proper documentation, usually a letter from a doctor or other mental health professional. Airlines are allowed to ask people traveling with emotional support animals for this documentation, but they are not required to.[201] These policies have led to soaring numbers of support pets on planes.

USA Today reports that United Airlines has seen a 75 percent increase in emotion support animals on flights–from 43,000 to 76,000–between 2016 and 2017. The rise has also contributed to a significant increase in onboard incidents.[202] The union representing United's flight attendants says many of these incidents include allergic reactions in other passengers and undesirable animal behaviors like aggressive behavior, biting, urination, and defecation.[203] This all contributed to United Airlines drawing the line when someone tried to bring a pet called Dexter on a flight leaving Newark. The airline refused not because Dexter is your typical four-legged emotional support animal but because Dexter is a peacock–and quite a large one at that.

This challenge pertains to whether United made the right call in changing its support pet policies after Dexter's aborted trip.

United's new policies require customers to confirm that the animal has been trained to behave properly in public and to acknowledge their responsibility for the animal's conduct. Customers must also provide the airline with 48 hours' notice, a health and vaccination form from a veterinarian, and a letter from a mental health professional stating the benefit received from the emotional support animal.[204] The 48-hour rule means that customers will have trouble boarding with their pets during emergency travel.

Do these changes seem fair? Consider that different airlines require different documentation in order to decide whether a pet is qualified as an emotional support animal. United and Delta Airlines require certain documentation, while American Airlines has other requirements. Some airlines don't allow emotional support pets onboard, period.[205] Should the airlines be consistent?

The preceding rules do not apply to service animals, which are legally defined as dogs "trained to do work or perform tasks for people with disabilities." These animals are protected by the Americans with Disabilities Act (ADA) and can go wherever their owners go. Service dogs receive specific training in order to be certified as such. A Seeing Eye dog, for example, is a carefully trained dog that serves as a travel tool for persons who have severe visual impairments or are blind. Emotional support animals are not required to go through the same training and certifications, a loophole that *National Geographic* reports some pet owners are abusing to avoid the airlines' surcharge of $125 or more for transporting regular pets.[206] A *CBS News* correspondent was actually able to purchase a support animal vest and accompanying mental health professional letter online without her cat even being evaluated. The registration took just five minutes and cost $150.[207]

This behavior is causing problems for those with legitimate service animals. Some are being harassed by fed-up and unsympathetic airline employees and passengers, and untrained emotional support pets have also attacked trained service animals during flights. An advocate for the blind told *CBS News*, "As a person who is blind, my access rights are being infringed upon when somebody passes off a fake service dog."[208]

SOLVING THE CHALLENGE

What would you do if you were United Airlines' CEO?

1. Do not implement the new rules. The airline should allow emotional support pets to travel unrestricted, just as service dogs do. Airlines should not be in the business of categorizing passengers' pets.
2. Implement the new rules. Emotional support pets are not service dogs and should be treated differently. The airline needs to ensure the safety of employees, passengers, and other animals during flight.
3. Refer this issue to regulators like the Department of Transportation instead of implementing your own rules. The government can address this issue by passing regulation that will consistently be enforced by all airlines.
4. Invent other options.

Uber Continuing Case connect

Learn about decision making at Uber, with an emphasis on how former CEO Travis Kalanick and current CEO Dara Khosrowshahi make decisions. Assess your ability to apply concepts discussed in this chapter to the case by going to Connect.

Organizing

8 Organizational Culture, Structure, and Design

Building Blocks of the Organization

©Olivier Renck/Aurora/Getty Images

After reading this chapter, you should be able to:

LO 8-1 Describe how managers align vision and strategies with the organization's culture and structure.

LO 8-2 Explain how to characterize an organization's culture.

LO 8-3 Describe the process of culture change in an organization.

LO 8-4 Compare the structures of for-profit, nonprofit, and mutual-benefit organizations.

LO 8-5 Identify the major elements of an organization.

LO 8-6 Describe the eight organizational structures.

LO 8-7 Identify the factors that affect the design of an organization's structure.

LO 8-8 Describe how to use the career readiness competencies of *understanding the business* and *personal adaptability* to assess an organization's internal context.

FORECAST *What's Ahead in This Chapter*

We discuss organizational cultures and structures, and how they should be aligned to coordinate employees in the pursuit of the organization's strategic goals. We then consider the three types of organizations and their seven basic elements. We next review seven types of organizational structures and consider five factors that should be considered when designing the structure of an organization. We conclude with a Career Corner that focuses on how to use the career readiness competencies of *understanding the business* and *personal adaptability* to improve your ability to assess an organization's internal context.

MANAGE U

How to Get Noticed in a New Job: Fitting into an Organization's Culture in the First 60 Days

"Once you are in the real world—and it doesn't make any difference if you are 22 or 62, starting your first job or your fifth," say former business columnists Jack and Suzy Welch, "the way to look great and get ahead is to overdeliver."[1]

Overdelivering means doing more than what is asked of you—not just doing the report your boss requests, for example, but doing the extra research to provide him or her with something truly impressive. "You must continue to 'sell yourself' after you are hired," says one human resources director. "Keep your boss informed of things you are working on, including projects others ask you to assist with."[2]

Among things you should do in the first 60 days are the following.[3]

Be Aware of the Power of First Impressions

Within three minutes of meeting someone new, people form an opinion about where the future of the relationship is headed, according to one study.[4] Journalist and author Malcolm Gladwell concluded that "Snap judgments are, first of all, enormously quick: they rely on the thinnest slices of experience . . . they are also unconscious."[5] Counter the possibility of someone else's bias in such a quick judgment by using your career readiness skills of social and emotional intelligence to put your best foot forward.

See How People Behave by Arriving Early and Staying Late

"Many aspects of a company's culture can be subtle and easy to overlook," writes one expert. "Instead, observe everything." Try coming in 30 minutes early and staying a little late just to observe how people operate—where they take their meals, for example. If a meal was part of your interview, you've probably picked up some clues about whether they regularly eat out or are mostly brown-bagging it at their desks.[6]

Network with People and Find Out How the Organization Works

Keep your networking skills at the ready; they represent a career readiness competency. During the first two weeks, get to know a few people and try to have lunch with them. Find out how the organization works, how people interact with the boss, what the corporate culture encourages and discourages. Walk the halls and get to know receptionists, mail room clerks, and office managers, who can help you learn the ropes. Your role here is to listen. Realize that you have a lot to learn when you're new.[7]

Ask for Advice

Be aware that those who seek advice are perceived as being more competent than those who do not.[8] Your proactive learning orientation will help you here; don't be afraid to ask co-workers for feedback as you start learning the job. At the end of 30 days, have a "How am I doing?" meeting with your boss.

Overdeliver

Because performance reviews for new hires generally take place at 60 to 90 days, you need to have accomplished enough—and preferably something big—to show your boss your potential. In other words, do as the Welches suggest: overdeliver.

For Discussion How does the preceding advice square with your past experiences in starting a new job? Are there things you wish you could have done differently?

8.1 Aligning Strategy, Culture, and Structure

THE BIG PICTURE

The study of organizing, the second of the four functions in the management process, begins with the study of organizational culture and structure, which managers must determine so as to implement a particular strategy. Organizational culture consists of the set of shared, taken-for-granted implicit assumptions that a group holds in the workplace. Organizational structure describes who reports to whom and who does what.

LO 8-1

Describe how managers align vision and strategies with the organization's culture and structure.

Organizational culture binds people to common norms and expectations just like glue binds pieces of materials into one. ©McGraw-Hill Education/Michael Scott, photographer

How important is *culture,* the "social glue" that binds together organizations?

"Culture and people are everything," says Brett Wilson, CEO of TubeMogul, a video advertising software company. "Nothing else matters, and our ability to stay ahead is a function of having the best people and moving faster than our competitors. . . . Creating an exceptional culture is the only way to build a sustainable competitive advantage."[9]

How an Organization's Culture and Structure Are Used to Implement Strategy

"A leader's job is to help inspire every employee to help execute strategy," says one report. "This requires consistently and constantly demonstrating, celebrating, and modeling the cultural traits that reinforce strategy."[10] Or, for better performance, perhaps the leader's style should even be *different* from the organization's culture (as we'll discuss later).[11]

Strategy, as we saw in Chapter 6, consists of the large-scale action plans that reflect the organization's vision and are used to set the direction for the organization. To implement a particular strategy, managers must determine the right kind of *organizational culture* and *organizational structure,* which mutually influence each other. *(See Figure 8.1.)*

The "I Wish . . ." feature illustrates what happened to John French when his employer failed to integrate strategy and culture.

I Wish...

...my company had integrated its corporate strategy and organizational culture.

John French. Courtesy John French

John French worked as a senior financial analyst for a medical group as part of a national health care system. While in this position, he witnessed severe resistance to change as the company attempted to reshape its culture.

It was necessary to change the culture of this health care company because the current culture was not valuing its employees. The company's competitor was located in the same area, and was constantly taking advantage of the undervalued employees at John's company. "Instead of promoting from within and cultivating talent, the way you get promoted here is by going to the competition and getting a raise," said John. John's company continued to lose some of its best employees because of their approach toward promotions. Consequently, people with little industry experience found themselves in management positions they were not qualified for.

In addition to failing to value its current employees, the company was struggling financially due to its culture. "We're a non-profit, and we had a very non-profit culture. Because of that, the company thought that it didn't need to focus on money. People would always say, 'It's for the patient,' but if you're bleeding money, you won't survive for the patient," said John.

Because of the lack of financial focus, the company continued to promote medical practitioners instead of businesspeople. This deepened the financial issues because the people who were managing the departments did not have business experience and were not concerned about the financial well-being of the company.

When John found himself in a management role after his manager left the company to work for the competition, he decided to bring in an analytics team to evaluate the company's finances. This did not go over well with the rest of the team. "We were able to link payments together and define how successful we were. And what we found was that we were actually overpaying our doctors. We were paying our doctors more than they were bringing in," said John. Of course, the doctors did not take well to this information, and they did not understand it from a financial perspective.

The medical group continued to lose money and talent by refusing to change its ways. John began to reevaluate his role within the company. He quickly realized that the culture was leading to the destruction of the company, and he no longer wanted to be a part of it.

After an unsuccessful meeting with Human Resources about an increase in pay, John left the company, where things have remained stagnant to this day.

Courtesy of John French

FIGURE 8.1

Drivers and flow of organizational culture

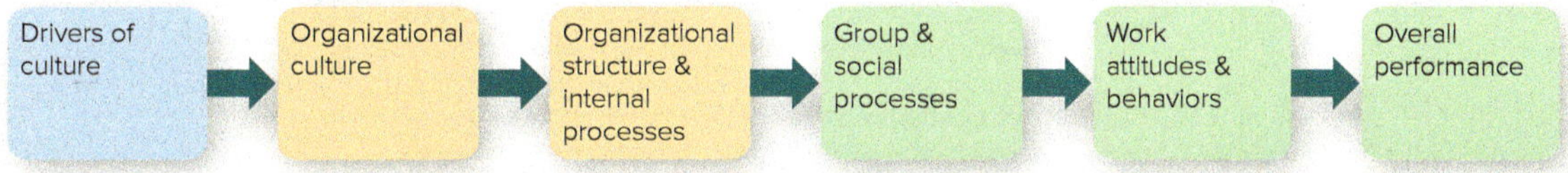

Realizing the Organizational Vision and Strategy: Get the Right Culture and the Right Structure

Let's consider these two concepts—organizational culture and organizational structure.

Organizational Culture: The Shared Assumptions That Affect How Work Gets Done

We described the concept of *culture* in Chapter 4 on global management as "the shared set of beliefs, values, knowledge, and patterns of behavior common to a group of people." Here we are talking about a specific kind of culture called an *organizational culture*.

According to scholar **Edgar Schein,** **organizational culture, sometimes called corporate culture, is defined as the set of shared, taken-for-granted implicit assumptions that a group holds and that determines how it perceives, thinks about, and reacts to its various environments.**[12] These are the beliefs and values shared among a group of people in the workplace that are passed on to new employees by way of socialization and mentoring, which significantly affect work outcomes at all levels.[13] As we said earlier, culture is the "social glue" that binds members of the organization together. Just as a human being has a personality—fun-loving, warm, uptight, competitive, or whatever—so an organization has a "personality," too, and that is its culture. The culture helps employees understand why the organization does what it does and how it intends to accomplish its long-term goals.

The cultural tone is often set in the hiring process. "The ultimate filter we use is that we only hire nice people," says Peter Miller, CEO of Optinose, a pharmaceutical company.[14] MuleSoft, a software company, looks for people with "high integrity, being a great team player, and they want to win as a company first, team second, individually third," says CEO Greg Schott.[15]

TubeMogul CEO Brett Wilson, mentioned earlier, also prefers nice people. "I . . . really value people who are kind to one another," he says. "That makes the workplace better, and they end up having a deeper sense of empathy with our clients." In addition, "we want a culture where people aren't afraid to make mistakes. . . . Our ability to win is a function of how innovative we are. So making mistakes is encouraged." Finally, he says, "it's a culture where we value the people who do what they say—they have a high 'do-to-say' ratio."[16]

Freewheeling culture. Mic, a New York City news website created by and for Millennials, which has 106 mostly Millennial employees, is described as having a "playful vibe."[17] Here CEO Chris Altchek *(right)* talks with an employee. At Mic, oversharing, acting entitled, and second-guessing the boss are the norm. Dogs wander between desks, some employees use a megaphone for impromptu announcements, others ride hoverboards into the kitchen for free snacks. Could the Mic culture work in, say, the labs of Pfizer Inc., the global pharmaceutical company, where drug discovery is a high-risk, costly endeavor? ©Jennifer S. Altman/The New York/Redux Pictures

Culture can vary considerably, with different organizations having differing emphases on risk taking, treatment of employees, teamwork, rules and regulations, conflict and criticism, and rewards.

As such, culture can have both positive and negative effects on employees and overall corporate performance. Zenefits, a San Francisco health-insurance brokerage start-up, for example, is being sued for actions associated with a *negative culture*. Its director of real estate and workplace services sent employees a note asking them to cut out using the headquarters stairwells for smoking, drinking, eating, and sex.[18]

Some other organizations, believing that the office has become "too nice," have embraced a culture known as "radical candor" or "front-stabbing," in which workers are encouraged "to drop the polite workplace veneer and speak frankly to each other no matter what," according to one report.[19] Still other companies go beyond candor to fraudulent behavior, such as the case of Volkswagen. The company admitted in 2015 that it cheated on its emission tests. Mitsubishi also admitted to 25 years of company engineers' intentionally manipulating fuel-economy tests.[20]

In addition, the elements that drive an organization's culture also vary. They may represent the values of the founder, the industry and business environment, the national culture, the organization's vision and strategies, and the behavior of leaders. *(See Table 8.1.)*

We thoroughly discuss organizational culture in Sections 8.2 and 8.3.

TABLE 8.1 What Drives an Organizational Culture?

• Founder's values
• Industry and business environment
• National culture
• Organization's vision and strategies
• Behavior of leaders

Organizational Structure: Who Reports to Whom and Who Does What **Organizational structure is a formal system of task and reporting relationships that coordinates and motivates an organization's members so that they can work together to achieve the organization's goals.** As we describe in Sections 8.4–8.6, organizational structure is concerned with who reports to whom and who specializes in what work.

Whether an organization is for-profit or nonprofit, the challenge for top managers is to align the organization's vision and strategies with its organizational culture and organizational structure, as shown in the two gold boxes in Figure 8.1.

Figure 8.1 shows that the consistency among these elements in turn impacts (see the three green boxes) group and social processes (discussed in Chapters 13–15), individual work attitudes and behaviors (discussed in Chapters 11–12), and the organization's overall performance. As you can see from the diagram, consistency across strategy, culture, and structure is expected to foster higher performance. •

EXAMPLE How Strategy Affects Culture and Culture Affects Structure: Cleveland Clinic Refocuses Its Continuous Improvement Strategy

The guiding principle at Cleveland Clinic, one of the largest research and teaching hospitals in the United States, is "Patients first."[21] To ensure that patients experience the best care and the best outcomes, the hospital needs practitioners who are at the top of their field but are not content with the status quo. So it recently undertook a new initiative to update its strategy of *continuous improvement*, in which all members of the organization are encouraged to make incremental improvements in all processes and services on an ongoing basis[22] (see Chapter 16). The idea this time was to "change the culture" by giving "everyone the opportunity to look at how they're doing their day-to-day jobs and where they could make improvements, reduce wastes, cut costs and improve the patient experience," the chief medical operations office said.[23]

The Strategy: Continuous Improvement The goal of Cleveland Clinic's continuous improvement strategy is "to create practices through which every caregiver is capable, empowered, and expected to make improvements every day." The Clinic is focusing on measuring and improving patient safety, patient quality, patient experience, caregiver experience, and affordability.[24] The reason for upgrading the continuous improvement program was not that practitioners didn't already value excellence; Cleveland's organizational culture is known for that. But as Dr. Lisa Yerian, medical director of continuous improvement, said, "People who are committed to excellence can create a lot of workarounds. They will go the extra mile but don't always think about how to go three miles fewer to deliver the same or better quality care."[25]

The Structure: A Matrix Cleveland Clinic itself is organized around individual organs and diseases rather than around clinical departments like most hospitals. Its continuous improvement department, launched in 2006 when the hospital first adopted continuous improvement, has since grown in size and in scope and now includes 32 members, some from industries outside the medical profession. Skilled in applying world-class quality improvement strategies, they are located in many different departments and institutes within the hospital, so they are able to work with teams that similarly cross functional lines in the organization.[26]

The Culture: A Commitment to Excellence The continuous improvement team has been able to strengthen the hospital's "patients first" culture in many tangible ways. It has reduced cancer patients' wait times for chemotherapy treatments, achieved faster set-up in the hospital's operating rooms, and dramatically reduced wait times in the emergency department so more patients are seen. In-patients and out-patients, as well as their caregivers and families, all have benefitted. In addition, the Decision Support Services (DSS) team, part of the finance division and an early participant in the newest continuous improvement effort, made permanent upgrades in its reporting process and changed its own culture. A brief project-status meeting every morning now gives every team member an opportunity to ask questions, air problems, and suggest solutions. As a result of these in-person check-ins, the volume of e-mail has dropped dramatically, team members feel more accountable to each other, and department costs have dropped more than 10 percent. Today, the DSS team members are helping to share what they learned about continuous improvement with teams in other areas of the organization.[27]

YOUR CALL

The continuous improvement model adopted by Cleveland Clinic integrates the hospital's vision, strategic goals, culture, and structure. Do you think this is hard to pull off in today's organizations? Why do you think Cleveland Clinic was successful?[28]

8.2 What Kind of Organizational Culture Will You Be Operating In?

THE BIG PICTURE

Organizational culture appears as three layers: observable artifacts, espoused values, and basic assumptions. Cultures can be classified into four types: clan, adhocracy, market, and hierarchy. Culture is transmitted to employees through symbols, stories, heroes, rites and rituals, and organizational socialization.

LO 8-2

Explain how to characterize an organization's culture.

Want to get ahead in the workplace but hate the idea of "office politics"?

You probably can't achieve the first without mastering the second. Although hard work and talent can take you a long way, "there is a point in everyone's career where politics becomes more important," says management professor Kathleen Kelley Reardon. You have to know the political climate of the company you work for, says Reardon, who is author of *The Secret Handshake* and *It's All Politics.*[29] "Don't be the last person to understand how people get promoted, how they get noticed, how certain projects come to attention. Don't be quick to trust. If you don't understand the political machinations, you're going to fail much more often."[30]

A great part of learning to negotiate the politics—that is, the different behavioral and psychological characteristics—of a particular workplace means learning to understand the organization's *culture.* The culture consists not only of the slightly quirky personalities you encounter but also all of an organization's normal way of doing business, as we'll explain.

The Three Levels of Organizational Culture

Organizational culture appears as three layers: (1) *observable artifacts*, (2) *espoused values*, and (3) *basic assumptions.*[31] Each level varies in terms of outward visibility and resistance to change, and each level influences another level.

Level 1: Observable Artifacts—Physical Manifestations of Culture

At the most visible level, organizational culture is expressed in *observable artifacts*—physical manifestations such as manner of dress, awards, myths and stories about the company, rituals and ceremonies, and decorations, as well as visible behavior exhibited by managers and employees.

Example: In a conference room reserved for sensitive discussions, online travel company Kayak has a 2-foot-high stuffed elephant named Annabelle—the "elephant in the room"—that is an artifact believed to bring forth more honest and constructive communications among employees.[32] (The expression "elephant in the room" is used in business and politics to mean an obvious truth that is either being ignored or going unaddressed.)

Although this is not a photo of Annabelle, you can see how a photo or stuffed animal can be used as an artifact to reflect an aspect of an organization's culture. ©McGraw-Hill Education

Level 2: Espoused Values—Explicitly Stated Values and Norms

Espoused values are the explicitly stated values and norms preferred by an organization, as may be put forth by the firm's founder or top managers.

Example: The founders of technology company Hewlett-Packard stressed the "HP Way," a collegial, egalitarian culture that gave as much authority and job security to employees as possible. Although managers may hope the values they espouse will directly influence employee behavior, employees don't always "walk the talk," frequently being more influenced by **enacted values**, which represent the values and norms actually exhibited in the organization.[33]

Another example: Leaders at retailer and health care company CVS Health recognized the gap between espoused values ("We sell health products") and enacted values ("We also sell tobacco products") and made a key strategic change to create alignment. A transformative moment came in early 2014 when CEO Larry Merlo announced that CVS would cease selling tobacco products by October 1. One year later, the company reported that the average smoker had purchased five fewer packs of cigarettes in states where CVS controlled at least 15 percent of the retail pharmacy market, amounting to an overall decrease of 95 million packs. In the same states, sales of nicotine patches rose 4 percent over the same period.[34]

Level 3: Basic Assumptions—Core Values of the Organization *Basic assumptions*, which are not observable, represent the core values of an organization's culture—those that are taken for granted and, as a result, are difficult to change.

Example: At insurance giant AIG, people worked so hard that, while employees commenting on Indeed.com generally call it a great place to work, one said, "The workplace culture is work hard. I didn't know anyone that worked 9:00-5:00. There were too many projects with tight deadlines to leave at 5:00."[35]

Another example: Many founders of start-ups hate rules and red tape. College Hunks Hauling Junk, for instance, was cofounded by Nick Friedman with no formal policies about dress code, vacation, sick days, and other things because he envisioned "a real-life Never Never Land where work is always fun, and the culture is always stress-free."[36] However, when the enterprise grew from a single cargo van to more than 50 franchises, the freewheeling spirit made employees lose focus, and client-service ratings, employee morale, and profitability all declined. The firm had to come up with rules and procedures while, at the same time, trying to "maintain a healthy balance of fun company culture with an accountable organization and team," Friedman said. Now more than 100 franchises strong, with $50 million in annual sales, the firm is riding high.[37]

Four Types of Organizational Culture: Clan, Adhocracy, Market, and Hierarchy

The competing values framework (CVF) provides a practical way for managers to understand, measure, and change organizational culture. The CVF, which has been validated by extensive research involving 1,100 companies, classifies organizational cultures into four types: (1) clan, (2) adhocracy, (3) market, and (4) hierarchy, as we'll explain.[38] *(See Figure 8.2.)*

Research leading to the development of the CVF found that organizational effectiveness varied along two dimensions:

- **The horizontal dimension–inward or outward focus?** This dimension expresses the extent to which an organization focuses its attention and efforts inward on internal dynamics and employees ("internal focus and integration") versus outward toward its external environment and its customers and shareholders ("external focus and differentiation").
- **The vertical dimension–flexibility or stability?** This dimension expresses the extent to which an organization prefers flexibility and discretion versus stability and control. Combining these two dimensions creates the four types of organizational culture based on different core values–namely, clan, adhocracy, market, and hierarchy.

FIGURE 8.2

Competing values framework

Source: Adapted from K.S. Cameron, R.E. Quinn, J. Degraff, and A.V. Thakor, Competing Values Leadership *(Northampton, MA: Edward Elgar, 2006), p. 32.*

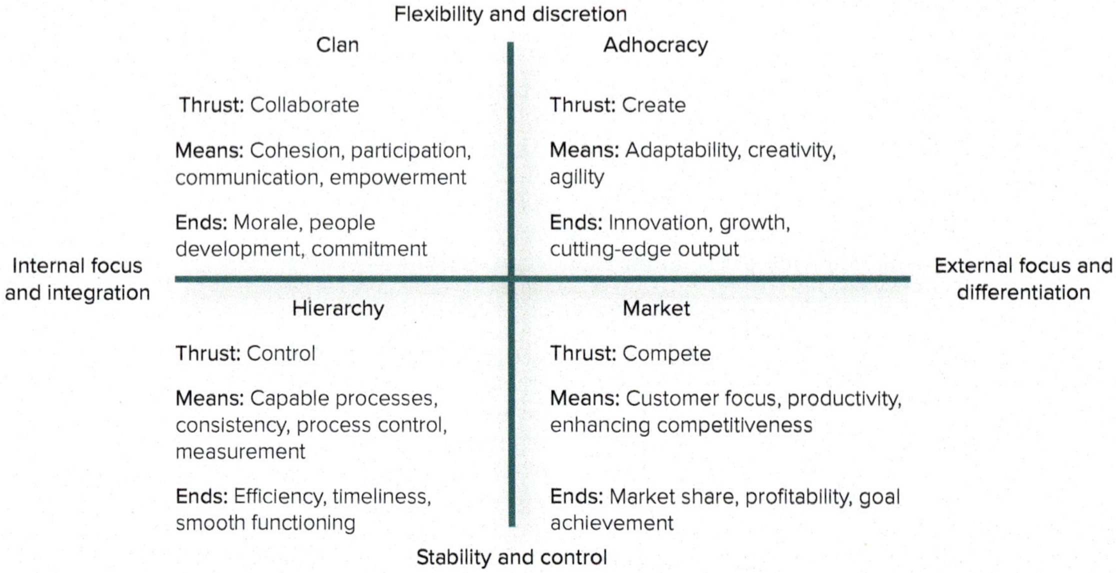

Each culture type has different characteristics, and while one type tends to dominate in any given organization, it is the mix of types that creates competitive advantage. We begin our discussion of culture types in the upper-left quadrant of the CVF.

1. Clan Culture: An Employee-Focused Culture Valuing Flexibility, Not Stability **A clan culture has an internal focus and values flexibility rather than stability and control.** Like a family-type organization, it encourages collaboration among employees, striving to encourage cohesion through consensus and job satisfaction and to increase commitment through employee involvement. Clan organizations devote considerable resources to hiring and developing their employees, and they view customers as partners.

Example: Property and casualty insurance company Acuity, *Fortune*'s No. 9 Best Company to Work For in 2017,[39] strongly endorses a clan culture. CEO Ben Salzmann believes "that if employees are given a fun, rewarding place to work where they can express their creativity, in return the firm will get innovation, diehard loyalty, and world-class customer service."[40] Employees have generous perks and are empowered to participate in the way the company is run. The end results are profitability and an enviably low turnover rate.[41]

2. Adhocracy Culture: A Risk-Taking Culture Valuing Flexibility **An adhocracy culture has an external focus and values flexibility.** Creation of new products and services is the strategic thrust of this culture, which attempts to create innovative products by being adaptable, creative, and quick to respond to changes in the marketplace. Employees are encouraged to take risks and experiment with new ways of getting things done. Adhocracy cultures are well suited for start-up companies, those in industries undergoing constant change, and those in mature industries that are in need of innovation to enhance growth.

Example: Baxter International, a giant Illinois-based manufacturer of medical products, values innovation enough to say it practically *is* culture. Recently appointed CEO José Almeida cut away several layers of the company's bureaucracy to make it easier for employees to communicate with peers around the organization and speed decision making. "Never disassociate innovation and culture," he says. "They are almost one and the same." Since his arrival, the company's stock has climbed 70 percent.[42]

Chick-fil-A culture. Among the quick-service restaurant's ways of engaging employees are hiring only nice people (harder than it sounds); hiring managers with people skills, not just functional skills; and closing stores on Sundays so employees can have family time. How would you classify Chick-fil-A's culture according to the competing values framework? ©St. Petersburg Times/Zuma Press Inc/Alamy Stock Photo

3. Market Culture: A Competitive Culture Valuing Profits over Employee Satisfaction

A market culture has a strong external focus and values stability and control. Because market cultures are focused on the external environment and driven by competition and a strong desire to deliver results, customers, productivity, and profits take precedence over employee development and satisfaction. Employees are expected to work hard, react fast, and deliver quality work on time; those who deliver results are rewarded.

Example: Uber, the ride-hailing company, has had such a culture, but its management allowed aggressively competitive and sometimes sexually harassing behavior to flourish within its freewheeling work environment, courting scandals from which the company is struggling to recover[43] even as its founder and CEO has been ousted.[44] Uber has also seen its reputation tarnished by drivers' bad behavior in some countries and its market clipped by legislators protecting local taxi industries in other locations such as London, British Columbia (Canada), Denmark, Italy, and Australia's Northern Territory.[45]

4. Hierarchy Culture: A Structured Culture Valuing Stability and Effectiveness

A hierarchy culture has an internal focus and values stability and control over flexibility. Companies with this kind of culture are apt to have a formalized, structured work environment aimed at achieving effectiveness through a variety of control mechanisms that measure efficiency, timeliness, and reliability in the creation and delivery of products.

This Amazon Distribution Center in Staffordshire, England relies on an internal focus to meet its delivery goals. ©SWNS/Alamy Stock Photo

Example: Amazon relies on the benefits of a hierarchical culture to effectively manage its vast shipping processes. A *Fortune* reporter commented that the company has achieved success by "sticking steadfastly–even boringly–to a few key principles. . . . Instead of focusing on competitors or technology shifts [a market culture orientation], they continually invest in getting a little bit better. In their core retail business, they grind out incremental improvements in delivery speed and product offerings while chipping away at prices."[46] Since purchasing Whole Foods in 2017, Amazon has been working to integrate its signature Amazon Prime service into the upscale grocery chain's operations to ease customer ordering, delivery, pickups, and returns.[47]

Are you curious about the type of culture that exists in a current or past employer? Do you wonder whether this culture is best suited to help the company achieve its strategic goals? The following self-assessment allows you to consider these questions.

SELF-ASSESSMENT 8.1

What Is the Organizational Culture at My Current Employer?

Please be prepared to answer these questions if your instructor has assigned Self-Assessment 8.1 in Connect.

1. How would you describe the organizational culture?
2. Do you think this type of culture is best suited to help the company achieve its strategic goals? Explain.

How Employees Learn Culture: Symbols, Stories, Heroes, Rites and Rituals, and Organizational Socialization

Culture is transmitted to employees in several ways, most often through such means as (1) *symbols*, (2) *stories*, (3) *heroes*, (4) *rites and rituals*, and (5) *organizational socialization*.[48]

1. Symbols

A symbol is an object or action that represents an idea or quality. With respect to culture, symbols are artifacts used to convey an organization's most important values. The Nike swish is an example.

Example: One of the most iconic products of IKEA, maker of inexpensive home furnishings, whose vision is "to create a better life for the many," is the LACK table, a 22-inch by 22-inch side table that sells for only $9.99.[49]

2. Stories

A story is a narrative based on true events, which is repeated—and sometimes embellished upon—to emphasize a particular value. Stories are oral histories that are told and retold by members about incidents in the organization's history.

Example: Marc Benioff is the founder and CEO of cloud computing business Salesforce.com, a San Francisco company known for its great sense of social responsibility and generosity (and rated No. 1 on *Fortune's* 2017 Best Companies to Work For list).[50] Its spirit of philanthropy is embodied in a story called the 1-1-1 rule that embodies its commitment to giving 1 percent of its product, 1 percent of its equity earnings, and 1 percent of employee work hours back to the community. So far that has meant donating $160 million to charity, volunteering 2.1 million hours of employees' time, and assisting 31,000 nonprofit organizations with free Salesforce technology.[51]

3. Heroes

A hero is a person whose accomplishments embody the values of the organization. IKEA employees are expected to work hard, inspired by an anecdote from their late Swedish founder, Invar Kamprad, in his 1976 "A Furniture Dealer's Testament." In that essay, he recounts how he was berated by his father for repeatedly failing to get out of bed to milk the cows on his family's farm. Then one day Kamprad got an alarm clock. "'Now by jiminy, I'm going to start a new life,' he determined, setting the alarm for twenty to six and removing the 'off button.'"[52] In Kamprad's obituary in 2018, *The Economist* noted, "Setbacks inspired him."[53]

4. Rites and Rituals

Rites and rituals are the activities and ceremonies, planned and unplanned, that celebrate important occasions and accomplishments in the organization's life. Military units and sports teams have long known the value of ceremonies handing out decorations and awards, but many companies have rites and rituals as well.

Example: Employee-owners of New Belgium Brewery in Fort Collins, Colorado, which makes Fat Tire Ale, are given a cruiser bicycle during their first year. After five years, they get a free brewery-hopping trip to Belgium, and after 10 years, a four-week paid sabbatical. (The company boasts a 93 percent employment retention rate.) "It's not just about making sure people get lots of perks," says cofounder and former CEO Kim Jordan. "It's about building a community."[54]

5. Organizational Socialization

Organizational socialization is defined as the process by which people learn the values, norms, and required behaviors that permit them to participate as members of an organization.[55] Converting from outsider into organizational insider may take weeks or even years and occurs in three phases, researcher Daniel Feldman suggests—before one is hired, when one is first taken on, and when one has been employed a while and is adjusting to the job.[56]

The first phase *(anticipatory socialization phase)* occurs before one joins the organization, when a person learns–from career advisors, from web sources, from current employees–what the organization's job needs and values are and how one's own needs, values, and skills might fit in. The second phase *(encounter phase)* takes place when a person is first hired and comes to learn what the organization is really like and how to adjust his or her expectations. The company may help to advance this socialization process through various familiarization programs (known as "onboarding" programs). The third phase *(change and acquisition phase)* comes about once the employee understands his or her work role and now must master the necessary skills and tasks and learn to adjust to the work group's values and norms. The company may advance this phase of socialization through goal setting, incentives, employee feedback, continued support, and ceremonies ("graduation") that celebrate completion of the process.

Example: New hires at New York University are partnered with a buddy during their first two months "to help welcome employees and reaffirm their decision to join NYU" as well as to provide a reliable contact for speedy answers on work practices and organizational culture. Among other characteristics, "the buddy should have a positive outlook on his/her work and use that perspective to help build self-confidence and loyalty in the new employee. The buddy should lead by example."[57]

The Importance of Culture

Many people believe culture powerfully shapes an organization's long-term success by enhancing its competitive advantage. A team of researchers tested this hypothesis with a meta-analysis (a statistical procedure combining data from multiple studies) of more than 38,000 organizational units–either organizations as a whole or departments in different organizations–and 616,000 individuals.[58] The results are shown below. *(See Figure 8.3.)*

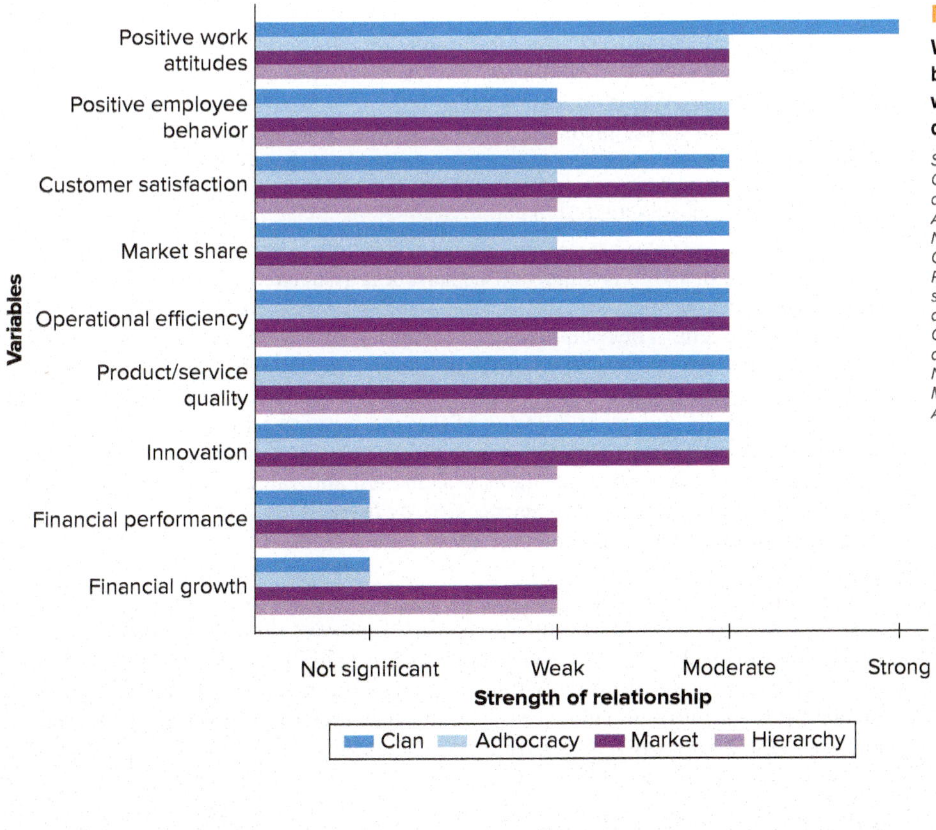

FIGURE 8.3

What organizational benefits are associated with what organizational cultures?

Source: Data taken from A. Y. Ou, C. Hartnell, A. Kinicki, E. Karam, and D. Choi, "Culture in Context: A Meta-Analysis of the Nomological Network of Organizational Culture." Presentation as part of symposium Connecting Culture and Context: Insights from Organizational Culture Theory and Research at the 2016 National Academy of Management meeting in Anaheim, California.

Results revealed that culture is positively associated with a variety of outcomes. Most relationships were of moderate strength, meaning they are important to today's managers. Closer examination of Figure 8.3 leads to the following six conclusions:

- **An organization's culture matters.** The type of organizational culture can be a source of competitive advantage.
- **Employees have more positive work attitudes when working in organizations with clan cultures.** Employees clearly prefer to work in organizations that value flexibility over stability and control, as well as those that are more concerned with satisfying the needs of employees than those of shareholders or customers.
- **Clan and market cultures are more likely to deliver higher customer satisfaction and market share.** We suspect this result holds because the positive employee attitudes associated with clan cultures motivate employees to provide better customer service.
- **Operational outcomes, quality, and innovation are more strongly related to clan, adhocracy, and market cultures than to hierarchical ones.** Managers should avoid the use of too many rules and procedures–hierarchical characteristics–when trying to improve these outcomes.
- **An organization's financial performance (profit and revenue growth) is related to market and hierarchy culture.** Clan and adhocracy cultures are not related to financial performance, so managers should not expect to see a direct increase in financial performance by encouraging these two types of culture. On the other hand, research suggests that developing market and hierarchical cultures can prompt higher financial performance.
- **Companies with market cultures tend to have more positive organizational outcomes.** Managers are encouraged to make their cultures more market oriented.

What Does It Mean to "Fit"? Anticipating a Job Interview

"What's your favorite movie?" the job interviewer asks you. "Your favorite website?" "What's the last book you read for fun?" "What makes you uncomfortable?"

These are the four most frequently asked interview questions used by hiring managers, according to a survey involving 285,000 kinds of interview questions.[59] For you as a job applicant, these questions might not seem to have much to do with your performance in previous jobs. But what the interviewer is trying to find out is how well you will *fit in*–what is called **person–organization (PO) fit**, which reflects the extent to which your personality and values match the climate and culture in an organization.[60]

A good fit of this kind is important because it is associated with more positive work attitudes and task performance, lower stress, and fewer expressions of intention to quit ("I'm gonna tell 'em, 'They can take this job and . . .'").[61] How well an applicant will fit in with the institution's organizational culture is considered a high priority by many interviewers. Indeed, more than 50 percent of the evaluators in one study considered "fit" to be the most important criterion of the interview process.[62]

How can you determine how well you might fit in before you go into a job interview? You should write down your strengths, weaknesses, and values–and then do the same for the organization you're interviewing with, by researching it online and talking with current employees. You can then prepare questions to ask the interviewer about how well you might fit.[63]

Example: If being recognized for hard work is important to you, ask the interviewer how the company rewards performance. If the answer doesn't show a strong link between performance and rewards ("Well, we don't really have a policy on that"), you'll probably have a low person-organization fit and won't be happy working there. Incidentally, a positive corporate culture that engages and motivates employees will help a company's bottom line, according to a study of car dealerships, but the reverse is not true–a company's success isn't enough to ensure a positive culture.[64]

8.3 The Process of Culture Change

THE BIG PICTURE

There are 12 ways a culture becomes established in an organization.

LO 8-3

Describe the process of culture change in an organization.

Changing organizational culture is essentially a teaching process–that is, a process in which members instruct each other about the organization's preferred values, beliefs, expectations, and behaviors. The process is accomplished by using one or more of the following 12 mechanisms.[65] These mechanisms represent levers that management pushes and pulls to create culture change. It's very important for managers to consider using a combination of these changes levers in order to create a culture that is aligned with their organizations' strategy.

Creating culture change involves pushing and pulling change levers in a desired direction. It is very similar to pushing and pulling these levers on a control panel of a lifting mechanism. In both cases, individuals push levers in order to produce a desired outcome. ©Neramit Buakaew/Shutterstock

1. Formal Statements

The first way to embed preferred culture is through the use of formal statements of organizational philosophy, mission, vision, and values, as well as materials used for recruiting, selecting, and socializing employees.

Example: Fashion website Polyvore has a distinct organizational culture embodied in the three statements posted on its website (1) "do a few things well," (2) "delight the user," and (3) "make an impact."[66] Walmart's website promotes four basic values that represent the core of the retailer's culture: (1) service to customers, (2) respect for the individual, (3) strive for excellence, and (4) act with integrity.[67]

2. Slogans and Sayings

The desirable corporate culture can be expressed in language, slogans, sayings, and acronyms.

Example: CEO Mary Berner used two slogans to create culture change at Cumulus Media Inc., the second-largest broadcaster in the United States with more than 454 stations. The acronym HABU reflects the company's focus on the "highest and best use" of resources. The slogan "The force" is short for "focused, responsible, collaborative, and empowered." To model support for these slogans, *The Wall Street Journal* reported that Berner "sold the corporate jet, consolidated duplicate internet-technology departments, and created a department to provide stations with market data and analytics on which to base local programming decisions."[68] What types of culture are reinforced by these slogans and changes?

Mary Berner has been CEO of Cumulus since 2015. She turned the company around financially by changing its culture. ©Scott Gries/Getty Images

3. Rites and Rituals

As we mentioned earlier, rites and rituals represent the planned and unplanned activities and ceremonies that are used to celebrate important events or achievements.

Example: OXO, an award-winning New York–based maker of office products and Good Grips brand kitchen tools, has adopted the universal design philosophy, meaning its products must be designed to be used by as many people as possible. In a ritual that reinforces this philosophy, employees collect gloves lost on the street for a display in the company's offices that's meant to remind everyone of "the different hands our products need to comfortably fit."[69]

4. Stories, Legends, and Myths

A story is a narrative about an actual event that happened within the organization and that helps to symbolize its vision and values to employees.

Example: Nike's reputation for innovation is reflected in the often-told story of cofounder Bill Bowerman's struggle to design a light running shoe that could grip an artificial surface well without spikes. Bowerman's wife Barbara tells what happened next: "We were making the waffles that morning and talking about [the track]. As one of the waffles came out, he said, 'You know, by turning it upside down—where the waffle part would come in contact with the track—I think that might work.' So he got up from the table and went tearing into his lab and got two cans of whatever it is you pour together to make the urethane, and poured them into the waffle iron."[70]

5. Leader Reactions to Crises

How top managers respond to critical incidents and organizational crises sends a clear cultural message.

Example: After three years of drought and lagging response by local politicians, the city of Cape Town, South Africa, with a population of almost 4 million people, faces the possibility of soon running out of water. Newly energized by the crisis, however, the governing party of the province has instituted tough restrictions on water use that have cut consumption by 60 percent and postponed Day Zero, the day the city is expected to have no water left. Mayor Ian Neilson urged citizens to continue conserving water even if seasonal rains bring needed reserves to the city's supply. Mmusi Maimane, leader of the governing party, thanked residents for responding "magnificently."[71]

6. Role Modeling, Training, and Coaching

Many companies provide structured training to provide an in-depth introduction to their organizational values. Others build learning into their culture.

Example: River Island is a family-run fashion retailer with 350 stores in the United Kingdom, the Middle East, Asia, and Europe and six websites handling transactions in four different currencies. Its management recently evaluated the company's performance feedback system and decided it needed to incorporate a larger role for continuous employee feedback and learning. "We have begun to prize learning," says Nebel Crohurst, the company's head of talent. "We now recognise the value in taking time to develop employees, role modeling and encouraging teams to continually develop their skills . . . If we're able to show externally that our culture supports career development and that we put our people at the forefront of the way we operate, then we have huge competitive advantage."[72]

7. Physical Design

There is constant experimenting to find the best office layout that will encourage employee productivity and send a strong message about the culture.

Example: A recent Work Environment Survey by a Capital One team found that employees of all ages value natural light, inspiring and creative artwork, adjustable furniture, and space for collaboration. Acknowledgement of local culture is also important. In the Capital One Plano TX facility, a workspace dedicated to digital product demos and formal and informal meetings is called "The Garage" because it houses a classic Chevrolet and picket fence, along with real garage doors to divide the space.[73]

8. Rewards, Titles, Promotions, and Bonuses

Rewards and status symbols are among the strongest ways to embed organizational culture.

Example: Change doesn't always go according to plan. United Airlines had been giving each eligible employee up to $300 per quarter when the company achieved the operational goals it had set. In early 2018, however, it announced a new system that would give out much larger prizes ranging all the way up to $40,000 in cash, as well as luxury cars and vacations, but to far fewer employees. Winners would be selected by lottery and would include one lucky winner of a $100,000 grand prize. The change angered employees, more than a thousand of whom signed an online petition in protest. Management quickly reversed itself and promised to reevaluate the program, though without committing to a timeline.[74]

9. Organizational Goals and Performance Criteria

Many organizations establish organizational goals and criteria for recruiting, selecting, developing, promoting, dismissing, and retiring people, all of which reinforce the desired organizational culture.

Example: Netflix has a corporate culture firmly focused on the expectation that employees are adults who can achieve their goals without complicated rules. Vacations are unlimited and the expense policy consists of just five words: "Act in Netflix's best interests." But former Chief Talent Officer Patty McCord, who helped build the company, says a great company needs to "eliminate the slackers, the laggards and the people who are just putting in his or her time."[75] The company's website therefore promises "no bell curves or rankings or quotas such as 'cut the bottom 10% every year,'" but it does say that "adequate performers will be given a generous severance package, so that we can find a star for that position."[76]

The wow culture. The "wow" factor that encourages Zappos's clan-based culture is partly created by encouraging employees to have fun at work. Is this a place you could stick with? ©Jared McMillen/Aurora Photos

10. Measurable and Controllable Activities

An organization's leaders can pay attention to, measure, and control a number of activities, processes, or outcomes that can foster a certain culture.

Example: Amazon, which has come under fire for putting too much pressure on its warehouse workers,[77] recently patented a wristband that can vibrate to alert workers when they are not performing productively. Although it is not in use, the device can collect information about where workers are and what they are doing.[78]

These activity tracking devices are a great example of how measurement can alter someone's behavior. ©Kelvin Wong/Shutterstock

11. Organizational Structure

The hierarchical structure found in most traditional organizations is more likely to reinforce a culture oriented toward control and authority compared with the flatter organization that eliminates management layers in favor of giving employees more power.

Example: Zappos recently adopted a radical experiment in organizational structure called *holacracy*, to encourage collaboration by eliminating workplace hierarchy—no titles and no bosses. Unfortunately, employees weren't sure how to get things done anymore, which resulted in such confusion that the company's 2015 turnover rate went from 20 percent to 30 percent.[79] Since then, however, turnover has stabilized once again, and the company remains committed to its newly flattened structure.[80]

12. Organizational Systems and Procedures

Companies are increasingly using electronic networks to increase collaboration among employees, to improve innovation, quality, and efficiency.

Example: A recent report by the McKinsey Global Institute revealed that 72 percent of the more than 4,000 large and small companies studied had adopted social tools like Slack, Yammer, Chatter, or Microsoft Teams to allow employees to communicate. Some explained that these innovative technologies were necessary for attracting younger workers.[81]

Organizational mergers entail the intergration of organizational systems and procedures across two or more organizations. This integration has important cultural implications. The "I'm Glad . . ." feature discusses Casey Walters' experience when his firm in the transporation industry merged with another company.

I'm Glad...

...management embraced an empowering culture during a merger.

Casey Walters is a legal counsel in the transportation industry. His company was involved in the merging of two companies that had completely different cultures. Casey witnessed resistance to change when the new company management had to decide which culture would be embraced for the company moving forward.

Casey Walters
Courtesy Casey Walters

Both companies belong to the same industry and offer the same services in the same area of the country, but they are run in very different ways. One company empowers its employees. The employees are asked to work toward a common goal, and management is willing to provide whatever resources needed to help them achieve the goal.

"On the other hand, the other company that was part of the merger said 'Here are the tasks that I want you to fulfill,' without sharing or collaborating with the employees about the end goal. It's very much task-oriented," said Casey.

Company management decided to transition the culture of the task-oriented company to the more empowered approach. "I have found it very interesting to see the difference in folks going above and beyond in the company where they feel empowered, as though they have ownership over not only the tasks but the goal, and that they play a part in the organization," said Casey, "rather than just ticking off boxes of the tasks that they've been assigned without knowing the bigger picture and how they are contributing to the overall success of the organization."

"I absolutely believe that this has been the right move for the company," said Casey, "but it hasn't come without growing pains and reluctance. With empowerment comes more responsibility."

Many employees of the previously task-driven company were resistant to the change, but once they saw the benefits of the new culture of empowerment, they embraced it. For example, one process that was affected by the new culture was the process of responding to subpoenas. Before, within the task-oriented company, employees would respond to every subpoena simply to check items off the list. In the empowered company, however, employees were expected to determine whether the subpoena had the power to compel disclosure rather than responding to every request addressed to the company. In short, the new deliberate and mindful process allows for a decrease in response by more than 75 percent, which saves time and money.

"There was reluctance to switch to this new process despite the anecdotal evidence that this would make your life much easier. But after we implemented it and addressed the employees' concerns, now they have a different pep in their step just based upon the fact that they are doing far less work," said Casey.

While the process of merging into one unified culture is complicated and takes time, Casey believes it will benefit the company in the long run.

Courtesy of Casey Walters

Don't Forget about Person–Organization Fit

Now that we have described the four key types of organizational culture and the mechanisms managers can use to change culture, it's time to reflect on your person-organization (PO) fit. Recall that PO fit reflects the extent to which your personality and values match the climate and culture in an organization. Your PO fit matters because it links to your work attitudes and performance.[82]

We have two activities for you to complete to measure your level of fit and see what you can do about it. The first is Self-Assessment 8.2, which measures your preference for the four types of culture in the CVF. The second is to answer the discussion questions associated with this assessment. You will be asked to conduct a gap analysis between the culture for a current or past employer and your preferred culture type. You can use this gap to make a plan of action for improving your PO fit. ●

SELF-ASSESSMENT 8.2

Assessing Your Preferred Type of Organizational Culture

This survey is designed to assess your preferred type of organizational culture. Please be prepared to answer these questions if your instructor has assigned Self-Assessment 8.2 in Connect.

1. In rank order, what are your preferred culture types? Are you surprised by the results?
2. Compute the gap between your preferred and actual culture types by subtracting your actual culture type score (Self-Assessment 8.1) from your preferred type score (Self-Assessment 8.2). Where are the largest gaps?
3. Make a plan to improve your person–organization fit. Focusing on your two largest culture types, identify what is causing the gaps. You will find it helpful to look at the survey items that measure these types.
4. Now use the 12 embedding mechanisms just discussed and suggest at least two things you can do to improve your level of fit.

8.4 Organizational Structure

THE BIG PICTURE

The organizational structure of the three types of organizations—for-profit, nonprofit, and mutual-benefit—may be expressed vertically or horizontally on an organization chart.

LO 8-4

Compare the structures of for-profit, nonprofit, and mutual-benefit organizations.

Once an organization's vision and strategy have been determined, as we stated at the beginning of this chapter, the challenge for top managers is, first, to create a culture that will motivate its members to work together and, second, a structure that will coordinate their actions to achieve the organization's strategic goals. Here let us begin to consider the second part—an organization's structure.

In Chapter 1, we defined an organization as a group of people who work together to achieve some specific purpose. According to **Chester I. Barnard's** classic definition, an **organization** is a system of consciously coordinated activities or forces of two or more people.[83] By this wording, a crew of two coordinating their activities to operate a commercial tuna fishing boat is just as much an organization as tuna companies Bumble Bee and StarKist with their thousands of employees.

The Organization: Three Types

As we stated in Chapter 1, there are three types of organizations classified according to the three different purposes for which they are formed:[84]

- **For-profit organizations.** These are formed to make money, or profits, by offering products or services.
- **Nonprofit organizations.** These are formed to offer services to some clients, not to make a profit (examples: hospitals, colleges).
- **Mutual-benefit organizations.** These are voluntary collectives whose purpose is to advance members' interests (examples: unions, trade associations).

Clearly, you might have an occupation (such as auditor or police officer) that is equally employable in any one of these three sectors. As a manager, however, you would be principally required to focus on different goals—making profits, delivering public services, or satisfying member needs—depending on the type of organization.

For-profit automakers are seeking growth by offering electric cars like this. They appeal to consumers who like cool technology, are environmentally conscious, or are frugal. There were 3.2 million electric cars on the global roadways. ©hans engbers/Alamy Stock photo

The Organization Chart

Whatever the size or type of organization, it can be represented in an organization chart. An **organization chart** is a box-and-lines illustration showing the formal lines of authority and the organization's official positions or work specializations. This is the family-tree-like pattern of boxes and lines posted on workplace walls and given to new hires, such as the following for a hospital. *(See Figure 8.4.)*

Two kinds of information that organization charts reveal about organizational structure are (1) the *vertical hierarchy of authority*, who reports to whom, and (2) the *horizontal specialization*, who specializes in what work.

FIGURE 8.4

Organization chart

Example for a hospital.

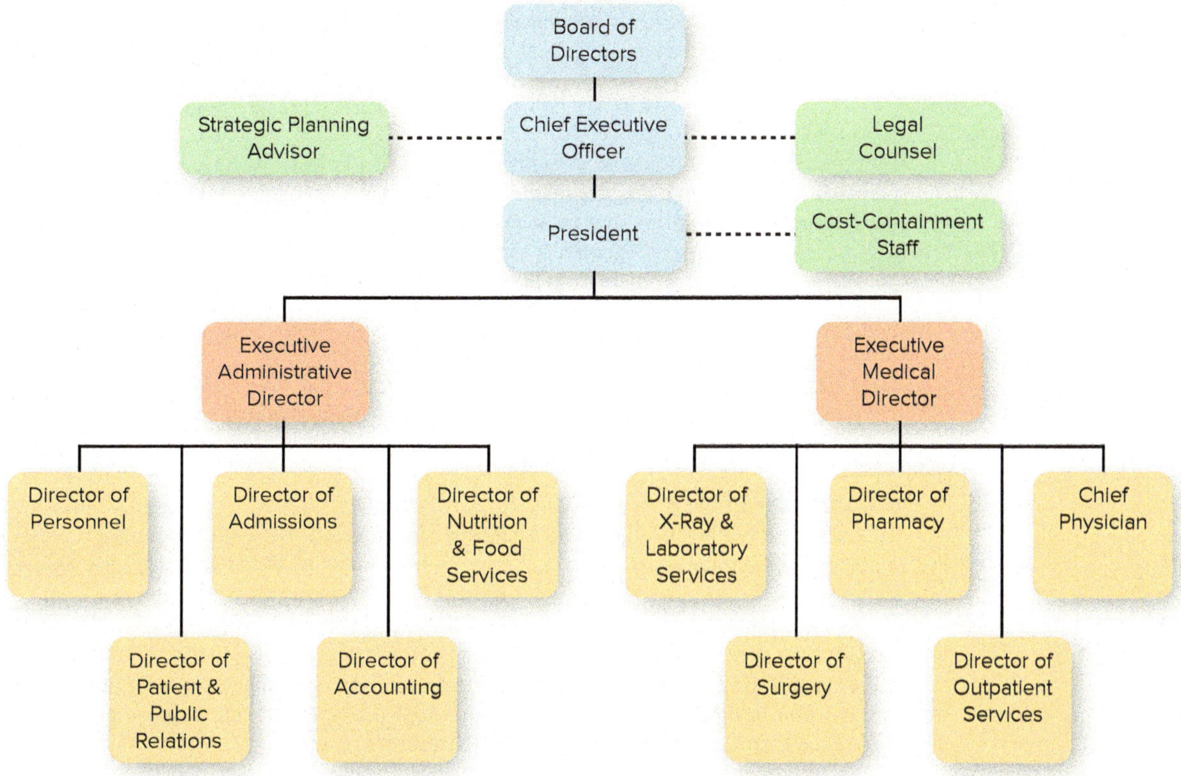

The Vertical Hierarchy of Authority: Who Reports to Whom A glance up and down an organization chart shows the *vertical hierarchy*, the chain of command. A formal vertical hierarchy also shows the official communication network—who talks to whom. In a simple two-person organization, the owner might communicate with just a secretary or an assistant. In a complex organization, the president talks principally to the vice presidents, who in turn talk to the assistant vice presidents, and so on.

The Horizontal Specialization: Who Specializes in What Work A glance to the left and right on the line of an organization chart shows the *horizontal specialization*, the different jobs or work specialization. The husband-and-wife partners in a two-person desktop-publishing firm might agree that one is the "outside person," handling sales, client relations, and finances and the other is the "inside person," handling production and research. A large firm might have vice presidents for each task—marketing, finance, and so on. ●

8.5 The Major Elements of an Organization

THE BIG PICTURE

Seven basic elements or features of an organization are described in this section.

LO 8-5

Identify the major elements of an organization.

Whether for-profit, nonprofit, or mutual-benefit, organizations have a number of elements in common. We discuss four proposed by an organizational psychologist, and then describe three others that most authorities agree on.

Common Elements of Organizations: Four Proposed by Edgar Schein

Organizational psychologist **Edgar Schein** proposed the four common elements of (1) *common purpose*, (2) *coordinated effort*, (3) *division of labor*, and (4) *hierarchy of authority*.[85] Let's consider these.

1. Common Purpose: The Means for Unifying Members

An organization without purpose soon begins to drift and become disorganized. **The common purpose unifies employees or members and gives everyone an understanding of the organization's reason for being.**

2. Coordinated Effort: Working Together for Common Purpose

The common purpose is realized through **coordinated effort, the coordination of individual efforts into a group or organizationwide effort.** Although it's true that individuals can make a difference, they cannot do everything by themselves.

3. Division of Labor: Work Specialization for Greater Efficiency

Division of labor, also known as *work specialization*, is the arrangement of having discrete parts of a task done by different people. Even a two-person crew operating a fishing boat probably has some work specialization—one steers the boat and the other works the nets. With division of labor, an organization can parcel out the entire complex work effort to be performed by specialists, resulting in greater efficiency.

4. Hierarchy of Authority: The Chain of Command

The hierarchy of authority, or *chain of command*, is a control mechanism for making sure the right people do the right things at the right time. If coordinated effort is to be achieved, some people—namely, managers—need to have more authority, or the right to direct the work of others. Even in member-owned organizations, some people have more authority than others, although their peers may have granted it to them.

In addition, authority is most effective when arranged in a hierarchy. Without tiers or ranks of authority, a lone manager would have to confer with everyone in his or her domain, making it difficult to get things done. Even in newer organizations that flatten the hierarchy, there still exists more than one level of management.[86] **A flat organization is defined as one with an organizational structure with few or no levels of middle management between top managers and those reporting to them.**

Finally, a principle stressed by early management scholars was that of **unity of command, in which an employee should report to no more than one manager in order to avoid** conflicting priorities and demands. Today, however, with advances in computer technology and networks, there are circumstances in which it makes sense for a person to communicate with more than one manager (as is true, for instance, with the organizational structure known as the matrix structure, as we'll describe).

Common Elements of Organizations: Three More That Most Authorities Agree On

To Schein's four common elements we add three others that most authorities agree on: (5) *span of control*, (6) *authority, responsibility, and delegation*, and (7) *centralization versus decentralization of authority*.

5. Span of Control: Narrow (or Tall) versus Wide (or Flat)

The span of control, or *span of management*, refers to the number of people reporting directly to a given manager.[87] There are two kinds of spans of control: narrow (or tall) and wide (or flat).

Narrow Span of Control This means a manager has a limited number of people reporting—three vice presidents reporting to a president, for example, instead of nine vice presidents. An organization is said to be *tall* when there are many levels with narrow spans of control.

Wide Span of Control This means a manager has several people reporting—a first-line supervisor may have 40 or more subordinates, if little hands-on supervision is required, as is the case in some assembly-line workplaces. An organization is said to be *flat* when there are only a few levels with wide spans of control.

Historically, spans of about 7 to 10 subordinates were considered best, but there is no consensus as to what is ideal. In general, when managers must be closely involved with their subordinates, as when the management duties are complex, they are advised to have a narrow span of control. This is why presidents tend to have only a handful of vice presidents reporting to them. By contrast, first-line supervisors directing subordinates with similar work tasks may have a wide span of control.

Today's emphasis on lean management staffs and more efficiency means that spans of control need to be as wide as possible while still providing adequate supervision. Wider spans also fit in with the trend toward allowing workers greater autonomy in decision making. Research suggests that, when aided by technology to communicate and monitor, a manager can oversee 30 employees or more.[88]

6. Authority, Responsibility, and Delegation: Line versus Staff Positions

Male sea lions have to battle other males to attain authority over the herd. In human organizations, however, authority is related to the management authority in the organization; it has nothing to do with the manager's fighting ability or personal characteristics. With authority goes *accountability, responsibility,* and the ability to *delegate* one's authority.

Accountability **Authority refers to the rights inherent in a managerial position to make decisions, give orders, and utilize resources.** (Authority is distinguished from *power*, which, as we discuss in Chapter 14, is the extent to which a person is able to influence others so they respond to orders.) In the military, of course, orders are given with the expectation that they will be obeyed, disobedience making one liable to a dishonorable discharge or imprisonment. In civilian organizations, disobeying orders may lead to less dire consequences (demotion or firing), but subordinates are still expected to accept that a higher-level manager has a legitimate right to issue orders.

Authority means **accountability—managers must report and justify work results to the managers above them.** Being accountable means you have the responsibility for performing assigned tasks.[89]

Responsibility With more authority comes more responsibility. **Responsibility is the obligation you have to perform the tasks assigned to you.** A car assembly-line worker has less authority and responsibility than a manager of the assembly line. Whereas the line worker is generally responsible for one specific task, such as installing a windshield, the manager has much greater responsibilities.

It is a sign of faulty job design when managers are given too much authority and not enough responsibility, in which case they may become abusive to subordinates in exerting authority.[90] Conversely, managers may not be given enough authority, so the job becomes difficult.

Delegation **Delegation is the process of assigning managerial authority and responsibility to managers and employees lower in the hierarchy.** To be more efficient, most managers are expected to delegate as much of their work as possible. However, many bosses get hung up on perfection, failing to realize that delegation is a necessary part of managing.

A smart rule is the "70% Rule": If the person you would like to perform the task is able to do it at least 70 percent as well as you can, you should delegate it. "Is it frustrating that the task won't be done with the same degree of perfection or perceived perfection that [you] could achieve?" asks one writer. "Sure! But let go of perfection."[91]

PRACTICAL ACTION How to Delegate Effectively

All managers must learn how to delegate—to assign management authority and responsibilities to people lower in the company hierarchy. Delegation also helps you avoid exhaustion from overwork. If, as a manager, you find yourself often behind, always taking work home, doing your subordinates' work for them, and constantly having employees seeking your approval before they can act, you're clearly not delegating well. If you lack even the time to train someone to take over tasks for you, reprioritize some tasks and find the time.[92]

How can you delegate more effectively? It's fine to start small. Here are some guidelines.[93]

Delegate Routine Tasks and Technical Matters Always try to delegate routine tasks and routine paperwork, keeping only the tasks that call for your input. When there are technical matters, let the experts handle them.

Delegate Tasks That Help Your Subordinates Grow Let your employees solve their own problems whenever possible. Let them try new things so they will grow in their jobs. Your success depends on theirs, so give them room to achieve.

Match Delegated Tasks to Your Subordinates' Skills and Abilities While recognizing that delegation involves some risk, make your assignments appropriate to the training, talent, skills, and motivation of your employees. Begin by asking your team members whether they can handle more work, and in what areas they would like to improve their skills or upgrade their responsibilities. Be sure you've given them the tools and clarity they need to get the job done, stay available for help and questions, but let your subordinates do what is now their job.[94]

Don't Delegate Confidential or Human Resource Matters Tasks that are confidential or that involve the evaluation, discipline, or counseling of subordinates should never be handed off to someone else.

Don't Delegate Emergencies By definition, an emergency is a crisis for which there is little time for solution and a high need for coordination within the organization. You should handle this yourself.

Don't Delegate Special Tasks That Your Boss Asked You to Do—Unless You Have His or Her Permission If your supervisor entrusts you with a special assignment, such as attending a particular meeting, don't delegate it unless you have permission to do so.

YOUR CALL

Managers fail to delegate for many reasons: An excessive need for perfection. A belief that only they should handle "special," "difficult," or "unusual" problems or clients. A wish to keep the parts of a job that are fun. A fear that others will think them lazy. A reluctance to let employees lower down in the hierarchy take risks. A worry that subordinates won't deliver. A concern that the subordinates will do a better job and show them up. Are any of these reasons that you might need to improve your skill at delegating? What are some others?

Regarding authority and responsibility, the organization chart distinguishes between two positions, line and staff. *(Refer back to Figure 8.4.)*

Line Position **Line managers have authority to make decisions and usually have people reporting to them.** Examples are the president, the vice presidents, the director of personnel, and the head of accounting. Line positions are indicated on the organization chart by a *solid line* (usually a vertical line).

Staff Position **Staff personnel have authority functions; they provide advice, recommendations, and research to line managers** (examples: specialists such as legal counsels and special advisers for mergers and acquisitions or strategic planning). Staff positions are indicated on the organization chart by a *dotted line* (usually a horizontal line).

7. Centralization versus Decentralization of Authority

Who makes the important decisions in an organization? That is what the question of centralization versus decentralization of authority is concerned with.

Centralized Authority **With centralized authority, important decisions are made by higher-level managers.** Very small companies tend to be the most centralized, although nearly all organizations have at least some authority concentrated at the top of the hierarchy. Kmart and McDonald's are examples of companies using this kind of authority.

An advantage in using centralized authority is that there is less duplication of work, because fewer employees perform the same task; rather, the task is often performed by a department of specialists. Another advantage of centralization is that procedures are uniform and thus easier to control; all purchasing, for example, may have to be put out to competitive bids.

Decentralized Authority **With decentralized authority, important decisions are made by middle-level and supervisory-level managers.** Here, obviously, power has been delegated throughout the organization. Among the companies using decentralized authority are General Motors and Harley-Davidson.

An advantage in having decentralized authority is that managers are encouraged to solve their own problems rather than to buck the decision to a higher level. In addition, decisions are made more quickly, which increases the organization's flexibility and efficiency. ●

8.6 Basic Types of Organizational Structures

THE BIG PICTURE

Eight types of organizational structures are simple, functional, divisional, matrix, horizontal, hollow, modular, and virtual.

LO 8-6

Describe the eight organizational structures.

As we'll see when we discuss job analysis in Chapter 9, companies create organizational structures in order to help employees do their jobs better. Because of this focus, structure and culture are often intertwined. When Google cofounder (with Sergey Brin) and CEO Larry Page was asked in 2011 about the biggest threat to his company, Page answered in a single word: "Google."

Now 20 years old, Google started out as a freewheeling company in which, as we mentioned, engineers were given time to experiment on their own projects, producing the famed Google's culture of innovation. The problem, however, was that the company grew so quickly (it's now more than 88,000 people) that decision making had become molasses-like. For instance, the two cofounders, who had been trained as engineers, had hired a professional manager, Eric Schmidt, to be CEO, but the three of them "had to agree before anything could be done," says one report. "The unwieldy management and glacial pace of decision making were particularly noticeable in [Silicon Valley], where start-ups overtake behemoths in months."[95]

In 2015, Google revamped its corporate structure into a conglomerate called Alphabet Inc., with individual operations headed by separate chief executives. The word *conglomerate* (defined as a large company that is doing business in different, quite unrelated areas–General Electric and Berkshire Hathaway are two examples) is unpopular with most companies today because critics think it spreads top management focus too widely.[96] However, for the Google founders, the purpose of Alphabet was not only to streamline the company's structure and decision-making processes, but also to bring more transparency into the company's operations to satisfy investors who, as one editorial explained it, "admired its cash-rich search businesses but complained that its other sidelines are hard to measure."[97] The reorganization separated the collection of traditional businesses most associated with Google–such as Search, Android, YouTube, and Google Maps–from more speculative "moonshot" ventures such as Calico (life extension), Google X (self-driving cars), Nest (smart-home devices), and Sidewalk (city infrastructure).[98]

Organizational design is concerned with designing the optimal structures of accountability and responsibility that an organization uses to execute its strategies. We can categorize organizational designs as three types: (1) traditional designs, (2) horizontal designs, and (3) designs that open boundaries between organizations.[99]

1. Traditional Designs: Simple, Functional, Divisional, and Matrix Structures

Traditional organizational designs tend to favor structures that rely on a vertical management hierarchy, with clear departmental boundaries and reporting arrangements, as follows.

FIGURE 8.5

Simple structure: An example

There is only one hierarchical level of management beneath the owner.

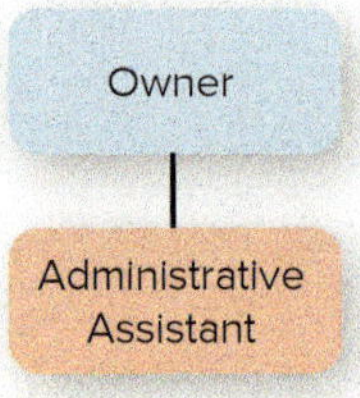

The Simple Structure: For the Small Firm

The first organizational form is the simple structure. This is the form often found in a firm's very early, entrepreneurial stages, when the organization is apt to reflect the desires and personality of the owner or founder. **An organization with a simple structure has authority centralized in a single person, a flat hierarchy, few rules, and low work specialization.** *(See Figure 8.5.)*

Hundreds of thousands of organizations are arranged according to a simple structure—for instance, small mom-and-pop firms running landscaping, construction, insurance sales, and similar businesses. Examples: Both Hewlett-Packard and Apple Computer began as two-man garage start-ups that later became large.

The Functional Structure: Grouping by Similar Work Specialties The second organizational form is the functional structure. **In a functional structure, people with similar occupational specialties are put together in formal groups.** This is a quite commonplace structure, seen in all kinds of organizations, for-profit and nonprofit. *(See Figure 8.6.)*

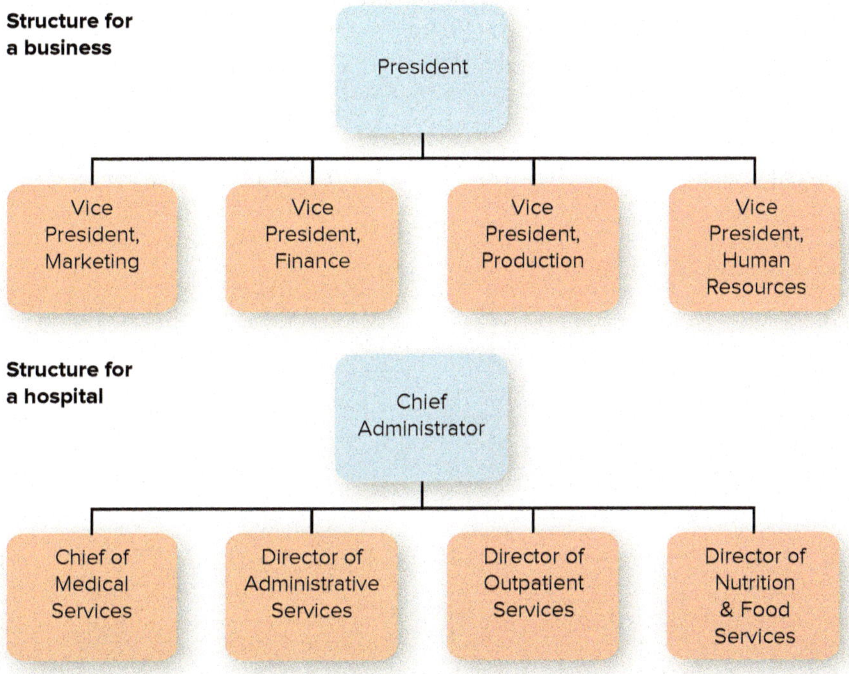

FIGURE 8.6

Functional structure: Two examples

This shows the functional structure for a business and for a hospital.

Examples: A manufacturing firm will often group people with similar work skills in a Marketing Department, others in a Production Department, others in Finance, and so on. A nonprofit educational institution might group employees according to work specialty under Faculty, Admissions, Maintenance, and so forth.

The Divisional Structure: Grouping by Similarity of Purpose The third organizational form is the divisional structure. **In a divisional structure, people with diverse occupational specialties are put together in formal groups by similar products or services, customers or clients, or geographic regions.** *(See Figure 8.7.)*

Product Divisions: Grouping by Similar Products or Services **Product divisions group activities around similar products or services.** Examples: The media giant Time Warner has different divisions for magazines, movies, recordings, cable television, and so on. The Warner Bros. part of the empire alone has divisions spanning movies and television, a broadcast network, retail stores, theaters, amusement parks, and music.

Customer Divisions: Grouping by Common Customers or Clients **Customer divisions tend to group activities around common customers or clients.** Examples: Ford Motor Co.

FIGURE 8.7

Divisional structure: Three examples

This shows product, customer, and geographic divisions.

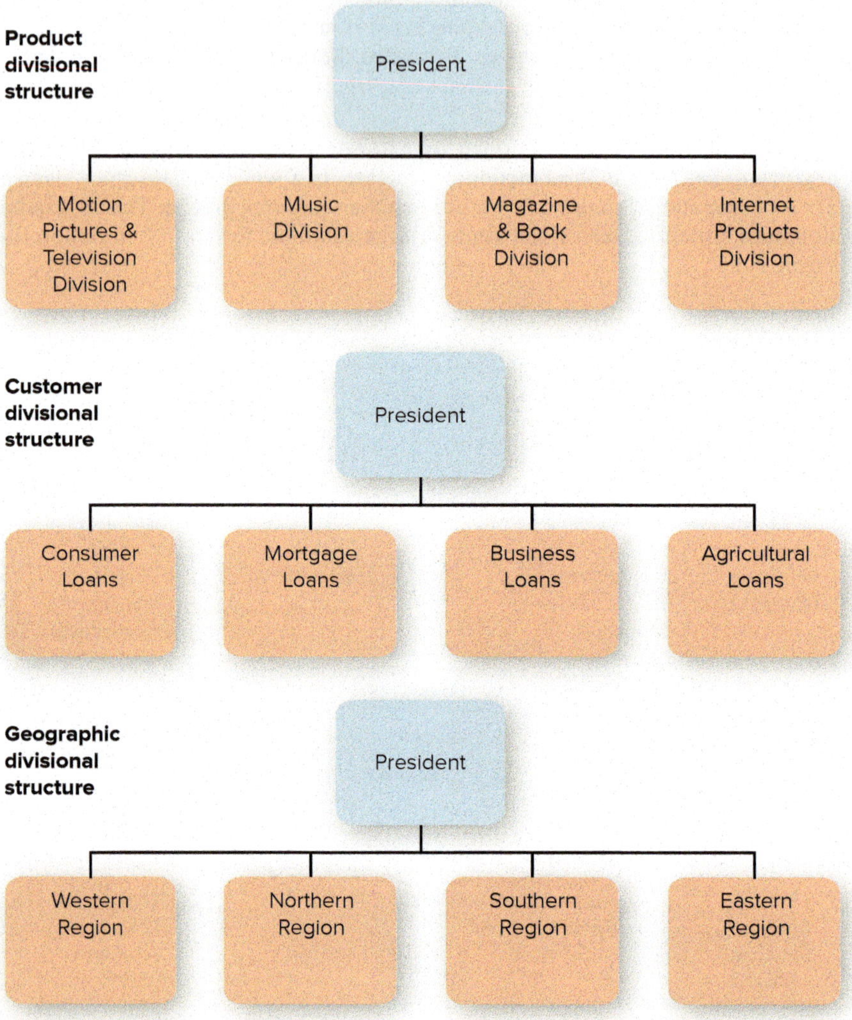

has separate divisions for passenger-car dealers, for large trucking customers, and for farm products customers. A savings and loan might be structured with divisions for making consumer loans, mortgage loans, business loans, and agricultural loans.

Geographic Divisions: Grouping by Regional Location **Geographic divisions group activities around defined regional locations.** Example: This arrangement is frequently used by government agencies. The Federal Reserve Bank, for instance, has 12 separate districts around the United States. The Internal Revenue Service also has several districts.

The Matrix Structure: A Grid of Functional and Divisional for Two Chains of Command

The fourth organizational form is the matrix structure. **In a matrix structure, an organization combines functional and divisional chains of command in a grid so that there are two command structures—vertical and horizontal.** The functional structure usually doesn't change—it is the organization's normal departments or divisions, such as Finance, Marketing, Production, and Research & Development. The divisional structure may vary—as by product, brand, customer, or geographic region. *(See Figure 8.8.)*

FIGURE 8.8

Matrix structure

An example of an arrangement that Ford might use.

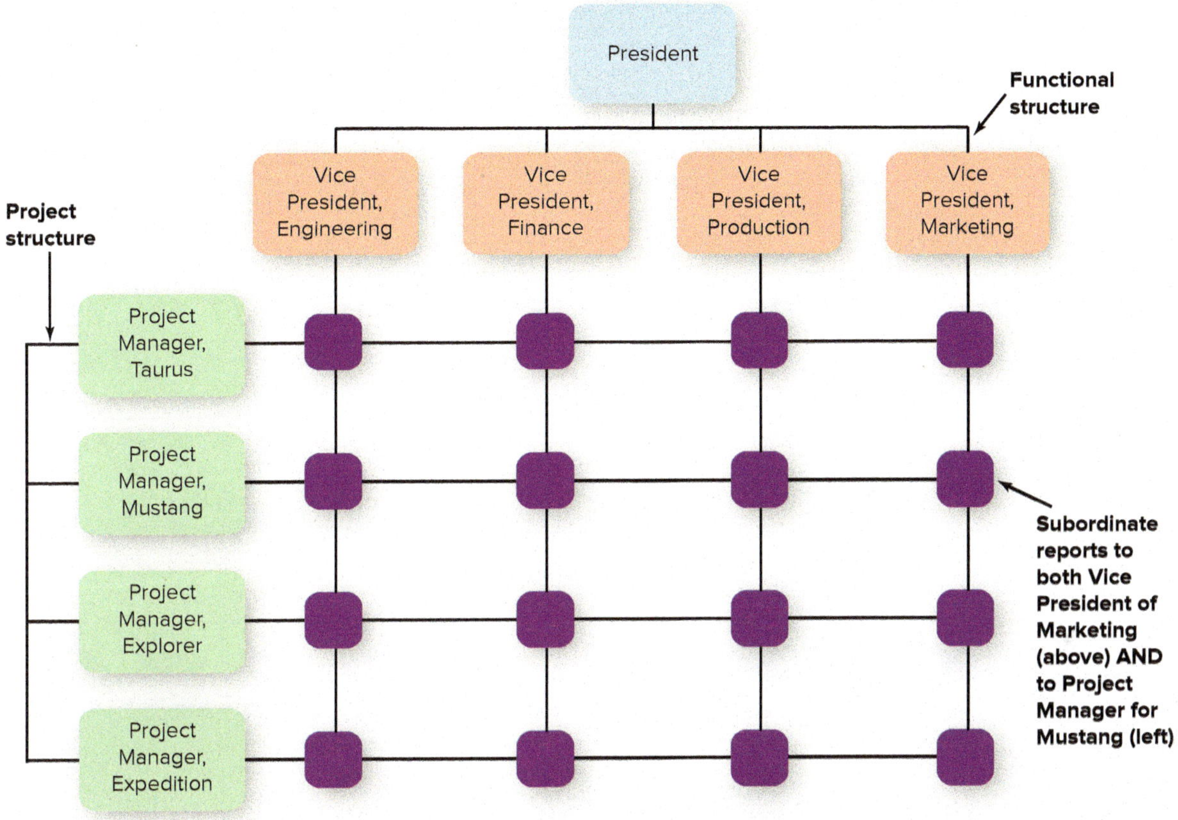

A hypothetical example, using Ford Motor Co.: The functional structure might be the departments of Engineering, Finance, Production, and Marketing, each headed by a vice president. Thus, the reporting arrangement is vertical. The divisional structure might be by product (the new models of Taurus, Mustang, Explorer, and Expedition, for example), each headed by a project manager. This reporting arrangement is horizontal. Thus, a marketing person, say, would report to *both* the vice president of marketing *and* the project manager for the Ford Mustang. Indeed, Ford Motor Co. used the matrix approach to create the Taurus and a newer version of the Mustang.

2. The Horizontal Design: Eliminating Functional Barriers to Solve Problems

The second organizational design is the horizontal design. **In a horizontal design, also called a team-based design, teams or workgroups, either temporary or permanent, are used to improve collaboration and work on shared tasks by breaking down internal boundaries.** For instance, when managers from different functional divisions are brought together in teams—known as cross-functional teams—to solve particular problems, the barriers between the divisions break down. The focus on narrow divisional interests yields to a common interest in solving the problems that brought them together. Yet team members still have their full-time functional work responsibilities and often still formally report to their own managers above them in the functional-division hierarchy. *(See Figure 8.9.)*

FIGURE 8.9

Horizontal design

This shows a mix of functional (vertical) and project-team (horizontal) arrangements.

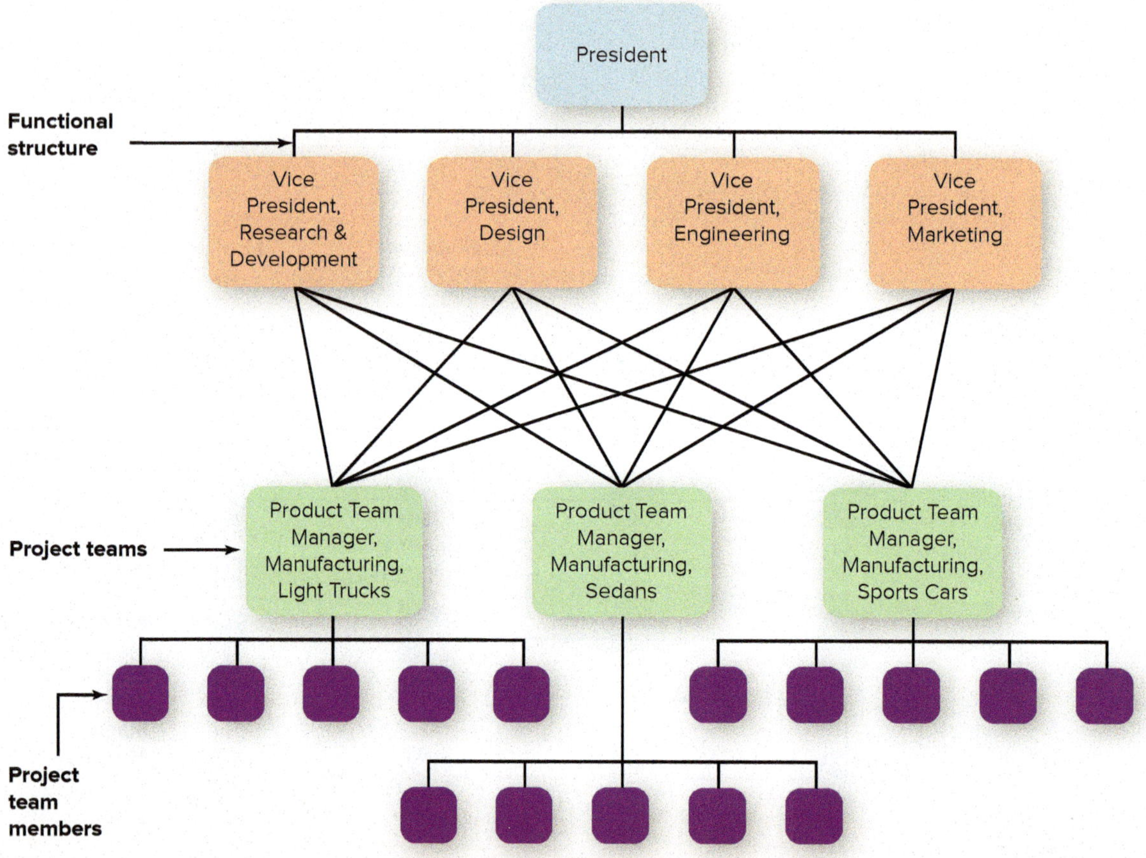

EXAMPLE Use of a Horizontal Design: Whole Foods Market

Upscale natural and organic-food grocery Whole Foods Market, recently purchased by Amazon, started out in 1980 as one store in Austin, Texas, and today has revenues of $15.7 billion and 477 stores in North America and the United Kingdom.[100] It remained one of *Fortune*'s "100 Best Companies to Work For" every year for 17 years (most recently as No. 75 in 2016).[101] Its management strategy is based not on hierarchy, but on autonomous profit centers of self-managed teams.

Decentralizing by Empowering Small Teams One of Whole Foods's core operating principles is that all work is teamwork. Thus, each store is organized into roughly eight self-managed teams, each with a designated team leader. The leaders in each store also operate as a team, as do the store leaders in each region, and the directors of the company's 11 regions operate as a team.

At the individual-store level, compensation is tied to team rather than individual performance, and performance measurements and individual pay schedules are open to all. Each team has the mission of improving the food for which it is responsible; is given wide flexibility in how it manages its responsibilities, hires and fires its members, and stocks its shelves; and is given a lot of power in how it responds to the changing tastes of local consumers.

A Steady Diet of Growth Whole Foods employees are given both the freedom to do the right thing for customers and the incentive to do the right thing for profits. The financial results of this business model are that Whole Foods is the most profitable food retailer in the United Sates, when measured by profit per square foot.[102]

Changes under Amazon So far it seems that Amazon is bringing mostly operational changes to Whole Foods, such as selectively cutting prices, testing an online ordering service with same-day delivery, allowing pick-up and return of Amazon orders in certain stores, and extending discounts and other benefits to Whole Foods shoppers who are Amazon Prime subscribers. The company has also sold Amazon products like the Echo and Kindle in pop-up stores staffed by Amazon employees at some Whole Foods locations. After the acquisition, Whole Foods' sales began by growing at a faster rate than before, and the grocery chain plans to hire more workers. But unless Amazon makes structural changes, it may not need to add more layers in the process.[103]

YOUR CALL

In designing new products, the horizontal design team approach, known as *concurrent engineering* or *integrated product development*, has been found to speed up design because all the specialists meet at once, instead of separately doing their own thing, then handing off the result to the next group of specialists. Why do you think a horizontal design would be better in a retail business such as groceries?

3. Designs That Open Boundaries between Organizations: Hollow, Modular, and Virtual Structures

The opposite of a bureaucracy, with its numerous barriers and divisions, a **boundaryless organization** is a fluid, highly adaptive organization whose members, linked by information technology, come together to collaborate on common tasks. The collaborators may include not only co-workers but also suppliers, customers, and even competitors. This means that the form of the business is ever-changing, and business relationships are informal.[104]

Three types of structures in this class of organizational design are *hollow, modular*, and *virtual* structures.

The Hollow Structure: Operating with a Central Core and Outsourcing Functions to Outside Vendors

In the **hollow structure**, often called the network structure, the organization has a central core of key functions and outsources other functions to vendors who can do them cheaper or faster. *(See Figure 8.10.)* A company with a hollow structure might retain such important core processes as design or marketing and outsource most other processes, such as human resources, warehousing, or distribution, thereby seeming to "hollow out" the organization.[105]

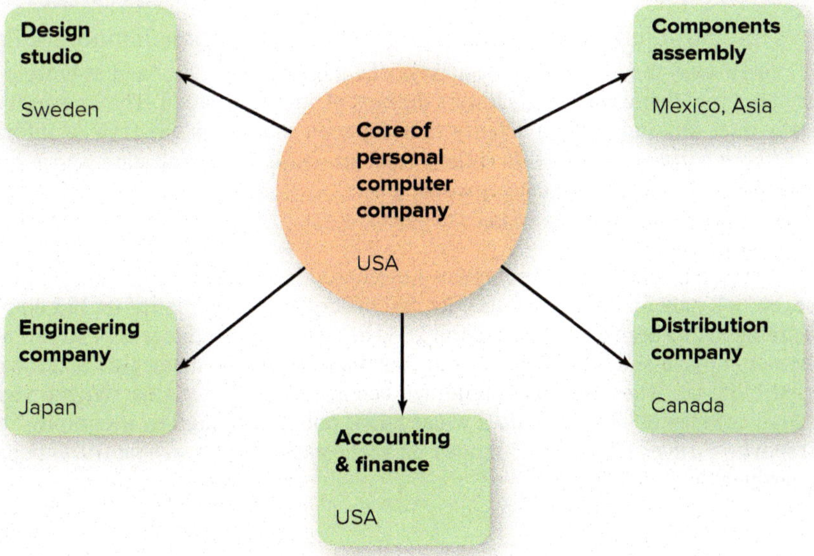

FIGURE 8.10

Hollow structure

This is an example of a personal computer company that outsources noncore processes to vendors.

Modular structure. The center section of Bombardier's eight-passenger Continental business jet is built in Ireland and is shipped to Wichita, Kansas, where it is assembled with 12 other major components in just four days. ©epa european presspoto agency b.v./Alamy Stock Photo

A firm with a hollow structure might operate with extensive, even worldwide operations, yet its basic core could remain small, thus keeping payrolls and overhead down. The glue that holds everything together is information technology, along with strategic alliances and contractual arrangements with supplier companies. An example of a hollow structure is EndoStim, the medical device start-up we described earlier.

The Modular Structure: Outsourcing Pieces of a Product to Outside Firms The modular structure differs from the hollow structure in that it is oriented around outsourcing certain *pieces of a product* rather than outsourcing certain *processes* (such as human resources or warehousing) of an organization. In a **modular structure**, **a firm assembles product chunks, or modules, provided by outside contractors.** One article compares this form of organization to "a collection of Lego bricks that can snap together."

An example of the modular structure is the massive 787 Dreamliner project, in which Boeing contracted with many suppliers, each responsible for one component or assembly, which were then integrated to make the aircraft. Another example is an eight-passenger business jet, the Continental, made by Bombardier (pronounced "bom-*bar*-dee-ay") of Wichita, Kansas. The Continental is designed in a dozen large modules, which are built in various places around the world. The cockpit and forward fuselage are built by Bombardier Montreal. The center section is built in Belfast, the wing by Mitsubishi in Japan, the stabilizers and rear fuselage by Aerospace Industrial Development in Taiwan, the landing gear by Messier-Dowty in Canada, and the tailcone by Hawker de Havilland in Australia. The engines are provided by General Electric and the avionics gear by Rockwell Collins, both companies in the United States. The 12 modules are shipped to Wichita, where the parts are snapped together in just four days.[106]

The Virtual Structure: An Internet-Connected Partner for a Temporary Project "Strip away the highfalutin' talk," says one industry observer, "and at bottom the Internet is a tool that dramatically lowers the cost of communication. That means it can radically alter any industry or activity that depends heavily on the flow of information."[107] One consequence of this is the **virtual structure**, **an organization whose members are geographically apart, usually working with e-mail and other forms of information technology, yet which generally appears to customers as a single, unified organization with a real physical location.**[108]

An example is web-services company Automattic Inc., which has a San Francisco office, but it's only for occasional use. Its real offices are the homes of its 123 employees working in 26 countries, 94 cities, and 28 U.S. states. Although occasionally employees hop on a plane and meet face to face, they mainly transmit messages via text-based internal blogs or, when misunderstandings occur, talk on the phone. With a virtual structure, companies can "tap into a wider talent pool not limited by geography," says one report. "Firms can also save money on real estate, though sizable travel budgets may partly offset that."[109]

8.7 Contingency Design: Factors in Creating the Best Structure

THE BIG PICTURE

Three factors that should be considered when determining the best organizational culture involve whether an organization's environment is mechanistic or organic, whether its environment stresses differentiation or integration, and how its strategy can affect its structure.

LO 8-7

Identify the factors that affect the design of an organization's structure.

What is the optimal size for an organization? How big is too big?

There is no one best form of structure for an organization. The choice of the best structure depends on a variety of contingency factors and internal organizational characteristics.[110] For example, the maker of Legos, Lego AS, is changing its structure because the current one "was created to cope with double-digit sales growth, but the company says it now has too many layers and overlapping business functions." Management feels this structure makes "it tougher to implement marketing strategies, slower to react to trends and disconnected from retailers."[111]

This section discusses how companies can more effectively structure themselves by using the concept of contingency organization design. According to the **contingency approach to organization design**, organizations are more effective when they are structured to fit the demands of the situation, and when the structure is aligned with the strategies and internal actions of the organization.

Three Factors to Be Considered in Designing an Organization's Structure

When managers are considering what organizational arrangements to choose from, such factors as stage of development are among the factors, or *contingencies,* they must consider. Recall from Chapter 2 that the *contingency approach* to management emphasizes that a manager's approach should vary according to—that is, be contingent on—the individual and environmental situation. Thus, the manager following the contingency approach simply asks, "What method is the best to use under these particular circumstances?"

Managers taking a contingency approach must consider the following factors in designing the best kind of structure for their particular organization at that particular time:

1. *Environment—mechanistic versus organic.*
2. *Environment—differentiation versus integration.*
3. *Link between strategy, culture, and structure.*

Could anyone do this? Hotel housekeepers, following the model of a mechanistic organization, are supposed to be able to make beds in no more than 3 minutes and ready an entire room within 24 minutes. The tasks are physically demanding, and the staff must be taught how to bend properly to make the work easier on the body. If you had this job, what would you do to vary the routine to avoid monotony—or would that sacrifice speed? ©Simon Dawson/Bloomberg/Getty Images

1. The Environment: Mechanistic versus Organic Organizations—the Burns and Stalker Model

Making beds—how hard could it be?

Actually, a hotel housecleaner may be expected to whip not just beds but entire rooms, 16–30 of them, into spick-and-span shape during an eight-hour shift. Here every job is broken down into the smallest of steps, with vacuuming, dusting, mopping, making beds, and so on expected to take about 20–24 minutes per room, according to time-motion studies. Making a neatly tucked bed should take no more than 3 minutes.[112] Marriott allows 30 minutes for tidying up a room and has developed a 66-step manual with very specific directions ("Wipe the nightstand's glass top with a blue rag, using the blue bottle. Wipe the phone and clock").[113]

Much of this kind of mundane hotel work exemplifies what British behavioral scientists **Tom Burns** and **G. M. Stalker** call a *mechanistic organization*, as opposed to an *organic organization*.[114] *(See Table 8.2.)*

TABLE 8.2 Mechanistic versus Organic Organizations

MECHANISTIC ORGANIZATIONS	ORGANIC ORGANIZATIONS
Centralized hierarchy of authority	Decentralized hierarchy of authority
Many rules and procedures	Few rules and procedures
Specialized tasks	Shared tasks
Formalized communication	Informal communication
Few teams or task forces	Many teams or task forces
Narrow span of control, taller structures	Wider span of control, flatter structures

Mechanistic Organizations: When Rigidity and Uniformity Work Best

In a **mechanistic organization**, **authority is centralized, tasks and rules are clearly specified, and employees are closely supervised.** Mechanistic organizations, then, are bureaucratic, with rigid rules and top-down communication. This kind of structure is effective in certain aspects of hotel work because the market demands uniform product quality and cleanliness.

In general, mechanistic design works best when an organization is operating in a stable environment. Yet new companies that have gone through a rough-and-tumble start-up period may decide to change their structures so that they are more mechanistic, with clear lines of authority.

Organic Organizations: When Looseness and Flexibility Work Best

In an **organic organization**, **authority is decentralized, there are fewer rules and procedures, and networks of employees are encouraged to cooperate and respond quickly to unexpected tasks.** Tom Peters and Robert Waterman called this kind of organization a "loose" structure.[115]

Organic organizations are sometimes termed "adhocracies" because they operate on an ad hoc basis, improvising as they go along. As you might expect, information-technology companies favor the organic arrangement because they constantly have to adjust to technological change. Companies that need to respond to fast-changing consumer tastes also favor organic arrangements.

Etsy, the quirky online craft marketplace, had been growing rapidly for a few years, adding staff and upgrading its trendy Brooklyn headquarters with garden walls and spaces reserved for yoga and meditation. The company increased employee salaries and offered generous benefits and perks, while maintaining a strong reputation that attracted heavy traffic to its website. In April 2015, it issued its initial public offering (IPO). But Etsy was spending as much as 24 percent of its revenue on general and administrative expenses (compared to, say, 10 percent at eBay) and it was losing money. In 2016, the board of directors announced a large layoff and replaced the CEO. The company changed its definition of "handmade," and its new CEO, Josh Silverman, simplified its focus from 15 measures to "the one metric that matters": gross merchandise sales. Some employees wonder whether the company's original idealism, which one investor said "does translate into growth," is being replaced by an imperative to simply sell merchandise. In other words, will its once organic organization become too mechanized for the company to retain its unorthodox, individualistic, and sometimes emotional culture? Time will tell. The company has given up its coveted status as a certified B Corp (granted by the nonprofit B Lab), but sales, revenues, and share price were all up dramatically in the fourth quarter of 2017. "We're getting a lot more done," said Silverman. "There's a lot more focus, a lot more urgency."[116]

SELF-ASSESSMENT 8.3

Assessing Your Organizational Structure Preference

This survey is designed to assess your preferred type of organizational structure. Please be prepared to answer these questions if your instructor has assigned Self-Assessment 8.3 in Connect.

1. Do you prefer a more mechanistic or organic structure? What do you think is the cause for this preference?
2. If you were interviewing for a job, what questions might you ask to determine if the company is more mechanistic or organic?

2. The Environment: Differentiation versus Integration—the Lawrence and Lorsch Model

Burns and Stalker's ideas were extended in the United States by Harvard University researchers **Paul R. Lawrence** and **Jay W. Lorsch.**[117] Instead of a *mechanistic-organic dimension*, however, they proposed a *differentiation-integration* dimension–forces that impelled the parts of an organization to move apart or to come together. The stability of the environment confronting the parts of the organization, according to Lawrence and Lorsch, determines the degree of differentiation or integration that is appropriate.

Differentiation: When Forces Push the Organization Apart

Differentiation is the tendency of the parts of an organization to disperse and fragment. The more subunits into which an organization breaks down, the more highly differentiated it is.

This impulse toward dispersal arises because of technical specialization and division of labor. As a result, specialists behave in specific, delimited ways, without coordinating with other parts of the organization. For example, a company producing dental floss, deodorants, and other personal-care products might have different product divisions, each with its own production facility and sales staff–a quite differentiated organization.

Integration: When Forces Pull the Organization Together

Integration is the tendency of the parts of an organization to draw together to achieve a common purpose. In a highly integrated organization, the specialists work together to achieve a common goal. The means for achieving this are a formal chain of command, standardization of rules and procedures, and use of cross-functional teams and computer networks so that there is frequent communication and coordination of the parts.

3. Linking Strategy, Culture, and Structure

We began this chapter by discussing why it makes sense that a company's organizational culture and organizational structure should be aligned with its vision and strategies. Thus, if the managers of an organization change its strategy, as gloStream did when it decided to add lots more people and put them under one roof instead of in a virtual network, they need to change the organization's culture and structure to support that strategy. Indeed, companies often begin by offering a single product or product line that requires only a simple structure, but as they grow and their strategies become more ambitious and elaborate, the culture and structure need to change to support those strategies.[118]

All the organizational cultures and structures described in this chapter are used today because all of them have advantages that make them appropriate for some cases and disadvantages that make them not useful for others. For example, the clear roles and strict hierarchy of an extremely mechanistic organization are clearly suitable in a system valuing careful routines and checks and balances, such as a nuclear power plant. A fast-moving start-up drawing on sources of expertise throughout the world may benefit from a more flexible culture and organic structure that lowers boundaries between functions and organizations.

8.8 Career Corner: Managing Your Career Readiness

Organizational culture and structure are important aspects of the internal context found in every organization. Recall from Chapter 4 that an organization's internal context represents the situational or environmental characteristics that influence employees' behavior.[119] Understanding the internal context of your organization helps you to fit in and display organizationally preferred behaviors, ultimately leading to higher job satisfaction, performance, and greater chances of promotability.[120] This section thus focuses on improving your ability to assess an organization's internal context.

LO 8-8

Describe how to use the career readiness competencies of *understanding the business* and *personal adaptability* to assess an organization's internal context.

We recommend an approach that uses two key career readiness competencies from the model shown below: *understanding the business* and *personal adaptability*.

FIGURE 8.11

Model of career readiness

©2018 Kinicki and Associates, Inc.

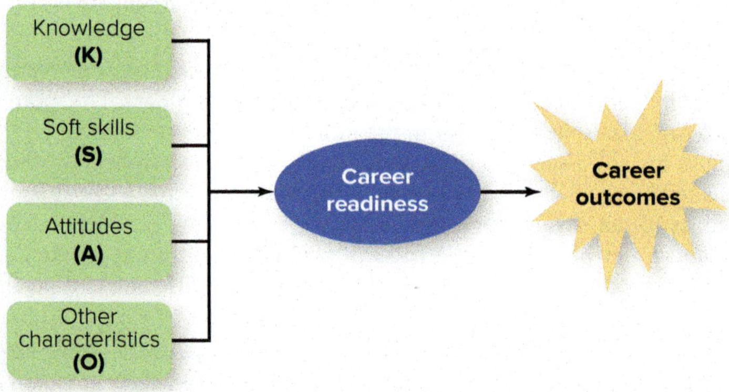

Understanding the Business and Where You "Fit" In

We are focusing on understanding the business and your level of fit after being hired. We recommend two steps for determining where you fit in a specific context and how you can adapt.[121]

Step 1: Assess Where and How You Fit in the Context. Use a current or past job to answer the following questions:

- What is the mission or purpose of my work unit?
- How does this work unit support corporate strategy, and what is at stake if we fail to achieve our goals?
- How long have my colleagues worked here and what is their background?
- What are the norms or expected ways of getting things done around here? What happens when someone violates one of these norms?
- Why did I take this job and what are my career expectations?
- What is my role in relationship to other roles in my work unit?
- How do I contribute to achievement of corporate strategies?

Next, brainstorm answers to the following questions. If you don't know the answers, seek input from colleagues or your boss.

- Where do I fit within the organization's structure? (It's important to understand reporting relationships across management levels.)
- What are the rules governing what we do and how we do it in this work unit? What is my view of these rules?
- What values define the culture? Are my values consistent with the organization's values?
- What are the characteristics of people in leadership roles? Do I like and admire these characteristics?

Step 2: How Can You Effectively Adapt? Answering the following questions will give you a plan for adapting to the current internal context.

- Based on my assessment of the organization's structure, how can I adapt to this context?
- Based on my assessment of the rules governing behavior, how can I adapt to this environment?
- Which of your values are consistent and inconsistent with the values of this organization? Am I willing to adapt? How might I do this?
- How might I adapt to the type of leadership in this organization?

Becoming More Adaptable

Personal adaptability is defined as the ability and willingness to adapt to changing situations. It represents an "other characteristic" in our model of career readiness that contributes to your performance and success because it allows you to remain productive during times of organizational change.[122] Try the following suggestions to increase your level of adaptability.

- **Focus on Being Optimistic.** Optimistic people see change as an opportunity. Because they therefore view work or career changes as challenges to be overcome, they have positive expectations about future events and confidence in their ability to adjust. Optimistic people tend not to whine. Rather, they attempt to change or influence a decision or they adapt and move on.[123]
- **Display a Proactive Learning Orientation.** A proactive learning orientation reflects your desire to learn and improve other career readiness competencies. This attitude keeps you focused on learning and initiating the behavior desired by an organization during times of change.
- **Be More Resourceful.** When faced with challenges, look for solutions not problems. Practice using project post mortems, discussed in Chapter 7, to find creative ideas for improving results. It also helps to create contingency plans that identify what you can do if Plan A doesn't work.
- **Take Ownership and Accept Responsibility.** This career readiness attitude is the willingness to accept responsibility for your actions. Adaptable people don't become "victim to external influences because they're proactive," according to a *Forbes* writer. He notes that, "To adapt to something new you must forego the old. Adaptable people don't hold grudges or eschew needlessly but instead absorb, understand and move on."[124] Indeed sound advice.
- **Expand Your Perspective by Asking Different Questions.** Asking new or novel questions helps to broaden your perspective when faced with a challenge. Most of us tend to ask questions that are too narrow. Try something like: "What surprises me about this situation? What are impossible options in this situation? What data am I ignoring?"[125]

Key Terms Used in This Chapter

accountability 301
adhocracy culture 288
authority 301
boundaryless organization 309
centralized authority 303
clan culture 288
common purpose 300
contingency approach to organizational design 311
coordinated effort 300
corporate culture 283
customer divisions 305
decentralized authority 303
delegation 302
differentiation 313
division of labor 300
divisional structure 305
enacted values 287
espoused values 286
flat organization 300
functional structure 305
geographic divisions 306
hero 290
hierarchy culture 289
hierarchy of authority 300
hollow structure 309
horizontal design 307
integration 313
line managers 303
market culture 289
matrix structure 306
mechanistic organization 312
modular structure 310
organic organization 312
organization 298
organization chart 298
organizational culture 283
organizational design 304
organizational socialization 290
organizational structure 285
person–organization (PO) fit 292
product divisions 305
responsibility 302
rites and rituals 290
simple structure 304
span of control 301
staff personnel 303
story 290
symbol 290
unity of command 300
virtual structure 310

Key Points

8.1 Aligning Strategy, Culture, and Structure

- Person–organization fit reflects the extent to which your personality and values match the climate and culture in an organization. A good fit is associated with more positive work attitudes and task performance, lower stress, and fewer intentions to quit.
- The challenge for top managers is to align the organization's vision and strategies with its organizational culture and organizational structure.
- Organizational culture is defined as the set of shared, taken-for-granted implicit assumptions that a group holds and that determines how it perceives, thinks about, and reacts to its various environments. The culture helps employees understand why the organization does what it does and how it intends to accomplish its long-term goals.
- Organizational structure is a formal system of task and reporting relationships that coordinates and motivates an organization's members so that they can work together to achieve the organization's goals.

8.2 What Kind of Organizational Culture Will You Be Operating In?

- Organizational culture appears as three layers. Level 1 is observable artifacts, the physical manifestations of culture. Level 2 is espoused values, explicitly stated values and norms preferred by an organization, although employees are frequently influenced by enacted values, which represent the values and norms actually exhibited in the organization. Level 3 consists of basic assumptions, the core values of the organization.
- According to one common methodology known as the *competing values framework*, organizational cultures can be classified into four types: (1) clan, which has an internal focus and values flexibility; (2) adhocracy, which has an external focus and values flexibility; (3) market, which has a strong external focus and values stability and control; and (4) hierarchy, which has an internal focus and values stability and control.
- Culture is transmitted to employees in symbols, stories, heroes, rites and rituals, and organizational socialization. A symbol is an object, an act, a quality, or an event that conveys meaning to others. A story is a narrative based on true events, which is repeated—and sometimes embellished on—to emphasize a particular value. A hero is a person whose accomplishments embody the values of the organization. Rites and rituals are the activities and ceremonies, planned and unplanned, that celebrate important occasions and accomplishments in the organization's life. Organizational socialization is defined as the process by which people learn the values, norms, and required behaviors that permit them to participate as members of an organization.

8.3 The Process of Culture Change

- The 12 mechanisms managers use to embed a culture in an organization are (1) formal statements; (2) slogans and sayings; (3) rites and rituals; (4) stories, legends, and myths; (5) leader reactions to crises; (6) role modeling, training, and coaching;

(7) physical design; (8) rewards, titles, promotions, and bonuses; (9) organizational goals and performance criteria; (10) measurable and controllable activities; (11) organizational structure; and (12) organizational systems and procedures.

8.4 Organizational Structure

- An organization is a system of consciously coordinated activities or forces of two or more people.
- There are three types of organizations classified according to the three different purposes for which they are formed: for-profit, nonprofit, and mutual-benefit.
- Whatever the size of an organization, it can be represented in an organization chart, a boxes-and-lines illustration showing the formal lines of authority and the organization's official positions or division of labor.
- Two kinds of information that organizations reveal about organizational structure are (1) the vertical hierarchy of authority, who reports to whom, and (2) the horizontal specialization, who specializes in what work.

8.5 The Major Elements of an Organization

- Organizations have seven elements. Four proposed by Edgar Schein are (1) common purpose, which unifies employees or members and gives everyone an understanding of the organization's reason for being; (2) coordinated effort, the coordination of individual efforts into a group or organizationwide effort; (3) division of labor, having discrete parts of a task done by different people; and (4) hierarchy of authority, a control mechanism for making sure the right people do the right things at the right time.
- Two other common elements are (5) span of control, which refers to the number of people reporting directly to a given manager, and (6) authority and accountability, responsibility, and delegation.
- Authority refers to the rights inherent in a managerial position to make decisions, give orders, and utilize resources. Accountability means that managers must report and justify work results to the managers above them. Responsibility is the obligation you have to perform the tasks assigned to you. Delegation is the process of assigning managerial authority and responsibility to managers and employees lower in the hierarchy.
- Regarding authority and responsibility, the organization chart distinguishes between two positions, line and staff. Line managers have authority to make decisions and usually have people reporting to them. Staff personnel have advisory functions; they provide advice, recommendations, and research to line managers.
- The final common element of organizations is (7) centralization versus decentralization of authority. With centralized authority, important decisions are made by higher-level managers. With decentralized authority, important decisions are made by middle-level and supervisory-level managers.

8.6 Basic Types of Organizational Structures

- Organizations may be arranged into eight types of structures. (1) In a simple structure, authority is centralized in a single person; this structure has a flat hierarchy, few rules, and low work specialization. (2) In a functional structure, people with similar occupational specialties are put together in formal groups. (3) In a divisional structure, people with diverse occupational specialties are put together in formal groups by similar products or services, customers or clients, or geographic regions. (4) In a matrix structure, an organization combines functional and divisional chains of command in grids so that there are two command structures—vertical and horizontal. (5) In a horizontal design or team-based design, teams or workgroups are used to improve horizontal relations and solve problems throughout the organization. A boundaryless organization is a fluid, highly adaptive organization whose members, linked by information technology, come together to collaborate on common tasks. Three designs that open boundaries between organizations are hollow, modular, and virtual structures. (6) In the hollow structure, often called the network structure, the organization has a central core of key functions and outsources other functions to vendors who can do them cheaper or faster. (7) In a modular structure, a firm assembles product chunks, or modules, provided by outside contractors. (8) The virtual structure is an organization whose members are geographically apart, usually working with e-mail and other forms of information technology, yet which generally appears to customers as a single, unified organization with a real physical location.

8.7 Contingency Design: Factors in Creating the Best Structure

- The process of fitting the organization to its environment is called contingency design. Managers taking a contingency approach must consider at least three factors in designing the best kind of structure for their organization at that particular time.
- The first is that an organization may be either mechanistic or organic. In a mechanistic organization, authority is centralized, tasks and rules are clearly specified, and employees are closely supervised. In an organic organization, authority is decentralized, there are fewer rules and procedures, and networks of employees are encouraged to cooperate and respond quickly to unexpected tasks.
- The second is that an organization may also be characterized by differentiation or integration. Differentiation is the tendency of the parts of an organization to disperse and fragment. Integration is

the tendency of the parts of an organization to draw together to achieve a common purpose.

- The third is the link between strategy, culture, and structure. If the managers of an organization change its strategy, they need to change the organization's culture and structure to support that strategy. Indeed, companies often begin by offering a single product or product line that requires only a simple structure, but as they grow and their strategies become more ambitious and elaborate, so the culture and structure need to change to support those strategies.

8.8 Career Corner: Managing Your Career Readiness

- You can improve your ability to assess an organization's internal context by using the career readiness competencies of *understanding the business* and *personal adaptability*.
- There is a two-step process for determining how you "fit" in a specific context.
- You can become more adaptable by being optimistic, displaying a proactive learning orientation, and being more resourceful.

Understanding the Chapter: What Do I Know?

1. To implement an organization's strategy, what are the two kinds of important areas that managers must determine?
2. How would you describe the four kinds of organizational cultures, according to the competing values framework?
3. Describe and explain the three levels of organizational culture.
4. What are five ways in which culture is transmitted to employees?
5. Name 12 mechanisms by which an organization's members teach each other preferred values, beliefs, expectations, and behaviors.
6. What are seven common elements of organizations?
7. Describe the four types of traditional organizational designs.
8. Explain what is meant by horizontal organizational designs.
9. What are three designs that open boundaries between organizations?
10. What are three factors to consider in designing an organization's structure?

Management in Action

Wells Fargo's Sales Culture Fails

The Company

How do you sell money? This is a fundamental challenge for retail banks, and Richard Kovacevich had a solution. He saw banks as stores, bankers as salespeople, and financial instruments as consumer products. Much like a deli worker asks if you'd like to upsize that combo or add dessert to your order, a banker should encourage you to add a credit card, savings account, or loan to your portfolio. Kovacevich called it "cross-selling," and he based it on the fact that customers with several accounts are much more profitable to a bank than customers with a single account. How many accounts should a customer have? Eight, according to the "Going for Gr-Eight" initiative he launched as CEO of Norwest in 1997. Why eight? Because, Kovacevich said, "It rhymes with GREAT!"[126]

SALES PRACTICES AT WELLS FARGO

Norwest merged with Wells Fargo in 1998; the bank retained the Wells Fargo name, and Kovacevich took the helm as president and CEO. He saw revenue growth as the bank's most important goal and cross-selling as the way to achieve it.[127] Bankers could earn between $500 and $2,000 in quarterly bonuses for hitting sales targets, and district managers could increase their annual compensation by up to $20,000. According to former Wells Fargo worker Scott Trainor, "If you could sell, you had a job."[128]

The strong sales culture transformed Wells Fargo's bottom line, as evidenced by a 67 percent increase in the bank's stock from 2006–2015.[129] Unfortunately, the culture had a dark side. Steven Schrodt, who worked at a Wells Fargo branch in Lincoln, Nebraska, before resigning due to severe sales pressure in 2012, remembers managers encouraging those who hadn't reached sales goals to open accounts for their family members and friends. Other former employees describe searching for potential customers at retirement homes and local bus stops.[130]

Bankers who grew tired of asking friends, family, and strangers for business adopted more covert tactics. One former Wells Fargo employee recalls the day he discovered a high-performing co-worker's secret formula. A customer had applied for a home equity loan and somehow also ended up with a $20,000 personal line of credit. "So then I realized how he was doing all his loans, because he was basically tagging on other loan products in the same application so they wouldn't really notice when they signed the documents."[131]

Problems started to emerge in 2009. At this point, Richard Kovacevich was gone, John Stumpf was president and CEO, and Kovacevich's sales culture was deeply embedded. To investigate potential problems in retail sales practices (RSPs) in the bank's branches, Wells Fargo established an internal task force in 2012. The task force concluded that the unethical behavior was due to a small set of "rogue" individual branch workers.[132] Wells Fargo subsequently fired more than 5,000 "rogue" bankers between 2013 and 2016.[133]

WELLS FARGO ADMITS TO FRAUD: BLAMES PROBLEM ON WORKERS, NOT CULTURE

In September 2016, the Office of the Comptroller of the Currency (OCC), the Consumer Financial Protection Bureau (CFPB), and the Los Angeles City Attorney publicly fined Wells Fargo $185 million for opening millions of bank accounts without customers' knowledge.[134, 135] The bank openly admitted to the fraud, but executives noted that Wells Fargo had official policies in place in their *Sales Quality Manual* requiring customers' consent "for each specific solution or service" and expressly prohibiting bankers from opening multiple accounts to increase incentive compensation.[136] In an interview with *The Wall Street Journal,* CEO Stumpf maintained "there was no incentive to do bad things" adding "the 1% that did it wrong, who we fired, terminated, in no way reflects our culture nor reflects the great work the other vast majority of the people do."[137] Former workers tell a different story.

While there was "no shortage of internal publications advising Wells employees on how to conduct themselves, including the *Wells Fargo Code of Ethics* and the *Wells Fargo Team Member Handbook,*"[138] the pressure inside branches was so intense that formal guidelines did little to deter underhanded sales tactics. In an interview with *NPR,* one former employee said bankers at her branch were expected to sell "a ridiculous amount of products" and that pressure and fraud occurred even at the bank's headquarters.[139] Former employees who worked at Wells between 2004 and 2011 told *NPR* the fraud was pervasive and that managers were heavily involved. One former banker recalled sitting at a conference table with her managers in a windowless, locked room and receiving a "formal warning" to sign. Her managers told her that bankers who didn't meet sales goals were not team players, and poor team members would be fired and forced to carry the mark on their permanent records.[140]

For bankers who did play by the rules, the outcome was bleak. "They ruined my life," says Bill Bado, a former Pennsylvania branch worker.[141] Bado repeatedly refused to open fraudulent bank accounts and credit cards, made calls to bank's ethics hotline, and even sent an e-mail to HR about his supervisors pressuring him to engage in unethical RSPs; just over a week after e-mailing HR, Bado was terminated for excessive tardiness. Another former employee lost her job after e-mailing Stumpf directly about the fraud; Stumpf has claimed he doesn't recall the e-mail.[142]

AFTERMATH

Stumpf resigned from Wells Fargo in October 2016, and Timothy Sloan took over as CEO. Sloan immediately discontinued labeling branches "stores" and overhauled the bank's incentive compensation plan, shifting the focus to customer satisfaction and drastically reducing the emphasis on sales goals. Sloan restructured the organization to fully centralize the bank's risk and HR functions, consolidating "much of the vast risk-control bureaucracy into a new office of ethics, oversight, and integrity, accountable to the board's risk committee."[143] And yet, in spite of Sloan's efforts, another scandal was brewing.

Earlier in 2016, executives at Wells Fargo had realized that hundreds of thousands of car loan customers had been charged for unnecessary auto insurance.[144] An internal report revealed that the costs of the gratuitous insurance resulted in auto loan defaults for more than 270,000 customers and the repossession of approximately 25,000 vehicles.[145] Federal probes into the insurance debacle shed light on yet another slew of internal issues with compliance, controls, and board oversight of operations at Wells Fargo.[146] In a report released in October 2017, OCC regulators slammed managers at Wells Fargo Dealer Services (the bank's auto loan unit) for ignoring customer complaints, failing to monitor contractors, and general laziness in responding to problems that had been unfolding since at least 2015.[147]

In July 2017, Wells Fargo publicly admitted it became aware of the auto insurance scandal a year prior. Interestingly, when the Senate Banking Committee asked, as part of the September 2016 hearings related to RSP fraud, if executives were "confident that this type of fraudulent activity does not exist" in other areas, the bank insisted problems were limited to individual employees in the community banking division.[148] Senator Sherrod Brown has since alleged that Wells Fargo "pure and simple lied to this committee–and lied to the public" in failing to disclose the auto insurance problems during the 2016 hearings.[149] Sloan has maintained there are fundamental differences between the RSP and auto insurance scandals, with only the former being fueled by sales incentives.[150]

Wells Fargo has experienced substantial losses in rankings, reputation, and bottom line.[151] Federal regulators continue to impose severe penalties and restrictions reflecting concerns with the bank's ability to manage potential operating risks.[152, 153]

FOR DISCUSSION

Problem-Solving Perspective

1. What is the underlying problem in this case from the regulators' perspective?
2. What role do you believe Wells Fargo's executive leadership played in the RSP and auto insurance scandals?
3. What do you think regulators should do to encourage permanent change in Wells Fargo's culture and prevent similar problems in the broader banking industry?

Application of Chapter Content

1. Using the competing values framework as a point of reference, how would you describe the organizational culture under CEO Kovacevich and under CEO Sloan? Provide examples to support your conclusions.
2. How do you think new branch employees learned the culture at Wells Fargo?
3. Describe how Wells Fargo can use the 12 mechanisms for culture change to drastically improve its culture.
4. Is Wells Fargo's structure more organic or mechanistic? Explain.
5. What is the most important lesson from this case? Discuss.

Legal/Ethical Challenge

Should Socializing outside Work Hours Be Mandatory?

Person-organization fit reflects the extent to which someone's personality and values match, or fit, and organization's culture and climate. Good fit is important for both employees and organizations. This challenge involves the cultural considerations of asking employees to socialize outside work hours. If socializing outside work is an expectation of new hires, then it becomes something to consider when applying for jobs.

Why would companies ask employees to socialize outside of work hours? There are a number of good reasons: (1) fostering comfort and relaxation among employees, (2) helping people de-stress after a hard day, (3) learning more about one's colleagues, and (4) building teamwork and unity.[154] All of these benefits should improve interpersonal relationships and potentially boost productivity and customer service.

If such requests are voluntary, however, then it is likely that fewer people will show up, thereby reducing the benefits. People who show up are more likely to be like-minded and share a common race and gender, as well as hobbies. For example, one employee described the in-group at their company as the folks who hunted and fished together outside of work.[155] Voluntary requests can thus serve as a subtle way of promoting homogeneity rather than diversity.

Moreover, voluntary requests potentially set up a situation in which people develop unequal social networks. This can have unfair career advantages for those who attend because people discuss work-related issues at such gatherings. In an interview, advertising executive Ian Mirmelstein said his career has suffered since he stopped attending work happy hours.[156]

It thus makes some sense to make it mandatory to socialize outside of work. Some companies accept this conclusion. Zappos did in the past, and other companies continue the practice today.

One woman told a reporter that there was an unwritten requirement at her employer that "employees were expected to spend extra money and time on group lunches and twice-weekly drinks. This kind of socializing was necessary in order to get ahead." She was not told about the requirement during the hiring process, and she now feels a lack of fit. Her problem with the expectation is that she has two children to pick up from school and she tries to save money by taking her lunch to work. In a recent performance appraisal, she was told, "I needed to be more of a team player." Her feedback was partly based on her lack of socializing outside of work.[157]

SOLVING THE CHALLENGE

What are your thoughts about making it mandatory to socialize outside of work hours?

1. I think it's a good idea. The benefits exceed the costs, and I don't agree that it fails to appreciate diversity. The socializing activities can be varied to fit the values and needs of diverse employees, thereby supporting diversity.
2. I don't like it. What employees do after work hours is their business, and companies should not infringe on them. Socializing outside work hours should be voluntary.
3. I believe that employers have no business interfering with how employees spend time outside of work. This means that I don't want either voluntary or mandatory requests about socializing outside of work hours. If people want to socialize outside work, let them arrange it on their own.
4. Invent other options.

Uber Continuing Case connect

Learn about the evolution of Uber's culture and how its structure has changed through the years by reading this case. Assess your ability to apply concepts discussed in this chapter to the case by going to Connect.

9 Human Resource Management

Getting the Right People for Managerial Success

©Olivier Renck/Aurora/Getty Images

After reading this chapter, you should be able to:

LO 9-1 Discuss the importance of strategic human resource management.

LO 9-2 Discuss ways to recruit and hire the right people.

LO 9-3 Outline common forms of compensation.

LO 9-4 Describe the processes used for orientation and learning and development.

LO 9-5 Discuss effective performance management and feedback techniques.

LO 9-6 List guidelines for handling promotions, transfers, discipline, and dismissals.

LO 9-7 Discuss legal considerations managers should be aware of.

LO 9-8 Describe labor-management issues and ways to work effectively with labor unions.

LO 9-9 Review the steps for becoming a better receiver of feedback.

FORECAST *What's Ahead in This Chapter*

This chapter considers human resource (HR) management—planning for, attracting, developing, and retaining an effective workforce. We consider how this subject fits in with the overall company strategy, how to evaluate current and future employee needs, and how to recruit and select qualified people. We describe the common forms of compensation, the processes used for orientation and learning and development, and how to assess employee performance and give feedback. We discuss guidelines for handling promotions and discipline, and workplace performance problems. We go over basic legal requirements and consider the role of labor unions. We conclude with a Career Corner that focuses on how to become a better receiver of feedback.

MANAGE U

How to Prepare for a Job Interview

Job candidates often make a few common mistakes in initial interviews. Here are some tips for using the career readiness competencies of career management, new media literacy, and communication skills to avoid them.

Be Prepared

Can you pronounce the name of the company with which you're interviewing? How about the name of the person who is going to interview you? Do you understand what the company makes or does, and the duties of the position for which you're interviewing? Do you know the company's competition? What new products or services are being offered? What are your greatest strengths and specific achievements? Your weaknesses? Research the company's website and any recent news articles and press releases about the firm. Identify strengths of yours that fit what the company does. When asked about your weaknesses, discuss how you recognized one, overcame a dilemma it posed, and were improved by it. Practice your answers, but not so much that you sound phony saying them.

Dress Right and Be On Time

Dress neatly and professionally for the interview. Make sure you know the exact location of the interview, and if possible, do a test run a day or so before, at about the same time of day as your interview, so you know how long it will take to get there on time. If unforeseeable circumstances arise and cause you to be late, call to inform your interviewer. When you arrive, be courteous to the receptionist and greet everyone who greets you. Silence your phone and don't take it out again until you've left the building.

Practice What to Say and What to Ask

Rehearse questions to ask the interviewer, such as the challenges for the position in the future and how success in the job will be defined. Don't make negative comments about your old company or boss. Rather, figure out the positives and convey what you learned and gained from your experience. If asked an inappropriate question (about age, marital status, whether you have children or plan to), politely say you don't believe the question is relevant to your qualifications. Be friendly and enthusiastic but not too personal.[1] Within 24 hours of the meeting, send an e-mail (with no misspellings or faulty grammar) thanking the interviewer and reiterating your interest in the position. If you think you messed up part of the interview, use the e-mail to smooth over your mistakes.[2]

Know What You Will Be Asked

More than 8 in 10 companies now routinely check job applicants' references, and 7 in 10 conduct background checks.[3] Some employers may ask for your GPA, especially if a job opening is highly competitive. If your grade point average is not as high as you would like, prepare an explanation.[4] Finally, be sure your social media profile is mostly private, and that whatever is public is limited, is not too personal, and would make your parents proud. More than 7 in 10 employers scrutinize job seekers' social media profiles, sometimes in search of personal information they are not allowed to ask about, such as whether you are married. While this kind of snooping—and particularly asking for your passwords—carries some legal risks for companies depending on state laws, unwary job applicants can still lose opportunities if their profiles don't reflect the kind of maturity the hiring company is looking for.[5] Don't let that happen to you.

For Discussion What kind of advice do you see here that you wish you'd followed in the past? What will you do differently next time?

9.1 Strategic Human Resource Management

THE BIG PICTURE

Human resource management consists of the activities managers perform to plan for, attract, develop, and retain an effective workforce. Planning the human resources needed consists of understanding current employee needs and predicting future employee needs.

LO 9-1

Discuss the importance of strategic human resource management.

How do you get hired by one of the top five workplaces for Millennials on *Fortune* magazine's list 2018—companies such as Ultimate Software, SalesForce, Edward Jones, Workday, and Kimley-Horn.[6]

You try to get to know someone in the company, suggests one guide.[7] You play up volunteer work on your résumé. You get ready to interview and interview and interview. And you do extensive research on the company—far more than just online research, such as by talking to customers.

And what kinds of benefits does an employee of a *Fortune* "Best" company get? At Google (now part of Alphabet), the Mountain View, California, search engine company (ranked No. 1 Best Company seven times in the last 10 years), you're entitled to eat in free gourmet cafeterias, have generous parental leave policies, get haircuts on site, work out at the gym, attend support group meetings and unconscious-bias workshops, have your laundry done free, and get virtual doctor visits. You may also be a candidate for millions of dollars in compensation incentives, special bonuses, and founders' awards.[8]

The reason for this exceptional treatment? It results in greater commitment and performance from employees,[9] which in turn fosters more profit according to a study of 250 companies. The researchers identified the top 6 percent that invested in the employee experience: technology, physical environment, and organizational culture. These companies included Adobe, Accenture, Facebook, and Microsoft, and they realized 4.2, 4.0, and 2.8 times the average profit, profit per employee, and revenue per employee, respectively, over the remaining 94 percent of the sample.[10] All told, investing in people leads to competitive advantage.

Human Resource Management: Managing an Organization's Most Important Resource

Human resource (HR) management consists of the activities managers perform to plan for, attract, develop, and retain an effective workforce. Whether it's McKinsey looking for entry-level business consultants, the U.S. Navy trying to fill its ranks, or churches trying to recruit priests and ministers, all organizations must deal with staffing.

The fact that the old personnel department is now called the human resources department is not just a cosmetic change. It is intended to suggest the importance of staffing to a company's success. Although talking about people as "resources" might seem to downgrade them to the same level as financial resources and material resources, in fact, people are an organization's most important resource.

Indeed, companies ranked in the top 10 on *Fortune* magazine's 2018 Best Companies list—which include Salesforce, Wegmans Food Markets, Ultimate Software, Boston Consulting Group, Edward Jones, Kimpton Hotels & Restaurants, Workday, Genentech, Hyatt, and Kimley-Horn—have discovered that putting employees first has been the foundation for their success[11] "If you're not thinking all the time about making every person valuable, you don't have a chance," says former General Electric head Jack Welch. "What's the alternative? Wasted minds? Uninvolved people? A labor force that's angry or bored? That doesn't make sense!"[12]

SELF-ASSESSMENT 9.1

Assessing the Quality of HR Practices

This survey is designed to assess the quality of HR practices at your current place of employment. If you are not currently working, consider a previous job when completing the survey. Please be prepared to answer these questions if your instructor has assigned Self-Assessment 9.1 in Connect.

1. How did you rate the quality of the company's HR practices?
2. Based on your responses, what advice would you give the senior HR leader about how to improve its HR practices? Be specific. What are the consequences of having poor-quality HR practices? Explain.

Clearly, companies listed among the best places to work become famous by offering progressive and valued programs, policies, and procedures. Are you curious to see if a current or past employer is one of these progressive companies? You can find out by taking Self-Assessment 9.1.

FIGURE 9.1
The strategic human resource management process

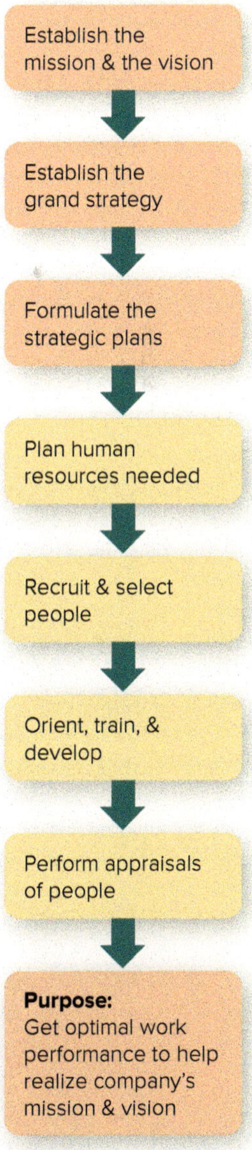

Human Resources as Part of Strategic Planning Some companies—those with flat management structures, for instance—have done away with HR departments entirely, letting the regular line managers handle these tasks. But most workers say they feel the absence of an in-house HR staff, especially when it comes to resolving pay problems and mediating employee disputes.[13] So what should organizations do in regard to investing in human resources? Based on research findings, we come down on the side that people are an organization's most important asset and it's important to invest in human resources. All told, studies show that companies have higher levels of employee satisfaction, financial performance, and service performance when the company has high-quality human resource practices and programs.[14] At many companies, human resources has become part of the strategic planning process. Thus, HR departments deal not only with employee paperwork and legal accountability—a very important area, as we describe in Section 9.7—but also with helping to support the organization's overall strategy.

Example: Is it important, as Wegmans' owners think, to have loyal, innovative, smart, passionate employees who will give their best to promote customer satisfaction (the grocery chain's mission)? Who, then, should be recruited? How should they be trained? What's the best way to evaluate and reward their performance? The answers to these questions should be consistent with the firm's strategic mission.

The purpose of the strategic human resource process, then—shown in the gold shaded boxes at right—is to get the optimal work performance that will help the company's mission and goals. *(See Figure 9.1.)*

Three concepts important in this view of human resource management are *human capital*, *knowledge workers*, and *social capital.*

Human Capital: Potential of Employee Knowledge and Actions New Brunswick Power, home of "Canada's Most Admired Corporate Culture," was facing dramatic changes in the energy industry, including climate change and the arrival of solar power, and economic and demographic changes in its local market of New Brunswick province as customers had energy choices for the first time. Says Sherry Thomson, the company's HR officer, "We needed to change the traditional culture of NB Power to be more agile, adjust our mindsets and engage our entire workforce in the effort so we could be our customers' first choice as new options became available to them." Thomson goes on, "The first challenge was confronting the mindset that HR's role was to be the 'employee advocate' versus a key *enabler* in driving business results. We needed to reposition and reframe ourselves in order to support and lead the transformation." Thomson achieved this by "stepping into the shoes of operational leaders [in order to] listen to their challenges and opportunities." Without that effort, she feels, "you don't get the invitation to partner in a way that's truly strategic." The relationships Thomson built, with the goal of engaging the entire workforce, have helped the company improve its earnings and discover many unsuspected new leaders among its employees who have helped continue the positive culture changes she sought.[15] **Human capital is the economic or productive potential of employee knowledge, experience, and actions.**

Scripps Health, a nonprofit health care system in San Diego and 45th on *Fortune*'s 2017 list of "Best Places to Work For," helps employees develop human capital by providing career coaching and college tuition reimbursement and scholarships. The company also offers a wide variety of internal courses, some taught by the CEO, that focus on employee development.[16]

It's also important to take responsibility for your own human capital. You may find this surprising, but a recent study showed that lack of sleep depletes your human capital and lowers performance.[17] To perform at their best, people need their full ration of sleep.

Knowledge Workers: Potential of Brain Workers **A knowledge worker is someone whose occupation is principally concerned with generating or interpreting information, as opposed to manual labor.** Knowledge workers add value to the organization by using their brains rather than their muscle and sweat, and as such they are the most common type of worker in 21st-century organizations.[18] Over the past three decades, automation has threatened a lot of routine jobs, but the rise of knowledge workers has been accelerating.

Social Capital: Potential of Strong and Cooperative Relationships **Social capital is the economic or productive potential of strong, trusting, and cooperative relationships.** It can help you land a job. For example, a national survey of recruiters revealed that 74 percent had found the highest-quality job applicants came through employee referrals. Employees hired through referrals also tend to stay longer at their jobs, a result of better person-organization fit.[19]

Social capital is also beneficial beyond the early stages of your career, particularly when you are developing trusting relationships with others. Trusting relationships lead to more job and business opportunities, faster advancement, greater capacity to innovate, and more status and authority.[20] Dora Moscoso, a project specialist with the Inter-American Development Bank, writes that networking is particularly valuable to entrepreneurs: "It is the social network of individuals whom entrepreneurs surround themselves with—mentors, peers, friends, family, and other entrepreneurs-that adds value and promotes trust, reciprocity, and cooperation."[21] All told, it pays to have a rich network of good relationships, and social capital helps makes this possible.

Planning the Human Resources Needed

When a building contractor, looking to hire someone for a few hours to dig ditches, drives by a group of idle day laborers standing on a street corner, is that a form of HR planning? Certainly it shows the contractor's awareness that a pool of laborers usually can be found in that spot. But what if the builder needs a lot of people with specialized training—to give him or her the competitive advantage that the strategic planning process demands?

Here we are concerned with something more than simply hiring people on an "as needed" basis. **Strategic human resource planning consists of developing a systematic, comprehensive strategy for (a) understanding current employee needs and (b) predicting future employee needs.** Let's consider these two parts.

Understanding Current Employee Needs To plan for the future, you must understand the present—what today's staffing picture looks like. This requires that you (or a trained specialist) first do a *job analysis* and from that write a *job description* and a *job specification.*[22]

- **Job analysis.** The purpose of **job analysis** is to determine, by observation and analysis, the basic elements of a job. Specialists who do this interview job occupants about what they do, observe the flow of work, and learn how results are accomplished. For example, UPS has specialists who ride with the couriers and time how long it takes to deliver a load of packages and note what problems are encountered (traffic jams, vicious dogs, recipients not home, and so on).
- **Job description and job specification.** Once the fundamentals of a job are understood, then you can write a **job description**, which summarizes what the holder of the job does and how and why he or she does it. Next you can write a **job specification**, which describes the minimum qualifications a person must have to perform the job successfully.

This process can produce some surprises. Jobs that might seem to require a college degree, for example, might not after all. Thus, the process of writing job analyses, descriptions, and specifications can help you avoid hiring people who are overqualified (and presumably more expensive) or underqualified (and thus not as productive) for a particular job.

In addition, by entering a job description and specification with their attendant characteristics into a database, an organization can use an applicant tracking system (ATS) to match keywords (nouns) on incoming résumés with the keywords describing the job.[23] Enterprise Rent-A-Car, for example, sorts through 50,000 candidates a month to identify those with a bachelor's degree, good driving record, and customer-service or leadership experience who might qualify for the company's management training program.[24]

What kind of job is this? A UPS driver's problems of driving in a big city—traffic, double parking, addressees not at home—are different from those of driving in rural areas, where there may be long stretches of boredom. Specialists in job analysis can interview drivers about their problems in order to write job descriptions that allow for varying circumstances. ©McGraw-Hill Education/John Flournoy, photographer

Predicting Future Employee Needs Job descriptions change, of course: Auto mechanics, for instance, now have to know how computer chips work in cars. (Current 7-Series BMWs and S-class Mercedes have about 100 processors apiece.) And new jobs are created: Who could have visualized the position of "e-commerce accountant" 10 years ago, for example?

As you might expect, predicting future employee needs means you have to become knowledgeable about the *staffing the organization might need* and the *likely sources for that staffing*:

- **The staffing the organization might need.** You could assume your organization won't change much. In that case, you can fairly easily predict that jobs will periodically become unoccupied (because of retirement, resignations, and so on) and that you'll need to pay the same salaries and meet the same criteria about minority hiring to fill them.

Better, however, to assume the organization will change. Thus, you need to understand the organization's vision and strategic plan so that the proper people can be hired to meet the future strategies and work. We discussed strategic plans in Chapter 6.

- **The likely sources for staffing.** You can recruit employees from either inside or outside the organization. In looking at those inside, you need to consider which employees are motivated, trainable, and promotable and what kind of training your organization might have to do. A device for organizing this kind of information is a **human resource inventory**, **a report listing your organization's employees by name, education, training, languages, and other important information.** In looking outside, you need to consider the availability of talent in your industry's and geographical area's labor pool, the training of people graduating from various schools, and such factors as what kinds of people are moving into your area. The U.S. Bureau of Labor Statistics and the U.S. Census Bureau issue reports on such matters.

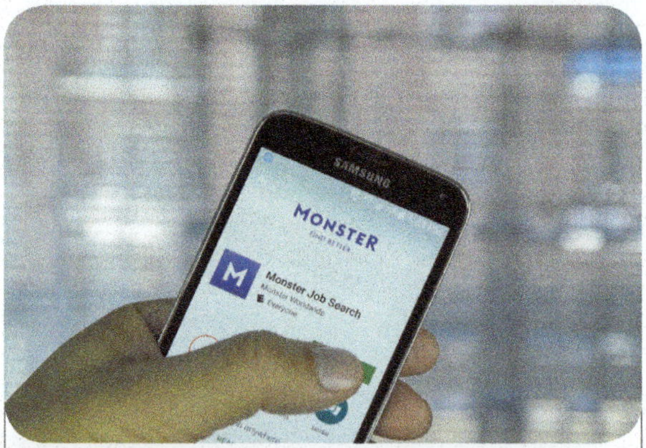

One way to attract potential employees. One of the first places companies are apt to look for potential employees is online, such as the social networking sites Facebook, LinkedIn, and Glassdoor, as well as Twitter (although sometimes searches can lead to discrimination against some candidates). Creative users also post unusual digital résumés featuring eye-catching graphics, YouTube videos, and PowerPoint slides on Pinterest, the popular online pin board for photos. As for job seekers, they can find useful job-hunting apps on Monster.com. Are you up to speed on these job-hunting advantages? ©dennizn/Shutterstock

9.2 Recruitment and Selection: Putting the Right People into the Right Jobs

THE BIG PICTURE

Qualified applicants for jobs may be recruited from inside or outside the organization. The task of choosing the best person is enhanced by such tools as reviewing candidates' application forms, résumés, and references; doing interviews, either structured or unstructured; and screening with ability, personality, performance, and other kinds of employment tests.

LO 9-2

Discuss ways to recruit and hire the right people.

"We know that 5% of your workforce produces 26% of your output, so you need to focus on hiring people who really make the difference," says San Francisco State University professor John Sullivan, an expert in human resources strategy. Hiring has become a science, Sullivan states, but most people doing the recruiting think it is still an art. "Most people in HR have no clue. We don't measure failed hires. There's no feedback loop."[25]

The tight labor market is making it harder for companies to find qualified employees. *The Wall Street Journal* reported that "Some firms are partnering with local school or unions while others are paying vacation costs, beefing up internship programs or adding new locations where labor isn't as scarce."[26] Let's consider in more detail this important HR function.

Recruitment: How to Attract Qualified Applicants

At some time nearly every organization has to think about how to find the right kind of people. **Recruiting is the process of locating and attracting qualified applicants for jobs open in the organization.** The word *qualified* is important: You want to find people whose skills, abilities, and characteristics are best suited to your organization. Recruiting is of two types: *internal* and *external.*

1. Internal Recruiting: Hiring from the Inside

Internal recruiting means making people already employed by the organization aware of job openings. Indeed, most vacant positions in organizations are filled through internal recruitment, mainly through **job posting, placing information about job vacancies and qualifications on bulletin boards, in newsletters, and on the organization's intranet.** This means employees need to take responsibility for managing their own careers (a career readiness skill we've discussed throughout the book). For instance, according to Kerry Bianchi, CEO of advertising technology company Visto, it's important for employees to work in more than one department in the organization, but "People think, 'if I put my head down someone will figure out what I want.' That's not real."[27] In one twist on recruiting from within, more firms are now *rehiring* former workers who had left (a tactic once frowned upon) because so many employers are having difficulty finding qualified people.[28]

2. External Recruiting: Hiring from the Outside

External recruiting means attracting job applicants from outside the organization. In years past, notices of job vacancies were placed through newspapers, employment agencies, executive recruiting firms, union hiring halls, college job-placement offices, and word of mouth. Today more than 90 percent of U.S. organizations use social networks to find new employees, with LinkedIn the most popular site by far. The Society for Human Resource Management even reports that 35 percent of employers are less likely to invite candidates without an online presence to come in for an interview.[29] While LinkedIn has far fewer users than

Facebook overall, 87 percent of recruiters use it to find candidates compared to only 55 percent for Facebook (not surprising considering the very different purposes and cultures of the two sites). Meanwhile, however, 83 percent of job seekers are Facebook users, while only 36 percent are on LinkedIn.[30]

Glassdoor, the job and recruitment site, reports that job seekers check an average of seven to eight recruitment websites during their search, and many Glassdoor users compare as many as seven different reviews of an organization before deciding what they think about it.

Both internal and external methods have advantages and disadvantages.[31] *(See Table 9.1.)*

TABLE 9.1 **Internal and External Recruiting: Advantages and Disadvantages**

INTERNAL RECRUITING	
ADVANTAGES	**DISADVANTAGES**
1. Employees tend to be inspired to greater effort and loyalty. Morale is enhanced because they realize that working hard and staying put can result in more opportunities. 2. The whole process of advertising, interviewing, and so on is cheaper. 3. There are fewer risks. Internal candidates are already known and are familiar with the organization.	1. Internal recruitment restricts the competition for positions and limits the pool of fresh talent and fresh viewpoints. 2. It may encourage employees to assume that longevity and seniority will automatically result in promotion. 3. Whenever a job is filled, it creates a vacancy elsewhere in the organization.
EXTERNAL RECRUITING	
ADVANTAGES	**DISADVANTAGES**
1. Applicants may have specialized knowledge and experience. 2. Applicants may have fresh viewpoints.	1. The recruitment process is more expensive and takes longer. 2. The risks are higher because the persons hired are less well known.

Which External Recruiting Methods Work Best? In general, the most effective sources are employee referrals, say human resource professionals, because, to protect their own reputations, employees are fairly careful about whom they recommend, and they know the qualifications of both the job and the prospective employee.[32] HR expert John Sullivan, mentioned earlier, states that this method is preferred by the better companies, which ask their own top-performing employees, "Who do you learn from? Who's better than you? Who mentors you?"[33]

Among some newer ideas: San Francisco–based BlueCrew is a tech-enabled employment agency focused on hiring for warehouse workers, forklift operators, and other blue-collar temporary employees.[34] Barclays, the international bank, uses a free mobile videogame called Stockfuse, a stock-trading game, to attract and evaluate job applicants.[35] A cloud-storage firm named Compose and an employment firm named Woo, both in northern California, arrange "blind dates" between job seekers and employers, using résumés that feature only a person's work, no names.[36] (The "I'm Glad ... feature describes how Sarah Cabou's health care company uses a similar approach.) GE Digital, located in Providence, Rhode Island, has stopped relying solely on people's credentials, instead using "competency-based selection" strategies that measure whether job applicants have the competencies to fill specific engineering roles.[37]

I'm Glad...

...my company is serious about its recruiting and selection processes.

Courtesy Sarah Cabou

Sarah Cabou is a senior market operations manager at a start-up health care company. Her company runs primary care clinics for geriatric patients, and the employee selection process is incredibly important given the type of work involved in being a health coach at the company.

"Geriatric patients come to our clinics and are seen by a doctor, but they also get a health coach who is a non-medical person who is trained in techniques like motivational interviewing and coaching skills to help our patients with behavioral change or whatever it is that might be a barrier to them achieving higher levels of health status," said Sarah.

Patients are also encouraged to participate in exercise classes like yoga and Tai Chi, and attend support groups and diabetic education classes among other activities.

"Our company is entirely based on interactions with our customers and patients in a health care setting that is a bit different from what most of our senior population has experienced. And that needs to be a really fantastic experience. This is entirely based on the person that sits with them—and that would be a health coach," said Sarah.

When the company opens a new clinic, a large-scale recruitment effort is launched. "We do not require health coaches to have a particular background, and this makes it really challenging to approach," said Sarah. "What we're hiring for is a certain culture match and a certain value profile. This makes looking at a résumé almost impossible to determine whether or not a person is a good fit for our company."

In order to cast a wide net, the company does "speed interviewing" to allow anyone who submitted a résumé to attend. The candidates participate in five-minute interviews with staff members who are trained to look for certain traits among the candidates. The interviewers ask the candidates what intrigued them about the job they applied for and what makes them think they might be a good fit.

Within those five minutes, the interviewer will decide whether the candidate will proceed to a full, one-on-one interview. "At first, I was taken aback by this process. How can we really get to know someone in five minutes enough to have them proceed to another interview? But I've been pleasantly shocked to find what you can know about a person in five minutes that you could never find from a résumé," said Sarah.

If the candidate is asked to participate in the second full interview, the staff will ask more behavioral-based questions and ask about past performance to determine if that person would be a good fit for the company. "We want the patient to have an amazing customer service experience from start to finish, and we can only do that through the right kind of people," said Sarah.

Courtesy of Sarah Cabou

How do you feel about the job you are in now, if you have one, or the last job you had? Do you feel like you are a "good fit" for the job? That is, do you like the work and does the work match your skills? Research shows that we are happier and more productive when our needs and skills fit the job requirements. If you would like to see whether or not you fit with your current (or last) job, complete Self-Assessment 9.2. You may find the results very interesting.

SELF-ASSESSMENT 9.2

Assessing Your Person–Job Fit

This survey is designed to assess your job fit. If you are not currently working, consider a previous job when completing the survey. Please be prepared to answer these questions if your instructor has assigned Self-Assessment 9.2 in Connect.

1. What is your level of fit?
2. Whether you have high or low fit, what are the main causes for your level of fit? Explain.
3. What questions might you ask a future recruiter to ensure a higher level of person–job fit? Be specific.

Realistic Job Previews **A realistic job preview (RJP) gives a candidate a picture of both positive and negative features of the job and the organization before he or she is hired.** This recruiting technique is very effective at reducing turnover within 30–90 days of employment.[38] For instance, hiring managers at the Hilton Baltimore demonstrate to housekeeping job applicants how to make a bed, then ask the applicants to do it themselves. With this realistic job preview, says Tishuana Hodge, regional director of HR, says, "We can see who is genuinely interested and physically up to the challenge."[39]

EXAMPLE The Changing Job Market: Millennials, the Gig Economy, and the Episodic Career

Young adults (Millennials and Gen Z—those born between 1981 and the mid-2000s) are said to be less focused on finding jobs that nourish the wallet than those that nourish the soul, less concerned with finding financial success than on making a difference, as we said at the start of Chapter 3. But will the economy and the job market cooperate?

The Gig Economy Most of the job growth among U.S. workers during the past decade has been not in traditional jobs, but rather in opportunities for independent contractors, through temporary services or on-call work. In this so-called *gig economy*, organizations contract with independent workers who are not employees for short-term engagements, and the burden of providing health insurance and the like falls on the workers themselves rather than on an employer.[40] Nearly half of all Millennial workers participate in the gig economy, and by 2027, such contract workers, who are often highly qualified, are expected to make up the majority of the workforce.[41]

Using contract workers saves employees a great deal of money. "Hiring experts for a specific project cuts overhead, ramp up time, hours spent interviewing and on-boarding permanent candidates, as well as long-term payroll expenses. All of these eliminated costs drop to your bottom line," according to the president of AXIOM Learning Solutions.[42]

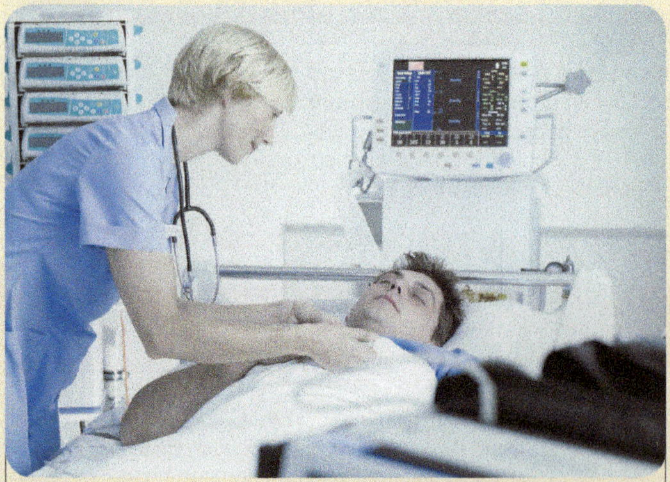

The shortage of health care workers has led to an increase in hiring independent contractors. Do you see any danger with this trend for health care providers? ©Martin Barraud/age fotostock

The Episodic Career Farai Chideya is the author of *The Episodic Career: How to Thrive at Work in the Age of Disruption.*[43] Because of decades of wage stagnation, the effects of the Great Recession, and "an incredible sense that perhaps the future will not be better than the past," she says, we have entered into the era of "the episodic career."[44] Surviving this challenge will require three qualities, she suggests: emotional resilience to deal with the unexpected, an understanding of the job market, and self-knowledge to effectively market your skills.

The Gig Economy's Dark Side Not everyone is convinced the gig economy is a good thing, however. Drivers for Lyft and Uber, for instance, earn little profit after spending their own money on auto insurance, repairs, fuel, depreciation, and other expenses.[45] Contract workers also lack benefits, promotion and career development opportunities, bargaining power, and the security of a steady cash flow.

Former U.S. Labor Secretary Robert Reich says the gig economy is changing "the whole employment relationship," and not for the better. Gig workers struggle to match their unpredictable income with the fixed costs of daily life, such as food and utilities. "They're on a downward escalator," he warns. Reich proposes adopting such economic supports for gig workers as income insurance to even out cash flows and portable benefits (tied to the worker, not the employer). But most important, he feels, is preventing people from falling into contract work in the first place: "If you believe, as I do, that the heart of the economy is a good job, with predictable wages and benefits, we are actually reducing the quality of life for millions of people," he concludes.[46]

YOUR CALL

What kind of skills could you bring to the gig economy? Would you prefer to be a contract worker or to be an employee? Why?

Selection: How to Choose the Best Person for the Job

Whether the recruitment process turns up a handful of job applicants or thousands, now you turn to the **selection process, the screening of job applicants to hire the best candidate.** Essentially, this becomes an exercise in *prediction*: How well will the candidate perform the job and how long will he or she stay?

Three types of selection tools are *background information, interviews*, and *employment tests*.

1. Background Information: Application Forms, Résumés, and Reference Checks

Application forms and résumés provide basic background information about job applicants, such as citizenship, education, work history, and certifications.

Unfortunately, a lot of résumé information consists of mild puffery and even outrageous fairy tales. A staggering 85 percent of job applicants lie on their résumés, a huge increase reported by a new study. One likely reason for the surge is that job seekers are trying to outsmart applicant tracking systems by doing whatever it takes to make sure key words in their résumés match the stated job requirements, whether they match the truth or not.[47] Other reasons include attempts to hide perceived deficiencies in technical or language skills, education, job history, or achievements, most of which are mistakes that can be cause for dismissal.[48] Regardless of the reason for misstating or lying, be aware that you can be fired for lying on a job application or résumé. We recommend honesty as the best policy.[49]

EXAMPLE Lies Job Applicants Have Told

Some of the most frequent lies job applicants tell on their résumés are about their education, employment history, achievements, and criminal or immigrant status. Here are a few real-world examples of what *not* to do.

Lies about Education Richard Clark falsely claimed, when he applied for a position at Coopers & Lybrand (Canada), that he had earned a doctorate. The lie went unchallenged and Clark was hired, but a few years later the company uncovered it while checking his qualifications before offering him a partnership. Clark was fired, sued for wrongful dismissal, and lost in court.[50] A better idea, if you feel your educational background is lacking, is to include other learning opportunities you've had, such as through volunteer work.

Lies about Employment History Another common fabrication attempts to cover gaps in employment history. In his application for a job as a sales rep for Jazz Forest Products, a lumber company, David Lura said he was currently winding down his own lumber business, but in fact he had closed it years before and had since worked in several other unrelated, low-level jobs. Lura was hired but he failed to close any sales, and after discovering he had lied about his job history, Jazz fired him. However, a Canadian court agreed with Lura that this lie was not serious enough to warrant dismissal.[51] Some people try to cover up taking years off to do child care, but it is better to explain than to hide these dates.[52] As you might expect, people also embellish their salary histories, job titles, and achievements on projects.

Lies about Both Largely due to unfilled openings at the U.S. Office of National Drug Control Policy, Taylor Weyeneth, then 23, rose rapidly to the position of deputy chief of staff. However, almost as quickly he resigned, after an investigation by *The Washington Post* in early 2018 revealed that he had lied on three separate résumés about having a master's degree (which he had never completed) and about his work at a law office, where a supervisor said he had actually been let go for not showing up. Weyeneth in fact had no professional experience other than as a campaign volunteer and had even lied about being president of his fraternity.[53]

YOUR CALL

Most employers compare résumé data to cover letters, check references, call alma maters, do background checks, sleuth on Google, and administer skills tests.[54] Now that you know that, would you lie on your résumé? Why or why not?

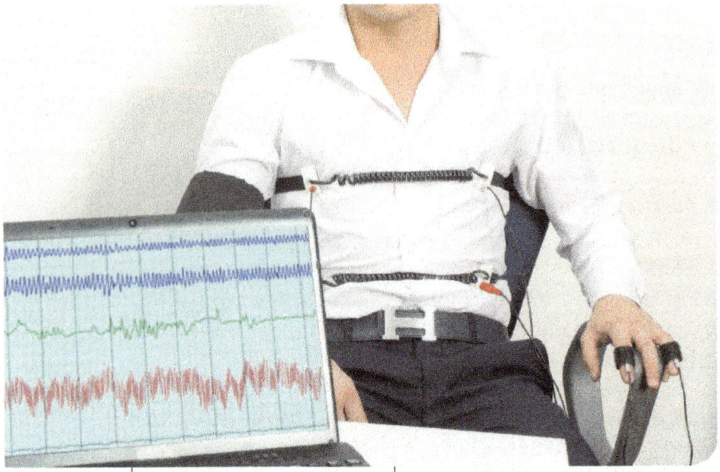

The Employee Polygraph Protection Act (1988) prohibits most private employers from using polygraphs during the hiring process. In contrast, federal, state, and local government agencies may use these tests. Would you be comfortable taking a polygraph test to obtain a government job?
©andreyuu/123RF

Many companies are finding conventional résumés not all that useful (because they don't quantify an applicant's accomplishments or are too full of fluff descriptors such as "outstanding" or "energetic") and are increasingly relying on professional networks such as LinkedIn, video profiles, or online quizzes to assess candidates.[55] Résumés are still popular and expected, however, and your cover letter matters too.[56]

While, under the law, people serving as references can answer any and all questions, including about protected information (like the applicant's age, race, or marital status) and can say anything else they want to (as long as it's true), hiring companies are still bound to use only legally allowed criteria for making employment decisions (*not* age, race, marital status, and so on). And some employers, perhaps fearful of lawsuits, enact policies to limit what their managers can say about former employees; for instance, some allow the person serving as a reference only to confirm the former employee's job title and dates of employment.[57] The information that is generally allowed includes the reason for departure and whether the employee would be rehired.[58] Obviously, in any job you want to leave a good name behind you.

Many employers also like to check applicants' credit references, although there is no evidence that people with weak credit scores are apt to be unqualified or dishonest employees. Several states have passed laws to curb the practice, often allowing it for jobs at certain levels or where required by law because of the position's financial responsibilities. In most states, prospective employers need the applicant's written consent to run a credit check in connection with a job offer.[59]

2. Interviewing: Unstructured, Situational, and Behavioral-Description The interview, which is the most commonly used employee-selection technique, may take place face to face, by videoconference, or—as is increasingly the case—via the Internet. (In-depth phone interviews of an hour or more are also frequently used.[60] However, face-to-face interviews have been perceived as being more fair and leading to higher job acceptance intentions than videoconferencing and telephone interviews.[61]) To help eliminate bias, interviews can be designed, conducted, and evaluated by a committee of three or more people.

The most commonly used employee-selection technique, interviewing, takes three forms: *unstructured interviews* and *two types of structured interviews*.[62]

Unstructured Interview Like an ordinary conversation, an **unstructured interview involves asking probing questions to find out what the applicant is like.** There is no fixed set of questions asked of all applicants and no systematic scoring procedure. As a result, the unstructured interview has been criticized as being overly subjective and apt to be influenced by the biases of the interviewer. Equally important, it is susceptible to legal attack because some questions may infringe on non-job-related matters such as privacy, diversity, or disability.[63] However, compared with the structured interview method, the unstructured interview has been found to provide a more accurate assessment of an applicant's job-related personality traits.[64]

Structured Interview Type 1: The Situational Interview The **structured interview involves asking each applicant the same questions and comparing their responses to a standardized set of answers.** The "I wish . . . " feature discusses Dena Baptiste's views about using structured interviews to hire retail employees.

I Wish...

...my company used a structured interview process.

Courtesy Dena Baptiste

Dena Baptiste, SHRM-SCP, worked as a Customer Relations Manager in the retail industry, and she believes her company could have done a better job ***selecting the right employees*** for the job.

As Dena points out, there is high employee turnover in the retail industry, and employers often take the "warm bodies" approach to hiring—that is, they work quickly to fill positions for the sake of filling them rather than taking time to meticulously select the candidates who best fit the company culture.

At Dena's company, managers would typically hire employees on the spot after one interview if they had a good personality or seemed motivated to do the job. This practice was particularly prevalent during busy selling seasons, like the winter holidays, when the company needed to make sure it was fully staffed for the shopping rush.

Employees who are hired quickly without much vetting often fail to stay with the company for an extended period. And the cycle continues when the company works to quickly fill those vacant positions in the same manner.

"I think it's important to have a structured interview process in place. I agree that somebody has to be a good fit and there are certain personality traits that are important, like being friendly and outgoing. But there has to be a standard process in place, and I really believe that there needs to be more than one person involved in the interview process," said Dena.

"Because retail has such high turnover, you have to move quickly, which is fine, but you still have to make the right decisions. If you're questioning a candidate and you have one manager who really likes that person and another manager who isn't sure, maybe you need to take a day to think about it instead of hiring the person because you need to fill a position. They should take the time to think about it, come back together and discuss it, and make a final decision," said Dena.

By having a solid interview and selection process in place, retail stores can work to combat high turnover and increase employee morale. In contrast, Dena noted that "When you have somebody who doesn't have the right temperament or personality, or doesn't really care all that much about the job, you get a drag on the employee morale, which can affect the whole team—and that can affect your customers. It's just not good for the organization as a whole."

Courtesy of Dena Baptiste

In one type of structured interview, the **situational interview, the interviewer focuses on hypothetical situations.** Example: "What would you do if you saw two of your people arguing loudly in the work area?" The idea here is to find out if the applicant can handle difficult situations that may arise on the job.

Structured Interview Type 2: The Behavioral-Description Interview In the second type of structured interview, the **behavioral-description interview, the interviewer explores what applicants have actually done in the past.** Example: "What was the best idea you ever sold to a supervisor, teacher, peer, or subordinate?" This question (the U.S. Army asked it of college students applying for its officer training program) is designed to assess the applicants' ability to influence others.

PRACTICAL ACTION — The Job Interview: What Employers Are Looking For

The Manage U feature at the beginning of the chapter talked about getting ready for a job interview. Here we add to those insights by taking you inside the interviewer's point of view.[65]

Before the Interview: Employers Define Their Needs and Review Applicants' Résumés. It's been said that looking to hire somebody is like going to the supermarket; the employer needs to have a list and know what he or she needs. Thus, the HR department will write out (or be told) what skills, traits, and qualities the job requires that the company is trying to fill. The interviewer will also look at the applicant's résumé or application to identify relevant experience, gaps, and discrepancies.

The Interviewer Prepares the Questions to Be Asked. The interviewer should use a structured approach that asks all candidates the same set of questions, so their answers can be compared. (This helps keep the company out of legal trouble, too, because it makes it more difficult for the interviewer to act on racial or gender bias.) In general, the questions should be designed to elicit the following types of information.

- **What drawbacks does the applicant's previous work experience show?** Examples: "Why are you leaving your current job, or why are you currently unemployed?"
- **Does the applicant have the knowledge and soft skills to do the job?** Examples: "Give an example where you came up with a creative solution." "Do you enjoy problem solving?" "Do you work well on a team?"
- **Can the applicant handle difficult situations?** Examples: "Tell me about an irate customer you handled." "Can you work without constant direction?"
- **Is the applicant willing to learn?** Examples: "Have you taken any extra classes, and why?" "How do you deal with change?" "What would you like to learn to do better?"
- **Will the applicant fit in with the organization's culture?** Examples: "Where do you see yourself in five years?" "How would your last supervisor describe you?" "How do you set goals for yourself?"

Interviewers Often Follow a Three-Scene Interview Scenario. The interview itself may follow a three-scene script.

- **Scene 1: The first three minutes—small talk and "compatibility" test.** The first scene is really a "compatibility test." It takes about three minutes and consists of exchanging small talk, giving the interviewer a chance to establish rapport and judge how well the candidate makes a first impression.

Note: First impressions are powerful. In a recent survey reported in the *Journal of Occupational and Organizational Psychology*, about 700 students participated in real job interviews of about half an hour each, after which 60 percent of the 166 interviewers said they had made up their minds about the candidate in 15 minutes or less. The rest made decisions within a few minutes of the interview's conclusion.[66]

- **Scene 2: The next 15–60 minutes—asking questions and listening to the applicant's "story."** In the next scene, the interviewer will ask you the questions he or she previously wrote out (and answer those that you have). A good interviewer will allow you, the interviewee, to do 70 percent–80 percent of the talking, and he or she will take notes to remember important points. Be aware that the interviewer's intuition can play a strong role in the hiring decision.
- **Scene 3: The final two minutes—closing the interview and setting up the next steps.** In the final minutes, the interviewer will listen to determine whether the candidate expresses interest in taking the job.

After the Interview. After you have left, the interviewer will probably write a short report making some sort of quantitative score of your qualifications and indicating reasons for the decision. If he or she decides to invite you back for a second interview (or pass you along to another interviewer), your references will also be checked.

YOUR CALL

What additional questions would you like to be asked that would showcase you as the best candidate? How would you work into the interview what you want to say?

3. Employment Tests: Ability, Personality, Performance, Integrity, and Others

Employment tests are legally considered to consist of any procedure used in the employment selection decision process, even application forms, interviews, and educational requirements.[67] The Equal Opportunity Employment Opportunity Commission lists "cognitive tests, personality tests, medical examinations, credit checks, and criminal background checks" among the common types.[68] Most types of employment testing are legal, including drug tests, though employers are obligated not to use results in ways that discriminate based on candidates' demographic or ethnic characteristics. Polygraphs, or lie detector tests, are generally not allowed, however.[69] Some major types of employment tests are the following.

Ability Tests *Ability tests* measure physical abilities, strength and stamina, mechanical ability, mental abilities, and clerical abilities. Intelligence or cognitive ability tests are also popular for predicting future executive performance, and perhaps with good reason. IBM's Supercomputer, Watson, recently performed an analysis of the personality traits of leading CEOs in industries including entertainment, finance, fashion, media, politics and found that intellect was one of the top two. (Altruism was the other.)[70] The military and law enforcement agencies test for physical qualifications, along with behavioral and educational abilities.

Performance Tests *Performance tests*, or *skills tests*, measure performance on actual job tasks—so-called job tryouts—as when computer programmers take a test on a particular programming language or middle managers work on a small sample project.[71] Some companies have an **assessment center, in which management candidates participate in activities for a few days while being assessed by evaluators.** A team of researchers examined the relative accuracy by which ability tests and assessment center results predicted who would be successful on the job. Although both tests were effective, assessment center tests were more effective.[72]

Personality Tests *Personality tests* measure such personality traits as emotional intelligence, social intelligence, resilience, personal adaptability, and need for achievement. Many of these represent competencies associated with career readiness. Career-assessment tests that help workers identify suitable jobs tend to be of this type.[73] One of the most famous personality tests, in existence for more than 75 years, is the 93-question Myers–Briggs Type Indicator, which has been translated into 25 languages and taken by millions of people around the world.[74] However, this and other personality tests, especially if like Myers-Briggs they were not designed for use in hiring decisions, need to be interpreted with caution because of the difficulty of measuring personality characteristics and of making a legal defense if the results are challenged.[75] In the last few years, their use has declined.[76]

EXAMPLE Personality Tests: Pros and Cons

Personality tests, if used, should be only one piece of the manager's hiring strategy. A recent analysis of selection procedures found that among the strategies that best predict future job performance is a general abilities test combined with an integrity test, one kind of personality test.[77]

Pros Those who support the use of personality tests in hiring believe they help identify candidates who could be good fits for the corporate culture, and those with personality traits that suggest superior performance in the job. They also feel tests help weed out those who may be dishonest and uncover the potential downsides of desired qualities like a strong work ethic (potentially poor response to stress) or high intelligence (potentially low emotional intelligence).[78]

Judy Weiniger is CEO of Weiniger Group and a believer in the use of personality tests. Because the tests ask repetitive questions to elicit the same information in different ways, she finds them reliable for helping identify candidates who will do well in different jobs based on their core personality traits, such as pinpointing people with strong social skills as potentially good sales reps. She also checks references and consults with her staff. "I think it would be very difficult to trick these tests and appear to be someone you're not," Weiniger says.[79]

Cons Those who disagree believe such tests are subjective, open to interpretation by people who are not trained to evaluate the results, and vulnerable to misuse by applicants who try to choose the answers they think the hiring company is looking for. Some also fear that personality tests can be discriminatory (some have caught the attention of the Equal Employment Opportunity Commission) and that they raise the potential for privacy violations.[80] Tests that appear to look for mental health characteristics may violate the Americans with Disabilities Act.[81]

The Myers & Briggs Foundation discourages reliance on the Myers-Briggs test, saying, "It is unethical and in many cases illegal to require job applicants to take the Indicator if the results will be used to screen out applicants. The administrator should not counsel a person to, or away from, a particular career, personal relationship or activity based solely upon type information."[82]

YOUR CALL

Would you be comfortable taking a personality test? Do you think it's better to honestly answer the questions or to provide ones that makes you appear more suited for the job? Explain.

Integrity Tests *Integrity tests* "assess attitudes and experiences related to a person's honesty, dependability, trustworthiness, reliability, and pro-social behavior."[83] The rationale for these tests is that people who do poorly on them may have low productivity or tend toward undesired work behaviors like theft, sabotage, and even violence. Overt integrity tests often ask specifically whether the applicant has ever engaged is illegal behavior. While integrity tests in general are easy to administer, it is also relatively easy for test takers to submit false responses.[84]

No drugs. Many jobs, such as those in warehousing and trucking, require that job applicants take a drug test to see if they test positive for marijuana, heroin, and other opioid drugs. However, many potential applicants simply skip tests they think they cannot pass. Do you think it's fair to force certain workers to take drug tests?
©Cultura/Getty Images

Drug and Alcohol Tests Companies are permitted to test job applicants for drug and alcohol use before making an offer, contingent to making an offer, and randomly after hiring, depending on state law. Job applicants cannot be tested selectively; either everyone who applies for a job must be tested or no one can be. Tests for the presence of drugs or alcohol can examine the person's urine, blood, hair, breath, saliva, or sweat. Marijuana use presents a complex problem because some states have legalized it for medical and/or recreational use, but the federal government has not.[85] Partly for this reason, and partly because unemployment has dropped over the last few years, putting pressure on companies to attract employees, drug testing for employment has been declining. Among companies that no longer conduct drug testing are Excellence Health Inc., AutoNation Inc., and the *Denver Post*.[86]

Reliability and Validity: Are the Tests Worth It?

With any kind of test, an important legal consideration is the test's **reliability—the degree to which a test measures the same thing consistently**—so that an individual's score remains about the same over time, assuming the characteristics being measured also remain the same.

Another legal consideration is the test's **validity—the test measures what it purports to measure and is free of bias.** If a test is supposed to predict performance, then the individual's actual performance should reflect his or her score on the test. Using an invalid test to hire people can lead to poor selection decisions. It can also create legal problems if the test is ever challenged in a court of law.

Geeks, Robots, and People Analytics: How AI Is Changing Recruiting

Artificial intelligence (AI) may still be a relatively new technology, but it is already changing many aspects of the recruitment and selection processes. Some AI programs can help with tasks as routine but time-consuming as scheduling interviews, screening and ranking candidates, creating job postings, and administering some kinds of ability tests. One AI company is working on a virtual assistant that can build a database of applicants' interactions with the hiring company to preserve information for future reference, and another builds models to help managers hire based on data about their current employees. AI can also help managers improve employee diversity and scan video interviews to analyze applicants' verbal and nonverbal communication for patterns and inconsistencies.[87]

9.3 Managing an Effective Workforce: Compensation and Benefits

THE BIG PICTURE

Managers must manage for compensation—which includes wages or salaries, incentives, and benefits.

LO 9-3

Outline common forms of compensation.

Do we work only for a paycheck? Many people do, of course. But money is only one form of compensation.

Compensation has three parts: (1) wages or salaries, (2) incentives, and (3) benefits. In different organizations one part may take on more importance than another. For instance, in some nonprofit organizations (education, government), salaries may not be large, but health and retirement benefits may outweigh that fact. In a high-technology start-up, the salary and benefits may actually be somewhat humble, but the promise of a large payoff in incentives, such as stock options or bonuses, may be quite attractive. Let's consider these three parts briefly. (We expand on them in Chapter 12, when we discuss ways to motivate employees.)

Wages or Salaries

Base pay consists of the basic wage or salary paid employees in exchange for doing their jobs. The basic compensation is determined by all kinds of economic factors: the prevailing pay levels in a particular industry and location, what competitors are paying, whether the jobs are unionized, if the jobs are hazardous, what the individual's level is in the organization, and how much experience he or she has.

Incentives

To attract high-performing employees and to induce those already employed to be more productive, many organizations offer incentives, such as commissions, bonuses, profit-sharing plans, and stock options. We discuss these in detail in Chapter 12.

Benefits

Benefits, or *fringe benefits*, are additional nonmonetary forms of compensation designed to enrich the lives of all employees in the organization, which are paid all or in part by the organization. We discuss benefits in more detail in Chapter 12, but examples are many: health insurance, dental insurance, life insurance, disability protection, retirement plans, holidays off, accumulated sick days and vacation days, recreation options, country club or health club memberships, family leave, discounts on company merchandise, counseling, credit unions, legal advice, and education reimbursement. For top executives, there may be "golden parachutes," generous severance pay for those who might be let go in the event the company is taken over by another company.

Communication is everything. Human resource managers need to keep these questions in mind: What good does it do a company to have attractive incentive plans if employees don't understand them? Will an employee exert the extra effort in pursuit of rewards if he or she doesn't know what the rewards are? ©ColorBlind Images/Blend Images LLC

Benefits are no small part of an organization's costs. In September 2017, private industry spent an average of $35.64 per hour worked in employment compensation, of which wages and salaries accounted for 68.3 percent and benefits for the remaining 31.7 percent.[88]

Managers should also be aware that men and women regard workplace benefits differently. Recent research by PriceWaterhouse showed that almost two-thirds of women respondants valued work-life balance as very important compared to only a little more than half of men. Women also valued "feeling like I can be myself" and having meaningful work slightly more than did men.[89] In another report, by MassMutual, men and women both chose vacation time and better 401(k) retirement plan matching as their top benefits, while women gave much higher value to tuition reimbursement than men did.[90]

9.4 Orientation and Learning and Development

THE BIG PICTURE

Two ways newcomers are helped to perform their jobs are through *orientation* to fit them into the job and through *learning and development* to upgrade employees' skills in their current position and develop them for future opportunities.

LO 9-4

Describe the processes used for orientation and learning and development.

On your first day of work at a new job, you will probably have to fill out a lot of forms. (Don't forget to bring your documentation—driver's license, Social Security card, perhaps passport—so you'll get the paperwork right and be paid on time.) After that, the process of orientation begins.

Today when a hire is made, companies often offer what is known as **onboarding**, **programs that help employees to integrate and transition to new jobs by making them familiar with corporate policies, procedures, cultures, and politics by clarifying work-role expectations and responsibilities.** This process also is referred to as employee socialization.[91] New software engineers hired at Facebook, for example, spend six weeks in an onboarding program called "Bootcamp." In it they are assigned a mentor and given a variety of tasks in specific "tracks" so they can learn about the company, its procedures, and best practices while doing real work (under close supervision, to avoid negatively affecting the site's more than 1 billion users). During these six weeks, the new employees gain enough first-hand, practical experience of the company's features and products to be able to choose the team on which they want to work. The program also allows them to bond with each other as well as network across the company. Ultimately, says Vlad Fedorov, the company's engineering director, "We want to set expectations that you're here to use your talents to be as impactful as possible. And we believe in you and here you're able to do it right from the start."[92]

The emphasis in onboarding, as we've said, is on "human capital." Why? Researchers have found that effective employee socialization enhances their job satisfaction and performance and reduces turnover.[93] The manager's tools for helping employees perform their jobs are *orientation and employee learning and development programs.*

Orientation: Helping Newcomers Learn the Ropes

The finalist candidate is offered the job, has accepted it, and has started work. Now he or she must begin, in that old sailor's phrase, to "learn the ropes." This is the start of **orientation**, **helping the newcomer fit smoothly into the job and the organization.**

Group training. In large companies, orientation and ongoing training are often conducted in group sessions led by a presenter while the employees follow along. What are the pros and cons of this approach? ©Rawpixel.com/Shutterstock

Helping New Employees Get Comfortable: The First Six Months "How well will I get along with other employees?" "What if I screw up on a project?" Going into a new job can produce a lot of uncertainty and anxiety. In part this is because, depending on the job, it may take 2–24 months for an average employee to be fully productive.[94]

The first six months on a job can be critical to how one performs over the long haul because that's when the psychological patterns are established. Thus, employers have discovered that it's far better to give newcomers a helping hand than to let them learn possibly inappropriate behavior that will be hard to undo later.[95]

The Desirable Characteristics of Orientation Like orientation week for new college students, the initial socialization period is designed to give new employees the information they need to be effective. In a large organization, orientation may be a formal, established process. In a small organization, it may be so informal that employees find themselves having to make most of the effort themselves.

Following orientation, the employee should emerge with information about three matters (much of which he or she may have acquired during the job-application process):

- **The job routine.** At minimum, the new employee needs to have learned what is required in the job for which he or she was hired, how the work will be evaluated, and who the immediate co-workers and managers are. This is basic.
- **The organization's mission and operations.** Certainly all managers need to know what the organization is about—its purpose, products or services, operations, and history. And it's now understood that low-level employees perform better if they, too, have this knowledge.
- **The organization's work rules and employee benefits.** A public utility's HR department may have a brochure explaining formalized work rules, overtime requirements, grievance procedures, and elaborate employee benefits. A technology start-up may be so fluid that many of these matters will not have been established yet. Even so, there are matters of law (such as those pertaining to sexual harassment) affecting work operations that every employee should be made aware of.

Learning and Development: Helping People Perform Better

Of course, in hiring, an employer always tries to select people whose qualifications match the requirements of the job. Quite often, however, there are gaps in what new employees need to know. These gaps are filled by learning and development (L&D) programs. The process has five steps, as shown below. *(See Figure 9.2.)* Typical areas for employee learning and development programs are customer service, safety, leadership, computer skills, quality initiatives, communications, human relations, ethics, diversity, and sexual harassment.

FIGURE 9.2

Five steps in the learning and development process

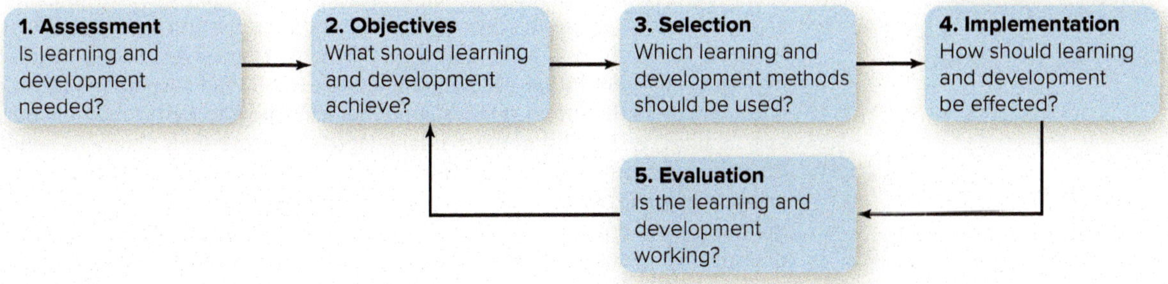

A recent report reveals that among Millennials, who are now the largest part of the U.S. workforce, training and development ranks as the workplace benefit they value most.[96] Some companies excel at L&D. For example, SAS, a global business software and services company headquartered in North Carolina, offers leadership programs, mentoring, and a career resource center. According to Shannon Heath, the company's senior communications specialist, "Knowledge workers never want to be stagnant. So SAS provides opportunities for growth to keep our employees challenged, motivated and engaged."[97] CyberCoders is a placement organization for the tech industry that offers an "incubator program" for its recruiters. Shane Lamb, the company's president, says, "We believe that equipping young professionals with the tools they need to build their business development and recruiting skill will lead to a long and successful career."[98]

At Estée Lauder, the cosmetics giant, learning and development opportunities include short-term special assignments, "stretch projects" that occupy a few hours a week in addition to the learner's regular workload, and temporary job swaps and job-sharing arrangements.[99] And at Yelp, to retain young account executives who have been carefully developed and are then sought out by competitors, managers act as mentors, stress the company's commitment to employee development, and promote from within. Optional L&D opportunities are always available to employees.[100] IBM uses artificial intelligence (AI) to analyze employees' profiles, training already undertaken, and expected career path to identify appropriate L&D programs for individuals, which can include animated simulations to provide coaching on desired behaviors.[101]

Some HR professionals believe most companies should be taking their L&D investments more seriously, however. Penny Asher, director of executive education at Open University Business School, says managers should realize that spending on effective L&D programs is less costly in the long run than failing to develop employees' capabilities across the organization. Employees at all levels expect it, she says. "These days, employees are demanding continuous learning and an investment in all the employee population rather than just picking up on the top tier of management. We are experiencing a fundamental shift that will affect every L&D department. . . . there has never been such pressure to get it right."[102]

The Different Types of Learning and Development There are all kinds of learning and development methods, and their effectiveness depends on whether facts or skills are being taught. If people are to learn *facts*—such as work rules or legal matters—lectures, videotapes, and workbooks are effective. If people are to learn *skills*—such as improving interpersonal relations or the use of new tools—then interactive techniques such as discussion, role-playing, case analysis, and simulations work better.

Another way to categorize L&D methods is to distinguish between on-the-job and off-the-job programs.

- **On-the-job learning and development.** On-the-job L&D takes place in the work setting while employees are performing job-related tasks. Four major methods are coaching, training positions, job rotation, and planned work activities.
- **Off-the-job learning and development.** Off-the-job L&D consists of classroom programs, workbooks, videos, and games and simulations. Today, of course, lots of off-the-job development consists of technology-enhanced learning—online learning, or e-learning. Virtual reality (VR) is an increasingly valuable L&D resource because it can simulate real situations and make learning more engaging, which translates into better results for retention and recall. Case Western University and Microsoft have partnered to train health care workers in human anatomy with a VR program called HoloLens.[103] Another VR initiative called MPathic helps medical students learn how to better read patients' and families' verbal and nonverbal language to improve their ability to handle difficult conversations.[104] Another relatively new approach is **microlearning**, or ***bite-size learning***, which segments learning into bite-size content, enabling a student to master one piece of learning before advancing to anything else. Most microlearning mixes video and interactive lessons that take under five minutes to complete and include a quiz.[105]

EXAMPLE Keller Williams Realty: Learning for Earning

"At Keller Williams University, we don't believe in learning for learning's sake; we believe in learning for earning's sake." Keller Williams Realty is a commission-based global real estate franchise company headquartered in Austin, Texas, with almost 177,000 agents in more than 900 regional offices around the world. Since 2014, it has been the largest such company in the world, with a strong commitment to educating, coaching, and developing its franchised associates. This drive to develop its agents is what the company believes not only sets it apart from competitors but also drives its steady growth and success.

Off-the-job learning and development. Your author, Angelo Kinicki, has conducted hundreds of educational classes off the job for executives around the world. Do you think managers can readily apply this knowledge back at work? ©stevecoleimages/Getty Images

In 2017, Keller Williams was named the top training organization in any industry worldwide by *Training* magazine (a professional development magazine for HR professionals). Among the criteria for the No. 1 designation are objective measures like the company's total budget for learning and development, that budget as a percent of company payroll, the number of L&D hours per program and per employee, and the results of several subjective measures and workplace surveys.

The company's learning and development tools and resources are available to agents at all levels of experience and are managed by the company's chief learning officer. The intention is to help all Keller Williams agents become experts in their particular markets, which can include luxury and commercial real estate and farm properties. The learning programs include Keller Williams University, which offers online multimedia training; skill building programs called MAPS Coaching; hundreds of onsite and virtual classroom training classes; special events including a "family reunion" convention; and several others. "For 35 years, Gary Keller has been saying we're a training and coaching organization disguised as a real estate company," said John Davis, CEO and president. "Thanks to his vision and commitment to investing in our people, we've been able to help our associates grow their businesses and create opportunities to fund their lives."

Keller Williams's new Mega Agent Expansion (MEA) program has helped more than 200 highly successful associates ("mega agents") expand their franchises into new markets by using class instruction, webinars, coaching, consulting, and mentoring to guide them. Learners complete the program with detailed business plans for their expansion efforts, new leadership skills, and needed expertise. A private social media community also allows them to share best practices with each other. As another benefit to the company, MEA helps it to retain these top agents. "For the first time," says Dianna Kokoszka, CEO of the MAPS coaching program, "individual agents can realize their dream of their brand stretching around the country or the world, all within Keller Williams."[106]

YOUR CALL

Keller Williams employees and agents average 82 hours of formal learning a year, almost seven hours a month. Do you think this is excessive? Can organizations spend too much on L&D? Explain.

You now have learned about the different HR programs and practices, such as recruiting, training, and compensation. Do careers in these fields interest you? Not everyone is suited for HR work, but it is very rewarding for some. The following self-assessment will help you decide whether or not a career in HR fits for you. •

SELF-ASSESSMENT 9.3 CAREER READINESS

Is a Career in HR Right for You?

This survey is designed to assess your skills and interests and determine if a career in human resources is right for you. Please be prepared to answer these questions if your instructor has assigned Self-Assessment 9.3 in Connect.

1. Are you suited for a career in human resources? Which specific aspect of human resources do you prefer?
2. Look at the top two areas of HR for which you tested as being best suited. Look over the descriptions of these fields and then identify what skills you need to have to be successful.
3. Even if you do not pursue a career in HR, which skills do you feel you should continue to develop? Explain.

9.5 Performance Appraisal

THE BIG PICTURE

Performance appraisal, assessing employee performance and providing them feedback, may be objective or subjective. Appraisals may be by peers, subordinates, customers, or oneself. Feedback may be formal or informal.

LO 9-5

Discuss effective performance management and feedback techniques.

Want to know how well your managers think you're doing at work? Be prepared to be disappointed: 60 percent of employees say they don't get adequate feedback, according to a 2015 study, and 43 percent say they don't get enough feedback to improve performance.[107] Feedback about how you're doing in your job is part of performance management.

Performance Management in Human Resources

No doubt you've had the experience at some point of having a sit-down with a superior, a boss or a teacher, who told you how well or poorly you were doing–a *performance appraisal.* A performance appraisal is a single event, as we discuss later in this section. Performance management, by contrast, is a powerful ongoing activity that has produced such spectacular results as 48 percent higher profitability, 22 percent higher productivity, 30 percent higher employee engagement scores, and 19 percent lower turnover.[108]

Performance management is defined as a set of processes and managerial behaviors that involve defining, monitoring, measuring, evaluating, and providing consequences for performance expectations.[109] It consists of four steps: (1) define performance, (2) monitor and evaluate performance, (3) review performance, and (4) provide consequences. *(See Figure 9.3.)*

FIGURE 9.3

Performance management: four steps

Source: Adapted from A. J. Kinicki, K. J. L. Jacobson, S. J. Peterson, and G. E. Prussia, "Development and Validation of the Performance Management Behavior Questionnaire," Personnel Psychology, *66 (2013), pp. 1–45.*

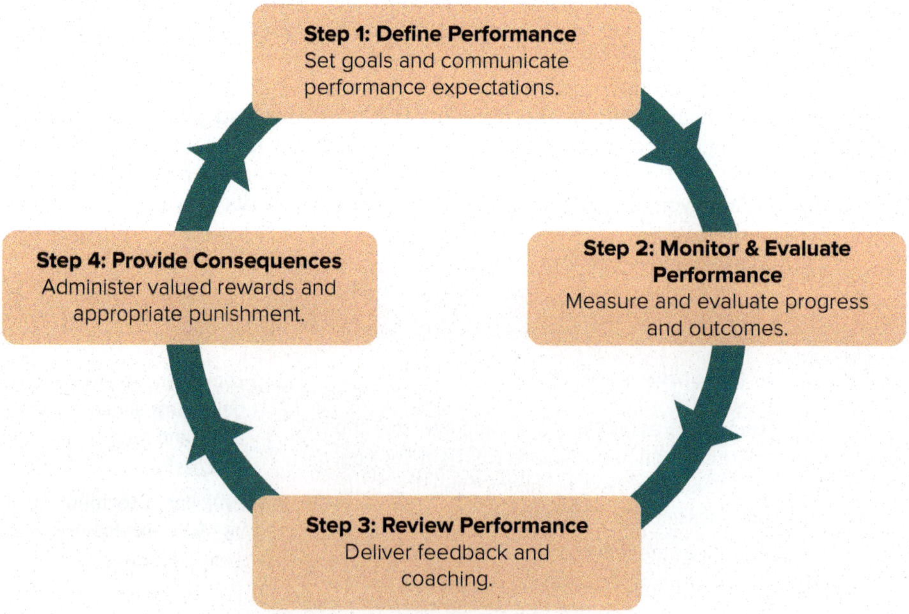

EXAMPLE Performance Management at Edward Jones

At almost 100 years old, St. Louis–based broker-dealer Edwards Jones & Co. is now the largest U.S. securities firm in terms of number of branches and salesforce. The company has 13,314 branches in the United States and Canada, mostly in small cities and towns, and employs nearly 16,000 financial advisors, who focus on selling mutual funds to nearly 7 million individual investors. Edward Jones has won a number of awards as a best place to work, a corporate equality proponent, a best workplace for women, and a top training company. It was ranked by *Fortune* as the 5th Best Place to Work For in the United States in 2017.[110] Here is a description of its performance management process (as defined by Figure 9.3).[111]

1. **Define performance.** Edward Jones generally hires and trains career changers and military veterans. It encourages them to build their financial advisor practice by adopting a four-step business planning process: Assess market and team; plan mission for three to five years; execute the plan; measure progress regularly. A set of proprietary planning tools and sample documents and a learning program are offered to develop skills such as collaboration, goal setting, and planning.
2. **Monitor and evaluate performance.** Several years ago, the company increased long-term performance expectations for its financial advisors. For example, advisors who were already exceeding expectations were expected to the increase their monthly production to $30,000 within 10 years of starting and $32,000 within 12 years. Those below expectations had goals of $20,000 a month at 5½ years and $22,000 at 6 years.
3. **Review performance.** Based on their current job descriptions, advisors are evaluated on their performance using a scale of 5, ranging from outstanding to unsatisfactory, against criteria like job knowledge, teamwork, decision making/problem solving, and leadership. Managers review their ratings with advisors and then give them an overall rating. Performance appraisal is seen as part of an ongoing, five-part circular process consisting of review, plan, develop, perform, and assess.
4. **Provide consequences.** Edward Jones advisors operate on a salary-plus-commission pay plan in which the proportion of earnings coming from commissions increases over time. High performers can be rewarded with bonuses, profit sharing, and travel awards; about 500 associates are also limited partners in the company. Low-performing individuals are given four months to improve, along with a performance improvement plan to help them get there.

YOUR CALL

What do you think about Edward Jones' performance management process? The financial goals for its financial advisors are considered low in comparison to those at competitors like Morgan Stanley and Wells Fargo Advisors, which tend to hire more experienced brokers. Do you think Edward Jones' performance goals are appropriate given the differences between it and other brokerages? Why or why not?

Performance management, which is often exerted through an organization's managers and human resources policies and practices, is a powerful means for improving individual, group, and organizational effectiveness.[112]

Performance Appraisals: Are They Worthwhile?

A **performance appraisal**, or *performance review*, **is a management process that consists of (1) assessing an employee's performance and (2) providing him or her with feedback.** Unlike performance management, which is an ongoing, interactive process between managers and employees, a performance appraisal is often dictated by a date on the calendar and can sometimes consist of a tense conversation that leaves both parties feeling unsatisfied.

Management expert W. Edwards Deming (see Chapter 2) felt that such reviews were actually harmful because people remember only the negative parts.[113] Ninety-five percent of managers in one study declared they were dissatisfied with their performance review/management systems.[114] No wonder, then, that some companies began dropping the practice altogether, although they soon learned that putting nothing in its place left employees without needed and indeed desired feedback about how they were doing on the job. Some companies went in the other direction, providing more frequent appraisals that would let managers and employees make faster "course corrections" and prevent performance problems from piling up. Among these companies are Gap, Pfizer, Cigna, and Procter & Gamble. Johnson & Johnson used to encourage managers to have five meetings a year in place of an annual review, in which, with each subordinate, they would focus on "goal setting, career discussion, a midyear performance review, a year-end appraisal, and a compensation review." Now the company is experimenting with a customized app that lets managers, employees, and their peers exchange feedback on a continuous basis and in real time.[115]

Deloitte, a global consulting firm, led the way in redesigning the performance review in 2015 after discovering, among other negatives, that the process in place was consuming nearly 2 million work hours a year, not nearly enough of which was spent in discussions of employees and their futures. After much internal research, the company came up with a streamlined system with three goals: (1) to recognize each individual's performance by (2) asking the person's manager four questions each quarter about what future actions he or she planned to take with respect to that employee, such as promote or flag as low-performing, and (3) to have managers check in with team members once a week. The overall aim of the revamped program is to gain not the "simplest" view of each employee, but the "richest."[116]

Accenture, Cigna, Microsoft, and Adobe are among the companies that have revamped their systems to encourage frequent or at least regular "check ins"; they are also abandoning rating or ranking systems they used in the past (see below). Adobe has boosted its stock price and reduced turnover by 30 percent since making the change.[117] Today, Deloitte continues to survey performance management and appraisal systems, and it reports that employees want regular feedback, likely influenced by the response mechanisms of social media, and that most companies are now able to obtain increasingly useful data for better HR decision making.[118]

In that context, let us take a look at performance appraisals, since they are still used frequently.

Two Kinds of Performance Appraisal: Objective and Subjective

There are two ways to evaluate an employee's performance—objectively and subjectively.

1. Objective Appraisals

Objective appraisals, also called *results appraisals*, are based on facts and are often numerical. In these kinds of appraisals, you would keep track of such matters as the numbers of products the employee sold in a month, customer complaints filed against an employee, miles of freight hauled, and the like.

There are two good reasons for having objective appraisals:

- **They measure desired results.** Objectively measuring desired results enables managers to focus employees on the important or preferred outcomes. Examples would be the number of cars sold by salespeople, the number of journal publications for professors, and the number of defects for a manufacturing plant.
- **They are harder to challenge legally.** Not being as subject to personal bias, objective appraisals are harder for employees to challenge on legal grounds, such as for age, gender, or racial discrimination.

2. Subjective Appraisals

Few employees can be adequately measured just by objective appraisals—hence the need for **subjective appraisals**, which are based on a manager's perceptions of an employee's (1) traits or (2) behaviors.

- **Trait appraisals.** *Trait appraisals* are ratings of such subjective attributes as "attitude," "initiative," and "leadership." Trait evaluations may be easy to create and use, but their validity is questionable because the evaluator's personal bias can affect the ratings.

- **Behavioral appraisals.** Behavioral appraisals measure specific, observable aspects of performance—being on time for work, for instance—although making the evaluation is still somewhat subjective. An example is the **behaviorally anchored rating scale (BARS)**, which rates employee gradations in performance according to scales of specific behaviors. For example, a five-point BARS rating scale about attendance might go from "Always early for work and has equipment ready to fully assume duties" to "Frequently late and often does not have equipment ready for going to work," with gradations in between.

"Here's the deal . . ." One of the most important tasks of being a manager is giving employees accurate information about their work performance. Which would you be more comfortable giving—objective appraisals or subjective appraisals? ©Asia Images Group/Getty Images

Who Should Make Performance Appraisals?

If one of your employees was putting on a good show of solving problems that, it turned out, she had actually *created* herself so that she could be an "office hero" and look good, how would you know about it? (This phenomenon has been dubbed "Munchausen—pronounced *MUN-chow-zen*—at work" because it resembles the rare psychological disorder in which sufferers seek attention by making up an illness.)[119] Most performance appraisals are done by managers; however, to add different perspectives, sometimes appraisal information is provided by other people knowledgeable about particular employees.

Peers, Subordinates, Customers, and Self

Among additional sources of information are co-workers and subordinates, customers and clients, and the employees themselves.

- **Peers and subordinates.** Co-workers, colleagues, and subordinates may well see different aspects of your performance. Such information can be useful for development, although it probably shouldn't be used for evaluation. (Many managers will resist soliciting such information about themselves, of course, fearing negative appraisals.)
- **Customers and clients.** Some organizations, such as restaurants and hotels, ask customers and clients for their appraisals of employees. Publishers ask authors to judge how well they are doing in handling the editing, production, and marketing of their books. Automobile dealerships may send follow-up questionnaires to car buyers.
- **Self-appraisals.** How would you rate your own performance in a job, knowing that it would go into your personnel file? Probably the bias would be toward the favorable. Nevertheless, *self-appraisals* help employees become involved in the whole evaluation process and may make them more receptive to feedback about areas needing improvement.

360-Degree Assessment: Appraisal by Multiple Sources

We said that performance appraisals may be done by peers, subordinates, customers, and oneself. Sometimes all these may be used in a technique called 360-degree assessment.

In a "theater in the round," the actors in a dramatic play are watched by an audience on all sides of them—360 degrees. Similarly, as a worker, you have many people watching you from all sides. Thus has arisen the idea of the **360-degree feedback appraisal**, or ***360-degree assessment***, in which employees are appraised not only by their managerial superiors but also by peers, subordinates, and sometimes clients, thus providing several perspectives.

Typically, an employee chooses evaluators from 6 to 12 other people to make evaluations, who then fill out anonymous forms, the results of which are tabulated by computer. The employee then goes over the results with his or her manager and together they put into place a long-term plan for performance goals.

All told, collecting performance information from multiple sources helps the person being evaluated get a broad view of his or her performance, and it highlights any biases and perceptual errors that are occurring. Finally, using multiple raters also makes it much more difficult for managers to unfairly favor or punish particular employees. According to one report, more than 85 percent of *Fortune* 500 companies use this method.[120] A recent study showed that this form of evaluation enhanced employees' ability and knowledge sharing.[121]

Forced Ranking: Grading on a Curve To increase performance, an estimated one-third of *Fortune* 500 companies have some variant of performance review systems known as forced ranking (or "rank and yank") systems.[122] In **forced ranking performance review systems**, all employees within a business unit are ranked against one another and grades are distributed along some sort of bell curve—just like students being graded in a college course. Top performers (such as the top 20 percent) are rewarded with bonuses and promotions; the worst performers (such as the bottom 20 percent) are given warnings or dismissed.

This type of performance review system is rapidly losing favor. Proponents of forced ranking say it encourages managers to identify and remove poor performers and structures a predetermined compensation curve, which enables them to reward top performers. However, opponents contend that the system eventually gets rid of talented as well as untalented people.[123] There may also be legal ramifications. A recent suit brought against Yahoo's media division claimed the company used forced ranking to discriminate against male employees.[124]

In addition, numeric ratings, rankings, and formal evaluations without positive feedback may produce the opposite of their intended results—namely, create a culture of *reduced* performance, according to recent neurological and psychological research.[125] When Accenture eliminated its ranking system, its CEO said, "We're going to evaluate you in your role, not vis-à-vis someone else who might work in Washington, who might work in Bangalore. It's irrelevant. It should be about you."[126] Finally, forced ranking systems—originally conceived at the turn of the 20th century to measure the performance of manual laborers and factory workers—seem inappropriate today, when more than 70 percent of workers are employed in service or knowledge-intensive jobs in which skills, attitudes, and abilities are hard to evaluate along a bell curve.

Effective Performance Feedback

As a manager, you may not feel comfortable about critiquing your employees' performance, especially when you have to convey criticism rather than praise. Nevertheless, giving performance feedback is one of the most important parts of the manager's job.

Think of yourself as a coach, as if you were managing a team of athletes, and remember to deliver at least one positive message to balance any negative feedback you must convey. Here are some suggestions:[127]

- *Take a problem-solving approach, avoid criticism, and treat employees with respect.* Recall the worst boss for whom you ever worked. How did you react to his or her method of giving feedback? Avoid criticism that might be taken personally.

Example: Don't say, "You're picking up that bag of cement wrong" (which both is personal and also criticizes by using the word *wrong*). Say, "Instead of bending at the waist, a good way to pick up something heavy is to bend your knees. That'll help save your back."

- *Be specific and direct in describing the employee's present performance and in identifying the improvement you desire.* Describe your subordinate's current performance in specific terms and concentrate on outcomes that are within his or her ability to improve.

It is important to remember that employees are unlikely to respond to constructive feedback unless they accept it. This underscores how important it is to deliver specific feedback in a way that does not cause defensiveness. We discuss the causes of defensive communication in Chapter 15. ©Antonio Guillem/Shutterstock

Example: Don't say, "You're always late turning in your sales reports." Say, "Instead of making calls on Thursday afternoon, why don't you take some of the time to do your sales reports so they'll be ready on Friday along with those of the other sales reps."

- *Get the employee's input.* In determining causes of a problem, listen to the employee and get his or her help in crafting a solution. Be thoughtful and compassionate.

Example: Don't say, "You've got to learn to get here by 9:00 a.m. every day." Say, "What changes do you think could be made so that your station is covered when people start calling at 9:00?"

- *Follow up.* Always check in with the employee later to be sure he or she has taken any corrective action you discussed and that you've made yourself available for any further questions or input.

Example: Don't say, "Why are you still turning in incomplete progress reports?" Say, "It's almost time for me to ask for your next progress report. Should we take a look at a draft of it together first?"

9.6 Managing Promotions, Transfers, Disciplining, and Dismissals

THE BIG PICTURE

As a manager, you'll have to manage employee replacement actions, as by promoting, transferring, demoting, laying off, or firing.

LO 9-6

List guidelines for handling promotions, transfers, discipline, and dismissals.

"The unemployment rate is an abstraction, an aggregation of bodiless data," writes journalist/novelist Walter Kirn, "but losing a job is a lived experience, written on the nerves. . . . Some blame themselves and some blame everybody. Still others, not knowing whom to blame, explode."[128]

Among the major–and most difficult–decisions you will make as a manager are those about employee movement within an organization: Whom should you let go? promote? transfer? discipline? All these matters go under the heading of *employee replacement.* And, incidentally, any time you need to deal with replacing an employee in a job, that's a time to reconsider the job description to see how it might be made more effective for the next person to occupy it.

As regards replacement, HR specialists distinguish between *turnover* (employee is replaced) and *attrition* (employee is not replaced), both of which occur when an employee leaves the company. Turnover occurs when an employee abandons, resigns, retires, or is terminated from a job, and the employer seeks to replace him or her. Attrition occurs when an employee retires or when the company eliminates his or her job, and the employer leaves the vacancy unfilled.[129] You'll have to deal with replacement whenever an employee quits, retires, becomes seriously ill, or dies. Or you may initiate the replacement action by promoting, transferring, demoting, laying off, or firing.

Promotion: Moving Upward

Promotion–moving an employee to a higher-level position–is the most obvious way to recognize that person's superior performance (apart from giving raises and bonuses). Three concerns are the following.

Fairness It's important that promotion be *fair.* The step upward must be deserved. It shouldn't be for reasons of nepotism, cronyism, or other kind of favoritism.

Nondiscrimination The promotion cannot discriminate on the basis of race, ethnicity, gender, age, or physical ability.

Others' Resentments If someone is promoted, someone else may be resentful about being passed over. As a manager, you may need to counsel the people left behind about their performance and their opportunities in the future. In fact, if you are passed over yourself, it is important not to let your anger build. Instead, gather your thoughts, then go in and talk to your boss and find out what qualities were lacking, suggests one report. You should also create a career action plan and look for ways to improve and showcase your knowledge, skills, and abilities. Don't forget to make your interest in advancement known.[130] Above all, don't give up. It may be that this was not the right opportunity for you and another will come when you least expect it.[131]

Transfer: Moving Sideways

Transfer is movement of an employee to a different job with *similar responsibility*. It may or may not mean a change in geographical location (which might be part of a promotion as well).

Employees might be transferred for four principal reasons: (1) to solve organizational problems by using their skills at another location; (2) to broaden their experience in being assigned to a different position; (3) to retain their interest and motivation by being presented with a new challenge; or (4) to solve some employee problems, such as personal differences with their bosses. Top Volkswagen managers considered implementing a mandatory rotation of key executives to new positions in order to disrupt what they perceived was "a culture of tolerance for breaking rules [that was] at the heart of its emissions crisis," according to *The Wall Street Journal*.[132] We also saw above that new employees at Estée Lauder and Facebook can rotate through different positions or departments as part of their company's learning and development process.

Disciplining and Demotion: The Threat of Moving Downward

Poorly performing employees may be given a warning or a reprimand and then disciplined. That is, they may be temporarily removed from their jobs, as when a police officer is placed on suspension or administrative leave—removed from his or her regular job in the field and perhaps given a paperwork job or told to stay away from work.

Alternatively, an employee may be demoted—that is, have his or her current responsibilities, pay, and perquisites taken away, as when a middle manager is demoted to a first-line manager. (Sometimes this may occur when a company is downsized, resulting in fewer higher-level management positions.)

Dismissal: Moving Out of the Organization

Dismissals are of three sorts: layoffs, downsizings, and firings. We will also describe exit interviews and nondisparagement agreements, which often go along with dismissals.

Layoffs The phrase being *laid off* tends to suggest that a person has been dismissed *temporarily*—as when a carmaker doesn't have enough orders to justify keeping its production employees—and may be recalled later when economic conditions improve. Layoffs are cited by many companies (recently Nordstrom, Sprint, and American Express) as needed to improve profitability, although research suggests they do not, in fact, improve profits.[133]

Downsizings A *downsizing* is a *permanent* dismissal; there is no rehiring later. An automaker discontinuing a line of cars or on the path to bankruptcy might permanently let go of its production employees.

Firings The phrase *being fired*, with all its euphemisms and synonyms—being "terminated," "separated," "let go," "sacked," "axed," "canned"—tends to mean that a person was dismissed *permanently "for cause"*: absenteeism, sloppy work habits, failure to perform satisfactorily, breaking the law, and the like. (A CEO "never gets fired," comments one writer dryly; rather, he or she leaves "to pursue other opportunities" or "spend more time with the family.")[134]

It used to be that managers could use their discretion about dismissals. Today, however, because of the changed legal climate, steps must be taken to avoid employees suing for "wrongful termination." That is, an employer has to carefully *document* the reasons for dismissals. You also need to take into account the fact that survivors in the company can suffer just as much as, if not more than, their colleagues who were let go.[135]

Incidentally, in terms of your own career, be aware that dismissals rarely come as a surprise. Most bosses are conflict-averse, and you may see the handwriting on the wall when your own manager begins to interact with you less.[136]

In some industries, such as those in information technology, "treating workers as if they are widgets to be used up and discarded is a central part of the revised relationship between employers and employees," in the view of one former employee of a Cambridge, Massachusetts, "digital sweatshop."[137] Start-ups are also quick to fire if new hires don't measure up quickly.[138]

The Practical Action box offers some suggestions for handling dismissals.

Fired. Being fired can be one of the most stressful events of one's life—more than the death of a close friend, separation from one's spouse over marital problems, or an injury requiring hospitalization. Some people who have been let go from their jobs suffer major health consequences. If you as a manager ever had to fire someone, what would you do to try to soften the blow? ©VGstockstudio/Shutterstock

PRACTICAL ACTION The Right Way to Handle a Dismissal

"Employment at will" is the governing principle of employment in the great majority of states, which means that anyone can be dismissed at any time for any reason at all—or for no reason.[139] Exceptions are whistle-blowers and people with employment contracts. Civil-rights laws also prohibit organizations' dismissing people for their gender, skin color, or physical or mental disability.[140]

Four suggestions for handling a dismissal follow.

Give the Employee a Chance First. If you're dealing with someone who has a problem with absenteeism, alcohol/drug dependency, or the like, articulate to that employee what's wrong with his or her performance; then set up a plan for improvement (which might include counseling). It's a good idea to get help from your HR department in such a case. Or if you're dealing with an employee who has a bad cultural or personality fit with the company—a buttoned-down, by-the-book style, say, that's at odds with your flexible, fast-moving organization—have a conversation about the mismatch and give the employee time to find a job elsewhere.[141]

Don't Delay the Dismissal, and Make Sure It's Completely Defensible. If improvements aren't forthcoming, don't carry the employee along because you feel sorry for him or her. Your first duty is to the performance of the organization. Make sure, however, that you've *documented* all the steps taken in advance of the dismissal. Also be sure that the steps taken follow the law and all important organizational policies. You should have a paper trail.[142]

Be Aware How Devastating a Dismissal Can Be. To the person being let go, the event can be as much of a blow as a divorce or a death in the family. Be compassionate but not emotional, and allow some silence to give the employee time to react.[143] Dismissals can also adversely affect those remaining with the company, who may feel guilty for not being fired, fearful of being fired, or worried about having to take on the fired person's workload. But if you have made the right decision, you have probably done everyone else on the team a favor by showing your commitment to maintaining a productive workplace.[144] Be sure you talk to your team members to discuss any issues that concern them (but without divulging details of the firing or your decision process).

Consider the Timing. On this score, current thinking is that the best day to lay people off is not Friday (the traditional day, when often managers didn't want to deal with other employees' reactions) and not Monday (when leaders may not have time to prepare for the aftermath) but rather the middle of the week, which gives former employees a chance to look for work before the week is over.[145]

Getting Ready to Survive a Job Loss. We hope you are never fired, but it is not a bad idea to protect yourself by being prepared. A few smart steps that rely on your career readiness skills are to build a personal brand by becoming known among your industry peers (try writing a blog or contributing articles on LinkedIn), to network both inside and outside the company, and to identify three companies or industries where your skills and abilities are valued and monitor them for hiring trends. Keep your résumé up to date, too, so you can start interviewing as soon as possible.[146]

Exit Interview and Nondisparagement Agreement

An exit interview is a formal conversation between a manager and a departing employee to find out why he or she is leaving and to learn about potential problems in the organization. For example, one company looked at the exit interviews of four employees and learned they all told the same story: Their manager "lacked critical leadership skills, such as showing appreciation, engendering commitment, and communicating vision and strategy," according to one article. Moreover, "the organization was promoting managers on the basis of technical rather than managerial skill."[147]

A departing employee may want to pound the desk during an exit interview and shout about all that went wrong, but that's not a good idea. "The last impression is the one people remember," suggests a *Wall Street Journal* article. "A graceful exit can burnish an employee's reputation and shore up valuable relationships. A bad one can do serious damage to both."[148]

A nondisparagement agreement is a contract between two parties that prohibits one party from criticizing the other; it is often used in severance agreements to prohibit former employees from criticizing their former employers. Employees who are laid off or whose jobs have been eliminated are often obliged to sign nondisparagement agreements in return for receiving severance pay—pay an employer may give a worker who leaves, such as the equivalent of two weeks of salary for each year he or she was employed. A nondisparagement clause at Abbott Laboratories in Libertyville, Illinois, reads "You agree to make every effort to maintain and protect the reputation of Abbott and its products and agents." However, some former Abbott employees say the provision "stopped them from speaking openly with elected officials or appearing at congressional hearings" about what they say was the misuse of temporary work visas (H-1B visas) to replace American workers with foreign-born workers, according to one account.[149]

9.7 The Legal Requirements of Human Resource Management

THE BIG PICTURE

Four areas of human resource law any manager needs to be aware of are labor relations, compensation and benefits, health and safety, and equal employment opportunity.

LO 9-7

Discuss legal considerations managers should be aware of.

Laws underlie all aspects of the human resource process discussed so far. Whatever your organization's human resource strategy, in the United States (and in U.S. divisions overseas) it has to operate within the environment of the American legal system. Four areas you need to be aware of are as follows. Some important laws are summarized in Table 9.2.

1. Labor Relations

The earliest laws affecting employee welfare had to do with unions, and they can still have important effects. Legislation passed in 1935 (the Wagner Act) resulted in the **National Labor Relations Board (NLRB)**, which enforces procedures whereby employees may vote to have a union and for collective bargaining. **Collective bargaining** consists of negotiations between management and employees about disputes over compensation, benefits, working conditions, and job security.

A 1947 law (the Taft-Hartley Act) allows the president of the United States to prevent or end a strike that threatens national security. (We discuss labor–management issues further in Section 9.8.)

2. Compensation and Benefits

The Social Security Act in 1935 established the U.S. retirement system. The passage of the **Fair Labor Standards Act** of 1938 established minimum living standards for workers engaged in interstate commerce, including provision of a federal minimum wage (currently $7.25 an hour; 29 states have higher minimums, 5 states do not have minimums) and a maximum workweek (now 40 hours, after which overtime must be paid), along with banning products from child labor. Salaried executive, administrative, and professional employees are exempt from overtime rules.

Proponents of a $15 minimum wage say it would help people pay their bills because existing minimum wages have not kept up with inflation, and it would create a fairer working environment because different states now pay wildly different minimums. Detractors say that the $15 figure is arbitrary and that a higher minimum would produce job losses, hurt low-skilled workers, have little effect on reducing poverty, and result in higher prices to consumers.[150]

3. Health and Safety

From miners risking tunnel cave-ins to cotton mill workers breathing lint, industry has always had dirty, dangerous jobs. Beginning with the Occupational Safety and Health Act (OSH Act) of 1970, a body of law has grown that requires organizations to provide employees with nonhazardous working conditions (most recently augmented by an update to the Toxic Substances Control Act of 1976).[151] Later laws extended health coverage, including 2010 health care reform legislation, which requires employees with more than 50 employees to provide health insurance.[152] (More than 60 percent of working-age Americans who signed up for Medicaid or a private health plan through the Affordable Care Act get health care they previously couldn't get.[153])

TABLE 9.2 Some Important Recent U.S. Federal Laws and Regulations Protecting Employees

YEAR	LAW OR REGULATION	PROVISIONS
Labor Relations		
1974	Privacy Act	Gives employees legal right to examine letters of reference concerning them
1986	Immigration Reform & Control Act	Requires employers to verify the eligibility for employment of all their new hires (including U.S. citizens)
2003	Sarbanes-Oxley Act	Prohibits employers from demoting or firing employees who raise accusations of fraud to a federal agency
Compensation and Benefits		
1974	Employee Retirement Income Security Act (ERISA)	Sets rules for managing pension plans; provides federal insurance to cover bankrupt plans
1993	Family and Medical Leave Act	Requires employers to provide 12 weeks of unpaid leave for medical and family reasons, including for childbirth, adoption, or family emergency
1996	Health Insurance Portability and Accountability Act (HIPPA)	Allows employees to switch health insurance plans when changing jobs and receive new coverage regardless of preexisting health conditions; prohibits group plans from dropping ill employees
2007	Fair Minimum Wage Act	Increased federal minimum wage to $7.25 per hour on July 24, 2009
Health and Safety		
1970	Occupational Safety and Health Act (OSHA)	Establishes minimum health and safety standards in organizations
1985	Consolidated Omnibus Budget Reconciliation Act (COBRA)	Requires an extension of health insurance benefits after termination
2010	Patient Protection and Affordable Care Act	Employers with more than 50 employees must provide health insurance
Equal Employment Opportunity		
1963	Equal Pay Act	Requires men and women be paid equally for performing equal work
1964, amended 1972	Civil Rights Act, Title VII	Prohibits discrimination on basis of race, color, religion, national origin, sex, or sexual orientation
1967, amended 1978 and 1986	Age Discrimination in Employment Act (ADEA)	Prohibits discrimination in employees over 40 years old; restricts mandatory retirement
1990	Americans with Disabilities Act (ADA)	Prohibits discrimination against essentially qualified employees with physical or mental disabilities or chronic illness; requires "reasonable accommodation" be provided so they can perform duties
1991	Civil Rights Act	Amends and clarifies Title VII, ADA, and other laws; permits suits against employers for punitive damages in cases of intentional discrimination

4. Equal Employment Opportunity

The effort to reduce discrimination in employment based on racial, ethnic, and religious bigotry and gender stereotypes began with Title VII of the Civil Rights Act of 1964. This established the **Equal Employment Opportunity Commission (EEOC)**, whose job is to enforce antidiscrimination and other employment-related laws. Title VII applies to all organizations or their agents engaged in an industry affecting interstate commerce that employs 15 or more employees. Contractors who wish to do business with the U.S. government (such as most colleges and universities, which receive federal funds) must be in compliance with various executive orders issued by the president covering antidiscrimination. Later laws prevented discrimination against older workers and people with physical and mental disabilities.

Workplace Discrimination, Affirmative Action, Sexual Harassment, and Bullying

Three important concepts covered by EEO laws are *workplace discrimination*, *affirmative action*, and *sexual harassment*, which we discuss in this section. We also consider *bullying*, which is *not* covered by equal employment opportunity (EEO) laws.

Workplace Discrimination **Workplace discrimination** occurs when employment decisions about people are made for reasons not relevant to the job, such as skin color or eye shape, gender, religion, national origin, and the like. Two fine points to be made here are that (1) although the law prohibits discrimination in all aspects of employment, it does not require an employer to extend *preferential treatment* because of race, color, religion, and so on and (2) employment decisions must be made on the basis of job-related criteria.

There are two types of workplace discrimination:

- *Adverse impact.* **Adverse impact** occurs when an organization uses an employment practice or procedure that results in unfavorable outcomes to a protected class (such as Hispanics) over another group of people (such as non-Hispanic whites). For example, requiring workers to have a college degree can inadvertently create adverse impact on Hispanics because fewer Hispanics graduate from college than whites. This example would not be a problem, however, if a college degree were required to perform the job. Another example is basing a person's starting salary on what he or she earned at a previous job. This can discriminate against women because they tend to make less money than men for the same level of experience and skills.

In recent years, pay discrepancies between women and men improved slightly, but as of 2016 women overall still earned only 80.5¢ to every $1 for a man, according to the Institute for Women's Policy Research. "If change continues at the same slow pace as it has done for the past fifty years, it will take 41 years–or until 2059[154]–for women to finally reach pay parity. For women of color, the rate of change is even slower: Hispanic women will have to wait until 2233[155] and Black women will wait until 2124[156] for equal pay." Of the most common occupations, the gender gap is widest for financial managers, followed by retail salespersons.[157] According to *HRMagazine*, pay discrepancies between men and women "is why a number of state and local legislators, including those in California and New York City, are moving to ban questions about job candidates' salary histories."[158]

- *Disparate treatment:* **Disparate treatment** results when employees from protected groups (such as disabled individuals) are intentionally treated differently. An example would be making a decision to give all international assignments to people with no disabilities because of the assumption that they won't need any special accommodations related to travel.

When an organization is found to have been practicing discrimination, the people discriminated against may sue for back pay and punitive damages. In 2017, among complaints to the EEOC, the most frequently cited basis for charges of discrimination was retaliation (49 percent), followed by race discrimination (34 percent); discrimination based on disability (32 percent); sex discrimination, including sexual harassment and pregnancy discrimination (30 percent); and discrimination based on age (22 percent): These percentages are greater than 100 percent because some charges allege multiple types of discrimination.[159]

Women are more likely to suffer from depression and anxiety compared to men, and one study suggests an important reason: U.S. women make significantly less money than their male counterparts, besides having to assume greater responsibility in child care and housework.[160]

Affirmative Action

Affirmative action focuses on achieving equality of opportunity within an organization. It tries to make up for past discrimination in employment by actively finding, hiring, and developing the talents of people from groups traditionally discriminated against. Steps include active recruitment, elimination of prejudicial questions in interviews, and establishment of minority hiring goals. It's important to note that EEO laws *do not* allow the use of hiring quotas.[161]

Affirmative action has created tremendous opportunities for women and minorities, but it has been resisted more by some white males who see it as working against their interests.[162] Affirmative action plans are more successful when employees view them as being fair and equitable and when whites are not prejudiced against people of color.[163] In addition, research shows that women and minorities hired on the basis of affirmative action felt stigmatized as unqualified and incompetent.[164]

Sexual Harassment

Sexual harassment consists of unwanted sexual attention that creates an adverse work environment. This means obscene gestures, sex-stereotyped jokes, sexually oriented posters and graffiti, suggestive remarks, unwanted dating pressure, physical nonsexual contact, unwanted touching, sexual propositions, threatening punishment unless sexual favors are given, obscene phone calls, and similar verbal or physical actions of a sexual nature.[165] The harassment may be

Sexual harassment. If this woman is unaware of the man ogling her legs, does that make his behavior acceptable? Or does it still contribute to an offensive work environment? ©Phanie/SuperStock

by a member of the opposite sex or a member of the same sex, by a manager, by a co-worker, or by an outsider. If the harasser is a manager or an agent of the organization, the organization itself can be sued, even if it had no knowledge of the situation.[166]

EXAMPLE Sexual Harassment at Work

Sexual harassment is never acceptable, but beginning in 2017, it has become less hidden. Men in fields ranging from sports to entertainment to politics to media and the arts were accused of groping, making sexually inappropriate comments, and even rape by women who at last felt empowered, if not compelled, to speak out.

In what *The New York Times* called "a seismic shift in what behavior is tolerated in the workplace," personified in a movement called #MeToo, scores of men, often high-profile figures with years of professional achievement behind them, were fired, suspended, or forced to resign or step down based on once hushed-up behavior in the recent, or not-so-recent, past. Some have admitted guilt and apologized; others have denied it. As of February 2018, the *Times* listed 71 such cases and promised the list would be updated as events continued to unfold.[167]

Sexual harassment is not a new behavior. It has occurred throughout history. Over the last two decades, psychologists attempted to understand its causes by studying men who harass or assault women. This research shows that male harassers "have different motivations yet typically share specific personality traits" that are amplified by having power, according to *The Wall Street Journal*. The two traits are *hostile masculinity* and *impersonal sexuality*. The *Journal* notes that "Men with 'hostile masculinity' find power over women to be a sexual turn-on. They feel anger at being rejected by a woman. . . . They justify their aggression and are often narcissists."[168] *Narcissism* consists of "a self-centered perspective, feelings of superiority, and a drive for personal power and glory."[169] Individuals with this trait have inflated views of themselves, fantasize about being in control of everything, and like to attract the admiration of others. It's thus not surprising that narcissists tend to emerge as leaders.[170] "Men with 'impersonal sexuality' prefer sex without intimacy or a close connection, which often leads them to seek promiscuous sex or multiple partners. Often, but not always, this type of person has had a difficult home environment as a child, with abuse or violence, or they had some anti-social tendencies as adolescents."[171]

YOUR CALL

Given that two personality traits are associated with sexual harassment, how can an organization stop it? Why do you think tolerance for the covering up of sexual harassment and other inappropriate or illegal behavior seems to be evaporating?

Two Types of Sexual Harassment There are two types of sexual harassment, both of which violate Title VII of the 1964 Civil Rights Act.

In the *quid pro quo harassment* type, the person to whom the unwanted sexual attention is directed is put in the position of jeopardizing being hired for a job or obtaining job benefits or opportunities unless he or she implicitly or explicitly acquiesces.

More typical is the *hostile environment* type, in which the person being sexually harassed doesn't risk economic harm but experiences an offensive or intimidating work environment. Anti-female remarks are particularly prevalent on social media.[172]

Table 9.3 presents some guidelines for preventing sexual harassment.

TABLE 9.3 Preventing Sexual Harassment

• Don't suggest or tolerate sexual favors for rewards related to work or promotion.
• Don't engage in uninvited touching, patting, or hugging of others' bodies.
• Don't make or tolerate sexually suggestive jokes, demeaning remarks, slurs, or obscene gestures or sounds.
• Don't display or accept sexual pictures in your workplace or write notes of a sexual nature.
• Don't laugh at others' sexually harassing words or behaviors.

What Managers Can Do To help prevent harassment from occurring, managers can make sure their companies have an effective sexual harassment policy in place. The policy should be shown to all current and new employees, who should be made to understand that neither sexual harassment nor covering up for an offender will not be tolerated under any circumstances.[173] A formal complaint procedure should be established, which should explain how charges will be investigated and resolved. Supervisors should be trained in Title VII requirements and the proper procedures to follow when charges occur. If charges occur, they should be investigated promptly and objectively, and if substantiated, the offender should be disciplined at once—no matter his or her rank in the company.

Bullying

Bullying is repeated mistreatment of one or more persons by one or more perpetrators; it is abusive physical, psychological, verbal, or nonverbal behavior that is threatening, humiliating, or intimidating. It can happen at work just as easily and as often as in the schoolyard.

Indeed, bullying on the job is now being experienced or has been experienced by 19 percent of employees, according to a recent survey. That is 30 million people; other estimates range even higher. Another 83 percent of workers have witnessed or been aware of it.[174] Bullying by supervisors that takes the form of forcing long hours on workers or yelling and behaving in a threatening way is more apt to occur in small

Bullying. A surprisingly common activity, bullying is apt to be verbal, involving shouting and name calling, or relational, including spreading malicious rumors and lies. In some cases, however, it can be physically aggressive, involving pinching or pushing. Perhaps as many as half of all employees have experienced some sort of bullying on the job. Have you? What did you do about it? ©Jetta Productions/The Image Bank/Getty Images businesses (50 or fewer employees), where the education level of bosses is often less high than in larger firms and where one person's bad behavior may have greater influence.[175]

Men account for 70 percent of workplace bullies, and women are 65 percent of the targets. Women are the bullies only 30 percent of the time, but most of their targets (67 percent) are also women.[176] Bullying can occur between colleagues, managers, and employees, but bosses are reported to be 61 percent of all workplace bullies.[177] Bullying on the job may be physically aggressive, such as pushing, pinching, or cornering someone. However, it is more apt to be verbal, including interrupting, shouting, swearing, and name calling. Or it may be relational, including malicious gossip, rumors, and lies that may cause someone to feel isolated or cut off. Bullying through technology (cyberbullying), such as Facebook, Twitter, or e-mail, accounts for about one in five incidents.[178]

The Effects of Bullying Unfortunately, many workplace bullies are quite charming and manipulative and so receive positive evaluations from their supervisors and achieve high levels of career success, according to one study.[179] "If people are politically skilled, they can do bad things really well," says one of the study authors.[180] Of course, that doesn't make this behavior right. Indeed, bullying can devastate a workplace.[181] According to the most recent report by the Workplace Bullying Institute, "40% of targets are believed to suffer adverse health consequences from bullying."[182] These can include anxiety, depression, and even panic attacks.[183]

Table 9.4 presents some guidelines for combating bullying. *(See Table 9.4.)*

TABLE 9.4 Beating Back the Bully

• **Recognize the mistreatment as bullying:** Don't blame yourself, and don't wait to respond. Stand up for yourself from the start. (Yes, this is hard to do.)
• **Stay calm and confident:** Don't feed the bully's sense of power by showing fear.
• **Don't strike back:** It might get you fired. Ask to be treated with fairness and respect.
• **Avoid being alone with the bully:** Make sure someone can hear your interactions. Or record them on your smartphone.
• **Document what is happening:** Specifically describe to the bully the effect he or she is having on your work and state that you will no longer tolerate it. Also document in writing the date and details (make hard copies of any emails, texts, or other written communications), describe the effect on your work, and indicate whether any witnesses were present.
• **Know your next steps:** Get others on your side. Seek advice from your manager and HR officer, and be ready to ask for a transfer or even seek a new job if all else fails.

Sources: A. Bruzzese, "Workplace Becomes New Schoolyard for Bullies," USA Today, *August 24, 2011, http://usatoday30.usatoday.com/money/jobcenter/workplace/bruzzese/2011-08-24-bully-bosses-overtake-workplace_n.htm (accessed June 6, 2016); K. V. Brown, "Far beyond School Playground, Bullying Common in Workplace,"* San Francisco Chronicle, *November 6, 2011, pp. A1, A10; Robert Half International, "6 Tips for Dealing with the Office Bully,"* The Arizona Republic, *November 29, 2015, p. 4E; G. James, "This Is Exactly What to Do if Your Boss Is a Bully,"* Inc., *February 22, 2018, https://www.inc.com/geoffrey-james/this-is-exactly-what-to-do-if-your-boss-is-a-bully.html?cid=search; S. Lucas, "Study: Bullied at Work? No Matter What You Do, You're Screwed,"* Inc., *February 23, 2017, https://www.inc.com/suzanne-lucas/study-bullied-at-work-no-matter-what-you-do-youre-screwed.html?cid=search; S. M. Heathfield, "How to Deal with a Bully at Work,"* The Balance, *September 30, 2017, https://www.thebalance.com/how-to-deal-with-a-bully-at-work-1917901.*

9.8 Labor–Management Issues

THE BIG PICTURE

We describe the process by which workers get a labor union to represent them and how unions and management negotiate a contract. This section also discusses the types of union and nonunion workplaces and right-to-work laws. It covers issues unions and management negotiate, such as compensation, cost-of-living adjustments, two-tier wage systems, and givebacks. It concludes by describing mediation and arbitration.

LO 9-8

Describe labor-management issues and ways to work effectively with labor unions.

Starting in 1943, James Smith worked his way up from washing dishes in the galley of a passenger train's dining car to waiter, earning tips on top of his wages of 36 cents an hour. The union job with the Brotherhood of Sleeping Car Porters, the first African American union, enabled him to go to college, and when he left the railroad he was hired as a civil engineer for the city of Los Angeles. "His story," says one report, "is emblematic of the role the railroads and a railroad union played in building a foundation for America's black middle class."[184] Unions also helped to grow the U.S. (and European) middle classes in general, bringing benefits to all, organized or not.

Labor unions are organizations of employees formed to protect and advance their members' interests by bargaining with management over job-related issues. The union movement is far less powerful that it was in the 1950s—indeed, its present membership is the lowest since 1916—but it is still a force in many sectors of the economy. *(See Table 9.5.)* Despite declining membership, about 60 percent of U.S. adults hold a favorable view of unions today, the highest in a decade and up sharply from less than 50 percent in 2015. Young adults hold more favorable views of unions (75 percent) than they do of business corporations (55 percent).[185]

TABLE 9.5 Snapshot of Today's U.S. Union Movement

Who's in a union (2017)?
• 10.7% of full-time U.S. workers—down from a high of 35.5% in 1945 but also up about a quarter million workers since 2016
• 6.5% of private-sector workers (7.6 million)
• 34.4% of public-sector workers (7.2 million)
• Most members, public sector: local government (40%), including teachers, police officers, and firefighters
• Most members, private sector: utilities (23%), transportation and warehousing (17%), telecommunications (16%), construction (14%)
• Union membership rate by gender: men (11%), women (10)
• Union membership rate by race and ethnicity: Blacks (13%), whites (11%), Asian Americans (9%), Hispanic Americans (9%)

Source: Bureau of Labor Statistics, "Union Members 2017," News Release, January 19, 2018, https://www.bls.gov/news.release/pdf/union2.pdf.

How Workers Organize

When workers in a particular organization decide to form a union, they first must get each worker to sign an *authorization card*, which designates a certain union as the workers' bargaining agent. When at least 30 percent of workers have signed cards, the union may ask the employer for official recognition.

Usually the employer refuses, at which point the union can petition the National Labor Relations Board (NLRB) to decide which union should become the *bargaining unit* that represents the workers, such as the Teamsters Union, United Auto Workers, American Federation of Teachers, or Service Employees International Union, as appropriate. (Some workers, however, are represented by unions you would never guess: Zookeepers, for instance, are represented by the Teamsters, which mainly organizes transportation workers. University of California, Berkeley, graduate student instructors are represented by the United Auto Workers.) An election is then held by the NLRB, and if 50 percent or more of the votes cast agree to unionization, the NLRB *certifies* the union as the workers' exclusive representative.

Have you ever been part of a union contract?
©Stockbyte/Getty Images

How Unions and Management Negotiate a Contract

Once a union is recognized as an official bargaining unit, its representatives can then meet with management's representatives to do collective bargaining—to negotiate pay and benefits and other work terms.

When agreement is reached with management, the union representatives take the collective bargaining results back to the members for *ratification*—they vote to accept or reject the contract negotiated by their leaders. If they vote yes, the union and management representatives sign a *negotiated labor-management contract*, which sets the general tone and terms under which labor and management agree to work together during the contract period.

The Issues Unions and Management Negotiate About

The key issues that labor and management negotiate are compensation, employee benefits, job security, work rules, hours, and safety matters. However, the first issue is usually the union security clause and management rights.

Union Security and Types of Workplaces

A key issue is, Who controls hiring policies and work assignments—labor or management? This involves the following matters:

- **The union security clause.** The basic underpinning of union security is the **union security clause**, the part of the labor–management agreement that states that employees who receive union benefits must join the union, or at least pay dues to it. In times past, a union would try to solidify the union security clause by getting management to agree to a *closed shop agreement*—which is illegal today—in which a company agreed it would hire only current union members for a given job.
- **Types of unionized and nonunionized workplaces.** The four basic kinds of workplaces are *closed shop*, *union shop*, *agency shop*, and *open shop*. *(See Table 9.6.)*
- **Right-to-work laws.** Individual states are allowed (under the 1947 Taft-Hartley Act) to pass legislation outlawing union and agency shops. As a result, 28 states have passed **right-to-work laws**, statutes that prohibit employees from being required to join a union as a condition of employment.

TABLE 9.6
Four Kinds of Workplace Labor Agreements

WORKPLACE	DEFINITION	STATUS
Closed shop	Employer may hire only workers for a job who are already in the union.	Illegal
Union shop	Workers aren't required to be union members when hired for a job but must join the union within a specified time.	Not allowed in 22 states (right-to-work states)
Agency shop	Workers must pay equivalent of union dues but aren't required to join the union.	Applies to public-sector teachers in some states, prohibited in others
Open shop	Workers may choose to join or not join a union.	Applies in 22 states (right-to-work states)

Business interests supporting such laws argue that forcing workers to join a union violates their rights and makes a state less attractive to businesses considering moving there. Union supporters say that states with such laws have overall lower wages and that all workers benefit from union gains, so everyone should be compelled to join.

The 28 work-to-right states are shown in dark blue in Figure 9.4.

Compensation: Wage Rates, COLA Clauses, and Givebacks

Unions strive to negotiate the highest wage rates possible, or to trade off higher wages for something else, such as better fringe benefits. Some issues involved with compensation are as follows:

- **Wage rates—same pay or different rates?** Wage rates subject to negotiation include overtime pay, different wages for different shifts, and bonuses. In the

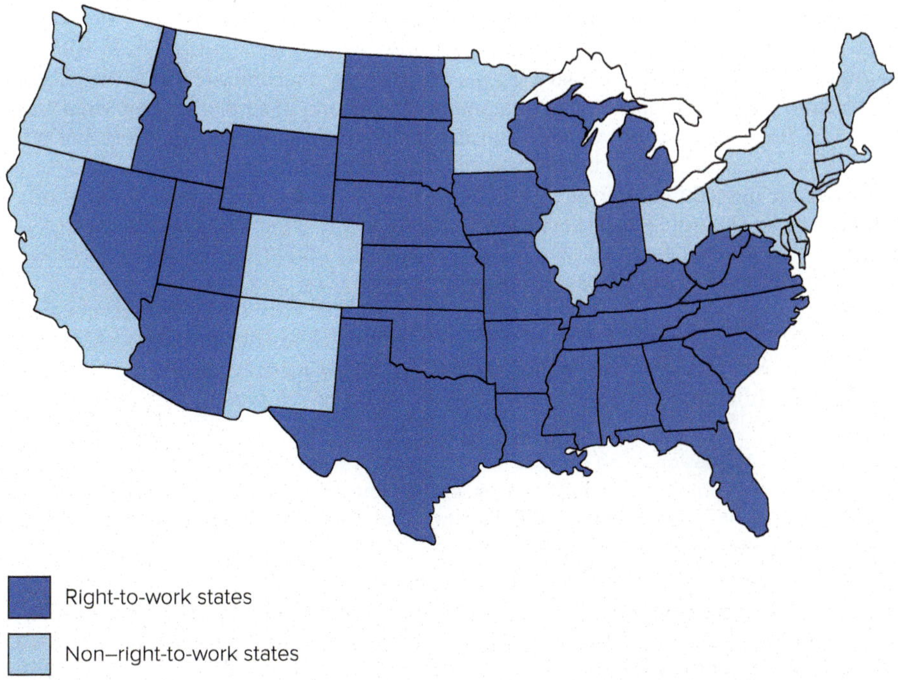

FIGURE 9.4
States with right-to-work laws
What kind of state do you live in? (Alaska and Hawaii are non–right-to-work states.)

past, unions tried to negotiate similar wage rates for unionized employees working in similar jobs for similar companies or similar industries. However, the pressure of competition abroad and deregulation at home has forced many unions to negotiate **two-tier wage contracts**, **in which new employees are paid less or receive lesser benefits than veteran employees have.**

Example: In 2011, when automakers began to create new jobs, new union hires were offered about half the pay ($14 an hour) that autoworkers were getting before ($28). Such two-tier wage systems can be attractive to employers, who are able to hire new workers at reduced wages, but they also benefit veteran union members, who experience no wage reduction. However, among autoworkers, at least, such contracts may be on the way out.[186] One study found that the two-tier setup wasn't, in fact, any more profitable for companies.[187]

- **Cost-of-living adjustment.** Because the cost of living is always going up (at least so far), unions often try to negotiate a **cost-of-living adjustment (COLA) clause**, **which during the period of the contract ties future wage increases to increases in the cost of living,** as measured by the U.S. Bureau of Labor Statistics's consumer price index (CPI). (An alternative is the *wage reopener clause*, which allows wage rates to be renegotiated at certain stated times during the life of the contract. Thus, a 10-year contract might be subject to renegotiation every two years.)
- **Givebacks.** During tough economic times, when a company (or, in the case of public employee unions, a municipality) is fighting for its very survival, management and labor may negotiate **givebacks**, **in which the union agrees to give up previous wage or benefit gains in return for something else.** Usually, the union seeks job security, as in a no-layoff policy.

Settling Labor–Management Disputes

Even when a collective-bargaining agreement and contract have been accepted by both sides, there may likely be ongoing differences that must be resolved. Sometimes differences lead to walkouts and strikes, or management may lock out employees. However, conflicts can be resolved through *grievance procedures* and *mediation* or *arbitration.*

Grievance Procedures

A grievance is a complaint by an employee that management has violated the terms of the labor–management agreement. Example: An employee may feel he or she is being asked to work too much overtime, is not getting his or her fair share of overtime, or is being unfairly passed over for promotion.

Grievance procedures are often handled initially by the union's *shop steward*, an official elected by the union membership who works at the company and represents the interests of unionized employees on a daily basis to the employees' immediate supervisors. If this process is not successful, the grievance may be carried to the union's chief shop steward and then to the union's grievance committee, who deal with their counterparts higher up in management.

If the grievance procedure is not successful, the two sides may decide to try to resolve their differences by one of two ways—*mediation* or *arbitration*.

Mediation

Mediation is the process in which a neutral third party, a *mediator*, listens to both sides in a dispute, makes suggestions, and encourages them to agree on a solution. Mediators may be lawyers or retired judges or specialists in various fields, such as conflict resolution or labor matters.

Arbitration

Arbitration is the process in which a neutral third party, an *arbitrator*, listens to both parties in a dispute and makes a decision that the parties have agreed will be binding on them. Arbitrators are often retired judges. Many corporations, including new tech start-ups, have vigorously embraced arbitration as a business tool with consumers and employees, and some for-profit colleges have even required it of their students, forbidding them from resolving their complaints through class-action suits (when a large number of plaintiffs with similar complaints band together to sue a company).[188] Critics, however, contend that forcing consumers to sign agreements that require arbitration and prevent lawsuits has the effect of biasing resolutions in favor of business and constitutes a "privatization of the justice system."[189]

Leo Kanne, head of Local 440 for the United Food & Commercial Workers International Union in Denison, Iowa, home of a Smithfield meat-processing plant, says plant workers earn enough to take their children to Pizza Ranch or maybe Dairy Queen every week and go on vacation once a year. "That's all these people want," he says. "Nobody is getting rich working in these plants." Word that a Chinese company had acquired Smithfield had everyone worried. Would they cut costs and not honor past labor agreements?[190] Considering these kinds of concerns, what is your feeling about labor unions? Self-Assessment 9.4 enables you to answer this question by assessing your general attitudes toward unions.

SELF-ASSESSMENT 9.4

Assessing Your Attitudes toward Unions

This survey is designed to assess your attitude toward unions. Please be prepared to answer these questions if your instructor has assigned Self-Assessment 9.4 in Connect.

1. Where do you stand on your attitude toward unions—positive, neutral, or negative?
2. What experiences or events in your life have led to your attitude toward unions? Describe. What do you think lies in the future for labor unions?
3. Why has there been growing dislike for unions in the United States?

New Ways to Advance Employee Interests From time to time, labor organizations take on new permutations. For instance, fast-food, construction, and contract workers are now able to more easily unionize, following a National Labor Relations Board decision that recognizes that the modern U.S. economy increasingly relies on shift work and temporary employees.[191] In 2015, carwash workers in Santa Fe, New Mexico, formed a workers committee (not a union), which is protected under the National Labor Relations Act from employer retaliation when employees are engaged in "concerted" activity to improve wages and conditions.[192] In 2016, Uber started a guild for its drivers in New York, which would provide limited benefits and protections, but would stop short of unionization and would not allow drivers to turn to the National Labor Relations Board to intervene on issues.[193] Finally, many employers are trying to advance workplace democracy by giving employees the chance to vote (as through digital survey tools such as TinyPulse and Know Your Company) "on issues from hiring to holiday parties," which, according to one report, "helps spark loyalty to the company."[194] ●

9.9 Career Corner: Managing Your Career Readiness

LO 9-9

Review the steps for becoming a better receiver of feedback.

"Feedback is the breakfast of champions," according to author, consultant, and management expert Dr. Blanchard. Blanchard is telling us that feedback is essential for success at any endeavor. The problem, however, is that people are not very good at either giving or receiving feedback, even though we continuously engage in these activities. A team of researchers found, for example, that individual performance *decreased* 38 percent of the time after receiving feedback.[195] We suspect this happens because most people have not been trained in how to provide effective feedback, and our brains are wired to resist negative feedback.[196] The brain identifies negative information faster than positive information and deems it more important in protecting us from harm.

One expert noted that this negativity bias "fosters or intensifies other unpleasant emotions, such as anger, sorrow, depression, guilt, and shame. It highlights past losses and failures, it downplays present abilities, and it exaggerates future obstacles."[197] All told, the brain produces a natural tendency to resist or explain away negative feedback.[198]

Our focus here is to help you become a better receiver of feedback, because it is essential for developing career readiness. Regardless of how feedback is delivered, nothing happens unless the receiver accepts the feedback and decides to do something with it.[199]

Becoming a Better Receiver

Becoming a better receiver takes some effort. Our model of career readiness reveals that you need to apply seven competencies: social intelligence, emotional intelligence, ownership/accepting responsibility, proactive learning orientation, positive approach, self-awareness, and openness to change. Use these competencies while putting the following steps into action:

Step 1: Identify Your Tendencies You have received feedback many times during your life and most likely developed patterns of responding. Do you tend to argue? Do you defend yourself and dispute the facts? Do you create a diversion and blame someone else? Do you smile but hide your anger? Do you have a knee-jerk response to reject feedback but then consider its merits at a later point in time? The career readiness

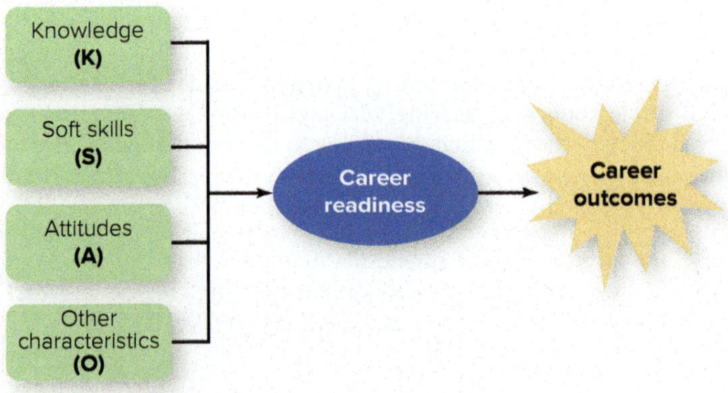

FIGURE 9.5

Model of career readiness

competency of taking ownership/accountability reminds us how important it is to take responsibility for our actions. This underscores the value of self-awareness, another career readiness competency, about our typical way of responding to negative feedback.[200]

Step 2: Engage in Active Listening Your brain's biology will jump into action upon receiving negative feedback. The amygdala, which acts like an alarm bell, suggests "threat," which in turn makes us hypervigilant to criticism and shuts down our ability to listen. This is unfortunate because it is essential to listen carefully and not interrupt when receiving negative feedback. Your goal during this process is to remain silent and strive to understand what is being communicated. Focus on determining whether what's being said is fact or opinion. That your work was poor quality is an opinion. That your report contained five misspelled words is a fact. Distinguishing facts from opinion during an interaction enables you to respond more effectively.

Now it's time to assess whether the information is accurate. It's essential to quiet the mind while assessing the accuracy of the feedback. This requires you to separate the delivery from the content in the message because so many people deliver feedback in a poor fashion: Judgmental feedback is less likely to be accepted.[201] It's hard to accept feedback that is delivered harshly or insensitively. But the message might be accurate.

Finally, consider the source.[202] What is the other person's intention in providing feedback? Is it to help you or to undermine your confidence? You surely will encounter both types of motives over the course of your life. The point is to listen and respond to those whose aim is to help you develop and improve.

Step 3: Resist Being Defensive **Defensiveness occurs when people perceive they are being attacked or threatened.** A neuroscience expert noted the amygdala "accesses emotional memories that identify a given stimulus as potentially threatening and triggers the emotional fear response that sets the fight-or-flight biobehavioral response in motion."[203] This in turn leads to defensive listening and destructive behaviors such as shutting down or being passive-aggressive, standing behind rules or policies, creating a diversion, or counterattacking.

Rather than trying to prove that the feedback giver is wrong about the feedback, it is essential to listen without preparing a reply. Let the person complete the message. Then it is helpful to ask questions such as, "I want to be sure I understand what you're saying. Do I have it right that you feel...?"[204] Asking questions quiets the amygdala and allows you to gain more insight about the threatening message.

Step 4: Ask for Feedback Your emotional triggers are less likely to be activated if you seek feedback rather than wait for it to be delivered. Look for opportunities to ask for bite-sized pieces of information about your behavior or performance as you work. Smaller doses are less threatening. A simple way is to ask someone for one thing you did well on a project and one thing that could be improved. Engaging in this behavior is also likely to improve your image because research shows that explicitly seeking performance feedback results in higher performance ratings.[205]

Step 5: Practice Being Mindful **Mindfulness is "the awareness that emerges through paying attention on purpose, in the present moment, and nonjudgmentally to the unfolding of experience moment by moment."**[206] Mindfulness also subdues the amygdala and allows you to hear feedback without getting caught up in emotions and internal stories about its meaning.[207] Meditation is a great method for increasing your general level of mindfulness. ●

Key Terms Used in This Chapter

360-degree feedback appraisal 347
adverse impact 356
affirmative action 357
arbitration 364
assessment center 337
base pay 339
behavioral-description interview 335
behaviorally anchored rating scale (BARS) 347
benefits 339
bullying 359
collective bargaining 354
compensation 339
cost-of-living adjustment (COLA) clause 364
defensiveness 367
disparate treatment 356
employment tests 336
Equal Employment Opportunity Commission (EEOC) 356
exit interview 353
external recruiting 329
Fair Labor Standards Act 354
forced ranking performance review systems 348
givebacks 364
grievance 364
human capital 326
human resource (HR) management 324
human resource inventory 328
internal recruiting 329
job analysis 327
job description 327
job specification 327
knowledge worker 326
labor unions 361
mediation 364
microlearning 342
mindfulness 367
National Labor Relations Board (NLRB) 354
nondisparagement agreement 353
objective appraisals 346
onboarding 340
orientation 340
performance appraisal 345
performance management 344
realistic job preview (RJP) 332
recruiting 329
reliability 338
right-to-work laws 362
selection process 333
sexual harassment 357
situational interview 335
social capital 326
strategic human resource planning 326
structured interview 334
subjective appraisals 346
two-tier wage contracts 364
union security clause 362
unstructured interview 334
validity 338
workplace discrimination 356

Key Points

9.1 Strategic Human Resource Management

- Human resource (HR) management consists of the activities managers perform to plan for, attract, develop, and retain an effective workforce. The purpose of the strategic human resource management process is to get the optimal work performance that will help realize the company's mission and vision.
- Three concepts important to human resource management are (1) human capital, the economic or productive potential of employee knowledge; (2) knowledge workers, people whose occupations are principally concerned with generating or interpreting information, as opposed to manual labor; and (3) social capital, the economic or productive potential of strong, trusting, and cooperative relationships.
- Strategic human resource planning consists of developing a systematic, comprehensive strategy for (1) understanding current employee needs and (2) predicting future employee needs.
- Understanding current employee needs requires first doing a job analysis to determine, by observation and analysis, the basic elements of a job. Then a job description can be written, which summarizes what the holder of the job does and how and why he or she does it. Next comes the job specification, which describes the minimum qualifications a person must have to perform the job successfully.
- Predicting employee needs means a manager must become knowledgeable about the staffing an organization might need and the likely sources of staffing, perhaps using a human resource inventory to organize this information.

9.2 Recruitment and Selection: Putting the Right People into the Right Jobs

- Recruiting is the process of locating and attracting qualified applicants for jobs open in the organization. Recruiting is of two types: internal and external.
- Internal recruiting means making people already employed by the organization aware of job openings, as through job postings.
- External recruiting means attracting job applicants from outside the organization. A useful approach is the realistic job preview, which gives a candidate a picture of both positive and negative features of the job and organization before he or she is hired.
- The selection process is the screening of job applicants to hire the best candidates. Three types of

selection tools are background information, interviewing, and employment tests.

- Background information is ascertained through application forms, résumés, and reference checks.
- Interviewing takes three forms. (1) The unstructured interview involves asking probing questions to find out what the applicant is like. (2) The structured interview involves asking each applicant the same questions and comparing his or her responses to a standardized set of answers. The first type of structured interview is the situational interview, in which the interview focuses on hypothetical situations. (3) The second type of structured interview is the behavioral-description interview, in which the interviewer explores what applicants have actually done in the past.
- Employment tests are legally considered to consist of any procedure used in the employment selection decision process, but the most common tests are ability tests, personality tests, performance tests, and integrity tests. Some companies have assessment centers, in which management candidates participate in activities for a few days while being assessed in performance tests by evaluators.
- Other tests include drug testing, polygraphs, and genetic screening. With any kind of test, an important legal consideration is the test's reliability, the degree to which a test measures the same thing consistently, and validity, whether the test measures what it purports to measure and is free of bias.

9.3 Managing an Effective Workforce: Compensation and Benefits

- Compensation has three parts: wages or salaries, incentives, and benefits.
- In the category of wages or salaries, the concept of base pay consists of the basic wage or salary paid employees in exchange for doing their jobs.
- Incentives include commissions, bonuses, profit-sharing plans, and stock options.
- Benefits are additional nonmonetary forms of compensation, such as health insurance, retirement plans, and family leave.

9.4 Orientation and Learning and Development

- Companies often perform what is known as onboarding, programs that help employees to integrate and transition to new jobs by making them familiar with corporate policies, procedures, cultures, and politics by clarifying work-role expectations and responsibilities.
- Two ways in which newcomers are helped to perform their jobs are through orientation and learning and development.
- Orientation consists of helping the newcomer fit smoothly into the job and organization. Following orientation, the employee should emerge with information about the job routine, the organization's mission and operations, and the organization's work rules and employee benefits.
- Learning and development entails a process for educating employees in the skills they need to do their jobs today and in the future.
- There are five steps in the learning and development process: (1) assessment, (2) objectives, (3) selection, (4) implementation, and (5) evaluation.

9.5 Performance Appraisal

- Performance management is defined as a set of processes and managerial behaviors that involve defining, monitoring, measuring, evaluating, and providing consequences for performance expectations. It consists of four steps: (1) define performance, (2) monitor and evaluate performance, (3) review performance, and (4) provide consequences.
- Performance appraisal consists of assessing an employee's performance and providing him or her with feedback. Appraisals are of two general types—objective and subjective.
- Two good reasons for having objective appraisals are that they measure results and they are harder to challenge legally. Objective appraisals are based on facts and are often numerical. An example is management by objectives.
- Subjective appraisals are based on a manager's perceptions of an employee's traits or behaviors. Trait appraisals are ratings of subjective attributes such as attitude and leadership. Behavioral appraisals measure specific, observable aspects of performance. Most performance appraisals are made by managers, but they may also be made by co-workers and subordinates, customers and clients, and employees themselves (self-appraisals). Sometimes all of these may be used, in a technique called the 360-degree feedback appraisal, in which employees are appraised not only by their managerial superiors but also by their peers, subordinates, and sometimes clients.
- In another evaluation technique, forced ranking performance review systems, all employees within a business unit are ranked against one another, and grades are distributed along some sort of bell curve.
- Performance feedback can be effected in two ways: (1) Formal appraisals are conducted at specific times throughout the year and are based on performance measures that have been established in advance. (2) Informal appraisals are conducted on an unscheduled basis and consist of less rigorous indications of employee performance.

9.6 Managing Promotions, Transfers, Disciplining, and Dismissals

- Managers must manage promotions, transfers, disciplining, and dismissals, which often involve replacing an employee with a new employee.
- As regards replacement, turnover must be distinguished from attrition. Turnover occurs when an employee abandons, resigns, retires, or is terminated from a job, and the employer seeks to

replace him or her. Attrition occurs when an employee retires or when the company eliminates his or her job, and the employer leaves the vacancy unfilled.

- In considering promotions, managers must be concerned about fairness, nondiscrimination, and other employees' resentment.
- Transfers, or moving employees to a different job with similar responsibility, may take place in order to solve organizational problems, broaden managers' experience, retain managers' interest and motivation, and solve some employee problems.
- Poor-performing employees may need to be disciplined or demoted.
- Dismissals may consist of layoffs, downsizings, or firings.
- An exit interview is a formal conversation between a manager and a departing employee to find out why he or she is leaving and to learn about potential problems in the organization. A nondisparagement agreement is a contract between two parties that prohibits one party from criticizing the other; it is often used in severance agreements to prohibit former employees from criticizing their former employers.

9.7 The Legal Requirements of Human Resource Management

- Four areas of human resource law that any manager needs to be aware of are labor relations, compensation and benefits, health and safety, and equal employment opportunity.
- Labor relations are dictated in part by the National Labor Relations Board, which enforces procedures whereby employees may vote to have a union and for collective bargaining. Collective bargaining consists of negotiations between management and employees about disputes over compensation, benefits, working conditions, and job security.
- Compensation and benefits are covered by the Social Security Act of 1935 and the Fair Labor Standards Act, which established minimum wage and overtime pay regulations.
- Health and safety are covered by the Occupational Safety and Health Act of 1970, among other laws.
- Equal employment opportunity is covered by the Equal Employment Opportunity Commission (EEOC), whose job it is to enforce antidiscrimination and other employment-related laws.
- Three important concepts covered by equal employment opportunity (EEO) are (1) discrimination, which occurs when people are hired or promoted—or denied hiring or promotion—for reasons not relevant to the job, such as skin color or national origin; (2) affirmative action, which focuses on achieving equality of opportunity within an organization; and (3) sexual harassment, which consists of unwanted sexual attention that creates an adverse work environment and which may be of two types—the quid pro quo type, which may cause direct economic injury, and the hostile environment type, in which the person being harassed experiences an offensive work environment.
- Another area of concern, though not covered by EEO laws, is bullying, repeated mistreatment by one or more perpetrators. Bullying is abusive physical, psychological, verbal, or nonverbal behavior that is threatening, humiliating, or intimidating.

9.8 Labor–Management Issues

- Labor unions are organizations of employees formed to protect and advance their members' interests by bargaining with management over job-related issues.
- Workers organize by signing authorization cards designating a certain union as their bargaining agent, and if enough cards are signed, the National Labor Relations Board will recognize the union as the bargaining unit. If 50 percent of workers agree, the NLRB certifies the union as the workers' exclusive representative. In negotiating a contract in collective bargaining, workers in the union must ratify the contract, after which union and management sign a negotiated labor–management contract.
- Among the issues unions negotiate are the union security clause, which states that workers must join the union or at least pay benefits to it.
- The four types of workplaces are closed shop (now illegal), union shop, agency shop, and open shop. Twenty-eight states have right-to-work laws that prohibit employees from being required to join a union as a condition of employment.
- Unions also negotiate wage rates, including two-tier wage contracts, with newer employees being paid less, and cost-of-living (COLA) adjustments giving wages that increase with the cost of living. Sometimes unions must negotiate givebacks, in which employees give up previous wage or benefit gains in return for something else.
- To avoid strikes, labor–management disputes may be resolved through grievance procedures or through mediation or arbitration.

9.9 Career Corner: Managing Your Career Readiness

- Becoming a better receiver of feedback requires using seven career readiness competencies: *social intelligence, emotional intelligence, ownership/accepting responsibility, proactive learning orientation, positive approach, self-awareness, and openness to change.*
- There are five steps to becoming a better receiver of feedback. They are: (1) identify your tendencies, (2) engage in active listening, (3) resist being defensive, (4) ask for feedback, and (5) practice being mindful.

Understanding the Chapter: What Do I Know?

1. What is human resource management and its purpose, and what are the three concepts important to it?
2. What is performance management, and what are the four steps in it?
3. Explain the two steps in strategic human resource planning.
4. What are the two types of recruiting, and how do the three types of selection tools work?
5. Differentiate among the three types of compensation.
6. Describe orientation, training, and development.
7. Explain the difference between objective and subjective performance appraisals, and describe 360-degree feedback appraisal, forced ranking, and formal versus informal performance feedback.
8. What are the four areas of human resource law a manager needs to be aware of?
9. Explain the concepts of discrimination, affirmative action, sexual harassment, and bullying.
10. What are the principal labor-management issues?

Management in Action

Difficulties Attracting and Retaining Human Capital in the Nursing Profession

Imagine a job that pays well above national averages and provides many opportunities for continuing education, specialization, and career advancement. It allows you to be active every day and to make a real difference in others' lives, along with the kind of scheduling flexibility some describe as "fantastic!"[208] Would you sign up? Strong salaries, lifelong learning opportunities, three-day workweeks, and meaningful work are common facets of a nursing career. And yet, hospitals consistently report nursing shortages stemming from both a lack of applicants and extremely high turnover rates. Turnover seems particularly high among newly minted registered nurses (RNs), with data suggesting approximately 18 percent–30 percent of new nurses quit their first job within a year.[209] With all the positives associated with the career, why do hospitals have such a hard time attracting and retaining nurses?

COMPENSATION

Nursing is one of the college majors with the highest starting salaries,[210] with new RNs earning an average of almost $60,000 annually. This salary is competitive when compared to the $49,000 overall average starting salary for new college graduates[211] and the U.S. median annual income of around $57,500.[212] RNs can earn six-figure annual incomes if they take night or overtime shifts or work as traveling nurses.[213,214]

But many RNs feel their salaries do not compensate them for the level of responsibility and the physical and emotional demands of the job.[215] One of the primary reasons cited for high nurse turnover, particularly in early careers, is that new nurses don't have a realistic understanding of job demands going in.[216] Many quickly recognize that good pay isn't enough to offset other job factors. As one nurse put it, "Nursing ain't for sissies, and if you choose nursing for the monetary benefits and not because you love the profession or love people, you will not stay."[217]

The gender pay gap is another compensation issue in the nursing profession. Although women account for 91 percent of nurses, female RNs earn between $4,000 and $17,000 less per year than their male colleagues.[218] Male RNs also enjoy significant career advancement and mobility advantages over female RNs, an effect described as a "glass escalator" that takes males in female-dominated professions "straight to the top" of the career ladder while their female counterparts spend their careers climbing lower rungs.[219]

INTERPERSONAL TREATMENT

It's not uncommon for nurses to experience verbal and physical abuse on the job. The mistreatment stems from three primary sources: doctors, other nurses, and patients.

The American Medical Association says doctors and nurses have an ethical obligation to ensure their working relationships with one another reflect a "common commitment to well-being" and are "based on mutual respect and trust."[220] In spite of this advice and the extensive training, skills, and knowledge nurses possess, they operate in an environment where doctors repeatedly question their competence. In a social media rant that went viral, Florida anesthesiologist Dr. David Glener said nurse practitioners were "useful but only as minions."[221] Physicians sometimes physically assault nurses. A Virginia nurse recalls a surgeon calling him "stupid" and throwing a bloody scalpel at him in the operating room because the nurse "didn't have a rare piece of equipment that he needed."[222]

Bullying is a problem among peers. Studies suggest that 45 percent of nurses have been bullied by other nurses. Nurse-on-nurse bullying isn't harmful just to the nurses who experience it—it's also detrimental to patient care. Said Renee Thompson (DNP, RN, CMSRN), "when you're being treated in a way that is making you feel badly, it stops the flow of information. When we're not freely communicating with members of the healthcare team, it ultimately affects outcomes."[223] In an interview with *Nurse.com*, Cole Edmonson (RN) added, "it's known that nurse bullying ultimately impacts the quality and safety of patient care being provided, as 75% of nurses state they are aware of errors in patient care or issues created when nurse bullying occurs."[224]

Patients are a third source of nurse mistreatment. Belinda Heimericks, executive director of the Missouri Nurses Association, says, "I suspect that if you ask nurses if they've been harassed by patients, a majority would say yes."[225] The reason? According to American Nurses Association President Pam Cipirano, nurses' caregiving roles often create the illusion, for patients, that nurses will comply with their demands. Cipriano says "the health care worker is expected to make a good situation out of a bad one," and patients sometimes assume nurses "should be able to tolerate whatever another human being dishes out at them" merely because those patients are under stress.[226] Abuse can also turn physical, with survey data suggesting that between 25 percent and 75 percent of nurses have suffered violence from patients, their visitors, or their families.[227]

INJURIES ON THE JOB

Nurses experience frequent and serious work-related injuries. The Bureau of Labor Statistics (BLS) indicates more than 35,000 injuries are reported annually among nursing employees, with most stemming from the daily work of moving and lifting patients.[228] In spite of a long-held tradition of teaching safe lifting techniques to nursing students, decades of data now show there is no safe technique for manually lifting patients.[229]

Some hospitals have invested in nursing staff's physical safety by purchasing specialized lifting equipment similar to that used to lift heavy parts in manufacturing facilities. Hospitals in Florida's Baptist Health System and the Department of Veterans Affairs have reduced nurses' lifting injuries by up to 80 percent since incorporating these machines, but industry experts say the majority of hospitals have not followed suit. According to James Collins, a research manager at the National Institute for Occupational Safety and Health, hospital workers feel frustrated with the progress being made toward nurse safety. Says Collins, "They've tried to persuade their bosses to launch major campaigns to prevent nurses from getting hurt lifting patients, but their pitch goes nowhere."[230] Some hospitals have been accused of trying to minimize or even hide data on injuries in response to questions about nurse safety.[231]

RESPONSES

Both patient outcomes and the bottom line suffer when nursing departments are understaffed.[232] Still, nurses continue to feel that hospital administrators undervalue them and treat them as disposable labor.[233] In response, some are resorting to collective action. In March 2018, the California Nurses Association announced that its 18,000 member RNs associated with the Kaiser Permanente health system had voted by an "overwhelming majority" to authorize negotiators to call a strike. Members of the union cited severe concerns with the low standards of care for patients and hospitals' "refusal to support a series of RN proposals that would enhance safe staffing and general patient care standards."[234]

FOR DISCUSSION

Problem-Solving Perspective

1. What is the underlying problem in this case from the perspective of a hospital administrator?
2. What role do you believe hospital administrators have played in contributing to nursing shortages and high nurse turnover?
3. What can hospitals do to increase nurse supply and retention rates?

Application of Chapter Content

1. What could hospitals do to create a realistic job preview before new nurses accept a position? How do you think this might help with nurse retention?
2. What type of training or development might hospitals offer to help reduce nurse turnover?
3. What steps could hospitals take to ensure male and female nurses are given equal opportunities in compensation and promotion decisions?
4. Do hospitals have a legal and/or ethical responsibility to invest more money in equipment to prevent work-related nursing injuries? Why or why not?
5. What do you think are the primary reasons nurses experience so much mistreatment on the job, and what can hospitals and nurses do to decrease these incidents?
6. Why do you think some nurses are resorting to collective action, and what do you think hospitals might do to proactively advance nurses' interests and avoid nursing strikes?

Legal/Ethical Challenge

Should Noncompete Agreements Be Legal?

This challenge considers the human resource policy of asking new hires to sign a noncompete agreement. Noncompete agreements are clauses "under which one party (usually an employee) agrees not to enter into or start a similar profession or trade in competition against another party (usually the employer)" for a specified period of time. In other words, the agreement prohibits the person signing it from working with another company that could be viewed as a competitor. The concept was born from the idea that an "employee might begin working for a competitor or starting a business, and gain competitive advantage by exploiting confidential information about their former employer's operations or trade secrets, or sensitive information such as customer/client lists, business practices, upcoming products, and marketing plans."[235]

Arthur Valdez was sued by Amazon.com Inc. for violating a noncompete agreement. Valdez was a supply chain and logistics executive for Amazon who was hired by Target. Target clearly competes against Amazon, and Valdez's agreement mandated an 18-month lag before he could take a new position with similar responsibilities. According to *The Wall Street Journal,* Amazon claims that "Mr. Valdez's new post will necessarily involve 'the disclosure and use of Amazon's confidential and proprietary information to Amazon's detriment and Target's advantage.'" Target denies that it wants confidential information about Amazon and says "this suit is without merit."[236]

Jessica Bell signed a noncompete agreement in a "stack of paperwork" she received when she joined Citrix software company in Raleigh, North Carolina. Bell, a single parent, got wind of potential layoffs at Citrix about two years into the job and began searching for employment at other companies. She started a position with Egnyte, a Silicon Valley-based tech firm that had recently opened a sales office in Raleigh. A few weeks into her new job, Bell and six other former Citrix employees working for Egnyte received letters from Citrix informing them that they were violating the noncompete clause. Egnyte filed suit against Citrix asking that the court rule the noncompete agreements were overly broad and therefore unenforceable.

Citrix countersued Egnyte and the seven employees, stating that Egnyte had hired the former Citrix workers "in order to engage in unfair competition with Citrix." Egnyte vowed to foot the legal bill for all seven employees and maintained that it hired them on the basis of talent, not to steal Citrix's intellectual property or customers. Bell said, "I certainly didn't think this would have implications and that they would have any control or power over my ability to feed my family essentially after I left Citrix."[237] She noted an obvious misunderstanding about what she was agreeing to when she signed Citrix's noncompete clause.

The use of noncompete agreements has nearly tripled since 2000, and their legality varies by state.[238] About 20 percent of U.S. workers have signed such agreements. Noncompete clauses have even extended to lower-level jobs; approximately 14 percent of employees who make less than $40,000 a year are bound by them.[239]

SOLVING THE CHALLENGE

Should companies be allowed to force employees to sign noncompete agreements?

1. Of course. Every company needs to protect its proprietary and confidential information.
2. In moderation. I agree that it makes sense to protect proprietary information like formulas, equations, trade secrets, and intellectual property for certain occupations or industries. But this should not apply to all jobs, such as working in a sandwich shop.
3. No. They should be against the law because they prohibit people from finding employment.
4. Invent other options. Explain.

Uber Continuing Case

Learn about Uber's human resource practices. Assess your ability to apply concepts discussed in this chapter to the case by going to Connect.

10 Organizational Change and Innovation

Lifelong Challenges for the Exceptional Manager

©Olivier Renck/Aurora/Getty Images

After reading this chapter, you should be able to:

LO 10-1 Discuss what managers should know about organizational change.

LO 10-2 Discuss three types of change, Lewin's change model, and the systems approach to change.

LO 10-3 Describe the purpose of organizational development.

LO 10-4 Describe the approaches toward innovation and components of an innovation system.

LO 10-5 Discuss ways managers can help employees overcome fear of change.

LO 10-6 Review the different ways to increase the career readiness competency of openness to change.

FORECAST *What's Ahead in This Chapter*

In this chapter, we consider the nature of change in organizations, including the two types of change—reactive and proactive—and the forces for change originating outside and inside the organization. Next we explore types and models of change. We then describe organizational development and discuss how you can manage employee fear and resistance to change. After discussing how to promote innovation within an organization, we conclude with a Career Corner that focuses on how to improve the career readiness competency of openness to change.

MANAGE U

How Can I Be More Creative at Work?

Do you think of yourself as creative? If you answered no, perhaps you thought the question was about whether you can draw, paint, compose music, design clothes, write poetry, or act in plays. But as creative and rewarding as those endeavors are, they are not the only ways in which your innate creativity can express itself. Neuroscience research shows that creative thought engages many different areas of the brain, and that the old right-brain/left-brain theory of the creative process has been a bit overrated.[1] That means that no matter how we think we're "wired," we all have the potential to be imaginative, innovative thinkers just by learning to look at things a little differently.

Creativity is a talent regularly sought by organizations. Indeed, one writer for *Psychology Today* says it is "at the heart of [the] essential skill set for the future."[2] There are many fun and simple ways you can leverage your career readiness competencies of proactive learning, positive approach, problem solving, and self-motivation to continually stretch and develop your own creative ability over time. Try a few of the following to increase four career readiness competencies that drive your creativity:

Proactive Learning

Nothing fires up the imagination like curiosity. Use your proactive learning skill to foster the habit of fearlessly asking questions about how everyday things work or where they come from and why.[3] Choose one or two questions at a time and look for answers in books, articles, nearby conferences or panel discussions, free or low-cost classes, podcasts, and TED Talks.[4] Your questions don't have to be about academic or work-related subjects, either. Learn a new sport. Take up a musical instrument. Join a chorus. As long as you're learning new things, you are keeping your creative muscle active. The Hope Lab, an organization dedicated to using technology to improve health outcomes for teens and young adults, has long maintained a culture of curiosity and innovation. One of the many ways it does so is by encouraging and helping pay for employees to take outside courses in everything from cooking to photography.[5]

Positive Approach

Positive feelings like gratitude, hope, joy, and empathy have been shown to build creative thinking.[6] You can actively cultivate these feelings with a little mindfulness. For instance, keep a "gratitude journal" by writing down one thing each day that you're grateful for, no matter how small. Elevate your capacity for joy by celebrating often, honoring even small events like a good grade on a test. Or, instead of wishing someone a happy birthday on social media and moving on, stop to make a phone call or take the person out for coffee or lunch. Reward yourself with a special meal if you've achieved a small milestone in your life. And don't sit still. Among its many benefits for physical health, exercise—even a simple bike ride or a walk outdoors—can also reinforce positive feelings.[7] Another aspect of positive approach is willingness to risk failure. "If you're not failing some of the time," says a writer in *Psychology Today*, "you're not stretching far enough outside of your comfort zone to keep learning and growing."[8] Stretching outside your comfort zone is what creativity is all about.

Problem Solving

Hone your creative problem-solving skills by looking for challenges you can practice solving now. You don't have to wait for your boss or professor to give you a difficult assignment to start becoming a better at this. Try learning to play chess, for instance. Its reliance on repeated patterns will strengthen your predictive abilities, and research has shown that chess players also demonstrate more than normal originality and flexibility of thought.[9] Not a fan of board games? Read detective novels by writers such as Agatha Christie or Sir Arthur Conan Doyle, still among the most widely read English-language writers of all time, or any of their more recent peers (search on Google or ask any librarian or bookseller). Or you can solve crosswords and other pencil-and-paper puzzles. All these activities will give your deductive and predictive powers a helpful workout.

Self-Motivation

Finally, setting creativity goals ignites the motivation to increase your level of creativity. A "personal creativity goal refers to the personal standard or aspiration that one's own job output should be creative," according to a team of creativity experts.[10] Setting a creativity goal will direct your attention and efforts at finding creative ways to perform your job. It will also impress your boss.

For Discussion Which of the above recommendations interest you? In what ways can you improve your creative skills, and what specific activities are you willing to commit to in order to increase your creativity?

10.1 The Nature of Change in Organizations

THE BIG PICTURE

Two types of change are reactive and proactive. Forces for change may consist of forces outside the organization—demographic characteristics; technological advancements; shareholder, customer, and market changes; and social and political pressures. Or they may be forces inside the organization—human resources concerns and managers' behavior.

LO 10-1

Discuss what managers should know about organizational change.

"Every journey starts with fear. . . . Do you know what fear stands for? False Evidence Appearing Real."[11]

Of course, not every fear rests on false evidence—often the evidence is very real indeed. But in an age of discontinuous change, we are all having to make our own new journeys. "There is a need to retool yourself," says the CEO of AT&T, "and you should not expect to stop."[12]

Fundamental Change: What Will You Be Called On to Deal With?

"It is hard to predict, especially the future," physicist Niels Bohr is supposed to have quipped.

But it is possible to identify and prepare for the future that has already happened, in the words of management theorist Peter Drucker.[13] Among the trends: Millennials will continue to be early adopters of new technology. Women will be a dominant force in the global marketplace. More people will move from rural to urban areas. Social networks will replace traditional institutions in driving change. Consumers will grow more informed, changing the power balance in the marketplace. A rising developing-world middle class will fuel global consumer spending. Spending on health and wellness will soar. Starting a new business will become easier. Niche markets will flourish. Cloud computing will do away with the brick-and-mortar office. Data will be critical for competitive advantage. Smart machines will get smarter.[14]

There are also some supertrends specifically shaping the future of business: (1) The marketplace is becoming more segmented; (2) competitors offering specialized solutions require us to get our products to market faster; (3) some companies are unable to survive disruptive innovation; (4) offshore suppliers are changing the way we work; and (5) knowledge, not information, is becoming the new competitive advantage.[15]

1. The Marketplace Is Becoming More Segmented and Moving toward More Niche Products In the recent past, managers could think in terms of mass markets—mass communication, mass behavior, and mass values. Now we have "demassification," with customer groups becoming segmented into smaller and more specialized groups responding to more narrowly targeted commercial messages.

These marketing messages may even be shaped and personalized by artificial intelligence technology, allowing bots, for instance, to engage in conversations with individually targeted consumers or small groups of consumers. Some suggest that this kind of customer-centric marketing can help create relationships that result in loyal customers and repeat business.[16]

Example: It is becoming increasingly easy to buy custom-made clothing at affordable prices. One New York City–based startup called Woodies, for example, offers high-quality men's cotton dress shirts (most under $100) and pants ($98–$145) online, made to order in return for a few basic size measurements. The company guarantees a perfect fit.[17]

2. More Competitors Are Offering Targeted Products, Requiring Faster Speed-to-Market Companies that take too long to commercialize their products may fail to capitalize on a narrow window of opportunity before competitors swoop in and pass them by," points out a *Forbes* writer.[18] Some of these competitors may be in and out of a market in a matter of days or months—like pop-up stores, "here today, gone tomorrow" retailers, such as those selling Halloween products.

Example: Virgin Group Ltd., headed by Sir Richard Branson, is known mainly for its music and airline businesses, but it has entered around 400 new businesses, one after the other—mobile phones, credit cards, hotels, games, trains, space flight, and cruise ships—and often very quickly. Virgin Comics, started in 2006, aimed at India's multibillion-dollar comics market, went from idea to public announcement in less than 11 months. In mid-2008, it restructured and changed its name to Liquid Comics.

Virgin train. A brainchild of British multiple entrepreneur Richard Branson, Virgin Trains was launched in 1997 to provide long-distance passenger services in the United Kingdom. Among Branson's many companies, perhaps 400 derivatives in all: Virgin Records, Virgin Mobile, Virgin Cola, Virgin Vodka, Virgin Car, and Virgin Galactic (for space tourism). Branson is quick to enter a new industry but also quick to get out if it isn't profitable. Branson's entrepreneurial approach: "Think, what's the most amazing way to do it?" ©Alvey & Towers Picture Library/Alamy Stock Photo

3. Some Traditional Companies May Not Survive Radical Change In *The Innovator's Dilemma: When New Technologies Cause Great Firms to Fail,* **Clayton M. Christensen**, a Harvard Business School professor, argues that when successful companies are confronted with a giant technological leap that transforms their markets, all choices are bad ones.

Indeed, he thinks, it's very difficult for an existing successful company to take full advantage of a technological breakthrough such as digitalization—what he calls **disruptive innovation, a process by which a product or service takes root initially in simple applications at the bottom of a market and then relentlessly moves up market, eventually displacing established competitors.**[19] Some companies that have the resources to survive disruption—to build "the next big thing"—often fail to do so.[20] Toys R Us is a good example.

EXAMPLE Radical Change: The Decline of Toys R Us

"Some organizations recognize faster than others that there are shifts in the ways customers want to be communicated with and the way customers want to purchase products. It probably took us a while." Thus, David Brandon, CEO of Toys R Us, reflected on one of the more obvious ways in which the once-powerful toy store chain failed to adapt and ultimately died.[21] The closing of nearly 800 U.S. stores, announced in early 2018, will end the chain's 70-year run.[22]

One observer suggests the company missed an opportunity to fill the gap between low-price suppliers such as Amazon and Target and local toy stores that don't compete on price but can provide personalized service. With an in-store experience little different from that of a "big box" store like Walmart and prices that weren't sufficiently competitive, Toys R Us couldn't protect itself against either type of competitor it faced. At the same time, it failed to capitalize on the digital capabilities others in its market were not providing, like apps to make product recommendations to shoppers or offer coupons while they were in the store. By the time the company finally developed an interactive game experience called Play Chaser to compete with Pokémon Go, it was too late to earn any benefit from it.[23]

Other contributors to the chain's downfall included opening too many stores, having stores that were too big, and carrying more than $5 billion in debt.[24] After declaring bankruptcy in the fall of 2017, with hopes of restructuring its way to recovery, Toys R Us experienced a 15 percent drop in sales over the crucial holiday shopping season and still faced paying millions of dollars a year in interest on its debts.[25] Already struggling with challenges from online retailers like Amazon and even the rise of mobile games and apps, it could no longer compete. Despite having a 15 percent share of the U.S. toy market, Toys R Us was finally forced to close its doors.[26]

YOUR CALL

Suppose an entrepreneur launching a new chain of toy stores asked for your advice about how to avoid the mistakes made by Toys R Us. What would you suggest, and why?

4. China, India, and Other Offshore Suppliers Are Changing the Way We Work As we said in Chapter 2, globalization and outsourcing are transforming whole industries and changing the way we work. China, India, Mexico, the Philippines, and other countries possess workers and even professionals willing to work twice as hard for half the pay, giving U.S. businesses substantial labor savings. While unquestionably some U.S. jobs have been lost, others have become more productive. Some engineers and salespeople, for example, have been liberated from routine tasks and can spend more time innovating and dealing with customers.

Example: Querétaro is not a place students would probably go for spring break, but it has become known for something not normally associated with Mexico: aircraft construction. U.S. aircraft makers from Bombardier to Cessna Aircraft to Hawker Beechcraft have various kinds of subassembly work there, where wages are lower but skill levels are not.[27]

But if some manufacturing jobs have moved cross-border, dozens of foreign manufacturers in aerospace, chemicals, and other industries are bringing jobs *to* the United States. British-based Rolls-Royce, for instance, makes diesel engines in South Carolina and employs 7,000 people in 26 U.S. states.[28] Siemens, a German company, makes power-plant turbines in North Carolina.[29] In addition, in 2015, the United States added roughly as many jobs due to foreign investment and U.S. companies returning from offshore as it lost to offshoring.[30]

5. Knowledge, Not Information, Is Becoming the New Competitive Advantage "Information is rapidly becoming a profitless commodity, and knowledge is becoming the new competitive advantage," says San Diego management consultant Karl Albrecht.[31]

That is, as information technology does more of the work formerly done by humans, even in high-tech areas (such as sorting data for relevance), many low-level employees previously thought of as knowledge workers are now being recognized as "data workers," who contribute very little added value to the processing of information. Unlike routine information handling, knowledge work is analytic and consists of problem solving and abstract reasoning—exactly the kind of task required of skillful managers, professionals, salespeople, and financial analysts. The rise of knowledge workers is accelerating despite the threat of automation, and indeed the number of people in knowledge-work jobs—nonroutine cognitive occupations—has more than doubled in the last 30 years and shows no sign of slowing down.[32]

Example: Middle-skill jobs like bookkeeping, clerical work, and repetitive assembly-line work are rapidly being taken over by automation, according to MIT economist David Autor. But higher-paying knowledge-work jobs, which require creativity and problem solving—often aided by computers—have grown rapidly, as have lower-skilled jobs that are resistant to automation.[33] Says a manager in one digital strategy company, "Modern workers are aware that, while job-specific training may quickly become obsolete, an ability to learn new skills will be valuable in a market that proves capable of drastically overhauling itself each year."[34]

Like reactive and proactive change, thunderstorms sometimes form unexpectedly and other times are predicted in advance. Proactively avoiding a thunderstorm is more likely to reduce harm from a storm.
©Jason Weingart Photography

Two Types of Change: Reactive and Proactive

Most CEOs, general managers, and senior public-sector leaders agree that incremental changes are no longer sufficient in a world that is operating in fundamentally different ways. Life in general, they say, is becoming more complex, and the firms that are able to manage that complexity are the ones that will survive in the long term.[35] Clearly, we are all in for an interesting ride.

As a manager, you will typically have to deal with two types of change: *reactive* and *proactive*.

1. Reactive Change: Responding to Unanticipated Problems and Opportunities

When managers talk about "putting out fires," they are talking about **reactive change**, **making changes in response to problems or opportunities as they arise.**

In response to a 2018 mass shooting at Marjory Stoneman Douglas High School in Parkland, Florida, several national retailers–including Dicks Sporting Goods, Walmart, and Cabela–changed their policy on gun sales, either raising the age to purchase a gun in their stores or limiting the types of weapons or accessories they will sell. In announcing the changes, the stores specifically referred to the deaths of 17 people, most of them students, in the Florida shooting.[36] At least a dozen other companies, from banks and insurance and technology companies to airlines and car rental firms, announced they were ending discount programs and other benefits they had offered NRA members for years.[37]

EXAMPLE Reactive Change: The BP Gulf of Mexico Blowout

Crises can happen quickly and without warning, and many companies have shown they don't deal with them well, as happened with Toyota's and GM's slow reactions in recalling defective vehicles. But for oil giant BP (formerly British Petroleum), the crisis was catastrophic—both for itself and most certainly for the United States.[38]

Crisis in the Gulf of Mexico In April 2010, an explosion on the BP drilling platform Deepwater Horizon in the Gulf of Mexico led to sinking of the rig, the loss of 11 lives, and the largest oil spill ever to happen in U.S. waters. Oil wells have emergency shutoff valves called blowout preventers, which can be triggered from the rig. The Deepwater Horizon, which floated 5,000 feet above the ocean floor, was equipped with this device, which nearly always works when wells surge out of control. However, it failed to operate on the day of the Gulf accident.

And what the rig did not have was a *backup* shutoff switch, a remote-control device that carries an acoustic signal through the water that can be activated as a last resort. Such acoustic backup triggers, which cost about $500,000, are not mandated by U.S. regulators, but they also haven't been tested under real-world conditions because major offshore oil-well blowouts are so rare. (Even so, Norway and Brazil require them, and some major oil companies, such as Royal Dutch Shell, carry them even when not mandated.)

BP Reacts As 2.5 million gallons of oil a day leaked from the open wellhead, the question was asked: Why wasn't BP prepared for such an accident? Eventually, the company capped the leak, but in the aftermath, BP pled guilty to federal felony charges and environmental law violations and was forced to sell almost $40 billion in assets to meet its liabilities, a move that cut its number of wells and platforms in half.[39] In the six years following, BP tried to settle with thousands of Gulf victims—from shrimpers to hotel owners—and deal with many dubious claims of businesses hundreds of miles from the Gulf, including a Florida escort service.[40] In 2016, a federal judge approved a $20 billion settlement to end the years of litigation.[41] In January 2018, the company announced that its 2017 compensation payments for the disaster would be $1.7 billion higher than anticipated, raising the total to about $65 billion.[42] In addition to the economic damage to the area, more than 1,400 dolphins and 1 million birds were killed in the disaster, while other effects on marine life in deeper waters are proving more difficult to measure.[43]

YOUR CALL

The BP blowout happened 21 years after the tanker Exxon *Valdez*'s catastrophic 1989 oil spill in the Gulf of Alaska, the effects of which are still being felt. Wasn't that enough time for oil companies to plan for major accidents? Why do you think BP was not more proactive in preparing for such events?

2. Proactive Change: Managing Anticipated Problems and Opportunities

In contrast to reactive change, **proactive change**, **or planned change, involves making carefully thought-out changes in anticipation of possible or expected problems or opportunities.**[44] In an interview with *Inc.* magazine, Brian Harper, CEO of a major mall developer, suggested that despite some publicized closings around the country, malls aren't dying out but rather are changing along with their customers in a fast-moving retail environment. Four strategies he says can help companies get ahead of change are to offer an outstanding customer experience, listen to customers to understand what they want and tailor the product or service to them, "know the difference between change and crisis," and embrace change instead of running from it.[45]

As we've stated, change can be hard, and the tools for survival are the career readiness competencies of personal adaptability and openness to change. We also know that organizations like to hire people who are adaptable and willing to accept change. How well do you think you fare in this regard? You can find out by taking Self-Assessment 10.1.

SELF-ASSESSMENT 10.1 CAREER READINESS

Assessing Your Openness to Change at Work

The following survey was designed to assess your attitudes toward change at work. Please be prepared to answer these questions if your instructor has assigned Self-Assessment 10.1 in Connect.

1. Where do you stand when it comes to your attitude toward change? Are you surprised by the results?
2. Based on your three lowest scoring survey items, how might you foster a more positive attitude toward change? Be specific.
3. What things might you say during an interview to demonstrate that you possess the career readiness competency of openness to change?

The Forces for Change Outside and Inside the Organization

How do managers know when their organizations need to change? The answers aren't clear-cut, but you can get clues by monitoring the forces for change—both outside and inside the organization. *(See Figure 10.1.)*

FIGURE 10.1

Forces for change outside and inside the organization

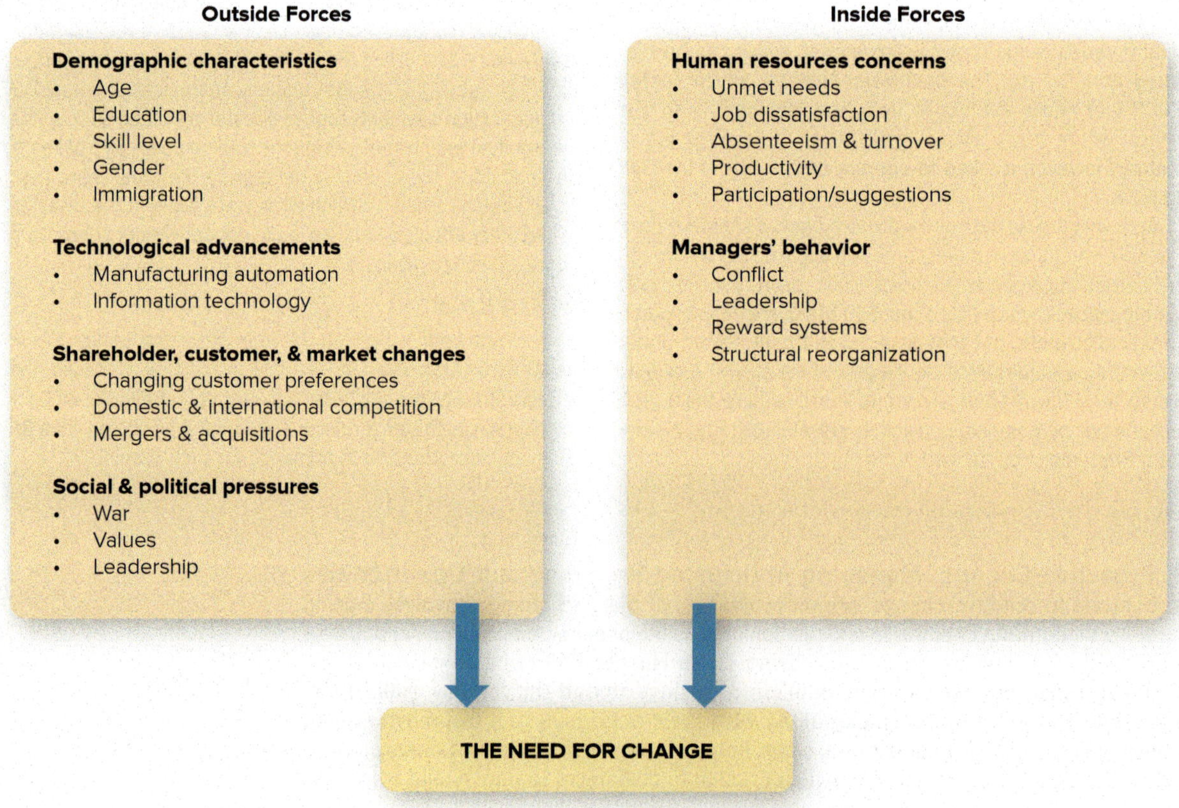

Forces Originating Outside the Organization External forces consist of four types, as follows.

1. Demographic Characteristics Earlier we discussed the demographic changes occurring among U.S. workers, with the labor force becoming more diverse. Example: For the first time since 1880, Americans ages 18 to 34 (Millennials) are more likely to be living with their parent(s) than in a household shared with a spouse or partner.[46] How might this affect their spending habits?

2. Technological Advancements **Technology is not just computer technology; it is any machine or process that enables an organization to gain a competitive advantage in changing materials used to produce a finished product.**

"We stand on the brink of a technological revolution that will fundamentally alter the way we live, work, and relate to one another," writes Klaus Schwab, executive chairman of the World Economic Forum. "In its scale, scope, and complexity, the transformation will be unlike anything humankind has experienced before."[47] This is the Fourth Industrial Revolution, characterized by "a fusion of technologies that is blurring the lines between the physical, digital, and biological spheres."

Example: GM's CEO Mary Barra told *The Wall Street Journal* that "In my 37 years at General Motors, the amount of technology is changing more than ever." In an attempt to develop fully electric vehicles that drive themselves, she further noted that "We've made cultural changes, we've changed where we do business, we're developing transformative technologies."[48]

EXAMPLE

From Ride Sharing to Self-driving Cars: Uber, Lyft, and the Upending of Transportation

"We think there's going to be more change in the world of mobility in the next five years than there has been in the last 50," says General Motors president Dan Ammann. The occasion was the announcement of GM's $500-million investment in Lyft, the ride-sharing service.[49]

Transportation Network Companies Just as technology has allowed the lodging-sharing service Airbnb (discussed in Chapter 1) to take business from hotels, so smartphones and apps have enabled on-demand "transportation network companies" (TNCs) such as Uber and Lyft to challenge the traditional taxi cab industry—and to threaten other transportation networks including municipal buses and subways. In cities around the world, these ride-sharing apps let people secure a ride on demand from a driver using his or her personal car. In some locations, however, such as London, Uber has been banned due to strong resistance from taxi drivers.[50]

Self-Driving Cars Many companies have invested in self-driving cars, from Tesla to Toyota, Ford, Fiat, Google (through its subsidiary Waymo), and Apple.[51] Even Uber joined the companies pouring billions of dollars into self-driving technology. But the March 2018 death of an Arizona pedestrian during the test-drive of an autonomous car, operating with a human backup driver and under perfect driving conditions, put Uber's program on hold and threw the future of self-driving cars into doubt.[52] In the wake of the accident, Arizona's governor suspended further testing by Uber in the state.[53] Critics point out not only that autonomous cars are imperfect navigators and slow to react, but also that they are vulnerable to hackers and perhaps, in the end, unnecessary.[54] Others call for a thorough rethinking not just of self-driving technology, but also of transportation policy and regulation.[55]

YOUR CALL

"This tragic incident makes clear that autonomous vehicle technology has a long way to go before it is truly safe for the passengers, pedestrians, and drivers who share America's roads," said Connecticut Senator Richard Blumenthal in a statement about the Arizona fatality. "In our haste to enable innovation, we cannot forget basic safety."[56] How safe do self-driving cars have to be before they can be deployed on the road? How would their use affect public transportation? The insurance industry?

3. Shareholder, Customer, and Market Changes Shareholders have begun to be more active in pressing for organizational change. Example: Some shareholders may form a **B corporation, or *benefit corporation*, in which the company is legally required to adhere to socially beneficial practices,** such as helping consumers, employees, or the environment. Among the leading B Corps in the United States are Patagonia, Eileen Fisher, Warby Parker, Reformation, Seventh Generation, and New Belgium Brewing.[57]

Customers are also becoming more demanding, being more inclined to take their business elsewhere if they do not get what they want from a given company.

Example: Millennials have been found to be more focused on app-based shopping options, like those offered by Starbucks, where many customers can preorder their beverages through their phones before picking them up. Millennials also prefer specialty stores to department stores, so stores like Macy's have been trying out "stores within a store."[58]

The global economy continues to influence the way U.S. companies have to do business.[59] Perhaps the most momentous recent example occurred in June 2016, when voters in the United Kingdom voted for a British exit ("Brexit") from the European Union, setting off shockwaves around the world and causing stock markets to fall off a cliff. Among the long-term results that may still be possible are trade restrictions from Europe that are harmful to Britain, a UK recession, the separation of Scotland and Northern Ireland from the UK, and efforts by other countries to leave the EU.[60]

4. Social and Political Pressures Social events can create great pressures.

Example: Poor diet choices, such as reliance on sugary sodas, have led to more than one in three U.S. adults and one in six children from ages 2 to 19 being obese, which in turn has contributed to an epidemic of type 2 diabetes.[61] Several big U.S. cities, including Philadelphia, Boulder, San Francisco, Seattle, and Berkeley, have already passed special taxes on soda, often against well-funded opposition from soda companies.[62] Many are watching the UK with interest. Its new two-tier soda tax, unlike others that are designed to raise revenue or discourage the purchase of soda, seems to actually be encouraging soda makers to reduce the sugar content of their products to avoid the tax.[63]

Forces Originating Inside the Organization

Internal forces affecting organizations may be subtle, such as low job satisfaction, or more dramatic, such as constant labor-management conflict. Internal forces may be of the two following types: *human resources concerns* and *managers' behavior.*

1. Human Resources Concerns Is there a gap between the employees' needs and desires and the organization's needs and desires? Job dissatisfaction–as expressed through high absenteeism and turnover–can be a major signal of the need for change. Organizations may respond by addressing job design, reducing employees' role conflicts, and dealing with work overload, to mention a few matters.

Example: After Foxconn's manufacturing facilities in China experienced some employee suicides attributed to unduly stressful working conditions, other Chinese companies like Pegatron implemented HR policies and practices to reduce employee hours and overtime. Pegatron, which operates an iPhone assembly facility outside Shanghai, requires employees to scan ID cards, use face scanners, and walk through turnstiles in order to monitor compliance with new overtime regulations.[64]

2. Managers' Behavior Excessive conflict between managers and employees or between a company and its customers is another indicator that change is needed. Perhaps there is a personality conflict, so that an employee transfer may be needed. Or perhaps some interpersonal training is required.

Example: Facebook's leadership decided to respond to tech blog Gizmodo's conclusion that "curators of Facebook's 'trending topics' feature suppressed news about conservative events and from conservative sources," according to *The Wall Street Journal.* The company is now training employees "to identify and check their political leanings."[65]

10.2 Types and Models of Change

THE BIG PICTURE

This section discusses the three types of change, from least threatening to most threatening: adaptive, innovative, and radically innovative. It also describes Lewin's three-stage change model: unfreezing, changing, and refreezing. Finally, it describes the systems approach to change: inputs, target elements of change, and outputs.

LO 10-2

Discuss three types of change, Lewin's change model, and the systems approach to change.

As we mentioned in Section 10.1, change may be forced upon an organization–reactive change, requiring you to make adjustments in response to problems or opportunities as they arise. This is exactly what happened to the U.S. Senate during the process to confirm Judge Kavanaugh to the Supreme Court in 2018. Or an organization may try to get out in front of changes–proactive change, or planned change, which involves making carefully thought-out changes in anticipation of possible problems or opportunities.

As a manager, particularly one working for an American organization, you may be pressured to provide short-term, quick-fix solutions. But when applied to organizational problems, this approach usually doesn't work: Quick-fix solutions have little staying power.

What, then, do we need to understand in order to effectively manage organizational change? In this section, we discuss the following:

- Three kinds of change.
- Lewin's change model.
- The systems approach to change.

Three Kinds of Change: From Least Threatening to Most Threatening

Whether organizational change is administrative or technological, it can be *adaptive*, *innovative*, or *radically innovative*, depending on (1) the degree of complexity, cost, and uncertainty and (2) its potential for generating employee resistance.[66]

Least Threatening: Adaptive Change—"We've Seen Stuff Like This Before"

Adaptive change is the reintroduction of a familiar practice–the implementation of a kind of change that has already been experienced within the same organization. This form of change is lowest in complexity, cost, and uncertainty. Because it is familiar, it is the least threatening to employees and thus will create the least resistance.

For example, during the annual Labor Day sale, a department store may ask its sales employees to work 12 hours a day instead of the usual 8. During tax-preparation time, the store's accounting department may imitate this same change in work hours. Although accounting employees are in a different department from sales employees, it's expected they wouldn't be terribly upset by the temporary change in hours because they've seen it in effect elsewhere in the store.

Somewhat Threatening: Innovative Change—"This Is Something New for This Company"

Innovative change is the introduction of a practice that is new to the organization. This form of change is characterized by moderate complexity, cost, and uncertainty. It is therefore apt to trigger some fear and resistance among employees.

For example, if a department store decides to adopt a new practice among its competitors by staying open 24 hours a day, requiring employees to work flexible schedules, it may be felt as moderately threatening.

Very Threatening: Radically Innovative Change—"This Is a Brand-New Thing in Our Industry"

Radically innovative change introduces a practice that is new to the industry. Because it is the most complex, costly, and uncertain, it will be felt as extremely threatening to managers' confidence and employees' job security and may well tear at the fabric of the organization.[67]

For example, Amazon is currently testing a new delivery system called Prime Air in Canada, the United Kingdom, and the Netherlands and recently ran its first U.S. test flight in California. The program uses drones to carry packages up to 5 pounds in 30 minutes or less. The goal, assuming regulatory approval that's still pending, is to safely operate the drones for a distance of 10 miles or more beyond the line of sight.[68]

Imagine the implications of companies using drones to distribute products.

Lewin's Change Model: Unfreezing, Changing, and Refreezing

Most theories of organizational change originated with the landmark work of social psychologist **Kurt Lewin**. Lewin developed a model with three stages–*unfreezing*, *changing*, and *refreezing*–to explain how to initiate, manage, and stabilize planned change.[69] *(See Figure 10.2.)*

FIGURE 10.2

Lewin's model of change

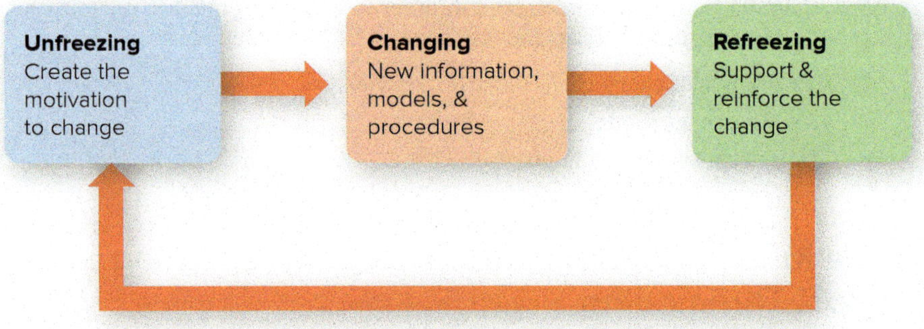

1. "Unfreezing": Creating the Motivation to Change

In the *unfreezing stage*, managers try to instill in employees the motivation to change, encouraging them to let go of attitudes and behaviors that are resistant to innovation. For this "unfreezing" to take place, employees need to become dissatisfied with the old way of doing things. Managers also need to reduce the barriers to change during this stage.

Example: Wireless handheld computers–personal digital assistants (PDAs)–are becoming established tools for health professionals, who use them to access patient records in hospital information systems. How well have they been accepted? Studies exploring nurses' perceptions about using PDAs in their daily patient practice found initial resistance, with some nurses concerned about the cost and short technological life cycle of these devices–the *unfreezing* stage.[70]

2. "Changing": Learning New Ways of Doing Things

In the *changing stage*, employees need to be given the tools for change: new information, new perspectives, new models of behavior. Managers can help here by providing benchmarking results, role models, mentors, experts, and training. Change is more likely to be accepted if employees possess the career readiness competencies of proactive learning orientation and openness to change.[71]

Example: In the *changing* stage, nurses learning PDAs were allowed to continue their manual patient-charting systems while learning the PDA-accessible versions, but only for a limited time to avoid adding to their already heavy workloads. They were assisted with educational programs to help them learn and implement the new technology, programs that also stressed the need to protect confidential patient records.

3. "Refreezing": Making the New Ways Normal In the *refreezing stage*, employees need to be helped to integrate the changed attitudes and behavior into their normal ways of doing things. Managers can assist by encouraging employees to exhibit the new change and then, through additional coaching and modeling, by reinforcing the employees in the desired change, as we'll discuss in Section 10.5.

Example: In the *refreezing* stage, as hospitals eliminated barriers that precluded the use of wireless networks, nurses learned to appreciate the usefulness of having a widely pervasive and portable technology, with its easier access to drug and diagnostic/laboratory reference applications and improved communications.

Eugene Lee describes how his employer in the aerospace/defense industry used Lewin's model to implement change in the "I'm glad . . ." feature.

I'm Glad...

...my company unfroze employees before implementing organizational change.

Eugene Lee is a supplier manager in the aerospace/defense industry. His company makes complex components for missiles and rockets, which can take up to two or three years per project to complete. The company underwent organizational change when a new division supply chain vice president was hired.

The new divisional vice president wanted to implement a more metrics-driven approach. He decided to unfreeze the organization by conducting an "all hands" meeting to set the tone. During his presentation to about 500 employees, he showed slides that explained all the company's relevant metrics and how they tied together with all departments and functions, like engineering, finance, and contracts. He explained the impact of early and late delivery dates, contract placement times, and pricing trends.

"This sounds like a really obvious thing, but we didn't actually have specific measurable targets before. What the new vice president did at this 'all hands' meeting was set the tone on how he would use this to advocate for our group and, essentially, make the other functions more accountable," said Eugene.

Accountability is important when collaboration across departments is needed to implement change. "When we have an issue, it's not strictly a supply chain issue. It's a program management issue. We might have had a design flaw from engineering that caused us to have to go back and rework materials. Or we might have had financing problems where we couldn't agree to certain terms with the supplier, and that caused a delay," said Eugene. "By focusing on metrics, we saw change in how we advocated our work, and we made other functions more accountable."

Another change entailed the introduction of ISTs, or integrated supplier teams. Eugene explained that, even for the same function, different managers didn't always communicate. "As an example, let's say this is a car company, and I happen to be the manager for tires. I buy tires for one car model, while the person next to me buys tires for another model. Even though we're both buying the same brand of tires, we don't communicate and don't understand the tire company's problems because we're devoted to our own product lines," he said.

The ISTs helped bridge communication gaps between functions. "We're going around cross-interviewing these ISTs and observing best practices and getting feedback from one another on how we should be operating. That gives us better collective bargaining advantage. It's almost like having mini consulting groups. It seems to be working well," said Eugene. "It's difficult to measure, but it created a viable best practices environment. I really appreciated this from the new leadership at the vice president level."

The company realized positive results within the first six months of the change. While there was some natural resistance to change, it was subtle. "I think a lot of people were on board to begin with because it gave us a common voice," said Eugene.

Courtesy Eugene Lee

Courtesy of Eugene Lee

A Systems Approach to Change

Change creates additional change–that's the lesson of systems theory. Promoting someone from one group to another, for instance, may change the employee interactions in both (as from cordial to argumentative, or the reverse). Adopting a team-based structure may require changing the compensation system to pay bonuses based on team rather than individual performance. A *systems approach* to change presupposes that any change, no matter how small, has a rippling effect throughout an organization.

A *system*, you'll recall from Chapter 2, is a set of interrelated parts that operate together to achieve a common purpose. The systems approach can be used to diagnose what to change and determine the success of the change effort.

The systems model of change consists of three parts: (1) *inputs*, (2) *target elements of change*, and (3) *outputs*. *(See Figure 10.3.)*

FIGURE 10.3

Systems model of change

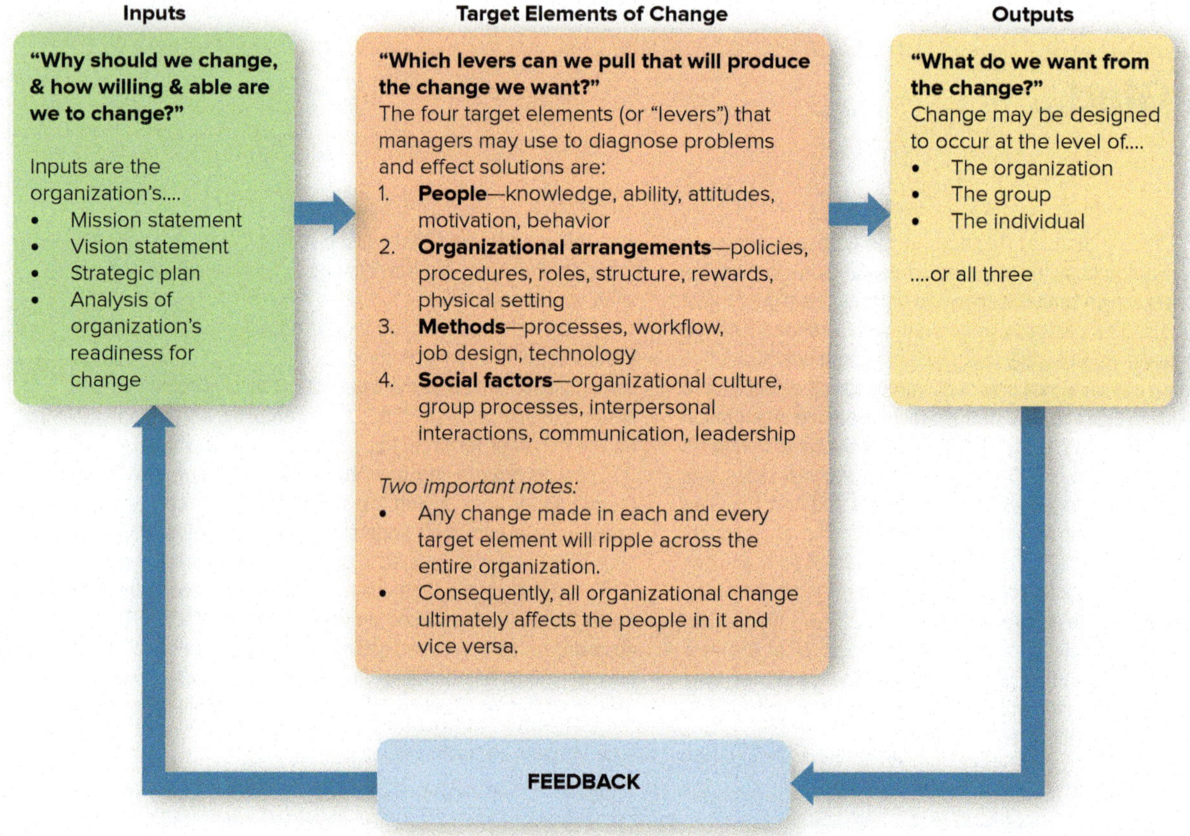

Source: Based on A. Kinicki and M. Fugate, Organizational Behavior: A Practical, Problem-Solving Approach *(New York: McGraw-Hill Education, 2016), Figure 16.4, p. 567, which was adapted from D. R. Fuqua and D. J. Kurpius, "Conceptual Models in Organizational Consultation,"* Journal of Counseling and Development, *July–August 1993, pp. 602–618; D. A. Nadler and M. L. Tushman, "Organizational Frame Bending: Principles for Managing Reorientation,"* Academy of Management Executive, *August 1989, pp. 194–203.*

Inputs: "Why Should We Change, and How Willing and Able Are We to Change?" "Why change?" A systems approach always begins with the question of why change is needed at all–what the problem is that needs to be solved. (Example: "Why change? Because our designers are giving us terrible products that we can't sell.")

Whatever the answer, the systems approach must make sure the desired changes align with the organization's *mission statement*, *vision statement*, and *strategic plan*–subjects we discussed in Chapter 5.[72]

A second question is "How willing and able are management and employees to make the necessary change?" **Readiness for change** **is defined as the beliefs, attitudes, and intentions of the organization's staff regarding the extent of the changes needed and how willing and able they are to implement them.**[73] Readiness has four components: (1) how strongly the company needs the proposed change, (2) how much the top managers support the change, (3) how capable employees are of handling it, and (4) how pessimistic or optimistic employees are about the consequences of the result.

Self-Assessment 10.2 will help you gauge your readiness for change. You can also use it to measure the readiness of an organization to which you belong.

SELF-ASSESSMENT 10.2 CAREER READINESS

What Is Your Readiness for Change?

If your instructor has assigned Self-Assessment 10.2 in Connect, think of a change at school, work, or another area of your life. Take Self-Assessment 10.2 to learn the extent of your readiness for change, or that of the organization in which the change needs to occur.

1. Of the four components, which is the lowest?
2. How do you think this result will affect the success of the particular change? Be specific.
3. Who seems to be most ready, you (components 1 and 2) or the organization (components 3 and 4)?
4. What things might you say during an interview to demonstrate that you possess the career readiness competency of personal adaptability?

Target Elements of Change: "Which Levers Can We Pull That Will Produce the Change We Want?" The target elements of change represent four levers that managers may use to diagnose problems (such as "Our designers are too inbred and don't look outside the company for ideas") and identify solutions (such as "We need new managers and new blood in the Design Group").

As Figure 10.3 shows, the four target elements of change (the four levers) are

1. People–their knowledge, ability, attitudes, motivation, and behavior.
2. Organizational arrangements–such as policies and procedures, roles, structure, rewards, and physical setting.
3. Methods–processes, work flow, job design, and technology.
4. Social factors–culture, group processes, interpersonal interactions, communication, and leadership.

Two things are important to realize:

- **Any change made in each and every target element will ripple across the entire organization.** For example, if a manager changes a system of *rewards* (part of the organizational arrangements) to reinforce team rather than individual performance, that change is apt to affect *organizational culture* (one of the social factors).
- **All organizational change ultimately affects the people in it and vice versa.** Thus, organizational change is more likely to succeed when managers carefully consider the prospective impact of a proposed change on the employees.

Outputs: "What Results Do We Want from the Change?" Outputs represent the desired goals of a change, which should be consistent with the organization's strategic plan. Results may occur at the organizational, group, or individual level (or all three) but will be most difficult to effect at the organizational level because changes will mostly likely affect a wide variety of target elements.

Feedback: "How Is the Change Working and What Alterations Need to Be Made?" Not all changes work out well, of course, and organizations need to monitor their success. This is done by comparing the status of an output such as employee or customer satisfaction before the change to the same measurable output sometime after the change has been implemented.

Force-Field Analysis: "Which Forces Facilitate Change and Which Resist It?" In most change situations being considered, there are forces acting for and against the change. **Force-field analysis** is a technique to determine which forces could facilitate a

proposed change and which forces could act against it. The first step is to identify the positive forces (called *thrusters*) and the negative forces (called *counterthrusters*). The second step is to remove the negative forces and then, if necessary, increase the positive forces. Although this may sound simple, it can be tricky to identify the forces at work.

Example: Procter & Gamble (P&G), maker of such household staples as Tide, Crest, and Gillette, recently reported that sales abroad were shrinking. Among the negative forces were the following: In countries overseas, the company had too many unprofitable products; smaller, nimbler rivals were taking away business; and currency fluctuations had made pricing difficult. Among the positive forces were these: P&G had extensive market data about customer needs, a strong enough financial position that it could forgo revenue in the short term, and an experienced management team that was ready to change. By exiting nearly 100 brands, narrowing its focus to 65 core brands, and forgoing sales in the short run, P&G could improve its profitability later. Thus, for example, in Mexico, the company shifted from selling cheap tissues to higher-priced variations, a move that cut sales but made the business more profitable.[74]

This Stora Enso paper plant in Eilenburg, Germany benefited from the strategic changes associated with using the systems model of change. What do you think is the most difficult aspect of applying this model at work? ©dpa picture alliance archive/Alamy Stock photo

Applying the Systems Model of Change

There are two different ways to apply the systems model of change. The first is as an aid during the strategic planning process. Once a group of managers identifies the organization's vision and strategic goals, group members can consider the target elements of change when developing action plans to support the accomplishment of goals. For example, Stora Enso, a pulp and paper manufacturer in Helsinki, Finland, was experiencing tremendous pressure to change due to reduced demand for paper and digitization. After seeking feedback from employees within different divisions and organizational layers (a social factor), the company decided to change its vision and goals (inputs). Management concluded that its "greatest opportunity lay in shifting the whole axis of the business to specialize in offerings made with renewable and bio-based materials."

To find growth opportunities, the company established a "Pathfinders" leadership team, which consisted of a dozen managers (organizational arrangement). This team was charged with identifying "sustainability opportunities that were falling between silos and, more broadly, to challenge the old ways of doing business" (people and social factors). Given the Pathfinders' success in creating organizational change, Stora Enso decided to replace them with 16 new members every year (people and method factors). The Pathfinders program became a vehicle to bring new perspectives into strategic decision making and morphed into "a program for identifying and developing change agents within the organization who would then serve as internal management consultants" (people, method, and social factors), according to the *Harvard Business Review*.[75]

The second application of the systems model uses it as a diagnostic framework to identify the causes of an organizational problem and propose solutions. We highlight this application by considering a consulting project conducted by your author, Angelo Kinicki. He was contacted by the CEO of a software company and asked to figure out why the presidents of three divisions were not collaborating with each other—the problem. It seemed two of the presidents had submitted the same proposal for a $4 million project to a potential customer. The software company did not get the work because the customer was appalled at having received two proposals from the same firm. Kinicki decided to interview employees by using a structured set of questions that pertained to each of the target elements of change. The interviews revealed that the lack of collaboration among division presidents was due to the reward system (an organizational arrangement), a competitive culture and poor communications (social factors), and poor work flow (a methods factor). Kinicki's recommendation was to change the reward system, restructure the organization, and redesign the work flow.

10.3 Organizational Development: What It Is, What It Can Do

THE BIG PICTURE

Organizational development (OD) is a set of techniques for implementing change, such as managing conflict, revitalizing organizations, and adapting to mergers. OD has three steps: diagnosis, intervention, and evaluation. Four factors have been found to make OD programs effective.

LO 10-3

Describe the purpose of organizational development.

Organizational development (OD) is a set of techniques for implementing planned change to make people and organizations more effective. Note the inclusion of people in this definition. OD focuses specifically on people in the change process. (Some scholars apply the term "organizational development" to techniques designed to improve *organizational* effectiveness and the term "change management" to techniques designed to improve *people* effectiveness–techniques that will help them, in one definition, to adopt "new mindsets, policies, practices, and behaviors to deliver organizational results.")[76]

Often OD is put into practice by a person known as a **change agent, a consultant with a background in behavioral sciences who can be a catalyst in helping organizations deal with old problems in new ways.** Other organizations actually employ organizational development specialists who help the company to lead and manage change.

What Can OD Be Used For?

OD can be used to address the following three matters.

1. Managing Conflict Conflict is inherent in most organizations. Sometimes an OD expert, perhaps in the guise of an executive coach, can help advise on how to improve relationships within the organization.

Example: Difficult co-workers can damage others' job performance and hurt a company's bottom line. Such "de-energizers" spread a dark cloud over everyone and leave you feeling deflated and depleted, says business professor Gretchen Spreitzer, who has done research in this area.[77] An organizational behavior specialist might be brought in to help buffer workers from the de-energizers by showing them how to limit interactions, make sure their own work is meaningful, and increase the time they spend with people who make them feel good, among other activities.

2. Revitalizing Organizations Information technology is wreaking such change that nearly all organizations these days are placed in the position of having to adopt new behaviors in order to resist decline. OD can help by opening communication, fostering innovation, and dealing with stress.

Example: For IBM, confronting the relentless advance of digital technology means confronting the question "Can you grow in the new businesses faster than your older, lucrative businesses decline?" The company is responding by hiring thousands of designers to challenge IBM's conventional thinking (such as coming up with a product idea and trying to sell it to customers) with new thinking (such as identifying users' needs as a starting point).[78]

3. Adapting to Mergers Mergers and acquisitions are associated with increased anxiety, stress, absenteeism, turnover, and decreased productivity.[79] Imagine how Whole Foods employees must have felt when the company was purchased for $13.7 billion by Amazon in 2017.[80] OD experts are often called upon in such situations to help integrate two firms with varying cultures, products, and procedures.

How OD Works

Like physicians, OD managers and consultants follow a medical-like model. (Or to use our more current formulation, they follow the rules of evidence-based management.) They approach the organization as if it were a sick patient, using *diagnosis, intervention,* and *evaluation*—"diagnosing" its ills, "prescribing" treatment or intervention, and "monitoring" or evaluating progress. If the evaluation shows that the procedure is not working effectively, the conclusions drawn are then applied (via a feedback loop) to refining the diagnosis, and the process starts again. *(See Figure 10.4.)*

FIGURE 10.4

The OD process

Sources: Adapted from W.L. French and C.H. Bell Jr., Organization Development: Behavioral Interventions for Organizational Improvement *(Englewood Cliffs, NJ: Prentice Hall. 1978); E. G Huse and T. G. Cummings,* Organizational Development and Change, *3rd ed. (St. Paul: West, 1985).*

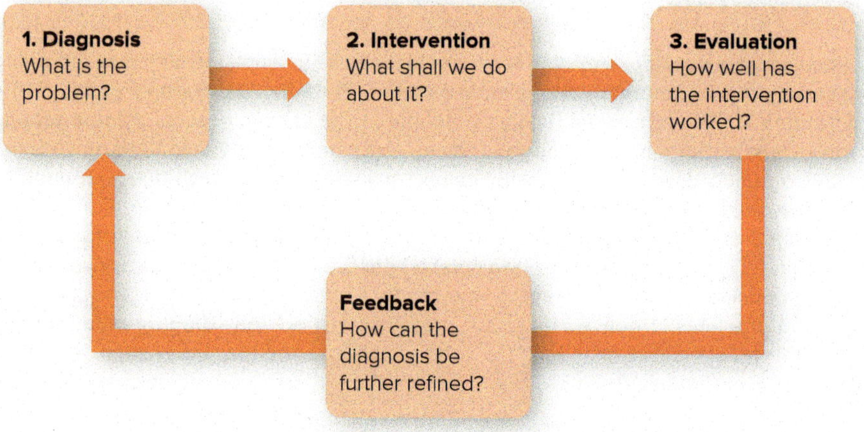

1. Diagnosis: What Is the Problem? To carry out the diagnosis, OD consultants or managers use some combination of questionnaires, surveys, interviews, meetings, records, and direct observation to ascertain people's attitudes and to identify problem areas. A problem is defined as a gap between an outcome or result desired by managers and the actual status of the outcome or result. For example, if your goal was to lose 10 pounds over 6 months and you only lost five, your problem is to lose five more pounds.

2. Intervention: What Shall We Do about It? "Treatment," or **intervention, is the attempt to correct the diagnosed problems.** Often this is done using the services of an OD consultant who works in conjunction with management teams. Some OD activities for implementing planned change are communicating survey results to employees to engage them in constructive problem solving, observing employee communication patterns and teaching them skills to improve them, helping group members learn to function as a team, stimulating better cohesiveness among several work groups, and improving work technology or organizational design. Coaching is often employed to improve interpersonal relationships and leadership. AT&T, for example, uses four different types of coaching: one-on-one coaching for executives, group coaching for second-level managers, one-on-one coaching for newly hired or promoted employees, and coaching based on 360-degree feedback for all employees.[81]

3. Evaluation: How Well Has the Intervention Worked? An OD program needs objective evaluation to see if it has done any good. Answers may lie in hard data about absenteeism, turnover, grievances, and profitability, which should be compared with earlier statistics. The change agent can use questionnaires, surveys, interviews, and the like to assess changes in employee attitudes.

4. Feedback: How Can the Diagnosis and Intervention Be Further Refined? If evaluation shows that the diagnosis was wrong or the intervention was not effective, the OD consultant or managers need to return to the beginning to rethink these two steps.

EXAMPLE Organizational Development: Using OD to Make Money in the Restaurant Business

If you own or manage a restaurant, how can you improve your chances of success? You could hire a change agent such as Eli Chait, who cofounded San Francisco–based Copilot Labs, a restaurant marketing analytics company that is now part of OpenTable.[82]

Diagnosis: "What Is the Problem?" Organizational development is often focused on "big wins" (such as merging two companies), but it can also be used in a small business like a restaurant where small or incremental wins are important. Thus, an owner might want to know "Which is more effective—promoting our happy hours or promoting our daily deals?"

Intervention: "What Shall We Do about It?" Analyzing sales data over 19 months for one restaurant, Copilot found that, in Chait's words, "happy hour contributes specifically to the hours of the day that are otherwise the slowest, driving critical off-peak [customer] traffic that is so important to restaurants. The deal traffic, however, is distributed across several periods of time, many of which are already busy," making it less effective.[83]

Evaluation: "How Well Has the Intervention Worked?" The outcome would seem to be foreshadowed by Copilot's research, but it would be up to the change agent to evaluate an activity's success when put into practice. There are all kinds of factors, after all, that can affect restaurant traffic. For instance, more data don't always translate into better customer service.[84] Some days are busier than others (Valentine's Day—busy; Super Bowl Sunday—not busy; Mother's Day—depends on the restaurant), when a promotion wouldn't be effective.[85]

Feedback: "How Can the Diagnosis and Intervention Be Further Refined?" Depending on the results of evaluation—namely, the profitability of the process according to the kind of promotions—the change agent might feel the diagnosis and intervention deserve a revisit. And the process would start over.

YOUR CALL

Do you think universities could do a better job educating students? How might the OD process be used to improve your educational experience?

The Effectiveness of OD

Among organizations that have practiced organizational development are American Airlines, B.F. Goodrich, General Electric, Honeywell, ITT, Procter & Gamble, Prudential, Texas Instruments, and Westinghouse Canada–companies covering a variety of industries.

Research has found that OD is most apt to be successful under the following circumstances.

1. Multiple Interventions OD success stories tend to use multiple interventions. Goal setting, feedback, recognition and rewards, training, participation, and challenging job design have had good results in improving performance and satisfaction.[86] Combined interventions have been found to work better than single interventions.[87]

2. Management Support OD is more likely to succeed when top managers give the OD program their support and are truly committed to the change process and the desired goals of the change program.[88] Using employee feedback during the change process is one way to demonstrate this support.[89]

3. Goals Geared to Both Short-and Long-Term Results Change programs are more successful when they are oriented toward achieving both short-term and long-term results. Managers should not engage in organizational change for the sake of change. Change efforts should produce positive results.[90]

4. OD Is Affected by Culture OD effectiveness is affected by cross-cultural considerations. Thus, an OD intervention that worked in one country should not be blindly applied to a similar situation in another country.[91] •

OD frequently focuses on improving work relationships among a team. Fostering happiness among team members like this requires effective managerial skills. Team work is discussed in Chapter 13. ©Image Source/Glow Images

10.4 Organizational Innovation

THE BIGGER PICTURE

Managers agree that the ability to innovate affects long-term success, and you will undoubtedly be asked to help your employer achieve this. This section provides insights into the ways organizations approach the goal of innovation. After discussing approaches toward innovation pursued by companies, we review the need to create an innovation system and summarize the influence of office design on innovation and performance.

LO 10-4

Describe the approaches toward innovation and components of an innovation system.

We live in a time of technological advancement that is creating transformative changes in the way we live, work, and play. Organizations are feeling both the opportunity and the pinch of this reality. Consider the situation faced by executives at Gap. Sales at the global retailer have slumped, and the company has too many stores. An industry expert further concluded, "Every retailer is competing for a shrinking pool of customers who lately spend more of their money on meals or services, such as manicures and travel. Still, they demand greater value and discounts from their clothing purchases." Although the company's chief executive promised to innovate, *Bloomberg Businessweek* reported, "10 months later, the transformation has yet to materialize. Sales have continued to disappoint."[92]

Is Gap an anomaly or is the need to innovate widespread? It's widespread! Results from a recent survey of 500 leaders showed that about 94 percent viewed innovation as key to their company's success. Sadly, only 14 percent of these executives had confidence in their organization's ability to drive innovation.[93]

Innovation "is the creation of something new that makes money; it finds a pathway to the consumer."[94] This definition underscores that innovations must be both novel and useful. We now take a closer look at innovation and the way organizations foster it. You will learn that innovation is more likely to occur when organizations create and support a system of innovation, which includes tailoring the characteristics of the physical environment to support innovation.

Approaches to Innovation

We can classify innovations by crossing their type with their focus, producing four distinct types. *(See Figure 10.5.)*

The Type of Innovation

Managers often need to improve a product or service they offer in response to competition or customer feedback. This response often amounts

FIGURE 10.5

Approaches toward innovation

Type of Innovation	Focus of Innovation: Improvement	Focus of Innovation: New Directions
Product	**Apple iPhone** • Eleven generations/versions since first introduced in June 2007	**Driverless Cars** • Major automobile manufacturers and Waymo
Process	**3-D Printing** • Alcoa's use of 3-D printing in its manufacturing process	**Home Construction** • Panelized homes

to a technological innovation. Or managers may need to improve the process by which a product is made or a service is offered. This need typically leads to a process improvement.

More specifically, a **product innovation is a change in the appearance or functionality/performance of a product or a service or the creation of a new one.** Apple has made 11 generations of iPhones that each added new features or functionality, such as camera features, screen size, and Siri voice control system. Apple has sold more than 1 billion iPhones around the world though 2017; in the first quarter of 2018, it sold more than 77 million more.[95] PepsiCo's creation of Mountain Dew Kickstart is another example: higher juice content, fewer calories, new flavors. This new drink has generated over $200 million in two years.[96]

A process innovation is a change in the way a product or a service is conceived, manufactured, or distributed. Alcoa's use of 3D printing in its manufacturing process of jet engine components is a great example. *Fortune* contrasted Alcoa's old and new manufacturing processes: "In the past, Alcoa built a die using a process called subtractive machining. It's similar to sculpture: Start with a material–in this case, steel–then whittle it down into the shape you need. Ten to 30 weeks later, the company ended up with a custom die that it would then use to cast the needed engine part. Today Alcoa pairs computer-aided design, or CAD, with 3-D printing to construct the die from a computer file, layer by layer. A process that once took half a year could be completed in two to eight weeks, allowing the company to dramatically increase its output." The new process reduced manufacturing costs by 25 percent.[97]

A three-D printer. Three-D printing, also known as additive manufacturing, is used to create a three-dimensional object by having a computer control the successive layers of material that comprise an object. Some people believe that 3-D printing will create a third industrial revolution.
©cookelma/Getty Images

The Focus of the Innovation

The focus continuum measures the scope of the innovation.

Improvement innovations enhance or upgrade an existing product, service, or process. These types of innovations are often incremental and are less likely to generate significant amounts of new revenue at one point in time. Barrick Gold Corp, is a good example. The mining company is using "Silicon Valley monitoring technology to mine more gold at cheaper rates while reducing injuries and pollution." Executive Chairman John Thornton told *Bloomberg Businessweek* that "literally every single aspect of the business should change." The company has reduced the cost of digging at its Cortez mine from $190 a ton to $140 using these innovations.[98]

In contrast, **new-direction innovations take a totally new or different approach to a product, service, process, or industry.** These innovations focus on creating new markets and customers and rely on developing breakthroughs and inventing things that didn't already exist. *Seasteading*–the creation of floating cities–is an example. The idea of creating floating cities is being led by the Seasteading Institute, based in San Francisco. The Institute's president views seasteading as "an opportunity to rewrite the rules that govern society." The Institute is currently focused on a floating island in French Polynesia and has a goal of building 12 more by 2020.[99]

The housing industry has experienced a new-direction innovation that changes the process of constructing homes. The traditional way of building a home is called "stick-built." Architectural plans are given to a general contractor, who then hires subcontractors to build the home in phases, starting with pouring the foundation and framing the structure. The process is time consuming, filled with quality issues, and expensive. The new alternative is "panelized homes," in which all components of a house are prefabricated at a climate-controlled factory and then shipped to the building site for construction. The weather-tight shell usually can be assembled in a matter days.[100] An

Building a panelized home. Note the section of a home being raised so that it can be assembled with additional prefabricated walls. As you can imagine, homes can be built more quickly using this innovative method of construction. ©AContadini/Getty Images

industry study compared results of these two constructions processes for a 2,600-square-foot home and found that panelized homes "required 26 percent less lumber, wasted 76 percent less materials, and needed just over a third of the man-hours that would be used in a comparable stick-built house.[101]

An Innovation System: The Supporting Forces for Innovation

Innovation won't happen as a matter of course. It takes dedicated effort and resources, and the process must be nurtured and supported. Organizations do this best by developing an innovation system. An **innovation system** **is "a coherent set of interdependent processes and structures that dictates how the company searches for novel problems and solutions, synthesizes ideas into a business concept and product designs, and selects which projects get funded."**[102] Research and practice have identified seven components of an innovation system: innovation strategy; committed leadership; innovative culture and climate; required structure and processes; necessary human capital; human resource policies, practices, and procedures; and appropriate resources.[103] *(See Figure 10.6.)* These must be aligned and integrated for innovation to blossom, hence the dual-headed arrows in Figure 10.6.

Create an Innovation Strategy Many companies fail in their improvement efforts because they lack an innovation strategy.[104] An *innovation strategy*, which amounts to a plan for being more innovative, requires a company to integrate its innovation activities into its business strategies. This integration encourages management to invest resources in innovation and generates employee commitment to innovation across the organization.

FIGURE 10.6
Components of an innovation system

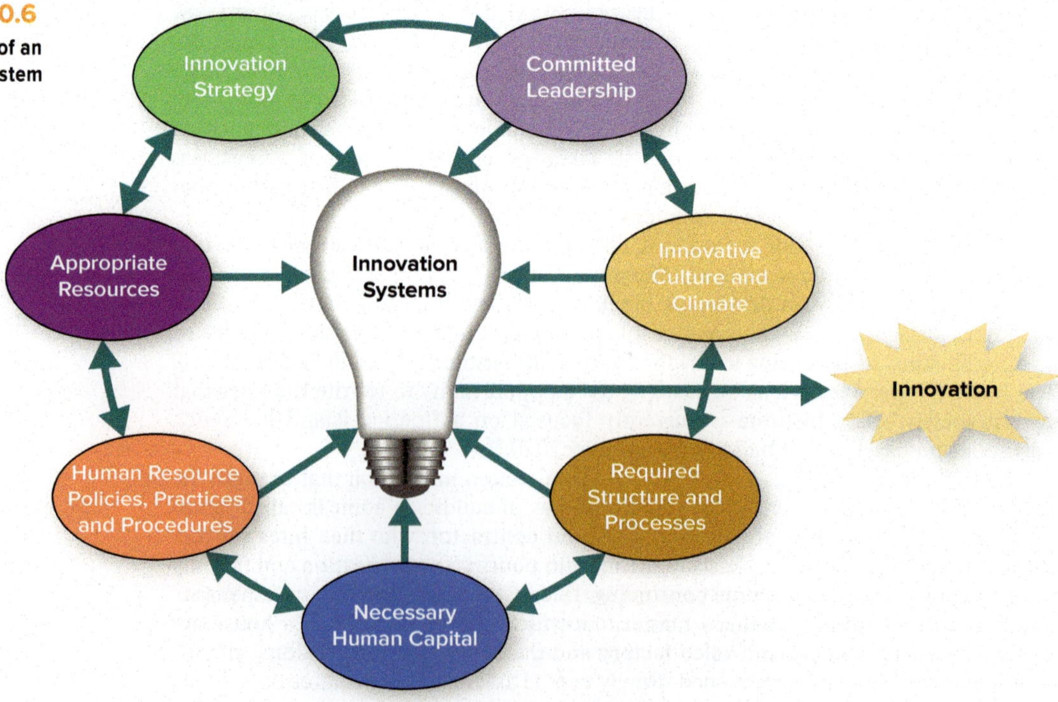

Corning is a diverse company that used its expertise in glassmaking to become a global manufacturer of specialty components needed for electronic displays, life sciences instruments, and telecommunications systems among others. According to a writer for the *Harvard Business Review*, "The company's business strategy focuses on selling 'keystone components' that significantly improve the performance of customers' complex system products. Executing this strategy requires Corning to be at the leading edge of glass and materials science so that it can solve exceptionally challenging problems for customers and discover new applications for its technologies. That requires heavy investments in long-term research.[105] The company spearheads these innovation efforts via a centralized R&D laboratory in upstate New York.

TABLE 10.1

The Most Innovative Companies

1. Apple
2. Netflix
3. Square
4. Tencent
5. Amazon
6. Patagonia
7. CVS Health
8. The Washington Post
9. Spotify
10. NBA
11. Marvel Studios
12. Instagram
13. Stitch Fix
14. SpaceX
15. Walmart

Source: "The World's 50 Most Innovative Companies 2018," Fast Company, https://www.fastcompany.com/most-innovative-companies/2018, accessed 3/27/18.

Commitment from Senior Leaders One of the biggest lessons we have learned from our consulting experience is that the achievement of strategic goals is unlikely without real commitment from senior leaders.[106] Former PepsiCo CEO Indra Nooyi knows this lesson well. She drove innovation by prioritizing design.

Nooyi hired Mauro Porcini from 3M to be PepsiCo's first chief design officer. Nooyi told an interviewer that Porcini "wanted resources, a design studio, and a seat at the table." She gave him all that. "Now our teams are pushing design through the entire system, from product creation, to packaging and labeling, to how a product looks on the shelf, to how consumers interact with it," she said.[107]

Foster an Innovative Culture and Climate A recent survey by the Boston Consulting Group identified risk-averse culture as the key obstacle to innovation.[108] Academic research also supports the conclusion that an innovative culture and climate are associated with the creation of new ideas and products.[109] These findings reflect the fact that innovation requires experimentation, failure, and risk taking, and these are all aspects of an organization'sculture.[110] Many senior leaders understand this link.

The legendary 3M Chairman William McKnight once said, "The best and hardest work is done in the spirit of adventure and challenge. . . . Mistakes will be made." Pixar President Ed Catmull has a similar viewpoint: "Mistakes aren't a necessary evil. They aren't evil at all. They are an inevitable consequence of doing something new . . . and should be seen as valuable."[111] See Table 10.1 for a list of *Fast Company* magazine's most innovative companies.

Have you worked for a company that has an innovative climate? Are you wondering what it takes to create such a climate? If yes, take the innovation climate Self-Assessment 10.3.

SELF-ASSESSMENT 10.3

How Innovative Is the Organizational Climate?

Please be prepared to answer these questions if your instructor has assigned Self-Assessment 10.3 in Connect.

1. What is the level of innovation? Are you surprised by the results? Explain.
2. Select the three lowest survey item scores. Use the content of these items to recommend what the company could do to become more innovative.

Required Structure and Processes Organizational structure and internal processes can promote innovation if they foster collaboration, cross-functional communication, and agility. Our earlier discussion of organizational design suggests that organic structures are better suited for innovation than mechanistic ones. For example, Juniper Networks, a leader in computer network integration, concluded that its "formal organizational structure was not conducive to the types of rich interactions and conversations required for innovation to thrive." Vince Molinaro, executive vice president of worldwide sales, commented, "We were not integrating diverse expertise and experience across engineering, infrastructure, and sales teams the way we could when we were a small company." Juniper changed its structure.[112]

The "I Wish . . ." feature illustrates what happened at Ashley Crow's employer when it failed to consider the processes associated with implementing an innovative idea.

I Wish...

...my company considered the components of an innovation system.

Ashley Crow is a supply chain project manager in the semiconductor manufacturing industry. The employees at her company have great ideas for ways to be innovative, but the ideas do not always come to fruition.

Courtesy Ashley Crow

One example of the company's struggle with innovation came when they tried to be proactive in staying ahead of government regulations. "Government regulations are changing all the time when it comes to what types of materials we can put into our products. There will be a new regulation coming out in a few years that puts a tighter limitation on what sorts of metals can go into our product," said Ashley.

In an attempt to be innovative and stay ahead of the competition, the managers decided to implement a change before the new mandate was official. "The company decided that, with this mandate coming down, we might as well make every single product free of any of the metals that would be restricted by the mandate. They decided they would do it today instead of waiting for the regulation to hit us. That way we already have the supply, we already have the manufacturing line, and we won't have to worry about it when this regulation hits," said Ashley.

While this seems like a great idea that could put the company out in front of the regulation and the competition, there were aspects of the process that were overlooked.

"The problem was that none of our suppliers actually had the capability to deliver that product. We asked for all of these brand new types of materials that do not exist in the marketplace. Our suppliers have not even developed them yet," said Ashley.

"But we went forward and put the order through the factory, and then the supplier came back to us and said they would be able to create it—in one year." This was an issue because Ashley's team had plans in place to create the new product line, but there was going to be a delay of up to a year to get the materials from the suppliers.

"They hadn't properly vetted the supplier or the supply prior to making the decision," said Ashley. While it is important to quickly harness creative ideas and innovate, the company needs to be realistic with their goals and expectations and carefully think through the implementation process.

Courtesy of Ashley Crow

Organizational processes are an organization's capabilities in management, internal processes, and technology that turn inputs into outcomes. Processes play a critical role in innovation. The design and consulting firm IDEO, for example, employs a unique process when it helps companies to innovate (see the Example box).

Crowdsourcing, defined as the practice of obtaining needed services, ideas, or content by soliciting contributions from a large group of people typically via the Internet, is being used by more companies to help innovate. For example, Anheuser-Busch used 25,000 online collaborators to help develop a golden-amber lager called Black Crown.[113] Richelieu Dennis, CEO of the cosmetics start-up Sundial Brands, calls customer input obtained through crowdsourcing "the most critical part of our marketing mix" and says it is responsible for the creation of one of the company's largest product lines.[114] To date, there has been limited research on the effectiveness of crowdsourcing. One recent study, however, showed that its use was positively associated with firm performance.[115]

EXAMPLE IDEO's Approach to Innovation

IDEO (pronounced "EYE-dee-oh") is a unique, award-winning, and highly respected and influential global design firm. It is responsible for such innovative products as the first mouse for Apple, heart defibrillators that walk a user through the steps, and TiVo's "thumbs up–thumbs down" button. An intense focus on end-user behavior is the foundation of all the company does and is embedded in the three steps of its design thinking. The steps are inspiration, ideation, and implementation.

- **Inspiration.** As defined by David Kelley, IDEO's legendary founder, inspiration is the problem or opportunity that motivates the search for solutions.
- **Ideation.** Ideation is the process of generating, developing, and testing ideas.
- **Implementation.** The final step, implementation, links the problem's solution to people's lives.

Observing user behavior and working with prototypes are important aspects of each step. They help IDEO's diverse problem-solving teams both define client problems and gauge the effectiveness of their solutions.

THINKING LIKE A DESIGNER

The company's consulting approach to products, services, processes, and strategy brings together what is desirable from a human point of view with what is technologically feasible and economically viable. It also allows people who are trained as designers to use creative tools to address a vast range of challenges. The goal: to tap into abilities we all have that are overlooked by more conventional problem-solving practices. Thinking like a designer relies on our ability "to be intuitive, to recognize patterns, to construct ideas that are emotionally meaningful as well as functional, and to express ourselves through means beyond words or symbols."[116]

DESIGN THINKING YOUR WAY TO INNOVATIVE SOLUTIONS

Beyond Product Design IDEO's design thinking has been so successful that many nonbusiness and nonproduct organizations are now engaging the company. For instance, FloodHelpNY is a "living platform" the company launched for the Center for NYC Neighborhoods to help New York City's homeowners assess their flood risk and take protective action, including researching flood insurance options. The program, funded by the Governor's Office of Storm Recovery, is an important resource for the nearly 400,000 New Yorkers currently at risk within the city's growing flood plain.[117] IDEO also worked with appliance maker Bosch, which operates one of the world's largest independent auto repair chains (17,000 locations worldwide), to create a digital service that allows smartphone users to book an appointment using their phone to have their car picked up, serviced, and brought back. The interface, called SWEETWORXX, also allows car owners to track the cost and progress of the work online. Launched in California, it is expected to roll out across the United States shortly.[118]

As an Organization IDEO has more than 700 employees in nine offices, both in major U.S. cities and overseas in London, Munich, Shanghai, and Tokyo.[119] The firm has an organic design, the result of merging four design companies. Its current structure builds on project teams and a flat hierarchy, in support of individual autonomy and creativity.[120]

YOUR CALL

What is appealing to you about IDEO? To what extent does IDEO's approach to design force companies to use the seven components of an innovation system (see Figure 10.6)? Explain.

Finally, a team of experts suggested that organizations can foster innovation by focusing on four agility techniques.[121]

1. **Place more emphasis on people than on processes and tools.** Innovation initiatives or projects should be built around motivated individuals who are empowered to get the job done and have the resources to do it.
2. **Be responsive to change rather than following a detailed plan.** It helps to create project plans, but don't spend large amounts of time trying to identify each and every task to be completed. Tasks frequently change as situations evolve. Teams thus need the freedom to diverge from project plans if the situation or customer requires it. GE is following this recommendation. Recently retired CEO Jeff Immelt encouraged employees to pivot to a new idea if an approach to innovating or solving problems wasn't working. He told a reporter from *Bloomberg Businessweek*, "We encourage people to try things, pivot, try them again. It's a better way to run the place than centralized command and control, process-laden."[122]
3. **Develop and test prototypes rather than focusing on documentation.** People learn more and are happier when they observe their ideas being applied in real

market conditions. Teams should experiment with products and services on a small scale to see whether customers like them. If they do, keep the new ideas; otherwise, it's back to the drawing board. For example, PepsiCo originally designed SunChips to be one-inch square and to break into pieces when eaten. When the company pilot-tested the product in focus groups, people said they preferred products that were smaller than one inch. PepsiCo concluded the chips were too big and changed its molds and production processes.[123]

4. **Collaborate with customers rather than adhering to rigid contracts.** Customers often don't know what they want. Adhering to fixed contracts and deliverables rather than adjusting to customer preferences can reduce innovation when employees get too focused on budgets and specifications. Constant collaboration with customers will keep work focused on what they ultimately value.[124]

Develop the Necessary Human Capital We defined human capital in Chapter 9 as the productive potential of an individual's knowledge and actions. Research has identified several employee characteristics that can help organizations innovate. For example, innovation has been positively associated with the individual characteristics associated with creativity, creative-thinking skills, intrinsic motivation, the quality of the relationship between managers and employees, and international work experience.[125]

Example: GE is aware of the need to develop human capital for innovation. The company has hired hundreds of software engineers to develop its analytic and Big Data capabilities. It is doing this in pursuit of the strategic goal of being a top-10 software company by 2020.[126]

Example: General Motors CEO Mary Barra is trying to increase innovation by hiring more executives with experience outside the firm. This action is the opposite of the company's tradition of promoting senior executives from within. According to *The Wall Street Journal*, "The shake-up reflects a desire to reshape a notoriously insular corporate culture with a tradition of grooming internal talent, including Ms. Barra, who joined GM as a college intern some three decades ago."[127]

Human Resource Policies, Practices, and Procedures Human resource policies, practices, and procedures need to be consistent with and reinforce the other six components of an innovation system. Companies that know this are more likely to be innovative and to have higher financial performance.[128] For example, the practice of bringing people from different disciplines together to both brainstorm and train is a good way to foster the collaboration needed for innovation. The University of Michigan's Biointerfaces Institute "locates materials scientists, chemical engineers, biomechanical engineers, and medical researchers near each other. The resulting collaborations led to the creation of a blood test that both captures and cultures cancer cells for speedier cancer diagnoses," according to a writer for *Training*.[129]

A company's performance management and incentive system are often at odds with an innovation culture and climate. For example, GE changed its well-known annual performance review process to make it more consistent with driving innovation and attracting younger software engineers. In the past, the company ranked all employees and then eliminated the bottom 10 percent. This process has been replaced with a more nurturing approach in which employees are coached by more experienced colleagues.[130] Companies also need to align their reward and recognition systems with innovation-related goals. Research shows that receipt of extrinsic rewards is associated with both creativity and innovation.[131]

Appropriate Resources Organizations need to put their money where their mouths are. If managers want innovation, they must dedicate resources to its development. Resources can include people, dollars, time, energy, knowledge, and focus. Heineken, for example, spent $2 million on training employees in beer basics to help them innovate.[132]

10.5 The Threat of Change: Managing Employee Fear and Resistance

THE BIG PICTURE

This section discusses the causes of resistance to change and the reasons employees fear change.

LO 10-5

Discuss ways managers can help employees overcome fear of change.

As we mentioned in Section 10.1, change may be forced upon an organization–*reactive* change, requiring you to make changes in response to problems or opportunities as they arise. Or an organization may try to get out in front of changes–*proactive* change, or planned change, which involves making carefully thought-out changes in anticipation of possible problems or opportunities.

What, then, are effective ways to manage organizational change and employees' fear and resistance to it? In this section, we discuss the following:

- The causes of resistance to change.
- Why employees resist change.

The Causes of Resistance to Change

Resistance to change is an emotional/behavioral response to real or imagined threats to an established work routine. Resistance can be as subtle as passive resignation and as overt as deliberate sabotage. As you will learn, change experts believe that resistance does not primarily reside within the individual but instead is a result of the context in which change occurs.[133]

Resistance can be considered to be the interaction of three causes. *(See Figure 10.7.)* They are

1. Employee characteristics.
2. Change agent characteristics.
3. The change agent–employee relationship.

For example, an employee's resistance is partly based on his or her perception of change, which is influenced by the attitudes and behaviors exhibited by the change agent and the level of trust between the change agent and the employee.

Let us consider these three sources.

FIGURE 10.7

A model of resistance to change

Source: Adapted from R. Kreitner and A. Kinicki. Organizational Behavior, *9th ed. (Burr Ridge, IL: McGraw-Hill/Irwin, 2010), p. 549.*

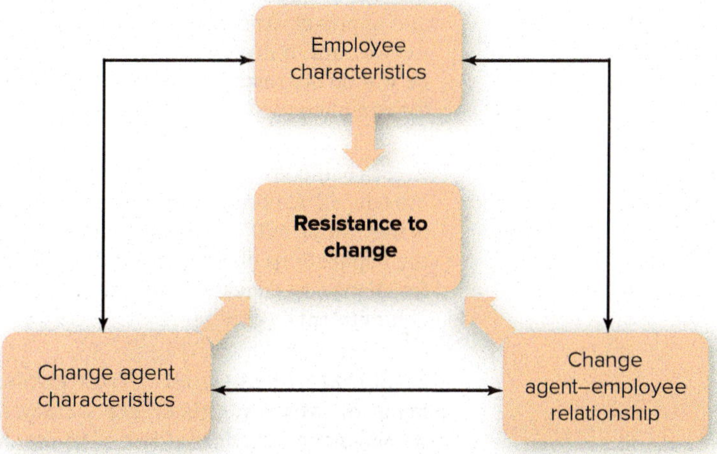

1. Employee Characteristics

The characteristics of a given employee consist of his or her individual differences (discussed in Chapter 11), actions and inactions, and perceptions of change. The next section discusses a variety of employee characteristics to resistance to change. One of them involves the career readiness competency of personal adaptability.[134] How adaptable are you? You can find out by taking Self-Assessment 10.4.

SELF-ASSESSMENT 10.4 CAREER READINESS

How Adaptable Are You?

The following survey was designed to assess your level of adaptability. Please be prepared to answer these questions if your instructor has assigned Self-Assessment 10.4 in Connect.

1. What is your level of adaptability? Are you surprised by the results?
2. Based on your scores, identify three things you can do to increase your level of adaptability. Explain.
3. What things might you say during an interview to demonstrate that you possess the career readiness competency of personal adaptability?

2. Change Agent Characteristics The characteristics of the change agent—the individual who is a catalyst in helping organizations change—also consist of his or her individual differences, experiences, actions and inactions, and perceptions of change. Such characteristics that might contribute to employee resistance to change include leadership style, personality, tactfulness, sense of timing, awareness of cultural traditions or group relationships, and ability to empathize with the employee's perspective.[135]

3. Change Agent–Employee Relationship As you might expect, resistance to change is reduced when change agents and employees have a trusting relationship—faith in each other's intentions. Mistrust, on the other hand, encourages secrecy, which begets deeper mistrust, and can doom an otherwise well-conceived change.[136]

Ten Reasons Employees Resist Change

Whether changes are adaptive, innovative, or radically innovative, employees may resist change for all kinds of reasons. Ten of the leading reasons for not accepting change are as follows.[137]

1. Individuals' Predisposition toward Change How people react to change depends a lot on how they learned to handle change and ambiguity as children. One person's parents may have been patient, flexible, and understanding, and from the time the child was weaned she may have learned there were positive compensations for the loss of immediate gratification. Thus, she will associate making changes with love and approval. Another person's parents may have been unreasonable and unyielding, forcing him to do things (piano lessons, for example) that he didn't want to do. Thus, he will be distrustful of making changes because he will associate them with demands for compliance.[138]

2. Surprise and Fear of the Unknown When radically different changes are introduced without warning—for example, without any official announcements—the office rumor mill will go into high gear, and affected employees will become fearful of the implications of the changes. It is essential for change leaders to explain the rationale for change, to educate people about the personal implications of change, and to garner commitment to change.[139]

3. Climate of Mistrust Trust involves reciprocal faith in others' intentions and behavior. Mistrust encourages secrecy, which causes deeper mistrust, putting even well-conceived changes at risk of failure. Managers who trust their employees make the change process an open, honest, and participative affair. All told, employees who feel fairly treated by managers during change are less likely to resist.[140]

4. Fear of Failure Intimidating changes on the job can cause employees to doubt their capabilities. Self-doubt erodes self-confidence and cripples personal growth and development.

5. Loss of Status or Job Security Administrative and technological changes that threaten to alter power bases or eliminate jobs—as often happens during corporate restructurings that threaten middle-management jobs—generally trigger strong resistance.

6. Peer Pressure Even people who are not themselves directly affected by impending changes may actively resist in order to protect the interests of their friends and co-workers.

These trees cannot resist the wind pressure. People are much different when it comes to change. While management might preach the need to change, like the wind blowing, people resist for a host of reasons. It is essential for managers to consider how they can overcome resistance to change when implementing something new. ©Chieh Cheng/Getty Images

7. Disruption of Cultural Traditions or Group Relationships Whenever individuals are transferred, promoted, or reassigned, it can disrupt existing cultural and group relationships.

Example: Traditionally, Sony Corp. promoted insiders to new positions. When an outsider, Howard Stringer, was named as the next chairman and CEO and six corporate officers were asked to resign, creating a majority board of foreigners, the former CEO, Nobuyuki Idei, worried the moves might engender strong employee resistance.[141]

8. Personality Conflicts Just as a friend can get away with telling us something we would resent hearing from an adversary, the personalities of change agents can breed resistance.

9. Lack of Tact or Poor Timing Introducing changes in an insensitive manner or at an awkward time can create employee resistance. Employees are more apt to accept changes when managers effectively explain their value, as, for example, in demonstrating their strategic purpose to the organization.

10. Nonreinforcing Reward Systems Employees are likely to resist when they can't see any positive rewards from proposed changes, as, for example, when one is asked to work longer hours without additional compensation.

Where do you stand on change? Are you open to change and embrace it, or do you have tendencies to resist? The following self-assessment assesses the extent to which you resist change, which is the opposite of the career readiness competency of openness to change. Given that employers are looking for people who accept and embrace change, this assessment provides you good feedback about your attitudes toward change. If your scores indicate resistance, you should consider what can be done to move your attitudes in a more positive direction. •

SELF-ASSESSMENT 10.5 CAREER READINESS

Assessing Your Resistance to Change

The following survey was designed to assess your resistance to change. Please be prepared to answer these questions if your instructor has assigned Self-Assessment 10.5 in Connect.

1. Are you more or less willing to accept change? Discuss.
2. Based on your scores, identify three things you can do to lower your resistance to change. These changes may involve new thoughts or beliefs or the display of new behaviors.
3. What might you say during an interview to demonstrate that you possess the career readiness competency of openness to change?

10.6 Career Corner: Managing Your Career Readiness

LO 10-6

Review the different ways to increase the career readiness competency of openness to change.

Openness to change is the career readiness competency most related to the concepts discussed in this chapter. It is an "other characteristic" from the model shown below and was defined in Table 1.2 as "flexibility when confronted with change, ability to see change as a challenge, and willingness to apply new ideas, processes, or directives." Employers desire this competency because of the constant need for organizations to adapt, change, and respond in novel or innovative ways to competitors. They know that openness to change supports employees' continuous learning and job satisfaction while reducing workplace annoyances and intentions to quit.[142] Openness to change is worth cultivating in yourself now and throughout your career.

So how can you become more open to change? What gets in your way? We answer these questions by first explaining the application of self-affirmation theory. We then review how self-compassion assists in promoting openness to change.

FIGURE 10.8

Model of career readiness

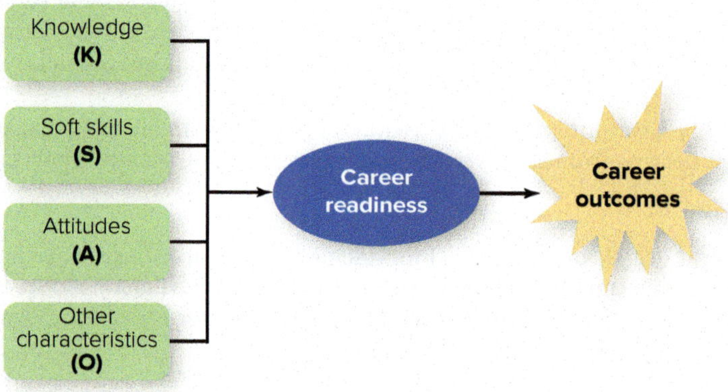

Applying Self-Affirmation Theory

When we speak of not being open to change, we are concerned about more than just organizational change or feedback from a boss or colleague. Your openness to change affects your social interactions with friends, colleagues, loved ones, and even strangers during controversial conversations on topics like politics, the value of unions, immigration policy, the #MeToo movement, and sexual preferences.[143]

What causes us to be close-minded about controversial topics or feedback about our behavior? Self-affirmation theory provides an answer. This theory is based on the premise that "people have a fundamental motivation to maintain self-integrity, a perception of themselves as good, virtuous, and able to predict and control important outcomes."[144] Two renowned psychologists note that a sense of integrity means people see themselves as "a good and appropriate person." They conclude, "Much research suggests that people have a 'psychological immune system' that initiates protective adaptations when an actual or impending threat is perceived."[145] The goal of these mechanisms is to restore self-worth.

It's the restoration of self-worth that inhibits openness to change. It occurs because we use defensive reactions such as rationalization, denial of responsibility, distortion of reality, excessive optimism, and discrediting of the source of information to protect our perceptions of self-integrity. As you can see, protecting our perceptions of self-worth chokes off openness to change, and these perceptions are based on our beliefs. The good news, however, is that research on this theory has firmly documented a technique for overcoming these defensive biases and opening our minds to change. It requires changing our beliefs with the use of "self-affirmations."

Self-affirmations are defined as positive statements "that can help you focus on goals, get rid of negative, self-defeating beliefs and program your subconscious mind."[146] They flip our close-minded thoughts from negativity to positivity. Sample affirmations include: "My work does not define me; I'm a good person," "I learn from mistakes," "I can accomplish whatever I put my mind to," "I love my job and know that I am making a difference," "I'm not perfect, but I stick to my values," "I'm ethical," and "I know I can do better, just like I did on the XYZ project."

Positive self-affirmations enhance our openness to change because they broaden our view of ourselves, which in turn reduces the need to defend ourselves in the face of a threat to self-integrity. If you want to increase your openness to either personal or work-related change, or to comments being made about a controversial subject such as immigration, try using self-affirmations when you feel threatened or get defensive. For example, if someone tells you that your views about immigration are naïve, tell yourself, "I am not an expert, but I am reasonably informed from reading and watching the news." If someone tells you your work was poor quality, tell yourself, "I expect to learn and do better in the future."

Practicing Self-Compassion

Dr. Christine Carter defines **self-compassion** as "gentleness with yourself." Here is what she had to say about using self-compassion to increase openness to self-development.

> We think that if we speak critically to ourselves, we will improve, but all the research shows with absolute certainty that self-criticism does not improve performance. It blocks your ability to learn from the situation and creates a stress response in which fight or flight are your only options. Personal growth is not on the menu when you are self-critical.[147]

Self-compassion can increase your openness to change or your career readiness competency of *positive approach* because it reduces your need to be perfect. It allows us to "give ourselves the same kindness and care we'd give to a good friend," according to psychologist Kristen Neff.[148] Self-compassion protects self-identity by allowing you to appreciate the difference between being a bad person and making a bad decision. As noted in *Psychology Today*, "When you have self-compassion, you understand that your worth is unconditional."[149] This in turn makes it easier to accept feedback from others, to consider alternative viewpoints from your own, to own up to your mistakes, and to empathize with others.[150]

Try the following suggestions in pursuit of more self-compassion:

1. **Self-kindness.** Replace perfectionism and self-judgement with forgiveness and kindness. Accept your imperfections and talk to yourself as you would to a loved-one.
2. **Remind yourself that you're not alone.** Psychotherapist Megan Bruneau reminds us that "to feel is to be human, and that whatever [we're] going through is also being experienced by millions of others. If we can recognize our shared humanity–that not one of us is perfect–we can begin to feel more connected to others, with a sense that we're all in this together."[151]
3. **Practice mindfulness meditation.** Mindfulness is a state of being present non-judgmentally. Meditation can help you achieve this state and avoid the negative thoughts that inhibit openness to change.[152]

Key Terms Used in This Chapter

adaptive change 383
B corporation 381
change agent 389
crowdsourcing 396
disruptive innovation 377
force-field analysis 387
innovation 392
innovation system 394
innovative change 383
intervention 390
organizational development (OD) 389
proactive change 379
process innovation 393
product innovation 393
radically innovative change 384
reactive change 379
readiness for change 386
resistance to change 399
self-affirmations 403
self-compassion 403
technology 381

Key Points

10.1 The Nature of Change in Organizations

- Among supertrends shaping the future of business: (1) The marketplace is becoming more segmented and moving toward more niche products. (2) More competitors are offering targeted products, requiring faster speed-to-market. (3) Some traditional companies may not survive radical change. (4) China, India, and other offshore suppliers are changing the way we work. (5) Knowledge, not information, is becoming the new competitive advantage.
- Two types of change are reactive and proactive. Reactive change is making changes in response to problems or opportunities as they arise. Proactive change involves making carefully thought-out changes in anticipation of possible or expected problems or opportunities.
- Forces for change may consist of forces outside the organization or inside it. (1) External forces consist of four types: demographic characteristics; technological advancements; shareholder, customer, and market changes; and social and political pressures. (2) Internal forces may be of two types: human resources concerns and managers' behavior.

10.2 Types and Models of Change

- Whether organizational change is administrative or technological, it can be adaptive, innovative, or radically innovative, depending on (1) the degree of complexity, cost, and uncertainty and (2) its potential for generating employee resistance.
- Adaptive change, the least threatening, is reintroduction of a familiar practice. Innovative change is the introduction of a practice that is new to the organization. Radically innovative change, the most threatening, involves introducing a practice that is new to the industry.
- Kurt Lewin's change model has three stages—unfreezing, changing, and refreezing—to explain how to initiate, manage, and stabilize planned change. (1) In the unfreezing stage, managers try to instill in employees the motivation to change. (2) In the changing stage, employees need to be given the tools for change, such as new information. (3) In the refreezing stage, employees need to be helped to integrate the changed attitudes and behavior into their normal behavior.
- A systems approach to change consists of three parts: inputs, target elements of change, and outputs, plus a feedback loop. (1) Inputs answer two questions: Why should we change? How willing and able are we to change? To answer the first question requires the organization's mission statement, vision statement, and strategic plan. To answer the second question requires knowing an organization's readiness for change—the staff's beliefs, attitudes, and intentions as to the extent of the changes needed and how willing and able they are to implement them. (2) Target elements of change represent the four levers that managers need to use to diagnose problems—people, organizational arrangements, methods, and social factors. (3) Outputs represent the desired goals of change, which should be consistent with the organization's strategic plan. (4) There is a feedback loop to determine how the change is working and what alterations need to be made.
- Force-field analysis is a technique to determine which forces could facilitate a proposed change and which forces could act against it.

10.3 Organizational Development: What It Is, What It Can Do

- Organizational development (OD) is a set of techniques for implementing planned change to make people and organizations more effective. Often OD is put into practice by a change agent, a consultant with a background in behavioral sciences who can be a catalyst in helping organizations deal with old problems in new ways. OD can be used to manage conflict, revitalize organizations, and adapt to mergers.
- The OD process follows a three-step process: (1) Diagnosis attempts to ascertain the problem. (2) Intervention is the attempt to correct the diagnosed problems. (3) Evaluation attempts to find out how well the intervention worked.
- Four factors that make OD work successfully are (1) multiple interventions are used, (2) top managers give the OD program their support, (3) goals are geared to both short- and long-term results, and (4) OD is affected by culture.

10.4 Organizational Innovation

- Innovation is the creation of something new and useful that gets commercialized.
- Crossing the types of innovation with the focus on the innovation results in four approaches to innovation.
- Innovation can produce new products or new processes and can vary in focus from improvement to new directions.
- An innovation system's seven components are (1) an innovation strategy; (2) commitment from senior leaders; (3) an innovative culture and climate; (4) required structure and processes; (5) necessary human capital; (6) appropriate resources; and (7) human resource policies, practices, and procedures.

10.5 The Threat of Change: Managing Employee Fear and Resistance

- Resistance to change is an emotional/behavioral response to real or imagined threats to an established work routine. Resistance can be considered to be the interaction of three causes: (1) employee characteristics, (2) change-agent characteristics, and (3) the change agent–employee relationship.
- Ten reasons employees resist change are as follows: (1) individuals' predisposition toward change, (2) surprise and fear of the unknown, (3) climate of mistrust, (4) fear of failure, (5) loss of status or job security, (6) peer pressure, (7) disruption of cultural traditions or group relationships, (8) personality conflicts, (9) lack of tact or poor timing, and (10) nonreinforcing reward systems.

10.6 Career Corner: Managing Your Career Readiness

- There are two key methods for improving your openness to change: self-affirmation theory and self-compassion.
- Self-affirmation theory reveals that openness to change is enhanced by replacing negative thoughts or beliefs about yourself with positive affirmations.
- You can increase self-compassion by practicing self-kindness, reminding yourself that you are not alone, and practicing mindfulness.

Understanding the Chapter: What Do I Know?

1. What are the two principal types of change?
2. Describe the four kinds of external forces of change and two kinds of internal forces of change.
3. How does Kurt Lewin's model of change work?
4. What is the organizational development process?
5. What's the difference between a product innovation and a process innovation?
6. Explain four approaches to innovation.
7. What are four steps for fostering innovation?
8. Employee resistance can be considered to be the interaction of what three causes?
9. There are 10 reasons employees resist change. What are they?
10. How can you increase the career competency of openness to change?

Management in Action

Chipotle Needs to Change

Chipotle Mexican Grill started in 1993 with a single restaurant and now operates in 2,400 locations, including in Canada, England, France, and Germany. The fast-food chain had approximately 60,000 employees and revenues of $4 billion in 2017.[153]

Steve Ells founded Chipotle and served as its CEO until 2018. Ells wanted to differentiate his brand from that of other fast-food chains, so he focused on fresh, high-quality raw ingredients free of antibiotics and pesticides. Meals were prepared using classic cooking methods and were served in choose-your-own style so diners could get the individual ingredients they preferred.[154]

Then the company's growth and profitability were stunted by outbreaks of foodborne illnesses. Customers were sickened by *E. coli*, norovirus, and salmonella at dozens of Chipotle restaurants around the United States between 2015 and 2016.[155] The restaurant's stock never recovered as shares fell nearly 60 percent between 2015 and 2018.[156] Let's examine what led to the burrito maker's fall from grace.

AS CHIPOTLE GREW, SO DID ITS PROBLEMS

Chipotle rose to greatness because customers were offered a straightforward set of options, food was prepared on site in an open kitchen, and diners felt they were eating something healthy. The company had success with this model early on, but the system started to crack as Chipotle grew. Inconsistent food preparation was the first stressor. The open kitchen proved a difficult model to scale, and poor food handling most likely led to the outbreak of foodborne illness. According to the *Chicago Tribune*, "Chipotle has been growing too quickly, and without a game plan." The restaurant chain was plagued by inconsistency and inefficiency.[157] Foodborne illnesses continued to haunt it almost two years after the initial outbreak. In 2017, "The rate of food poisoning reports attributed to Chipotle continues to be multiples higher than peers," said *Business Insider*.[158] These statistics are especially troubling for a brand that prides itself as providing "Food with Integrity."

The restaurant's menu reflects another crack in its vision and strategies. Chipotle offers burritos, tacos, burrito bowls, and salads. This simple menu attracted customers for over a decade but is now seen as "stale," according to an analyst with the *Tribune*.[159] Ells began offering queso in September 2017 in an attempt to spice up Chipotle's menu. The results were not promising. Only 15 percent of orders included queso, compared to the 40 percent of orders that included guacamole. *Business Insider* reported that queso-related traffic died off after peaking the first week the new item was available.[160]

These problems have created opportunities for other fast-casual restaurants such as Qdoba and Moes, which are opening locations all over the United States. According to a UBS analyst, ". . . these concepts are exhibiting significant growth rates while also increasing competition for attractive market/site selection." Chipotle's once unquestionable market leadership is on shaky ground.

CHIPOTLE'S NEW CEO WAS SUCCESSFUL AT TACO BELL

Chipotle named Brian Niccol CEO in 2018. Niccol had been Taco Bell's chief marketing officer from 2011 to 2015 before taking over as its CEO.[161] He was hired at Chipotle because of the successful turnaround he had overseen at Taco Bell.

A disgruntled customer had filed a lawsuit in 2011 alleging Taco Bell's taco mixture was more filler than beef. The suit was later withdrawn, but it took a toll on Taco Bell's reputation and sales. Niccol's change efforts focused on repositioning the chain as a youthful lifestyle brand. He did this by welcoming ideas from restaurant employees and introduced new menu items, including breakfast.[162] These changes produced impressive results. Taco Bell posted an average of 4 percent sales growth during Niccol's time as CEO.[163] The fast-food chain also beat out Pizza Hut and KFC as the most successful restaurant in the Yum Brands portfolio.[164]

NICCOL'S CHALLENGE AT CHIPOTLE

Niccol faces three challenges at Chipotle. The first is the menu and potential resistance to changing it from the company's senior leadership. The second is increased competition taking advantage of the company's past problems, and the third relates to Chipotle's food preparation practices and their contribution to foodborne illness.

Niccol first needs to address Chipotle's menu problem. According to a *CNNMoney* analyst, "They need something that gets people talking about the brand again." The analyst says that Chipotle should consider adding new menu items such as nachos or frozen margaritas. Niccol may be positively disposed to this suggestion because he was also the architect of Taco Bell's positive move to offer breakfast and Doritos Locos tacos.[165] Other analysts have concerns about the company venturing too far from its core offerings.[166]

Those who are skeptical about changing the menu include Chipotle's founder and current executive chair, Steve Ells. Ells still yields significant power and is known as a hands-on leader and perfectionist, according to *The Wall Street Journal*.[167] He told *The New York Times*, "It's not like you can put a whole new thing up on the menu board and—like at a typical fast-food place."[168] This view is supported by Ells's earlier strategic failure of adding queso to the menu.

Niccol is likely to experience resistance to some of his ideas because Ells does not believe Chipotle is like Taco Bell. Chipotle is more vulnerable to suppliers' changes in the price of items such as avocados and chicken. Other fast-food brands can push increased costs to franchises—something Chipotle does not have. Ells also refuses to compromise on quality as part of any change. "I don't think you're going to see a situation where someone says, 'To hell with food with integrity. We're going to buy cheap commodity meat now and really turn this thing around,'" he told the *Times*.[169]

Chipotle's second challenge is increased competition, and the biggest threat here is Panera. Panera is outside Chipotle's cuisine niche, but it is competing with its promise of fresh, additive-free ingredients. It also has an exhaustive menu that rotates seasonally. Chipotle customers who are tired of its "big-four" menu will easily find a Panera nearby; *Business Insider* reports that 87 percent of Chipotles compete with a Panera Bread within a 10-minute drive.[170]

Niccol will have to do more than change Chipotle's menu if he wants to compete with Panera. He needs to address his third challenge, which is stopping people from getting foodborne illnesses at his restaurants. The new CEO might accomplish this by slowing the chain's growth and focusing on safer operations. For example, each of Chipotle's approximately 2,400 locations does its own prep work, such as washing lettuce and chopping tomatoes.[171] Although this practice is part of Chipotle's operational vision, an analyst from the *Tribune* suggested that "[Chipotle managers have] to keep to their core values . . .but need to find a way to be more consistent and efficient." The analyst recommended that Chipotle wash and prep food in a central location and send it out to nearby stores.[172]

Such a food preparation change will significantly alter Chipotle's restaurant structure. Customers may no longer walk into a restaurant and see employees grilling meat and chopping vegetables behind the food line. This setup has been part of the chain's vision and heritage and represents something Ells holds near and dear. "Niccol will likely face an uphill battle in uprooting some of that heritage, as he's stepping into a role occupied by a founder for the past 25 years," said an analyst to *Business Insider*.[173] Can Niccol inspire change and save Chipotle?

FOR DISCUSSION

Problem-Solving Perspective

1. What is the underlying problem in this case from CEO Brian Niccol's perspective?
2. What are some of the causes of this problem?

Application of Chapter Content

1. What type of change does Niccol need to inspire—reactive or proactive? Explain.
2. Using Figure 10.1, describe what forces for change exist both inside and outside Chipotle.
3. Does Chipotle need adaptive, innovative or radically innovative change? Explain.
4. Utilize Lewin's model of change (Figure 10.2) as a blueprint and describe how Niccol can inspire change at Chipotle.
5. Think about the outbreak of food-borne illness at Chipotle and utilize the organizational development process (Figure 10.4) to remedy the issue.
6. Does Niccol need to bring product or process innovation to Chipotle? Explain.

Legal/Ethical Challenge

Did L'Oreal Go Too Far in Firing Its Patent Lawyer?

Patents give companies competitive advantage. They create legal protection for products and can be used for marketing purposes. They are most frequently pursued by innovative firms, particularly in high-tech industries. For example, IBM, Samsung, and Canon were the three top patent recipients in the United States in 2016, 2015, and 2014.[174] The U.S. Patent and Trademark Office issued 298,407 patents in 2015.[175]

This challenge deals with L'Oreal's firing of Steven Trzaska. Trzaska was a patent lawyer in charge of a team that examined the work of the company's researchers to decide whether it contained patentable work product. The team then submitted patent applications when appropriate. L'Oreal spends about $1 billion a year on research and development while employing 4,000 people in research labs around the world. The company is clearly committed to innovating its product offerings.

Trzaska filed a lawsuit against L'Oreal, claiming he was let go for "refusing to make filings for dubious inventions just so the company could fill an annual quota." He said L'Oreal had "ordered him to apply for at least 40 patents last year to help fill a companywide global quota of 500 applications. The company sought to post on its cosmetics packaging that the contents were 'patent pending,' thus increasing their allure to consumers, according to the lawsuit."[176] The company denies the charges and plans to vigorously fight them.

The U.S. Patent Office is trying to enhance its evaluation process because it feels many applications cover vague ideas that are not real inventions. Trzaska said L'Oreal was interested in improving the quality of its applications, but "a review by an outside organization had found 'the vast majority of its inventions were of low or poor quality,'" according to the lawsuit. This in turn led L'Oreal researchers to submit fewer ideas for potential application and Trzaska's team to reject more. All told, submitted applications declined and reduced the chance of achieving the company's global patent goals.

The lawsuit claims that Trzaska was fired "for his refusal to draft and file patent applications for proposed inventions which were not patentable" and for his failure to allow his team members to file such applications.[177]

SOLVING THE CHALLENGE

How would you rule if you were a judge evaluating this case?

1. I would side with the company. It's not Trzaska's job to be a gatekeeper. Let the U.S. Patent Office make those decisions. Trzaska's role is to help the company acquire patents for its products, and he was jeopardizing future sales by taking an unduly hard stance about patentable work. Further, the company's goal specified the number of applications, not the number accepted.
2. I would side with Trzaska. He took a stand on the quality of submissions for patent applications. The company should focus on the quality of ideas submitted rather than on the work of Trzaska's team. What is Trzaska supposed to do when people submit poor ideas?
3. I'm not sure who is right or wrong, but I don't like the idea of setting goals for innovation such as the number of patent applications submitted.
4. Invent other options.

Uber Continuing Case connect

Learn about the forces for change at Uber, how the company is a force for change to competitors, and why employees are resisting change. Assess your ability to apply concepts discussed in this chapter to the case by going to Connect.

Leading

PART 5 • LEADING

11 Managing Individual Differences and Behavior

Supervising People as People

©Olivier Renck/Aurora/Getty Images

After reading this chapter, you should be able to:

LO 11-1 Describe the importance of personality and individual traits in the hiring process.

LO 11-2 Explain the effects of values and attitudes on employee behavior.

LO 11-3 Describe the way perception can cloud judgment.

LO 11-4 Explain how managers can deal with employee attitudes.

LO 11-5 Identify trends in workplace diversity that managers should be aware of.

LO 11-6 Discuss the sources of workplace stress and ways to reduce it.

LO 11-7 Describe how to develop the career readiness competencies of positive approach and emotional intelligence.

FORECAST *What's Ahead in This Chapter*

This first of five chapters on leadership discusses how to manage for individual differences and behaviors. We describe personality and individual behavior; values, attitudes, and behavior; and specific work-related attitudes and behaviors managers need to be aware of. We next discuss distortions in perception and consider what stress does to individuals. We conclude with a Career Corner that focuses on the career readiness competencies of a *positive approach* and *emotional intelligence*.

MANAGE U

How to Make a Positive First Impression at Work

The power of perception is so well known that we consciously try to manage other people's perceptions to ensure their first impression of us is a positive one. As we'll see below, some of the influences on others' perceptions of us that we can't control are unconscious biases about race, age, and gender; the weight of internal influences like the kind of day someone is having (called the fundamental attribution error); the inclination to be influenced by the most recent event or person encountered (the recency error); and the tendency to weigh early information most heavily (the primacy effect). And thanks to the confirmation bias, "people see what they expect to see."[1] But still, a great deal of someone's first impression of you is yours to control.

Creating positive first impressions is important in job or client interviews and other social situations. A writer for *The Wall Street Journal* noted that "A growing body of research shows the snap judgments people make about others' trustworthiness are wrong more often than most people think. These first impressions are formed in milliseconds based on instinctive responses in the brain's emotion-processing center, the amygdala."[2] The good news is that you can influence these perceptions by using the following suggestions and your career readiness skills of positive approach and self-awareness.

Be Prepared

We've recommended before that you should be ready to ask and answer questions in job interviews. When meeting new co-workers, subordinates, clients, or company executives, the same advice applies. There's no substitute for the confidence you'll gain from having done your homework.

Stand (or Sit) Straight and Smile

Your body language conveys your confidence and invites others to feel confident in you as well. Lift your chin and straighten your back.[3] Dropping your shoulders and keeping them relaxed can improve the tone of your voice to further support the positive image you want to portray. Smiling suggests a friendly and open personality most people can readily warm to.

Look for Common Ground

It's only natural for us to like people who are similar to us in some way. Even a small link like a common interest in sports, music, or travel can help form a bond that will allow more positive associations to form as you communicate. Asking a few polite questions to uncover such common ground (making small talk) indicates your interest in the other person. "The better you make the other person feel, the more they'll be inclined to have a positive impression of you."[4]

Keep Up the Good Work

Once you've landed a job or a client account, continue solidifying the good impression you've made by being consistently reliable, prompt, humble, willing to learn, open to new experiences, and eager to be part of the team. Ask for help when you need it and say thank you when it's given.[5]

If All Else Fails

Sometimes, despite our efforts, we fail to show our best selves. Perhaps we fumble the answer to an interview question, show up for a work event in the wrong clothes, or tell a crowd of new co-workers a joke that falls flat. An unqualified disaster? It doesn't have to be. Experts suggest giving yourself a little time to recover and then taking steps to remedy the negative impression by explaining what happened, presenting plenty of strong evidence in your favor, and asking for a second chance. Be prepared to spend time repairing the relationship, but don't give up.[6]

For Discussion Have you ever felt like you got off on the wrong foot with a new acquaintance or co-worker? What did each of you do to try to repair the situation?

11.1 Personality and Individual Behavior

THE BIG PICTURE

Personality consists of stable psychological and behavioral attributes that give you your identity. We describe five personality dimensions and five personality traits that managers need to be aware of to understand workplace behavior.

LO 11-1

Describe the importance of personality and individual traits in the hiring process.

In this and the next four chapters, we discuss the third management function (after planning and organizing)—namely, leading. *Leading,* as we said in Chapter 1, is defined as *motivating, directing, and otherwise influencing people to work hard to achieve the organization's goals.*

How would you describe yourself? Are you outgoing? aggressive? sociable? tense? passive? lazy? quiet? Whatever the combination of traits, which result from the interaction of your genes and your environment, they constitute your personality. More formally, **personality consists of the stable psychological traits and behavioral attributes that give a person his or her identity.**[7] As a manager, you need to understand personality attributes because they affect how people perceive and act within the organization.[8]

The Big Five Personality Dimensions

In recent years, the many personality dimensions have been distilled into a list of factors known as the Big Five.[9] **The Big Five personality dimensions are (1) extroversion, (2) agreeableness, (3) conscientiousness, (4) emotional stability, and (5) openness to experience.**

- **Extroversion.** How outgoing, talkative, sociable, and assertive a person is.
- **Agreeableness.** How trusting, good-natured, cooperative, and soft-hearted someone is.
- **Conscientiousness.** How dependable, responsible, achievement-oriented, and persistent someone is.
- **Emotional stability.** How relaxed, secure, and unworried a person is.
- **Openness to experience.** How intellectual, imaginative, curious, and broad-minded someone is.

Pre-employment psychometric testing, which includes personality testing, has grown into an industry estimated to be worth $2 billion a year, fueled by employers' increased desire to identify candidates in all fields with the career readiness skills they seek.[10] For example, "We've seen a rise in companies wanting to test the soft skills of information technology candidates, which usually has been a certification-only assessment of hard skills," said Mike Hudy, a vice president at Shaker, an assessment company.[11] Companies use these tests, believing that hiring decisions will be more accurate and predictive of high performers. But are they? Turns out conscientiousness has the most consistent relationships with important outcomes such as task performance, leadership behavior, supervisor-rated liking, resilience, and lower unemployment.[12] Do you wonder whether your personality has affected your behavior at work?

Sociable and assertive. Does it take a certain kind of personality to be a good salesperson? Have you ever known people who were quiet, unassuming, even shy but who were nevertheless very persistent and persuasive—that is, good salespeople? ©Dave and Les Jacobs/Blend Images/Alamy Stock Photo

Where do you think you stand in terms of the Big Five? You can find out by completing Self-Assessment 11.1.

SELF-ASSESSMENT 11.1 CAREER READINESS

Where Do You Stand on the Big Five Dimensions of Personality?

This survey is designed to assess your personality, using the Big Five index. Please be prepared to answer these questions if your instructor has assigned Self-Assessment 11.1 in Connect.

1. What is your personality profile, according to the Big Five?
2. Which of the Big Five is most likely going to help you achieve good grades in your classes and gain employment after graduation?
3. What things might you say during an interview to demonstrate that you have self-awareness regarding your personality?

Core Self-Evaluations

A core self-evaluation (CSE) represents a broad personality trait comprising four positive individual traits: (1) *self-efficacy*, (2) *self-esteem*, (3) *locus of control*, and (4) *emotional stability*. Managers need to be aware of these personality traits as they are related to employees work attitudes, performance, and behavior.[13]

1. Self-Efficacy: "I Can/Can't Do This Task"

Self-efficacy is the **belief in one's personal ability to do a task.** This is about your personal belief that you have what it takes to successfully complete a specified task in a specific situation This characteristic has been expanded into a broader motivational trait labeled generalized self-efficacy. **Generalized self-efficacy** represents **"individuals' perception of their ability to perform across a variety of different situations."**[14] It is a career readiness competency desired by employers.

Have you noticed that those who are confident about their ability tend to succeed, whereas those preoccupied with failure tend not to? Indeed, high expectations of self-efficacy have been linked with all kinds of positives, including academic and work performance, lower burnout, and motivation.[15] One study found that the sales performance of life-insurance agents was much better among those with high self-efficacy.[16] A meta-analysis involving 21,616 people also found a significant positive correlation between self-efficacy and job performance.[17]

Among the implications for managers are the following:

- **Assign jobs accordingly.** Complex, challenging, and autonomous jobs tend to enhance people's perceptions of their self-efficacy. Boring, tedious jobs generally do the opposite.
- **Develop employees' self-efficacy and generalized self-efficacy.** Self-efficacy is a quality that can be nurtured. Employees with low self-efficacy need lots of constructive pointers and positive feedback.[18] Goal difficulty needs to match individuals' perceived self-efficacy, but goals can be made more challenging as performance improves.[19] Small successes need to be rewarded. Employees' expectations can be improved through guided experiences, mentoring, and role modeling.[20] It's also important to monitor employees' generalized self-efficacy because it impacts all aspects of our lives. For example, low generalized self-efficacy can foster **learned helplessness, the debilitating lack of faith in your ability to control your environment.**[21] Managers certainly don't want this to happen. It also is related to your job satisfaction and task performance.[22]

Self-efficacy. Former Marine Corps Staff Sgt. Charlie Linville, 30, shown here (left) with his climbing partner, Tim Medvetz. Linville reached the 29,029-foot summit of Mt. Everest in May 2016, becoming the first combat-wounded veteran to do so. He had already conquered some of the highest peaks in the world on one leg. He was injured while defusing bombs in Afghanistan in 2011, when an explosive device detonated, leading to the amputation of his right leg below the knee. Do you have a personal belief that you can succeed at great things? ©Niranjan Shrestha/AP Images

What is your level of generalized self-efficacy? Find out by taking Self-Assessment 11.2. Results may enhance your confidence at achieving both your personal and work-related goals. For example, German university students with low self-efficacy tended to display higher levels of career indecision.[23]

SELF-ASSESSMENT 11.2 CAREER READINESS

What Is Your Level of Generalized Self-Efficacy?

This survey is designed to assess your generalized self-efficacy. Please be prepared to answer these questions if your instructor has assigned Self-Assessment 11.2 in Connect.

1. What is your level of generalized self-efficacy?
2. Examine the three lowest item score and determine the issues that are lowering your level of efficacy. What might you do to improve your generalized self-efficacy based on this determination.
3. What things might you say during an interview to demonstrate that you have possess the career readiness competency of generalized self-efficacy?

2. Self-Esteem: "I Like/Dislike Myself" How worthwhile, capable, and acceptable do you think you are? The answer to this question is an indicator of your **self-esteem**, **the extent to which people like or dislike themselves, their overall self-evaluation.**[24] Research offers some interesting insights about how high or low self-esteem can affect people and organizations.

- **People with high self-esteem.** Compared with people with low self-esteem, people with high self-esteem are more apt to handle failure better and to become leaders. They also are less likely to be depressed and less likely to engage in counterproductive behavior at work.[25] However, when faced with pressure situations, high-self-esteem people have been found to become egotistical and boastful.[26]

- **People with low self-esteem.** Conversely, low-self-esteem people confronted with failure have been found to have focused on their weaknesses and to have had primarily negative thoughts.[27] Moreover, they are more dependent on others and are more apt to be influenced by them and to be less likely to take independent positions.

Can self-esteem be improved? According to one study, "low self-esteem can be raised more by having the person think of *desirable* characteristics *possessed* rather than of undesirable characteristics from which he or she is free."[28] Some ways in which managers can build employee self-esteem are shown below. *(See Table 11.1.)*

TABLE 11.1

Some Ways That Managers Can Boost Employee Self-Esteem

• Reinforce employees' positive attributes and skills.
• Provide positive feedback whenever possible.
• Break larger projects into smaller tasks and projects.
• Express confidence in employees' abilities to complete their tasks.
• Provide coaching whenever employees are seen to be struggling to complete tasks.

3. Locus of Control: "I Am/Am Not the Captain of My Fate"

As we discussed briefly in Chapter 1, **locus of control** **indicates how much people believe they control their fate through their own efforts.** If you have an *internal locus of control,* you believe you control your own destiny. If you have an *external locus of control,* you believe external forces control you.

Research shows internals and externals have important workplace differences. Internals exhibit less anxiety, greater work motivation, and stronger expectations that effort leads to performance. They also obtain higher salaries.[29] Most importantly, one's internal locus of control can be improved by providing more job autonomy.[30]

These findings have two important implications for managers:

- **Expect different degrees of structure and compliance for each type.** Employees with internal locus of control will probably resist close managerial supervision. Hence, they should probably be placed in jobs requiring high initiative and lower compliance. By contrast, employees with external locus of control might do better in highly structured jobs requiring greater compliance.
- **Employ different reward systems for each type.** Since internals seem to have a greater belief that their actions have a direct effect on the consequences of that action, internals likely would prefer and respond more productively to incentives such as merit pay or sales commissions. (We discuss incentive compensation systems in Chapter 12.)

4. Emotional Stability: "I'm Fairly Secure/Insecure When Working under Pressure"

Emotional stability **is the extent to which people feel secure and unworried and how likely they are to experience negative emotions under pressure.** People with low levels of emotional stability are prone to anxiety and tend to view the world negatively, whereas people with high levels tend to show better job performance.

Emotional Intelligence: Understanding Your Emotions and the Emotions of Others

Emotional intelligence (EI or EQ) has been defined as "the ability to carry out accurate reasoning about emotions and the ability to use emotions and emotional knowledge to enhance thought."[31] Said another way, **emotional intelligence is the ability to monitor your and others' feelings and to use this information to guide your thinking and actions.** It is a career readiness competency desired by employers and was first introduced in 1909. Since that time some claim it to be the secret elixir to happiness and higher performance. Are you curious if research supports such lofty conclusions?

What Do We Know about EI?

Recent research underscores the importance of developing higher EI, but it does not confirm its lofty expectations. EI was moderately associated with (1) better social relations and well-being, (2) job satisfaction, (3) better emotional control, (4) conscientiousness and self-efficacy, (5) organizational citizenship behavior, and (6) self-rated performance. Interestingly, EI was not found to be a driver of supervisory ratings of performance.[32] **Daniel Goleman**, a psychologist who popularized the trait of EI, concluded that EI is composed of four key components: self-awareness, self-management, social awareness, and relationship management.[33] *(See Table 11.2.)*

TABLE 11.2
The Traits of Emotional Intelligence

1. *Self-awareness.* The most essential trait. This is the ability to read your own emotions and gauge your moods accurately, so you know how you're affecting others.
2. *Self-management.* This is the ability to control your emotions and act with honesty and integrity in reliable and adaptable ways. You can leave occasional bad moods outside the office.
3. *Social awareness.* This includes empathy, allowing you to show others that you care, and organizational intuition, so you keenly understand how your emotions and actions affect others.
4. *Relationship management.* This is the ability to communicate clearly and convincingly, disarm conflicts, and build strong personal bonds.

Sources: For a current review, see S. Côté, "Enhancing Managerial Effectiveness via Four Core Facets of Emotional Intelligence: Self-Awareness, Social Perception, Emotion Understanding, and Emotion Regulation," Organizational Dynamics, *July–September 2017, pp. 140–147; D. Joseph, J. Jin, D. Newman, and E. O'Boyle, "Why Does Self-Reported Emotional Intelligence Predict Job Performance? A Meta-Analytic Investigation of Mixed EI,"* Journal of Applied Psychology, *March 2015, pp. 298–342.*

Can You Raise Your EI?

Is there any way to raise your own emotional intelligence, to sharpen your career readiness? Although parts of EI represent stable traits that are not readily changed, other aspects, such as using empathy, can be developed.[34] Two suggestions for improvement are as follows:

- **Develop awareness of your EI level.** Becoming aware of your level of emotional intelligence is the first step. The self-assessment on the following page can be used for this purpose.
- **Learn about areas needing improvement.** The next step is to learn more about those EI aspects in which improvement is needed. For example, to improve your skills at using empathy, find articles on the topic and try to implement their recommendations. One such article suggests that empathy in communications is enhanced by trying to (1) understand how others feel about what they are communicating and (2) gaining appreciation of what people want from an exchange.[35] The Practical Action box illustrates how apps are used to develop EI. •

SELF-ASSESSMENT 11.3 CAREER READINESS

What Is Your Level of Emotional Intelligence?

The following survey is designed to assess your emotional intelligence. Please be prepared to answer these questions if your instructor has assigned Self-Assessment 11.3 in Connect.

1. How do you stand on the five dimensions of emotional intelligence?
2. Use the scores from the items to identify your strengths and liabilities.
3. Identify two ways you can increase your emotional intelligence.
4. What things might you say during an interview to demonstrate that you possess the career readiness competency of emotional intelligence?

PRACTICAL ACTION Using Technology to Develop Emotional Intelligence

Emotional intelligence (EI) is one of the most important skills a job candidate can have. Studies suggest that around 90 percent of top performers have high levels of EI,[36] and 71 percent of hiring managers and HR professionals would choose an applicant with high EI over one with high IQ.[37]

Empathy is a key component of EI.[38] To empathize means to understand and even experience others' perspectives and feelings.[39] Empathy drives performance, increases engagement, helps us build relationships, decreases turnover, improves customer service, and fosters teamwork.[40]

Many experts believe we can develop our EI. But until recently, suggestions have consisted mostly of generic advice such as "develop an understanding of your own emotions"[41] or "put yourself in the other person's shoes."[42] Emerging technology is providing more immersive, and therefore realistic, methods for increasing EI.

Corporate Use of Artificial Intelligence (AI)

The Wall Street Journal reported that more than 40 percent of employers across the globe have used artificial intelligence tools to analyze employees' emotions. Ultimate Software Group Inc., which developed the AI tool *Xander*, said it "can determine whether an employee feels optimistic, confused or angry, and provide insights to help manage teams."[43]

Empathy Training

The *Translator* app, currently in development, wants to help employees increase their "empathy muscle." Users provide personal information including gender, sexual orientation, and race to create an identity profile. The app then designs lessons—including audio exercises, games, and virtual-reality (VR) experiences—to teach users about other identities that are different from their own. For example, a white male worker might experience, through virtual reality (VR), what it feels like to be a woman of color in a board meeting, including being called "honey" and having others ask her to get coffee because they assume she's a secretary.[44]

Random App of Kindness (RAKi) is a free app that consists of mini-games designed to improve specific aspects of users' empathy. These include emotion recognition, response inhibition, and caring for others' needs. The app takes interventions that have previously been used to increase empathy in face-to-face settings and translates them into easily accessible smartphone games.[45]

YOUR CALL

Do you believe that AI, simulations, and games can help increase employees' emotional intelligence? Do you think you could be a more empathetic person? What can you do to develop this skill?

11.2 Values, Attitudes, and Behavior

THE BIG PICTURE

Organizational behavior (OB) considers how to better understand and manage people at work. In this section, we discuss individual values and attitudes and how they affect people's actions and judgments.

LO 11-2

Explain the effects of values and attitudes on employee behavior.

If you look at a company's annual report or at a brochure from its corporate communications department, you are apt to be given a picture of its *formal aspects*: Goals. Policies. Hierarchy. Structure.

Could you exert effective leadership if the formal aspects were all you knew about the company? What about the *informal aspects*? Values. Attitudes. Personalities. Perceptions. Conflicts. Culture. Clearly, you need to know about these hidden, "messy" characteristics as well. *(See Figure 11.1, left.)*

FIGURE 11.1

Formal and informal aspects of an organization

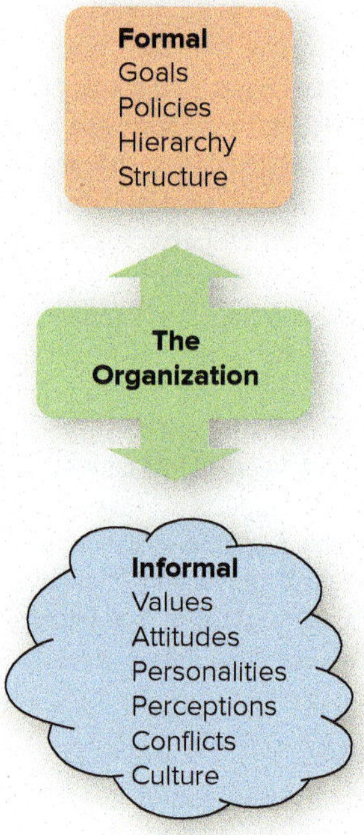

Organizational Behavior: Trying to Explain and Predict Workplace Behavior

The informal aspects are the focus of the interdisciplinary field known as **organizational behavior (OB), which is dedicated to better understanding and managing people at work.** In particular, OB tries to help managers not only *explain* workplace behavior but also *predict* it, so that they can better lead and motivate their employees to perform productively. OB looks at two areas:

- **Individual behavior.** This is the subject of this chapter. We discuss such individual attributes as values, attitudes, personality, perception, and learning.
- **Group behavior.** This is the subject of later chapters, particularly Chapter 13, where we discuss norms, roles, and teams.

Let's begin by considering individual values, attitudes, and behavior.

Values: What Are Your Consistent Beliefs and Feelings about *All* Things?

Values are abstract ideals that guide one's thinking and behavior across all situations.[46] Lifelong behavior patterns are dictated by values that are fairly well set by the time people are in their early teens. After that, however, one's values can be reshaped by significant life-altering events, such as having a child, undergoing a business failure, or surviving the death of a loved one, a war, or a serious health threat.

From a manager's point of view, it's helpful to know that values represent the ideals that underlie how we behave at work. Ideals such as concern for others, self-enhancement, independence, and security are common values in the workplace.[47] Managers who understand an employee's values are better suited to assign them to meaningful projects and to help avoid conflicts between work activities and personal values.[48]

Attitudes: What Are Your Consistent Beliefs and Feelings about *Specific* Things?

Values are abstract ideals—global beliefs and feelings—that are directed toward all objects, people, or events. Values tend to be consistent both over time and over related situations.

By contrast, attitudes are beliefs and feelings that are directed toward *specific* objects, people, or events. More formally, an **attitude is defined as a learned predisposition toward a given object.**[49] It is important for you to understand the components of attitudes because attitudes directly influence our behavior.[50]

Example: Job satisfaction is moderately associated with performance and strongly related to turnover.[51] Unhappy workers are less likely to demonstrate high performance, while happy workers are less likely to quit. This is why it is important for managers to track employees' attitudes and to understand their causes. For example, a happiness survey conducted by Robert Half, the recruitment firm, found that most Millennial employees (now aged 18 to 34) are happy at work and confirmed that happiness is related to higher productivity.[52] A similar study by LinkedIn found that, unlike older workers, 18- to 24-year-olds hold beliefs about the value of sharing, likely learned from their use of social media, that lead them to rely on friendships at work for boosts to their happiness, motivation, and productivity.[53]

The Three Components of Attitudes: Affective, Cognitive, and Behavioral

Attitudes have three components—*affective, cognitive,* and *behavioral.*[54]

- **The affective component—"I feel."** **The affective component of an attitude consists of the feelings or emotions one has about a situation.** How do you *feel* about people who talk loudly on cell-phones in restaurants? If you feel annoyed or angry, you're expressing negative emotions, or affect. (If you're indifferent, your attitude is neutral.)
- **The cognitive component—"I believe."** **The cognitive component of an attitude consists of the beliefs and knowledge one has about a situation.** What do you *think* about people in restaurants talking on cell-phones? Is what they're doing inconsiderate, acceptable, even admirable (because it shows they're productive)? Your answer reflects your beliefs or ideas about the situation.
- **The behavioral component—"I intend."** **The behavioral component of an attitude, also known as the intentional component, is how one intends or expects to behave toward a situation.** What would you *intend to do* if a person talked loudly on a cell-phone at the table next to you? Your action may reflect your negative or positive feelings (affective), your negative or positive beliefs (cognitive), and your intention or lack of intention to do anything (behavioral).

All three components are often manifested at any given time. For example, if you call a corporation and get one of those telephone-tree menus ("For customer service, press 1 . . .") that never seem to connect you to a human being, you might be so irritated that you would say

- "I hate being given the runaround." [*affective component—your feelings*]
- "That company doesn't know how to take care of customers." [*cognitive component—your perceptions*]
- "I'll never call them again." [*behavioral component—your intentions*]

A *Positive Approach* is one of the career readiness competencies desired by employers.[55] We defined this attitude in Chapter 1 as the "willingness to accept developmental feedback, to try and suggest new ideas, and to maintain a positive attitude at work." You can see why employers want to hire new graduates with this attitude. Where do you think you stand? Find out by taking Self-Assessment 11.4.

When Attitudes and Reality Collide: Consistency and Cognitive Dissonance One of the last things you want, probably, is to be accused of hypocrisy—to be criticized for saying one thing and doing another. Like most people, you no doubt want to maintain consistency between your attitudes and your behavior.

SELF-ASSESSMENT 11.4 CAREER READINESS

Do You Have a Positive Approach at Work?

The following survey is designed to assess the extent you possess a positive approach or attitude at work. Please be prepared to answer these questions if your instructor has assigned Self-Assessment 11.4 in Connect.

1. How do you stand on the two dimensions underlying a positive approach?
2. Based on individual item scores, identify one strength and one weaknesses for the dimensions of positive attitude and feedback seeking and acceptance. Now discuss the actions you might take to enhance your weaknesses.
3. What things might you say in an interview to demonstrate that you possess this career readiness competency?

But what if a strongly held attitude bumps up against a harsh reality that contradicts it? Suppose you're extremely concerned about getting AIDS, which you believe you might get from contact with body fluids, including blood. Then you're in a life-threatening auto accident in a third-world country and require surgery and blood transfusions—including transfusions of blood from (possibly AIDS-infected) strangers in a blood bank. Do you reject the blood to remain consistent with your beliefs about getting AIDS?

In 1957, social psychologist **Leon Festinger** proposed the term **cognitive dissonance** **to describe the psychological discomfort a person experiences between his or her cognitive attitude and incompatible behavior.**[56] Because people are uncomfortable with inconsistency, Festinger theorized, they will seek to reduce the "dissonance," or tension, of the inconsistency. How they deal with the discomfort, he suggested, depends on three factors:

- **Importance.** How important are the elements creating the dissonance? Most people can put up with some ambiguities in life. For example, many drivers don't think obeying speed limits is very important, even though they profess to be law-abiding citizens. People eat greasy foods, even though they know that ultimately those foods may contribute to heart disease.
- **Control.** How much control does one have over the matters that create dissonance? A juror may not like the idea of voting the death penalty but believe that he or she has no choice but to follow the law in the case. A taxpayer may object to his taxes being spent on, say, special-interest corporate welfare for a particular company but not feel that he can withhold taxes.
- **Rewards.** What rewards are at stake in the dissonance? You're apt to cling to old ideas in the face of new evidence if you have a lot invested emotionally or financially in those ideas. If you're a police officer who worked 20 years to prove a particular suspect guilty of murder, you're not apt to be very accepting of contradictory evidence after all that time.

The Practical Action box below provides an example of three key methods Festinger suggested to reduce cognitive dissonance.

PRACTICAL ACTION Using Cognitive Reframing to Reduce Cognitive Dissonance

College students feel a lot of pressure to be bright, intellectual, and capable of juggling all their newfound freedoms and responsibilities. But many also experience high levels of stress as they try to keep it all together. For those who struggle with additional, often invisible stressors such as anxiety, depression, and cognitive challenges and learning disabilities like dyslexia and attention deficit/hyperactivity disorder (ADHD), navigating the college experience can feel downright overwhelming.[57] The negative thoughts, feelings, and inner dialogue that often accompany these experiences can lead to further stress and can affect students' ability to succeed in college.[58]

How can you reduce the cognitive dissonance you experience as a result of high performance expectations coupled with high stress in college? You can use a therapeutic technique called cognitive reframing (or cognitive restructuring) to identify, challenge, and modify negative thoughts.[59] Learning to reframe destructive thoughts is a critical life skill and will help you lower your stress and achieve a more balanced, realistic perspective on the challenges you face and your ability to master them.[60]

Give Yourself Some Advice

Self-made billionaire Richard Branson struggled so much with dyslexia in high school that he dropped out. Now Branson is part of the global charity *Made By Dyslexia*, which aims to help people reframe dyslexia "as a positive influence in their lives."[61] Branson suggests people struggling with cognitive differences write a letter to their younger selves explaining that the challenges they face are assets and unique capabilities rather than flaws. In Branson's letter to his teenage self, he says to "use your alternative ways of thinking to be creative and think bigger."[62]

Ask Yourself a Few Questions

Another useful technique for reframing your thoughts is called the ABCDEs of Cognitive Restructuring.[63] When you begin to feel like you aren't good enough, smart enough, or capable enough to succeed in college because of stress or invisible challenges, use this five-step process:

A Name the event or problem. For example:

I have four exams in one week and my grades are important to me. I don't know how to tackle the challenge of studying in order to earn a high grade on all the exams.

B List your beliefs about the event or problem.

I don't have enough time to study for all these exams. I will either need to focus on studying for one or two and accept poor performance on the others, or study just enough for each exam to get passing grades on all four.

C Identify the consequences of your beliefs.

I won't earn the grades I want to earn in all four courses and my GPA will drop. This can reduce my ability to get a good job.

D Formulate a counterargument to your initial thoughts and beliefs. Pessimistic thoughts are generally overreactions, so the first step is to correct inaccurate or distorted thoughts.

I have not considered creative methods for studying and performing well on all my exams. I may not be able to assemble thorough study guides for all four, but I know others in my classes are in the same boat, and we may be able to combine our materials and work as a group to study for these exams. I could also ask my professors for advice on narrowing down the content for studying. The worst-case scenario is that I don't earn As on all four exams and I use this experience to learn to prepare earlier for future exams. One bad exam grade may not mean I am unable to earn a high final course grade or find a good job after graduation.

E Describe how energized and empowered you feel at the moment.

I'm motivated to do as well as I can on these exams. I got into college and have made it this far. There is no reason I can't continue to be a successful student and go on to have a great career.

These questions will help you to identify destructive thought patterns, evaluate their merit, neutralize those that are unrealistic, and work to find solutions to the things causing your stress.

YOUR CALL

Do you struggle with high levels of stress because of your workload, responsibilities, a cognitive difference, or some other invisible challenge such as anxiety or depression that sometimes gets the better of your self-esteem? Which of the preceding suggestions would help you to reframe your experiences in a more positive light?

Behavior: How Values and Attitudes Affect People's Actions and Judgments

Values (global) and attitudes (specific) are generally in harmony, but not always. For example, a manager may put a positive *value* on helpful behavior (global) yet may have a negative *attitude* toward helping an unethical co-worker (specific). Together, however, values and attitudes influence people's workplace **behavior—their actions and judgments.** ●

11.3 Perception and Individual Behavior

THE BIG PICTURE

Perception, a four-step process, can be skewed by five types of distortion: stereotyping, implicit bias, the halo effect, the recency effect, and causal attribution. We also consider the self-fulfilling prophecy, which can affect our judgment as well.

LO 11-3

Describe the way perception can cloud judgment.

If you were a smoker, which warning on a cigarette pack would make you think more about quitting? "Smoking seriously harms you and others around you"? A blunt "Smoking kills"? Or a stark graphic image showing decaying teeth?

This is the kind of decision public health authorities in various countries are wrestling with. (One study found that highly graphic images about the negative effects of smoking had the greatest impact on smokers' intentions to quit.)[64] These officials, in other words, are trying to decide how *perception* might influence behavior.

The Four Steps in the Perceptual Process

Perception is the process of interpreting and understanding one's environment. The process of perception is complex, but it can be boiled down to four steps.[65] *(See Figure 11.2.)*

FIGURE 11.2 The four steps in the perceptual process

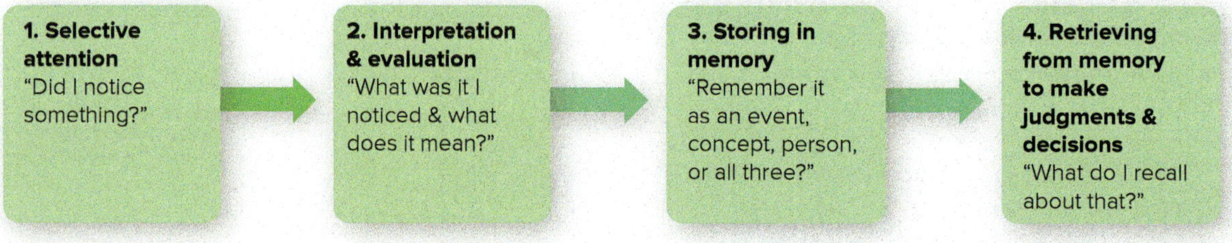

In this book, we are less concerned about the theoretical steps in perception than in how perception is distorted, since this has considerable bearing on the manager's judgment and job. In any one of the four stages of the perception process, misunderstandings or errors in judgment can occur. Perceptual errors can lead to mistakes that can be damaging to yourself, other people, and your organization.

Five Distortions in Perception

Although there are other types of distortion in perception, we will describe the following: (1) *stereotyping*, (2) *implicit bias*, (3) the *halo effect*, (4) the *recency effect*, and (5) *causal attribution*.

1. Stereotyping: "Those Sorts of People Are Pretty Much the Same" If you're a tall African American man, do people make remarks about basketball players? If you're of Irish descent, do people believe you drink a lot? If you're Jewish, do people think you're money-oriented? If you're a woman, do people think you're automatically nurturing? All these are stereotypes. **Stereotyping** is the tendency to attribute to an individual the characteristics one believes are typical of the group to which that individual belongs.[66]

Principal areas of stereotyping that should be of concern to you as a manager are (1) *sex-role stereotypes*, (2) *age stereotypes*, and (3) *race/ethnicity stereotypes*. (People with disabilities, discussed in Section 11.5, are also apt to be stereotyped.)

Sex-Role Stereotypes A *sex-role stereotype* is the belief that differing traits and abilities make males and females particularly well suited to different roles. Thus, for example, people tend to prefer male bosses (33 percent) to female bosses (20 percent) in a new job, according to a recent Gallup poll, even though the public generally views women as being every bit as capable as men at being leaders, according to Pew Research.[67] (Reverse bias can occur when managers fighting bias against women overdo it and discriminate against men.)[68] Another recent study demonstrated that entrepreneurs displaying stereotypically female traits (warmth, sensitivity, and emotionality) were less likely to have a proposal accepted by venture capitalists than those exhibiting masculine traits (forcefulness, aggressiveness, and assertiveness).[69]

A summary of research revealed that

- Women perceive more sex-based mistreatment then men, and racial minorities similarly perceive more race-based mistreatment than Whites. On the positive side, however, perceptions of sex and race differences have been decreasing over time.[70]
- Women have a harder time than men in being perceived as effective leaders. (The exception: Women were seen as more effective when the organization faced a crisis and needed a turnaround.)
- Women of color are more negatively affected by sex-role stereotypes than are white women or men in general.[71]

Another Pew study of more than 4,500 U.S. adults found that most believe in various gender differences: "87% believe men and women express their feelings differently, 76% believe they have different physical abilities, 68% think they have different personal interests or hobbies and 64% believe they take different approaches to parenting." In contrast, only 37 percent appear to believe men's and women's workplace skills differ.[72]

Age Stereotypes Another example of an inaccurate stereotype is the belief that older workers are less motivated, more resistant to change, less trusting, less healthy, and more likely to have problems with work-life balance. A recent study refuted all these negative beliefs about age.[73] While such beliefs can still create problems, a report by the Transamerica Center for Retirement Studies found that more than half the nation's baby boomers plan to work beyond the age of 65, and perhaps even indefinitely, thanks in large part to financial worries associated with the high cost of medical care and the fragility of Social Security and other benefits. In fact, the labor force of workers aged 65 to 75 and up is expected to grow faster through 2024 than any other, between 4.5 and 6.4 per year, according to the U.S. Bureau of Labor Statistics.[74]

The New York Times recently reported on several companies that prize their older workers. One of these is Lee Spring, a Brooklyn-based firm that gave a valued factory technician an office job at age 57 to relieve him of the need to stand and lift all day. The employee's insights were valuable to the company's younger engineers, who had never worked on the factory floor, and they in turn taught him about design and software. Lee Spring received an Age Smart Employer Award by entering a competition run by Columbia University's Aging Center. The Center's program, which had 100 applicants in 2017 (twice as many as in 2016), identifies employers that are setting new standards by adjusting training, scheduling, and job demands for older workers. They include a military shipbuilder, an accounting firm, a film production company, and Steelcase, the office furniture maker.[75]

Race/Ethnicity Stereotypes Consider the stereotypes Dr. Sutton-Ramsey encountered while tending to an emergency room patient at Bellevue Hospital in Manhattan. When the doctor, who is African American, entered the patient's room, the patient's mother "demanded that a physician come in," according to *The Wall Street Journal.* "Well, you've got one, I'm here," said Dr. Sutton-Ramsey. The mother did not believe him and asked to see the physician in charge. The supervisor, who also is black, entered and asked how to be of assistance. "The patient ended up refusing medical care and left the emergency room."[76]

Studies of race-based stereotypes have demonstrated that people of color experienced more perceived discrimination and less psychological support than whites.[77] Perceived racial discrimination was also associated with more negative work attitudes, physical health, psychological health, and organizational citizenship behavior.[78] Among the experiences whites tend to take for granted at work that people of color may not experience are being consistently in the racial majority, having plenty of roles models of their own race, being heard in meetings without having to assert themselves, making mistakes without other people offering race-related excuses for them, succeeding without being hailed as an example of "progress," not being asked to present the "white perspective" on a problem, and not having to worry about whether race will impede their career.[79]

2. Implicit Bias: "I Really Don't Think I'm Biased, but I Just Have a Feeling about Some People" More than 85% of Americans consider themselves to be unprejudiced, but researchers conclude that most hold some degree of implicit racial bias.[80]

Explicit bias reflects attitudes or beliefs endorsed at a conscious level—for example, "I don't let any teenage black men wearing hoodies come into my store; they might hold me up." **Implicit bias** **is the attitudes or beliefs that affect our understanding, actions, and decisions in an unconscious manner**—for example, from several New York City police officers, "We had to shoot him, he seemed to be reaching for a gun." (This was the 1999 shooting of Guinean immigrant Amadou Diallo, who was killed when police fired 41 rounds as he pulled out his wallet.)[81]

Implicit bias has come into the forefront of public discussion with the rise in the number of deaths of African Americans at the hands of the police in Ferguson, Missouri; Cleveland; New York; Baton Rouge; Chicago; Charlotte, North Carolina; Baltimore; Cincinnati; Falcon Heights, Minnesota; Tulsa; and Sacramento, among others. In some cases the shootings were filmed; in several, the police were not convicted or not charged.[82] But implicit bias also appears to affect employment-related decisions. A recent study showed that racism led to discriminatory decisions in hiring and performance evaluations. Ageism also was found to impact discriminatory hiring decisions.[83]

If changing explicit bias is difficult, taking steps to root out implicit bias is even harder. Nevertheless, police departments, in particular, are taking great steps forward, requiring intergroup contact, positive feedback, clear norms of behavior, and similar matters.[84]

3. The Halo Effect: "One Trait Tells Me All I Need to Know" We often use faces as markers for gender, race, and age, but face and body characteristics can lead us to fall back on cultural stereotypes. For example, height has been associated with perceptions of prosperity—high income—and occupational success. Excess weight can be stereotypically associated with negative traits such as laziness, incompetence, and lack of discipline.[85] These examples illustrate the **halo effect**, **in which we form an impression of an individual based on a single trait.** (The phenomenon is also called the *horn-and-halo effect* because not only can a single positive trait be generalized into an array of positive traits, but the reverse is also true.)

As if we needed additional proof that life is unfair, it has been shown that attractive people generally are treated better than unattractive people. Attractive members of Congress get more TV coverage, and attractive political candidates win more often.[86] Attractive students have higher expectations by teachers in terms of academic achievement.[87] Attractive employees are generally paid higher salaries than unattractive ones are, and attractive CEOs are paid more than less appealing CEOs.[88] (Male CEOs also tend to be taller—6 feet compared to an average man's 5-feet-10.5 inches, in one Swedish study.)[89] Clearly, however, if a manager fails to look at *all* of an individual's traits, he or she has no right to complain if that employee doesn't work out.

EXAMPLE The Halo Effect: Does Body Weight Weigh Down Careers?

Lulu Hunt Peters was an overweight child and, by early adulthood, weighed 220 pounds. She earned a medical degree from the University of California–Berkeley and dropped 70 pounds by adopting a strict low-calorie diet. Her book, *Diet & Health: With Key to the Calories*, sold millions of copies and became the first ever weight-loss book to make the best-seller list. All this happened before the year 1920.[90]

Peters' writings introduced a novel concept to a nation that had most recently been concerned that its citizens didn't have *enough* to eat during wartime. Her message was that being overweight was bad and resulted from individual choices to eat too much and exercise too little.[91] Peters saw obesity as shameful and believed dieting and remaining thin were signs of self-control. Her book even suggested that people who were unable to resist the temptations of food were likely to be immoral in their other behavior as well.[92] Around this same time, in the early 20th century, Hollywood began to adopt similar ideals, and to this day the Western preference for thinness remains.

Does Higher Weight Equate to Lower Competence? According to research, organizational decision makers use weight as a substitute for evaluating personal factors that predict work motivation, behavior, and ability. Specifically, there is a strong tendency to equate higher weight with laziness, sloppiness, unprofessionalism and lower levels of intelligence, conscientiousness, self-discipline, productivity, and competence.[93] In short, organizations view overweight applicants and workers as less capable and less desirable.[94]

These generalizations about weight affect workers in virtually every aspect of organizational life. Overweight applicants are less likely to be hired for jobs, particularly those that are customer-facing.[95] Managers evaluate overweight workers more negatively than thin workers and judge them as less viable for supervisory and leadership roles.[96] Workers who carry more weight make less money and are less likely to receive promotions than their thinner counterparts with equal qualifications.[97] Clearly, body weight activates a halo effect.

The Halo Misperception Discrimination against overweight individuals stems largely from the misconception that body size is always the result of poor personal choices.[98] In truth, body size tells us very little in the absence of information about a person's genetics, general health profile, bone structure, and many other factors.

YOUR CALL

Do you allow weight to influence your judgments about others' abilities and characteristics? How can you suppress this bias in your role as a manager?

Handsomely compensated. This attractive group of people are more likely to be paid better than unattractive workers. Do you think this is fair? Why do you think this bias occurs and what can be done to stop it? ©Monkey Business Images/Shutterstock

4. The Recency Effect: "The Most Recent Impressions Are the Ones That Count" The **recency effect** is the tendency to remember recent information better than earlier information, perhaps because when you activate your recall, the later recollections are still present in working memory. You see this misperception often operating among investors (even professionals), who are more likely to buy a stock if they see something about it in the news or if it has a high one-day return.[99]

5. Causal Attributions **Causal attribution** is the activity of inferring causes for observed behavior. Rightly or wrongly, we constantly formulate cause-and-effect explanations for our own and others' behavior. Attributional statements such as the following are common: "Joe drinks too much because he has no willpower, but I need a few drinks after work because I'm under a lot of pressure."

Even though our causal attributions tend to be self-serving and are often invalid, it's important to understand how people formulate attributions because they profoundly affect organizational behavior. For example, a supervisor who attributes an employee's poor performance to a lack of effort might reprimand that person. However, training might be deemed necessary if the supervisor attributes the poor performance to a lack of ability.

As a manager, you need to be alert to two attributional tendencies that can distort one's interpretation of observed behavior—the *fundamental attribution bias* and the *self-serving bias*.

- **Fundamental attribution bias.** In the **fundamental attribution bias**, people attribute another person's behavior to his or her personal characteristics rather than to situational factors.

  Example: A study of manufacturing employees found that top managers attributed the cause of industrial back pain to individuals, whereas workers attributed it to the environment.[100]

- **Self-serving bias.** In the **self-serving bias**, people tend to take more personal responsibility for success than for failure.

  Examples: You get an A on an exam and conclude that it's due to your level of studying. Had you received a poor grade, you would more likely conclude that the professor wrote a poor exam or didn't effectively teach the subject matter. Another example occurs in car accidents, when both parties tend to blame the other driver.[101]

The Self-Fulfilling Prophecy, or Pygmalion Effect

The **self-fulfilling prophecy**, also known as the *Pygmalion* ("pig-*mail*-yun") *effect*, describes the phenomenon in which people's expectations of themselves or others lead them to behave in ways that make those expectations come true.

Expectations are important. An example is a waiter who expects some poorly dressed customers to be stingy tippers, who therefore gives them poor service and so gets the result he or she expected—a much lower tip than usual. Research has shown that by raising managers' expectations for individuals performing a wide variety of tasks, higher levels of achievement and productivity can be achieved.[102]

The lesson for you as a manager is that when you expect employees to perform badly, they probably will, and when you expect them to perform well, they probably will. (In the G. B. Shaw play *Pygmalion*, a speech coach bets he can get a lower-class girl to change her accent and her demeanor so that she can pass herself off as a duchess. In six months, she successfully "passes" in high society, having assumed the attributes of a woman of sensitivity and taste.)

Research in a variety of industries and occupations shows that the effect of the self-fulfilling prophecy can be quite strong.[103] That is, managerial expectations powerfully influence employee behavior and performance. Among the things managers can do to create positive performance expectations: Recognize that everyone has the potential to increase his or her performance. Introduce new employees as if they have outstanding potential. Encourage employees to visualize the successful execution of tasks. Help them master key skills.[104]

EXAMPLE "What's within You Is Stronger Than What's in Your Way"

Erik Weihenmayer was diagnosed with an eye disease called juvenile retinoschisis at age 4; by his freshman year of high school, he was completely blind. He recalls that, at the time, "I was afraid that I wasn't going to be able to participate in life."[105] But instead of shielding him from opportunities, his parents encouraged him to take up all the activities his peers were tackling.[106] Weihenmayer became captain of his high school wrestling team and went on to represent Connecticut in the National Junior Freestyle Wrestling Championships.[107] He also realized that the keen tactile senses he'd developed due to the loss of his sight made him especially suited for rock climbing, a hobby that eventually blossomed into a lifelong passion.

In 2001, Weihenmayer became the first blind person to summit Mount Everest.[108] Although Himalayan experts strongly discouraged him from attempting the climb because of his blindness, he persisted. He recalls, "They were judging me on the basis of one thing that they knew about me and that was being blind. But they didn't realize that there are a dozen other attributes that contribute to whether you're a good mountaineer or not."[109] Weihenmayer acknowledges that life isn't always easy but believes strongly that "People have the inner resources to become anything they want to be. Challenge just becomes the vehicle for tapping into those inner resources."[110] By 2008, he had earned the distinction of being one of only a few hundred people in history to complete the seven summits, meaning he has climbed to the top of the highest mountain on each of the seven continents.[111]

Weihenmayer is the cofounder of an organization called *No Barriers*, which aims to help those with challenges live rich and meaningful lives.[112] He believes that all of us should make the conscious decision to do the things that make us uncomfortable and live our most extraordinary lives, in spite of our fears or the beliefs we often allow to limit us.[113] He receives many letters from parents of children who are blind or have other disabilities, asking for guidance. His advice? "The key is to really have tremendously high expectations and to teach kids how to be self-sufficient and confident and give them the skills that they need to succeed."[114]

YOUR CALL

Have you allowed yourself to be limited by certain expectations? What is something you've wanted to do but have been afraid to try because you don't believe you can? What advice do you think Erik Weihenmayer would give you?

Erik Weihenmayer, the first blind person to succeed in climbing to the top of Mt. Everest. Do you think Erik ever doubted his ability to climb the mountain? ©A7A collection/Photo 12/ Alamy Stock Photo

11.4 Work-Related Attitudes and Behaviors Managers Need to Deal With

THE BIG PICTURE

Attitudes are important because they affect behavior. Managers need to be alert to the key work-related attitudes having to do with engagement, job satisfaction, and organizational commitment. Among the types of employee behavior they should attend to are their on-the-job performance and productivity, absenteeism and turnover, organizational citizenship behaviors, and counterproductive work behaviors.

LO 11-4

Explain how managers can deal with employee attitudes.

"Keep the employees happy," we often hear. It's true that attitudes are important, the reason being that *attitudes affect behavior.* But is keeping employees happy all that managers need to know to get results? We discuss motivation for performance in the next chapter. Here, let us consider what managers need to know about key work-related attitudes and behaviors.

Three types of attitudes managers are particularly interested in are (1) *employee engagement,* (2) *job satisfaction,* and (3) *organizational commitment.*

1. Employee Engagement: How Connected Are You to Your Work?

Research on job involvement has evolved into the study of an individual difference called **employee engagement**, **defined as a "mental state in which a person performing a work activity is full immersed in the activity, feeling full of energy and enthusiasm for the work."**[115] Employers, consultants, and academics have actively studied the causes and consequences of employee engagement given its potential for increasing individual, group, and organizational performance.[116] Let's consider what we've learned.

How Much of the U.S. Workforce Is Actively Engaged? The U.S. workforce appears to be achieving at above the global average. Consulting firm Aon Hewitt has tracked data on employee engagement around the globe for over 15 years, studying millions of employees. Recent figures for North America (of which the United States is the largest component) are shown in Table 11.3.[117] The U.S. workforce leads several regions but is outpaced by Latin America and Africa-Middle East.

What Contributes to Employee Engagement? Here are some key drivers of employee engagement, both personal and situational.

TABLE 11.3

Employee Engagement around the World

LOCATION OF EMPLOYEES	PERCENT OF HIGHLY OR MODERATELY ENGAGED EMPLOYEES
1. The World	62%
2. North America	66
3. Europe	57
4. Asia Pacific	64
5. Latin America	71
6. Africa-Middle East	67

Person Factors

- Personality.
- Positive psychological capital.
- Human and social capital.[118]

Situation Factors

- Job characteristics. People are engaged when their work contains variety and when they receive timely feedback about performance.
- Leadership. People are more engaged when their manager is supportive and maintains a positive, trusting relationship with them.[119]
- Organizational climate can range from positive and inspiring to negative and depleting. Positive climates obviously foster engagement.
- Stressors. **Stressors are environmental characteristics that cause stress.** Engagement is higher when employees are not confronted with a lot of stressors.[120]

What Outcomes Are Associated with Employee Engagement? Consulting firms such as Gallup, Hewitt Associates, and Blessing White have been in the forefront of collecting proprietary data supporting the practical value of employee engagement. For example, Gallup estimates that an organization whose employees are highly engaged can achieve 12 percent higher customer satisfaction/loyalty, 18 percent more productivity, and 12 percent greater profitability.[121] Other recent academic studies similarly showed a positive relationship between employee engagement, performance, and physical and psychological well-being and corporate-level financial performance and customer satisfaction.[122]

Now that you know engagement is correlated with performance at work, try Self-Assessment 11.5 to measure your level of engagement in your studies. Can you improve your performance in the classroom?

Can Managers Increase Employee Engagement? Yes, according to a systematic review of 20 studies. The researchers found four types of interventions that managers can use to positively influence employee engagement.[123] They are:

1. *Personal resource building* interventions, which "focus on increasing individuals' self-perceived positive attributes and strengths, often by developing self-efficacy, resilience or optimism."
2. *Job resource building* interventions, which "focus on increasing resources in the work environment such as autonomy, social support, and feedback."
3. *Leadership training* interventions, which "involve knowledge and skill building workshops for managers."
4. *Health promotion* interventions, which "encourage employees to adopt and sustain healthier lifestyles and reduce and manage stress."[124]

SELF-ASSESSMENT 11.5 CAREER READINESS

To What Extent Are You Engaged in Your Studies?

The following survey was designed to assess your level of engagement in your studies. Please be prepared to answer these questions if your instructor has assigned Self-Assessment 11.5 in Connect.

1. What is your level of engagement?
2. Find your three lowest-rated items. Based on the content of these items, what can you do to improve your level of engagement? Hint: Doing this requires you to identify the cause of the low ratings for each item.
3. What might you say during an interview to demonstrate that you possess the career readiness competency of self-motivation?

2. Job Satisfaction: How Much Do You Like or Dislike Your Job?

Job satisfaction is the extent to which you feel positive or negative about various aspects of your work. Most people don't like everything about their jobs. Their overall satisfaction depends on how they feel about several components, such as *work*, *pay*, *promotions*, *co-workers*, and *supervision*.[125] Among the key correlates of job satisfaction are stronger motivation, job involvement, organizational commitment, and life satisfaction and less absenteeism, tardiness, turnover, and perceived stress.[126]

A recent study by the Society for Human Resource Management indicates that an impressively high 89 percent of U.S. employees are satisfied with their jobs and are "moderately engaged."[127] But what is the relationship between job satisfaction and job performance—does more satisfaction cause better performance, or does better performance cause more satisfaction? This is a subject of much debate among management scholars.[128] One comprehensive study found that (1) job satisfaction and performance are moderately related, meaning that employee job satisfaction is a key work attitude managers should consider when trying to increase performance, but (2) the relationship between satisfaction and performance is complex and it seems that both variables influence each other through a host of individual differences and work-environment characteristics.[129]

How satisfied are you with the job you are in now, if you have one, or the last job you had? You can find out by taking Self-Assessment 11.6.

SELF-ASSESSMENT 11.6

How Satisfied Are You with Your Present Job?

The following survey was designed to assess how satisfied you are with your current job, or a previous job, if you're not presently working. Please be prepared to answer these questions if your instructor has assigned Self-Assessment 11.6 in Connect.

1. What is your level of satisfaction with recognition, compensation, and supervision?
2. If you have low to medium satisfaction with any aspect of the job, identify what can be done to increase your job satisfaction. Be sure to consider what you can do, what your boss might do, or what the organization might do. Be specific.

3. Organizational Commitment: How Much Do You Identify with Your Organization?

Organizational commitment reflects the extent to which an employee identifies with an organization and is committed to its goals. For instance, women's commitment to work is often called into question thanks to longstanding biases. "Pregnant women and mothers are assumed to be less committed to their careers, and every time they leave the office or ask for any flexibility, that commitment is further called into question," says Anne Marie Slaughter, former director of policy planning at the U.S. State Department.[130] Research shows a significant positive relationship between organizational commitment and job satisfaction, performance, turnover, and organizational citizenship behavior—discussed in the next section.[131] Thus, if managers are able to increase job satisfaction, employees may show higher levels of commitment, which in turn can elicit higher performance and lower employee turnover.[132]

Important Workplace Behaviors

Why, as a manager, do you need to learn how to manage individual differences? The answer, as you might expect, is so that you can influence employees' behavior. Among the types of behavior are (1) *performance and productivity*, (2) *absenteeism and turnover*, (3) *organizational citizenship behaviors*, and (4) *counterproductive work behaviors*.

1. Performance and Productivity Every job has certain expectations, but in some jobs performance and productivity are easier to define than in others. How many contacts should a telemarketing sales rep make in a day? How many sales should he or she close? Often a job of this nature will have a history of accomplishments (from what previous job holders have attained), so that it is possible to quantify performance behavior.

However, an advertising agency account executive handling major clients such as a carmaker or a beverage manufacturer may go months before landing this kind of big account. Or a researcher in a pharmaceutical company may take years to develop a promising new prescription drug.

In short, the method of evaluating performance must match the job being done.

2. Absenteeism and Turnover Should you be suspicious of every instance of absenteeism? Of course, some absences—illness, death in the family, or jury duty, for example—are legitimate. However, a lot of no-show behavior is related to job dissatisfaction.[133] One study of 700 managers found that 20 percent called in sick simply because they didn't feel like going to work that day. The top three reasons for employees taking bogus sick days are for doing personal errands, catching up on sleep, and relaxing.[134]

Absenteeism may be a precursor to turnover, which, as we saw in Chapter 9, is when an employee abandons, resigns, retires, or is terminated from a job. Every organization experiences some turnover, as employees leave for reasons of family, better job prospects, or retirement. However, except in low-skill industries, a continual revolving door of new employees is usually not a good sign, since replacement and training are expensive. The Society for Human Resource Management recently estimated the average dollar cost of hiring a new employee to be $4,129 and put the time investment at 42 days.[135] That dollar amount may be a conservative estimate; other studies, including a review of 11 research papers on the subject, have suggested the cost of replacing a highly skilled employee can be as high as two times the employee's annual salary.[136]

Experience demonstrates five practical ways to reduce turnover: (1) Base hiring decisions on the extent to which an applicant's values fit the organization's values. (2) Provide post-hiring support, which is referred to as onboarding. As we mentioned in Chapter 9, onboarding programs help employees to integrate and transition to new jobs by making them familiar with corporate policies, procedures, culture, and politics by clarifying work-role expectations and responsibilities.[137] (3) Focus on enhancing employee engagement. (4) Incorporate realistic job previews (RJPs, discussed in Chapter 9) into the hiring process. (5) Offer employees benefits, such as flexible work hours (discussed in Chapter 12), that meet their needs and values.[138]

3. Organizational Citizenship Behaviors **Organizational citizenship behaviors (OCBs) are those employee behaviors that are not directly part of employees' job descriptions—that exceed their work-role requirements.** Examples, according to one description, include "such gestures as constructive statements about the department, expression of personal interest in the work of others, suggestions for improvement, training new people, respect for the spirit as well as the letter of housekeeping rules, care for organizational property, and punctuality and attendance well beyond standard or enforceable levels."[139] Research demonstrates a significant and moderately positive correlation between organizational citizenship behaviors and job satisfaction, productivity, efficiency, and customer satisfaction.[140]

Thriving employees. Zingerman's, an Ann Arbor, Michigan, community of food-related businesses, encourages employees to thrive through such devices as sharing information and experimenting with ways to solve problems on their own. Employees with high job satisfaction can help organizations grow. Courtesy of Zingerman's Community of Businesses

4. Counterproductive Work Behaviors The flip side of organizational citizenship behaviors would seem to be what are called **counterproductive work behaviors (CWBs)**, types of behavior that harm employees and the organization as a whole. Such behaviors may include absenteeism and tardiness, drug and alcohol abuse, and disciplinary problems but also extend beyond them to more serious acts such as accidents, sabotage, sexual harassment, violence, theft, and white-collar crime.[141] Some 96 percent of workers say they have experienced uncivil behavior, and 98 percent have witnessed it.[142]

Clearly, if an employee engages in some kind of CWB, the organization needs to respond quickly and appropriately, defining the specific behaviors that are unacceptable and the requirements for acceptable behavior. The problem, however, is that managers and co-workers do not have adequate opportunity to observe CWBs.[143] That's why it is more desirable to take preventive measures. One way is to screen for CWB during the hiring process. For instance, it's been found that applicants scoring higher on cognitive ability (intelligence) tests are less likely to be involved in violence and property damage after they are hired.[144] Employees are also less likely to engage in CWB if they have satisfying jobs that offer autonomy or that don't require them to supervise too many people.[145]

EXAMPLE The Toxic Workplace: "Rudeness Is Like the Common Cold"

Incivility. Rudeness. Jerks at work. They're all forms of counterproductive work behaviors or CWBs, and they're the bane of the office.

"Nothing is more costly to an organization's culture than a toxic employee," says management professor Christine Porath. "Rudeness is like the common cold—it's contagious, spreads quickly, and anyone can be a carrier."[146] Researcher Trevor Foulk concurs. "If someone is rude to me" he says, "it is likely that in my next interaction I will be rude to whomever I am talking to. You respond to their rudeness with your own rudeness."[147]

Sapping Energy and Productivity Management professor Gretchen Spreitzer believes that difficult co-workers are "de-energizers" who spread their dispiriting attitude to others. "They leave you feeling depleted, fatigued, and exhausted."[148] A recent study supported this conclusion. People experiencing incivility from a co-worker ended up with fewer resources for controlling their own impulses later on. The more someone had to interact with a de-energizer, the more likely that person was rude to others.[149]

Examples of incivility include snippy remarks, interruptions, eye-rolling, and berating another employee for being late.[150] Toxic bosses may demoralize employees by such actions as "walking away from a conversation because they lose interest; answering calls in the middle of meetings without leaving the room; openly mocking people by pointing out their flaws or personality quirks in front of others," and similar incivilities, says Porath.[151]

The Price of Incivility People who engage in negative and harmful behavior can hurt an organization's bottom line.[152] In fact, "avoiding a toxic employee can save a company more than twice as much as bringing on a star performer—specifically, avoiding a toxic worker was worth about $12,500 in turnover costs," says one writer reporting on the study "Toxic Workers."[153]

Another academic study demonstrated that the costs of incivility are diminishing creativity, deteriorating performance and team spirit, and fleeing customers. "Employees are less creative when they feel disrespected, and many get fed up and leave," according to the authors. "About half deliberately decrease their effort or lower the quality of their work. And incivility damages customer relationships."[154] What's more, recent research suggests that it only takes *one* uncivil co-worker to cause feelings of isolation, job insecurity, and even health problems in others.[155]

Spotting the Toxic Office You'll know you're working in a toxic office when you see employees "congregate in hush-hush circles around cubicles after meetings to put a negative spin on what just transpired," says one report. Or when managers withhold information or employees feel it's not safe to offer their ideas, creativity, or inputs. And you'll know it's really time to update your résumé when people around you start breaking down and experiencing health issues.[156]

YOUR CALL

If you were working in a toxic workplace and had to stay there for a while, what would you do to try to make things better?

11.5 The New Diversified Workforce

THE BIG PICTURE

One of today's most important management challenges is working with stakeholders of all sorts who vary widely in diversity—in age, gender, race, religion, ethnicity, sexual orientation, capabilities, and socioeconomic background. Managers should also be aware of the differences between internal and external dimensions of diversity and barriers to diversity.

LO 11-5

Identify trends in workplace diversity that managers should be aware of.

Might you hold a few preconceptions that are worth examining? Here's a reality check:

- **Assumption: Illegal immigrants dramatically affect the U.S. economy.** No, says the American Immigration Council. Undocumented immigrants represent only 5 percent of the civilian workforce.[157]
- **Assumption: Customer bias favoring white men has just about disappeared.** Unfortunately not, suggests a study of college students, which found that people give higher ratings for customer satisfaction to white men than to women and members of minorities.[158]
- **Assumption: Young workers earn less than they used to.** Yes, evidently. The wages for young college graduates have recovered ground lost since the recession but have risen to only 1.4 percent above 2000 levels, which may reflect a wider problem of wage stagnation across all workers.[159]

The United States is becoming more diverse in its ethnic, racial, gender, and age makeup. Among the trends the Pew Research Center anticipates will shape the United States (and even the world) in the next few decades are (1) a reduction (already taking place) in immigration to the United States from Mexico, (2) an increase in immigration from Asian countries, (3) racially diverse Millennials maturing, (4) a growing share of women in "top leadership jobs" and a continued narrowing of the gender wage gap, (5) a decline in the number of two-parent households, (6) a drop in the share of middle-class households, and (7) a rise in the number of people who describe themselves as unaffiliated with any organized religion.[160]

Diversity may have its benefits, but it can also be an important management challenge. Let's consider this.

The beauty of this flower bed lies in its diversity of colors, shapes, and smells. Employee diversity is similarly celebrated by embracing differences among people. ©hailin/Shutterstock

How to Think about Diversity: Which Differences Are Important?

Diversity represents all the ways people are unlike and alike—the differences and similarities in age, gender, race, religion, ethnicity, sexual orientation, capabilities, and socioeconomic background. Note here that diversity is not synonymous with differences. Rather, it encompasses both differences and similarities. This means that as a manager you need to manage both simultaneously.

FIGURE 11.3 **The diversity wheel**

Four layers of diversity

Source: From Diverse Teams at *Work by Lee Gardenswartz and Anita Rowe. Copyright 2003, Society for Human Resource Management, Alexandria, VA.*

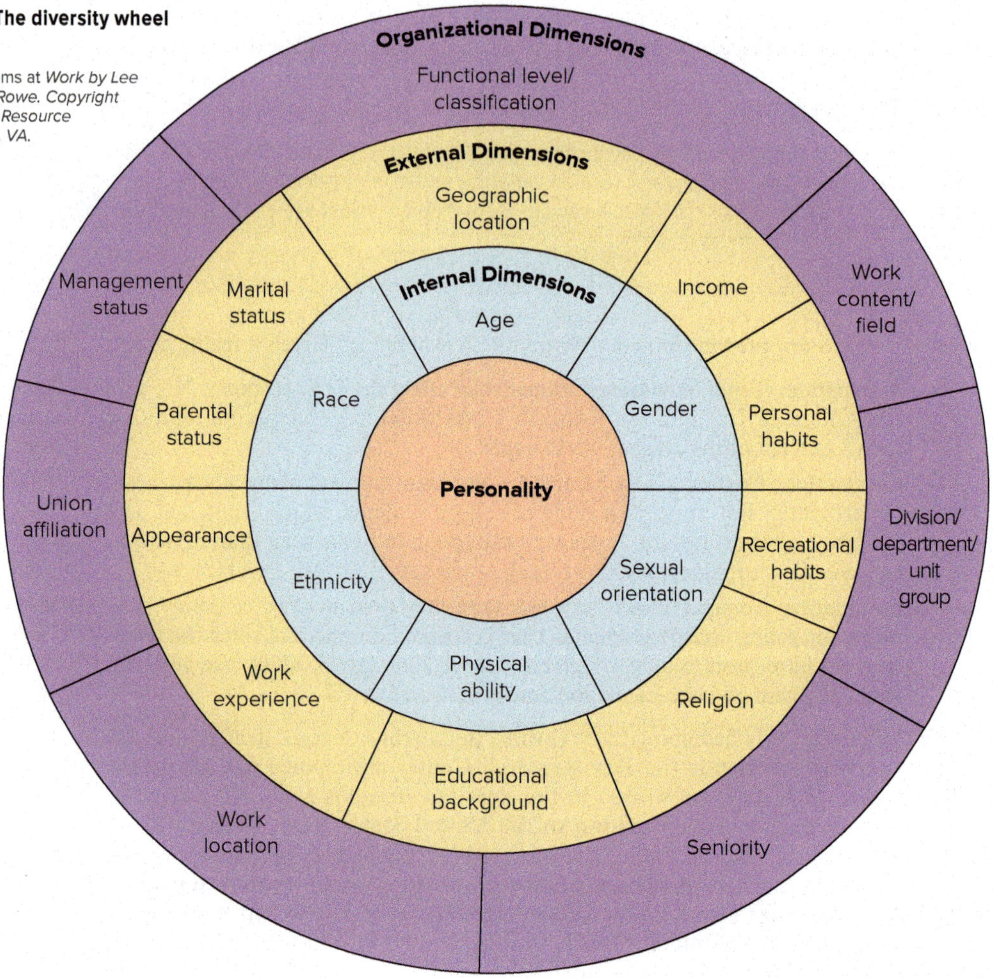

To help distinguish the important ways in which people differ, diversity experts Lee Gardenswartz and Anita Rowe have identified a "diversity wheel" consisting of four layers of diversity: (1) *personality*, (2) *internal dimensions*, (3) *external dimensions, and* (4) *organizational dimensions. (See Figure 11.3.)*

Let's consider these four layers:

Personality

At the center of the diversity wheel is personality. It is at the center because, as we said in Section 11.1, *personality* is defined as the stable physical and mental characteristics responsible for a person's identity.

Internal Dimensions

Internal dimensions of diversity are those human differences that exert a powerful, sustained effect throughout every stage of our lives: gender, age, ethnicity, race, sexual orientation, and physical abilities.[161] These are referred to as the *primary* dimensions of diversity because they are not within our control, for the most part. Yet they strongly influence our attitudes, expectations, and assumptions about other people, which in turn influence our own behavior.

What characterizes internal dimensions of diversity is that they are visible and salient in people. And precisely because these characteristics are so visible, they may be associated with certain stereotypes—for instance, that black people work in menial jobs.

Example: In a 2014 television interview, then-President Barack Obama recalled how, while waiting outside a restaurant after dinner, he had been handed car keys to fetch a vehicle from valet parking. Michelle Obama recounted that while visiting a Target store as First Lady, she was asked by another shopper to get something off a high shelf. (She added, "These incidents in the black community, this is the regular course of life.")[162]

External Dimensions **External dimensions of diversity include an element of choice; they consist of the personal characteristics that people acquire, discard, or modify throughout their lives:** educational background, marital status, parental status, religion, income, geographic location, work experience, recreational habits, appearance, and personal habits. They are referred to as the *secondary* dimensions of diversity because we have a greater ability to influence or control them than we do internal dimensions.

These external dimensions also exert a significant influence on our perceptions, behavior, and attitudes. If you are not a believer in the Muslim religion, for example, you may not perceive the importance of some of its practices–as Abercrombie and Fitch subsidiary Hollister did not, which told college student Hani Khan that she had to remove her hijab (Islamic headscarf) to work at its San Mateo, California, store, then fired her when she refused. The Equal Employment Opportunity Commission sued the company on Khan's behalf, on the grounds that a headscarf did not affect her job performance.[163]

Organizational Dimensions Organizational dimensions include management status, union affiliation, work location, seniority, work content, and division or department.

Trends in Workforce Diversity

How is the U.S. workforce apt to become more diverse in the 21st century? Let's examine five categories on the internal dimension–*age, gender, race/ethnicity, sexual orientation*, and *physical/mental abilities*–and one category on the external dimension, *educational level.*

Age: More Older People in the Workforce By the time you read this, Millennials will have replaced baby boomers as the largest adult generation in the United States.[164] Yet they will find many older workers working alongside them. The proportion of employed workers over 65 rose from 12.8 to 16.8 percent from 2000 to 2016, growing to nearly 9 million people, of whom only a little more than a third (36.1 percent) are working part-time. Most older workers are in management, sales, and office and administrative support positions. And although men account for less than half the 65-and-over age cohort, they make up 55 percent of the workforce in their age group.[165]

Not only are older workers staying in the workforce longer, but a trend called "unretirement" is also becoming more common, say economists.[166] Recent studies have found that, thanks to longer life spans, less physical labor on the job, and better health, somewhere between 25 and 40 percent of workers who retire eventually return to the workforce, full- or part-time. While income is sometimes the reason, an economist from Harvard Medical School found three other motivators in data from a national study: a sense of purpose, mental stimulation, and social engagement.[167]

Diversity enriches. A diverse population in a company can provide ideas, experience, and points of view that strengthen the business culture. What has been your experience, if any, with a diverse workplace? ©The Businessman/Alamy Stock Photo

One 69-year-old project manager who returned to the workforce to take a part-time job with a small company after two years of retirement said, "As long as somebody wants me, I have a lot to contribute." A social worker who retired at 63 from a crushing workload in a child protection agency had a life-changing realization 18 months later. "It hit me like a thunderbolt, how much I missed social work. That's who I was." She returned to her profession, working on-call two days a week.[168]

Do you have much experience being around older people? How do you feel about the idea of working with them? To find out, try Self-Assessment 11.7.

SELF-ASSESSMENT 11.7 CAREER READINESS

What Are Your Attitudes about Working with Older Employees?

The following survey was designed to assess your attitudes about working with older employees. Please be prepared to answer these questions if your instructor has assigned Self-Assessment 11.7 in Connect.

1. What is the quality of your relationships with older employees? How about your satisfaction with working with older people?
2. How might the quality of relationships with older employees affect your performance and promotability?
3. What things might you say during an interview to demonstrate that you can work with people of all ages?

Gender: More Women Working Since the 1960s, women have been flooding into the workplace in great numbers; their share of the workforce is expected to increase to 47.2 percent in 2024, whereas men's is expected to decline from 53.2 percent to 52.8 percent in the same period.[169] Seven in 10 women with children under 18 are working, most of them full-time.[170] In addition, more businesses are now owned by women; women currently own 10 million businesses, earning about $1.4 trillion annually.[171] Finally, women are gaining some ground in the top rungs of business. In 2018, women held 24 CEO positions in the Standard & Poor's 500 companies.[172]

But the pay gap between women and men still persists, and it affects women with children in particular.[173] This is alarming because "mothers are the primary or sole earners for 40 percent of households with children under 18 today, compared with 11 percent in 1960."[174] As of 2015, U.S. women earned on average only 83 percent of what men earn, according to research by the Pew Center. Women aged 25 to 34 fared slightly better, earning 90 percent of what men in this age group were paid.[175] Factors contributing to the gap's persistence include the fact that more women than men interrupt their careers to care for children or other family members, women's underrepresentation in high-paying jobs, and gender discrimination. The pay gap is higher for women with children, and this "motherhood penalty" has either held steady over time or even grown.[176]

Following the lead of Australia, Germany, and Iceland, the British government has taken a big step toward solving a similar problem, which research by PricewaterhouseCoopers indicates could otherwise take almost 100 years to fix if left alone. New legislation requires UK companies with more than 250 employees to publish annual reports of salary differences between men and women, publicly revealing the gender gap in order to force corrections to be made. "This is a game-changer," said the policy manager of a British women's rights organization.[177]

The obstacles to women's progress are collectively known as the **glass ceiling—the metaphor for an invisible barrier preventing women and minorities from being promoted to top executive jobs.** Women are more likely than men to complete a college degree by the time they are 29,[178] so what factors are holding women back? Three are negative stereotypes, lack of mentors, and limited experience in line or general management.[179] Among the strategies suggested for fighting gender discrimination: getting more women on corporate governing boards, increasing the diversity of the applicant pool, evaluating work assignments to ensure they are fairly distributed, making everyone's salary public, mentoring, and helping with work-life management.[180]

Interestingly, however, peers, managers, direct reports, and judges/trained observers rated women executives as more effective than men. Men also rated themselves as more effective than women evaluated themselves.[181] And a number of studies have found that companies with more women executives have better financial performance. One such study, by the Credit Suisse Research Institute, concluded that "the higher the percentage of women in top management, the greater the excess returns for shareholders."[182] We discuss women in leadership further in Chapter 14 and women and communication in Chapter 15.

Race and Ethnicity: More People of Color in the Workforce The non-Hispanic white population is projected to peak in 2024, then to slowly decrease. Whites are projected to change from 77.5 percent in 2014 to 68.5 percent in 2060, African Americans from 13.2 percent to 14.3 percent, Asians from 5.4 percent to 9.3 percent, Hispanics or Latinos from 17.4 percent to 28.6 percent, and American Indian/Alaskan Native from 1.2 percent to 1.5 percent.[183] People of color have hit the glass ceiling, with whites holding more of the managerial and professional jobs. In addition, two other trends show that U.S. businesses need to do a lot better by minority populations.

First, minorities tend to earn less than whites. Median household income in 2016 was $39,490 for African Americans and $47,675 for Hispanics. It was $65,041 for non-Hispanic whites. (Asians had the highest median income, at $81,431.)[184]

Second, a number of studies have shown that minorities experienced more perceived discrimination, racism-related stress, and less psychological support than whites did.[185]

Sexual Orientation: LGBTQ People Become More Visible It is difficult to accurately estimate the number of people in the United States who identify as part of the LGBT (lesbian, gay, bisexual, transgender) community. One likely reason is that surveys on the topic have used different definitions of the terms and asked inconsistent questions.[186] Another is the possibility that negative attitudes about non-normative sexuality have made people reluctant to identify themselves as LGBT.[187] A recent Gallup poll found 4.1 percent of the population so identified, or about 10 million people, up from 8.3 million in 2012.[188] A fifth term, Q for "queer," is sometimes added as a deliberately ambiguous umbrella term.[189]

Transgender is a term for people whose sense of their gender differs from what is expected based on the sex characteristics with which they are born.[190] That is, these are the estimated 0.03 percent of the population who feel their bodies and genders do not match, that the gender label they received at birth does not fit.[191] They may use labels such as *gender fluid* and *nonbinary*.

People in the United States have become far more tolerant of gay and lesbian behavior over time, with 63 percent saying in 2016 that society should accept homosexuality, up from 51 percent 10 years before.[192] No doubt things will change further, since the U.S. Supreme Court made it clear in June 2015 that marriage is no longer *solely* a legal union between a man and a woman. "The right to marry is a fundamental right inherent in the liberty of the person," Justice Anthony Kennedy wrote (in *Obergefell v. Hodges*) in support of the majority ruling that states may not refuse to marry same-sex couples. "Under the Due Process and Equal Protection Clauses of the Fourteenth Amendment couples of the same sex may not be deprived of that right and that liberty."[193]

Meanwhile the pay gap that used to hold for gay and bisexual men has disappeared, and according to one report, gay men now earn on average 10 percent *more* than straight men in similar employment.[194] While studies are inconclusive, it appears that lesbian women have enjoyed a pay advantage over straight women (though not over men of any sexual orientation) and continue to do so, possibly because of career choices they make and the fact that women earn lower salaries overall.[195]

Provisions of the Affordable Care Act made it illegal for federally funded health care providers to discriminate against the LGBT community, but one-third of transgender people reported in a recent study that they had experienced at least one negative interaction with a health care provider, ranging from denial of treatment to physical assault.[196] And, despite the changing social and legal landscape, "between 11 percent and 28 percent of LGB workers report losing a promotion simply because of their sexual orientation, and 27 percent of transgender workers report being fired, not hired, or denied a promotion in the past year."[197] Forty-two percent of LGBT people in a recent study reported using "vague language" to discuss their relationships, and 37 percent said they had hidden such a relationship to avoid being discriminated against. "When you're perceived as feminine–whether you're a woman or a gay man," said one gay man at a *Fortune* 500 company, "you get excluded from relationships that improve your career."[198]

People with Differing Physical and Mental Abilities About 5.67 million people, or 1.9 percent of the U.S. population, have a physical or mental disability, according to the U.S. Census Bureau.[199] However, only about 30 percent of those between 16 and 64 are employed, and they earn far less than those without a disability (monthly median income of $1,961 compared to $2,724).[200]

Since 1992 the **Americans with Disabilities Act (ADA), has prohibited discrimination against people with disabilities** and requires organizations to reasonably accommodate an individual's disabilities.[201] But in a recent survey of more than 3,000 supervisors by the nonprofit Kessler Foundation, only 28 percent of respondents said their organizations have disability hiring goals. One problem the supervisors reported was their perception that upper management was less committed to providing the training and accommodations that would be required for employees who required them.[202] Yet, according to Helena Berger, president of American Association of People with Disabilities, "having a disability may make you a better problem solver. You may be more innovative."[203]

Disability. Everyone recognizes the wheelchair as signifying that a person has a disability, but other disabilities are not easily identified—and may not invite understanding. Do you think that mental disabilities, for example, should be accommodated in employment? If you were subject to mood swings, do you think that would prevent you from doing your job effectively? ©Huntstock/ Brand X Pictures/Getty Images

Educational Levels: Mismatches between Education and Workforce Needs Two important mismatches between education and workplace are these:

- **College graduates may be in jobs for which they are overqualified.** According to one researcher, about a quarter of all college graduates are overqualified for their jobs. In other words, a great many college graduates are **underemployed**—working at jobs that require less education than they have. This number is reassuringly lower than earlier estimates of nearly half of all college grads, and the situation will be temporary for many, who will earn more as they gain more experience in their fields. But the pay gap between those who are in poor-fit and good-fit jobs appears to have grown and is now nearly 50%, according to this research.[204]
- **High-school dropouts and others may not have the literacy skills needed for many jobs.** A recent study found that 7 percent of all people in the United States between the ages of 16 and 24 had dropped out of high school in 2014.[205] Men make up 55 percent of such dropouts. If, as has been alleged, more than two-thirds of the American workforce reads below ninth-grade level, that is a problem for employers, because about 70 percent of the on-the-job reading materials are written at or above that level.[206]

Barriers to Diversity

Some barriers are erected by diverse people themselves. In the main, however, most barriers are put in their paths by organizations.[207] When we speak of "the organization's barriers," we are, of course, referring to the *people* in the organization—especially those who may have been there for a while—who are resistant to making it more diverse.

Resistance to change, which was discussed in Chapter 10, is an attitude that all managers come up against from time to time, and resistance to diversity is simply one variation. It may be expressed in the following six ways.

1. Stereotypes and Prejudices **Ethnocentrism** is the belief that your native country, culture, language, abilities, or behavior is superior to those of another culture. When differences are viewed as being weaknesses—which is what many stereotypes and prejudices ultimately come down to—this may be expressed as a concern that diversity hiring will lead to a sacrifice in competence and quality.

2. Fear of Discrimination against Majority Group Members Some employees are afraid that attempts to achieve greater diversity in their organization will result in bias against the majority group—that more black or Asian employees will be promoted to fire captain or police lieutenant, for example, over the heads of supposedly more qualified whites. Google recently fired an engineering employee for writing a long memo, which was soon made public, about why women (in his view) are not inherently suited for jobs in technology. The fired employee has sued Google, claiming the company discriminates against conservative white men.[208] A similar case happened with a white recruiter from YouTube. He claimed the company retaliated "against him after he complained that the video site discriminated against white and Asian male applicants in favor of hiring blacks, Hispanics and women." Alphabet Inc., parent company of Google and YouTube, told *The Wall Street Journal* that it would defend itself in both cases.[209]

3. Resistance to Diversity Program Priorities Some companies, such as PepsiCo, IBM, and Deloitte & Touche, have taken aggressive diversity approaches, such as offering special classes teaching tolerance for diversity and seminars in how to get

Woman manager. On the job she might be a high-powered manager of scores of people, but at home she may still be expected to be the principal manager of an important few—the children. ©Liam Norris/Getty Images

along.[210] Some employees may see diversity programs as distracting them from the organization's "real work." In addition, they may be resentful of diversity-promoting policies that are reinforced through special criteria in the organization's performance appraisals and reward systems.

4. A Negative Diversity Climate **Diversity climate** is a subcomponent of an organization's overall climate and is defined as the employees' aggregate "perceptions about the organization's diversity-related formal structure characteristics and informal values."[211] Diversity climate is positive when employees view the organization as being fair to all types of employees, which promotes employee loyalty and overall firm performance.[212] It also enhances psychological safety. **Psychological safety** reflects the extent to which people feel free to express their ideas and beliefs without fear of negative consequences.[213] The "I'm Glad . . . " box on the next page illustrates how one manager created a positive diversity climate.

5. Lack of Support for Family Demands In 2016, 50.7 million U.S. children lived in families with two parents.[214] In 60.6 percent of such families, both parents worked; in 20.8 percent, only the father worked; and in 5.3 percent, only the mother worked.[215] Yet in a great many households, it is still women who primarily take care of children, as well as other domestic chores. When organizations aren't supportive in offering flexibility in hours and job responsibilities, these women may find it difficult to work evenings and weekends or to take overnight business trips. A few

I'm glad...

...my manager embraced diversity and fostered inclusiveness.

Courtesy Brenton Smith

Brenton Smith served as the vice president for a real estate company. The manager of this company excelled at embracing diversity by listening to all his employees' ideas and opinions when making decisions.

The manager was 65 years old, and he had been working in the industry for a long time. During Brenton's time with the company, it was also employing two young interns. One of the interns was from Japan, and the other was from South Korea.

"The interns were very quiet the first couple of weeks, but as time went on, they would voice their opinions more," said Brenton. Part of the reason was the manager's openness to hearing everyone's thoughts, no matter their age or cultural differences. The manager created an environment where everyone felt safe expressing their opinions and confident that their ideas were being heard.

One example of Brenton's manager embracing the ideas of all his employees came when the team was planning a presentation to secure a big deal. "Our manager was using the same template that was always used for pitching presentations. We had it all written up and ready to go, and then one of the interns came to talk to me and said he thought we should change the presentation," said Brenton. The intern from Japan thought technology should be incorporated into the presentation. He also thought the message would be better received if he presented alongside the manager to add some variety, rather than just having the manager read alone from the slide deck.

"I agreed with him and told him that I thought he should present the idea to our manager. So he went to the manager's office and presented his idea for the presentation," said Brenton. "The manager listened intently to the idea, which was an entirely different viewpoint since the intern was from Japan and had a different way of doing business."

The manager liked the intern's idea, but he did not make a final decision until he ran it past the rest of the team. He called the employees into his office to take a vote. A majority voted to proceed with the intern's new idea for the presentation.

"The deal was successful, and to this day the company still uses that presentation technique," said Brenton. Because Brenton's manager includes every one of his employees in his decision-making process—no matter their age, race, or culture—he is able to build on all of their strengths to improve company processes and procedures.

Courtesy of Brenton Smith

companies—such as Starbucks, McDonald's, IBM, AT&T, and Walmart—have begun offering or improving existing paid family leave policies, a benefit 94 percent of respondents recently told a Pew Center survey they thought would help families. Yet the United States remains the only industrialized country without mandatory paid leave for parents.[216]

6. A Hostile Work Environment for Diverse Employees Hostile work environments are characterized by sexual, racial, and age harassment and can be in violation of Equal Employment Opportunity law, such as Title VII of the Civil Rights Act.[217] Whether perpetrated against women, men, older individuals, or LGBTQ people, hostile environments are demeaning, unethical, and appropriately called "work environment pollution." A recent example involved former Fox anchor Gretchen Carlson. She filed a complaint saying she was fired because she refused to sleep with Fox News CEO Roger Ailes, who was later also fired for sexual harassment. Data from the U.S. Equal Employment Opportunity Commission revealed that almost half the 27,000 harassment complaints it received in 2017 involved sex.[218] You certainly won't get employees' best work if they believe the work environment is hostile toward them.

Ultimate Software is a good example (see next page) of a company that has attempted to effectively manage diversity by overcoming these six barriers. ●

EXAMPLE PEOPLE FIRST AT ULTIMATE SOFTWARE

Ultimate Software consistently earns a top spot on *Fortune* magazine's list of the *Best Places to Work* for diversity and for women, African Americans, and Hispanics, and Latinos.[219] The company specializes in cloud-based people management solutions and prides itself on putting "People First" in an inclusive environment that fosters respect for every employee.[220] According to Ultimate's website, "We have always believed that diversity drives innovation, creativity, and business success."[221] Here are some of the ways Ultimate is winning at diversity management.

Health and Family Benefits Ultimate pays 100 percent of its employees' health care premiums (medical, dental, vision), including coverage for costly fertility treatments. These benefits extend to families, including same-sex married couples. Employees enjoy paid maternity/paternity/adoption leave, and unlimited paid time off means they can worry less about taking time away from work to address personal or family needs. Ultimate provides $300 a year per child to help cover the costs of extracurricular activities for employees' kids.[222]

Communities of Interest The company prides itself on its four unique Communities of Interest. These informal groups give employees opportunities for socializing, professional networking, and community service, and they provide professional development, diversity trainings (such as on transgender sensitivities), and peer-support groups for minorities in leadership positions.[223] All the communities are inclusive, meaning that anyone who considers him- or herself an "ally" of the individuals represented in the groups is welcome to join. The communities are:

- PrideUS (People Respecting Individual Differences Empower Ultimate Software): promotes an environment that feels safe and welcoming for all workers, particularly those who identify as LGBTQ+.
- Women in Leadership: aims to help women at Ultimate achieve their maximum potential. Women account for about 50 percent of Ultimate's workforce, and almost half are in leadership positions.
- UltiVETS: formed to provide support for active military, veterans, and their friends and families.
- UltiHOPE: provides resources for employees and caregivers whose lives have been touched by cancer, including current cancer patients and cancer survivors.

Members also volunteer and raise money for nonprofit organizations and ally communities. For example, Ultimate's PrideUS group partnered with the Miami HEAT to sponsor the annual *Loud and Proud Dance Party* in South Florida, an event celebrating life and diversity for the LGBTQ+ community.[224] The *Women in Leadership* group sponsors the "Athena Scholarship," which gives two $20,000 college scholarships each year to daughters of Ultimate employees who are pursuing college careers in technology or who demonstrate superior leadership skills in their schools or communities.[225]

Technology Ultimate promotes diversity and fosters inclusion in its workplace through cutting-edge technology. Its main cloud-based offering, UltiPro, aims to help other companies do the same. UltiPro's advantage is that it integrates virtually all a company's HR needs into one seamless, inclusive platform that simplifies and elevates performance management using cutting-edge data capabilities. It provides managers with up-to-date, unbiased information needed for employment decisions, and it keeps employees on track toward their performance and career goals by recommending, and often providing, necessary trainings and professional development opportunities. The platform supports the unique cultural, fiscal, language, and legal/compliance needs for multiple users in multiple locations across the country or globe.[226]

Ultipro is designed to help companies clear many common diversity management hurdles. Its business intelligence tools can capture rich data across multiple levels to assess whether the organization is meeting strategic diversity goals.[227] Its intuitive design and cultural adaptability make it user-friendly for workers of all ages, digital competencies, and backgrounds. Its reliance on quantifiable metrics reduces the influence of unconscious biases in decision-making.[228] The platform also overcomes social networking barriers separating diverse workers by identifying, recommending, and facilitating connections and mentorships between employees.[229] Finally, its *UltiPro Perception* tool helps mitigate one of the key diversity management issues in organizations by giving employees an accessible and anonymous way to voice needs, concerns, and opinions to upper management.[230]

YOUR CALL

Which of an organization's diversity management initiatives will be most important to you when you are interviewing for jobs? To what extent would Ultimate's diversity programs help recruit the best talent?

11.6 Understanding Stress and Individual Behavior

THE BIG PICTURE

Stress is what people feel when enduring extraordinary demands or opportunities and are not sure how to handle them. There are six sources of stress: individual differences, individual task, individual role, group, organizational, and nonwork demands. We describe some consequences of stress and discuss three methods organizations use to reduce it.

LO 11-6

Discuss the sources of workplace stress and ways to reduce it.

Stress is the tension people feel when they are facing or enduring extraordinary demands, constraints, or opportunities and are uncertain about their ability to handle them effectively.[231] Stress is the feeling of tension and pressure; the source of stress is called a *stressor.*

Although stress, and our response to it, are highly personal events, nearly 44 percent of working U.S. adults in a recent Harvard poll reported that their current job is stressful enough to affect their health, and most of them think those effects are negative. Other data confirms that more than one in three U.S. workers experiences stress related to the job, often caused by situations like overwork, unpredictable schedules and night shifts, unsafe work places, low wages, layoffs of colleagues, conflict at work, and family worries like the need to care for ill relatives while working. Almost 1 million people are absent from the U.S. workplace each day due to stress-related factors.[232]

The Toll of Workplace Stress

The U.S. Centers for Disease Control (CDC) report that U.S. workers are now spending 8 percent more time on the job than they did 20 years ago, and 13 percent are also holding down a second job.[233] Almost three-quarters (73 percent) of workers reportedly regularly experience some psychological symptoms of stress, and 77 percent report regular physical symptoms. Such stress is estimated to cost U.S. employers $30 billion a year in lost productivity alone,[234] and as much as $300 billion a year when the costs of health care and absenteeism are factored in.[235]

Stress can cause conflicts and distraction at work; make you fatigued all the time; and generate problems like insomnia, backaches, headaches, and chest pain.[236] More than one in four workers (26 percent) report feeling "often burned out or stressed" by work.[237] At the same time, according to the director of the Harvard poll cited earlier, "almost half of people who work are at a workplace that has no workplace health program."[238]

Workplace stress diminishes positive emotions, job satisfaction, organizational commitment, and job performance and increases alcohol and illicit drug use, sleeplessness, overeating, and job turnover.[239] Indeed, historically researchers have generally believed that there is an *inverted U-shaped relationship* between stress and performance. That is, low levels of stress lead to low performance (because people are not "charged up" to perform), but high levels of stress also lead to an energy-sapping fight-or-flight response that produces low performance. Optimal performance, according to this hypothesis, results when people experience moderate levels of stress.

Stress kills! The effects of stress cumulate over our lives, making it essential to address the stressors in your life. Stressors do not generally disappear on their own. ©Christopher Robbins/Image Source

While a moderate amount of stress can have some health and behavioral benefits,[240] excess or negative stress reveals itself in three kinds of symptoms:

- **Physiological signs.** Lesser physiological signs are sweaty palms, restlessness, backaches, headaches, upset stomach, and nausea. More serious signs are hypertension and heart attacks.
- **Psychological signs.** Psychological symptoms include forgetfulness, boredom, irritability, nervousness, anger, anxiety, hostility, and depression.
- **Behavioral signs.** Behavioral symptoms include sleeplessness, changes in eating habits, and increased smoking/alcohol/drug abuse.[241] Stress may be revealed through reduced performance and job satisfaction.

If stress is extreme, burnout can result. **Burnout** is a state of emotional, mental, and even physical exhaustion, expressed as listlessness, indifference, or frustration. Clearly, the greatest consequence for the organization is reduced productivity. Overstressed employees are apt to call in sick, miss deadlines, take longer lunch breaks, and show indifference to performance. However, some may put in great numbers of hours at work, making an unusual number of mistakes or getting less accomplished than before. They may also feel mentally and emotionally drained, or alienated or underappreciated.[242]

How Does Stress Work?

Stress has both physical and emotional components. Physically, according to Canadian researcher Hans Selye, considered the father of the modern concept of stress, stress is "the nonspecific response of the body to any demand made upon it."[243] Emotionally, stress has been defined as the feeling of being overwhelmed, "the perception that events or circumstances have challenged, or exceeded, a person's ability to cope."[244]

Stressors can be *hassles*, or simple irritants, such as misplacing or losing things, having concerns about one's physical appearance, and having too many things to do. For example, a frustrating morning commute was found to create stress and impair performance.[245] Stressors can also be *crises*, such as responding to a hurricane, tornado, or school shooting. Or they can be *strong stressors*, which can dramatically strain a person's ability to adapt—extreme physical discomfort, such as chronic severe back pain.

Stressors can be both *negative* and *positive*. That is, being fired or getting divorced can be a great source of stress, but so can being promoted or getting married. As Selye writes, "It is immaterial whether the agent or the situation we face is pleasant or unpleasant; all that counts is the intensity of the demand for adjustment and adaptation."[246] In addition, Selye distinguished between bad stress (what he called "distress"), in which the result of the stressor can be anxiety and illness, and good stress ("eustress," pronounced *yu stress*), which can stimulate a person to better coping and adaptation, such as performing well on a test.[247] In this discussion, however, we are mainly concerned with how stress negatively affects people and their performance.

The Sources of Job-Related Stress

There are six sources of stress on the job: (1) *demands created by individual differences*, (2) *individual task demands*, (3) *individual role demands*, (4) *work-life balance*, (5) *group demands*, and (6) *organizational demands.*

1. Demands Created by Individual Differences: The Stress Created by Genetic or Personality Characteristics Some people are born worriers, those with a gene mutation (known as BDNF) that Yale researchers identify with people who chronically obsess over negative thoughts.[248] Others arc impatient, hurried, deadline-ridden, competitive types with the personality characteristic known as **Type A behavior pattern**, meaning they are involved in a chronic, determined struggle to accomplish more in less time.[249] Type A behavior has been associated with increased performance in the work of professors, students, and life insurance brokers.[250] However, it also has been associated with greater cardiovascular activity and higher blood pressure, as well as to heart disease, especially for individuals who showed strong feelings of anger, hostility, and aggression.[251]

2. Individual Task Demands: The Stress Created by the Job Itself Some occupations are more stressful than others.[252] Being a retail store manager, for instance, can be quite stressful for some people.[253] But being a home-based blogger, paid on a piecework basis to generate news and comment, may mean working long hours to the point of exhaustion.[254] Jobs that require "emotional labor"—pretending to be cheerful or smiling all the time, no matter how you feel—can be particularly demanding.[255]

Low-level jobs can be more stressful than high-level jobs because employees often have less control over their lives and thus have less work satisfaction. Being a barista, day care teacher, hotel concierge, or purchasing agent, jobs that don't usually pay very well, can be quite stressful.[256]

3. Individual Role Demands: The Stress Created by Others' Expectations of You **Roles are sets of behaviors that people expect of occupants of a position.** Stress may come about because of *role overload*, *role conflict*, and *role ambiguity*.

- **Role overload.** Role overload occurs when others' expectations exceed your ability. Example: If you as a student are carrying a full course load plus working two-thirds time plus trying to have a social life, you know what role overload is—and what stress is. Similar things happen to managers and workers.
- **Role conflict.** Role conflict occurs when someone feels torn by the different expectations of important people in one's life. Example: Your supervisor says the company needs you to stay late to meet an important deadline, but your family expects you to be present for your child's birthday party.
- **Role ambiguity.** Role ambiguity occurs when others' expectations are unknown. Example: You find your job description and the criteria for promotion vague, a complaint often voiced by newcomers to an organization.

Jobs with high task and role demands but low levels of personal control are particularly troublesome. In these cases, people are likely to find that their efforts to complete work activities are blocked, resulting in persistent stress, discomfort, and burnout. The problem is that individuals do not have the resources, power, or authority to influence the way the work gets done or the timelines for completion.[257] A seven-year study of people working in jobs with low control and high job demands experienced a "15.4% increase in the odds of death compared to low job demands. For those in high control jobs, high demands are associated with a 34% decrease in the odds of death compared to low job demands."[258]

4. Work-Family Conflict **Work–life conflict occurs when the demands or pressures from work and family domains are mutually incompatible.**[259] Work and family can conflict in two ways: Work responsibilities can interfere with family life, and family demands can interfere with work responsibilities.[260]

For instance, an employee who is caring for an aging mother skips a department meeting to take his mother to a doctor's appointment (family interferes with work). Perhaps another day he works late to finish a report on time and has to reschedule his mother's follow-up appointment (work interferes with family).

Both these types of conflicts matter, because their effects spill over both at home and at work. *(See Table 11.4.)* From a management perspective, we recommend that organizations strive to reduce stressors, increase

Have you ever felt like this person? Many jobs are stressful, some because people's lives are at stake (military personnel, firefighters, police officers), some because they are highly deadline-driven (event coordinators, public relations executives). What techniques do you use to manage stress? Do you ever just ignore it and plow through your daily activities? ©Comstock/Stockbyte/Getty Images

TABLE 11.4

Negative Consequences of Conflicts among Work, Family, and Other Life Domains

Source: Adapted from F. T. Amstad, L. L. Meier, U. Fasel, A. Elfering, and N. K. Semmer, "A Meta-Analysis of Work-Family Conflict and Various Outcomes with a Special Emphasis on Cross-Domain versus Matching Domain Relations," Journal of Occupational Health Psychology, *16, no. 2 (2011), pp. 151–169.*

WORK INTERFERES WITH FAMILY	FAMILY INTERFERES WITH WORK	OUTCOMES LINKED TO LIFE MORE GENERALLY
Job satisfaction	Marital satisfaction	Life satisfaction
Intentions to quit	Family satisfaction	Health problems
Absenteeism	Family-related strain	Depression
Job performance	Family-related performance	Substance use/abuse

employee engagement, and implement wellness programs to assist employees in balancing their work and family demands.[261] Wellness programs are discussed in the next section. Companies like Deloitte, TIAA, and Cisco have implemented gender-neutral parental-leave policies to help parents balance responsibilities associated with a newborn. Deloitte, for example, allows employees to take "as many as 16 weeks off to care for a new baby regardless of the staffer's gender or which parent would be the primary caregiver."[262]

5. Group Demands: The Stress Created by Co-workers and Managers Even if you don't particularly care for the work you do but like the people you work with, that feeling can be a great source of satisfaction and prevent stress. When people don't get along, that can be a great stressor. Even if you have stress under control, a co-worker's stress might bother you, diminishing productivity.[263]

In addition, managers can create stress for employees. A boss who consistently engages in workplace behaviors like overt self-promotion, unwillingness to listen, a tendency to make unreasonable demands, lying, unfair decision making, and a general lack of ethics can become a source of stress.[264] Alice Guo describes how her boss created stress in the "I Wish . . . ." feature.

I Wish...

...my manager alleviated my work-related stress.

Alice Guo is a senior manager of international business development in the education industry. She enjoys her role within the company, but she underwent a lot of work-related stress when she first started.

Courtesy Alice Guo

Unfortunately for Alice, her manager did not provide a lot of clarity around the expectations of her position. "As a new employee, you need to be trained and you need to be provided enough information to navigate the new work environment. And the communication is key," said Alice. "However, what I encountered when I started my job was that the communication with my supervisor was not enough. My supervisor didn't have a direct style of communication, so I often misinterpreted the feedback he gave me."

As Alice struggled to learn the ins and outs of her new job, her manager did not give her direct feedback to indicate she was missing expectations. She thought she was being successful in her new role, until she saw her first-quarter performance review.

"I was shocked to receive a negative response. I realized that, after almost two months of working there, not only was I not doing what they expected of me, but there was a lot of information about the job that I should have been given but I had never received," said Alice. Her role was new to the company, so a clear job description was never created or relayed to her. Her superiors never checked to make sure she received the proper training or knew what the goals and expectations were for her role. She had to learn and navigate the new role on her own.

Because of poor communication and unclear expectations, Alice had to figure out a way to turn her performance around and prove to her manager that she was capable of doing her job. This put her under a considerable amount of stress.

"Because I was new to the company, it was hard for me to approach my supervisor. There were times that I didn't trust him because I didn't know whether he was saying the right thing and whether he was doing it intentionally or not. The feedback he was giving me was inconsistent with my performance review, so there was some mistrust," said Alice. "I worked hard over the holidays, which was really stressful, and I didn't know if I was going to keep my job."

After almost a month of working extra hours and undergoing plenty of workplace stress, Alice was able to work with her supervisor to establish trust and better communication. "It was a good experience to reflect on the certain things that I should avoid if I ever became a manager," said Alice.

Courtesy of Alice Guo

6. Organizational Demands: The Stress Created by the Environment and Culture The physical environments of some jobs are great sources of stress: poultry processing, asbestos removal, coal mining, fire fighting, police work, ambulance driving, and so on. Even white-collar work can take place in a stressful environment, with poor lighting, too much noise, improper placement of furniture, and lack of privacy.

An organizational culture that puts high-pressure work demands on employees will fuel the stress response. One stressor that companies are beginning to recognize as a two-edged sword is the way in which communication technologies make it possible for even corporate employees to be on call around the clock, able or even encouraged to answer e-mails and other messages at night, on the weekend, and even on vacation. To counter the stress-inducing effects of never getting away from the office, PricewaterhouseCoopers uses a pop-up note to remind employees that they're checking their work e-mail on the weekend,[265] and health care consulting firm Vynamic discourages employees from both sending and responding to e-mails between 10 at night and 7 in the morning. "Stress was showing up as a challenge for our team—an area that we weren't really making improvements on," said CEO Dan Calista. "Through some conversations about the abundance of e-mail and the always-being-on nature of our jobs, we realized that this could be a great opportunity to create a structured way to disconnect on a regular basis, not just for vacations."[266]

European companies have taken stronger action. Volkswagen blocks after-hours e-mails to employees' phones, and Daimler deletes e-mails sent to employees who are on vacation.[267] Porsche is considering following their example by returning out-of-hours e-mails to the senders. Said one executive in favor of the change, "To read and reply to e-mails from the boss during the evenings is unpaid working time which increases stress—that's just not acceptable."[268] France has gone even farther, effectively banning work e-mails during certain after-work hours for companies with more than 50 employees, adopting a new "right to disconnect" law similar to one already enacted in Germany in 2014.[269]

Reducing Stressors in the Organization

There are all kinds of **buffers, or administrative changes, that managers can make to reduce stressors and improve employee well-being.**[270] This section reviews six recommendations, starting with attempts to help people develop their resilience.

- **Build resilience.** *Resilience* represents the capacity to consistently bounce back from adversity and to sustain yourself when confronted with challenges. It is a career readiness competency desired by employers. Do you think people are born resilient, or is it something that is learned over time? The consensus is that it represents a capacity that is developed over time.[271] Consider the example of inventor James Dyson. Dyson spent five years testing more than 5,000 versions of what he hoped would be a better vacuum cleaner that operated on the same principle as a cyclone. Today, his company, named after him, markets the Dual Cyclone bagless vacuum and almost 60 other products and is worth $4.8 billion.[272]

Resilience assists you in achieving goals by encouraging positive thinking in the face of setbacks and challenges. That is one reason it represents a career readiness competency desired by employers. To what extent do you possess the career readiness competency of resilience? Find out by taking Self-Assessment 11.8.

SELF-ASSESSMENT 11.8 CAREER READINESS

What Is Your Level of Resilience?

The following survey was designed to assess your level of resilience. Please be prepared to answer these questions if your instructor has assigned Self-Assessment 11.8 in Connect.

1. What is your level of resilience?
2. Looking at your item scores, identify the three areas you scored lowest. Now, propose one idea for improving each these aspects of resilience. Be specific.
3. What things might you say during an interview to demonstrate that you possess this career readiness competency?

Some strategies for building resilience are practicing mindfulness, which helps reduce stress, learning how to prioritize incoming information so you will process it more effectively and make better decisions, taking frequent short breaks from work to restore your focus, and mentally detaching from problems so you can respond to them rather than reacting emotionally.[273] Other recommendations include practicing optimism, using cognitive reframing when faced with challenges, remembering your comebacks from adversity, supporting others, and getting the proper amount of sleep.[274]

- **Roll out employee assistance programs.** **Employee assistance programs (EAPs) include a host of programs aimed at helping employees to cope with stress, burnout, substance abuse, health-related problems, family and marital issues, and any general problem that negatively influences job performance.**[275]
- **Recommend a holistic wellness approach.** **A holistic wellness program focuses on self-responsibility, nutritional awareness, relaxation techniques, physical fitness, and environmental awareness.** This approach goes beyond stress reduction by encouraging employees to try to balance physical, mental, and social well-being by accepting personal responsibility for developing and adhering to a health promotion program. Google's wellness program is discussed in the Example box.

EXAMPLE Corporate Wellness Programs

It's hard to find an article on successful corporate wellness programs that doesn't mention Google. The company's approach has become a gold standard against which other companies measure success in this arena.[276] Google clearly cares about its employees' well-being and quality of life. Here are some of the statements Google makes to its employees with its wellness initiatives:

We Want Employees to Feel Good Google offers a variety of onsite services to help employees feel better when they're not at their best, including physicians, physical therapists, and chiropractors.[277] Some managers reward employees with massage credits to cash in with one of the onsite masseurs, and the company encourages those in need of some extra zzz's to take a snooze in one of its nap pods.[278]

Google encourages employees to be proactive about their health with perks like reduced health insurance premiums for those who pursue fitness and a host of opportunities to do so during the workday. Googlers have access to free fitness centers, exercise classes, and bicycles and are encouraged to play

De-stressing. Experts say that exercise can be a tremendous stress reliever. Many companies maintain physical-fitness centers not only as an employee perk but also because they realize that exercise helps to improve stamina and endurance while reducing tension. ©Ariel Skelley/Blend Images LLC

intramural sports. Standing desks keep employees up and active, and workplace showers make workers feel more comfortable after riding bikes to work or breaking a sweat during workday exercise.[279]

We Want Employees to Eat Well Working at Google means having access to three healthy meals a day, plus healthy snacks, for free. The corporate office houses more than 30 eateries that serve a variety of entrees, juices, and snack options.[280] Color-coding nudges employees to make good choices; green or transparent containers hold healthier options like vegetables, and red or opaque ones hold options like croutons and cookies.[281] One employee said having the food options "saves me time and money, and helps me build relationships with my colleagues."[282]

We Want Employees to Have Fun and Learn New Things Google employees get to have fun at work. They have access to LEGO stations, ping-pong tables, bowling alleys, and arcade machines and can travel between floors using slides instead of elevators or stairs.[283] Those who want to learn something new can take classes in things like cooking, guitar, and coding.[284]

We Want Employees to Stress Less Google does its part to ensure its employees are able to manage the stresses of daily life. There's a mindfulness meditation program for those who want to meditate and a concierge service that runs errands so employees have fewer demands to satisfy outside work.[285] Google tries to take care of life's bigger worries too. Surviving spouses receive 50 percent of their deceased loved one's salary for 10 years, and each child gets $1,000 per month.[286] Employees also have access to financial planning services and advisors to help them plan for the future.[287]

How Google Overcomes Challenges Other Companies Face About 70 percent of employers offer some type of wellness benefits for employees, but one of their biggest challenges is getting employees to actually use them. A recent study explains that employees don't want to take the extra time outside work to improve their well-being.[288] What makes Google a corporate wellness superstar is its willingness to weave wellness opportunities into employees' daily work lives.[289] Rather than offering benefits employees have to access in their limited free time, Google puts wellness at the forefront of the organization's everyday culture. This means employees actually take advantage of the programs, which translates into tremendous gains for both workers and the company. As one reporter notes, "What Google demonstrates with its all-encompassing benefits package is that employee wellness is achieved with a well-rounded, expertly crafted effort to improve employee quality of life. Employee happiness is achieved through wellness, wellness is achieved through happiness, and ultimately, that happiness benefits everyone, including Google."[290]

YOUR CALL

Which of Google's wellness perks are most appealing to you? How important will a corporate wellness program be for you when you are choosing an employer?

- **Create a supportive environment.** Job stress often results because employees work under poor supervision and lack freedom. Wherever possible, it's better to keep the organizational environment less formal, more personal, and more supportive of employees. Mentors can also help reduce stress.[291] Some companies are helping employees relieve financial worries by paying them small amounts of money as an incentive to set cash aside in an emergency fund.[292]
- **Make jobs interesting.** Stress also results when jobs are routinized and boring. It's better to try to structure jobs so that they allow employees some freedom and variety.
- **Make career counseling available.** Companies such as IBM make career planning available, which reduces the stress that comes when employees don't know what their career options are and where they're headed.

11-7 Career Corner: Managing Your Career Readiness

LO 11-7

Describe how to develop the career readiness competencies of positive approach and emotional intelligence.

This chapter has implications for developing at least six competencies associated with our model of career readiness *(see Figure 11.4)*: self-awareness, generalized self-efficacy, social intelligence, emotional intelligence, positive approach, and resilience. This section focuses on developing the attitude of positive approach and the emotional intelligence soft skill of self-management.

FIGURE 11.4

Model of career readiness

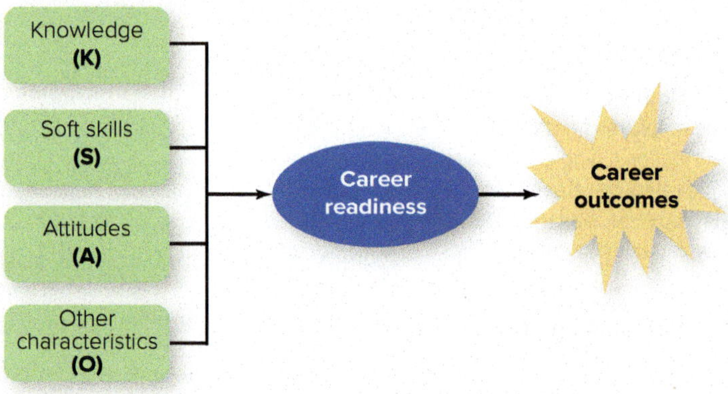

Fostering a Positive Approach

A *positive approach* represents a willingness to accept developmental feedback, to try and suggest new ideas, and to maintain a positive attitude at work. Maintaining a positive approach is hard given the hustle and bustle of life and employers' increased expectations for employees. We recommend a two-step approach for developing a positive approach.

Step 1: Identify potentially bad attitudes. We all have bad days or stressful moments. The purpose of this step is to identify the types of negative behaviors that tend to crop up when you have a bad day or a stressful moment. This awareness can help you replace potentially negative behaviors with positive ones. Answer the following questions.[293]

- Are you a *porcupine*? Porcupines send out verbal and nonverbal messages that say, "Stay away from me."
- Are you an *entangler*? Entanglers want to involve others in their interests. They push their concerns and want to be heard, noticed, and listened to.
- Are you a *debater*? Debaters like to argue even if there is no issue to debate.
- Are you a *complainer*? Complainers point out the problems in a situation but rarely provide solutions of their own.
- Are you a *blamer*? Blamers are like complainers but point out negatives aimed at a particular individual.
- Are you a *stink bomb thrower*? Stink bomb throwers like to make sarcastic or cynical remarks, use nonverbal gestures of disgust or annoyance, and sometimes yell or slam things.

Based on your answers, which bad behaviors do you tend to exhibit? Now consider how these behaviors may be perceived by others. It won't be positive. How can you catch yourself starting to behave in these negative ways? Finally, what can you do to replace these negative tendencies with positive ones? Be specific.

Step 2: Identify "good attitude" behaviors. This step aims to assist you in breaking down the concept of "good attitudes" into specific behaviors. Once you identify the behaviors, your task is to focus on displaying them at work. Follow these recommendations:[294]

- Begin by defining what it means to have a good attitude. Think of people you know who display great attitudes. Next, generate a list of the characteristics they possess and the positive behaviors they exhibit at work.
- Take the first item on your list and break it down into smaller behavioral components. Describe it; then describe it some more. For example, if being "pleasant to others" is an exemplar of a good attitude, describe what this looks like. A pleasant person says hello to all colleagues. Describing this further leads to, "She walks over to each person's desk in the morning and says, 'Hello, did you have a good evening?'" Describing it further shows that this person occasionally brings breakfast treats such as sweet rolls to share.
- Repeat the above step for each item on your "good attitude" list.
- Review the list of detailed behaviors and identify any themes. Are there any recurring behaviors, expressions, or gestures?
- Select a minimum of three behavioral themes or specific behaviors you want to focus on over the next two weeks. Consider situations in which these behaviors might be exhibited.
- Exhibit the targeted behaviors in the targeted situations. Observe how people react to you when you exhibit these positive behaviors. If the reaction is not positive, consider why.
- Repeat the last two steps for another set of behaviors.

Self-Managing Your Emotions

Self-management reflects the ability to control your emotions and act with honesty and integrity in reliable and adaptable ways. Here are some tips for enhancing this ability.[295]

- **Identify your emotional triggers and physiological responses.** What words, sayings, or situations cause your emotions to ramp up? Do you get nervous before a presentation or when meeting strangers? Keeping a journal is good way to identify your emotional triggers. Simply take a few minutes during the day to jot down your feelings and what caused them. For example, one of your authors knows that he tends to react emotionally when people use judgmental or derogatory words to describe other people or when someone is lying. His body lets him know because he feels flushed or his heart starts to beat faster. This awareness enables him to notice his "emotionality" and to focus on reducing it.
- **Engage in emotional regulation.** Pausing and reflecting is a good solution. When you sense heightened emotions, stop and take a couple of deep breaths. This will relax the emotional brain and engage the thinking brain, thereby allowing you to react in a less emotional manner.[296]
- **Channel your emotions.** Letting off steam is fine; just be sure to do it at the right place and time. Venting with a trusted friend is more effective than yelling at someone at work. Exercise is another way to fend off the potential stressors and emotions associated with being busy or overburdened. ●

Key Terms Used in This Chapter

- affective component of an attitude 417
- Americans with Disabilities Act (ADA) 436
- attitude 417
- behavior 419
- behavioral component of an attitude 417
- Big Five personality dimensions 410
- buffers 445
- burnout 442
- causal attribution 424
- cognitive component of an attitude 417
- cognitive dissonance 418
- core self-evaluation (CSE) 411
- counterproductive work behaviors (CWBs) 430
- diversity 431
- diversity climate 438
- emotional intelligence 414
- emotional stability 413
- employee assistance programs (EAPs) 446
- employee engagement 426
- ethnocentrism 437
- external dimensions of diversity 433
- fundamental attribution bias 424
- generalized self-efficacy 411
- glass ceiling 435
- halo effect 422
- holistic wellness program 446
- implicit bias 422
- internal dimensions of diversity 432
- job satisfaction 428
- learned helplessness 411
- locus of control 413
- organizational behavior (OB) 416
- organizational citizenship behaviors (OCBs) 429
- organizational commitment 428
- perception 420
- personality 410
- psychological safety 438
- recency effect 424
- roles 443
- self-efficacy 411
- self-esteem 412
- self-fulfilling prophecy 424
- self-serving bias 424
- stereotyping 420
- stress 441
- stressors 427
- transgender 435
- Type A behavior pattern 442
- underemployed 437
- values 416
- work–life conflict 443

Key Points

11.1 Personality and Individual Behavior

- Personality consists of the stable psychological traits and behavioral attributes that give a person his or her identity. There are five personality dimensions and five personality traits that managers need to be aware of to understand workplace behavior.
- The Big Five personality dimensions are extroversion, agreeableness, conscientiousness, emotional stability, and openness to experience. Extroversion, an outgoing personality, is associated with success for managers and salespeople. Conscientiousness, or a dependable personality, is correlated with successful job performance. A person who scores well on conscientiousness may be a proactive personality, someone who is more apt to take initiative and persevere to influence the environment.
- A core self-evaluation represents a broad personality trait comprising four positive individual traits: (1) Self-efficacy is the belief in one's personal ability to do a task. Low self-efficacy is associated with learned helplessness, the debilitating lack of faith in one's ability to control one's environment. (2) Self-esteem is the extent to which people like or dislike themselves. (3) Locus of control indicates how much people believe they control their fate through their own efforts. (4) Emotional stability is the extent to which people feel secure and unworried and how likely they are to experience negative emotions under pressure.
- Emotional intelligence is defined as the ability to monitor your and others' feelings and use this information to guide your thinking and actions.

11.2 Values, Attitudes, and Behavior

- Organizational behavior (OB) is dedicated to better understanding and managing people at work. OB looks at two areas: individual behavior (discussed in this chapter) and group behavior (discussed in later chapters).
- Values must be distinguished from attitudes and from behavior. Values are abstract ideals that guide one's thinking and behavior across all situations.
- Attitudes are defined as learned predispositions toward a given object. Attitudes have three components. The affective component consists of the feelings or emotions one has about a situation. The cognitive component consists of the beliefs and knowledge one has about a situation. The behavioral component is how one intends or expects to behave toward a situation.

- When attitudes and reality collide, the result may be cognitive dissonance, the psychological discomfort a person experiences between his or her cognitive attitude and incompatible behavior. Cognitive dissonance depends on three factors: importance, control, and rewards. The ways to reduce cognitive dissonance are to change your attitude and/or your behavior, belittle the importance of the inconsistent behavior, or find consonant elements that outweigh the dissonant ones.

11.3 Perception and Individual Behavior

- Perception is the process of interpreting and understanding one's environment. There are five distortions of perception. They are: (1) stereotyping, the tendency to attribute to an individual the characteristics one believes are typical of the group to which that individual belongs; (2) implicit bias, which refers to the attitudes or beliefs that affect our understanding, actions, and decisions in an unconscious manner; (3) the halo effect, the forming of an impression of an individual based on a single trait; and (4) the recency effect, the tendency to remember recent information better than earlier information.; and (5) causal attribution, the activity of inferring causes for observed behavior. Two attributional tendencies that can distort one's interpretation of observed behavior are the fundamental attribution bias, in which people attribute another person's behavior to his or her personal characteristics rather than to situational factors, and the self-serving bias, in which people tend to take more personal responsibility for success than for failure.
- The self-fulfilling prophecy (Pygmalion effect) describes the phenomenon in which people's expectations of themselves or others lead them to behave in ways that make those expectations come true.

11.4 Work-Related Attitudes and Behaviors Managers Need to Deal With

- Managers need to be alert to work-related attitudes having to do with (1) employee engagement, an individual's involvement, satisfaction, and enthusiasm for work; (2) job satisfaction, the extent to which you feel positive or negative about various aspects of your work; and (3) organizational commitment, reflecting the extent to which an employee identifies with an organization and is committed to its goals.
- Among the types of behavior that managers need to influence are (1) performance and productivity; (2) absenteeism, when an employee doesn't show up for work, and turnover, when employees leave their jobs; (3) organizational citizenship behaviors, those employee behaviors that are not directly part of employees' job descriptions—that exceed their work-role requirements; and (4) counterproductive work behaviors, behaviors that harm employees and the organization as a whole.

11.5 The New Diversified Workforce

- Diversity represents all the ways people are alike and unlike—the differences and similarities in age, gender, race, religion, ethnicity, sexual orientation, capabilities, and socioeconomic background.
- There are two dimensions of diversity: (1) Internal dimensions of diversity are those human differences that exert a powerful, sustained effect throughout every stage of our lives: gender, ethnicity, race, physical abilities, age, and sexual orientation. (2) External dimensions of diversity consist of the personal characteristics that people acquire, discard, or modify throughout their lives: personal habits, educational background, religion, income, marital status, and the like.
- By now the vocabulary surrounding LGBT issues has changed considerably. Transgender is an umbrella term for people whose sense of their gender differs from what is expected based on the sex characteristics with which they are born. LGBT isn't considered inclusive enough to suit many people today, and the rubric has been expanded to LGBTQ, in which "Q" can stand for "queer" or for "questioning."
- There are five categories in the internal dimension and one category in the external dimension in which the U.S. workforce is becoming more diverse.
- There are six ways in which employees and managers may express resistance to diversity: (1) Some express stereotypes and prejudices based on ethnocentrism, the belief that one's native country, culture, language, abilities, or behavior is superior to that of another country. (2) Some employees are afraid of discrimination against majority group members. (3) Some employees see diversity programs as distracting them from the organization's supposed "real work." (4) There may be a negative diversity climate, defined as the employees' aggregate perceptions about the organization's diversity-related formal structure characteristics and informal values and their feelings of psychological safety, the extent to which they feel free to express ideas without negative consequences. (5) Organizations may not be supportive of flexible hours and other matters that can help employees cope with family demands. (6) Organizations may show lack of support for career-building steps for diverse employees.

11.6 Understanding Stress and Individual Behavior

- Stress is the tension people feel when they are facing or enduring extraordinary demands, constraints, or opportunities and are uncertain about their ability to handle them effectively. Stress is the feeling of tension and pressure; the source of stress is called a stressor.

- There are six sources of stress on the job: (1) Demands created by individual differences may arise from a Type A behavior pattern, meaning people have the personality characteristic that involves them in a chronic, determined struggle to accomplish more in less time. (2) Individual task demands are the stresses created by the job itself. (3) Individual role demands are the stresses created by other people's expectations of you. Roles are sets of behaviors that people expect of occupants of a position. Stress may come about because of role overload, role conflict, or role ambiguity. Work-life conflict falls in this category. (4) Group demands are the stresses created by co-workers and managers. (5) Organizational demands are the stresses created by the environment and culture of the organization. (6) Nonwork demands are the stresses created by forces outside the organization, such as money problems or divorce.
- Positive stress can be constructive. Negative stress can result in poor-quality work; such stress is revealed through physiological, psychological, or behavioral signs. One sign is burnout, a state of emotional, mental, and even physical exhaustion. Stress can lead to alcohol and other drug abuse.
- There are buffers, or administrative changes, that managers can make to reduce the stressors that lead to employee burnout, such as adding extra staff or giving employees more power to make decisions. Some general organizational strategies for reducing unhealthy stressors are to roll out employee assistance programs, recommend a holistic wellness approach, create a supportive environment, make jobs interesting, and make career counseling available.

11.7 Career Corner: Managing Your Career Readiness

- A two-step approach is used to develop a positive approach at work. The first is to identify the types of negative behaviors that crop up during bad or stressful days. The second step is to identify and exhibit "good attitude" behaviors.
- You can increase your emotional intelligence by developing the ability to manage emotions. Three tips are: (1) identify your emotional triggers and physiological response, (2) engage in emotional regulation, and (3) channel your emotions.

Understanding the Chapter: What Do I Know?

1. What are the Big Five personality dimensions?
2. What are four personality traits managers need to be aware of to understand workplace behavior?
3. How is emotional intelligence defined?
4. How do you distinguish values from attitudes and behavior?
5. What is the process of perception?
6. What are five types of distortion in perception, and what is the Pygmalion effect?
7. What are three work-related attitudes managers need to be conscious of?
8. What are four types of behavior that managers need to influence?
9. Explain the two dimensions of diversity.
10. What are six sources of stress on the job?

Management in Action

Does the Financial Services Industry Lack Diversity?

Professionals in the financial services industry (FSI) tend to be Caucasian and male.[297] Women, for example, represent approximately 29 percent of senior managers in financial services, and Asians and African Americans account for only about 8 percent, and 6 percent, respectively.[298] Further, the proportion of women and racial and ethnic minorities in upper management has remained largely unchanged in the past decade. While Asians and Hispanics have seen slight increases in upward mobility, women have seen no movement, and African Americans have actually lost ground.[299]

BARRIERS AND STRUGGLES

There are four explanations for the scarcity of women and minorities in financial services. First, research shows that we are socially conditioned to equate financial acumen with being male. A recent study from Yale and Columbia looked at a popular online platform that financial planners use to seek stock market advice, with users identifying by only their screen names. Results revealed that both male and female users gravitated toward financial advice from people they assumed were male. Specifically, users were far less likely to value advice from those with ambiguous or feminine names, such as Lee or Mary, and far more likely to value advice from those with masculine names like Matthew.[300]

Second, women and minorities don't grow up viewing a career in the FSI as an option. This may be due to the fact that women and minorities have historically had little representation in the industry. Financial professional Cameo Robinson said, "When you don't see other people who look like you, you start to wonder: Can I really do this? Is this something that I can be successful in?"[301]

Third, many women and minorities in the FSI perceive an unfair climate in their organizations. One example developed into a 2016 lawsuit by a former managing director for Bank of America. She alleges that her pay was significantly lower than her male colleagues' and that the bank treated female employees as "second class citizens."[302] A female executive vice president at Pacific Investment Management Company (Pimco) recently filed suit against her employer for sex- and age-based discrimination and for retaliation when she voiced her concerns. Among her assertions is that "Pimco has admitted in numerous internal documents dating back to at least 2011 that it has an 'unconscious bias' against women."[303]

Fourth, there is evidence of systemic bias against women and minorities in the FSI. In 2017 MetLife and Wells Fargo both settled class-action lawsuits related to racial discrimination, for $32.5 million and $35.5 million respectively.[304] According to one reporter, court documents show "MetLife's 'discriminatory' management assessments, training, and selection practices 'systematically and disproportionately' excluded African Americans from branch management-feeder positions"[305] that lead to higher levels in the company. The suit against Wells Fargo alleged the bank's "teaming and account distribution policies and practices exclude African-Americans from lucrative teams and client account distributions and segregate its workforce by race."[306] Finally, a recent industry-wide study revealed that female financial advisors receive significantly harsher punishment for wrongdoing than their white male colleagues.[307]

A NORM OF SILENCE

Discrimination issues such as those mentioned earlier rarely end up in court, despite their frequency and severity. Where's the public outcry analogous to the recent "Me Too" movement? A couple of facts about the FSI provide insight.

First, the EEOC does not require companies to publicize firm-level diversity data.[308] Only 3 percent of *Fortune* 500 companies shared their complete diversity data with the public in 2017.[309] Proponents in the FSI suggest that releasing this data would force financial institutions to address their diversity problems more aggressively.[310] Data on female and minority career progression and turnover—including who is and is not promoted, who quits, why they quit, and where they go afterwards—would also provide the industry with a more fine-grained understanding of the root causes of its diversity problems.[311] The diversity-challenged tech industry has seen a push for more transparency in recent years, with companies like Google, Facebook, Apple, and Intel now publicizing diversity data and encouraging others to do the same.[312] However, most major financial institutions still elect not to release this information.

Second, most FSI professionals sign mandatory arbitration agreements as a condition of employment.[313] These agreements oblige workers to settle all disputes with their employers in private arbitration proceedings, effectively preventing information about discrimination from ever reaching the public.

"Hazard pay premiums" also reinforce systemic silence. Financial jobs carry substantial personal financial risk, but many professionals are willing to sacrifice fair treatment for a chance at enormous personal gains. According to Joni Hersch, professor of law and economics at Vanderbilt Law School, "The problem with these industries is that the prize is so big at the top . . . If you successfully compete and advance, the payoff is huge, and that keeps people motivated to keep putting out effort and not complain about the working conditions."[314]

LACK OF DIVERSITY HAS CONSEQUENCES

The industry's lack of diversity has profound implications for consumers. Specifically, women and minorities in society are less likely to seek out the opportunity to build wealth because they don't see themselves represented in the industry's ranks. Clients have difficulty building trusting relationships with financial professionals who can't fully empathize with their backgrounds and values. People want advice from advisors they can relate to on a personal level, and for many U.S. adults, this archetype doesn't exist in FSI.[315]

Panelists at the 2016 Securities Industry and Financial Markets Association (SIFMA) meeting called for diversity and inclusion as a "business imperative," citing numerous advantages for both organizations and consumers.[316] Congresswoman Terri Sewell, a member of the House Financial Services Committee, said at the meeting, "The success of our nation's financial sector hinges on its most important asset—our people," stressing that real change and innovation would require the FSI to start hiring people with diverse "experience and voices."[317] Representative Maxine Waters has called the state of diversity in the FSI "unacceptable" adding that "diverse representation in the management of these institutions is essential in order to ensure that all consumers have fair access to credit, capital and banking and financial services."[318]

FOR DISCUSSION

Problem-Solving Perspective

1. What is the underlying problem in this case from the FSI's perspective?
2. What role do you believe financial service industry leaders have had in allowing the lack of progress toward increasing diversity and inclusion?
3. What, if anything, do you believe the government should do to encourage more understanding of, and progress toward solving, the industry's diversity problems?

Application of Chapter Content

1. How would you characterize the diversity climate and the overall work environment for women and minorities in the FSI?
2. What do you think have been the primary drivers of a lack of diversity in the FSI?
3. What role do you think stereotypes and prejudices have played in women's and minorities' struggle to break the glass ceiling in the FSI?
4. What strategies do you suggest the FSI use to fight discrimination against women and minorities?
5. How might financial services institutions create more supportive environments for their female and minority workers?

Legal/Ethical Challenge

Should Airlines Accommodate Oversized People?

Traveling on an airplane can be extra difficult for overweight and tall people. The width of an average airplane seat has decreased from 18.5 inches in the early 2000s to around 17 inches or less.[319] Given individual differences in hip width, this can be a problem, particularly for women. The Civilian American and European Surface Anthropometry Resource Project (Caesar) investigated the issue, backed by funding from a consortium of scientific research organizations and engineering and aerospace companies.

The Caesar project measured more than 4,000 people from the United States and Europe and uncovered the following: "The hip breadth of men in the 95th percentile of the population, i.e., on the very big side, measures 17.6 inches." This means that 95% of all men can fit into a standard Airbus seat. In contrast, females face a different situation. According to Caesar's report, "the hip breadth of women in the 90th percentile is 19.2 inches, and those in the 95th percentile have hips measuring 22.4 inches."[320] The core skeletal system is the reason for the difference between men and women. Females simply have a larger pelvis than men.

Seat pitch, the distance between seat backs, also is decreasing. This makes for less leg room for all people. The typical seat pitch in Economy class has narrowed to 31 inches, with some airlines offering as little as 28 inches of leg room.[321]

Do you think airlines should be bound by minimum seat size and leg room standards? The advocacy group Flyers Rights has campaigned for federally regulated seat sizes, citing concerns such as inability to quickly evacuate aircraft and health hazards like deep vein thrombosis.[322] Although there are currently no such regulations in the United States, federal judges recently ordered the Federal Aviation Administration (FAA) to review commercial airline seat sizes and pitch.[323] Some people believe that forcing airlines to establish bigger, standard seat sizes ultimately increases fares. Industry group Airlines for America opposes the idea, for instance. "The group notes that the FAA should regulate seat size for safety, but should not substitute its judgments for market forces on what people are willing to pay."[324]

The trends are clear. In general, airlines are adding seats while decreasing seat width and pitch. These changes clearly affect taller, wider, and heavier individuals and may even pose health risks to passengers. Samoa Air is resolving this issue by charging fees based on passengers' weight. Does this seem ethical?

The question to consider is whether seat width and pitch should be regulated by law or determined by market forces.

SOLVING THE CHALLENGE

1. I recommend creating a national standard for airline seats based on the average passenger as opposed to using gender as part of the computation. I would

standardize seat width based on passengers' average hip size. I would also standardize seat pitch so that it accommodates passengers' average height. Once this is done, I would charge passengers a special fee for more space.

2. Let market forces determine the design of airplanes and fares. The government should stay out of this issue. For example, Bombardier's CS100 expanded seat width to 18.5 inches and included 19 inches for the middle seat. The airline maker did this to compete against smaller seats offered in planes made by Airbus and Boeing.[325]
3. Because women, on average, have larger hip breadth than men, it is not fair to base fees on the size of a seat. This would disadvantage women. I would standardize seat width based on the average size of women. People can pay extra fees if they want additional seat width or pitch.
4. Invent other options.

Uber Continuing Case

Learn about personality traits held by Uber founder and former CEO Travis Kalancik and current CEO Dara Khosrowshahi. Assess your ability to apply concepts discussed in this chapter to the case by going to Connect.

12 Motivating Employees

Achieving Superior Performance in the Workplace

©Olivier Renck/Aurora/Getty Images

After reading this chapter, you should be able to:

LO 12-1 Explain the role of motivation in accomplishing goals.

LO 12-2 Identify the needs that motivate most employees.

LO 12-3 Discuss similarities and differences among three process theories.

LO 12-4 Compare different ways to design jobs.

LO 12-5 Discuss how to use four types of reinforcement.

LO 12-6 Discuss the role of compensation in motivating employees.

LO 12-7 Describe how to develop the career readiness competency of self-motivation.

FORECAST *What's Ahead in This Chapter*

This chapter discusses motivation from four perspectives: content (theories by Maslow, McClelland, Deci and Ryan, and Herzberg), process (equity, expectancy, and goal-setting theories), job design, and reinforcement. We then consider rewards for motivating performance, and conclude with a Career Corner that focuses on how to enhance the career readiness competency of self-motivation.

MANAGE U

Managing for Motivation: Building Your Own Motivation

Are you putting something off right now because you just haven't felt inspired to tackle it? Self-motivation is critical for work success because it drives performance, particularly in work situations where you're expected to apply good work habits and focus in order to be productive without constant supervision.[1] Consider that self-motivated employees at the Hay Group, a global management and consulting firm, were 43 percent more productive than employees with low motivation.[2] This finding supports employers' desire to hire people with the career readiness competency of self-motivation. You certainly want to possess this attitude.

Here are some suggestions for honing your self-motivation (and getting to that task you've been putting off).[3]

1. Reframe your reason. Perhaps you've having trouble accomplishing an objective because you haven't thought through why you're really aiming for it. A goal to look for a job in a particular field because one of your friends is or because someone said it was exciting may not be enough to ignite your inner drive. Try reframing the goal in terms that invoke your own values rather than someone else's: "I want to work in marketing because I think it's a good match for my new media, communication, and social intelligence skills."[4]

2. Be realistic. Realistic goals aren't necessarily easy ones; the American Psychological Association reports that when we set goals that are challenging, we're 90 percent more likely to achieve them.[5] Realistic goals are specific. "I want to get a good job in an exciting field" is broad. "I want to get an entry-level job with a marketing research company" is specific and, therefore, realistic.

3. Set interim goals. At the same time, you shouldn't set yourself up to try accomplishing a big goal in one grand gesture. Break your big goal down into smaller ones, each with a date attached, to lay out a plan of smaller steps you can follow that all lead in the same direction. "I will draft my résumé by the end of this month," and "During the two weeks after that, I will ask three people to critique and proofread it for me," are good interim goals toward your ultimate objective of finding an entry-level marketing job.

4. Celebrate ongoing achievements. Applaud yourself for reaching each of the milestones you've set. Few things are as motivating as rewards, and since each step you accomplish in your plan is bringing you closer to your big goal, each is worth a celebration. Treat yourself to something you've wanted or take time off to do something that's fun. You've earned it.

5. Hold yourself accountable. It's one thing to celebrate success, but if there are no consequences for failure, motivation can drag. A mentor who encourages you and checks in on your progress can give your forward momentum a regular boost. No mentor? Create your own by simply letting a friend know your goal and keeping that person up to date as you proceed through your plan. A Dominican University professor recently studied 149 adults of all ages in businesses and other organizations in the United States and abroad. She found that well over 70 percent of those who used a weekly e-mail to report their goal achievement to a friend either completely accomplished their goal or got more than halfway there. Of those who didn't check in with anyone, only 35 percent achieved as much.[6]

6. Envision success. While you should anticipate setbacks (and forgive yourself for them), keeping the finish line in mind and regularly imagining yourself crossing it will soon become a mental habit that reinforces your positive approach and builds your professionalism and work ethic.

7. Create a "brag book." Start a journal that contains notes about your successes. This aids your recall of "rock star performance," which in turn fuels your self-confidence.[7] Self-confidence drives self-motivation and the associated desire to complete your short- and long-term projects. It also provides behavioral examples of your performance and career readiness competencies to discuss during job interviews.

For Discussion Are you currently using any of these strategies? If not, which ones can you adopt now to achieve your most immediate goals?

12.1 Motivating for Performance

THE BIG PICTURE

Motivation is defined as the psychological processes that arouse and direct people's goal-directed behavior. There are four major perspectives that offer different explanations for how to motivate employees. They are content theories, process theories, job design, and reinforcement theory.

LO 12-1

Explain the role of motivation in accomplishing goals.

What would make you rise a half hour earlier than usual to ensure you got to work on time—and to perform your best once there?

Among the possible inducements (such as those offered by SAS, Google, and Salesforce): free snacks and free meals, onsite laundry, Friday afternoons off, child care assistance, freedom to paint your walls, tuition reimbursement, career counseling, and having your dog at work. How about repayment of your student loan—there's a big one! (Only 3 percent to 4 percent of companies currently offer it, but large employers like Staples, PricewaterhouseCoopers, and Live Nation are joining them, and a recent survey says nearly three of four employers are considering or planning to do so soon.)[8] How about getting paid to live near your job? (Housing subsidies are sometimes offered to attract new hires to high-rent areas like Silicon Valley.)[9]

Whether employment rates are high or low, there are always companies, industries, and occupations in which employers feel they need to bend over backward to retain their human capital.

Motivation: What It Is, Why It's Important

Why do people do the things they do? The answer is this: They are mainly motivated to fulfill their wants and needs.

What Is Motivation and How Does It Work?

Motivation may be defined as the psychological processes that arouse and direct goal-directed behavior.[10] Motivation is difficult to understand because you can't actually see it or know it in another person; it must be *inferred* from one's behavior. Nevertheless, it's imperative that you as a manager understand the process of motivation if you are to guide employees in accomplishing your organization's objectives.

The way motivation works actually is complex, the result of multiple *personal and contextual factors. (See Figure 12.1.)*

FIGURE 12.1

An integrated model of motivation

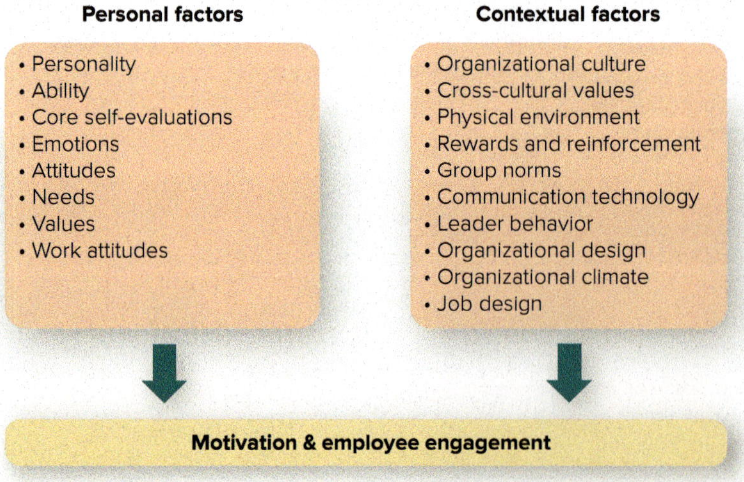

The individual personal factors that employees bring to the workplace range from personality to attitudes, many of which we described in Chapter 11. The contextual factors include organizational culture, cross-cultural values, the physical environment, and other matters we discuss in this chapter and the next. Both categories of factors influence an employee's level of motivation and engagement at work.

However, motivation can also be expressed in a simple model—namely, that people have certain *needs* that *motivate* them to perform specific *behaviors* for which they receive *rewards* that *feed back* and satisfy the original need. *(See Figure 12.2.)*

FIGURE 12.2 A simple model of motivation

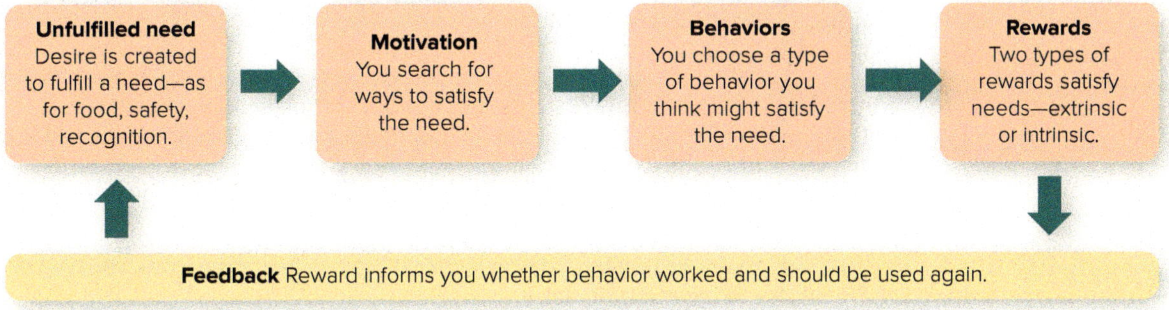

For example, as an hourly worker you desire more money (need), which impels you (motivates you) to work more hours (behavior), which provides you with more money (reward) and informs you (feedback loop) that working more hours will fulfill your need for more money in the future.

Rewards (as well as motivation itself) are of two types—*extrinsic* and *intrinsic.*[11] Managers can use both to encourage better work performance.

- **Extrinsic rewards—a reward given by others.** An **extrinsic reward is the payoff, such as money, a person receives from others for performing a particular task.** Motivation is driven by receiving a valued reward from another person or entity.

  Example: Companies are trying to reduce health care costs by paying employees to lose weight.[12] (Some firms are asking their employees to pay higher insurance premiums to spur them to take off pounds, but that has not been found to be a strong enough motivation. "Financial incentives can work well—if they are separated from insurance premiums," suggests one team of researchers.)[13]

  Another example: Companies like Uber Technologies Inc., McDonald's Corp, and Outback Steakhouse are implementing apps that allow employees to gain near-instant access to their earned wages. The payment plan enables employees to avoid high-interest loans and can improve employee attendance and tenure, according to *The Wall Street Journal.*[14]

- **Intrinsic rewards—a reward given to yourself.** An **intrinsic reward is the satisfaction, such as a feeling of accomplishment, a person receives from performing the particular task itself.** An intrinsic reward is an internal reward; the payoff comes from pleasing yourself.

  Example: When Debbie Feit, a senior copywriter at MARS, a Southfield, Michigan-based marketing agency, was given a month-long paid sabbatical at a charitable organization of her choice, she chose to donate her time writing marketing materials and completing grant applications for children's mental health organizations. "MARS could have just sent money to the organization," Feit says, "but instead they also devoted my time to something I felt passionate about. I was very touched by the experience."[15]

SELF-ASSESSMENT 12.1 CAREER READINESS

Are You More Interested in Extrinsic or Intrinsic Rewards?

The following survey was designed to assess extrinsic and intrinsic motivation. Please be prepared to answer these questions if your instructor has assigned Self-Assessment 12.1 in Connect.

1. What is more important to you, extrinsic or intrinsic rewards? Are you surprised by the results?
2. How can you use the results to increase your motivation to obtain good grades in your classes?
3. What might you say during an interview to demonstrate your self-awareness regarding the rewards that motivate you?

We all are motivated by a combination of extrinsic and intrinsic rewards. Which type of reward is more valuable to you? Answering this question can help you generate self-motivation and higher performance while also increasing the career readiness competency of self-awareness.

Why Is Motivation Important? It seems obvious that organizations would want to motivate their employees to be more productive. But motivation also plays a role in influencing a host of outcomes, including employee engagement, organizational citizenship, absenteeism, and service quality.[16] In order of importance, you as a manager want to motivate people to:

1. **Join your organization.** You need to instill in talented prospective workers the desire to come to work for you.
2. **Stay with your organization.** Whether you are in good economic times or bad, you always want to be able to retain good people.
3. **Show up for work at your organization.** In many organizations, absenteeism and lateness are tremendous problems.
4. **Be engaged while at your organization.** Engaged employees produce higher-quality work and better customer service.
5. **Do extra for your organization.** You hope your employees will perform extra tasks above and beyond the call of duty (be organizational "good citizens").

The Four Major Perspectives on Motivation: An Overview

There is no theory accepted by everyone as to what motivates people. In this chapter, therefore, we present the four principal perspectives. From these, you may be able to select what ideas seem most workable to you. The four perspectives on motivation are (1) *content*, (2) *process*, (3) *job design*, and (4) *reinforcement*, as described in the following four main sections.

Following is a quick overview of these perspectives and the theories that utilize each one.

1. ***Content theories*** emphasize needs as motivators.
   - *Maslow's hierarchy of needs* has five levels to be met in order.
   - *McClelland's acquired needs theory* posits three needs, for achievement affiliation, and power.
   - *Deci and Ryan's self-determination theory* assumes people seek innate needs of competence, autonomy, and relatedness in order to grow.
   - *Herzberg's two-factor theory* differentiates hygiene and motivators that determine work satisfaction and dissatisfaction.
2. ***Process theories*** focus on the thoughts and perceptions that motivate behavior.
   - *Equity/justice theory* proposes that people seek fairness and justice in their interactions and relationships.
   - *Expectancy theory* says people are motivated by how much they want something and how likely they think it is they will get it.
   - *Goal-setting theory* says goals that are specific, challenging, and achievable will motivate behavior.
3. ***Job design theories*** focus on designing jobs that lead to employee satisfaction and performance.
   - *Scientific management theory* attempted to fit people to jobs by reducing the number of tasks workers had to perform to achieve a goal.
   - *Job enlargement and job enrichment* are ways to fit jobs to people by offering more variety, challenges, and responsibility.
   - *The job characteristics model* is an outgrowth of job enrichment that traces the effect of five job characteristics on employees' psychological states and work outcomes.
4. ***Reinforcement theory*** is based on the notion that motivation is a function of behavioral consequences and not unmet needs. •

12.2 Content Perspectives on Employee Motivation

THE BIG PICTURE

Content perspectives are theories emphasizing the needs that motivate people. Needs are defined as physiological or psychological deficiencies that arouse behavior. The content perspective includes four theories: Maslow's hierarchy of needs, McClelland's acquired needs theory, Deci and Ryan's self-determination theory, and Herzberg's two-factor theory.

LO 12-2

Identify the needs that motivate most employees.

Content perspectives, also known as ***need-based perspectives,*** **are theories that emphasize the needs that motivate people.** Content theorists ask, "What kind of needs motivate employees in the workplace?" **Needs are defined as physiological or psychological deficiencies that arouse behavior.** They can be strong or weak, and because they are influenced by environmental factors, they can vary over time and from place to place.

In addition to McGregor's Theory X/Theory Y (see Chapter 2), content perspectives include four theories:

- Maslow's hierarchy of needs theory.
- McClelland's acquired needs theory.
- Deci and Ryan's self-determination theory.
- Herzberg's two-factor theory.

Maslow's Hierarchy of Needs Theory: Five Levels

In 1943, one of the first researchers to study motivation, Brandeis University psychology professor **Abraham Maslow** (mentioned previously in Chapter 2), put forth his **hierarchy of needs theory, which proposes that people are motivated by five levels of needs: (1) physiological, (2) safety, (3) love, (4) esteem, and (5) self-actualization.**[17] *(See Figure 12.3.)*

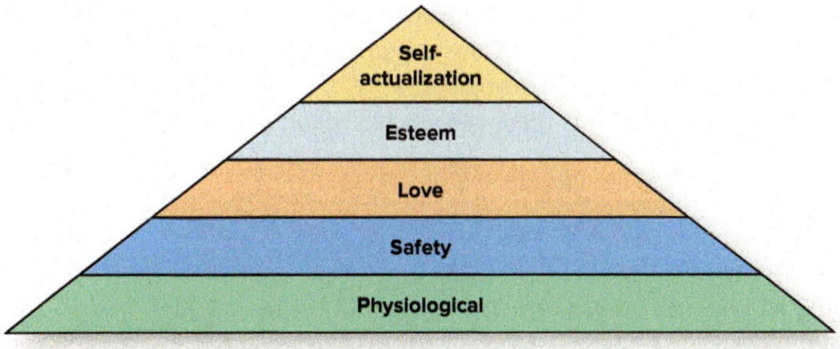

1. **Physiological need—the most basic human physical need:** Need for food, clothing, shelter, comfort, self-preservation. *Workplace example: these are covered by wages.*
2. **Safety need:** Need for physical safety, emotional security, avoidance of violence. *Workplace examples: health insurance, job security, work safety rules, pension plans satisfy this need.*
3. **Love need:** Need for love, friendship, affection. *Workplace examples: office parties, company softball teams, management retreats.*
4. **Esteem need:** Need for self-respect, status, reputation, recognition, self-confidence. *Workplace examples: bonuses, promotions, awards.*
5. **Self-actualization need—the highest level need:** Need for self-fulfillment: increasing competence, using abilities to the fullest. *Workplace example: sabbatical leave to further personal growth.*

FIGURE 12.3

Maslow's hierarchy of needs

The Five Levels of Needs In proposing this hierarchy of five needs, ranging from basic to highest level, Maslow suggested that needs are never completely satisfied. That is, our actions are aimed at fulfilling the "deprived" needs, the needs that remain unsatisfied at any point in time. Thus, for example, once you have achieved safety (security), which is the second most basic need, you will then seek to fulfill the third most basic need–love (belongingness).

EXAMPLE The "Chief Emotion Officer": A Hotel CEO Applies Maslow's Hierarchy to Employees, Customers, and Investors

Chip Conley founded and led the boutique hotel company Joie de Vivre (JDV) for nearly 24 years.[18] JDV's mission statement is "creating opportunities to celebrate the joy of life." In *Peak: How Great Companies Get Their Mojo from Maslow*, Conley describes how JDV used Maslow's theory to motivate the business's three key stakeholders—employees, customers, and investors—by tapping into the power of self-actualization to create peak performance.[19]

Leaders act as CEOs—"chief emotion officers"—says Conley.[20] Drawing on the notion that emotions are just as contagious as the flu virus, Conley believes that you can spread positive emotions in the same way. Thus, for example, every senior management meeting ends with a leader describing someone in the organization who has done outstanding work, and then an executive is dispatched to thank that person.[21]

Motivating Employees In applying the Maslow pyramid to employees, says Conley, "the basic need that a job satisfies is money. Toward the middle are needs like recognition for a job well done, and at the top are needs like meaning and creative expression."[22]

Thus, housekeepers, who represent half a hotel's workers, were gathered in small groups and asked what the hotels would look like if they weren't there each day. Following their answers (unvacuumed carpets, piled-up trash, bathrooms filled with wet towels), they were then asked to come up with alternative names for housekeeping. Some responses: "serenity keepers," "clutter busters," "the peace-of-mind police."

From this exercise, workers developed a sense of how the customer experience would not be the same without them.[23] And that, says Conley, "gets to a sense of meaning in your work that satisfies that high-level human motivation." Addressing the highest-level need gives employees "a sense that the job helps them become the best people they can be."[24]

Motivating Customers Many hotels offer clean, safe accommodations. JDV designs each of its 30 hotels to "flatter and vindicate a different category of customers' distinct self-image," says Conley. Thus, in San Francisco, the Hotel Rex's tweedy décor and Jack London touches appeal to urbane literary types. The corridors feature quotations by novelists John Steinbeck and Dashiell Hammett, the bar is called the Vicious Circle (a reference to the famed New York Algonquin literary hangout), and the lobby is stuffed with books and 1920s art.[25] The Vitale's fitness-conscious services and minimalist design target "the kind of bourgeois bohemian who might like *Dwell Magazine*."[26]

Motivating Investors Although most investors focus on a "returns-driven relationship" (bottom of the pyramid), some have higher motivations. They are driven not by the deal "but rather [by] an interesting, worthwhile deal," which JDV attempts to provide.[27]

YOUR CALL

Part of the appeal of Maslow's hierarchy, says social psychologist Douglas Kenrick of Arizona State University, is that the pyramid "captures a complicated idea in a very simple way."[28] Do you agree? How do you think managers at large organizations can use this theory?

Using the Hierarchy of Needs Theory to Motivate Employees Research does not clearly support Maslow's theory, although it remains popular among managers. Still, the importance of Maslow's contribution is that he showed that workers have needs beyond that of just earning a paycheck. To the extent the organization permits, managers should first try to meet employees' level 1 and level 2 needs, of course, so that employees won't be preoccupied with them. This is exactly what Amazon did in 2018 by raising the minimum wage of all its workers to at least $15 per hour. Then, however, organizations need to give employees a chance to fulfill their higher-level needs in ways that also advance the goals of the organization.[29]

McClelland's Acquired Needs Theory: Achievement, Affiliation, and Power

David McClelland, a well-known psychologist, investigated the needs for affiliation and power and as a consequence proposed the **acquired needs theory**, which states that three needs—achievement, affiliation, and power—are major motives determining people's behavior in the workplace.[30] McClelland believes that we are not born with our needs; rather, we learn them from the culture–from our life experiences.

The Three Needs Managers are encouraged to recognize three needs in themselves and others and to attempt to create work environments that are responsive to them. The three needs, one of which tends to be dominant in each of us, are as follows. *(See Figure 12.4.)*

- **Need for achievement–"I need to excel at tasks."** This is the desire to excel, to do something better or more efficiently, to solve problems, to achieve excellence in challenging tasks.
- **Need for affiliation–"I need close relationships."** This is the desire for friendly and warm relations with other people.
- **Need for power–"I need to control others."** This is the desire to be responsible for other people, to influence their behavior or to control them.[31]

McClelland identifies two forms of the need for power–personal and institutional.

The negative kind is the need for *personal power,* as expressed in the desire to dominate others, and involves manipulating people for one's own gratification.

The positive kind, characteristic of top managers and leaders, is the desire for *institutional power*, as expressed in the need to solve problems that further organizational goals.

Where do you think you stand in terms of being motivated by these three needs? You can find out by completing Self-Assessment 12.2.

FIGURE 12.4
McClelland's three needs

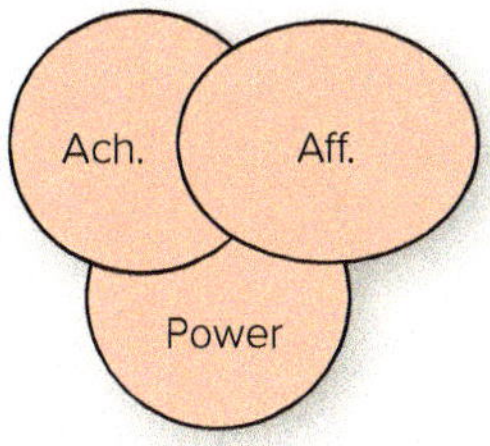

A "well-balanced" individual: achievement, affiliation, and power are of equal size.

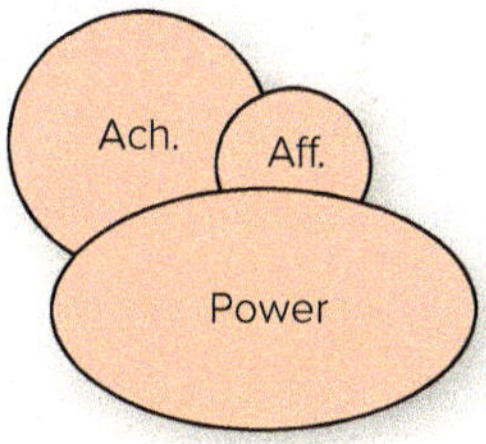

A "control freak" individual: achievement is normal, but affiliation is small and power is large.

SELF-ASSESSMENT 12.2 CAREER READINESS

Assessing Your Acquired Needs

The following survey was designed to assess your motivation in terms of acquired needs. Please be prepared to answer these questions if your instructor has assigned Self-Assessment 12.2 in Connect.

1. What is the order of your most important needs? Are you surprised by this result?
2. Given that achievement and power needs are associated with career advancement, how might you increase these two need states?
3. What might you say during an interview to demonstrate that you have a high need for achievement?

Using Acquired Needs Theory to Motivate Employees You can apply acquired needs theory by appealing to the preferences associated with each need when you (1) set goals, (2) provide feedback, (3) assign tasks, and (4) design the job.[32] Let's consider how you can apply this theory.

Need for Achievement People motivated by the *need for achievement* prefer working on challenging, but not impossible, tasks or projects. They like situations in which good performance relies on effort and ability rather than luck, and they like to be rewarded for their efforts. High achievers also want to receive a fair and balanced amount of positive and negative feedback. This enables them to improve their performance.

Need for Power If you, like most effective managers, have a *high need for power*, that means you enjoy being in control of people and events and being recognized for this responsibility. Accordingly, your preference would probably be for work that allows you to control or have an effect on people and be publicly recognized for your accomplishments.

Need for Affiliation If you tend to seek social approval and satisfying personal relationships, you may have a *high need for affiliation*. In that case, you may not be the most efficient manager because at times you will have to make decisions that will make people resent you. Instead, you will tend to prefer work, such as sales, that provides for personal relationships and social approval.

Deci and Ryan's Self-Determination Theory: Competence, Autonomy, and Relatedness

Developed by **Edward Deci** (pronounced "*Dee*-see") and **Richard Ryan,** psychologists at the University of Rochester, **self-determination theory** assumes that people are driven to try to grow and attain fulfillment, with their behavior and well-being influenced by three innate needs: competence, autonomy, and relatedness.[33]

Focus on Intrinsic Motivation Self-determination theory focuses primarily on intrinsic motivation and rewards (such as feeling independent) rather than on extrinsic motivation and rewards (such as money or fame). Intrinsic motivation is longer lasting than extrinsic motivation and has a more positive impact on task performance.[34]

The Three Innate Needs To achieve psychological growth, according to the theory, people need to satisfy the three innate (that is, inborn) needs of competence, autonomy, and relatedness:

1. **Competence—"I want to feel a sense of mastery."** People need to feel qualified, knowledgeable, and capable of completing a goal or task and to learn different skills.
2. **Autonomy—"I want to feel independent and able to influence my environment."** People need to feel they have freedom and the discretion to determine what they want to do and how they want to do it.
3. **Relatedness—"I want to feel connected to other people."** People need to feel a sense of belonging, of attachment to others.

Using Self-Determination Theory to Motivate Employees Managers can apply this theory by engaging in leader behavior that fosters the experience of competence, autonomy, and relatedness.[35] Following are some specific suggestions:

- **Competence.** Managers like Della Jerkan can provide tangible resources, time, contacts, and coaching to improve employee competence, making sure that employees have the knowledge and information they need to perform their jobs. The "I'm glad . . ." feature on the next page illustrates how Della followed this recommendation. Example: To increase competence, Mascoma Savings Bank in Lebanon, New Hampshire, partners with local universities to offer its employees learning opportunities that go beyond what the company itself can make available to them.[36]
- **Autonomy.** To enhance feelings of autonomy, managers can develop trust with their employees and empower them by delegating meaningful tasks to them.

I'm glad...

...I fostered employees' sense of competence.

Courtesy Della Jerkan

Della Jerkan worked as an assistant manager at a clothing boutique. She was given the difficult task of managing other employees close to her age. "I wasn't that much older than those employees, and I sometimes think that if you're not much older or highly experienced in the field that you're in, people might not take you seriously. I tried really hard to treat them kindly. It sounds simple, but I think it's an important thing to implement when you're supervising other people or trying to train them or get them to do a good job. I think it makes them feel valued. You're starting off on the right foot," said Della.

A difficult, but necessary, part of managing the employees at the boutique was delegating tasks. "I tried to give the employees a sense of responsibility instead of saying 'You must do this and you must do that.' I tried to instill that these are important daily tasks that need to get done in order for our business to run efficiently," said Della.

She made it a point to be sure that tasks were evenly distributed in terms of quantity and quality. "I wanted to make sure I evenly divided the tasks among them and make sure they all had a similar level of responsibility, so none of them felt like they weren't good at something since I didn't give them a certain task."

Delegating didn't come easy to Della, however. "When I was in college, I used to hate group projects because I felt like it was hard to get people to perform at the level you expected of them. So I would just do all the work myself."

But when Della became the assistant manager at the boutique, it was nearly impossible for her to manage everything on her own. "There was no way I could check inventory, label prices, clean the store, and run the cash register at the same time. I tried my best to make sure all of the employees split these tasks evenly," she said. "I would complete tasks like counting the cash drawer, which my manager only entrusted me to do, and then I would delegate the tasks like filling shelves and organizing the displays to the other employees."

Once Della had earned the employees' trust, she was able to delegate tasks without having to micromanage their work every day. "I feel like micromanaging someone makes them feel less valued and trusted. You don't want them to feel like you're watching over their shoulder, but it's also understandable that supervisors and managers want things done a certain way," said Della.

She explained that you don't want to give employees minimal instructions and send them on their way, but rather you want to give them enough detail to instill the confidence to try things on their own. Some of the employees were young and had little to no experience in the retail industry, so they needed additional guidance at first to help them build confidence before being given the freedom to manage themselves.

Courtesy of Della Jerkan

Example: Results-only work environments (ROWE) are focused on results rather than on when or how the work is done, which gives employees a great deal of freedom. Gap adopted this strategy a few years ago, and one manager says, "I have never seen my employees happier, while at the same time having a rise in productivity."[37]

- **Relatedness.** Many companies use camaraderie to foster relatedness. Example: Salesforce.com is number one on *Fortune*'s 2018 list of the world's best places to work with good reason. Says one employee, "This is an extraordinary, special place that really cares about their employees, customers, and community alike. We are strongly encouraged to give back to the community. I have done everything from working in a soup kitchen to working in a children's hospital in Morocco—all supported by the company."[38]

Are you feeling motivated in this course? To what extent does the instructor for this course satisfy your needs for competence, autonomy, and relatedness? You can find out by taking Self-Assessment 12.3.

SELF-ASSESSMENT 12.3 CAREER READINESS

Assessing Your Needs for Self-Determination

The following survey was designed to assess the extent to which an instructor is satisfying your needs for self-determination. Please be prepared to answer these questions if your instructor has assigned Self-Assessment 12.3 in Connect.

1. Are your needs being met? Do the results make sense in terms of your level of motivation in this course?
2. Based on the results, identify two things you might do to increase your motivation.
3. What might you say during an interview to demonstrate your self-awareness of your needs for competence, autonomy, and relatedness?

Herzberg's Two-Factor Theory: From Dissatisfying Factors to Satisfying Factors

Frederick Herzberg arrived at his needs-based theory as a result of a landmark study of 203 accountants and engineers who were interviewed to determine the factors responsible for job satisfaction and dissatisfaction.[39] Job satisfaction was more frequently associated with achievement, recognition, characteristics of the work, responsibility, and advancement. Job dissatisfaction was more often associated with working conditions, pay and security, company policies, supervisors, and interpersonal relationships. The result was Herzberg's **two-factor theory**, **which proposed that work satisfaction and dissatisfaction arise from two different factors—work satisfaction from *motivating factors* and work dissatisfaction from *hygiene factors*.**

Hygiene Factors versus Motivating Factors In Herzberg's theory, the hygiene factors are the lower-level needs, and the motivating factors are the higher-level needs. The two areas are separated by a zone in which employees are neither satisfied nor dissatisfied. *(See Figure 12.5.)*

How much do you want? Would a big desk in a big office with a view represent the tangible realization of managerial success for you? Would this motivate you to excel at work? ©Adventtr/Getty Images

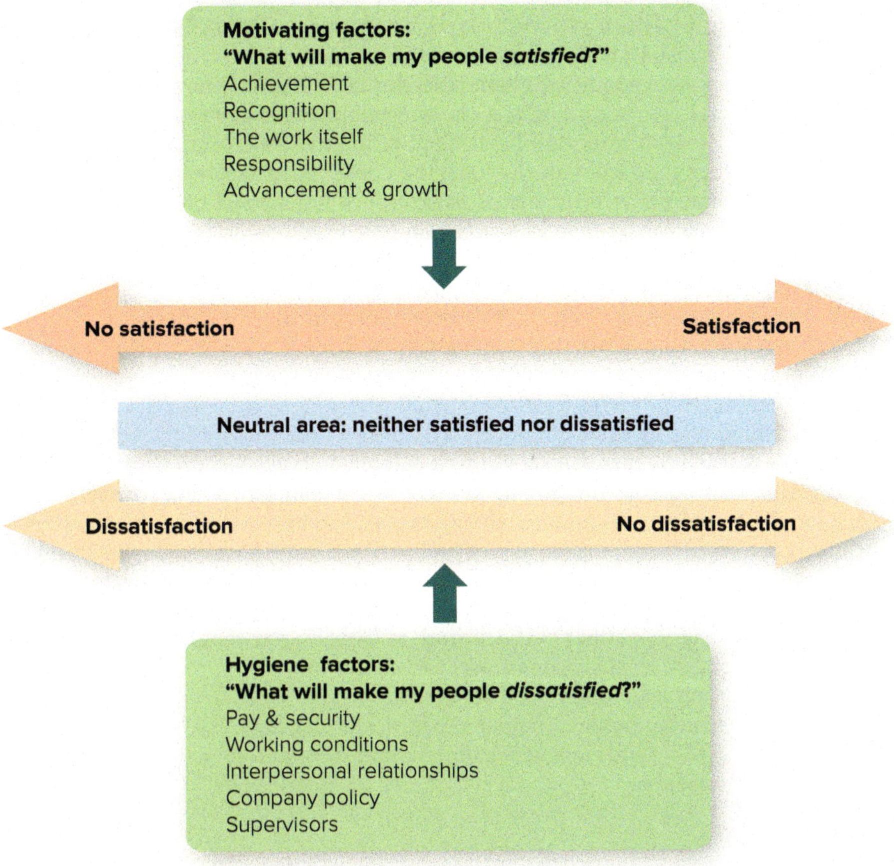

FIGURE 12.5

Herzberg's two-factor theory: satisfaction versus dissatisfaction

- **Hygiene factors—"Why are my people dissatisfied?"** The lower-level needs, **hygiene factors**, are factors associated with job dissatisfaction—such as salary, working conditions, interpersonal relationships, and company policy—all of which affect the job context in which people work.

  We believe you can satisfy and motivate people by providing good hygiene factors. The Container Store, regularly rated as one of the top companies to work for by *Fortune* (No. 93 in 2018), is a good example. The company offers paid time off, sick days, and health insurance to part-timers, and its rate of full-time employee turnover, about 16%, is far lower than the industry average of 74.9%.[40]

- **Motivating factors—"What will make my people satisfied?"** The higher-level needs, **motivating factors**, or simply *motivators*, are factors associated with job *satisfaction*—such as achievement, recognition, responsibility, and advancement—all of which affect the job content or the rewards of work performance. Motivating factors—challenges, opportunities, recognition—must be instituted, Herzberg believed, to spur superior work performance.

  An example of a motivating factor would be to give workers more control over their work. When Southwest Airlines decided not to charge passengers for shipping their luggage (though many competitors had long done so), one reason was to avoid turning flight attendants into baggage handlers, as passengers tried to stuff more and more carry-on luggage into overhead bins—which would have made the flight attendants unhappy and in turn made passengers unhappy. "We want our employees to feel that their job [is] a calling," said Southwest CEO Garry Kelly. "And the people who most have to feel that way are the ones closest to the customer."[41]

Using Two-Factor Theory to Motivate Employees During the Great Recession, with fewer jobs available, many people felt they were stuck in jobs they disliked—only 39 percent said they were happy with their positions in 2009, according to a survey by the Conference Board.[42] In the midst of a strong economic recovery in 2017, in contrast, a SHRM survey of 44 factors in job satisfaction found 89 percent of U.S. employees somewhat or very satisfied with the jobs; the contributing factor cited by the largest percentage of these survey respondents was "respectful treatment of all employees at all levels."[43] Employee engagement is declining in developed countries, however, according to a global survey by Aon Hewitt, a global management consulting company. "The rise in populist movements like those in the U.S., the U.K., and other regions is creating angst within organizations as they anticipate the potential for a decrease in free labor flow. Along with rapid advances in technology, which are increasingly threatening job security, fewer employees are engaged," says the survey report, "and we expect this trend to continue."[44]

There will always be some employees who dislike their jobs, but the basic lesson of Herzberg's research is that you should first eliminate dissatisfaction (hygiene factors), making sure that working conditions, pay levels, and company policies are reasonable. You should then concentrate on spurring motivation by providing opportunities for achievement, recognition, responsibility, and personal growth (motivating factors).

Positive hygiene factors include allowing pets at work; offering video game arcades, fitness classes, and intramural sports (volleyball, soccer); and providing a library of free movies, books, and magazines.[45] If you work at Google, you could also have a college reimbursement plan, legal aid, and travel assistance—and if you die, the company will pay your family half your salary for a decade.[46]

The four needs theories are compared below. *(See Figure 12.6.)* Note how acquired needs theory (McClelland) and self-determination theory (Deci and Ryan) focus only on higher-level needs. ●

FIGURE 12.6 **A comparison of needs and satisfaction theories: Maslow hierarchy of needs, McClelland acquired needs, Deci and Ryan self-determination, and Herzberg two-factor**

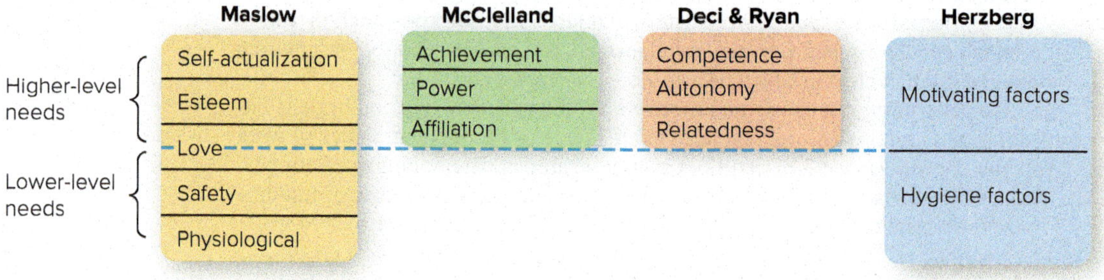

12.3 Process Perspectives on Employee Motivation

THE BIG PICTURE

Process perspectives, which are concerned with the thought processes by which people decide how to act, have three viewpoints: equity/justice theory, expectancy theory, and goal-setting theory.

LO 12-3

Discuss similarities and differences among three process theories.

Process perspectives are concerned with the thought processes by which people decide how to act—how employees choose behavior to meet their needs. Whereas need-based perspectives simply try to understand employee needs, process perspectives go further and try to understand why employees have different needs, what behaviors they select to satisfy them, and how they decide if their choices were successful.

In this section we discuss three process perspectives on motivation:

- Equity/justice theory
- Expectancy theory
- Goal-setting theory

Equity/Justice Theory: How Fairly Do You Think You're Being Treated in Relation to Others?

Fairness—or, perhaps equally important, the *perception* of fairness—can be a big issue in organizations. For example, if, as a salesperson for Target, you received a 10 percent bonus for doubling your sales, would that be enough? What if other Target salespeople received 15 percent?

Equity theory is a model of motivation that explains how people strive for *fairness* and *justice* in social exchanges or give-and-take relationships. Pioneered by psychologist **J. Stacey Adams,** equity theory is based on the idea that employees are motivated to see fairness in the rewards they expect for task performance and are motivated to resolve feelings of injustice.[47] We will discuss Adams's ideas and their application, then discuss the extension of equity theory into what is called *justice theory*. We conclude by discussing how to motivate employees with both equity and justice theory.

Equity theory is based on *cognitive dissonance* (see Chapter 11), the psychological discomfort people experience between their cognitive attitude and incompatible behavior—a discomfort that, it's suggested, motivates them to take action to maintain consistency between their beliefs and their behavior. Accordingly, when we are victimized by unfair social exchanges ("I was *way* overcharged for that car repair!"), our resulting cognitive dissonance prompts us to correct the situation—whether it's slightly changing our attitude or behavior ("That shop is going to get my worst rating on Yelp") or, at the extreme, committing sabotage or workplace violence.

Example: The typical U.S. adult believes a CEO earns $1 million in annual pay, whereas the actual median compensation is about $10.3 million. Regardless, most people (74 percent) believe CEOs are paid too much relative to the average worker.[48] How, then, might employees respond to knowing that the average pay for CEOs in 2017 began at around 100 times their median worker's pay (in the energy industry) and could go as high as nearly 669 times the salary of the median worker (in the retail industry)?[49] Some experts suggest that such imbalances are partly responsible for the $600 billion that is stolen annually in U.S. workplaces, or roughly $4,500 per employee.[50]

The Elements of Equity Theory: Comparing Your Inputs and Outputs with Those of Others The key elements in equity theory are *inputs*, *outputs (rewards)*, and *comparisons*. *(See Figure 12.7.)*

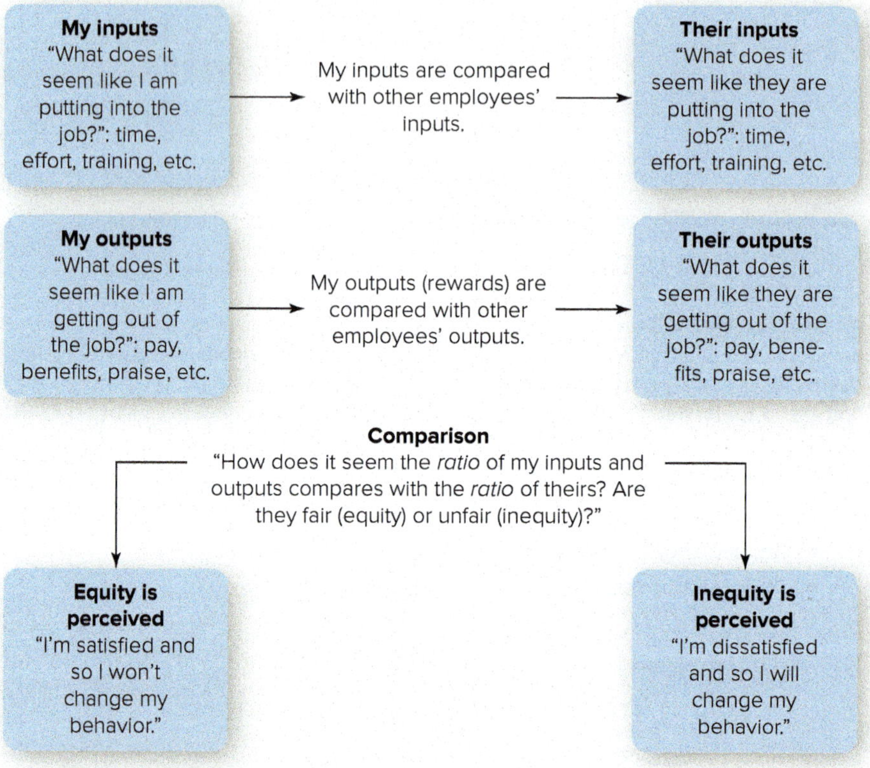

FIGURE 12.7
Equity theory
How people perceive they are being fairly or unfairly rewarded.

- **Inputs—"What do you think you're putting into the job?"** The inputs that people perceive they give to an organization are their time, effort, training, experience, intelligence, creativity, seniority, status, and so on.
- **Outputs or rewards—"What do you think you're getting out of the job?"** The outputs are the rewards that people receive from an organization: pay, benefits, praise, recognition, bonuses, promotions, status perquisites (corner office with a view, say, or private parking space), and so on.
- **Comparison—"How do you think your ratio of inputs and rewards compares with those of others?"** Equity theory suggests that people compare the *ratio* of their own outcomes to inputs against the *ratio* of someone else's outcomes to inputs. When employees compare the ratio of their inputs and outputs (rewards) with those of others—whether co-workers within the organization or even other people in similar jobs outside it—they then make a judgment about fairness. Either they perceive there is *equity*, and so they are satisfied with the ratio and don't change their behavior, or they perceive there is *inequity*, and so they feel resentful and act to change the inequity.[51]

Using Equity Theory to Motivate Employees Adams suggests that employees who feel they are being underrewarded will respond to the perceived inequity in one or more negative ways, as by reducing their inputs ("I'm just going to do the minimum required"), trying to change the outputs or rewards they receive ("If they won't give me a raise, I'll just take stuff"), distorting the inequity ("They've never paid me what I'm worth"), changing the object of comparison ("They think I don't work as hard as Bob? He's a slacker compared to Sid"), or leaving the situation ("I'm outta here!"). By contrast, employees who think they are treated fairly are more likely to support organizational change, more apt to cooperate in group settings, and less apt to turn to arbitration and the courts to remedy real or imagined wrongs.

The Elements of Justice Theory: Distributive, Procedural, and Interactional Beginning in the later 1970s, researchers in equity theory began to expand into an area called *organizational justice,* which is concerned with the extent to which people perceive they are treated fairly at work. Three different components of organizational justice have been identified: *distributive, procedural,* and *interactional.*[52]

- **Distributive justice—"How fairly are rewards being given out?"** **Distributive justice** reflects the perceived fairness of how resources and rewards are distributed or allocated.
- **Procedural justice—"How fair is the process for handing out rewards?"** **Procedural justice** is defined as the perceived fairness of the process and procedures used to make allocation decisions.
- **Interactional justice—"How fairly am I being treated when rewards are given out?"** **Interactional justice** relates to the "quality of the interpersonal treatment people receive when procedures are implemented."[53] This form of justice is not about how decision making or procedures are perceived but rather with whether people themselves believe they are being treated fairly when decisions are implemented. Fair interpersonal treatment necessitates that managers communicate truthfully and treat people with courtesy and respect.

SELF-ASSESSMENT 12.4

Measuring Perceived Fair Interpersonal Treatment

The following survey was designed to assess the extent to which you are experiencing fair interpersonal treatment at work. Please be prepared to answer these questions if your instructor has assigned Self-Assessment 12.4 in Connect.

1. Are you being treated equitably?
2. Based on examining the three lowest scoring items, what could your manager do to improve your perceptions of equity?
3. What can you do to increase your perceptions of fair interpersonal treatment?

Using Equity and Justice Theories to Motivate Employees Employees often may feel quite strongly about what they perceive to be an inequitable or unjust work situation. Often the source of their frustration is pay; one Gallup poll revealed that 51 percent of Americans felt they were underpaid.[54]

Your knowledge of equity and justice theories will allow you to hear out and better understand employee concerns. As an employee yourself, you can motivate other workers by clearly understanding and communicating their opportunities to improve their situations. You can communicate reasonable expectations and make sure objective measures for rewards are well understood.

Five practical lessons can be drawn from equity and justice theories, as follows.

1. Employee Perceptions Are What Count No matter how fair management thinks the organization's policies, procedures, and reward system are, each employee's perception of the equity of those factors is what counts.

Example: In 2018, a woman randomly shot and wounded three YouTube employees at company headquarters in California before killing herself, apparently in protest against what she believed were efforts to censor the videos she posted on YouTube and thus limit her ability to earn income. The woman was one of the website's community of content creators, who share in the ad revenue YouTube earns from the material they create and post. She had been told by the company that some of her content was inappropriate, and at least one video had been age-restricted by YouTube.[55]

2. Employees Want a Voice in Decisions That Affect Them Managers benefit by allowing employees to participate in making decisions about important work outcomes. In general, employees' perceptions of procedural justice are enhanced when they have a voice in the decision-making process.[56] **Voice is defined as "employees' upward expression of challenging but constructive opinions, concerns, or ideas on work-related issues to their managers."[57]**

Managers are encouraged to seek employee input on organizational changes that are likely to affect the workforce. This conclusion was supported by survey results for the IBM Institute for Business Value and IBM Smarter Workforce Institute. Findings showed that 83 percent of employees desired a voice in improving customer issues, product perceptions, and opportunities for improving the work environment.[58] Starbucks also made changes based on employees' voice. The company decided to give employees two pay raises in 2018 partly in response to baristas' complaints about being underpaid.[59]

3. Employees Should Be Given an Appeals Process Employees who are given the opportunity to appeal decisions that affect their welfare enhance the perceptions of distributive and procedural justice.

4. Leader Behavior Matters Employees' perceptions of justice are strongly influenced by the leadership behavior exhibited by their managers (leadership is discussed in Chapter 14). Thus, it is important for managers to consider the justice-related implications of their decisions, actions, and public communications.[60]

Example: John Mackey, co-CEO of Whole Foods, believes companies have "a higher purpose that goes beyond making money," and as one sign of his commitment to fairness, he has capped his own salary, which is 19 times as much as the average Whole Foods worker earns.[61] Compare this to the CEO pay ratios cited above.

5. A Climate for Justice Makes a Difference Managers need to pay attention to the organization's climate for justice. For example, an aggregation of 38 research studies demonstrated that an organization's climate for justice was significantly related to team performance.[62] Researchers also believe a climate of justice can significantly influence the type of customer service provided by employees. In turn, this level of service is likely to influence customers' perceptions of "fair service" and their subsequent loyalty and satisfaction.

The discussion of equity/justice theory has important implications for your own career. For example, you could work to resolve negative inequity by asking for a raise or a promotion (raising your outputs) or by working fewer hours or exerting less effort (reducing inputs). You could also resolve the inequity cognitively, by adjusting your perceptions as to the value of your salary or other benefits (outcomes) or the value of the actual work done by you or your co-workers (inputs).

EXAMPLE Transparency at Buffer

The Western world has long abided by an unwritten rule about pay—that talking openly about your salary is a bad thing.[63] But there is a movement brewing, particularly in tech, toward a more open culture as companies learn that when pay is transparent, employees feel a sense of fairness and are happier on the job.[64] Buffer Technology takes this transparency to a whole new level and is reaping many benefits.

Pay Transparency at Buffer Buffer Technology started making all its employees' salaries public in 2013. CEO Joel Giascogne said the process began with an open dialogue among team members about the salary each member should make and why. This helped the company to think critically about the processes being used to determine individuals' compensation. Soon after, Buffer started publishing everyone's salaries on a spreadsheet.[65]

Buffer has since increased from 10 to 80 (mostly remote) employees and has continued to evolve its pay transparency.[66] The company uses an openly accessible formula to calculate and explain each employee's specific salary. It accounts for employees' local cost of living, experience level, loyalty (employees receive a 5 percent raise for each year with the company), and value of their specific role. Employees receive an additional $3,000 in salary for each dependent.[67] Buffer continuously monitors its pay formula and updates it to ensure it remains easy for all employees to understand, interpret, and apply.[68] The company also values transparency for its potential workforce. Its website includes a "Transparent Salary Calculator" so that people can see what they'd likely make if they got a job at Buffer.[69]

Buffer receives frequent accolades for its commitment to pay transparency, but also criticism for the absence of performance in its salary equation, a practice that contradicts justice theory. Justice theory is based on the idea that employees should receive rewards commensurate with their performance. A salary system that doesn't account for performance differences between workers falls short on this key component of justice.

Transparency in All Things One of Buffer's core values is to "default to transparency," which it does with complete openness regarding salaries, company data, and its own successes and failures. According to one reporter, "They have gone far beyond the call of duty when it comes to being honest about what they're up to, in good times and bad."[70] It's easy to find information on Buffer's website about almost everything that's happening in the company, including real-time revenue stats, pricing, fundraising details, and diversity metrics. For employees, every e-mail in the system is completely accessible to every team member.

How Transparency Pays Off Giascogne says Buffer's policy of transparency pays off in many ways. First, people are much less consumed with money and politics. They know what's going on in the company, how much money everyone makes, and why they make it, so they spend less time thinking, ruminating, and talking about it.[71]

Second, the transparency actually encourages open conversations when people feel undervalued. Giascone says that while it's inevitable in any organization that some will feel undervalued or jealous of others' pay, the company's commitment to transparency means that workers feel comfortable voicing their discontent early, and they know they can challenge and discuss issues with their managers before resentments set in.[72] According to management researcher David Burkus, "When salary information is transparent, it doesn't mean people will agree with all of it. But it does mean they have recourse. It gives you a chance to disagree with the system, then use your disagreement to make a positive change in the company's pay structure."[73]

Finally, the transparency policy has benefited Buffer as an organization because people are drawn to its reputation for openness and fairness. Job applications doubled in the month after Buffer went public with salaries, and the quality of the applicants has also increased dramatically.[74]

One Buffer employee said the transparency "breaks down silos" and that "overall, transparency at Buffer has helped to shape and define our culture for the better. It helps remove a lot of bias and ambiguity from things like our hiring and promotion process. And of course, transparent e-mail democratizes access to information."[75]

YOUR CALL

What do you think about Buffer's approach toward transparency? Can you identify any drawbacks? Do you want to work for an organization that values open access to information?

Expectancy Theory: How Much Do You Want and How Likely Are You to Get It?

Introduced by **Victor Vroom**, **expectancy theory boils down to deciding how much effort to exert in a specific task situation.** This choice is based on a two-stage sequence of expectations—moving from effort to performance and then from performance to outcomes.[76]

The Three Elements: Expectancy, Instrumentality, and Valence

What determines how willing you (or an employee) are to work hard at tasks important to the success of the organization? The answer, says Vroom, is that you will do what you *can* do when you *want* to.

Your motivation, according to expectancy theory, involves the relationship between your *effort*, your *performance*, and the desirability of the *outcomes* (such as pay or recognition) you receive for your performance. These relationships, which are shown in the following drawing, are affected by the three elements of *expectancy*, *instrumentality*, and *valence*. *(See Figure 12.8.)*

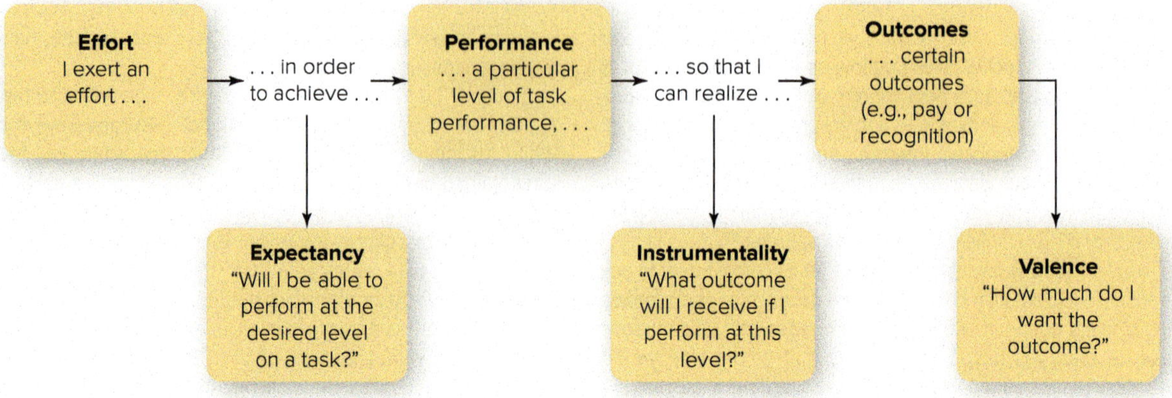

FIGURE 12.8
Expectancy theory: the major elements

1. Expectancy—"Will I Be Able to Perform at the Desired Level on a Task?" **Expectancy is the belief that a particular level of effort will lead to a particular level of performance.** This is called the *effort-to-performance expectancy.*

Example: If you believe that putting in more hours studying for this class will result in a higher grade, then you have high effort-to-performance expectancy. That is, you believe that your efforts will matter.

2. Instrumentality—"What Outcome Will I Receive if I Perform at This Level?" **Instrumentality is the expectation that successful performance of the task will lead to the outcome desired.** This is called the *performance-to-reward expectancy.*

Example: Tesla Inc. created a very high instrumentality between performance and pay for CEO Elon Musk. The pay plan "entails a 10-year grant of stock options that would vest in 12 tranches [a tranch is a portion of overall performance], each with shares equal to 1% of the company's total shares outstanding as of Jan. 21, 2018. A tranche would vest only if a pair of milestones are achieved, one based on market value, the other on a measure of revenue or profit. . . . Mr. Musk could net billions of dollars even if he achieves just a few of the milestones. . . . Tesla said that if none of the tranches are achieved, Mr. Musk wouldn't receive any compensation."[77]

3. Valence—"How Much Do I Want the Outcome?" **Valence is value, the importance a worker assigns to the possible outcome or reward.**

Example: Human resource management firm Kronos decided to use vacation time as a reward after finding that talented job applicants were losing interest in the company because they already had four to five weeks of vacation and it offered only three. So the company followed Netflix's lead by offering an open system in which there is no set limit on vacation days. "Individuals work things out in consultation with their supervisors," according to the *Harvard Business Review*. Kronos notes that the policy has enhanced recruiting and employee engagement, and employees are not taking off significantly more days than they did before. Voluntary turnover also dropped after implementation of the policy.[78]

For your motivation to be high, you must be high on all three elements—expectancy, instrumentality, and valence. If any element is low, your motivation goes down.

Using Expectancy Theory to Motivate Employees

The principal problem with expectancy theory is that it is complex. Even so, the underlying logic is understandable, and research supports its use as a motivational tool.[79]

When attempting to motivate employees, managers should ask the following questions:

- **What rewards do your employees value?** As a manager, you need to get to know your employees and determine what rewards (outcomes) they value, such as pay raises or recognition.

- **What are the job objectives and the performance level you desire?** You need to clearly define the performance objectives and determine what performance level or behavior you want so that you can tell your employees what they need to do to attain the rewards.
- **Are the rewards linked to performance?** You want to reward high performance, of course. Thus, employees must be aware that *X* level of performance within *Y* period of time will result in *Z* kinds of rewards. In a team context, however, research shows that it is best to use a combination of individual and team-based rewards.[80]
- **Do employees believe you will deliver the right rewards for the right performance?** Your credibility is on the line here. Your employees must believe that you have the power, the ability, and the will to give them the rewards you promise for the performance you are requesting.

EXAMPLE Reducing the F's: Applying Expectancy Theory to Failing Students

"A highly skilled CEO is hard to find," observes a business writer. "Highly paid CEOs, however, are everywhere you look."[81]

Indeed, the mass media are full of stories about top managers who don't produce results but are still rewarded (such as the 17 top executives at Toys "R" Us who received millions in bonuses after the company filed for bankruptcy).[82] Where's the inducement to deliver superior performance when you're going to be rewarded anyway?[83]

Maybe we can learn from high school.

Fewer F's As a principal in Arizona high schools, Dr. Tim Richard used a motivational program called Celebration/Remediation to improve student grades. For instance, at 3,000-student Westwood High School in Mesa, which had 1,200 failing pupils, the number of students with F grades dropped to 900 within the first few months of adopting the program. At Poston Butte High School, the number of students with one or more F's was reduced from 555 to 262 in nine weeks. San Tan Foothills High School saw the rate of students who were failing at least one class drop from 40 percent to 12 percent.[84] "Once we changed the culture by bringing on Celebration/Remediation . . . ," Richard said, "the kids have completely embraced it."[85]

Celebration or Remediation? The program works like this: Students who are passing all their classes get a 25- to 30-minute daily break for "celebration time" with friends. "But those who have even one F must stay inside for 'remediation,'" and the time is instead devoted to "extra study, help from peer tutors, or meetings with teachers," Richard told the *Arizona Republic*.[86]

Richard believes the key to motivating students is to link a highly valued reward—socializing with friends outside—with grades. Socializing includes not only hanging out, but also eating snacks, playing organized games, and listening and dancing to music. "You really appreciate celebration after you have been in remediation," said Ivana Baltazar, a 17-year-old senior who raised her grade in economics from an F to a B after receiving help through the program. Students who prefer to skip socializing can use the extra time for schoolwork. "I've stayed before just to catch up and get some of the stress out from the AP classes that I'm taking. So I feel like it's a good time to just cool down," said San Tan Foothills student Paola Lopez.[87]

YOUR CALL

The tricky part, observes Westwood student tutor Joseph Leung, is addressing expectancy—"getting people out of the mindset that they can't succeed. . . . A lot of times they just haven't done their homework. I try to help them understand that the difference between a person passing and failing is their work ethic."[88] For top executives in business, expectancy doesn't seem to be a problem; rather, it's instrumentality and valence. How could you apply Richard's program to reward performance in business?

Goal-Setting Theory: Objectives Should Be Specific and Challenging but Achievable

We have been considering the importance of goal setting since first introducing the topic in Chapter 5. **Goal-setting theory suggests that employees can be motivated by goals that are specific and challenging but achievable.** According to psychologists **Edwin Locke** and **Gary Latham**, who developed the theory, it is natural for people to set and strive for goals; however, the goal-setting process is useful only if people *understand* and *accept* the goals.

The Four Motivational Mechanisms of Goal-Setting Theory Goal setting helps motivate you by doing the following:

1. It Directs Your Attention Goal setting directs your attention toward goal-relevant tasks and away from irrelevant ones.

2. It Regulates the Effort Expended The effort you expend is generally proportional to the goal's difficulty and time deadlines.

3. It Increases Your Persistence Goal setting makes obstacles become challenges to be overcome, not reasons to fail.

4. It Fosters Use of Strategies and Action Plans The use of strategies and action plans make it more likely that you will realize success.

Stretch goals Companies committed to break-out growth sometimes adopt **stretch goals**, which are goals beyond what they actually expect to achieve. Rationales for stretching include forcing people out of their comfort zones to achieve more, building their confidence when they succeed, insulating the company against future setbacks, and accepting the challenge of higher performance standards.[89] Companies like Google, Boeing, Apple, and 3M, have all reported success with wildly daring objectives. Google says such goals "can tend to attract the best people and create the most exciting work environments . . . stretch goals are the building blocks for remarkable achievements in the long term."[90]

Other managers find, however, that this type of goal has drawbacks and should be used with care. For example, stretch goals can demotivate employees because they set aims that seem unattainable, they can encourage unethical behavior as employees try to reach the goals in whatever way they can, and they can lead companies to take unnecessary risks.[91] For example, many people believe that the use of stretch goals contributed to the emissions scandal at Volkswagen.[92] Two recent studies seem to confirm that stretch goals "generate large attainment discrepancies that increase willingness to take risks, undermine goal commitment, and generate lower risk-adjusted performance."[93]

Two Types of Goal Orientations The concept of goal orientation proposes that we may have one of two reasons for trying to achieve a goal depending on our orientation. The **learning goal orientation** sees goals as a way of developing competence through the acquisition of new skills, while the **performance goal orientation** sees them as a way of demonstrating and validating a competence we already have by seeking the approval of others. Research on these goal preferences suggests that people with a strong learning goal orientation appreciate opportunities to enhance their skills, such as through training, performance feedback, and the assignment of challenging tasks, while those with a strong performance orientation may be less willing to take on new challenges for fear of failure and may set lower goals for themselves to avoid making themselves vulnerable to criticism. The learning goal orientation is generally the better of the two for jobs that call for creativity, willingness to embrace new ideas or adapt to new environments, making effective use of performance feedback, and taking a proactive, problem-solving approach. In a separate study the performance goal orientation was found to be "either unrelated or negatively related to performance" on the job.[94]

The possibility of failure is always present, but those with a strong performance orientation may find that it holds them back professionally because it lets them settle for achieving less. Among those who faced and overcame their fear of failure–and indeed the reality of failure–are Beyoncé, who at age 9 lost a singing competition that would have brought her a recording contract; Thomas Edison, who famously said that failing thousands of times was simply a way of discovering what would not work; fashion designer Donna Karan ("I failed draping!"); and best-selling writer Stephen King, who from his teen years saved his rejection slips in order to motivate himself to keep trying. Michael Jordan has said, "I've missed more than 9,000 shots in my career. I've lost almost 300 games. Twenty-six times I've been trusted to take the game winning shot and missed. I've failed over and over and over again in my life. And that is why I succeed." For those who fear failing lest they be judged, Theodore Roosevelt had this to say, "It is not the critic who counts" but rather the doer of deeds, "who at the best knows in the end the triumph of high achievement, and who at the worst, if he fails, at least fails while daring greatly, so that his place shall never be with those cold and timid souls who neither know victory nor defeat."[95]

You may recall that a proactive learning orientation is a career readiness competency desired by employers: It's the same type of attitude as a learning goal orientation. We provided Self-Assessment 5.3 to assess the extent to which you possess this competency.

Some Practical Results of Goal-Setting Theory A *goal* is defined as an objective that a person is trying to accomplish through his or her efforts. Goal-setting experts Locke and Latham proposed the following recommendations when implementing a goal-setting program.[96] To result in high motivation and performance, according to recent research, goals must have a number of characteristics, as follows.

1. Goals Should Be Specific Goals that are specific and difficult lead to higher performance than general goals like "Do your best" or "Improve performance." This is why it is essential to set specific, challenging goals. Goals such as "Sell as many cars as you can" or "Be nicer to customers" are too vague. Instead, goals need to be specific—usually meaning *quantitative,* as in "Boost your revenues 25 percent" and "Cut absenteeism by 10 percent."[97] Pacific Gas & Electric adheres to this recommendation. Specific goals include: "the time it takes to dispatch and respond to a call in the gas organization; the amount of time it takes to onboard new supervisors to their role and have them be productive; the number of work errors and subsequent time and costs for rework."[98]

2. Certain Conditions Are Necessary for Goal Setting to Work People must have the ability and resources needed to achieve the goal, and they need to be committed to the goal. Goal commitment can be fostered by allowing employees to participate in the process of establishing goals.

3. Goals Should Be Linked to Action Plans An action plan outlines the activities or tasks that need to be accomplished in order to obtain a goal and reminds us of what we should be working on. Both individuals (such as college students) and organizations are more likely to achieve their goals when they develop detailed action plans.[99]

Example: Teams of employees at Tornier, a medical device manufacturer in Amsterdam, meet every 45, 60, or 90 days to create action plans for completing their goals. Implementation of the plans can take between 6 and 18 months, depending on the complexity of the goal.[100]

4. Performance Feedback and Participation in Deciding How to Achieve Goals Are Necessary but Not Sufficient for Goal Setting to Work Feedback and participation enhance performance only when they lead employees to set and commit to a specific, difficult goal.

Example: Take Jim's Formal Wear, a tuxedo wholesaler in Illinois. "Once a week," says one report, "employees meet with their teams to discuss their efforts and what changes should be made the next week. Employees frequently suggest ways to improve efficiency or save money, such as reusing shipping boxes and hangers."[101] Goals lead to higher performance when you use feedback and participation to stay focused and committed to a specific goal. Some of the preceding recommendations are embodied in the advice we presented in Chapter 5—namely, that goals should be SMART: specific, measurable, attainable, results-oriented, and having target dates. ●

12.4 Job Design Perspectives on Motivation

THE BIG PICTURE

Job design, the division of an organization's work among employees, applies motivational theories to jobs to increase performance and satisfaction. The traditional approach to job design is to fit people to the jobs; the modern way is to fit the jobs to the people, using job enrichment and approaches that are based on Herzberg's landmark two-factor theory, discussed earlier in this chapter. The job characteristics model offers five job attributes for better work outcomes.

LO 12-4

Compare different ways to design jobs.

About half of workers reported in a recent year that their current job was stagnant.[102] Is there anything that can be done about this?

Job design is (1) the division of an organization's work among its employees and (2) the application of motivational theories to jobs to increase satisfaction and performance. There are two different approaches to job design—one traditional, one modern—that can be taken in deciding how to design jobs. The traditional way is *fitting people to jobs*; the modern way is *fitting jobs to people.*[103]

Fitting People to Jobs

Fitting people to jobs is based on the assumption that people will gradually adapt to any work situation. Even so, jobs must still be tailored so that nearly anyone can do them. This is the approach often taken with assembly-line jobs and jobs involving routine tasks. For managers the main challenge becomes "How can we make the worker most compatible with the work?"

One technique is **scientific management, the process of reducing the number of tasks a worker performs.** When a job is stripped down to its simplest elements, it enables a worker to focus on doing more of the same task, thus increasing employee efficiency and productivity. This may be especially useful, for instance, in designing jobs for mentally disadvantaged workers, such as those jobs run by Goodwill Industries. However, research shows that simplified, repetitive jobs lead to job dissatisfaction, poor mental health, and a low sense of accomplishment and personal growth.[104]

Fitting Jobs to People

Fitting jobs to people is based on the assumption that people are underutilized at work and that they want more variety, challenges, and responsibility. This philosophy, an outgrowth of Herzberg's theory, is one of the reasons for the popularity of work teams in the United States. The main challenge for managers is "How can we make the work most compatible with the worker so as to produce both high performance and high job satisfaction?"

Two techniques for this type of job design are (1) *job enlargement* and (2) *job enrichment.*

Job Enlargement: Putting More Variety into a Job

The opposite of scientific management, **job enlargement consists of increasing the number of tasks in a job to increase variety and motivation.** For instance, the job of installing flat screens in television sets could be enlarged to include installation of the circuit boards as well.

Although proponents claim job enlargement can improve employee satisfaction, motivation, and quality of production, research suggests job enlargement by itself won't have a significant and lasting positive effect on job performance. After all, working at two boring tasks instead of one doesn't add up to a challenging job. Instead, job enlargement is just one tool of many that should be considered in job design.[105]

Job Enrichment: Putting More Responsibility and Other Motivating Factors into a Job Job enrichment is the practical application of Frederick Herzberg's two-factor motivator-hygiene theory of job satisfaction.[106] Specifically, **job enrichment consists of building into a job such motivating factors as responsibility, achievement, recognition, stimulating work, and advancement.**

However, instead of the job-enlargement technique of simply giving employees additional tasks of similar difficulty (known as *horizontal loading*), with job enrichment employees are given more responsibility (known as *vertical loading*).

Intuit, for example, encourages employees "to spend 10% of their working time on projects and ideas of their own, even if they are not related to their assignments." The company has found that this practice has led to the creation of several successful new products.[107]

The Job Characteristics Model: Five Job Attributes for Better Work Outcomes

Developed by researchers **J. Richard Hackman** and **Greg Oldham**, the job characteristics model of design is an outgrowth of job enrichment.[108] The **job characteristics model consists of (a) five core job characteristics that affect (b) three critical psychological states of an employee that in turn affect (c) work outcomes—the employee's motivation, performance, and satisfaction.** The model is illustrated below. *(See Figure 12.9.)*

FIGURE 12.9 **The job characteristics model**

Source: From J. Richard Hackman and Greg R. Oldham, Work Redesign, *1e ©1980.*

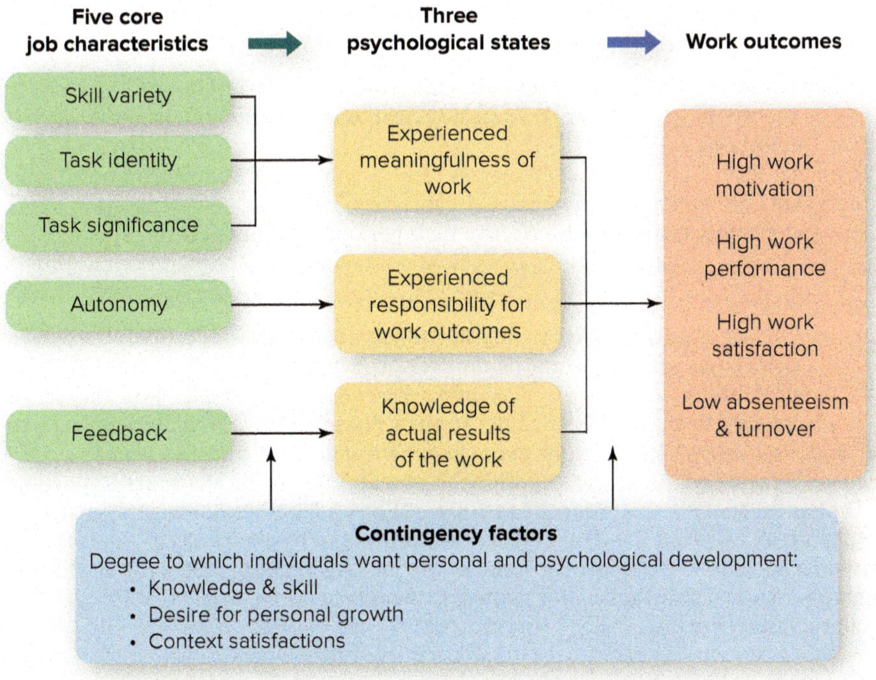

Five Job Characteristics The five core job characteristics are *skill variety, task identity, task significance, autonomy*, and *feedback*, as follows.

She appears to be immersed in her work. Effective job design can do the same thing for you. ©Inmagineasia/Getty Images

1. Skill Variety—"How Many Different Skills Does Your Job Require?" *Skill variety* describes the extent to which a job requires a person to use a wide range of different skills and abilities.

Example: The skill variety required by an executive chef is higher than that for a coffeehouse barista.

2. Task Identity—"How Many Different Tasks Are Required to Complete the Work?" *Task identity* describes the extent to which a job requires a worker to perform all the tasks needed to complete the job from beginning to end.

Example: The task identity for a craftsperson who goes through all the steps to build a stained-glass church window is higher than it is for an assembly-line worker who installs just the windshields on cars.

3. Task Significance—"How Many Other People Are Affected by Your Job?" *Task significance* describes the extent to which a job affects the lives of other people, whether inside or outside the organization.

Example: A technician who is responsible for keeping a hospital's electronic equipment in working order has higher task significance than a person wiping down cars in a carwash.

4. Autonomy—"How Much Discretion Does Your Job Give You?" *Autonomy* describes the extent to which a job allows an employee to make choices about scheduling different tasks and deciding how to perform them.

Example: College-textbook salespeople have lots of leeway in planning which campuses and professors to call on. Thus, they have higher autonomy than do toll-takers on a bridge, whose actions are determined by the flow of vehicles.

5. Feedback—"How Much Do You Find Out How Well You're Doing?" *Feedback* describes the extent to which workers receive clear, direct information about how well they are performing the job.

Example: Professional basketball players receive immediate feedback on how many of their shots are going into the basket. Engineers working on new weapons systems may go years before learning how effective their performance has been.

How the Model Works According to the job characteristics model, these five core characteristics affect a worker's motivation because they affect three critical psychological states: *meaningfulness of work, responsibility for results*, and *knowledge of results*. (Refer to Figure 12.9 again.) In turn, these positive psychological states fuel *high motivation, high performance, high satisfaction*, and *low absenteeism and turnover*. Research shows that experienced meaningfulness is the most important psychological state.[109] Consider the feelings of Shirali Patel, Cybersecurity manager at Raaytheon. She told *The Wall Street Journal* that the best part of her job is that it allows her to "help defend against some of the most advanced threats the world currently faces: cyber attacks and network threats against critical data and IT infrastructure."[110]

One other element—shown at the bottom of Figure 12.9—needs to be discussed: *contingency factors*. This refers to the degree to which a person wants personal and psychological development. Job design works when employees are motivated; to be so, they must have three attributes: (1) necessary knowledge and skill, (2) desire for personal growth, and (3) context satisfactions—that is, the right physical working conditions, pay, and supervision.

Job design works. But keep in mind that it is not for everyone. It is more likely to work when people have the required knowledge and skills, when they want to develop, and when they are satisfied with their jobs.[111]

Applying the Job Characteristics Model

There are three major steps to follow when applying the model.

- **Diagnose the work environment to see whether a problem exists.** Hackman and Oldham developed a self-report instrument for managers to use called the *job diagnostic survey*. This will indicate whether an individual's so-called motivating potential score (MPS)—the amount of internal work motivation associated with a specific job—is high or low.
- **Determine whether job redesign is appropriate.** If a person's MPS is low, an attempt should be made to determine which of the core job characteristics is causing the problem. You should next decide whether job redesign is appropriate for a given group of employees. Job design is most likely to work in a participative environment in which employees have the necessary knowledge and skills.
- **Consider how to redesign the job.** Here you try to increase those core job characteristics that are lower than national norms.

Example: Employers want to save on health costs by helping employees with diabetes, heart disease, and similar chronic conditions avoid emergency room visits and hospital admissions. However, primary care doctors, who could help patients manage their conditions (as by reminding diabetics to monitor their blood-glucose levels daily), are being expected to handle a rapidly growing volume of administrative tasks and see ever more patients a day, sometimes as many as one every 11 minutes. As a result, they often "have one eye on the patient, and one eye on the clock."[112]

The proposed solution? Redesign the job by rewarding primary care doctors for spending more time with patients.[113] (Some perils to avoid: complex compensation designs, poor alignment of goals, and lack of defined, actionable measures, all of which can lead to unintended consequences and failure.)[114]

EXAMPLE Do Job Characteristics Matter in the Modern Workforce?

Lessons from the job characteristics model (JCM) are alive and well, according to an Internet search of what makes employees happy, motivated, productive, and committed. Employees and organizations thrive when a few key principles are woven into jobs, and these are echoed in the JCM. Here's how successful organizations are currently putting the JCM to use.

Making Jobs Meaningful Job meaningfulness "is consistently and overwhelmingly ranked by employees as one of the most important factors driving job satisfaction," according to the *Chicago Tribune*. "It's the linchpin of qualities that make for a valuable employee: motivation, job performance, and a desire to show up and stay."[115] One way organizations are increasing meaningfulness is by allowing workers to use a variety of their skills on the job. At Vodori, a digital marketing firm, workers (or "Vodorians" as they refer to themselves) are encouraged to be nimble. Vodori facilitates this by providing frequent opportunities for employees to learn new skills, work on varied projects, and engage with tasks that are far outside their job descriptions.[116] This decreases boredom and also helps workers feel their talents are being fully utilized and appreciated.

Jobs that allow workers to engage with projects from start to finish also foster a sense of meaning. At Spotify, work is performed by eight-person units called "squads." These squads are responsible for products from planning through production cycles, giving unit members the opportunity to see a project through from ideation to implementation.[117]

Workers also want to know that what they do has impact. In reality, many jobs can feel monotonous and mundane. Take call-center workers whose job was to cold-call University of Michigan alumni to ask for scholarship funding. Repetitive and often unrewarding work, perhaps. But a study found that after these workers had spent 10 minutes chatting with students who directly benefited from the call center's efforts, they stayed on the phone with alumni 142 percent longer and revenues grew 171 percent. The employees could see the meaningful impact their work was having on people's lives, and this drastically enhanced their work outcomes.[118]

Giving Employees Responsibility People prefer the discretion to make decisions on their own because micromanagement makes us feel like babies who can't be trusted.[119] Giving employees freedom signals that they are important and makes them feel more personally responsible for the outcomes of projects they're working on.

Hubspot is a marketing and sales platform that has recently been ranked among the best tech companies, and best overall companies, to work for. Hubspot's chief people officer Katie Burke says autonomy is very important in their company. "We give people a lot of clear direction on our end goals . . . we tell them where we want them to end up, we give them the destination, but we don't prescribe Google Maps style or Waze style exactly how they should actually get there."[120] Marcus Andrews, a principal product manager at the company, appreciates this autonomy. He says, "There's as much help from your managers or teams as you want and guidance, but you really have autonomy to take [a project] in the direction that you want."[121]

Letting Workers Know How They're Doing and How They Can Improve Employees want to be good at their jobs. We want to know what we're doing well, where we are struggling, and how we can get better when we aren't hitting the mark. Feedback, provided in the right way, helps satisfy these desires.

At Cargill, a Minneapolis-based food producer and distributor, feedback has become critical to daily operations and success. The company introduced the "Everyday Performance Management" system to infuse daily organizational interactions with encouragement and feedback from management. Managers are trained to give feedback that is constructive and that helps employees to move forward. The result? About 70 percent of the workers at Cargill feel the continuous feedback has enhanced their professional development and perceptions of being valued by the organization.[122]

YOUR CALL

Which of these job characteristics are most important to you? How might you facilitate things like meaningfulness, responsibility, and feedback as a manager?

12.5 Reinforcement Perspectives on Motivation

THE BIG PICTURE

Reinforcement theory suggests behavior will be repeated if it has positive consequences and won't be if it has negative consequences. There are four types of reinforcement: positive reinforcement, negative reinforcement, extinction, and punishment. This section also describes how to use some reinforcement techniques to modify employee behavior.

LO 12-5

Discuss how to use four types of reinforcement.

Reinforcement evades the issue of people's needs and thinking processes in relation to motivation, as we described under the need-based and process perspectives. Instead, the reinforcement perspective, which was pioneered by **Edward L. Thorndike** and **B. F. Skinner**, is concerned with how the consequences of a certain behavior affect that behavior in the future.[123]

Skinner was the father of *operant conditioning*, the process of controlling behavior by manipulating its consequences. Operant conditioning rests on Thorndike's **law of effect,** which says behavior with favorable consequences tends to be repeated, while behavior with unfavorable consequences tends to disappear.[124]

From these underpinnings has come **reinforcement theory**, which attempts to explain behavior change by suggesting that behavior with positive consequences tends to be repeated, whereas behavior with negative consequences tends not to be repeated. The use of reinforcement theory to change human behavior is called *behavior modification.*

The Four Types of Reinforcement: Positive, Negative, Extinction, and Punishment

Reinforcement is anything that causes a given behavior to be repeated or inhibited, whether praising a child for cleaning his or her room or scolding a child for leaving a tricycle in the driveway.

There are four types of reinforcement: (1) *positive reinforcement,* (2) *negative reinforcement,* (3) *extinction,* and (4) *punishment. (See Figure 12.10.)*

Positive Reinforcement: Strengthens Behavior

Positive reinforcement is the use of positive consequences to strengthen a particular behavior.

Example: A supervisor who has asked an insurance salesperson to sell more policies might reward successful performance by saying, "It's great that you exceeded your sales quota, and you'll get a bonus for it. Maybe next time you'll sell even more and will become a member of the Circle of 100 Top Sellers and win a trip to Paris as well." Note the rewards: praise, more money, recognition, awards. Presumably this will *strengthen* the behavior and the sales rep will work even harder in the coming months.

Negative Reinforcement: Also Strengthens Behavior

Negative reinforcement is the process of strengthening a behavior by withdrawing something negative.

Example: A supervisor who has been nagging a salesperson might say, "Well, so you exceeded your quota" and stop the nagging. Note the neutral statement; there is no praise but also no longer any negative statements. This could cause the sales rep to *maintain* his or her existing behavior.

Extinction: Weakens Behavior

Extinction is the weakening of behavior by ignoring it or making sure it is not reinforced.

Example: You fail to pick up a cell phone call from a solicitor because you want the person to stop calling. By ignoring the call, you hope the person on the other end will give up trying to reach you.

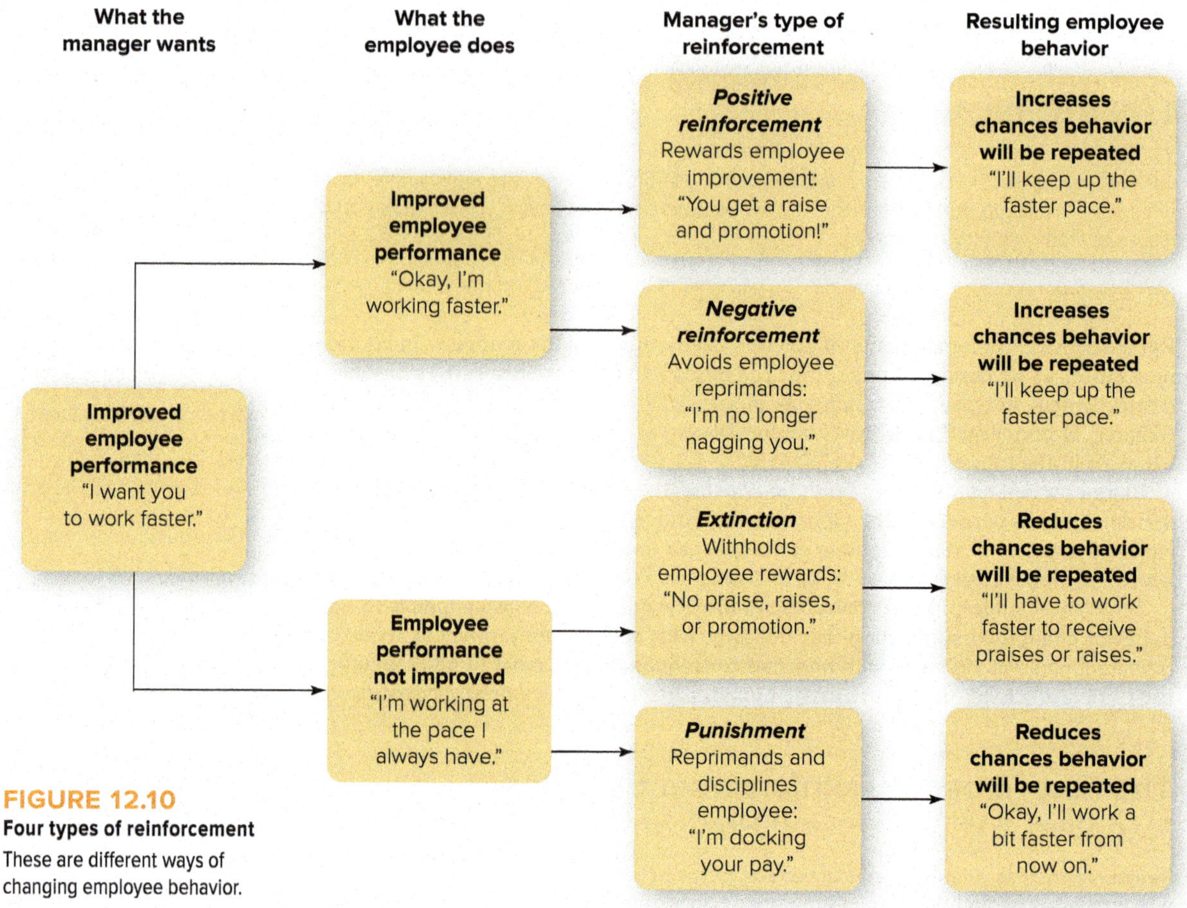

FIGURE 12.10
Four types of reinforcement
These are different ways of changing employee behavior.

Punishment: Also Weakens Behavior **Punishment** is the process of weakening behavior by presenting something negative or withdrawing something positive.

Example: The U.S. Department of Transportation now fines airlines up to $27,500 per passenger for planes left on the tarmac for more than three hours. This policy reduced reported cases from 535 to 12 in the first year it was implemented.[125] Airline lobbying groups are now pressing the Trump administration to roll back the rule, however, among other passenger protections.[126] The "I Wish . . . " feature illustrates how a manager used fear as a motivational tool. Do you think it's a good strategy to use fear to motivate employees?

Using Reinforcement to Motivate Employees

The following are some guidelines for using two types of reinforcement—positive reinforcement and punishment.

Positive Reinforcement There are several aspects of positive reinforcement, which should definitely be part of your toolkit of managerial skills:

- **Reward only desirable behavior.** You should give rewards to your employees only when they show *desirable* behavior. Thus, for example, you should give praise to employees not for showing up for work on time (an expected part of any job) but for showing up early.

I Wish...

...my manager used positive reinforcement rather than punishment.

Jon Ivanhoe worked in the customer services department of a health care services company. His manager was unsuccessful in motivating employees with his use of fear tactics.

During Jon's time in this position, the health care company bought out another company that would allow for new technology to be integrated into the organization, with online solutions that focused on patient–physician interactions. At the time, this was emerging new technology in the industry.

Courtesy Jon Ivanhoe

With the acquisition of the technology company came a new general manager (GM) for that division. His responsibility was to oversee all the professional services. Very early in his tenure, the GM called a large meeting for the entire business unit.

"Not just my customer services unit, but the entire business unit got to meet this new GM. And he was a smart guy, but he was also egotistical and abrasive. We observed that he was very autocratic in his management style," said Jon. "He was abrupt in his decision-making process. He certainly wasn't very collaborative."

What stood out most to Jon in this meeting was what the GM said to the team when they sat down to look at their business model. Jon's business unit was not growing quickly, whereas the new technology company they just acquired had a huge growth rate. "Right off the bat this GM came in and said, directly to the entire team, 'You guys are not growing, and we're probably going to be getting rid of your business.'"

Jon's business unit hung on in various forms for eight more years, so the GM's statement was not entirely true. "What it served to do was try to put a certain level of fear into the sales, account management, and product management parts of our business to either facilitate a shift in innovation or create a pipeline that would accelerate more sales," said Jon. "I thought it was interesting that this was the way he went about trying to motivate us. It was really demotivating us instead. What I saw over a period of time was that we lost some software developers to other projects. We started seeing our business get pulled apart."

Jon admitted that the fear tactics caused him to be frustrated, disengaged, and angry rather than motivated. When his business unit began to unravel, he had to ask himself, "Was this meant to be all along, or is this a self-fulfilling prophecy?" If the GM was hoping that his fear tactics would motivate the employees to prove him wrong, he was unsuccessful.

Courtesy of Jon Ivanhoe

- **Give rewards as soon as possible.** You should give a reward as soon as possible after the desirable behavior appears. Thus, you should give praise to an early-arriving employee as soon as he or she arrives, not later in the week.
- **Be clear about what behavior is desired.** Clear communication is everything. You should tell employees exactly what kinds of work behaviors are desirable, and you should tell everyone exactly what he or she must do to earn rewards.
- **Have different rewards and recognize individual differences.** Recognizing that different people respond to different kinds of rewards, you should have different rewards available. Thus, you might give a word of praise verbally to one person, text or e-mail a line or two to another person, or send a hand-scrawled note to another.

Punishment Unquestionably there will be times when you'll need to threaten or administer an unpleasant consequence to stop an employee's undesirable behavior. Sometimes it's best to address a problem by combining punishment with positive reinforcement. Some suggestions for using punishment are as follows.

- **Punish only undesirable behavior.** You should give punishment only when employees show frequent *undesirable* behavior. Otherwise, employees may come to view you negatively, as a tyrannical boss. Thus, for example, you should reprimand employees who show up, say, a half hour late for work but not 5 or 10 minutes late.

Punishment. What do you feel if you see a police car with lights and siren coming up behind you? Would getting a $260 speeding ticket change your behavior? What if it happened several times? Yet consider also other, presumably stronger, forms of governmental punishment that are supposed to act as deterrents to bad behavior. Does the possibility of the death penalty really deter homicides? Why or why not? ©Hill Street Studios/Blend Images LLC

- **Give reprimands or disciplinary actions as soon as possible.** You should mete out punishment as soon as possible after the undesirable behavior occurs. Thus, you should give a reprimand to a late-arriving employee as soon as he or she arrives.
- **Be clear about what behavior is undesirable.** Tell employees exactly what kinds of work behaviors are undesirable and make sure the severity of the disciplinary action or reprimand matches the severity of the behavior. A manager should not, for example, dock an hourly employee's pay if he or she is only 5 or 10 minutes late for work.
- **Administer punishment in private.** You would hate to have your boss chew you out in front of your subordinates, and the people who report to you also shouldn't be reprimanded in public, which would lead only to resentments that may have nothing to do with an employee's infractions.
- **Combine punishment and positive reinforcement.** If you're reprimanding an employee, be sure to also say what he or she is doing right and state what rewards the employee might be eligible for. For example, while reprimanding someone for being late, say that a perfect attendance record over the next few months will put that employee in line for a raise or promotion. ●

12.6 Using Compensation, Nonmonetary Incentives, and Other Rewards to Motivate: In Search of the Positive Work Environment

THE BIG PICTURE

Compensation, the main motivator of performance, includes pay for performance, bonuses, profit sharing, gainsharing, stock options, and pay for knowledge. Other, nonmonetary incentives address needs that aren't being met, such as work–life balance, growth in skills, positive work environment, and meaning in work.

LO 12-6

Discuss the role of compensation in motivating employees.

Here let us consider the principal tools found in the modern workplace to motivate employees to perform—and to perform at the height of their abilities. We begin with various forms of compensation. We then address nonmonetary incentives: employees' (1) *need for work-life balance*, (2) *need to expand their skills*, (3) *need for a positive work environment*, and (4) *need to matter—to find meaning in their work.*

Would you, as a young professional, be willing to take a $7,600 pay cut for a better quality of work life? That's what most Millennial professionals said, in a recent study by Fidelity Investments.[127] Most said they wouldn't mind taking a hefty pay cut "if it meant improved work-life balance, career development, company culture, and purposeful work," according to one report.[128]

Is Money the Best Motivator?

Whatever happened to good old money as a motivator?

Most workers rate having a caring boss higher than they value monetary benefits, according to several surveys.[129] A recent Jobvite survey of 2,287 U.S. adults showed that about 50 percent were willing to take a 10 percent pay cut to work at a job they found meaningful.[130] In a week-long experiment at an Intel plant in Israel, workers chose either a pizza voucher or a compliment from the boss more often than they opted for cash as a productivity bonus, and by the end of the week, those getting the monetary award were posting a 6.5 percent *decline* in productivity.[131] Clearly, then, motivating doesn't just involve money.

Motivation and Compensation

Most people are paid an hourly wage or a weekly or monthly salary. Both of these are easy for organizations to administer, of course. But by itself a wage or a salary gives an employee little incentive to work hard. Incentive compensation plans try to do so, although no single plan will boost the performance of all employees. (Indeed, a *Wall Street Journal* analysis found that none of 2015's highest-paid CEOs ran one of the 10 best-performing companies. Only three of those executives headed a firm ranked among the top 10 percent in total shareholder return.)[132]

Characteristics of the Best Incentive Compensation Plans In accordance with most of the theories of motivation we described earlier, for incentive plans to work, certain criteria are advisable, as follows. (1) Rewards must be linked to performance and be measurable. (2) The rewards must satisfy individual needs. (3) The rewards must be agreed on by manager and employees. (4) The rewards must be believable and achievable by employees.

Popular Incentive Compensation Plans In what way would you like to be rewarded for your efforts? Some of the most well-known incentive compensation plans are *pay for performance, bonuses, profit sharing, gainsharing, stock options,* and *pay for knowledge.*

- **Pay for performance.** Also known as *merit pay,* **pay for performance** bases pay on one's results. Thus, different salaried employees might get different pay raises and other rewards (such as promotions) depending on their overall job performance.

  Examples: One standard pay-for-performance plan is payment according to a **piece rate**, in which employees are paid according to how much output they produce, as is often used with farm workers picking fruits or vegetables. Piece-rate employers must comply with state and federal minimum wage laws.[133] Another is the **sales commission**, in which sales representatives are paid a percentage of the earnings the company made from their sales, so that the more they sell, the more they are paid. The financial services company Edward Jones pays its employees a salary plus commissions on sales for the first four years and then commissions only, on a scale that increases from 9 percent to 40 percent over time.[134]

- **Bonuses.** **Bonuses** are cash awards given to employees who achieve specific performance objectives.

  Example: The department store Nieman Marcus pays its salespeople a percentage of the earnings from the goods they sell.

- **Profit sharing.** **Profit sharing** is the distribution to employees of a percentage of the company's profits.

  Example: In one T-shirt and sweatshirt manufacturing company, 10 percent of pretax profits are distributed to employees every month, and more is given out at the end of the year. Distributions are apportioned according to such criteria as performance, attendance, and lateness for individual employees. Companies that are largely or entirely employee-owned, such as Publix Supermarkets and W.L. Gore & Associates, also use profit sharing in their compensation plans.[135]

- **Gainsharing.** **Gainsharing** is the distribution of savings or "gains" to groups of employees who reduced costs and increased measurable productivity. Gainsharing has been applied in a variety of industries, from manufacturing to nonprofit, and is said to be used in more than a quarter of *Fortune* 1,000 companies, as well as many small to mid-size businesses.[136] In one version (the so-called *Scanlon plan*), a portion of any cost savings, usually 75 percent, is distributed to employees.

  Example: The Progressive Corporation, one of the nation's largest insurance providers, has adopted a performance-based gainsharing plan open to all officers and employees (except temps). The plan calculates payments by multiplying paid earnings by a target percentage (a figure between 1 percent and 150 percent that varies by position) and by a performance factor.[137]

- **Stock options.** With **stock options**, certain employees are given the right to buy stock at a future date for a discounted price. Among the largest U.S. companies granting stock options to their employees are Nordstrom, Whole Foods, Aflac, The Cheesecake Factory, and Genentech.[138] The motivator here is that employees holding stock options will supposedly work hard to make the company's stock rise so that they can obtain it at a cheaper price.

- **Pay for knowledge.** Also known as *skill-based pay,* **pay for knowledge** ties employee pay to the number of job-relevant skills or academic degrees they earn.[139]

  Example: The teaching profession is a time-honored instance of this incentive, in which elementary and secondary teachers are encouraged to increase their salaries by earning further college credit. However, firms such as FedEx also have pay-for-knowledge plans.

Motivation as a small business owner. Pizza chef Tony Gemignani demonstrates the proper technique for making pizza. Gemignani, who worked in and studied many U.S. pizza parlors, was inspired by a 2000 visit to Italy to learn how to make award-winning char-spotted, soft-centered Neapolitan pizza, a learning process that took seven years and involved grinding his own sausage and pulling his own mozzarella. Opening his own restaurant in 2009 showed that he had read the market correctly for American public taste and love of choices. Coupling good food with a flair for the dramatic (restaurant decor featuring metal sculptures resembling tribal tattoos, for instance), Gemignani and his partners opened Pizza Rock, which now has several California and Nevada stores.[140] For some people, like Gemignani, the only way to merge motivation and compensation is to own and manage their own business. What factors or incentives motivate you to work hard? ©Eric Risberg/AP Images

Nonmonetary Ways of Motivating Employees

Employees who can behave autonomously, solve problems, and take the initiative are apt to be the very ones who will leave if they find their own needs aren't being met—namely, (1) the need for work-life balance, (2) the need to expand their skills, (3) the need for a positive work environment, and (4) the need to matter—to find meaning in their work.

The Need for Work–Life Balance For more than half of men and women in a 2013 Accenture survey, work-life balance was the key determinant of career success—ahead of money, recognition, autonomy, or making a difference.[141] In another survey, 46 percent of employees said work-life balance was the thing they valued most when looking for a new job (second only to salary, cited by 57 percent). According to Pew Research, Millennials in particular are apt to say the most important things in life are "being a good parent" (52 percent) and "having a successful marriage" (30 percent), rather than "having a high-paying career" (15 percent).[142] These studies support the Boston Consulting Group's decision to spend over $100 million for a computer system "to make work schedules more predictable in a 24/7 industry."[143]

Among the employer offerings designed to cater to the desire for work-life balance (at least for some employees) are *work-life benefits*, *flex-time*, and *vacation/sabbatical time*.

- **Work-life benefits.** **Work–life benefits are employer-sponsored benefit programs or initiatives designed to help all employees balance work life with home life.**[144] The purpose of such benefits is to remove barriers that make it hard for people to strike a balance between their work and personal lives, such as allowing parents time off to take care of sick children. The worst obstacles to work-life balance, according to one survey, are *bad bosses*—defined as "demanding, overbearing, and mean." Constant work beyond standard business hours and inflexible scheduling tied for second. Third were incompetent colleagues and long commutes.[145]

Work-life benefits include helping employees with day care costs or even establishing onsite centers; offering domestic-partner benefits; giving job-protected leave for new parents; and providing technology, such as mobile phones and laptops, to enable parents to work at home.[146] (Unfortunately, the workplace culture often tends to discourage paid leave for parents, particularly fathers.)[147]

How good are U.S. employers at making work-life benefits available? The United States actually ranks fairly low on this feature—29th out of 36 on a list of countries with the best work-life balance.[148] And although two-thirds (67 percent) of HR professionals *think* their employees have a balanced work life, according to one survey, among employees themselves nearly half (45 percent) still crave more time each week for personal activities.[149]

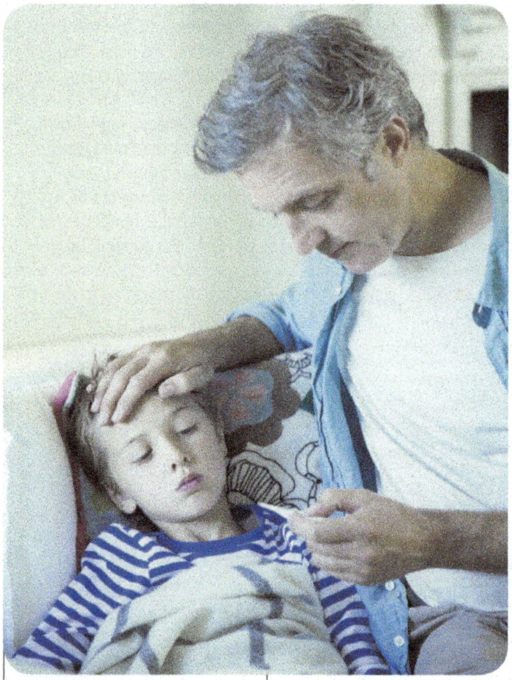

Balancing work with life. Work factors don't always allow for life factors—sick children, school appointments, family emergencies, problems with aging parents, medical appointments, and other personal matters. People around the world are urging employees to ease the single-minded focus on jobs by introducing more flexibility and balance into their lives—work-life balance. What are the top three nonwork concerns that you might have to deal with that you hope your employer might accommodate for you?
©Paul Bradbury/Getty Images

- **Flex-time.** *Flex-time* is a characteristic of the flexible workplace—including part-time work, flex-time, a compressed workweek, job sharing, and telecommuting. Among the top 10 companies offering flex-time arrangements are AT&T, United Healthcare Group, Kaplan, and Hilton Worldwide.[150]

  In one flex-time experiment, in which employees were told they could work wherever and whenever they chose as long as projects were completed on time and goals were met, such employees not only met their goals (as well as did a control group) but were sleeping better, less stressed, and less interested in leaving the organization a year later.[151]
- **Vacations and sabbaticals.** It used to be a badge of honor for Citigroup's junior bankers to put in 100-hour work weeks. Now, says CEO Michael Corbat, "I want people to have family lives, personal lives." Recently, the bank unveiled a program that lets young employees take a long sabbatical—an extended vacation—during which the Citigroup volunteers are paid 60 percent of their salary and take a year off to do charitable work helping, say, businesses develop growth plans in Kenya.[152]

Some of the companies offering paid sabbaticals to U.S. employees are Genentech, the Boston Consulting Group, The Container Store, Klimpton Hotels and Restaurants, REI, PricewaterhouseCoopers, and Autodesk.[153]

About 4 percent of American corporations, most of them technology firms, offer *unlimited* paid time off.[154] Whatever the arrangement, the aim, of course, is to enable employees to reenergize themselves but also, it is hoped, to cement their loyalty to the organization.[155] (Ironically, however, most employees with unlimited time off are unlikely to use much of it—and if they quit or get fired, they will not get a payout for unused vacation days.)

The Need to Expand Skills According to a recent Gallup poll, "87% of millennials rate 'professional or career growth and development opportunities' as important to them in a job—far more than the 69% of non-millennials who say the same."[156] Young workers in particular, having watched their parents undergo downsizing, are apt to view a job as a way of gaining skills that will enable them to earn a decent living in the future. Employers have another point of view: They see it as developing *human capital*, which, as we saw in Chapter 9, is the economic or protective potential of employee knowledge, experience, and actions.

Learning opportunities can take three forms:

- **Studying co-workers.** Managers can see that workers are matched with co-workers from whom they can learn, allowing them, for instance, to "shadow" (watch and imitate) workers in other jobs or be in interdepartmental task forces.
- **Tuition reimbursement.** There can also be tuition reimbursement for part-time study at a college or university.
- **Learning and development.** According to *Training* magazine, U.S. companies spent a record $93.6 billion on employee learning and development in 2016, representing the largest annual increase in 31 years.[157] Although instructor-led classrooms are still the dominant training method, 28.6 percent of learning hours were spent on online or other computer-based programs, including virtual classrooms and webcasts. Blended learning techniques accounted for about 35 percent of learning hours, and nearly 4 percent were conducted via mobile devices.[158]

The Need for a Positive Work Environment Wanting to work in a positive environment begins with the idea of well-being. **Well-being is the combined impact of five elements—positive emotions, engagement, relationships, meaning, and achievement (PERMA),** according to renowned psychologist Martin Seligman.[159] There is one essential consideration to remember about these elements: We must pursue them for their own sake, not as a means to obtain another outcome. In other words, well-being comes about by freely pursuing one or more of the five elements in PERMA.

Flourishing represents the extent to which our lives contain PERMA. When we flourish, our lives result in "goodness . . . growth, and resilience."[160] We should all strive to flourish because of its association with other positive outcomes, like lower cardiovascular risk, lower levels of inflammation, longer life, better sleep, and positive mental health.[161] Unfortunately, many people are not flourishing. For example, a recent survey of 160,000 people around the world revealed that 33 percent reported above-average stress.[162] U.S. data further showed that a majority of people lose sleep because of work-related stress and many people are abusing painkillers to combat it. Painkiller abuse costs employers about $25.5 billion a year in absenteeism and lost productivity.[163]

By contrast, positive emotions *broaden* your perspective about how to overcome challenges in your life—joy, for instance, is more likely to lead you to envision creative ideas during a brainstorming session. Positive emotions also *build* on themselves, resulting in a spreading of positive emotions within yourself and those around you.[164]

What is it that employers can do to create a positive work environment? One simple suggestion is to encourage managers and co-workers to express gratitude. The following Practical Action box explains how this can be done.

PRACTICAL ACTION How Managers Can Encourage Gratitude

Psychology professor and author Robert Emmons says that gratitude is a "basic human requirement."[165] People need to receive recognition and appreciation for the contributions they make.[166] Since we spend the majority of our waking hours at our jobs, this makes encouraging gratitude in the workplace vital, and studies suggest that gratitude increases job satisfaction, work productivity, and physical/mental health.[167] As one reporter put it, "Gratitude is the grease that makes working with others easier."[168] Here are some suggestions for encouraging gratitude with your friends and colleagues.

Be Specific One of the best ways to show others sincere appreciation is to give them praise that is specific and tied to how they have helped you or the organization achieve its goals.[169] Says Dr. Wayne Nemeroff of PsyMax Solutions, "Recall a particular situation and describe a specific behavior; acknowledge the impact the behavior or action had on the group or the project or the action or on you."[170]

Lucid Software created a corporate gratitude flowchart to show gratitude to its employees. Rather than generic praise, the diagram contains a personalized message of gratitude for each employee written by the manager. Each note expresses specifically what the employee does to contribute to the company, and every employee receives a copy of the full flowchart at the end of the year.[171]

Use Gratitude to Build Relationships Gratitude not only bolsters individual employees' confidence, it also helps build partnerships across organizational boundaries.

The sales and service teams at Blinds.com came up with the "traveling department trophy" that it awards each month to the partner group that has made a noticeable impact. The trophy includes a "thank you breakfast" offering an opportunity for networking and relationship-building across divisions that may not otherwise interact.[172]

Go Public Expressions of gratitude are particularly special when you give them to your co-workers.[173] Public accolades satisfy our social and esteem needs and serve as examples to others of the kinds of work behaviors the organization values. Furthermore, studies suggest that just witnessing expressions of gratitude, even if you are not the one being praised, is enough to generate positive benefits of gratefulness.[174] Clearly, public recognition can be a useful tool.

Encourage Peer-to-Peer Gratitude Some evidence suggests it may be more important for workers to be thanked by their peers than by their managers. Such praise may hold more weight because peers are highly familiar with what it takes to do the job well.[175]

Laszlo Bock, former senior VP of people operations at Google, created a digital tool called gThanks that Google employees could use to thank each other for their contributions to the company. Any worker could show gratitude to any other worker, and Bock often printed the messages of thanks and hung them outside his office.[176]

Make It Easy for Others to Practice Gratitude Gratitude needs to be easy to practice if you want to inject it into your organization's culture. One company suggested keeping blank thank-you notes at the front desk that employees could grab whenever they wanted to send a note of thanks to another employee.[177]

Organizations can also make it easier for customers to show gratitude to employees. Disney introduced the hashtag #CastCompliment for visitors to use to recognize any outstanding experiences they've had with cast members (employees) while at the park. Employees' bosses then retweet the comments with the employees' photographs.[178]

Recognize the Power of Praise Praise is a powerful tool no matter how you show it. Research suggests that it takes three positive comments to outweigh the impact of a single negative comment we receive.[179] Even if employees aren't performing as well as you'd like, it may be worthwhile to consider praising the things they *are* doing well instead of criticizing them for faults. We are more likely to repeat good behavior, and also be motivated to improve, when our efforts and contributions are recognized and appreciated.[180]

Southwest Airlines recognizes the power of praise. The company's CEO gives a weekly "shout out" to an employee who has done an outstanding job, and Southwest's magazine features a story about an exemplary employee each month.[181]

YOUR CALL

Can you recall a time when someone expressed sincere gratitude for your contributions to a project? How did this make you feel? What creative suggestions can you come up with to encourage more gratitude in your organization?

Two other suggestions involve the creation of a positive physical setting and a thoughtful boss. Let us consider each of these suggestions.

- **Positive Physical Settings.** The cubicle, according to new research, is stifling the creativity and morale of many workers, and the bias of modern-day office designers for open spaces and neutral colors is leading to employee complaints that their workplaces are too noisy or too bland. Some businesses, such as advertising giant Grey Group in New York, have even moved beyond cubicles to completely open offices, which at Grey required a business psychologist to hold "space therapy" sessions to ease employee concerns.[182]

  "The key to successful workspaces is to empower individuals by giving them choices that allow control over their work environment," says a *Harvard Business Review* article.[183] That's especially key when it comes to keeping employees happy.

EXAMPLE Successful Workspaces

As we said, the traditional private office has yielded to cubicles and more recently to open-plan offices with few or no walls. (Indeed, Facebook hired a world-famous architect to design an office that is a single room stretching 10 acres and accommodating several thousand engineers.)[184]

Distractions or Performance? Although crowding people together can promote cooperative behavior, it also, of course, leads to lack of privacy and increased distractions, which can stifle creativity, dampen morale, and lead to diminished individual and organizational performance.[185]

"There is no such thing as something that works for everybody," says Alan Hedge, a professor of environmental analysis at Cornell University.[186] An 8-foot-by-8-foot cubicle may not be a good visual trigger for human brains, and companies wanting to improve creativity and productivity may need to think about giving office employees better things to look at.[187]

YOUR CALL

Although 70 percent of today's organizations have open-plan offices, other designs are now being tried that go beyond the "open" and "closed" models and can balance people's wishes for privacy against the competing desire for collaboration.[188] "The emerging trend is the hybrid approach," says one workplace strategist, "which includes about a 15% to 30% closed plan with a variety of other work areas to supplement just sitting at a desk."[189] What kind of office surroundings would work best for you?

- **Thoughtful bosses.** It's said that "people don't leave jobs, they leave managers," points out a *Forbes* writer, citing evidence of a survey from the United Kingdom in which 42 percent of 1,374 employees left a job because of a bad boss and almost a third felt their present boss was a bad manager.[190] A Gallup study also found that about 50 percent of the 7,200 adults surveyed left a job "to get away from their manager."[191] Some of these employees were well paid, but is this enough?

The Need to Matter—Finding Meaning in Work Workers now want to be with an organization that allows them to feel they matter. A recent research study reported in *Frontiers in Psychology* found that workers in a broad range of job categories and salary levels were willing to take a 32 percent cut in pay in order to do more meaningful work. In another study of almost 250 people in the United States, jobs that were considered meaningful included teaching, writing, nursing, being an artist, and working for a nonprofit.[192] In a recent *Forbes* list of "the 25 most meaningful jobs that pay well," the top five were in the medical professions.[193]

World War II concentration camp survivor Viktor Frankl, author of *Man's Search for Meaning*, strongly believed that "striving to find a meaning in one's life is the primary motivational force" for people.[194] In other words, it is the drive to find meaning in our lives that instills in us a sense of purpose and motivation to pursue goals. A legendary story is told of the cleaner at NASA who, when President Kennedy asked him what his job was, replied, "I'm helping to put a man on the moon."[195]

Meaningfulness, then, is the sense of "belonging to and serving something that you believe is bigger than the self."[196] What follows are three suggestions for building meaning into your life.

1. **Identify activities you love doing.** Try to do more of these activities or find ways to build them into your work role.

   Example: Employees at St. Jude Children's Research Hospital in Memphis embody this suggestion. They truly enjoy participating in the St. Jude Marathon weekend because it raises money for the children being treated at the hospital. One employee, a cancer survivor, commented, "Each year it provides me with another opportunity to give back so that we can help countless other children have anniversaries of their own."[197]

2. **Find a way to build your natural strengths into your personal and work life.** Want to be more engaged with your school, work, and leisure activities? Take the time to list your highest strengths, your weaknesses, which strengths you use on a daily basis–and find what you can do to incorporate your strengths into your school, work, and leisure activities.

3. **Go out and help someone.** Research shows that people derive a sense of meaningfulness from helping others, that it creates an upward spiral of positivity.[198]

Example: Salesforce.com encourages this result by giving employees 56 hours a year to volunteer within their communities.[199] ●

12.7 Career Corner: Managing Your Career Readiness

LO 12-7

Describe how to develop the career readiness competency of self-motivation.

This chapter has clear implications for developing the career readiness attitude of self-motivation. It is an attitude within the career readiness model shown below (see Figure 12.11.) The competency of self-motivation is defined as the ability to work productively without constant direction, instruction, and praise. It also includes the ability to establish and maintain good work habits and consistent focus on organizational goals and personal development. Practicing self-management is a great way to take a structured approach to increasing your self-motivation.

FIGURE 12.11

Model of career readiness

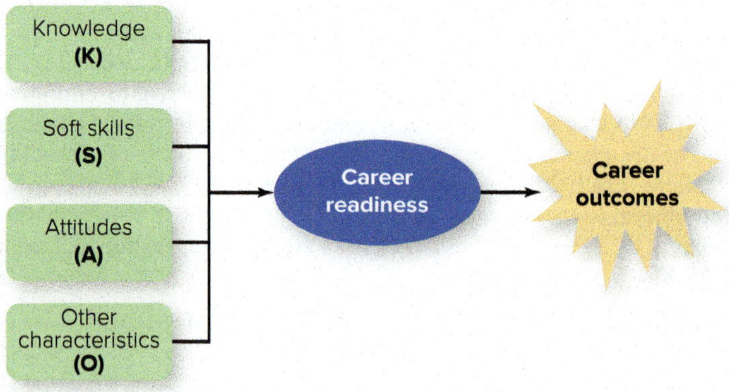

Self-management entails more than just controlling your emotions. Effective self-management skills "help you efficiently communicate with co-workers, management and customers, make right decisions, plan your working time, and keep your body healthy," according to a business writer.[200] The essence of self-management is understanding who you are, what you want in life, what you want to accomplish during your life-long journey, and then making it all happen. This pursuit of your dreams or goals is what drives the self-motivation employers are looking for. The following six steps will help you apply the principles of self-management on a daily basis.

1. Identify Your "Wildly Important" Long-Term Goal

Your goal can be as long term as a personal vision statement, or as short term such as getting a job after graduation that fits your needs and values and pays a decent salary. The wildly important goal is your "north star" or guiding purpose. Writing it down becomes a reminder of how you should spend your time in both the short and long term. For example, one of your authors guides his life around the vision of "leading a life that influences the lives of others." This goal fuels his motivation to continue to write textbooks because he believes they can influence the lives of people like you.

State your Wildly Important Goal in terms of the SMART framework we discussed in Chapter 5. Recall that SMART goals are specific, measurable, attainable, results-oriented and contain target dates. Your author might state his goal as, "Complete revisions of my textbooks according to schedule and budget over the next ten years." You might have a job-related goal such as, "Obtain a job within three months after graduation that pays $50,000 and is consistent with my values and desires."

2. Break Your Wildly Important Goal into Short-Term Goals

Research tells us you are more likely to achieve your Wildly Important Goal if you break it down into smaller bite-size goals. For example, if your most important long-term goal is to get a good job after graduation, this step entails identifying the major milestones you must accomplish to make that happen. They might include outcomes like: maintain a GPA of 3.0, increase my career readiness, obtain an internship, become a student leader in one organization, gain work experience in my functional field of study, obtain funds to pay tuition, and network with professionals in my field of study.

3. Create a "To-Do" List for Accomplishing Your Short-Term Goals

A "to-do" list identifies the daily activities needed to achieve your short-term goals. It is your detailed plan for achieving them. You may want to use task management software to help create and organize your tasks. For example, one of your authors has a "higher-level" task list that spans outcomes he wants to achieve for the next year. He then creates more immediate task lists every month that guide his behavior.

4. Prioritize the Tasks

A to-do list can get overwhelming if you don't organize it. Organize by prioritizing the tasks in the order in which you need to complete them. Prioritizing in this way enables you to schedule your time to maximize your efficiency and smooth your achievement of interdependent tasks. There is one common error to avoid during this step. Research shows that people tend to work on "easy to complete" tasks rather than harder ones as a task list grows. This strategy actually makes you less productive because easier tasks are generally not as important as more difficult or time-consuming tasks.[201] One useful suggestion is to rank the tasks from (1) for low importance to (5) for high importance.

5. Create a Time Schedule

It's time to establish start and stop dates for each task once you have made your task list. Dates enable you to organize your schedule and monitor your progress. Here again you may find it useful to employ task management software.

6. Work the Plan, Reward Yourself, and Adjust as Needed

The best-laid plans generally have unforeseen inhibitors like illness, a car breakdown, or a crashed computer. Be flexible while working your task plan. Finally, make the process fun by rewarding yourself for achieving various milestones. The reward should be something you value. One of your authors uses golf as his reward for completing his designated tasks.

Key Terms Used in This Chapter

acquired needs theory 463
bonuses 488
content perspectives 461
distributive justice 471
equity theory 469
expectancy 474
expectancy theory 473
extinction 483
extrinsic reward 459
flourishing 491
gainsharing 488
goal-setting theory 475
hierarchy of needs theory 461
hygiene factors 467
instrumentality 474
interactional justice 471
intrinsic reward 459
job characteristics model 479
job design 478
job enlargement 478
job enrichment 479
law of effect 483
learning goal orientation 476
meaningfulness 493
motivating factors 467
motivation 458
needs 461
negative reinforcement 483
pay for knowledge 488
pay for performance 488
performance goal orientation 476
piece rate 488
positive reinforcement 483
procedural justice 471
process perspectives 469
profit sharing 488
punishment 484
reinforcement 483
reinforcement theory 483
sales commission 488
scientific management 478
self-determination theory 464
stock options 488
stretch goals 476
two-factor theory 466
valence 474
voice 472
well-being 491
work–life benefits 489

Key Points

12.1 Motivating for Performance

- Motivation is defined as the psychological processes that arouse and direct goal-directed behavior.
- In a simple model of motivation, people have certain needs that motivate them to perform specific behaviors for which they receive rewards that feed back and satisfy the original need.
- Rewards are of two types: (1) An extrinsic reward is the payoff, such as money, a person receives from others for performing a particular task. (2) An intrinsic reward is the satisfaction, such as a feeling of accomplishment, that a person receives from performing the particular task itself.
- As a manager, you want to motivate people to do things that will benefit your organization—join it, stay with it, show up for work at it, perform better for it, and do extra for it.
- Four major perspectives on motivation are (1) content, (2) process, (3) job design, and (4) reinforcement.

12.2 Content Perspectives on Employee Motivation

- Content perspectives or need-based perspectives emphasize the needs that motivate people. Needs are defined as physiological or psychological deficiencies that arouse behavior.
- Besides the McGregor Theory X/Theory Y (Chapter 2), need-based perspectives include (1) the hierarchy of needs theory, (2) the acquired needs theory, (3) the self-determination theory, and (4) the two-factor theory.
- The hierarchy of needs theory proposes that people are motivated by five levels of need: physiological, safety, love, esteem, and self-actualization needs.
- The acquired needs theory states that three needs—achievement, affiliation, and power—are major motives determining people's behavior in the workplace.
- The self-determination theory assumes that people are driven to try to grow and attain fulfillment, with their behavior and well-being influenced by three innate needs: competence, autonomy, and relatedness.
- The two-factor theory proposes that work satisfaction and dissatisfaction arise from two different factors: work satisfaction from so-called motivating factors, and work dissatisfaction from so-called hygiene factors.
- Hygiene factors, the lower-level needs, are factors associated with job dissatisfaction—such as salary and working conditions—which affect the environment in which people work. Motivating factors, the higher-level needs, are factors associated with job satisfaction—such as achievement and advancement—which affect the rewards of work performance.

12.3 Process Perspectives on Employee Motivation

- Process perspectives are concerned with the thought processes by which people decide how to act. Three process perspectives on motivation are (1) equity theory, (2) expectancy theory, and (3) goal-setting theory.

- Equity theory focuses on employee perceptions as to how fairly they think they are being treated compared with others.
- The key elements in equity theory are inputs, outputs (rewards), and comparisons. (1) With inputs, employees consider what they are putting into the job in time, effort, and so on. (2) With outputs or rewards, employees consider what they think they're getting out of the job in terms of pay, praise, and so on. (3) With comparison, employees compare the ratio of their own outcomes to inputs against the ratio of someone else's outcomes to inputs.
- Equity theory has expanded into an area called organizational justice, which is concerned with the extent to which people perceive they are treated fairly at work. Three different components of organizational justice have been identified. Distributive justice reflects the perceived fairness of how resources and rewards are distributed or allocated. Procedural justice is defines as the perceived fairness of the process and procedures used to make allocation decisions. Interactional justice relates to the quality of the interpersonal treatment people receive when procedures are implemented.
- Five practical lessons of equity and justice theories are that employee perceptions are what count, employee participation helps, having an appeal process helps, leader behavior matters, and a climate for justice makes a difference.
- Expectancy theory is based on three concepts: expectancy, instrumentality, and valence of rewards. (1) Expectancy is the belief that a particular level of effort will lead to a particular level of performance. (2) Instrumentality is the expectation that successful performance of the task will lead to the outcome desired. (3) Valence is the value, the importance a worker assigns to the possible outcome or reward.
- When attempting to motivate employees, according to the logic of expectancy theory, managers should ascertain what rewards employees value, what job objectives and performance level they desire, whether there are rewards linked to performance, and whether employees believe managers will deliver the right rewards for the right performance.
- Goal-setting theory suggests that employees can be motivated by goals that are specific and challenging but achievable and linked to action plans.
- In addition, the theory suggests that goals should be set jointly with the employee, be measurable, and have a target date for accomplishment and that employees should receive feedback and rewards.

12.4 Job Design Perspectives on Motivation

- Job design is, first, the division of an organization's work among its employees and, second, the application of motivational theories to jobs to increase satisfaction and performance.
- Two approaches to job design are fitting people to jobs (the traditional approach) and fitting jobs to people.
- Fitting jobs to people assumes people are underutilized and want more variety. Two techniques for this type of job design include (1) job enlargement, increasing the number of tasks in a job to increase variety and motivation, and (2) job enrichment, building into a job such motivating factors as responsibility, achievement, recognition, stimulating work, and advancement.
- An outgrowth of job enrichment is the job characteristics model, which consists of (a) five core job characteristics that affect (b) three critical psychological states of an employee that in turn affect (c) work outcomes—the employee's motivation, performance, and satisfaction.
- The five core job characteristics are (1) skill variety—how many different skills a job requires; (2) task identity—how many different tasks are required to complete the work; (3) task significance—how many other people are affected by the job; (4) autonomy—how much discretion the job allows the worker; and (5) feedback—how much employees find out how well they're doing.
- Three major steps to follow when applying the job characteristics model are (1) diagnose the work environment to see if a problem exists, (2) determine whether job redesign is appropriate, and (3) consider how to redesign the job.

12.5 Reinforcement Perspectives on Motivation

- Reinforcement theory attempts to explain behavior change by suggesting that behavior with positive consequences tends to be repeated whereas behavior with negative consequences tends not to be repeated. Reinforcement is anything that causes a given behavior to be repeated or inhibited. The theory rests on Thorndike's law of effect, which says behavior with favorable consequences tends to be repeated, while behavior with unfavorable consequences tends to disappear. The use of reinforcement theory to change human behavior is called behavior modification.
- There are four types of reinforcement. (1) Positive reinforcement is the use of positive consequences to strengthen a particular behavior. (2) Negative reinforcement is the process of strengthening a behavior by withdrawing something negative. (3) Extinction is the weakening of behavior by ignoring it or making sure it is not reinforced. (4) Punishment is the process of weakening behavior by presenting something negative or withdrawing something positive.
- In using positive reinforcement to motivate employees, managers should reward only desirable behavior, give rewards as soon as possible, be clear about what behavior is desired, and have different rewards and recognize individual differences.

- In using punishment, managers should punish only undesirable behavior, give reprimands or disciplinary actions as soon as possible, be clear about what behavior is undesirable, administer punishment in private, and combine punishment and positive reinforcement.

12.6 Using Compensation and Other Rewards to Motivate

- Compensation is only one form of motivator. For incentive compensation plans for work, rewards must be linked to performance and be measurable; they must satisfy individual needs; they must be agreed on by manager and employee; and they must be perceived as being equitable, believable, and achievable by employees.
- Popular incentive compensation plans are the following. (1) Pay for performance bases pay on one's results. One kind is payment according to piece rate, in which employees are paid according to how much output they produce. Another is the sales commission, in which sales representatives are paid a percentage of the earnings the company made from their sales. (2) Bonuses are cash awards given to employees who achieve specific performance objectives. (3) Profit sharing is the distribution to employees of a percentage of the company's profits. (4) Gainsharing is the distribution of savings or "gains" to groups of employees who reduced costs and increased measurable productivity. (5) Stock options allow certain employees to buy stock at a future date for a discounted price. (6) Pay for knowledge ties employee pay to the number of job-relevant skills or academic degrees they earn.
- There are also nonmonetary ways of compensating employees. Some employees will leave because they feel the need for work–life balance, the need to expand their skills, and the need to matter. To retain such employees, nonmonetary incentives have been introduced, such as the flexible workplace.
- Other incentives that keep employees from leaving are thoughtfulness by employees' managers, work–life benefits such as day care, attractive surroundings, skill-building and educational opportunities, and work sabbaticals.

12.7 Career Corner: Managing Your Career Readiness

- Self-motivation is increased by applying six steps of self-management.
- The six steps of self-management include the following: (1) Identify your wildly important long-term goal. (2) Break your wildly important goal into short-term goals. (3) Create a "to do" list for accomplishing your short-term goals. (4) Prioritize the tasks you need to complete. (5) Create a time schedule for completing tasks. (6) Work the plan, reward yourself, and adjust as needed.

Understanding the Chapter: What Do I Know?

1. What is motivation, and how does it work?
2. What are the four major perspectives on motivation?
3. Briefly describe the four content perspectives discussed in this chapter: hierarchy of needs theory, acquired needs theory, self-determination theory, and two-factor theory.
4. What are the principal elements of the three process perspectives: equity theory, expectancy theory, and goal-setting theory?
5. What is the definition of job design, and what are two techniques of job design?
6. Describe the five job attributes of the job characteristics model.
7. What are the four types of reinforcement?
8. What are six incentive compensation plans?
9. Discuss some nonmonetary ways of motivating employees.
10. Explain a process for using self-management to enhance the career readiness competency of self-motivation.

Management in Action

Motivation Challenges in the Fast-Food World

Fast-food jobs—frying potatoes and flipping burgers in hot, cramped spaces for troves of impatient customers—are generally viewed as temporary gigs filled primarily by teenagers wanting extra spending money. In turn, fast-food companies needn't worry about paying living wages, making work meaningful, or providing opportunities for growth because workers won't stick around long enough for these things to matter. This was true as recently as the 1980s, when the majority of fast-food workers were teenagers. But today, 75 percent of workers are at least 20 years old, and one-third have their own children.[202] Industry employees now describe "unbearable" work environments that include low pay, harsh physical and emotional conditions, and rapidly changing technology, combined with insufficient staff levels and training.[203] Evidence suggests the fast-food industry hasn't done much to change its approach to motivating workers, despite its changing landscape and consistent revenue growth in the last 15 years.[204]

A DAY IN THE LIFE OF A FAST-FOOD WORKER

There are four key reasons fast-food work doesn't motivate employees. First, these jobs are designed with few motivating characteristics, with one study describing them as "low-skilled, alienating, standardized, and highly routinized."[205] Some tasks are so repetitive that restaurants are exploring whether robots can do them.[206] There are also few opportunities for advancement.[207] Data indicate about 90 percent of fast-food workers occupy frontline jobs (cook, cashier), with most of the remaining 10 percent in low-level supervisory positions. Only 2 percent of fast-food jobs are upper-level managerial, professional, or technical roles, compared with 31 percent of the jobs in the United States.[208] One former fast-food worker says, "I spent four years working at McDonald's . . . I never advanced up the rungs, never was a manager, never achieved anything of significance in my time there."[209] Industry spokespersons tout opportunities for hard-working employees to become top managers and even franchisees, but most workers' lifetime earnings would barely cover the $750,000+ required to open a franchise.[210]

Second, fast-food workers perceive strong pay inequity. Most earn minimum wage, and restaurants keep the majority of their workforce part-time to avoid paying benefits. Over half of fast-food workers rely on some form of governmental assistance, and many earn extra hours by splitting their time across multiple restaurants.[211] Terrence Wise told a reporter about the intricate bus-hopping route he'd devised to travel between his jobs at a Burger King and a McDonald's in Kansas City, adding that he was sometimes lucky enough to get two 8-hour shifts in a single day. Wise still earned $8 per hour after 11 years with Burger King.[212] U.S. fast-food workers earn an average hourly wage of $9.09, meaning that even 40 hours a week wouldn't put a family of three above the poverty line. While fast-food CEOs have earned increasingly higher pay over the years, employees' wages have remained stagnant.[213] Recently, workers at restaurants including Papa John's, McDonald's, Jimmy John's, Chipotle, Taco Bell, and Carl's Jr. have filed wage-theft suits. These suits allege that employers intentionally underpaid them by failing to pay overtime, taking illegal deductions, forcing people to work off the clock, or paying below-minimum wages.[214]

Third, people often mistreat fast-food employees. According to one former worker, "Customers always wait in the wings, ready to scream, throw drinks and use racial slurs over a lack of ketchup."[215] A Starbucks' barista described her job as "incredibly tiresome" because "we're getting screamed at by customers for not being fast enough, so we try to go fast, and we mess up the money, or we mess up the drinks, and then we get yelled at for messing up the money and messing up the drinks."[216] Shantel Walker, a 30+ year Papa John's veteran, said "customers . . . don't see the retaliatory measures happening behind that counter . . . they don't see your hours getting cut and cut. They don't see your boss talking to you like you're worthless."[217]

Fourth, high-pressure fast-food environments present physical safety hazards for workers. In 2015, employees filed federal complaints against McDonald's for unsafe work environments, saying understaffing meant employees were pressured to cook food too quickly and without adequate time to mop up messes or to allow fryers to cool before changing oil. The employees said this led to falls and burn injuries and that restaurants didn't provide even basic first-aid supplies, often instructing them to treat burns with condiments.[218]

INDUSTRY OUTCOMES

Employees and organizations in this industry have experienced two key outcomes. First, workers suffer stress-related health problems. Studies show fast-food workers experience more stress than others in equally demanding careers because of their jobs' characteristic absence of both job security and control.[219] Further, the emotional labor of constantly pretending to be happy and engaged with customers, regardless of what's happening behind the counter, leads to job dissatisfaction, burnout, and even substance abuse. One long-time worker says she uses illicit drugs to decrease the stress she experiences from the "fake feelings" she has to exhibit on the job. National surveys indicate over 17 percent of food service workers use illegal substances—a higher rate of drug abuse than any other industry.[220]

Second, the industry is facing record-high turnover rates. Recent data indicate a 150 percent turnover rate in fast food—the highest ever recorded in the industry's history.[221] Some blame restaurants' rapid introduction of new technologies (delivery services, self-ordering kiosks, mobile ordering). Adapting to new technologies takes time, and many restaurants aren't providing the necessary training resources to ensure workers feel they can use the tools proficiently.[222] McDonald's CEO Steve Easterbrook said, "It's going to get increasingly challenging to attract the talent you want into your business . . . and then you've got to work really hard through training and development to retain them."[223]

SMALL IMPROVEMENTS

Recent grassroots campaigns and nonprofits such as Fight for $15 and Fast Food Justice have had at least small positive impacts on the industry. For example, although fast-food workers still can't unionize, new laws in cities like San Francisco, Seattle, and New York are helping workers organize, and some cities have enacted wage protections and scheduling requirements to give employees more job stability and predictability.[224] New York City Comptroller Scott Stringer sees the improvements as part of a larger movement of "economic justice" that he hopes will spread to fast-food organizations across the country.[225]

FOR DISCUSSION

Problem-Solving Perspective

1. What is the underlying problem in this case from the fast-food industry's perspective?
2. What are the causes of this problem?
3. If you were a consultant to a food industry CEO, what recommendations would you make for fixing this problem?

Application of Chapter Content

1. What are the major motivation issues at play in the fast-food industry according to the major needs-based theories of motivation (Maslow's hierarchy, McClellands's acquired needs, and Deci and Ryan's self-determination)?
2. What would Herzberg's theory say about hygiene and motivating factors present in fast-food industry jobs?
3. What do you think are the major drivers of the equity issues faced by fast food employees?
4. How might expectancy theory alleviate some of the problems related to high turnover rates in the fast-food industry?
5. Use the job characteristics model to assess fast-food jobs and suggest how they might be improved to increase their motivating potential.

Legal/Ethical Challenge

Are Workplace Wellness Programs Using Proper Motivational Tools?

Workplace wellness programs (WWPs) aim to motivate employees to live healthier lifestyles. Companies encourage participation by offering insurance premium discounts, cash prizes, health club memberships, and other rewards to employees who (1) participate in the programs and (2) reach certain health goals, including smoking cessation, weight loss, and blood glucose and blood pressure reduction.[226] More than two-thirds of U.S. employers currently offer wellness programs.[227] Proponents believe WWPs ultimately save companies money by making employees healthier, thereby reducing the likelihood that employees will file costly medical claims.[228] This challenge looks at the use of health outcome-based rewards in voluntary WWPs.

Employees who choose to participate in voluntary WWPs provide personal medical data and undergo periodic health assessments to track their progress. One popular tool is the health risk appraisal, a questionnaire that gathers information about personal medical history, lifestyle choices, physiological metrics (weight, height), and family disease history, all of which are used to create a risk profile and plan of recommendations for the employee to address their health risks. Another commonly used tool, biometric screening, benchmarks and tracks employee data such as weight, body mass index (BMI), blood pressure, cardiovascular fitness, cholesterol, and blood glucose.[229]

One concern with WWPs is the risk of exposing workers' private medical data. Employers are typically prohibited from basing employment decisions on medical information. The Americans with Disabilities Act and the Genetic Information Nondiscrimination Act regulate how much personal medical data, if any, an employer is allowed to ask for, and the Health Insurance Portability and Accountability Act (HIPAA) sets strict standards for storage and access to individual health data. But wellness program vendors are often exempt from these provisions because many are not considered health care providers. Vendors may even sell health data to third parties and thus expose employees to the risk of unlawful disclosure and use of their data.

Another concern is that WWPs tie employee rewards to metrics that can be (1) inaccurate and/or (2) uncontrollable. For example, many WWPs use fitness trackers to monitor employees' daily step counts and exercise frequency. But studies show that fitness trackers provide highly inaccurate and unreliable data.[230] Other popular incentives include weight loss and blood pressure/blood glucose reduction, but these metrics can fluctuate drastically in a single day and also depend on the reliability of the specific instruments used to measure them. Rewards tied to reductions in body mass index (BMI) are problematic because this measurement fails to account for factors such as muscle mass, body frame, and pregnancy, leaving otherwise highly fit employees at risk of being categorized as overweight or obese.[231]

The metrics used in WWPs also fail to account for factors that participants may have little to no control over. Eating healthier and exercising more are positive choices with health benefits for many people, but these practices aren't a surefire way to reduce weight and blood pressure/blood glucose in every participant. Certain medical conditions make meeting these goals extremely difficult, even with exemplary lifestyle choices.

The challenge is to decide whether organizations should tie employee rewards to employee health outcomes in voluntary WWPs.

SOLVING THE CHALLENGE

1. I am not in favor of tying employee rewards to health outcomes. Collecting and protecting employee medical information presents substantial risks including possible data breaches. Employees should have equal access to low-cost, quality health care, regardless of their personal health information, risk profiles, or health improvements. I would keep the programs voluntary and not administer rewards.
2. I think it's a good idea to tie rewards to employee health outcomes and to include waivers for employees to sign to authorize the release of their health information when they opt in to WWPs. Those who can improve their health-related outcomes should be rewarded for helping reduce the employer's health care costs.
3. I think it is a good idea to tie rewards to employee health outcomes, provided those outcomes can be measured reliably and accurately. Also, it is only fair to reward people for meeting goals they are actually able to control. Increasing stress-relieving practices such as meditation may be a more realistic goal for someone with hypertension than blood-pressure reduction. Employers should work with employees to come up with realistic, achievable, personalized goals.
4. Invent other options.

Uber Continuing Case

Learn how Uber has attempted to motivate both its drivers and nondrivers. You will see the application of several theories and concepts from this chapter. Assess your ability to apply the management concepts discussed in this chapter to the case by going to Connect.

13 Groups and Teams

Increasing Cooperation, Reducing Conflict

©Olivier Renck/Aurora/Getty Images

After reading this chapter, you should be able to:

LO 13-1 Identify the characteristics of groups and teams.

LO 13-2 Describe the development of groups and teams.

LO 13-3 Discuss ways managers can build effective teams.

LO 13-4 Describe ways managers can deal successfully with conflict.

LO 13-5 Describe how to develop the career readiness competency of teamwork/collaboration.

FORECAST *What's Ahead in This Chapter*

In this chapter, we consider groups versus teams and discuss different kinds of teams. We describe how groups evolve into teams and discuss how managers can build effective teams. We also consider the nature of conflict, both good and bad. We conclude with a Career Corner that focuses on developing the career readiness competency of teamwork/collaboration.

MANAGE U

Effectively Managing Team Conflict

Have you ever worked with a group or team that agreed about everything? Probably not. Everyone comes to a group project or assignment with different experiences, different ideas, and different expectations. Ideally, those differences bring out everyone's creative side and lead to a great conclusion, but often conflicts arise that take a little effort to overcome. Here are some suggestions for handling group conflict at school and at work that will help you hone your career readiness competencies of oral communication, teamwork/collaboration, leadership, and social intelligence.[1]

Ask a Lot of Questions

To resolve a conflict between group members, you first need to get an accurate idea of what the disagreement is about, find out what everyone thinks about it, and gather as many suggestions for resolving the conflict as you can. Before you decide that you have the one and only answer, individually ask team members what they think, and especially what they want to achieve. Try to understand what is driving their behavior in the conflict.

Frame the Conflict around Behavior, not Personalities

No one likes being attacked or criticized just because they disagree. Instead of saying, "You're holding everything up, Chris, because you're so stubborn," which is an attack on Chris's personality, try saying, "If you would please hear everyone out before you make up your mind, Chris, we'll be able to put more options on the table." This moves the focus to a behavior Chris can change and identifies the benefit to the group from doing so. If others in the group are having personality conflicts among themselves, encourage them to adopt this strategy, too, and to reframe their complaints to focus on changing behaviors and not personality.

Remind Team Members About the Group Norms

Norms establish accepted ways of behaving, and they can make or break a group. We suggest you take the time to establish group norms shortly after forming. Remind everyone that your current project or assignment requires them to put forth their best and most cooperative efforts at working together in order to achieve your collective goal. This entails setting norms of taking responsibility for tasks, keeping on schedule, and not interrupting others in team meetings. It's also helpful to encourage team members to focus on what they have in common, including the ultimate goal, rather than on their differences.

Choose Your Words with Care

Ever heard the phrase that you catch more bees with honey than vinegar? The point is that words matter when it comes to conflict. Saying, "Christa, this work stinks, I'd get better work from a high school student," is likely to create defensiveness and conflict. You want to stay away from evaluative statement like this and replace them with specific, descriptive words. "Christa, your report had five computational errors, was two days late, and had five typos." Describe rather than evaluate.

You also want to avoid absolutes like *always* and *never*. "Jose, you never complete your team assignments on time," or "Rashad, you are always late to meetings." Absolutes are rarely true and they foster defensiveness and conflict.

There is a big difference between saying, "You want to redraft the whole report *but* I want to stay on schedule," and saying, "You want to redraft the whole report *and* I want to stay on schedule." The first suggests your goals aren't compatible; the second says both sides have merit and compromise is possible.

Remember Conflict Can Be Productive

It's tempting to avoid or even fear conflict because open disagreement can be uncomfortable. But conflict isn't always bad. If we all thought alike, new ideas would be rare indeed. Look for the reasons behind the conflict. Is it about procedures or processes that can be adjusted, about personalities, which you can encourage people to work around in the short term, or about different ways of approaching the solution? The latter can be a gold mine of creativity for the group if you practice handling conflict effectively.

For Discussion Think back to a conflict that occurred in a group or team to which you belong. What was the real cause of the disagreement, and how was it resolved? Would you do anything differently if you could?

13.1 Groups versus Teams

THE BIG PICTURE

Teamwork promises to be a cornerstone of future management. A team is different from a group. A group typically is management-directed, a team self-directed. Groups may be formal, created to do productive work, or informal, created for friendship. Work teams engage in collective work requiring coordinated effort. Other types of teams are project teams, cross-functional teams, self-managed teams, and virtual teams.

LO 13-1

Identify the characteristics of groups and teams.

Over a quarter century ago, management philosopher Peter Drucker predicted that future organizations would not only be flatter and information-based but also organized around teamwork–and that has certainly come to pass.[2]

In fact, your ability to work well as a team member is a career readiness competency desired by employers and it can affect your job opportunities and success, as well as influencing the kind of employers that might appeal to you. Jenny Gottstein is director of games at The Go Game, a company that builds interactive games to promote team-building in large organizations including Facebook, Google, and American Express. "We're seeing companies use their strong corporate culture as a bargaining chip to recruit the best and brightest talent. When applying for jobs, millennial employees are not only assessing their salary and benefits, but also whether or not they relate to the working environment, and enjoy rolling up their sleeves next to their peers. As a result of this culture shift, team-building is being used as a marketing and recruitment tool."[3]

When you take a job in an organization, the chances are you won't be working alone. You'll be working with others in situations requiring teamwork. A recent survey of 1,300 companies found that people spend more than 50 percent of their time working in teams. Unfortunately, these same individuals reported that only 27 percent of their teams performed at high levels a majority of the time. Forty-three percent believed their teams performed optimally less than half the time.[4] Clearly, teamwork is essential for organizational success, as the table below shows. *(See Table 13.1.)*

TABLE 13.1 **Why Teamwork Is Important**

THE IMPROVEMENTS	EXAMPLE
Increased productivity	At one GE factory, teamwork resulted in a workforce that was 20% more productive than comparable GE workforces elsewhere.
Increased speed	Guidant Corp., maker of lifesaving medical devices, halved the time it took to get products to market.
Reduced costs	Boeing used teamwork to develop the 777 at costs far less than normal.
Improved quality	Westinghouse used teamwork to improve quality performance in its truck and trailer division and within its electronic components division.
Reduced destructive internal competition	Men's Wearhouse fired a salesman who wasn't sharing walk-in customer traffic, and total clothing sales volume among all salespeople increased significantly.
Improved workplace cohesiveness	Cisco Systems told executives they would gain or lose 30% of their bonuses based on how well they worked with peers and in three years had record profits.

Groups and Teams: How Do They Differ?

Aren't a group of people and a team of people the same thing? By and large, no. One is a collection of people, the other a powerful unit of collective performance. One is typically management directed, the other self-directed.

Consider the differences, as follows.

What a Group Is: A Collection of People Performing as Individuals

A **group** is defined as (1) two or more freely interacting individuals who (2) share norms, (3) share goals, and (4) have a common identity.[5] A group is different from a crowd, a transitory collection of people who don't interact with one another, such as a crowd gathering on a sidewalk to watch a fire. And it is different from an organization, such as a labor union, which is so large that members also don't interact.

An example of a work group would be a collection of 10 employees meeting to exchange information about various companies' policies on wages and hours.

What a Team Is: A Collection of People with Common Commitment

McKinsey & Company management consultants Jon R. Katzenbach and Douglas K. Smith say it is a mistake to use the terms *group* and *team* interchangeably. Successful teams, they say, tend to take on a life of their own. Thus, a **team** is defined as a small group of people with complementary skills who are committed to a common purpose, performance goals, and approach for which they hold themselves mutually accountable.[6] "The essence of a team is common commitment," say Katzenbach and Smith. "Without it, groups perform as individuals; with it, they become a powerful unit of collective performance."[7]

An example of a team is a collection of 2–10 employees who are studying industry pay scales, with the goal of making recommendations for adjusting pay grades within their own company.

Xero, an award-winning maker of accounting software for small businesses, relies on a welcoming, family-like environment to motivate employee teams to keep sight of their common commitment in the midst of the company's rapid global growth. The president of Xero USA, Keri Gohman, says, "Often I've joined companies when you walk in the door, and you think 'What's the culture, how do I need to adjust my style so that I can be successful?' . . . but Xero's just been a place where everyone is uniquely encouraged to be themselves."[8]

Teamwork is a soft skills career readiness competency desired by employers. It is defined as the ability to work effectively with and build collaborative relationships with diverse people, work within a team structure, and manage interpersonal conflict. How do you feel about working in teams? Would you prefer to work alone? You can examine your attitude toward teamwork by completing Self-Assessment 13.1.

SELF-ASSESSMENT 13.1 CAREER READINESS

Attitudes toward Teamwork

The following survey was designed to assess your attitude toward teamwork. Please be prepared to answer these questions if your instructor has assigned Self-Assessment 13.1 in Connect.

1. What is your attitude toward teamwork?
2. If you do not have a positive teamwork attitude, consider the reason and identify what you might do to foster a more positive attitude.
3. What might you say during an interview to demonstrate that you possess the competency of teamwork/collaboration?

Formal versus Informal Groups

Groups can be either formal or informal.[9]

- Formal groups—created to accomplish specific goals. **A formal group is a group assigned by organizations or its managers to accomplish specific goals.** A formal group may be a division, a department, a work group, or a committee. It may be permanent or temporary. In general, people are assigned to them according to their skills and the organization's requirements.
- Informal groups—created for friendship. **An informal group is a group formed by people whose overriding purpose is getting together for friendship or a common interest.** An informal group may be simply a collection of friends who hang out with one another, such as those who take coffee breaks together, or it may be as organized as a prayer breakfast, a bowling team, a service club, a company "alumni group" (for example, former Apple employees), or a voluntary organization.

What's important for you as a manager to know is that informal groups can advance or undercut the plans of formal groups. The formal organization may make efforts, say, to speed up the plant assembly line or to institute workplace reforms. But these attempts may be sabotaged through the informal networks of workers who gossip over e-mails and informal gatherings, such as meeting after work for a beer.[10]

However, interestingly, informal groups can also be highly productive—even more so than formal groups.

EXAMPLE — Informal Groups and Informal Learning: Sharing Knowledge in the Lunchroom and on Social Media

As a manager, what would you think if you saw employees making brief conversation near the lunchroom coffeepot? Are they talking about the season finale of their favorite show, or is something more productive taking place? Office kitchens have been hidden out of sight for generations, an unloved necessity kept stark to make sure workers didn't linger, says the *Los Angeles Times*. Companies are now seeing office kitchens in a new light. Kitchens are being turned into showplaces intended to boost morale, encourage collaboration, and create a learning environment.[11] Why the change of heart?

Workplace Learning: Mostly Informal Research has found that 70 percent of workplace learning is informal.[12] Organizations are taking notice of this phenomenon. For example, Siemens managers have placed overhead projectors and empty pads of paper in the lunchroom to facilitate the exchange of information.[13] The highest-performing Google employees teach and support those employees looking to improve. Google certainly has the resources to afford fancy training programs. The company instead opts for peer-to-peer training in order to foster a culture of learning that values continuous development and the sharing of knowledge and expertise.[14]

Talking it out. Ever worked in a job in which you got a lot of informal training through conversations over coffee? Could this be done with social networking? ©Jacobs Stock Photography/Photodisc/Getty Images

Online Peer-to-Peer Networks What about when employees are in far-flung places? "Sales reps are out in the field and they're kind of on islands," pointed out an Indianapolis software-firm executive. "It's a challenge to keep everyone connected."[15] So when the 75 reps started overwhelming the sales-support staff with questions about product details and client information, the company created a website on which the reps could post and answer questions in an informal peer-to-peer learning setting.[16] These types of portals can also be used for employees in distant locations to tell each other personal and professional stories to share experiences. Research has shown that when people talk informally, 65 percent of the time they are telling stories. So providing an online venue for storytelling can be quite effective.[17]

YOUR CALL

Can games (such as the online multiplayer game *Second Life*) or other social media (Facebook, Twitter, Instagram, etc.) be used to foster informal workplace collaboration? How about allowing employees to BYOD—"bring your own device" to work, such as their own smartphone or tablet?[18]

Types of Teams

Different types of teams have different characteristics. We can differentiate some typical teams according to their

1. Purpose.
2. Duration.
3. Level of member commitment.

Work Teams

A company's audit team and a professional sports team have several things in common. Like all work teams, they have a clear purpose that all members share. These teams are usually permanent, and members must give their complete commitment to the team's purpose in order for the team to succeed.

Project Teams

If you have ever completed a team project for a class, you have been part of a project team. Project teams at work are assembled to solve a particular problem or complete a specific task, such as brainstorming new marketing ideas for one of the company's products. Members can meet just once or work together for many years, depending on the nature of the assignment, and they may meet virtually or face to face. They can come from the same or different departments or functional areas, and while serving on the project team, they continue to fulfill their primary responsibilities.

Cross-Functional Teams

Cross-functional teams are designed to include members from different areas within an organization, such as finance, operations, and sales. Cross-functional teams can serve any purpose, they can be work teams or project teams, and their assignment can be long- or short-term. Brian Walker, CEO of furniture maker Herman Miller, described how his company uses cross-functional teams to work on new-product design:

> *We're big believers in putting teams together. . . . We're very willing to move folks around between departments. In our design process, for example, we deliberately create tension by putting together a cross-functional team that includes people from manufacturing, finance, research, ergonomics, marketing and sales. The manufacturing guys want something they know they can make easily and fits their processes. The salespeople want what their customers have been asking for. The tension comes from finding the right balance, being willing to follow those creative leaps to the new place, and convincing the organization it's worth the risk.*[19]

Herman Miller's cross-functional team in Japan consists of people from sales, marketing, and operations, and it recently moved to a newly designed "living office" space that allows for both collaboration and privacy.[20]

Working as a team. This group of employees seems to be acting like a team. We see everyone actively focused on the task at hand. Have you experienced the difference in working for a group versus for a team? How would you describe the key differences? ©Gregory Kramer/Getty Images

Self-Managed Teams

Self-managed teams are defined as groups of workers who are given administrative oversight for their task domains. Experts estimate about 80 percent of *Fortune* 1,000 and 81 percent of manufacturing firms use self-managed teams.[21] They are expected to foster increased productivity and employee quality of work life because employees are delegated greater authority and granted increased autonomy.[22]

The most common chores of today's self-managed teams are work scheduling and customer interaction, and the least common are hiring and firing. Most self-managed teams are also found at the shop-floor level in factory settings, although some experts predict growth of the practice in service operations and even management ranks.

Self-managed teams have been found to have a positive effect on productivity and attitudes of self-responsibility and control, although there is no significant effect on job satisfaction and organizational commitment.[23]

Research also shows self-managed teams are most effective when some guidance is provided by a leader and when the team has supportive technology.[24] Although these conclusions don't qualify as a sweeping endorsement of self-managed teams, experts expect a trend toward such teams in North America because of a strong cultural bias in favor of direct participation.

Virtual Teams **Virtual teams work together over time and distance via electronic media to combine effort and achieve common goals.** Given technological advances, they are growing in popularity. In a recent survey of nearly 1,400 respondents in 80 countries, 85 percent reported working on at least one virtual team, and most worked on more than one such team. Nearly half reported that their teams consisted of people from different countries or cultures.[25]

Advocates say virtual teams are very flexible and efficient because they are driven by information and skills, not by time and location. People with needed information and/or skills can be team members, regardless of where or when they actually do their work.[26] Nevertheless, virtual teams have pros and cons like every other type of team.

Virtual teams and distributed workers present many potential benefits: reduced real estate costs (limited or no office space); ability to leverage diverse knowledge, skills, and experience across geography and time (you don't have to have an SAP expert in every office); ability to share knowledge of diverse markets; and reduced commuting and travel expenses. The flexibility often afforded by virtual teams also can reduce work-life conflicts for employees, which some employers contend makes it easier for them to attract and retain talent.[27]

Virtual teams have challenges, too. It is more difficult for them than for face-to-face teams to establish team cohesion, work satisfaction, trust, cooperative behavior, and commitment to team goals.[28] Thus, virtual teams should be used with caution. It should be no surprise that building team relationships is more difficult when members are geographically distributed. This hurdle and time zone differences are challenges reported by nearly 50 percent of companies using virtual teams. Members of virtual teams also reported being unable to observe the nonverbal cues of other members and experiencing a lack of collegiality.[29] These challenges apply to virtual teams more generally, as does the difficulty of leading such teams.[30] When virtual teams cross country borders, cultural differences, holidays, time zones, and local laws and customs also can cause problems.

Working virtually. Technology not only allows people to communicate where, when, and with whom they wish, but it also allows many people and organizations to work without offices. What are the advantages and disadvantages for you personally of telecommuting and virtual work? ©Image Source/ Getty Images

PRACTICAL ACTION Best Practices for Virtual Teams

We put together a collection of eight practices to help focus your efforts and accelerate your success as a member or leader of a virtual team.

1. **Adapt your communications.** Learn how the various remote workers function, including their preferences for e-mail, texts, and phone calls. It often is advisable to have regularly scheduled contact using technology such as telepresence robots, chat apps, and video conferencing (such as Skype).[31] Be strategic and talk to the right people at the right times about the right topics. Don't just blanket everybody via e-mail—focus your message.
2. **Have fun.** Use your company's intranet or other technology to keep distributed workers connected. Acknowledging birthdays and recognizing accomplishments are especially important for those who are not regularly in the office. Also consider having a "Funday Friday" when the team shares best and worst vacation stories, plays the competitive quiz game Kahoot!, or does chair yoga.[32]
3. **Build trust.** Building trust takes effort; it doesn't happen magically. It is fostered by having face-to-face meetings at least once a year and by getting to know each other. Team-building activities can be built into the annual agenda. Sharing personal information (hobbies, family information) and displaying flexibility in dealing with technological or geographic challenges can engender trust.[33]
4. **Be a good partner.** Often, members of virtual teams are not direct employees of your employer but are independent contractors. Nevertheless, your success and that of your team depend on them. *Treat them like true partners and not hired help.* You need them, and presumably they need you.
5. **Share information.** Effective virtual teams don't hoard information. Resources and information should flow freely, and communication should be transparent. Shared file sites in the cloud (on Google Docs, Dropbox, and other platforms) can serve as information hubs for all team members.[34]
6. **Document the work.** If team members work in different time zones, some projects can receive attention around the clock as they are handed off from one zone to the next. Doing this effectively requires that both senders and receivers clearly specify what they have completed and what they need in each transfer.
7. **Select individuals who can thrive.** "The best virtual workers tend to be those who thrive in interdependent work relationships . . . [and] are self-reliant and self-motivated. . . . Those who tend to struggle in virtual team situations are people who wait for instructions and want to be told what to do."[35] Consider bringing on potential hires as freelancers before extending an offer for long-term employment. This approach helps ensure they develop rapport with colleagues and succeed in a nontraditional work environment.[36]
8. **Use your communication skills.** Because so much communication is written, virtual team members should write in-easy-to-understand and to-the-point language. Responsiveness is also key in order to maintain trust, even if that response is as simple as "Sounds good to me!"[37]

Researchers and consultants agree about one aspect of virtual teams—*there is no substitute for face-to-face contact.* Meeting in person is especially beneficial early in virtual team development, and team leaders are encouraged to meet even more frequently with key members. Face-to-face interactions can be as simple as lunch, water-cooler conversations, social events, or periodic meetings. Whatever the case, such interactions enable people to get familiar with each other and build credibility, trust, and understanding. This reduces misunderstandings and makes subsequent virtual interactions more efficient and effective, and it increases job performance and reduces conflict and intentions to quit.[38]

Face-to-face interactions enable people to get real-time feedback, forge meaningful and real connections, and get a better sense of what others actually think and feel.[39] Moreover, virtual teams cannot succeed without some additional and old-fashioned factors, such as effective decision making, good communication, training, a clear mission and specific objectives, effective leadership, schedules, and deadlines.[40] Underlying many of these is one of the truly essential elements to effective teams of all types—trust. ●

13.2 Stages of Group and Team Development

THE BIG PICTURE

Groups can evolve into teams by going through five stages of development: forming, storming, norming, performing, and adjourning. They can also develop if they are forced to change in response to a crisis. We'll look at both these processes.

LO 13-2

Describe the development of groups and teams.

FIGURE 13.1

Five stages of group and team development

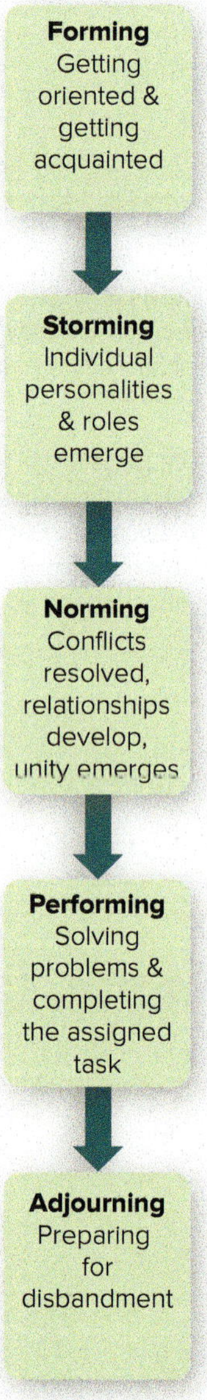

Tuckman's Five-Stage Model

Managers often talk of products and organizations going through stages of development, from birth to maturity to decline. Groups and teams go through the same thing. One theory proposes five stages of development: *forming*, *storming*, *norming*, *performing*, and *adjourning*.[41] *(See Figure 13.1.)*

Let us consider these stages in which groups may evolve into teams—bearing in mind that the stages often aren't of the same duration or intensity or even necessarily always in this sequence.

Stage 1: Forming—"Why Are We Here?"

The first stage, **forming**, **is the process of getting oriented and getting acquainted.** This stage is characterized by a high degree of uncertainty as members try to break the ice and figure out who is in charge and what the group's goals are. For example, if you were to become part of a team that is to work on a class project, the question for you as an individual would be "How do I fit in here?" For the group, the question is "Why are we here?"[42]

At this point, mutual trust is low, and there is a good deal of holding back to see who takes charge and how. Conflict at this stage may actually be beneficial, leading to increased creativity.[43] At this juncture, if the formal leader (such as the class instructor or a supervisor) does not assert his or her authority, an emergent leader will eventually step in to fill the group's need for leadership and direction. During this stage, leaders should allow time for people to become acquainted and to socialize.

Stage 2: Storming—"Why Are We Fighting over Who's in Charge and Who Does What?"

The second stage, **storming**, **is characterized by the emergence of individual personalities and roles and conflicts within the group.** For you as an individual, the question is "What's my role here?" For the group, the issue is "Why are we fighting over who's in charge and who does what?" This stage may be of short duration or painfully long, depending on the goal clarity and the commitment and maturity of the members.

This is a time of testing. Individuals test the leader's policies and assumptions as they try to determine how they fit into the power structure. Subgroups take shape, and subtle forms of rebellion, such as procrastination, occur. Many groups stall in stage 2 because power politics may erupt into open rebellion.

In this stage, the leader should encourage members to suggest ideas, voice disagreements, and work through their conflicts about tasks and goals.

Stage 3: Norming—"Can We Agree on Roles and Work as a Team?"

In the third stage, **norming**, **conflicts are resolved, close relationships develop, and unity and harmony emerge.** For individuals, the main issue is "What do the others expect me to do?" For the group, the issue is "Can we agree on roles and work as a team?" Note, then, that the *group* may now evolve into a *team.*

Teams set guidelines related to what members will do together and how they will do it. The teams consider such matters as attendance at meetings, being late, use of cell phones and laptops during meetings, and what to do when someone misses a team assignment.

Groups that make it through stage 2 generally do so because a respected member other than the leader challenges the group to resolve its power struggles so something can be accomplished. Questions about authority are resolved through unemotional, matter-of-fact group discussion. A feeling of team spirit is experienced because members believe they have found their proper roles. **Group cohesiveness, a "we feeling" binding group members together,** is the principal by-product of stage 3.[44]

This stage generally does not last long. Here the leader should emphasize unity and help identify team goals and values.

Stage 4: Performing—"Can We Do the Job Properly?"

In **performing, members concentrate on solving problems and completing the assigned task.** For individuals, the question here is "How can I best perform my role?" For the group/team, the issue is "Can we do the job properly?" During this stage, the leader should allow members the empowerment they need to work on tasks.

Turning teamwork into action. This group of students is participating in a science fair in Athens, Greece. The group clearly is in the performing stage of group development. Does it appear that all participants are equally engaged in dealing with the task at hand? If you were a member of this group, what would you do to motivate all members to actively participate in completing the task?
©Melanie Stetson Freeman/AP Images

Stage 5: Adjourning—"Can We Help Members Transition Out?"

In the final stage, **adjourning, members prepare for disbandment.** Having worked so hard to get along and get something done, many members feel a compelling sense of loss. For the individual, the question now is "What's next?" For the team, the issue is "Can we help members transition out?"

The leader can help ease the transition by rituals celebrating "the end" and "new beginnings." Parties, award ceremonies, graduations, or mock funerals can provide the needed punctuation at the end of a significant teamwork project. The leader can emphasize valuable lessons learned in group dynamics to prepare everyone for future group and team efforts.

Is Tuckman's Model Accurate?

Although research does not support the notion that groups can't perform until the performing stage, both academics and practitioners agree that groups have a life cycle.[45] Research also tells us that high-performing teams successfully navigating the process of group or team development tend to display productive energy toward getting things done.[46] Do your current teams at work or school display this productive energy? You can find out by completing Self-Assessment 13.2.

SELF-ASSESSMENT 13.2

Assessing Your Team's Productive Energy

The following survey was designed to assess your team's productive energy. Please be prepared to answer these questions if your instructor has assigned Self-Assessment 13.2 in Connect.

1. To what extent does the team display productive energy? Are you surprised by the results?
2. Based on your survey scores, what can be done to improve the level of energy being displayed by the team? Be specific.
3. What would the survey suggest that you should do next time you are the leader of a work or school project team?

Punctuated Equilibrium

Groups don't always follow the distinct stages of Tuckman's model. In another type of group development, called **punctuated equilibrium**, **they establish periods of stable functioning until an event causes a dramatic change in norms, roles, and/or objectives. The group then establishes and maintains new norms of functioning, returning to equilibrium.** *(See Figure 13.2.)* Punctuated equilibrium often occurs in the wake of unexpected change.[47] Since a slim majority of voters in the UK voted in 2016 in favor of leaving the European Union, for example, the 27 remaining member countries will face major changes in the economic and political stability of the 26-year-old economic and trade group. An 18-month transition period has been negotiated, but alterations in the way they trade, share resources, and maintain peaceful borders are expected to develop over many years as the EU remakes itself following the loss of one of Europe's largest economies, officially scheduled for March 29, 2019.[48] In the world of retailing, Walmart's low-price approach was a change that revolutionized an industry. Companies and teams that can adapt will realize tremendous new opportunities, but those that don't often find themselves obsolete. Punctuated equilibrium can drive significant change, development, and opportunity. ●

FIGURE 13.2

Punctuated equilibrium

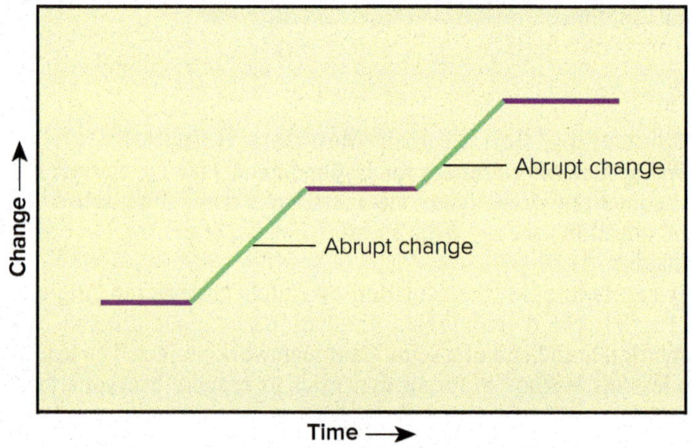

13.3 Building Effective Teams

THE BIG PICTURE

To build a group into a high-performance team, managers must consider matters of collaboration, trust, performance goals and feedback, motivation through mutual accountability and interdependence, team composition, roles, norms, and team processes.

LO 13-3

Discuss ways managers can build effective teams.

"What is a high-performance team?" Current research and practice suggest seven attributes: shared leadership, shared accountability, sense of common purpose, trust and open communication, clear role expectations, early conflict resolution, collaboration, and effective team processes.[49] Thus, as a future manager, the first thing you have to realize is that building a high-performance team is going to require some work. But the payoff will be a stronger, better-performing work unit.[50]

The most essential considerations in building a group into an effective team are (1) *collaboration*, (2) *trust*, (3) *performance goals and feedback*, (4) *motivation through mutual accountability and interdependency*, (5) *composition*, (6) *roles*, (7) *norms*, and (8) *effective team processes*.

1. Collaboration—the Foundation of Teamwork

Collaboration is the act of sharing information and coordinating efforts to achieve a collective outcome. As you might expect, teams are more effective when members collaborate.[51] Collaboration is the secret sauce enabling teams to produce more than the sum of their parts.[52] Many factors can influence collaboration, including how teams are rewarded.[53] For example, Whole Foods reinforces teamwork in its team-based structure by focusing rewards on team rather than individual performance.[54]

A recent and exhaustive survey by Google was aimed at discovering what made the best of its hundreds of work teams successful. The researchers found that the company's highest-performing teams shared two characteristic behaviors: (1) Everyone on the team spoke in about equal proportion, meaning that no one hogged the floor or held comments back, and (2) members were very good at interpreting other members' feelings based on their tone of voice and nonverbal cues. These characteristics led to unusually high levels of collaboration and success.[55] Other influential factors were the dependability of team members, clear goals, work that had impact and meaning, and psychological safety (freedom from judgment).[56]

Getting team members to collaborate is not easy. "Employees have to set aside the desire to be the person who is right in every discussion, and focus on helping the team find the right answer," says author Mike Steib. Team members also need to "engage in the productive conflict, the listening and debating, that help you get to the right answer," according to Steib.[57] Team leaders and managers can reinforce these behaviors by modeling them and by structuring the work to avoid unproductive collaboration.[58] They also might want to play happy music around the office. A recent experiment showed that people exposed to happy music ("Yellow Submarine" by the Beatles, "Walking on Sunshine" by Katrina and the Waves, "Brown Eyed Girl" by Van Morrison, and the theme song from "Happy Days") had more positive moods, which in turn led to greater cooperative behavior.[59]

The "I'm glad . . ." feature describes how Tulsi Rao's boss creates collaboration among teams. She builds teams around the strengths of individual team members.

I'm glad...
...my manager fosters collaboration.

Courtesy Tulsi Rao

Tulsi Rao is the director of marketing and patient experience at an orthopedic clinic. Her manager is great at putting together high-performing work teams.

Tulsi's company has had three CEOs in three years, but the third CEO has proven to be a great fit. She sets clear goals for her employees, inspires individual team members, acknowledges individual weaknesses and builds on individual strengths, encourages autonomy, and takes time to learn about all of her employees on a personal and professional level.

By putting all of these positive managerial traits together, Tulsi's manager is able to build high-performing work teams.

"We have a team that is put together to identify future projects, like a business development committee. Typically, when you think about building such a team, you think of including the CEO, the COO, marketing, and sales, but my manager has taken it out of that shell, and she looks at who the boots on the ground are," said Tulsi.

"In our setting, these are the physical therapists that work with the patients, who see them in and out every day. It's the athletic trainers who work with the various school teams that we work with. So she pulls in people that, traditionally, wouldn't necessarily be a part of a business development team. She identifies their role in the organization as a whole, and she also hones in on their individual strengths," said Tulsi.

For example, the athletic training supervisor has an eye for attracting customers like high school students and their parents since he works with them on a daily basis. He is able to share his information and his unique perspective with the team.

"The CEO looks at things from a nontraditional perspective, not just looking at your education and your job function in the organization but really looking at who can offer the perspective we need in order to make this an effective team," said Tulsi. "She believes in inspiring individual team members and helping them understand how their work is adding to the whole process."

In addition to using team members' strengths to their advantage, Tulsi's manager encourages team bonding outside of work to build strong relationships. When you pair all of these things with a clearly stated, unified goal, the team is able to find its group identity and work together for the same cause.

Courtesy Tulsi Rao

2. Trust: "We Need to Have Reciprocal Faith in Each Other"

Trust is defined as reciprocal faith in others' intentions and behaviors. The word *reciprocal* emphasizes the give-and-take aspect of trust—that is, we tend to give what we get: Trust begets trust, distrust begets distrust. Trust is based on *credibility*—how believable you are based on your past acts of integrity and follow-through on your promises. Four decades of research supports a positive relationship between team members' trust and team performance.[60]

"The best way to engage employees is to build a culture of trust," says Jenny Gottstein of The Go Game. "A team that trusts each other and respects everyone's contribution can make significant cognitive leaps when innovating or problem-solving."[61]

EXAMPLE Building Trust Starts with Leader Behavior

Building a culture of trust starts with the leader of the team or work-unit. For the company as a whole, that leader is the CEO. Showing vulnerability is one of the simplest ways to foster trust. Consider the case of Uber CEO Dara Khosrowshahi. Khosrowshahi wrote a parting memo in 2017 when he was leaving Expedia. In it, he said, "I have to tell you, I am scared."[62] What was he scared of? Leaving Expedia after 12 years to run a struggling organization like Uber, something that may strike fear in any human being.

Take Responsibility for Your Mistakes When leaders admit to making mistakes, they are creating an opportunity to earn respect, strengthen their teams, and lead by example. This ultimately builds a culture of trust.[63] Karl Kangur, founder and CEO of content marketing solution MRR Media, is not afraid to admit his errors and even views them as learning opportunities. "I'm very open with the team about times that I've made mistakes. This helps me avoid making the same mistakes and shows the rest of the team that we're all equal," says Kangur.[64] "You have to be forgiving of mistakes and ready to transition each one into a learning experience," agrees Adam Steele, owner and operator of link-building company Loganix. "I like to set a standard by using our own company blog to discuss the times I've messed up big time but, more importantly, what I've learned from them."[65]

Ask for Help Some leaders view asking for help from employees as a weakness, but it is actually a strength. The most emotionally connected leaders let their employees know when they need assistance. Trust is then recognized as a two-way street, allowing employees to communicate more openly with their leaders and teammates.[66] "Asking for help from others can rally your team around shared goals, and it breeds an environment that's conducive to productive collaboration," says Carey Rome, CEO of Cypress Resources. Leaders are also demonstrating their trust in an employee's abilities when they seek his or her particular expertise. That trust can then become a great motivator and push the employee to excel even further.[67] Research has shown that asking for help also increases trust and cooperation in teams because it stimulates oxytocin production.[68] Oxytocin, known as the "trust molecule," is that warm and fuzzy feeling you get when you feel really good about someone.[69]

YOUR CALL

Do you see showing vulnerability as a strength or weakness? Are there times when you feel your feelings of vulnerability should be hidden? Why or why not?

The importance of trust. David A. Ferucci (center), with two IBM colleagues, led a team of artificial intelligence researchers that programmed a computing system named Watson to compete on the game show *Jeopardy*, whose host, Alex Trebeck, is shown in 2011 talking about the upcoming event. Watson beat the previous (human) grand champions. All successful teams operate within a climate of trust. (left): ©Suzanne DeChillo/The New York Times/Redux Pictures; (right): ©Seth Wenig/AP Images

3. Performance Goals and Feedback

As an individual, you no doubt prefer to have measurable goals and to have feedback about your performance. The same is true with teams. Teams are not just collections of individuals. They are individuals organized for a collective purpose. That purpose needs to be defined in terms of specific, measurable performance goals with continual feedback to tell team members how well they are doing.[70]

An obvious example is the teams you see on television at Indianapolis or Daytona Beach during automobile racing. When the driver guides the race car off the track to make a pit stop, a team of people quickly jack up the car to change tires, refuel the tank, and clean the windshield—all in a matter of seconds. The performance goal is to have

Cooperation and collaboration. A crew swarms over a car driven by A. J. Allmendinger during a pit stop in the NASCAR 2014 Sprint Cup All-Star Race at Watkins Glen, New York. Cereal maker General Mills was able to cut the time workers changed a production line for a Betty Crocker product from 4.5 hours to just 12 minutes by adapting ideas in efficiency and high performance from a NASCAR pit crew working at blinding speed.

the car back on the track as quickly as possible. The number of seconds of elapsed time—and the driver's place among competitors once back in the race—tells the team how well they are doing.

4. Motivation through Mutual Accountability and Interdependence

Do you work harder when you're alone or when you're in a group? When clear performance goals exist, when the work is considered meaningful, when members believe their efforts matter, and when they don't feel they are being exploited by others—this kind of culture supports teamwork.[71] Being mutually accountable to other members of the team rather than to a supervisor makes members feel mutual trust and commitment—a key part in motivating members for team effort. Mutual accountability is fostered by having team "members share accountability for the work, authority over how goals are met, discretion over resource use, and ownership of information and knowledge related to the work."[72]

Do you like it when your performance is contingent on someone else's efforts? Your answer reflects your experience with team member interdependence. **Team member interdependence** **reveals the extent to which team members rely on common task-related team inputs, such as resources, information, goals, and rewards, and the amount of interpersonal interactions needed to complete the work.**[73] A recent study of more than 7,000 teams showed that interdependence affects team functioning, which in turn influences team performance.[74] The key takeaway from this study is reinforcement of the need for team leaders to monitor the quality of team member interdependence.

5. Team Composition

Team composition **reflects the collection of jobs, personalities, values, knowledge, experience, and skills of team members.** The concept is related to our discussion of workforce diversity in Chapter 11. You learned that diversity is good for business and that it must be effectively managed. The same is true for team composition.[75]

For example, a recent study examining the characteristics of effective teams at Cisco found that one of the top three such qualities was members' conviction that their values were shared.[76] This is a feeling you've probably experienced as a member of a team or club built around common interests.

The most important idea to remember is that team member composition should fit the responsibilities of the team. Fit enhances effectiveness and misfit impedes it.[77] Let's consider a few examples.

Teams perform better when members have a high tolerance for uncertainty (a personality trait) during the early stages of team development (forming and storming). This same finding applies to self-managed and virtual teams, due to their relative lack of imposed direction and face-to-face communication.[78] Research also shows that teams with members who possess greater diversity in the way they solve problems had higher performance than teams with a uniform or consistent approach to problem-solving.[79] Finally, in the university context, top management teams (presidents, vice presidents, and chancellors) who were more diverse in terms of educational and disciplinary backgrounds generated more funding for research and improved school reputations.[80]

6. Roles: How Team Members Are Expected to Behave

Roles are socially determined expectations of how individuals should behave in a specific position. As a team member, your role is to play a part in helping the team reach its goals. Members develop their roles based on the expectations of the team, of the organization, and of themselves, and they may do different things. You, for instance, might be a team leader. Others might do some of the work tasks. Still others might communicate with other teams.[81]

Two types of team roles are task and maintenance. *(See Table 13.2.)*

TABLE 13.2
Task and Maintenance Roles

TASK ROLES	DESCRIPTION
Initiator	Suggests new goals or ideas
Information seeker/giver	Clarifies key issues
Opinion seeker/giver	Clarifies pertinent values
Elaborator	Promotes greater understanding through examples or exploration of implications
Coordinator	Pulls together ideas and suggestions
Orienter	Keeps group headed toward its stated goal(s)
Evaluator	Tests group's accomplishments with various criteria such as logic and practicality
Energizer	Prods group to move along or to accomplish more
Procedural technician	Performs routine duties (handing out materials or rearranging seats)
Recorder	Performs a "group memory" function by documenting discussion and outcomes

(Continued)

TABLE 13.2
Task and Maintenance Roles (*Continued*)

MAINTENANCE ROLES	DESCRIPTION
Encourager	Fosters group solidarity by accepting and praising various points of view
Harmonizer	Mediates conflict through reconciliation or humor
Compromiser	Helps resolve conflict by meeting others halfway
Gatekeeper	Encourages all group members to participate
Standard setter	Evaluates the quality of group processes
Commentator	Records and comments on group processes/dynamics
Follower	Serves as a passive audience

Adapted from discussion in K.D. Bonno and P. Shoats, "Functional Roles of Group Members," Journal of Social Issues, *Spring 1948, 41–49.*

Task Roles: Getting the Work Done

A **task role**, or *task-oriented role,* **consists of behavior that concentrates on getting the team's tasks done.** Task roles keep the team on track and get the work done. If you stand up in a team meeting and say, "What is the real issue here? We don't seem to be getting anywhere," you are performing a task role.

Examples: Coordinators, who pull together ideas and suggestions; orienters, who keep teams headed toward their stated goals; initiators, who suggest new goals or ideas; and energizers, who prod people to move along or accomplish more are all playing task roles.

Maintenance Roles: Keeping the Team Together

A **maintenance role, or relationship-oriented role, consists of behavior that fosters constructive relationships among team members.** Maintenance roles foster positive working relationship among team members. If someone at a team meeting says, "Let's hear from those who oppose this plan," he or she is playing a maintenance role.

Examples are encouragers, who foster group solidarity by praising various viewpoints; standard setters, who evaluate the quality of group processes; harmonizers, who mediate conflict through reconciliation or humor; and compromisers, who help resolve conflict by meeting others "halfway."

7. Norms: Unwritten Rules for Team Members

Norms are more encompassing than roles. **Norms are general guidelines or rules of behavior that most group or team members follow.** Norms point out the boundaries between acceptable and unacceptable behavior.[82] Although some norms can be made explicit, typically they are unwritten and seldom discussed openly; nevertheless, they have a powerful influence on group and organizational behavior.

Why Norms Are Enforced: Four Reasons

Norms tend to be enforced by group or team members for four reasons:[83]

- **To help the group survive—"Don't do anything that will hurt us."** Norms are enforced to help the group, team, or organization survive.

Example: The manager of your team or group might compliment you because you've made sure it has the right emergency equipment.

- **To clarify role expectations—"You have to go along to get along."** Norms are also enforced to help clarify or simplify role expectations.

  Example: At one time, new members of Congress wanting to buck the system by which important committee appointments were given to those with the most seniority were advised to "go along to get along"—go along with the rules in order to get along in their congressional careers.

- **To help individuals avoid embarrassing situations—"Don't call attention to yourself."** Norms are enforced to help group or team members avoid embarrassing themselves.

  Examples: You might be ridiculed by fellow team members for dominating the discussion during a report to top management ("Be a team player, not a show-off"). Or you might be told not to discuss religion or politics with customers, whose views might differ from yours.

- **To emphasize the group's important values and identity—"We're known for being special."** Finally, norms are enforced to emphasize the group's, team's, or organization's central values or to enhance its unique identity.

  Examples: Nordstrom's department store chain emphasizes the great lengths to which it goes in customer service. Some colleges give an annual award to the instructor whom students vote best teacher.

PRACTICAL ACTION How to Build Effective Team Norms

High-performing teams use the power of team norms to overcome challenges and obstacles.[84] Team norms allow a team to increase collective performance through healthy debate and clarity of purpose and roles, which in turn lead to high performance.[85] The following suggestions can help any team to build effective team norms.

Look to the Past for What Worked Effective norms propel a team toward effective group dynamics and performance, whereas ineffective ones become an anchor. Identifying earlier team practices that worked is a good way to establish preferred norms. Simply think about great teams you participated on and consider the various norms that guided their efforts. What made that team so great? Do the same for an ineffective team on which you worked. This exercise provides you with a list of practices that did and did not work. You can then rank them by their significance to the current tasks at hand. For example, Missouri's Department of Elementary and Secondary Education encourages school district teams to rank effective past practices by importance when deciding which to use on new teams.[86]

Break Down Norms into Behaviors Once you have a list of norms, convert them to measurable behaviors. For example, the norm of encouraging equal participation in meetings results in the behavior of soliciting input from everyone when making a team decision.[87] This recommendation was taken to heart by Dan Levy, Facebook's global small business team director. "I end every meeting and most conversations with requests for feedback either in the meeting or via e-mail," he said. It's important to remember that it takes time for norms to take effect. Levy's norm of asking for feedback during meetings wasn't an instant success. He had to ask for input from team members for months before people felt comfortable sharing.[88]

Accountability Is Key Accountability plays a key role in setting normative expectations. Norms are unlikely to take hold if there is no accountability.[89] Creating a system to police behavior can actually be fun! Imagine serving on a team that has restricted the use of phones during meetings. How might this be enforced? One team observed by *Harvard Business Review* mandated a $5 penalty for each time someone got distracted by his or her phone. The $5 was put in a "norm bucket." The team used some of the resulting fund to go out for drinks at the end of the year and donated the remainder to charity.[90]

YOUR CALL

How well do you think an organization could incorporate all the suggestions listed here for creating effective team norms? What other strategies do you think contribute to the adoption of effective norms?

8. Effective Team Processes

Teams, like individuals, get things done by turning inputs into desired outputs. High-performing teams accomplish this task by using effective team processes. **Team processes** are "members' interdependent acts that convert inputs to outcomes through cognitive, verbal, and behavioral activities directed toward organizing taskwork to achieve collective goals."[91] There are three additional activities teams can use to improve team processes, beyond the seven just discussed.

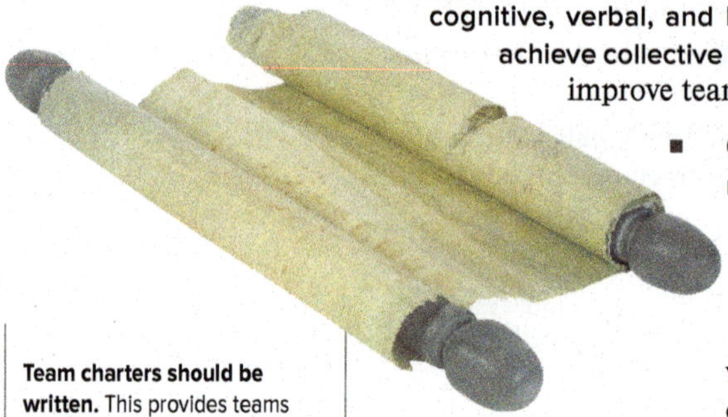

Team charters should be written. This provides teams with written documentation regarding norms and other operational agreements. ©Ingram Publishing/Alamy Stock Photo

- **Create a team charter.** A **team charter** outlines how a team will manage teamwork activities. It "represents an agreement among members as to how the team will work as an empowered partnership in making binding decisions and sharing accountability for delivering quality products/services that meet user/customer needs in a timely and cost-efficient way."[92] Your author Angelo Kinicki requires teams in his classes to create charters. He does this because research shows team charters are associated with higher, sustained performance, particularly for teams that are low on team conscientiousness.[93]
- **Engage in team reflexivity.** **Team reflexivity** is a process in which team members collectively reflect on the team's objectives, strategies, and processes and adapt accordingly."[94] It helps improve team performance and reduce team members' burnout because it provides them a sense of control and support. From a management perspective, teams must be given the time to engage in reflexivity.
- **Give team members a voice.** **Team voice** reflects the extent to which team members feel free to "engage in the expression of constructive opinions, concerns, or ideas about work-related issues."[95] Google's research on high-performing teams showed that team voice fostered a feeling of psychological safety, which is essential for innovation.[96]

Putting It All Together

Thus far in this chapter, we have considered the things that make groups and teams both effective and ineffective. We hope you understand that creating and leading a high performance team takes planning and skill. The first step in improving a team's performance, however, involves an assessment of its effectiveness.

So how can you determine whether a team is effective? A group's output surely is one indicator, but there are others that are more "team process oriented." You can get an idea of these process-oriented indicators by taking Self-Assessment 13.3. •

SELF-ASSESSMENT 13.3

Assessing Team Effectiveness

The following survey was designed to assess the overall effectiveness of a team's internal processes. Please be prepared to answer these questions if your instructor has assigned Self-Assessment 13.3 in Connect.

1. How effective is the team?
2. What aspects of the team's internal processes are most in need of positive development?
3. Based on your survey scores, what are three recommendations for improving the team's internal processes? Be specific.

13.4 Managing Conflict

THE BIG PICTURE

Conflict, an enduring feature of the workplace, is a process in which one party perceives that its interests are being opposed or negatively affected by another party. Conflict can be negative (bad) or functional (good). Indeed, either too much or too little conflict can affect performance. This section identifies four sources of conflict in organizations and describes four ways to stimulate constructive conflict.

LO 13-4

Describe ways managers can deal successfully with conflict.

Mistakes, pressure-cooker deadlines, increased workloads, demands for higher productivity, and other kinds of stress—all contribute to on-the-job conflict.[97] Most people envision *conflict* as meaning shouting and fighting, but as a manager you will encounter more subtle, nonviolent forms: opposition, criticism, arguments. Thus, a definition of conflict seems fairly mild: **Conflict** is a process in which one party perceives that its interests are being opposed or negatively affected by another party.[98]

Conflict is a natural aspect of life. A place to begin our discussion of conflict is to consider the two types of conflict—dysfunctional and functional.

The Nature of Conflict: Disagreement Is Normal

Conflict is simply disagreement, a perfectly normal state of affairs. Conflicts may take many forms: between individuals, between an individual and a group, between groups, within a group, and between an organization and its environment.

Although all of us might wish to live lives free of conflict, it is now recognized that certain kinds of conflict can actually be beneficial. Let us therefore distinguish between *dysfunctional conflict* (bad) and *functional conflict* (good).

- **Dysfunctional conflict—bad for organizations.** From the standpoint of the organization, **dysfunctional conflict** is conflict that hinders the organization's performance or threatens its interests. For example, Emily Cho, vice president at Korean Air, created dysfunctional conflict by throwing water in the face of an advertising agency employee during a meeting. As a manager, you need to do what you can to remove dysfunctional conflict, sometimes called negative conflict. In the case of Emily Cho, her father, Cho Yang-ho, chairman of Hanjin Group and Korean Air, apologized for her behavior and encouraged her to resign.[99] The "I Wish ..." feature illustrates what can happen when dysfunctional conflict is not effectively managed.
- **Functional conflict—good for organizations.** The good kind of conflict is **functional conflict,** which benefits the main purposes of the organization and serves its interests.[100] This type of conflict is also called productive conflict and occurs "when team members openly discuss disagreements and divergent perspectives without fear, anxiety, or perceived threat."[101] For instance, Facebook's recent acknowledgement that the personal data of 87 million users was improperly accessed by marketing and political consulting firms raised multiple questions for the company. Public anger and mistrust brought founder and CEO Mark Zuckerberg before a wary Congress to testify about the company's security procedures and transparency. It seems possible that the result will be revamped internal policies and perhaps even new government regulations that will make the company a more trusted platform for its nearly 1.5 billion daily users worldwide.[102]

The ability to effectively work with others is a career readiness competency desired by employees. Do you see yourself as easy to get along with and relatively conflict free? Self-Assessment 13.4 was designed to answer this question. It assesses the extent to which your work relationships contain dysfunctional or functional conflict.

I Wish...

...I was able to manage interpersonal conflict more effectively.

Tim Blankenship was a finance manager for the health care and outsourcing departments of his company. He could have managed the interpersonal conflict between two of his employees better by being more involved in the beginning stages of the project.

Courtesy Tim Blankenship

As the finance manager, Tim recruited two financial analysts from his team to reengineer their annual budgeting process. He tasked the two employees with this project in order to reduce the amount of time the team spent on it so they could free up more time for other strategic initiatives.

One of the financial analysts was in her mid-30s with a lot of finance experience, and the other was in her mid-20s, fresh out of college and new to the company. "One of the things about the older employee is that she would pretend to understand your request, and she really leaned on mimicking her colleagues to see what they would do in a situation to get their work done. And then the younger employee, being green and fresh-faced, had good ideas but she had no organizational savvy to be able to execute on those ideas," said Tim.

Conflict arose when the younger employee would present new ideas and the older employee would shoot them down. The older employee fell back on her own experience at other companies and refused to listen to new ideas, which quickly frustrated the younger employee. The project stalled since they could not come to an agreement, and the team had to fall back on the existing process in order to move forward. A lot of time was lost on the project.

"I didn't do a good job of mapping out the right timeline," said Tim. "We needed about four months to plan out the budget, and we used about four to six weeks of that time trying to figure out how we were going to redo this process. It made me look bad as the new manager in the group because our employees were working extra time and staying late to catch up on this annual budgeting process."

Reflecting on his experience, Tim would take time to think through both employees' personalities and skills gaps before setting them loose on the project. "If I were to go back and do it again, I would probably sit in on the first few meetings to help validate the younger employee's ideas in front of the older employee, and tell the older employee that she has the right experience and organizational contacts to make these changes happen," said Tim.

By being involved early in the process and giving encouragement and direction, Tim could have better managed the employees to avoid the interpersonal conflict that spoiled the reengineering of the budgeting process.

Courtesy of Tim Blankenship

SELF-ASSESSMENT 13.4

Interpersonal Conflict Tendencies

If your instructor has assigned Self-Assessment 13.4 in Connect, you will learn how well you get along with others at work and/or school.

1. Does your score match your perception of yourself?
2. The assessment measures how well you get along with others and how they treat you; both are sources of conflict. If you were to improve the measure, what other factors do you think should be included?

Can Too Little or Too Much Conflict Affect Performance?

It's tempting to think that a conflict-free work group is a happy work group, as indeed it may be. But is it a productive group? In the 1970s, social scientists specializing in organizational behavior introduced the revolutionary idea that organizations could suffer from *too little* or *too much* conflict. Neither scenario is good.

- **Too little conflict–inactivity.** Work groups, departments, or organizations that experience too little conflict tend to be plagued by apathy, lack of creativity, indecision, and missed deadlines. The result is that organizational performance suffers.

- **Too much conflict—warfare.** Excessive conflict, on the other hand, can erode organizational performance because of political infighting, dissatisfaction, lack of teamwork, and turnover. Workplace aggression and violence are manifestations of excessive conflict.[103]

Thus, it seems that a moderate level of conflict can induce creativity and initiative,[104] thereby raising performance, as shown in the diagram below. *(See Figure 13.3.)* As you might expect, however, what constitutes "moderate" will vary among managers.

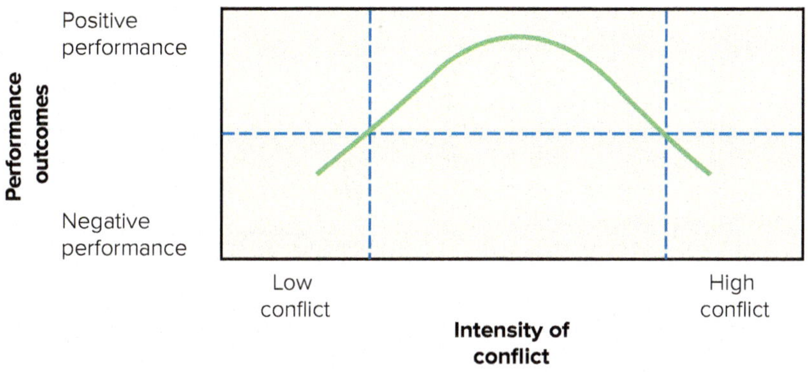

FIGURE 13.3

The relationship between intensity of conflict and performance outcomes

Too little conflict or too much conflict causes performance to suffer.

Source: Derived from L. D. Brown, Managing Conflict at Organizational Interfaces *(Englewood Cliffs, NJ: Prentice-Hall, 1983).*

Three Kinds of Conflict: Personality, Intergroup, and Cross-Cultural

There are a variety of sources of conflict—so-called *conflict triggers*. Three of the principal ones are (1) *between personalities*, (2) *between groups*, and (3) *between cultures*. By understanding these, you'll be better able to take charge and manage the conflicts rather than letting the conflicts take you by surprise and manage you.

1. Personality Conflicts: Clashes Because of Personal Dislikes or Disagreements

We've all had confrontations, weak or strong, with people because we disagreed with them or disliked their personalities, such as their opinions, their behavior, their looks, whatever. **Personality conflict is defined as interpersonal opposition based on personal dislike or disagreement.** Such conflicts often begin with instances of *workplace incivility*, or employees' lack of regard for each other, which, if not curtailed, can diminish job satisfaction, health, and levels of customer service.[105] Unfortunately, personality conflicts are quite common. A recent report found that 62 percent of employees reported experiencing rude treatment by a colleague at least once a month in 2016, compared to 49 percent in 1998 and 55 percent in 2011.[106] A summary of research on stress found that 28 percent of workers cited "people issues" as a leading cause of stress at work.[107]

2. Intergroup Conflicts: Clashes among Work Groups, Teams, and Departments

The downside of collaboration, or the "we" feeling discussed earlier, is that it can translate into "we versus them." This produces conflict among work groups, teams, and departments within an organization.

Some ways in which intergroup conflicts are expressed are as follows:

- **Inconsistent goals or reward systems—when people pursue different objectives.** It's natural for people in functional organizations to be pursuing different objectives and to be rewarded accordingly, but this means that conflict is practically built into the system.

TABLE 13.3
Ways to Build Cross-Cultural Relationships

1. Be a good listener.
2. Be sensitive to others' needs.
3. Be cooperative, not overly competitive.
4. Advocate inclusive (participative) leadership.
5. Compromise rather than dominate.
6. Build rapport through conversations.
7. Be compassionate and understanding.
8. Avoid conflict by emphasizing harmony.
9. Nurture others (develop and mentor).

Source: Adapted from R. L. Tung, "American Expatriates Abroad: From Neophytes to Cosmopolitans," Journal of World Business, *Summer 1998, table 6, p. 136.*

- **Ambiguous jurisdictions—when job boundaries are unclear.** "That's not my job and those aren't my responsibilities." "Those resources belong to me because I need them as part of my job." When task responsibilities are unclear, that can often lead to conflict. This cause was partly to blame for the altercation between a store manager and two African American nonpaying guests at a Philadelphia Starbucks in 2018. The manager called police when the two guests, who were waiting to meet a friend, refused to leave. The guests were arrested. The manager's decision to call police stemmed from the company's lack of policy regarding treatment of lingering nonpaying guests.[108]
- **Status differences—when there are inconsistencies in power and influence.** It can happen that people who are lower in status according to the organization chart actually have disproportionate power over those theoretically above them, which can lead to conflicts.

3. Multicultural Conflicts: Clashes between Cultures With cross-border mergers, joint ventures, and international alliances common features of the global economy, there are frequent opportunities for clashes between cultures. Often success or failure, when business is being conducted across cultures, arises from dealing with differing assumptions about how to think and act.

One study of 409 expatriates (14 percent of them female) working for U.S. and Canadian multinational firms in 51 countries identified nine specific ways to facilitate interaction with host-country nationals, the results of which are shown at left. *(See Table 13.3.)* Note that "Be a good listener" tops the list—the very thing lacking in so many U.S. managers, who are criticized for being blunt to the point of insensitivity.[109] Looking beyond your own cultural lens and resolving not to make assumptions are other suggestions.[110] To avoid conflict through misunderstanding when you are speaking in public to a diverse or international audience, the need for sensitivity to your hearers suggests sticking to your native language, avoiding jokes that can misfire, and paring away slang and jargon.[111]

How to Stimulate Constructive Conflict

As a manager you are being paid not just to manage conflict but even to create some, where it's constructive and appropriate, in order to stimulate performance. Constructive conflict, if carefully monitored, can be very productive under a number of circumstances: when your work group seems afflicted with inertia and apathy, resulting in low performance; when there's a lack of new ideas and resistance to change; when there seem to be a lot of yes-men and yes-women (expressing groupthink) in the work unit; when there's high employee turnover; or when managers seem unduly concerned with peace, cooperation, compromise, consensus, and their own popularity rather than in achieving work objectives.

The following four strategies are used to stimulate constructive conflict.

1. Spur Competition among Employees Competition is, of course, a form of conflict, but competition is often healthy in spurring people to produce higher results. Thus, a company will often put its salespeople in competition with one another by offering bonuses and awards for achievement—a trip to a Caribbean resort, say, for the top performer of the year.

2. Change the Organization's Culture and Procedures Competition may also be established by making deliberate and highly publicized moves to change the corporate culture—by announcing to employees that the organization is now going to be more innovative and reward original thinking and unorthodox ideas. Procedures, such as paperwork sign-off processes, can also be revamped. Results can be reinforced in visible ways through announcements of bonuses, raises, and promotions.

3. Bring in Outsiders for New Perspectives Without "new blood," organizations can become inbred and resistant to change. This is why managers often bring in outsiders—people from a different unit of the organization, new hires from competing companies, or consultants. With their different backgrounds, attitudes, or management styles, these outsiders can bring a new perspective and can shake things up.

4. Use Programmed Conflict: Devil's Advocacy and the Dialectic Method **Programmed conflict is designed to elicit different opinions without inciting people's personal feelings.** Sometimes decision-making groups become so bogged down in details and procedures that nothing of substance gets done. The idea here is to get people, through role-playing, to defend or criticize ideas based on relevant facts rather than on personal feelings and preferences.

Top employee. Companies frequently stimulate constructive competition among employees to produce better performance. Top salespeople, for instance, may be rewarded with a trip to a resort. Do you think you would do well in a company that makes you compete with others to produce higher results? ©Tony Tallec/Alamy Stock Photo

The method for getting people to engage in this debate of ideas is to do disciplined role-playing, for which two proven methods are available: *devil's advocacy* and the *dialectic method.* These two methods work as follows:

- Devil's advocacy—role-playing criticism to test whether a proposal is workable. **Devil's advocacy is the process of assigning someone to play the role of critic to** voice possible objections to a proposal and thereby generate critical thinking and reality testing.

  Periodically role-playing devil's advocate has a beneficial side effect in that it is great training for developing analytical and communicative skills. However, it's a good idea to rotate the job so no one person develops a negative reputation.
- The dialectic method—role-playing two sides of a proposal to test whether it is workable. Requiring a bit more skill training than devil's advocacy does, the **dialectic method is the process of having two people or groups play opposing roles in a debate in order to better understand a proposal.** After the structured debate, managers are more equipped to make an intelligent decision.[112]

PRACTICAL ACTION Playing the Devil's Advocate

Research shows that teams effectively utilizing devil's advocates perform better than those who don't.[113] So what happens when you are chosen as the team's opposing viewpoint? How can you be critical of the team's ideas without upsetting your colleagues? Here are four tips for successfully playing this important role.

1. **Listen closely.** You need to actively listen to someone's idea before potentially disagreeing with it. That means paying attention and making sure the idea-sharer knows you are listening.[114] For example, repeat the idea you just heard in your own words before providing your opposing viewpoint.

This is called paraphrasing. Colleagues are more receptive to feedback when they believe you are truly hearing them.[115]

2. **It's not a game of gotcha.** Devil's advocacy should be framed as a way to stimulate constructive conflict, not generate resentment. The goal is not to be an adversary. Rather, it is to reduce uncertainty and inspire learning.[116] The airing of differing opinions should be heard by the rest of the team as a nonthreatening, alternate way to evaluate solutions to an issue.[117] The devil's advocate helps bring up issues that might otherwise be ignored. Sometimes that leads to discrediting an idea, which is fine.[118]
3. **Stay positive.** Research reveals that teams perform worse when an opposing opinion is seen as confrontational. Divergent opinions should be presented in a constructive way so they will not be taken personally or emotionally.[119] For example, try to find something meaningful about an idea and comment on that before you introduce your opposing viewpoint. Colleagues are more receptive to your point of view if they believe you've listened to them with an open mind.[120]
4. **Don't beat a dead horse.** Your goal is not to win a debate, so don't dwell once you've made your point. If the team is not convinced by your argument the first two times, repeating your point probably won't change things.[121] What it may do is cause frustration and dysfunctional conflict with your colleagues. Let it go!

Five Basic Behaviors to Help You Better Handle Conflict

Whatever kind of organization you work for, you'll always benefit from knowing how to manage conflict. There are five basic behaviors that enable you to work on disagreements and keep them from flaring into out-of-control personality conflicts: *openness*, *equality*, *empathy*, *supportiveness*, and *positiveness*.[122]

1. Openness State your views openly and honesty, not trying to disguise the real object of your disagreement. Look at the conflict as a way to better understand the situation and find a solution. Concentrate on identifying the problem and taking a problem-solving approach.

2. Equality Treat the other's status and ideas as equal to yours, allowing that person time to completely express his or her opinions. Evaluate all ideas fairly and logically, without regard to ownership.

3. Empathy Try to connect with the other person's feelings and point of view, showing you are truly listening by using such expressions as "I suspect you are disappointed in . . ."

4. Supportiveness Let the other person know you want to find a resolution that will benefit you both. Describe the specifics you have difficulty understanding, without evaluating or judging them. Support the other person's position when it makes sense to do so.

5. Positiveness Be positive about the other person and your relationship. Express your willingness to work toward a resolution that will be feasible for everyone.

Before beginning to try to adopt these behaviors preparatory to dealing with a dispute, you should also try to be aware of your customary conflict-handling style with Self-Assessment 13.5 on the next page.

Dealing with Disagreements: Five Conflict-Handling Styles

Even if you're at the top of your game as a manager, working with groups and teams of people will now and then put you in the middle of disagreements, sometimes even destructive conflict. There are five conflict-handling styles, or techniques, you can use for handling disagreements with individuals: *avoiding, obliging, dominating, compromising*, and *integrating*.[123] Figure 13.4 shows how each of the styles can be distinguished from the others by the parties' relative concern for others (on the x-axis) and for themselves (on the y-axis).

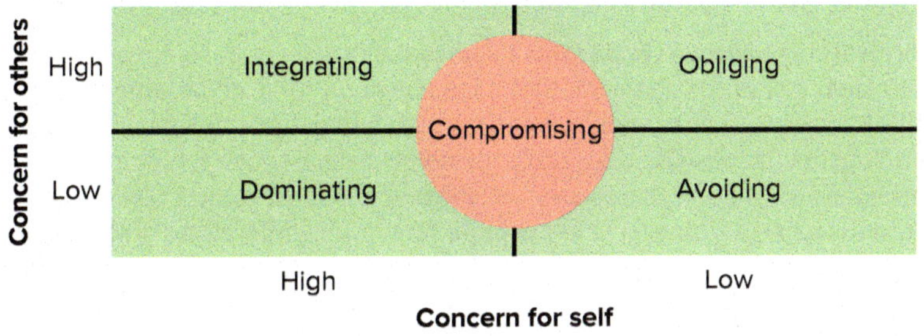

FIGURE 13.4

Five common conflict-handling styles

Source: From M. A. Rahim, "A Strategy for Managing Conflict in Complex Organizations," Human Relations, *1985, p. 84.*

Avoiding—*Avoiding* is ignoring or suppressing a conflict. It is appropriate for trivial issues, when emotions are high and a cooling-off period is needed, or when the cost of confrontation outweighs the benefits of resolving the conflict.

Obliging—An obliging or accommodating manager allows the desires of the other party to prevail. This style may be appropriate when it's possible to eventually get something in return or when the issue isn't important to you.

Dominating—Also known as "forcing," *dominating* is simply ordering an outcome, when a manager relies on his or her formal authority and power to resolve a conflict. It is appropriate when an unpopular solution must be implemented and when it's not important that others commit to your viewpoint.

Compromising—In *compromising*, both parties give up something to gain something. It is appropriate when both sides have opposite goals or possess equal power.

Integrating—In this collaborative style, the manager strives to confront the issue and cooperatively identify the problem, generating and weighing alternatives and selecting a solution. It is appropriate for complex issues plagued by misunderstanding. •

SELF-ASSESSMENT 13.5 CAREER READINESS

What Is Your Conflict-Management Style?

The following exercise is designed to determine your conflict-handling style. Please be prepared to answer these questions if your instructor has assigned Self-Assessment 13.5 in Connect.

1. Were you surprised by the results? Why or why not? Explain.
2. Were the scores for your primary and backup conflict-handling styles relatively similar, or was there a large gap? What does this imply? Discuss.
3. Is your conflict-handling style one that can be used in many different conflict scenarios? Explain.
4. What things might you say during an interview to demonstrate that you possess the ability to manage conflict?

13.5 Career Corner: Managing Your Career Readiness

Effectively working in groups and teams requires the use of several competencies from the model of career readiness shown below. *(See Figure 13.5.)* You can improve your teamwork skills by using the competencies of oral communications, teamwork/collaboration, social intelligence, a positive approach, professionalism/work ethic, and a service to others orientation. Of these, teamwork/collaboration is most closely tied to concepts and models discussed in this chapter. Let's explore how you can develop skills associated with this competency.

FIGURE 13.5

Model of career readiness

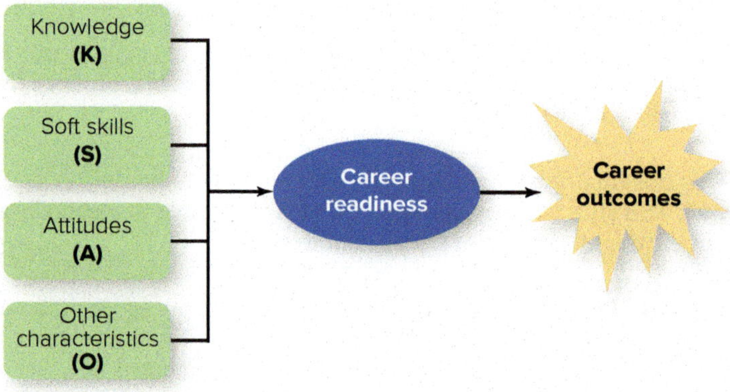

Become a More Effective Team Member

Teamwork requires a group of people to integrate their efforts in the pursuit of achieving a common goal. Below are four actions you can employ to become a better team member.

1. **Commit to the team.** Vince Lombardi, considered one of the all-time best coaches in professional football, lived this philosophy. He said, "Individual commitment to a group effort–that is what makes a team work, a company work, a society work, a civilization work." We all know that one player cannot do it all in team sports. Great players, such as LeBron James, formerly from the Cleveland Cavaliers, are strategic in their approach toward teamwork. They realize that their job is to help team members raise their level of play while also inspiring and motivating them to achieve specific goals. It's the same at school and work. Consider your school project teams as an opportunity to apply your best talents toward the goal of increasing the team's overall grade. Commitment to a team comes down to your willingness to put the needs of others over self-interests. Yes, you may sacrifice some individual recognition in this process, but the team benefits. The key action here is the willingness to focus on the greater good of the team.[124]
2. **Support team members.** Author Will Smith states, "If you're not making someone else's life better, then you're wasting your time. Your life will become better by making other lives better." This sentiment is precisely what it means to be a good teammate. You can provide emotional support in the form of the time you take to listen to and discuss personal matters with others. Instrumental

support might entail showing someone how to complete a task or learn a new skill. It also means putting in extra hours to help the team achieve its goals. Sharing information and providing positive feedback are other forms of support. While your goal in supporting others should not be to expect something in return, you will find that the norm of reciprocity motivates others to put in more effort to help the team or you down the line. The norm of reciprocity is a powerful social norm by which we feel obligated to return favors or assistance after people have provided favors or assistance to us.[125]

3. **Bring positive emotions to the team.** Leave criticism and negativity outside team meetings. They are toxic and reinforce others' tendency to complain. In contrast, positive emotions such as happiness, gratefulness, and kindness create upward spirals of positivity in others. Positive emotions in team meetings make people feel welcome and truly part of the team, which in turn fosters improved performance.[126]
4. **Lead by example.** Demonstrate the behaviors you desire in others. If you want full commitment to team goals, commit to them yourself. If you want people to come prepared to team meetings, come overprepared. Show your colleagues that you are willing to go the extra mile to help the team achieve its goals. Like positive emotions, leadership by example creates a positive contagion motivating others to participate and increase their performance.[127]

Become a More Effective Collaborator

Earlier we defined *collaboration* as the act of sharing information and coordinating efforts to achieve a collective outcome. Collaboration is essential for teamwork, but it isn't the same thing as teamwork. Teamwork requires some formal structure such as a team leader, agendas for meetings, and organization. Collaboration is more spontaneous, less structured, and less hierarchical. You don't need an agenda item that says "collaborate." Here are some tips for becoming a more effective collaborator.

1. **Listen and learn.** Author Ken Blanchard said it well: "None of us is as smart as all of us." You can't get the best from people if you don't encourage them to share their ideas, opinions, and beliefs. You may not agree with them, but people need to be heard. Remember that sharing different perspectives is essential for collaboration.[128] Listening is the flip side of talking. Active listening requires effort and motivation. You can improve your listening by: withholding judgment, asking questions, showing respect, keeping your concentration and focus in the present moment, and remaining quiet.[129]
2. **Be open-minded.** You can't collaborate if you aren't open to others' ideas. You won't get the benefit of your teammates' experience and knowledge if you fail to consider their input. Being open also requires you to stop trying to impress others by having the best or brightest ideas. Just contribute what you can and let the team decide what ideas work best.[130] ●

Key Terms Used in This Chapter

adjourning 511
collaboration 513
conflict 521
cross-functional teams 507
devil's advocacy 525
dialectic method 525
dysfunctional conflict 521
formal group 506
forming 510
functional conflict 521
group 505
group cohesiveness 511
informal group 506
maintenance role 518
norming 510
norms 518
performing 511
personality conflict 523
programmed conflict 525
punctuated equilibrium 512
roles 517
self-managed teams 507
storming 510
task role 518
team 505
team charter 520
team composition 516
team member interdependence 516
team processes 520
team reflexivity 520
team voice 520
trust 514
virtual teams 508

Key Points

13.1 Groups versus Teams

- Groups and teams are different—a group is typically management-directed, a team self-directed. A group is defined as two or more freely interacting individuals who share collective norms, share collective goals, and have a common identity. A team is defined as a small group of people with complementary skills who are committed to a common purpose, performance goals, and approach for which they hold themselves mutually accountable.
- Groups may be either formal, established to do something productive for the organization and headed by a leader, or informal, formed by people seeking friendship with no officially appointed leader.
- Teams are of various types, but one of the most important is the work team, which engages in collective work requiring coordinated effort. A project team may also be a cross-functional team, staffed with specialists pursuing a common objective.
- Three other types of teams are continuous improvement teams, consisting of small groups of volunteers or workers and supervisors who meet intermittently to discuss workplace and quality-related problems; self-managed teams, defined as groups of workers given administrative oversight for their task domains; and virtual teams, which work together over time and distance via electronic media to combine effort and achieve common goals.

13.2 Stages of Group and Team Development

- A group may evolve into a team through five stages. (1) Forming is the process of getting oriented and getting acquainted. (2) Storming is characterized by the emergence of individual personalities and roles and conflicts within the group. (3) In norming, conflicts are resolved, close relationships develop, and unity and harmony emerge. (4) In performing, members concentrate on solving problems and completing the assigned task. (5) In adjourning, members prepare for disbandment.
- A group can also develop by means of punctuated equilibrium, in which it establishes periods of stable functioning until an event causes a dramatic change in norms, roles, and/or objectives. The group then establishes and maintains new norms of functioning, returning to equilibrium.

13.3 Building Effective Teams

- There are eight considerations managers must take into account in building a group into an effective team. (1) They must ensure individuals are collaborating, or systematically integrating their efforts to achieve a collective objective. (2) They must establish a climate of trust, or reciprocal faith in others' intentions and behaviors. (3) They must establish measurable performance goals and have feedback about members' performance.
- (4) They must motivate members by making them mutually accountable to one another. (5) They must consider team composition.
- (6) They must consider the role each team member must play. A role is defined as the socially determined expectation of how an individual should behave in a specific position. Two types of team roles are task and maintenance. A task role consists of behavior that concentrates on getting the team's tasks done. A maintenance role consists of behavior that fosters constructive relationships among team members.
- (7) They must consider team norms, the general guidelines or rules of behavior that most group or team members follow. Norms tend to be enforced by group or team members for four reasons: to help the group survive, to clarify role expectations, to help individuals avoid embarrassing situations, and to emphasize the group's important values and identity.

13.4 Managing Conflict

- Conflict is a process in which one party perceives that its interests are being opposed or negatively affected by another party. Conflict can be dysfunctional, or negative. However, constructive, or functional, conflict benefits the main purposes of the organization and serves its interests. Too little conflict can lead to inactivity; too much conflict can lead to warfare.
- Four devices for stimulating constructive conflict are (1) spurring competition among employees, (2) changing the organization's culture and procedures, (3) bringing in outsiders for new perspectives, and (4) using programmed conflict to elicit different opinions without inciting people's personal feelings.
- Two methods used in programmed conflict are (1) devil's advocacy, in which someone is assigned to play the role of critic to voice possible objections to a proposal, and (2) the dialectic method, in which two people or groups play opposing roles in a debate in order to better understand a proposal. Five basic behaviors enable you to work on disagreements and keep them from flaring into out-of-control personality conflicts: openness, equality, empathy, supportiveness, and positiveness.

13.5 Career Corner: Managing Your Career Readiness

- Working in groups requires the use of several career readiness competencies, including oral communications, teamwork/collaboration, social intelligence, a positive approach, professionalism/work ethic, and a service to others.
- You can become a better team member by committing to the team, supporting team members, bringing positive emotions to the team, and leading by example.
- You can become a better collaborator by listening and learning and being open-minded.

Understanding the Chapter: What Do I Know?

1. How do groups and teams differ?
2. What's the difference between formal groups and informal groups?
3. Describe four types of work teams.
4. What are the stages of group and team development?
5. Explain the eight most essential considerations in building a group into an effective team.
6. How do functional and dysfunctional conflict differ?
7. How would you go about stimulating constructive conflict?
8. What are devil's advocacy and the dialectic method?
9. What are five basic behaviors to help you better handle conflict?
10. How can I become a better team member?

Management in Action

IBM Wants Its Employees Back in the Office

International Business Machines Corporation (IBM) started in the early 1900s as a manufacturer of machinery such as commercial scales, industrial time recorders, and meat and cheese slicers.[131] The company invented the first personal computer (PC) in 1981. The PC was a landmark in transitioning the use of computers from the military and government to the desks of everyday people.[132] IBM made a major strategic move into services and software when it sold its PC division to Lenovo in 2004.[133] The company had 380,000 employees and revenues of more than $78 billion in 2017.[134]

IBM has experienced 20 consecutive quarters of declining revenue. It also missed analysts' revenue expectations in 2017,[135] and the stock lost approximately 30 percent of its value between 2013 and 2018.[136] Although CEO Virginia "Ginni" Rometty attributes these results to "her selling off legacy businesses and to unavoidable currency hits,"[137] others think that group dynamics and teleworking are partly a cause.

THE COMPANY SAYS ITS TEAMS CAN'T KEEP UP

CEO Rometty "is on a protracted mission to make IBM a cloud-based 'solutions' business,"[138] but the transformation is having trouble keeping up with "the competitive tech marketplace that has become significantly more agile and nimble over the past decade," said an analyst to *NBC News*.[139] IBM was already a distant third to Amazon and Microsoft in cloud computing and was losing ground to Google as of 2017.[140]

What's slowing the company down? Some IBM executives blame a lack of team collaboration and innovation due to teleworking. Chief Financial Officer Martin Schroeter told investors in 2016 that it's about "get[ting] the teams back together as opposed to so spread out," saying that remote working is not doing IBM any favors when it comes to being agile.[141]

This is an interesting conclusion given that IBM was a pioneer of remote work, according to *The Wall Street Journal*.[142] More than 40 percent of IBM's workforce in 173 countries worked remotely in 2009.[143] The company's own Smarter Workplace Institute stated in 2014 that remote workers "tend to be happier, less stressed, more productive, more engaged with their jobs and teams, and believe that their companies are more innovative as a result of flexible work arrangements."[144] IBM again boasted in 2017 that "telework works" in its Smarter Workforce Blog.[145]

IBM gave a surprising ultimatum to thousands of employees a week after the blog was written: Come back to the office in the next 30 days, or leave the company.[146] The organization also released a statement to *CNN Technology* saying, "In many fields, such as software development and digital marketing, the nature of work is changing, which requires new ways of working. . . . We are bringing small, self-directed agile teams in these fields together."[147]

IBM's decision may be grounded in science, especially when it comes to collaboration, creativity, and trust. Studies show that proximity boosts collaborative efficiency, according to *The Atlantic*: Collaborative efficiency is the speed at which a group successfully solves a problem.[148] IBM wants to see more collaborative efficiency. The company's VP of Communications, Carrie Altieri, told the *Huffington Post* that "For areas of the business where heavy collaboration and co-creation are key for time to market like development or marketing, we want those employees working together."[149]

Some experts also say that working in close proximity has a positive effect on creativity and trust. An IBM team needs to exhibit functional conflict in order to be creative, according to *Inc.* magazine. Functional conflict is based on the premise that teammates can argue passionately about a topic without letting it become personal and emotional. This ability depends on the existence of significant trust among team members, which *Inc.* argues can primarily be gained in face-to-face interactions.[150]

IT'S ALL IN THE PROCESS!

Critics say IBM got it wrong and that team processes are the issue, not working remotely. "Unfortunately, the move is just smoke in mirrors; it's an illusion that they've made progress when all they've really done is shuffled people around into different boxes," said a *Forbes* consultant. He believes having a set of consistently enforced virtual norms trumps the need to be located in the same space (co-location).[151] Virtual norms can include check-ins by team members. A daily meeting (or even two) might be required to ensure team cohesiveness, according to an expert at *Entrepreneur Media*. Frequent meetings also provide an opportunity for teams to lay down some goals and expectations for each team member and ensure that those expectations are being met. This check-in will promote shared accountability, particularly in remote teams.[152]

IS COLOCATION THE RIGHT SOLUTION?

Some experts, such as Stephane Kasriel, the chief executive of Upwork, contend IBM's decision will backfire and adversely affect team morale and corporate performance.[153] Ron Favali is a prime example. Favali is a 15-year IBM marketing veteran who has spent the last 12 years working from a home office outside Tampa, Florida. His team uses IBM's Sametime instant messaging voice and video chat software to stay connected and on-task, despite being scattered across three states. Favali may not be able to move to Atlanta, Austin, Boston, Chicago, New York, or San Francisco—all locations to which IBM "invited" its marketing team to relocate. His morale dropped so much after the directive that he told *Fox Business* he is leaving the company.[154]

Kasriel believes IBM's move will cause other talented employees to leave, ultimately diminishing the quality of its teams. He says that IBM's " . . . best talent will easily find new jobs with companies that are more open to remote work."[155] All told, the loss of talent will put IBM further behind its competitors.

A mass exodus of talent would recall the fall of another giant. Yahoo CEO Marissa Mayer decided to discontinue remote working in 2013.[156] That decision " . . . didn't really help Yahoo," said Sara Sutton, the founder and CEO of Flexjobs.com.[157] Mayer was ranked by *CNBC* as the "least likable" CEO in technology after the decision.[158]

What would you do if you were Ginni Rometty?

FOR DISCUSSION

Problem-Solving Perspective

1. What is the underlying problem in this case from the perspective of CEO Ginni Rometty? a senior leader from human resources?
2. What are the causes of this problem?
3. What advice would you offer to solve the problem? Explain.

Application of Chapter Content

1. What are some virtual best practices IBM could have employed for its remote teams? Explain.
2. Whether or not employees are colocated, describe how IBM can build effective teams.
3. How could IBM stimulate functional or constructive conflict in its virtual teams? Explain.
4. IBM's leadership and many in its workforce may not agree on how to address the company's lagging revenues. What conflict handling style is IBM leadership utilizing to address the conflict?

Legal/Ethical Challenge

When Employees Smoke Marijuana Socially: A Manager's Quandary

This challenge examines issues that may arise when co-workers smoke marijuana together outside work. We first provide background on the legalities of using marijuana before reviewing the case

Legalities of Using Marijuana

Nine states have legalized recreational marijuana use as of 2018: Alaska, California, Colorado, Maine, Massachusetts, Nevada, Oregon, Vermont, and Washington. Another 20 allow for medical marijuana use. Both recreational and medical marijuana use are still deemed illegal by the federal government, however.[159] This means that employers are generally not looking the other way when it comes to using marijuana. *CBS News* reports that most employers screen employees for marijuana use, even in states where it is permissible. Some states that allow for marijuana use have pushed back. For example, Maine enacted a law in 2018 protecting employees from discrimination solely on the basis of marijuana use.[160]

The Case

You work in a state where it is illegal to use marijuana recreationally, and your employer has a zero-tolerance policy regarding the use of drugs. You also are a supervisor at a telephone call center and have very positive relationships with members of your work team and your manager. Blake is a member of your work team.

Blake invited you to his birthday party at his home, and you happily agreed to attend. During the party, you walked out to the backyard to get some fresh air and noticed that Blake and several other employees of your company were smoking marijuana: None of these individuals have prescriptions for medical marijuana. You have been told on several occasions by members of your own work team that these same individuals have used marijuana at other social events.

Although Blake is a member of your work team, the other smokers are not. You don't really feel any need to tell management about these people smoking pot because you have never noticed their being impaired at work. At the same time, you feel conflicted because your employer takes a hard stand against the use of any drugs. If the company found out that you knew about their smoking, it would adversely affect your career. The company expects managers to act with honesty and integrity and to be forthright with senior management.

The following week you receive an e-mail from the vice president of human resources to evaluate Blake for a promotion to a supervisory position. Blake is one of three people being considered. You have a great relationship with the VP, but you know he takes a hard line on drug use. At the same time, you believe Blake is a good employee, but you wonder whether his smoking marijuana shows bad judgment for someone being considered for a managerial position at the company. As you close the VP's e-mail, you begin to consider how to respond.

SOLVING THE CHALLENGE

As Blake's supervisor, what would you do?

1. I would not tell the vice president of human resources about Blake's drug use. He's doing a good job and I have not seen any impairment.
2. I would tell the vice president of human resources about the incident in which I observed Blake smoking marijuana, but I also would reinforce that he is a good performer. My gut feeling is that I need to honor the company's zero-tolerance policy on drug use.
3. I would talk to Blake. I would explain my predicament and then ask him about the frequency of his drug use. If Blake promised to stop smoking marijuana, I would not tell the vice president of human resources about the incident.
4. Invent other options. Discuss.

Uber Continuing Case connect

Learn how Uber has set up teams in each city in which it operates. Assess your ability to apply the management concepts discussed in this chapter to the case by going to Connect.

14

Power, Influence, and Leadership

From Becoming a Manager to Becoming a Leader

©Olivier Renck/Aurora/Getty Images

After reading this chapter, you should be able to:

LO 14-1 Describe managers' appropriate use of power and influence.

LO 14-2 Identify traits and characteristics of successful leaders.

LO 14-3 Identify behaviors of successful leaders.

LO 14-4 Describe situational leadership.

LO 14-5 Describe transformational leadership and its effects on employees.

LO 14-6 Compare three additional perspectives on leadership.

LO 14-7 Explain how to develop the career readiness competency of self-awareness.

FORECAST *What's Ahead in This Chapter*

How do leaders use their power and influence to get results? This chapter considers this question. We discuss the sources of a leader's power and how leaders use persuasion to influence people. We then consider the following approaches to leadership: trait, behavioral, situational, transformational, and three additional perspectives. We conclude with a Career Corner that focuses on developing the career readiness competency of self-awareness.

MANAGE U

Improving Your Leadership Skills

According to one company's chief research executive writing in *Inc.* magazine, "Leadership is the art of execution. It's the art of getting things done."[1] This chapter introduces you to a number of insightful theories about leadership. For now, "getting things done" by leading others is a good place to begin thinking about what kind of leader you are and might become.

Here are some suggestions for improving your career readiness competency of leadership.

1. Discover your leadership style. We all develop a style of leading that is based on personal characteristics, traits, gender, interpersonal skills, and utilization of power and influence skills.[2] Identifying your leadership style is thus an ongoing process that evolves as you acquire more experience and responsibility in the workplace. You can think of this process as simply discovering what your strengths are over time and developing some flexible ways to use them in helping others achieve goals.[3] We include five self-assessments in this chapter to help you gain an understanding about your leadership style.

2. Adopt a proactive learning orientation. This suggestion follows naturally from the first one. Becoming a leader is a process that never actually ends,[4] which means you need to keep learning about your industry, yourself, your skills, and your strengths and weaknesses as you move through your career. Take classes or courses online, network with peers and mentors, ask questions, stay open-minded, seek challenging opportunities, and look outside your industry occasionally for ideas and practices you can adapt to your own leadership toolkit. A proactive learning orientation is a career readiness competency desired by employers.

3. Recognize that there is no single best way to lead. As motivational speaker and writer Jack Canfield says, "True leaders understand that they have the opportunity and ability to respond differently to every situation. When events arise, whether they're good or bad, leaders see these events as neutral. But they see their response to these events as crucial."[5] You will need to adapt your leadership strategy to each situation that calls for it, or, as Tesla's CEO Elon Musk says, "I move myself to where the biggest problem is."[6]

4. Show your followers that you value them. Delegate responsibility to those you lead and earn their respect by modeling ethical behavior. Always give credit where it is due, praise in public and criticize in private, and ask for help when you need it. Don't be stingy with compliments and encouragement.[7] Work on building trust with your team, too, by communicating with honesty and truth, being an attentive listener and a positive thinker, and accepting the responsibility that comes with being the leader.[8]

5. Practice mindfulness. You can reduce stress and worry, sharpen your focus, and make more thoughtful decisions by adopting the habit of mindfulness, which means focusing your awareness on the present and on acceptance of your feelings and thoughts.[9] Mindfulness becomes easier through meditation, which you can practice with simple techniques for as little as 5 or 10 minutes a day.[10] Mindfulness also helps you lead others through tough times and crises by enabling you to communicate calm, purposefulness, and positivity.

For Discussion One business writer suggests it's time for business leaders to abandon an old "rule" of leadership that says "great leaders work alone."[11] Do you agree that effective leadership should include motivating, developing, and encouraging others? Why or why not?

14.1 The Nature of Leadership: The Role of Power and Influence

THE BIG PICTURE

Leadership skills are needed to create and communicate a company's vision, strategies, and goals as well as to execute on these plans and goals. This section highlights the way successful managers use power and influence to achieve these ends and describes five sources of power and nine influence tactics they use to lead others. Leaders use the power of persuasion to get others to follow them. Five approaches to leadership are described in the next five sections.

LO 14-1

Describe managers' appropriate use of power and influence.

Leadership. What is it? Is it a skill anyone can develop? How important is it to organizational success?

Leadership is the ability to influence employees to voluntarily pursue organizational goals.[12] "Leadership" is a broad term, as this definition implies. It can describe a formal position in an organization, which usually carries a title like CEO or CFO, or an informal role, such as that played by an expert whose opinion in some area we value.

Although not everyone is suited to being a good leader, evidence shows that people can be trained to be more effective leaders.[13] In response, more companies are using management development programs to build a pipeline of leadership talent. They also provide leadership coaching to targeted employees. **Leadership coaching is "about enhancing a person's abilities and skills to lead and to help the organization meet its operational objectives.** It's about boosting the person's ability to perform as a leader and to achieve the vision," according to one expert.[14] It is estimated that U.S. companies spent $14 billion on coaching in 2016.[15]

Effective leadership matters! A recent study spanning 60 years and more than 18,000 firm-years showed that CEO behavior significantly impacted organizational performance.[16] Don't take this study to mean effective leadership only matters at the top. Other research reinforces the value of fostering effective leadership at all organizational levels.

Let's begin our study of leadership by considering the difference between leading and managing and the role of power and influence skills.

What Is the Difference between Leading and Managing?

Bernard Bass, a leadership expert, concluded that "leaders manage and managers lead, but the two activities are not synonymous."[17] Broadly speaking, managers typically perform functions associated with planning, investigating, organizing, and control, and leaders focus on influencing others. Leaders inspire others, provide emotional support, and try to get employees to rally around a common goal. Leaders also play a key role in *creating* a vision and strategic plan for an organization. Managers, in turn, are charged with *implementing* the vision and plan. We can draw several conclusions from this division of labor.

First, good leaders are not necessarily good managers, and good managers are not necessarily good leaders. Second, effective leadership requires effective managerial skills at some level. For example, United Airlines former CEO, Jeff Smisek, resigned due to managerial deficiencies that produced labor problems, poor customer service, and poor financial results.[18] In contrast, both Tim Cook, CEO of Apple, and Mary Dillon, CEO of Ulta Beauty, are recognized for their use of good managerial skills when implementing corporate strategies.[19]

TABLE 14.1
Characteristics of Managers and Leaders

BEING A MANAGER MEANS . . .	BEING A LEADER MEANS . . .
Planning, organizing, directing, controlling	Being visionary
Executing plans and delivering goods and services	Being inspiring, setting the tone, and articulating the vision
Managing resources	Managing people
Being conscientious	Being inspirational (charismatic)
Acting responsibly	Acting decisively
Putting customers first—responding to and acting for customers	Putting people first—responding to and acting for followers
Mistakes can happen when managers don't appreciate people are the key resource, underlead by treating people like other resources, or fail to be held accountable	Mistakes can happen when leaders choose the wrong goal, direction, or inspiration; overlead; or fail to implement the vision

Source: Adapted from P. Lorenzi, "Managing for the Common Good: Prosocial Leadership," Organizational Dynamics *33, no. 3 (2004), p. 286.*

Managers conduct planning, organizing, directing, and control. Leaders inspire, encourage, and rally others to achieve great goals. Managers implement a company's vision and strategic plan. Leaders create and articulate that vision and plan. Table 14.1 summarizes the key characteristics of managers and leaders.

Do you want to lead others or understand what makes a leader tick? Then take the following self-assessment. It provides feedback on your readiness to assume a leadership role and can help you consider how to prepare for a formal leadership position.

SELF-ASSESSMENT 14.1 CAREER READINESS

Assessing Your Readiness to Assume the Leadership Role

The following survey was designed to assess your readiness to assume the leadership role. Be prepared to answer these questions if your instructor has assigned Self-Assessment 14.3 in Connect.

1. What is your level of readiness? Are you surprised by the results?
2. Looking at the three highest- and lowest-rated items in the survey, what can you do to increase your readiness to lead? Think of specific actions you can take right now.
3. What things might you say during an interview to demonstrate that you are ready to lead?

Managerial Leadership: Can You Be *Both* a Manager and a Leader?

Absolutely. The latest thinking is that individuals are able to exhibit a broad array of the contrasting behaviors shown in Table 14.1 (a concept called *behavioral complexity*).[20] Thus, in the workplace, many people are capable of exhibiting **managerial leadership**,

defined as "the process of influencing others to understand and agree about what needs to be done and the process of facilitating individual and collective efforts to accomplish shared objectives."[21] Here, the "influencing" part is leadership and the "facilitating" part is management.

Managerial leadership may be demonstrated not only by managers appointed to their positions, but also by those who exercise leadership on a daily basis but don't carry formal management titles (such as certain co-workers on a team).

Coping with Complexity versus Coping with Change: The Thoughts of John Kotter

In considering management versus leadership, retired Harvard Business School professor **John Kotter** suggests that one is not better than the other, that in fact they are *complementary* systems of action. The difference is that . . .

- *Management* is about coping with *complexity*.
- *Leadership* is about coping with *change*.[22]

Let's consider these differences.

Being a Manager: Coping with Complexity Management is necessary because complex organizations, especially the large ones that so much dominate the economic landscape, tend to become chaotic unless there is good management.[23]

Being a Leader: Coping with Change As the business world has become more competitive and volatile, doing things the same way as last year (or doing it 5 percent better) is no longer a formula for success. More changes are required for survival—hence the need for leadership.

Five Sources of Power

Power is the ability to marshal human, informational, and other resources to get something done. Defined this way, power is all about influencing others. The more influence you have, the more powerful you are, and vice versa.

Global leaders. Leadership impacts the security, sustainability, and well-being of our planet. These leaders of the Group of 20 major economies clearly impact our lives in many ways. The purpose of the meeting taking place here was to determine how advanced and emerging economies can create mutually beneficial growth strategies. ©Sean Gallup/ Getty Images

To really understand leadership, we need to understand the concept of power and authority. *Authority* is the right to perform or command; it comes with the job. In contrast, *power* is the extent to which a person is able to influence others so they respond to requests.

People who pursue **personalized power—power directed at helping oneself—as a way of enhancing their own selfish ends may give the word *power* a bad name.** However, there is another kind of power, **socialized power—power directed at helping others.** This is the kind of power you hear in expressions such as "My goal is to have a powerful impact on my community."[24]

Within organizations there are typically five sources of power leaders may draw on: *legitimate*, *reward*, *coercive*, *expert*, and *referent*.

1. Legitimate Power: Influencing Behavior Because of One's Formal Position

Legitimate power, which all managers have, is power that results from managers' formal positions within the organization. All managers have legitimate power over their employees, deriving from their position, whether it's a construction boss, ad account supervisor, sales manager, or CEO. This power may be exerted both positively or negatively—as praise or as criticism, for example.

2. Reward Power: Influencing Behavior by Promising or Giving Rewards

Reward power, which all managers have, is power that results from managers' authority to reward their subordinates. Rewards can range from praise to pay raises, from recognition to promotions.

Example: The top-performing employees at Home Mortgage Alliance, a mortgage lender based in Denver and a "top small workplace" in 2018, are rewarded with a vacation trip each year. Recent destinations have included Hawaii and Mexico.[25]

3. Coercive Power: Influencing Behavior by Threatening or Giving Punishment

Coercive power, which all managers have, results from managers' authority to punish their subordinates. Punishment can range from verbal or written reprimands to demotions to terminations. In some lines of work, fines and suspensions may be used. Coercive power has to be used judiciously, of course, since a manager who is seen as being constantly negative will produce a lot of resentment among employees. Before Alan Mulally took over at Ford Motor Co., for instance, the expectation fostered by a culture of blame at the firm was that any manager who had bad news to report would be fired. Mulally's corrective action was to say a manager *had* a problem, not that he or she *was* the problem.[26]

4. Expert Power: Influencing Behavior Because of One's Expertise

Expert power is power resulting from one's specialized information or expertise. Expertise, or special knowledge, can be mundane, such as knowing the work schedules and assignments of the people who report to you. Or it can be sophisticated, such as having computer or medical knowledge. Administrative assistants may have expert power because, for example, they have been in a job a long time and know all the necessary contacts. CEOs may have expert power because they have knowledge not shared with many others.

5. Referent Power: Influencing Behavior Because of One's Personal Attraction

Referent power is power deriving from one's personal attraction. As we will see later in this chapter (under the discussion of transformational leadership, Section 14.5), this kind of power characterizes strong, visionary leaders who are able to persuade their followers through their charisma. Referent power may be associated with managers, but it is more likely to be characteristic of leaders.

Now that you've learned about the five bases of power, complete Self-Assessment 14.2 to identify which bases you prefer to use. Answering the associated questions will help you understand how the various forms of power can both help and hurt you when trying to influence others.

SELF-ASSESSMENT 14.2 CAREER READINESS

What Kind of Power Do I Prefer?

If your instructor has assigned Self-Assessment 14.2 in Connect, you will learn which bases of power you prefer to use.

1. Which of the five bases of power do you prefer to use?
2. Describe how this form of power helps you at school, at work, and in social situations.
3. Which of the five bases is your least preferred? What are the implications for you at school, at work, and in social situations?
4. What things might you say during an interview to demonstrate that you understand how to use power when influencing others?

Common Influence Tactics

Influence tactics are conscious efforts to affect and change behaviors in others. The nine most common ways people try to get their bosses, co-workers, and subordinates to do what they want are listed in Table 14.2, beginning with the most frequently used.

These are considered *generic* influence tactics because they characterize social influence as we use it in all directions. Research has also shown this ranking to be fairly consistent regardless of whether the direction of influence is downward, upward, or lateral.

Hard versus Soft Tactics

Some refer to the first five influence tactics—rational persuasion, inspirational appeals, consultation, ingratiation, and personal appeals—as *"soft" tactics* **because they are friendlier than, and not as coercive as, the last four tactics—** exchange, coalition, pressure, and legitimating tactics, which are *"hard" tactics* **because they exert more overt pressure.**

Which Influence Tactics Do You Prefer?

When you read the list of tactics, each probably meant something to you. Which do you most commonly use? Knowing the answer can help you better choose the appropriate tactic for any given situation and

Influence tactics. In mid-2015 Taylor Swift asserted her immense power and influence and successfully changed one of Apple's policies. Before the launch of Apple Music, the company said it intended not to compensate musicians for their music used during the free trial of its new subscription service. Swift, who often speaks on behalf of other musicians, threatened to withhold her new album from Apple, now the largest single retailer of music. She said, "We don't ask for free iPhones. Please don't ask us to provide you with our music for no compensation." Apple quickly changed its policy and compensated musicians for the use of their work during the free trial and since. Which tactics (and bases of power) did Swift use to influence Apple? ©Mike Coppola/Getty Images

TABLE 14.2 Nine Common Influence Tactics

INFLUENCE TACTIC	DESCRIPTION	EXAMPLE
1. Rational persuasion	Trying to convince someone with reason, logic, or facts	As CEO, Allan Mullally reversed the negative meeting culture at Ford Motor Co.—and its financial fortunes—by encouraging open and honest discussion and collaboration focused on finding solutions rather than placing blame.[27]
2. Inspirational appeals	Trying to build enthusiasm by appealing to others' emotions, ideals, or values	The late Steve Jobs's understanding that people want to fulfill their dreams, not just purchase products, continues to inform every design and marketing decision at Apple, the company he founded.[28]
3. Consultation	Getting others to participate in planning, decision making, and changes	"I end up asking a lot of questions," says Nike's CEO, Mark Parker. Known for encouraging and seeking ideas from even junior members of management, Parker deliberately avoids a micro managing style.[29]
4. Ingratiation	Getting someone in a good mood prior to making a request	This is being friendly and helpful and using praise, flattery, or humor.[30]
5. Personal appeals	Referring to friendship and loyalty when making a request or asking a friend to do a favor	Employees who volunteer might make a personal appeal to colleagues to donate time, clothing, or money to a cause.[31]
6. Exchange	Making explicit or implied promises and trading favors	This type of exchange is sometimes called a quid pro quo ("this for that"). For example, President Trump has proposed that Congress approve a physical wall at the Mexican border in exchange for his agreement to extend the threatened DACA program protecting young immigrants.[32] Leaders must be careful not to allow favoritism and coercion to evolve, however.[33]
7. Coalition tactics	Getting others to support your efforts to persuade someone	Cory Booker, U.S. Senator from New Jersey, credits coalition leadership with the economic revival of Newark during his past job as mayor: "None of these accomplishments happened because of one individual's effort. They happened because, in Newark, we brought together new coalitions of grassroots neighborhood groups and elected leaders, nonprofits and business groups, labor unions and leaders in the capital markets, developers and philanthropists. I am proud of the unity that was forged in Newark—it's proof, to me, that people will rally around bold goals and, in turn, achieve significant progress."[34]
8. Pressure	Demanding compliance or using intimidation or threats	Chinese philosopher Lao-Tzu wrote, "The highest type of ruler is one of whose existence the people are barely aware. Next comes one whom they love and praise. Next comes one whom they fear. Next comes one whom they despise and defy."[35]
9. Legitimating tactics	Basing a request on authority or right, organizational rules or policies, or explicit/implied support from superiors	In 2018 Senator Tammy Duckworth of Illinois became the first U.S. senator to give birth while in office. She easily won passage of a resolution allowing legislators to bring children under one year of age to the senate floor, enabling her to cast an important vote within days of her daughter's birth.[36]

Source: Descriptions of these influence tactics are based on D. Kipnis, S. Schmidt, and I. Wilkinson, "Intraorganizational Influence Tactics: Exploration in Getting One's Way," Journal of Applied Psychology, *August 1980, pp. 440–452; and Table 1 in G. Yukl, C. M. Falbe, and J. Y. Youn, "Patterns of Influence Behavior for Managers,* Group & Organization Management, *March 1993, pp. 5–28.*

thus increase the chance of achieving your desired outcome. You can enhance your self-awareness about the career readiness competency of leadership by completing Self-Assessment 14.3.

SELF-ASSESSMENT 14.3 CAREER READINESS

Which Influence Tactics Do I Use?

If your instructor has assigned Self-Assessment 14.3 in Connect, you will learn which of the nine influence tactics you use and in what order of frequency.

1. Is your rational persuasion score the highest? Regardless, give some specific examples of ways you use this tactic.
2. Which tactic is your least preferred (lowest score)? Provide examples of situations when and how you may use this tactic.
3. What might you say during an interview to demonstrate that you understand how to use these nine tactics to influence others?

Match Tactics to Influence Outcomes

Research and practice provide some useful lessons about the relative effectiveness of influence tactics.

- **Rely on the core.** *Core influence tactics*—rational persuasion, consultation, collaboration, and inspirational appeals—are most effective at building commitment.
- **Be authentic.** Don't try to be someone else. Be authentic to your values and beliefs.
- **Consult rather than legitimate.** Some employees are more apt to accept change when managers rely on a consultative strategy and are more likely to resist change when managers use a legitimating tactic.
- **"Ingratiation" is not a good long-term strategy.** Ingratiation improved short-term sales goal achievement but reduced it in the long term in a study of salespeople. Glad handing may help today's sales but not tomorrow's.
- **Be subtle.** Subtle flattery and agreement with the other person's opinion (both forms of ingratiation) were shown to increase the likelihood that executives would win recommendation to sit on boards of directors.
- **Learn to influence.** Research with corporate managers of a supermarket chain showed that influence tactics can be taught and learned. Managers who received 360-degree feedback on two occasions regarding their influence tactics showed an increased use of core influence tactics.

You'll need to understand *and* effectively apply a range of influence tactics to be effective. But you can learn and improve influence tactics to move resisters to compliance and move those who are compliant to commitment.

An Integrated Model of Leadership

Figure 14.1 provides an overview of what you will learn in this chapter. It presents an integrated model of leadership. Starting at the far right of the model, you see that leadership effectiveness is the outcome we want to explain. The center of the model shows this outcome is influenced by four types of leadership behavior: *task-oriented*, *relationship-oriented*, *passive*, and *transformational*: Passive leadership is bad and should be avoided. In turn, our ability to effectively engage in these leader behaviors is affected by traits, gender, and leadership skills (the left side of the model).

FIGURE 14.1 An integrated model of leadership

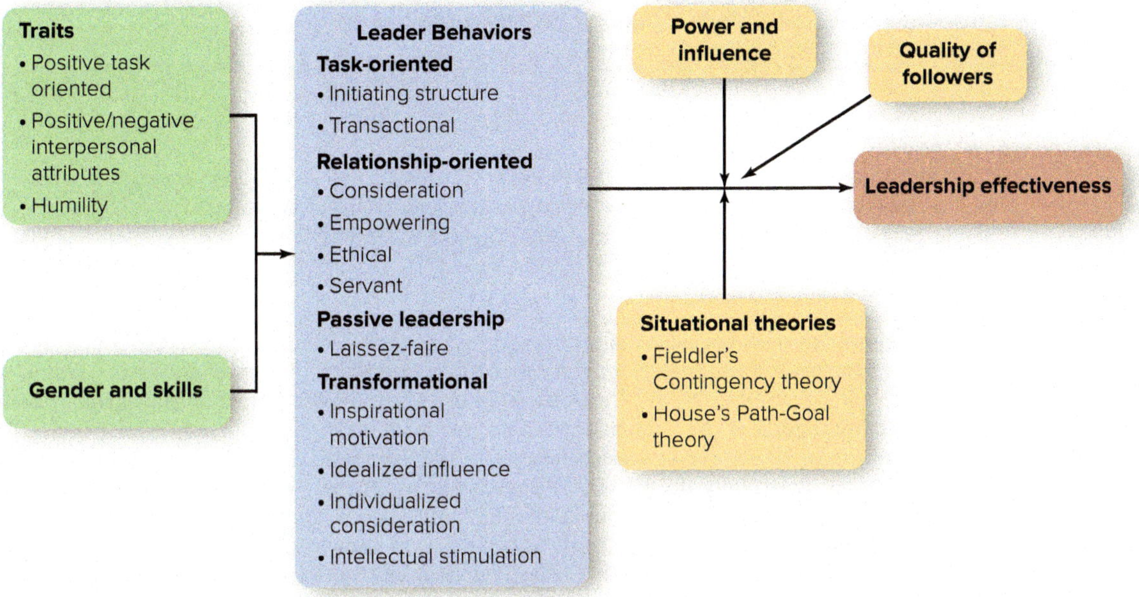

Moreover, Figure 14.1 shows that the relationship between leader behavior and leadership effectiveness is affected by three other considerations: power and influence, quality of followers, and situational factors. For example, people with more power and strong influence skills are better suited to execute the three positive types of leader behavior in a more effective manner. Similarly, you will be more effective if you exhibit the three positive leader behaviors at the right time. Different situations call for different leader behaviors. This chapter helps you understand when to change your leadership style and behavior. •

14.2 Trait Approaches: Do Leaders Have Distinctive Traits and Personal Characteristics?

THE BIG PICTURE

Trait approaches attempt to identify distinctive characteristics that account for the effectiveness of leaders. We describe (1) positive task-oriented traits and positive/negative interpersonal attributes (narcissism, Machiavellianism, psychopathy) and (2) some results of gender studies.

LO 14-2

Identify traits and characteristics of successful leaders.

Consider a leader called one of "the most powerful women in business" by *Fortune* magazine, a former CIA operations officer, graduate of University Pennsylvania's Wharton School, and one-time official in the White House Office of Management and Budget and later the Pentagon, who has led one of the world's largest defense contractors since 2013. "Performance speaks for itself," she says. "Results are, at the end of the day, all that really do matter."[37] That leader is Phebe Novakovic, CEO of General Dynamics. She seems to embody the traits of (1) dominance, (2) intelligence, (3) self-confidence, (4) high energy, and (5) task-relevant knowledge.

These are the five traits that researcher **Ralph Stogdill** in 1948 concluded were typical of successful leaders.[38] Stogdill is one of many contributors to **trait approaches to leadership, which attempt to identify distinctive characteristics that account for the effectiveness of leaders.**[39]

Positive Task-Oriented Traits and Positive/Negative Interpersonal Attributes

Traits play a central role in how we perceive leaders, and they ultimately affect leadership effectiveness.[40] This is why researchers have attempted to identify a more complete list of traits that differentiate leaders from followers. Table 14.3 shows an expanded list of both positive *and* negative interpersonal attributes often found in leaders.[41] Notice the inclusion of the Big Five traits we discussed in Chapter 11 as positive attributes.

Leadership at TOMS. Texas native Blake Mycoskie is the founder of TOMS shoes and several other global businesses based on his "One for one"® premise: that every purchase, whether of shoes, eye wear, coffee, or a handbag, should help someone in need. Among other achievements, his companies have donated 60 million pairs of shoes, restored eyesight to almost half a million people, and provided safe water and childbirth services to thousands.[42] What positive leadership traits do you think Mycoskie possesses? ©Aristidis Vafeiadakis/Zuma Press, Inc/ Alamy Stock Photo

TABLE 14.3
Key Task-Oriented Traits and Interpersonal Attributes

POSITIVE TASK-ORIENTED TRAITS	POSITIVE/NEGATIVE INTERPERSONAL ATTRIBUTES
• Intelligence	• Extraversion (+)
• Conscientiousness	• Agreeableness (+)
• Open to experience	• Emotional intelligence (+)
• Emotional stability	• Narcissism (−)
• Positive affect	• Machiavellianism (−)
	• Psychopathy (−)

We have discussed most positive interpersonal attributes elsewhere, but we need to describe the negative, or "dark side," traits of some leaders: narcissism, Machiavellianism, and psychopathy. You want to avoid displaying these negative traits because they have a strong negative association with employees' mental health.[43]

- **Narcissism** is defined as "a self-centered perspective, feelings of superiority, and a drive for personal power and glory."[44] Narcissists have inflated views of themselves, seek to attract the admiration of others, and fantasize about being in control of everything. Although passionate and charismatic, narcissistic leaders may provoke counterproductive work behaviors in others, such as strong resentments and resistance.[45] They also tend to act more narcissistically when they perceive that someone has treated them unfairly.[46]
- **Machiavellianism.** Inspired by the pessimistic beliefs of Niccolò Machiavelli, a philosopher and writer (*The Prince*) in the Italian Renaissance, **Machiavellianism** (pronounced "mah-kyah-*vel*-yahn-izm") displays a cynical view of human nature and condones opportunistic and unethical ways of manipulating people, putting results over principles. This view is manifested in such expressions as "All people lie to get what they want" and "You have to cheat to get ahead." Like narcissism, Machiavellianism is also associated with counterproductive work behaviors, especially as people begin to understand that they are being coldly manipulated.
- **Psychopathy.** **Psychopathy** ("sigh-*kop*-a-thee") is characterized by lack of concern for others, impulsive behavior, and a dearth of remorse when the psychopath's actions harm others. Not surprisingly, a person with a psychopathic personality can be a truly toxic influence in the workplace.

If you have a propensity for any of these, you need to know that the expression of "dark side" traits tends to result in career derailment—being demoted or fired.[47]

Leadership at Turing Pharmaceuticals. Martin Shkreli (seated, center), founder and former CEO of Turing Pharmaceuticals, tried to build a business strategy of purchasing the rights to inexpensive but life-saving prescription drugs and raising their prices to dizzying heights. Public response was swift and devastatingly negative; meanwhile, Shkreli has pleaded not guilty to fraud charges associated with other firms he managed. Does he sound like an effective leader? ©Tom Williams/CQ Roll Call/Newscom

What Do We Know about Gender and Leadership?

The increase in the number of women in the workforce has generated much interest in understanding the similarities and differences between female and male leaders.

Sheryl Sandberg. Named in 2014 the ninth most powerful woman in the world by *Forbes* and the 10th most powerful woman in business by *Fortune*, Sandberg is the chief operating officer (COO) and business face of Facebook. She's also a passionate advocate for women achieving more top corporate leadership jobs. As she told a Barnard College graduating class, "A world where men ran half our homes and women ran half our institutions would be just a much greater world." ©Simon Dawson/Bloomberg/Getty Images

Fact versus Fiction: What Are the Basic Statistics? Women make up more than half the workforce and more than half of all college students in the United States.[48] There were 32 women CEOs leading *Fortune* 500 companies in 2017, a tiny number but more than ever before.[49] The popular press has promoted the idea that companies have significantly higher financial performance when females are members of what is called the upper echelon, which includes the CEO and the top management team team (TMT).[50] Research tells us, however, that this conclusion is somewhat overstated. A recent academic meta-analysis summarizing 146 studies from 33 different countries uncovered two positive conclusions about the percentage of females in a company's upper echelon: (1) "there is no cumulative . . . evidence of long-term performance declines for firms that have more females in their upper echelons" and (2) "there are small but dependably positive associations of female representation in CEO positions and TMTs with long-term value creation."[51]

Do Men and Women Vary in Terms of Leadership Style and Effectiveness? The answer is yes based on the following research results:

- Men were observed to display more task leadership and women more relationship leadership.[52]
- Women used a more democratic or participative style than men, and men used a more autocratic and directive style.[53]
- A study conducted by the BI Norwegian Business School of nearly 3,000 managers' personalities and characteristics concluded that on almost every criterion, women performed better than men. Women ranked ahead of men in initiative and communication, openness and innovation, sociability and supportiveness, and methodical approach to management and goal setting. Men were rated better at dealing with stress and remaining emotionally stable. According to one of the study's coauthors, women "are decidedly more suited to management positions than their male counterparts. If decision-makers ignore this truth, they could effectively be employing less qualified leaders and impairing productivity."[54]
- Peers, managers, direct reports, and judges/trained observers rated women executives as more effective than men. Men also rated themselves as more effective than women evaluated themselves.[55]
- One study of 10,000 global leaders conducted by Development Dimensions International (DDI) found almost no differences between men and women in their levels of hard or soft skills.[56] Another study, by DDI and the Conference Board, found only a few differences, notably in confidence levels.[57] An article combining the results of these two studies drew these broad conclusions from the data:

  1. Women leaders are less confident than men and less likely to rate themselves highly.
  2. Women and men are very similar on management skills like "building high-performance cultures; engaging employees; cultivating a customer-focused culture; creating alignment and accountability; enhancing organizational talent; building strategic partnerships and relationships, driving process innovation and driving efficiency." Says DDI's vice president, "The disparity in gender diversity has little to do with competence levels."[58]

Are There Social Forces Working against Women Leaders? Yes, according to these data.

- There are more women leaders in health care, education, and retail industries than in consumer products, transportation, tech, energy, and automotive industries. But nowhere do their numbers approach their proportion in the overall population, and women managers are also less likely to get plum assignments or international experience.[59] Why do these differences in leadership opportunities persist? A new Pew Research study of the gender attitudes of more than 4,500 U.S. adults suggests that social attitudes "shape how women are viewed in the workplace and whether or not women's ambition to reach leadership positions is supported." For instance, although most people actually don't see gender differences in workplace behavior and success, among those who do, 61 percent of men believe the differences are due to biology, while 65 percent of women say they come from society's differing expectations of men and women.[60]
- Another factor the Pew study identified is that U.S. adults value attractiveness (35 percent) and empathy/nurturing (30 percent) most in women, with only 9 percent valuing ambition and leadership. Highly valued in men are "honesty and morality" (33 percent), followed by professional and financial success (23 percent). Almost 3 in 10 respondents to the study actually said women should *not* have ambition, leadership, or assertive traits. More believed women face pressure to be involved parents than believed men do (77 percent versus 49 percent). More than half the women surveyed (52 percent) felt they were under pressure to be successful in their careers, while only 38 percent of men thought women faced this stress.[61]
- Studies of more than 37,000 managers showed that the display of "ineffective interpersonal behaviors were slightly less frequent among female managers but slightly more damaging to women than men when present."[62]
- Female CEOs receive more scrutiny than male CEOs, according to an 18-year dataset of activist investors. An activist investor is a shareholder who owns more than 5 percent of a public company's voting stock and desires to change management practices. Results showed that "female CEOs are more likely than male CEOs to come under threat from activist investors, and also are more likely to have simultaneous threats from multiple activist investors."[63] Female CEOs clearly experience greater monitoring and pressure from activist investors than do male CEOs.

EXAMPLE Great Leaders Worldwide

Canada's Justin Trudeau Although he is the son of an earlier and long-time prime minister, Canada's popular leader Justin Trudeau came to politics by an unusual route. He has been a teacher, a bouncer, the leader of a nonprofit organization, and even an occasional actor. As prime minister, he has won praise for championing the rights of women and Canada's indigenous population (his cabinet contains more than 50 percent women and minorities and includes an openly gay politician, a member who is blind, Sikhs, and Aboriginals), for highlighting his role as a husband and father, and for leading the country with grace and skill. He is also, as journalist Noah Richler described, "kind of fun to watch," whether he's riding a unicycle, sporting his *Hitchhiker's Guide to the Galaxy* T-shirt, or marching in a gay pride parade wearing socks that signal the end of Ramadan. Trudeau has said he has a "deep conviction that you cannot do this job unless you stay connected to the people . . . and that means being close enough that they can feel close to you."[64]

His humility, optimism, and willingness to admit mistakes and to open dialogues with those who disagree with him reflect a high degree of emotional intelligence. As one Canadian observer says of Trudeau, "The very skills the prime minister honed as a teacher and third-sector leader are key to his ability to motivate and react with agility—not just his caucus but Canadians and other global leaders. The successful teacher and senior leader has an ability to parse diverse threads, read situations, motivations, and personalities, and respond in real time. An increasingly in-demand skill amidst huge change."[65]

Justin Trudeau. Prime Minister of Canada Justin Trudeau (in green) participates in a Pride Parade in Vancouver, Canada.
©Sergei Bachlakov/Shutterstock

Germany's Angela Merkel Angela Merkel, long-time chancellor of Germany, grew up in the communist-controlled sector of a divided country struggling to overcome the horrors of World War II and its disastrous defeat. A chemist by training, who also served as environmental minister, she is now the longest-term leader in Europe and one of the most powerful women on the planet. Deputy Finance Minister Jens Spahn notes that Merkel is calm and rational in solving problems, saying, "She works like a scientist: she reads lots, assesses the facts and doesn't have preconceptions."[66] Her generally cautious and low-key approach has helped her lead her reunified country through globalization, enormous economic and technological change, and a worldwide financial crisis. This disciplined realist also took the lead in offering shelter to more than 1 million Muslim and other refugees who crossed Germany's border in 2015, an act for which UN High Commissioner on Refugees Filippo Grandi said Germany exemplified an international role model.[67]

Angela Merkel. Federal Chancellor of Germany Angela Merkel.
©Thomas Frey/imageBROKER/Alamy Stock Photo

Though some are critical of her humane and generous stance and even suggest it could lead to her political downfall, Merkel herself says, "In many regions war and terror prevail. States disintegrate. For many years we have read about this. We have heard about it. We have seen it on TV. But we had not yet sufficiently understood that what happens in Aleppo and Mosul can affect Essen or Stuttgart. We have to face that now."[68]

YOUR CALL

What leadership traits do you think Justin Trudeau exhibits? What leadership traits does Angela Merkel seem to have? Which do they share, and how do they differ? What might account for any differences?

Are Knowledge and Skills Important?

Knowledge and skills are extremely important! A team of researchers identified four basic skills leaders need. *(See Table 14.4.)*

So What Do We Know about Leadership Traits?

Trait theory offers us four conclusions.

1. **We cannot ignore the implications of leadership traits.** Traits play a central role in the way we perceive leaders, and they do ultimately affect leadership effectiveness.[73] For instance, focus, confidence, transparency, and integrity were among the top traits listed in a survey of current business leaders, along with patience, openness, and generosity.[74]

TABLE 14.4

Four Basic Skills for Leaders

WHAT LEADERS NEED	AND WHY
Cognitive abilities to identify problems and their causes in rapidly changing situations	Leaders must sometimes devise effective solutions in short time spans with limited information. One situation requiring quick action that many managers will likely face is a data breach. Says Ralph de la Vega, president & CEO, AT&T Mobile & Business Solutions, "There are only two kinds of companies today . . . those that have experienced a data breach and those that will be breached."[69]
Interpersonal skills to influence and persuade others	Leaders need to work well with diverse people. Alan Colberg, president and CEO of Assurant, says civility is one of a handful of key interpersonal skills in every career. The others he cites are the abilities to build relationships, conscientiousness, and integrity.[70]
Business skills to maximize the use of organizational assets	Leaders increasingly need business skills as they advance up through an organization. Three valuable but often-overlooked skills that most people can develop with a little effort are mindfulness, curiosity, and optimism.[71]
Conceptual skills to draft an organization's mission, vision, strategies, and implementation plans	Conceptual skills matter most for individuals in the top ranks in an organization. Entrepreneurs may have their conceptual skills tested on a regular basis. Sara Blakely's father regularly asked her, "What have you failed at this week?" After repeated setbacks, she eventually came up with the line of slimming intimate wear she called Spanx.[72]

Source: Adapted from T. V. Mumford, M. A. Campion, and F. P. Morgeson, "Leadership Skills Strataplex: Leadership Skill Requirements across Organizational Levels," Leadership Quarterly, *2007, pp. 154–166.*

More specifically, many companies attempt to define leadership traits important for their context. BNSF Railway Company, for example, identified the traits it wanted leaders to exhibit (such as questioning, listening, and being mindful) in pursuit of its sales goals. The company then designed a leadership development program to help its employees learn and apply these traits.[75]

2. **The positive and "dark triad" traits suggest the qualities you should cultivate and avoid if you want to assume a leadership role in the future.** Martha Stewart, founder of a several successful business ventures, admits to being a "maniacal" micromanager, for instance, who needs to "understand every part of the business to be able to maximise those businesses."[76] Personality tests and other trait assessments can help evaluate your strengths and weaknesses on these traits. The website for this book contains a host of tests you can take for this purpose.
3. **Organizations may want to include personality and trait assessments in their selection and evaluation processes.** Among the growing number of companies using psychometric testing are Citigroup, ExxonMobil, Ford Motor, Procter & Gamble, Hewlett-Packard (HP), and J.P. Morgan.[77]
4. **Cross-cultural competency is an increasingly valued task-oriented trait.** It's also a career readiness competency. As more companies expand their international operations and hire more culturally diverse people for domestic operations in the United States, they want to enhance employees' global mind-set.[78] **A global mind-set is your belief in your ability to influence dissimilar others in a global context.** •

14.3 Behavioral Approaches: Do Leaders Show Distinctive Patterns of Behavior?

THE BIG PICTURE

Behavioral leadership approaches try to determine unique behaviors displayed by effective leaders. These approaches can be divided into four categories, the first three of which are discussed in this section: (1) task-oriented behavior, (2) relationship-oriented behavior, (3) passive behavior, and (4) transformational behavior (discussed in Section 14.5).

LO 14-3

Identify behaviors of successful leaders.

The Integrated Model of Leadership shown in Figure 14.1 showed that a leader's traits, gender, and skills directly affect the choice of four categories of leader behavior. The focus of those interested in **behavioral leadership approaches** **is to determine the key behaviors displayed by effective leaders.** These approaches identified four categories of leader behavior:

- Task-oriented behavior.
- Relationship-oriented behavior.
- Passive behavior.
- Transformational behavior (discussed in Section 14.5).

Much of what we know about task-oriented and relationship-oriented behaviors is based on research done at The Ohio State University and University of Michigan.

Task-Oriented Leader Behaviors: Initiating-Structure Leadership and Transactional Leadership

The primary purpose of **task-oriented leadership behaviors** **is to ensure that people, equipment, and other resources are used in an efficient way to accomplish the mission of a group or organization.**[79] Examples of task-oriented behaviors are planning, clarifying, monitoring, and problem solving. However, two kinds are particularly important: (1) *initiating-structure leadership* and (2) *transactional leadership*.[80]

Men of steel. What kind of leadership behavior is appropriate for directing these kinds of workers—the kind that directs them how to complete the task or the kind that develops good worker–boss relationships? ©Steve Dunwell/Photolibrary/Getty Images

Initiating-Structure Leadership: "Here's What We Do to Get the Job Done"

Initiating-structure leadership is leader behavior that organizes and defines—that is, "initiates the structure for"—what employees should be doing to maximize output. Clearly, this is a very task-oriented approach.

Example: Meg Whitman, CEO of HP, likes to use initiating structure. *Fortune* reported that she is a "punctuality zealot, she'd chide staff for starting meetings a couple of minutes later. Some managers were put off when she personally checked their travel schedules."[81]

David Miliband, president and CEO of the nonprofit International Rescue Committee, echoes the "get the job done" mindset when he says, "Whatever is going on, your number-one responsibility is to have a mind-set at work that says, 'We can solve this.'"[82]

Transactional Leadership: "Here's What We Do to Get the Job Done, and Here Are the Rewards"

As a manager, your power stems from your ability to provide rewards (and threaten reprimands) in exchange for your subordinates' doing the work. When you do this, you are performing **transactional leadership, focusing on clarifying employees' roles and task requirements and providing rewards and punishments contingent on performance.** Like initiating-structure leadership, transactional leadership also encompasses setting goals and monitoring progress.[83]

Example: Nick Saban, head football coach at University of Alabama, has put together an impressive winning streak in his more than 10 years in the job, matching the record for most championships by a college football coach since 1936 and consistently being ranked number one in the Associated Press's weekly poll. He makes good use of the transactional leader's ability to reward team members with wins. "I enjoy seeing if I can get somebody to respond," he says, "even if they're a little bit abnormal and abstract in how they view the world. Well, how can I reach this person to get them to do things that are going to benefit them, but also benefit the organization?"[84]

Initiating-structure leadership has a moderately strong positive relationship with leadership effectiveness, according to research.[85] Transaction leadership also has a positive association with leader effectiveness and group performance.[86]

Relationship-Oriented Leader Behavior: Consideration, Empowerment, Ethical Leadership, and Servant Leadership

Relationship-oriented leadership is primarily concerned with the leader's interactions with his or her people. The emphasis is on enhancing employees' skills and creating positive work relationships among co-workers and between the leader and the led. Such leaders often act as mentors, providing career advice, giving employees assignments that will broaden their skills, and empowering them to make their own decisions.[87] One of the simplest and best ways to engage relationship-leadership is to ask open questions and listen attentively.[88]

There are four kinds of relationship-oriented behaviors:

- Consideration
- Empowering leadership
- Ethical leadership
- Servant-leadership

Consideration: "The Concerns and Needs of My Employees Are Highly Important"

Consideration is leader behavior that is concerned with group members' needs and desires and that is directed at creating mutual respect or trust. This is an important type of behavior to use in addition to task leadership because it promotes social interactions and identification with the team and leader. Considerate leader behavior has a moderately strong positive relationship with measures of leadership effectiveness.[89]

The most effective leaders use different blends of task-oriented behavior and consideration when interacting with others. To what extent do you think you do this when interacting with school or work colleagues? You can answer this question by taking Self-Assessment 14.4.

SELF-ASSESSMENT 14.4 CAREER READINESS

Assessing Your Task- and Relationship-Oriented Leader Behavior

The following survey was designed to evaluate your own leader behavior. Please be prepared to answer these questions if your instructor has assigned Self-Assessment 14.4 in Connect.

1. Do you prefer to use task or relationship leadership? Why do you think this is the case?
2. Look at the items for the two lowest scored items for initiating structure and consideration and then identify how you can increase the extent to which you display both types of leadership.
3. What things might you say during an interview to demonstrate that you can be both task and relationship-oriented in your approach toward leading others?

Empowering Leadership: "I Want My Employees to Feel They Have Control over Their Work"

Empowering leadership represents the extent to which a leader creates perceptions of psychological empowerment in others. Psychological empowerment is employees' belief that they have control over their work. Empowering leadership was found to have positive effects on performance, organizational citizenship behavior, and creativity for individuals and teams.[90] Let's see how this process works.

Increasing employee psychological empowerment requires four kinds of behaviors—leading for (1) meaningfulness, (2) self-determination, (3) competence, and (4) progress.

- **Leading for meaningfulness: inspiring and modeling desirable behaviors.** Managers lead for meaningfulness by *inspiring* their employees and *modeling* desired behaviors. Example: Employees may be helped to identify their passions at work by the leader's creating an exciting organizational vision that employees can connect with emotionally. "True leadership," according to Sheryl Sandberg, Facebook's COO, "stems from individuality that is honestly and sometimes imperfectly expressed . . . Leaders should strive for authenticity over perfection."[91]
- **Leading for self-determination: delegating meaningful tasks.** Managers can lead for employee self-determination by *delegating* meaningful tasks to them. Delegation is most effective when managers can truly let go. "Leadership is about making others better as a result of your presence," says Sandberg, "and making sure that impact lasts in your absence."[92]
- **Leading for competence: supporting and coaching employees.** It goes without saying that employees need to have the necessary knowledge to perform their jobs. Accomplishing this goal involves managers' *supporting* and *coaching* their employees. When Sandberg joined Facebook as COO, she stopped at hundreds of employees' desks to introduce herself, letting them know that she was willing to engage with and learn from them. She enjoys asking questions and encouraging debate.[93]
- **Leading for progress: monitoring and rewarding employees.** Sandberg is widely credited with spurring many companies to take a more compassionate view of employees facing difficult family crises such as illness and death. She suffered the sudden loss of her husband in 2015, and in 2017 she challenged companies to improve their stingy policies. "I think we need to do better for the people who work for us, and I think what companies need to understand is that this is not a

trade-off. People should not have to choose between being a great employee and a mother, sister, a wife, a father. But if we invest in people, they invest in us, and this stuff is good for everyone."[94] Managers lead for progress by *monitoring* and *rewarding* others. We discussed how to do this in Chapter 12.

Ethical Leadership: "I Am Ready to Do the Right Thing"

Ethical leadership represents normatively appropriate behavior that focuses on being a moral role model. This includes communicating ethical values to others, rewarding ethical behavior, and treating followers with care and concern.[95]

Ethical leadership is clearly driven by personal factors related to our beliefs and values. It also has a reciprocal relationship with an organization's culture and climate. In other words, an ethical culture and climate promote ethical leadership, and ethical leadership in turn promotes an ethical culture and climate. Such leadership is positively related to employee job satisfaction, organizational commitment, organizational citizenship behavior, motivation, and task performance.[96] It also is negatively associated with job stress, counterproductive work behavior, and intentions to quit.[97] It appears that ethical leadership has many positive benefits.

EXAMPLE Lauren Bush Lauren's Empowering, Values-Driven Leadership at FEED

Lauren Bush Lauren, founder of FEED. ©Eamonn McCormack/Wireimage/Getty Images

Lauren Bush Lauren, or "LBL," witnessed devastating poverty during her travels as an undergraduate student spokesperson for the United Nations World Food Program and decided to make it her life's work to end world hunger.[98] She cofounded FEED to focus on food-deprived, school-aged children across the globe.[99] The company sells bags, T-shirts, and towels, and each item features a stenciled number to indicate how many meals it provides. For example, a consumer's purchase of FEED's original and most popular product, the burlap FEED 1 bag, feeds one school child for one year.[100]

Here are the ways LBL empowers others to accomplish FEED's mission:

1. **Empowering teammates.** LBL credits much of FEED's success to the people on her team. She believes the best way to do business is to find talented people and get out of their way. She says, "The most important thing you can do when starting a business is surround yourself with smart people who know a lot more than you do in certain realms."[101] In FEED's early days, LBL realized the

company was on the verge of bankruptcy due to shipping costs. She met with an accountant at UPS and quickly learned she knew nothing about supply chain management—so she hired the accountant to manage FEED's supply chain.[102]

2. **Empowering consumers.** LBL knows that ending world hunger requires large-scale participation. Feed empowers consumers to be part of the solution by attaching tangible donations to each product they purchase. LBL designed FEED to appeal to Millennials' desire to be involved in meaningful endeavors, saying "What Feed does is give individuals a way to participate in very big, overwhelming world issues in a way that's fun, creative, accessible and easy."[103]
3. **Empowering those in need.** FEED's business model strives to empower everyone in its supply chain, including its manufacturers. The company makes all its products under fair-labor conditions and partners with artisans in food-insecure countries so people in need can earn a living manufacturing FEED's items.[104] FEED also aims to empower the children it serves. LBL describes meeting a little girl in Rwanda who was receiving a free daily meal through FEED. The girl told LBL she wanted to be the first female president of Rwanda.[105] As the company website states, "When a child is given a free, nutritious school lunch, it can break the cycle of poverty she was born into and empower her to change her own life."[106]

LBL believes the best way to succeed in a socially focused enterprise is to combine your passion with a cause you truly care about. She created FEED by blending her love of fashion and design with her passion for ending world hunger.[107] She also notes the importance of choosing partners who share your organization's values; she has turned down opportunities to sell FEED's products in stores whose values didn't align with her own.[108]

FEED has donated more than 100 million meals to date. Says LBL, "I have learned so much about being a leader over the last ten years of starting and growing FEED. I have made many mistakes along the way, but each has been an incredible learning opportunity. And every day, I try to lead from a place where the mission and founding intention behind FEED is my driving force and north star."[109]

YOUR CALL

How is LBL's leadership both ethical and empowering? How do ethics and empowerment combine to make FEED so successful in accomplishing its mission?

Servant-Leadership: "I Want to Serve Others and the Organization, Not Myself" The term *servant leadership*, coined by Robert Greenleaf in 1970, reflects not only his onetime background as a management researcher for AT&T but also his views as a lifelong philosopher and devout Quaker.[110] **Servant-leadership focuses on providing increased service to others—meeting the goals of both followers and the organization—rather than to yourself.** CEOs Mike DeFrino from Kimpton Hotels and Marc Benioff from Salesforce.com are servant leaders (see the Example feature below).

EXAMPLE Servant-Leadership: Leaders Who Work for the Led

Who are some successful servant-leaders?

A Listener First Mike DeFrino defines servant-leadership as "the ability to both serve and lead and to do so without expecting anything back." DeFrino is the CEO of Kimpton Hotels & Restaurants, and because he believes that "most of the intelligence in the organization is much closer to the ground than the corner office," around his employees he is a dedicated listener rather than a talker.[111]

A Representative of All Stakeholders Salesforce chair and CEO Marc Benioff believes CEOs can change the world by serving not only their shareholders but also their employees, business partners, local communities, and the planet. His 1-1-1 philanthropy model harnesses Salesforce's resources to generate social impact. The organization donates 1 percent of its products, equity, and employees' time, and more than 3,000 companies have joined the cause.[112] Benioff says CEOs "have to understand that they represent their stakeholders, all of them. They need to be able to speak and act on behalf of them."[113]

YOUR CALL

Understandably, servant-leadership is popular with employees. How do you think servant-leadership helps these companies to be successful? Do you think there any situations in which servant-leadership would *not* be appropriate?

Servant-leadership is not a quick-fix approach to leadership. Rather, it is a long-term approach to life and work. Ten characteristics of the servant-leader are shown in Table 14.5. You can't go wrong by trying to adopt these characteristics.

TABLE 14.5
Ten Characteristics of the Servant-Leader

1.	Focus on listening
2.	Ability to empathize with others' feelings
3.	Focus on healing suffering
4.	Self-awareness of strengths and weaknesses
5.	Use of persuasion rather than positional authority to influence others
6.	Broad-based conceptual thinking
7.	Ability to foresee future outcomes
8.	Believe they are stewards of their employees and resources
9.	Commitment to the growth of people
10.	Drive to build community within and outside the organization

Source: From L. C. Spears, "Introduction: Servant-Leadership and the Greenleaf Legacy," in L. C. Spears (Ed.), Reflections on Leadership: How Robert K. Greenleaf's Theory of Servant-Leadership Influenced Today's Top Management *(New York: John Wiley & Sons, 1995), pp. 1–14.*

Employees whose manager displays the characteristics shown in Table 14.5 are likely to be happier, more productive, more creative, and more willing to go above and beyond their customary duties.[114] The following self-assessment measures the extent to which you possess a serving orientation. Results from the assessment will enhance your understanding of what it takes to really be a servant-leader, and they provide insight into the career readiness competency of service/others orientation.

SELF-ASSESSMENT 14.5 CAREER READINESS

Assessing Your Servant Orientation

The following survey is designed to assess the extent to which you possess a servant orientation. Please be prepared to answer these questions if your instructor has assigned Self-Assessment 14.5 in Connect.

1. To what extent do you possess a servant orientation? Are you surprised by the results?
2. How might you demonstrate more servant-leadership in your teams at work or school? Be specific.
3. What things might you say during an interview to demonstrate that you possess the career readiness competency of service/others orientation?

Passive Leadership: The Lack of Leadership Skills

Passive leadership is a form of leadership behavior characterized by a lack of leadership skills. For example, in the type of passive leadership called the *management-by-exception* style, managers do not intervene until problems are brought to their attention or until the problems become serious enough to demand action.[115]

Another passive type is **laissez-faire leadership**, **a form of "leadership" characterized by a general failure to take responsibility for leading.** Not taking responsibility can hardly be considered leadership (although it often seems to be manifested by CEOs whose companies get in trouble, as when they say, "I had no idea about the criminal behavior of my subordinates"). Interestingly, laissez-faire ("*lay*-zay fair") leadership is seen more in men than women.[116]

Examples of laissez-faire leadership are seen in various kinds of failure—failing to deal with conflict, to coach employees on difficult assignments, to help set performance goals, to give performance feedback, to deal with bullying, and so on. This passive leadership has a huge negative impact on employee perceptions of leaders—outweighing their *positive* perceptions of contributions by initiating structure, transactional, and consideration forms of leadership.[117]

Passive leadership. Do you really hate to get involved in conflict, like the man looking out the window? Passive leadership like this does not lead to positive outcomes. Have you ever been managed by a passive leader? Were you happy in this situation? ©Digital Vision/ Photodisc/Getty Images

So What Do We Know about the Behavioral Approaches?

Two key conclusions we may take away from the behavioral approaches are the following:

1. **A leader's behavior is more important than his or her traits.** It is important to train managers on the various forms of task and relationship leadership, and to avoid passive leadership.
2. **There is no type of leader behavior that is best suited for all situations.** Effective leaders learn how to match their behavior to the situation at hand. We discuss how to do this in the next section. •

14.4 Situational Approaches: Does Leadership Vary with the Situation?

THE BIG PICTURE

Effective leadership behavior depends on the situation at hand, say believers in two contingency approaches: Fiedler's contingency leadership model and House's path–goal leadership model.

LO 14-4

Describe situational leadership.

Perhaps leadership is not characterized by universally important traits or behaviors. There is no one best style that will work in all situations. This is the point of view of proponents of the **situational approach** (or *contingency approach*) to leadership, who believe that effective leadership behavior depends on the situation at hand. That is, as situations change, different styles become appropriate.

Let's consider two situational approaches: (1) the *contingency leadership model* by Fiedler and (2) the *path-goal leadership model* by House.

1. The Contingency Leadership Model: Fiedler's Approach

The oldest model of the contingency approach to leadership was developed by **Fred Fiedler** and his associates in 1951.[118] The **contingency leadership model** determines if a leader's style is (1) task-oriented or (2) relationship-oriented and if that style is effective for the situation at hand. Fiedler's work was based on 80 studies conducted over 30 years.

Two Leadership Orientations: Tasks versus Relationships Are you task-oriented or relationship-oriented? That is, are you more concerned with task accomplishment or with people?

To find out, you or your employees would fill out a questionnaire (known as the least preferred co-worker, or LPC, scale), in which you think of the co-worker you least enjoyed working with and rate him or her according to an eight-point scale of 16 pairs of opposite characteristics (such as friendly/unfriendly, tense/relaxed, efficient/inefficient). The higher the score, the more the relationship-oriented the respondent; the lower the score, the more task-oriented.

Do you care more about getting things done or having harmonious relationships with others? ©Ingram Publishing

The Three Dimensions of Situational Control Once the leadership orientation is known, then you determine *situational control*–how much control and influence a leader has in the immediate work environment.

There are three dimensions of situational control: *leader-member relations*, *task structure*, and *position power*.

- **Leader-member relations–"Do my subordinates accept me as a leader?"** This dimension, the most important component of situational control, reflects the extent to which a leader has or doesn't have the support, loyalty, and trust of the work group.
- **Task structure–"Do my subordinates perform unambiguous, easily understood tasks?"** This dimension refers to the extent to which tasks are routine, unambiguous, and easily understood. The more structured the jobs, the more influence a leader has.
- **Position power–"Do I have power to reward and punish?"** This dimension refers to how much power a leader has to make work assignments and reward and punish. More power equals more control and influence.

For each dimension, the amount of control can be *high,* in which case the leader's decisions will produce predictable results because he or she has the ability to influence work outcomes. Or it can be *low*, in which case the leader doesn't have that kind of predictability or influence. By combining the three different dimensions with different high/low ratings, we have eight different leadership situations. These are represented in the diagram below. *(See Figure 14.2.)*

FIGURE 14.2 **Representation of Fiedler's contingency model**

Situational Control	High-Control Situations			Moderate-Control Situations				Low-Control Situations
Leader-member relations	Good	Good	Good	Good	Poor	Poor	Poor	Poor
Task structure	High	High	Low	Low	High	High	Low	Low
Position power	Strong	Weak	Strong	Weak	Strong	Weak	Strong	Weak
Situation	1	11	111	1V	V	V1	V11	V111
Optimal Leadership Style	**Task-Motivated Leadership**			**Relationship-Motivated Leadership**				**Task-Motivated Leadership**

Source: Adapted from F. E. Fiedler, "Situational Control and a Dynamic Theory of Leadership," in B. King, S. Streufert, and F. E. Fiedler (Eds.), Managerial Control and Organizational Democracy *(New York: John Wiley & Sons, 1978), p. 114.*

Which Style Is Most Effective? Neither leadership style is effective all the time, Fiedler's research concludes, although each is right in certain situations.

- **When task-oriented style is best.** The task-oriented style works best in either *high-control* or *low-control* situations.

  Example of a *high-control* situation (leader decisions produce predictable results because he or she can influence work outcomes): Suppose you were supervising parking-control officers ticketing cars parked illegally in expired meter zones, bus zones, and the like. You have (1) high leader-member relations because your subordinates are highly supportive of you and (2) high task structure because their jobs are clearly defined. (3) You have high position control because you have complete authority to evaluate their performance and dole out punishment and rewards. Thus, a task-oriented style would be best.

  Example of a *low-control* situation (leader decisions can't produce predictable results because he or she can't really influence outcomes): Suppose you were a high school principal trying to clean up graffiti on your private-school campus, helped only by students you can find after school. You might have (1) low leader-member relations because many people might not see the need for the goal. (2) The task structure might also be low because people might see many different ways to achieve the goal. And (3) your position power would be low because the committee is voluntary and people are free to leave. In this low-control situation, a task-oriented style would also be best.

- **When relationship-oriented style is best.** The relationship-oriented style works best in situations of *moderate control.*

  Example: Suppose you were working in a government job supervising a group of firefighters fighting wildfires. You might have (1) low leader-member relations if you are promoted over others in the group but (2) high task structure, because the job is fairly well defined. (3) You might have low position power, because the rigidity of the civil-service job prohibits you from doing much in the way of rewarding and punishing. Thus, in this moderate-control situation, relationship-oriented leadership would be most effective.

What do you do if your leadership orientation does not match the situation? Then, says Fiedler, it's better to try to move leaders into suitable situations rather than try to alter their personalities to fit the situations.[119] Fiedler does not believe that people can change their basic leadership style.

2. The Path–Goal Leadership Model: House's Approach

A second situational approach, advanced by **Robert House** in the 1970s and revised by him in 1996, is the **path–goal leadership model, which holds that the effective leader makes available to followers desirable rewards in the workplace and increases their motivation by clarifying the *paths*, or behavior, that will help them achieve those *goals* and providing them with support.** A successful leader thus helps followers by tying meaningful rewards to goal accomplishment, reducing barriers, and providing support, so as to increase "the number and kinds of personal payoffs to subordinates for work-goal attainment."[120]

Numerous studies testing various predictions from House's original path-goal theory provided mixed results.[121] As a consequence, he proposed a new model, a graphical version of which is shown below. *(See Figure 14.3.)*

FIGURE 14.3

General representation of House's revised path–goal theory

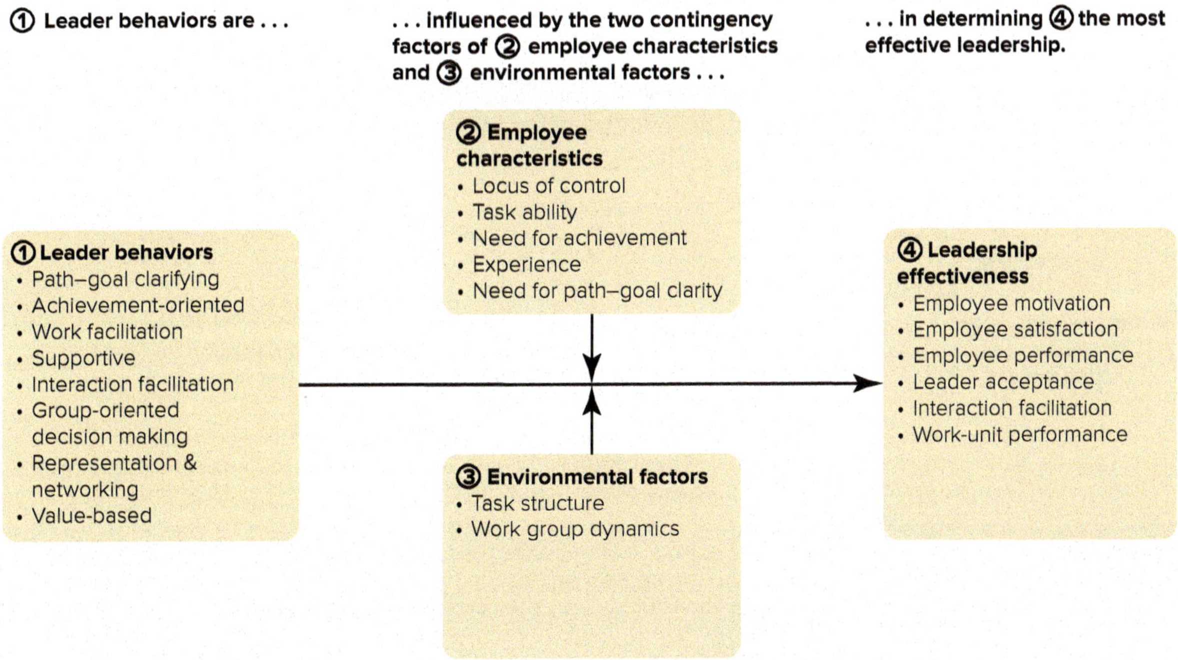

What Determines Leadership Effectiveness: Employee Characteristics and Environmental Factors Affect Leader Behavior Two contingency factors, or variables—*employee characteristics* and *environmental factors*—cause some *leadership behaviors* to be more effective than others.

- **Employee characteristics.** Five employee characteristics are locus of control (described in Chapter 11), task ability, need for achievement, experience, and need for path-goal clarity.
- **Environmental factors.** Two environmental factors are task structure (independent versus interdependent tasks) and work group dynamics.
- **Leader behaviors.** Originally, House proposed that there were four leader behaviors, or leadership styles—*directive* ("Here's what's expected of you and here's how to do it"), *supportive* ("I want things to be pleasant, since everyone's about equal here"), *participative* ("I want your suggestions in order to help me make decisions"), and *achievement-oriented* ("I'm confident you can accomplish the following great things"). The revised theory expands the number of leader behaviors from four to eight. *(See Table 14.6.)*

TABLE 14.6 **Eight Leadership Styles of the Revised Path–Goal Theory**

STYLE OF LEADER BEHAVIORS	DESCRIPTION OF BEHAVIOR TOWARD EMPLOYEES
1. Path–goal clarifying ("Here's what's expected of you and here's how to do it.")	Clarify performance goals. Provide guidance on how employees can complete tasks. Clarify performance standards and expectations. Use positive and negative rewards contingent on performance.
2. Achievement-oriented ("I'm confident you can accomplish the following great things.")	Set challenging goals. Emphasize excellence. Demonstrate confidence in employee abilities.
3. Work facilitation ("Here's the goal, and here's what I can do to help you achieve it.")	Plan, schedule, organize, and coordinate work. Provide mentoring, coaching, counseling, and feedback to assist employees in developing their skills. Eliminate roadblocks. Provide resources. Empower employees to take actions and make decisions.
4. Supportive ("I want things to be pleasant, since everyone's about equal here.")	Treats others as equals. Show concern for well-being and needs. Be friendly and approachable.
5. Interaction facilitation ("Let's see how we can all work together to accomplish our goals.")	Emphasize collaboration and teamwork. Encourage close employee relationships and sharing of minority opinions. Facilitate communication; resolve disputes.
6. Group-oriented decision making ("I want your suggestions in order to help me make decisions.")	Pose problems rather than solutions to work group. Encourage members to participate in decision making. Provide necessary information to the group for analysis. Involve knowledgeable employees in decision making.
7. Representation and networking ("I've got a great bunch of people working for me, whom you'll probably want to meet.")	Present work group in positive light to others. Maintain positive relationships with influential others. Participate in organization-wide social functions and ceremonies. Do unconditional favors for others.
8. Value-based ("We're destined to accomplish great things.")	Establish a vision, display passion for it, and support its accomplishment. Communicate high performance expectations and confidence in others' abilities to meet their goals. Give frequent positive feedback. Demonstrate self-confidence.

Source: Adapted from R. J. House, "Path–Goal Theory of Leadership: Lessons, Legacy, and a Reformulated Theory," Leadership Quarterly, *Autumn 1996, pp. 323–352.*

Coleaders. David Byttow (left) and Chrys Bader are cofounders of San Francisco–based Secret, an app that allows people to share messages anonymously with their friends. Which of the eight path–goal leadership styles would you expect to find dominating this organization? ©David Paul Morris/Bloomberg/Getty Images

Thus, for example, employees with an internal locus of control are more likely to prefer achievement-oriented leadership or group-oriented decision making (formerly participative) leadership because they believe they have control over the work environment. The same is true for employees with high task ability and experience.

Employees with an external locus of control, however, tend to view the environment as uncontrollable, so they prefer the structure provided by supportive or path–goal clarifying (formerly directive) leadership. The same is probably true of inexperienced employees.

Besides expanding the styles of leader behavior from four to eight, House's revision of his theory also puts more emphasis on the need for leaders to foster intrinsic motivation through empowerment. Finally, his revised theory stresses the concept of shared leadership, the idea that employees do not have to be supervisors or managers to engage in leader behavior but rather may share leadership among all employees of the organization.

So What Do We Know about the Situational Approaches?

There have not been enough direct tests of House's revised path–goal theory using appropriate research methods and statistical procedures to draw overall conclusions.[122] Research on transformational leadership, however, which is discussed in Section 14.5, is supportive of the revised model.[123]

Applying situational leadership theory is not easy. In any leadership role, you will encounter many different situations, and there is no one best style for managing all of them. In addition, we all tend to rely on behaviors that have worked for us in the past even if the situation we face suggests we should change. We justify our actions by reasoning that we are doing what we are good at, but in fact we are vulnerable to our own biases about what we think works and what doesn't.

Although further research is needed on the new model, we can offer several important implications for managers:[124]

- **Use more than one leadership style.** Effective leaders possess and use more than one style of leadership. Thus, you are encouraged to study the eight styles offered in path–goal theory so that you can try new leader behaviors when a situation calls for them.
- **Help employees achieve their goals.** Leaders should guide and coach employees in achieving their goals by clarifying the path and removing obstacles to accomplishing them. Effective coaching was found to increase employees' performance.[125]
- **Managers need to alter their leadership behavior for each situation.** A small set of employee characteristics (ability, experience, and need for independence) and environmental factors (task characteristics of autonomy, variety, and significance) are relevant contingency factors, and managers should modify their leadership style to fit them. The career readiness competencies of emotional and social intelligence are helpful tools for doing so.
- **Provide what people and teams need to succeed.** View your role as providing others with whatever they need to achieve their goals. For some it could be encouragement, and for others it could be direction and coaching. ●

PRACTICAL ACTION Applying Situational Theories

How can you make situational theories work for you? A team of researchers proposed a general strategy managers can use across a variety of situations. It has five steps.[126] We explain how to implement the steps by using the examples of a head coach of a sports team and a sales manager.

- **Step 1: Identify important outcomes.** Managers must first identify the goals they want to achieve. For example, the head coach may have games to win or avoiding injury to key players, whereas a sales manager's goal might be to increase sales by 10 percent or reduce customers' complaints by half.
- **Step 2: Identify relevant leadership behaviors.** Next managers need to identify the specific types of behaviors that may be appropriate for the situation at hand. The list in Table 14.6 is a good starting point. A head coach in a championship game, for instance, might focus on achievement-oriented and work-facilitation behaviors. In contrast, a sales manager might find path-goal–clarifying, work-facilitation, and supportive behaviors more relevant for the sales team. Don't try to use all available leadership behaviors. Rather, select the one or two that appear most helpful.
- **Step 3: Identify situational conditions.** Fiedler and House both identify a set of potential contingency factors to consider, but there may be other practical considerations. For example, a star quarterback on a football team may be injured, which might require the team to adopt a different strategy for winning the game. Similarly, the need to manage a virtual sales team with members from around the world will affect the types of leadership most effective in this context.
- **Step 4: Match leadership to the conditions at hand.** There are too many possible situational conditions for us to provide specific advice. This means you should use your knowledge about management and employee behavior to find the best match between your leadership styles and behaviors and the situation at hand. The coach whose star quarterback is injured might use supportive and values-based behaviors to instill confidence that the team can win with a different quarterback. Our sales manager also might find it useful to use the empowering leadership associated with work-facilitation behaviors and avoid directive leadership.
- **Step 5: Decide how to make the match.** Managers can use guidelines from either contingency theory or path-goal theory: change the person in the leadership role or change his or her behavior. It is not possible to change the head coach in a championship game. This means the head coach needs to change his or her style or behavior to meet the specific challenge. In contrast, the organization employing the sales manager might move him or her to another position because the individual is too directive and does not like to empower others. Or the sales manager could change his or her behavior, if possible.

14.5 The Uses of Transformational Leadership

THE BIG PICTURE

Four key behaviors of transformational leaders in affecting employees are they inspire motivation, inspire trust, encourage excellence, and stimulate them intellectually.

LO 14-5

Describe transformational leadership and its effects on employees.

We have considered the major traditional approaches to understanding leadership—the trait, behavioral, and situational approaches. But newer approaches seem to offer something more by trying to determine what factors inspire and motivate people to perform beyond their normal levels.

One recent approach proposed by **Bernard Bass and Bruce Avolio,** known as **full-range leadership**, suggests that leadership behavior varies along a full range of leadership styles, from passive (*laissez-faire*) "leadership" at one extreme, through transactional leadership, to transformational leadership at the other extreme.[127] As we stated, passive leadership is not leadership, but transactional and transformational leadership behaviors are both positive aspects of being a good leader.[128] We considered transactional leadership in Section 14.3. Here let's consider transformational leadership.

Transformational Leaders

Transformational leadership transforms employees to pursue organizational goals over self-interests. Transformational leaders, in one description, "engender trust, seek to develop leadership in others, exhibit self-sacrifice, and serve as moral agents, focusing themselves and followers on objectives that transcend the more immediate needs of the work group."[129] Whereas transactional leaders try to get people to do *ordinary* things, transformational leaders encourage their people to do *exceptional* things—significantly higher levels of intrinsic motivation, trust, commitment, and loyalty—that can produce significant organizational change and results.

Transformational leaders are influenced by two factors:

- **Individual characteristics.** The personalities of such leaders tend to be more extroverted, agreeable, proactive, and open to change than nontransformational leaders. (Female leaders tend to use transformational leadership more than male leaders do.)[130]
- **Organizational culture.** Adaptive, flexible organizational cultures are more likely than are rigid, bureaucratic cultures to foster transformational leadership.

The Best Leaders Are Both Transactional and Transformational

It's important to note that transactional leadership is an essential *prerequisite* to effective leadership, and the best leaders learn to display both transactional and transformational styles of leadership to some degree. Indeed, research suggests that transformational leadership leads to superior performance when it "augments," or adds to, transactional leadership.[131]

EXAMPLE The Superior Performance of Both a Transactional and Transformational Leader: PepsiCo's Former CEO, Indra Nooyi

PepsiCo's Indra Nooyi, the company's first female CEO, ranks number two on *Fortune*'s 2017 most powerful women list.[132] She uses a mix of transactional and transformational leadership.

An Early Lesson in Task Performance As a young girl growing up in India, Nooyi competed against her sister every day as their mother asked them each to imagine herself a different world leader, deliver a campaign speech, and then wait to see which had won her mother's "vote." This "incredibly formative experience" taught Nooyi that she could become anything she wanted to be.[133]

Long Term: Healthier Food Nooyi's vision of "Performance with Purpose" sent the company on a decade-long path of developing healthier products.[134] Starbucks CEO Howard Schultz described her as "way ahead of her competitors," with health-conscious moves such as buying Tropicana and Quaker Oats and removing trans fats from PepsiCo's products.[135] Nooyi doubled down on her vision by establishing PepsiCo's goals to further reduce sugar, salt, and saturated fat by 2025 and to improve water efficiency and reduce greenhouse gas emissions in the company's production processes.[136]

Short Term: Stay Profitable In addition to using transformational leadership in pursuit of "Performance with Purpose," Nooyi uses transactional leadership to maximize short-term profits and shareholder value. PepsiCo has seen soda sales, stock, and profits fluctuate, and Nooyi has fielded criticism for what some have called "feel-good nonsense." But recent data shows that PepsiCo has outperformed its quarterly expectations consistently since 2016. Nooyi said, "I have the results to show for long term management and the scars to show for short term management," adding that companies should recognize that "investments in future impact, community, employees, and customers result in sustainable, impressive growth that trumps the often fleeting or unstable results that come with solely chasing short-term performance."[137]

YOUR CALL

What unique individual characteristics are displayed by Nooyi? What other types of leader behavior has she exhibited?

Four Key Behaviors of Transformational Leaders

Whereas transactional leaders are dispassionate, transformational leaders excite passion, inspiring and empowering people to look beyond their own interests to the interests of the organization. They appeal to their followers' self-concepts—their values and personal identity—to create changes in their goals, values, needs, beliefs, and aspirations.

Transformational leaders have four key kinds of behavior that affect followers.[138]

1. Inspirational Motivation: "Let Me Share a Vision That Transcends Us All"

Transformational leaders have **charisma** (**"kar-*riz*-muh"), a form of interpersonal attraction that inspires acceptance and support.** At one time, **charismatic leadership—which was assumed to be an individual inspirational and motivational characteristic of particular leaders,** much like other trait-theory characteristics—was viewed as a category of its own, but now it is considered part of transformational leadership.[139] Someone with charisma, then, is more able to persuade and influence people and to make others feel comfortable and at ease than someone without charisma.[140]

A transformational leader inspires motivation by offering an agenda, a grand design, an ultimate goal—in short, a *vision,* "a realistic, credible, attractive future" for the organization, as leadership expert Burt Nanus calls it.[141] John Hennessy, former president of Stanford University and current chair of Google's parent company Alphabet, believes that inspirational motivation is a critical skill for effective leadership. He concluded that "'The ability to tell appropriate, compelling and inspiring stories,' is essential. Describing work as a journey shared among colleagues helps bring employees together in a common cause."[142]

Examples: Civil rights leader Martin Luther King Jr. had a vision—a "dream," as he put it—of racial equality. Candy Lightner, founder of Mothers Against Drunk Driving, had a vision of getting rid of alcohol-related car crashes. Apple Computer's

Steve Jobs had a vision of developing an "insanely great" desktop computer. To recruit John Scully, who was CEO of Pepsi at the time, Jobs asked, "Do you want to sell sugared water the rest of your life, or do you want a chance to change the world?"[143]

2. Idealized Influence: "We Are Here to Do the Right Thing" Transformational leaders are able to inspire trust in their followers because they express their integrity by being consistent, single-minded, and persistent in pursuit of their goal. Not only do they display high ethical standards and act as models of desirable values, but they are also able to make sacrifices for the greater good.

Martin Luther King Jr. Civil rights leader Martin Luther King was an inspiration to millions of people. Here he is addressing people during the March on Washington at the Lincoln Memorial. This is where he gave his famous "I Have a Dream" speech. Do you think charismatic business leaders like King are able to be more successful than more conventional and conservative managers? ©Agence France Presse/Central Press/Getty Images

Example: Dr. Donald Hopkins, a physician at the Carter Center in Atlanta, GA, has devoted his life to improving public health, beginning with his efforts as a young man to help eradicate smallpox from the world. Now 76, Hopkins is still fighting to eliminate Guinea worm disease, a debilitating but preventable illness that lingers in only two countries, Chad and Ethiopia. His work to educate and motivate not only local communities but also world leaders has improved and saved the lives of countless people. Former president Jimmy Carter considers him a hero.[144]

3. Individualized Consideration: "You Have the Opportunity Here to Grow and Excel" Transformational leaders don't just express concern for subordinates' well-being. They actively encourage them to grow and to excel by giving them challenging work, more responsibility, empowerment, and one-on-one mentoring.

Example: Meg Whitman, former CEO of HP, decided to reduce barriers between herself and employees. Shortly after taking over for Mark Hurd, "she peeled off the smoke-tinted window film that shielded the C-suite from view and tore down fencing around the executive parking lot. As someone who never had a corner office—or any office-at eBay, she moved everyone to cubicles and plunked down in one herself. Getting staff to open up was like pulling teeth," Whitman said.[145]

The "I'm Glad..." feature describes how Josh Margulies used individualized consideration to influence a team of marketing employees.

I'm glad...

...I understood the value of using individualized consideration.

Josh Margulies worked as a director of marketing and product marketing for a health care company. He used strong influence tactics to convince the company to change its brand.

Courtesy Josh Margulies

The company was a start-up that had been running for three years with the brand developed by the company's founders. "The brand looked unpolished," said Josh. "My goal was to take the company through an entire brand revision, to reshape the brand identity for everything from the logo to colors and fonts."

Josh was new to the staff of about eight employees when he took on this rebranding project. "All the people there were founders who were very partial to their brand, so it was a huge task to get them to see the value of taking it to the next level and getting them to understand why the things they were doing with the current brand were incorrect," said Josh.

One of the first things Josh wanted to change was the logo, which was red. Josh felt red was an inappropriate color for a health care company. The color was all over the company's website, including the navigation buttons, which was a problem since red is a color associated with stopping, not going.

Josh sat down with the team and went through every aspect of the brand to understand what they had intended when they originally created it and what they wanted to convey with the new look. It was a challenging process.

"The brand was their baby. They had founded it and created it. Everything they had done had been from the heart and very personal. I couldn't just go in and tell them their logo was trash. I had to show understanding and empathy to prove that I understood the passion for their brand and why it was so important to them," said Josh. He paired his empathy and understanding with expertise in building brands in order to influence the founders of the company to make a change.

"Through focus groups and one-on-one meetings, they understood that what they thought they were showing with their brand was not truly what they were showing. They were more open to making these changes once they realized the perceived message and value that they were sharing as opposed to the actual message that was coming across," said Josh.

The new, more professional brand gave the founders the confidence they needed to raise money and eventually sell their business.

Courtesy of Josh Margulies

4. Intellectual Stimulation: "Let Me Describe the Great Challenges We Can Conquer Together" Transformational leaders are gifted at communicating the organization's strengths, weaknesses, opportunities, and threats so that subordinates develop a new sense of purpose. Employees become less apt to view problems as insurmountable or "that's not my department." Instead they learn to view them as personal challenges that they are responsible for overcoming, to question the status quo, and to seek creative solutions.

Example: John Mackey is CEO and cofounder of Whole Foods, and a founder of the Conscious Capitalism movement, dedicated to "doing business with purpose."[146] He feels the organic food industry hasn't gone far enough to address social issues like responsible use of water and energy and fair labor standards for migrant workers. So he instituted a rating system to measure such practices, believing Whole Foods should play a role in pointing out and correcting gaps. Organic farmers protested the new system, calling it expensive and burdensome, but Mackey made only a few changes to it. "I am absolutely a contrarian," he said of his decision. "You need dissonance, and you need someone who is challenging things. Otherwise you get stuck."[147]

Have you worked for a transformational leader? The following self-assessment measures the extent to which a current or former manager used transformational leadership. Taking the assessment provides a good idea about the specific behaviors you need to exhibit if you want to lead in a transformational manner.

SELF-ASSESSMENT 14.6

Assessing Your Boss's Transformational Leadership

Please be prepared to answer these questions if your instructor has assigned Self-Assessment 14.6 in Connect.

1. What could your manager have done to be more transformational?
2. What three behaviors can you exhibit to increase your application of transformational leadership?

So What Do We Know about Transformational Leadership?

It works! Research shows that transformational leadership is associated with many positive outcomes such as increased organizational, team, and individual performance; job satisfaction; employee identification with their leaders and with their immediate work groups; employee engagement; and intrinsic motivation.[148]

There are three practical applications of transformational leadership.

1. It Can Be Used to Train Employees at Any Level. Not just top managers but employees at any level can be trained to be more transactional and transformational.[149] It is best to couple this training with developmental coaching and job challenges.[150]

2. You Can Prepare and Practice Being Transformational The simplest way to practice is to write down ideas for exhibiting the four key behaviors of transformational leadership–inspirational motivation, idealized influence, individualized consideration, and intellectual stimulation–the next time you attend a team meeting at school or work. For example, you might inspire your teammates by highlighting the benefits of doing a good job, by building the team's confidence in their ability to complete the assignment, and by telling the team you believe in them. You can drive idealized influence by explaining your role or commitment to working on the assignment and modeling high-performance behaviors. Show individualized consideration by describing the resources and support available to the team, by demonstrating a supportive attitude to everyone, and by recognizing people for their accomplishments. Finally, describing the team's challenges, explaining the tasks or goals everyone needs to achieve, and highlighting why successfully completing the assignment will help the team can foster intellectual stimulation.

3. It Should be Used for Ethical Reasons While ethical transformational leaders enable employees to enhance their self-concepts, unethical ones select or produce obedient, dependent, and compliant followers.

To better ensure positive results from transformational leadership, top managers should follow the practices shown below. *(See Table 14.7.)* ●

TABLE 14.7

The Ethical Things Top Managers Should Do to Be Effective Transformational Leaders

• **Employ a code of ethics.** The company should create and enforce a clearly stated code of ethics.
• **Choose the right people.** Recruit, select, and promote people who display ethical behavior.
• **Make performance expectations reflect employee treatment.** Develop performance expectations around the treatment of employees; these expectations can be assessed in the performance-appraisal process.
• **Demonstrate commitment to diversity.** Train employees to value diversity.
• **Reward high moral conduct.** Identify, reward, and publicly praise employees who exemplify high moral conduct.

Source: These recommendations were derived from J. M. Howell and B. J. Avolio, "The Ethics of Charismatic Leadership: Submission or Liberation?" The Executive, *May 1992, pp. 43–54.*

14.6 Three Additional Perspectives

THE BIG PICTURE

Two other kinds of leadership are the *leader–member exchange model*, which emphasizes that leaders have different sorts of relationships with different subordinates, and *leading with humility*, grounded in the belief that something exists that is greater than ourselves. A third perspective is the role of followers in the leadership process.

LO 14-6

Compare three additional perspectives on leadership.

Two additional kinds of leadership deserve discussion: (1) the *leader-member exchange (LMX) model of leadership* and (2) *leading with humility.*

Leader–Member Exchange Leadership: Having Different Relationships with Different Subordinates

Proposed by **George Graen** and **Fred Dansereau,** the **leader–member exchange (LMX) model of leadership emphasizes that leaders have different sorts of relationships with different subordinates.**[151] Unlike other models we've described, which focus on the behaviors or traits of leaders or followers, the LMX model looks at the *quality* of relationships between managers and subordinates. Also, unlike other models, which presuppose stable relationships between leaders and followers, the LMX model assumes each manager-subordinate relationship is unique. This model is one of the most researched approaches to studying leadership, and it has significant practical implications for managers and employees.

In-Group Exchange versus Out-Group Exchange

The unique relationship, which supposedly results from the leader's attempt to delegate and assign work roles, can produce two types of leader-member exchange interactions.[152]

- **In-group exchange: trust and respect.** In the *in-group exchange*, the relationship between leader and follower becomes a partnership characterized by mutual trust, respect and liking, and a sense of common fates. Subordinates may receive special assignments and special privileges.
- **Out-group exchange: lack of trust and respect.** In the *out-group exchange*, leaders are characterized as overseers who fail to create a sense of mutual trust, respect, or common fate. Subordinates receive less of the manager's time and attention than those in in-group exchange relationships.

What type of exchange do you have with your manager? The quality of the relationship between you and your boss matters. Not only does it predict your job satisfaction and happiness, but it also is related to turnover. You can assess the quality of the relationship with a current or former boss by completing Self-Assessment 14.7.

SELF-ASSESSMENT 14.7

Assessing Your Leader–Member Exchange

The following survey was designed to assess the quality of your leader–member exchange. Please be prepared to answer these questions if your instructor has assigned Self-Assessment 14.7 in Connect.

1. Where do you stand on the different dimensions underlying leader–member exchange? Are you surprised by the results?
2. Do you think the quality of your leader–member exchange is impacting your job satisfaction or performance? Explain.
3. Based on your survey scores, how might you improve the quality of your relationship with your boss? Be specific.

Is the LMX Model Useful? Yes! Consider that a high LMX is associated with individual-level behavioral outcomes like task performance, turnover, organizational citizenship, counterproductive behavior, and attitudinal outcomes such as organizational commitment, job satisfaction, and justice.[153] More importantly, a recent study showed that task, relationship, and transformational leadership all have their positive effects on employees via their immediate impact on the quality of an LMX. This led a team of researchers to conclude that "If leaders want to serve as a catalyst for high levels of follower performance, our results suggest that they need to focus on one particular follower perception."[154] This is important because it tells us that "the effectiveness of any given leadership behavior is likely to be influenced by the followers' perceptions of their relationship with their leader, such that followers with good relationships with their leader will respond more positively in terms of performance to a given leadership behavior, compared to followers with poor relationship with their leader."[155]

The key takeaway for you is to take ownership of bad relationships with bosses. You should not expect your boss to change if you have a poor relationship. This is exactly what Mary Wright experienced with her boss (see the "I wish ..." feature below). You should change your behavior toward your boss instead, and then your boss may reciprocate. One expert suggested two generic practices: First, "It pays to figure out what motivates your boss . . . find ways to help her talk about her successes." Second, for bosses who like control, give "lots of information about what you're doing and offer choices about next steps so he can make the decision."[156]

I Wish...

...I had known about the impact of a poor LMX: I do now!

Mary Wright worked as a process engineer in an automotive facility under a plant manager who elicited fear rather than respect from his subordinates.

Courtesy Mary Wright

The manager would degrade employees in front of their peers, even going so far as to call some employees unkind names. "It makes you lose the drive and joy for your job," said Mary.

The manager had a negative attitude about everything, and he did not foster collaboration. "He always said 'Figure it out and tell me what the problem is.' He was just looking for someone to blame. He didn't want us to collaborate or work together to solve problems," said Mary.

"The company had expectations of quality products and a certain amount of scraps. We had these milestones that we were trying to meet, and when we failed to meet them we had to figure out who messed up. That was the mentality all the time—not 'What is the problem and how can we fix it?' but 'Who messed up?' and 'We better change this so it doesn't happen again,'" said Mary.

The manager did not listen to his subordinates' opinions or ideas, either. He exerted his authority and expected his subordinates to do what he told them to, with no questions asked.

Most employees felt they did not have the authority to challenge the manager, so they kept their heads down and did their work without confronting him. Some employees tried to speak up at meetings, but it only caused fighting and tension.

Mary believes an attitude shift from the manager would have been enough to elicit respect rather than fear from his employees.

"Instead of being negative, he could have said, 'Okay, this happened. I understand that this is money that is wasted and product that we can't sell, but let's work together as a team and figure this out.' Instead of having such a negative attitude about it, using a positive spin to encourage us to work together and try to fix it would have really helped," said Mary.

"Looking back, I think this was one of the greatest learning experiences I've had in my career because it really taught me that 90 percent of finding a new job is finding a good boss," said Mary.

Courtesy of Mary Wright

The Power of Humility

Humility is a relatively stable trait grounded in the belief that "something greater than the self exists."[157] Although some think it is a sign of weakness or low self-esteem, nothing could be further from the truth.

Satya Nadella. The CEO of Microsoft is one of *Time* magazine's most influential people of 2018 and the author of a new book about his so-far successful plans for reviving the giant tech company's fortunes. But he told Microsoft's outgoing CEO Steve Ballmer that he would accept the top position "only if you want me to." Nadella brings to the job what one writer calls "a different style, a different humility." Bill Gates called him "humble, forward-looking and pragmatic." Says Nadella himself, "I think empathy is everything."[158]
©Chesnot/Getty Images News/ Getty Images

Humble leaders tend to display five key qualities valued by employees: high self-awareness, openness to feedback, appreciation of others, low self-focus, and appreciation of the greater good.[159] Lazlo Bock, Google's former senior vice president of people operations, said humility is one of the traits he's looking for in new hires. He concluded that "it is not just humility in creating space for others to contribute, it's intellectual humility. Without humility, you are unable to learn."[160]

Although the scientific study of humility is relatively new, it has shown proven benefits for this trait. One recent study of about 100 small to medium U.S. tech companies found that those with humble CEOs also had more collaborative top managers who were readier to share information with others. Another study of 161 teams found that humility is actually contagious. Employees who were more open to advice and feedback and more willing to own up to mistakes turned out to have humble leaders.[161] Another study, however, examined 72 works teams and more than 350 individual employees from 11 tech companies in China over a three-month period. The researchers found that followers were likely to adopt the behaviors of a humble leader only in situations of low power distance. That is, when power distance was relatively high and followers expected their leaders to show dominance, they mistrusted humble leaders and did not feel psychologically safe about expressing their opinions or taking risks.[162]

What can we conclude about humility in the context of managing others? First, try to be more humble by changing the focus of your accomplishment from "me" to "we." Share credit with others, but by all means be authentic. Don't try to fake humility.[163] Second, try to spend more time asking questions and less time talking about yourself or telling people what to do.[164] Third, an organization's culture can promote humility. Employee-owned construction company TDIndustries does so with its agreed-upon set of cultural norms: "No rank in the room, everyone participates—no one dominates, and listen as an ally." Employees also strive to be on a first-name basis with everyone.[165]

Followers: What Do They Want, How Can They Help?

Is the quality of leadership dependent on the qualities of the followers being led? So it seems. Leaders and followers need each other, and the quality of the relationship determines how we behave as followers.[166]

What Do Followers Want in Their Leaders? Research shows that followers seek and admire leaders who create feelings of

- **Significance.** Such leaders make followers feel that what they do at work is important and meaningful.
- **Community.** These leaders create a sense of unity that encourages followers to treat others with respect and to work together in pursuit of organizational goals.
- **Excitement.** The leaders make people feel energetic and engaged at work.[167]

What Do Leaders Want in Their Followers? Followers vary, of course, in their level of compliance with a leader, with *helpers* (most compliant) showing deference to their leaders, *independents* (less compliant) distancing themselves, and *rebels* (least compliant) showing divergence.[168]

Leaders clearly benefit from having helpers (and, to some extent, independents). They want followers who are productive, reliable, honest, cooperative, proactive, and flexible. They do not want followers who are reluctant to take the lead on projects, fail to generate ideas, are unwilling to collaborate, withhold information, provide inaccurate feedback, or hide the truth.[169]

We give some suggestions on how to be a better follower–and enhance your own career prospects–in the following Practical Action box. •

PRACTICAL ACTION How to Be a Good Leader by Being a Good Follower

Changing business culture and the increasing power of technology have shifted the relationship between leaders and followers. Good followers today don't simply follow. They are empowered to let leaders know when things are going in the wrong direction.

Here's how you can become an intelligent follower. These same skills can make you a good leader, too.[170]

1. **Understand what motivates people.** Learn about what co-workers, customers, and bosses want, and what drives them to do their best work (or to prevent others from working well). It sounds obvious, but don't overlook the value of asking your boss how you can best communicate with each other and how often.
2. **Choose your battles.** You can't win at everything, but you can choose where to invest your time and energy. Learn how to get along with co-workers, subordinates, and bosses who are similar to you as well as with those who are different.
3. **Be brave.** Don't be afraid to tell your boss—diplomatically—when you think he or she may be wrong and to offer intelligent alternatives. Helpful feedback is always valuable, and remember to be supportive when things are going well.
4. **Work collaboratively.** Being a good team player, meeting your goals, and letting the team take credit when appropriate can go a long way toward bringing out the best in others, including your boss when you are in a follower role. Also keep your boss informed; no one likes being caught by surprise.
5. **Think critically.** Develop your ability to ask the right questions, raise intelligent challenges, and maintain your own competence and motivation.

YOUR CALL

Although it's always in your and the leader's best interest if you become a good follower, sometimes the two of you may differ so completely in habits, dislikes, and so on that you may simply have to look for opportunities outside your present work situation. Do you think you've been a good follower in past jobs?

14.7 Career Corner: Managing Your Career Readiness

LO 14-7

Explain how to develop the career readiness competency of self-awareness.

This chapter demonstrated that leadership is a concept with much breadth and depth. You learned that it affects all aspects of organizational effectiveness, thus requiring the combined use of 14 career readiness competencies from the model shown below: understanding the business, critical thinking/problem solving, oral/written communication, leadership, social intelligence, networking, emotional intelligence, self-motivation, professionalism/work ethic, personal adaptability, self-awareness, service/others orientation, openness to change, and generalized self-efficacy. *(See Figure 14.4.)*

FIGURE 14.4

Model of career readiness

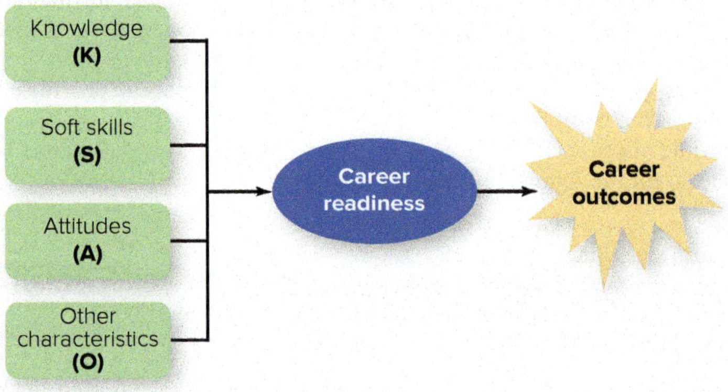

We obviously can't discuss here how to develop all these competencies. To make this section more manageable we focus on the critically important competency of *self-awareness.*

Becoming More Self-Aware

Developing self-awareness is not just an intellectual exercise. It entails understanding who you are and what you stand for. It requires thinking about your life vision, values, personality, needs, behavioral tendencies, and social skills. One expert summarized the power of self-awareness by concluding that it provides "the ability to lead with a sense of purpose, authenticity, openness, and trust. It explains our successes and our failures. And by giving us a better understanding of who we are, self-awareness lets us better understand what we need most from other people, to complement our own deficiencies in leadership."[171] You can become more self-aware by taking the following actions:

1. **Take the time to reflect.** Most of us are so busy accomplishing our daily activities or short-term goals that we leave ourselves no time to reflect and learn. This pattern gets tasks done but can prevent our learning the new skills needed for more difficult assignments or promotions. However, it's the people who are motivated to learn and change who are more likely to be noticed for promotions and leadership roles.[172] You can build intentional reflection into your life by considering the following questions on a regular basis:

   - What happened?
   - What did I learn in general?
   - What did I learn about me?
   - What will I do to improve in the future?[173]

Try recording your answers in a journal. Research shows that this practice will increase your critical thinking and self-reflection.[174] You need to choose the frequency of journaling, but once a week is a minimum. Your author Angelo Kinicki has his students journal on a daily basis and then submit a weekly summary. Students find it invaluable.

2. **Write down your priorities.** All good leaders identify what must get done and then allocate time and resources to get those goals accomplished. Self-awareness begins with identifying your top priorities for the next day, week, month, and year. The clarity you can gain from this practice enables you to target your efforts and resources on things that truly matter. It also helps you make decisions that support important goals while minimizing time spent on activities that are not consistent with your primary interests.[175]
3. **Learn your strengths and weaknesses.** Completing self-assessments like the ones featured in this textbook and studying the feedback is a good first step. Because self-assessments can be positively biased, you should also ask family, friends, colleagues, and mentors for feedback. They observe you on a regular basis and can be a good source of information, especially when you let them know it's safe to give you really honest feedback. If there is a particular behavior you really want to change, ask a trusted person to let you know every time you exhibit it.
4. **Avoid the Dunning-Kruger effect.** Consider the following statements: "If I was just intelligent, I'd be okay. But I am fiercely intelligent, which most people find very threatening" (actress Sharon Stone). "People the world over recognize me as a great spiritual leader" (actor Steven Seagal). Most overly gifted people do not go around boasting like this. You never heard Albert Einstein, for example, tell people that he was "fiercely intelligent."

The **Dunning-Kruger effect** was developed by two psychology professors–Dr. David Dunning and Dr. Justin Kruger. It is **"a cognitive bias whereby people who are incompetent at something are unable to recognize their own incompetence. And not only do they fail to recognize their incompetence, they're also likely to feel confident that they actually are competent."** Consider this effect in light of results from an online quiz asking 10,000 people how they react to constructive criticism. Only 39 percent said they deal with constructive criticism by considering the cause of that feedback. It's possible that the other 61 percent are caught up in the Dunning-Kruger effect.

The point is that this bias will detract from your ability to recognize your weaknesses, which then prevents you from correcting them. Seeking regular feedback and focusing on a proactive learning orientation are two ways to overcome the Dunning-Kruger effect.[176] At Microsoft, for example, CEO Satya Nadella "and his senior leadership team are adamant that the company's ultimate success depends on how well every employee embraces what they have dubbed a 'learning mindset,' one that demands more listening than talking."[177] Sounds like Dunning-Kruger better run for cover at Microsoft! ●

Key Terms Used in This Chapter

behavioral leadership approaches 550
charisma 564
charismatic leadership 564
coercive power 539
consideration 551
contingency leadership model 557
Dunning-Kruger effect 573
empowering leadership 552
ethical leadership 553
expert power 539
full-range leadership 563
global mind-set 549
influence tactics 540
initiating-structure leadership 551
laissez-faire leadership 556
leader–member exchange (LMX) model of leadership 568
leadership 536
leadership coaching 536
legitimate power 539
Machiavellianism 545
managerial leadership 537
narcissism 545
passive leadership 555
path–goal leadership model 559
personalized power 539
power 538
psychological empowerment 552
psychopathy 545
referent power 539
relationship-oriented leadership 551
reward power 539
servant-leadership 554
situational approach 557
socialized power 539
task-oriented leadership behaviors 550
trait approaches to leadership 544
transactional leadership 551
transformational leadership 563

Key Points

14.1 The Nature of Leadership: The Role of Power and Influence

- Leadership is the ability to influence employees to voluntarily pursue organizational goals. Power is the ability to marshal human, informational, and other resources to get something done.
- To understand leadership, we must understand authority and power. Authority is the right to perform or command; it comes with the manager's job. People may pursue personalized power, power directed at helping oneself, or, better, they may pursue socialized power, power directed at helping others.
- Within an organization there are typically five sources of power leaders may draw on; all managers have the first three. (1) Legitimate power is power that results from managers' formal positions within the organization. (2) Reward power is power that results from managers' authority to reward their subordinates. (3) Coercive power results from managers' authority to punish their subordinates. (4) Expert power is power resulting from one's specialized information or expertise. (5) Referent power is power deriving from one's personal attraction.
- There are nine influence tactics for trying to get others to do something you want, ranging from most used to least used tactics as follows: rational persuasion, inspirational appeals, consultation, ingratiating tactics, personal appeals, exchange tactics, coalition tactics, pressure tactics, and legitimating tactics.
- Four principal approaches or perspectives on leadership, as discussed in the rest of the chapter, are (1) trait, (2) behavioral, (3) situational, and (4) transformational.

14.2 Trait Approaches: Do Leaders Have Distinctive Traits and Personal Characteristics?

- Trait approaches to leadership attempt to identify distinctive characteristics that account for the effectiveness of leaders.
- Four positive task-oriented traits are (1) intelligence, (2) consciousness, (3) openness to experience, and (4) emotional stability. These traits in turn can be expanded into a list of both positive and negative interpersonal attributes often found in leaders. Among the positive attributes are extraversion, agreeableness, and communication skills. Among the negative attributes are narcissism, Machiavellianism, and psychopathy.
- Women occupy a growing but still very small number of CEO and top-management positions in the United States. Men have been observed to display more task leadership and women more relationship leadership. Women used a more democratic or participative style than men, and female leadership was associated with more communication, openness, and sociability. Peers, managers, direct reports, and judges/trained observers rated women executives as more effective than men. Social forces still hinder women's progress in attaining leadership roles.

14.3 Behavioral Approaches: Do Leaders Show Distinctive Patterns of Behavior?

- Behavioral leadership approaches try to determine the unique behaviors displayed by effective leaders. Three categories are task-oriented behavior, relationship-oriented behavior, and transformational behavior (discussed in Section 14.5).

- Task-oriented behaviors are those that ensure that people, equipment, and other resources are used in an efficient way to accomplish the mission of a group or organization. Two types of task-oriented behaviors are (1) initiating-structure leadership, leader behavior that organizes and defines what employers should be doing to maximize output, and (2) transactional leadership, which focuses on clarifying employees' roles and task requirements and providing rewards and punishments contingent on performance.
- Relationship-oriented leadership is primarily concerned with the leader's interaction with his or her people. There are four kinds of relationship-oriented behaviors: (1) consideration, (2) empowering leadership, (3) ethical leadership, and (4) servant-leadership.
- Consideration is leader behavior that is concerned with group members' needs and desires and that is directed at creating mutual respect or trust.
- Empowering leadership represents the extent to which a leader creates perceptions of psychological empowerment in others. Psychological empowerment is employees' belief that they have control over their work. Increasing employee psychological empowerment requires four kinds of behaviors—leading for (1) meaningfulness, (2) self-determination, (3) competence, and (4) progress. Leading for meaningfulness is inspiring and modeling desirable behaviors. Leading for self-determination is delegating meaningful tasks. Leading for competence is supporting and coaching employees. Leading for progress is monitoring and rewarding employees. One technique used to empower employees is participative management, the process of involving employees in setting goals, making decisions, solving problems, and making changes in the organization.
- Ethical leadership represents normatively appropriate behavior that focuses on being a moral role model. This includes communicating ethical values to others, rewarding ethical behavior, and treating followers with care and concern.
- Servant-leadership focuses on providing increased service to others—meeting the goals of both followers and the organization—rather than to oneself.
- Passive leadership is a form of leadership behavior characterized by a lack of leadership skills. One type of passive leadership is laissez-faire leadership, a form of "leadership" characterized by a general failure to take responsibility for leading.
- Two conclusions that can be drawn from behavioral approaches are that (1) a leader's behavior is more important than his or her traits and (2) there is no one best style of leadership.

14.4 Situational Approaches: Does Leadership Vary with the Situation?

- Proponents of the situational approach (or contingency approach) to leadership believe that effective leadership behavior depends on the situation at hand—that as situations change, different styles become effective. Two contingency approaches are described: the Fiedler contingency leadership model and the path–goal leadership model.
- The Fiedler contingency leadership model determines if a leader's style is task-oriented or relationship-oriented and if that style is effective for the situation at hand. Once it is determined whether a leader is more oriented toward tasks or toward people, then it's necessary to determine how much control and influence a leader has in the immediate work environment.
- The three dimensions of situational control are leader-member relations, which reflect the extent to which a leader has the support of the work group; the task structure, which reflects the extent to which tasks are routine and easily understood; and position power, which reflects how much power a leader has to reward and punish and make work assignments.
- For each dimension, the leader's control may be high or low. A task-oriented style has been found to work best in either high-control or low-control situations; the relationship-oriented style is best in situations of moderate control.
- The House path–goal leadership model, in its revised form, holds that the effective leader clarifies paths through which subordinates can achieve goals and provides them with support. Two variables, employee characteristics and environmental factors, cause one or more leadership behaviors—which House expanded to eight from his original four—to be more effective than others.

14.5 The Uses of Transformational Leadership

- Full-range leadership describes leadership along a range of styles (from passive to transactional to transformational), with the most effective being transactional/transformational leaders.
- Transformational leadership transforms employees to pursue goals over self-interests. Transformational leaders are influenced by two factors: (1) Their personalities tend to be more extroverted, agreeable, and proactive. (2) Organizational cultures are more apt to be adaptive and flexible.
- The best leaders are both transactional and transformational. Four key behaviors of transformational leaders in affecting employees are they inspire motivation, inspire trust, encourage excellence, and stimulate them intellectually.
- Transformational leadership has three implications. (1) It can improve results for both individuals and groups. (2) It can be used to train employees at any level. (3) It can be used by both ethical or unethical leaders.

14.6 Three Additional Perspectives

- The leader–member exchange (LMX) model of leadership emphasizes that leaders have different sorts of relationships with different subordinates.
- Humble leaders tend to display five key qualities valued by employees: high self-awareness, openness to feedback, appreciation of others, low self-focus, and appreciation of the greater good.
- Whatever their type, leaders need followers who vary in compliance from helpers to independents to rebels. Leaders want followers who are productive, reliable, honest, cooperative, proactive, and flexible. They do not want followers who are reluctant to take the lead on projects, fail to generate ideas, are unwilling to collaborate, withhold information, provide inaccurate feedback, or hide the truth.

14.7 Career Corner: Managing Your Career Readiness

- Becoming a more effective leader requires the application of 14 career readiness competencies: understanding the business, critical thinking/problem solving, oral/written communication, leadership, social intelligence, networking, emotional intelligence, self-motivation, professionalism/work ethic, personal adaptability, self-awareness, service/others orientation, openness to change, and generalized self-efficacy.
- You can become more self-aware by taking the following four actions: (1) Take the time to reflect. (2) Write down your priorities. (3) Learn your strengths and weaknesses. (4) Avoid the Dunning-Kruger effect.

Understanding the Chapter: What Do I Know?

1. What is the difference between being a manager and being a leader?
2. What are five sources of power?
3. In brief, what are five approaches to leadership described in this chapter?
4. What are some positive task-oriented traits and positive/negative interpersonal attributes?
5. Explain the two types of task-oriented behavior.
6. Describe the three types of relationship-oriented behaviors.
7. Briefly discuss the two types of situational leadership approaches.
8. What are key constituents of transformational leadership?
9. Explain how the leader-member exchange (LMX) model works.
10. How can I become more self-aware?

Management in Action

VA TURNAROUND: A WAITING GAME

The U.S. Department of Veterans Affairs (VA) is "the most comprehensive system of assistance for Veterans of any nation in the world."[178] The VA includes more than 1,200 outpatient and medical centers and provides health care, benefits, and burials for more than 9 million U.S. veterans each year. The agency's mission is "to care for those 'who shall have borne the battle' and for their families and survivors," and its $185+ million budget aims to ensure that those who have served in the U.S. military have timely access to high quality health care and benefits.[179] The VA has had major problems fulfilling these duties in recent years.[180]

THE VA STRUGGLES TO MEET ITS MISSION

In 2014, news broke exposing a "systemic" scheduling problem that was jeopardizing veterans' ability to access health care at VA medical centers across the country. An independent investigation found that facilities in multiple states had backlogs of thousands of veterans waiting for physician appointments, with average wait times exceeding 100 days. Facilities also were falsifying records to make it seem that their veterans were receiving care much faster than they actually were.[181]

President Obama acted quickly, and Congress and the White House passed the $16 billion Veterans Access, Choice, and Accountability Act of 2014 (Choice Act) to infuse the VA system with the resources it needed to hire additional doctors, nurses, and staff to manage and speed up the claims process and reduce its backlog.[182] VA Secretary Eric Shineski resigned and Bob McDonald, U.S. Army Veteran and former Procter & Gamble CEO, took charge.[183] Dr. David Shulkin also joined the turnaround efforts as VA

Undersecretary of Health. One veteran described the task ahead of them as "trying to right a ship that's on fire and is taking on water," but McDonald vowed to repair the agency's wounds.[184] He took pride in being accessible, and Gulf War vet Ron Brown described exchanging frequent phone calls with him, saying, "There has never been a time that I've contacted Secretary Bob that he has never responded to me. He has never not returned an email, or even a text message."[185] Others praised the work ethic McDonald brought to the VA and the overall responsiveness within the agency once he took charge.[186]

In 2016, two years after the Choice Act had injected billions of dollars into the VA system, the Commission on Care issued a report suggesting the money had been improperly managed and that little had been done to solve the backlogs and wait times. Findings further revealed that the number of new VA hires did not increase beyond what it would have been without the $2.5 billion, and there appeared to be no logical system in place for assigning staff to VA facilities.[187] The hospitals with the greatest need weren't necessarily getting the greatest amount of new hires, and wait times did not decrease in VA medical centers that received new hires.[188]

Both McDonald and Shulkin suggested that people not focus on wait times as the most important metric of health care success.[189] Instead, McDonald often touted veterans' satisfaction with their health care "experience" as a more suitable measure. He infamously said "When you go to Disney, do they measure the number of hours you wait in line? . . . What's important is, what's your satisfaction with the experience?"[190] But as House Representative Paul Ryan noted, satisfaction with the experience of seeing a doctor is moot if you never get an actual appointment. Further criticisms included rumors of retaliation against whistleblowers in the system, growing wait times, and McDonald's appointment of a doctor at the scandal-ridden Phoenix VA medical center who had a history of negligence and mismanagement.[191]

SERVICE-LEVEL PROBLEMS PERSIST

President Trump fired McDonald in 2017 and elevated Undersecretary David Shulkin to be VA Secretary.[192] Soon after, a series of anonymous complaints about the Washington, DC, VA facility prompted a new investigation.[193] A 2018 report exposed alarming safety concerns, including physicians' inability to get necessary supplies for procedures, inadequate sterilization of equipment, and an egregious lack of financial oversight.[194] Doctors described running across the street to a private hospital to borrow supplies mid-surgery, and the facility kept thousands of boxes of patients' medical records unsecured in warehouses, the basement, and a dumpster. Hospital staff had tracked only about half the patient safety issues resulting from supply issues between 2014 and 2016, and the incidents that were tracked were often reported inaccurately to minimize their severity. Further, the facility had purchased about $92 million worth of medical supplies, much of which was found collecting dust in warehouses, without "proper controls to ensure the purchases were necessary and cost-effective."[195] VA inspector general Michael Missal said "it was difficult to pinpoint precisely how the conditions described in this report could have persisted at the medical center for so many years" but felt strongly that "senior leaders at all levels had a responsibility to ensure that patients were not placed at risk." He suggested that top leadership at the VA had created a "climate of complacency."[196]

The report also found that VA officials at virtually all levels, including those at program offices that had been under Shulkin's direct control, had known for several years about "serious, persistent deficiencies," and didn't act. In a response, Shulkin acknowledged that problems in the VA system were "systemic" but that he "did not recall" ever receiving notification about the issues at the DC facility.[197] The 2018 report blamed the issues on "unwillingness or inability of leaders to take responsibility for the effectiveness of their programs and operations" and a "sense of futility" at all levels in the VA about making substantive changes to the system.[198] It further stated that "leaders frequently abrogated individual responsibility and deflected blame to others . . . despite the many warnings and ongoing indicators of serious problems, leaders failed to engage in meaningful interventions of effective remediation."[199]

Shulkin left the VA in March 2018. The White House says he resigned; Shulkin says he was fired.[200] Trump nominated presidential physician Rear Admiral Ronny Jackson to replace Shulkin as VA Secretary, and troves of accusations about Jackson's conduct and ethics quickly followed. Current and former staff members accused him of being "the most unethical person I have ever worked with," and "incapable of not losing his temper."[201] Others characterized Jackson as an excessive drinker and said he often prescribed inordinately large supplies of opioid medications for White House staff. Jackson was said to often belittle his staff members, who saw him as an abusive person with an explosive personality.[202] President Trump remained steadfast in his support of Jackson as the nominee, calling him "one of the finest people I have ever met."[203] But multiple government officials, including President Trump, acknowledged that Jackson lacked the experience necessary for directing a governmental agency or large organization, with one reporter noting that "he doesn't understand the work or the people who do it, and that's not how effective leadership models are built in any industry."[204] By April 2018, Jackson had withdrawn himself from the nomination.

WHAT'S NEXT?

In spite of all the problems plaguing the VA system, doctors and nurses at many facilities have managed to continue providing veterans with care that is "comparable or better in clinical quality to care in the private sector."[205] Inspector General Missal said this is "largely due to the efforts of many dedicated health care providers that overcame service deficiencies to ensure patients received needed care."[206] But thousands of veterans never get the chance to receive that care, and access to health services remains "the biggest problem across the board," according to veterans' attorney Katrina Eagle.[207]

According to one reporter, "The VA deserves a competent and experienced leader, with the policy background and management ability to steer it through these troubled times. The next secretary of Veterans Affairs will have to confront a number of policy dilemmas relating to disability ratings and payments, VA infrastructure and bureaucracy issues."[208] The reporter added, "For the sake of the country's veterans, we can only hope that the next nominee will be open to a variety of policy options and have the management experience to lead the department to accomplish them."[209]

FOR DISCUSSION

Problem-Solving Perspective

1. What is the underlying problem in this case from the VA secretary's perspective?
2. What are the causes of this problem?
3. What recommendations would you make to the Department of Veterans Affairs for fixing this problem?

Application of Chapter Content

1. From the perspective of trait theories, how would you evaluate the VA leaders discussed in the case? Which traits did each of the leaders possess? Which traits were they lacking?
2. What skills would you suggest as most important for the next VA secretary to possess? Do you think any of the previous VA leaders displayed these skills?
3. Evaluate both McDonald and Shulkin according to their task-oriented and relationship-oriented leadership behaviors. In which areas do you think each succeeded? In which areas do you think each failed?
4. How would transformational leadership theory suggest the next VA secretary approach the task of turning around the struggling agency?

Legal/Ethical Challenge

SHOULD STARBUCKS HAVE A CORPORATE LOITERING POLICY?

Starbucks launched a multimillion-dollar global brand campaign in 2014 called "Meet Me at Starbucks." The ad focused not on coffee, but instead on the idea that Starbucks stores were a great place to socialize, whether to catch up with friends, conduct business, or hold a group meeting.[210] But is it OK to hang out at Starbucks if you aren't buying anything?

Starbucks doesn't have a corporate policy on loitering. Instead, individual stores set their own rules about whether people can sit inside or use the restroom for free; at some locations, the answer is no.[211] This was the case at a Philadelphia Starbucks where two black men were recently arrested for trespassing and disturbance. Business partners Donte Robinson and Rashon Nelson were waiting to meet with an associate when one of them asked to use the restroom. They hadn't purchased anything, and the store manager called the police after the men refused to leave. A video of Robinson and Nelson being taken away in handcuffs went viral and sparked public outrage and accusations of racial profiling.[212]

Starbucks CEO Kevin Johnson apologized publicly for the incident and flew to Philadelphia to meet with Robinson and Nelson in person.[213] The men settled with Starbucks for an undisclosed amount plus an offer of a free college education through the company's partnership with Arizona State University. They also settled with the city of Philadelphia for a symbolic $1 each and a promise that the city would start a $200,000 entrepreneurship program for its public high school students.[214]

The Philadelphia location did have a no-loitering policy, but the guidelines for whether police should be engaged to enforce rules vary by region and may be difficult for managers to interpret. Johnson said that threats and serious disturbances may warrant law enforcement, but that the Philadelphia manager's decision to call the police in this situation was "completely inappropriate."[215] Starbucks did not publicly discipline the manager, although a corporate spokesperson said she was no longer employed by Starbucks as part of a "mutual decision."[216] The company closed more than 8,000 of its U.S. locations for a day to conduct training on racial and other unconscious biases.[217]

Starbucks has not announced any changes to its corporate policy (or lack thereof) on loitering. Do you think the company should implement a company wide loitering policy?

SOLVING THE CHALLENGE

What would you do if you were CEO of Starbucks?

1. I am not in favor of Starbucks instituting a corporate loitering policy. Decisions on how to manage customers and when to involve police should be made by store-level leadership, not corporate executives. Some locations are busier than others and should be able to decide whether nonpaying customers are taking up space that would otherwise go to paying customers. Managers should also have the discretion to call the police when they feel it's appropriate. A single bad decision by one store manager shouldn't represent the entire company, and most managers know how to apply these types of policies in a fair and nondiscriminatory fashion. The additional bias training will help prevent similar incidents from occurring in the future.
2. I think it's a good idea for Starbucks to have a corporate loitering policy. This type of leadership should come from the top of the organization and set the tone for what's important to the company. A corporate policy would provide clearer guidance to store managers on how to handle nonpaying customers and would also protect the company from liability due to store managers making bad decisions. Starbucks should also provide clear and consistent guidelines for managers on when it's appropriate to call law enforcement.
3. I think it might be a good idea for Starbucks to have a corporate loitering policy, provided the policy does not lead to the appearance of discrimination and allows Starbucks to maintain its identity as a socially responsible, warm, welcoming place to spend time with others. For example, the policy could state that loitering is welcomed as long as there are no paying customers waiting for a seat. If paying customers don't have anywhere to sit, then nonpaying customers should leave to make room for them. I think all employees should participate in unconscious-bias training to ensure the policy is applied fairly and consistently.
4. Invent other options.

Uber Continuing Case connect

Learn about the contrasting leadership traits and behaviors used by Uber's former CEO Travis Kalanick and current CEO Dara Khosrowshahi. Assess your ability to apply the management concepts discussed in this chapter to the case by going to Connect.

15 Interpersonal and Organizational Communication

Mastering the Exchange of Information

©Olivier Renck/Aurora/Getty Images

After reading this chapter, you should be able to:

LO 15-1 Describe the communication process.

LO 15-2 Compare communication channels and appropriate ways for managers to use them.

LO 15-3 Identify barriers to communication and ways managers can overcome them.

LO 15-4 Discuss how managers can successfully use social media to communicate.

LO 15-5 Identify ways for managers to improve their listening, writing, and speaking skills.

LO 15-6 Review the techniques for improving the career readiness competency of networking.

FORECAST *What's Ahead in This Chapter*

This chapter describes the process of transferring information and understanding between individuals and groups. It also describes several communication barriers—physical, personal, cross-cultural, nonverbal, and gender differences. It shows how you can use different channels and patterns of communication, both formal and informal, to your advantage. It discusses how managers use information technology to communicate more effectively. We also provide recommendations for becoming a better listener, writer, and speaker. We conclude with a Career Corner that focuses on developing the career readiness competency of networking.

MANAGE U

Improving Your Use of Empathy

Have you ever had a conversation that left you worried or unsatisfied because you could tell the other person didn't really understand what you were feeling? One of the key components of effective communication is empathy, the ability to perceive and share other people's feelings. It's part of the career readiness skill of emotional intelligence and represents a natural human ability everyone has, and one that you can actively improve.

Empathy will help you gain a better and more accurate understanding of what's really going on when you communicate with others at work—what they need, what they're feeling, why they're saying what they're saying, and even what they aren't saying. That, in turn, will help shape your response and make you a better communicator with stronger work and personal relationships. In fact, the Consortium for Research on Emotional Intelligence in Organizations has traced a link between empathy and sales success and other types of superior performance, especially in teams.[1]

Empathy also improves your leadership and your ability to defuse conflict.[2] It should be easy to see that someone who conveys empathy and understanding toward others will more easily earn their respect and thus be better able to lead and direct them. And your ability to resolve conflict ultimately depends on your being able to see what matters to all the parties and what each side hopes to achieve.

Empathy can even improve your performance in job interviews by helping you understand what the interviewer needs in a new hire. In this way, you can show why you're the right one for the job.[3]

Here are some suggestions for developing empathy and strengthening your emotional intelligence in the process.[4]

Practice Your Best Listening Skills Interrupting others, or even thinking about how you're going to respond instead of actually listening to what's being said, prevents you from focusing on the other person and their message. Checking your phone during in person conversations also limits you ability to focus on what is being said.

Observe Nonverbal Cues Pay attention to the speaker's body language, facial expression, and tone of voice. Are these giving a message that contradicts the words being spoken? Try to find out why. Watch your own nonverbal behavior, too. For instance, maintain comfortable eye contact while listening and speaking.

Ask Yourself, "What You Would Do in the Other Person's Place?" If you're having trouble understanding where someone is coming from, try asking yourself what you would do if the situation were reversed and you were in that person's shoes. This imagined swap is the essence of empathy because it lets you perceive and feel what the other person is seeing, hearing, and feeling.

Know Your Audience Whether you're making a presentation to a group or speaking one-on-one, be sure you understand how much your audience already knows about the topic on which you're speaking. Use that knowledge to avoid overexplaining or leaving people in the dark.

Smile Smiling doesn't just automatically raise your own spirits (try it and see). It also makes you look friendlier and more open to others' views and ideas. Showing genuine interest in others is a hallmark of empathy.

For Discussion One way to put these suggestions into practice is to challenge yourself to have a substantive conversation in which you really connect with someone you consider difficult to communicate with or with whom you frequently disagree. Can you make a plan to try this? Which tips will be most helpful to you?

15.1 The Communication Process: What It Is, How It Works

THE BIG PICTURE

Communication is the transfer of information and understanding from one person to another. The process involves sender, message, and receiver; encoding and decoding; the medium; feedback; and "noise," or interference. Managers need to tailor their communication to the appropriate medium (rich or lean) for the appropriate situation.

LO 15-1

Describe the communication process.

How good a communicator do you think you are? A survey of 200 U.S. employers and 4,200 graduating seniors revealed that while nearly 80 percent of the college students in the survey believed they were competent in both oral and written communication, only 42 percent of employers thought students were correct about their oral skills, and only 56 percent said students had good writing skills.[5]

Communication Defined: The Transfer of Information and Understanding

Researchers have begun to examine communication as a form of social information processing, in which receivers interpret messages by cognitively processing them. This work has led to development of a perceptual model of communication that depicts it as a process in which receivers create meaning in their own minds.[6]

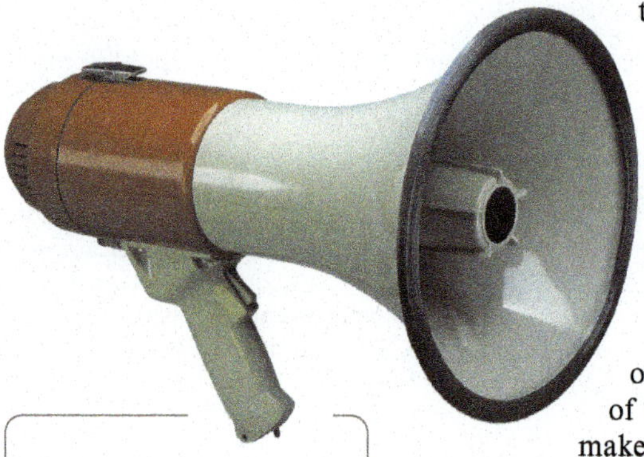

You don't have to shout to communicate. ©Comstock Images/ Alamy Stock Photo

Communication—the transfer of information and understanding from one person to another—is an activity that you as a manager will have to do a lot. The fact that managers do a lot of communicating doesn't mean they're necessarily good at it—that is, that they are efficient or effective. You are an *efficient communicator* when you can transmit your message accurately in the least time. You are an *effective communicator* when your intended message is accurately understood by the other person. Thus, you may well be efficient in sending a group of people a reprimand by e-mail. But it may not be effective if it makes them angry so that they can't absorb its meaning.

The "I'm glad . . ." feature below illustrates how Donna Mostrom reacted to positive communication from her manager. These skills are a good role model for managers.

I'm glad...

...my manager was an effective communicator.

Donna Mostrom worked as an assistant vice president in the supply chain department of a beauty consumer-packaged goods company. Her manager was a good listener, he gave constructive criticism, and he partnered with Donna to solve problems.

"He was completely honest with me, and I loved it. Before I even started the job, he told me all the pros and cons about the company culture, so I went in with my eyes open. And he told me all the things he would do specifically to help me succeed," said Donna.

When meeting with Donna, the manager let her talk first so all her questions were answered during the allotted time. He listened and tried never to interrupt her. If they did run out of time to address Donna's questions during the meeting, he never kept Donna past the time. Instead, he rescheduled another meeting to address her questions.

Her manager always made sure that Donna had a clear understanding. "He never sent me all the way back to the drawing board. It was never an impossible ask. There was always a confirmation that I understood what he was asking for or what he needed," said Donna.

"He was always incredibly accessible. If he was traveling, he would jump on the phone. He was very thorough in his responses, and he would make sure I had whatever was needed. But he always put the focus on me and my needs before bringing up his own needs," said Donna. "He would always go over the positives. If he wanted me to change anything, he would say, 'I really like this, but *this* is actually what I'm looking for. What do you think?' It was never a directive. He was never demanding that I do something."

Courtesy Donna Mostrom

Donna's manager was able to build trust by being honest and direct, by listening before speaking, and by being accessible. Once a good working relationship had been built, Donna was confident that he would work with her to solve problems rather than just directing her to complete tasks.

For example, Donna once suggested to her manager that she travel to each of the company's plants to meet face-to-face with the plant workers when they rolled out a new training process. While this was different from what the company normally did, Donna's manager was willing to partner with her to come up with a creative solution. The initiative was a success.

"People really liked him and had a lot of respect for him," said Donna. The manager's effective communication skills went a long way with his employees.

Courtesy of Donna Mostrom

How the Communication Process Works

Communication has been said to be a process consisting of "a sender transmitting a message through media to a receiver who responds."[7] A diagram of this communication process is shown below. *(See Figure 15.1.)* Let's take a look at its different parts.

Sender, Message, and Receiver

The **sender** is the person wanting to share information—called a message—and the **receiver** is the person for whom the message is intended, as follows.

Sender ⟶ Message ⟶ Receiver

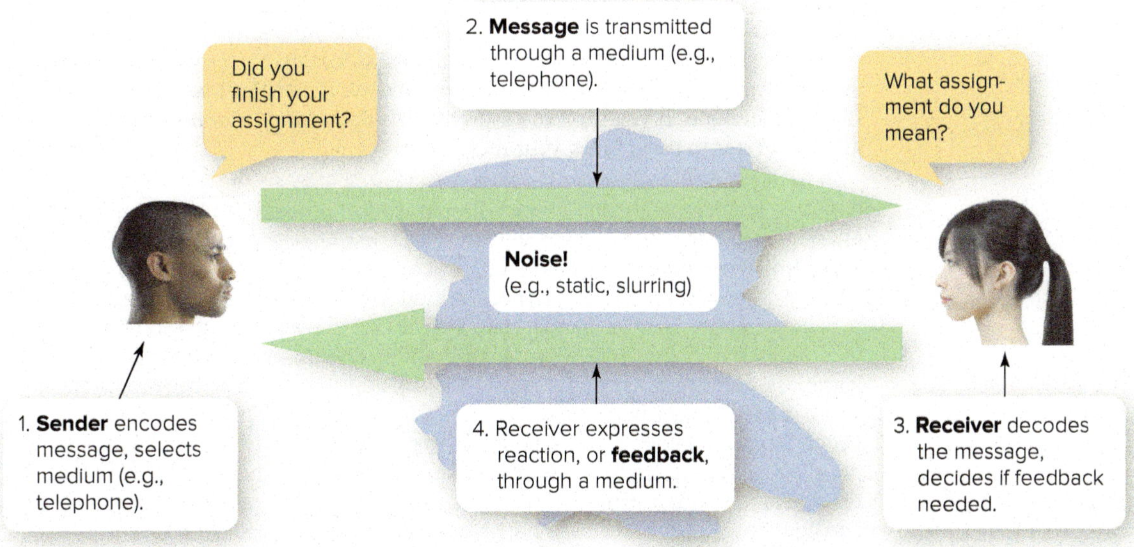

FIGURE 15.1 **The communication process**

"Noise" is not just noise or loud background sounds but any disturbance that interferes with transmission—static, fadeout, distracting facial expressions, an uncomfortable meeting site, competing voices, and so on.

(male): ©Fuse/Getty Images; (female): ©Takayuki/Shutterstock

Encoding and Decoding Of course, the process isn't as simple as just sender/message/receiver. If you were an old-fashioned telegraph operator using Morse code to send a message over a telegraph line, you would first have to encode the message, and the receiver would have to decode it. But the same is true when you are sending the message by voice to another person in the same room and have to decide what language to speak in and what terms to use, and when you are texting a friend and can choose your words, your abbreviations and even an emoji or two.

Encoding **is translating a message into understandable symbols or language.** **Decoding** **is interpreting and trying to make sense of the message.** Thus, the communication process is now

Sender **[Encoding]** → Message → **[Decoding]** Receiver

The Medium The means by which you as a communicator send a message is important, whether it is typing a text or an e-mail, hand-scrawling a note, or communicating by voice in person or by phone or videoconference. This means is the **medium**, **the pathway by which a message travels:**

Sender [Encoding] → Message **[Medium]** Message → [Decoding] Receiver

Feedback "Flight 123, do you copy?" In the movies, that's what you hear the flight controller say when radioing the pilot of a troubled aircraft to see whether he or she received ("copied") the previous message. And the pilot may radio back, "Roger, Houston, I copy." This acknowledgment is an example of **feedback**, **whereby the receiver expresses his or her reaction to the sender's message.**

Sender [Encoding] → Message [Medium] Message → [Decoding] Receiver

[Feedback] Message

Feedback is essential in communication so that the person sending the message can know whether the receiver understood it in the same way the sender intended—and whether he or she agrees with it. It is an essential component of communication accuracy and can be facilitated by paraphrasing. **Paraphrasing** **occurs when people restate in their own words the crux of what they heard or read.** It clarifies that a message was accurately understood. If you want to ensure that someone understands something you said, ask him or her to paraphrase your message.

Noise Unfortunately, the entire communication process can be disrupted at several different points by **noise**—**any disturbance that interferes with the transmission of a message.** Noise can occur in the medium, of course, in the form of static in a radio transmission, fadeout on a cell phone, or loud music when you're trying to talk in a restaurant. Laptops, for example, are a source of noise when used by college students to take notes during lectures. A growing body of research shows that "college students learn less when they use computers or laptops during lectures. They also tend to earn worse grades," according to *The New York Times.* The decrease in learning is thought to occur "because students can type faster than they can write," which results in the lecturer's words going "right to the students typing fingers without stopping in their brains for substantive processing."[8] In contrast, writing by hand requires students to process and condense spoken words so they can record their thoughts on paper.

Further, noise can occur in the encoding or decoding, as when people from different cultures stumble over each other's languages. One of your authors—Angelo Kinicki—was consulting in Asia and found, for instance, that his suggestion that Asian managers "touch base" (a baseball reference) with their colleagues drew blank looks. We discuss cross-cultural barriers to communication later in the chapter.

Even within the same culture, we can encounter semantic problems (problems that revolve around the meaning of words). When a supervisor tells you, "We need to get this done right away," what does it mean? Does "We" mean just you? You and your co-workers? Or you, your co-workers, and the boss? Does "right away" mean today, tomorrow, or next week?

Another language barrier is jargon. **Jargon is terminology specific to a particular profession or group.** (Example: "The HR VP wants the RFP to go out ASAP." Translation: "The vice president of human resources wants the request for proposal to go out as soon as possible.") *Buzzwords* are designed to impress rather than inform. (Example: "Could our teams interface on the ad campaign that went viral, and then circle back with the boss?")[9] Noise also occurs in *nonverbal communication* (discussed later in this chapter), when our physical movements and our words send different messages.

EXAMPLE Secrecy and Silence

Volkswagen Volkswagen's fortunes have been imperiled after the 2015 revelation that about 11 million of its diesel cars were equipped with the means to cheat federal emissions tests. CEO Mattias Mueller blames the company's "culture of silence" for preventing employees at many levels from speaking out about "Dieselgate." Volkswagen's former CEO Martin Winterkorn even received a memo about "irregularities" in the cars' emissions but reportedly did nothing.[10] The scheme went on for about 10 years before a U.S. nonprofit group discovered what was going on.[11]

Volkswagen admitted in 2017 that executives had lied to and misled the Environmental Protection Agency about certain vehicles' compliance with U.S. emissions standards.[12] The company pleaded guilty to three felony counts and agreed to pay a $2.8 billion criminal fine. The automaker also agreed to pay another $1.5 billion civil penalty to settle environmental, customs, and financial claims.[13]

Theranos Secrecy was an operational mandate at Theranos Inc., a biomedical testing company founded by former CEO Elizabeth Holmes. Different departments had separate key cards for entry, and the company's chemists and engineers were discouraged from discussing their work, even with one another. The resulting "silo" effect prevented staff from collaborating to solve problems with the company's blood-testing products, which failed to live up to Holmes's public claims that they would be innovative.

Holmes continued to deny problems with Theranos products, even as multiple investigations into the company began. She falsely claimed that a 2015 product recall ordered by the Food and Drug Administration was voluntary and even gave inaccurate presentations to employees. Employees didn't

Martin Winterkorn. Dr. Martin Winterkorn resigned as Volkswagen's CEO in September 2015 after the Environmental Protection Agency began investigating emission test issues. ©Bernhard Classen/Alamy Stock Photo

Elizabeth Holmes. Elizabeth Holmes, CEO of Theranos, speaking to *Fortune*'s Most Powerful Women Conference. Neither Holmes or Theranos admitted or denied the SEC's allegations. ©Krista Kennell/Shutterstock

actually learn the extent of the company's troubles until investigators' reports were released to the press.[14] Holmes settled fraud charges with the Securities and Exchange Commission in 2018 by giving up 18.9 million Theranos shares and paying a $500,000 fine. She was also barred from running a public company for 10 years.[15] The former CEO still faces a separate civil suit initiated by Theranos investors.[16]

YOUR CALL

In terms of the communications process modeled in Figure 15.1, do you think a "culture of silence" can constitute a form of noise? What about the "silo" effect? At what other point or points in the communication model do you think silence and secrecy can interfere with communication?

Selecting the Right Medium for Effective Communication

All kinds of communication tools are available to managers, ranging from one-to-one face-to-face conversation all the way to use of the mass media. However, managers need to know how to use the right tool for the right condition—when to use e-mail or when to meet face-to-face, for example. Should you congratulate a team for exceeding its goals by addressing the group in person, sending an e-mail, posting an announcement near the office coffee machine—or all three? What medium would you select for delivering a reprimand?

All media have their own advantages and disadvantages, and there are a few different criteria to consider when choosing the right medium.[17] For instance, texts and tweets require the writer to be brief and precise, and like e-mails (which generally are brief), they provide a record of the communication that in-person and phone communication don't. They can also be sent almost without regard to time-zone differences. But unlike voice, video call, and in-person messages, written communications often fail to convey nuances of meaning through tone of voice and body language, and thus they can more easily be misinterpreted. Many a manager has discovered that a simple phone call can cut through layers of misinterpreted e-mails.

We can generally categorize differences between communication media in terms of whether a given medium is *rich* or *lean.* What does this mean?

Is a Medium Rich or Lean in Information?

Media richness indicates how well a particular medium conveys information and promotes learning. That is, the "richer" a medium is, the better it is at conveying information.[18] The term *media richness* was proposed by respected organizational theorists Richard Daft and Robert Lengel as part of their contingency model for media selection.[19]

Types of media can be positioned along a continuum ranging from high to low media richness, as shown in Figure 15.2.

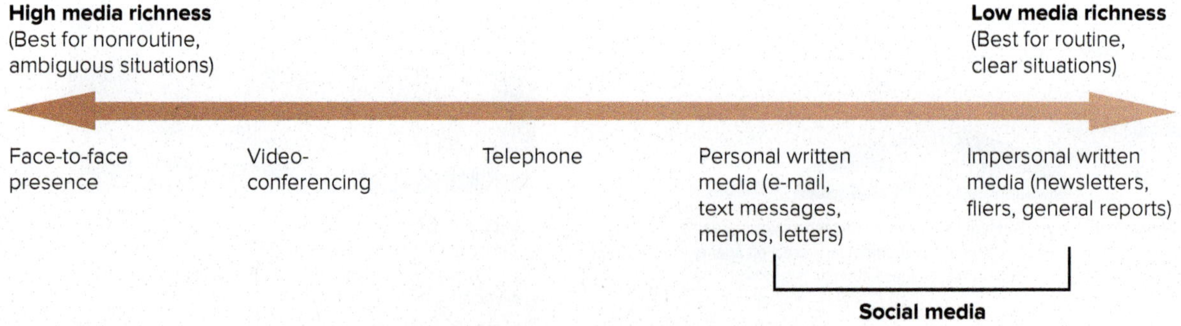

FIGURE 15.2 Contingency model of media selection

Face-to-face communication, also the most personal form of communication, is the richest. It allows the receiver of the message to observe multiple cues, such as body language and tone of voice. It allows the sender to get immediate feedback, to see how well the receiver comprehended the message. At the other end of the media richness scale, impersonal written media are just the reverse—only one cue and no feedback—making them low in richness.

As you might expect, people have preferences for the type of medium they like to use, and they have different perceptions of the richness of the same medium.[20] Males and people with extroverted and agreeable personality characteristics tend to use media high in richness. Contrary to stereotypes, age has no impact on media richness preference.[21] What are your preferences?

Matching the Appropriate Medium to the Appropriate Situation

In general, the following guidelines are useful.[22]

Rich Medium: Best for Nonroutine Situations and to Avoid Oversimplification A *rich* medium is more effective with nonroutine situations. Examples: In what way would you like your boss to inform you of a nonroutine change, like the introduction of a new employee benefit? Via a memo tacked on the bulletin board (a lean medium)? Or via a face-to-face meeting or phone call (a rich medium)?

The danger of using a rich medium for routine matters (such as monthly sales reports) is that it results in information *overloading*—the delivery of more information than necessary.

Lean Medium: Best for Routine Situations and to Avoid Overloading A *lean* medium is more effective in routine situations. Examples: In what manner would you as a sales manager like to get routine monthly sales reports from your 50 sales reps? Via time-consuming phone calls (a somewhat rich medium)? Or via e-mails or text messages (a somewhat lean medium)? The danger of using a lean medium for nonroutine matters (such as an announcement of a company reorganization) is that it results in information *oversimplification*—it doesn't provide enough of the information the receiver needs and wants.

E-mail and social media like Facebook, LinkedIn, and Twitter vary in media richness, being leaner if they impersonally blanket a large audience and are anonymous (or posted under a screen name), and richer if they mix personal textual and video information that prompts quick conversational feedback.[23] We discuss social media in Section 15.4 ●

15.2 How Managers Fit into the Communication Process

THE BIG PICTURE

Formal communication channels follow the chain of command, which is of three types—vertical, horizontal, and external. Informal communication channels develop outside the organization's formal structure. One type is the grapevine. Another, face-to-face communication, builds trust and depends heavily on managers' effective listening skills.

LO 15-2

Compare communication channels and appropriate ways for managers to use them.

If you've ever had a low-level job in nearly any kind of organization, you know that there is generally a hierarchy of management between you and the organization's president, director, or CEO. If you had a suggestion that you wanted him or her to hear, you doubtless had to go up through management channels. That's formal communication. However, you may have run into that top manager in the elevator. Or in the restroom. Or in a line at the bank. You could have voiced your suggestion casually then. That's informal communication.

Formal Communication Channels: Up, Down, Sideways, and Outward

Formal communication channels are recognized as official. The organization chart we described in Chapter 8 indicates how official communications–memos, letters, reports, announcements–are supposed to be routed.

Formal communication is of three types: (1) *vertical*–meaning upward and downward, (2) *horizontal*–meaning laterally (sideways), and (3) *external*–meaning outside the organization.

1. Vertical Communication: Up and Down the Chain of Command

Vertical communication is the flow of messages up and down the hierarchy within the organization: bosses communicating with subordinates, subordinates communicating with bosses. As you might expect, the more management levels through which a message passes, the more it is prone to some distortion.

- **Downward communication–from top to bottom. Downward communication flows from a higher level to a lower level (or levels).** In small organizations, top-down communication may be delivered face-to-face. In larger organizations, it's delivered via meetings, e-mail, official memos, company publications, and town hall meetings. American health care company DaVita invites all its employees every eight weeks to "participate in a company-wide phone call with the company's 'mayor,' CEO Kent Thiry. Teammates dial in to hear about the state of the company, and ask questions about any subject they choose."[24]
- **Upward communication–from bottom to top. Upward communication flows from a lower level to a higher level(s).** Often, this type of communication is from a subordinate to his or her immediate manager, who in turn will relay it up to the next level, if necessary. Effective upward communication depends on an atmosphere of trust. Employees are less likely to pass on bad news when they don't trust the boss.

Types of downward and upward communication are shown below. *(See Table 15.1.)*

Upward bound. How do you communicate with a manager two or three levels above you in the organization's hierarchy? You can send a memo through channels. Or you can watch for informal opportunities like this when a manager heads for a cup of coffee. ©Jacobs Stock Photography/Getty Images

TABLE 15.1 **Types of Downward and Upward Communication**

Downward Communication

Most downward communication involves one of the following kinds of information:

- Instructions related to particular job tasks. Example (supervisor to subordinate): "The store will close Monday for inventory. All employees are expected to participate."
- Explanations about the relationship between two or more tasks. Example: A manager may request an employee to complete a task ahead of schedule because another department needs the output before it can begin working on a critical task.
- Explanations of the organization's policies, practices, and procedures. Example: "The human resources department sends an e-mail blast about new benefits or procedures for taking vacations."
- A manager's feedback about a subordinate's performance. Example: "You missed the project deadline by two days, which impacted the team's ability to meet the customer's needs. Let's discuss the reason for this."
- Attempts to encourage a sense of mission and dedication to the organization's goals. Example: "Manager calls team meeting to discuss how the team is contributing to company's strategic goals."

Upward Communication

Most upward communication involves the following kinds of information:

- Reports of progress on current projects. Example: "We are three hours behind in taking inventory. What can we do to catch up?"
- Reports of unsolved problems requiring help from people higher up. Example: "We can't complete our tasks because we need input from another department."
- New developments affecting the work unit. Example: "Two employees want to take vacation the same week. How would you like to handle this?"
- Suggestions for improvements. Example: "Can you help me interpret results on this spreadheet?"
- Reports on employee attitudes and efficiency. Example: "Our customer satisfaction scores have gone down over the last year. Let's schedule a department meeting to create a plan of action."

Sources: Adapted from D. Katz and R. Kahn, The Social Psychology of Organizations *(New York: Wiley, 1966); and E. Planty and W. Machaver, "Upward Communications: A Project in Executive Development,"* Personnel *28 (1952), pp. 304–318.*

2. Horizontal Communication: Within and between Work Units

Horizontal communication flows within and between work units; its main purpose is coordination. As a manager, you will spend perhaps as much as a third of your time in this form of communication—consulting with colleagues and co-workers at the same level as you within the organization. In this kind of sideways communication, you will be sharing information, coordinating tasks, solving problems, resolving conflicts, and getting the support of your peers. Horizontal communication is encouraged through the use of meetings, committees, task forces, and matrix structures.

Horizontal communication can be impeded in three ways: (1) by specialization that makes people focus on only their jobs; (2) by rivalry between workers or work units, which prevents sharing of information; and (3) by lack of encouragement from management.

3. External Communication: Outside the Organization

External communication flows between people inside and outside the organization. This form of communication is increasingly important because organizations desire to communicate with other stakeholders—customers, suppliers, shareholders, or other owners—in pursuit of their strategic goals. Small business owners particularly rely on external communication to help grow their businesses. A recent study, for example, revealed that small business owners tended to seek input or counsel from two sources: peers in the same community or online from a peer they had never met.[25]

Informal Communication Channels

Informal communication channels develop outside the formal structure and do not follow the chain of command—they are more spontaneous, can skip management levels, and can cut across lines of authority.

Two types of informal channels are (1) the *grapevine* and (2) *face-to-face communication.*

The Grapevine **The grapevine is the unofficial communication system of the informal organization,** a network of in-person and online gossip and rumor. Workplace gossip can be positive or negative, and it serves important functions.[26] For example, research shows that the grapevine delivers as much as 70 percent of all organizational communication, although only a little more than half of executives understand that the rumor mill is more active when official communication is lacking. In a recent series of interviews with 1,100 employees in a range of industries, almost half said that when official and unofficial communications conflict, they are more likely to believe the grapevine. Written or online company communications, such as e-mails and newsletters, edged out the grapevine, but only slightly; 51 percent of those interviewed said they trusted a newsletter more than rumor.[27]

As U.S. legislators debated a contentious plan to make changes in the VA Choice program that some feared would ease privatization of community-based health services to veterans, the House committee chair Republican Phil Roe told reporters he had "heard through the grapevine" that Democratic minority leader Nancy Pelosi might give it support she had earlier withheld.[28]

Face-to-Face Communication Despite the entrenched use of quick and efficient electronic communication in our lives, face-to-face conversation is still justifiably a major part of most people's work day. Employees value authentic human contact with the boss and welcome the implication that their manager cares about them. Face time builds relationships and trust, shows respect for employees as individuals, and thus is highly motivating. Netflix CEO Reed Hastings doesn't have an office at all. "I just had no need for it," he says. "It is better for me to be meeting people all around the building."[29] And as one writer noted, while Millennials may spend a lot of time texting, a major reason is that they're making plans to get together in person.[30]

Some basic principles apply to making the most of face-to-face communication in the work environment.[31]

1. **Make time for face-to-face.** Rather than hoping to catch people at random, schedule time with individual employees, and make sure you'll both be free of distractions (including cell phones) for the few minutes your interaction will take. This is not the moment to multi-task.
2. **Listen more and talk less.** Listen not just to the words the other person is saying, but also to the emotional content behind the words. Make eye contact and observe body language. This will help you be empathetic, a topic discussed in the last section of this chapter. When it's your turn to speak, be brief. If your message is specific or factual, prepare your facts and outline your thoughts ahead of time. Expect questions and be prepared with answers.
3. **Deliver good news up front; lead in to bad.** Happy tidings don't require a long build-up. Bad news and controversial decisions, however, may go over better if you build up to them by explaining the situation, identifying factors you can't control, and giving the other side of the argument its due.
4. **Hold employee town hall meetings.** For in-person meetings with groups of employees, "town hall" meetings, often held monthly or quarterly, usually consist of a presentation by managers and an open question-and-answer session. Be available for informal conversations with individuals afterward. Town hall meetings are a great way for politicians to communicate with their constituents.[32] DaVita, for example, "holds town hall meetings to build a stronger culture around idea sharing . . . that directly impacts the pipeline of projects being worked on."[33]

A town hall meeting. U.S. President Barack Obama (left) and Facebook CEO Mark Zuckerberg (right) talk to Facebook employees at a town hall meeting at corporate headquarters in Palo Alto, California. Why would a president of the U.S. want to participate in such events? ©Justin Sullivan/Getty Images

5. **Use webcasts when you can't be there.** You can still achieve face time even if your employees work remotely. Use webcasts, video conferencing, or a social video portal to communicate with geographically dispersed people. It is important to ensure, however, that the technical aspects of these communications are arranged prior to using them. Keep communications direct and personal. If possible, try to make sure everyone has the same communication experience. That is, try to avoid having meetings that mix in-person and remote attendees. •

PRACTICAL ACTION How to Streamline Meetings

Managers spend a great deal of time in meetings, and much of it may be counterproductive. A survey of 182 senior managers in a range of industries revealed that 71 percent viewed their meetings as unproductive and inefficient.[34] Meetings can also be costly. Wasted time in meetings costs companies more than $37 billion each year, according to *Inc.* magazine.[35] Here are some ways to make sure the meetings you run or attend, whether virtually or in person, are as effective as possible.[36]

What to Do as a Meeting Leader

1. **Set a clear goal and communicate it beforehand.** Before you call a meeting, ask yourself what specific task or tasks you want the meeting to accomplish. Write these down in the form of an agenda with time limits for each point, leaving brief time slots for attendees' input and discussion. Creating an agenda does more than keep you on track; it helps others know what they should prepare for the meeting, saving valuable time.[37]
2. **Invite the appropriate people.** The list of attendees needs to fit the task at hand. Participants should be there for a clear purpose and should possess the necessary knowledge expertise to participate.[38]
3. **Start and end on time.** Respect other people's time commitments. Be the first in the meeting room and start when you said you would. Stick to the time limits you've allowed for each agenda item, and keep your eye on the clock. Learn how to gently but firmly cut off unproductive discussion. ("Thanks for your contribution, Jay. Let's quickly hear from one more person before we move on to the next point.")
4. **Keep it short or provide breaks.** The brain likes its rations in small bites. For the first 30 minutes of a meeting, roughly 84 percent of attendees will be engaged, but by minute 45, this is down to 64 percent. Longer meetings are sometimes necessary to tackle more complex issues, though. Regular breaks of 5 to 10 minutes should be provided in these instances for people to make a call or check e-mails. This also reduces anxiety in the room.[39] Aaron Sapiro, CEO of digital agency Huge Inc., took a more radical approach to meeting times. He replaced 30-minute meetings with meetings lasting five minutes, and he uses desk-side "drive-bys" to accommodate people who want to meet with him.[40]
5. **Save your opinion for last.** Once a leader states his or her opinion, there is a good chance the group will support it even if they do not agree. You should ensure that everyone's thoughts on a matter are presented before providing your own. Many times the group will come around to your point of view, making it unnecessary to chime in early.[41]
6. **Follow up.** Within 24 hours of the meeting, clarify results and expectations by sending attendees a summary of decisions made, tasks to be performed, and who is to perform them and when.

What to Do as a Meeting Participant

1. **Prepare but stay flexible.** Respond promptly to the meeting invitation. Read the agenda (ask for one if you don't receive it ahead of time), and be prepared with any facts or data you may be called upon to present. You should also prepare to be flexible because meetings don't always go as planned. For example, if you have 15 minutes scheduled to present, prepare both a full presentation and a shortened one in case your time is limited.[42]
2. **Be on time.** Showing up late is disrespectful and disruptive. It can also make the meeting run over time if the leader decides to wait for you.
3. **Participate intelligently.** Expect to contribute to the meeting, but make sure your contributions are brief, professional, and on point. Ask questions that start with "how" and "what" rather than "why." These types of questions don't put people on the defensive or delve into fact finding. Instead, they encourage colleagues to open up and think expansively.[43]
4. **Follow up.** If you came away from the meeting with a to-do list, be sure you act on it in a timely way so the goals of the meeting can be achieved. You may even be able to avoid having to attend another meeting to go over the same agenda all over again.

YOUR CALL

Do you think it makes sense to have a policy that all meetings must end in five minutes? Why? Do you have any additional suggestions about making meetings more effective?

15.3 Barriers to Communication

THE BIG PICTURE

We describe several barriers to communication. Physical barriers include sound, time, and space. Personal barriers include variations in communication skills, processing and interpreting information, trustworthiness and credibility, ego strength, listening skills, judging others, and generational considerations. Cross-cultural barriers are a greater challenge as more jobs include interactions with others around the globe. Nonverbal communication can present a barrier if it conflicts with the spoken message. Finally, gender differences can present barriers but can be overcome.

LO 15-3

Identify barriers to communication and ways managers can overcome them.

If you have ever been served the wrong drink because the server couldn't hear you in a noisy restaurant, clicked on a broken web link, missed your boarding call because the airport's public address system was full of static, or taken offense at a text you later found you misinterpreted, you've experienced a barrier to communication. Some barriers occur within the communication process itself, as shown below. (*See Table 15.2.*) We'll look at several types—physical, personal, cross-cultural, nonverbal, and gender differences.

TABLE 15.2 **Some Barriers That Happen within the Communication Process**

All it takes is one blocked step in the communication process for communication to fail. Consider the following.

- **Sender barrier—no message gets sent.** Example: If a manager has an idea but is afraid to voice it because he or she fears criticism, then obviously no message gets sent.
- **Encoding barrier—the message is not expressed correctly.** Example: If people have a different first language the meaning of words can be misinterpreted.
- **Medium barrier—the communication channel is blocked.** Example: When a computer network is down, the network is an example of a blocked medium.
- **Decoding barrier—the recipient doesn't understand the message.** Example: You pulled an all-nighter traveling back from spring break and today your brain is fuzzy and unfocused during class lectures.
- **Receiver barrier—no message gets received.** Example: Because you were texting during a class lecture, you weren't listening when the professor announced a new assignment due to tomorrow.
- **Feedback barrier—the recipient doesn't respond enough.** Example: You give someone driving directions, but since they only nod their heads and don't repeat the directions back to you, you don't really know whether you were understood.

1. Physical Barriers: Sound, Time, Space

Try shouting at someone over the roar of earth-moving machinery on a construction site and you know what physical communication barriers are. Other such barriers are time-zone differences, telephone-line static, and crashed computers. Office design can be a physical barrier, too, if it isolates people in cubicles. But privacy does have advantages.

Open offices like this can be noisy and lead to distractions. Have you ever worked in an open office? Did you like it? ©Monkey Business Images/Shutterstock

Open-plan offices are intended to bring even the most introverted people together in accessible, shared spaces designed to encourage conversation and collaboration. Such floor plans can provide workspaces that are uniformly bright and airy, are cheap to construct, and make it easier to include others in impromptu meetings and discussions. But they can also make it hard for people to concentrate. They can be noisy and full of distractions, and people may feel unable to escape being "on" all day because they have less privacy than they would like. Open-plan environments can also encourage employees to keep tabs on each other's comings and goings, which can be a source of stress for some.[44]

Recent research by Oxford Economics seems to argue for cubicles over open-plan space. When 1,200 employees and managers were asked about the workplace amenity they valued most, almost 7 in 10 (68 percent) rated the ability to work without distractions among their top three. For perspective, consider that only 7 percent of respondents valued free food and day care.[45] These employees may be on to something. The University of California Irvine conducted a recent study showing that "it takes an average of 23 minutes and 15 seconds to get back to the task" after you've been interrupted.[46]

Amazon hopes its new headquarters in downtown Seattle will be an enabler of communication. The ambitious complex will consist of a collection of buildings centered around three high-tech greenhouses filled with 3,000 species of plants, many of which are endangered or even extinct in the wild. The greenhouse "spheres" will bring the outdoors in and offer treehouse-style meeting rooms, suspension bridges, walls made of vines, and an indoor creek. "The whole idea," says the project's lead architect, "was to get people to think more creatively."[47]

2. Personal Barriers: Individual Attributes That Hinder Communication

"Is it them or is it me?" How often have you wondered, when someone has shown a surprising response to something you said, how the miscommunication happened? Let's examine seven personal barriers that contribute to miscommunication.

Variable Skills in Communicating Effectively A recent study by Altos Origin found that employees spend 40 percent of their work time on internal e-mails that "add no value to the company."[48] Some people are simply better communicators than others. They have the vocabulary, the writing ability, the speaking skills, the facial expressions, the eye contact, the dramatic ability, the "gift of gab," and the social skills to express themselves in a superior way. But better communication skills can be learned.[49] The final section in this chapter discusses a variety of ways you can improve your communication effectiveness.

Variations in the Way We Process and Interpret Information Are you from a working-class or a privileged background? Are you from a particular ethnic group? Because communication is a perceptual process in which people use different frames of reference and experiences to interpret the world around them, they are selective about what things have meaning to them and what don't. These differences affect what we say and what we think we hear. Some believe technology is changing the very way we communicate, with clicks and swipes substituting for words as people engage in multiple conversations at once, only one of which might be taking place in person.[50]

What differentiates effective communicators, according to communications expert Zamira Jones, is their understanding that ensuring the receiver's correct interpretation of the intended message is up to the sender. "Effective communication is defined by the receiver. If your receiver fails to understand your message, it is your fault, not theirs."[51]

Variations in Trustworthiness and Credibility Without trust between you and the other person, communication is apt to be flawed. Instead of communicating, both of you will be concentrating on defensive tactics, not the meaning of the message being exchanged. In the end, low trust damages communication, which in turn reduces outcomes like job satisfaction, creativity, collaboration, and performance.[52]

The solution, says writer Martin Zwilling, is to work on relationships first. "When people are listening to someone with confidence and trust, there is a predisposition to hear the message and agree."[53]

Oversized Egos Our egos—our pride, our self-esteem, even arrogance—are a fourth barrier. Egos can cause political battles, turf wars, and the passionate pursuit of power, credit, and resources. They influence the way we treat each other and how receptive we are to being influenced by others.

Too much ego—the trait of narcissism—is a handicap, but so is too little. Some successful leaders and communicators are what one expert calls "productive narcissists," such as Bill Gates and Steve Jobs.[54] But for most of us, a little perspective on our ego is in order. Most of the time, it's not about us, and that's a good thing.[55,56] When asked later about his motives for announcing, toward the end of the 2016 presidential campaign, that the FBI was taking a controversial second look at e-mails sent by candidate Hillary Clinton (an inquiry that quickly proved groundless), former FBI director James Comey told *The New York Times,* "I thought I knew the right way to do it, and in hindsight, especially with great feedback from my family, I don't think I did."[57]

Faulty Listening Skills Do you find your mind wandering over the course of a day? Do you forget people's names shortly after meeting them? These are signs of mindlessness. **Mindlessness is a state of reduced attention. It is expressed in behavior that is rigid, or thoughtless.**[58] Life's dynamics put all of us into occasional states of mindlessness. Our brains simply can't keep up with all the stimuli we receive, according to noted psychiatrist Edward Hallowell. "Never in history has the human brain been asked to track so many data points," Hallowell says. He believes overloading of our brains is a primary cause of poor listening and poor performance at school and work. "We're simply expecting more of our brains than they have the energy to handle."[59]

Another barrier to listening, ironically, is cell phones. If we're looking at our screens all the time, how can we really be listening to those who are right before us?[60]

Tendency to Judge Others' Messages Some people assume the phrase "Black Lives Matter" is meant to imply that only black lives matter, while others believe the rejoinder "All Lives Matter" is intended to negate the value of black lives. The point is that we all have a natural tendency, according to psychologist Carl Rogers, to judge others' statements from our own point of view (especially if we have strong feelings about the issue).[61]

Generational Differences If you've tried to teach an older relative how to text or use Facebook, you may have some appreciation for how difficult it can be for older generations to adapt to new technologies. On the other hand, U.S. Senator Bernie Sanders, 77, maintains an active Twitter feed with almost 8 million followers.[62]

With office norms generally becoming less formal as younger people move into the workplace, a preference has grown for the ease of text and e-mail, which can easily reach many people with the same message.[63] You may not be surprised to learn that a European telecom company found the voice-call function was only the fifth most frequently used app on most people's cell phones.[64] Kevin Castle, a 30-something chief technology officer at Technossus in Irvine, California, even keeps his office phone in a cabinet, unplugged, believing that being respectful of others' needs means e-mailing first before making a potentially intrusive phone call.[65]

And for Brit Morin, CEO and founder of Brit + Co., a media and e-commerce platform based in San Francisco, e-mail is outdated. Morin says, "Half my team doesn't use email anymore. . . . The Gen X and older generations–they're not adopting Slack [an internal communications platform] and they're missing out on a lot of community and information that might be useful in their jobs."[66]

But those who want to communicate effectively across generations might keep in mind the advice of one company founder and CEO writing in *Inc.* magazine. Says Alison David, "the most effective way to communicate with Millennials is to follow the same best practices for communicating with every generation."[67] Principles like being clear and concise, practicing empathy, avoiding information overload, and using communication to help people solve problems don't change.

3. Cross-Cultural Barriers

Culture "encompasses the ideas, values, practices, and material objects that allow a group of people, even an entire society, to carry out their collective lives in relative order and harmony."[68]

Because the norms and beliefs of our culture are so deeply ingrained in our thoughts and behaviors, culture naturally affects the way we communicate, both with those who share that culture and especially with those from other cultures. One obvious reason is that language differences often exist. For example, jokes and humor are very much linked to culture.[69] One of your authors found that good American jokes don't necessarily get laughs in Europe, Asia, and Scandinavia. Even the United States and Great Britain, whose cultures share many elements, are often said to be "two countries divided by a common language" (an ironic observation often attributed to the British playwright George Bernard Shaw).

Other causes of cultural differences that can impede communication are nonverbal signs and symbols (such as crossed fingers or thumbs-up, which mean very different things around the world), prejudice and bias, religious and other beliefs, and the tendency to value our own culture above all others, called *ethnocentrism*.[70]

This barrier has been partially overcome via cross-cultural communication training.[71] In Brooklyn, New York, for example, where the population of Chinese immigrants has increased 50 percent over the last generation, Midwood Ambulance, a private ambulance company run by an Italian American family, recently began hiring Chinese-speaking health care workers to staff three ambulances with lettering in Chinese and English on their sides. The response was so positive that three more ambulances have been ordered. "The fact that I can speak their language was a tremendous help," said Jason Lau, a medical technician who helped deliver a Chinese couple's baby on the way to the hospital.[72] Help with training is available from the American Ambulance Association, which just published its first handbook for cross-cultural communication. The handbook cites barriers to communication, key communication tips for EMTs and paramedics, and cultural norms to be aware of.[73]

Cross-cultural training is particularly important for expatriates, or employees working abroad. Success in such assignments can hinge on the employee's adaptability and cultural awareness. Preparation is the key. A U.S. executive for a coffee company recently received 50 hours of language training for an assignment in the Netherlands, even though English is widely spoken there. The payoff? "I do not take the [Dutch] cultural norm of the direct and very honest communication style personally," the executive said. "Therefore, I do not overreact to questions or communications that others may find offensive or confrontational. This has helped me build very positive relationships, as I assume positive intent regarding the content of the communication, and never get side-tracked based on the style of communication."[74]

EXAMPLE Personal and Cross-Cultural Barriers to Communication Can Adversely Affect an Organization

Dirty Image Dove came under fire for posting an advertisement on its Facebook page showing a black woman removing a dark-brown T-shirt to reveal a woman who had become white after using Dove body lotion. The Unilever-owned brand admitted it had "missed the mark" by insinuating that black means dirty and white means clean, but the damage had been done. Dove's image actually ended up in need of cleaning as thousands of social media users accused the company of racism and called for a boycott of its products.[75]

An Anti-Semitic Toad Wendy's decided to post an image of a frog styled with red hair on its Twitter account to match its company logo. What's wrong with a toad? The company chose to spotlight Pepe the Frog, an image the Anti-Defamation League has deemed a hate symbol. Pepe wasn't always known as a controversial amphibian. He started out as an Internet meme for sad situations but was hijacked by extremist groups to represent bigotry and anti-Semitism. Wendy's quickly deleted the tweet, but the company was hammered on social media for not keeping up with the times.[76]

Hold the Bacon! Great Britain's largest supermarket chain, Tesco, placed Pringles chips under a banner reading "Ramadan Mubarak" ("Happy Ramadan" in Arabic) at one of its Liverpool stores.[77] Ramadan is the holiest month in Islam.[78] The problem was that Tesco advertised bacon-flavored chips, and Islam strictly forbids the consumption of pork products. The store is a couple of blocks from Whitechapel's East London Mosque, one of the largest Muslim places of worship in Europe, so the gaffe did not go unnoticed. The marketing initiative triggered outrage and accusations of cultural insensitivity on social media. The company quickly apologized, saying, "We apologise for the mistake, which was made in one store in London. These Pringles cans have now been moved."[79]

YOUR CALL

How would you attempt to recover from a personal or cross-cultural gaffe? What can you do to avoid cross-cultural gaffes?

4. Nonverbal Communication: How Unwritten and Unspoken Messages May Mislead

Nonverbal communication consists of messages sent outside of the written or spoken word. We primarily express nonverbal communication through (1) *eye contact*, (2) *facial expressions*, (3) *body movements and gestures*, and (4) *touch*.[80] Some research suggests that about 55 percent of what we communicate is transmitted nonverbally.[81]

1. Eye Contact Westerners use eye contact to signal the beginning and end of a conversation, to reflect interest and attention, and to convey both honesty and respect. Most people from Western cultures tend to avoid eye contact when conveying bad news or negative feedback. Asians, however, lower their eyes to show respect, while members of Latin cultures do so to show remorse.[82] Interpreting these nonverbal communications as evasive behavior will lead to misunderstanding.[83]

2. Facial Expressions You're probably used to thinking that smiling represents warmth, happiness, or friendship, whereas frowning represents dissatisfaction or anger. But people in some cultures are less openly demonstrative than people in the United States.[84] The Japanese, for example, feel those in the United States smile too much and too broadly. They themselves may smile, slightly, when angry or embarrassed, as well as when happy. One study showed photographs of facial expressions to thousands of people in 44 countries. Among the findings were that, in cultures with low uncertainty avoidance (see Chapter 4), people judged smiling faces as indicating untrustworthiness and possibly even lower intelligence. "Grinning without cause is not a skill Russians possess or feel compelled to cultivate," says a report on the study. "There's even a Russian proverb that translates, roughly, to '*laughing for no reason is a sign of stupidity.*'"[85] One U.S. novelist reported in *The New York Times* that when she smiled too much during a visit to Hong Kong, the woman she was speaking to stepped away from her in alarm.[86]

Bored or tired? People's behavior doesn't always reflect what's going on around them. It may reflect what's going on *inside* of them. Perhaps this man on the right was up late the night before with a sick child or working to meet a project deadline. Even so, when speaking, you need to watch your audience for their reactions. ©Mediaphotos/Getty Images

3. Body Movements and Gestures Open body positions, such as leaning slightly backward, express openness, warmth, closeness, and availability for communication. Closed body positions, such as folded arms or crossed legs, represent defensiveness. Angling your body away from the other person generally makes you look un-interested.[87] You can use these conclusions to improve communications with others.

An experimental study demonstrated the power of using positive, defensive, or no hand gestures when communicating. Participants were shown a video of a leader giving a speech while displaying either positive (community hands–palms facing up, humility–hands clasped at waist level, and steepling–hands form a steeple with fingertips touching), defensive (hands in pockets, crossed arms, hands clasped behind the back), or no hand gestures (keeping hands at one's side). They then rated the extent to which they liked the leader and their positive emotions toward the person. Results showed that people had more positive reactions and emotions toward leaders employing positive hand gestures.[88]

But keep in mind that interpretations of body language can depend on context and culture. For instance, waving your hand with your palm facing away from you means "good-bye" in the United States but "come here" in Korea.[89]

4. Touch Norms for touching vary significantly around the world. For example, kissing on the cheek, patting on the shoulder, and embracing may be appropriate in the United States, but many people in Asia find these actions offensive. These type of behaviors are in appropriate in the Middle East.[90]

Western women tend to use touching of other women to show friendship or sympathy, whereas men are less likely to touch other men and more likely to associate being touched with sexual behavior.[91] Other cultures are often more conservative about the use of touch between men and women.[92]

The table below gives some suggestions for better nonverbal communication skills. *(See Table 15.3.)* It's important to remember that these recommendations may vary across cultures.

TABLE 15.3

Improving Nonverbal Communication Skills

You can practice these skills by watching TV with the sound off and interpreting people's emotions and interactions.

DO . . .	DON'T . . .
Maintain eye contact	Look away from the speaker
Lean toward the speaker	Turn away from the speaker
Speak at a moderate rate	Speak too quickly or slowly
Speak in a quiet, reassuring tone	Speak in an unpleasant tone
Smile and show animation	Yawn excessively
Occasionally nod your head in agreement	Close your eyes
Be aware of your facial expressions	Lick your lips, bite your nails, play with your hair

Source: Adapted from P. Preston, "Nonverbal Communication: Do You Really Say What You Mean?" Journal of Healthcare Management, *March–April 2005, pp. 83–86.*

Exchange of views? Men and women have different communication styles. How effective do you think you are at communicating with the opposite sex?
©monkeybusinessimages/Getty Images

5. Gender Differences

Women and men process language in different parts of the brain, so perhaps it's not surprising that gender differences in communication exist.[93] A recent series of more than 100,000 interviews with male and female executives revealed some of these differences. For instance, women view questioning as their best contribution and use questions to spark ideas, build consensus, and show concern for others. Men think women ask too many questions. They tend to interpret them as barriers to progress or signs of overly controlling behavior.[94]

Many women often feel excluded during meetings and discussions, while about 90 percent of men feel women have equal opportunities to contribute. Both have a point; women prefer to be asked to participate, while men assume someone who doesn't voluntarily speak up simply has nothing to say.[95]

Because stress heightens different hormones in men and in women, men tend to withdraw and isolate themselves when problem solving, whereas women seek out others for support and can interpret men's withdrawing as lack of caring.[96]

Some possible general differences in communication between genders are summarized below. *(See Table 15.4.)* Note, however, that these don't apply in all cases, which would constitute stereotyping.

TABLE 15.4 **Gender and Communication Differences: How Do Men and Women Differ?**

COMMUNICATION CHARACTERISTIC	MEN	WOMEN
Taking credit	Greater use of "I" statements (e.g., "I did this" and "I did that"); more likely to boast about their achievements	Greater use of "We" statements, (e.g., "We did this" and "We did that"); less likely to boast about their achievements
Displaying confidence	Less likely to indicate that they are uncertain about an issue	Mostly likely to indicate a lack of certainty about an issue
Being polite	More likely to appear certain and definitive	Greater use of qualifiers and hedging
Focus of messaging	Focused on self and more likely to mention "Me" or "I"	Focused on other person and more likely to mention "We" or "You"
Talking patterns	More apt to interrupt women and talk over others	Less apt to interrupt men and talk over others
Listening	More likely to take in words and content, less likely to use positive overlaps such as "Yea" or "I see" to demonstrate listening	More likely to hear words and the emotions behind them, more likely to use positive overlaps such as "I agree" or "That's right" to demonstrate listening
Nonverbal patterns	Less expressive (e.g., smile less) and focus more on words than nonverbal cues, less likely to touch	More expressive (e.g., smile more) and skilled at deciphering nonverbal cues, more likely to touch
Answering questions	Quick and to the point	Tend to provide more information than needed
Using emoticons	Use emoticons more often to express sarcasm and banter	Use smiling and laughing emoticons more than men

Source: Derived from A. Nelson and C.D. Brown, The Gender Communication Handbook *(San Francisco, CA: Pfeiffer, 2012); and D. Tannen,* You Just Don't Understand: Women and Men in Conversation *(New York: Ballantine Books, 1990).*

Deborah Tannen recommends that everyone become aware of how differing linguistic styles affect our perceptions and judgments. A **linguistic style** is a person's characteristic speaking patterns—pacing, pausing, directness, word choice, and use of questions, jokes, stories, apologies, and similar devices. For example, in a meeting, regardless of gender, "those who are comfortable speaking up in groups, who need little or no silence before raising their hands, or who speak out easily without waiting to be recognized are more apt to be heard," she says. "Those who refrain from talking until it's clear that the previous speaker is finished, who wait to be recognized, and who are inclined to link their comments to those of others will do fine at a meeting where everyone else is following the same rules but will have a hard time getting heard in a meeting with people whose styles are more like the first pattern."[97] •

PRACTICAL ACTION Improving Communications between Men and Women

Men and women may speak the same language, but they sure communicate differently. This can lead to gender-based miscommunication.[98] It is important to improve communication between men and women because women account for nearly half the workforce and fill nearly 2 of 10 management positions, according to *American City Business Journals*.[99] Here are four ways to bridge the gender communications gap.

1. **Make sure task instructions are clear.** Women tend to ask more questions before beginning work, while men usually roll up their sleeves and jump in. Men may view asking questions as a sign of weakness and lack of confidence, but women believe it is a way to validate data before starting a task. Male bosses need to suspend judgment when listening to females and recognize that questioning can lead to improved performance. Female bosses, on the other hand, shouldn't assume a male colleague knows enough to complete a job just because he didn't ask anything. Instead, they should confirm that male colleagues have enough information to complete their tasks.[100]

2. **Balance how much you need to say.** Men tend to prioritize productivity and efficiency in their conversations, while women may use communication to explore and organize thoughts. Male colleagues should understand that their female counterparts aren't always looking for solutions—so don't jump to one unless asked. Female colleagues should understand that their male counterparts have a lower tolerance for excessive details. Get to the point sooner rather than later, if possible.[101]

3. **Strike a happy medium between relationships and power.** The sexes impose authority differently. Women are more collaborative, while men routinely challenge and expect to be challenged. These differences don't mesh well when exposed to each other. Women may see their male colleagues as bullies and insecure when they come on strong. Men, in contrast, may see their women counterparts as lacking confidence or conviction because they work so hard to get buy-in. The solution is for both sexes to meet halfway. Men should try to be more collaborative, while women ought to take charge more often.[102]

4. **Recognize that we all don't listen the same way.** Women believe good listening skills include making eye contact with the speaker, whereas their male colleagues may not. Men often engage in limited eye contact and nonverbal feedback while listening. According to *Forbes*, women often erroneously cite this lack of eye contact as evidence that, frustratingly, their male bosses don't value their input. The solution requires effort from both sides. Men should strive to make eye contact and utilize nonverbal feedback during a conversation so their female colleagues can confirm they are being heard and understood. Women, in turn, should feel at ease that their male colleagues are listening, even if they don't show it.[103]

YOUR CALL

What do you think are the biggest challenges in cross-gender communication? Do you think both males and females should flex to the tendencies of the other gender?

15.4 Social Media and Management

THE BIG PICTURE

We discuss social media and their use by employees and managers. We look at the impact of social media on managers' and organizations' effectiveness, including applications to recruiting, productivity, sales, innovation, and reputation management. We also consider the costs of social media use, such as the effects of cyberloafing and the need to manage e-mail, as well as growing concerns about security and privacy. We look at the use of texting in organizations and, finally, at the implications for managers of setting social media policy.

LO 15-4

Discuss how managers can successfully use social media to communicate.

Social media, which use web-based and mobile technologies to generate interactive dialogue with members of a network, are woven into every aspect of our lives. We begin our exploration of these technologies by documenting their general use. We then examine the effects of social media on managerial and organizational effectiveness, review the downside of social media, discuss the key impacts of texting on management and organizational behavior, and discuss the need for organizations to develop social media policies.

Social Media Has Changed the Fabric of Our Lives

The widespread use of social media is changing our personal lives and the very nature of how businesses operate and the principles of management. A recent survey of 9,200 travelers across 31 countries, for example, provides insight into the impact of social media in our lives. Eighty-one percent reported that they would rather travel with their mobile devices than with a loved one.[104] From a business perspective, Facebook's new live streaming feature may not yet rival its main social media site in popularity, but it has already attracted small business users who compare its features and benefits with that of Periscope, a similar application from Twitter. Despite some differences, both channels allow business managers to reach and interact with customers in new ways.[105] Researchers suggest that application of such tools can increase a company's brand awareness and sales.[106]

Besides the business application of social media, they affect our lives in countless other ways. Consider, for example, when Republican representatives cut off the live television feed in the House at the end of a legislative session in June 2016. The Democrats who had been pressing for a vote on gun control legislation refused to leave the chamber and used Periscope to stream their impromptu sit-in via cell phone. They held their ground for about 36 hours as C-SPAN picked up the feed and the legislators' protest went viral.[107] And, with undoubtedly profound implications for law enforcement, gun control, and race relations in the United States, Diamond Reynolds stunned the world in 2016 when she live-streamed on Facebook the fatal shooting by police of her boyfriend, Philandro Castile, who had been pulled over for a broken tail light and died in the emergency room. Within a few days, the video had been viewed 3.2 million times on Reynolds's page alone.[108]

What does data suggest about the use of social media? Figure 15.3 shows the usage of various social networks across all age groups. Those between the ages of 18–29 use social media more than any other group, and those over 60 the least. All told, however, it appears all age groups use these tools, underscoring the need for managers to use social media tools with employees of all ages.

A recent survey of more than 3,500 professionals in France, Germany, Japan, Spain, the UK, and the United States documented their use of mobile devices at work. Results showed

- 60 percent check or send personal e-mail at least once a day.
- 57 percent send personal text messages at least once a day.
- 53 percent make personal voice calls at least once a day.
- 50 percent check or use social media at least once a day.[109]

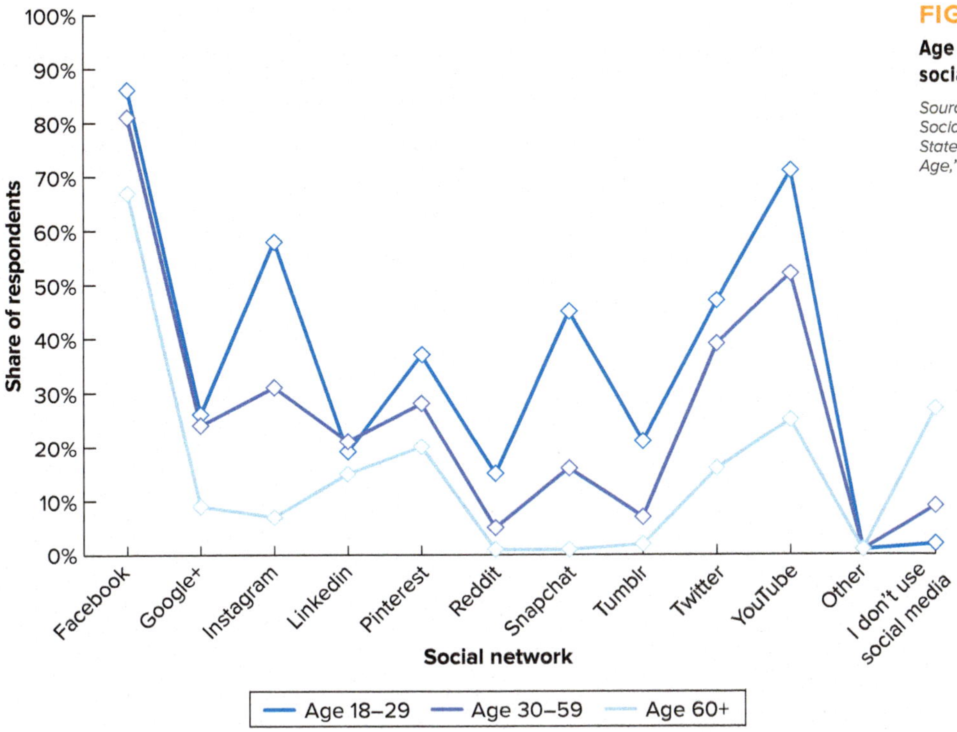

FIGURE 15.3

Age distribution at the top social networks

Source: "Research of Selected Social Networks in the United States as of February 2017, by Age," Statista, *2018.*

It's no wonder, then, that the communications capabilities of social media continue to grow and expand and that managers need to keep up with their increasing potential.

Moreover, those whose businesses are global, for instance, are using social medial platforms to reach audiences in developing countries around the world. And it's not just a matter of mastering Facebook or Twitter; in fact, some overseas governments actively block their citizens' access to Western media channels. Instead, adapting to local conditions also means knowing, for instance, that "the largest social network in China is QQ, Orkut is widely used in India and Brazil, Kontakte is strong in Russia, Hi5 is the leading network in Peru, and Maktoob is the choice throughout the Arab world."[110]

Social Media and Managerial and Organizational Effectiveness

With their ease of use, speed, and potentially huge audiences, social media have increasing applications for managers' and organizations' effectiveness. We will look at social media use in employment recruiting, employee and employer productivity, sales, innovation, and corporate reputation.

Employment Recruiting About 92 percent of companies today use social media for recruiting,[111] especially for recruiting "passive" job candidates–that is, those who aren't actively looking for a new job. Although Facebook and LinkedIn have 2 billion and 500 million users, respectively, recruiters prefer LinkedIn. A national survey of recruiters revealed that 87 percent used LinkedIn versus 55 percent for Facebook.[112] Nearly half of recruiters say they use texting to reach job candidates and hiring managers alike.[113] "'People don't want to have that ten-minute [phone] conversation any more if they could just reply with a quick text,' said Kirby Cuniffe, chief executive of staffing firm Aegis Worldwide LLC."[114]

Craig Fisher, head of employer brand at software firm CA Technologies and CEO of TalentNet, agrees that it's easier to find people with specific skill sets with social media tools. Managers should be savvy, however. Says Fisher, they should "keep good content flowing that is helpful to their social communities and avoid just 'asking' all the time, so that when candidates see these ads and check out the company, they see a helpful resource and interesting culture."[115]

On the job applicant's side, 59 percent used social media to conduct research on companies of interest, and they preferred Facebook (67 percent) over Twitter (35 percent).[116] As you probably know, most company websites have a "Jobs" or "Employment" tab where interested job seekers can search and apply for open positions. Beyond this fairly simple interaction, you also can customize your searches on job posting sites like Monster and Indeed.com and apply directly to the hiring firm, attaching résumés, writing samples, links to blogs and videos, and other pertinent information. Companies can also post jobs on industry-specific hosting and social networking platforms, like GitHub (software developers), Dribble (web designers),[117] and Mediabistro (media professionals). More than 60,000 jobs are tweeted on Monster every day.[118] And according to Career Builder's website, 52 percent of companies check out potential hires' social media pages, including their sometimes unguarded profiles on Facebook and LinkedIn.[119]

PRACTICAL ACTION Building Your Personal Social Media Brand

Employers are increasingly relying on social media to hire new talent. A CareerBuilder survey of more than 2,300 hiring managers and human resources professionals in 2017 found that 70 percent of employers used social media to screen candidates before hiring. This was up significantly from 60 percent in 2016. More than 54 percent of these employers found content on social media that caused them not to hire a candidate.[120] So how can you stand out in the crowd in a good way? You may want to start by referring back to Chapter 6's Manage U feature, where we discussed the development of an effective social media strategy. Here are some additional tips for managing your online brand.

1. **Optimize your profile at LinkedIn and industry-specific networking sites.** Make sure you list timely, accurate information about your current and recent jobs. It's also important to demonstrate your increasing level of experience or broadening set of skills in your job descriptions. Remember to fill out every section of your profile with key words important to recruiters in your industry and to provide a unique headline that briefly describes what makes you so special.[121] Sometimes networking sites won't allow you to provide a more detailed picture of your personal brand. So you may want to consider developing your own professional-looking website. This allows you to further control your message to potential employers.

2. **Follow the companies that interest you.** Start by conducting Internet research on a set of potential employers. Look for organizations that operate in disciplines you are studying or have a personal interest in. You can start broad and then narrow it down, targeting employers that really mesh with your interests. Then use social media and networking sites to follow these companies and find or ask for connections to people who work there.[122] Adding these connections to your network demonstrates your interest in the firm and also allows you to find out more about the company's culture and future plans. Effective networking takes time, so be patient.

3. **Participate in industry-related chat rooms and discussion groups.** It is worth the effort to positively contribute to ongoing online conversations because it raises your profile and introduces your name to new connections. You can even consider starting an industry-specific blog, if you're really an expert. Don't feel intimidated if you are still a novice. Asking intelligent questions can help your networking efforts, even if you're still learning the ropes.

4. **Edit your general online social presence.** Your overall presence on Facebook, Instagram, Twitter, LinkedIn, and other sites should not cause a negative first impression. You don't necessarily need a professional photo shoot; just delete any embarrassing old photos and make sure what is there represents a mature and responsible individual. Also delete embarrassing tweets or other social media postings.[123] When deciding what to keep and what to delete, always think, "Would I want this to appear on the evening news?"

YOUR CALL

Think of 8 to 10 companies in an industry you'd like to work in. What kind of online brand do you think recruiters at those companies are looking for?

Social media can also lead to hiring discrimination (by revealing applicants' religious affiliation, age, family composition, or sexual orientation). Says Craig Fisher of TalentNet, "anything that is public information is fair game in researching prospective candidates. When those candidates become applicants, the rules change a bit." At the same time, "you just can't use that information in consideration of employment if it is a protected characteristic."[124]

Employee Productivity While overuse of and even addiction to social media exist and can cause serious problems,[125] there seems little doubt that social media tools at work, used appropriately, can make communication by and among employees more productive. In fact, productivity is a driving force behind the use of all forms of technology at work, including social media. The key for employees, managers, and employers is to harness the speed and reach of social media to enhance individual performance.

Results like reduced turnover, higher performance, increased job satisfaction, and greater creativity and collaboration are common findings in research about the effects of social media.[126] Employees who work remotely are particular beneficiaries of social media's communications capabilities. Customized scheduling, organizing, networking, document sharing, messaging, and other digital communication options help relieve them of the need to commute, attend routine meetings, and be distracted by colleagues.[127] Digital productivity tools that control e-mail, organize links and contacts, prioritize tasks, and even edit prose can help remote workers stay focused and organized so they can meet deadlines and enjoy work-life balance.[128]

At the same time, managers need to remember that employees don't have to be in touch all the time, no matter how easy it is. There is plenty of evidence that everyone should unplug from e-mail and social media on a regular basis, if not during every evening, weekend, and vacation.[129] Concerned that productivity was actually suffering, health care consulting firm Vynamic began discouraging employees from sending e-mails between 11 p.m. and 7 a.m. Monday through Friday and all day on weekends. Job satisfaction is up since the change took place.[130]

Work-life balance. As this family knows, vacations are good for everyone. Research shows that everyone needs some down time. It also helps to give our electronic devices a break as well. ©David Buffington/Blend Images LLC

How often do you use social media while at work? Do you think it is helping or hindering your performance? You can find out by completing Self-Assessment 15.1.

SELF-ASSESSMENT 15.1 CAREER READINESS

To What Extent Are You Effectively Using Online Social Networking at Work?

The following survey was designed to assess how well you are using social networking in your job. Please be prepared to answer these questions if your instructor has assigned Self-Assessment 15.1 in Connect.

1. To what extent are social media helping or hurting your performance at work?
2. Based on your survey scores, what can you do to more effectively use social media at work? Be specific.
3. What things might you say during an interview to demonstrate that you possess the career readiness competency of *new media* literacy?

Employer Productivity Companies of all sizes and in all industries believe in the benefits of social media, including their ability to keep employees engaged and satisfied, and therefore productive. Novartis, the pharmaceutical giant, uses social media games to teach employees about its products, reaching 600 workers around the world and logging a 12 percent jump in employee satisfaction as a result. Volkswagen Ireland encouraged its 125 workers to collaborate better by adopting Workplace, a Facebook platform designed for this purpose. Efficiency has risen, says the firm, and fewer e-mails are being sent.[131] If used effectively, social media allow companies to reap many of the benefits listed in Table 15.5.

TABLE 15.5
Social Media Benefits for Employers

BENEFIT	DESCRIPTION
Connect in real time over distance	Employees, customers, communities, suppliers, prospective talent, and many others can communicate as needed and while work is being completed.
Collaborate within and outside organization	Linking sources of knowledge is a means for realizing the potential of employee diversity and enhancing productivity. Social media are by definition a way of connecting people virtually, so their effective implementation benefits virtual teamwork.
Expand boundaries	Social networks can become critical means for organizational innovation and effectiveness, allowing them to utilize knowledge, skills, and experience of people outside (not employed by) the organization.

Source: Adapted from L. McFarland and R. Ployhart, "Social Media: A Contextual Framework to Guide Research and Practice," Journal of Applied Psychology, *2015, pp. 1653–1677.*

The essence of social media is *connectivity*. If deployed effectively, social media enable businesses to do the following:

- **Connect with key stakeholders.** The use of social media allows you to connect in real time and over distances with many customers, suppliers, employees, potential talent, and other key stakeholders.
- **Connect with varied sources of expertise inside the organization.** We've seen such connectivity demonstrated in virtual teams, redefining conventional organizational

boundaries and drawing on different sources of talent, knowledge, and experience throughout the organization.

- **Connect with varied sources of expertise outside the organization.** Social media can cross organizational boundaries and connect with outsiders to help in problem solving. An example is *crowdsourcing*, as we'll see below. A variant is *crowdfunding*, raising money via online sources.

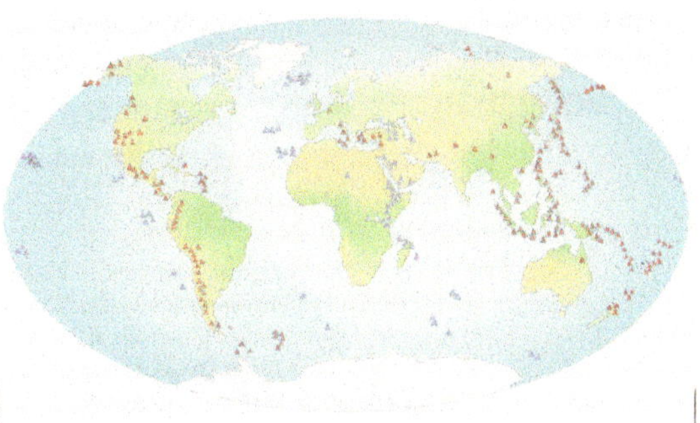

Social media enables people to instantly communicate with others around the world. ©Dorling Kindersley/Getty Images

On the other hand, if not managed effectively, social media can create many legal, financial, and human resource risks.[132] For instance, each employee who plays fantasy football loses about one hour a week of work time.[133] The price tag for productivity lost to fantasy football was $17 billion in 2016.[134]

Social Media and Innovation: Crowdsourcing

If you are looking for an innovative solution to a problem, you might conclude that the more people you have thinking about the problem, the more potential ideas will be generated. That's the idea behind **crowdsourcing, using the Internet and social media to enlist a group outside the organization for help solving a problem.** The strategy has drawn a lot of attention, especially for its use in fundraising (crowdfunding) on such sites as Kickstarter, but it has a mixed record of success.[135]

Some crowdsourcing efforts are organized as competitions, with teams volunteering to solve a problem by a certain deadline and win a cash prize. New York's Metropolitan Transportation Authority recently ran a contest, which it called a "genius challenge," to solicit the public's ideas for fixing the city's aging subway system. The agency received more than 400 submissions from people in 23 countries and says it will "absolutely follow up on" the eight winning ideas, whose contributors shared a $1 million prize.[136] Some companies recruit temporary or contingent workers through crowdsourcing and pay them for their time and efforts whether or not they succeed.[137] Critics say, however, that large groups of people working on a problem have been shown to produce only average results; they advise hiring real experts to get the job done.[138]

A recent study of 20,000 organizations that tried crowdsourcing found that successful efforts had two features in common. First, the managers behind them were proactive in that they encouraged contributors to submit ideas by posting their own ideas first and inviting public comment, opening the conversation and giving potential collaborators needed insight into the organization and its needs. Second, the managers were reactive in responding publicly to the contributions they received, validating the contributors and encouraging still more to come forward because they felt confident their ideas would be heard.[139]

Because more and more companies are exploring the use of social media to enhance the product development process, researchers are starting to quantitatively study its benefits. Although it is too soon to make a definitive conclusion, results from a global study of the product development process in more than 660 companies is enlightening. The researchers concluded "despite the promise, the expected positive results are frequently not realized in practice. . . . We believe that social media provides a game-changing opportunity for companies that learn how to exploit it. But taking advantage of the opportunity requires more than having a Facebook presence with a loyal base of 'friends' who say they 'like' you. In order to use social media for innovation, organizations need clear strategies and objectives."[140]

Social Media and Sales and Brand Recognition

Is it logical to expect that an "effective" social media presence generates customers and brand recognition? Yes, for the following reasons:

1. Social media can increase product/service awareness and generate customer inquiries.
2. Social media can enhance relationships with customers.

3. Social media can increase the ability to reach customers on a global scale.
4. For small or local businesses, social media can foster co-promotion of local businesses and the image of small businesses in the area.[141]
5. Social media can foster consumers' conversations about brands.[142]

Promoting green. This 2009 Volkswagen AG Jetta TDI was named Green Car of the Year by the *Green Car Journal* in 2008. Do you think this designation helped promote sales of the vehicle? ©Armando Arorizo/Bloomberg/Getty Images

Don't assume that the mere use of social media automatically results in more sales and brand recognition. Recent research suggests that social media won't create positive outcomes unless two conditions are present.[143] First, the company must possess both competence in social media skills and technology and commitment in the form of dedicated resources. Second, a successful social media strategy requires consumers or customers with social media skills. A PR specialist writing in *Forbes* suggests companies should also make sure their messages are relevant, timely, and surprising and that marketers should track their results to learn what works.[144]

UnderArmour scored a big success with its "I Will What I Want" videos of female athletes on YouTube, for example. These brief films were intended to "[empower] women of all shapes and sizes to get moving and not let anyone hold them back." One notable entry in the series, drawing more than 7.5 million views, featured rising ballet star Misty Copeland, the first African American dancer to be promoted to principal dancer at American Ballet Theater.[145] TOMS Shoes was another social media winner, with an Instagram campaign in which the socially conscious company promised to donate one pair of shoes for every photo someone posted of their own bare feet. Almost 300,000 pairs were donated as a result of the drive.[146] Also popular on Instagram is GoPro's regular showcasing of user-generated content. Action-camera enthusiasts are invited to post their own photos for the company's popular Photo of the Day opportunity.[147]

Misty Copeland. Misty Copeland performing "Giselle" at the Metropolitan Opera House. ©Hiroyuki Ito/Getty Images

EXAMPLE TD Bank Dominates Social Media

Toronto-Dominion Bank (TD) may be the 11th largest bank in the United States,[148] but its social media performance is second to none. The changing banking landscape has motivated a significant change in the way financial institutions such as TD promote their brands. "The shift of banks' customers to mobile and online transactions has caused them to devise new strategies—which includes having a sophisticated social media plan," said Bryan Segal, the former CEO of Engagement Labs.[149] Engagement Labs uses data obtained through social media feeds to offer social media data, analytics, and reports for organizations that are engaging on social networks.[150]

TD wants customers to know it still cares about them, even if increasingly more transactions are done online or through automated teller machines (ATMs) instead of inside the branch. For example, TD launched a social media campaign in 2014 known as #TDThanksYou. The bank surprised millions of North American customers with personalized gifts when they visited branch ATMs. Customers were selected by their local branch representatives who knew their personal stories. For example, a Toronto woman who was the sole caregiver for her Alzheimer's-diagnosed husband was provided with a trip to England to visit her daughter and caregiving support for her husband. Customers' emotional reactions at the ATM were caught on video and posted on Twitter via the TDThanksYou hashtag. One video garnered nearly 24 million views.[151]

TD reinforces its customer service brand by using Facebook and Twitter to correspond with account holders in almost real time. For example, the bank answers customer posts on Facebook in just over an hour; its average Twitter response rate is around 46 minutes. One of the bank's primary competitors, JPMorgan Chase, takes about 10 hours to respond to social media inquiries, according to an analysis by Engagement Labs.[152] TD also uses social media as a means to educate. The bank has conducted thousands of financial education classes for customers and noncustomers since 2014, according to *American Banker*.[153] It even has an online "WOW! Zone" that helps kids and teens develop strong financial skills.[154]

These social media efforts have put TD Bank at the top of the Engagement Labs' rankings for both Facebook and Twitter, ahead of competitors such as Bank of America and Wells Fargo.[155]

YOUR CALL

Are there potential drawbacks to having a robust social media presence as TD Bank does? If so, what are they?

Social Media and Reputation Some companies have been very successful at using social media to build and protect their reputations online. The benefits are real.[156] Research with KLM Royal Dutch Airline showed that customers who engaged with the company online had more positive perceptions about its reputation.[157]

One of the biggest dangers managers face is negative comments about the organization posted by disgruntled customers or even employees. Some tips for defusing these and limiting the harm they can do are:[158]

1. **Create and enforce a social media policy for employees.** We'll discuss social media policies in more detail. At a minimum, your policy should limit what employees can say on the organization's web pages and ensure that all posted content meets the highest ethical standards.
2. **Appoint experienced managers to monitor your social media presence and respond quickly and appropriately to negative posts.** Vitamin Water waited 24 hours before responding to customers voicing anger on Facebook about its new flavor.[159] A Mississippi woman received an insensitive e-mail from her state representative about her problems getting medical supplies for her diabetic child. She posted the legislator's crass response on Facebook, where it went viral.[160] A great deal of damage can occur online in a short time, and all of it in the public eye.
3. **Acknowledge there is a problem.** Gracefully accepting that someone has a genuine issue with the organization, its product or service, or its posts—even if the problem is a misunderstanding on his or her part—can go a long way toward defusing bad feelings. If the organization is in error, the appropriate manager should say so and apologize.

4. **Take the conversation offline if necessary.** If a customer refuses to be satisfied, take the conversation to a private sphere such as phone or e-mail. Not only will this keep it out of the public eye and prevent further damage to the brand but the individualized attention may also reduce the customer's ire.

A company's reputation is affected by posts made by current and former employees. Sites like Glassdoor.com, for instance, allow people to publicly (and anonymously) rate their employers on criteria like salary, benefits, work-life balance, career advancement possibilities, and even the quality of the employment interview. Firms that are confident they have happy employees can encourage them to spread the buzz about office parties, outings, and incentives and rewards on corporate websites, social media, and blogs, building the company's image as a good place to work.[161]

Cyberloafing is not always as obvious as a person sleeping on a park bench. It can occur in subtle ways, such as a person texting a friend about dinner plans while at work.
©Michael Heim/123RF

Downsides of Social Media

It's fair to say the digital age and rise of social media have introduced almost as many difficulties as efficiencies into people's lives. Some of these problems relate to cyberloafing, security breaches, privacy concerns, and the volume of e-mail.

Cyberloafing

Lost productivity due to **cyberloafing—using the Internet at work for personal use**—is a primary concern for employers in their adoption of social media. Some studies put the cost at $85 billion per year and report that employees spend 60 percent–80 percent of their time at work pretending to do actual or legitimate work. It also exposes companies to computer viruses and uses up bandwidth.[162] How do employees waste time on social media?

- 50 percent are talking on a cell phone or texting.
- 39 percent are surfing the Internet.
- 38 percent are on social media.
- 23 percent are sending personal e-mail.[163]

Then there is shopping online while at work. A survey by CareerBuilder found that on average 47 percent of workers planned to shop online.[164,165]

Software tools can reduce cyberloafing. One program developed by researchers at Arizona State University restricts the websites employees are allowed to access from work, the length of time they are permitted to spend there, or both. The program "significantly" reduced cyberloafing at the company where it was installed. The lead researcher advises that managers engage employees in decisions about how to use such tools, however, both to make sure rules are fair and to make employees feel like "part of the conversation."[166]

Another consideration for managers is that most employees can and do bring their own devices to work and so are perfectly capable of bypassing controls installed on office computers. And, say some observers who think reports of cyberloafing's extent are exaggerated, taking an online break from work might not be such a bad thing. It can reduce stress and improve concentration. The key, again, is fairness in setting and upholding policies about social media use, which we discuss below.[167]

Phubbing and FOMO

Microaggressions, or acts of unconscious bias, include a number of seemingly tiny but repeated actions, like interrupting others, mispronouncing or mistaking someone's name, and avoiding eye contact. A particular form of microaggression is called *phubbing*, for phone snubbing or ignoring those present in order to pay attention to a mobile phone. The urge to phub others springs from the fear of missing out—**FOMO—or of being out of touch with something happening in our social network,**[168] a growing phenomenon although research shows that conversations are actually less rewarding for both parties when interrupted by one person's texting.[169]

A recent study by professors at Baylor University found that employees who were phubbed by their manager felt they could no longer trust that manager to keep promises or treat them fairly, which led to negative effects on their psychological preparedness to work and, predictably, on their job satisfaction and job performance as well.[170] Phubbing tends to be more common among younger people, who are more intimately connected to their phones, and among men, who view interruptions as less onerous than do women.[171] Even if unused, a cell phone on the table can make people feel less connected to those they are with.[172] Phubbing doesn't have to recur, however. The phubbed should calmly explain how they feel, and phubbers should use empathy to understand the harm their microaggression is doing to their communications and their relationships.[173]

Psychologists have demonstrated that FOMO causes anxiety. A recent study examined college students' anxiety levels after giving up their phones for one hour. Light users of smartphones experienced no increases in anxiety, while moderate users showed signs of increased anxiety after 25 minutes without a phone. These levels of anxiety stayed steady for the remaining time of the hour-long study. Heavy users, in contrast, revealed heightened anxiety after 10 phone-free minutes, and their level of anxiety increased over time.[174]

FOMO is exacerbated by our habits, such as paying attention to our phones during sleep hours. "One study found that 40 percent of students reported waking at night to answer phone calls, and 47 percent woke to answer text messages." Psychologists demonstrated that "people of all generations seem to have succumbed to the phenomenon."[175] The "I Wish . . ." feature discusses Tracy Liebsohn's experience with FOMO.

I Wish...
...I didn't have FOMO.

Tracy Leibsohn is a senior project manager in the consumer products industry. After being promoted from intern to her current position, she was given a company cell phone so that she could access her work e-mail on the go. While this made her e-mail more accessible to her, it caused her work life to creep into her personal life. She spends about 80 percent of her workday answering e-mails.

Courtesy Tracy Leibsohn

"I have a work cell phone and I can get e-mail on it. I think that's pretty common for most people. And it's tempting on the weekends or in the middle of the night or first thing in the morning to look at your phone and see what you have on your plate and what e-mails came through when you weren't at work," said Tracy.

"From a work–life balance standpoint, being able to access e-mail at home and having it readily available is a blessing and a curse at the same time," said Tracy. "It's really nice to not have to power up your computer and sit down at a desk—you have access all the time, and you keep up on what's going on if you're out of town or not in the office. But at the same time, it can create unnecessary anxiety when you should really be offline rather than feeling obligated to sit and check your phone."

The thought of knowing that she has unread e-mails piling up in her inbox gives Tracy anxiety. In order to reduce the anxiety, she checks her e-mail, whether it is at night, in the morning, or even while she is on vacation.

"About a year ago, I was on vacation out of the country for a week. I was on paid time off and shouldn't have to check my work e-mail, but I brought my work phone with me because I didn't want to miss anything urgent," said Tracy. "I caught myself checking and responding to e-mail several times throughout the vacation. I was with my husband, and he was very frustrated that I was supposed to be relaxing but instead my head was in two different places because I was stressed about what was going on at work."

"Looking back, the issue that I was responding to and was stressed about probably could have waited, but it caused me to be distracted from vacation because I was trying to stay connected to work," said Tracy.

Courtesy of Tracy Leibsohn

Psychologist Adam Alter offers a solution. He notes that "there is no silver bullet solution, and going cold turkey is nearly impossible. It's really about sustainable use. The best thing we can do is to section off parts of our lives from technology to keep them sacred and tech-free."[176] An example is leaving your phone outside your bedroom at night or turning it off when eating with others.

Security: Guarding against Cyberthreats **Security is defined as a system of safeguards for protecting information technology against disasters, system failures, and unauthorized access that result in damage or loss.** Security is a continuing challenge, with computer and cell-phone users constantly having to deal with threats ranging from malicious software (malware) that tries to trick people into yielding passwords and personal information to viruses that can destroy or corrupt data.[177] According to the Norton *Cyber Crime Report for 2017*, nearly 980 million people in 20 countries were victims of cybercrime in 2017, with an average cost per person of $142 and three full days to deal with the effects. More than four in five consumers believe cybercrime is, in fact, a crime and should be prosecuted as such, but 42 percent find it acceptable to commit "morally questionable online behaviors in certain circumstances,"[178] which may help explain why employees are often called the weakest link in a company's defense against the threat. Even app-laden personal cell phones brought to the workplace can introduce a grave risk to a company's security.[179]

Biggest hack. Gary McKinnon arrives at the High Courts in London to appeal his extradition to the United States. He is a Scottish systems administrator and was accused of conducting the biggest U.S. military hack of all time. The British government blocked his extradition order to the U.S. Do you think governments around the world should prosecute hackers like McKinnon to the fullest extent? ©John Stillwell/PA Images/Alamy Stock Photo

Citing recent cyberattacks on major companies like Equifax, Verizon, and Target, *Harvard Business Review* noted that "attackers didn't need to break down a wall of ones and zeros, or sabotage a piece of sophisticated hardware; instead they simply needed to take advantage of predictably poor user behavior."[180] Such behavior crosses generations; younger workers are just as likely as their older peers to ignore or underuse common safeguards.[181] For example, one in four Millennials use the same password for all their accounts, while only 10 percent of Boomers do.[182] A motivating strategy called "social proof" can help nudge employees toward safer online behavior at work by showing or informing them of how others act in the same circumstances and then giving them the tools and education they need to follow suit.[183]

The key to protecting digital communication systems against fraud, hackers, identity theft, and other threats is prevention. The table below presents some ways to protect yourself. *(See Table 15.6.)* The federal government also offers valuable advice at the FCC's website.[184]

TABLE 15.6

Protecting against Security and Privacy Breaches on the Internet

- **Don't use passwords that can be easily guessed.** Use weird combinations of letters, numbers, and punctuation, and mix uppercase and lowercase, along with special characters such as !, #, and %.
- **Don't use the same password for multiple sites.** Avoid using the same password at different sites, since if hackers or scammers obtain one account, they potentially have your entire online life.
- **Don't reveal sensitive information on social networking sites.** Even people who set their profiles to Facebook's strictest privacy settings may find sensitive information leaked all over the web.
- **Be careful about free and illegal downloads.** File-sharing programs often contain spyware, as do sites containing free and illegal songs, movies, and TV shows.
- **Be mindful of liability issues.** Employers routinely monitor employee e-mail for offensive messages or risky material that may expose them to lawsuits.
- **Keep antivirus software updated.** The antivirus software on your computer won't protect you forever. Visit the antivirus software maker's website and enable the automatic update features.

Source: Derived from B. K. Williams and S. C. Sawyer, Using Information Technology: A Practical Introduction, *11th ed. (New York: McGraw-Hill Education, 2015), pp. 94, 100, 101, 357, 478.*

Privacy: Keeping Things to Yourself **Privacy is the right of people not to reveal information about themselves.** Threats to privacy can range from name migration, as when a company sells its customer list to another company, to online snooping, to government prying and spying. A potentially devastating violation of privacy is **identity theft, in which thieves hijack your name and identity and use your good credit rating to get cash or buy things.** Many of the cautions in Table 15.6 apply here, too.

The most important thing to know about online and social media privacy is that, as the recent misuse of Facebook users' personal data indicates,[185] nothing posted is ever truly private.[186] In some cases, Internet users are their own worst enemies, posting compromising images and information about themselves on social networking sites that may be available to, say, potential employers. Others, like the Mississippi representative mentioned previously whose unhelpful response to a constituent in need went viral, disastrously fail to think before they post. It has wisely been said that if you wouldn't want to see something on the front page of the newspaper or the evening news, don't post it.

As for privacy at work, "Generally in the workplace, there isn't a right to privacy," according to Melissa Ventrone, a privacy attorney.[187] Monitoring of electronic communications is widespread. In most circumstances, employers are permitted to monitor—that is, read—their employees' e-mail and track their Internet use, and two-thirds of those in a recent survey said they did so.[188] More than a quarter of all employers in the survey also said they had fired someone for "e-mail misuse," and more than 7 in 10 have disciplined employees for social media gaffes.[189] And your privacy rights may be limited when you are using your employer's computer and other equipment.[190] Monitoring can become a source of bias, however, and determined employees can often get around monitoring tools and devices, sometimes weakening the organization's security protocols in the process.[191] And at least two dozen class-action lawsuits have been filed in Illinois, claiming employers violated the state's Biometric Information Privacy Act.[192]

The Need to Manage E-Mail Employees tend to have a love-hate relationship with e-mail. We love that we can send and receive e-mail 24/7 from anywhere. But we hate the fact that the average worker can receive hundreds of e-mails a day, and the fact that most of us can handle no more than a few dozen in that time. While texting, social networking, and other forms of electronic and digital communication have begun to reduce the dominance of e-mail, it's predicted that the number of e-mail users worldwide will continue to grow, reaching nearly 4.1 billion people (or 52 percent of the world's population) by 2021. One reason is that so many other communications applications, as well as online shopping sites, require a valid e-mail address for access.[193]

Table 15.7 on the next page provides some practical tips for handling e-mail.

Managerial Implications of Texting

Common sense says that a colleague or customer standing in front of you or talking to you by phone or videoconference deserves your full and immediate attention, while the person texting you about your plans for the evening can wait. But texting does have some legitimate workplace applications. How can managers best make use of its capabilities?

Many feel that those who deal directly with customers should not be texting at work. A cashier, a crossing guard, a customer service rep, and a salesperson—not to mention a cab or bus driver—are good examples of employees whose phones should be tucked in a bag or a drawer at all times.[194] At the same time, some very limited use of texting for personal reasons at work, in the right time and place, can be a big help in increasing work-life balance and relieving stress.[195]

If texting is an integral part of your workplace communications—not least because it can reduce costs and eliminate the time phone customers spend waiting on hold[196]—ideally it should be covered under the organization's social media policy (discussed next). Who participates in or initiates group messages, for instance? How quickly are people expected to reply to texts? For what purposes can texts be sent, and to whom?

TABLE 15.7
Tips for Better E-mail Handling

- **Turn off all noncritical notifications and unsubscribe from newsletters.** An important first step is to reduce the amount of unnecessary e-mail you get.
- **Set aside one or two 15-minute periods each day to review e-mail.** Don't check it compulsively, and try not to read or send e-mails before or after work hours. About 40% of Gen X and Gen Y employees say they do so, but intrusions into off-work hours can disrupt work–life balance.
- **Treat all e-mail as confidential.** See the discussion of privacy above. Also think twice about including other people in your message who may not need to read it.
- **Be brief and professional, and proofread (twice).** Keep your message as short as possible and avoid spelling, grammatical, and other errors, especially in people's names and titles. Save emojis for personal messages.
- **Remember that not every topic belongs on e-mail.** Complicated or controversial topics may be better discussed on the phone or in person to avoid misunderstandings.
- **Remember that e-mails represent business records.** E-mails can become the subject of disclosure in lawsuits. Be careful what you write; it may be used against you or your company in a court of law.

Sources: S. M. Wich, "Court Report: E-Mail Undermined Defense to FMLA Claim," HRMagazine, *June/July 2017, p. 20; Money (Contributor),* Forbes, *April 7, 2015, "Why Checking Email after Work Is Bad for Your Career—and Health,"* Fortune, *http://fortune.com/2015/04/07/why-checking-email-after-work-is-bad-for-your-career-and-health-2/ (accessed July 2016); A. Samuel "How I Tamed the Email Beast at Work,"* The Wall Street Journal, *March 14, 2016, http://www.wsj.com/articles/how-i-tamed-the-email-beast-at-work-1457921533 (accessed July 2016); A. Fridman, "How to Stop Email Distractions at Work,"* Inc., *June 23, 2016, http://www.inc.com/adam-fridman/how-to-stop-email-distractions-at-work.html (accessed July 2016).*

Here are a few tips for making the most of texting for work purposes:[197]

1. **As with all social media tools, strictly limit your use for personal reasons during the work day.** It helps to let your friends and family know you will not respond while at work.
2. **Text only important messages.** Avoid using texting for routine information, and make it clear in your message why it is urgent. As always, be brief. If you must deliver bad news, be courteous and do it over the phone or in person.
3. **Avoid texting during meetings.** Not only is it rude to text during a meeting; it's likely the people you might need to text will be in the meeting with you, so there should be no problem with leaving your phone behind.
4. **Don't use abbreviations or emojis.** Abbreviations like "omw" and "btw" look unprofessional in a business message and can confuse some readers. Save emojis for texts with family and friends.
5. **As always, proofread.** Read every message before sending, and be especially alert for potential miscommunication instigated by auto-correct features.

Managerial Considerations in Creating Social Media Policies

The purpose of a social media policy at work is not to completely close off employees' access to personal e-mails and texts or even to shopping websites. Many employees already feel guilty if they need to deal with personal messages at work but say they would quit their job if their ability to do at least some personal tasks during the workday were restricted.[198] And while as much as half of social media use during work hours may be taking place for nonwork reasons, many employees do use social media for constructive work purposes, such as making and nurturing professional connections and seeking solutions to problems from those both inside and outside the organization.[199]

Social Media Policy A **social media policy** describes the who, how, when, and for what purposes of social media use, and the consequences for noncompliance. Such a policy can not only clarify expectations and relieve guilt, but also prevent impulsive or abusive posts and messages that can damage an organization's or an individual's reputation. The essential elements of an effective social media policy are outlined in Table 15.8.

TABLE 15.8 Seven Elements of an Effective Social Media Policy

Applies the same standards across all posts and platforms. Employees should understand that they represent their company wherever they post, not only on professional networks like LinkedIn but also on sites more generally used for personal expression such as Twitter and Instagram. The same standards should thus apply everywhere.
Identifies sites employees may use at work. Depending on the company's goals, it may want to limit employees' social media use during the workday to specific sites.
Informs employees of terms of use and conditions of the platforms they'll be using. Violations of terms can limit the employer's future access to the site.
Identifies who may speak for the company and for what purpose. If the employer maintains a corporate Facebook page or Twitter feed, for example, only specified employees should be empowered to post there.
Clarifies the distinction between personal and work-related posts. Remind employees that their personal posts can affect their professional life.
Requires professional behavior online. Managers and employees alike should be cautioned against cyberbullying and the unfair or discriminatory use of any information about others they may find online.
Upholds confidentiality. Internal complaints and conflicts should never be aired online where partners, clients, and competitors can read about them. Proprietary information should never be disclosed in any forum, including on the Internet.
Discourages anonymous posts. If the content of a post or message meets the highest standards of professionalism and respect for others, it should not need to be anonymous. At the same time, employees should be encouraged to clarify when they are speaking on behalf of the company and when they are not.
Specifies the consequences of violations. Employees should understand what is at risk if they violate the company's social media policy and whether they will be disciplined, receive training, or even be dismissed.

Sources: Based on Aria Solar, "5 Key Components to an Agile Social Media Policy for Employees (and 3 Brands Doing It Right)," Getbambu.com, January 9, 2018, https://getbambu.com/blog/social-media-policy-for-employees/; Forbes Human Resources Council, "Why Your Business Needs a Social Media Policy and Eight Things It Should Cover," Forbes, May 25, 2017, *https://www.forbes.com/sites/forbeshumanresourcescouncil/2017/05/25/why-your-business-needs-a-social-media-policy-and-eight-things-it-should-cover/#2cab409b5264; "Six Elements of a Good Social Media Policy,"* PowerDMS, *July 6, 2017, https://www.powerdms.com/blog/six-elements-good-social-media-policy/.*

The Example box describes selected elements of several companies' current social media policies.

EXAMPLE A Sampling of Social Media Policies

Here are selected provisions from some prominent companies' social media policies.[200]

At IBM, employees may say in their posts that they work for the company, but they must make it clear that they speak for themselves and not the organization. They are also not permitted to use IBM logos or trademarks unless authorized by the company.[201] IBM does not state what disciplinary action may result as a consequence of violating its social media policy.

Best Buy believes responsibility to the organization does not end when "you are off the clock." For example, employees are prohibited from posting anything discriminatory on social media, whether related to the organization or not. Best Buy defines categories of discrimination quite broadly to include "age, sex, race, color, creed, religion, ethnicity, sexual orientation, gender identity, national origin, citizenship, disability, or marital status." An employee can be fired for violating Best

Buy's social media policy, whether or not the posting is on company-sponsored social media.[202]

McDonald's tells its employees to "Be cautious and do not disclose confidential information in any online forum, such as a blog or any form of social media." Employees who violate this are subject to disciplinary action, up to and including termination of employment.[203]

Walmart asks its associates to "consider using company established channels for job-specific issues."[204] The world's largest private employer[205] encourages team members to utilize Walmart's "Open Door Process" or WalmartOne.com instead of posting anything on Facebook or Instagram. Walmart also asks employees not to respond to customer inquiries or comments directed at the company on social media without explicit approval.[206]

The *Washington Post* wants its employees to remember that "*Washington Post* journalists are always *Washington Post* journalists." They are advised to refrain from "writing, tweeting or posting anything—including photographs or video—that could objectively be perceived as reflecting political, racial, sexist, religious or other bias or favoritism."[207] The *Post* extended its social media policy in 2017 to prohibit employees from "disparaging the products and services of the *Post*'s advertisers, subscribers, competitors, business partners or vendors." The Washington Post Newspaper Guild, which represents the paper's newsroom members, has protested this addition to the social media policy as overly protective of advertisers.[208]

Intel utilizes a "disclose, protect, and use common sense" methodology. For example, the chipmaker asks employees to:

- Disclose that their social media posts about Intel are their own personal opinions.
- Protect the organization by not sharing confidential information.
- Use common sense by refraining from boasting that their products are smarter, faster, or higher-performing than competitors (there are Federal Trade Commission mandates about that).

Intel's social media policy extends to nonemployees, including contingent workers and affiliated agencies. If these parties are found to "consistently and repeatedly . . . make false or misleading statements about Intel, Intel products, or Intel Services . . ." the company may discontinue its relationship with them.[209]

YOUR CALL

One writer says that since employees today are unable to fully separate their personal posts from the reputation of their organization, each one is, in effect, "a mouthpiece, a critic, a supporter, a case in point, an endorsement, a walking billboard."[210] Do you agree or disagree? Do you think having a social media policy can effectively mitigate the dangers of allowing employees to fill these roles?

Assessing an Organization's Social Media Readiness Consider the social media readiness of an organization to which you belong. Self-Assessment 15.2 helps you assess leadership's attitude toward social media, such as

- How supportive management is of creating communities.
- How well the culture fosters collaboration and knowledge sharing.
- How widely social media is used to collaborate.

With this knowledge you can determine how well your own attitudes fit with those of the organization, and it may even unveil opportunities for you to improve the organization's readiness. •

SELF-ASSESSMENT 15.2

Assessing Social Media Readiness

Please be prepared to answer these questions if your instructor has assigned Self-Assessment 15.2 in Connect.

1. To what extent is the organization ready for capitalizing on social media?
2. Based on the results, what recommendations would you make to management about improving the value of social media within the company? Be specific.

15.5 Improving Communication Effectiveness

THE BIG PICTURE

We describe how you can be a more effective listener, as in learning to concentrate on the content of a message, communicating nondefensively, and employing empathy. We offer four tips for becoming a more effective writer. Finally, we discuss how to be an effective speaker through three steps.

LO 15-5

Identify ways for managers to improve their listening, writing, and speaking skills.

Given that research suggests managers spend more than 75 percent of their time communicating and that poor communication is estimated to cost organizations more than $9.3 billion annually,[211] it's no surprise that written and verbal communications skills are key career readiness competencies desired by employers.[212]

How would you assess your communication skills? Do you think you are better than most? Do you know when it's time to stop talking during a job interview? An applicant for the job of vice president at water utility Aqua America Inc. did not. She spent 25 minutes answering the CEO's first interview question. The CEO told *The Wall Street Journal*, "I felt like I was being filibustered. . . . There should be no need for verbal diarrhea."[213] He did not hire the person. You can check out your communication skills by completing the following self-assessment. If your score is lower than you prefer, seek out ideas for improving your skills.

SELF-ASSESSMENT 15.3 CAREER READINESS

Assessing My Communication Competence

This scale measures your communication competence. Please be prepared to answer these questions if your instructor has assigned Self-Assessment 15.3 in Connect.

1. Are you surprised by the results? Explain.
2. Based on your scores, what are your top three strengths and your three biggest weaknesses?
3. How might you use your strengths more effectively in your role as a student?
4. What might you say or do during an interview to demonstrate that you possess the career readiness competency of oral/written communication?

Let's see how you can be more effective at the essential communication skills.

Nondefensive Communication

Using evaluative or judgmental comments such as "Your work is terrible" or "You're always late for meetings" spurs defensiveness, which can lead to **defensive communication**—**either aggressive, attacking, angry communication or passive, withdrawing communication.** The better alternative is **nondefensive communication**—**communication that is assertive, direct, and powerful.**

You may be surprised to learn that defensiveness is often triggered by nothing more than a poor choice of words or nonverbal posture during interactions. In the language of behavior modification, these triggers are *antecedents* of defensiveness. For example, using absolutes like "always" or "never" is very likely to create a defensive response. Try to avoid using absolutes because they are rarely true. You can instead increase your communication competence by avoiding the defensive antecedents and employing the positive antecedents of nondefensive communication shown in Table 15.9.

TABLE 15.9 Antecedents of Defensive and Nondefensive Communication

TOWARD DEFENSIVENESS		TOWARD NONDEFENSIVENESS	
STYLE	**EXAMPLE**	**STYLE**	**EXAMPLE**
Evaluative	*"Your work is sloppy."*	**Descriptive**	*"Your work was two days late."*
Controlling	*"You need to . . ."*	**Problem solving**	*"What do you think are the causes of the missed deadline?"*
Strategizing	*"I'd like you to agree with me during the meeting so that we can overcome any challenges."*	**Straightforward**	*"Vote your conscience at the meeting. You can agree or disagree with my proposal."*
Neutral	*"Don't worry about missing the deadline it's no big deal."*	**Empathetic**	*"I sense you are disappointed about missing the deadline. Let's figure out how we can get back on schedule."*
Superior	*"Listen to me, I've worked here 20 years."*	**Equal**	*"Let's figure out the causes of the missed deadline together."*
Certain	*"We tried this idea in the past. It just doesn't work."*	**Honest and open**	*Using I-messages: "I am angry about the way you spoke to the customer because our department looked unresponsive."*

Based on J. R. Gibb, "Defensive Communication," Journal of Communication, *1961, pp. 141–148; and "Reach Out: Effective Communication,"* Sunday Business Post, *April 14, 2013.*

Communicating nondefensively begins with making sure your emotions are in check. Don't have important conversations when you are emotional. Other actions include framing your message into terms that acknowledge the receiver's point of view, freeing yourself of prejudice and bias, asking good questions and actively listening to responses, and being honest about your intentions. Your communications will be more effective and nondefensive when you communicate with the intention of helping others.[214]

Given that we want you to learn how to promote nondefensive communication, we encourage you to complete Self-Assessment 15.4. It assesses whether a current or past work environment is supportive of nondefensive communication.

SELF-ASSESSMENT 15.4

Does Your Organization Have a Supportive or Defensive Communication Climate?

The following survey was designed to assess the supportive and defensive communication climate of your organization. Please be prepared to answer these questions if your instructor has assigned Self-Assessment 15.4 in Connect.

1. Where does the work environment stand in terms of having a supportive or defensive communication climate?
2. Based on your survey scores, what advice would you give to management in order to promote a more supportive communication climate? Be specific.
3. Considering your project teams at school, what can you do to create a more supportive communication climate in these teams?

Using Empathy

Although researchers propose multiple types of empathy, the general consensus is that, as described in the Manage U feature at the start of the chapter, **empathy is the ability to recognize and understand another person's feelings and thoughts.**[215] It is a reflective technique that fosters open communication. Empathy works for managers because it is not the same thing as uncritically accepting others' words and behavior; rather, it relies on a conscious effort to understand the emotional impact of our own words and behavior.[216]

Psychologist Paul Ekman's research shows that your ability to be empathetic is dependent on using three distinct types of empathy: cognitive empathy, emotional empathy, and compassionate empathy.

- **Cognitive empathy.** Having cognitive empathy means you can "identify how another person feels and consider what they may be thinking."
- **Emotional empathy.** Emotional empathy is the ability to "physically feel what another feels."
- **Compassionate empathy.** With compassionate empathy we "not only grasp a person's predicament and feel their feelings, but we're moved to help in some way." Ekman says this form of empathy is dependent on first mastering your cognitive and emotional empathy.[217]

Experience tells us that you won't be able to use these types of empathy if you are not mindful. You may recall from Chapter 1, that mindfulness is defined as "the awareness that emerges through paying attention on purpose, in the present moment, and nonjudgmentally to the unfolding of experience moment by moment."[218] Mindfulness assists you in placing your attention on the feelings and emotions others are displaying both verbally and nonverbally. You can increase your mindfulness during conversations by first setting an intention to stay in the present moment. You then can attempt to pause before responding, make friendly eye contact, and strive to be kind and nonjudgmental.[219] These actions will enhance your active listening, which fosters the ability to engage in cognitive and emotional empathy. Therapist Margaret Cullen suggests that the simplest way to improve your empathetic skills is by "taking the time to remember 'the common humanity of the other person.'"[220]

Using empathy. Does the sales representative on the right appear empathetic toward the customer's complaint about returning an appliance? How might empathy be displayed in this context?
©Allesalltag/Alamy Stock Photo

Empathy leads to more effective communication and interaction because people feel heard.[221] In fact, medical students in the United States are increasingly being trained to use empathy when talking with patients, and the admissions test for medical school will now include questions designed to test applicants' existing understanding of psychology and human behavior. "Empathy is a cognitive attribute, not a personality trait," says Mohammadreza Hojat, a research professor of psychiatry at Jefferson Medical College.[222]

Being an Effective Listener

"Listening is the single most important and underrated skill in business, in social media, and in life. It's something we can always improve on," says Dave Kerpen, founder and CEO of social media software firm Likeable Local.[223] Richard Branson, entrepreneurial founder and CEO of the Virgin Group, agrees. The lesson he learned from his father was "Listen more than you speak. Nobody learned anything by hearing themselves speak."[224]

Actively listening, truly listening, requires more than just hearing, which is merely the physical component. **Active listening is the process of actively decoding and interpreting verbal messages.** Active listening requires full attention and processing of information, which hearing does not.

There is general consensus that listening is a cornerstone skill of communication competence. In studies that support this conclusion, active listening made receivers feel more understood. It also led people to conclude that their conversations were more helpful, sensitive, and supportive.[225] Clearly, active listening yields positive outcomes.

Unfortunately, many of us think we are good listeners when evidence suggests just the opposite. For example, researchers estimate that typical listeners retain only 20 percent–50 percent of what they hear.[226]

Why do you think we miss or lose so much of what we hear? One reason is that we have the cognitive capacity to process words at a much higher rate than people speak. This means our cognitive processes are being underutilized, leading to daydreaming and distractions. Noise is another reason. A third reason, and one you can control, is your motivation to listen and your listening style. It takes effort to actively listen. You won't be a better listener unless you are motivated to become one.

Understand me. What's the recipe for effective listening—for really finding out what someone has to say? Probably it is *listen, watch, write, think, question.* What do you do to fight lapses in concentration if you're tired or bored? You suppress negative thoughts, ignore distractions about the speaker's style of delivery or body language, and encourage the speaker with eye contact, an interested expression, and an attentive posture. This will make you more involved and interested in the subject matter. ©Image Source/Stockbyte/Getty Images

Understand Your Listening Style—or Styles

You can improve your communication competence by understanding your typical listening style. There are four styles:[227]

1. **Active—I'm fully invested.** Active listeners are "all in." They are motivated to listen and give full attention when others are talking. They focus on what is being communicated and expend energy by participating in the discussion. They put their phone away, withhold judgment, and listen silently. They also use positive body language, such as leaning in or making direct eye contact, to convey their interest.[228]
2. **Involved—I'm partially invested.** Involved listeners devote only some of their attention and energy to listening. They reflect on what is being said and half-halfheartedly participate in the discussion. Their nonverbal cues can show interest and noninterest in the same conversation. If you tend to check your texts while having a meal with friends, you may be only an involved listener in the real-life

interaction. Next time try having everyone put his or her phone in the center of the table until the check arrives.

3. **Passive–It's not my responsibility to listen.** Passive listeners are not equal partners in a speaking-listening exchange. They assume the speaker is responsible for the quality of the interaction and believe their role is to passively take in information. Passive listeners will display attentiveness, but they can fake it at times. Overall, they don't expend much motivation or energy in receiving and decoding messages. Is this your listening style during course lectures?
4. **Detached–I'm uninterested.** Detached listeners tend to withdraw from the interaction. They appear inattentive, bored, distracted, and uninterested. They may start using mobile devices during the speaking-listening exchange. Their body language will reflect lack of interest, such as slumping and avoiding direct eye contact. It is all too easy to tune out an unimaginative PowerPoint presentation during a meeting, for example.

Do you think you are an effective listener? Effective listening is an essential skill associated with the career readiness competencies of social and emotional intelligence. If you want to increase these competencies, feedback regarding your listening habits will be valuable. You can get this feedback by completing Self-Assessment 15.5.

SELF-ASSESSMENT 15.5 CAREER READINESS

Assessing Your Listening Style

The following survey was designed to assess the overall strength of your listening skills. Please be prepared to answer these questions if your instructor has assigned Self-Assessment 15.5 in Connect.

1. Is your listening style detached, passive, or involved? Based on your survey scores, what can you do to become more of an involved listener? Be specific.
2. Think of two ways you can practice better listening in your teams at work or school. Be specific.
3. What can you say or do during an interview to display your listening skills?

Concentrate on the Content of the Message

Effective listening is a learned skill, so it takes energy and desire to develop it. Basically, however, it comes down to *paying attention to the content of the message.* Following are some suggestions for increasing your listening skills, which you can practice in your college lectures and seminars. *(See Table 15.10.)*

Being an Effective Writer

Writing is an essential career readiness and management skill, all the more so because e-mail and texting have replaced the telephone in so much of business communication. Taking a business writing class can be a major advantage. (Indeed, as a manager, you may have to identify employees who need writing training.) Following are some tips for writing business communications more effectively.

Start with Your Purpose

Rather than building up to the point, if you are delivering routine or positive news you should start by telling your purpose and stating what you expect of the reader. Along the same lines, when e-mailing, make sure the subject line clearly expresses your reason for writing. For instance, "Who is available Thursday afternoon?" does not inform the reader of your topic as well as "Davis project meeting moved to Thursday 3 p.m." does.

TABLE 15.10 Tips for Effective Listening

1.	**Show respect.** Give everyone the opportunity to explain his or her ideas without interrupting. Actively try to help the sender convey his or her message. Use eye contact to show your interest.
2.	**Listen from the first sentence.** Turn off your internal thoughts and whatever you were thinking about prior to the interaction. Also turn off or silence and put away your phone.
3.	**Be mindful.** Stay in the moment and focus on the sender. Don't try to figure out what the speaker is *going* to say or mentally compose your response. Avoid multitasking while someone is speaking.
4.	**Keep quiet.** You have two ears and one mouth; use them accordingly. Try to use the 80/20 rule: Your conversational partner should speak 80% of the time, and you should speak 20%.
5.	**Ask good questions.** Asking relevant questions clarifies what is being said and demonstrates that you are listening and working to understand.
6.	**Paraphrase and summarize.** Paraphrasing amounts to repeating back to someone what you just heard that person say. Summarizing is used to integrate or consolidate an entire conversation. Both these techniques enhance communication accuracy because they help ensure you are correctly understanding the messages.
7.	**Remember what was said.** Either take notes or make an effort to log critical information into your mental computer.
8.	**Involve your body.** Use nonverbal cues to demonstrate interest and involvement.

Sources: Based on G. Itzchakov and A. N. Kluger, "The Listening Circle: A Simple Tool to Enhance Listening and Reduce Extremism Among Employees," Organizational Dynamics, *October-December 2017, pp. 220–226; J. Keyser, "Active Listening Leads to Business Success,"* T+D, *July 2013, pp. 26–28; Kathy Lockwood, "Are You Listening,* Forbes, *August 24, 2017, https://www.forbes.com/sites/forbescoachescouncil/2017/08/24/are-you-listening/#18378dbb7298.*

Write Simply, Concisely, and Directly Short and sweet is the key.[229] Keep your words simple and use short words, sentences, and phrases. Be direct instead of vague, and use active rather than passive voice. (Directness, active voice: "Please call a meeting for Wednesday." Vagueness, passive voice: "It is suggested that a meeting be called for Wednesday.")

Know Your Audience Send your message to all who need the information it contains, but *only* to those people. Resist the urge to include everyone, and be especially careful, in responding to messages, to think before you click "Reply All." If you are feeling emotional as you write, don't click "Send" at all but instead save your draft, take a break of at least a few hours, and go back to it later. Your feelings may have changed and your communication, and your relationships, will likely be better for it.

Don't Show Ignorance of the Basics Texting has made many people more relaxed about spelling and grammar rules. Although this is fine among friends, as a manager you'll need to create a more favorable impression in your writing. Besides using spelling and grammar checkers, proofread your writing before sending it on. Check people's names and titles in particular, and be especially aware that auto-correct features can make incorrect assumptions about what you meant to say.

Some other tips are shown on the next page. *(See Table 15.11.)*

Being an Effective Speaker

We speak in many different circumstances, from one-on-one conversations, to meetings, to formal presentations. In terms of personal oral communication, most of the best advice comes under the heading of listening because effective listening governs the amount and content of the talking you need to do.[230]

TABLE 15.11

Rules for Business Writing, Both Online and Offline

DON'T . . .
1. Begin an e-mail with "Hey." "Hi" or "Hello" is more appropriate.
2. Use abbreviations or emojis.
DO . . .
3. Spell words correctly.
4. Use complete sentences.
5. Use proper capitalization and punctuation.
6. Use active voice versus passive.
7. Use first/second person (we/you) rather than third person (it/they/them/one).
8. Use short, simple sentences with fewer adjectives and adverbs.

Sources: Derived from J. Arrowood, "Write in Plain Language," Training, *January/February 2017, p. 22; G. Leibowitz, "6 Tips for Writing Emotionally Intelligent Emails,"* Inc., *http://www.inc.com/glenn-leibowitz/how-to-write-emotionally-intelligent-emails.html (accessed July 2016).*

The ability to talk to a room full of people–to make an oral presentation–is one of the greatest skills you can have. And in case you think you don't have this skill, "everyone has public speaking ability," according to one writer for the London Speaker Bureau. It's simply that some people are more practiced because they have the opportunity to use it more than others.[231]

While 20 percent of more than 2,000 working U.S. professionals in a recent survey said they take almost any steps to avoid public speaking, 70 percent agreed that the ability to make a skillful presentation was "critical" to their careers. And even more said they would like to be better at it.[232] In fact, reports of how widespread fear of public speaking is are probably exaggerated; it's possible that as much as 75 percent of the population shares this fear.[233] Some people find public speaking a stimulating challenge and an opportunity to showcase their professional skills and reputation.

However you feel or think you feel about public speaking, there is no doubt you'll have to call upon your presentation skills during your career. You can find some good models in the many TED talks available online.[234,235] And you can do away with a great deal of anxiety about speaking in public by knowing what and how to prepare. For instance, ask ahead of time about who the audience will be, how much time you will be allowed, what technology might be available for incorporating audio or visual material, who else may be speaking, and whether there will be a question-and-answer session afterward. Arrive early and check the room to be sure promised equipment is in place and working. As for the content of your presentation, Dale Carnegie's classic advice still holds: (1) Tell them what you're going to say. (2) Say it. (3) Tell them what you said.[236]

1. Tell Them What You're Going to Say The introduction should take 5 percent–15 percent of your speaking time, and it should prepare the audience for the rest of the speech. Avoid jokes and such tired phrases as "I'm honored to be with you here today. . . ." Because everything in your speech should be relevant, be bold and go right to the point with a "grabber" such as a personal story or compelling comparison that attracts listeners' attention and prepares them to follow you closely.[237] For example:

Predictor for success. Enjoying public speaking and being good at it are the top predictors of success and upward mobility. How might you develop these skills? ©Blend Images/Alamy Stock Photo

"Good afternoon. You may not have thought much about identity theft, and neither did I until my identity was stolen–twice. Today I'll describe how our supposedly private credit, health, employment, and other records are vulnerable to theft and how you can protect yourself."

2. Say It The main body of the speech takes up 75 percent–90 percent of your time. The most important thing to realize is that your audience won't remember more than a few points anyway. Choose them carefully and cover them as succinctly as possible.

Needless to say, your success rests largely on how well you deliver this part of the speech. Be sure you have done your homework. Speak about what you know best, understand your audience's point of view and preconceptions, and check and recheck your facts. These preparatory steps enhance your confidence and ensure you have credibility with your listeners.

When you practice this part of your presentation, be particularly attentive to transitions during the main body of the speech. Listening differs from reading in that the listener has only one chance to get your meaning. Thus, be sure you constantly provide your listeners with guidelines and transitional phrases so they can see where you're going. Example:

"There are five ways the security of your supposedly private files can be compromised. The first way is . . . The second way happens when . . . "

3. Tell Them What You Said The end might take 5 percent–10 percent of your time. Many professional speakers consider the conclusion to be as important as the introduction, so don't drop the ball here. You need a solid, strong, persuasive wrap-up.

Use some sort of signal phrase that cues your listeners that you are heading into your wind-up. Examples:

"Let's review the main points . . ."
"In conclusion, what CAN you do to protect against unauthorized invasion of your private files? I point out five main steps. One . . ."

Give some thought to the last thing you will say. It should be strongly upbeat, a call to action, a thought for the day, a little story, a quotation. Examples:

"I want to leave you with one last thought . . ."
"Finally, let me close by sharing something that happened to me . . ."
"As Albert Einstein said, 'Imagination is more important than knowledge.'"

Then say, "Thank you," and stop. ●

15.6 Career Corner: Managing Your Career Readiness

LO 15-6

Review the techniques for improving the career readiness competency of networking.

Communication is a career readiness competency that requires the application of 12 competencies from the model of career readiness shown below (see Figure 15.4). You can improve your communication skills by recognizing the need to also develop the following competencies: new media literacy, oral/written communication, teamwork/collaboration, leadership, social intelligence, networking, emotional intelligence, self-motivation, positive approach, career management, self-awareness, and generalized self-efficacy.

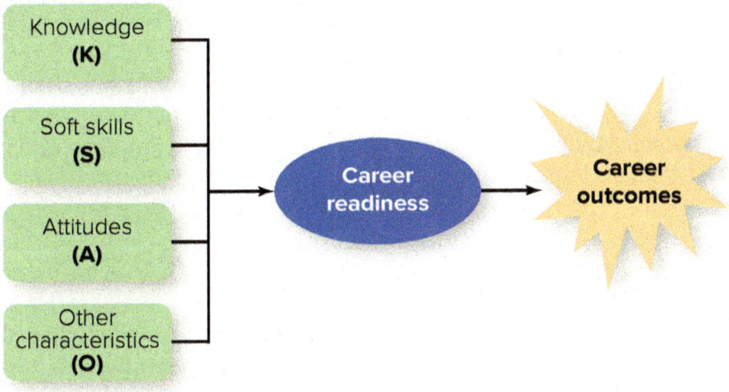

FIGURE 15.4

Model of career readiness

We are going to focus on the competency of networking because it plays a key role in getting a job after graduation and requires good communication skills. Networking is the ability to build and maintain a strong, broad professional network of relationships. It typically requires developing and using contacts from one context in another.

Improve Your Face-to-Face Networking Skills

We're sure you've heard the phrase, "It's not what you know, it's who you know." A recent survey of 3,000 people supported this conclusion. Results showed that 85 percent of the respondents had found their jobs via networking.[238] Unfortunately, many of us dislike networking and even view it as "insincere and manipulative, even slightly unethical," according to *The Wall Street Journal*.[239] We suspect these negative feelings are partly driven by the fact that "many of us aren't sure where to start, what to say when we connect with someone or how to maintain that relationship."[240] Even though there is some art and science to networking, we believe the following four tips can improve your networking competencies.

Create a Positive Mindset A negative attitude about networking is a roadblock to developing this competency. Pursue a more positive attitude by eliminating the thought that networking is a game. Networking is more enjoyable when it is driven by your authentic intention to develop genuine relationships, rather than being something required for getting a job. Strive to view networking as a vehicle to make more friends and connect with people with similar interests. This mindset is more likely to take you further with the relationship because it creates shared bonding rather than the pursuit of self-interests. When meeting someone for the first time, keep it light, look for common interests, and demonstrate "true" interest.[241]

Identify Your Career Goals Before doing any networking, you need to be clear about your goals and plans. Establish a 5- to 10-year career goal and then develop a high-level action plan for accomplishing it. Say, for example, that your 5-year goal is to be employed in a job in which you supervise at least five employees and make $150,000. Now write down what goals you need to meet in years 1–4 to meet this overall goal. Try to identify a few people who can kickstart or accelerate the achievement of this goal. They can be people you know or second-degree acquaintances of people you know. These individuals should become targets of your networking. If you don't know anyone, then your task is to find social outlets where you can meet these types of people.[242]

Network with a Purpose Have a purpose for attending networking events. Do you want to reconnect with friends and acquaintances, or do you want to meet new people? What type of people do you want to meet? We encourage you to look for people with common interests who can help you and people whom you can help.[243] Research shows that networkers tend to spend the majority of their time with people they already know, so we encourage you to avoid putting pressure on yourself to meet strangers. In support of this conclusion, *The Wall Street Journal* reported that "a wealth of research suggests that your less-cultivated business acquaintances, or 'weak ties,' have more information, opportunities and potential introductions to share with you than either your close contacts or total strangers."[244]

Build Personal Connections The key is to draw people into meaningful conversations. People will remember more about you if the conversation is meaningful and has some degree of emotionality. For example, you probably won't be remembered if you lead with: So where do you work? Where are you from? Do live nearby? You'll get a more positive response by asking insightful or interesting questions. One consultant suggested using questions such as, "Have you been working on anything exciting recently?" or "Any exciting plans this summer?"[245] To create emotionality in the conversation, you might ask, "What was the highlight of your day?" or "What's keeping you awake at night?"[246] By asking good questions you not only create a positive first impression, but you might cause the other person to learn something that helps him or her grow.

Be Mindful It's worth emphasizing the need to be mindful when communicating with others. For example, you might think it's fine to interrupt a conversation with someone to answer your phone, but others might think differently. Try your best to avoid phubbing and FOMO. Maintain eye contact with those with whom you are conversing, and avoid the tendency to let wandering eyes survey the room for the next person you want to meet. That's an easy way to send the message that the person in front of you is not important.

Follow-Up Be sure to follow up with those individuals you found particularly interesting or would like to see again. Use whatever medium of communication you deem relevant. While texting and e-mail are fast, we have had very positive experiences when we've written a handwritten note of appreciation.[247]

Key Terms Used in This Chapter

active listening 618
communication 582
crowdsourcing 605
culture 595
cyberloafing 608
decoding 584
defensive communication 615
downward communication 588
empathy 617
encoding 584
external communication 589
feedback 584
FOMO 608
formal communication channels 588
grapevine 590
horizontal communication 589
identity theft 611
informal communication channels 589
jargon 585
linguistic style 599
media richness 586
medium 584
microaggressions 608
mindlessness 594
noise 584
nondefensive communication 615
nonverbal communication 596
paraphrasing 584
privacy 611
receiver 583
security 610
sender 583
social media 600
social media policy 613
upward communication 588

Key Points

15.1 The Communication Process: What It Is, How It Works

- Communication is the transfer of information and understanding from one person to another. The process involves sender, message, and receiver; encoding and decoding; the medium; feedback; and dealing with "noise."
- The sender is the person wanting to share information. The information is called a message. The receiver is the person for whom the message is intended. Encoding is translating a message into understandable symbols or language. Decoding is interpreting and trying to make sense of the message. The medium is the pathway by which a message travels. Feedback is the process in which a receiver expresses his or her reaction to the sender's message.
- The entire communication process can be disrupted at any point by noise, defined as any disturbance that interferes with the transmission of a message.
- For effective communication, a manager must select the right medium. Media richness indicates how well a particular medium conveys information and promotes learning. The richer a medium is, the better it is at conveying information. Face-to-face presence is the richest; an advertising flyer would be one of the lowest. A rich medium is best for nonroutine situations and to avoid oversimplification. A lean medium is best for routine situations and to avoid overloading.

15.2 How Managers Fit into the Communication Process

- Communication channels may be formal or informal.
- Formal communication channels follow the chain of command and are recognized as official. Formal communication is of three types: (1) Vertical communication is the flow of messages up and down the organizational hierarchy. (2) Horizontal communication flows within and between work units; its main purpose is coordination. (3) External communication flows between people inside and outside the organization.
- Informal communication channels develop outside the formal structure and do not follow the chain of command. Two aspects of informal channels are the grapevine and face-to-face communication. (1) The grapevine is the unofficial communication system of the informal organization. The grapevine is faster than formal channels, is always operating, but is not always accurate, (2) Face-to-face communication builds trust between managers and employees. Managers should set aside time for such communication and hone their listening skills.

15.3 Barriers to Communication

- Barriers to communication are of five types: (1) Physical barriers are exemplified by walls, background noise, and time-zone differences. (2) Personal barriers are individual attributes that hinder communication. (3) Cross-cultural barriers are more common in view of globalization. (4) Nonverbal barriers often arise in cross-cultural communication and when verbal and nonverbal messages conflict. (5) Gender differences result in part from bias and assumptions that can be overcome.
- Nine personal barriers are (1) variable skills in communicating effectively, (2) variations in frames of reference and experiences that affect how information is interpreted, (3) variations in trustworthiness and credibility, (4) oversized egos, (5) faulty listening skills, (6) tendency to judge others' messages, (7) inability to listen with

understanding, (8) stereotypes (oversimplified beliefs about a certain group of people) and prejudices, and (9) nonverbal communication (messages sent outside of the written or spoken word, including body language).

- Six ways in which nonverbal communication is expressed are through (1) eye contact, (2) facial expressions, (3) body movements and gestures, (4) touch, (5) setting, and (6) time.

15.4 Social Media and Management

- Social media contribute heavily to employee and employer productivity. They are widely used in employment recruiting and have applications in organizational innovation (via crowdsourcing), in sales, and in reputation management.
- Social media have costs as well. Cyberloafing—the personal use of computers and digital devices at work—costs organizations time and money. FOMO, or fear of missing out, can lead people to ignore those present in order to constantly monitor their phones. It is associated with anxiety. Security issues arise when careless or disgruntled employees put the organization's online environment at risk. Everyone must take responsibility for ensuring the privacy of his or her own and the organization's information and communication. Finally, controlling the flow of e-mail is a challenge for many.
- Texting's organizational applications and use may be growing, but personal texts should be strictly limited during the workday.
- Managers should engage employees in the creation of fair and effective social media policy to ensure social media tools are consistently put to constructive work purposes.

15.5 Improving Communication Effectiveness

- Nondefensive communication is essential for effective communication. Table 15.9 provides suggestions for communicating nondefensively.
- Three types of empathy are cognitive, in which you identify with others' feelings; emotional, in which you physically feel what others feel; and compassionate, in which you are moved to help others based on their feelings.

  People tend to rely on one or more of the following listening styles: active—I'm fully invested, involved—I'm partially invested, passive—It's not my responsibility to listen, and detached—I'm uninterested. Active listening, the process of actively decoding and interpreting verbal messages, requires full attention and processing of information. To become a good listener, you should concentrate on the content of the message, not delivery; ask questions and summarize the speaker's remarks; listen for ideas; resist distractions and show interest; and give the speaker a fair hearing.
- To become an effective writer, start with your purpose. Write simply, concisely, and directly. Know your audience, and follow basic spelling and grammar rules for appropriately formal communication.
- To become an effective speaker, study successful models, know your subject, and prepare and rehearse ahead of time. For the presentation itself, follow three simple rules. Tell people what you're going to say. Say it. Tell them what you said.

15.6 Career Corner: Managing Your Career Readiness

- Becoming a more effective communicator requires the application of 12 career readiness competencies. They are: new media literacy, oral/written communication, teamwork/collaboration, leadership, social intelligence, networking, emotional intelligence, self-motivation, positive approach, career management, self-awareness, and generalized self-efficacy.
- You can develop your networking competency by following six recommendations: (1) Create a positive mindset. (2) Identify your career goals. (3) Network with a purpose. (4) Build personal connections. (5) Be mindful. (6) Follow up.

Understanding the Chapter: What Do I Know?

1. Explain the communications process.
2. What are some common sources of noise in communication?
3. Explain the differences between formal and informal communication channels.
4. What are the five types of barriers to communication and examples of each?
5. Explain how social media can contribute to employee productivity.
6. How does social media make employers more productive?
7. What are some of the costs of social media in organizations?
8. Describe the managerial implications of texting at work.
9. What should managers know about creating a social media policy?
10. Explain the five listening styles and how to be a good listener.

Management in Action

Fyre and Fury

Imagine "a world of surreal experiences and inspired curiosity that touches the sweet spot between imagination and possibility . . . a place where the tropical sun shines all day, and our celebrations ignite the night."[248] This is a snippet from the marketing campaign for Fyre Fest, a luxury concert event that 20-something socialite/entrepreneur Billy McFarland and rapper Ja Rule conceptualized when they discovered the beautiful Bahamas' Exuma Islands in October 2016. McFarland had no experience producing live music festivals, but he had plenty of connections, knew how to raise money, and understood the power of messaging.[249]

Fyre Festival took off on social media less than two months later when Kendall Jenner, Bella Hadid, Emily Ratajkowski, and other influencers simultaneously Instagrammed the event's first advertisement. The video featured crystal-blue waters, yachts, and supermodels "frolicking and dancing on a beach."[250] Ticket packages ranged from $1,500 to $400,000 and included promises of luxury beach villas, treasure hunts, white-glove concierge services, and the finest gourmet food and drinks from famed restaurateur Stephen Starr—all on the private Exuma island of Fyre Cay that had once belonged to the late drug lord Pablo Escobar. The social media campaign was a massive success, and thousands of adventurous concertgoers quickly cashed in on the chance to be part of the extravaganza. What they got was anything but.[251]

FYRE FESTIVAL GOES DOWN IN FLAMES

On Thursday, April 27, 2017, throngs of excited festivalgoers began arriving in the Exumas. Organizers had arranged first-class transportation between the airport and the festival and a white-glove service to deliver attendees' luggage straight to their reserved luxury villas. Instead, attendees rode on packed school buses to an unfinished, gravel-covered development plot speckled with emergency-relief tents. There was nary a villa, concierge, shower, or gourmet meal in sight.[252] There were no celebrity sightings and no musicians because McFarland and his team, seeing disaster ahead, had already secretly alerted them to stay away. McFarland had sent no such messages to the rest of the attendees, who arrived to dashed dreams.[253]

Event staff told attendees, "It's every man for himself," as they rushed to grab tents in a free-for-all.[254] "They had no way to communicate with anybody," said one attendee, who remembers McFarland standing atop a table frantically yelling instructions at the crowd.[255] Another recalls "everyone you spoke to had a different answer and no one knew who was in charge . . . there were no [phone] chargers or electricity outlets . . . and there was barely service."[256] Attendees who weren't lucky enough to find hotel rooms on the island or transportation back to the airport slept on soaking wet mattresses and dined on sliced bread and cheese. They found their luggage piled inside a giant shipping container and searched for their bags in the darkness with cell phone lights. The event was a complete and utter disaster.

Thousands of ticketholders eventually made their way off the island in a mass exodus marked by hunger, exhaustion, bewilderment, and anger. The only direct communication they received from the organizers was a single e-mail saying, "The festival is being postponed until we can further assess if and when we are able to create the high-quality experience we envisioned."[257] Fyre organizers took to social media in the days that followed, blaming the weather and the Exumas' poor infrastructure for the fiasco.[258] In reality, McFarland had tried to plan an unprecedented event on an undeveloped construction lot. He failed his team, vendors, attendees, and the people of the Bahamas.

WHERE DID THINGS GO WRONG?

A big event starts with a big idea—a concept for a theme, audience, and experience. A fairly standard process is then used to plan the event. Organizers first calculate a realistic idea of their financial resources, aligning all subsequent decisions with this budget. Second comes logistics, which include searching for a venue; ensuring that the venue provides a safe and suitable infrastructure; securing any necessary additions, upgrades, and permits; contracting with vendors (caterers, service staff, security, sanitation companies); and booking talent (musicians, performers). Third, and only after logistics are in place, organizers develop and distribute marketing materials and use those to sell admission. The process requires experience, expertise, and a constant flow of communication among various stakeholders.[259] McFarland did things his own way. He began by paying models and influencers hundreds of thousands of dollars to advertise a fantasy; sold tickets to said fantasy; and repeatedly ignored information indicating that he didn't have the time, money, or expertise to pull it off.

The island of Fyre Cay didn't exist, nor did the lavish villas people had booked through the festival's website, and McFarland had repeatedly failed to find production firms that would execute the event on his terms. One executive recalls a familiar scene: "They [production companies] would say 'It's going to cost, like, $5 million to stage this thing,' and the Fyre guys would say, 'No, it'll cost $300,000.' There was a complete detachment from reality."[260] Six weeks before the event, "Nothing had been done. . . . Festival vendors weren't in place, no stage had been rented, transportation had not been arranged," according to former Fyre talent producer Chloe Gordon. Planners warned McFarland and his team that they didn't have the money to put on the event they had advertised and should instead roll tickets over to a 2018 event and begin planning it immediately. Gordon recalls a Fyre executive responding, "Let's just do it and be legends, man." She quit a week later.[261]

Rumors began to circulate among entertainment industry professionals in the weeks before the festival, and on April 2, *The Wall Street Journal* reported growing concerns about the event. Vendors, contractors, and artists were severing ties when they didn't receive payment, and ticketholders were still in the dark about logistics.[262] Maude Etkin, an interior designer and ticketholder from Manhattan, says Fyre hadn't responded to e-mails for weeks.[263] Through it all, McFarland continued to promote Fyre Festival as a top-notch experience through his website and social media platforms, hanging onto his fantasy until the bitter end.

TRIAL BY FYRE

To date, vendors, employees, and attendees have filed at least nine multi-million-dollar class-action lawsuits against McFarland and the Fyre organization, citing fraud, breach of contract, and negligent misrepresentation. McFarland took a plea deal in March 2018, admitting to two counts of wire fraud, forfeiting $27 million, and agreeing to federal prison time.[264]

The Bahamian Ministry of Tourism issued statements after the event in an attempt to salvage its reputation, saying, "We want to ensure that all stakeholders and guests know of the development and infrastructural capacity of this island" and, "It is our hope that the Fyre Festival visitors would consider returning to the Islands of the Bahamas in the future to truly experience all of our beauty."[265]

FOR DISCUSSION

Problem-Solving Perspective

1. What is the underlying problem in this case from an event-planning perspective?
2. What were the causes of this problem?
3. What recommendations would you make to someone trying to execute a similar idea in the future?

Application of Chapter Content

1. What kinds of vertical and horizontal communication errors did McFarland make while attempting to plan the festival?
2. What do you see as the biggest barriers to communication in this situation?
3. How did McFarland's background and lack of experience affect the way he processed the messages he received during planning?
4. Would you say McFarland was ultimately effective or ineffective at using social media? Explain.
5. Do you think McFarland could have successfully executed this event if he had been a better communicator? What, specifically, would have to change?

Legal/Ethical Challenge

Was ESPN Fair in Firing Curt Schilling for His Social Media Post?

Curt Schilling is a six-time professional baseball All-Star. His career record of 216-146 and his incredible 11-2 postseason performance earned him legendary status and helped him land a job at ESPN in 2010. He was fired from the network in April 2016 after sharing a Facebook post.

Schilling is perhaps as well known for his lack of tact as he is for his ability to command a baseball game, and ESPN seemed to tolerate his often politically charged comments during his tenure. According to Alex Reimer, a *Forbes* reporter, ESPN did not discipline Schilling for "railing against the theory of evolution on Twitter or for saying in March that Hillary Clinton should be 'buried under a jail' if she shared classified information on her private email server."[266] Just before Schilling made the comment about Clinton, ESPN had issued a companywide e-mail directing employees to abstain from "political editorializing, personal attacks or 'drive-by' comments regarding the candidates and their campaigns." Schilling said the e-mail went to his spam folder.[267] ESPN had, however, suspended him in 2015 after he tweeted a meme about Muslim extremists and Nazis.

Schilling's ultimate firing was due to his sharing an anti-transgender image along with some commentary. The image showed an overweight man wearing a wig and women's clothing with parts of the T-shirt cut out to expose his breasts. It says: "LET HIM IN! to the restroom with your daughter or else you're a narrow-minded, judgmental, unloving racist bigot who needs to die."[268] Schilling added his own comments about the rights of transgender people that ESPN found offensive.

The *New York Daily News* reported that "Schilling's remarks were in support of a North Carolina law that bars people in the state from using a bathroom other than the one for their biological gender."[269] According to *The New York Times*, ESPN issued a statement saying it is an inclusive company and that Schilling's "conduct was unacceptable."[270]

Schilling claims he isn't "transphobic or homophobic and 'wouldn't care' if his son wanted to be a woman."[271] He also commented, on a personal blog, "Let's make one thing clear right upfront. If you get offended by ANYTHING in this post, that's your fault, all yours."[272] Schilling, in turn, has been very critical of ESPN since his dismissal.

SOLVING THE CHALLENGE

Do you think it was fair for ESPN to fire Curt Schilling for expressing his views on social media?

1. No. ESPN was displaying political correctness rather than supporting its employee's right to express his views about transgender bathroom rights. He should be reinstated.
2. Yes. ESPN told its employees not to make political statements and Schilling clearly ignored this recommendation. People in the broadcasting industry need to be very careful when communicating.
3. Invent other options.

Uber Continuing Case connect

Learn how Uber communicates with several of its key constituents such as customers and employees. Assess your ability to apply the management concepts discussed in this chapter to the case by going to Connect.

Controlling

PART 6 • CONTROLLING

16 Control Systems and Quality Management

Techniques for Enhancing Organizational Effectiveness

©Olivier Renck/Aurora/Getty Images

After reading this chapter, you should be able to:

LO 16-1 Describe control as a managerial function.

LO 16-2 Explain how successful companies implement controls.

LO 16-3 Discuss the purpose of the balanced scorecard and strategy maps in measuring performance.

LO 16-4 Describe financial tools managers should know.

LO 16-5 Explain the total quality management process.

LO 16-6 Identify barriers to effective control and ways managers can overcome them.

LO 16-7 Describe the manager's role in increasing productivity.

LO 16-8 Discuss the process for managing career readiness and review five tips for managing your career.

FORECAST *What's Ahead in This Chapter*

The final management function, control, is monitoring performance, comparing it with goals, and taking corrective action as needed. We define *managing for performance* and explain its importance. We then identify six reasons for the need of management control, explain the steps in the control process, and describe three types of control managers use. Next we cover levels and areas of control and financial tools for control, as well as ways to control the supply chain and special considerations for service organizations. We discuss the balanced scorecard and total quality management (TQM). We describe the four keys to successful control, five barriers to successful control, and review how managers can influence productivity. We conclude with a Career Corner that focuses on the career readiness competency of career management.

MANAGE U

Using a Mentor to Exercise Control in Your Career

Mentoring is the process of forming and maintaining intensive and lasting developmental relationships between a variety of developers (people who provide career and psychosocial support) and a junior person (the protégé).[1] Mentors are experienced, knowledgeable, and trusted people willing to coach you throughout the passages of your career. You may find your mentor through networking or a personal introduction; he or she will usually be someone active in your field or industry and familiar with the issues professionals in it face.

Having a mentor is a uniquely valuable career development opportunity, but it also offers a way for you to benchmark, or compare, yourself to someone more experienced and discover the skills or topics you need to work on in order to measure up. As this chapter shows, organizations frequently use benchmarking strategies to make course corrections to their own performance and to develop their employees.

Because of their status in the organization or industry, mentors are, by definition, busy people. You may meet with your mentor regularly or only a few times, but you want to both be respectful and get the most from the opportunity. Here are a few strategies for making the collaboration successful for both of you.[2]

Set Goals Identify specific goals you want to achieve in the relationship—and in each meeting or conversation—and let your mentor know what they are so you can work toward them together. You've learned in this course that goals are motivating; they also give you a way to measure your progress and correct course as needed. Being a protégé is an active process; your mentor is not going to do your work for you. You need to know what you want and go after it.

Come Prepared Do your homework before meeting or talking with your mentor. If you want advice on writing a report, send a draft beforehand and be ready to discuss it. If your mentor recommends an action, take that step before checking in to discuss what happened as a result. Ask lots of questions, but first make sure you truly can't answer or research them on your own and that they draw on your mentor's unique knowledge and experience.

Stay Open-Minded You can feel free to disagree with your mentor, but bring solid information and good ideas to any debate and respectfully evaluate your mentor's input. Be ready to accept your mentor's feedback even if it's sometimes critical; such individual coaching can be the most valuable part of your experience as a mentee because it gives you the tools you need to grow. Finally, remember to fight off the Dunning-Kruger effect we discussed in Chapter 14.

Respect Your Mentor's Time Commit to the relationship, because it's up to you, not your mentor, to make it work. Show up for all meetings, and start and end on time to avoid taking advantage of your mentor's generosity. Limit contacts between sessions for the same reason; ask what's acceptable if, for instance, you want to e-mail a brief question for a quick yes-no answer. *Always* say thank you.

Know When It's Not Working Sometimes a mentoring relationship doesn't work out because the mentor can't provide the right kind of help or doesn't have the time to commit. If that's the case, and if you're sure you've done all you could to make the collaboration succeed, it's time to gracefully let your mentor know you are ready to step out on your own, with gratitude for all that he or she has offered you. Later, analyze what you believe you really need in a mentor, and try looking for someone closer to your ideal.

For Discussion A mentoring relationship is a two-way street. When you reach out to a potential mentor, what can you offer in return for the coaching and expertise? Make a list of ideas, considering what your age, cultural background, goals, and outside interests might contribute to the collaboration.

16.1 Control: When Managers Monitor Performance

THE BIG PICTURE

Controlling is monitoring performance, comparing it with goals, and taking corrective action. This section describes six reasons control is needed and four steps in the control process.

LO 16-1

Describe control as a managerial function.

Control is making something happen the way it was planned to happen. **Controlling is defined as monitoring performance, comparing it with goals, and taking corrective action as needed.** Controlling is the fourth management function, along with planning, organizing, and leading, and its purpose is plain: to make sure that performance meets objectives.

- **Planning** is setting goals and deciding how to achieve them.
- **Organizing** is arranging tasks, people, and other resources to accomplish the work.
- **Leading** is motivating people to work hard to achieve the organization's goals.
- **Controlling** is concerned with seeing that the right things happen at the right time in the right way.

All these functions affect one another and in turn affect an organization's performance and productivity. *(See Figure 16.1.)*

FIGURE 16.1 Controlling for effective performance

What you as a manager do to get things done, with controlling shown in relation to the three other management functions. (These are not lockstep; all four functions happen concurrently.)

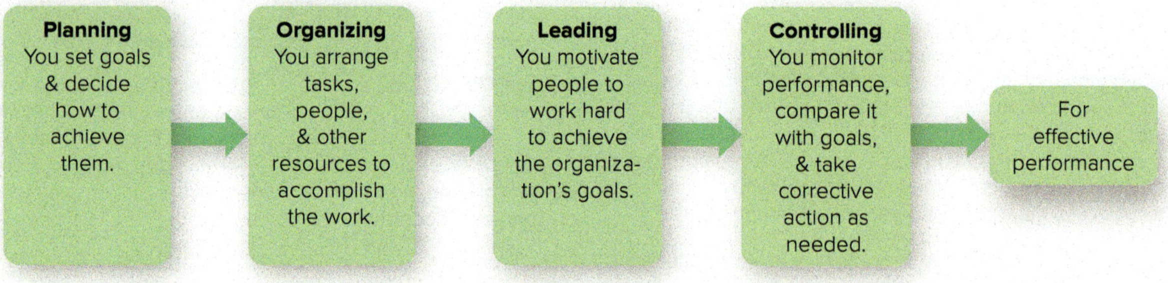

Why Is Control Needed?

Lack of control mechanisms can lead to problems for both managers and companies. For example, in the wake of at least 11 reported deaths and dozens of injuries, more than 100 million autos have been recalled in the United States and worldwide due to faulty airbags manufactured by Takata, a Japanese auto parts maker.[3] As the scope of the recall continued to grow, first Takata's CEO resigned and then, in 2017, the company pleaded guilty to deception and filed for bankruptcy. Between penalties and restitution payments, it was expected to owe about $1 billion.[4] Could greater control have helped avoid or reduce the consequences of these situations? Of course. Control can save lives!

There are six reasons control is needed.

1. To Adapt to Change and Uncertainty Markets shift. Consumer tastes change. New competitors appear. Technologies are reborn. New materials are invented.

Control matters. The National Highway Traffic Safety Administration (NHTSA) concluded that the airbag recall from 14 different automakers is the largest and most complex in U.S. history. The airbags, which were made by Takata, involved car models from 2002 through 2015. The purpose of a management control system is to prevent mistakes, errors, and design flaws from reaching consumers. ©Jochen Tack/Alamy Stock Photo

Government regulations are altered. All organizations must deal with these kinds of environmental changes and uncertainties. Control systems can help managers anticipate, monitor, and react to these changes.

Example: FedEx and UPS experienced unknown demand during the 2017 holiday seasons. They employed extensive control processes to accommodate this uncertain demand while avoiding delivery delays and lost packages. Patrick Fitzgerald, senior vice president at FedEx, noted that the company has a "'pretty good idea' of how many items it will receive ahead of Christmas, along with where it will need to deploy trucks and planes, thanks to ongoing contact with retailers." He also said that the company does extensive monitoring so that it can "be clear in setting expectations on how much our networks can handle on any given day."[5] Atlanta-based UPS planned to use "ready teams" in cities such as Atlanta, Denver, and Houston to accommodate the excessive demand. The company also asked drivers to work more hours and hired 95,000 seasonal workers.[6]

2. To Discover Irregularities and Errors

Small problems can mushroom into big ones. Cost overruns, manufacturing defects, employee turnover, bookkeeping errors, and customer dissatisfaction are all matters that may be tolerable in the short run. But in the long run, they can bring about even the downfall of an organization.

Example: *The New York Times* recently revealed that long before a self-driving Uber vehicle killed a pedestrian in Arizona in 2018, the cars were requiring human intervention much more frequently than self-driving cars being tested by other companies such as Waymo (a division of Google). For instance, Waymo cars drove almost 5,600 miles before the driver had to take the wheel. Uber's target was 13 miles without a human assist, and it was not meeting that goal.[7]

3. To Reduce Costs, Increase Productivity, or Add Value

Control systems can reduce labor costs, eliminate waste, increase output, and increase product delivery cycles. In addition, controls can help add value to a product so that customers will be more inclined to choose them over rival products.

Example: Simple changes to an office environment can change employee attitudes and have a positive impact on productivity.[8] The use of color, arrangement of space, type of seating and lighting, and presence or absence of music can all affect productivity, perhaps by as much as 20 percent. Control mechanisms to monitor the results of such changes can be as simple as periodic employee satisfaction surveys.[9]

4. To Detect Opportunities and Increase Innovation Hot-selling products. Competitive prices on materials. Changing population trends. New overseas markets. Controls can help alert managers to innovative opportunities that might have otherwise gone unnoticed.[10]

Example: Uniqlo, the big Asian apparel retailer, is locked in competition for global market share with "fast fashion" clothiers Zara (from Spain), H&M (Sweden), and online stores. Like those at most businesses, Uniqlo managers look at a monthly metric called EBIDTA, earnings before interest, depreciation, taxes, and amortization, to gauge their success in each new market they enter.[11]

5. To Provide Performance Feedback Can you improve without feedback? When a company becomes larger or when it merges with another company, it may find it has several product lines, materials-purchasing policies, customer bases, and worker needs that conflict with each other. Controls help managers coordinate these various elements by providing feedback.[12]

Example: Global companies like Pepsi-Cola must manage broad and diverse arrays of brands and products at locations around the world. To ensure the same high level of quality everywhere despite dealing with a virtual army of suppliers, Pepsi relies on an interlocking set of sustainability and quality control policies covering everything from ingredients to packaging. It must abide by regulations imposed by the U.S. Food and Drug Administration and by agencies around the globe, including the European Food Safety Authority and Health Canada, for instance.[13]

Feedback also has a control function for individuals and teams, and the quality of this feedback affects employee attitudes and performance.[14] Will Newman discusses this perspective in the "I'm Glad . . ." feature.

I'm glad...

...my company made employees feel valued and engaged by regularly monitoring performance.

Will Newman worked as a financial advisor for a financial services company that created a culture of high morale and engagement by **regularly monitoring employee performance** and providing feedback.

Courtesy Will Newman

"Company leadership really did a great job of making all employees feel involved and valued. There were all sorts of initiatives that you could get involved in—not just for your current role, but for your future with the company. You really had a voice in what you were doing and where the company was going," said Will.

The company had a program that allowed employees to nominate one another for exceptional performance. The winners received $250 gift cards if their managers could validate the outstanding performance called out by their peers. This was another practice that led employees to feel valued because their good performance was being noticed.

Another important practice that increased employee engagement was the use of performance reviews. "They were huge on having us create our own mid-year plan and year-end plan to take control of our own performance and our own career path. It was very open-ended. They wanted us to tell them what we wanted to do, what we were doing well, what we wanted to work on, and how they could help us. Because of this, crew engagement was fantastic, and overall, morale was improved," said Will.

The leadership team would monitor calls and e-mails and then sit down with employees to review them. "It would be a way to ask 'What do you think you did well on that? What do you think you could have improved on?' It focused on helping the employee get the most out of the review," said Will. Leadership made sure to follow up with helpful feedback for each employee so they could learn from their mistakes and improve at their job.

Because managers regularly reviewed employee performance and provided meaningful feedback, employees felt actively engaged and valued by their colleagues and managers. They knew their work was important if leadership was active and concerned enough to invest in each individual.

Will was able to apply the positive experience he had with this company when he started his own company, Newman's Financial Planning, which is a fee-only registered advisory firm in the state of Arizona.

Courtesy of Will Newman

FIGURE 16.2
Six reasons control is needed

6. To Decentralize Decision Making and Facilitate Teamwork Controls allow top management to decentralize decision making at lower levels within the organization and to encourage employees to work together in teams. Facing a possible shortage of doctors in some areas of medicine, for instance, health care professionals are anticipating a rise in teamwork, small group practices, and the delegation of some routine patient services to nurse practitioners.[15] Controls, including secure digital patient records, will be important in ensuring high-quality and personalized care.

The six reasons control is needed are summarized above. *(See Figure 16.2.)*

Steps in the Control Process

Control systems may be altered to fit specific situations, but generally they follow the same steps. The four **control process steps** are **(1) establish standards; (2) measure performance; (3) compare performance to standards; and (4) take corrective action, if necessary.** *(See Figure 16.3.)*

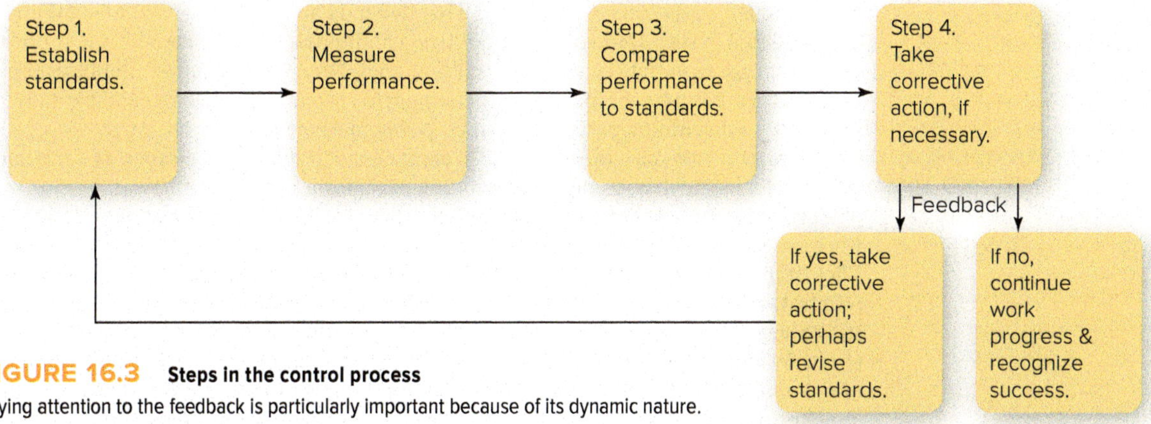

FIGURE 16.3 **Steps in the control process**
Paying attention to the feedback is particularly important because of its dynamic nature.

Let's consider these four steps.

1. Establish Standards: "What Is the Outcome We Want?" **A control standard, or *performance standard* or simply *standard*, is the desired performance level for a given goal.** Standards may be narrow or broad, and they can be set for almost anything, although they are best measured when they can be made quantifiable.

Nonprofit institutions might have standards for level of charitable contributions, number of students or volunteers retained, or degree of legal compliance. For-profit organizations might have standards of financial performance, employee hiring, manufacturing defects, percentage increase in market share, percentage reduction in costs, number of customer complaints, and return on investment. Service organizations may look at number of customers, clients, or patients served; time spent with each; and resulting level of satisfaction. More subjective standards, such as level of employee satisfaction, can also be set, although they may have to be expressed more quantifiably in terms of, say, reduced absenteeism and sick days and increased job applications.

One technique for establishing standards is to use *the balanced scorecard*, as we explain later in this chapter.

2. Measure Performance: "What Is the Actual Outcome We Got?" The second step in the control process is to measure performance, such as by number of products sold, units produced, time to completion, or cost per item sold.[16]

Example: This is harder than you think. Consider the example of measuring the length of a marathon. Kimberly Nickel thought she ran a personal best of 4 hours 37 minutes in the PNC Milwaukee Marathon. She proudly posted a selfie on Facebook showing the medal she received. Later that day, however, she received a note from race organizers indicating that "the 26.2 mile course had been laid out incorrectly, making it about 0.8 miles too short and disqualifying the race as an official or certified marathon."[17] Nickel sadly took down the posted photos.

Performance data are usually obtained from five sources: (1) employee behavior and deliverables, (2) peer input or observations, (3) customer feedback, (4) managerial evaluations, and (5) output from a production process.

3. Compare Performance to Standards: "How Do the Desired and Actual Outcomes Differ?" The third step in the control process is to compare measured performance against the standards established. Most managers are delighted with performance that exceeds standards, which becomes an occasion for handing out bonuses, promotions, and perhaps offices with a view. For performance that is below standards, they need to ask: Is the deviation from performance significant? The greater the difference between desired and actual performance, the greater the need for action.

How much deviation is acceptable? That depends on *the range of variation* built in to the standards in step 1. In voting for political candidates, for instance, there is supposed to be no range of variation; as the expression goes, "every vote counts." In political polling, however, a range of 3 percent–4 percent error is considered an acceptable range of variation. In machining parts for the solar-powered space probe Juno, currently orbiting Jupiter after a five-year journey, NASA engineers could tolerate a range of variation a good deal smaller than someone machining parts for a power lawnmower.

Employees and managers use control charts to monitor the amount of variation in a work process. **Control charts are a visual statistical tool used for quality control purposes.** They help managers set upper and lower quality limits on a process and then monitor (control) performance in order to keep it within these limits, correcting course if results stray above the upper or below the lower limit over time.[18] Managers construct control charts by looking at historical data for the process they want to measure, such as number of tax returns completed by a CPA firm per week, tons of steel produced by a manufacturer per day, or dollar volume of charitable contributions solicited by a nonprofit during a month-long fund drive. They then use that information to establish the normal or desired performance and its allowable upper and lower limits. *(See Figure 16.4.)* Each of these flows has a separate horizontal line on the chart, which also functions as a timeline.[19] When a process goes "out of control"—that is, when it exceeds either the upper or the lower limit—management takes note and investigates. Some variations may be routine or expected, such as a rise in the volume of toy orders before the holiday shopping season or an uptick in charitable donations following a natural disaster. But other

FIGURE 16.4 **Sample control chart for completing assigned readings**

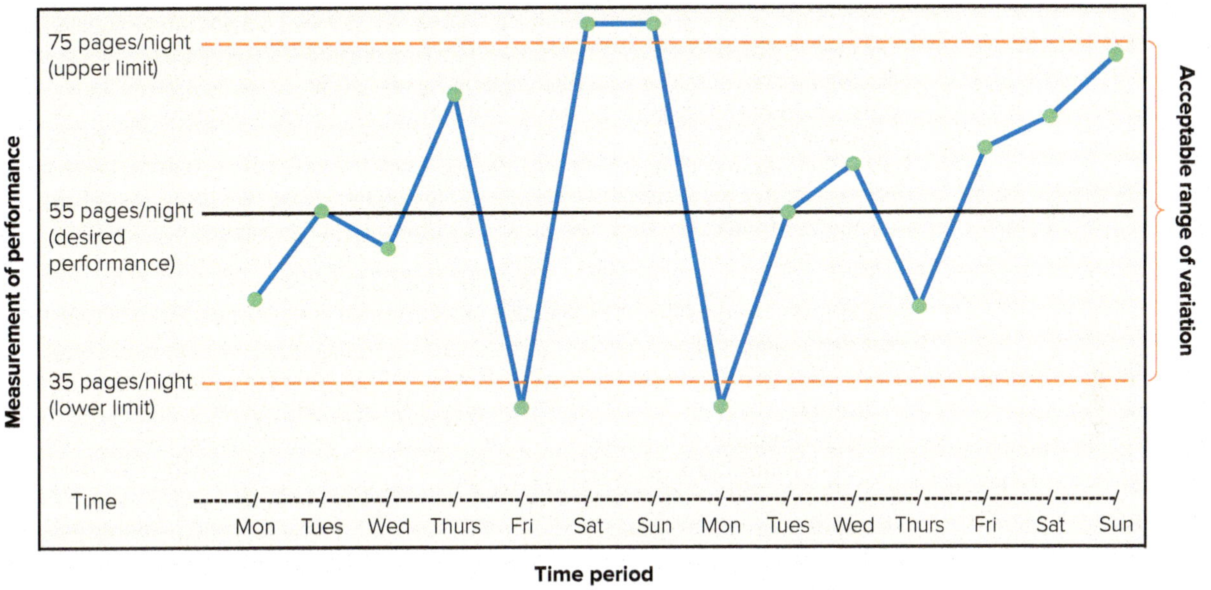

variations, such as a sudden drop in production because a machine has broken down or a large number of employees are out ill, will show up on a control chart as deviations and indicate an "out of control" situation that requires attention.

To understand how control charts work, we created one that you can use to monitor your progress in studying for finals. For example, suppose your experience reveals that in order to complete the assigned reading for all your courses before finals, you need to read 55 pages a night for the next two weeks. Fifty-five pages a night is your desired performance, and depending on how efficiently you can make up for lost time, you

Control and space flight. The Juno space probe was built by Lockheed Martin and is operated by NASA. It began an orbit of Jupiter in July 2016 and is expected to conduct a 20-month scientific investigation. It uses highly sophisticated equipment to measure the planet's gravity field, magnetic field, and polar magnetosphere. This type of equipment requires extraordinary levels of accuracy. Source: NASA/JPL-Caltech might set 35 pages as your acceptable lower limit and 75 as your upper limit. We created the control chart by drawing three horizontal lines with your upper limit on top, your lower limit on the bottom, and your desired rate of 55 pages a night in the middle. The timeline of two weeks is shown at the bottom of the chart. To put it to use, simply mark the number of pages you read each night as a point on the chart, and then connect the dots. Looking at Figure 16.4, you can see that the student exhibited acceptable performance from Monday through Thursday of the first week. Friday's reading was below acceptable limits, which the student made up for by exceeding the upper limit of 75 pages a day on Saturday and Sunday. This was followed by a substandard performance on Monday and then reading levels within acceptable limits the rest of the week.

The range of variation is often incorporated in computer systems into a principle called management by exception. **Management by exception is a control principle that states that managers should be informed of a situation only if data show a significant deviation from standards.**

4. Take Corrective Action, If Necessary: "What Changes Should We Make to Obtain Desirable Outcomes?" This step concerns *feedback*–modifying, if necessary, the control process according to the results or effects. This might be a dynamic process that will produce different effects every time you put the system to use. There are three possibilities here: (1) Make no changes. (2) Recognize and reinforce positive performance. (3) Take action to correct negative performance.

When performance meets or exceeds the standards set, managers should give rewards, ranging from giving a verbal "Job well done" to more substantial payoffs such as raises, bonuses, and promotions to reinforce good behavior.

When performance falls significantly short of the standard, managers should carefully examine the reasons and take the appropriate action. Sometimes the standards themselves were unrealistic, owing to changing conditions, in which case the standards need to be altered. Sometimes employees haven't been given the resources for achieving the standards. And sometimes the employees may need more attention from management as a way of signaling that their efforts have been insufficient in fulfilling their part of the job bargain.

EXAMPLE Steps in the Control Process: What's Expected of UPS Drivers?

Helping younger drivers train for successful careers has been a priority for UPS. The company designed a high-tech training center called Integrad[20] around research showing how people learn from video games and smartphones.

Integrad's curriculum consists of a one-week experiential learning course enhanced by virtual-reality simulations so drivers can practice delivery methods without ever leaving the building. UPS says, "The intent of the simulations [is] to help students identify potential hazards by visualizing other vehicles, pedestrians, traffic signs and signals, the basis of what a driver needs to drive defensively." Drivers also have an opportunity to practice delivery methods in a realistic setting on an outside course called "Clarkville, USA." The course mimics a small town "arrayed with small houses, street signs and even a dog bowl to alert drivers of the presence of a dog."[21]

Integrad operates 10 sites in eight different U.S. states, in addition to locations in Germany and the United Kingdom. The program has so far trained approximately 12,000 drivers in "safe work methods, safe driving methods, customer service methods, training in using the handheld computer (DIAD—acronym for Delivery Information Acquisition Device) for recording delivery information, proper package selection, and UPS history."[22]

UPS utilizes the control process after drivers have completed the Integrad program to ensure the program's learning objectives continue to be met. The company establishes standards for routine tasks, such as number of pickups and deliveries in an hour. It then measures drivers' performance and compares it with the standards, taking corrective action, if necessary. Consider this example from its Louisville, Kentucky operations.

ESTABLISHING STANDARDS

UPS establishes standards for its drivers that project the number of miles driven, deliveries, and pickups. A typical day for a driver in Louisville might include driving 60 miles to make 125 deliveries.[23]

MEASURING PERFORMANCE

UPS managers get a constant stream of feedback about drivers' performance from the DIAD device and from two onboard computer systems. On-Road Integrated Optimization and Navigation (ORION) optimizes the drivers' routes, and Telematics relays information about how often drivers back up and whether they are wearing seat belts. "Everything the driver does is being measured," says the company's business manager in Louisville.[24]

COMPARING PERFORMANCE TO STANDARDS

UPS managers compare a driver's performance (miles driven and number of pickups and deliveries) with the standards that were set for his or her particular route. A range of variation may be allowed to take into account issues like winter or summer driving or traffic conditions that slow productivity.

TAKING CORRECTIVE ACTION

If a driver fails to perform to the standards set, UPS can take corrective actions ranging from mentoring and development to termination.[25]

YOUR CALL

The UPS controls were devised by industrial engineers based on experience. Do you think the same kinds of controls could be established for, say, filling out tax forms for H&R Block?

Types of Controls

There are three types of control: feedforward, concurrent, and feedback. They vary based on timing.

Feedforward Control **Feedforward control focuses on preventing future problems.** It does this by collecting performance information about past performance and then planning to avoid pitfalls or roadblocks prior to starting a task or project, essentially helping people learn from mistakes.[26] Southwest Airlines' top two HR executives recently told a radio host that employees at the company who make a mistake on the customer's behalf are coached or retrained instead of being punished.[27]

Concurrent Control **Concurrent control entails collecting performance information in real time.** This enables managers to determine if employee behavior and organizational processes conform to regulations and standards. Corrective action can then be taken immediately when performance is not meeting expectations. For instance, trucking companies use GPS tracking to monitor "where company vehicles go, when they get there and how fast they move between destinations. It helps managers plan more efficient routes and alerts drivers to adjust routes in the event of an accident ahead. It also encourages employees to stay on task rather than running personal errands."[28]

Technology is typically used for concurrent control. Word-processing software is a good example. It immediately lets us know when we misspell words or use incorrect grammar. Corporate online monitoring of our e-mail and Internet use is another example of concurrent control.

Feedback Control This form of control is extensively used by supervisors and managers. **Feedback control amounts to collecting performance information after a task or project is done.** This information then is used to correct or improve future performance. Classic examples include receiving test scores a week after taking the test, receiving customer feedback after purchasing a product, receiving student ratings of a teaching performance weeks after teaching a class, rating the quality of a movie after watching it, and participating in a performance review at work.

Stop lights clearly serve as a control mechanism. Would you drive through a yellow light if a police officer was sitting on a motorcycle near the light? I guess it would depend on how far away you were from the light and how fast you were going. Without question, however, the officer represents another type of cue that affects behavior.
©Stella Photography/Shutterstock

The problem with feedback control is that it occurs too late. For instance, if an instructor is doing a bad job in the classroom, he or she needs to make changes right away. Learning 10 weeks later that his or her performance was ineffective does not help current students. The same is true when it comes to customer satisfaction and quality. On the positive side, many people want feedback, and late is better than never.

IBM recognized the limitations of providing feedback in annual performance reviews. The company scrapped its 10-year-old system, called Personal Business Commitments, and replaced it with one called Checkpoint. The new system requires employees to set short-term goals, and managers provide quarterly feedback on their progress.[29] ●

Small business. What type of control is most important for small businesses? Do you think employees in small companies, such as a garden pots store, need less control than employees in large companies? ©Don Mason/Getty Images

16.2 Levels and Areas of Control

THE BIG PICTURE

This section describes three levels of control—strategic, tactical, and operational—and six areas of control: physical, human, informational, financial, structural (bureaucratic and decentralized), and cultural. We also look at the supply chain and special considerations for control mechanisms in service firms.

LO 16-2

Explain how successful companies implement controls.

How are you going to apply the steps of control to your own management area? Let's look at this in several ways: First, you need to consider the *level* of management at which you operate–top, middle, or first level. Second, you need to consider the *areas* that you draw on for resources–physical, human, information, and/or financial. Finally, we look at the *type of firm*. If you manage a manufacturing firm, you will have *supply chain* issues that require controls at many points, while if your firm is a service provider, you still require controls, but of a different type.

Levels of Control: Strategic, Tactical, and Operational

There are three levels of control, which correspond to the three principal managerial levels: *strategic* planning by top managers, *tactical* planning by middle managers, and *operational* planning by first-line (supervisory) managers and team leaders.

1. Strategic Control by Top Managers

Strategic control is monitoring performance to ensure that strategic plans are being implemented and taking corrective action as needed. Strategic control is mainly performed by top managers, those at the CEO and VP levels, who have an organizationwide perspective.[30]

For example, General Electric's legendary CEO Jack Welch vastly increased the company's market value during his 20-year tenure. He embraced change; believed managers should facilitate, not complicate; embodied energy and vision; and insisted on operating on the basis of facts. Focus and follow-up were hallmarks of his management style.[31]

2. Tactical Control by Middle Managers

Tactical control is monitoring performance to ensure that tactical plans—those at the divisional or departmental level—are being implemented and taking corrective action as needed. Tactical control is done mainly by middle managers, those with such titles as "division head," "plant manager," and "branch sales manager." Reporting is done on a weekly or monthly basis.

3. Operational Control by First-Line Managers

Operational control is monitoring performance to ensure that operational plans—day-to-day goals—are being implemented and taking corrective action as needed. Operational control is done mainly by first-line managers, those with titles such as "department head" or "supervisor." It also includes team leaders. Reporting is done on a daily basis.

Considerable interaction occurs among the three levels, with lower-level managers providing information upward and upper-level managers checking on some of the more critical aspects of plan implementation below them.

Six Areas of Control

The six areas of organizational control are *physical, human, informational, financial, structural,* and *cultural.*

1. Physical Area

The physical area includes buildings, equipment, and tangible products.

Examples: Equipment controls monitor the use of computers, cars, HVAC equipment, and other machinery. The speedometer in your car is a physical control. Quality controls ensure that products are being built according to certain acceptable standards. Inventory-management controls keep track of how many products are in stock, how many will be needed, and what their delivery dates are. If you have ever searched for a popular item on Amazon.com, for instance, you may have seen a notification like "Only 5 left in stock (more on the way)." The company's sophisticated inventory controls supply the information that makes these notifications possible. Lowe's, a home improvement retailer, is experimenting with robot inventory checkers that roam the aisles, deftly avoiding shoppers while scanning product bar codes on the shelves.[32]

2. Human Resources Area The controls used to monitor employees include personality tests and drug testing for hiring, performance tests during training, performance evaluations to measure work productivity, and employee surveys to assess job satisfaction, engagement, and leadership. Adidas human resource function has expanded its role and likely its control functions as well, as the following Example box describes.

EXAMPLE Adidas Cares about Fair Labor Practices

Adidas is known for its athletic shoes, clothing, and accessories, but what may go unnoticed is its reputation for superb workplace standards. As Europe's largest sportswear manufacturer with more than 53,000 employees,[33] Adidas again earned accreditation by the Fair Labor Association (FLA) in October 2017 for its commitment to upholding fair labor standards in its supply chains. The company was first accredited by FLA in 2005.[34]

The FLA was established in 1999 to "combine the efforts of business, civil society organizations, and colleges and universities to promote and protect workers' rights and to improve working conditions globally through adherence to international standards."[35] Organizations that affiliate with the FLA "commit to upholding international labor standards throughout their supply chains..." This commitment is evaluated by the FLA Board of Directors during an initial multi-year evaluation, with reaccreditation assessments conducted regularly thereafter.[36]

Adidas has been the subject of FLA's praise for many reasons, most importantly its platform for submission of employee grievances and its comprehensive approach to preventing labor violations in its supply chain. Adidas takes employee grievances very seriously. It offers a short message service (SMS) system in countries such as Indonesia, Vietnam, Cambodia, and China through which employees can confidentially text their grievances to suppliers, allowing both the suppliers and Adidas to review trends and stay informed. For example, more than 5,000 SMS-based grievances were submitted in China alone during a six-month period in 2016.[37]

Adidas also takes an active role in responding to grievances. It often follows up by checking that workers in specific locations are being treated fairly and that the work environment is safe and healthy. Warning letters are issued if problems are found, and the Adidas sourcing team will be directed to stop working with the factory if they are not remedied. Moreover, the company will immediately stop working with a factory if serious issues, such as life-threatening safety problems, are found. Adidas will also notify the local government of such violations at suppliers' factories.[38]

Adidas is also committed to preventing labor violations in its supply chain of about 800 independent factories in more than 55 countries. The company has a Social and Environmental Affairs (SEA) team that commissions independent auditors to verify supplier compliance with the company's supply chain code of conduct.[39] Suppliers that have not been approved by the diverse SEA team of 70 engineers, lawyers, HR managers and environmental auditors[40] cannot be utilized. Adidas also supports its suppliers with training, either by Adidas' own staff or by third-party providers. The training covers topics such as workplace standards, sustainable compliance, and supplier self-assessment methods.[41]

YOUR CALL

How do you think Adidas' fair labor practices affect its employees, local communities, and the brand as a whole? Has your image of Adidas changed now that you've read about its practices?

3. Informational Area Production schedules, sales forecasts, environmental impact statements, analyses of competition, and public relations briefings all are controls on an organization's various information resources. Among the factors that will govern a decision about whether a high-speed passenger-rail line is to be built in Oregon, for instance, is an environmental impact statement being prepared by the state's Department of Transportation.[42]

4. Financial Area Are bills being paid on time? How much money is owed by customers? How much money is owed to suppliers? Is there enough cash on hand to meet payroll obligations? What are the debt-repayment schedules? What is the advertising budget? Clearly, the organization's financial controls are important because they can affect the preceding three areas. If Oregon's high-speed rail line becomes a reality, one of the major tasks for project managers will be controlling the cost of building it, which estimates say could rise as high as $4.5 billion.[43]

5. Structural Area A company's structure functions as a control mechanism by specifying a chain of command (identifying who reports to whom) and officially sanctioned communication channels. Two examples are *bureaucratic control* and *decentralized control.*

- **Bureaucratic control.** **Bureaucratic control is an approach to organizational control that is characterized by use of rules, regulations, and formal authority to guide performance.** This form of control attempts to elicit employee compliance, using strict rules, a rigid hierarchy, well-defined job descriptions, and administrative mechanisms such as budgets, performance appraisals, and compensation schemes (external rewards to get results). The foremost example of use of bureaucratic control is the traditional military organization.

  Bureaucratic control works well in organizations in which the tasks are explicit and certain. While rigid, it can be an effective means of ensuring that performance standards are being met. However, it may not be effective if people are looking for ways to stay out of trouble by simply following the rules, or if they try to beat the system by manipulating performance reports, or if they try to actively resist bureaucratic constraints.
- **Decentralized control.** **Decentralized control is an approach to organizational control that is characterized by informal and organic structural arrangements,** the opposite of bureaucratic control. This form of control aims to get increased employee commitment, using the corporate culture, group norms, and workers taking responsibility for their performance. Decentralized control is found in companies with a relatively flat organization.

6. Cultural Area The company's culture is an informal method of control. It influences the work process and levels of performance through the set of accepted norms and behaviors that develop as a result of the values and beliefs that constitute an organization's culture. If an organization's culture values innovation and collaboration, as at many tech start-ups, for instance, then employees are likely to be evaluated on the basis of how much they engage in collaborative activities and enhance or create new products.

Bureaucratic control. In businesses such as construction of large subdivisions, tasks are explicit and certain, and employees are expected to perform them the same way each time. However, a small contractor, such as one building custom houses, need not be bureaucratic. Source: Photo by Lynn Betts, USDA Natural Resources Conservation Service

Controlling the Supply Chain

The supply chain is the sequence of suppliers that contribute to creating and delivering a product, from raw materials to production to final buyers. Supply chains are a major cost center for most companies, and the way firms structure the distribution of their products can have enormous financial impact. In recognition of this impact, companies are paying closer attention to the sourcing, shipping, and warehousing of their products and of the ingredients and component parts they require. Many organizations are creating specialized supply chain departments that look specifically at cost and quality control in these areas and the way they contribute to the cost and quality of finished products. Managing supply chain functions has become so important that some academic management departments now offer undergraduate and master's degrees in supply chain management, including at Arizona State University, for example.

Poor supply chain control recently plagued Kentucky Fried Chicken's UK operations. Problems resulted in the temporary closure of half the company's 900 restaurants due to an interruption in its supply of chickens. "The chicken crossed the road," said the company's website. "Just not to our restaurants." The incident arose from the chain's decision to switch its delivery contractor from Bidvest, a South African company, to DHL, based in Germany. DHL in turn said "operational issues" had caused the delays.[44] Customers were not amused, but KFC won back some goodwill with a humorous ad showing Colonel Sanders with an empty bucket and a mischievous rearrangement of its name that suggested a profane word.[45] Britain is KFC's fifth-largest market, worth almost $25 billion a year.[46]

At Target, with annual sales in the $75 billion range,[47] the supply chain has evolved with advances in online shopping. Where the goal was once to deliver goods from suppliers to regional warehouses in a straight line, now, says the company's CIO, Mike McNamara, "All of our inventory is available to all our guests, all the time. We will ship from a point to a guest that makes the most economic sense, or gives the guest the shortest lead time. That means that the thing that was once linear is now a network."[48]

Amazon has been experimenting with using drones as "the delivery truck of the future." The company hopes drones will someday be able to accurately deliver packages weighing up to five pounds ("the vast majority of the things we sell at Amazon") within 30 minutes in both cities and rural areas. It warns that drones won't become a reality anytime soon, however.[49]

Control in Service Firms

Service providers, such as income-tax preparers, hospitals and dental practices, consultants, accountants, hair and nail salons, stockbrokers, hotels, and airlines, differ from manufacturers in several ways. The most obvious is that service companies cannot hold any inventory of their services, which are intangible; instead, they provide these services only on demand. Your new haircut does not exist until you sit down in the stylist's chair, for example.

Another difference is that service firms usually develop a personal, if temporary, relationship with their client or customer. Your haircut or flu shot is provided only to you, in other words, and the seat you buy on a plane heading to Amsterdam can be filled only by you. Some services are highly perishable. If you don't show up for your flight to Amsterdam, your ability to occupy that particular seat on that particular plane vanishes forever, along with your chance to sleep in the hotel room you reserved at your destination. The education you acquire in college is another example of the personal nature of service; that education is yours alone.[50]

The U.S. service industry has grown considerably in the last few decades as a great deal of manufacturing activity has moved overseas. Before World War II, there were about two service-industry jobs for every manufacturing job in the United States. Today the ratio of service to manufacturing employment is almost seven to one.[51]

Because services are provided by humans (for the most part), everything we have outlined in this chapter that relates to measuring and controlling employee behavior applies to the role of control in service organizations. Clearly, training and education affect the quality of any service. Health care organizations operate under high control standards, for example, as evidenced by the many years of education and training required to obtain a license to practice medicine or dentistry. The same holds for the practice of law. Ongoing training and certification are a form of control for airline pilots, tax accountants (CPAs), teachers, physical therapists, and personal trainers.

16.3 The Balanced Scorecard and Strategy Maps

THE BIG PICTURE

The balanced scorecard helps managers establish goals and measures for four strategic perspectives. A visual representation of the relationships among balanced scorecard perspectives is the strategy map.

LO 16-3

Discuss the purpose of the balanced scorecard and strategy maps in measuring performance.

Wouldn't you, as a top manager, like to have displayed in easy-to-read graphics all the information on sales, orders, and the like assembled from data pulled in real-time from corporate software? The technology exists and it has a name: a *dashboard*, like the instrument panel in a car.

Bob Parsons, founder of GoDaddy, believed in dashboards. "Measure everything of significance. Anything that is measured and watched improves," he said.[52]

Throughout this book we have stressed the importance of *evidence-based management*—the use of real-world data rather than fads and hunches in making management decisions. When properly done, the dashboard is an example of the important tools that make this kind of management possible. The balanced scorecard is another.

The Balanced Scorecard: A Dashboard-like View of the Organization

Robert Kaplan is a professor of accounting at the Harvard Business School and a leading authority on strategic performance measurement. David Norton is co-founder of Balanced Scorecard Collaborative. Kaplan and Norton developed what they call the **balanced scorecard, which gives top managers a fast but comprehensive view of the organization via four indicators: (1) customer satisfaction, (2) internal processes, (3) innovation and improvement activities, and (4) financial measures.**

"Think of the balanced scorecard as the dials and indicators in an airplane cockpit," write Kaplan and Norton. For a pilot, "reliance on one instrument can be fatal. Similarly, the complexity of managing an organization today requires that managers be able to view performance in several areas simultaneously."[53] It is not enough, say Kaplan and Norton, to simply measure financial performance, such as sales figures and return on investment. Operational matters, such as customer satisfaction, are equally important.[54]

The Balanced Scorecard: Four "Perspectives"

The balanced scorecard establishes (a) *goals* and (b) *performance measures* according to four "perspectives," or areas—*financial, customer, internal business,* and *innovation and learning. (See Figure 16.5.)*

1. Financial Perspective: "How Do We Look to Shareholders?" Corporate financial strategies and goals generally fall into two buckets: revenue growth and productivity growth. Revenue growth goals might focus on increasing revenue from both new and existing customers. Equipment manufacturer John Deere, for instance, is pursuing new revenue by developing software services that provide information and guidance to farmers in the field. It is doing this to offset a recent 5 percent decrease in revenue.[55] Productivity metrics like revenue per employee or total output produced divided by number of employees are common organization-level goals. We can also measure productivity in terms of costs. For example, Bob Evans Farms Inc. is closing 27 underperforming restaurants in an attempt to decrease costs and improve profitability.[56]

FIGURE 16.5 The balanced scorecard: Four perspectives

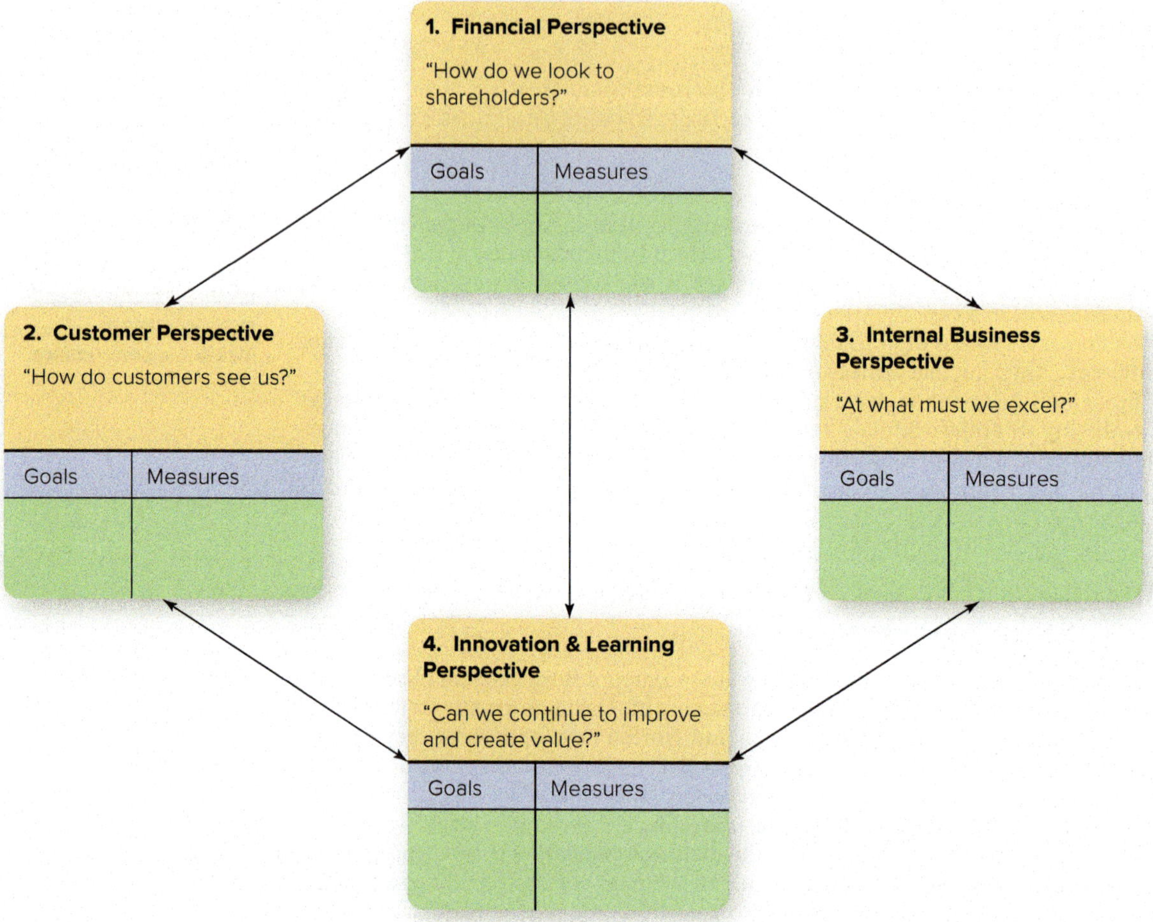

Source: Adapted from R. S. Kaplan and D. P. Norton, "The Balanced Scorecard—Measures That Drive Performance," Harvard Business Review, *January–February 1992, pp. 71–79.*

2. Customer Perspective: "How Do Customers See Us?" Many companies view customers as one of their most important constituents. The balanced scorecard translates this belief into measures such as market share, customer acquisition, customer retention, customer satisfaction/loyalty, product/service quality, response time (the time between order and delivery), and percentage of bids won.

Sunnybrook Health Sciences Centre, part of the University of Toronto Faculty of Medicine, has 1.2 million patient visits a year. The four "quality of care" goals in its balanced scorecard all relate to the ways in which its constituents—patients and partners—experience the organization. The goals are:

- **Goal 1:** Improve the patient experience and outcomes through inter-professional, high quality care.
- **Goal 2:** Focus on the highest levels of specialized care in support of our Academic Health Sciences Centre definition.
- **Goal 3:** Work with system partners and government to build an integrated delivery system in support of our communities and our Academic Health Sciences Centre definition.

- **Goal 4:** Achieving excellence in clinical care associated with our strategic priorities.[57]

3. Internal Business Perspective: "At What Must We Excel?" The internal business perspective focuses on "what the organization must excel at" to effectively meet its financial objectives and customers' expectations. A team of researchers identified four critical high-level internal processes that managers are encouraged to measure and manage:

1. Innovation.
2. Customer service and satisfaction.
3. Operational excellence, which includes safety and quality.
4. Good corporate citizenship.[58]

These processes influence productivity, efficiency, quality, safety, and a host of other internal metrics. Companies tend to adopt continuous improvement programs in pursuit of upgrades to their internal processes.

Example: Seven in 10 people in the United States who need a life-saving bone marrow or cord blood transplant do not have a suitable donor within their families. That's where the "Be the Match Registry," run by the nonprofit National Marrow Donor Program (NMDP), comes into play, with more than 10.5 million registered potential donors. When the NMDP recently resolved to double its annual transplant rate, its managers realized the organization needed a new strategic plan. After consulting with other nonprofits and health care organizations, it chose the balanced scorecard approach for its ability to incorporate powerful quality-management strategies as well improve internal processes. Improvements that have already been made at NMDP include reduced time to find matches, increased global brand awareness and donor recruitment, earlier referrals from physicians, and lower medical costs for patients and families.[59]

4. Innovation and Learning Perspective: "Can We Continue to Improve and Create Value?" Learning and growth of employees are the foundation for all other goals in the balanced scorecard. The idea here is that capable and motivated employees, who possess the resources and culture needed to get the job done, will provide higher-quality products and services in a more efficient manner. Making this happen requires a commitment to invest in progressive human resource practices and technology. Typical metrics in this perspective are employee satisfaction/engagement, employee retention, employee productivity, training budget per employee, technology utilization, and organizational climate and culture. Many are tracked with employee surveys to gauge attitudes and opinions.

Example: Tolko Industries Ltd. is a family-owned Canadian forest products company that faced the need to change its strategy when the housing market in the United States, its largest source of sales, went into a sudden decline. Its managers knew they also needed to reenergize and secure the buy-in of the company's 3,500 employees, who worked in 22 business units across Canada. Recent layoffs had depressed morale, and employee retention was suffering. The company adopted the balanced scorecard approach as a "living plan" with a multi-year time horizon and began by developing a new vision, mission statement, and strategy. Once top managers were focused on the new strategy, a "train the trainer" exercise was introduced to help employees become familiar with the changes and understand, with the help of a strategy map developed in the process, that "this is how we will be doing business."[60]

To what extent is/was your current or past employer committed to the innovation and learning of its employees? You can find out by completing Self-Assessment 16.1.

SELF-ASSESSMENT 16.1

Assessing the Innovation and Learning Perspective of the Balanced Scorecard

The following survey was designed to assess the innovation and learning perspective of the balanced scorecard. Please be prepared to answer these questions if your instructor has assigned Self-Assessment 16.1 in Connect.

1. Where does the company stand in terms of commitment to innovation and learning? Are you surprised by the results?
2. Use the three highest and lowest scores to identify the strengths and weaknesses of this company's commitment to innovation and learning.
3. Based on your answer to question 2, provide three suggestions for what management could do to improve its commitment to innovation and learning.

Strategy Mapping: Visual Representation of the Path to Organizational Effectiveness

Have you ever worked for a company that failed to effectively communicate its vision and strategic plan? If yes, then you know how it feels to be disengaged because you don't know how your work contributes to organizational effectiveness. Kaplan and Norton recognized this common problem and developed a tool called a strategy map.

A **strategy map** is a **"visual representation of a company's critical objectives and the crucial relationships among them that drive organizational performance."** Maps show relationships among a company's strategic goals. This helps employees understand how their work contributes to their employer's overall success.[61] They also provide insight into how an organization creates value to its key constituents. For example, a map informs others about the knowledge, skills, and systems that employees should possess (innovation and learning perspective) to innovate and build internal capabilities (internal business perspective) that deliver value to customers (customer perspective), which eventually creates higher shareholder value (financial perspective).

We created an illustrative strategy map in Figure 16.5. Starting with learning and growth, the arrows in the diagram show the logic that connects goals to internal processes, to customers, to financial goals, and finally to the long-term goal of providing shareholder value. For example, you can see that organizational culture affects the internal process goals related to innovation, operational improvements, and good corporate citizenship. This causal structure provides a strategic road map of how the company plans to achieve organizational effectiveness.

You can also detect which of the four perspectives is most important by counting the number of goals in each perspective. For this sample map, there are four, five, eight, and four goals for the financial, customer, internal processes, and learning and growth perspectives, respectively. You can also see that internal process goals affect eight other goals—count the number of arrows coming from internal process goals. All told, the beauty of a strategy map is that it enables leaders to present a strategic road map to employees on one page. It also provides a clear statement about the criteria used to assess organizational effectiveness.

There is one final benefit to strategy maps. They serve as the starting point for any organization that wants to implement goal cascading or management by objectives. For example, your author Angelo Kinicki has worked with several organizations that cascaded a top-level strategy map like the one shown in Figure 16.6 down three to four organizational levels. He is currently consulting with a firm that has created individual level scorecards for all its roughly 3,000 employees.[62]

FIGURE 16.6 **Sample strategy map for Dr Pepper Snapple Group**

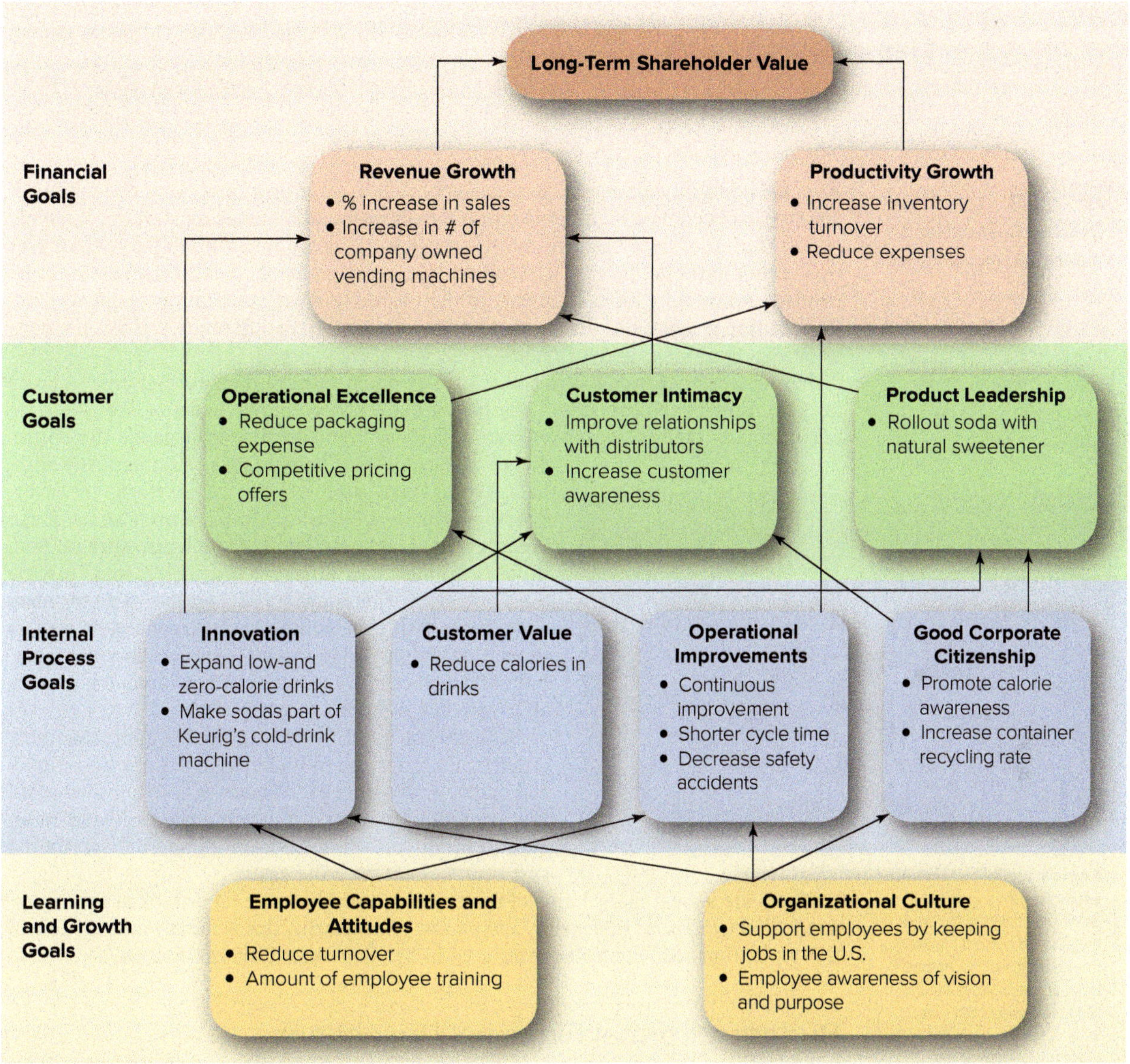

Sources: This map was based on information in "Dr Pepper Snapple Group to Boost Container Recycling, and More. . . ," TheShelbyReport.com, *February 12, 2016; C. Choi, "Dr Pepper to Test Naturally Sweetened Sodas,"* FoodManufacturing.com, *February 13, 2014; A. Gasparro and M. Esterl, "Keurig Reels in Dr Pepper for Its Coming Soda Machine,"* TheWallStreetJournal.com, *January 7, 2015; S. Frizell, "Coke and Pepsi Pledge to Cut Calories,"* Time.com, *September 23, 2014; M. Esterl, "How Dr Pepper Cuts Costs. And Then Cuts Costs Some More,"* The Wall Street Journal, *February 16, 2016, p. R2; "Vision—Call to Breakthrough ACTION,"* DrPepperSnappleGroup.com *(accessed May 12, 2016).*

16.4 Some Financial Tools for Control

THE BIG PICTURE

Financial controls are especially important. These include budgets, financial statements, and audits.

LO 16-4

Describe financial tools managers should know.

At some point in your career, you may very well be your own boss. That doesn't mean you have to become a high-flying entrepreneur or found an amazing start-up. It simply means that in today's "gig economy," young workers are much more likely than ever before to join the millions of U.S. adults who work on-demand as freelancers or independent contractors for at least part of their working life. (Exact numbers are very difficult to find because different surveys define these workers differently.[63] If this happens to be you, knowledge about financial tools will serve you well.)

Hiring freelancers can save companies as much as a third of normal payroll costs because most freelancers aren't eligible for expensive employee benefits like paid time off, company medical coverage, and pensions.[64] Nor do they experience the convenience of having their income taxes automatically withheld from their pay. At the same time, however, freelancers enjoy the freedom to work from home, make their own hours, choose their assignments, work on multiple assignments in different industries, and, yes, be their own boss. That includes being responsible for managing their cash flow and business expenses, as well as for setting money aside to pay their own income taxes, both of which can be a challenge when income is seasonable, variable, or both.

Financial control and contract employees. Five young co-workers meeting to discuss a project. One or more are likely freelancers given the increasing trend of companies hiring them. Hiring freelancers can save labor costs, but it also can leave those freelancers feeling outside the normal comings and goings of the work environment. ©Ingram Publishing

With this in mind, you can probably appreciate how important it is for you to understand the basics of financial controls. Whether as the manager of your own small "gig economy" business or as a manager on staff in an organization, you will need to monitor finances and be sure revenues are covering costs.

There are a great many kinds of financial controls, but here let us look at the following: *budgets*, *financial statements*, and *audits*. (Necessarily, this is merely an overview of this topic. Financial controls are covered in detail in other business courses.)

Budgets: Formal Financial Projections

A budget is a formal financial projection. It states an organization's planned activities for a given period of time in quantitative terms, such as dollars, hours, or number of products. Budgets are prepared not only for the organization as a whole but also for the divisions and departments within it. The point of a budget is to provide a yardstick against which managers can judge how well they are controlling monetary expenditures.

Various software tools are also available to help you manage personal or freelance budgeting, such as QuickBooks and apps like Mint and Venmo.[65]

Historically, managers have used three budget-planning approaches. Two of them—the planning programming budgeting system and zero base budgeting—are no longer favored and are now infrequently used. The dominant approach today is incremental budgeting.[66]

Incremental Budgeting

Incremental budgeting allocates increased or decreased funds to a department by using the last budget period as a reference point; only incremental changes in the budget request are reviewed. One difficulty is that incremental budgets tend to lock departments into stable spending arrangements; they are not flexible in meeting environmental demands. Another difficulty is that a department may engage in many activities—some more important than others—but it's not easy to sort out how well managers performed at the various activities. Thus, the department activities and the yearly budget increases take on lives of their own.

Fixed versus Variable Budgets

In general, we can identify two types of incremental budgets: *fixed* and *variable.*

- **Fixed budgets—where resources are allocated on a single estimate of costs.** Also known as a *static budget*, a **fixed budget** **allocates resources on the basis of a single estimate of costs.** That is, there is only one set of expenses; the budget does not allow for adjustment over time. For example, you might have a budget of $50,000 for buying equipment in a given year—no matter how much you may need equipment exceeding that amount.
- **Variable budgets—where resources are varied in proportion with various levels of activity.** Also known as a *flexible budget*, a **variable budget** **allows the allocation of resources to vary in proportion with various levels of activity.** That is, the budget can be adjusted over time to accommodate pertinent changes in the environment. For example, you might have a budget that allows you to hire temporary workers or lease temporary equipment if production exceeds certain levels. As a freelancer, you might set up your budget to allow for the unexpected, like the purchase of a second monitor for your laptop if you accept an assignment that requires it.

Financial Statements: Summarizing the Organization's Financial Status

A financial statement is a summary of some aspect of an organization's financial status. The information contained in such a statement is essential in helping managers maintain financial control over the organization.

There are two basic types of financial statements: the *balance sheet* and the *income statement.*

The Balance Sheet: Picture of Organization's Financial Worth for a Specific Point in Time

A balance sheet summarizes an organization's overall financial worth—that is, assets and liabilities—at a specific point in time.

Assets are the resources that an organization controls; they consist of current assets and fixed assets. *Current assets* are cash and other assets that are readily convertible to cash within one year's time. Examples are inventory, sales for which payment has not been received (accounts receivable), and U.S. Treasury bills or money market mutual funds. *Fixed assets* are property, buildings, equipment, and the like that have a useful life that exceeds one year but that are usually harder to convert to cash. *Liabilities* are claims, or debts, by suppliers, lenders, and other nonowners of the organization against a company's assets. If you are a member of the gig economy, the quarterly estimated federal and local taxes you will need to pay on your annual income are a financial liability of your business.

Many entrepreneurs believe that cash is king when it comes to running a business.
©3D Vector/Shutterstock

The Income Statement: Picture of Organization's Financial Results for a Specified Period of Time

The balance sheet depicts the organization's overall financial worth at a specific point in time. By contrast, the **income statement** **summarizes an organization's financial results—revenues and expenses—over a specified period of time,** such as a quarter or a year.

TABLE 16.1
Sample Profit and Loss Statements

LACI, THE COMPUTER DOCTOR PROFIT & LOSS JANUARY 1 THROUGH DECEMBER 31, 2016		
Income:		Jan 1–Dec 31, 16
Sales		481,219.00
Services Income		23,050.00
Total Income		504,269.00
Parts and Materials	45,711.60	
Gross Profit		458,557.40
Expenses:		
Bank Service Charges		150.00
Charitable Donations		2,000.00
Dues and Subscriptions		1,520.88
Insurance:		
General Liability Insurance	1,925.00	
Workman's Compensation Insurance	1,016.00	
Total Insurance Expense:		2,941.00
Payroll Taxes:		
Payroll 941	13,992.76	
Federal Unemployment Tax	103.00	
State Unemployment Tax	210.00	
Total Payroll Taxes:		14,305.76
Payroll:		
Officer Wages	150,000.00	
Salary and Wages	49,896.50	
Total Payroll:		199,896.50
Accounting and Legal		1,402.75
Automobile Expenses:		
Maintenance	140.16	
Gas	1,012.92	
License	828.31	
Total Automobile Expenses:		1,981.39
Office Rent		24,000.00
Office supplies		1,775.00
Repairs and Maintenance		285.19
Telephone and Internet		1,856.25
Utilities		2,085.09
TOTAL EXPENSE:		254,199.81
NET INCOME:		204,357.59

Source: Angelo Kinicki

You will need to understand an income statement if you end up self-employed or start a business. We created a sample profit and loss statement for a two-person operation consisting of an owner and one employee *(see Table 16.1)*. The company is doing quite well with $204,357 of net income, computed by subtracting total expenses from gross profit. You can also see the types of expenses that confront any small business. You have expenses for insurance, payroll and payroll taxes, accounting, auto, rent, supplies, and other expenses.

Audits: External versus Internal

When you think of auditors, do you think of grim-faced accountants looking through a company's books to catch embezzlers and other cheats? That's one function of auditing, but besides verifying the accuracy and fairness of financial statements, the audit also is intended to be a tool for management decision making. **Audits are formal verifications of an organization's financial and operational systems.**

You can imagine that audits of medium and large companies entail collecting, analyzing, and interpreting large amounts of information. Because of this, more and more companies are using data analytics to conduct audits; we discussed data analytics in Chapter 7. Regarding the use of analytics, one expert concluded, "The use of analytics in the audit process results in better audit planning, focus, and recommendations."[67]

Audits are of two types—*external* and *internal.*

Accountants at the Academy Awards? Sam Rockwell on the left with Frances McDormand holding their Academy Awards in 2017. Every year since 1929 the secret ballots for Oscar nominees voted on by members of the Academy of Motion Picture Arts and Sciences have been tabulated by accountants from the firm now knows as PricewaterhouseCoopers. The accounting firm takes this task very seriously. Accounting is an important business function because investors depend on independent auditors to verify that a company's finances are what they are purported to be. ©Albert L. Ortega/WireImage/Getty Images

External Audits—Financial Appraisals by Outside Financial Experts An **external audit** **is a formal verification of an organization's financial accounts and statements by outside experts.** The auditors are certified public accountants (CPAs) who work for an accounting firm (such as PricewaterhouseCoopers) that is independent of the organization being audited. Their task is to verify that the organization, in preparing its financial statements and in determining its assets and liabilities, followed generally accepted accounting principles.[68]

Internal Audits—Financial Appraisals by Inside Financial Experts An **internal audit** **is a verification of an organization's financial accounts and statements by the organization's own professional staff.** Their jobs are the same as those of outside experts—to verify the accuracy of the organization's records and operating activities. Internal audits also help uncover inefficiencies and thus help managers evaluate the performance of their control systems.

When Citigroup recently had to issue $330 million in refunds to about 1.75 million credit card holders, it did so to correct "methodological issues" in calculating the annual interest rate its customers had been charged. The error was caught in a routine audit required by the CARD Act, a relatively new federal law. The bank apologized to customers, who received an average refund of $190, and described the error in its annual report, which was sent to the Securities and Exchange Commission.[69]

We end this section on financial tools in a more personal manner by assessing your financial literacy. This is an important assessment in light of the *The Wall Street Journal*'s conclusion that "there's a financial-literacy crisis in the U.S. And it is probably even worse than it seems."[70] A recent survey of 1,400 adults, for instance, showed that seven in 10 Americans delay financial decisions due to "lack of confidence in money matters and not having the right mind-set."[71] This creates stress and lowers productivity and well-being. Some companies, such as Aetna Inc. and SunTrust Banks Inc., recognize the importance of this issue and have provided money-management classes.[72] Self-Assessment 16.2 evaluates your knowledge in matters associated with interest-bearing accounts, investments, inflation, pensions, creditworthiness, and insurance. It's a fun way to find out if your financial literacy is up to speed. •

SELF-ASSESSMENT 16.2 CAREER READINESS

Assessing Your Financial Literacy

The following survey was designed to assess your financial literacy. Please be prepared to answer these questions if your instructor has assigned Self-Assessment 16.2 in Connect.

1. Where do you stand in terms of financial literacy?
2. Look at the statements you got incorrect, and identify the specific aspects of financial knowledge that you may be lacking.
3. What can you say during an interview to demonstrate that you possess financial literacy? Be specific.

16.5 Total Quality Management

THE BIG PICTURE

Total quality management (TQM) is dedicated to continuous quality improvement, training, and customer satisfaction. Two core principles are people orientation and improvement orientation. Some techniques for improving quality are employee involvement, benchmarking, outsourcing, reduced cycle time, and statistical process control.

LO 16-5

Explain the total quality management process.

Bristol Tennessee Essential Services (BTES), an electrical utility whose 68 employees serve 33,000 customers, was the 2017 winner of the coveted Baldrige Award.[73] This award is "given by the President of the United States to businesses and to education, health care, and nonprofit organizations that apply and are judged to be outstanding in seven areas of performance excellence." The seven areas are leadership; strategy; customers; measurement, analysis, and knowledge management; workforce; operations; and results.[74]

BTES counts reliability as a key goal and more than meets it. For the past three years, the company has exceeded its benchmark goal of containing power outages to less than 60 minutes per customer per year, easily outperforming the industry average of 90 to 100 minutes. One means for meeting this goal is the company's database of outage factors, which employees discuss at daily and weekly meetings. High reliability and BTES's help desk and customer service line have brought customer satisfaction to nearly 100 percent, but the company doesn't take that for granted. Senior leaders review all customer feedback at weekly meetings of the Continuous Improvement Team.[75]

Over the last 40 years, BTES has also saved its customers a total of about $70 million by constantly monitoring and controlling costs, investing in employee training, and integrating its fiber optic system. The company outperforms the industry in terms of preparedness, with a sustained performance rate of 99.99 percent. Its employee retention rate is even higher—a remarkable 100 percent. Three-quarters of employees have perfect attendance (compared to an industry average of less than 20 percent). Only two safety accidents have cost the company workdays in the last 35 years, and its maintenance and operating expenses are lower than those of comparable companies. The company's annual revenue has grown to about $112 million.[76]

As we saw in Chapter 2, two strategies for ensuring quality are *quality control*, the strategy for minimizing errors by managing each stage of production, and *quality assurance*, focusing on the performance of workers and urging them to strive for "zero defects."

Quality control at Midway. MidwayUSA is a privately held retailer of hunting and outdoor-related products. Its business requires the accurate application of management control systems. Here we see the outbound shipping lanes of a large system of conveyors the company uses to manage distribution of its products from the receiving docks to the UPS trucks. In order to maintain accuracy and efficiency, the company relies on a variety of tools associated with total quality management. ©MidwayUSA

Deming Management: The Contributions of W. Edwards Deming to Improved Quality

Previously, Frederick Taylor's scientific management philosophy, designed to maximize worker productivity, had been widely instituted. But by the 1950s, scientific management had led to organizations that were rigid and unresponsive to both employees and customers. **W. Edwards Deming's** challenge, known as **Deming management**, proposed ideas for making organizations more responsive, more democratic, and less wasteful. These included the following principles.

1. Quality Should Be Aimed at the Needs of the Consumer "The consumer is the most important part of the production line," Deming wrote.[77] Thus, the efforts of individual workers in providing the product or service should be directed toward meeting the needs and expectations of the ultimate user.

2. Companies Should Aim at Improving the System, Not Blaming Workers Deming suggested that U.S. managers were more concerned with blaming problems on individual workers rather than on the organization's structure, culture, technology, work rules, and management–that is, "the system." By treating employees well, listening to their views and suggestions, Deming felt, managers could bring about improvements in products and services.

3. Improved Quality Leads to Increased Market Share, Increased Company Prospects, and Increased Employment When companies work to improve the quality of goods and services, they produce less waste, experience fewer delays, and are more efficient. Lower prices and superior quality lead to greater market share, which in turn leads to improved business prospects and consequently increased employment.

4. Quality Can Be Improved on the Basis of Hard Data, Using the PDCA Cycle Deming suggested that quality could be improved by acting on the basis of hard data. The process for doing this came to be known as the **PDCA cycle,** a Plan-Do-Check-Act cycle using observed data for continuous improvement of operations. *(See Figure 16.7.)* Like the steps in the control process in Figure 16.3, step 3 ("Check") is a *feedback* step, in which performance is compared to goals. Feedback is instrumental to control.

Core TQM Principles: Deliver Customer Value and Strive for Continuous Improvement

Total quality management (TQM) is defined as a comprehensive approach—led by top management and supported throughout the organization—dedicated to continuous quality improvement, training, and customer satisfaction. TQM is not easy to achieve. Ayesha Al Mehairbi, for example, discusses the challenges of pursuing continuous improvement in a plastics solutions company.

I Wish...

...my company were focused on continuously improving work processes.

Ayesha Al Mehairbi is a budget and cost control manager for a creative plastics solutions company. While quality is ingrained as part of the culture at Ayesha's company, she believes several processes need improvement in order for the company to continue producing quality products and services.

Courtesy Ayesha Al Mehairbi

Ayesha's company measures quality internally and externally. Internally, the company seeks feedback from its employees every two years through the use of surveys. The company hires an external provider to run a comprehensive survey to look into the company's performance to meet the employees' expectations in different focus areas like management and leadership, processes, support services, and seeks for suggestions and improvements. This provides an opportunity for employee feedback to be heard and acted on. Management then creates an action plan from the survey feedback and works to implement any necessary changes.

Externally, the company is continuously looking to outperform the industry's benchmark in different areas like cost-optimization strategies, financial performance, efficiency, and excellence programs. It also provides surveys to its external customers to receive feedback on its service.

While the company strives to produce quality products, Ayesha believes that in order for it to continuously deliver the best products, certain internal processes need to be improved.

"I think one of the challenges that we're facing is that the market dynamic is quite fast, and we aren't as fast keeping up with the changes around us," said Ayesha. "Because of the size of our company, and some of the old practices we have, we aren't able to move as quickly as we'd like."

Her company has several dated and lengthy processes in place that get in the way of continuously improving products. "We tend to have a lot of processes and procedures within the company, so it takes too long to get a change started, approved, and completed," said Ayesha. "This prevents the company from being able to implement change rapidly. It just takes too much time. Sometimes we are just not as dynamic in terms of processes and procedures."

A tight budget limits the ability to pour resources into all the departments that need improvement. On top of that, the global culture sometimes impedes the change process as well.

"We are international, so we have multiple nationalities working for the same company. Some of the employees like change and others don't, depending on their culture and where they're coming from," said Ayesha. "It is a challenge to get people to accept the change and adopt it. We tend to have some resistance."

While the company stresses quality, it will have to improve some of its processes in order to maintain a high standard. Without such improvements, the quality of the products could decline.
Courtesy of Ayesha Al Mehairbi

In Chapter 2, we said there are four components to TQM:

1. Make continuous improvement a priority.
2. Get every employee involved.
3. Listen to and learn from customers and employees.
4. Use accurate standards to identify and eliminate problems.

These may be summarized as **two core principles of TQM—namely, (1) people orientation—everyone involved with the organization should focus on delivering value to customers—and (2) improvement orientation—everyone should work on continuously improving the work processes.**[78] Let's look at these further.

1. People Orientation—Focusing Everyone on Delivering Customer Value

Organizations adopting TQM value people as their most important resource—both those who create a product or service and those who receive it. Thus, not only are employees given more decision-making power, so are suppliers and customers.

This people orientation operates under the following assumptions.

- **Delivering customer value is most important.** The purpose of TQM is to focus people, resources, and work processes to deliver products or services that create value for customers. Toyota is a long-time practitioner of TQM; its Lexus plant in Georgetown, Kentucky, its largest vehicle manufacturing plant worldwide, produces more than half a million cars a year.[79] The 750 employees who worked on the first Lexus line to be built in the United States received millions of hours of special sensory training "so they could see, hear, feel and smell what a Lexus should be." Some repeatedly took apart and rebuilt a small fleet of cars to understand thousands of parts, and they studied with master craftsmen in Japan.[80]

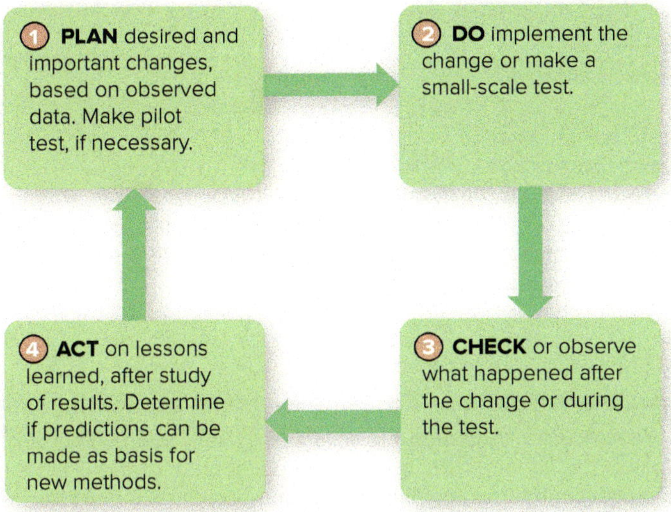

FIGURE 16.7

The PDCA cycle: Plan-Do-Check-Act

The four steps continuously follow each other, resulting in continuous improvement.

Source: From W. Edwards Deming, Out of the Crisis, Plan Do Study Act Cycle, *Massachusetts Institute of Technology, 2000, p. 88.*

- **People will focus on quality if given empowerment.** TQM assumes that employees (and often suppliers and customers) will concentrate on making quality improvements if given the decision-making power to do so. The reasoning here is that the people actually involved with the product or service are in the best position to detect opportunities for quality improvements. In support of this conclusion, research shows lack of employee involvement as the biggest obstacle to successful TQM implementation.[81]
- **TQM requires training, teamwork, and cross-functional efforts.** Employees and suppliers need to be well trained, and they must work in teams. Teamwork is considered important because many quality problems are spread across functional areas. For example, if cell-phone design specialists conferred with marketing specialists (as well as customers and suppliers), they would find that the challenge of using a cell phone for older people is pushing 11 tiny buttons to call a phone number.

EXAMPLE Hyundai Takes On the Luxury Car Market

The Hyundai Motor Co. is well known for its economical automobiles, but it has now taken the luxury car market by storm with the introduction of its Genesis brand in 2016. The South Korean carmaker's luxury line of vehicles supplanted Audi, BMW, Lexus, and Porsche to top *Consumer Reports'* 2018 annual ranking of automotive brands.[82] How did a company that manufactures no-frills compact vehicles outdo established German and Japanese luxury brands? The answer lies in Hyundai's ability to create a high-quality vehicle that earns high marks from its owners.[83]

Things weren't always smooth sailing for the Genesis. It was first introduced to the market under the Hyundai label in 2008. Poor quality resulted in sales dropping from 264,000 to 90,000 vehicles two years later.[84] These results caught the attention of Hyundai's chair and CEO, Chung Mong Koo. Mong Koo is known for demanding unwavering obedience from his employees. "His orders and initiatives are carried out swiftly, meticulously and without question," according to *Fortune*.[85] Mong Koo sent a memo telling factory managers that poor quality would no longer be tolerated and reinforced this directive by visiting factories himself, looking for quality-control problems. For example, he asked a factory worker to open an engine hood during one of these visits and quickly saw that all the bolts inside were different colors. After the factory manager was publicly reprimanded, all the bolts were properly painted black.[86]

Mong Koo also increased the size of Hyundai's quality-control department from 100 to 1,000 people. He asked this expanded team to thoroughly expect each and every vehicle, down to the bolts. This was not their only mandate, however. Quality-control engineers were expected to solicit feedback from employees on how to improve quality.[87] A CEO who demanded obedience from all had made an important exception—quality issues can and should be questioned by everyone in the organization.[88]

Hyundai's change in quality-control protocol seems to be producing results. The 2017 Genesis was awarded second place in the J.D. Power Initial Quality Study. The study is based on responses from nearly 80,000 purchasers and ranks brands by the number of flaws found by owners of new cars during the first 90 days. Genesis received a score of 77 problems per 100 owners, compared to the industry average of 97. Fellow South Korean automaker Kia took first place with a score of 72.[89]

YOUR CALL

Hyundai still trails Kia in the J.D. Power quality rankings. What do you think the company can do to improve even more? Is it a coincidence that two South Korean automakers have topped the quality rankings?

2. Improvement Orientation—Focusing Everyone on Continuously Improving Work Processes Although big schemes, grand designs, and crash programs have their place, the lesson of the quality movement from overseas is that the way to success is through continuous, small improvements. **Continuous improvement** is defined as ongoing, small, incremental improvements in all parts of an organization—all products, services, functional areas, and work processes. Kia Motors, the Korean car maker that has sold autos in the United States for about 20 years, has worked hard to establish a reputation for quality. Its Global Command and Control Center monitors live feeds from all its assembly plants in real time from South Korea, and production is limited to 7 million cars a year to ensure that quality remains high. Said one industry analyst about Kia's parent firm Hyundai, "All the people I meet at Hyundai are hell-bent on making sure quality is getting better all the time. This special mind-set . . . says that 'we will be best at what we do, wherever we go and whatever it takes.'"[90]

This improvement orientation focuses on increasing operational performance and makes the following assumptions.[91]

- **It's less expensive to do it right the first time.** TQM assumes that it's better to do things right the first time than to do costly reworking. To be sure, creating high-quality products and services requires a costly investment in training, equipment, and tools, for example. But it is less expensive than dealing with poor quality and the poor customer relationships that result.
- **It's better to make small improvements all the time.** This is the assumption that continuous improvement must be an everyday matter, that no improvement is too small, that there must be an ongoing effort to make things better a little bit at a time all the time. At Daimler, for instance, finished cars are packed so tightly together in storage yards that it's difficult for workers to read the RFID (radio frequency identification) tags used to control inventory. That's where drones come in, reading the tags quickly and inexpensively and at any hour when humans are not in the lot. The next small improvement? Smaller drones.[92]
- **Accurate standards must be followed to eliminate small variations.** TQM emphasizes the collection of accurate data throughout every stage of the work process. It also stresses the use of accurate standards (such as benchmarking) to evaluate progress and eliminate small variations, which are the source of many quality defects.
- **There must be strong commitment from top management.** Employees and suppliers won't focus on making small, incremental improvements unless managers go beyond lip service to support high-quality work, as do the top managers at Ritz-Carlton, Amazon.com, and Ace Hardware.

Kaizen is a Japanese philosophy of small continuous improvement that seeks to involve everyone at every level of the organization in the process of identifying opportunities and implementing and testing solutions.[93] It offers advantages for large and small companies alike, whether manufacturers or service firms, as the Example box shows.

Continuous improvement. Instead of making a walkway or street by laying bricks one at a time, how about using something like this? Dave Dyer of Swiss firm ABB Consulting points to this brick-laying machine as a great example of continuous improvement, one of the two core principles of TQM. The operators, he writes, "feed the bricks into the machine via gravity, there are no moving parts, and the path is laid as the machine moves. It's amazing!" What examples of continuous improvement can you think of? ©epa european pressphoto agency b.v./Alamy Stock Photo

EXAMPLE Kaizen Principles in Action

Herman Miller, the U.S. manufacturer of office equipment and chairs, has increased productivity 500 percent and quality 1,000 percent in the years since adopting Kaizen methods. The company's renowned Aeron chairs are now produced in 17 seconds, compared to 82 before Kaizen.[94]

At Studio 904, a Seattle hair salon, Kaizen principles led to a change in workflow so that everyone on staff can provide all styling services. Thus, customers no longer have to wait for each step during their visit to be performed by a dedicated stylist who may be working with more than one client at a time.[95]

Wagamama, a trendy UK restaurant chain expanding to the United States, saw early adoption of technology as the improvement identified by Kaizen principles. The company was years ahead of its competition in building customer-focused digital solutions. For example, its Qkr! app allows customers to split the bill with friends by paying for specific menu items on their iOS and Android phones. Wagamama has issued wireless handheld devices to staff for taking diners' orders and accepting payments and is now moving most of its tools to a cloud-based system.[96]

Boeing utilizes Kaizen principles in the building of its 737 aircraft at its Renton production facility near Seattle, Washington.[97] The company solicits feedback from its assembly workers on ways to improve efficiency during repeated Kaizen meetings. These meetings also address environmental considerations, such as the reduction of greenhouse gases during aircraft production.[98] Kaizen principles have greatly improved Boeing's aircraft production speed, which is important since it fiercely competes on this dimension with rival Airbus. Airbus actually achieved record aircraft production in 2017 with 718 jets delivered, but it was still outshone by Boeing, which delivered 763. This is a significant improvement for Boeing because it was producing only 420 jets a year in 2012.[99]

YOUR CALL

Some recommended tips for implementing Kaizen methods include actively looking for unconventional ideas, thinking about how to do something instead of why it can't be done, and avoiding both excuses and perfection.[100] Do you think this is good advice for Herman Miller, Studio 904, Wagamama, and Boeing? Why or why not?

Applying TQM to Services

Manufacturing industries provide tangible products (think jars of baby food); service industries provide intangible products (think child care services). Manufactured products can be stored (such as dental floss in a warehouse); services generally need to be consumed immediately (such as dental hygiene services). Services tend to require a good deal of people effort (although some services can be provided by machines, such as vending machines and ATMs). Finally, services are generally provided at locations and times convenient for customers; that is, customers are much more involved in the delivery of services than they are in the delivery of manufactured products.

One clear prerequisite for providing excellent service is effective training. Isadore Sharp, founder and chair of Four Seasons Hotels and Resorts, recently experienced outstanding room service while visiting one of the chain's new facilities, in a location where few employees could have been expected to have prior experience of hospitality industry standards. When he asked the server where she had learned to perform so well, she replied, "They let me take everything home for me to practice with my family."[101] It takes more than training, however, to provide high-quality service.[102]

EXAMPLE Service Excellence

A customer experience study conducted in 2017 found that 8 in 10 consumers are willing to switch companies due to poor customer service.[103] So how can companies keep a loyal customer following? Consider the practices used by two companies known for providing great customer service: Nordstrom and Trader Joe's.

NORDSTROM

Nordstrom operates 373 stores in the United States and Canada.[104] Nordstrom's ". . . superior customer service is . . . [a] factor that positions it more defensively against competition at the mall and online," according to *Yahoo! Finance*.[105]

Nordstrom's competitive advantage starts with using employee empowerment to elicit employees' creativity. The department store chain's code of conduct directs employees to "Use your best judgement."[106] This idea makes it clear that empowerment is not just a benefit of working at Nordstrom, it's *your job*. Nordstrom asks its employees to come up with creative solutions to issues that couldn't be fully covered by a predetermined set of policies.[107] For example, a woman lost her wedding ring while trying on clothes at a Nordstrom in North Carolina. A store security worker saw her crawling on the sales floor under the racks and came to help. They both searched for the ring but could not find it. So the Nordstrom employee then asked two building-services workers to open the bags of the store's vacuum cleaners, where they found the shiny diamond.[108]

Going the extra mile at work doesn't mean your employees are providing a personal touch for customers at the expense of their own job satisfaction, however. In fact, empowerment tends to increase employee satisfaction, which is one reason Nordstrom has made *Fortune*'s "Best Place to Work" list for 20 consecutive years.[109]

Nordstrom also uses technology to compete, especially with online retailers. The store is striving for "digital parity," which is the idea that every business, whether online or brick and mortar, needs to be as good as the best purely online companies. For example, Nordstrom is implementing mobile technology that allows customers to pay for their purchases wherever they are in the store. So a customer can pay for shoes after trying them on without waiting in line. Nordstrom understands that you don't have to wait in line to pay when you are shopping online, so why wait in a store?[110]

TRADER JOE'S

Trader Joe's was ranked first in the supermarket category of the 2016 American Customer Satisfaction Index (ACSI) Retail Report[111] and second in the 2017 version, behind Publix.[112] Market Force also conducted a survey of more than 10,000 grocery store shoppers based on food quality, checkout speed, value, and customer service in which Trader Joe's rounded out the top three in the final rankings.[113]

Trade Joe's operates more than 470 grocery stores nationwide[114] and made a name for itself selling hipster-yuppie snacks like wild salmon jerky and $2 wines.[115] The chain stays competitive by quickly reacting to its customers' needs. Managers are called captains (employees are the crew) and spend most of their days on the retail floor, wearing Hawaiian shirts and interacting with customers. If a customer asks about a product, the captain or crew member instantly brings the product, opens it, and indulges in a taste test with the customer to see whether they like it. Trader Joe's also refunds the price of any product customers are not satisfied with, even if it has been opened.[116]

Allowing captains to spend their time on the retail floor also allows them to learn about customer needs and quickly react to them instead of asking customers to send their feedback to a call center. For example, a Trader Joe's in Nevada decided to stock up on a customer's favorite soy ice-cream cookie. Another location in Phoenix decided to open earlier than the company standard hour of 9 am so its local community could shop at a time that was convenient for them.[117]

YOUR CALL

Do you think Nordstrom's and Trader Joe's approaches to customer service can compete with online shopping? Why or why not?

Perhaps you're beginning to see how judging the quality of services is a different animal from judging the quality of manufactured goods, because it comes down to meeting the customer's *satisfaction*, which may be a matter of *perception*. (After all, some hotel guests, restaurant diners, and supermarket patrons, for example, are more easily satisfied than others.)

Some people view college students as customers. Do you? For those schools that care about the quality of what they offer, it is important to assess student satisfaction with the college or university as a whole. If you are curious about your level of satisfaction with your college or university, then complete Self-Assessment 16.3.

SELF-ASSESSMENT 16.3

Assessing Your Satisfaction with Your College or University Experience

The following survey was designed to assess the extent to which you are satisfied with your college experience. Please be prepared to answer these questions if your instructor has assigned Self-Assessment 16.3 in Connect.

1. What is your level of satisfaction? Are you surprised by the results?
2. Based on your scores, identify three things that your college or university might do to improve student satisfaction. Be specific.
3. Are students really customers? Explain your rationale.

Some TQM Tools, Techniques, and Standards

Several tools and techniques are available for improving quality. We described benchmarking in Chapter 10. Here we describe *outsourcing, reduced cycle time, statistical process control, Six Sigma, and quality standards ISO 9000 and ISO 14000.*

Outsourcing: Let Outsiders Handle It **Outsourcing** (discussed in detail in Chapter 4) **is the subcontracting of services and operations to an outside vendor.** Usually, this is done to reduce costs or increase productivity.[118] Outsourcing short-term and project work to freelance or contract workers in the so-called gig economy also saves companies many employee-related expenses.

Outsourcing is also being done by many state and local governments, which, under the banner known as privatization, have subcontracted traditional government services such as fire protection, correctional services, and medical services. As many as 1.5 million U.S. jobs were reportedly outsourced in 2016.[119]

Reduced Cycle Time: Increasing the Speed of Work Processes Another TQM technique is the emphasis on increasing the speed with which an organization's operations and processes can be performed. This is known as **reduced cycle time**, **or reduction in steps in a work process,** such as fewer authorization steps required to grant a contract to a supplier. The point is to improve the organization's performance by eliminating wasteful motions, barriers between departments, unnecessary procedural steps, and the like.

At Ralph Lauren, a recent slowdown in sales and an increase in inventory prompted the company to look for ways to reduce production time for its high-fashion products from 15 months to 9, which will help it better match supply to demand, reduce excess inventory, and lower the volume of goods that need to be sold at marked-down prices.[120]

Bar-code scanners, not the type used at checkout counters to track inventory, are increasingly used to decrease the time it takes for employees to select, pack, and ship products. Exel Logistics, for example, found that bar-code scanners decreased the rate of assembling orders by 10 percent–20 percent.[121]

Statistical Process Control: Taking Periodic Random Samples As the pages of this book were being printed, instruments called densitometers and colorimeters were used to measure ink density and trueness of color, taking samples of printed pages at fixed intervals. This is an ongoing check for quality control.

All kinds of products require periodic inspection during their manufacture: hamburger meat, breakfast cereal, flashlight batteries, wine, and so on. The tool often used for this is **statistical process control**, **a statistical technique that uses periodic random samples from production runs to see if quality is being maintained within a standard range of acceptability.** If quality is not acceptable, production is stopped to allow corrective measures.

Statistical process control is the technique that McDonald's uses, for example, to make sure that the quality of its burgers is always the same, no matter where in the world they are served. Companies such as Intel and Motorola use statistical process control to ensure the reliability and quality of their products.

Six Sigma and Lean Six Sigma: Data-Driven Ways to Eliminate Defects *Sigma* is the Greek letter statisticians use to define a standard deviation. In the quality-improvement process known as Six Sigma, the higher the sigma, the fewer the deviations from the norm—that is, the fewer the defects. Developed by Motorola in 1985, Six Sigma has since been embraced by General Electric, Allied Signal, American Express, 3M, and other companies.[122] There are two variations, *Six Sigma* and *Lean Six Sigma*.

- **Six Sigma.** **Six Sigma** **is a rigorous statistical analysis process that reduces defects in manufacturing and service-related processes.** By testing thousands of variables and eliminating guesswork, a company using the technique attempts to improve quality and reduce waste to the point where errors nearly vanish. In everything from product design to manufacturing to billing, the attainment of Six Sigma means there are no more than 3.4 defects per million products or procedures.[123]

  Six Sigma may also be thought of as a philosophy—to reduce variation in your company's business and make customer-focused, data-driven decisions. The method preaches the use of Define, Measure, Analyze, Improve, and Control (DMAIC). Team leaders may be awarded a Six Sigma "black belt" for applying DMAIC.

- **Lean Six Sigma.** More recently, companies are using an approach known as **Lean Six Sigma**, **which focuses on problem solving and performance improvement—speed with excellence—of a well-defined project.**[124]

3M Company's latest five-year plan includes improvements to its supply chain and an increased focus on Lean Six Sigma in order to bring about "improved customer service, operational efficiencies, and an increased cash flow."[125]

Six Sigma and Lean Six Sigma may not be perfect because they cannot compensate for human error or control events outside a company.[126] Still, they let managers approach problems with the assumption that there's a data-oriented, tangible way to approach problem solving.

ISO 9000 and ISO 14000: Meeting Standards of Independent Auditors If you're a sales representative for Du Pont, a U.S. chemical company, how will your overseas clients know your products have the quality they are expecting? If you're a purchasing agent for an Ohio-based tire company, how can you tell whether the synthetic rubber you're buying overseas is adequate?

At one time, buyers and sellers simply had to rely on a supplier's past reputation or personal assurances. In 1987, the International Organization for Standardization (ISO), based in Geneva, Switzerland, created a set of quality standards known as the 9000 series. There are two such standards:

- **ISO 9000.** **The ISO 9000 series consists of quality-control procedures companies must install—from purchasing to manufacturing to inventory to shipping—that can be audited by independent quality-control experts, or "registrars."** The goal is to reduce flaws in manufacturing and improve productivity by adopting eight "big picture" Quality Management Principles:
  - Customer focus.
  - Leadership.
  - Involvement of people.
  - Process approach.
  - System approach to management.
  - Continual improvement.
  - Factual approach to decision making.
  - Mutually beneficial supplier relationships.[127]

  Companies must document their ISO 9000 procedures and train their employees to use them. The ISO 9000 series of standards was expanded to include ISO 9001:2008. "ISO 9001 is the only standard within the ISO 9000 family that an organization can become certified against, because it is the standard that defines the requirements of having a Quality Management System."[128] Member organizations in 161 countries contribute to the development of ISO standards.[129]
- **ISO 14000.** **The ISO 14000 series extends the concept, identifying standards for environmental performance.** ISO 14000 dictates standards for documenting a company's management of pollution, efficient use of raw materials, and reduction of the firm's impact on the environment.

Takeaways from TQM Research

TQM principles have been used by thousands of organizations through the years. Although companies do not always use the tools, techniques, and processes as suggested by experts, a team of researchers concluded that the vast majority of TQM adopters follow its general principles, which in turn fosters improved operational performance.[130] Researchers also identified four key inhibitors to successfully implementing TQM: (1) the failure to provide evidence supporting previous improvement activities, (2) the lack of a champion who is responsible for leading the implementation, (3) the inability to measure or track results of the program, and (4) the failure to develop a culture of quality or continuous learning.[131] Managers need to overcome these roadblocks for TQM to deliver its intended benefits.

16.6 Managing Control Effectively

THE BIG PICTURE

This section describes four keys to successful control and five barriers to successful control.

LO 16-6

Identify barriers to effective control and ways managers can overcome them.

How do you as a manager make a control system successful, and how do you identify and deal with barriers to control? We consider these topics next.

The Keys to Successful Control Systems

Successful control systems have a number of common characteristics: (1) They are strategic and results oriented. (2) They are timely, accurate, and objective. (3) They are realistic, positive, and understandable and they encourage self-control. (4) They are flexible.

1. They Are Strategic and Results Oriented Control systems support strategic plans and are concentrated on significant activities that will make a real difference to the organization. Thus, when managers are developing strategic plans for achieving strategic goals, that is the point at which they should pay attention to developing control standards that will measure how well the plans are being achieved.[132]

Example: Companies whose strategies include a commitment to sustainable methods can be guided by standards set by the Sustainability Accounting Standards Board, which sets reporting guidelines for "[disclosing] sustainability performance information to stakeholders."[133]

2. They Are Timely, Accurate, and Objective Good control systems—like good information of any kind—should be

- **Timely—meaning when needed.** The information should not necessarily be delivered quickly, but it should be delivered at an appropriate or specific time, such as every week or every month. And it certainly should be often enough to allow employees and managers to take corrective action for any deviations.
- **Accurate—meaning correct.** Accuracy is paramount, if decision mistakes are to be avoided. Inaccurate sales figures may lead managers to mistakenly cut or increase sales promotion budgets. Inaccurate production costs may lead to faulty pricing of a product.
- **Objective—meaning impartial.** Objectivity means control systems are impartial and fair. Although information can be inaccurate for all kinds of reasons (faulty communication, unknown data, and so on), information that is not objective is inaccurate for a special reason: It is biased or prejudiced. Control systems need to be considered unbiased for everyone involved so that they will be respected for their fundamental purpose—enhancing performance.

3. They Are Realistic, Positive, and Understandable and Encourage Self-Control Control systems have to focus on working for the people who will have to live with them. Thus, they operate best when they are made acceptable to the organization's members who are guided by them.[134] Thus, they should

- **Be realistic.** They should incorporate realistic expectations. If employees feel performance results are too difficult, they are apt to ignore or sabotage the performance system.

- **Be positive.** They should emphasize development and improvement. They should avoid emphasizing punishment and reprimand.
- **Be understandable.** They should fit the people involved, be kept as simple as possible, and present data in understandable terms. They should avoid complicated computer printouts and statistics.
- **Encourage self-control.** They should encourage good communication and mutual participation. They should not be the basis for creating distrust between employees and managers.

4. They Are Flexible

Control systems must leave room for individual judgment, so that they can be modified when necessary to meet new requirements.

Barriers to Control Success

Among the several barriers to a successful control system are the following.

1. Too Much Control

Some organizations, particularly bureaucratic ones, try to exert too much control. They may try to regulate employee behavior in everything from dress code to timing of coffee breaks. This leads to micromanagement, which frustrates employees and may lead them to ignore or try to sabotage the control process.

Among the telltale signs that you (or your boss) might be a micromanager, someone who is unable to delegate tasks and decisions and insists on taking an inappropriately detailed focus on subordinates' work, are

1. Working excessive hours and weekends and skipping vacation.
2. Checking everyone's work because no one else can do things right.
3. Needing to be copied on and approve everything.
4. Requiring others to continually check in and be constantly available.
5. Having to hire new people all the time because turnover is so high.[135]

Micromanagement is a form of over-control that is counterproductive for several reasons. Employees are more effective and achieve greater job satisfaction if they feel empowered to use their own judgment as far as possible to get the job done. And micromanagers can become bottlenecks who actually slow the flow of work and decisions, if not stop it altogether. Some solutions, if you recognize yourself in this profile, are to start by delegating small decisions, recognizing that the worst-case scenario you likely imagine if you let go is probably not going to happen, and accepting that some degree of uncertainty is inevitable in management, and in life.[136]

Another helpful strategy is to give employees regular opportunities to discuss expectations, so they feel empowered to act independently. At the online discount clearinghouse called FatWallet, for instance, employees and managers meet quarterly to evaluate successes and failures and to reset goals as needed. Bridge Worldwide, a marketing agency, makes many everyday decisions by allowing employees to vote.[137]

2. Too Little Employee Participation

As highlighted by W. Edwards Deming, which was discussed in Chapter 2, employee participation can enhance productivity. Involving employees in both the planning and the execution of control systems can bring legitimacy to the process and heighten employee morale.

3. Overemphasis on Means Instead of Ends

We said that control activities should be strategic and results oriented. They are not ends in themselves but the means to eliminating problems. Too much emphasis on accountability for weekly production quotas, for example, can lead production supervisors to push their workers and equipment too hard, resulting in absenteeism and machine breakdowns. Or it can lead to game playing—"beating the system"—as managers and employees manipulate data to seem to fulfill short-run goals instead of the organization's strategic plan.

4. Overemphasis on Paperwork A specific kind of misdirection of effort is management emphasis on getting reports done, to the exclusion of other performance activity. Reports are not the be-all and end-all. Undue emphasis on reports can lead to too much focus on quantification of results and even to falsification of data. Note that going paperless, while laudable, does not reduce the risk of over-focusing on reporting.

5. Overemphasis on One Instead of Multiple Approaches One type or method of control may not be enough. By having multiple control activities and information systems, an organization can have multiple performance indicators, thereby increasing accuracy and objectivity. A recent study found that control systems affect each other and thus must be integrated.[138]

These gamblers are enjoying the slot machine, but are they being controlled by the casino? Casinos establish the payout ratio on slot machines. As a player, you can't control when you will lose or win, but established payout ratios guarantee that someone will win at some point. Do you enjoy gambling? ©nd3000/iStock/Getty Images

16.7 Managing for Productivity

THE BIG PICTURE

The purpose of a manager is to make decisions about the four management functions—planning, organizing, leading, and controlling—to get people to achieve productivity and realize results. Productivity is defined by the formula of outputs divided by inputs for a specified period of time. Productivity matters because it determines whether the organization will make a profit or even survive.

LO 16-7

Describe the manager's role in increasing productivity.

In Chapter 1, we pointed out that as a manager in the 21st century you will operate in a complex environment in which you will need to deal with seven challenges—managing for (1) competitive advantage, (2) diversity, (3) globalization, (4) information technology, (5) ethical standards, (6) sustainability, and (7) your own happiness and life goals.

Within this dynamic world, you will draw on the practical and theoretical knowledge described in this book to make decisions about the four management functions of planning, organizing, leading, and controlling. The purpose is to get the people reporting to you *to achieve productivity and realize results*. This process is diagrammed below, pulling together the main topics of this book. *(See Figure 16.8.)*

FIGURE 16.8

Managing for productivity and results

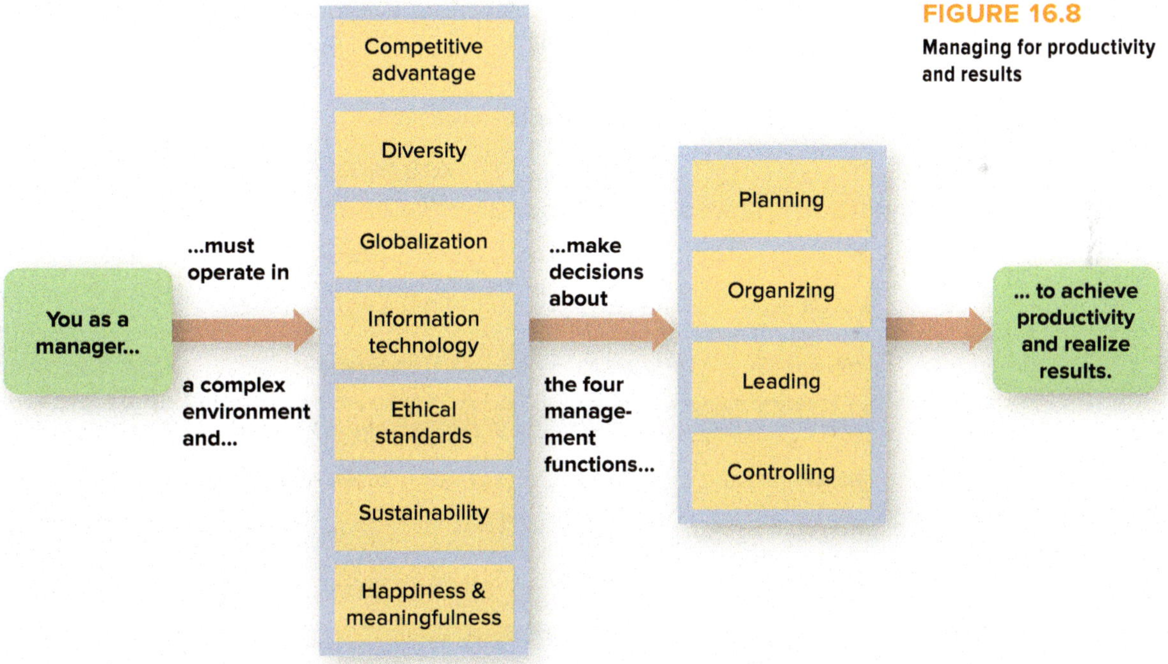

What Is Productivity?

Productivity can be applied at any level, whether for you as an individual, for the work unit you're managing, or for the organization you work for. Productivity is defined by the formula of *outputs divided by inputs* for a specified period of time. Outputs are all the goods and services produced. Inputs are not only labor but also capital, materials, and energy. That is,

$$\text{Productivity} = \frac{\text{Outputs}}{\text{Inputs}} \quad \text{or} \quad \frac{\text{Goods} + \text{Services}}{\text{Labor} + \text{Capital} + \text{Materials} + \text{Energy}}$$

What does this mean to you as a manager? It means that you can increase overall productivity by making substitutions or increasing the efficiency of any one element: labor, capital, materials, energy. For instance, you can increase the efficiency of labor by substituting capital in the form of equipment or machinery, as in employing a backhoe instead of laborers with shovels to dig a hole.[139] Or you can increase the efficiency of materials inputs by expanding their uses, as when lumber mills discovered they could sell not only boards but also sawdust and wood chips for use in gardens. Or you can increase the efficiency of energy by putting solar panels on a factory roof so the organization won't have to buy so much electrical power from utility companies.

Why Is Increasing Productivity Important?

The more goods and services that are produced and made easily available to us and for export, the higher our standard of living. Increasing the gross domestic product (GDP)—the total dollar value of all the goods and services produced in the United States—depends on raising productivity, as well as on a growing workforce.

Table 16.2 shows the GDP for the U.S. and 11 other countries in 2017 and 2018 (projected). India is poised to show the highest growth, closely followed by China and, farther behind, by Sweden and Singapore.[140]

The U.S. Productivity Track Record During the 1960s, productivity in the United States averaged a hefty 2.9 percent a year, then sank to a disappointing 1.5 percent right up until 1995. Because the decline in productivity no longer allowed

TABLE 16.2 Global Gross Domestic Product (GDP)

COUNTRY	2017	2018 PROJECTED GDP (IN BILLIONS)	%GDP GROWTH
Brazil	1556.44	1608.74	1.05%
Canada	1530.7	1595.5	2.056%
China	12,263.43	13,3338.23	6%
Denmark	314.274	327.117	2%
France	2537.92	2609.06	1.486%
Germany	3591.69	3697.31	1.358%
India	2487.94	2724.76	7.598%
Singapore	304.097	313.439	2.465%
Sweden	530.293	543.93	2.51%
United Kingdom	2885.48	2999.29	2.21%
United States	19,294.99	20,145.05	2.375%
Venezuela	149.508	109.036	−3%

Note: All numbers shown in billions of US dollars.

Sources: *"2018 Economic Statistics and Indicators," http://www.economywatch.com/economic-statistics/year/2018/; "2017 Economic Statistics and Indicators," http://www.economywatch.com/economic-statistics/year/2017/ (accessed May 7, 2018).*

the improvement in wages and living standards that had benefited so many U.S. workers in the 1960s, millions of people took second jobs or worked longer hours to keep from falling behind. From 1995 to 2000, however, during the longest economic boom in U.S. history, the productivity rate jumped to 2.5 percent annually, as the total output of goods and services rose faster than the total hours needed to produce them. From the business cycle peak in the first quarter of 2001 to the end of 2007, productivity grew at an annual rate of 2.7 percent.[141]

Then came the recession year 2008, when it fell to 2 percent. Then, from the fourth quarter of 2008 to the fourth quarter of 2009, productivity rose 5.4 percent—"a turnaround unprecedented in modern history," said *Newsweek*; it also rose an impressive 4.1 percent in 2010.[142] Recently, however, productivity has been declining globally, not only in developed economies such as the United States, Japan, and Europe but also in China, which had been growing rapidly for some time. Productivity has even been zero or negative in some countries. Gains in productivity are expected to remain small for the short term.[143] Productivity growth in the United States was actually negative in 2016 after growing from 2010 through 2015.[144]

Advances in technology can significantly contribute to increases in productivity. For instance, turbine technology has enabled windfarms like this one to increase the power they generate at a lower cost.
©Comstock Images/Alamy Stock Photo

Globalization, which has made national economies far more interconnected and dependent on one another, helps increase the ripple effects of any country's economic downturns on its neighbors and trading partners. Climate change is also affecting productivity as extreme weather becomes more common, bringing droughts, floods, and other uncommon events to areas unused to dealing with them.[145]

The Role of Information Technology In the last decade wages have stagnated for most workers, even as productivity gains from information technology—automation and the Internet, shareware, cloud computing, and other communication technologies, for example—have slowed. Financial rewards for tech innovation have been concentrated among a very few inventors and entrepreneurs, while wage gains in the United States, Canada, Europe, and Japan remain low.[146]

Some observers say the problem is not a lack of productivity growth but a measurement error. New technologies are difficult to value, and new companies that charge users nothing and try to earn revenue from advertising (that users can sometimes avoid) are entering a new world we may be incorrectly assessing with old tools.[147]

In particular, many companies have implemented **enterprise resource planning (ERP) software systems, information systems for integrating virtually all aspects of a business,** helping managers stay on top of the latest developments.

What Processes Can I Use to Increase Productivity?

Benchmarking **Benchmarking is a way to measure something against a standard, the benchmark.** Companies use internal benchmarks to set performance standards, competitive benchmarking to assess themselves against their competitors, and strategic benchmarking when they are ready to look outside their industry, such as when adopting Six Sigma, to learn from world-class performers wherever they are.[148]

As a personal tool, benchmarking is a useful way to measure your own growth as an employee and eventually as a manager. At the most basic level, for instance, you can look at colleagues and fellow team members who are valued by the organization and measure your own performance against theirs. What is each person particularly good at? Perhaps someone in your group is always asked to prepare the project report because he has excellent writing skills. Or you may notice a manager who is always the first one in the room for a scheduled meeting, ready to start on time and prepared with an insightful question. As we mentioned at the beginning of this chapter, you can also think of your mentor as someone against whose (likely high) standards of performance and expertise you can benchmark yourself.

Using these benchmarks as gauges to measure your own growth and development at work, you can look for ways to improve your technical and interpersonal skills.

Best Practices

Best practices are "a set of guidelines, ethics or ideas that represent the most efficient or prudent course of action."[149] Companies often develop best practices internally through managers' and employees' positive experiences on the job, and they sometimes adopt the strategies with which other companies have succeeded in similar situations. For example, teams were found to have higher performance when they established a process of regularly meeting to discuss work processes or best practices.[150] Some best practices are guided by laws and regulations; for instance, companies may not ask job applicants questions that would allow hiring managers to discriminate based on race or ethnicity, sex, age, or religion. So a best practice in hiring is to know the law and ask only allowed questions.

Many of the suggestions in this book's "Manage U," "Practical Action," and "Career Corner" features represent best practices you can adopt as you polish your career readiness skills and prepare for a career, whether or not you aspire to a management position. If you are fortunate enough to work with a mentor in the future, you will surely learn many more best practices.

Managing Individual Productivity

Individual employees, managers, and organizations all share responsibility for increasing individual productivity. Individuals contribute by proactively bringing their skills, energy, talents, and motivation to work on a daily basis. They also can increase productivity by engaging in self-development and organizational citizenship. This is most likely to happen, however, when employees work for supportive and talented managers. This is where managers enter the productivity equation.

Managers need to bring their "best selves" to work just like any other employee. In addition, they can use many of the concepts, tools, and techniques discussed throughout this book to help develop their managerial and leadership skills. Managerial behavior is a key input to individual productivity. We believe it is essential for managers to take a learning orientation toward their jobs. This implies that managers will attempt to continuously improve their leadership skills. This might involve taking courses at a local college or university, enrolling in company-sponsored training programs, obtaining advice from an executive coach or mentor, or reading relevant books.

Organizations contribute to individual productivity by providing positive work environments and cultures that promote employee engagement, satisfaction, and flourishing. This ultimately involves investing in training and development for all employees. Companies can also invest in information technology that helps people to reduce distractions and focus on completing tasks. Cloud computing tools, for example, are a way to reduce manual tasks, share responsibility, and eliminate most paperwork.[151] At the same time, however, technology has so successfully decreased the cost of interactions (following a principle known as Metcalfe's law) that the number of messages like phone calls, e-mails, texts, and IMs we send and receive has risen dramatically; one study estimates managers receive more than 30,000 such messages a year (about 115 every working day).[152] Whether these effects of technology are really a boost to productivity may be up to the individual manager. •

16.8 Career Corner: Managing Your Career Readiness

LO 16-8

Discuss the process for managing career readiness and review five tips for managing your career.

We've all heard stories of successful people who did not follow a structured or intentional path to their careers, but they are the exception, not the rule. Most successful people do not sit back and wait for opportunities to present themselves. They are more likely to pursue a proactive approach to career management.

Control plays a critical role in the career readiness competency of career management, which represents the proactive management of your career and the seeking of opportunities for professional development. We look at Figure 16.9 to discuss this relationship. You will learn that managing your career entails using many of the ideas discussed in previous Career Corner features.

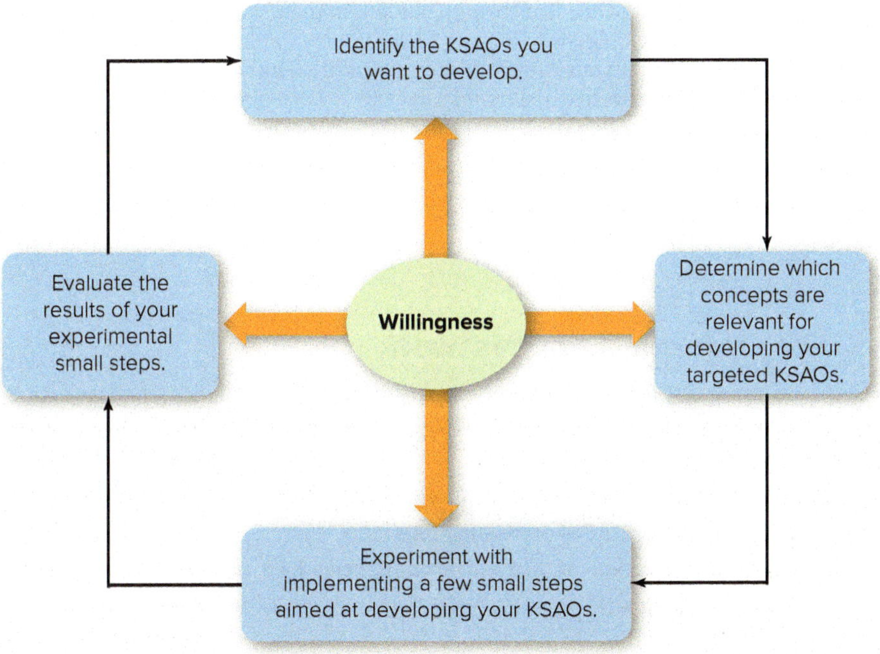

FIGURE 16.9

Process for managing career readiness

Both the control process and the process for managing career readiness begin with identifying what you want to accomplish. In so doing, recognize that a job and a career are not the same thing. Jobs are something we do to earn money, they tend to be temporary, and they are in service of someone or something else. Some people are perfectly happy with a job. In contrast, your career belongs to you and lasts a lifetime. You own it, manage it, nurture it, and create it to fit your values and needs.[153] Careers are what we do in pursuit of our own needs and fulfillment rather than someone else's. This distinction underscores the importance of using the career readiness competencies of ownership/accepting responsibility, self-motivation, self-awareness, and openness to change to manage your career.

Many college students do not have a clear vision for their career. They are more focused on getting a decent job after graduation. If this is true for you, then we suggest starting the career management process by focusing on finding a job that fits your values, needs, and financial objectives. Regardless of whether you are pursuing your dream job or not, you still need to be concerned about your career readiness because employers want people with these skills. So how do you proceed?

Using the process shown in Figure 16.9, start by identifying a small set of career readiness competencies from the categories of Knowledge, Skills, Attitudes, and Other Characteristics (KSAOs) shown in Table 1.2 and discussed throughout this textbook. This decision gets you started on creating a development plan. Next, consult the Career Corner sections in this textbook to design small developmental experiments. Finally, engage the control process by monitoring, evaluating, and rewarding your progress.

Here are five more generic tips for managing your career. They go far beyond having a good résumé.[154]

1. Make Every Day Count

Every action you display at work is a paint stroke on the canvas of your brand. If you want people to perceive you as a motivated, skilled, passionate, and career-ready employee, then act that way. Improving your self-management skills, which were discussed in the Career Corner for Chapter 12, is a good starting point. We then recommend that you brush up your time management skills. They are essential for handling the workload and competing priorities you will experience in your first job.[155] We want to warn you about one time management mistake that can affect your long-term success. People who focus on completing easy, short-term tasks were found to be less effective in the long term. The short-term sense of accomplishment leads people to ignore the critically more important and difficult activities that produce long-term success.[156]

2. Stay Informed and Network

It's really important to stay abreast of changes in your field and industry. Look for new trends, changing regulations, best practices, and applications of new technology. You can do this by:

- Becoming active in professional organizations.
- Attending workshops or training programs.
- Enrolling in online or face-to-face college classes.[157]

Network by using the suggestions presented in the Career Corner for Chapter 15.

3. Promote Yourself

The goal of self-promotion is to inform others about your value and potential impact on organizational goals. Don't confuse this with grandstanding or overtly boasting about your greatness. Use humility. You also should not assume that your good work will always be recognized and publicized, or you'll be disappointed. Here are some suggestions for effective self-promotion:[158]

- Discuss your accomplishments and the specific actions you took to make them happen. Focus on facts and figures rather than personality to avoid a perception of self-interest.
- Discuss the benefits your actions had on your team, department, or division. This forces you to take a "big picture" perspective, which also minimizes the impression of self-interest.

- Discuss how others contributed to the accomplishments. Sharing the limelight reinforces that you are a team player, which is another career readiness competency.

4. Roll with Change and Disruption

Careers rarely follow an organized trajectory. It's more likely your career will have tributaries, roundabouts, and personal diversions. Experts suggest that people change jobs 10 to 15 times over a career, with an average of 12.[159] These changes are either voluntary, such as moving for a better opportunity, or involuntary, such as being fired or laid off. If you move voluntarily, congratulations! You now have the opportunity to reinvent yourself. If the departure is not by choice, you'll likely feel disappointed, angry, or humiliated. Give yourself time to recover. Job loss is one of the most stressful life events we experience.[160] It's essential to learn from the situation and put bitterness behind you. No recruiter wants to hear job applicants bad-mouth previous employers.

5. Small Things Matter during Interviews

The best résumé, experience, and career readiness will not withstand interpersonal blunders that occur during the recruitment process. Jobvite's 2017 national survey of 831 recruiters identified the following deal-breakers:

- "Being rude to the receptionist or other support staff (85%), checking your phone (71%), showing up late (58%), and bad hygiene (52%) are the top bad behaviors to automatically disqualify a candidate during an interview. . . .
- "Dressing too casually for an interview can be a deal-breaker for nearly 1 in 4 recruiters."[161]

Epilogue: The Keys to Your Managerial Success

THE BIG PICTURE

As we end the book, this section describes some life lessons to take away.

We have come to the end of the book, our last chance to offer some suggestions to take with you that we hope will benefit you in the coming years. Following are some life lessons pulled from various sources that can make you a "keeper" in an organization and help you be successful.

- **Adopt a proactive approach to life-long learning.** Life in general is not going to become less complex. This requires all of us to continue to grow and develop if we want to be active, positive contributors to our families, work environments, communities, and society at large.
- **Find your passion and follow it.** Jane Chen is the founder and CEO of Embrace Innovations, which markets to developing countries a line of inexpensive, portable incubators for premature babies. Chen's inspiration is the great medieval and Renaissance cathedrals in Europe. Unlikely? Not really. These architectural wonders, which took generations to build, were created by people inspired to contribute to something greater than themselves, even if they would not live to see it.[162] Find something that inspires you, that you love to do, and do it vigorously.
- **Encourage self-discovery, and be realistic.** To stay ahead of the pack, you need to develop self-awareness, have an active mind, and be willing to grow and change. Legendary designer Diane von Furstenberg recalls the lesson she learned from early mistakes that reduced her control over her business and diluted her brand: "Your worst moments are your best souvenirs."[163]
- **Every situation is different, so be flexible.** No principle, no theory will apply under all circumstances. Industries, cultures, supervisors, employees, and customers will vary. It's not a sign of weakness to be willing to change something that isn't working or to try something new.[164] Justin Tobin, founder and president of consultancy firm DDG, credits his mother with teaching him that "experimentation leads to the discovery of a unique identity and that everything in life and work is completely subjective. What one person likes, another might not, and that's not only okay, it's encouraged inside innovative organizations."[165]
- **Focus on career readiness.** Today we live and work in a team universe. Try getting feedback on your interpersonal skills from friends, colleagues, and team members, and develop a plan for improvement. Even nonverbal communication is a people skill. Dave Kerpen, CEO of Likeable Local, once made an important contact with someone who started a conversation with him at a crowded event because he was wearing distinctive orange shoes. Now Kerpen wears orange shoes every day.[166]
- **Learn how to develop leadership skills.** Every company should invest in the leadership development of its managers if it is to improve the quality of its future leaders. But you can also work to develop your own leadership skills. For instance, offer to help others, take the initiative when action is needed (sometimes called being a self-starter), and don't be afraid to ask for more responsibility to demonstrate what you're capable of.[167] Another life lesson: If you set the bar high, even if you don't reach it, you end up in a pretty good place—that is, achieving a pretty high mark.

- **Treat people as if they matter, because they do.** If you treat employees, colleagues, and customers with dignity, they respond accordingly. Bryce Drew, head coach of the Valparaiso men's basketball team, the Crusaders, says this about his players: "The person is more important than the result. We're going to recruit families. We're going to recruit players that want to be part of our family here. That's how we live our daily life and that's how we treat our team. I think when people sign on to come here, they know they're coming to be more than basketball players. They're coming to be cared for and develop into men."[168]
- **Draw employees and peers into your management process.** The old top-down, command-and-control model of organization is moving toward a flattened, networked kind of structure. Managers now work more often with peers, where lines of authority aren't always clear or don't exist, so that one's persuasive powers become key. Power has devolved to front-line employees who are closest to the customer and to small, focused, self-managed teams that have latitude to pursue new ideas. Ask them what they think are the best ways to get things done.[169]
- **Keep your cool, and take yourself lightly.** The more unflappable you appear in difficult circumstances, the more you'll be admired by your bosses and co-workers. Having a sense of humor helps. The renowned British physicist and author Stephen Hawking spent his career looking for the answers to almost impenetrable questions like, "Where did the universe come from?" and "How will it end?" Yet he was famously witty and relished the opportunity to appear as himself on popular TV shows like *The Simpsons*, *Star Trek: The Next Generation*, and *The Big Bang Theory*, appearances that he said made him more famous than his complex theories about the universe.[170]
- **Go with the flow, and stay positive.** Life has its ebbs and flows. You'll have good times and bad. During this journey, don't focus too heavily on negative events and thoughts. Negative thoughts rob you of positive energy and your ability to perform at your best. In contrast, a positive approach toward life is more likely to help you flourish.[171]

I wish you the very best of luck. Follow your dreams and enjoy the journey!

Angelo Kinicki

Key Terms Used in This Chapter

audits 652
balance sheet 651
balanced scorecard 645
benchmarking 669
best practices 670
budget 650
bureaucratic control 643
concurrent control 639
continuous improvement 658
control chart 636
control process steps 635
control standard 635
controlling 632
decentralized control 643
Deming management 655
enterprise resource planning (ERP) 669
external audit 653
feedback control 639
feedforward control 639
financial statement 651
fixed budget 651
income statement 651
incremental budgeting 650
internal audit 653
ISO 9000 series 663
ISO 14000 series 663
Kaizen 658
Lean Six Sigma 662
management by exception 638
operational control 641
outsourcing 661
PDCA cycle 655
reduced cycle time 661
Six Sigma 662
statistical process control 662
strategic control 641
strategy map 648
supply chain 643
tactical control 641
total quality management (TQM) 655
two core principles of TQM 656
variable budget 651

Key Points

16.1 Control: When Managers Monitor Performance

- Controlling is defined as monitoring performance, comparing it with goals, and taking corrective action as needed.
- There are six reasons that control is needed: (1) to adapt to change and uncertainty; (2) to discover irregularities and errors; (3) to reduce costs, increase productivity, or add value; (4) to detect opportunities; (5) to deal with complexity; and (6) to decentralize decision making and facilitate teamwork.
- There are four control process steps. (1) The first step is to set standards. A control standard is the desired performance level for a given goal. (2) The second step is to measure performance, based on written reports, oral reports, and personal observation. (3) The third step is to compare measured performance against the standards established. (4) The fourth step is to take corrective action, if necessary, if there is negative performance.

16.2 Levels and Areas of Control

- In applying the steps and types of control, managers need to consider (1) the level of management at which they operate, (2) the areas they can draw on for resources, and (3) the style of control philosophy.
- There are three levels of control, corresponding to the three principal managerial levels. (1) Strategic control, done by top managers, is monitoring performance to ensure that strategic plans are being implemented. (2) Tactical control, done by middle managers, is monitoring performance to ensure that tactical plans are being implemented. (3) Operational control, done by first-level or supervisory managers, is monitoring performance to ensure that day-to-day goals are being implemented.
- Most organizations have six areas that they can draw on for resources. (1) The physical area includes buildings, equipment, and tangible products; these use equipment control, inventory-management control, and quality controls. (2) The human resources area uses personality tests, drug tests, performance tests, employee surveys, and the like as controls to monitor people. (3) The informational area uses production schedules, sales forecasts, environmental impact statements, and the like to monitor the organization's various resources. (4) The financial area uses various kinds of financial controls, as we discuss in Section 16.4. (5) The structural area uses hierarchical or other arrangements such as bureaucratic control, which is characterized by use of rules, regulations, and formal authority to guide performance, or decentralized control, which is characterized by informal and organic structural arrangements. (6) The cultural area influences the work process and levels of performance through the set of norms that develop as a result of the values and beliefs that constitute an organization's culture.

16.3 The Balanced Scorecard and Strategy Maps

- To establish standards, managers often use the balanced scorecard, which provides a fast but comprehensive view of the organization via four indicators: (1) financial measures, (2) customer satisfaction, (3) internal processes, and (4) innovation and improvement activities.

- The strategy map, a visual representation of the four perspectives of the balanced scorecard—financial, customer, internal business, and innovation and learning—enables managers to communicate their goals so that everyone in the company can understand how their jobs are linked to the overall objectives of the organization.

16.4 Some Financial Tools for Control

- Financial controls include (1) budgets, (2) financial statements, and (3) audits.
- A budget is a formal financial projection. The most important budget-planning approach is incremental budgeting, which allocates increased or decreased funds to a department by using the last budget period as a reference point; only incremental changes in the budget request are reviewed. Budgets are either fixed, which allocate resources on the basis of a single estimate of costs, or variable, which allow resource allocation to vary in proportion with various levels of activity.
- A financial statement is a summary of some aspect of an organization's financial status. One type, the balance sheet, summarizes an organization's overall financial worth—assets and liabilities—at a specific point in time. The other type, the income statement, summarizes an organization's financial results—revenues and expenses—over a specified period of time.
- Audits are formal verifications of an organization's financial and operational systems. Audits are of two types. An external audit is formal verification of an organization's financial accounts and statements by outside experts. An internal audit is a verification of an organization's financial accounts and statements by the organization's own professional staff.

16.5 Total Quality Management

- Much of the impetus for quality improvement came from W. Edwards Deming, whose philosophy, known as Deming management, proposed ideas for making organizations more responsive, more democratic, and less wasteful.
- Among the principles of Deming management are (1) quality should be aimed at the needs of the consumer; (2) companies should aim at improving the system, not blaming workers; (3) improved quality leads to increased market share, increased company prospects, and increased employment; and (4) quality can be improved on the basis of hard data, using the PDCA, or Plan-Do-Check-Act, cycle.
- Total quality management (TQM) is defined as a comprehensive approach—led by top management and supported throughout the organization—dedicated to continuous quality improvement (such as through Kaizen), training, and customer satisfaction. The two core principles of TQM are people orientation and improvement orientation.
- In the people orientation, everyone involved with the organization is asked to focus on delivering value to customers, focusing on quality. TQM requires training, teamwork, and cross-functional efforts.
- In the improvement orientation, everyone involved with the organization is supposed to make ongoing, small, incremental improvements in all parts of the organization. This orientation assumes that it's less expensive to do things right the first time, to do small improvements all the time, and to follow accurate standards to eliminate small variations.
- Several techniques are available for improving quality. (1) Outsourcing is the subcontracting of services and operations to an outside vendor. (2) Reduced cycle time consists of reducing the number of steps in a work process. (3) Statistical process control is a statistical technique that uses periodic random samples from production runs to see if quality is being maintained within a standard range of acceptability. (4) Six Sigma is a rigorous statistical analysis process that reduces defects in manufacturing and service-related processes. (5) ISO 9000 consists of quality-control procedures companies must install—from purchasing to manufacturing to inventory to shipping—that can be audited by independent quality-control experts, or "registrars." ISO 14000 extends the concept to environmental performance.

16.6 Managing Control Effectively

- Successful control systems have four common characteristics: (1) They are strategic and results oriented. (2) They are timely, accurate, and objective. (3) They are realistic, positive, and understandable and they encourage self-control. (4) They are flexible.
- Among the barriers to a successful control system are the following: (1) Organizations may exert too much control. (2) There may be too little employee participation. (3) The organization may overemphasize means instead of ends. (4) There may be an overemphasis on paperwork. (5) There may be an overemphasis on one approach instead of multiple approaches.

16.7 Managing for Productivity

- A manager has to deal with six challenges—managing for competitive advantage, diversity, globalization, information technology, ethical standards, sustainability, and his or her own happiness and meaningfulness.
- Managers must make decisions about the four management functions—planning, organizing, leading, and controlling—to get people to achieve productivity and realize results.
- Productivity is defined by the formula "outputs divided by inputs for a specified period of time." Productivity matters because it determines whether the organization will make a profit or even survive.
- Much of productivity growth is thought to result from the implementation of information technology, including enterprise resource planning (ERP) systems, though wages in most industrialized countries have not kept up. Productivity depends on control.

16.8 Career Corner: Managing Your Career Readiness

- Developing the competency of career management requires the application of four additional career readiness competencies: ownership/accepting responsibility, self-motivation, self-awareness, and openness to change.
- Figure 16.9 displays a four-step process for managing career readiness.
- Five generic tips help you manage your career: (1) Make every day count. (2) Stay informed and network. (3) Promote yourself. (4) Roll with change and disruption. (5) Small things matter during interviews.

Understanding the Chapter: What Do I Know?

1. What is control, and what are six reasons control is needed?
2. Explain the steps in the control process, and describe the three levels of control.
3. Distinguish among the six areas of organizational control: physical, human, informational, financial, structural, and cultural.
4. Explain the four indicators of the balanced scorecard, and state what a strategy map is.
5. What are four mechanisms of success for measurement-managed firms and four barriers to effective measurement?
6. Define *incremental budgeting*, and give some examples of types of budgets.
7. Explain the following financial tools used for control: financial statement, balance sheet, income statement, and audits (both external and internal).
8. Discuss total quality management, its two core principles, and the concept of continuous improvement.
9. Explain the following TQM tools and techniques: reduced cycle time, the ISO 9000 series, the ISO 14000 series, statistical process control, and Six Sigma and Lean Six Sigma.
10. What is the formula for defining productivity?

Management in Action

Is Tesla Out of Control?

Tesla started in 2003 and specializes in electric cars, battery energy storage, and solar panels. The company had more than 37,000 employees and revenues of over $11 billion in 2017.[172] Tesla revolutionized the electric car industry when it introduced the fully electric, plug-in Model S sports sedan in 2013. The Model S was named "Car of the Century" by *Car and Driver* magazine in 2015.[173]

Tesla's Model S started at well over $70,000, with some models costing more than $100,000.[174] Tesla added a more affordable Model 3 at around $35,000 to its lineup in 2017.[175]

Tesla's finances struggled since introducing the Model 3. The company's net losses grew from $773 million in 2016 to $2.24 billion in 2017.[176] Moody's downgraded the company's credit rating based on fears that it could run out of money by the end of 2018.[177] What happened?

TESLA'S MANUFACTURING PROBLEMS

Manufacturing of the Model 3 has been "hell," according to Musk.[178] The vehicle is taking too long to make, and it has a high defect rate.

Tesla's production line couldn't keep up with the demand for approximately 400,000 Model 3s between 2017 and 2018. The company has been operating out of a former GM/Toyota joint venture plant in California with a capacity to produce 400,000 cars annually. Tesla could barely get a quarter of that production in 2017 as it resorted to pulling cars off the production line and finishing them by hand.[179]

Tesla's production line is suffering from too much automation, according to *Business Insider*. Most car manufacturers automate stamping, painting, and welding, but Musk decided to automate even more.[180] He directed that final vehicle assembly, including putting parts inside the vehicle, be completed by robots. "It's remarkable how much can be done by just beating up robots ... adding additional robots at choke points and just making lines go really, really fast," he said in 2017.[181] To his surprise, automation actually slowed production. "Automation in final assembly doesn't work," said a Wall Street analyst. For example, Japanese carmakers actually limit automation because it is costly and negatively impacts quality.[182] Tesla experienced this firsthand. Musk's robots couldn't get the final assembly sequencing right, delaying assembly and prompting manual refinishes.[183]

The robots also haven't saved the company any money. Tesla was able to reduce the number of workers on its production line due to automation, but it had to hire more expensive engineers to manage and program its robots. This does not even take into account the expense associated with redoing assembly that robots couldn't get right in the first place.[184]

Model 3s coming off the production line were defective. According to the *LA Times*, "Online Tesla forums are rife with comments from some of those lucky enough to have the car in hand. They're griping about dead batteries, leaking tail lamps, protruding headlights, door rattles, and body panels that don't line up—and in many cases, they've got photos to back it up."[185]

The delays and poor production quality are creating a cash problem for Tesla. It can't sell cars it hasn't produced, yet *Bloomberg* reported that the company spent nearly half a million dollars every hour of 2017. "Whether [Tesla] can last another 10 months or a year, [Musk] needs money, and quickly," said Kevin Tynan, a senior analyst with Bloomberg Intelligence. Tynan estimated Tesla will be required to raise at least $2 billion in fresh capital by mid-2018.[186] Musk disagreed, tweeting "Tesla will be profitable & cash flow positive in Q3 & Q4 [2018], so obviously no need to raise money."[187]

Musk's ambition has been praised in the past, but Tesla's worsening financial position is raising more and more questions. The company has lost $4.6 billion since going public in 2010.

MUSK IS TRYING TO TAKE CONTROL

Tesla's plan is to take greater control of its manufacturing line in order to increase production and reduce expenses. Musk admitted in 2018 that Tesla overly relied on robots in production telling *CBS*, "...excessive automation at Tesla was a mistake. To be precise, my mistake. Humans are underrated."[188] Musk believes more humans need to oversee vehicle assembly, starting with him. The CEO is spending day and night at the Tesla factory (even sleeping in the conference room) so he can realize errors in production and solve them in real time.[189] Tesla employees may not be too thrilled. Musk describes himself not only as micromanager, but as a "nano-manager" (*micro-* means a thousandth of something, while *nano-* means a billionth). "I have [obsessive-compulsive disorder] OCD on product-related issues," he told *The Wall Street Journal*. "I always see what's ... wrong ... I never see what's right."[190]

Musk says that direct oversight has allowed him to "unlock some of the critical things that were holding [Tesla] back."[191] His first move was to temporarily shut down the entire Model 3 production line in April 2018. Tesla's spokesperson termed the shutdown as "planned downtime" to "improve automation and systemically address bottlenecks in order to increase production rates."[192] Critics believed Musk was wrong to put the line on hold. "Periodic shutdowns of hours or a day are not uncommon during pre-launch pilot build. They are unheard of in regular production, where [Musk] supposedly is," said a former General Motors vice chairman.[193]

What Musk did not put on hold were his expectations for production. Tesla committed to increasing production from 5,000 to 6,000 cars a week by June 2018, according to *USA Today*.[194] The investor community is skeptical of this lofty goal, especially since Musk has a history of failing to deliver. For example, he said in 2017 that Tesla would churn out 5,000 Model 3s by year's end but only delivered 2,700.[195]

Musk plans to get to 6,000 cars a week by producing them day and night. Tesla is adding another production shift at its manufacturing plant, transitioning to 24/7 operations. The company is hiring 400 workers a week for several weeks in order to cover this new shift.[196] Some analysts don't think this is a wise move as most U.S. auto plants at established automakers only operate two eight-hour shifts. This is because supplying a plant with parts and keeping the equipment in peak operation is difficult when running around the clock. "There's diminishing returns when running 24/7," said an executive analyst with *CNNMoney*. Running an additional shift also has financial implications for Tesla. The additional hires will surely put more pressure on its finances.[197]

Musk's response is to tighten the purse strings elsewhere. He is planning an audit to save expenses where possible, says *The Detroit News*. "I have asked the Tesla finance team to comb through every expense worldwide, no matter how small, and cut everything that doesn't have a strong value justification," he wrote in a 2018 e-mail to Tesla employees. "All capital or other expenditures above a million dollars, or where a set of related expenses may accumulate to a million dollars over the next 12 months, should be considered on hold until explicitly approved by me," said the CEO.[198]

Can Musk get Tesla under control before it runs out of cash?

FOR DISCUSSION

Problem-Solving Perspective

1. What is the underlying problem in this case from the perspective of CEO Elon Musk?
2. What are the causes of the problem?
3. What is your evaluation of Musk's approach for solving the problem?

Application of Chapter Content

1. Is Musk implementing feedforward, concurrent, or feedback control to solve production issues? Explain.
2. Which areas of organizational control are part of Tesla's plan to remedy issues with the Model 3? Provide examples.
3. Create a balanced scorecard to give Musk a view of Tesla. Utilize all four perspectives.

4. What type of an audit is Musk utilizing? Explain.
5. Is Musk exhibiting the two core principles of total quality management? Why or why not?
6. Which barriers to control success are exhibited by Tesla? Provide examples.

Legal/Ethical Challenge

Should Companies Use GPS to Track Employees?

More companies are using GPS apps to track the whereabouts of their employees for productivity and safety-related reasons. A 2017 study showed that nearly a third of employees were tracked via GPS by their employers.[199]

Employee tracking is growing in both the commercial and government sectors. For example, the city of Park Hills, Missouri, installed GPS devices in 2018 on city-owned vehicles, including some police cruisers. The city administrator believed the tracking devices would lead to "better-spent drive time, improvement of the safety of city employees, improvement of job performance, [and] improvement of services provided to the community. . . . " The system is not very expensive. The GPS devices were provided for free with the city signing a two-year contract and paying a $200 monthly subscription fee.[200]

GPS tracking can apply after an employee's shift is over. If a worker takes an employer-owned vehicle home at night or over the weekend, it might continue sending its location. Tracking devices on mobile phones may also continue broadcasting an employee's location during time off.[201] One in 10 employees responded to a QuickBooks survey saying that they were, in fact, being tracked 24 hours a day, confirming concerns of around-the-clock tracking.[202]

Employees out in the field may not be the only ones being tracked in the future. Amazon was granted patents for the design of warehouse tracking wristbands in 2018. The company currently has its warehouse "pickers" stand in front of shelves and move items into bins, tracking each product with a handheld barcode scanner. Amazon says the wristbands will speed up the fulfillment process by freeing up employees' hands from scanners and their eyes from computer screens. This isn't the only information the company can track though. Any wearable can collect personal information about an employee, even unintentionally. "They could gather detailed information about a worker's every move–when they go to the restroom, if they slow down at certain times of day, how often they stop and rest," according to *CNNMoney.*[203]

The legal landscape around tracking employees is "very vague," said Lew Maltby, the president of the National Workrights Institute. Federal privacy laws do not explicitly bar businesses from using GPS to track their employees. So an employee's chances of success in court will depend on different factors, including whether or not consent was given to be tracked and whether the device being tracked belongs to them or the company. "It's essentially whatever shocks the judge," said Maltby.[204]

SOLVING THE CHALLENGE

What would you do if you were the CEO of a company and your managers proposed an employee GPS tracking system?

1. The company needs to use all means to ensure employee productivity and safety. Employees need to provide consent, as a condition of employment, to being tracked when using company vehicles and/or electronic devices at any time of the day. If you are in possession of company property, the company needs to know what you are up to. Let's implement the tracking system.
2. The company should not be tracking employees, on or off the clock, as this is an invasion of privacy. The last thing we need to do is play Big Brother and demoralize our workforce. Let's find other ways to ensure productivity and safety.
3. Employee productivity and safety is important, but needs to be balanced with privacy concerns. Employees should consent to being tracked while on the clock, but once they've clocked out the tracking system should be disabled. Let's implement a limited tracking system.
4. Invent other options.

Uber Continuing Case connect

Learn about Uber's use of control mechanisms on its drivers to encourage service quality. Assess your ability to apply the management concepts discussed in this chapter to the case by going to Connect.

LEARNING MODULE 2

The Project Planner's Toolkit

Flowcharts, Gantt Charts, and Break-Even Analysis

THE BIG PICTURE

Three tools used in project planning, which was covered in Chapter 5, are flowcharts, Gantt charts, and break-even analysis.

Project planning may begin (in the definition stage) as a back-of-the-envelope kind of process, but the client will expect a good deal more for the time and money being invested. Fortunately, there are various planning and monitoring tools that give the planning and execution of projects more precision. Three tools in the planner's toolkit are (1) flowcharts, (2) Gantt charts, and (3) break-even analysis.

Tool #1: Flowcharts—for Showing Event Sequences and Alternate Decision Scenarios

A *flowchart* is a useful graphical tool for representing the sequence of events required to complete a project and for laying out "what-if" scenarios. Flowcharts have been used for decades by computer programmers and systems analysts to make a graphical "road map," as it were, of the flow of tasks required. These professionals use their own special symbols (indicating "input/output," "magnetic disk," and the like), but there is no need for you to make the process complicated. Generally, only three symbols are needed: (1) an oval for the "beginning" and "end," (2) a box for a major activity, and (3) a diamond for a "yes or no" decision. *(See Figure A.1, next page.)*

Computer programs such as iGrafx's ABC FlowCharter are available for constructing flowcharts. You can also use the drawing program in word processing programs such as Microsoft Word.

Benefits

Flowcharts have two benefits:

- **Planning straightforward activities.** A flowchart can be quite helpful for planning ordinary activities–figuring out the best way to buy textbooks or a car, for example. It is also a straightforward way of indicating the sequence of events in, say, thinking out a new enterprise that you would then turn into a business plan.
- **Depicting alternate scenarios.** A flowchart is also useful for laying out "what-if" scenarios–as in if you answer "yes" to a decision question you should follow Plan A, if you answer "no" you should follow Plan B.

Limitations

Flowcharts have two limitations:

- **No time indication.** They don't show the amounts of time required to accomplish the various activities in a project. In building a house, the foundation might take only a couple of days, but the rough carpentry might take weeks. These time differences can't be represented graphically on a flowchart (although you could make a notation).

FIGURE A.1 **Flowchart: website, print, or television?**

Example of a flowchart for improving a company's advertising.

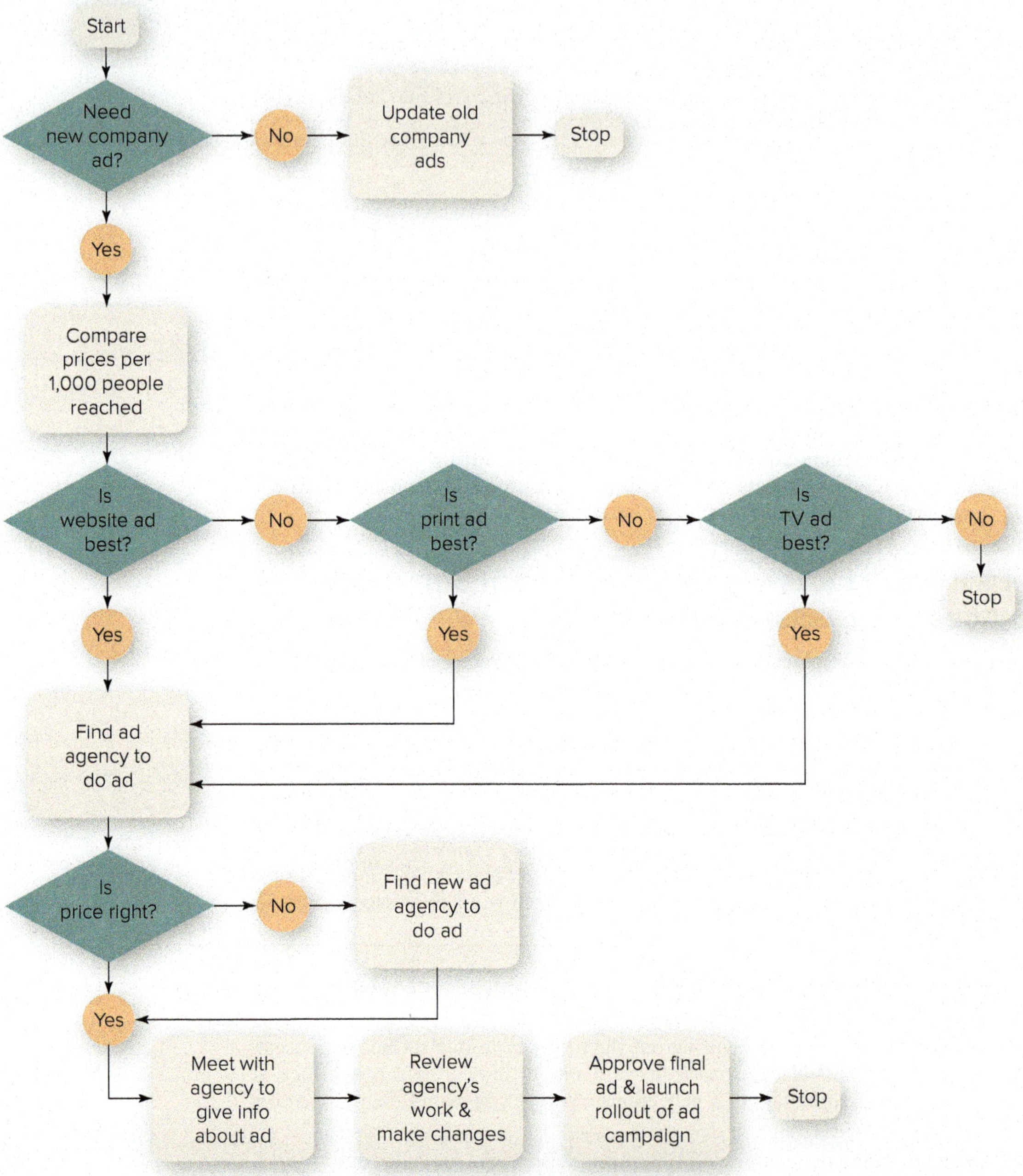

- **Not good for complex projects.** They aren't useful for showing projects consisting of several activities that must all be worked on at the same time. An example would be getting ready for football season's opening game, by which time the players have to be trained, the field readied, the programs printed, the band rehearsed, the ticket sellers recruited, and so on. These separate activities might each be represented on their own flowcharts, of course. But to try to express them all together all at once would produce a flowchart that would be unwieldy, even unworkable.

Tool #2: Gantt Charts—Visual Time Schedules for Work Tasks

We have mentioned how important deadlines are to making a project happen. Unlike a flowchart, a Gantt chart can graphically indicate deadlines.

The Gantt chart was developed by **Henry L. Gantt,** a member of the school of scientific management (discussed in Chapter 2). **A *Gantt chart* is a kind of time schedule–a specialized bar chart that shows the relationship between the kind of work tasks planned and their scheduled completion dates.** *(See Figure A.2, below.)*

A number of software packages can help you create and modify Gantt charts on your computer. Examples are CA-SuperProject, Microsoft Project, Primavera SureTrak Project Manager, and TurboProject Professional.

Benefits

There are three benefits to using a Gantt chart:

- **Express time lines visually.** Unlike flowcharts, Gantt charts allow you to indicate visually the time to be spent on each activity.
- **Compare proposed and actual progress.** A Gantt chart may be used to compare planned time to complete a task with actual time taken to complete it, so that you can see how far ahead or behind schedule you are for the entire project. This enables you to make adjustments so as to hold to the final target dates.
- **Simplicity.** There is nothing difficult about creating a Gantt chart. You express the time across the top and the tasks down along the left side. As Figure A.2 shows, you can make use of this device while still in college to help schedule and monitor the work you need to do to meet course requirements and deadlines (for papers, projects, tests).

Limitations

Gantt charts have two limitations:

- **Not useful for large, complex projects.** Although a Gantt chart can express the interrelations among the activities of relatively small projects, it becomes cumbersome and unwieldy when used for large, complex projects. More sophisticated management planning tools may be needed, such as PERT networks.

FIGURE A.2 Gantt chart for designing a website

This shows the tasks accomplished and the time planned for remaining tasks to build a company website.

Accomplished: ||||||||

Planned: \\\\\\\\

<table>
<tr><th>Stage of development</th><th>Week 1</th><th>Week 2</th><th>Week 3</th><th>Week 4</th><th>Week 5</th></tr>
<tr><td>1. Examine competitors' websites</td><td>||||||||||||||
||||||||</td><td>|||||||||</td><td></td><td></td><td></td></tr>
<tr><td>2. Get information for your website</td><td>||||||||||||||
||||||||</td><td>||||||||||||||
||||||||</td><td></td><td></td><td></td></tr>
<tr><td>3. Learn Web-authoring software</td><td></td><td>||||||||||||||
||||||||</td><td>||||||||||||||
||||||||</td><td></td><td></td></tr>
<tr><td>4. Create (design) your website</td><td></td><td></td><td>\\\\\\\\</td><td>\\\\\\\\\\\\\\
\\</td><td>\\\\</td></tr>
<tr><td>5. "Publish" (put) website online</td><td></td><td></td><td></td><td></td><td>\\\\\\\\\\\\</td></tr>
</table>

- **Time assumptions are subjective.** The time assumptions expressed may be purely subjective; there is no range between "optimistic" and "pessimistic" of the time needed to accomplish a given task.

Tool #3: Break-Even Analysis—How Many Items Must You Sell to Turn a Profit?

Break-even analysis **is a way of identifying how much revenue is needed to cover the total costs of developing and selling a product.** Let's walk through the computation of a break-even analysis, referring to the illustration. *(See Figure A.3.)* We assume you are an apparel manufacturer making shirts or blouses. Start in the lower-right corner of the diagram on the following page and follow the circled numbers as you read the descriptions below.

① *Fixed costs (green area):* Once you start up a business, whether you sell anything or not, you'll have expenses that won't vary much, such as rent, insurance, taxes, and perhaps salaries. These are called *fixed costs,* **expenses that don't change regardless of your sales or output.** Fixed costs are a function of time—they are expenses you have to pay out on a regular basis, such as weekly, monthly, or yearly. Here the chart shows the fixed costs (green area) are $600,000 per year no matter how many sales units (of shirts or blouses) you sell.

② *Variable costs (blue area):* Now suppose you start producing and selling a product, such as blouses or shirts. At this point you'll be paying for materials, supplies, labor, sales commissions, and delivery expenses. These are called *variable costs,* **expenses that vary directly depending on the numbers of the product that you produce and sell.** (After all, making more shirts will cost you more in cloth, for example.) Variable costs, then, are a function of volume—they go up and down depending on the number of products you make or sell. Here the variable costs (blue area) are relatively small if you sell only a few thousand shirts but they go up tremendously if you sell, say, 70,000 shirts.

③ *Total costs (first right upward-sloping line—green plus blue area added together):* The sum of the fixed costs and the variable costs equals the total costs (the green and blue areas together). This is indicated by the line that slopes upward to the right from $600,000 to $3,000,000.

④ *Total sales revenue (second right upward-sloping line):* This is the total dollars received from the sale of however many units you sell. The sales revenue varies depending on the number of units you sell. Thus, for example, if you sell 30,000 shirts, you'll receive $1,800,000 in revenue. If you sell 40,000 shirts, you'll receive somewhat more than $2,400,000 in revenue.

⑤ *Break-even point (intersection of dashed lines):* Finding this point is the purpose of this whole exercise. **The** *break-even point* **is the amount of sales revenue at which there is no profit but also no loss to your company.** On the graph, this occurs where the "Total sales revenues" line crosses the "Total costs" line, as we've indicated here where the dashed lines meet. This means that you must sell 30,000 shirts and receive $1,800,000 in revenue in order to recoup your total costs (fixed plus variable). Important note: Here is where pricing the shirts becomes important. If you raise the price per shirt, you may be able to make the same amount of money (hit your break-even point) by selling fewer of them—but that may be harder to do because customers may resist buying at the higher price.

⑥ *Loss (red area):* If you fail to sell enough shirts at the right price (the break-even point), you will suffer a loss. *Loss* **means your total costs exceed your total sales revenue.** As the chart shows, here you are literally "in the red"—you've lost money.

⑦ *Profit (black area):* Here you are literally "in the black"—you've made money. All the shirts you sell beyond the break-even point constitute a profit. *Profit* **is the amount by which total revenue exceeds total costs.** The more shirts you sell, of course, the greater the profit.

The kind of break-even analysis demonstrated here is known as the *graphic method.* The same thing can also be done algebraically.

FIGURE A.3 **Break-even analysis**

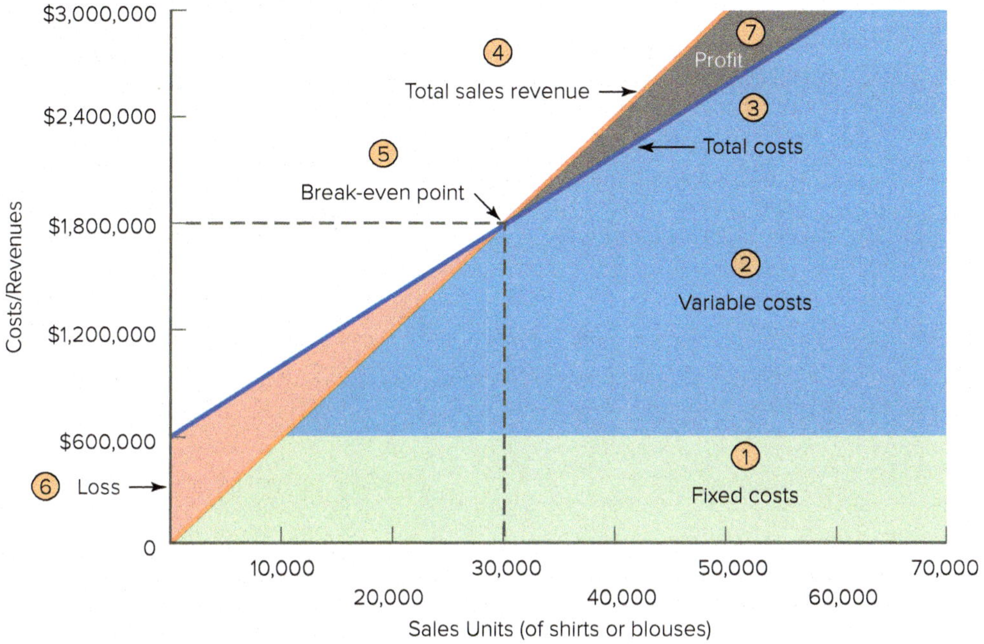

Benefits Break-even analysis has two benefits:

- **For doing future "what-if" alternate scenarios of costs, prices, and sales.** This tool allows you to vary the different possible costs, prices, and sales quantities to do rough "what-if" scenarios to determine possible pricing and sales goals. Since the numbers are interrelated, if you change one, the others will change also.
- **For analyzing the profitability of past projects.** While break-even analysis is usually used as a tool for future projects, it can also be used retroactively to find out whether the goal of profitability was really achieved, since costs may well have changed during the course of the project. In addition, you can use it to determine the impact of cutting costs once profits flow.

EXAMPLE Break-Even Analysis: Why Do Airfares Vary So Much?

Why do some airlines charge four times more than others for a flight of the same distance?

There are several reasons, but break-even analysis enters into it.

United Airlines's average cost for flying a passenger 1 mile in a recent year was 11.7 cents, whereas Southwest's was 7.7 cents. Those are the break-even costs. What they charged beyond that was their profit.

Why the difference? One reason, according to a study by the U.S. Department of Transportation, is that Southwest's expenses are lower. United flies more long routes than short ones, so its costs are stretched out over more miles, making its costs for flying shorter routes higher than Southwest's.

Another factor affecting airfares is the type of passengers flying a particular route—whether they are high-fare-paying business travelers or more price-conscious leisure travelers. Business travelers often don't mind paying a lot (they are reimbursed by their companies), and those routes (such as Chicago to Cincinnati) tend to have more first-class seats, which drives up the average price. Flights to vacation spots (such as Las Vegas) usually have more low-price seats because people aren't willing to pay a lot for pleasure travel. Also, nonstop flight fares often cost more than flights with connections.

Limitations Break-even analysis is not a cure-all.

- **It oversimplifies.** In the real world, things don't happen as neatly as this model implies. For instance, fixed and variable costs are not always so readily distinguishable. Or fixed costs may change as the number of sales units goes up. And not all customers may pay the same price (some may get discounts).
- **The assumptions may be faulty.** On paper, the formula may work perfectly for identifying a product's profitability. But what if customers find the prices too high? Or what if sales figures are outrageously optimistic? In the marketplace, your price and sales forecasts may really be only good guesses.

CHAPTER 1

1. NACE Staff, "Employers Rate Career Competencies, New Hire Proficiency," December 11, 2017, www.naceweb.org/career-readiness/competencies/employers-rate-career-competencies-new-hire-proficiency; M. Tarpey, "The Skills You Need for the Jobs of the Future," February 16, 2017, www.careerbuilder.com/advice/the-skills-you-need-for-the-jobs-of-the-future.

2. K. Armstrong, "At Keller Demo Day, Six Student Teams Pitch Their Companies," *New Jersey Tech Weekly*, August 24, 2017, http://njtechweekly.com/art/3393-at-keller-demo-day-six-student-teams-pitch-their-companies/.

3. P. Ingrassia, "How GM's Mary Barra Does It," *Fortune*, September 9, 2016, http://fortune.com/mary-barra-general-motors-essay/.

4. B. Vlasi, "G.M. Chief Mary Barra Is Named Chairwoman, Affirming Her Leadership," *The New York Times*, January 5, 2016, p. B3.

5. A. Hartmans, "The Fabulous Life of Amazon CEO Jeff Bezos, the Second Richest Person in the World," *BusinessInsider.com*, May 15, 2017, http://www.businessinsider.com/amazon-founder-ceo-jeff-bezos-early-life-2017-5.

6. R. Barker, "No, Management Is *Not* a Profession," *Harvard Business Review*, July–August 2010, pp. 52–60.

7. M. P. Follett, quoted in J. F. Stoner and R. E. Freeman, *Management*, 5th ed. (Englewood Cliffs, NJ: Prentice Hall, 1992), p. 6.

8. S. McChrystal, *Team of Teams* (New York: Penguin Publishing Group, 2015).

9. J. Stewart, "After a Massive Blackout Atlanta's Airport Faces a Logistical Nightmare," *Wired*, December 18, 2017, https://www.wired.com/story/atlanta-airport-blackout-flights/.

10. "Delta Baggage Operations Return to Normal After ATL Outage," December 20, 2017, http://news.delta.com/delta-baggage-operations-return-normal-after-atl-outage.

11. E. C. McLaughlin, T. Smith, and M. Savidge, "Thousands Trying to Get Out of Atlanta after Lights Went Out at Hartsfield Airport," *CNN*, December 18, 2017, http://www.cnn.com/2017/12/18/us/atlanta-airport-power-outage/index.html.

12. A. Blinder and R. Fausset, "Atlanta's Airport Has Power Again, but Many Passengers Are Stranded," *The New York Times*, December 18, 2017, https://www.nytimes.com/2017/12/18/us/atlanta-airport-blackout.html?_r=1.

13. K. Rosenblatt, "Atlanta Power Outage Highlights a Larger Problem with Aging U.S. Airports," *NBC News*, December 21, 2017, https://www.nbcnews.com/storyline/airplane-mode/atlanta-power-outage-highlights-larger-problem-aging-u-s-airports-n831246.

14. T. Cullen, "Delta CEO Wants Georgia Power Company to Pay for Losses after Atlanta Airport Outage," *Daily News*, December 21, 2017, http://www.nydailynews.com/news/national/delta-ceo-reimbursement-altanta-airport-outage-losses-article-1.3713151.

15. Bureau of Labor Statistics, "Usual Weekly Earnings of Wage and Salary Workers, Third Quarter 2017," *News Release*, October 18, 2017, www.bls.gov/news.release/pdf/wkyeng.pdf (accessed January 4, 2018).

16. Bureau of Labor Statistics, "Usual Weekly Earnings of Wage and Salary Workers, Third Quarter 2017," *News Release*, October 18, 2017, www.bls.gov/news.release/pdf/wkyeng.pdf (accessed January 4, 2018).

17. S. Choe, "Top 10 Highest Paid CEOs in 2016," *USA Today*, https://www.usatoday.com/story/money/2017/05/23/ceo-pay-highest-paid-chief-executive-officers-2016/339079001/.

18. G. Donnelly, "Top CEOs Make More in Two Days than an Average Employee Does in One Year," *fortune.com*, July 20, 2017, http://fortune.com/2017/07/20/ceo-pay-ratio-2016/

19. "Chief Executive Officer Salaries," *Salary.com*, January 2016, www1.salary.com/Chief-Executive-Officer-salary.html; and Bureau of Labor Statistics, "Top Executives," *Occupational Outlook Handbook*, December 17, 2015, www.bls.gov/ooh/Management/Top-executives.htm (both accessed January 25, 2016).

20. E. Hoyt, "34 Weird (But Cool) College Majors," *fastweb*, June 23, 2017, https://www.fastweb.com/career-planning/articles/the-35-weird-but-cool-college-majors.

21. B. Schwartz, "Rethinking Work," *The New York Times*, August 30, 2015, pp. SR-1, SR-4. Schwartz is the author of *Why We Work* (New York: Simon & Schuster, 2015).

22. 2013 CareerBuilder survey, reported in D. Auerbach, "Mentors Helpful at Every Career Stage," *Reno Gazette-Journal*, February 9, 2014, p. 10F. See also S. Burn, "Why You Should Be a Mentor," *Forbes*, May 20, 2015, www.forbes.com/sites/chicceo/2015/05/20/why-you-should-be-a-mentor/#2c7ec51424d0.

23. P. Drucker, reported in R. L. Knowdell, "A Model for Managers in the Future Workplace: Symphony Conductor," *The Futurist*, June–July 1998, p. 22.

24. "20 First Line Manager Salaries," *careerbliss*, https://www.careerbliss.com/first-line-manager/salaries/ (accessed January 9, 2018).

25. Susan L. Solomon, interviewed by A. Wolfe, "Susan L. Solomon," *The Wall Street Journal*, February 6–7, 2016, p. C11; and "Susan L. Solomon," New York Stem Cell Foundation, http://nyscf.org/about-us/boards-councils/board-of-directors/item/228-susan-l-solomon-chief-executive-officer (accessed January 5, 2017).

26. G. Guilford, "30 Firms Earn Half the Total Profit Made by All US Public Companies," *Quartz*, July 28, 2017, https://qz.com/1040046/30-firms-earn-half-the-total-profit-made-by-all-us-public-companies/.

27. "Quick Facts About Nonprofits," National Center for Charitable Statistics, http://nccs.urban.org/data-statistics/quick-facts-about-nonprofits.

28. "Directory of Charities and Nonprofit Organizations," *GuideStar*, http://www.guidestar.org/NonprofitDirectory.aspx?cat=7&subcat=39&p=1.

29. H. Mintzberg, *The Nature of Managerial Work* (New York: Harper & Row, 1973).

30. H. Mintzberg, *The Nature of Managerial Work* (New York: Harper & Row, 1973).

31. Ed Reilly, quoted in W. J. Holstein, "Attention-Juggling in the High-Tech Office," *The New York Times*, June 4, 2006, sec. 3, p. 9.

32. J. J. Deal, "Always On, Never Done? Don't Blame the Smartphone," Center for Creative Leadership, April 2015, www.ccl.org/leadership/pdf/research/AlwaysOn.pdf.

33. M. Ward, "A Brief History of the 8-hour Workday, Which Changed How Americans Work," *CNBC*, May 3, 2017, https://www.cnbc.com/2017/05/03/how-the-8-hour-workday-changed-how-americans-work.html.

34. N. Bowles, "Concept of Work/Life Balance on Its Way to Being Obsolete," *San Francisco Chronicle*, November 2, 2013, pp. D1, D3; and H. L. Gray, "7 Tips for Work-Life Balance as an Entrepreneur," February 11, 2016, www.huffingtonpost.com/haley-lynn-gray/7-tips-for-work-life-balance-as-an-entrepreneur_b_9206250.html.

35. J. Kabat-Zinn, "Mindfulness-Based Interventions in Context: Past, Present, and Future," *Clinical Psychology: Science and Practice*, Summer 2003, p. 145.

36. "Multitasking: Switching Costs," American Psychological Association, http://www.apa.org/research/action/multitask.aspx.

37. E. Halliwell, "When the MindGoes Dark," *Mindful*, February 2018, pp. 40–49; and U. R. Hülsheger, J. W. B. Lang, F. Depenbrock, C. Fehmann, F. R. H. Zilstra, and H. J. E. M. Alberts, "The Power of Presence: The Role of Mindfulness at Work for Daily Levels and Change Trajectories of Psychological Detachment and Sleep Quality," *Journal of Applied Psychology*, November 2014, pp. 1113–1128.

38. C. Comaford, "Why Mindfulness and Meditation Matter in Leadership," *Forbes*, March 13, 2016, https://www.forbes.com/sites/christinecomaford/2016/03/13/why-mindfulness-and-meditation-matter-in-leadership/2/#53707eb54e6b.

39. M. Tabaka, "9 Unusual Ways to Improve Your Short-Term Memory, Ranked by Weirdness," *Inc.*, June 26, 2017, https://www.inc.com/marla-tabaka/forgetfulness-is-just-annoying-9-unusual-ways-to-improve-your-memory.html.

40. M. Levin, "Why Google, Nike, and Apple Love Mindfulness Training, and How You Can Easily Love It Too," *Inc.*, June 12, 2017, https://www.inc.com/marissa-levin/why-google-nike-and-apple-love-mindfulness-training-and-how-you-can-easily-love-.html;"Mindfulness for Managers: Feeling Good is Good for Business," *TOPMBA*, November 14, 2016, https://www.topmba.com/jobs/career-trends/mindfulness-managers-feeling-good-good-business.
41. "Mindfulness for Managers: Feeling Good is Good for Business," *TOPMBA*, November 14, 2016, https://www.topmba.com/jobs/career-trends/mindfulness-managers-feeling-good-good-business.
42. "Mindfulness for Managers: Feeling Good is Good for Business," *TOPMBA*, November 14, 2016, https://www.topmba.com/jobs/career-trends/mindfulness-managers-feeling-good-good-business.
43. C. Comaford, "Why Mindfulness and Meditation Matter in Leadership," *Forbes*, March 13, 2016, https://www.forbes.com/sites/christinecomaford/2016/03/13/why-mindfulness-and-meditation-matter-in-leadership/2/#53707eb54e6b.
44. K. Swisher, "Google CEO Sundar Pichai Canceled An All-hands Meeting about Gender Controversy Due to Employee Worries of Online Harassment," *Recode*, August 10, 2017, https://www.recode.net/2017/8/10/16128380/google-cancels-all-hands-meeting-controversy-memo.
45. R. L. Zweigenhaft and G. W. Domhoff, *The New CEOs: Women, African American, Latino, and Asian American Leaders of Fortune 500 Companies* (Lanham, MD: Rowman & Littlefield, 2011).
46. "Women CEOs Speak," Korn Ferry Institute, November 2017, https://engage.kornferry.com/Global/fileLib/Women_CEOs_speak/KF-Rockefeller-Women-CEOs-Speak-Nov_2017.
47. R. L. Katz, "Skills of an Effective Administrator," *Harvard Business Review*, September–October, 1974, p. 94. Also see M. K. De Vries, "Decoding the Team Conundrum: The Eight Roles Executives Play," *Organizational Dynamics*, Vol. 36, No. 1 (2007), pp. 28–44.
48. B. Vlasic, "New GM Chief Is Company Woman, Born to It," *The New York Times*, December 11, 2013, pp. A1, A3.
49. Dan Akerson, quoted in R. Wright and H. Foy, "GM Beats Rivals to Put Woman in Driving Seat," *Financial Times*, December 11, 2013, p. 1.
50. Vlasic, "New GM Chief Is Company Woman, Born to It."
51. Gary Cowger, who mentored Barra, quoted in D.-A. Durbin and T. Krishner, "Mary Barra, a Child of GM, Prepares to Lead It," *AP*, December 24, 2013, http://bigstory.ap.org/article/mary-barra-child-gm-prepares-lead-it (accessed February 27, 2016).
52. Barra, quoted in Vlasic, "New GM Chief Is Company Woman, Born to It."
53. J. Bennett and S. Murray, "Longtime Insider Is GM's First Female CEO," *The Wall Street Journal*, December 11, 2013, pp. A1, A10.
54. M. Spector and C. M. Matthews, "GM Admits to Criminal Wrongdoing," *The Wall Street Journal*, September 18, 2015, pp. B1, B2; M. Spector, "GM Does a U-Turn in Ignition-Switch Case Motion," *The New York Times*, October 7, 2015, p. B4; G. Nagesh and J. S. Lublin, "Investors Yet to Value GM Changes," *The Wall Street Journal*, February 1, 2016, www.wsj.com/articles/investors-yet-to-value-gm-changes-1454371679 (accessed February 12, 2016).
55. G. Nagesh, "GM's Long-Haul Plan," *The Wall Street Journal*, October 26, 2015, p. R2; Nagesh and Lublin, "Investors Yet to Value GM Changes"; and B. Vlasic, "Buoyed by North America, GM Posts $9.7 Billion Profit for 2015," *The New York Times*, February 4, 2016, p. B2.
56. Dan Akerson, quoted in Vlasic, "New GM Chief Is Company Woman, Born to It."
57. Vlasic, "New GM Chief Is Company Woman, Born to It."
58. Durbin and Krishner, "Mary Barra, a Child of GM, Prepares to Lead It."
59. J. Bruce, "Why Soft Skills Matter and the Top 3 You Need," *Forbes*, March 10, 2017, https://www.forbes.com/sites/janbruce/2017/03/10/why-soft-skills-matter-and-the-top-3-you-need/#4d9fe62276f3.
60. M. Eggleston, " Millennials Need Soft Skills Training," *Training Industry*, July 21, 2014, https://www.trainingindustry.com/blog/performance-management/millennials-need-soft-skills-training/.
61. M. Huppert, "3 Business Leaders Share the Most Important Soft Skills They Look for in a New Hire," *LinkedIn*, October 18, 2017, https://business.linkedin.com/talent-solutions/blog/recruiting-tips/2017/3-business-leaders-share-the-most-important-soft-skills-they-look-for-in-a-hire.
62. J. Bruce, "Why Soft Skills Matter And The Top 3 You Need," *Forbes*, March 10, 2017, https://www.forbes.com/sites/janbruce/2017/03/10/why-soft-skills-matter-and-the-top-3-you-need/#4d9fe62276f3.
63. "Interpersonal Skills for Managers," American Management Association, http://www.amanet.org/training/seminars/interpersonal-skills-for-managers.aspx#how_will_you_benefit.
64. A. Kalish, "11 Cheap Online Classes You Can Take to Improve Your Interpersonal Skills," *The Muse*, https://www.themuse.com/advice/11-cheap-online-classes-you-can-take-to-improve-your-interpersonal-skills.
65. CEO recruiter, quoted in Colvin, "Catch a Rising Star."
66. Colvin, "Catch a Rising Star."
67. M. Csikszentmihalyi, *Flow: The Psychology of Optimal Experience* (New York: Harper Collins, 1990); *Beyond Boredom and Anxiety* (San Francisco: Jossey-Bass, 1975); and *Creativity: Flow and the Psychology of Discovery and Invention* (New York: Harper Perennial, 1996).
68. Interview with Brian Chesky by A. Kessler, "The 'Sharing Economy' and Its Enemies," *The Wall Street Journal*, January 18–19, 2014, p. A11.
69. Airbnb, *Fast Company*, https://www.fastcompany.com/company/airbnb (accessed Jan 4, 2017); J. Weed, "Airbnb Grows to a Million Rooms and Hotel Rivals Are Quiet, for Now," *The New York Times*, May 11, 2015, p. B4; M. B. Weiner, "Home Sharing Seems to Be Here to Stay," *San Francisco Chronicle*, August 30, 2015, p. L4; C. Elliott, "Big Hotels' Plan to Win Customers from Airbnb," *Fortune.com*, January 27, 2016, http://fortune.com/2016/01/27/big-hotels-airbnb (accessed February 9, 2016); and M. della Cava, "Beyoncé's 'Super' $10,000-a-Night Airbnb Digs," *USA Today*, February 8, 2016, www.usatoday.com/story/tech/news/2016/02/08/beyonces-super-10000-night-airbnb-digs/80032066 (accessed February 9, 2016).
70. Weiner, "Home Sharing Seems to Be Here to Stay."
71. Weed, "Airbnb Grows to a Million Rooms, and Hotel Rivals Are Quiet, for Now."
72. Elliott, "Big Hotels' Plan to Win Customers from Airbnb"; C. Jones, "New App Creates Pop-up Social Networks at Hotels," *Reno Gazette-Journal*, January 26, 2015, p. 5B, reprinted from *USA Today;* B. Prunty, "Hotels Make an Extra Effort to Ensure Guests a Good Night's Sleep," *The New York Times*, July 21, 2015, p. B4; M. C. White, "Hotels Remake Rooms for a More Casual Style of Work," *The New York Times*, September 8, 2015, p. B5; N. Trejos, "The Incredible Shrinking Hotel Room," *Reno Gazette-Journal*, September 20, 2015, p. 4U, reprinted from *USA Today;* and J. Kell, "Hilton Debuts New Chain to Win over Millennials," *Fortune.com*, January 25, 2016, http://fortune.com/2016/01/25/hilton-new-chain-millennials (accessed February 9, 2016).
73. See J. W. O'Neill and Y. Ouyang, *From Air Mattresses to Unregulated Business: An Analysis of the Other Side of Airbnb*, Pennsylvania State University, January 2016, https://fortunedotcom.files.wordpress.com/2016/01/pennstate_airbnbreport_.pdf (accessed February 10, 2016). See also C. Elliott, "Airbnb Runs 'Illegal Hotels,' Hotel Industry Study Claims," *Fortune.com*, January 20, 2016, http://fortune.com/2016/01/20/airbnb-illegal-hotels-study (accessed February 10, 2016).
74. B. Carson, "Airbnb's New Apartment Brand Lands $200 Million Investment," *Forbes*, December 18, 2017, https://www.forbes.com/sites/bizcarson/2017/12/18/airbnbs-apartment-brand-niido-investment/#6835b9f50492.
75. K. Schwab, " The Fourth Industrial Revolution: What It Means, How to Respond," *World Economic Forum*, January 14, 2016, https://www.weforum.org/agenda/2016/01/the-fourth-industrial-revolution-what-it-means-and-how-to-respond/.
76. J. S. Lublin and V. Fuhrmans, "CEOs Gird for a Year of Disruption," *The Wall Street Journal*, January 4, 2018, p. B7.
77. "Retail E-commerce Sales in the United States from 2016 to 2022 (in million U.S. dollars)," *Statista*, https://www.statista.com/statistics/272391/us-retail-e-commerce-sales-forecast/; M. Lindner, "E-commerce Is Expected to Grow to 17% of US Retail Sales by 2022," *Digital Commerce 360*, August 9, 2017, https://www.

digitalcommerce360.com/2017/08/09/e-commerce-grow-17-us-retail-sales-2022/.

78. See Forrester Research, "112 Results for 'Disruption' in Everything," https://www.forrester.com/search?range=504001&N=204=0%200&tmtxt=+disruption&page=1 (accessed February 10, 2016).

79. "The Exponential Growth of Data," *inside BIGDATA,* February 16, 2017, https://insidebigdata.com/2017/02/16/the-exponential-growth-of-data/.

80. Voucher Cloud, reported in "How Much Data Is Created Daily?" *Storage Servers,* February 6, 2016, https://storageservers.wordpress.com/2016/02/06/how-much-data-is-created-daily (accessed February 10, 2016).

81. A. Williams, "Will Robots Take Our Children's Jobs?" *The New York Times,* December 11, 2017, https://www.nytimes.com/2017/12/11/style/robots-jobs-children.html; C. C. Miller, " Evidence That Robots Are Winning the Race for American Jobs," *The UpShot,* March 28, 2017, https://www.nytimes.com/2017/03/28/upshot/evidence-that-robots-are-winning-the-race-for-american-jobs.html.

82. R. Sharma, "No, That Robot Will Not Steal Your Job," *The New York Times,* October 7, 2017, https://www.nytimes.com/2017/10/07/opinion/sunday/no-that-robot-will-not-steal-your-job.html.

83. S. Lohr, "Robots Will Take Jobs, but Not as Fast as Some Fear, New Report Says," *The New York Times,* January 12, 2017, https://www.nytimes.com/2017/01/12/technology/robots-will-take-jobs-but-not-as-fast-as-some-fear-new-report-says.html.

84. See R. Torten, C. Reaiche, and E. L. Caraballo, "Teleworking in the New Milleneum," *The Journal of Developing Areas,* 2016, pp. 317–326; and R. S. Gajendran, D. A. Harrison, and K. Delaney-Klinger, "Are Telecommuters Remotely Good Citizens? Unpacking Telecommuting's Effects on Performance via I-Deals and Job Resources," *Personnel Psychology,* Summer 2015, pp. 353–393.

85. G. Lõpez, and K. Bialik, "Key Findings about U.S. Immigrants," *Pew Research Center,* May 3, 2017, http://www.pewresearch.org/fact-tank/2017/05/03/key-findings-about-u-s-immigrants/.

86. S. L. Colby and J. M. Ortman, "Projections of the Size and Composition of the U.S. Population: 2014 to 2060," *Current Population Reports,* March 2015, U.S. Census Bureau, Figure 1, https://www.census.gov/content/dam/Census/library/publications/2015/demo/p25-1143.pdf (accessed February 10, 2016).

87. Colby and Ortman, "Projections of the Size and Composition of the U.S. Population: 2014 to 2060," Table 2.

88. Colby and Ortman, "Projections of the Size and Composition of the U.S. Population: 2014 to 2060," Table 1.

89. A. Simone, "The 'How Are You?' Culture Clash," *The New York Times,* January 20, 2014, p. A15.

90. D. Tannen, "Greetings, from Around the World," letter, *The New York Times,* January 24, 2014, p. A24.

91. N. Saval, "Globalisation: The Rise and Fall of an Idea that Swept the World," *The Guardian,* July 14, 2017, https://www.theguardian.com/world/2017/jul/14/globalisation-the-rise-and-fall-of-an-idea-that-swept-the-world.

92. P. Wiseman, and M. Crutsinger, "IMF, World Bank Push Back against Globalization's Detractors," *Business Insider,* October 14, 2017, http://www.businessinsider.com/ap-imf-world-bank-push-back-against-globalizations-detractors-2017-10.

93. See N. Bloom and J. Van Reenan, "Why Do Management Practices Differ across Firms and Countries?" *Journal of Economic Perspectives,* Vol. 24, No. 1 (2010), pp. 203–224.

94. B. Zycher, "The Volkswagen Emissions Scandal and the Bureaucratic Pursuit Of Power," *Investor's Business Daily,* October 18, 2017, https://www.investors.com/politics/commentary/the-volkswagen-emissions-scandal-and-the-bureaucratic-pursuit-of-power/; C. Atiyeh, "Everything You Need to Know About the VW-Diesel Emissions Scandal," *Car and Driver,* October 24, 2017, https://blog.caranddriver.com/everything-you-need-to-know-about-the-vw-diesel-emissions-scandal/

95. D. Rushe, "Oliver Schmidt Jailed for Seven Years for Volkswagen Emissions Scam," *The Guardian,* December 17, 2017, https://www.theguardian.com/business/2017/dec/06/oliver-schmidt-jailed-volkswagen-emissions-scam-seven-years.

96. J. Kantor, and M. Twohey, "Harvey Weinstein Paid Off Sexual Harassment Accusers for Decades," *The New York Times,* October 5, 2017, https://www.nytimes.com/2017/10/05/us/harvey-weinstein-harassment-allegations.html?mtrref=undefined.

97. F. Pirani, "From Weinstein to Lauer: A Timeline of 2017's Sexual Harassment Scandals," *AJC.com,* December 19, 2017, http://www.ajc.com/news/world/from-weinstein-lauer-timeline-2017-sexual-harassment-scandals/qBKJmUSZRJqgOzeB9yN2JK/.

98. M. Kouchaki and I. H. Smith, "The Morning Morality Effect: The Influence of Time of Day on Unethical Behavior," *Psychological Science,* January 2014, pp. 95–102.

99. J. Roberts and D. Wasieleski, "Moral Reasoning in Computer-Based Task Environments: Exploring the Interplay between Cognitive and Technological Factors on Individuals' Propensity to Break Rules," *Journal of Business Ethics,* October 2012, pp. 355–376.

100. D. Schaffhauser, "9 in 10 Students Admit to Cheating in College, Suspect Faculty Do the Same," *Campus Technology,* February 23, 2017, https://campustechnology.com/articles/2017/02/23/9-in-10-students-admit-to-cheating-in-college-suspect-faculty-do-the-same.aspx

101. See "Ethics Pays," *EthicalSystems.org,* http://ethicalsystems.org/content/ethics-pays (accessed February 21, 2016).

102. A. Tugend, "In Life and Business, Learning to Be Ethical," *The New York Times,* January 11, 2014, p. B5.

103. A. E. Tenbrunsel, University of Notre Dame, quoted in Tugend, "In Life and Business, Learning to Be Ethical."

104. T. L. Friedman, *Hot, Flat, and Crowded: Why We Need a Green Revolution—and How It Can Renew America* (New York: Picador, 2009).

105. A. Gore, *An Inconvenient Truth* (Emmaus, PA: Rodale, 2006). See also A. Gore, *The Future: Six Drivers of Global Change* (New York: Random House, 2013).

106. This definition of *sustainability* was developed in 1987 by the World Commission on Environment and Development.

107. See J. Kaeser, "Industry Must Lead on Climate Change," *The New York Times,* September 22, 2015, p. A27.

108. "Sustainable Solutions for the World's Biggest Challenges," *Fortune,* September 15, 2017, p. 52.

109 J. Aaker, Stanford Graduate School of Business, quoted in C. B. Parker, "Stanford Research: The Meaningful Life Is a Road Worth Traveling," *Stanford Report,* January 1, 2014, http://news.stanford.edu/news/2014/january/meaningful-happy-life-010114.html (accessed February 3, 2016). The study is R. F. Baumeister, K. D. Vohs, J. L. Aaker, and E. N. Garbinsky, "Some Key Differences between a Happy Life and a Meaningful Life," *Journal of Positive Psychology,* Vol. 8, No. 6 (2013), pp. 505–516.

110. M. E. P. Seligman, *Flourish* (New York: Free Press, 2011), p. 17.

111. See M. Seligman, *Flourish* (New York: Free Press, 2011).

112. R. Levering, "The 100 Best Companies to Work for 2016," *Fortune,* March 15, 2016, pp. 143–165.

113. M. E. P. Seligman, *Flourish* (New York: Free Press, 2011).

114. M. C. Bush and S. Lewis-Kulin, "100 Best Companies to Work for 2017," *Fortune,* March 15, 2017, p. 86.

115. "2017 Most Attractive Employer Rankings," *The Future of Talent: Advertising Supplement to the Wall Street Journal,* 2017, p. 4.

116. See "Falling Short? College Learning and Career Success," *Hart Research Associates,* 2015.

117. Jennifer Grasz, "Forty Percent of Employers Plan to Hire Full-Time, Permanent Employees in 2017, Career Builder's Annual Job Forecast Finds," January 6, 2017, http://www.careerbuilder.com/share/aboutus/pressreleasesdetail.aspx?sd=1%2F6%2F2017&id=pr983&ed=12%2F31%2F2017; Mary Clarke, "Addressing the Soft Skills Crisis," *Strategic HR Review,* July 2016, pp. 137–139.

118. See "Job Outlook 2016: Attributes Employers Want to See on New College Graduates' Resumes," 2016, Job Outlook 2016: National Association of Colleges and Employers, http://www.naceweb.org/

s11182015/employers-look-for--in-new-hires.aspx; "Watch the skills gap," 2016, http://www.adeccousa.com/employers/resources/skills-gap-in-the-american-workforce; and M. Elliott, "5 Skills College Grads Need to Get a Job," *USA Today,* 2015, http://www.usatoday.com/story/money/personalfinance/2015/05/03/cheat-sheet-skills-college-grads-job/26574631.

119. See Alex Gray, "Goodbye, Maths and English. Hello, Teamwork and Communication?" February 16, 2017, http://ewn.co.za/2017/02/16/goodbye-maths-and-english-hello-teamwork-and-communication.

120. K. Davidson, "Employers Find 'Soft Skills' Like Critical Thinking in Short Supply," *The Wall Street Journal*, August 30, 2016, http://www.wsj.com/articles/employers-find-soft-skills-like-critical-thinking-in-short-supply-1472549400?mod=trending_now_3.

121. Büler, *The Future of Talent: Advertising Supplement to the Wall Street Journal*, 2017, p. 21.

122. See "Future Work Skills 2020," Institute for the Future for the University of Phoenix Research Institute, 2011, p. 13, http://www.iftf.org/uploads/media/SR-1382A_UPRI_future_work_skills_sm.pdf.

123. See L. Pinto and D. Ramalheira, "Perceived Employability of Business Graduates: The Effect of Academic Performance and Extracurricular Activities," *Journal of Vocational Behavior,* 2017, pp. 165–178.

124. K. Davidson, "Hard to Find: Workers with Good 'Soft Skills'," *The Wall Street Journal*, August 31, 2016, pp. B1, B6.

125. See S. Dawkins, A. W. Tian, A. Newman, and A. Martin, "Psychological Ownership: A Review and Research Agenda," *Journal of Organizational Behavior*, 2017, pp. 163–183.

126. T. Williams, "7 Core Competencies Shape Career Readiness for College Graduates," January 12, 2016, https://www.goodcall.com/news/7-core-competencies-shape-career-readiness-for-college-graduates-03909.

127. See M. Jay, "The Secrets of Resilience," *The Wall Street Journal,* November 11-12, 2017, pp. C1–C2.

128. M. Faller, "Glory and Grit," *ASU Thrive Magazine,* Fall 2017, pp 18–22.

129. M. Jay, *Supernormal: The Untold Story of Adversity and Resilience* (New York: Hachette Book Group, 2017).

130. See B. Tulgan, *Bridging the Soft Skills Gap* (Hoboken, New Jersey: John Wiley, 2015) and L. Gillin, *10 Soft Skills You Need* (Dover, Delaware: Global Courseware, 2015).

131. See S. Bates and S. Miller, "The Class of 2017: Ready to Work," *HR Magazine,* August 2017, p. 8; and "The Difference Between an Internship & a Co-Op," October 29, 2017, https://www.thebalance.com/whats-the-difference-between-an-internship-and-a-coop-1987135.

132. Additional insights can be found in W. Enelow, "Charting Your Course," *HR Magazine,* September 2017, pp. 20–21; and S. Shellenbarger, "Don't Feel Stuck: It's Time to Update Your Career Blueprint," *The Wall Street Journal,* February 15, 2017, p. A9.

133. "Major League Baseball," *Wikipedia,* https://en.wikipedia.org/wiki/Major_League_Baseball, last updated January 2, 2018.

134. "MLB Advanced Media," *Wikipedia,* https://en.wikipedia.org/wiki/MLB_Advanced_Media, last updated on December 2, 2017.

135. See R. Bachman and B. Costa, "Baseball's Rainmaker Forced Out After Alleged Misconduct," *The Wall Street Journal,* December 21, 2017, https://www.wsj.com/articles/baseballs-rainmaker-forced-out-after-alleged-misconduct-1513882805.

136. K. Draper, "MLB Executive Bob Bowman Ousted for Inappropriate Behavior," *Boston.com,* December 21, 2017, https://www.boston.com/sports/mlb/2017/12/21/mlb-executive-bob-bowman-ousted-for-inappropriate-behavior.

137. K. Draper, "Bob Bowman, Major League Baseball's Digital Mastermind, Steps Down," *The New York Times,* November 6, 2017, https://nyti.ms/2j6beGk.

138. K. Draper, "Bob Bowman, Major League Baseball's Digital Mastermind, Steps Down," *The New York Times,* November 6, 2017, https://nyti.ms/2j6beGk.

139. C. Calcaterra, "Former MLBAM Head Bob Bowman Was Forced Out Over Workplace Misconduct," December 21, 2017, http://mlb.nbcsports.com/2017/12/21/former-mlbam-head-bob-bowman-was-forced-out-over-workplace-misconduct.

140. FanBoy, "Could Bob Bowman Be the Next CEO of Disney?" August 31, 2016, https://www.laughingplace.com/w/articles/2016/08/31/bob-bowman-next-ceo-disney; and C. Romo, "Bob Bowman Should Have Been the Next MLB Commissioner," https://www.sporttechie.com/bob-bowman-should-have-been-the-next-mlb-commissioner.

141. R. Bachman and B. Costa, "Baseball's Rainmaker Forced Out After Alleged Misconduct," *The Wall Street Journal,* December 21, 2017, https://www.wsj.com/articles/baseballs-rainmaker-forced-out-after-alleged-misconduct-1513882805.

142. R. Bachman and B. Costa, "Baseball's Rainmaker Forced Out After Alleged Misconduct," *The Wall Street Journal,* December 21, 2017, https://www.wsj.com/articles/baseballs-rainmaker-forced-out-after-alleged-misconduct-1513882805.

143. R. Bachman and B. Costa, "Baseball's Rainmaker Forced Out After Alleged Misconduct," *The Wall Street Journal,* December 21, 2017, https://www.wsj.com/articles/baseballs-rainmaker-forced-out-after-alleged-misconduct-1513882805.

144. R. Bachman and B. Costa, "Baseball's Rainmaker Forced Out After Alleged Misconduct," *The Wall Street Journal,* December 21, 2017, https://www.wsj.com/articles/baseballs-rainmaker-forced-out-after-alleged-misconduct-1513882805.

145. J. Terranova, "MLB Accused of Hiding Exec's Misdeeds for Years as Billions Poured In," December 21, 2017, https://nypost.com/2017/12/21/mlb-executive-left-after-years-of-inappropriate-behavior.

146. R. Bachman and B. Costa, "Baseball's Rainmaker Forced Out After Alleged Misconduct," *The Wall Street Journal,* December 21, 2017, https://www.wsj.com/articles/baseballs-rainmaker-forced-out-after-alleged-misconduct-1513882805.

CHAPTER 2

1. I. Leung, "The Tech Industry Is Getting Very People and Culture Focused, Here's Why," *Forbes,* August 5, 2017, https://www.forbes.com/sites/irisleung/2017/08/05/the-tech-industry-is-getting-very-people-and-culture-focused-heres-why/#9db558e57b84.

2. I. Leung, "The Tech Industry Is Getting Very People and Culture Focused, Here's Why," *Forbes,* August 5, 2017, https://www.forbes.com/sites/irisleung/2017/08/05/the-tech-industry-is-getting-very-people-and-culture-focused-heres-why/#9db558e57b84.

3. "Seventy Percent of College Students Work While Enrolled, New Georgetown University Research Finds," Georgetown University Center on Education and the Workforce, October 28, 2015, https://cew.georgetown.edu/wp-content/uploads/Press-release-WorkingLearners__FINAL.pdf.

4. "Recreational Equipment, Inc (REI)," *Great Place to Work,* http://reviews.greatplacetowork.com/recreational-equipment-inc-rei (accessed January 22, 2018).

5. Tom Peters, quoted in J. A. Byrne, "The Man Who Invented Management," *BusinessWeek,* November 28, 2005, www.businessweek.com/stories/2005-11-27/the-man-who-invented-management (accessed January 22, 2016).

6. Byrne, "The Man Who Invented Management." See also R. Karlgaard, "Peter Drucker on Leadership," *Forbes.com,* November 19, 2004, www.forbes.com/2004/11/19/cz_rk_1119drucker.html.

7. C. M. Christensen and M. E. Raynor, "Why Hard-Nosed Executives Should Care about Management Theory," *Harvard Business Review,* September 2003, pp. 67–74.

8. Christensen and Raynor, "Why Hard-Nosed Executives Should Care about Management Theory," p. 68.

9. S. L. Montgomery and D. Chirot, quoted in F. Zakaria, "Something in the Air," *The New York Times Book Review*, August 23, 2015, pp. 14–15. Montgomery and Chirot are authors of *The Shape of the New: Four Big Ideas and How They Made the Modern World* (Princeton, NJ: Princeton University Press, 2015).

10. See D. K. Berman, "The No-Boss Company," *The Wall Street Journal*, October 27, 2015, p. 3.
11. "Holacracy and Self-Organization," *Zappos Insights*, https://www.zapposinsights.com/about/holacracy (accessed January 22, 2018).
12. J. Reingold, "How a Radical Shift Left Zappos Reeling," *Fortune*, March 4, 2016, http://fortune.com/zappos-tony-hsieh-holacracy/.
13. Z. Guzman, "Zappos CEO Tony Hsieh on Getting Rid of Managers: What I Wish I'd Done Differently," *CNBC*, September 13, 2016, https://www.cnbc.com/2016/09/13/zappos-ceo-tony-hsieh-the-thing-i-regret-about-getting-rid-of-managers.html.
14. J. Reingold, "How a Radical Shift Left Zappos Reeling," *Fortune*, March 4, 2016, http://fortune.com/zappos-tony-hsieh-holacracy/.
15. For more on the history of management, see W. Kiechel III, "The Management Century," *Harvard Business Review*, November 2012, pp. 62–75.
16. See G. D. Babcock and R. Trautschold, *The Taylor System in Franklin Management*, 2nd ed. (New York: Engineering Magazine Co., 1917).
17. L. C. Prieto and T. A. Phipps, "Re-Discovering Charles Clinton Spaulding's 'The Administration of Big Business,'" *Journal of Management History*, 2016, pp. 73–90.
18. L. C. Prieto and T. A. Phipps, "Re-Discovering Charles Clinton Spaulding's 'The Administration of Big Business,'" *Journal of Management History*, 2016, p. 82.
19. See N. Bloom, R. Sadun, and J. Van Reenen, "Does Management Really Work?" *Harvard Business Review*, November 2012, pp. 76–82.
20. B. Rice, "The Hawthorne Defect: Persistence of a Flawed Theory," *Psychology Today*, February 1982, pp. 70–74.
21. A. Maslow, "A Theory of Human Motivation," *Psychological Review*, July 1943, pp. 370–396.
22. D. McGregor, *The Human Side of Enterprise* (New York: McGraw-Hill, 1960).
23. A. Singh, "Why Open-Plan Offices Don't Work (And Some Alternatives That Do)," *arch daily*, November 23, 2017, https://www.archdaily.com/884192/why-open-plan-offices-dont-work-and-some-alternatives-that-do.
24. The history of the office workplace is described in N. Saval, *Cubed: A Secret History of the Workplace* (New York: Doubleday, 2014).
25. M. Konnikova, "The Open Office Trap," *The New Yorker*, January 7, 2014, www.newyorker.com/business/currency/the-open-office-trap.
26. K. Sehgal, "It's Time to Bring Back the Office Cubicle," *Fortune*, January 18, 2017, http://fortune.com/2017/01/18/i-hate-open-offices/.
27. S. Shellenbarger, "Why You Can't Concentrate at Work," *The Wall Street Journal*, May 9, 2017, https://www.wsj.com/articles/why-you-cant-concentrate-at-work-1494342840.
28. G. James, "Open-Plan Offices Kill Productivity, According to Science," *Inc.*, May 18, 2017, https://www.inc.com/geoffrey-james/science-just-proved-that-open-plan-offices-destroy-productivity.html.
29. D. Baer, "More Evidence That Open Offices Make People Less Social," *The Cut*, September 19, 2016, https://www.thecut.com/2016/09/more-evidence-that-open-offices-make-people-less-social.html.
30. G. Marks, "Some Apple Employees May Quit Over New 'Open' Office Plan," *The Washington Post*, August 18, 2017, https://www.mercurynews.com/2017/08/17/some-apple-employees-may-quit-over-new-open-office-plan/.
31. See J. Corsello and D. Minor, "Want to be More Productive? Sit Next to Someone Who Is," *Harvard Business Review*, February 14, 2017, https://hbr.org/2017/02/want-to-be-more-productive-sit-next-to-someone-who-is.
32. J. Lombardo, "Intel's Operations Management Strategy: 10 Decisions, Productivity," *Panmore Institute*, April 22, 2017, http://panmore.com/intel-operations-management-strategy-10-decisions-productivity.
33. J. O. Bergman and J. Smialek, "Thaler, Famed for 'Nudge' Theory, Wins Nobel Economics Prize," *Bloomberg*, October 9, 2017, https://www.bloomberg.com/news/articles/2017-10-09/richard-h-thaler-wins-2017-nobel-economics-prize.
34. Social and Behavioral Sciences Team, *Annual Report* (Washington, DC: Executive Office of the President, National Science and Technology Council, September 2015).
35. J. Levitz, "To Recruit Workers, Manufacturers Go to Parents' Nights," *The Wall Street Journal*, December 17, 2017, https://www.wsj.com/articles/to-recruit-workers-manufacturers-go-to-parents-nights-1513425600?mod=searchresults&page=1&pos=9.
36. "The Top Gurus," *The Wall Street Journal*, May 5, 2008, p. B6.
37. G. Hamel, with B. Breen, *The Future of Management* (Boston: Harvard Business School Press, 2007), p. 6.
38. G. Hamel, "Break Free!" *Fortune*, September 19, 2007, http://money.cnn.com/magazines/fortune/fortune_archive/2007/10/01/100352608/index.htm (accessed March 14, 2016).
39. J. Pfeffer and R. I. Sutton, "Profiting from Evidence-Based Management," *Strategy & Leadership*, Vol. 34, No. 2 (2006), pp. 35–42. See also J. Pfeffer and R. I. Sutton, "Evidence-Based Management," *Harvard Business Review*, January 2006, pp. 63–74.
40. Y. Vilner, "These Companies Are Shaping The Face of Big Data," *Inc.*, September 30, 2016, https://www.inc.com/yoav-vilner/these-companies-are-shaping-the-face-of-big-data.html?cid=search.
41. R. Bean and J. Stephen, "5 Ways Big Data and AI Will Impact Life Sciences Firms in 2018," *Forbes*, December 21, 2017, https://www.forbes.com/sites/ciocentral/2017/12/21/5-ways-big-data-and-ai-will-impact-life-sciences-firms-in-2018/#5f86bc283c8e.
42. J. Paine, "Big Data in Marketing: 5 Use Cases," *Inc.*, November 25, 2017, https://www.inc.com/james-paine/5-ways-big-data-is-changing-marketing.html?cid=search.
43. J. Paine, "How Big Data Is Disrupting the Travel Industry," *Inc.*, October 31, 2017, https://www.inc.com/james-paine/3-ways-big-data-is-disrupting-travel-industry.html.
44. Y. Vilner, "How Big Data Analytics May Help Governments Protect Us," *Inc.*, June 27, 2017, https://www.inc.com/yoav-vilner/how-big-data-analytics-may-help-governments-protect-us.html?cid=search.
45. B. Marr, "3 Massive Big Data Problems Everyone Should Know About," *Forbes*, June 15, 2017, https://www.forbes.com/sites/bernardmarr/2017/06/15/3-massive-big-data-problems-everyone-should-know-about/#286d2cdf6186.
46. "Six Sigma–Its Origin and Meaning," *Six Sigma*, https://www.6sigma.us/six-sigma-articles/six-sigma-its-origin-and-meaning/ (accessed January 22, 2018).
47. "Lean Six Sigma Success Stories in the Food Industry," *goleansixsigma.com*, https://goleansixsigma.com/lean-six-sigma-success-stories-in-the-food-industry/ (accessed January 22, 2018).
48. "Lean Six Sigma Success Stories in the Retail Industry," *goleansixsigma.com*, https://goleansixsigma.com/lean-six-sigma-success-stories-in-the-retail-industry/ (accessed January 22, 2018).
49. "ISO 9000," *Reference for Business*, http://www.referenceforbusiness.com/small/Inc-Mail/ISO-9000.html (accessed January 22, 2018).
50. "ISO 9000–Quality Management," *ISO, International Organization for Standardization*, 2018, https://www.iso.org/iso-9001-quality-management.html (accessed January 22).
51. Mark Feffer, "8 Tips for Creating a Learning Culture," *HR Magazine*, August 2017, pp. 50–54
52. D. Jones, "5 Tips for Building a Learning Culture in Your Workplace," *The Balance*, January 17, 2018, https://www.thebalance.com/building-learning-culture-3878190.
53. A. Garvin, "Building a Learning Organization," *Harvard Business Review*, July/August 1993, pp. 78–91; and T. Kelly, "Measuring Informal Learning: Encourage a Learning Culture and Track It!" *Training Industry*, March 21, 2014, www.trainingindustry.com/professional-education/articles/measuring-informal-learning.aspx (accessed January 23, 2016).
54. See H. W. Shin, J. C. Picken, and G. G. Dess, "Revisiting the Learning Organization: How to Create It," *Organizational Dynamics*, January-March 2017, pp. 46–56.
55. See K. Gutierrez, "The Google Way of Building a Strong Learning Culture," *SH!FT*, April 5, 2016, https://www.shiftelearning.com/blog/building-learning-culture; and C. Aranda, J. Arellano, and A. Davila,

"Organizational Learning in Target Setting," *Academy of Management Journal,* June 2017, pp. 1189–1211.

56. R. J. Grossman, "A Culture of Learning," *HR Magazine,* May 2015, p. 37.

57. B. Scudamore, "5 Ways to Foster a Culture of Learning (And Why It Matters)," *Inc.,* August 17, 2017, https://www.inc.com/brian-scudamore/why-this-company-asks-employees-to-imagine-the-imp.html?cid=search.

58. J. Miller, "Why a Culture of Learning Should Be Built from the Top Down," *Inc.,* October 17, 2017, https://www.inc.com/jeff-miller/68-percent-of-employees-want-to-learn-from-their-ceos-which-means-its-time-to-teach.html.

59. K. Kolo, "Virtual Reality: The Next Generation of Education, Learning and Training," *Forbes,* December 13, 2017, https://www.forbes.com/sites/forbesagencycouncil/2017/12/13/virtual-reality-the-next-generation-of-education-learning-and-training/#71ade55e733f.

60. S. M. Heathfield, "4 Tips to Make Training and Development Work," *The Balance,* November 7, 2016, https://www.thebalance.com/employee-training-transfer-tips-1919302.

61. D. Jones, "5 Tips for Building a Learning Culture in Your Workplace," *The Balance,* January 17, 2018, https://www.thebalance.com/building-learning-culture-3878190.

62. Pfeffer and Sutton, "Profiting from Evidence-Based Management."

63. S. Bawany, "The CEO's Role in Developing a Learning Organization," *EDA,* April 1, 2016, https://www.executivedevelopment.com/the-ceos-role-in-developing-a-learning-organization/.

64. R. Jana, "Inspiration from Emerging Economies," *Business Week,* March 23 and 30, 2009, p. 41.

65. See A. L. Kristof-Brown, R. D. Zimmerman, and E. C. Johnson, "Consequences of Individuals' Fit at Work: A Meta-Analysis of Perrson-Job, Person-Organization, Person-Group, and Person-Supervisor Fit," *Personnel Psychology,* Summer 2005, pp. 281–342.

66. See Good.Co Team, "Job Seekers: Stop Creeping on Your Ex Online and Start Doing This Instead," February 19, 2014, https://good.co/blog/job-seekers-digital-research.

67. This list was partially based on H. Huhman, "7 Things to Research Before Any Job Interview," August 29, 2014, https://www.glassdoor.com/blog/7-research-job-interview; and Good.Co Team, "20 Things Recruiters Want, But Won't Tell You (HR Insider)," July 28, 2014, https://good.co/blog/things-recruiters-want-from-candidates-interview.

68. "Sears," *Wikipedia,* https://en.wikipedia.org/wiki/Sears (accessed January 23, 2018).

69. K. Bhasin and L. Lambert, "The Long, Hard, Unprecedented Fall of Sears," *Bloomberg,* May 8, 2017, https://www.bloomberg.com/news/articles/2017-05-08/the-long-hard-unprecedented-fall-of-sears.

70. J. Creswell, "The Incredible Shrinking Sears," *The New York Times,* August 11, 2017, https://www.nytimes.com/2017/08/11/business/the-incredible-shrinking-sears.html.

71. C. Jones, "Sears and Kmart Might Not Have Enough Money to Stock Their Shelves," *USA Today,* March 21, 2017, https://www.usatoday.com/story/money/business/2017/03/21/sears-says-substantial-doubt-can-stay-business/99479726/.

72. "Eddie Lampert," *Wikipedia,* https://en.wikipedia.org/wiki/Eddie_Lampert (accessed January 23, 2018).

73. J. Bowman, "The Problem with Sears Holdings Isn't Tesla, Uber, or Amazon," *fool.com,* March 6, 2016, https://www.fool.com/investing/general/2016/03/06/the-problem-with-sears-holdings-isnt-tesla-uber-or.aspx.

74. L. Kaye, "How Sears Became the Worst Retailer, and Company, in America," *triplepundit.com,* July 22, 2013, https://www.triplepundit.com/2013/07/sears-worst-retailer-company-america/.

75. P. Andersen, "Sears and JC Penney: Bad Management or Sign Of The Times?" *Forbes,* January 28, 2014, https://www.forbes.com/sites/investor/2014/01/28/sears-and-jc-penney-bad-management-or-sign-of-the-times/#20a63d73f60e.

76. See: J. Creswell, "The Incredible Shrinking Sears," *The New York Times,* August 11, 2017, https://www.nytimes.com/2017/08/11/business/the-incredible-shrinking-sears.html; J. Bowman, "The Problem with Sears Holdings Isn't Tesla, Uber, or Amazon," *fool.com,* March 6, 2016, https://www.fool.com/investing/general/2016/03/06/the-problem-with-sears-holdings-isnt-tesla-uber-or.aspx

77. J. Creswell, "The Incredible Shrinking Sears," *The New York Times,* August 11, 2017, https://www.nytimes.com/2017/08/11/business/the-incredible-shrinking-sears.html.

78. J. Creswell, "The Incredible Shrinking Sears," *The New York Times,* August 11, 2017, https://www.nytimes.com/2017/08/11/business/the-incredible-shrinking-sears.html.

79. H. Peterson, "Sears is on the Brink of Catastrophe as Store Closures Loom and Top Execs Flee the Company," *Business Insider,* December 3, 2016, http://www.businessinsider.com/sears-problems-loom-large-2016-12.

80. H. Peterson, "Sears Is Teetering on the Edge of Bankruptcy and Kmart Could Be Its First Casualty," *Business Insider,* December 16, 2017, http://www.businessinsider.com/sears-kmart-bankruptcy-talk-resurfaces-as-year-ends-2017-12.

81. H. Peterson, "Sears is Teetering on the Edge of Bankruptcy and Kmart Could Be Its First Casualty," *Business Insider,* December 16, 2017, http://www.businessinsider.com/sears-kmart-bankruptcy-talk-resurfaces-as-year-ends-2017-12.

82. C. Jones, "Sears and Kmart Might Not Have Enough Money to Stock Their Shelves," *USA Today,* March 21, 2017, https://www.usatoday.com/story/money/business/2017/03/21/sears-says-substantial-doubt-can-stay-business/99479726/ .

83. C. Isidore, "Sears Had a Miserable, Miserable Christmas," *CNN Money,* January 10, 2018, http://money.cnn.com/2018/01/10/news/companies/sears-sales-plunge-cost-cuts/index.html.

84. Creswell, "The Incredible Shrinking Sears," *The New York Times,* August 11, 2017, https://www.nytimes.com/2017/08/11/business/the-incredible-shrinking-sears.html.

85. J. Creswell, "The Incredible Shrinking Sears," *The New York Times,* August 11, 2017, https://www.nytimes.com/2017/08/11/business/the-incredible-shrinking-sears.html.

CHAPTER 3

1. See A. T. Myer, C. N. Thoroughgood, and S. Mohammed, "Complementary or Competing Climates? Examining the Interactive Effects of Service and Ethical Climates on Company-Level Financial Performance," *Journal of Applied Psychology,* August 2016, pp. 1178–1190.

2. See M. Kouchaki, "How Wells Fargo's Fake Accounts Scandal Got So Bad," *Fortune,* September 15, 2016, http://fortune.com/2016/09/15/wells-fargo-scandal/; P. Conti-Brown, "Why Wells Fargo Might Not Survive Its Fake Accounts Scandal," *Fortune,* August 31, 2017, http://fortune.com/2017/08/31/wells-fargo-fake-accounts-scandal-2017-tim-sloan/.

3. M. Mazzilli, "Wells Fargo Sees No End Yet to Sales Scandal Costs, Gets Tax Boost," *Reuters,* January 12, 2018, https://www.reuters.com/article/us-wells-fargo-results/wells-fargo-sees-no-end-yet-to-sales-scandal-costs-gets-tax-boost-idUSKBN1F11LE.

4. The antecedents of climate are discussed by C. Ostroff, A. Kinicki, and R. S. Muhammad, "Organizational Culture and Climate," in I. B. Weiner, N. W. Schmitt, and S. Highhouse, *Handbook of Psychology Vol. 12: Industrial and Organizational Psychology* (Hoboken, NJ: John Wiley & Sons, 2013), pp. 643–676.

5. See M. Thakrar, "Six Ways to Live Your Values and Create a More Ethical Workplace," *Forbes,* November 4, 2017, https://www.forbes.com/sites/forbescoachescouncil/2017/11/14/six-ways-to-live-your-values-and-create-a-more-ethical-workplace/#3d4400a82a92; C. McLaverty and A. McKee, "What You Can Do to Improve Ethics at Your Company," *Harvard Business Review,* December 29, 2016, https://hbr.org/2016/12/what-you-can-do-to-improve-ethics-at-your-company.

6. J. Wicks, quoted in G. Rifkin, "Making a Profit and a Difference," *The New York Times,* October 5, 2006, p. C5.

7. See for example, G. Kaul and T. Duggan, "Mindful Diners' Quest for Fair Trade," *San Francisco Chronicle,* September 8, 2015, pp. A1, A8, A9.

8. Jon Miller, interviewed by W. Henisz, "Big Business and the New Norm: Doing Good at the Core, Not the Periphery," *Knowledge@Wharton,* March 21, 2014, http://knowledge.wharton.upenn.edu/article/big-business-can-fix-world (accessed February 16, 2016).

9. Rob Michalak, reported in D. Gelles, "Gobble Up, but Still Doing Good for the World," *The New York Times,* August 23, 2015, p. BU-3.

10. J. Garofoli, "Box to Donate Its Product to Nonprofits," *San Francisco Chronicle,* May 28, 2014, pp. C1, C6.

11. J. Hidalgo, "Better World Books Distribution Center Plans to Hire 100 Workers," *Reno Gazette-Journal,* January 15, 2016, pp. 7A, 8A.

12. For various definitions of Generation Y and Generation Z, see W. J. Schroer, "Generations X, Y, Z, and the Others—Cont'd," *The Social Librarian,* www.socialmarketing.org/newsletter/features/generation3.htm (accessed February 14, 2016).

13. P. A. Argenti, "Corporate Ethics in the Era of Millennials," *NPR,* August 24, 2016, https://www.npr.org/sections/13.7/2016/08/24/490811156/corporate-ethics-in-the-era-of-millennials.

14. J. Wingard, "How Companies Are Managing the Millennial Generation," *Knowledge@Wharton,* March 5, 2015, http://knowledge.wharton.upenn.edu/article/how-companies-should-manage-millennials (accessed February 16, 2016).

15. S. Landrum, "Millennials and Quality: The Search for a Better Everything," *Forbes,* April 14, 2017, https://www.forbes.com/sites/sarahlandrum/2017/04/14/millennials-and-quality-the-search-for-a-better-everything/#9393567347a7.

16. H. Park, J. M. Twenge, and P. M. Greenfield, "The Great Recession: Implications for Adolescent Values and Behavior," *Social Psychological and Personality Science* 5, no. 3. (2014), pp. 310–318.

17. J. Wingard, "How Companies Are Managing the Millennial Generation," *Knowledge@Wharton,* March 5, 2015, http://knowledge.wharton.upenn.edu/article/how-companies-should-manage-millennials (accessed February 16, 2016); K. Fagan, "Survivors: New Life Comes with Healing," *San Francisco Chronicle,* September 6, 2015, pp. A1, A12–A13.

18. J. Goodnight, quoted in D. A. Kaplan, "The Best Company to Work For," *Fortune*, February 8, 2010, pp. 56–64.

19. *Fortune 100 Best,* http://fortune.com/best-companies/sas/.

20. *NCEO National Center for Employee Ownership,* https://www.nceo.org/articles/employee-ownership-100 (accessed January 24, 2018).

21. "Company Overview of Facebook, Inc.," *Bloomberg,* accessed February 6, 2018, https://www.bloomberg.com/research/stocks/private/board.asp?privcapId=20765463.

22. P. Houdek, "Rewards for Falling Off a Horse: Bad Corporate Governance Is Enabling Managers to Receive Pay for Luck," *Organizational Dynamics,* July–September 2017, pp. 189–194.

23. K. Elsesser, "The Truth about Women's Impact on Corporate Boards (It's Not Good News)," *Forbes,* June 23, 2016, https://www.forbes.com/sites/kimelsesser/2016/06/23/the-truth-about-womens-impact-on-corporate-boards-its-not-good-news/#5ca473375ecb.

24. "Catalyst, Pyramid: Women in S&P 500 Companies," January 17, 2018, http://www.catalyst.org/knowledge/sp-pyramids-methodology.

25. M. B. Sauter and S. Stebbins, "America's Most Hated Companies," *Yahoo Finance,* January 10, 2017, https://finance.yahoo.com/news/america-most-hated-companies-110032495.html.

26. G. Bhalla, "Soulful Leadership Is Vital for Customer Well-Being," *Forbes,* April 26, 2017, https://www.forbes.com/sites/forbescoachescouncil/2017/04/26/soulful-leadership-is-vital-for-customer-well-being/#77331be5b611.

27. See I. Schenkler, "United Airlines Should've Known That Blaming the Victim Always Backfires," *Fortune,* April 13, 2017, http://fortune.com/2017/04/13/united-airlines-ceo-response-david-dao/; J. Creswell and S. Maheshwari, "United Grapples with PR Crisis over Videos of Man Being Dragged off Plane," *The New York Times*, April 11, 2017, https://www.nytimes.com/2017/04/11/business/united-airline-passenger-overbooked-flights.html.

28. J. Creswell and S. Maheshwari, "United Grapples with PR Crisis over Videos of Man Being Dragged off Plane," *The New York Times,* April 11, 2017, https://www.nytimes.com/2017/04/11/business/united-airline-passenger-overbooked-flights.html.

29. J. Creswell and S. Maheshwari, "United Grapples with PR Crisis over Videos of Man Being Dragged off Plane," *The New York Times,* April 11, 2017, https://www.nytimes.com/2017/04/11/business/united-airline-passenger-overbooked-flights.html.

30. J. Creswell and S. Maheshwari, "United Grapples with PR Crisis over Videos of Man Being Dragged off Plane," *The New York Times,* April 11, 2017, https://www.nytimes.com/2017/04/11/business/united-airline-passenger-overbooked-flights.html.

31. G. Bhalla, "Soulful Leadership Is Vital for Customer Well-Being," *Forbes,* April 26, 2017, https://www.forbes.com/sites/forbescoachescouncil/2017/04/26/soulful-leadership-is-vital-for-customer-well-being/#77331be5b611.

32. See, for example, M. Gottfried, "E-Commerce Is behind Pier 1's Dive," *The Wall Street Journal,* December 18, 2015, p. C8; S. Kapner, S. Nassauer, and L. Stevens, "Malls Reel as Web Roars," *The Wall Street Journal,* December 24, 2015, pp. A1, A2.

33. H. Tabuchi, "Stores Suffer from a Shift of Behavior in Buyers," *The New York Times,* August 14, 2015, B1. For more on this subject, see J. Hamblin, "Buy Experiences, Not Things," *The Atlantic,* October 7, 2014, www.theatlantic.com/business/archive/2014/10/buy-experiences/381132 (accessed March 7, 2016).

34. "Kayak Paddle Achieves Sought-After Aesthetics Using Carbon Fiber Recycled from Aircraft Production," RTP Company, accessed February 6, 2018, https://www.rtpcompany.com/kayak-paddle/.

35. United States Department of Labor: Bureau of Labor Statistics, https://www.bls.gov/news.release/union2.nr0.htm.

36. *United States Department of Labor: Bureau of Labor Statistics,* https://www.bls.gov/news.release/union2.nr0.htm.

37. *United States Department of Labor: Bureau of Labor Statistics,* https://www.bls.gov/news.release/union2.nr0.htm.

38. "Town Is Reeling after New Factory Shuts Its Doors," *San Francisco Chronicle,* November 8, 2013, p. D4, reprinted from *The New York Times.*

39. M. Day, "More than 100 Cities Start Courting Amazon for Its HQ2," *Chicago Tribune,* September 15, 2017, http://www.chicagotribune.com/business/ct-amazon-hq2-bidders-20170915-story.html.

40. N. Wingfield, "Amazon Chooses 20 Finalists for Second Headquarters," January 18, 2018, https://www.nytimes.com/2018/01/18/technology/amazon-finalists-headquarters.html; C. V. Bagli, "Amazon Names Newark and New York City as 'HQ2' Finalists," *The New York Times,* January 18, 2018, https://www.nytimes.com/2018/01/18/nyregion/amazon-headquarters-finalists.html.

41. N. Wingfield, "Amazon Chooses 20 Finalists for Second Headquarters," January 18, 2018, https://www.nytimes.com/2018/01/18/technology/amazon-finalists-headquarters.html; C. V. Bagli, "Amazon Names Newark and New York City as 'HQ2' Finalists," *The New York Times,* January 18, 2018, https://www.nytimes.com/2018/01/18/nyregion/amazon-headquarters-finalists.html.

42. Wingfield, "Amazon Chooses 20 Finalists for Second Headquarters," January 18, 2018, https://www.nytimes.com/2018/01/18/technology/amazon-finalists-headquarters.html.

43. B. Casselman, "Promising Billions to Amazon: Is It a Good Deal for Cities?" *The New York Times,* January 26, 2018, https://www.nytimes.com/2018/01/26/business/economy/amazon-finalists-incentives.html.

44. Casselman, "Promising Billions to Amazon: Is It a Good Deal for Cities?" *The New York Times,* January 26, 2018, https://www.nytimes.com/2018/01/26/business/economy/amazon-finalists-incentives.html.

45. D. Shepardson, "U.S. Commercial Drone Use to Expand Tenfold by 2021: Government Agency," *Reuters,* March 21, 2017, https://www.reuters.com/article/us-usa-drones/u-s-commercial-drone-use-to-expand-tenfold-by-2021-government-agency-idUSKBN16S2NM.

46. M. Gay, "Cities Move to Curb Carriages," *The Wall Street Journal,* March 24, 2014, p. A3; N. N. Grynbaum, "City Announces Deal on Carriage Horses in Central Park," *The New York Times,* January 18, 2016, p. A18.

47. M. Vultaggio, "Why Is Everyone Wearing Black Dresses on the 2018 Golden Globes' Red Carpet?" *Newsweek,* January 7, 2018, http://www.newsweek.com/black-dresses-golden-globes-2018-red-carpet-773428.
48. Center for Poverty Research: University of California, Davis https://poverty.ucdavis.edu/faq/what-current-poverty-rate-united-states.
49. "Labor Productivity and Costs," Bureau of Labor Statistics, accessed February 6, 2018, https://www.bls.gov/lpc/prodybar.htm.
50. D. Kopf, " US Productivity Growth Is Negative and Economists Aren't Sure Why," *Quartz,* March 31, 2017, https://qz.com/946675/us-productivity-growth-was-negative-in-2016-and-economists-arent-sure-why/.
51. M. Hanlon, "The Golden Quarter," *Aeon Magazine,* December 2014, https://aeon.co/essays/has-progress-in-science-and-technology-come-to-a-halt (accessed March 3, 2016).
52. Robert J. Gordon, reported in A. Davidson, "Do Technological Advances Determine the Health of Our Economy?" *The New York Times Magazine,* February 21, 2016, pp. 16–20.
53. Hanlon, "The Golden Quarter," *Aeon Magazine,* December 2014, https://aeon.co/essays/has-progress-in-science-and-technology-come-to-a-halt (accessed March 3, 2016).
54. B. Marr, "The Internet of Things (IOT) Will Be Massive in 2018: Here Are the 4 Predictions from IBM," *Forbes,* January 4, 2018, https://www.forbes.com/sites/bernardmarr/2018/01/04/the-internet-of-things-iot-will-be-massive-in-2018-here-are-the-4-predictions-from-ibm/#18a76560edd3.
55. "Gartner Says 8.4 Billion Connected 'Things' Will Be in Use in 2017, up 31 Percent from 2016," *Gartner,* February 7, 2017, https://www.gartner.com/newsroom/id/3598917.
56. See D. Palmer, "An Internet of Things 'Crime Harvest' Is Coming unless Security Problems Are Fixed," *ZDNet,* January 25, 2018, http://www.zdnet.com/article/an-internet-of-things-crime-harvest-is-coming-unless-security-problems-are-fixed/; A. Meola, "What Is the Internet of Things (IoT)?" *Business Insider,* December 19, 2016, http://www.businessinsider.com/what-is-the-internet-of-things-definition-2016-8.
57. R. Smithers, "Strangers Can Talk to Your Child through 'Connected' Toys, Investigation Finds," *The Guardian,* November 14, 2017, https://www.theguardian.com/technology/2017/nov/14/retailers-urged-to-withdraw-toys-that-allow-hackers-to-talk-to-children.
58. "Business Is Embracing Internet of Things as Most Important Technology, Says New Study," *Forbes,* January 16, 2018, https://www.forbes.com/sites/forbespr/2018/01/16/business-is-embracing-internet-of-things-as-most-important-technology-says-new-study/2/#3373cdcd578e.
59. See "The First Study of Self-Driving Car Crash Rates Suggests They Are Safer," *Fast Company,* January 11, 2016, https://www.fastcompany.com/3055356/the-first-study-of-self-driving-car-crash-rates-suggests-they-are-safer; "Driverless Cars Will Not Save Cities from Either Traffic or Infrastructure Expense," *The Economist,* January 20, 2018, p. 68.
60. J. Weiland and A. Crow, "How Safe Are Self-Driving Cars?" *HuffPost,* May 2, 2017, https://www.huffingtonpost.com/entry/how-safe-are-self-driving-cars_us_5908ba48e4b03b105b44bc6b.
61. D. Bennett, "'Peak Car' and the Beginning of the End of the Commute," *Bloomberg Businessweek,* November 13, 2013, www.bloomberg.com/bw/articles/2013-11-13/peak-car-and-the-beginning-of-the-end-of-the-commute (accessed February 19, 2016).
62. D. Pitt, Associated Press, "Piano Stores Closing as Fewer Children Taking Up Instrument," *Nevada Appeal,* January 4, 2015, p. C7.
63. Associated Press, "Casinos Woo Coveted Millennials with Tattoos, Mixed Martial Arts," *San Francisco Chronicle,* February 6, 2016, p. A6.
64. See S. Miller, "Americans Show Less Acceptance of LGBTQ People, Survey Says," *Arizona Republic,* January 26, 2018, p. 2B.
65. M. Robinson, J. Berke, and S. Gould, "This Map Shows Every State That Has Legalized Marijuana," *Business Insider,* January 23, 2018, http://www.businessinsider.com/legal-marijuana-states-2018-1.
66. See M. McMillen, "Is Drinking Diet Soda a Health Risk?" *webmd health news,* May 5, 2017, https://www.webmd.com/diet/news/20170505/diet-soda-health-risks.
67. Y. Alcindor, "Killer Diseases Creeping Back," *USA Today,* April 7, 2014, p. 1A; Y. Alcindor, "Diseases Get Second Life," *USA Today,* April 7, 2014, p. 5A.
68. See "Adult Obesity Facts," Centers for Disease Control and Prevention, August 29, 2017, https://www.cdc.gov/obesity/data/adult.html.
69. M. Schweitzer and E. E. Levine, "The Affective and Interpersonal Consequences of Obesity," *Organizational Behavior and Human Decision Processes* 127 (2015), pp. 66–84.
70. B. Wolf, "9 Fast Food Trends for 2016," *QSR Magazine,* January 2016, https://www.qsrmagazine.com/reports/9-fast-food-trends-2016 (accessed February 20, 2016).
71. G. Toppo and P. Overberg, "1-Person Households Grow More Common," *USA Today,* August 28, 2013, p. 3A; N. Shah, "'Baby Bust' Starts to Ease," *The Wall Street Journal,* September 5, 2013, p. B3; Pew Research Center tabulations of U.S. Census data, in "Fewer Putting a Ring on It," *USA Today,* March 25, 2014, p. 1A.
72. S. Colby and J. Ortman, "Projections of the Size and Composition of the U.S. Population: 2014 to 2060," United States Census Bureau, March 2015, https://census.gov/content/dam/Census/library/publications/2015/demo/p25-1143.pdf.
73. M. Meehan, "The Top Trends Shaping Business for 2017," *Forbes,* December 15, 2016, https://www.forbes.com/sites/marymeehan/2016/12/15/the-top-trends-shaping-business-for-2017/#4fce41646a8a.
74. E. Lipton and B. Meier, "Under Trump, Coal Mining Gets New Life on U.S. Lands," *The New York Times,* August 6, 2016, https://www.nytimes.com/2017/08/06/us/politics/under-trump-coal-mining-gets-new-life-on-us-lands.html.
75. GAO, U.S. Government Accountability Office, accessed October 2, 2018, https://www.gao.gov/key_issues/climate_change_funding_management/issue_summar.
76. *Clements Worldwide,* accessed October 2, 2018, https://www.clements.com/sites/default/files/resources/The-Most-Litigious-Countries-in-the-World.pdf.
77. L. Elliott, "Brexit Is a Rejection of Globalization," *The Guardian,* June 26, 2016, https://www.theguardian.com/business/2016/jun/26/brexit-is-the-rejection-of-globalisation.
78. "Google Pressed on Searches," *San Francisco Chronicle,* April 1, 2014, p. D2.
79. M. Scott, "Google Takes New Steps to Comply with European Privacy Ruling," *The New York Times,* February 12, 2016, p. B3.
80. K. Wiggins, S. Bodoni, and J. Hodges, "Google Girds for England Battle over 'Right to Be Forgotten,'" *BusinessDay,* January 19, 2018, https://www.businesslive.co.za/bd/world/europe/2018-01-19-google-girds-for-england-battle-over-right-to-be-forgotten/.
81. T. Warren, "Uber Loses Its License to Operate in London," *The Verge,* September 22, 2017, https://www.theverge.com/2017/9/22/16349070/uber-london-tfl-license.
82. L. Josephs, "International Tourism Is Booming, but Not to the U.S." *CNBC,* January 17, 2018, https://www.cnbc.com/2018/01/17/international-tourism-is-booming-but-not-to-the-us.html.
83. S. Saul, "As Flow of Foreign Students Wanes, U.S. Universities Feel the Sting," *The New York Times,* January 2, 2018, https://www.nytimes.com/2018/01/02/us/international-enrollment-drop.html.
84. Data from Secretary of Education Arne Duncan, reported in D. Skorton and G. Altschuler, "America's Foreign Language Deficit," *Forbes,* August 27, 2012, www.forbes.com/sites/collegeprose/2012/08/27/americas-foreign-language-deficit/#51f2b679382f (accessed February 20, 2016).
85. A. Friedman, "America's Lacking Language Skills," *The Atlantic,* May 10, 2015, www.theatlantic.com/education/archive/2015/05/filling-americas-language-education-potholes/392876/ (accessed February 20, 2016).
86. See D. Mulkeen, "Bribery and International Business: What Role Does Culture Play?" *Communicaid,* January 3, 2016, https://www.communicaid.com/cross-cultural-training/blog/bribery-international-business-what-role-does-culture-play/; K. Gerasimova, "The Critical Role of Ethics and Culture in Business Globalization," *gothamCulture,*

September 29, 2016, https://gothamculture.com/2016/09/29/critical-role-ethics-culture-business-globalization/.

87. Survey of 764 employees by Stroz Friedberg, *On the Pulse: Information Security Risk in American Business*, January 2014, www.strozfriedberg.com/wp-content/uploads/2014/01/Stroz-Friedberg_On-the-Pulse_Information-Security-in-American-Business.pdf.

88. L. T. Hosmer, *The Ethics of Management* (Homewood, IL: Irwin, 1987). See also S. Welch, "The Uh-Oh Feeling," *O Magazine,* November 2007, pp. 117–120.

89. M. Spector and A. Harder, "VW's U.S. Chief Apologizes, Says Engineers at Fault," *The Wall Street Journal,* October 9, 2015, pp. B1, B2.

90. C. Atiyeh, "Everything You Need to Know about the VW Diesel-Emissions Scandal," *Car and Driver,* October 24, 2017, https://blog.caranddriver.com/everything-you-need-to-know-about-the-vw-diesel-emissions-scandal/.

91. C. Atiyeh, "Everything You Need to Know about the VW Diesel-Emissions Scandal," *Car and Driver,* October 24, 2017, https://blog.caranddriver.com/everything-you-need-to-know-about-the-vw-diesel-emissions-scandal/.

92. B. Zycher, "The Volkswagen Emissions Scandal and the Bureaucratic Pursuit of Power," *Investors Business Daily,* October 18, 2017, https://www.investors.com/politics/commentary/the-volkswagen-emissions-scandal-and-the-bureaucratic-pursuit-of-power/.

93. E. D. Lawrence, "VW Executive Pleads Guilty in Emissions Scandal," *USA Today,* August 4, 2017, https://www.usatoday.com/story/money/cars/2017/08/04/vw-executive-pleads-guilty-emissions-scandal/539754001/.

94. B. Lysaght and C. Remondini, "Volkswagen's Stock Rebound Leaves Daimler and BMW in the Dust," *Bloomberg,* December 18, 2018, https://www.bloomberg.com/news/articles/2017-12-19/volkswagen-s-stock-rebound-leaves-daimler-and-bmw-in-the-dust.

95. E. Behrmann, "Volkswagen Apologizes for Testing of Diesel Fumes on Monkeys," *Bloomberg,* January 28, 2018, https://www.bloomberg.com/news/articles/2018-01-28/volkswagen-apologizes-for-testing-of-diesel-fumes-on-monkeys.

96. *Falling Short? College Learning and Career Success. Selected Findings from Online Surveys of Employers and College Students Conducted on Behalf of the Association of American Colleges & Universities,* January 20, 2015, Hart Research Associates, Washington, DC, https://www.aacu.org/leap/public-opinion-research/2015-survey-results (accessed March 8, 2016).

97. See J. McGregor, "Ethical Misconduct, by the Numbers," *The Washington Post,* February 4, 2014, https://www.washingtonpost.com/news/on-leadership/wp/2014/02/04/ethical-misconduct-by-the-numbers/?utm_term=.c5b5cdaadd6f.

98. "Is Your Doctor on a Drug Maker's Payroll?" editorial, *USA Today,* February 21, 2014, p. 6A.

99. See A. Schwatz, "The 5 Most Common Unethical Behaviors in the Workplace," January 26, 2015, https://www.bizjournals.com/philadelphia/blog/guest-comment/2015/01/most-common-unethical-behaviors-in-the.html.

100. L. M. Katz, "Monitoring Employee Productivity: Proceed with Caution," *SHRM Society for Human Resource Management,* June 1, 2015, https://www.shrm.org/hr-today/news/hr-magazine/pages/0615-employee-monitoring.aspx.

101. B. J. Tepper, "Consequences of Abusive Supervision," *Academy of Management Journal,* volume 43, issue 2, April 2000, p. 178.

102. See R. Vogel, and M. S. Mitchell, "The Motivational Effects of Diminished Self-Esteem for Employees Who Experience Abusive Supervision," *Journal of Management,* September 2017, pp. 2218–2251; J. D. Mackey, R. E. Frieder, J. R. Brees, and M. J. Martinko, "Abusive Supervision: A Meta-Analysis and Empirical Review," *Journal of Management,* July 2017, pp. 1940–1965.

103. See J. Murray, "5 Ways to Protect Your Business from Employee Theft," *The Balance,* February 14, 2017, https://www.thebalance.com/protect-business-from-employee-theft-3573209.

104. See Y. Zhang and T. C. Bednall, "Antecedents of Abusive Supervision: A Meta-Analytic Review," *Journal of Business Ethics,* December 2016, pp. 455–471.

105. M. S. Mitchell, M. D. Baer, M. L. Ambrose, R. Folger, and N. F. Palmer, "Cheating under Pressure: A Self-Protection Model of Workplace Cheating Behavior," *Journal of Applied Psychology,* January 2018, p. 54.

106. See "8 Astonishing Stats on Academic Cheating," *Open Education Database,* accessed January 30, 2018, http://oedb.org/ilibrarian/8-astonishing-stats-on-academic-cheating.

107. R. Pérez-Peña, "Studies Find More Students Cheating, With High Achievers No Exception," *The New York Times,* September 7, 2012, http://www.nytimes.com/2012/09/08/education/studies-show-more-students-cheat-even-high-achievers.html.

108. See M. S. Mitchell, M. D. Baer, M. L. Ambrose, R. Folger, and N. F. Palmer, "Cheating under Pressure: A Self-Protection Model of Workplace Cheating Behavior," *Journal of Applied Psychology,* January 2018, pp. 54–73.

109. See A. Schwatz, "The 5 Most Common Unethical Behaviors in the Workplace," January 26, 2015, https://www.bizjournals.com/philadelphia/blog/guest-comment/2015/01/most-common-unethical-behaviors-in-the.html.

110. B. Kabanoff, "Equity, Equality, Power, and Conflict," *Academy of Management Review,* April 1991, pp. 416–441.

111. Example given by accounting professor D. Jordan Lowe, in "Making Ethical Decisions: Mood Matters," November 13, 2015, W. P. Carey School of Business, Arizona State University, http://research.wpcarey.asu.edu/accounting/making-ethical-decisions-mood-matters.

112. D. Fritzsche and H. Baker, "Linking Management Behavior to Ethical Philosophy: An Empirical Investigation," *Academy of Management Journal,* March 1984, pp. 166–175.

113. J. P. Dietrich, A. L. Van Gaest, S. A. Strickland, and M. R. Arkoosh, "The Impact of Temperature Stress and Pesticide Exposure on Mortality and Disease Susceptibility of Endangered Pacific Salmon," *Chemosphere,* February 19, 2014, www.ncbi.nlm.nih.gov/pubmed/24559935 (accessed March 31, 2016).

114. Privacy Rights Clearinghouse, "Workplace Privacy and Employee Monitoring," revised January 2016, www.privacyrights.org/workplace-privacy-and-employee-monitoring (accessed March 31, 2016).

115. B. Van Voris, "SAC's Mathew Martoma Seeks Freedom in Appeals Court Bid," *Bloomberg Businessweek,* October 28, 2015, www.bloomberg.com/news/articles/2015-10-28/sac-s-mathew-martoma-seeks-freedom-in-appeals-court-bid (accessed February 20, 2016).

116. W. Pavlo, "White Collar Cases to Watch in 2017," *Forbes,* January 5, 2017, https://www.forbes.com/sites/walterpavlo/2017/01/05/white-collar-cases-to-watch-in-2017/#739083b12d04.

117. See S. Clifford and C. Moynihan, "Martin Shkreli Is Found Guilty of Fraud," *The New York Times,* August 4, 2017, https://www.nytimes.com/2017/08/04/business/dealbook/martin-shkreli-guilty.html; M. Abadi, "Martin Shkreli Is in Prison—and Could Face a Harsher Punishment when He's Sentenced for Securities Fraud Next Year," *Business Insider,* September 14, 2017, http://www.businessinsider.com/martin-shkreli-inmate-facebook-post-2017-9.

118. F. Norris, "Goodbye to Reforms of 2002," *The New York Times,* November 6, 2009, pp. B1, B6.

119. See "Has Sarbanes-Oxley Failed?" *The New York Times,* July 24, 2012, www.nytimes.com/roomfordebate/2012/07/24/has-sarbanes-oxley-failed?action=click&module=Search&region=searchResults%230&version=&url=http%3A%2F%2Fquery.nytimes.com%2Fsearch%2Fsitesearch%2F%23%2FSarbOx%2F (accessed March 31, 2016).

120. L. Moyer, "Monsanto Will Pay $80 Million to SEC," *The New York Times,* February 10, 2016, p. B3.

121. F. J. Evans, quoted in C. S. Stewart, "A Question of Ethics: How to Teach Them?" *The New York Times,* March 21, 2004, sec. 3, p. 11.

122. See W. R. Hason, J. R. Moore, C. Bachleda, A. Canterbury, C. Franco Jr., A. Marion, and C. Schreiber, "Theory of Moral Development of Business Students: Case Studies in Brazil, North America, and

Morocco," *Academy of Management Learning & Education,* September 2017, pp. 393–414.
123. S. H. E. Costa and R. David, "Goldman, JPMorgan Said to Fire 30 Analysts for Cheating on Tests," *BloombergBusiness*, October 16, 2015, www.bloomberg.com/news/articles/2015-10-16/goldman-sachs-said-to-dismiss-20-analysts-for-cheating-on-tests (accessed March 8, 2016).
124. L. Kohlberg, "Moral Stages and Moralization: The Cognitive Developmental Approach," in T. Lickona, ed., *Moral Development and Behavior: Theory, Research, and Social Issues* (New York: Holt, Rinehart and Winston, 1976), pp. 31–53; and J. W. Graham, "Leadership, Moral Development and Citizenship Behavior," *Business Ethics Quarterly,* January 1995, pp. 43–54.
125. Adapted in part from W. E. Stead, D. L. Worrell, and J. Garner Stead, "An Integrative Model for Understanding and Managing Ethical Behavior in Business Organizations," *Journal of Business Ethics,* March 1990, pp. 233–242. Also see D. Lange, "A Multidimensional Conceptualization of Organizational Corruption Control," *Academy of Management Review,* July 2008, pp. 710–729; and M. J. Pearsall and A. P. J. Ellis, "Thick as Thieves: The Effects of Ethical Orientation and Psychological Safety on Unethical Team Behavior," *Journal of Applied Psychology* 96 (2011), pp. 401–411.
126. D. Meinert, "Creating an Ethical Workplace," *Society for Human Resource Management,* April 1, 2014, https://www.shrm.org/hr-today/news/hr-magazine/pages/0414-ethical-workplace-culture.aspx.
127. T. R. Mitchell, D. Daniels, H. Hopper, J. George-Falvy, and G. R. Ferris, "Perceived Correlates of Illegal Behavior in Organizations," *Journal of Business Ethics,* April 1996, pp. 439–455.
128. "Whistle-Blower Law Protects Outside Consults, Too," *San Francisco Chronicle,* March 5, 2014, p. A6.
129. "How to File a Safety and Health Complaint," Occupational Safety and Health Administration, accessed February 7, 2018, https://www.osha.gov/workers/file_complaint.html.
130. https://www.irs.gov/compliance/whistleblower-informant-award (accessed January 26, 2018).
131. "The Age of the Whistleblower," *The Economist,* December 5, 2015, www.economist.com/news/business/21679455-life-getting-better-those-who-expose-wrongdoing-companies-continue-fight (accessed February 24, 2016).
132. Ethics Resource Center, *National Business Ethics Survey of the U.S. Workforce,* 2013 (Arlington, VA: Ethics Resource Center, 2014).
133. See B. Protess, "He Leaked a Photo of Rick Perry Hugging a Coal Executive. Then He Lost His Job," *The New York Times,* January 17, 2018, https://www.nytimes.com/2018/01/17/business/rick-perry-energy-photographer.html; S. Neuman, "Photographer Says He Lost His Job after Leaking Pictures of Rick Perry and Coal CEO," *NPR,* January 18, 2018, https://www.npr.org/sections/thetwo-way/2018/01/18/578791199/photographer-says-he-lost-his-job-after-leaking-pictures-of-rick-perry-and-coal.
134. M. Hand, "Releasing This Picture Got a Department of Energy Photographer Fired. He Doesn't Regret It," *Think Progress,* January 22, 2018, https://thinkprogress.org/energy-department-whistleblower-b1c6606a5c67/.
135. See B. Protess, "He Leaked a Photo of Rick Perry Hugging a Coal Executive. Then He Lost His Job," *The New York Times,* January 17, 2018, https://www.nytimes.com/2018/01/17/business/rick-perry-energy-photographer.html; S. Neuman, "Photographer Says He Lost His Job after Leaking Pictures of Rick Perry and Coal CEO," *NPR,* January 18, 2018, https://www.npr.org/sections/thetwo-way/2018/01/18/578791199/photographer-says-he-lost-his-job-after-leaking-pictures-of-rick-perry-and-coal.
136. "Whistleblowers Are More Important Than Ever in Keeping Our Nation Unified under the Rule of Law," *Whistleblower Aid,* accessed February 6, 2018, *https://whistlebloweraid.org/.*
137. M. Hand, "Releasing This Picture Got a Department of Energy Photographer Fired. He Doesn't Regret It," *Think Progress,* January 22, 2018, https://thinkprogress.org/energy-department-whistleblower-b1c6606a5c67/.
138. A. Tugend, "Opting to Blow the Whistle or Choosing to Walk Away," *The New York Times,* September 21, 2013, p. B5.
139. S. Lebowitz, "On the 10th Anniversary of TOMS, Its Founder Talks Stepping Down, Bringing in Private Equity, and Why Giving Away Shoes Provides a Competitive Advantage," *Business Insider,* June 15, 2016, http://www.businessinsider.com/toms-blake-mycoskie-talks-growing-a-business-while-balancing-profit-with-purpose-2016-6.
140. N. F. Taylor, "What Is Corporate Social Responsibility?" *Business News Daily,* June 19, 2015, www.businessnewsdaily.com/4679-corporate-social-responsibility.html (accessed February 23, 2016).
141. A. B. Carroll, "Managing Ethically with Global Stakeholders: A Present and Future Challenge," *Academy of Management Executive,* May 2004, p. 118. Also see A. B. Carroll, "Corporate Social Responsibility: The Centerpiece of Competing and Complementary Frameworks," *Organizational Dynamics,* April–June 2015, pp. 87–96.
142. See "How Emerging Multinationals Are Embracing Social Responsibility," *Knowledge@Wharton,* November 12, 2015, http://knowledge.wharton.upenn.edu/article/why-emerging-multinationals-are-embracing-social-responsibility (accessed February 24, 2016).
143. M. Friedman, *Capitalism and Freedom* (Chicago: University of Chicago Press, 1962). See also S. Gallagher, "A Strategic Response to Friedman's Critique of Business Ethics," *Journal of Business Strategy,* January 2005, pp. 55–60.
144. P. Samuelson, "Love That Corporation," *Mountain Bell Magazine,* Spring 1971.
145. See S. Hafenbrädl and D. Waeger, "Ideology and the Micro-Foundations of CSR: Why Executives Believe in the Business Case for CSR and How This Affects Their CSR Engagements," *Academy of Management Journal,* August 2017, pp. 1582–1606; O. Farooq, D. E. Rupp, and M. Farooq, "The Multiple Pathways through which Internal and External Corporate Social Responsibility Influence Organizational Identification and Multifoci Outcomes: The Moderating Role of Cultural and Social Orientations," *Academy of Management Journal,* June 2017, pp. 954–985.
146. D. Pontefract, "Salesforce CEO Marc Benioff Says the Business of Business Is Improving the State of the World," *Forbes,* January 7, 2017, https://www.forbes.com/sites/danpontefract/2017/01/07/salesforce-ceo-marc-benioff-says-the-business-of-business-is-improving-the-state-of-the-world/#3b4190ee7eb0.
147. "Sustainable Company/Sustainable World: Salesforce.com Sustainability Report FY2012," *Salesforce.com,* San Francisco, www.salesforce.com/assets/pdf/misc/SustainabilityReport.pdf (accessed February 24, 2016). See also J. Temple, "Salesforce's Philosophy: Share," *San Francisco Chronicle,* November 18, 2013, pp. A1, A9; J. Garofoli, "Big Push for Tech to Fight Poverty," *San Francisco Chronicle,* March 7, 2014, pp. A1, A11.
148. "STEM Education," *salesforce.org,* accessed February 7, 2018, http://www.salesforce.org/grants/stem-education/.
149. D. Gallagher, "Making It Rain at Salesforce.com," *The Wall Street Journal,* February 26, 2015, p. C8.
150. L. Saad and J. M. Jones, "U.S. Concern about Global Warming at Eight-Year High," *Gallup News,* March 16, 2016, http://news.gallup.com/poll/190010/concern-global-warming-eight-year-high.aspx.
151. Intergovernmental Panel on Climate Change, United Nations, *Climate Change 2013: The Physical Science Basis—Summary for Policymakers*, September 28, 2013, www.climatechange2013.org/images/report/WG1AR5_SPM_FINAL.pdf (accessed February 23, 2016).
152. Definitions adapted from U.S. Environmental Protection Agency, "Climate Change: Basic Information," February 23, 2016, https://www3.epa.gov/climatechange/basics/ (accessed February 23, 2016).
153. M. Hume, *Why We Disagree about Climate Change: Understanding Controversy, Inaction, and Opportunity* (Cambridge, UK: Cambridge University Press, 2010).
154. C. Davenport, "Threat to Bottom Line Spurs Action on Climate," *The New York Times,* January 24, 2014, pp. A1, A21.
155. See The Coca-Cola Company, "2020 Sustainability Goals: Progress Update," August 17, 2017, http://www.coca-colacompany.com/stories/sustainability/2017/2020-sustainability-goals.

156. See "Green Evolution: How Business Is Joining the Environmental Movement," *Knowledge@Wharton,* December 10, 2015, http://knowledge.wharton.upenn.edu/article/green-evolution-how-business-is-joining-the-environmental-vanguard (accessed February 23, 2016).
157. A. G. Robinson and D. M. Schroeder, "Greener and Cheaper," *The Wall Street Journal,* March 23, 2009, p. R4; R. Farzad, "The Scrappiest Car Manufacturer in America," *Bloomberg Businessweek,* June 6, 2011, pp. 68–74.
158. D. Palmquist, "Conservancy Science at Dow's Freeport, TX, Site," The Nature Conservancy, www.nature.org/science-in-action/science-features/dow-analyses.xml (accessed March 31, 2016).
159. Gretchen Daily, quoted in C. Lochhead, "Ecologists Try in Quiet Ways to Save the Planet," *San Francisco Chronicle,* January 5, 2014, pp. A1, A8.
160. R. LeBlanc, "E-Waste Recycling Facts and Figures," *the balance,* March 26, 2017, https://www.thebalance.com/e-waste-recycling-facts-and-figures-2878189.
161. R. LeBlanc, "E-Waste Recycling Facts and Figures," *the balance,* March 26, 2017, https://www.thebalance.com/e-waste-recycling-facts-and-figures-2878189.
162. Intergovernmental Panel on Climate Change, United Nations, "Climate Change 2014: Impacts, Adaptation, and Vulnerability—Summary for Policymakers," March 31, 2014, http://ipcc-wg2.gov/AR5/images/uploads/IPCC_WG2AR5_SPM_Approved.pdf (accessed February 23, 2016). See account of this report in J. Gillis, "U.N. Says Lag in Confronting Climate Woes Will Be Costly," *The New York Times,* January 17, 2014, p. A8.
163. See also W. Mauldin, "Nations Delay Climate Pledges," *The Wall Street Journal,* August 24, 2015, p. A9; "Proof That a Price on Carbon Works," editorial, *The New York Times,* January 19, 2016, p. A22; M. Urban and L. Deegan, "T-Shirt Weather in the Arctic," *The New York Times,* February 6, 2016, p. A21.
164. "#2 Bill Gates," *Forbes,* https://www.forbes.com/profile/bill-gates/#757fdb7d689f (accessed October 3, 2018).
165. C. Clifford, "These 14 Billionaires Just Promised to Give Away More than Half of Their Money Like Bill Gates and Warren Buffett," *cnbc,* May 31, 2017, https://www.cnbc.com/2017/05/31/14-billionaires-signed-bill-gates-and-warren-buffetts-giving-pledge.html.
166. "The 2016 Deloitte Millennial Survey: Winning over the Next Generation of Leaders," Deloitte, https://www2.deloitte.com/content/dam/Deloitte/global/Documents/About-Deloitte/gx-millenial-survey-2016-exec-summary.pdf (accessed January 17, 2018).
167. "Increasing Employee Reporting Free from Retaliation," *ECI Ethics and Compliance Initiative,* http://www.ethics.org/ecihome/research/nbes/nbes-reports/reporting-retaliation (accessed January 17, 2018).
168. "Is Good Still Growing?" 2017 Conscious Consumer Spending Index, *Good Must Grow,* http://www.goodmustgrow.com/ (accessed January 17, 2018).
169. M. Whittaker, "Ethical Investing Continues to Grow," *U.S. News and World Report,* January 27, 2017 https://money.usnews.com/investing/articles/2017-01-27/ethical-investing-continues-to-grow.
170. K. Jiang, J. Hu, Y. Hong, H. Liao, and S. Liu, "Do It Well and Do It Right: The Impact of Service Climate and Ethical Climate on Business Performance and the Boundary Conditions," *Journal of Applied Psychology,* November 2016, pp. 1553–1568.
171. A. Nusca, "Equifax Stock Has Plunged 18.4% since It Revealed Massive Breach," *Fortune,* September 11, 2017, http://fortune.com/2017/09/11/equifax-stock-cybersecurity-breach/.
172. E. Winkler, "Wynn Resorts Is Test of Tolerance," *The Wall Street Journal,* January 30, 2018, p. B12.
173. P. Georgescu, "Doing the Right Thing Is Just Profitable," *Forbes,* July 26, 2017, https://www.forbes.com/sites/petergeorgescu/2017/07/26/doing-the-right-thing-is-just-profitable/#257bfc4b7488, July 26, 2018; "The Just 100 America's Best Corporate Citizens," *Forbes,* https://www.forbes.com/just-companies/#74a99aff2bf0.
174. H. Syse of the Peace Research Institute, Oslo, Norway, quoted in "Special Report on Business Ethics: Enhancing Corporate Governance," press release, *Knowledge@Wharton,* February 25, 2016, http://knowledge.wharton.upenn.edu/special-report/special-report-on-business-ethics-enhancing-corporate-governance/?utm_source=kw_newsletter&utm_medium=email&utm_campaign=2016-02-25 (accessed February 26, 2016). The report is "Special Report on Business Ethics: Enhancing Corporate Governance," February 2016, *Knowledge@Wharton* and AKO Foundation, http://d1c25a6gwz7q5e.cloudfront.net/reports/2016-02-25-Enhancing-Corporate-Governance.pdf (accessed February 26, 2016).
175. D. Barton and M. Wiseman, "Where Boards Fall Short," *Harvard Business Review,* January–February 2015, pp. 99–104; T. Lee, "Directors Need Directions," *San Francisco Chronicle,* February 28, 2016, pp. D1, D6.
176. K. S. Nash, J. S. Lublin, and A. Andriotis, "Boards Scramble to Defuse Cyberrisks," *The Wall Street Journal,* January 11, 2018, pp. B1, B6.
177. See "Fox Says It Was Aware of Bill O'Reilly's Harassment Settlement when It Extended His Contract," *Fortune,* October 21, 2017, http://fortune.com/2017/10/21/fox-aware-bill-oreilly-harassment-settlement-extended-contract/; L. Shen, "The 10 Biggest Business Scandals of 2017," *Fortune,* December 31, 2017, http://fortune.com/2017/12/31/biggest-corporate-scandals-misconduct-2017-pr/.
178. R. Hurley, "Trust Me," *The Wall Street Journal,* October 24, 2011, p. R4.
179. These suggestions were partly based on K. Quindlen, "19 Easy and Immediate Ways You Can Live a More Ethical Life," *Thought Catalog,* August 18, 2015, https://thoughtcatalog.com/kim-quindlen/2015/08/19-easy-and-immediate-ways-you-can-live-a-more-ethical-life.
180. B. L. Fredrickson, *Positivity* (New York: Three Rivers Press, 2009), p. 70.
181. "5 'Life Hacks' to Live More Ethically in 2017," *The Ethics Centre,* January 11, 2017, http://www.ethics.org.au/on-ethics/blog/january-2017/5-life-hacks-to-live-more-ethically-in-2017.
182. "5 'Life Hacks' to Live More Ethically in 2017," *The Ethics Centre,* January 11, 2017, http://www.ethics.org.au/on-ethics/blog/january-2017/5-life-hacks-to-live-more-ethically-in-2017.
183. "5 'Life Hacks' to Live More Ethically in 2017," *The Ethics Centre,* January 11, 2017, http://www.ethics.org.au/on-ethics/blog/january-2017/5-life-hacks-to-live-more-ethically-in-2017.
184. K. Quindlen, "19 Easy and Immediate Ways You Can Live a More Ethical Life," *Thought Catalog,* August 18, 2015, https://thoughtcatalog.com/kim-quindlen/2015/08/19-easy-and-immediate-ways-you-can-live-a-more-ethical-life.
185. The last two suggestions were taken from R. Amster, "9 Tips to Help You Strengthen Your Integrity," *Success,* August 16, 2017, https://www.success.com/article/9-tips-to-help-you-strengthen-your-integrity/.
186. Quindlen, "19 Easy and Immediate Ways You Can Live a More Ethical Life," *Thought Catalog,* August 18, 2015, https://thoughtcatalog.com/kim-quindlen/2015/08/19-easy-and-immediate-ways-you-can-live-a-more-ethical-life.
187. H. Chavez, "10 Ways to Become a More Ethical Consumer," *Life Hack,* http://www.lifehack.org/414951/10-ways-to-become-a-more-ethical-consumer (accessed October 3, 2018).
188. "What is the NCAA?" *NCAA,* www.ncaa.org/about/resources/media-center/ncaa-101/what-ncaa (accessed January 12, 2018).
189. "National Collegiate Athletic Association." *Encyclopaedia Britannica online,* Encyclopedia Britannica Inc., n.d. (accessed January 12, 2018).
190. "Amateurism," *NCAA,* www.ncaa.org/amateurism (accessed January 12, 2018).
191. "NCAA Rules and Regulations Guidebook." *NCAA,* www.ncaa.org/sites/default/files/mf-f-michigan-tech-booster-club.pdf (accessed January 11, 2018).
192. "Amateurism." *NCAA,* www.ncaa.org/amateurism (accessed January 18, 2018).

193. M. Tracy and R. Ruiz, "In College Basketball Scandal, Follow the Money . . . and the Shoes," *The New York Times,* September 27, 2017, www.nytimes.com/2017/09/27/sports/ncaabasketball/adidas-pitino-louisville.html.

194. J. Bauer-Wolf, "Black Eye for College Basketball." *Inside Higher Ed,* September 27, 2017, www.insidehighered.com/news/2017/09/27/corruption-charges-are-huge-moment-college-basketball.

195. C. Barnewall, "NBA's 'One-and-Done' Rule May Be on Its Way Out, But What Will Replace It?" *CBS Sports*, November 17, 2017, www.cbssports.com/nba/news/nbas-one-and-done-rule-may-be-on-its-way-out-but-what-will-replace-it/.

196. R. Morello, "What Is the Job of an Assistant Basketball Coach?" *Houston Chronicle*, n.d., work.chron.com/job-assistant-basketball-coach-25728.html.

197. D. Ridpath, "The NCAA Needs to Get Tougher on Corrupt Coaches." *Fortune*, October 3, 2017, fortune.com/2017/10/03/ncaa-basketball-bribery-scandal-rick-pitino/.

198. B. Pascoe, C. Schmidt, and C. Prendergast, "Wildcats Assistant Book Richardson Facing Up to 60 Years if Convicted in Basketball Bribery Scandal," *Arizona Daily Star*, September 27, 2017, www.tucson.com/sports/arizonawildcats/basketball/wildcats-assistant-book-richardson-facing-up-to-years-if-convicted/article_0ac3d4ae-a2c3-11e7-8234-472ac626eb67.html.

199. M. Titus, "An FBI Sting Operation Just Exposed College Basketball's Worst-Kept Secret." *The Ringer*, September 26, 2017, www.theringer.com/2017/9/26/16371360/fbi-sting-operation-assistant-coach-arrests-scandal.

200. J. Branch, "Here, There and Everywhere: Assistant Coaches," *The New York Times*, March 15, 2013, www.nytimes.com/2013/03/16/sports/ncaabasketball/theyre-here-there-and-everywhere-college-basketball-assistants.html.

201. J. Bauer-Wolf, "Black Eye for College Basketball," *Inside Higher Ed,* September 27, 2017, www.insidehighered.com/news/2017/09/27/corruption-charges-are-huge-moment-college-basketball.

202. J. Bauer-Wolf, "Black Eye for College Basketball," *Inside Higher Ed,* September 27, 2017, www.insidehighered.com/news/2017/09/27/corruption-charges-are-huge-moment-college-basketball.

203. B. Pascoe, C. Schmidt, and C. Prendergast, "Wildcats Assistant Book Richardson Facing Up to 60 Years if Convicted in Basketball Bribery Scandal," *Arizona Daily Star*, September 27, 2017, www.tucson.com/sports/arizonawildcats/basketball/wildcats-assistant-book-richardson-facing-up-to-years-if-convicted/article_0ac3d4ae-a2c3-11e7-8234-472ac626eb67.html.

204. M. Galloway, "KU Basketball's Bill Self Speaks Out on 'Dark Week' for College Hoops," *The Topeka Capital-Journal*, September 28, 2017, www.cjonline.com/sports/hawkzone/2017-09-28/ku-basketball-s-bill-self-speaks-out-dark-week-college-hoops.

205. S. Axson, "Louisville Head Coach Rick Pitino Officially Fired," *Sports Illustrated*, October 16, 2017, www.si.com/college-basketball/2017/10/16/louisville-rick-pitino-fired.

206. S. Ryan, "Federal Corruption Investigation Rocks College Basketball," *Chicago Tribune*, September 26, 2017, www.chicagotribune.com/sports/college/ct-ncaa-basketball-coaches-fraud-corruption-20170926-story.html.

207. T. Winter, and P. McCausland, "Federal Bribery Indictments Unsealed Against NCAA Coaches," *NBC News*, November 9, 2017, www.nbcnews.com/news/sports/federal-bribery-indictments-unsealed-against-ncaa-coaches-n819156.

208. J. Bilas, "Why the College Basketball Scandal Won't Get Fixed until the NCAA Pays Athletes," *ESPN,* September 28, 2017, www.espn.com/mens-college-basketball/story/_/id/20841877/until-ncaa-solves-money-problem-pays-athletes-problems-continue.

209. M. Galloway, "KU Basketball's Bill Self Speaks Out on 'Dark Week' for College Hoops," *The Topeka Capital-Journal*, September 28, 2017, www.cjonline.com/sports/hawkzone/2017-09-28/ku-basketball-s-bill-self-speaks-out-dark-week-college-hoops.

210. D. Ridpath, "The NCAA Needs to Get Tougher on Corrupt Coaches," *Fortune*, 3 October 3, 2017, fortune.com/2017/10/03/ncaa-basketball-bribery-scandal-rick-pitino/.

211. D. Ridpath, "The NCAA Needs to Get Tougher on Corrupt Coaches," *Fortune*, 3 October 3, 2017, fortune.com/2017/10/03/ncaa-basketball-bribery-scandal-rick-pitino/.

212. Pascoe, Schmidt, and Prendergast, "Wildcats Assistant Book Richardson Facing Up to 60 Years if Convicted in Basketball Bribery Scandal," *Arizona Daily Star*, September 27, 2017, www.tucson.com/sports/arizonawildcats/basketball/wildcats-assistant-book-richardson-facing-up-to-years-if-convicted/article_0ac3d4ae-a2c3-11e7-8234-472ac626eb67.html.

213. K. Boone, "Oklahoma State Fires Associate Head Coach Lamont Evans amid FBI Investigation," *CBS Sports*, September 28, 2017, www.cbssports.com/college-basketball/news/oklahoma-state-fires-associate-head-coach-lamont-evans-amid-fbi-investigation/.

214. T. Green, "Auburn Assistant Chuck Person Facing 6 Federal Charges Including Corruption," *Alabama Local News*, September 27, 2017, www.al.com/auburnbasketball/index.ssf/2017/09/auburn_assistant_chuck_person.html.

215. F. Fraschilla, "A Coach's View of the Complicated College Basketball Landscape," *ESPN*, November 11, 2017, www.espn.com/mens-college-basketball/story/_/id/21330638/a-coach-view-complicated-college-basketball-landscape.

216. Bauer-Wolf, "Black Eye for College Basketball," *Inside Higher Ed,* September 27, 2017, www.insidehighered.com/news/2017/09/27/corruption-charges-are-huge-moment-college-basketball.

217. J. Bilas, "Why the College Basketball Scandal Won't Get Fixed until the NCAA Pays Athletes," *ESPN,* September 28, 2017, www.espn.com/mens-college-basketball/story/_/id/20841877/until-ncaa-solves-money-problem-pays-athletes-problems-continue.

218. F. Fraschilla, "A Coach's View of the Complicated College Basketball Landscape," *ESPN*, November 11, 2017, www.espn.com/mens-college-basketball/story/_/id/21330638/a-coach-view-complicated-college-basketball-landscape.

219. L. Schnell, "Indictments in College Basketball Fraud Scheme Only Just the Beginning," *USA Today*, 26 Sept. 2017, www.usatoday.com/story/sports/ncaab/2017/09/26/indictments-college-basketball-fraud-scheme-only-just-beginning/705183001/.

220. A. Kamenetz, "A New Look at the Lasting Consequences of Student Debt," *NPR,* April 4, 2017, www.npr.org/sections/ed/2017/04/04/522456671/a-new-look-at-the-lasting-consequences-of-student-debt

221. J. Mitchell, "How to Apply for Student-Debt Forgiveness for Victims of School Fraud," January 20, 2016, http://blogs.wsj.com/briefly/2016/01/20/student-debt-forgiveness-for-victims-of-school-fraud-at-a-glance/

222. D. Douglas-Gabriel, "Trump Administration Is Sitting on Tens of Thousands of Student Debt Forgiveness Claims," *Washington Post,* July 27, 2017, www.washingtonpost.com/news/grade-point/wp/2017/07/27/trump-administration-is-sitting-on-tens-of-thousands-of-student-debt-forgiveness-claims/?utm_term=.d739612fa7ea

223. J. Mitchell, "Thousands Want Student Loans Cancelled," *The Wall Street Journal,* January 21, 2016, p. A3.

CHAPTER 4

1. See Caz, "9 Ways to Prepare and Protect Yourself before Working Abroad," *YTravel,* April 16, 2017, https://www.ytravelblog.com/9-ways-prepare-protect-working-abroad/; A. Shaw, "15 Things You Need to Know about Working Abroad," *The Muse,* accessed February 12, 2018, https://www.themuse.com/advice/15-things-you-need-to-know-about-working-abroad; E. Preske, "9 Steps to Get You Ready to Move Abroad," *Travel+ Leisure,* January 14, 2018, http://www.travelandleisure.com/travel-tips/how-to-prepare-to-move-abroad; A. Cain, "4 Things You Need to Do to Secure a Job Abroad," *Business Insider,* September 30, 2017, http://www.businessinsider.com/how-to-get-a-job-abroad-2017-9/#do-your-research-1; "4 Magic Tips on Working Abroad," *goabroad.com,* accessed

February 19, 2018, https://www.goabroad.com/articles/jobs-abroad/4-magic-tips-on-working-abroad; "5 Tips for Expats Living and Working Abroad," *Clements Worldwide,* accessed February 19, 2018, https://www.clements.com/resources/articles/Five-Tips-for-Living-and-Working-Abroad.

2. M. Sosby and L. League, "The 5 Things You'll Gain by Working Abroad Early in Your Career," *Fast Company*, January 12, 2016, https://www.fastcompany.com/3055265/the-5-things-youll-gain-by-working-abroad-early-in-your-career.

3. K. Amadeo, "U.S. Import Statistics and Issues," *The Balance*, April 19, 2017, https://www.thebalance.com/u-s-imports-statistics-and-issues-3306260.

4. "Poll: Americans Prefer Low Prices to Items 'Made in the USA,'" *Chicago Tribune*, April 14, 2016, http://www.chicagotribune.com/business/ct-americans-prices-vs-made-in-usa-20160414-story.html.

5. A. Petroff, "Britain Crashes Out of World's Top 5 Economies," *CNN Money*, November 22, 2017, http://money.cnn.com/2017/11/22/news/economy/uk-france-biggest-economies-in-the-world/index.html.

6. L. M. Segarra, "These Are the Richest Countries in the World," *Fortune,* November 17, 2017, http://fortune.com/2017/11/17/richest-country-in-the-world/.

7. *2018 Index of Economic Freedom,* https://www.heritage.org/index/ranking (accessed October 3, 2018).

8. See the related discussion in J. McGregor and S. Hamm, "Managing the Global Workforce," *BusinessWeek,* January 28, 2008, p. 34; and C. Boles, "Last Call? Gates Pushes Globalism in Remarks," *The Wall Street Journal,* March 13, 2008, p. B3.

9. "Number of Smartphone Users in the United States from 2010 to 2022 (in millions)," *Statista*, https://www.statista.com/statistics/201182/forecast-of-smartphone-users-in-the-us/ (accessed February 19, 2018).

10. "Internet Usage Statistics, The Internet Big Picture," *Internet World Stats*, https://www.internetworldstats.com/stats.htm (accessed February 19, 2018).

11. "E-Commerce Sales as Percentage of Total Retail Sales in Selected Countries in 2017," *Statista*, https://www.statista.com/statistics/255083/online-sales-as-share-of-total-retail-sales-in-selected-countries/ (accessed February 19, 2018).

12. M. Corkery and N. Wingfield, "Amazon Asked for Patience. Remarkably, Wall Street Complied," *The New York Times*, https://www.nytimes.com/2018/02/04/technology/amazon-asked-for-patience-remarkably-wall-street-complied.html (accessed February 4, 2018).

13. See "Company Overview," *Alibaba Group,* accessed February 12, 2018, http://www.alibabagroup.com/en/about/overview (accessed February 19, 2018); "What Is Alibaba?" *The Wall Street Journal,* http://projects.wsj.com/alibaba/ (accessed February 12, 2018).

14. "What Is Alibaba?" *The Wall Street Journal*, http://projects.wsj.com/alibaba/ (accessed February 12, 2018).

15. J. Russell, "Alibaba Will Soon Begin Selling Cars Using These Gigantic Vending Machines," *Tech Crunch*, December 14, 2017, https://techcrunch.com/2017/12/14/alibaba-car-vending-machines/.

16. P. R. La Monica, "Here's Why People Want Kroger to Partner with Alibaba," *CNN Money*, January 25, 2018, http://money.cnn.com/2018/01/25/investing/kroger-alibaba/index.html.

17. R. M. Kantor, quoted in K. Maney, "Economy Embraces Truly Global Workplace," *USA Today,* December 31, 1998, pp. 1B, 2B.

18. M. Collins, "The Pros and Cons of Globalization," *Forbes,* May 6, 2015, www.forbes.com/sites/mikecollins/2015/05/06/the-pros-and-cons-of-globalization (accessed March 7, 2016).

19. J. Kuepper, " Globalization and Its Impact On Economic Growth," *The Balance*, June 19, 2017, https://www.thebalance.com/globalization-and-its-impact-on-economic-growth-1978843.

20. B. Snavely, "Foreign Automakers Vie to Appear More American," *USA Today*, July 12, 2017, https://www.usatoday.com/story/money/cars/2017/07/11/foreign-automakers-american/467049001/.

21. B. Vlasic, "After Years of Growth, Automakers Are Cutting U.S. Jobs," *The New York Times*, July 4, 2017, https://www.nytimes.com/2017/07/04/business/automaker-jobs-trump.html.

22. G. Easterbrook, "The Boom Is Nigh," *Newsweek,* February 22, 2010, pp. 48–49.

23. J. Bucki, "Pros and Cons of Outsourcing," *The Balance*, February 4, 2018, https://www.thebalance.com/top-6-outsourcing-disadvantages-2533780.

24. D. Patel, "The Pros and Cons of Outsourcing," *Forbes*, July 17, 2017, https://www.forbes.com/sites/deeppatel/2017/07/17/the-pros-and-cons-of-outsourcing-and-the-effect-on-company-culture/2/#110a95726087.

25. N. Negroponte, quoted in Maney, "Economy Embraces Truly Global Workplace." See also S. Fidler, "Globalization: Battered but Not Beaten," *The Wall Street Journal,* January 21, 2015, p. A6.

26. See D. Cimilluca, "Mergers Set a Record as Firms Bulk Up," *The Wall Street Journal,* December 21, 2015, p. A10.

27. B. Gomes-Casseres, "What the Big Mergers of 2017 Tell Us about 2018," *Harvard Business Review*, January 2, 2018, https://hbr.org/2017/12/what-the-big-mergers-of-2017-tell-us-about-2018.

28. A. Kacik, " Healthcare Mega-Mergers Dominate 2017," *Modern Healthcare*, December 26, 2018, http://www.modernhealthcare.com/article/20171226/NEWS/171229957.

29. B. Gomes-Casseres, "What the Big Mergers of 2017 Tell Us about 2018," *Harvard Business Review*, January 2, 2018, https://hbr.org/2017/12/what-the-big-mergers-of-2017-tell-us-about-2018.

30. B. Gomes-Casseres, "What the Big Mergers of 2017 Tell Us about 2018," *Harvard Business Review*, January 2, 2018, https://hbr.org/2017/12/what-the-big-mergers-of-2017-tell-us-about-2018.

31. "How Mergers Damage the Economy," editorial, *The New York Times,* November 1, 2015, p. SR-10.

32. See editorial, "Beer Industry Harmed by Purchase of Distributors," *Reno Gazette-Journal,* October 30, 2015, p. 6A, reprinted from *USA Today.*

33. P. McDonald, quoted in M. L. Levin, "Global Experience Makes Candidates More Marketable," *The Wall Street Journal,* September 11, 2007, p. B6.

34. K. Zimmerman, "Is It Possible for Millennials to Find Jobs Abroad?" *Forbes*, November 24, 2016, https://www.forbes.com/sites/kaytiezimmerman/2016/11/24/is-it-possible-for-millennials-to-find-jobs-abroad/#34d1d9151cc6.

35. M. Sosby and L. League, "The 5 Things You'll Gain by Working Abroad Early in Your Career," *Fast Company*, January 12, 2016, https://www.fastcompany.com/3055265/the-5-things-youll-gain-by-working-abroad-early-in-your-career.

36. R. C. Carter, senior vice president for human resources at A&E Television Networks, quoted in H. Chura, "A Year Abroad (or 3) as a Career Move," *The New York Times,* February 26, 2006, www.nytimes.com/2006/02/25/business/worldbusiness/25abroad.html?pagewanted=all&_r=0 (accessed March 9, 2016).

37. See A. Davies, D. Fidler, and M. Gorbis, "Future Work Skills," Institute for the Future for the University of Phoenix Research Institute, 2011, p. 9, http://www.iftf.org/futureworkskills.

38. "The Biggest Companies in the World in 2015," *The Telegraph,* July 22, 2015, www.telegraph.co.uk/business/2016/02/11/the-biggest-companies-in-the-world-in-2015/toyota-car (accessed March 10, 2016).

39. B. Herman, "The U.S. Companies with the Most Cash Parked Overseas," *Axios*, December 4, 2017, https://www.axios.com/the-us-companies-with-the-most-cash-parked-overseas-1513388347-50edfdb5-863f-48fa-a99b-2dc7f3985227.html.

40. M. Hanbury, "11 American Companies That Are No Longer American," *Business Insider*, January 13, 2018, http://www.businessinsider.com/american-companies-that-are-no-longer-american-2017-6/#ben-and-jerrys-2.

41. See T. Andreas, "The Scope of Polycentric Governance Analysis and Resulting Challenges," *Journal of Self-Governance and Management Economics,* 2017, pp. 52–82; D. G. Schmidt, "Geocentric Ethics: Using Bicultural Skills to Develop Global Organizational Culture," *Journal of International Business Ethics,* 2016, pp. 16–28.

42. See S. Correa and A-M. Parente-Laverde, "Consumer Ethnocentrism, Country Image and Local Brand Preference: The Case of

the Columbian Textile, Apparel and Leather Industry," *Global Business Review,* October 2017, pp. 1111–1123.

43. S. Gould and A. Villas-Boas, "Here's Where All the Components of Your iPhone Come From," *Business Insider*, April 12, 2016, http://www.businessinsider.com/where-iphone-parts-come-from-2016-4.

44. See J. Dunn, "Netflix Now Has More Subscribers Internationally Than in the US," *Business Insider,* July 18, 2017, http://www.businessinsider.com/netflix-subscribers-international-vs-us-earnings-chart-2017-7; F. Di Pietro, "How Netflix Inc. Is Overcoming This Key Obstacle to Its International Expansion," *The Motley Fool,* May 19, 2017, https://www.fool.com/investing/2017/05/09/how-netflix-inc-is-overcoming-this-key-obstacle-to.aspx.

45. N. Purnell, "Apple Makes iPhone Push in India," *The Wall Street Journal,* January 21, 2016, p. B4.

46. P. Rana, "Ikea's India Bet Hits Thicket of Rules," *The Wall Street Journal,* February 24, 2016, pp. A1, A14.

47. "Here's Why Amazon Is Expanding in Australia," *Forbes*, May 19, 2017, https://www.forbes.com/sites/greatspeculations/2017/05/09/heres-why-amazon-is-expanding-in-australia/#6752ec141043.

48. D. Kiley, "Forget Mexico: Ford Moving Focus Production from U.S. to China, with Eye on Profitability," *Forbes*, June 20, 2017, https://www.forbes.com/sites/davidkiley5/2017/06/20/ford-will-move-focus-production-from-michigan-to-china/2/#12e4c80b5ea6.

49. See J. Zhu and S. Jiang, "China Sovereign Wealth Fund CIC Plans More U.S. Investments: Chairman," *Reuters,* January 16, 2017, https://www.reuters.com/article/us-china-us-cn-invst/china-sovereign-wealth-fund-cic-plans-more-u-s-investments-chairman-idUSKBN1500S1; C. Ming and B. Lo, "Countries Are 'Specifically Targeting' China with 'Protectionism,' Official Says," *CNBC,* January 5, 2018, https://www.cnbc.com/2018/01/15/china-wealth-fund-faces-protectionism-says-cic-president.html.

50. C. Ming and B. Lo, "Countries Are 'Specifically Targeting' China with 'Protectionism,' Official Says," *CNBC,* January 5, 2018, https://www.cnbc.com/2018/01/15/china-wealth-fund-faces-protectionism-says-cic-president.html.

51. H. Moser and S. Montalbano, "Why Made-in-USA Fashion Is Turning Heads," *Industry Week*, January 18, 2018, http://www.industryweek.com/economy/why-made-usa-fashion-turning-heads.

52. R. Sharrow, "Kevin Plank: Under Armour's New City Garage Innovation Center Will Help Spur Manufacturing," *Baltimore Business Journal*, June 28, 2016, https://www.bizjournals.com/baltimore/news/2016/06/28/kevin-plankunder-armours-new-city-garage.html.

53. D. Cave, "As Ties with China Unravel, U.S. Companies Head to Mexico," *The New York Times,* June 1, 2014, p. A6.

54. See H. Long, " U.S. Has Lost 5 Million Manufacturing Jobs since 2000," *CNN Money,* March 29, 2016, http://money.cnn.com/2016/03/29/news/economy/us-manufacturing-jobs/index.html; K. Amadeo, "How Outsourcing Jobs Affects the U.S. Economy," *The Balance,* March 30, 2017, https://www.thebalance.com/how-outsourcing-jobs-affects-the-u-s-economy-3306279.

55. K. Bahler, "Americans See Job Outsourcing as Biggest Threat to U.S. Workers," *Money,* October 6, 2016, http://time.com/money/4521151/job-outsourcing-report/.

56. "Jobs Overseas Outsourcing Statistics," *Statistic Brain Research Institute,* www.statisticbrain.com/outsourcing-statistics-by-country (accessed March 14, 2016).

57. See A. Kiersz, "The 20 Best Jobs of the Future," *Business Insider,* January 22, 2014, www.businessinsider.com/best-jobs-of-the-future-2014-1; M. Grothaus, "The Top Jobs in 10 Years Might Not Be What You Expect," *Fast Company,* May 18, 2015, www.fastcompany.com/3046277/the-new-rules-of-work/the-top-jobs-in-10-years-might-not-be-what-you-expect; *The Future of Jobs: Employment, Skills, and Workforce Strategy for the Fourth Industrial Revolution,* World Economic Forum, January 2016, www3.weforum.org/docs/WEF_FOJ_Executive_Summary_Jobs.pdf.

58. K. Amadeo, "How Outsourcing Jobs Affects the U.S. Economy," *The Balance*, March 30, 2017, https://www.thebalance.com/how-outsourcing-jobs-affects-the-u-s-economy-3306279.

59. "Here's How Your Degree, and Your Skills, Can Impact Your Salary," *IN*, September 28, 2017, https://www.linkedin.com/jobs/blog/how-education-impacts-salary.

60. E. Aston, "Why Students Drop Out of College, and How We Can Do Something About It," *HuffPost*, January 16, 2018, https://www.huffingtonpost.com/entry/why-most-students-drop-out-of-college-and-how-we-can_us_5a5d9f77e4b01ccdd48b5f46.

61. B. Farrow, "For American Franchisors to Succeed Overseas, They Have to Be Open to Change," *Entrepreneur*, July 12, 2017, https://www.entrepreneur.com/article/296218.

62. "Company Overview of Shanghai General Motors Co., Ltd.," *Bloomberg*, https://www.bloomberg.com/research/stocks/private/snapshot.asp?privcapId=5477465 (accessed February 19, 2018).

63. "Changan Ford Automobile Co., Ltd., (CAF) Assembly Plant 3," *Ford,* https://corporate.ford.com/company/plant-detail-pages/changan-ford-automobile-co-ltd-CAF-assembly-plant-3.html (accessed February 19, 2018).

64. See E. Wolff, "Trump Imposes Tariffs on Solar Imports," *Politico,* January 22, 2018, https://www.politico.com/story/2018/01/22/trump-solar-tariffs-china-357612; A. Behsudi, "Trump Delivers Dose of 'America First' Ahead of Davos," *Politico,* January 22, 2018, https://www.politico.com/story/2018/01/22/trump-imports-trade-303859.

65. See C. Capozzi, "What Is the Difference between Tariffs Import Quotas," *Bizfluent,* September 25, 2017, https://bizfluent.com/info-8458339-difference-between-tariffs-import-quotas.html.

66. "U.S. Department of Commerce Self-Initiates Historic Antidumping and Countervailing Duty Investigations on Common Alloy Aluminum Sheet from China," *Commerce.Gov*, November 28, 2017, https://www.commerce.gov/news/press-releases/2017/11/us-department-commerce-self-initiates-historic-antidumping-and.

67. P. Baker, "U.S. Will Restore Full Relations with Cuba, Erasing a Last Trace of Cold War Hostility," *The New York Times,* December 18, 2014, p. A1; A. Mallin, "President Obama and the First Family Arrive in Cuba for Historic Visit," *ABC News,* March 20, 2016, http://abcnews.go.com/US/president-obama-family-arrive-cuba-historic-visit/story?id=37791583 (accessed March 31, 2016).

68. A. Gomez, "Trump Cracks Down on U.S. Business and Travel to Cuba. Here's What's Changing," *USA Today*, November 8, 2018, https://www.usatoday.com/story/news/world/2017/11/08/trump-cracks-down-u-s-business-and-travel-cuba/843419001/.

69. T. Zhao, "Why an Oil Embargo Won't Stop North Korea," *CNN*, December 1, 2017, https://www.cnn.com/2017/12/01/opinions/china-north-korea-oil-embargo/index.html.

70. M. Mozur, "Trump Can't Stop Trade With North Korea. But He Does Have Options," *The New York Times*, September 4, 2017, https://www.nytimes.com/2017/09/04/business/trump-china-north-korea-trade.html.

71. These definitions are found in "What Are Embargoes and Sanctions?" New York District Export Council, www.newyorkdec.org/what-are-embargoes-and-sanctions.html (accessed March 13, 2016).

72. N. Turak, "Trump to Agree to New Russia Sanctions But Impact Will Be Minimal, Analysts Predict," *CNBC*, January 29, 2018, https://www.cnbc.com/2018/01/29/new-us-russia-sanctions-trump-to-comply-but-impact-will-be-minimal.html.

73. J. Bhagwati, *Protectionism* (Cambridge, MA: MIT Press, 1988).

74. S. Ben-Achour, "The Real Reason We Talk about NAFTA So Much," *Business Insider*, March 23, 2017, http://www.businessinsider.com/did-nafta-cost-or-create-jobs-2017-3.

75. G. Finch, J. Warren and T. Coulter, "Frankfurt Is the Big Winner in Battle for Brexit Bankers," *Bloomberg*, September 28, 2017, https://www.bloomberg.com/graphics/2017-brexit-bankers/.

76. "The U.K. Will Make Concessions to EU Banks to Keep Them in London after Brexit," *Fortune*, December 20, 2017, http://fortune.com/2017/12/20/uk-boe-eu-banks-brexit/.

77. A. Hunt and B. Wheeler, "Brexit: All You Need to Know about the UK Leaving the EU," *BBC*, February 12, 2018, http://www.bbc.com/news/uk-politics-32810887.

78. J. Wingrove, A. Mayeda, and E. Martin, "All Eyes on U.S. After Week of Cautious Optimism in Nafta Talks," *Bloomberg Businessweek*, January 29, 2018, https://www.bloomberg.com/news/articles/2018-01-29/u-s-set-to-give-signal-as-nafta-bartering-suggests-progress.

79. J. Wingrove, A Mayeda, and E. Martin, "All Eyes on U.S. after Week of Cautious Optimism in Nafta Talks," *Bloomberg Politics*, January 29, 2018, https://www.bloomberg.com/news/articles/2018-01-29/u-s-set-to-give-signal-as-nafta-bartering-suggests-progress.

80. N. Barkin and Y. Bayoumy, "On Eve of Trump Trip, EU Leaders Warn against Nationalism," *Reuters*, January 24, 2018, https://www.reuters.com/article/us-davos-meeting-europe/on-eve-of-trump-trip-eu-leaders-warn-against-nationalism-idUSKBN1FD28T?il=0.

81. K. Tausche, "Can the US Rejoin TPP? Yes—with Permission," *CNBC*, January 26, 2018, https://www.cnbc.com/2018/01/26/can-the-us-rejoin-tpp-yes–with-permission.html.

82. World Bank, *Global Economic Prospects: Potential Macroeconomic Implications of the Trans-Pacific Partnership Agreement*, January 2016, www.worldbank.org/content/dam/Worldbank/GEP/GEP2016a/Global-Economic-Prospects-January-2016-Implications-Trans-Pacific-Partnership-Agreement.pdf (accessed March 12, 2016).

83. J. Papier, "The Incredible Shrinking Dollar," *PWJohnson Wealth Management*, www.pwjohnson.com/resources/articles/falling_dollar.pdf (accessed April 15, 2016).

84. "Compare Cost of Living between Cities," *Expatistan*, accessed February 13, 2018, https://www.expatistan.com/cost-of-living.

85. W. Bello, "The BRICS: Challengers to the Global Status Quo," *Foreign Policy in Focus*, August 29, 2014, http://fpif.org/brics-challengers-global-status-quo (accessed March 11, 2016).

86. See P. Gillespie, "Russia and China Have Had Enough of Western Banking," *CNN Money*, May 4, 2015, http://money.cnn.com/2015/05/04/news/economy/russia-approves-brics-reserve-bank-imf (accessed March 11, 2016).

87. C. A. Kupchan, "The World in 2050: When the 5 Largest Economies Are the BRICs and Us," *The Atlantic*, February 17, 2012, www.theatlantic.com/business/archive/2012/02/the-world-in-2050-when-the-5-largest-economies-are-the-brics-and-us/253160 (accessed March 11, 2016).

88. I. Bremmer, "The Mixed Fortunes of the BRICS Countries, in 5 Facts," *Time*, September 1, 2017, http://time.com/4923837/brics-summit-xiamen-mixed-fortunes/.

89. I. Bremmer, "The Mixed Fortunes of the BRICS Countries, in 5 Facts," *Time*, September 1, 2017, http://time.com/4923837/brics-summit-xiamen-mixed-fortunes/.

90. P. Pajpai, "The World's Top 10 Economies," *Investopedia*, July 7, 2017, https://www.investopedia.com/articles/investing/022415/worlds-top-10-economies.asp.

91. "Brazil: Country at a Glance," *The World Bank*, www.worldbank.org/en/country/brazil (accessed March 13, 2016).

92. K. Allen, "Brazil's Economy Slumps to 25-Year Low," *The Guardian*, March 3, 2016, www.theguardian.com/business/2016/mar/03/brazil-economy-low-oil-prices-inflation (accessed March 13, 2016).

93. I. Bremmer, "The Mixed Fortunes of the BRICS Countries, in 5 Facts," *Time*, September 1, 2017, http://time.com/4923837/brics-summit-xiamen-mixed-fortunes/.

94. O. Guo, "Aiming at China's Armpits: When Foreign Brands Misfire," *The New York Times*, February 2, 2018, https://www.nytimes.com/2018/02/02/business/china-consumers-deodorant.html.

95. "How Cultures Collide," *Psychology Today*, July 1976, p. 69.

96. N. Kathirvel and I.M.C. Febiula, "Understanding the Aspects of Cultural Shock in International Business Arena," *International Journal of Information, Business and Management*, May 2016, pp. 105–115. Also see F. Fitzpatrick, "Taking the 'Culture' Out of 'Culture Shock'—A Critical Review of Literature on Cross-Cultural Adjustment in International Relocations," *Critical Perspectives on International Business; Bradford*, 2017, pp. 278–296.

97. A summary of cross-cultural research is provided by M. J. Gelfand, Z. Aycan, M. Erez, and K. Leung, "Cross-Cultural Industrial Organizational Psychology and Organizational Behavior: A Hundred-Year Journey," *Journal of Applied Psychology*, March 2017, pp. 514–529.

98. For complete details, see G. Hofstede, *Culture's Consequences: International Differences in Work-Related Values*, abridged ed. (Newbury Park, CA: Sage, 1984).

99. M. Javidan and R. J. House, "Cultural Acumen for the Global Manager: Lessons from Project GLOBE," *Organizational Dynamics*, Spring 2001, pp. 289–305; R. J. House, P. J. Hanges, M. Javidan, P. W. Dorfman, and V. Gupta, eds., *Culture, Leadership, and Organizations: The GLOBE Study of 62 Societies* (Thousand Oaks, CA: Sage, 2004); M. Javidan, P. W. Dorfman, M. S. de Luque, and R. J. House, "In the Eye of the Beholder: Cross Cultural Lessons in Leadership from Project GLOBE," *Academy of Management Perspectives*, February 2006, pp. 67–90.

100. J. Marcus and H. Le, "Interactive Effects of Levels of Individualism–Collectivism on Cooperation: A Meta-Analysis," *Journal of Organizational Behavior*, August 2013, pp. 813–834.

101. B. S. Reiche, P. Cardona, Y.-T. Lee et al., "Why Do Managers Engage in Trustworthy Behavior? A Multilevel Cross-Cultural Study in 18 Countries," *Personnel Psychology*, Vol. 67, No. 1 (2014), pp. 61–98.

102. S. Davis, "The State of Global Leadership Development," *Training*, July/August 2015, pp. 52–55.

103. "How Many Languages Are There in the World?" *Ethnologue*, https://www.ethnologue.com/guides/how-many-languages (accessed February 13, 2018); T. Neeley, "Global Business Speaks English," *Harvard Business Review*, May 2012, https://hbr.org/2012/05/global-business-speaks-english.

104. T. Neeley, "Global Business Speaks English," *Harvard Business Review*, May 2012, https://hbr.org/2012/05/global-business-speaks-english.

105. S. Fisher, "The 7 Best Free Language Learning Apps," *The Balance*, September 8, 2017, https://www.thebalance.com/the-7-best-free-language-learning-apps-1357060.

106. See A. Sorokowska, P. Sorokowski, P. Hilpert, K. Cantarero, T. Frackowiak, K. Almadi et al., "Preferred Interpersonal Distances: A Global Comparison," *Journal of Cross-Cultural Psychology*, 2017, pp. 577–592.

107. Kari Heistad, CEO of Culture Coach International, quoted in E. Maltby, "Expanding Abroad? Avoid Cultural Gaffes," *The Wall Street Journal*, January 19, 2010, p. B5.

108. See D. Marsh, *Doing Business in the Middle East* (London: Little, Brown Book Group, 2015).

109. K. Seong-Kon, writing in *The Korea Herald*, summarized in "A Society That Needs No Appointment," *The Week*, May 29, 2009, p. 14.

110. See C. Tam and T. Oliveira, "Understanding Mobile Banking Individual Performance: The DeLone & McLean Model and the Moderating Effects of Individual Culture," *Internet Research*, 2017, pp. 538–562.

111. See M. Daskin, "Linking Polychronicity to Hotel Frontline Employees' Job Outcomes: Do Control Variables Make a Difference," *EuroMed Journal of Business*, 2016, pp. 162–180.

112. See J. Berg, "8 Things Planners Should Know about International Meetings," *Bizbash*, January 22, 2016, https://www.bizbash.com/8-things-planners-should-know-about-international-meetings/new-york/story/31675/#.WoMs_kxFx9B; H. Jacobs, "I Forgot One Thing on My Trip to Japan—and Now I Have to Apologize to Every Person I Meet," *Business Insider*, January 17, 2017, http://www.businessinsider.com/japan-business-culture-etiquette-bring-business-cards-2017-1.

113. See G. A. Smith, "A Growing Share of Americans Say It's Not Necessary to Believe in God to Be Moral," *Pew Research Center*, October 16, 2017, http://www.pewresearch.org/fact-tank/2017/10/16/a-growing-share-of-americans-say-its-not-necessary-to-believe-in-god-to-be-moral/; "America's Changing Religious Landscape," Pew Research Center, May 12, 2015, http://www.pewforum.org/2015/05/12/americas-changing-religious-landscape/.

114. E. Green, "The Non-Religious States of America," *The Atlantic*, September 6, 2017, https://www.theatlantic.com/politics/archive/2017/09/no-religion-states-prri/538821/.

115. "Venezuela Wins Expropriation Cases in US Supreme Court, Paris Court of Appeals & ICSID," *Bilaterals.org*, May 2, 2017, https://www.bilaterals.org/?venezuela-wins-expropriation-cases.

116. "20 Countries where Bribery in Business Is Common Practice," *worldatlas*, accessed February 13, 2018, https://www.worldatlas.com/articles/20-countries-where-bribery-in-business-is-common-practice.html.

117. R. Abrams, "Retailers Like H&M and Walmart Fall Short of Pledges to Overseas Workers," *The New York Times*, May 31, 2016, https://www.nytimes.com/2016/05/31/business/international/top-retailers-fall-short-of-commitments-to-overseas-workers.html.

118. Estimate by the International Labor Organization, reported in T. Lee, "Tech Joins Slavery Fight," *San Francisco Chronicle,* January 31, 2016, pp. D1, D3.

119. See "Number of U.S. Citizens Living Abroad," *Wikipedia*, https://en.wikipedia.org/wiki/American_diaspora, last updated on February 11, 2018.

120. R. Feintzeig, "After Stints Abroad, Re-Entry Can Be Hard," *The Wall Street Journal,* September 18, 2013, p. B6.

121. See H-J. Lee, H. Chei, C. Miska, and G. K. Stahl, "Looking Out or Looking Up: Gender Differences in Expatriate Turnover Intentions," *Cross Cultural & Strategic Management,* 2017, pp. 288–309; C. Jonasson, J. Lauring, J. Selmer, and J-L. Trembath, "Job Resources and Demands for Expatriate Academics: Linking Teacher-Student Relations, Intercultural Adjustment, and Job Satisfaction," *Journal of Global Mobility,* 2017, pp. 5–21.

122. I. Urbina, "In Buying Cheap Clothes, U.S. Flouts Own Counsel," *The New York Times,* December 23, 2013, pp. A1, A6.

123. See A. Breitenmoser and B. Bader, "Repatriation Outcomes Affecting Corporate ROI: A Critical Review and Future Agenda," *Management Quarterly Review,* June 2016, pp. 195–234.

124. P. Basca, "Become a Better Leader with These 5 Cultural-Awareness Tips," *Entrepreneur Network,* September 14, 2015, https://www.entrepreneur.com/article/250546.

125. J. W. Traphagan, "A Simple Way to Raise Your Cultural Awareness at Work," *Fast Company,* May 20, 2015, https://www.fastcompany.com/3043687/a-simple-way-to-raise-your-cultural-awareness-at-work.

126. G. Johns, "Advances in the Treatment of Context in Organizational Research," in F. P. Morgeson, H. Aguinis, and S. J. Ashford, eds., *Annual Review of Organizational Psychology and Organizational Behavior* (Palo Alto: CA, Annual Reviews, 2017), pp. 21–46.

127. B. Tulgan, *Bridging the Soft Skills Gap* (Hoboken, NJ: John Wiley & Sons, 2015).

128. These suggestions were based on I. Sommerdorf, "60 Ways to Improve Your Cultural Awareness," *Odyssey,* April 26, 2016, https://www.theodysseyonline.com/60-ways-to-improve-your-cultural-awareness.

129. Supportive research can be found in M. M. Chao, R. Takeuchi, and J.-L. Farh, "Enhancing Cultural Intelligence: The Roles of Implicit Culture Beliefs and Adjustment," *Personnel Psychology,* 2017, pp. 257–292.

130. "Didi Chuxing," *Wikipedia,* last updated on January 16, 2018, https://en.wikipedia.org/wiki/Didi_Chuxing.

131. J. Hong, "How China's Ride-Hailing King DiDi Is Taking over the World before Uber Can," *Forbes*, August 3, 2017, https://www.forbes.com/sites/jinshanhong/2017/08/03/how-chinas-ride-hailing-king-didi-is-taking-over-the-world-before-uber-can/#2cdd14fd3fd8.

132. "Look Out Uber—China's Didi Just Raised $4 Billion to Go Global in the Ride-Hailing Battle," *Fortune*, December 21, 2017, http://fortune.com/2017/12/21/uber-didi-4-billion-ride-hailing-global/.

133. "China's Didi Cashes Up to Go Global in Next Stage of Uber Battle," *Bloomberg.com*, December 20, 2017, https://www.bloomberg.com/news/articles/2017-12-21/china-s-didi-raises-more-than-4-billion-in-new-funding-round.

134. "China's Didi Targets Taiwan Expansion with Franchising Model," *Bloomberg.com,* December 19, 2017, https://www.bloomberg.com/news/articles/2017-12-19/china-s-didi-targets-taiwan-expansion-with-franchising-model.

135. "China's Didi Chuxing Will Buy Control of Brazil's 99," *Fortune*, January 4, 2018, http://fortune.com/2018/01/03/china-didi-chuxing-99-latin-america-uber/.

136. Y. Kubota, "In Uber-Didi War, Brazil Is Latest Battlefield," *The Wall Street Journal*, January 4, 2018, https://www.wsj.com/articles/in-uber-didi-war-brazil-is-latest-battlefield-1515062277.

137. J. Love and H. Somerville, "Uber's Chinese Rival Didi Chuxing to Enter Mexico Next Year," *Reuters*, December 8, 2017, https://www.reuters.com/article/us-didi-mexico-exclusive/exclusive-ubers-chinese-rival-didi-chuxing-to-enter-mexico-next-year-sources-idUSKBN1E12XU.

138. S. Pham, "Uber's Big Chinese Rival Didi Is Buying Brazilian Startup 99," *CNNMoney*, January 4, 2018, http://money.cnn.com/2018/01/04/technology/didi-99-acquisition-uber-brazil/index.html.

139. A. Fitzpatrick, "Uber Lost $750 Million in Second Quarter of 2016," *Time*, August 25, 2016. http://time.com/4465901/uber-china-losses/.

140. "World Cup Bribes, Death Threats: Corrupt World of FIFA," *USA Today*, November 20, 2017, https://www.usatoday.com/story/sports/soccer/2017/11/20/world-cup-bribes-death-threats-corrupt-world-of-fifa/107864644/.

141. G. Dunbar, "FIFA Corruption Culture Exposed in Trials," *Chicago Tribune*, December 22, 2017, http://www.chicagotribune.com/90minutes/ct-90mins-fifa-corruption-culture-exposed-in-trials-20171222-story.html.

142. B. Chandler and M. Adlem, "Bribery, Corruption and Fraud in the Middle East," First Middle East Bribery, Corruption and Fraud survey, 2014.

CHAPTER 5

1. See M. Caldwell, "Making It between College and Your First Job," *The Balance,* June 30, 2017, https://www.thebalance.com/making-it-between-college-and-your-first-job-2386193; "Make a Career Plan," *ge/cd MIT Global Education and Career Development,* accessed February 22, 2018, https://gecd.mit.edu/explore-careers/career-first-steps/make-career-plan; "7 Steps to Become a Better Planner," *The Ripenists,* http://www.theripenists.com/7-steps-become-better-planner/ (accessed February 22, 2018).

2. M. Caldwell, "Making It between College and Your First Job," *The Balance,* June 30, 2017, https://www.thebalance.com/making-it-between-college-and-your-first-job-2386193.

3. Mark Zuckerberg, quoted in S. Murphy Kelly, "Facebook Changes Its 'Move Fast and Break Things' Motto," *Mashable,* April 30, 2014, http://mashable.com/2014/04/30/facebooks-new-mantra-move-fast-with-stability/#.4Lfi3bl7sqW (accessed March 19, 2016). See also S. Fiergerman, "Are Facebook's 'Move Fast and Break Things' Days Over?" *Mashable,* March 13, 2013, http://mashable.com/2014/03/13/facebook-move-fast-break-things/#XUbMhtL5H8qJ (accessed March 19, 2016).

4. R. Kreitner, *Management,* 11th ed. (Boston: Houghton Mifflin, 2008), p. 147.

5. "Half of Millennials Plan to Start a Business in the Next 3 Years," *PR Newswire,* accessed February 22, 2018, https://www.prnewswire.com/news-releases/half-of-millennials-plan-to-start-a-business-in-the-next-3-years-300465835.html.

6. G. Yara, "Firm Makes Hidden Doors for Homes," *Mesa Republic,* February 17, 2018, pp. 3,4, 6.

7. "Fenty Beauty by Rihanna," *fentybeauty.com,* https://www.fentybeauty.com/about-fenty (accessed February 22, 2018); A. Gumbs, "Rihanna Is Killing It as an Entrepreneur with Fenty Beauty," *Black Enterprise*, January 29, 2018, http://www.blackenterprise.com/rihanna-entrepreneur-fenty-beauty/; K. Hays, "Fenty Beauty Sales on Track to Outstrip Kylie Cosmetics, KKW Beauty," *WWD,* January 26, 2018, http://wwd.com/business-news/financial/rihanna-fenty-beauty-sales-on-track-to-outstrip-kylie-jenner-cosmetics-kim-kardashian-beauty-11127361/.

8. A. A. Thompson Jr. and A. J. Strickland III, *Strategic Management: Concepts and Cases,* 13th ed. (New York: McGraw-Hill/Irwin, 2003).

9. D. J. Collis and M. G. Rukstad, "Can You Say What Your Strategy Is?" *Harvard Business Review,* April 2008, pp. 82–90.

10. See M. Keynes, "Making Planning Work: Insights from Business Development," *International Journal of Entrepreneurship and Innovative Management,* 2018, pp. 33–56; M. S. Ridwan, "Planning Practices: A Multiple Case Study in the High-Performing Banks," *Journal of Organizational Change Management,* 2017, pp. 487–500.
11. See R. L. Martin, "The Big Lie of Strategic Planning," *Harvard Business Review,* January–February 2014, pp. 79–84.
12. H. Mintzberg, "The Strategy Concept II: Another Look at Why Organizations Need Strategies," *California Management Review,* Vol. 30, No. 1 (1987), pp. 25–32.
13. G. Hamel, with B. Breen, *The Future of Management* (Boston: Harvard Business School Press, 2007), p. 191.
14. P. Cohan, "Five Commandments for Faster Growth," *Knowledge@Wharton,* March 9, 2016, http://knowledge.wharton.upenn.edu/article/five-commandments-for-faster-growth (accessed March 27, 2016).
15. V. Yee, "Where Did You Want That Pizza? In the Park, between the Trees," *The New York Times,* October 6, 2013, p. News-21; J. Brustein, "People Want More Takeout, Ordered Online," *San Francisco Chronicle,* February 24, 2014, pp. D1, D3.
16. S. Berfield, "New Vending Machines Offer Fresher Items," *San Francisco Chronicle,* February 16, 2014, p. C3.
17. A. Wexler, "Taxify Overtakes Uber in Africa," *The Wall Street Journal,* September 17, 2018, p. B4.
18. E. Bernstein, "An Emotion We Need More of," *The Wall Street Journal,* March 22, 2016, pp. D1, D4.
19. P. F. Drucker, *The Practice of Management* (New York: Harper & Row, 1954), p. 122.
20. T. A. Stewart, "A Refreshing Change: Vision Statements That Make Sense," *Fortune,* September 30, 1996, pp. 195–196.
21. "Coca-Cola at a Glance: Infographic," *Coca Cola Journey,* accessed February 26, 2018, http://www.coca-colacompany.com/our-company/infographic-coca-cola-at-a-glance.
22. "Mission, Vision & Values," *Coca Cola Journey,* accessed February 26, 2018, http://www.coca-colacompany.com/our-company/mission-vision-values; "Mission Statement: Dedicated to Creating the Most Epic Entertainment Experiences . . . Ever," *Blizzard Entertainment,* http://us.blizzard.com/en-us/company/about/mission.html (accessed February 26, 2018).
23. See C. Christensen, "How Will You Measure Your Life?" *Harvard Business Review,* July–August 2010, pp. 46–51.
24. Adapted from H. L. Rossi, "7 Core Values Statements That Inspire," *Fortune.com,* March 13, 2015, http://fortune.com/2015/03/13/company-slogans/ (accessed March 21, 2016).
25. Eric Johnson, quoted in Rossi, "7 Core Values Statements That Inspire."
26. P. J. Below, G. L. Morrisey, and B. L. Acomb, *The Executive Guide to Strategic Planning* (San Francisco: Jossey-Bass, 1987), p. 2.
27. "Five Strategic Actions," *The Coca-Cola Company,* April 27, 2016, http://www.coca-colacompany.com/stories/five-strategic-actions.
28. "Our Way Forward: How We're Keeping People at the Heart of Our Business," *Coca-Cola Journey,* February 7, 2017, http://www.coca-colacompany.com/stories/our-way-forward.
29. L. Bossidy and R. Charan, *Execution: The Discipline of Getting Things Done* (New York: Crown Business, 2002), p. 227.
30. See "The World's Most Admired Companies," *Fortune,* http://fortune.com/worlds-most-admired-companies/ (accessed February 26, 2018); "Southwest Airlines Reports Record Fourth Quarter and Annual Profit; 45th Consecutive Year of Profitability," *Yahoo Finance,* https://finance.yahoo.com/news/southwest-airlines-reports-record-fourth-113000600.html (accessed February 26, 2018).
31. "Southwest Airlines Careers," *Southwest.com,* https://www.southwest.com/html/about-southwest/careers/index.html (accessed February 26, 2018).
32. "Southwest Airlines Employees Earn $543 Million in 2017 ProfitSharing," *Business Insider,* February 8, 2018, http://markets.businessinsider.com/news/stocks/southwest-airlines-employees-earn-543-million-in-2017-profitsharing-1001741366.
33. B. Spiegel, "What Kind of Planes Does Southwest Airlines Fly?" *USA Today,* http://traveltips.usatoday.com/kind-planes-southwest-airlines-fly-62394.html (accessed February 26, 2018).
34. D. Gilbertson, "Southwest Airlines: Hawaii Flights Could Begin This Year," *USA Today,* https://www.usatoday.com/story/travel/flights/todayinthesky/2018/01/25/southwest-airlines-hawaii-flights-could-begin-year/1068025001/ (accessed February 26, 2018).
35. "Southwest Airlines Reports Record Fourth Quarter and Annual Profit; 45th Consecutive Year of Profitability," *Yahoo Finance,* January 25, 2018, https://finance.yahoo.com/news/southwest-airlines-reports-record-fourth-113000600.html.
36. See D. Green, "L.L. Bean Just Changed Its Return Policy—But There's a Huge Loophole for Some Customers," *Business Insider,* February 9, 2018, http://www.businessinsider.com/how-to-return-ll-bean-items-after-policy-change-2018-2; J. Amatulli, "Forever 21 Just Quietly Changed Its Return Policy for the Better," *HuffPost,* January 18, 2017, https://www.huffingtonpost.com/entry/forever-21-just-quietly-changed-their-return-policy-for-the-better_us_587f9fc6e4b0c147f0bc44b2.
37. J. Amos, "Elon Musk's Falcon Heavy Rocket Launches Successfully," *BBC,* February 7, 2018, http://www.bbc.com/news/science-environment-42969020.
38. B. Kesling and D. Nissenbaum, "Goal to Slash Wait Times Was 'Unrealistic,' Aide Said," *The Wall Street Journal,* May 24–25, 2014, p. A4.
39. See S. Ovide, "Snapchat Seems Confused about Its Mission," *Bloomberg,* November 29, 2017, https://www.bloomberg.com/gadfly/articles/2017-11-29/snapchat-appears-confused-about-what-it-wants-to-be; K. Benner, "Snapchat User Growth Disappoints in Another Down Quarter," *The New York Times,* November 7, 2017, https://www.nytimes.com/2017/11/07/technology/snap-earnings.html; E. Bary, "Snap Judgment: Why Investors Aren't Yet Buying Snapchat's Vision," *Barron's,* October 4, 2017, https://www.barrons.com/articles/snap-stock-earnings-guidance-1507133723?mg=prod/accounts-barrons.
40. S. McNeal, "Teens Are Losing It Over Snapchat's Unpopular App Redesign," *Buzzfeed News,* February 9, 2018, https://www.buzzfeed.com/stephaniemcneal/people-totally-hate-the-new-snapchat-update-and-are-vowing?utm_term=.dke9PWba1#.vxAWQN6JG.
41. P. F. Drucker, *The Practice of Management* (New York: Harper & Row, 1954).
42. G. Latham, G. Seijts, and J. Slocum, "The Goal Setting and Goal Orientation Labyrinth: Effective Ways for Increasing Employee Performance," *Organizational Dynamics,* October–December 2016, p. 275.
43. See M. P. E. Cunha, L. Giustiniano, A. Rego, and S. Clegg, "Mission Impossible? The Paradoxes of Stretch Goal Setting," *Management Learning,* 2017, pp. 140–157; G. Latham, G. Seijts, and J. Slocum, "The Goal Setting and Goal Orientation Labyrinth: Effective Ways for Increasing Employee Performance," *Organizational Dynamics,* October–December 2016, pp. 271–277.
44. M. A. Wolfson, S. I. Tannenbaum, J. E. Mathieu, and M. T. Maynard, "A Cross-Level Investigation of Informal Field-Based Learning and Performance Improvements." *Journal of Applied Psychology,* January 2018, p. 17.
45. See A. Fox, "Put Plans into Action," *HRMagazine,* April 2013, pp. 27–31.
46. See S. S. Wang, "Never Procrastinate Again," *The Wall Street Journal,* September 1, 2015, pp. D1, D2.
47. See G. Latham, G. Seijts, and J. Slocum, "The Goal Setting and Goal Orientation Labyrinth: Effective Ways for Increasing Employee Performance," *Organizational Dynamics,* October–December 2016, pp 271–277.
48. R. Rodgers and J. E. Hunter, "Impact of Management by Objectives on Organizational Productivity," *Journal of Applied Psychology,* April 1991, pp. 322–336; M. Johansen and D. P. Hawes, "The Effect of the Tasks Middle Managers Perform on Organizational Performance," *Public Administration Quarterly,* Fall 2016, pp. 580–616.
49. This example was taken from a graphic illustration by A. Kinicki and is used for training managers in cascading; copyright ©2016 by Kinicki

and Associates Inc. For more on goal cascading, see A. J. Kinicki, K. J. L. Jacobson, B. M. Galvin, and G. E. Prussia, "A Multilevel Systems Model of Leadership," *Journal of Leadership & Organizational Studies,* May 2011, pp. 133–149.

50. See "Small Businesses Comprise What Share of the U.S. Economy?" *SBA,* https://www.sba.gov/sites/default/files/FAQ_Sept_2012.pdf (accessed February 26, 2018); " Small Business GDP: Update 2002-2010," *SBA,* https://www.sba.gov/content/small-business-gdp-update-2002-2010 (accessed February 26, 2018).

51. See T. Gabriel, "Eager to Create Blue-Collar Jobs, a Small Business Struggles," *The New York Times,* September 3, 2017, https://www.nytimes.com/2017/09/03/us/quillen-small-business-michigan.html?action=click&contentCollection=Reader%20Center&module=RelatedCoverage&region=Marginalia&pgtype=article; and A. Gregory, "10 Powerful Steps to Achieve Your Small Business Goals," *The Balance,* December 26, 2017, https://www.thebalance.com/powerful-goal-setting-steps-2951854.

52. K. Korosec, "Why Tesla Model 3 Deliveries Missed the Mark," *Fortune,* January 3, 2018, http://fortune.com/2018/01/03/why-tesla-model-3-deliveries-missed-the-mark/.

53. R. Ferris, "We Still Don't Know How Many Model 3 Cars Tesla Is Making," *CNBC,* February 8, 2018, https://www.cnbc.com/2018/02/08/we-still-dont-know-how-many-model-3-cars-tesla-is-making.html.

54. J. Stewart, "Tesla Delays Its Model 3 Production Goals—Again," *Wired,* January 3, 2018, https://www.wired.com/story/musk-model-3-tesla-production-delays-january/.

55. J. Stewart, "Tesla Delays Its Model 3 Production Goals—Again," *Wired,* January 3, 2018, https://www.wired.com/story/musk-model-3-tesla-production-delays-january/.

56. R. Nolan, "How to Be More Proactive: A Step-By-Step Guide," *Goalcast,* September 2, 2016, https://www.goalcast.com/2016/09/02/how-to-be-more-proactive-step-step-guide.

57. "The Future of Talent: MARS," Advertising Supplement to *The Wall Street Journal,* 2017, p. 30.

58. These recommendations were derived from R. Nolan, "How to Be More Proactive: A Step-By-Step Guide," *Goalcast,* September 2, 2016, https://www.goalcast.com/2016/09/02/how-to-be-more-proactive-step-step-guide.

59. The structure of this exercise was partially based on B. Tulgan, *Bridging the Soft Skills Gap* (Hoboken, New Jersey: John Wiley & Sons, 2015).

60. These suggestions were based on S. Pavlina, "Suspending Judgment," June 3, 2010, https://www.stevepavlina.com/blog/2010/06/suspending-judgment.

61. "Our History," *About Fender Musical Instruments*, 2017, https://www.fender.com/pages/about.

62. Nusca, "Amped and Revamped," *Fortune*, December 1, 2017, 26–29.

63. K. Bhasin, "Don't Give Up on the Guitar. Fender Is Begging You," *Bloomberg*, November 21, 2016,https://www.bloomberg.com/news/articles/2016-11-21/don-t-give-up-on-the-guitar-fender-is-begging-you.

64. J. P. Titlow, "How Fender Is Reinventing Online Guitar Lessons For The Age Of Distraction," *Fast Company*, July 6, 2017, http://www.fastcompany.com/40437554/fender-reinvents-online-guitar-lessons-for-the-digitally-distracted.

65. Nusca, "Amped and Revamped," *Fortune*, December 1, 2017, 26–29.

66. J. P. Titlow, "How Fender Is Reinventing Online Guitar Lessons for the Age of Distraction," *Fast Company,* July 6, 2017, http://www.fastcompany.com/40437554/fender-reinvents-online-guitar-lessons-for-the-digitally-distracted.

67. M. DeBord, "I Spent a Few Months Using Fender's Online Guitar-Learning Tool—and I Was Surprised by How Much I Learned," *Business Insider*, December 28, 2017, http://www.businessinsider.com/fender-play-review-2017-10.

68. K. Bhasin, "Don't Give Up on the Guitar. Fender Is Begging You," *Bloomberg*, November 21, 2016, https://www.bloomberg.com/news/articles/2016-11-21/don-t-give-up-on-the-guitar-fender-is-begging-you.

69. K. Bhasin, "Don't Give Up on the Guitar. Fender Is Begging You," *Bloomberg*, November 21, 2016, https://www.bloomberg.com/news/articles/2016-11-21/don-t-give-up-on-the-guitar-fender-is-begging-you.

70. J. P. Titlow, "How Fender Is Reinventing Online Guitar Lessons for the Age of Distraction," *Fast Company,* July 6, 2017, http://www.fastcompany.com/40437554/fender-reinvents-online-guitar-lessons-for-the-digitally-distracted.

71. K. Bhasin, "Don't Give Up on the Guitar. Fender Is Begging You," *Bloomberg*, November 21, 2016, https://www.bloomberg.com/news/articles/2016-11-21/don-t-give-up-on-the-guitar-fender-is-begging-you.

72. A. LaVito, "Online Shopping Sales Hit a Record during the Holiday Season," *CNBC*, January 16, 2018, https://www.cnbc.com/2018/01/16/online-shopping-sales-hit-a-record-during-the-holiday-season.html.

73. K. Bhasin, "Don't Give Up on the Guitar. Fender Is Begging You," *Bloomberg*, November 21, 2016, https://www.bloomberg.com/news/articles/2016-11-21/don-t-give-up-on-the-guitar-fender-is-begging-you.

74. J. D. Rockoff, "Pfizer Ends Hunt for Drugs to Treat Alzheimer's and Parkinson's," *The Wall Street Journal*, January 6, 2018, https://www.wsj.com/articles/pfizer-ends-hunt-for-drugs-to-treat-alzheimers-and-parkinsons-1515267654.

75. "Pharma Giant Pfizer Pulls Out of Research into Alzheimer's," *BBC News*, January 10, 2018, http://www.bbc.com/news/health-42633871.

76. D. Crow, "Big Pharma Efforts on Alzheimer's Tested by Pfizer Exit," *Financial Times*, January 18, 2018, https://www.ft.com/content/c4e1241e-f731-11e7-88f7-5465a6ce1a00.

77. J. D. Rockoff, "Pfizer Ends Hunt for Drugs to Treat Alzheimer's and Parkinson's," *The Wall Street Journal*, January 6, 2018, https://www.wsj.com/articles/pfizer-ends-hunt-for-drugs-to-treat-alzheimers-and-parkinsons-1515267654.

78. "Mission & Purpose," Pfizer, 2018, http://www.pfizer.com/careers/en/mission-purpose (accessed January 22, 2018).

79. D. Crow, "Big Pharma Efforts on Alzheimer's Tested by Pfizer Exit," *Financial Times*, January 18, 2018, https://www.ft.com/content/c4e1241e-f731-11e7-88f7-5465a6ce1a00.

80. D. Crow, "Big Pharma Efforts on Alzheimer's Tested by Pfizer Exit," *Financial Times*, January 18, 2018, https://www.ft.com/content/c4e1241e-f731-11e7-88f7-5465a6ce1a00.

CHAPTER 6

1. "Sneaky Veg, About," https://www.sneakyveg.com/about/ (accessed March 5, 2018); K. Cook, "15 Inspiring Examples of Small Business Branding," *HubSpot,* https://blog.hubspot.com/marketing/inspiring-examples-of-small-business-branding (accessed March 5, 2018).

2. "The Future of Talent," *Advertising Supplement to The Wall Street Journal,* 2017, p. 23.

3. M. Sweetwood, "8 Reasons a Powerful Personal Brand Will Make You Successful," *Entrepreneur,* March 27, 2017, https://www.entrepreneur.com/article/289278.

4. L. Lake, "How to Write Your Personal Branding Statement," *The Balance,* June 10, 2017, https://www.thebalance.com/how-to-write-your-personal-branding-statement-2295809.

5. E. Gross, "10 Ways to Build Your Personal Brand (and Why You Should)," *Skillcrush,* October 24, 2016, https://skillcrush.com/2015/02/20/10-ways-build-personal-brand/.

6. G. Colvin, "There's No Quit in Michael Porter," *Fortune,* October 29, 2012, pp. 162–166.

7. M. E. Porter, "What Is Strategy?" *Harvard Business Review,* November–December 1996, pp. 61–78. Porter has updated his 1979 paper on competitive forces in M. E. Porter, "The Five Competitive Forces That Shape Strategy," *Harvard Business Review,* January 2008, pp. 79–93.

8. M. E. Porter, "What Is Strategy?" *Harvard Business Review,* November–December 1996, pp. 61–78.

9. G. Petro, "Amazon's Acquisition of Whole Foods Is about Two Things: Data and Product," *Forbes,* August 2, 2017, https://www.forbes.com/sites/gregpetro/2017/08/02/amazons-acquisition-of-whole-foods-is-about-two-things-data-and-product/#cf3be62a8084; "Volvo, Autoliv Form Driverless Car Joint Venture," *Phys.org,* September 6, 2016, https://phys.org/news/2016-09-volvo-autoliv-driverless-car-joint.html.

10. P. Anderson, "McGraw-Hill and iFlipd Pilot a Weekly Textbook Rental Program," *Publishing Perspectives,* August 25, 2017, https://publishingperspectives.com/2017/08/mcgraw-hill-iflipd-ebook-print-textbook-rental.

11. S. Taneja, M. G. Pryor, and M. Hayek, "Leaping Innovation Barriers to Small Business Longevity," *Journal of Business Strategy,* 2016, pp. 44–51; G.N. Powell and K. A. Eddleston, "Family Involvement in the Firm, Family-to-Business Support, and Entrepreneurial Outcomes: An Exploration," *Journal of Small Business Management,* October 2017, pp. 614–631.

12. L. van Scheers and M. K. Makhitha, "Are Small and Medium Enterprises (SMEs) Planning for Strategic Marketing in South Africa?" *Foundations of Management,* 2016, pp. 243–250.

13. C. O'Brien, "Evernote's 5% Problem Offers a Cautionary Lesson to Tech Companies," *redhat,* January 5, 2016, https://venturebeat.com/2016/01/05/evernotes-5-problem-offers-a-cautionary-lesson-to-tech-companies/; A. Taylor, "Why Do the Best Companies in the World Use Strategic Planning?" *Strategy Management Consulting,* January 8, 2018, http://www.smestrategy.net/blog/why-do-the-best-companies-in-the-world-use-strategic-planning.

14. A. Turnbull, "We Hired a Business Coach, and Here's What Happened," *Groove,* January 7, 2016, https://www.groovehq.com/blog/hiring-a-business-coach; A. Taylor, "Why Do the Best Companies in the World Use Strategic Planning?" *Strategy Management Consulting,* January 8, 2018, http://www.smestrategy.net/blog/why-do-the-best-companies-in-the-world-use-strategic-planning.

15. N. Shirouzu, "Toyoda Rues Excessive Profit Focus," *The Wall Street Journal,* March 2, 2010, p. B3. Also see K. Linebaugh, D. Searcey, and N. Shirouzu, "Secretive Culture Led Toyota Astray," *The Wall Street Journal,* February 10, 2010, pp. A1, A6.

16. "Corporate Vision and Financial Objectives," Macy's Inc., https://www.macysinc.com/about-us/corporate-vision-philosophy-financial-objectives/default.aspx (accessed March 5, 2018); "Policies/Positions," Macy's Inc., https://www.macysinc.com/about-us/policies-positions/overview/default.aspx (accessed March 5, 2018).

17. P. Wahba, "Can America's Department Stores Survive?" *Fortune,* February 21, 2017, http://fortune.com/2017/02/21/department-stores-future-macys-sears/; N. Bomey, "Macys Announces 5,000 Job Cuts, 7 New Store Closures," *USA Today,* January 4, 2018, https://usat.ly/2lUugxd; C. Reagan and L. Picker, "It's More Than Amazon: Why Retail Is in Distress Now," *CNBC,* May 5, 2017, https://www.cnbc.com/2017/05/05/its-more-than-amazon-why-retail-is-in-distress-now.html.

18. A. Kurtz and R. Abrams, "Jeff Gennette to Succeed Terry Lundgren as Macys Chief," *The New York Times,* June 23, 2016, https://www.nytimes.com/2016/06/24/business/jeff-gennette-to-replace-terry-lundgren-as-macys-chief.html.

19. A. Kurtz and R. Abrams. "Jeff Gennette to Succeed Terry Lundgren as Macys Chief," *The New York Times,* June 23, 2016, https://www.nytimes.com/2016/06/24/business/jeff-gennette-to-replace-terry-lundgren-as-macys-chief.html; and S. Kapner, "Macy's Hires eBay Executive amid Management Shakeup," *The Wall Street Journal,* August 21, 2017, https://www.wsj.com/articles/macys-hires-ebay-executive-amid-management-shakeup-1503348301.

20. A. Kinicki, K. Jacobson, B. Galvin, and G. Prussia, "A Multilevel Systems Model of Leadership," *Journal of Leadership & Organizational Studies,* May 2011, pp. 133–149.

21. C. R. Breer, R. F. Lusch, and M. A. Hitt, "A Service Perspective for Human Capital Resources: A Critical Base for Strategy Implementation," *Academy of Management,* May 2017, pp. 137–158.

22. P. Wahba, "Why Macy's Departing Chairman Thinks the Chain Has Turned a Corner," *Fortune,* January 19, 2018, http://fortune.com/2018/01/19/macys-lundgren/; L. Dignan, "Macy's, Kohl's, Blue Apron Share One Thing: Fear of Being Amazon-ed," *ZDNet,* August 10, 2017, http://www.zdnet.com/article/macys-kohls-blue-apron-share-one-thing-fear-of-being-amazon-ed/.

23. Dignan, "Macy's, Kohl's, Blue Apron Share One Thing: Fear of Being Amazon-ed," *ZDNet,* August 10, 2017, http://www.zdnet.com/article/macys-kohls-blue-apron-share-one-thing-fear-of-being-amazon-ed/.

24. L. Thomas, "Macys Reports Stronger Holiday Sales, but Not Enough to Ward Off Dismal 2017," *CNBC,* January 4, 2018, https://www.cnbc.com/2018/01/04/macys-holiday-sales-stronger-but-not-enough-to-ward-off-dismal-2017.html.

25. N. Tajitsu, "Toyota Forecasts Tough Outlook for U.S. Sales, Yen Boost to Overall Profit," *Reuters,* November 6, 2017, https://www.reuters.com/article/us-toyota-results/toyota-forecasts-tough-outlook-for-u-s-sales-yen-boost-to-overall-profit-idUSKBN1D70JC.

26. M. Kawai, "Monozukuri Supporting Toyota's Competitiveness," *Toyota Global,* February 6, 2018, http://www.toyota-global.com/pages/contents/investors/financial_result/2018/pdf/q3/competitiveness.pdf.

27. "Top Ten Most Reliable 2017 Cars," JD Power, October 4, 2017, http://www.jdpower.com/cars/articles/top-10-most-reliable-2017-cars.

28. O. Jurevicius, "SWOT Analysis of Toyota," *Strategic Management Insight,* December 10, 2016, https://www.strategicmanagementinsight.com/swot-analyses/toyota-swot-analysis.html.

29. J. Dudovskiy, "Toyota SWOT Analysis," *Research Methodology,* January 23, 2016, https://research-methodology.net/toyota-swot-analysis/.

30. O. Jurevicius, "SWOT Analysis of Toyota," *Strategic Management Insight,* December 10, 2016, https://www.strategicmanagementinsight.com/swot-analyses/toyota-swot-analysis.html.

31. "Voluntary Recalls," *Toyota USA Newsroom,* http://toyotanews.pressroom.toyota.com/section_display.cfm?section_id=639 (accessed March 5, 2018).

32. J. Dudovskiy, "Toyota SWOT Analysis," *Research Methodology,* January 23, 2016, https://research-methodology.net/toyota-swot-analysis/.

33. O. Jurevicius, "SWOT Analysis of Toyota," *Strategic Management Insight,* December 10, 2016, https://www.strategicmanagementinsight.com/swot-analyses/toyota-swot-analysis.html.

34. A. Shah, "Toyota Seeks India Sales Boost with Aspirational, Global-Spec Models," *Reuters,* February 7, 2018, https://www.reuters.com/article/us-india-autoshow-toyota/toyota-seeks-india-sales-boost-with-aspirational-global-spec-models-idUSKBN1FR1BR.

35. S. Glinton, "Automakers Say Trump's Anti-NAFTA Push Could Upend Their Industry," *NPR,* February 26, 2018, https://www.npr.org/2018/02/26/583943580/automakers-say-trumps-anti-nafta-push-could-upend-their-industry.

36. O. Jurevicius, "SWOT Analysis of Toyota," *Strategic Management Insight,* December 10, 2016, https://www.strategicmanagementinsight.com/swot-analyses/toyota-swot-analysis.html.

37. C. Said, "Shuddle 'Uber for Kids' Service Reaches End of Road," *San Francisco Chronicle,* April 14, 2016, https://www.sfchronicle.com/business/article/Shuddle-Uber-for-kids-service-reaches-end-7249450.php.

38. J. B. Barney, "Firm Resources and Sustained Competitive Advantage," *Journal of Management* 19 (1991), pp. 99–120.

39. C. Said, "Shuddle 'Uber for Kids' Service Reaches End of Road," *San Francisco Chronicle,* April 14, 2016, https://www.sfchronicle.com/business/article/Shuddle-Uber-for-kids-service-reaches-end-7249450.php.

40. D. Clark and R. McMillan, "Giants Tighten Grip on Internet Economy," *The Wall Street Journal,* November 6, 2011, pp. B1, B4; F. Manjoo, "'Frightful 5' to Dominate Digital Life a Long Time," *The New York Times,* January 21, 2016, pp. B1, B7. See also J. Graham, "Top Stories of 2015," *Reno Gazette-Journal,* January 2, 2016, p. 5B, reprinted from *USA Today;* the article reports that the companies dominating the 2015 tech headlines were Amazon, Apple, Facebook, and Google.

41. D. Clark and R. McMillan, "Giants Tighten Grip on Internet Economy," *The Wall Street Journal,* November 6, 2011, pp. B1, B4.

42. F. Manjoo, "'Frightful 5' to Dominate Digital Life a Long Time," *The New York Times,* January 21, 2016, pp. B1, B7.

43. M. Anderson, "As Amazon Turns 20, a Look at Its Biggest Bets," *Reno Gazette-Journal,* July 19, 2015, pp. 1D, 5D.

44. F. Manjoo, "'Frightful 5' to Dominate Digital Life a Long Time," *The New York Times,* January 21, 2016, pp. B1, B7.

45. M. Wolff, "The End of Yahoo Is Justly Near," *Reno Gazette-Journal,* December 21, 2016, p. 4B, reprinted from *USA Today.*

CHAPTER NOTES

46. Anshu Sharma, quoted in C. Mims, "Why Companies Are Being Disrupted," *The Wall Street Journal*, January 25, 2016, p. B4.

47. For forecasting related to public policy and political polling, see "Why Even the Best Forecasters Sometimes Miss the Mark," *Knowledge@Wharton*, April 19, 2016, http://knowledge.wharton.upenn.edu/article/why-even-the-best-forecasters- sometimes-miss-the-mark (accessed April 24, 2016).

48. S. Banker, "The Supply Chain Implications of the Houston Flood," *Forbes*, August 29, 2017, https://www.forbes.com/sites/stevebanker/2017/08/29/the-supply-chain-implications-of-the-houston-flood/#4d4b8e882c22.

49. N. Bomey, "UPS, FedEx Halt Delivery to Major Areas of Texas, Louisiana amid Storm," *USA Today*, August 29, 2017, https://www.usatoday.com/story/money/2017/08/29/ups-fedex-usps-hurricane-harvey-amazon/613027001/.

50. N. Bomey, "UPS, FedEx Halt Delivery to Major Areas of Texas, Louisiana amid Storm," *USA Today*, August 29, 2017, https://www.usatoday.com/story/money/2017/08/29/ups-fedex-usps-hurricane-harvey-amazon/613027001/.

51. W. Risher, "How FedEx Is Coping with Hurricane Harvey's Impact," *Transport Topics*, August 29, 2017, http://www.ttnews.com/articles/how-fedex-coping-hurricane-harveys-impact.

52. N. Bomey, "UPS, FedEx Halt Delivery to Major Areas of Texas, Louisiana amid Storm," *USA Today*, August 29, 2017, https://www.usatoday.com/story/money/2017/08/29/ups-fedex-usps-hurricane-harvey-amazon/613027001/.

53. C. Goldwasser, "Benchmarking: People Make the Process," *Management Review*, June 1995, p. 40.

54. "Benchmarking," *Bain & Company*, November 7, 2017, www.bain.com/publications/articles/management-tools-benchmarking.aspx.

55. J. Spacey, "12 Examples of Benchmarking," *Simplicable*, July 4, 2017, https://simplicable.com/new/benchmarking.

56. "Etsy, Inc. Reports First Quarter 2017 Financial Results," *Etsy Investor Relations*, May 2, 2017, https://investors.etsy.com/news-and-events/press-releases/2017/05-02-2017-211356003.

57. A. Balakrishnan, "Etsy Shares Seesaw Despite Better-than-Expected Quarterly Sales," *CNBC*, November 6, 2017, https://www.cnbc.com/2017/11/06/etsy-earnings-q3-2017.html.

58. A. Balakrishnan, "Etsy Shares Seesaw Despite Better-than-Expected Quarterly Sales," *CNBC*, November 6, 2017, https://www.cnbc.com/2017/11/06/etsy-earnings-q3-2017.html.

59. H. Tabuchi, "Etsy Welcomes Manufacturers to Artisanal Fold," *The New York Times*, September 14, 2015, pp. B1, B2. See also A. Larocca, "Etsy Wants to Crochet Its Cake and Eat It Too," *New York Magazine*, April 4–17, 2016, pp. 39–45.

60. S. Elliott, "Still Ticking, Timex Nods to Heritage in a Fast World," *The New York Times*, January 22, 2014, p. B6.

61. "Timex, Share Your Style," *Timex*, https://www.timex.com/as-seen-in.html (accessed March 5, 2018).

62. B. Sisario and K. Russell, "Sales Hold Steady for a Radically Changed Music Industry," *The New York Times*, March 25, 2016, pp. B1, B7.

63. H. Karp, "Streaming Gives Music Industry a Lift," *The Wall Street Journal*, April 13, 2016, p. B4.

64. Applications of the technique can be found in L. Norton, "4 Lessons to Learn from Declining Business Models: How to Prevent Your Organization from Going Extinct," *HRNews*, March 27, 2017; G. Genoveva and T. S. Siam, "Analysis of Marketing Strategy and Competitive Advantage," *The International Journal of Economic Perspectives*, 2017, pp. 1571–1579.

65. A. Kasi, "BCG Matrix of Dell," *BCG*, April 1, 2017, http://bcgmatrixanalysis.com/bcg-matrix-of-dell/.

66. M. Johnson, "15 of the Best Mergers & Acquisitions of 2017," *Nasdaq*, December 29, 2017, https://www.nasdaq.com/article/15-of-the-best-mergers-acquisitions-of-2017-cm898464.

67. M. Johnson, "15 of the Best Mergers & Acquisitions of 2017," *Nasdaq*, December 29, 2017, https://www.nasdaq.com/article/15-of-the-best-mergers-acquisitions-of-2017-cm898464.

68. F. A. Hanssen, "Vertical Integration during the Hollywood Studio Era," *Journal of Law & Economics*, August 2010, pp. 519–543.

69. K. Favaro, "Vertical Integration 2.0: An Old Strategy Makes a Comeback," *Strategy+Business*, May 6, 2015, www.strategy-business.com/blog/Vertical-Integration-2-0-An-Old-Strategy-Makes-a-Comeback?gko=41fe1 (accessed April 26, 2016).

70. M. E. Porter, *Competitive Strategy* (New York: The Free Press, 1980). See also M. E. Porter, "The Five Competitive Forces That Shape Strategy," *Harvard Business Review*, January 2008, pp. 79–93.

71. See R. Greenspan, "Starbucks Coffee's Five Forces Analysis (Porter's Model)," *Panmore Institute*, January 31, 2017, http://panmore.com/starbucks-coffee-five-forces-analysis-porters-model; M. Farber, "Dunkin' Donuts Is Considering a Name Change," *Fortune*, August 4, 2017, http://fortune.com/2017/08/04/dunkin-donuts-name-change/.

72. "Supplier Diversity Program," *Starbucks*, https://www.starbucks.com/responsibility/sourcing/suppliers (accessed March 5, 2018).

73. A. Mceachern, "Loyalty Case Study: Starbucks Rewards," *Smile.io*, July 24, 2017, https://blog.smile.io/loyalty-case-study-starbucks-rewards.

74. P. Mourdoukoutas, "Competition Is Catching Up, as Starbucks Buzz Cools Off," *Forbes*, July 29, 2017, https://www.forbes.com/sites/panosmourdoukoutas/2017/07/29/competition-is-catching-up-as-starbucks-buzz-cools-off/#4a57c4752962.

75. L. Myler, "How Differentiation Strategies Can Get You to Pay 4,400 Times More for a Commodity," *Forbes*, November 23, 2016, https://www.forbes.com/sites/larrymyler/2016/11/23/how-differentiation-strategies-can-get-you-to-pay-4400-times-more-for-a-commodity/#769b94dc4413.

76. J. K. Willcox, "With Redbox on Demand, Kiosk Company Gives Streaming a Second Shot," *Consumer Reports*, February 16, 2018, https://www.consumerreports.org/streaming-video-services/with-redbox-on-demand-kiosk-company-gives-streaming-another-shot/.

77. S. Saltzman, "How Lush Is Winning at Both Online and Brick-and-Mortar Beauty Retail," *Fashionista*, August 28, 2017, https://fashionista.com/2017/08/lush-cosmetics-business-strategy.

78. B. W. Barry, "A Beginner's Guide to Strategic Planning," *The Futurist*, April 1998, pp. 33–36; from B. W. Barry, *Strategic Planning Workbook for Nonprofit Organizations*, revised and updated (St. Paul, MN: Amherst H. Wilder Foundation, 1997).

79. L. Bossidy and Ram Charan, with C. Burck, *Execution: The Discipline of Getting Things Done* (New York: Crown Business, 2002).

80. Results can be found in "Wanted: Employees Who Get Things Done," *HR Magazine*, January 2008, p. 10.

81. J. Muller, "Ford Fires CEO Mark Fields; Former Steelcase Chief Jim Hackett to Take Over," *Forbes*, May 21, 2017, https://www.forbes.com/sites/joannmuller/2017/05/21/ford-fires-ceo-mark-fields-former-steelcase-chief-jim-hackett-to-take-over/#7466b65979dc.

82. R. Kaplan and D. Norton, "Mastering the Management System," *Harvard Business Review*, January 2008, pp. 66–77.

83. P. Economy, "Salesforce, Facebook, Google, Costco, and Starbucks among 50 Best Places to Work in 2017," *Inc.*, July 6, 2017, https://www.inc.com/peter-economy/salesforce-facebook-google-costco-and-starbucks-am.html.

84. "Costco Has Great Benefits," *Costco.com*, https://www.costco.com/benefits.html (accessed March 5, 2018).

85. J. Ho, "How McDonald's, Costco, and IKEA Can Help You Discover the Perfect Business Model," *Inc.*, May 17, 2017, https://www.inc.com/jackelyn-ho/happy-with-your-business-model-mcdonalds-and-ikea-might-just-change-your-mind.html?cid=search.

86. K. Taylor, "Costco Is Beating Walmart and Amazon with the 'Best Business Model' in Retail," *Business Insider*, February 22, 2016, http://www.businessinsider.com/why-costcos-business-model-is-so-great-2016-2.

87. Execution is also discussed by C. Montgomery, "Putting Leadership Back into Strategy," *Harvard Business Review*, January 2008, pp. 54–60; J. Lorsch and R. Clark, "Leading from the Boardroom," *Harvard Business Review*, April 2008, pp. 105–111.

88. J. Zenger and J. Folkman, "4 Ways to Be More Effective at Execution," *Harvard Business Review,* May 23, 2016, https://hbr.org/2016/05/4-ways-to-be-more-effective-at-execution.

89. J. Zenger and J. Folkman, "4 Ways to Be More Effective at Execution," *Harvard Business Review,* May 23, 2016, https://hbr.org/2016/05/4-ways-to-be-more-effective-at-execution.

90. C. Ong, "5 Key Steps for Successful Strategy Execution," *Envisio,* September 14, 2017, http://www.envisio.com/blog/5-key-steps-for-successful-strategy-execution.

91. J. Zenger and J. Folkman, "4 Ways to Be More Effective at Execution," *Harvard Business Review,* May 23, 2016, https://hbr.org/2016/05/4-ways-to-be-more-effective-at-execution.

92. "A Simple Guide to Becoming a Better Business Strategist," *Macquarie,* December 12, 2016, https://www.macquarie.com/au/advisers/expertise/smart-practice/6-ways-you-can-improve-your-strategic-thinking.

93. N. Bowman, "4 Ways to Improve Your Strategic Thinking Skills," *Harvard Business Review,* December 27, 2016, https://hbr.org/2016/12/4-ways-to-improve-your-strategic-thinking-skills.

94. These suggestions were based on J. Sullivan, "6 Ways to Screen Job Candidates for Strategic Thinking," *Harvard Business Review,* December 13, 2016, https://hbr.org/2016/12/6-ways-to-screen-job-candidates-for-strategic-thinking.

95. D. Lacy, "Talent Management: Understand Your Employer's Business to Become Strategic Partner," *Dresser & Associates,* 2018, www.dresserassociates.com/knowledge-center/talent-management/Understand-Your-Employers-Business.php#.

96. "A Simple Guide to Becoming a Better Business Strategist," *Macquarie,* December 12, 2016, https://www.macquarie.com/au/advisers/expertise/smart-practice/6-ways-you-can-improve-your-strategic-thinking.

97. See the description in "Six Thinking Hats," *The De Bono Group,* www.debonogroup.com/six-thinking-hats.php (accessed March 11, 2018).

98. "Fact Sheet," General Electric, August 1, 2017, https://www.ge.com/about-us/fact-sheet.

99. C. Gasparino and B. Schwartz, "Neutron Jack Welch Is Going Nuclear over GE Meltdown," *Fox Business*, January 19, 2018, http://www.foxbusiness.com/markets/2018/01/19/neutron-jack-welch-is-going-nuclear-over-ge-meltdown.html.

100. "Jeff Immelt," *Wikipedia,* https://en.wikipedia.org/wiki/Jeff_Immelt (accessed February 5, 2018).

101. "Jeff Immelt," *Wikipedia,* https://en.wikipedia.org/wiki/Jeff_Immelt (accessed February 5, 2018).

102. D. Bennett, "How GE Went from American Icon to Astonishing Mess," *Bloomberg*, February 1, 2018, https://www.bloomberg.com/news/features/2018-02-01/how-ge-went-from-american-icon-to-astonishing-mess.

103. T. Franck, "GE Will Likely Be Dropped from the Dow, Deutsche Bank Predicts," *CNBC,* January 31, 2018, https://www.cnbc.com/2018/01/31/ge-will-likely-be-dropped-from-the-dow-deutsche-bank-predicts.html.

104. A. Raghavan and K. Kranhold, "GE Unveils $9.5 Billion Deal to Acquire U.K.'s Amersham," *The Wall Street Journal,* October 10, 2003, https://www.wsj.com/articles/SB106574018488408500.

105. A. Stratton, "A Timeline of Jeff Immelt's Tenure as GE's CEO," *The Wall Street Journal,* June 12, 2017, https://www.wsj.com/articles/a-timeline-of-jeff-immelts-tenure-as-ges-ceo-1497276816.

106. D. Bennett, "How GE Went from American Icon to Astonishing Mess," *Bloomberg*, February 1, 2018, https://www.bloomberg.com/news/features/2018-02-01/how-ge-went-from-american-icon-to-astonishing-mess.

107. A. Scott, "GE Shifts Strategy, Financial Targets for Digital Business after Missteps," *Reuters*, August 30, 2017, https://www.reuters.com/article/us-ge-digital-outlook-insight/ge-shifts-strategy-financial-targets-for-digital-business-after-missteps-idUSKCN1B80CB.

108. "GE Completes Acquisition of Alstom Power and Grid Businesses," *GE Newsroom*, November 3, 2015, https://www.genewsroom.com/press-releases/ge-completes-acquisition-alstom-power-and-grid-businesses-282204.

109. "GE Completes Acquisition of Alstom Power and Grid Businesses," *GE Newsroom*, November 3, 2015, https://www.genewsroom.com/press-releases/ge-completes-acquisition-alstom-power-and-grid-businesses-282204.

110. "Aviation History," *GE Aviation*, https://www.geaviation.com/company/aviation-history (accessed February 7, 2018).

111. G. Bradt, "GE's Impending Breakup's Underlying Root Cause: The Need for a Single Overarching Strategy," *Forbes*, January 18, 2018, https://www.forbes.com/sites/georgebradt/2018/01/17/ges-impending-breakups-underlying-root-cause-the-need-for-a-single-overarching-strategy/#13f19516fc0b.

112. T. Gryta, J. S. Lublin, and D. Benoit, "'Success Theater' Masked Rot at GE," *The Wall Street Journal*, February 22, 2018, p. A8.

113. D. Bennett, "How GE Went from American Icon to Astonishing Mess," *Bloomberg*, February 1, 2018, https://www.bloomberg.com/news/features/2018-02-01/how-ge-went-from-american-icon-to-astonishing-mess.

114. C. Gasparino, "GE CEO Feud: Welch vs. Immelt," *Fox Business*, January10, 2018, www.foxbusiness.com/markets/2018/01/10/ge-ceo-feud-welch-vs-immelt.html.

115. D. Bennett, "How GE Went from American Icon to Astonishing Mess," *Bloomberg*, February 01, 2018, https://www.bloomberg.com/news/features/2018-02-01/how-ge-went-from-american-icon-to-astonishing-mess.

116. R. D'Aveni, "General Electric Should Defy Wall Street Pressure to Break Up," *Forbes,* January 19, 2018, https://www.forbes.com/sites/richarddaveni/2018/01/19/now-is-the-worst-time-for-ge-to-break-up/#6b415c292f0d.

117. "Flannery Unveils His Strategy to Revive GE," *The Economist*, November 16, 2017, https://www.economist.com/news/business/21731412-newish-bosss-plan-focused-slashing-costs-sharpening-culture-and-shrinking.

118. D. Bennett, "How GE Went from American Icon to Astonishing Mess," *Bloomberg*, February 1, 2018, https://www.bloomberg.com/news/features/2018-02-01/how-ge-went-from-american-icon-to-astonishing-mess.

119. R. D'Aveni, "General Electric Should Defy Wall Street Pressure to Break Up," *Forbes,* January 19, 2018, https://www.forbes.com/sites/richarddaveni/2018/01/19/now-is-the-worst-time-for-ge-to-break-up/#6b415c292f0d.

120. M. Korn and C. Rexrode, "Banks Pay Big Bucks for Top Billing on College Campuses," *The Wall Street Journal*, January 28, 2018, https://www.wsj.com/articles/banks-pay-big-bucks-for-top-billing-on-college-campuses-1517148001.

121. A. Carrns, "Count Bank Overdraft Fees as a Holiday Expense, Too," *The New York Times*, January 5, 2018, https://www.nytimes.com/2018/01/05/your-money/bank-overdraft-fees.html.

122. M. Korn and C. Rexrode, "Banks Pay Big Bucks for Top Billing on College Campuses," *The Wall Street Journal*, January 28, 2018, https://www.wsj.com/articles/banks-pay-big-bucks-for-top-billing-on-college-campuses-1517148001.

123. M. Korn and C. Rexrode, "Banks Pay Big Bucks for Top Billing on College Campuses," *The Wall Street Journal*, January 28, 2018, https://www.wsj.com/articles/banks-pay-big-bucks-for-top-billing-on-college-campuses-1517148001.

124. "U.S. Bank Student Checking Account," *U.S. Bank,* 2018, https://www.usbank.com/student-banking/student-accounts-and-cards/student-checking.html (accessed January 30, 2018).

125. M. Korn and C. Rexrode, "Banks Pay Big Bucks for Top Billing on College Campuses," *The Wall Street Journal*, January 28, 2018, https://www.wsj.com/articles/banks-pay-big-bucks-for-top-billing-on-college-campuses-1517148001.

126. M. Jarzemsky, "Cuomo Probes Cards' School Ties," *The Wall Street Journal,* September 4, 2010, https://www.wsj.com/articles/SB10001424052748704855104575470040614786402.

127. J. Silver-Greenberg and M.Pilon, "Cards Return to School," *The Wall Street Journal,* May 7, 2011, https://www.wsj.com/articles/SB10001424052748704322804576303652621312770.

LEARNING MODULE 1

1. B. Blake, "Do You Have That Entrepreneurship 'It' Factor? Find Out Here," *Forbes*, https://www.forbes.com/sites/brockblake/2018/02/10/do-you-have-that-entrepreneurship-it-factor-find-out-here/#23f02a394cf5.

2. S. Stahl, "Five Steps to Pivoting into Entrepreneurship," *Forbes*, November 21, 2017, https://www.forbes.com/sites/ashleystahl/2017/11/21/five-steps-to-pivoting-into-entrepreneurship/#7d5f6507545c.

3. M. Murmann, "The Startups Most Likely to Succeed Have Technical Founders Who Quickly Hire Businesspeople," *Harvard Business Review*, November 6, 2017, https://hbr.org/2017/11/the-startups-most-likely-to-succeed-have-technical-founders-who-quickly-hire-businesspeople.

4. M. R. Sheradsky, "Why Pursuing Entrepreneurship Is a Wise Move for Motivated Founders," *Forbes*, March 19, 2018, https://www.forbes.com/sites/theyec/2018/03/19/why-pursuing-entrepreneurship-is-a-wise-move-for-motivated-founders/#7bdeb86bc776.

5. R. A. Friedman, "The Trouble with Being the Boss," *The Wall Street Journal*, February 9, 2018, p. M4.

6. L. Kim, "11 Most Famous Entrepreneurs of All Time (and What Made Them Wildly Rich)," *Inc.*, April 30, 2015, https://www.inc.com/larry-kim/11-most-famous-entrepreneurs-of-all-time-and-what-made-them-wildly-rich.html.

7. T. Loudenback, "Tesla Shareholders Just Approved a $2.6 Billion Stock Option Plan for Elon Musk—Here's How He Spends His $20 Billion Fortune," *Business Insider*, March 21, 2018, http://www.businessinsider.com/tesla-elon-musk-net-worth-2017-10.

8. "Elon Musk," *Wikipedia*, last updated on March 27, 2018, https://en.wikipedia.org/wiki/Elon_Musk.

9. R. K. Jain, "Entrepreneurial Competencies: A Meta-Analysis and Comprehensive Conceptualization for Future Research," *Vision*, 2011, p. 128.

10. Boston BBB, "The Difference between Entrepreneurs and the Self-Employed," *Malden Patch*, September 12, 2013, https://patch.com/massachusetts/malden/the-difference-between-entrepreneurs-and-the-selfemployed_0bb9c4b9.

11. A. Vance, "Time for Microsoft to Tap Its Inner Google," *Bloomberg Businessweek*, February 10–16, 2014, pp. 8–9; D. Clark, M. Langley, and S. Ovide, "Microsoft's CEO Pick: From India to Insider," *The Wall Street Journal*, February 1–2, 2014, pp. A1, A2.

12. R. Branson, "Richard Branson on Intrapreneurs," *Entrepreneur.com*, accessed February 28, 2016; A. Bruzzese, "Entrepreneurialism at Work," *Arizona Republic*, January 15, 2014, p. CL-1.

13. N. Singer, "The Watched Lab of Dr. Bell," *The New York Times*, February 16, 2014, pp. BU-1, BU-4, BU-5.

14. Boston BBB, "The Difference between Entrepreneurs and the Self-Employed," *Malden Patch*, September 12, 2013, https://patch.com/massachusetts/malden/the-difference-between-entrepreneurs-and-the-selfemployed_0bb9c4b9.

15. "The Distinction between Entrepreneurship and Self-Employment," *Kenyaplex*, November 3, 2017, https://www.kenyaplex.com/resources/13730-the-distinction-between-entrepreneurship-and-self-employment.aspx.

16. N. Mavindidze, "Entrepreneurship vs Self-Employment," *The Herald*, March 27, 2018, https://www.herald.co.zw/entrepreneurship-vs-self-employment.

17. "Elon Musk," *Wikipedia*, last updated on March 27, 2018, https://en.wikipedia.org/wiki/Elon_Musk.

18. N. Mavindidze, "Entrepreneurship vs Self-Employment," *The Herald*, March 27, 2018, https://www.herald.co.zw/entrepreneurship-vs-self-employment.

19. "The Distinction between Entrepreneurship and Self-Employment," *Kenyaplex*, November 3, 2017, https://www.kenyaplex.com/resources/13730-the-distinction-between-entrepreneurship-and-self-employment.aspx.

20. H. Brandstätter, "Personality Aspects of Entrepreneurship: A Look at Five Meta-Analyses," *Personality and Individual Differences*, August 2011, pp. 222–230; R. K. Jain, "Entrepreneurial Competencies: A Meta-Analysis and Comprehensive Conceptualization for Future Research," *Vision*, 2011, pp. 127–152.

21. R. K. Jain, "Entrepreneurial Competencies: A Meta-Analysis and Comprehensive Conceptualization for Future Research," *Vision*, 2011, p. 134.

22. H. Brandstätter, "Personality Aspects of Entrepreneurship: A Look at Five Meta-Analyses," *Personality and Individual Differences*, August 2011, pp. 222–230; R. K. Jain, "Entrepreneurial Competencies: A Meta-Analysis and Comprehensive Conceptualization for Future Research," *Vision*, 2011, pp. 127–152.

23. T. Butler, "Hiring An Entrepreneurial Leader," *Harvard Business Review*, March–April 2017, pp. 85–93.

24. H. Kanapi, "15 Entrepreneurship Statistics That You Should Know," *FitSmallBusiness*, July 30, 2017, https://fitsmallbusiness.com/entrepreneurship-statistics.

25. Definition by Paul Graham, head of business accelerator Y Combinator, cited in N. Robehmed, "What Is a Startup?" *Forbes*, December 16, 2013, www.forbes.com/sites/natalierobehmed/2013/12/16/what-is-a-strartup/print.

26. B. Carson, "The 17 Best New Startups That Have Launched This Year," *Business Insider*, July 15, 2017,

27. J. Mannes, "VoiceOps Launches to Put Insights in the Hands of Managers Coaching Sales Reps," *TechCrunch*, April 12, 2017, https://techcrunch.com/2017/04/12/voiceops-launches-to-put-insights-in-the-hands-of-managers-coaching-sales-reps/.

28. M. Kosoff, "These 15 Startups Didn't Exist 5 Years Ago—Now They're Worth Billions," *Business Insider*, December 10, 2015, http://www.businessinsider.com/these-startups-didnt-exist-5-years-ago-now-theyre-worth-billions-2015-12.

29. "Frequently Asked Questions," U.S. Small Business Administration Office of Advocacy, June 2016, http://www.sba.gov/sites/default/files/advocacy/SB-FAQ-2016_WEB.pdf.

30. "Frequently Asked Questions," U.S. Small Business Administration Office of Advocacy, January 2011, http://www.sba.gov/advo.

31. "Data Release," *Sageworks*, December 8, 2017, https://www.sageworks.com/data-releases/state-small-business-entering-2018.

32. "Frequently Asked Questions," U.S. Small Business Administration Office of Advocacy, June 2016, http://www.sba.gov/sites/default/files/advocacy/SB-FAQ-2016_WEB.pdf.

33. T. Seth, "Standard of Living: Meaning, Factor and Other Details," *Economics Discussion*, http://www.economicsdiscussion.net/articles/standard-of-living-meaning-factor-and-other-details/1453 (accessed March 29, 2018).

34. S. Singer, M. Herrington, and E. Menipaz, "Global Report 2017/18," *Global Entrepreneurship Monitor*, 2018, http://gemconsortium.org/report.

35. A. Vance, "Polymath Who Dreams Up More Contraptions than Edison," *Bloomberg Businessweek*, October 26–November 1, 2015, pp. 57–61.

36. D. Crimmins, "Lowell Wood—The Quiet Genius," *Roots of Wealth*, January 11, 2016, https://www.rootsofwealth.com/lowell-wood-the-quiet-genius.

37. "Top 10 Sources of Business Ideas & Opportunities for 2018," *ProfitableVenture*, 2018, https://www.profitableventure.com/sources-of-business-ideas.

38. B. Ansberry, "An Entrepreneur with Autism Finds His Path," *The Wall Street Journal*, November 27, 2017, pp. R1–R2.

39. A. Vance, "Celtic Tigers," *Bloomberg Businessweek*, August 7, 2017, p. 39.

40. S. Ward, "7 Ways to Discover a Winning Business Idea," *The Balance*, November 25, 2016, https://www.thebalance.com/create-winning-business-ideas-2947249.

41. I. Morris, "Apple Responds to iPhone Slowdown Complaints and Offers Solutions," *Forbes*, December 28, 2017, https://www.forbes.com/sites/ianmorris/2017/12/28/apple-responds-to-iphone-slowdown-complaints-and-offers-solutions/#5da610db79ee.

42. F. J. Greene and C. Hopp, "Research: Writing a Business Plan Makes Your Startup More Likely to Succeed," *Harvard Business Review,* July 14, 2017, https://hbr.org/2017/07/research-writing-a-business-plan-makes-your-startup-more-likely-to-succeed.

43. S. Robbins, "Why You Must Have a Business Plan," *Entrepreneur,* https://www.entrepreneur.com/article/74194 (accessed March 30, 2018).

44. F. J. Greene and C. Hopp, "Research: Writing a Business Plan Makes Your Startup More Likely to Succeed," *Harvard Business Review,* July 14, 2017, https://hbr.org/2017/07/research-writing-a-business-plan-makes-your-startup-more-likely-to-succeed.

45. F. J. Greene and C. Hopp, "Are Formal Planners More Likely to Achieve New Venture Viability? A Counterfactual Model and Analysis," *Strategic Entrepreneurial Journal,* March 2017, pp. 36–60.

46. S. Ward, "One-Page Business Plan Templates," *The Balance,* April 10, 2017, https://www.thebalance.com/one-page-business-plan-templates-4135972; N. Parsons, "How to Write a One-Page Business Plan," *Bplans,* https://articles.bplans.com/how-to-write-a-one-page-business-plan (accessed March 30, 2018).

47. P. Hull, "10 Essential Business Plan Components," *Forbes,* February 21, 2013, https://www.forbes.com/sites/patrickhull/2013/02/21/10-essential-business-plan-components; "7 Elements of a Business Plan," Quickbooks, 2017, https://quickbooks.intuit.com/r/business-planning/7-elements-business-plan.

48. S. Caramela, "How to Choose the Best Legal Structure for Your *Business," Business News Daily,* January 29, 2018, https://www.businessnewsdaily.com/8163-choose-legal-business-structure.html; and "IRS Business Structures," *Internal Revenue Service,* last updated December 14, 2017, https://www.irs.gov/businesses/small-businesses-self-employed/business-structures.

49. "Sole Proprietorships," *Internal Revenue Service,* last updated March 13, 2018, https://www.irs.gov/businesses/small-businesses-self-employed/sole-proprietorships.

50. "Partnerships," *Internal Revenue Service,* last updated on March 2, 2018, https://www.irs.gov/businesses/small-businesses-self-employed/partnerships.

51. M. Symonds, "Why Entrepreneurship Isn't Just a Kid's Game," *Forbes,* March 23, 2018, https://www.forbes.com/sites/mattsymonds/2018/03/23/why-entrepreneurship-isnt-just-a-kids-game/#4d25ae69638c.

52. S. Caramela, "How to Choose the Best Legal Structure for Your Business," *Business News Daily,* January 29, 2018, https://www.businessnewsdaily.com/8163-choose-legal-business-structure.html.

53. S. Caramela, "How to Choose the Best Legal Structure for Your Business," *Business News Daily,* January 29, 2018, https://www.businessnewsdaily.com/8163-choose-legal-business-structure.html; "Forming a Corporation," *Internal Revenue Service,* last updated December 15, 2017, https://www.irs.gov/businesses/small-businesses-self-employed/forming-a-corporation.

54. "Forming a Corporation," *Internal Revenue Service,* last updated December 15, 2017, https://www.irs.gov/businesses/small-businesses-self-employed/forming-a-corporation.

55. "S Corporations," *Internal Revenue Service,* last updated October 6, 2016, https://www.irs.gov/businesses/small-businesses-self-employed/s-corporations.

56. "2017 Mid-Year Economic Report," *National Small Business Association,* 2017, http://www.nsba.biz/wp-content/uploads/2017/09/Mid-Year-Economic-Report-2017.pdf.

57. H. R. Johnson, "What Is an LLC (Limited Liability Company)?" *Legal Zoom,* https://www.legalzoom.com/articles/what-is-a-limited-liability-company-llc?kid=0f29ecc7-72c8-4a58-8f23-4c2193ac028c&utm_source=google&utm_medium=cpc&utm_term=what_is_an_llc&utm_content=247005141740&utm_campaign=BIZ_|_LLC&gclid=CjwKCAjwwPfVBRBiEiwAdkM0HYjZQSz6F3Q_BaPhdbJeQSC_ftIBJhH6mpreIPmnln-JVyOxl1OH5_BoC92sQAvD_BwE (accessed March 30, 2018).

58. "2017 Mid-Year Economic Report," *National Small Business Association,* 2017, http://www.nsba.biz/wp-content/uploads/2017/09/Mid-Year-Economic-Report-2017.pdf.

59. G. Schmid, "17 Statistics Every Business Owner Needs to Be Well Aware of," *Fundera Ledger,* July 19, 2017, https://www.fundera.com/blog/small-business-statistics.

60. "2017 Mid-Year Economic Report," *National Small Business Association,* http://www.nsba.biz/wp-content/uploads/2017/09/Mid-Year-Economic-Report-2017.pdf (accessed April 12, 2018).

61. "2017 Mid-Year Economic Report," *National Small Business Association,* 2017, http://www.nsba.biz/wp-content/uploads/2017/09/Mid-Year-Economic-Report-2017.pdf.

62. "2017 Mid-Year Economic Report," *National Small Business Association,* 2017, http://www.nsba.biz/wp-content/uploads/2017/09/Mid-Year-Economic-Report-2017.pdf.

63. "About the SBA," *U.S. Small Business Association,* https://www.sba.gov/about-sba/what-we-do/mission (accessed April 2, 1018).

64. "About the SBA," *U.S. Small Business Association,* https://www.sba.gov/about-sba/what-we-do/history (accessed April 2, 1018).

65. "7 Sources of Start-Up Financing," *bdc,* https://www.bdc.ca/en/articles-tools/start-buy-business/start-business/pages/start-up-financing-sources.aspx (accessed April 2, 1018).

66. "How Venture Capitalists Really Assess a Pitch," *Harvard Business Review,* May–June 2017, https://hbr.org/2017/05/how-venture-capitalists-really-assess-a-pitch.

67. "7 Sources of Start-Up Financing," *bdc,* https://www.bdc.ca/en/articles-tools/start-buy-business/start-business/pages/start-up-financing-sources.aspx (accessed April 2, 2018).

68. "How Venture Capitalists Really Assess a Pitch," *Harvard Business Review,* May–June 2017, https://hbr.org/2017/05/how-venture-capitalists-really-assess-a-pitch.

69. "What Is Crowd Investing?" *SyndicateRoom,* https://www.syndicateroom.com/crowd-investing (accessed April 2, 2018).

70. C. Hartnell, A. Kinicki, L. Lambert, M. Fugate, and P. Corner, "Do Similarities or Differences between CEO Leadership and Organizational Culture Have a More Positive Effect on Firm Performance? A Test of Competing Predictions," *Journal of Applied Psychology* 101 (2016), 846–861.

71. A. Y. Ou, C. Hartnell, A. Kinicki, E. Kram, and Choi, "Culture in Context: A Meta-Analysis of the Nomological Network of Organizational Culture," Presentation at Connecting Culture and Context: Insights from Organizational Culture Theory and Research, 2016 National Academy of Management meeting, Anaheim, California.

CHAPTER 7

1. B. Taylor, "How Coca-Cola, Netflix, and Amazon Learn from Failure," *Harvard Business Review,* November 10, 2017, https://hbr.org/2017/11/how-coca-cola-netflix-and-amazon-learn-from-failure.

2. L. Quinto, "Critical Thinking Starts with an Open Mind," *EDA,* October 3, 2016, https://www.executivedevelopment.com/critical-thinking-starts-open-mind/.

3. K. Hedges, "How to Keep an Open Mind," *Forbes,* December 17, 2015, https://www.forbes.com/sites/work-in-progress/2015/12/17/how-to-keep-an-open-mind/3/#6c44903046ac.

4. P. Hopper and K. Sakuja, "A 4-Step Process to Help Senior Teams Prioritize Decisions," *Harvard Business Review,* March 27, 2017, https://hbr.org/2017/03/a-4-step-process-to-help-senior-teams-prioritize-decisions.

5. M. Myatt, "6 Tips for Making Better Decision," *Forbes,* March 28, 2012, https://www.forbes.com/sites/mikemyatt/2012/03/.../6-tips-for-making-better-decisions.

6. D. Kaplan, "Starbucks: The Art of Endless Transformation," *Inc.,* June 2014, pp. 82–86, 128.

7. "Starbucks Company Statistics," *Statistics Brain,* August 12, 2013, www.statisticbrain.com/starbucks-company-statistics (accessed June 13, 2014).

8. H. Schultz, quoted in J. H. Ostdick, "Rekindling the Heart & Soul of Starbucks," *Success,* www.success.com/article/rekindling-the-heart-soul-of-starbucks (accessed May 2, 2016).

9. J. Jargon, "Starbucks CEO to Focus on Digital," *The Wall Street Journal,* January 30, 2014, p. B6; B. Gruley and L. Patton, "The Arabica Project," *Bloomberg Businessweek,* February 17–23, 2014, pp. 64–69; B. Horovitz, "Starbucks Serving Alcohol at More Locations," *USA Today,* March 21, 2014, p. 5B; Associated Press, "Boutique Coffee Shops Jolt Chains to Step Up Game," *San Francisco Chronicle,* March 26, 2016, p. D2.

10. B. Horowitz, "Starbucks Climbs to No. 2 in Sales," *Reno Gazette-Journal,* March 21, 2015, p. 4B, reprinted from *USA Today.*

11. B. Kowitt, "Howard Schultz Has Something Left to Prove," *Fortune,* June 8, 2017, http://fortune.com/2017/06/08/fortune-500-starbucks-howard-schultz/.

12. W. Duggan, "Starbucks Is Brewing Up a Comeback," *U.S. News & World Report,* April 21, 2017, https://money.usnews.com/investing/articles/2017-04-21/starbucks-corporation-sbux-is-brewing-up-a-comeback.

13. B. Horowitz, "Why People Love to Love-Hate Starbucks," *USA Today,* February 12, 2014, p. 2A.

14. D. Kahneman, *Thinking, Fast and Slow* (New York: Farrar, Straus and Giroux, 2011), pp. 20–22.

15. Book review of Kahneman, *Thinking, Fast and Slow,* by J. Holt, "Two Brains Running," *The New York Times,* November 25, 2011, www.nytimes.com/2011/11/27/books/review/thinking-fast-and-slow-by-daniel-kahneman-book-review.html?_r=0 (accessed May 3, 2016).

16. "Wean Wall Street Off Its Gambling Addictions," editorial, *USA Today,* March 1, 2010, p. 15A.

17. Chip Heath, quoted in J. Rae-Dupree, "Innovative Minds Don't Think Alike," *The New York Times,* December 30, 2007, business section, p. 3.

18. G. Tett, *The Silo Effect: The Peril of Expertise and the Promise of Breaking Down Barriers* (Boston: Little, Brown, 2015).

19. A. Farnham, "Teaching Creativity Tricks to Buttoned-Down Executives," *Fortune,* January 10, 1994, pp. 94–100.

20. H. A. Simon, *Administrative Behavior,* 3rd ed. (New York: Free Press, 1996); H. A. Simon, "Making Management Decisions: The Role of Intuition and Emotion," *The Academy of Management Executive,* February 1987, pp. 57–63.

21. D. Farrell and F. Grieg, "How Falling Gas Prices Fuel the Consumer: Evidence from 25 Million People," JPMorgan Chase & Co. Institute, October 2015, https://www.jpmorganchase.com/content/dam/jpmorganchase/en/legacy/corporate/institute/document/jpmc-institute-gas-report.pdf (accessed May 7, 2016).

22. J. Brustein and S. Soper, "Who's Alexa?" *Bloomberg Businessweek,* May 2–May 8, 2016, pp. 31–33.

23. J. Wortham, "Once Just a Site with Funny Cat Pictures, and Now a Web Empire," *The New York Times,* June 14, 2010, pp. B1, B8.

24. D. Kahneman and G. Klein, "Conditions for Intuitive Expertise: A Failure to Disagree," *American Psychologist,* September 2009, pp. 515–526.

25. H. Asvoll, "Developing a Framework of Reflective, Intuitive Knowing in Innovation Management," *Academy of Strategic Management Journal,* 2017, pp. 1-22.

26. A. Jackson, "Elon Musk Uses This 6-Step Process to Make Decisions," *Inc.,* November 16, 2017, https://www.inc.com/business-insider/how-elon-musk-makes-decisions-rolling-stone.html.

27. D. Straus, "How to Learn the 1 Skill That Comes Naturally to Elon Musk, Jeff Bezos and Nikola Tesla," *Inc.,* August 2, 2017, https://www.inc.com/david-straus/how-to-learn-the-1-skill-that-comes-naturally-to-e.html.

28. S. Lewin, "'Crazy Things Can Come True': Elon Musk Reacts to Falcon Heavy Launch Success," *Space.com,* February 7, 2018, https://www.space.com/39618-elon-musk-falcon-heavy-spacex-reaction.html.

29. S. Lewin, "'Crazy Things Can Come True': Elon Musk Reacts to Falcon Heavy Launch Success," *Space.com,* February 7, 2018, https://www.space.com/39618-elon-musk-falcon-heavy-spacex-reaction.html.

30. R. Umoh, "Steve Jobs and Albert Einstein Both Attributed Their Extraordinary Success to This Personality Trait," *CNBC,* June 29, 2017, https://www.cnbc.com/2017/06/29/steve-jobs-and-albert-einstein-both-attributed-their-extraordinary-success-to-this-personality-trait.html.

31. R. Umoh, "Steve Jobs and Albert Einstein Both Attributed Their Extraordinary success to This Personality Trait," *CNBC,* June 29, 2017, https://www.cnbc.com/2017/06/29/steve-jobs-and-albert-einstein-both-attributed-their-extraordinary-success-to-this-personality-trait.html.

32. R. Umoh, "Steve Jobs and Albert Einstein Both Attributed Their Extraordinary Success to This Personality Trait," *CNBC,* June 29, 2017, https://www.cnbc.com/2017/06/29/steve-jobs-and-albert-einstein-both-attributed-their-extraordinary-success-to-this-personality-trait.html.

33. E. Dane and M. G. Pratt, "Exploring Intuition and Its Role in Managerial Decision Making," *Academy of Management Review,* January 2007, pp. 33–54.

34. I. Gallo, S. Sood, T. C. Mann, and T. Gilovich, "The Heart and the Head: On Choosing Experiences Intuitively and Possessions Deliberately," *Journal of Behavioral Decision Making,* July 2017, pp. 754–768.

35. Advice attributed to Sunny Vanderbeck of Satori Capital, Dallas, in V. Harnish, "Finding the Route to Growth," *Fortune,* May 18, 2014, p. 45.

36. Courage and intuition are discussed by K. K. Reardon, "Courage as a Skill," *Harvard Business Review,* March 2007, pp. 51–56.

37. M. Oshin, "Elon Musk's '3-Step' First Principles Thinking: How to Think and Solve Difficult Problems Like a Genius," *The Mission,* August 30, 2017, https://medium.com/the-mission/elon-musks-3-step-first-principles-thinking-how-to-think-and-solve-difficult-problems-like-a-ba1e73a9f6c0.

38. M. Oshin, "Elon Musk's '3-Step' First Principles Thinking: How to Think and Solve Difficult Problems Like a Genius," *The Mission,* August 30, 2017, https://medium.com/the-mission/elon-musks-3-step-first-principles-thinking-how-to-think-and-solve-difficult-problems-like-a-ba1e73a9f6c0.

39. D. Straus, "How to Learn the 1 Skill That Comes Naturally to Elon Musk, Jeff Bezos and Nikola Tesla," *Inc.,* August 2, 2017, https://www.inc.com/david-straus/how-to-learn-the-1-skill-that-comes-naturally-to-e.html.

40. A. Blinder, "Mine Chief Is Sentenced in Conspiracy over Safety," *The New York Times,* April 7, 2016, pp. A12, A17; B. McLean, "Poison Pill," *Vanity Fair,* February 2016, pp. 106–109, 142–144.

41. J. Kauflin, "The 10 Biggest CEO Departures of 2017," *Forbes,* December 14, 2017, https://www.forbes.com/sites/jeffkauflin/2017/12/14/the-10-biggest-ceo-departures-of-2017/#47a1d7e60ae7.

42. M. Astor, "Florida Legislator's Aide Is Fired after He Calls Parkland Students 'Actors,'" *The New York Times,* February 20, 2018, https://www.nytimes.com/2018/02/20/us/florida-shooting-benjamin-kelly-actors.html.

43. K. Rivera and P. Karlsson, "CEOs Are Getting Fired for Ethical Lapses More Than They Used to," *Harvard Business Review,* June 6, 2017, https://hbr.org/2017/06/ceos-are-getting-fired-for-ethical-lapses-more-than-they-used-to.

44. M. J. Quade, R. L. Greenbaum, and O. V. Petrenko, "'I Don't Want to be Near You, Unless . . . ': The Interactive Effect of Unethical Behavior and Performance onto Relationship Conflict and Workplace Ostracism," *Personnel Psychology,* 2017, pp. 675–709.

45. M. J. Lupoli, L. Jampol, and C. Oveis, "Lying Because We Care: Compassion Increases Prosocial Lying," *Journal of Experimental Psychology,* 2017, pp. 1026–1042; Y. Liu, S. Zhao, R. Li, L. Zhou, and F. Tian, "The Relationship between Organizational Identification and Internal Whistle-Blowing: The Joint Moderating Effects of Perceived Ethical Climate and Proactive Personality," *Review of Managerial Science,* January 2018, pp. 113–134.

46. C. Clifford, "These 14 Billionaires Just Promised to Give Away More Than Half of Their Money Like Bill Gates and Warren Buffett," *CNBC,* May 31, 2017, https://www.cnbc.com/2017/05/31/14-billionaires-signed-bill-gates-and-warren-buffetts-giving-pledge.html.

47. "A Commitment to Philanthropy," *The Giving Pledge,* accessed March 6, 2018, https://givingpledge.org/.

48. C. McNamara, "Complete Guide to Ethics Management: An Ethics Toolkit for Managers," www.mapnp.org/library/ethics/ethxgde.htm (accessed June 14, 2014).

49. D. Meinert, "Creating an Ethical Culture," *HR Magazine*, April 2014, pp. 23–27.
50. Warby Parker cofounder Neil Blumenthal, quoted in L. Philip, "Warby Parker's Philanthropic Vision," *Philadelphia Style*, August 29, 2012, http://phillystylemag.com/warby-parker-philanthropy-vision-spring (accessed May 9, 2016).
51. C. E. Bagley, "The Ethical Leader's Decision Tree," *Harvard Business Review*, February 2003, pp. 18–19.
52. C. E. Bagley, "The Ethical Leader's Decision Tree," *Harvard Business Review*, February 2003, p. 19.
53. C. E. Bagley, "The Ethical Leader's Decision Tree," *Harvard Business Review*, February 2003, p. 19.
54. The website YourMorals.org studies morality and values, offering questionnaires for readers to fill out. Some of the results are described in J. Haidt, *The Righteous Mind: Why Good People Are Divided by Politics and Religion* (New York: Random House, 2012).
55. M. Harrell and L. Barbato, "Great Managers Still Matter: The Evolution of Google's Project Oxygen," *RE: Work*, February 27, 2018, https://rework.withgoogle.com/blog/the-evolution-of-project-oxygen/.
56. B. Hall, "Google's Project Oxygen Pumps Fresh Air into Management," *TheStreet*, February 11, 2014, https://www.thestreet.com/story/12328981/1/googles-project-oxygen-pumps-fresh-air-into-management.html (accessed May 20, 2016).
57. M. Harrell and L. Barbato, "Great Managers Still Matter: The Evolution of Google's Project Oxygen," *RE: Work*, February 27, 2018, https://rework.withgoogle.com/blog/the-evolution-of-project-oxygen/.
58. J. Pfeffer and R. I. Sutton, "Profiting from Evidence-Based Management," *Strategy & Leadership* 34, no. 2 (2006), pp. 35–42.
59. Pfeffer's recent book, *Leadership BS: Fixing Workplaces and Careers One Truth at a Time* (New York: HarperCollins, 2015).
60. J. Pfeffer and R. I. Sutton, "Profiting from Evidence-Based Management," *Strategy & Leadership* 34, no. 2 (2006), pp. 35–42.
61. J. Wortham, "In Tech, Starting Up by Failing," *The New York Times*, January 18, 2012, pp. B1, B6.
62. Reported in A. Shontell, "The Tech 'Titanic': How Red-Hot Startup Fab raised $330 Million and Then Went Bust," *Business Insider*, February 6, 2015, www.businessinsider.com/how-billion-dollar-startup-fab-died-2015-2 (accessed May 9, 2016).
63. C. Garling, "Excessive Hype Does Promising Products No Favors," *San Francisco Chronicle*, September 27, 2013, p. C5.
64. "Are CEOs Less Ethical Than in the Past?" *Strategy&*, accessed March 6, 2018, https://www.strategyand.pwc.com/ceosuccess.
65. Bryant, "Google's Quest to Build a Better Boss."
66. J. Pfeffer and R. I. Sutton, "Profiting from Evidence-Based Management," *Strategy & Leadership* 34, no. 2 (2006), pp. 35–42.
67. L. Garfield, "6 Before-and-After Transformations of Dead Shopping Malls That Were Given New Lives," *Business Insider*, April 1, 2017, http://www.businessinsider.com/dead-shopping-malls-transformations-2017-3#after-undergoing-a-facelift-the-building-re-opened-as-the-global-mall-at-the-crossings-in-2013-its-now-a-satellite-campus-of-nashville-state-community-college-and-includes-617000-square-feet-of-retail-space-a-recreation-center-classrooms-a-library-and-an-.
68. J. Pfeffer and R. I. Sutton, "Profiting from Evidence-Based Management," *Strategy & Leadership* 34, no. 2 (2006), pp. 66–67.
69. G. Loveman, "Diamonds in the Data Mine," *Harvard Business Review*, May 2003, pp. 109–113. See also T. Davenport, L. Prusak, and B. Strong, "Putting Ideas to Work," *The Wall Street Journal*, March 10, 2008, p. R11.
70. T. H. Davenport, "Competing on Analytics," *Harvard Business Review*, January 2006, pp. 99–107.
71. S. Baker, "How Much Is That Worker Worth?" *BusinessWeek*, March 23 & 30, 2009, pp. 46–48.
72. D. Robson, "Considered a Data Dinosaur, a Sport Is Trying an Analytic Approach," *The New York Times*, August 14, 2015, p. B8.
73. M. Lewis, *Moneyball: The Art of Winning an Unfair Game* (New York: W.W. Norton, 2004). For comment on the Oakland A's and *Moneyball*, see J. Manuel, "Majoring in Moneyball," *Baseball America Features*, December 23, 2003, www.baseballamerica.com/today/features/031223collegemoneyball.html.
74. G. Ferrari-King, "Most Advanced Analytics Teams in Sports," *Bleacher Report*, October 6, 2016, http://bleacherreport.com/articles/2667799-most-advanced-analytics-teams-in-sports.
75. B. Cohen, "Remaking Basketball the Warriors' Way," *The Wall Street Journal*, April 7, 2016, pp. A1, A12; M. Johnson, "Now NBA Defenses Got Turned Inside Out," *The Wall Street Journal*, March 2, 2015, p. B8.
76. Lacob, quoted in Schoenfeld, "Team Building."
77. A. Hirsch, "Falcons Making Modern Analytics a Priority in 2016," *AtlantaFalcons.com*, April 21, 2016, http://www.atlantafalcons.com/news/blog/article-1/Falcons-Making-Modern-Analytics-a-Priority-in-2016/a67cc515-e8d0-4cdc-9038-fd3bdb7b7099.
78. "The Atlanta Falcons Sleep Performance Program | FusionHealth," *YouTube.com*, accessed March 7, 2018, https://www.youtube.com/watch?v=SHDEkZT0x2g.
79. G. Ferrari-King, "Most Advanced Analytics Teams in Sports," *Bleacher Report*, October 6, 2016, http://bleacherreport.com/articles/2667799-most-advanced-analytics-teams-in-sports.
80. T. H. Davenport, "Competing on Analytics," *Harvard Business Review*, January 2006, pp. 99–107.
81. G. Bensinger and L. Stevens, "Delivery Startup to Get Funding from UPS," *The Wall Street Journal*, February 24, 2016, p. B6.
82. "UPS Explores Drone Deliveries of Life-Saving Medicines," *Phys Org*, May 9, 2016, http://phys.org/news/2016-05-ups-explores-drone-deliveries-life-saving.html (accessed May 13, 2016).
83. T. H. Davenport, "Competing on Analytics," *Harvard Business Review*, January 2006, pp. 99–107.
84. A. Cave, "What Will We Do When The World's Data Hits 163 Zettabytes In 2025?" *Forbes*, April 13, 2017, https://www.forbes.com/sites/andrewcave/2017/04/13/what-will-we-do-when-the-worlds-data-hits-163-zettabytes-in-2025/#5eb2e78b349a.
85. J. Thomas, "Where Is the World Supposed to Put All of Its Data?" *Forbes.com*, February 17, 2015, www.forbes.com/sites/ibm/2015/02/17/where-is-the-world-supposed-to-put-all-of-its-data/#33e2a986112c (accessed May 13, 2016).
86. A. Brust, "Big Data: Defining Its Definition," *ZDNet*, March 1, 2012, www.zdnet.com/article/big-data-defining-its-definition/ (accessed May 13, 2016).
87. S. Lohr, "Amid the Flood, a Catchphrase Is Born," *The New York Times*, August 12, 2012, p. BU-3.
88. M. S. Malone, "The Big-Data Future Has Arrived," *The Wall Street Journal*, February 23, 2016, p. A17.
89. McKinsey Global Institute report, May 2011, quoted in J. Temple, "Big Data Can Lead to Big Breakthroughs in Research," *San Francisco Chronicle*, December 9, 2011, www.sfgate.com/cgi-bin/article.cgi?f=/c/a/2011/12/08/BUDC1M9I8A.DTL (accessed June 14, 2014).
90. "Big Data Executive Survey 2018," *New Vantage Partners*, http://newvantage.com/wp-content/uploads/2018/01/Big-Data-Executive-Survey-2018-Findings.pdf (accessed March 7, 2018).
91. T. H. Davenport, "Analytics 3.0," *Harvard Business Review*, December 2013, pp. 65–72.
92. J. Temple, "Big Data Can Lead to Big Breakthroughs in Research," *San Francisco Chronicle*, December 9, 2011, www.sfgate.com/cgi-bin/article.cgi?f=/c/a/2011/12/08/BUDC1M9I8A.DTL (accessed June 14, 2014).
93. M. Wilson, "Infiniti Research: Four Hot Retail Trends," *CSA*, February 26, 2018, https://www.chainstoreage.com/store-spaces/infiniti-research-four-hot-retail-trends/.
94. "Should Hiring Be Based on Gut—or Data?" *Knowledge@Wharton*, August 24, 2015, http://knowledge.wharton.upenn.edu/article/should-hiring-be-based-on-gut-or-data (accessed May 13, 2016); M. Luca, J. Kleinberg, and S. Mullainathan, "Algorithms Need Managers, Too," *Harvard Business Review*, January–February 2016, pp. 97–101.
95. B. Aslan, "To All Recruiters—Use Machine Learning to Hire Better Candidates," *Medium*, June 8, 2016, https://medium.com/@

deadlocked_d/to-all-recruiters-use-machine-learning-to-hire-better-candidates-c5aad22f3319.

96. R. E. Silverman, "Bosses Tap Big Data to Flag Workers' Ills," *The Wall Street Journal*, February 17, 2016, pp. B1, B7.

97. J. Markoff, "Government Aims to Build a 'Data Eye in the Sky,'" *The New York Times*, October 11, 2011, p. D1.

98. B. Sisario, "Discography Site Charms Album Fans," *The New York Times*, December 30, 2015, pp. B1, B4; B. Sisario, "Going to the Ends of the Earth to Get the Most Out of Music," *The New York Times*, June 8, 2015, pp. B1, B4.

99. S. Ember, "As Digital Upends TV Viewing, Data Reigns," *The New York Times*, May 12, 2015, pp. B1, B6; "How Data Analytics Is Shaping What You Watch," *Knowledge@Wharton*, September 3, 2015, http://knowledge.wharton.upenn.edu/article/how-data-analytics-is-shaping-what-you-watch/ (accessed May 13, 2016).

100. A. Alter and K. Russell, "Moneyball for Book Publishers, Tracking the Way We Read," *The New York Times*, March 15, 2016, pp. B1, B6.

101. R. Bean, "Bloomberg's Data Initiative: Big Data for Social Good in 2018," *Forbes*, January 2, 2018, https://www.forbes.com/sites/ciocentral/2018/01/02/bloombergs-data-initiative-big-data-for-social-good-in-2018/#26d0d793a441; "Data for Health," *Bloomberg Philanthropies*, https://www.bloomberg.org/program/public-health/data-health/#problem (accessed March 8, 2018).

102. L. Currey Post, "Big Data Helps UK National Health Service Lower Costs, Improve Treatments," *Forbes*, February 7, 2018, https://www.forbes.com/sites/oracle/2018/02/07/big-data-helps-uk-national-health-service-lower-costs-improve-treatments/#45021d4a58e3.

103. M. S. Malone, "The Big-Data Future Has Arrived," *The Wall Street Journal*, February 23, 2016, p. A17; L. Landro, "Mining Malpractice Data to Make Health Care Safer," *The Wall Street Journal*, May 10, 2016, p. D3.

104. "FACT SHEET: Launching the Data-Driven Justice Initiative: Disrupting the Cycle of Incarceration," The White House: Office of the Press Secretary, June 30, 2016, https://obamawhitehouse.archives.gov/the-press-office/2016/06/30/fact-sheet-launching-data-driven-justice-initiative-disrupting-cycle.

105. C. Mims, "Easy-to-Use Yelp and Google Hold Pointers to Fix Balky Governments," *The Wall Street Journal*, May 9, 2016, pp. B1, B5.

106. M. Madden and L. Rainee, "Americans' Attitudes about Privacy, Security, and Surveillance," *Pew Research Center*, May 20, 2015, www.pewinternet.org/2015/05/20/americans-attitudes-about-privacy-security-and-surveillance (accessed May 15, 2016).

107. D. Borak and K. Vasel, "The Equifax Hack Could Be Worse Than We Thought," *CNN Money*, February 10, 2018, http://money.cnn.com/2018/02/09/pf/equifax-hack-senate-disclosure/index.html.

108. T. Fox-Brewster, "A Brief History of Equifax Security Fails," *Forbes*, September 8, 2017, https://www.forbes.com/sites/thomasbrewster/2017/09/08/equifax-data-breach-history/#48e79e4b677c.

109. L. Hay Newman, "Equifax Officially Has No Excuse," *Wired*, September 14, 2017, https://www.wired.com/story/equifax-breach-no-excuse/.

110. P. Rucker, "Exclusive: U.S. Consumer Protection Official Puts Equifax Probe on Ice—Sources," *Reuters*, February 4, 2018, https://www.reuters.com/article/us-usa-equifax-cfpb/exclusive-u-s-consumer-protection-official-puts-equifax-probe-on-ice-sources-idUSKBN1FP0IZ.

111. D. Lindorff, "Five Months after Equifax Hack, Social Security Still Relies on Discredited Firm," *Salon*, January 8, 2018, https://www.salon.com/2018/01/08/five-months-after-equifax-hack-social-security-still-relies-on-discredited-firm/.

112. D. Fischer, "Big Data Is Overrated Compared to Human Ingenuity," *Forbes*, January 17, 2018, https://www.forbes.com/sites/forbestechcouncil/2018/01/17/big-data-is-overrated-compared-to-human-ingenuity/2/#4af0187c76e5.

113. The discussion of styles was based on material contained in A. J. Rowe and R. O. Mason, *Managing with Style: A Guide to Understanding, Assessing and Improving Decision Making* (San Francisco: Jossey-Bass, 1987), pp. 1–17.

114. I. Salisbury, "This Is Jeff Bezos' Best Advice about Making Big Decisions," *Money*, April 13, 2017, http://time.com/money/4738244/bezos-decision-making-fast/.

115. J. Cao, "IBM's Rometty Sees AI Changing, Not Eliminating, Future Jobs," *Bloomberg Technology*, September 13, 2017, https://www.bloomberg.com/news/articles/2017-09-13/ibm-s-rometty-sees-ai-changing-not-eliminating-future-jobs; H. Merry, "InterConnect Keynote: Ginni Rometty, Watson Cloud," *IBM*, March 21, 2017, https://www.ibm.com/blogs/internet-of-things/ginni-rometty-interconnect-cloud/.

116. E. Lytkina Botelho, K. Rosenkoetter Powell, S. Kincaid, and D. Wang, "What Sets Successful CEOs Apart," *Harvard Business Review*, May–June 2017, https://hbr.org/2017/05/what-sets-successful-ceos-apart.

117. R. Makgosa and O. Sangodoyin, "Retail Market Segmentation: The Use of Consumer Decision-Making Styles, Overall Satisfaction and Demographics," *The International Review of Retail*, February 2018, pp. 64–91.

118. D. Kahnemann and A. Tversky, "Judgment under Uncertainty: Heuristics and Biases," *Science* 185 (1974), pp. 1124–1131; A. Tversky and D. Kahneman, "The Belief in the Law of Numbers," *Psychological Bulletin* 76 (1971), pp. 105–110; D. R. Bobocel and J. P. Meyer, "Escalating Commitment to a Failing Course of Action: Separating the Roles of Choice and Justification," *Journal of Applied Psychology*, June 1994, pp. 360–363.

119. K. Breuninger, "The Odds of Winning Those Record Powerball, Mega Millions Jackpots Are beyond Slim," *CNBC*, January 5, 2018, https://www.cnbc.com/2018/01/05/odds-of-winning-a-lottery-jackpot-are-worse-than-you-expect.html.

120. N. Hertz, "Why We Make Bad Decisions," *The New York Times*, October 20, 2013, p. SR-6.

121. S. Borenstein, "Disasters Often Stem from Hubris," *The Arizona Republic*, July 10, 2010, p. A4.

122. D. Kahneman, "The Surety of Fools," *The New York Times Magazine*, October 19, 2011, pp. 30–33, 62.

123. S. Li, Y. Sun, and Y. Wang, "50% Off or Buy One, Get One Free? Frame Preference as a Function of Consumable Nature in Dairy Products," *Journal of Social Psychology* 147 (2007), pp. 413–421.

124. S. Benartzi, "How People Err in Estimating Their Spending in Retirement," *The Wall Street Journal*, March 28, 2016, p. R4.

125. K. Johnson, "U.S. Spent $86 Million on Plane Never Flown," *USA Today*, March 30, 2016, https://www.usatoday.com/story/news/politics/2016/03/30/pentagon-dea-afghanistan/82432898/.

126. J. Ross and B. M. Staw, "Organizational Escalation and Exit: Lessons from the Shoreham Nuclear Power Plant," *Academy of Management Journal*, August 1993, pp. 701–732.

127. C. Metz, "Paul Allen Wants to Teach Machines Common Sense," *The New York Times*, February 28, 2018, https://www.nytimes.com/2018/02/28/technology/paul-allen-ai-common-sense.html.

128. "AI Drives Better Business Decisions," *MIT Technology Review*, June 20, 2016, https://www.technologyreview.com/s/601732/ai-drives-better-business-decisions/.

129. "AI Drives Better Business Decisions," *MIT Technology Review*, June 20, 2016, https://www.technologyreview.com/s/601732/ai-drives-better-business-decisions/.

130. "Apple and Amazon's Moves in Health Signal a Coming Transformation," *The Economist*, February 3, 2018, https://www.economist.com/news/business/21736193-worlds-biggest-tech-firms-see-opportunity-health-care-which-could-mean-empowered.

131. A. Agrawal, J. Gans, and A. Goldfarb, "How AI Will Change the Way We Make Decisions," *Harvard Business Review*, July 26, 2017, https://hbr.org/2017/07/how-ai-will-change-the-way-we-make-decisions.

132. T. Simonite, "Two Giants of AI Team Up to Head Off the Robot Apocalypse," *Wired*, July 7, 2017, https://www.wired.com/story/two-giants-of-ai-team-up-to-head-off-the-robot-apocalypse/.

133. T. Simonite, "Two Giants of AI Team Up to Head Off the Robot Apocalypse," *Wired,* July 7, 2017, https://www.wired.com/story/two-giants-of-ai-team-up-to-head-off-the-robot-apocalypse/.

134. "AI Drives Better Business Decisions," *MIT Technology Review,* June 20, 2016, https://www.technologyreview.com/s/601732/ai-drives-better-business-decisions/.

135. "AI Drives Better Business Decisions," *MIT Technology Review,* June 20, 2016, https://www.technologyreview.com/s/601732/ai-drives-better-business-decisions/.

136. "Artificial Intelligence Is the Future of Growth," *Accenture,* accessed March 8, 2018, https://www.accenture.com/us-en/insight-artificial-intelligence-future-growth.

137. T. Simonite, "Two Giants of AI Team Up to Head Off the Robot Apocalypse," *Wired,* July 7, 2017, https://www.wired.com/story/two-giants-of-ai-team-up-to-head-off-the-robot-apocalypse/.

138. C. Clifford, "Top A.I. Experts Warn of a 'Black Mirror'-esque Future with Swarms of Micro-Drones and Autonomous Weapons," *CNBC,* February 21, 2018, https://www.cnbc.com/2018/02/21/openai-oxford-and-cambridge-ai-experts-warn-of-autonomous-weapons.html.

139. R. Varshneya, "Three Ways Business Leaders Can Use AI Right Now," *Inc.,* February 23, 2018, https://www.inc.com/rahul-varshneya/three-ways-business-leaders-can-use-ai-right-now.html.

140. F. Tepper, "You Can Text SFMOMA and It Will Respond with Art on Demand," *techcrunch.com,* July 10, 2017, https://techcrunch.com/2017/07/10/you-can-text-sfmoma-and-it-will-respond-with-art-on-demand/.

141. "How Artificial Intelligence Can Eliminate Bias and Improve HR Operations," *Forbes* Human Resources Council, October 3, 2017, https://www.forbes.com/sites/forbeshumanresourcescouncil/2017/10/03/how-artificial-intelligence-can-eliminate-bias-and-improve-hr-operations/#78ae3e834573.

142. C. Clifford, "Steve Wozniak Explains Why He Used to Agree with Elon Musk, Stephen Hawking on A.I.—But Now He Doesn't," *CNBC,* February 23, 2018, https://www.cnbc.com/2018/02/23/steve-wozniak-doesnt-agree-with-elon-musk-stephen-hawking-on-a-i.html.

143. C. Metz, "Good News: A.I. Is Getting Cheaper. That's Also Bad News," *The New York Times,* February 20, 2018, https://www.nytimes.com/2018/02/20/technology/artificial-intelligence-risks.html.

144. C. Clifford, "Top A.I. Experts Warn of a 'Black Mirror'-esque Future with Swarms of Micro-Drones and Autonomous Weapons," *CNBC,* February 21, 2018, https://www.cnbc.com/2018/02/21/openai-oxford-and-cambridge-ai-experts-warn-of-autonomous-weapons.html.

145. C. Metz, "Good News: A.I. Is Getting Cheaper. That's Also Bad News," *The New York Times,* February 20, 2018, https://www.nytimes.com/2018/02/20/technology/artificial-intelligence-risks.html.

146. C. Clifford, "Top A.I. Experts Warn of a 'Black Mirror'-esque Future with Swarms of Micro-Drones and Autonomous Weapons," *CNBC,* February 21, 2018, https://www.cnbc.com/2018/02/21/openai-oxford-and-cambridge-ai-experts-warn-of-autonomous-weapons.html.

147. T. Simonite, "Two Giants of AI Team Up to Head Off the Robot Apocalypse," *Wired,* July 7, 2017, https://www.wired.com/story/two-giants-of-ai-team-up-to-head-off-the-robot-apocalypse/.

148. C. Clifford, "Steve Wozniak Explains Why He Used to Agree with Elon Musk, Stephen Hawking on A.I.—But Now He Doesn't," *CNBC,* February 23, 2018, https://www.cnbc.com/2018/02/23/steve-wozniak-doesnt-agree-with-elon-musk-stephen-hawking-on-a-i.html.

149. G. W. Hill, "Group versus Individual Performance: Are $n + 1$ Heads Better Than 1?" *Psychological Bulletin,* May 1982, pp. 517–539. Also see W. T. H. Koh, "Heterogeneous Expertise and Collective Decision-Making," *Social Choice and Welfare,* April 2008, pp. 457–473.

150. N. F. R. Maier, "Assets and Liabilities in Group Problem Solving: The Need for Integrative Function," *Psychological Review* 74 (1967), pp. 239–249.

151. N. F. R. Maier, "Assets and Liabilities in Group Problem Solving: The Need for Integrative Function," *Psychological Review* 74 (1967), pp. 239–249.

152. S. Cain, "The Rise of the New Groupthink," *The New York Times,* January 15, 2012, pp. WR1, WR6; J. Lehrer, "Groupthink," *The New Yorker,* January 30, 2012, pp. 22–27.

153. Methods for increasing group consensus were investigated by R. L. Priem, D. A. Harrison, and N. K. Muir, "Structured Conflict and Consensus Outcomes in Group Decision Making," *Journal of Management,* December 22, 1995, pp. 691–710.

154. I. Janis, *Groupthink,* 2nd ed. (Boston: Houghton Mifflin, 1982), p. 9. See also K. D. Lassila, "A Brief History of Groupthink," *Yale Alumni Magazine,* January–February 2008, pp. 59–61, www.philosophy-religion.org/handouts/pdfs/BRIEF-HISTORY_GROUPTHINK.pdf (accessed August 10, 2016).

155. J. Sonnenfeld, "Another Suicidal Board? How DuPont's Directors Failed Ellen Kullman," *Fortune,* October 15, 2015, http://fortune.com/2015/10/13/dupont-board-ellen-kullman/?iid=sr-link7#160 (accessed September 14, 2016).

156. A. Bruzzese, "Keep Remote Workers in the Loop," *Arizona Republic,* March 2, 2011.

157. I. Janis, *Groupthink,* 2nd ed. (Boston: Houghton Mifflin, 1982), pp. 174–175.

158. Surowiecki, quoted in Kemper, "Senate Intelligence Report: Groupthink Viewed as Culprit in Move to War"; J. A. LePine, "Adaptation of Teams in Response to Unforeseen Change: Effects of Goal Difficulty and Team Composition in Terms of Cognitive Ability and Goal Orientation," *Journal of Applied Psychology* 90 (2005), pp. 1153–1167.

159. C. R. Sunstein and R. Hastie, "How to Defeat Groupthink: Five Solutions," *Fortune,* January 13, 2015, http://fortune.com/2015/01/13/groupthink-solutions-information-failure/?iid=sr-link2#160 (accessed September 14, 2016).

160. D. L. Gladstein and N. P. Reilly, "Group Decision Making under Threat: The Tycoon Game," *Academy of Management Journal,* September 1985, pp. 613–627.

161. These conclusions were based on the following studies: J. H. Davis, "Some Compelling Intuitions about Group Consensus Decisions, Theoretical and Empirical Research, and Interpersonal Aggregation Phenomena: Selected Examples, 1950–1990," *Organizational Behavior and Human Decision Processes,* June 1992, pp. 3–38; and J. A. Sniezek, "Groups under Uncertainty: An Examination of Confidence in Group Decision Making," *Organizational Behavior and Human Decision Processes,* June 1992, pp. 124–155.

162. M. W. Blenko, M. C. Mankins, and P. Rogers, "The Decision-Driven Organization," *Harvard Business Review,* June 2010, pp. 55–62.

163. T. Rogers, "How to Design Small Decision Groups," *Amazing Applications of Probability and Statistics,* www.intuitor.com/statistics/SmallGroups.html (accessed June 12, 2016).

164. Supporting results can be found in J. R. Hollenbeck, D. R. Ilgen, D. J. Sego, J. Hedlund, D. A. Major, and J. Phillips, "Multilevel Theory of Team Decision Making: Decision Performance in Teams Incorporating Distributed Expertise," *Journal of Applied Psychology,* April 1995, pp. 292–316.

165. D. H. Gruenfeld, E. A. Mannix, K. Y. Williams, and M. A. Neale, "Group Composition and Decision Making: How Member Familiarity and Information Distribution Affect Process and Performance," *Organizational Behavior and Human Decision Processes,* July 1996, pp. 1–15.

166. P. L. McLeod, R. S. Baron, M. W. Marti, and K. Yoon, "The Eyes Have It: Minority Influence in Face-to-Face and Computer-Mediated Group Discussions," *Journal of Applied Psychology* 82 (1997), pp. 706–718.

167. Results can be found in C. K. W. De Dreu and M. A. West, "Minority Dissent and Team Innovation: The Importance of Participation in Decision Making," *Journal of Applied Psychology,* December 2001, pp. 1191–1201.

168. G. M. Parker, *Team Players and Teamwork: The New Competitive Business Strategy* (San Francisco: Jossey-Bass, 1990).
169. These recommendations were obtained from G. M. Parker, *Team Players and Teamwork: The New Competitive Business Strategy* (San Francisco: Jossey-Bass, 1990).
170. A. F. Osborn, *Applied Imagination: Principles and Procedures of Creative Thinking,* 3rd ed. (New York: Scribner's, 1979). For an example of how brainstorming works, see P. Croce, "Think Brighter," *FSB,* January 2006, p. 35.
171. M. Oppezzo and D. L. Schwartz, "Give Your Ideas Some Legs: The Positive Effect of Walking on Creative Thinking," *Journal of Experimental Psychology: Learning, Memory, and Cognition* 40, no. 4 (2014), pp. 1142–1152.
172. W. H. Cooper, R. Brent Gallupe, S. Pallard, and J. Cadsby, "Some Liberating Effects of Anonymous Electronic Brainstorming," *Small Group Research,* April 1998, pp. 147–178.
173. See K. Eaton, "Finding the Right App to Unblock Those Creative Juices," *The New York Times,* February 27, 2014, p. B9.
174. D. Meinert, "Brainstorming Gone Bad," *HR Magazine,* April 2016, p. 14.
175. G. Katzenstein, "The Debate on Structured Debate: Toward a Unified Theory," *Organizational Behavior and Human Decision Processes,* June 1996, pp. 316–332.
176. P. Chen, "How to Hold a Productive Post-Mortem Meeting," *Forbes,* October 31, 2016, https://www.forbes.com/sites/forbestechcouncil/2016/10/31/how-to-hold-a-productive-post-mortem-meeting/2/#29bb22c077cf; J. Fleming, "How to Conduct a Project Post-Mortem," *Bizfluent,* September 26, 2017, https://bizfluent.com/how-8421062-conduct-project-postmortem.html.
177. L. B. Black, "What I Learned about Creativity from Pixar's Ed Catmull," *The Next Web,* October 2, 2014, https://thenextweb.com/dd/2014/10/02/learned-creativity-pixars-ed-catmull/.
178. B. Tulgan, *Bridging The Soft Skills Gap: How to Teach the Missing Basics to Today's Young Talent* (Hoboken, NJ: John Wiley & Sons, 2015).
179. B. Tulgan, *Bridging The Soft Skills Gap: How to Teach the Missing Basics to Today's Young Talent* (Hoboken, NJ: John Wiley & Sons, 2015).
180. The idea for this exercise was based on B. Tulgan, *Bridging The Soft Skills Gap: How to Teach the Missing Basics to Today's Young Talent* (Hoboken, NJ: John Wiley & Sons, 2015).
181. These steps were based on M. Myatt, "6 Tips for Making Better Decisions," *Forbes,* March 28, 2012, https://www.forbes.com/sites/mikemyatt/2012/03/28/6-tips-for-making-better-decisions/#4206b32634dc.
182. These questions were based on L. Liaros, "Explaining Your Decision Making Process," *Interview Tips,* https://everydayinterviewtips.com/explaining-your-decision-making-process-during-an-interview/ (accessed March 19, 2018); L. Liaros, "How to Show You Have Quick Decision Making Skills," *Everyday Interview Tips,* https://everydayinterviewtips.com/how-to-show-you-have-quick-decision-making-skills/ (accessed March 19, 2018); L. Liaros, "Using Instincts vs Data to Make Decisions," *Everyday Interview Tips,* https://everydayinterviewtips.com/using-instinct-data-to-make-decisions/ (accessed March 19, 2018).
183. "New York City Transit—History and Chronology," *Metropolitan Transportation Authority,* http://web.mta.info/nyct/facts/ffhist.htm (accessed February 13, 2018).
184. B. Rosenthal, E. Fitzsimmons, and M. LaForgia, "How Politics and Bad Decisions Starved New York's Subways," *The New York Times,* November 18, 2017, https://www.nytimes.com/2017/11/18/nyregion/new-york-subway-system-failure-delays.html.
185. B. Rosenthal, E. Fitzsimmons, and M. LaForgia, "How Politics and Bad Decisions Starved New York's Subways," *The New York Times,* November 18, 2017, https://www.nytimes.com/2017/11/18/nyregion/new-york-subway-system-failure-delays.html.
186. V. Barone, "MTAs Next Transit Chief Sees a Path toward a Healthy System," *amNewYork,* December 11, 2017, https://www.amny.com/transit/mta-s-incoming-transit-president-is-convinced-the-system-can-be-fixed-1.15407269.
187. *A Bold Direction for Leading Transportation in The Next 100 Years* (New York: MTA Transportation Reinvention Commission, 2014).
188. *A Bold Direction for Leading Transportation in The Next 100 Years* (New York: MTA Transportation Reinvention Commission, 2014).
189. A. Siff, "MTA Shelves Plan to Modernize Subway Stations amid Criticism," *NBC New York,* January 25, 2018, https://www.nbcnewyork.com/news/local/MTA-Postpones-Plan-Modernize-Subway-Stations-Cuomo-De-Blasio-470926353.html.
190. K. Lovett, "MTA Wrote $4.9M Check to Three Upstate Ski Centers," *NY Daily News,* July 10, 2017, http://www.nydailynews.com/news/politics/mta-wrote-4-9m-check-upstate-ski-centers-article-1.3313757.
191. B. Rosenthal, E. Fitzsimmons, and M. LaForgia, "How Politics and Bad Decisions Starved New York's Subways," *The New York Times,* November 18, 2017, https://www.nytimes.com/2017/11/18/nyregion/new-york-subway-system-failure-delays.html
192. "Congestion Pricing: Driving in Manhattan Could Soon Cost $11.52," *CBS News,* January 19, 2018, https://www.cbsnews.com/news/congestion-pricing-manhattan-drivers-could-soon-pay-more-tolls/.
193. E. Fitzsimmons, "Cuomo Declares a State of Emergency for New York City Subways," *The New York Times,* June 29, 2017, https://www.nytimes.com/2017/06/29/nyregion/cuomo-declares-a-state-of-emergency-for-the-subway.html.
194. R. Yancey, "State Lawmakers Must Approve a Subway Plan: Riders," *amNewYork,* February 12, 2018, https://www.amny.com/transit/subway-bus-budget-1.16723747.
195. J. Lartney, "Can the British Man Who Saved Toronto's Subway Help New York City?" *The Guardian,* December 29, 2017, https://www.theguardian.com/us-news/2017/dec/29/can-the-british-man-who-saved-torontos-subway-help-new-york-city.
196. V. Barone, "MTA's Next Transit Chief Sees a Path toward a Healthy System," *amNewYork,* December 11, 2017, https://www.amny.com/transit/mta-s-incoming-transit-president-is-convinced-the-system-can-be-fixed-1.15407269.
197. V. Barone, "MTA's Next Transit Chief Sees a Path toward a Healthy System," *amNewYork,* December 11, 2017, https://www.amny.com/transit/mta-s-incoming-transit-president-is-convinced-the-system-can-be-fixed-1.15407269.
198. A. Siff, "MTA Shelves Plan to Modernize Subway Stations amid Criticism," *NBC New York,* January 25, 2018, https://www.nbcnewyork.com/news/local/MTA-Postpones-Plan-Modernize-Subway-Stations-Cuomo-De-Blasio-470926353.html.
199. P. Berger, "New Transit Boss Vows To Shake Up Ailing System," *The Wall Street Journal,* January 22, 2018, https://www.wsj.com/articles/new-transit-boss-vows-to-shake-up-ailing-system-1516666863.
200. P. Berger, "New N.Y.C. Transit Head, Obsessive About Detail, Takes Charge," *The Wall Street Journal,* January 29, 2018, https://www.wsj.com/articles/new-n-y-c-transit-head-obsessive-about-detail-takes-charge-1517230800.
201. T. Llamas, G. Wagschal, A. Paparella, C. Lopez, K. Reller, L. Effron, and C. Ferguson, "Some Pet Owners Game the Emotional Support Animal System to Fly Pets for Free," *ABC News,* April 3, 2015, http://abcnews.go.com/Health/pet-owners-game-emotional-support-animal-system-fly/story?id=30064532.
202. B. Jansen, "Following Peacock Fiasco, United Airlines Tightens Policy for Comfort Animals," *USA Today,* February 2, 2018, https://www.usatoday.com/story/travel/2018/02/01/united-joins-delta-updating-policies-deal-flood-comfort-animals/1086683001/.
203. L. Zumbach, "United Tightens Rules for Emotional Support Animals," *Chicago Tribune,* February 1, 2018, http://www.chicagotribune.com/business/ct-biz-united-tightens-rules-emotional-support-animals-0202-story.html.
204. L. Zumbach, "United Tightens Rules for Emotional Support Animals," *Chicago Tribune,* February 1, 2018, http://www.chicagotribune.com/business/ct-biz-united-tightens-rules-emotional-support-animals-0202-story.html.

205. M. Matousek, "Here's How Airlines Decide If a Pet Qualifies as an Emotional Support Animal," *Business Insider,* January 31, 2018, http://www.businessinsider.com/airline-rules-for-emotional-support-animals-2018-1.
206. S. Gibbens, "Can Peacocks Be Emotional Support Animals? Its Complicated," *National Geographic,* January 31, 2018, https://news.nationalgeographic.com/2018/01/woman-brings-peacock-plane-emotional-support-animal-explained-spd/.
207. A. McCarren, "Delta Bites Back over Too Many Emotional Support Animals on Board," *WUSA,* January 19, 2018, http://www.wusa9.com/article/news/local/delta-bites-back-over-too-many-emotional-support-animals-on-board/509562359.
208. D. Leonhardt, "It's Time to End the Scam of Flying Pets," *The New York Times,* February 4, 2018, https://www.nytimes.com/2018/02/04/opinion/flying-pets-scam-peacock.html.

CHAPTER 8

1. J. Welch and S. Welch, "Dear Graduate . . . ," *BusinessWeek,* June 19, 2006, p. 100.
2. Bonnie Scherry, director of corporate HR at G&A Partners, quoted in M. Tarpey, "How to Get Noticed by Your Boss," *Reno Gazette-Journal,* September 6, 2015, p. 4D.
3. S. Timlin, "How to Make Your First 90 Days in a New Job a Success," *Hays Recruiting,* June 21, 2017, https://social.hays.com/2017/06/21/first-90-days-in-a-new-job; J. Bianchi, "How to Ace Your New Job in the First 90 Days," *Forbes,* June 11, 2104; https://www.forbes.com/forbes/welcome/?toURL=https://www.forbes.com/sites/learnvest/2014/06/11/how-to-ace-your-new-job-in-the-first-90-days/&refURL=https://www.google.com/&referrer=https://www.google.com/.
4. M. Sunnafrank and A. Ramirez Jr., "At First Sight: Persistent Relational Effects of Get-Acquainted Conversations," *Journal of Social and Personal Relationships,* June 1, 2004, pp. 361–379.
5. S. M. Heathfield, "Why 'Blink' Matters: The Power of First Impressions," *The Balance,* October 24, 20116, https://www.thebalance.com/why-blink-matters-the-power-of-first-impressions-1919374.
6. S. McCord, "4 Sneaky Ways to Determine Company Culture in an Interview," *The Muse,* accessed March 19, 2018, https://www.themuse.com/advice/4-sneaky-ways-to-determine-company-culture-in-an-interview.
7. K. Madden, "Start New Job on the Right Foot," *Reno Gazette-Journal,* March 18, 2012, p. 1-J.
8. A. W. Brooks, F. Gino, and M. E. Schweitzer, "Smart People Ask for (My) Advice: Seeking Advice Boosts Perceptions of Competence," *Management Science,* June 2015, pp. 1421–1435.
9. Brett Wilson, interviewed by A. Bryant, "It's All in the Follow-Through," *The New York Times,* May 25, 2014, p. BU-2.
10. C. R. Mainardi, "How CEOs Get Strategy Wrong, and How They Can Get It Right," *The Wall Street Journal,* May 23, 2016, p. R8.
11. C. A. Hartnell, A. J. Kinicki, L. S. Lambert, M. Fugate, and P. D. Corner, "Do Similarities or Differences between CEO Leadership and Organizational Culture Have a More Positive Effect on Firm Performance? A Test of Competing Predictions," *Journal of Applied Psychology,* June 2016, pp. 846–861.
12. E. H. Schein, "Culture: The Missing Concept in Organization Studies," *Administrative Science Quarterly,* June 1996, p. 236.
13. B. Schneider, V. González-Roma, C. Ostroff, and M. A. West, "Organizational Climate and Culture: Reflections on the History of the Constructs in the Journal of Applied Psychology, *Journal of Applied Psychology,* March 2017, pp. 469–482.
14. P. Miller, interviewed by A. Bryant, "To Work Here, Win the 'Nice' Vote," *The New York Times,* July 19, 2015, p. BU-2.
15. G. Schott, interviewed by A. Bryant, "The Threats to a Positive Workplace," *The New York Times,* August 30, 2015, p. BU-2.
16. Brett Wilson, quoted in A. Bryant, "It's All in the Follow-Through," *The New York Times,* May 25, 2014, p. BU-2.
17. B. Widdicombe, "Staff's Young. So's the Boss. Problem?" *The New York Times,* March 20, 2016, pp. ST-1, ST-13.
18. R. Winkler, "Zenefits Warned Employees on Risqué Behavior," *The Wall Street Journal,* February 23, 2016, p. B4.
19. R. Feintzeig, "When 'Nice' Is a Four-Letter Word," *The Wall Street Journal,* December 31, 2015, pp. D1, D3.
20. J. Ewing, "VW Investigation Focus to Include Managers Who Turned a Blind Eye," *The New York Times,* October 26, 2016, p. B3; W. Boston, "VW Still a Work in Progress," *The Wall Street Journal,* February 24, 2016, p. B7; J. Soble, "Mitsubishi Discloses It Cheated on Fuel Test," *The New York Times,* April 21, 2016, pp. B1, B2; "Mitsubishi Cheating Scandal Expands to More Models," *San Francisco Chronicle,* May 12, 2016, p. C6, reprinted from *The New York Times.*
21. "Patients," *Cleveland Clinic,* http://portals.clevelandclinic.org/ungc/Patients (accessed March 19, 2018).
22. "Continuous Improvement," *myclevelnadclinic.org,* https://my.clevelandclinic.org/departments/clinical-transformation/depts/continuous-improvement (accessed March 19, 2018).
23. D. Drickhamer, "Transforming Healthcare: What Matters Most? How the Cleveland Clinic Is Cultivating a Problem-Solving Mindset and Building a Culture of Improvement," *Lean Enterprise Institute,* May 28, 2015, https://www.lean.org/common/display/?o=2982.
24. "Continuous Improvement," *myclevelnadclinic.org,* https://my.clevelandclinic.org/departments/clinical-transformation/depts/continuous-improvement (accessed March 19, 2018).
25. D. Drickhamer, "Transforming Healthcare: What Matters Most? How the Cleveland Clinic Is Cultivating a Problem-Solving Mindset and Building a Culture of Improvement," *Lean Enterprise Institute,* May 28, 2015, https://www.lean.org/common/display/?o=2982.
26. "Continuous Improvement," *myclevelnadclinic.org,* accessed March 19, 2018, https://my.clevelandclinic.org/departments/clinical-transformation/depts/continuous-improvement (accessed March 19, 2018).
27. D. Drickhamer, "Transforming Healthcare: What Matters Most? How the Cleveland Clinic Is Cultivating a Problem-Solving Mindset and Building a Culture of Improvement," *Lean Enterprise Institute,* May 28, 2015, https://www.lean.org/common/display/?o=2982.
28. "Continuous Improvement," *myclevelnadclinic.org,* https://my.clevelandclinic.org/departments/clinical-transformation/depts/continuous-improvement (accessed March 19, 2018).
29. K. K. Reardon, *The Secret Handshake: Mastering the Politics of the Business Inner Circle* (New York: Doubleday, 2002).
30. K. K. Reardon, interviewed by J. Vishnevsky, "Ask the Expert: Kathleen Kelley Reardon," *U.S. News & World Report,* July 25, 2005, p. EE10. See also T. Bradberry, "6 Powerful Ways to Win at Office Politics," *Huffington Post,* December 31, 2015, www.huffingtonpost.com/dr-travis-bradberry/6-powerful-ways-to-win-at_b_8870506.html (accessed May 17, 2016).
31. E. H. Schein, *Organizational Culture and Leadership,* 2nd ed. (San Francisco: Jossey-Bass, 1992).
32. C. Suddath, "Inside the Elephant Room," *Bloomberg Businessweek,* December 16, 2012, pp. 84–85.
33. M. C. Imd, J. S. Harrison, R. E. Hoskisson, and K. J. Imd, "Walking the Talk: A Multistakeholder Exploration of Organizational Authenticity, Employee Productivity, and Post-Merger Performance," *Academy of Management Perspectives* 28, no. 1 (2014), pp. 38–56.
34. "We Quit Tobacco, Here's What Happened Next," *CVS Health,* https://cvshealth.com/thought-leadership/cvs-health-research-institute/we-quit-tobacco-heres-what-happened-next (accessed March 14, 2018).
35. "AIG Culture Reviews: Accounting," *Indeed,* https://www.indeed.com/cmp/AIG/reviews?fcountry=ALL&ftopic=culture&fjobcat=accounting (accessed March 14, 2018).
36. Nick Friedman, quoted in B. Haislip, "When Entrepreneurs Realize 'Anything Goes' Has to Go," *The Wall Street Journal,* June 12, 2014, p. R4.
37. T. Heath, "Duo behind College Hunks Moving Company Ditch a Digital Path for Old-School Success," *Chicago Tribune,* August 1, 2016, http://www.chicagotribune.com/business/ct-college-hunks-moving-company-success-heath-20160801-story.html.

38. A thorough description of the competing values framework is provided in K. S. Cameron, R. E. Quinn, J. Degraff, and A. V. Thakor, *Creating Values Leadership* (Northhampton, MA: Edward Elgar, 2006). See also C. A. Hartnell, A. Y. Ou, and A. Kinicki, "Organizational Culture and Organizational Effectiveness: A Meta-Analytic Investigation of the Competing Values Framework's Theoretical Suppositions," *Journal of Applied Psychology* 96, no. 4 (2011), pp. 677–694.

39. "9—Acuity," *Fortune*, "100 Best Companies to Work For," http://fortune.com/best-companies/2017/acuity/ (accessed March 14, 2018).

40. B. Salzman, quoted in "Acuity: Job Requirement: Have Fun at Work," *Fortune*, March 15, 2016, p. 30.

41. "9—Acuity," *Fortune*, "100 Best Companies to Work For," http://fortune.com/best-companies/2017/acuity/ (accessed March 14, 2018).

42. S. Gharib, "This CEO Believes That Innovation and Culture Are One and the Same," *Fortune*, February 14, 2018, http://fortune.com/2018/02/14/baxter-international-jose-almeida/?iid=sr-link4.

43. S. Kaplan, "4 Steps Every Company Must Take to Avoid Replicating Uber's Toxic Culture," *Inc.*, June 16, 2017, https://www.inc.com/soren-kaplan/4-steps-every-company-must-take-to-avoid-replicating-ubers-toxic-culture.html?cid=search.

44. S. Kaplan, "4 Steps Every Company Must Take to Avoid Replicating Uber's Toxic Culture," *Inc.*, June 16, 2017, https://www.inc.com/soren-kaplan/4-steps-every-company-must-take-to-avoid-replicating-ubers-toxic-culture.html?cid=search.

45. A. Rhodes, "Uber: Which Countries Have Banned the Controversial Taxi App," *Independent*, September 22, 2017, http://www.independent.co.uk/travel/news-and-advice/uber-ban-countries-where-world-taxi-app-europe-taxi-us-states-china-asia-legal-a7707436.html; G. Smith, "How Uber's Tumultuous History in London Resulted in It Being Banned," *Fortune*, September 22, 2017, http://fortune.com/2017/09/22/uber-banned-london-timeline-history/.

46. D. McGinn, "The Numbers in Jeff Bezos's Head," *Harvard Business Review*, November 2014, p. 58.

47. N. Wingfield, "Bit by Bit, Whole Foods Gets an Amazon Touch," *The New York Times*, March 1, 2018, https://www.nytimes.com/2018/03/01/technology/bit-by-bit-whole-foods-gets-an-amazon-touch.html.

48. T. E. Deal and A. A. Kennedy, *Corporate Cultures: The Rites and Rituals of Corporate Life* (Reading, MA: Addison-Wesley, 1982), p. 22. See also T. E. Deal and A.A. Kennedy, *The New Corporate Cultures: Revitalizing the Workplace after Downsizing, Mergers, and Reengineering* (Cambridge, MA: Perseus, 2000).

49. "Lack Table," *IKEA*, https://www.ikea.com/us/en/catalog/products/40104270/ (accessed March 19, 2018).

50. "Salesforce," *Fortune*, http://fortune.com/best-companies/salesforce/ (accessed March 19, 2018).

51. J. Cox, "A View from the Top: How Salesforce's Tony Prophet Is Championing Equality in Silicon Valley," *Independent*, June 14, 2017, https://www.independent.co.uk/news/business/analysis-and-features/a-view-from-the-top-salesforce-tony-prophet-silicon-valley-tech-chief-equality-officer-diversity-a7775831.html.

52. Ingvar Kamprad, quoted in L. Collins, "House Perfect," p. 60.

53. "Obituary: Ingvar Kamprad Died on January 27th," *The Economist*, February 8, 2018, https://www.economist.com/news/obituary/21736501-founder-ikea-furniture-empire-was-91-obituary-ingvar-kamprad-died-january-27th.

54. T. Loudenback, "Why Employee-Owned New Belgium Brewing Gives Workers Bikes, Travel Vouchers, and Paid Sabbaticals on Their Work Anniversaries," *Business Insider*, June 17, 2016, http://www.businessinsider.com/new-belgium-brewery-employee-perks-2016-6.

55. J. Van Maanen, "Breaking In: Socialization to Work," in R. Dubin, ed., *Handbook of Work, Organization, and Society* (Chicago: Rand-McNally, 1976), p. 67.

56. D. C. Feldman, "The Multiple Socialization of Organization Members," *Academy of Management Review*, April 1981, pp. 309–381.

57. "New Employee Onboarding: Buddy Guidelines," *nyu.edu*, https://www.nyu.edu/content/dam/nyu/hr/documents/managerguides/BuddyGuidelines.pdf (accessed March 19, 2018).

58. A. Y. Ou, C. Hartnell, A. Kinicki, E. Karam, and D. Choi, "Culture in Context: A Meta-Analysis of the Nomological Network of Organizational Culture," presentation as part of symposium Connecting Culture and Context: Insights from Organizational Culture Theory and Research at the 2016 National Academy of Management meeting in Anaheim, California.

59. Survey by employment website Glassdoor, reported in L. Hill, "Only BFFs Need Apply," *Bloomberg Businessweek*, January 7–13, 2013, pp. 63–65.

60. L. Hill, "Job Applicants' Cultural Fit Can Trump Qualifications," *Bloomberg Businessweek*, January 3, 2013, www.businessweek.com/articles/2013-01-03/job-applicants-cultural-fit-can-trump-qualifications (accessed May 16, 2016).

61. A. L. Kristof-Brown, R. D. Zimmerman, and E. C. Johnson, "Consequences of Individuals' Fit at Work: A Meta-Analysis of Person-Job, Person-Organization, Person-Group, and Person-Supervisor Fit," *Personnel Psychology*, Summer 2005, pp. 281–342; A. L. Kristoff-Brown, J. Y. Seong, D. S. Degeest, W-W. Park, and D-S. Hong, "Collective Fit Perceptions: A Multilevel Investigation of Person-Group Fit with Individual-Level and Team-Level Outcomes," *Journal of Organizational Behavior*, October 2014, pp. 969–989.

62. L. Rivera, "Hiring as Cultural Matching: The Case of Elite Professional Service Firms," *American Sociological Review*, December 2012, pp. 999–1022.

63. A. Kinicki, "'Fitting in' Important at Workplace," *Arizona Republic*, June 8, 2015, www.azcentral.com/story/money/business/career/2015/06/07/fitting-important-workplace/28592961/ (accessed May 18, 2016); C. Boho, "How to Find the Right Cultural Fit," *Arizona Republic*, November 15, 2015, p. 4E.

64. A. S. Boyce, L. R. G. Nieminen, M. A. Gillespie, A. M. Ryan, and D. R. Denison, "Which Comes First, Organizational Culture or Performance? A Longitudinal Study of Causal Priority with Automobile Dealerships," *Journal of Organizational Behavior*, April 2015, pp. 339–359.

65. The mechanisms are based on material contained in E. H. Schein, "The Role of the Founder in Creating Organizational Culture," *Organizational Dynamics*, Summer 1983, pp. 13–28.

66. "Our Values," *Polyvore*, https://www.polyvore.com/cgi/about.team (accessed March 19, 2018).

67. "Working at Walmart," *Walmart*, https://corporate.walmart.com/our-story/working-at-walmart (accessed March 19, 2018).

68. H. Karp, "CEO Aims to Revive Broadcaster," *The Wall Street Journal*, May 6, 2016, p. B2.

69. "About Us," *OXO*, https://www.oxo.com/our-philosophy (accessed March 19, 2018).

70. H. Peterson, "The Bizarre Inspiration behind Nike's First Pair of Running Shoes," *Business Insider*, July 6, 2015, http://www.businessinsider.com/nikes-first-running-shoes-were-made-in-a-waffle-iron-2015-7.

71. M. Winsor, "Cape Town May 'Completely' Avert 'Day Zero' Water Crisis, Officials Say," *ABC*, March 8, 2018, http://abcnews.go.com/International/cape-town-completely-avert-day-officials/story?id=53607900.

72. "How River Island Thrived from Creating a Feedback-Friendly Culture," *Management Today*, March 8, 2018, https://www.managementtoday.co.uk/river-island-thrived-creating-feedback-friendly-culture/any-other-business/article/1458889; "About Us," River Island, https://us.riverisland.com/inside-river-island/about-us (accessed March 19, 2018).

73. D. Schawbel, " Billy Baker and Michelle Cleverdon: Why Your Workplace Design Matters," *Forbes*, August 29, 2017, https://www.forbes.com/sites/danschawbel/2017/08/29/billy-baker-and-michelle-cleverdon-why-your-workplace-design-matters/2/#4b5d0e9b5f3b

74. S. Bomkamp and L. Zumbach, "United Walks Back New Bonus Lottery System That Angered Employees," *Chicago Tribune*, March 8, 2018, http://www.chicagotribune.com/business/ct-biz-united-bonus-lottery-20180306-story.html.

75. J. Cowan, "What Netflix's Corporate Culture Can Teach Us about Hiring—and Firing," *Canadian Business*, June 9, 2017, http://www.

canadianbusiness.com/leadership/netflix-chief-talent-officer-patty-mccord/.
76. "Netflix Culture," *jobs.netflix.com,* https://jobs.netflix.com/culture (accessed March 19, 2018).
77. L. Rittenhouse, "Amazon Warehouse Employees' Message to Jeff Bezos—We Are Not Robots," *The Street,* September 29, 2017, https://www.thestreet.com/story/14312539/1/amazon-warehouse-employees-discuss-grueling-work.html.
78. "Labour-Monitoring Technologies Raise Efficiency—and Hard Questions," *The Economist,* March 1, 2018, https://www.economist.com/news/finance-and-economics/21737507-pushing-back-against-controlling-bosses-leaves-workers-more-likely-be-replaced.
79. J. Useem, "Are Bosses Necessary?" *The Atlantic,* October 2015, pp. 28–32; D. K. Berman, "The No-Boss Company," *The Wall Street Journal,* October 27, 2015, p. R3; and B. Lam, "Why Are So Many Zappos Employees Leaving?" *The Atlantic,* January 15, 2016, www.theatlantic.com/business/archive/2016/01/zappos-holacracy-hierarchy/424173 (accessed May 25, 2016).
80. C. Cancialosi, "Preserving a Culture People Love as Your Company Grows: Lessons from Zappos," *Forbes,* May 30, 2017, https://www.forbes.com/sites/chriscancialosi/2017/05/30/preserving-a-culture-people-love-as-your-company-grows-lessons-from-zappos/#46b51f65712b; "Holacracy and Self-Organization," *Zappos Insights,* https://www.zapposinsights.com/about/holacracy (accessed March 19, 2018).
81. P. Leonardi and T. Neeley, "What Managers Need to Know about Social Tools," *Harvard Business Review,* November–December 2017, https://hbr.org/2017/11/what-managers-need-to-know-about-social-tools.
82. S. Shellenbarger, "A Checklist Before You Quit," *The Wall Street Journal,* January 3, 2018, p. A9; A H. Deng, C-H. Wu, K. Leung, and Y. Guan, "Depletion from Self-Regulation: A Resource-Based Account of the Effect of Value Incongruence," *Personnel Psychology,* 2016, pp. 431–465.
83. C. I. Barnard, *The Functions of the Executive* (Cambridge, MA: Harvard University Press, 1938), p. 73.
84. P. M. Blau and W. R. Scott, *Formal Organizations* (San Francisco: Chandler, 1962).
85. E. H. Schein, *Organizational Psychology,* 3rd ed. (Englewood Cliffs, NJ: Prentice-Hall, 1980).
86. J. P. Friesen, A. C. Kay, R. P. Eibach, and A. D. Galinsky, "Seeking Structure in Social Organization: Compensatory Control and the Psychological Advantages of Hierarchy," *Journal of Personality and Social Psychology* 106 (2014), pp. 590–609. This work on hierarchies existing within flat organizations is also described in M. Hutson, "Espousing Equality, but Embracing a Hierarchy," *The New York Times,* June 22, 2014, p. BU-3.
87. For an overview of the span of control concept, see D. D. Van Fleet and A. G. Bedeian, "A History of the Span of Management," *Academy of Management Review,* July 1977, pp. 356–372.
88. Research by V. Smeets and F. Warzynski, "Too Many Theories, Too Few Facts? What the Data Tell Us about the Link between Span of Control, Compensation, and Career Dynamics," *Labour Economics, Special Issue on Firms and Employees* 15 (2008). The study was reported in G. Anders, "Overseeing More Employees—With Fewer Managers," *The Wall Street Journal,* March 24, 2008, p. B6.
89. Accountability is thoroughly discussed by A. T. Hall, D. D. Frink, and M. R. Buckley, "An Accountability Account: A Review and Synthesis of the Theoretical and Empirical Research on Felt Accountability," *Journal of Organizational Behavior,* 2017, pp. 204–224.
90. T. A. Stewart, "CEOs See Clout Shifting," *Fortune,* November 6, 1989, p. 66.
91. J. Schleckser, "When to Delegate? Try the 70 Percent Rule," *Inc.,* August 14, 2014, www.inc.com/jim-schleckser/the-70-rule-when-to-delegate.html (accessed May 25, 2016).
92. J. Craven, " Great Leaders Perfect the Art of Delegation," *Forbes,* February 21, 2018, https://www.forbes.com/sites/forbescoachescouncil/2018/02/21/great-leaders-perfect-the-art-of-delegation/#681b47971eb2; A. Acton, "Delegation Is a CEO's Secret Weapon: Here's How to Do It Right," *Forbes,* August 15, 2017, https://www.forbes.com/sites/annabelacton/2017/08/15/effective-delegation-is-a-ceos-secret-weapon-heres-how-to-do-it-right/#8ffca20433d1.
93. J. Craven, " Great Leaders Perfect the Art of Delegation," *Forbes,* February 21, 2018, https://www.forbes.com/sites/forbescoachescouncil/2018/02/21/great-leaders-perfect-the-art-of-delegation/#681b47971eb2; A. Acton, "Delegation Is a CEO's Secret Weapon: Here's How to Do It Right," *Forbes,* August 15, 2017, https://www.forbes.com/sites/annabelacton/2017/08/15/effective-delegation-is-a-ceos-secret-weapon-heres-how-to-do-it-right/#8ffca20433d1; D. Finkel, "Use This Little-Known Delegation Trick to Get Stuff Done the Right Way," *Inc.,* February 21, 2018, https://www.inc.com/david-finkel/use-this-little-known-delegation-trick-to-get-stuff-done-right-way.html?cid=search.
94. J. Craven, " Great Leaders Perfect the Art of Delegation," *Forbes,* February 21, 2018, https://www.forbes.com/sites/forbescoachescouncil/2018/02/21/great-leaders-perfect-the-art-of-delegation/#681b47971eb2; A. Acton, "Delegation Is a CEO's Secret Weapon: Here's How to Do It Right," *Forbes,* August 15, 2017, https://www.forbes.com/sites/annabelacton/2017/08/15/effective-delegation-is-a-ceos-secret-weapon-heres-how-to-do-it-right/#8ffca20433d1; D. Finkel, "Use This Little-Known Delegation Trick to Get Stuff Done the Right Way," *Inc.,* February 21, 2018, https://www.inc.com/david-finkel/use-this-little-known-delegation-trick-to-get-stuff-done-right-way.html?cid=search.
95. C. C. Miller, "Google's Chief Works to Trim a Bloated Ship," *The New York Times,* November 10, 2011, pp. A1, A3. See also Lee, "Google Redoes Rules to Keep Its 'Googliness.'"
96. L. Hoffman, "The Conglomerate Is Embraced by Google," *The Wall Street Journal,* August 12, 2015, p. C4.
97. Editorial, "A Is for Alphabet," *San Francisco Chronicle,* August 12, 2015, p. A11.
98. F. Manjoo, "Google Seeks New Horizons: A Reorganization Gives the Founders Room to Dream Big beyond Search," *The New York Times,* August 11, 2015, pp. B1, B4.
99. This section was adapted from R. Kreitner and A. Kinicki, *Organizational Behavior,* 10th ed. (New York: McGraw-Hill/Irwin, 2013), pp. 503–508.
100. D. Thompson, "The Amazon-ification of Whole Foods," *The Atlantic,* February 8, 2018, https://www.theatlantic.com/business/archive/2018/02/whole-foods-two-hour-delivery-amazon/552821/; "Company Info," *Whole Foods Market,* http://www.wholefoodsmarket.com/company-info (accessed March 19, 2018).
101. R. Levering, "The 100 Best Companies to Work For," *Fortune,* March 15, 2016, pp. 141–166.
102. A. Gasparro, "Natural Grocers Lose Vigor," *The Wall Street Journal,* April 10, 2014, pp. B1, B2; B. Kowitt, "Whole Foods Takes Over America," *Fortune,* April 28, 2014, pp. 70–77.
103. K. Taylor, "Here Are All the Changes Amazon Is Making to Whole Foods," *Business Insider,* March 2, 2018, http://www.businessinsider.com/amazon-changes-whole-foods-2017-9; D. Thompson, "The Amazon-ification of Whole Foods," *The Atlantic,* February 8, 2018, https://www.theatlantic.com/business/archive/2018/02/whole-foods-two-hour-delivery-amazon/552821/; H. Peterson, "Amazon Is Transforming Whole Foods into a Tech Store," *Business Insider,* November 16, 2017, http://www.businessinsider.com/amazon-whole-foods-tech-pop-ups-2017-11.
104. Adapted from "Boundaryless," *Encyclopedia of Small Business,* ed. K. Hillstrom and L. C. Hillstrom (Farmington Hills, MI: Thomson Gale, 2002; and Seattle, WA: eNotes.com, 2006), http://business.enotes.com/small-business-encyclopedia/boundaryless (accessed June 20, 2014).
105. N. Anand and R. L. Daft, "What Is the Right Organization Design?" *Organizational Dynamics* 36 (2007), pp. 329–344.
106. S. Siekman, "The Snap-Together Business Jet," *Fortune,* January 21, 2002, http://archive.fortune.com/magazines/fortune/fortune_archive/2002/01/21/316585/index.htm (accessed May 25, 2016);

N. Anand and R. L. Daft, "What Is the Right Organization Design?" *Organizational Dynamics* 36 (2007), p. 336.

107. M. J. Mandel and R. D. Hof, "Rethinking the Internet," *Business-Week,* March 26, 2001, p. 118.

108. See the related discussion in E. E. Makarius and B. Z. Larson, "Changing the Perspective of Virtual Work: Building Virtual Intelligence at the Individual Level," *Academy of Management Review,* 2017, pp. 159–178.

109. R. E. Silverman, "Step into the Office-Less Company," *The Wall Street Journal,* September 4, 2012, p. B6.

110. S. J. G. Girod and S. Karim, "Restructure or Reconfigure," *Harvard Business Review,* March–April 2017, pp. 128–132.

111. S. Chaudhuri, "Lego Hits Brick Wall as Digital Play Grows," *The Wall Street Journal,* September 6, 2017, p. A1.

112. S. Monson, "Maid to Order," *Seattle Times,* April 16, 2006, http://old.seattletimes.com/html/businesstechnology/2002932996_hospitality16.html (accessed June 23, 2016).

113. H. Touryalai, "Ready, Set, Clean! Secrets to Cleaning a Marriott Hotel Room," *Forbes,* June 26, 2013, www.forbes.com/sites/halahtouryalai/2013/06/26/ready-set-clean-secrets-to-cleaning-a-marriott-hotel-room/#36bc03aa7d0f (accessed May 25, 2016).

114. T. Burns and G. M. Stalker, *The Management of Innovation* (London: Tavistock, 1961). See also W. D. Sine, H. Mitsuhashi, and D. A. Kirsch, "Revisiting Burns and Stalker: Formal Structure and New Venture Performance in Emerging Economic Sectors," *Academy of Management Journal,* February 2006, pp. 121–132.

115. T. J. Peters and R. H. Waterman, *In Search of Excellence* (New York: Harper & Row, 1982).

116. M. Chafkin and J. Cao, "The Barbarians Are at Etsy's Hand-Hewn, Responsibly Sourced Gates," *Bloomberg Businessweek,* May 18, 2017, https://www.bloomberg.com/news/features/2017-05-18/the-barbarians-are-at-etsy-s-hand-hewn-responsibly-sourced-gates; A. Lashinsky, "How Etsy's New CEO Threw Out All of the Company's Key Metrics, Except One," *Fortune,* March 5, 2018, http://fortune.com/2018/03/05/how-etsys-new-ceo-threw-out-all-of-the-companys-key-metrics-except-one/; D. Gelles, "Inside the Revolution at Etsy," *The New York Times,* November 25, 2017, https://www.nytimes.com/2017/11/25/business/etsy-josh-silverman.html.

117. P. R. Lawrence and J. W. Lorsch, *Organization and Environment* (Homewood, IL: Irwin, 1967).

118. A. D. Chandler Jr., *Strategy and Structure: Chapters in the History of the Industrial Enterprise* (Cambridge, MA: MIT Press, 1962).

119. G. Johns, "Advances in the Treatment of Context in Organizational Research," in F. P. Morgeson, H. Aguinis, and S. J. Ashford (eds.), *Annual Review of Organizational Psychology and Organizational Behavior* (Palo Alto, CA: Annual Reviews, 2017), pp. 21–46.

120. Y. W. Chung, "The Role of Person-Organization Fit and Perceived Organizational Support in the Relationship between Workplace Ostracism and Behavioral Outcomes," *Australian Journal of Management,* May 2017, pp. 328–349; J. Hu, S. J. Wayne, T. N. Bauer, B. Erdogan, and R. C. Liden, "Self and Senior Executive Perceptions of Fit and Performance: A Time-Lagges Examination of Newly-Hired Executives," *Human Relations*, June 2016, pp. 1259–1286.

121. These two steps were based on material in B. Talgan, *Bridging the Soft Skills Gap: How to Teach the Missing Basics to Today's Young Talent* (Hoboken, NJ: John Wiley & Sons, 2015).

122. M. Fugate, A. J. Kinicki, and B. E. Ashforth, "Employability: A Psycho-Social Construct, Its Dimensions, and Applications," *Journal of Vocational Behavior,* 2004, pp. 14–38.

123. M. Fugate, A. J. Kinicki, and B. E. Ashforth, "Employability: A Psycho-Social Construct, Its Dimensions, and Applications," *Journal of Vocational Behavior,* 2004, pp. 14–38; J. Boss, "14 Signs of an Adaptable Person," *Forbes,* September 3, 2015, https://www.forbes.com/sites/jeffboss/2015/09/03/14-signs-of-an-adaptable-person/#51b03aad16ea.

124. J. Boss, "14 Signs of an Adaptable Person," *Forbes,* September 3, 2015, https://www.forbes.com/sites/jeffboss/2015/09/03/14-signs-of-an-adaptable-person/#51b03aad16ea.

125. J. G. Berger, "4 Steps to Becoming More Adaptable to Change," *Fast Company,* March 9, 2015, https://www.fastcompany.com/3043294/4-steps-to-becoming-more-adaptable-to-change.

126. B. Mclean, "How Wells Fargo's Cutthroat Corporate Culture Allegedly Drove Bankers to Fraud," *Vanity Fair,* May 31, 2017, www.vanityfair.com/news/2017/05/wells-fargo-corporate-culture-fraud.

127. B. Mclean, "How Wells Fargo's Cutthroat Corporate Culture Allegedly Drove Bankers to Fraud," *Vanity Fair,* May 31, 2017, www.vanityfair.com/news/2017/05/wells-fargo-corporate-culture-fraud.

128. E. Glazer, "How Wells Fargo's High-Pressure Sales Culture Spiraled Out of Control," *The Wall Street Journal*, September 16, 2016, www.wsj.com/articles/how-wells-fargos-high-pressure-sales-culture-spiraled-out-of-control-1474053044.

129. C. Arnold, "Former Wells Fargo Employees Describe Toxic Sales Culture, Even at HQ," *NPR,* October 4, 2016, www.npr.org/2016/10/04/496508361/former-wells-fargo-employees-describe-toxic-sales-culture-even-at-hq.

130. E. Glazer, "How Wells Fargo's High-Pressure Sales Culture Spiraled Out of Control," *The Wall Street Journal*, September 16, 2016, www.wsj.com/articles/how-wells-fargos-high-pressure-sales-culture-spiraled-out-of-control-1474053044.

131. C. Arnold, "Former Wells Fargo Employees Describe Toxic Sales Culture, Even at HQ," *NPR,* October 4, 2016, www.npr.org/2016/10/04/496508361/former-wells-fargo-employees-describe-toxic-sales-culture-even-at-hq.

132. E. Glazer, "How Wells Fargo's High-Pressure Sales Culture Spiraled Out of Control," *The Wall Street Journal*, September 16, 2016, www.wsj.com/articles/how-wells-fargos-high-pressure-sales-culture-spiraled-out-of-control-1474053044.

133. M. Egan, "5,300 Wells Fargo Employees Fired Over 2 Million Phony Accounts," *CNN Money,* September 9, 2016, http://money.cnn.com/2016/09/08/investing/wells-fargo-created-phony-accounts-bank-fees/index.html.

134. K. McCoy, "Wells Fargo Fined $185M for Fake Accounts; 5300 Were Fired," *USA Today,* September 8, 2016, www.usatoday.com/story/money/2016/09/08/wells-fargo-fined-185m-over-unauthorized-accounts/90003212/.

135. E. Glazer and A. Prang, "Wells Fargo Names New Regulatory Executive," *The Wall Street Journal,* January 30, 2018, www.wsj.com/articles/wells-fargo-names-new-regulatory-executive-1517332921.

136. E. Glazer, "How Wells Fargo's High-Pressure Sales Culture Spiraled Out of Control," *The Wall Street Journal*, September 16, 2016, www.wsj.com/articles/how-wells-fargos-high-pressure-sales-culture-spiraled-out-of-control-1474053044.

137. E. Glazer and C. Rexrode, "Big U.S. Retail Bank Operations under Scrutiny after Wells Scandal," *The Wall Street Journal*, October 25, 2016, www.wsj.com/articles/big-u-s-retail-bank-operations-under-scrutiny-follow-wells-scandal-1477400747.

138. B. Mclean, "How Wells Fargo's Cutthroat Corporate Culture Allegedly Drove Bankers to Fraud," *Vanity Fair,* May 31, 2017, www.vanityfair.com/news/2017/05/wells-fargo-corporate-culture-fraud.

139. C. Arnold, "Former Wells Fargo Employees Describe Toxic Sales Culture, Even at HQ," *NPR,* October 4, 2016, www.npr.org/2016/10/04/496508361/former-wells-fargo-employees-describe-toxic-sales-culture-even-at-hq.

140. C. Arnold, "Former Wells Fargo Employees Describe Toxic Sales Culture, Even at HQ," *NPR,* October 4, 2016, www.npr.org/2016/10/04/496508361/former-wells-fargo-employees-describe-toxic-sales-culture-even-at-hq.

141. M. Egan, "I Called the Wells Fargo Ethics Line and Was Fired," *CNN Money*, September 21, 2016, www.money.cnn.com/2016/09/21/investing/wells-fargo-fired-workers-retaliation-fake-accounts/index.html.

142. M. Egan, "I Called the Wells Fargo Ethics Line and was Fired," *CNN Money*, September 21, 2016, www.money.cnn.com/2016/09/21/investing/wells-fargo-fired-workers-retaliation-fake-accounts/index.html.

143. "Wells Fargo Takes on Culture Change in Wake of Scandal," *CEB Global*, June 13, 2017, www.cebglobal.com/talentdaily/wells-fargo-takes-on-culture-change-in-wake-of-scandal/.

144. M. Egan, "Wells Fargo Accused of Lying to Congress about Auto Insurance Scandal," *CNN Money*, October 3, 2017, www.money.cnn.com/2017/10/03/investing/wells-fargo-lie-congress-hearing-auto-insurance/index.html.

145. G. Morgenson, "Regulator Blasts Wells Fargo for Deceptive Auto Insurance Program," *New York Times*, October 20, 2017, www.nytimes.com/2017/10/20/business/wells-fargo-auto-insurance-comptroller.html.

146. G. Morgenson, "Wells Fargo, Awash in Scandal, Faces Violations Over Car Insurance Refunds," *New York Times*, August 7, 2017, www.nytimes.com/2017/08/07/business/wells-fargo-insurance.html.

147. G. Morgenson, "Regulator Blasts Wells Fargo for Deceptive Auto Insurance Program," *New York Times*, October 20, 2017, www.nytimes.com/2017/10/20/business/wells-fargo-auto-insurance-comptroller.html.

148. M. Egan, "Wells Fargo Accused of Lying to Congress about Auto Insurance Scandal," *CNN Money*, October 3, 2017, www.money.cnn.com/2017/10/03/investing/wells-fargo-lie-congress-hearing-auto-insurance/index.html.

149. M. Egan, "Wells Fargo Accused of Lying to Congress about Auto Insurance Scandal," *CNN Money*, October 3, 2017, www.money.cnn.com/2017/10/03/investing/wells-fargo-lie-congress-hearing-auto-insurance/index.html.

150. M. Egan, "Wells Fargo Accused of Lying to Congress about Auto Insurance Scandal," *CNN Money*, October 3, 2017, www.money.cnn.com/2017/10/03/investing/wells-fargo-lie-congress-hearing-auto-insurance/index.html.

151. G. Colvin, "Inside Wells Fargo's Plan to Fix Its Culture Post-Scandal," *Fortune*, June 11, 2017, www.fortune.com/2017/06/11/wells-fargo-scandal-culture/.

152. A. Held, "Fed Slaps Unusual Penalty on Wells Fargo following 'Widespread Consumer Abuses,'" *NPR*, February 3, 2018, www.npr.org/sections/thetwo-way/2018/02/03/583014020/fed-slaps-unusual-penalty-on-wells-fargo-following-widespread-consumer-abuses.

153. E. Glazer, "Wells Fargo Earns New Ire from Bank Overseers," *The Wall Street Journal*, January 5, 2018, www.wsj.com/articles/wells-fargo-earns-new-ire-from-bank-overseers-1515187163.

154. S. Marks, "Should Company Outings Be Mandatory?" November 5, 2012, https://www.recruiter.com/i/should-company-outings-be-mandatory/

155. C. Beaton, "Bringing Work to the Bar: How to Put Fair Limits on the After-Work Hang," *Transparency*, August 3, 2017, https://transparency.kununu.com/how-to-put-fair-limits-to-socializing-after-work.

156. R. Gale, "Drinking With Co-Workers: Sexual Harassment Is Not the Only Reason We Should Rethink Pairing Drinks and Work," *Slate*, February 27, 2018, https://slate.com/human-interest/2018/02/harassment-isnt-the-only-reason-we-should-rethink-drinking-at-work.html

157. M. Kendall, "What's So Bad about Mandatory Work Socializing?" *qz.com*, February 24, 2016, http://qz.com/623260/whats-so-bad-about-mandatory-workplace-socializing/

CHAPTER 9

1. N. P. Podsakoff, S. W. Whiting, P. M. Podsakoff, and P. Mishra, "Effects of Organizational Citizenship Behaviors on Selection Decisions in Employment Interviews," *Journal of Applied Psychology* 96 (2011), pp. 310–326; A. Stahl, "4 Common Mistakes to Avoid in Job Interviews," *Forbes*, February 28, 2017, https://www.forbes.com/sites/ashleystahl/2017/02/28/4-common-mistakes-to-avoid-in-job-interviews/#31e97f20bd2c; L. Ryan, "Ten Mistakes 90% of Job Seekers Make," *Forbes*, January 5, 2017, https://www.forbes.com/sites/lizryan/2017/01/05/ten-mistakes-90-of-job-seekers-make/#5b8c94622f49.

2. V. Oliver, "Blew the Job Interview? There's Still Hope," *San Francisco Chronicle*, July 11, 2014, p. C2.

3. A. Doyle, "Will Employers Check Your References?" *The Balance*, November 21, 2017, https://www.thebalance.com/will-employers-check-your-references-2060797; B. Goldberg, "Majority of Employers Background Check Employees . . . Here's Why," *Career Builder*, November 17, 2016, https://www.careerbuilder.com/advice/majority-of-employers-background-check-employees.

4. R. Reshwan, "Does GPA Matter When Applying for a Job?" *U.S. News & World Report*, April 26, 2016, https://money.usnews.com/money/blogs/outside-voices-careers/articles/2016-04-26/does-gpa-matter-when-applying-for-a-job.

5. L. Salm, "70% of Employers Are Snooping Candidates' Social Media Profiles," *Career Builder*, June 15, 2017, https://www.careerbuilder.com/advice/social-media-survey-2017; J. Hyman, "NBC Reignites Privacy Debate by Requiring Job Seekers' Social Media Passwords," *Workforce*, August 1, 2017, http://www.workforce.com/2017/08/01/nbc-reignites-privacy-debate-requiring-job-seekers-social-media-passwords/.

6. See C. Austin, "The 10 Best Workplaces for Millenials," June 26, 2018, http://fortune.com/2018/06/26/10-best-workplaces-for-millennials.

7. A. Fisher, "How to Get Hired by a 'Best' Company," *Fortune*, February 4, 2008, p. 96.

8. M. C. Bush and S. Lewis-Kulin, "100 Best Companies to Work For 2017," *Fortune*, pp. 79–84.

9. J. Korff, T. Biemann, and S. C. Voelpel, "Differentiating HR Systems' Impact: Moderating Effects of Age on the HR System-Work Outcome Association," *Journal of Organizational Behavior*, 2017, pp. 415–438.

10. "Talent Investing in Employees Pays Off," *Harvard Business Review*, July–August 2017, p. 26.

11. "100 Best Companies to Work For," *Fortune*, 2018, http://fortune.com/best-companies/list.

12. J. Welch, quoted in N. M. Tichy and S. Herman, *Control Your Destiny or Someone Else Will: How Jack Welch Is Making General Electric the World's Most Competitive Corporation* (New York: Doubleday, 1993), p. 251.

13. L. Weber and R. Feintzeig, "Is It a Dream or a Drag? Companies without HR," *The Wall Street Journal*, April 9, 2014, pp. B1, B7.

14. R. R. Kehoe and C. J.Collins, "Human Resource Management and Unit Performance in Knowledge-Intensive Work," *Journal of Applied Psychology*, 2017, pp. 1222–1236; J. Korff, T. Biemann, and S. C. Voelpel, "Human Resource Management Systems and Work Attitudes: The Mediating Role of Future Time Perspective," *Journal of Organizational Behavior*, 2017, pp. 45–67.

15. J. Wasserman, "HR: Earning a Strategic Seat at the Transformation Table," *Fortune*, March 4, 2018, https://www.forbes.com/sites/johnkotter/2018/03/04/hr-earning-a-strategic-seat-at-the-transformation-table/#6d0d89737b62.

16. "Scripps Health," *Fortune 100 Best Companies to Work For*, 2017, http://fortune.com/best-companies/list/filtered?searchByName=scripps%20health.

17. M. Feffer, "New Connections," *HR Magazine*, April 2015, pp. 46–52.

18. L. Rainie, "Incentives—and Pressures—for U.S. Workers in a 'Knowledge Economy,'" *Pew Research Center*, March 23, 2016, www.pewresearch.org/fact-tank/2016/03/23/incentives-and-pressures-for-u-s-workers-in-a-knowledge-economy (accessed June 1, 2016).

19. C. M. Barnes, K. Jiang, and D. P. Lepak, "Sabotaging the Benefits of Our Own Human Capital: Work Unit Characteristics and Sleep," *Journal of Applied Psychology*, February 2016, pp. 209–221.

20. T. Casciaro, F. Gino, and M. Kouchake, "Managing Yourself: Learn to Love Networking," *Harvard Business Review*, May 2016, pp. 104–107.

21. K. Weisul, "Why Social Capital Is Key to Entrepreneurs' Success," *Inc.*, February 15, 2017, https://www.inc.com/kimberly-weisul/why-social-capital-key-entrepreneurs-success.html?cid=search.

22. R. E. Ployhart, N. Schmitt, and N. T. Tippins, "Solving the Supremet Problem: 100 Years of Selection and Recruitment," *Journal of Applied Psychology*, 2017, pp. 291–304.

23. L. Rangel, "The Easy How-to Guide to Formatting Resumes for Applicant Tracking Systems," *LinkedIn,* https://premium.linkedin.com/jobsearch/articles/the-easy-how-to-guide-for-formatting-resumes-for-applicant-tracking-systems (accessed March 20, 2018).
24. T. S. Bernard, "Job Hunting in the Digital Age," *The New York Times,* April 10, 2016, Education Life section, p. 19.
25. J. Sullivan, interviewed by N. Waller, "The Key to Making Sure You Hire the Best Performers," *The Wall Street Journal,* June 2, 2016, p. B6.
26. R. Simon, "Recruiting Workers Involves More Work," *The Wall Street Journal,* February 22, 2018, p. B4.
27. S. Harrington, "How This CEO Shakes Up Linear Hiring Practices," *Forbes,* December 29, 2017, https://www.forbes.com/sites/samantha-harrington/2017/12/29/how-this-ceo-shakes-up-linear-hiring-practices/#32c5c3c0361c.
28. "More Firms Rehiring Workers Who Left," *San Francisco Chronicle,* April 1, 2016, p. C3, reprinted from *Pittsburgh Post-Gazette.* See also L. Gellman, "Ex-Employees: Gone, Not Forgotten," *The Wall Street Journal,* February 22, 2016, p. R8.
29. D. Graham, "Ready, Set, Switch—Shape Up Your Social Media," *Forbes,* February 20, 2018, https://www.forbes.com/sites/dawngraham/2018/02/20/ready-set-switch-shape-up-your-social-media/#1b97ab116f2d.
30. "8 Social Media Statistics You Need to Know If You're in Recruitment—Infographic," *Talent Works,* September 27, 2017, https://www.talent-works.com/2017/09/27/social-media-recruitment/.
31. E. Krell, "Look Outside or Seek Within?" *HR Magazine,* January/February 2016, pp. 61–64.
32. Respondents to the Society for Human Resource Management's *2007 E-Recruiting Survey* reported that employee referrals generated the highest quality of job candidates and best return on investment for their organization. See T. Minton-Eversole, "E-Recruitment Comes of Age, Survey Says," *HR Magazine,* August 2007, p. 34.
33. J. Sullivan, interviewed by N. Waller, "The Key to Making Sure You Hire the Best Performers," *The Wall Street Journal,* June 2, 2016, p. B6.
34. C. Said, "BlueCrew Applies Tech to Fill Blue-Collar Jobs," *San Francisco Chronicle,* March 2, 2016, pp. C1, C6.
35. S. E. Needleman, "Play This Game and Win a Job!" *The Wall Street Journal,* March 14, 2016, www.wsj.com/articles/play-this-game-and-win-a-job-1457921553 (accessed June 4, 2016).
36. R. Feintzeig, "With 'Blind Hiring,' It's Not Who You Are, It's What You Know," *The Wall Street Journal,* January 6, 2016, pp. B1, B4; W. Lee, "Woo Sets Up Blind Dates for Workers, Employers," *San Francisco Chronicle,* March 4, 2016, pp. C1, C3.
37. J. Arnold, "Hiring For Skills, Not Pedigree," *HRMagazine,* March 2018, pp. 45–50.
38. J. M. Phillips, "Effects of Realistic Job Previews on Multiple Organizational Outcomes: A Meta-Analysis," *Academy of Management Journal,* December 1998, pp. 673–690.
39. M. A. Tucker, "Show and Tell," *HR Magazine,* January 2012, pp. 51–53.
40. N. Irwin, "Job Growth in Past Decade Was in Temp and Contract," *The New York Times,* March 31, 2015, p. A3. See also K. Pender, "How Contractors and Employees Differ," *San Francisco Chronicle,* September 20, 2015, pp. D1, D3; S. Westly, "A Third Definition of Contractors and Employees," *San Francisco Chronicle,* February 21, 2016, p. E6.
41. J. Wertz, " Why the Gig Economy Can Be Essential to Business Growth," *Forbes,* January 23, 2018, https://www.forbes.com/sites/jiawertz/2018/01/23/why-the-gig-economy-can-be-essential-to-business-growth/#54f2bc582580.
42. J. Wertz, " Why the Gig Economy Can Be Essential to Business Growth," *Forbes,* January 23, 2018, https://www.forbes.com/sites/jiawertz/2018/01/23/why-the-gig-economy-can-be-essential-to-business-growth/#54f2bc582580.
43. F. Chideya, *The Episodic Career: How to Thrive at Work in the Age of Disruption* (New York: Atria, 2016).
44. F. Chideya, interviewed by D. Graham, "'The Episodic Career': Navigating Today's Job Market," *Knowledge@Wharton,* February 3, 2016, http://knowledge.wharton.upenn.edu/article/episodic-career-navigating-todays-job-market (accessed June 15, 2016).
45. E. Sherman, " The Gig Economy Won't Save Workers at $3.37 an Hour," *Forbes,* March 3, 2018, https://www.forbes.com/sites/eriksherman/2018/03/03/the-gig-economy-wont-save-workers-at-3-37-an-hour/#1a0594cd47a1.
46. C. O'Donovan, "Former US Labor Secretary Robert Reich Says the Gig Economy Can Be a 'Nightmare'," *BuzzFeed,* August 2, 2016, https://www.buzzfeed.com/carolineodonovan/former-us-labor-secretary-robert-reich-says-the-gig-economy?utm_term=.ehNqgZjy6#.wf2aEQRAp.
47. J. T. O'Donnell, "85 Percent of Job Applicants Lie on Resumes. Here's How to Spot a Dishonest Candidate," *Inc.,* August 15, 2017, https://www.inc.com/jt-odonnell/staggering-85-of-job-applicants-lying-on-resumes-.html.
48. C. Dondas, "Lies in Your Resume That Will Get You Fired...," *allwomenstalk,* accessed March 20, 2018, http://money.allwomenstalk.com/lies-in-your-resume-that-will-get-you-fired.
49. See D. Winterton, "Is It Legal for My Employer to Fire Me for Lying on a Job Application or Resume?" *Legal Match,* April 11, 2018, https://www.legalmatch.com/law-library/article/lying-on-a-job-application-or-resume.html.
50. H. Levitt, "Lying on Your Resumé Isn't Always Sure Fire Cause for Firing," *Financial Post,* October 19, 2016, http://business.financialpost.com/executive/careers/lying-on-your-resume-isnt-always-sure-fire-cause-for-firing.
51. H. Levitt, "Lying on Your Resumé Isn't Always Sure Fire Cause for Firing," *Financial Post,* October 19, 2016, http://business.financialpost.com/executive/careers/lying-on-your-resume-isnt-always-sure-fire-cause-for-firing.
52. P. Cohen, "Perils of a Gap in the Resume," *The New York Times,* May 20, 2016, pp. B1, B6.
53. E. Relman, "A 24-Year-Old Trump Appointee Who Held a Top Drug Policy Job Despite Having no Relevant Experience Quit after an Investigation into His Credentials," *Business Insider,* January 25, 2018, http://www.businessinsider.com/taylor-weyeneth-office-of-national-drug-control-policy-lied-on-resume-2018-1; R. O'Harrow Jr., "Trump's 24-Year-Old Drug Policy Appointee to Step Down by Month's End," *The Washington Post,* January 24, 2018, https://www.washingtonpost.com/investigations/trumps-24-year-old-drug-policy-appointee-to-step-down-by-months-end/2018/01/24/77ce5656-0159-11e8-8acf-ad2991367d9d_story.html?utm_term=.8316fdaec237.
54. "Lying on Your Resume? Here's How You'll Get Caught," *Glassdoor,* September 15, 2017, https://www.glassdoor.com/blog/lying-on-your-resume/.
55. R. E. Silverman, "No More Resumes, Say Some Firms," *The Wall Street Journal,* January 24, 2012, p. B6.
56. A. Green, "How Employers Decide Whether to Interview You," *U.S. News & World Report,* September 18, 2017, https://money.usnews.com/money/blogs/outside-voices-careers/articles/2017-09-18/how-employers-decide-whether-to-interview-you.
57. P. W. Barada, "What Can Former Employers Legally Say about Me?" *Monster,* accessed March 20, 2018, https://www.monster.com/career-advice/article/what-can-employers-legally-say.
58. A. Assad, "What Is HR Allowed to Ask From Previous Employers?" *Chron,* accessed March 20, 2018, http://work.chron.com/hr-allowed-ask-previous-employers-22431.html.
59. A. Waterfield, "Credit Checks for Employees and Applicants: Are They Worth It?" *Bloomberg BNA,* August 3, 2017, https://www.bna.com/credit-checks-employees-b73014462639/.
60. S. E. Needleman, "The New Trouble on the Line," *The Wall Street Journal,* June 2, 2009, pp. B7, B10; K. Tyler, "Who You Gonna Call?" *HR Magazine,* April 2014, pp. 65–67.
61. D. S. Chapman, K. L. Uggerslev, and J. Webster, "Applicant Reactions Face-to-Face and Technology-Mediated Interviews: A Field Investigation," *Journal of Applied Psychology* 88 (2003), pp. 944–953.
62. J. Levashina and M. A. Campion, "Measuring Faking in the Employment Interview: Development and Validation of an Interview Faking

Behavior Scale," *Journal of Applied Psychology,* November 2007, pp. 1638–1656.

63. E. D. Pursell, M. A. Campion, and S. R. Gaylord, "Structured Interviewing: Avoiding Selection Problems," *Personnel Journal,* November 1980; J. Levashina, C. J. Hartwell, F. P. Morgeson, and M. A. Campion, "The Structured Employment Interview: Narrative and Quantitative Review of the Research Literature," *Personnel Psychology* 67, no. 1 (2014), pp. 241–293.

64. M. C. Blackman, "Personality Judgment and the Utility of the Unstructured Employment Interview," *Basic and Applied Social Psychology* 24 (2002), pp. 241–250. See also B. W. Swider, M. R. Barrick, T. B. Harris, and A. C. Stoverink, "Managing and Creating an Image in the Interview: The Role of Interviewee Initial Impressions," *Journal of Applied Psychology* 96 (2011), pp. 1275–1288.

65. L. Ryan, "12 Qualities Employers Look for when They're Hiring," *Forbes,* March 2, 2016, https://www.forbes.com/sites/lizryan/2016/03/02/12-qualities-employers-look-for-when-theyre-hiring/#23a539982c24; K. Grice, "Former Google Recruiter: This Is How to Improve Your Interviews," *Fast Company,* March 12, 2018, https://www.fastcompany.com/40540524/former-google-recruiter-this-is-how-to-improve-your-interviews; M. Ward, "The 5 Soft Skills That Will Get You Hired—and How to Learn Them," *CNBC,* April 26, 2017, https://www.cnbc.com/2017/04/26/the-5-soft-skills-that-will-get-you-hired--and-how-to-learn-them.html.

66. N. Zipkin, "How Long Does It Take to Decide on a Job Candidate? The Answer May Surprise You," *Entrepreneur,* June 7, 2015, https://www.entrepreneur.com/article/246948.

67. "Employment Testing," *Wikipedia,* July 21, 2017, https://en.wikipedia.org/wiki/employment_testing.

68. "Employment Tests and Selection Procedures," *The U.S. Equal Employment Opportunity Commission,* https://www.eeoc.gov/policy/docs/factemployment_procedures.html (accessed March 21, 2018).

69. A. Doyle, "Types of Pre-Employment Tests," *The Balance,* October 14, 2017, https://www.thebalance.com/types-of-pre-employment-tests-2059812.

70. L. Chierotti, "What Are the Top 2 Personality Traits of Leaders Across All Major Industries? IBM Supercomputer Watson Has the Results," *Inc.,* July 6, 2017, https://www.inc.com/logan-chierotti/supercomputer-discovers-top-2-personality-traits-o.html?cid=search.

71. On the subject of job tryouts, see M. Mullenweb, "The CEO of Automattic on Holding 'Auditions' to Build a Strong Team," *Harvard Business Review,* April 2014, pp. 39–42.

72. P. R. Sackett, O. R. Shewach, and H. N. Keiser, "Assessment Center versus Cognitive Ability Tests: Challenging the Conventional Wisdom on Criterion-Related Validity," *Journal of Applied Psychology,* 2017, pp. 1435–1447.

73. J. Hodges, "a) Doctor b) Builder c) Cop d) HELP!" *The Wall Street Journal,* April 22, 2010, p. D2.

74. S. Rust, "Obituary: Physicist Who Developed World-Renowned Personality Test—and Saved Einstein from Drowning," *Oxford Mail,* http://www.oxfordmail.co.uk/news/16086520.OBITUARY_Physicist_who_developed_world_renowned_personality_test_and_saved_Einstein_from_drowning/ (accessed March 21, 2018).

75. "Are Resumes Passé? Enter the EQ Test," *Knowledge@Wharton,* June 18, 2014, http://knowledge.wharton.upenn.edu/article/resumes-passe-enter-eq- test (accessed June 5, 2016); D. Meinert, "Heads Up!" *HR Magazine,* June 2015, pp. 88–98.

76. H. O'Neill, "Is the Cult of Personality Testing Still Dominating the Hiring Process . . . and Should It Be?" *Mighty Recruiter,* March 1, 2017, https://www.mightyrecruiter.com/blog/cult-of-personality-testing/.

77. T. Wen, "The New Way Your Personality Could Be Holding You Back," *BBC,* August 21, 2017, http://www.bbc.com/capital/story/20170818-the-new-way-your-personality-could-be-holding-you-back.

78. "Biggest Pros and Cons of Personality Tests as Hiring Tools," *Inc.,* August 7, 2017, https://www.inc.com/workpop/picking-the-best-candidate-according-to-science-sh.html?cid=search.

79. H. O'Neill, "Is the Cult of Personality Testing Still Dominating the Hiring Process . . . and Should It Be?" *Mighty Recruiter,* March 1, 2017, https://www.mightyrecruiter.com/blog/cult-of-personality-testing/.

80. "Biggest Pros and Cons of Personality Tests as Hiring Tools," *Inc.,* August 7, 2017, https://www.inc.com/workpop/picking-the-best-candidate-according-to-science-sh.html?cid=search.

81. C. O'Neil, "Personality Tests Are Failing American Workers," *The Charlotte Observer,* January 20, 2018, http://www.charlotteobserver.com/opinion/op-ed/article195668439.html.

82. "Ethical Guidelines," *The Myers & Briggs Foundation,* http://www.myersbriggs.org/myers-and-briggs-foundation/ethical-use-of-the-mbti-instrument/ethical-guidelines.htm?bhcp=1 (accessed March 21, 2018).

83. "Types of Employment Tests," *Society for Industrial and Organizational Psychology,* http://www.siop.org/workplace/employment%20testing/testtypes.aspx (accessed March 21, 2018).

84. "Types of Employment Tests," *Society for Industrial and Organizational Psychology,* http://www.siop.org/workplace/employment%20testing/testtypes.aspx (accessed March 21, 2018); "Assessment and Selection," *OPM,* https://www.opm.gov/policy-data-oversight/assessment-and-selection/other-assessment-methods/integrityhonesty-tests/ (accessed March 21, 2018).

85. A. Doyle, "Things You Should Know About Pre-Employment Drug Testing," *The Balance,* March 15, 2018, https://www.thebalance.com/drug-and-alcohol-tests-for-employment-2060409.

86. R. Greenfield and J. Kaplan, "The Coming Decline of the Employment Drug Test," *Bloomberg,* March 5, 2018, https://www.bloomberg.com/news/articles/2018-03-05/the-coming-decline-of-the-employment-drug-test.

87. R. Seseri, "How AI Is Changing the Game for Recruiting," *Forbes,* January 29, 2018, https://www.forbes.com/sites/valleyvoices/2018/01/29/how-ai-is-changing-the-game-for-recruiting/#54b6f1551aa2; J. Alsever, "How AI Is Changing Your Job Hunt," *Fortune,* May 19, 2017, http://fortune.com/2017/05/19/ai-changing-jobs-hiring-recruiting/.

88. "Employer Costs for Employee Compensation," news release text, Bureau of Labor Statistics, https://www.bls.gov/news.release/ecec.nr0.htm (accessed March 21, 2018).

89. "Work-Life 3.0: Understanding How We'll Work Next," *pwc,* https://www.pwc.com/us/en/industry/entertainment-media/publications/consumer-intelligence-series/assets/pwc-consumer-intelligence-series-future-of-work-june-2016.pdf (accessed March 21, 2018).

90. L. Dixon, "Do Benefits Preferences Differ by Gender?" *Talent Economy,* September 14, 2016, http://www.talenteconomy.io/2016/09/14/benefits-preferences-differ-gender/.

91. T. D. Allen, L. T. Eby, G. T. Chao, and T. N. Bauer, "Taking Stock of Two Relational Aspects of Organizational Life: Tracing the History and Shaping the Future of Socialization and Mentoring Research," *Journal of Applied Psychology,* 2017, pp. 324–337.

92. R. Feloni, "Facebook Engineering Director Describes What It's Like to Go through the Company's 6-Week Engineer Bootcamp," *Business Insider,* March 2, 2016, http://www.businessinsider.com/inside-facebook-engineer-bootcamp-2016-3.

93. A. M. Ellis, S. S. Nifadkar, T. N. Bauer, and B. Erdogan, "Newcomer Adjustment: Examining the Role of Managers' Perception of Newcomer Proactive Behavior during Organizational Socialization," *Journal of Applied Psychology,* 2017, pp. 993–1001; L. G. E. Smith, N. Gillespie, V. J. Callan, T. W. Fitzsimmons, and N. Paulsen, "Injunctive and Descriptive Logics during Newcomer Socialization: The Impact on Organizational Identification, Trustworthiness, and Self-Efficacy," *Journal of Organizational Behavior,* 2017, pp. 487–511.

94. K. Oakes, "How Long Does It Take to Get Fully Productive?" *Training Industry Quarterly,* Winter 2012, pp. 40–41.

95. G. R. Jones, "Organizational Socialization as Information Processing Activity: A Life History Analysis," *Human Organization* 42, no. 4 (1983), pp. 314–320.

96. E. P. Wilson, "How Leading Tech Companies Use Learning & Development to Engage Employees," *Medium,* March 28, 2016, https://

medium.com/tradecraft-traction/how-leading-tech-companies-use-learning-development-to-engage-employees-662fe35fcb3a.

97. I. Thottam, "10 Companies with Awesome Training and Development Programs," *Monster*, https://www.monster.com/career-advice/article/companies-with-awesome-training-development-programs (accessed March 21, 2018).

98. I. Thottam, "10 Companies with Awesome Training and Development Programs," *Monster*, https://www.monster.com/career-advice/article/companies-with-awesome-training-development-programs (accessed March 21, 2018).

99. "Learning and Development," Estee Lauder Companies, https://www.elcompanies.com/talent/working-here/learning-and-development (accessed March 21, 2018).

100. E. P. Wilson, "How Leading Tech Companies Use Learning & Development to Engage Employees," *Medium*, March 28, 2016, https://medium.com/tradecraft-traction/how-leading-tech-companies-use-learning-development-to-engage-employees-662fe35fcb3a.

101. P. Cappelli and A. Tavis, "The New Rules of Talent Management," *Harvard Business Review*, March–April 2018, https://hbr.org/2018/03/the-new-rules-of-talent-management.

102. K. Higginbottom, "Learning and Development Not Valued by Organizations," *Forbes*, May 5, 2017, https://www.forbes.com/sites/karenhigginbottom/2017/05/05/learning-and-development-not-valued-by-organizations/#312189d86acb.

103. M. Goeden, "How 4 Industries Are Using Virtual Reality to Train Employees," *eLearning Industry*, November 8, 2017, https://elearningindustry.com/using-virtual-reality-to-train-employees-4-industries.

104. M. Goeden, "How 4 Industries Are Using Virtual Reality to Train Employees," *eLearning Industry*, November 8, 2017, https://elearningindustry.com/using-virtual-reality-to-train-employees-4-industries.

105. Saunderson, "Learning Technology Paves the Way for Change"; L. Kolodny, "A New Way to Train Workers, One Small Bite at a Time," *The Wall Street Journal*, March 14, 2016, p. R6; A. M. Paul, "How to Make Microlearning Matter," *SHRM*, May 1, 2016, https://www.shrm.org/publications/hrmagazine/editorialcontent/2016/ 0516/pages/0516-microlearning.aspx (accessed June 5, 2016).

106. L. Freifeld, "Training Magazine Ranks 2017 Training Top 125 Organizations," *Training*, January 31, 2017, https://trainingmag.com/training-magazine-ranks-2017-training-top-125-organizations; "Canada's Best Employers, #273 Keller Williams Realty," *Forbes*, https://www.forbes.com/companies/keller-williams-realty/ (accessed March 21, 2018); "A Real Estate Powerhouse," *Keller Williams*, http://www.kw.com/kw/careers-in-real-estate.html (accessed March 21, 2018); "Keller Williams Inducted into Training Magazine's Hall of Fame," *Business Wire*, https://www.businesswire.com/news/home/20180213006268/en/Keller-Williams-Inducted-Training-Magazine's-Hall-Fame (accessed March 21, 2018); "Keller Williams Named Top Training Organization Worldwide," *Keller Williams*, January 31, 2017, https://blog.kw.com/keller-williams-named-top-training-organization-worldwide; "Tap into the Real Estate Industry's Brightest Minds and Top Producers," *Keller Williams*, http://www.kw.com/kw/education.html (accessed March 21, 2018); and L. Freifeld, "Keller Williams Is at Home at No. 1," *Training*, https://trainingmag.com/trgmag-article/keller-williams-home-no-1 (accessed March 21, 2018).

107. Study by consulting firm Watson Wyatt Worldwide (now Towers Watson), reported in M. Ipe, "Feedback Essential for Employee Growth," *Arizona Republic*, October 2, 2015, www.azcentral.com/story/money/business/jobs/2015/10/02/feedback-essential-employee-growth/73044324 (accessed June 6, 2016).

108. C. Groscurth. "Great Managers Can Fix Broken Performance Management Systems," *Gallup Business Journal*, June 14, 2015, www.gallup.com/businessjournal/183770/great-managers-fix-broken-performance-management-systems.aspx (accessed June 13, 2016).

109. Adapted from A. J. Kinicki, K. J. L. Jacobson, S. J. Peterson, and G. E. Prussia, "Development and Validation of the Performance Management Behavior Questionnaire," *Personnel Psychology* 66 (2013), pp. 1–45.

110. M. C. Bush and S. Lewis-Kulin, "100 Best Companies to Work For 2017," *Fortune*, March 15, 2017, pp. 79–136.

111. See "Committed to Helping Our Customers," Edward Jones, http://careers.edwardjones.com/explore-edward-jones/about.html (accessed March 21, 2018); "Edward Jones Financial Advisor Performance Appraisal," *Slideshare*, https://www.slideshare.net/billmohamed41/edward-jones-financial-advisor-performance-appraisal (accessed March 21, 2018); C. Mucciolo, "Edward Jones Raises FA Production Expectations," *Wealth Management Magazine*, April 29, 2010, http://www.wealthmanagement.com/news/edward-jones-raises-fa-production-expectations; "There's No Substitute for a Plan," *Edward Jones*, https://www.fa-mag.com/userfiles/ads_2017/Edward_Jones_LG_March_2017/EJ_Whitepaper_Business_Planning_Final.pdf (accessed March 21, 2018); "Financial Advisor Compensation Package," Edward Jones, http://careers.edwardjones.com/explore-opportunities/new-financial-advisors/compensation/compensation.html (accessed March 21, 2018); J. Horowitz, "Edward Jones Boosts Broker Count, But Commissions Plummet," *Advisor Hub*, January 12, 2017, https://advisorhub.com/edward-jones-boosts-broker-count-commissions-plummet/; J. Horowitz, "Edward Jones Noses Ahead of Morgan Stanley to Boast Biggest Brokerage Force," *Advisor Hub*, November 10, 2017, https://advisorhub.com/edward-jones-noses-ahead-morgan-stanley-boast-biggest-brokerage-force/.

112. A. S. DeNisi and K. R. Murphy, "Performance Appraisal and Performance Management: 100 Years of Progress?" *Journal of Applied Psychology*, 2017, pp. 421–433.

113. W. E. Deming, reported by D. S. Perrin, in P. Downs, "Bringing Back Employee Reviews," *The New York Times*, June 26, 2014, p. B5.

114. CEB Global, reported in D. Wilkie, "Is the Annual Performance Review Dead?" *HR Magazine*, October 2015, pp. 11–12.

115. P. Cappelli and A. Tavis, "The New Rules of Talent Management," *Harvard Business Review*, March–April 2018, https://hbr.org/2018/03/the-new-rules-of-talent-management.

116. M. Buckingham and A. Goodall, "Reinventing Performance Management," *Harvard Business Review*, April 2015, https://hbr.org/2015/04/reinventing-performance-management.

117. "Break Free from Performance Management Shackles: Companies That Are Paving the Way," *business.com*, February 22, 2017, https://www.business.com/articles/performance-management-companies-that-are-breaking-free/.

118. N. Sloan, D. Agarwal, S. Garr, and K. Pastakia, "Performance Management: Playing a Winning Hand," *Deloitte*, February 28, 2017, https://www2.deloitte.com/insights/us/en/focus/human-capital-trends/2017/redesigning-performance-management.html.

119. The term "Munchausen at work" was created by Georgia Institute of Technology business professor Nathan Bennett. See N. Bennett, "Munchausen at Work," *Harvard Business Review*, November 16, 2007, pp. 24–25.

120. S. M. Heathfield, "60 Degree Feedback: See the Good, the Bad and the Ugly," *The Balance*, January 4, 2018, https://www.thebalance.com/360-degree-feedback-information-1917537.

121. K. Y. Kim, L. Atwater, P. C. Patel, and J. W. Smither, "Multisource Feedback, Human Capital, and the Financial Performance of Organizations," *Journal of Applied Psychology*, 2016, pp. 1569–1584.

122. A. Przystanski, "Performance Ranking Re-enters Legal Spotlight," *Namely*, February 10, 2016, https://hrnews.namely.com/hrnews/blog/2016/2/10/performance-ranking-re-enters-legal-spotlight.

123. Meinert, "Reinventing Reviews."

124. A. Smith, "Yahoo's Forced Ranking Raises Legal Questions about Ratings," Society for Human Resource Management, February 4, 2016, https://www.shrm.org/resourcesandtools/legal-and-compliance/employment-law/pages/yahoo-forced-ranking.aspx.

125. D. Rock and B. Jones, "Why More and More Companies Are Ditching Performance Ratings," *Harvard Business Review*, September 8, 2015, https://hbr.org/2015/09/why-more-and-more-companies-are-ditching-performance-ratings (accessed June 6, 2016); R. Feintzeig, "The Trouble with Grading Employees," *The Wall Street Journal*, April 22, 2015, pp. B1, B7.

126. "Break Free from Performance Management Shackles: Companies That Are Paving the Way," *business.com,* February 22, 2017, https://www.business.com/articles/performance-management-companies-that-are-breaking-free/.
127. G. Leibowitz, "6 Ways Truly Effective Leaders Deliver Feedback," *Inc.,* February 13, 2018, https://www.inc.com/glenn-leibowitz/6-ways-truly-effective-leaders-deliver-feedback.html?cid=search; P. Gasca, "Want o Deliver Effective Feedback? Try the 'You Suck Sandwich' Approach," *Inc.,* February 26, 2018, https://www.inc.com/peter-gasca/deliver-feedback-like-a-ninja-with-a-you-suck-sandwich.html?cid=search; J. Peterson, "Want to Be a Better Leader? Start by Giving Useful Feedback—Here's How," *Inc.,* January 12, 2018, https://www.inc.com/joel-peterson/3-ways-to-give-constructive-feedback-that-actually-works.html?cid=search; M. Schneider, "3 Steps to Give Tough but Effective Feedback to Your Employees," *Inc,* September 27, 2017, https://www.inc.com/michael-schneider/3-steps-to-give-tough-but-effective-feedback-to-your-employees.html?cid=search.
128. Definitions adapted from R. Mayhew, "Employee Turnover vs. Attrition," *Chron,* http://smallbusiness.chron.com/employee-turnover-vs-attrition-15846.html (accessed June 7, 2016).
129. Definitions adapted from R. Mayhew, "Employee Turnover vs. Attrition," *Chron,* http://smallbusiness.chron.com/employee-turnover-vs-attrition-15846.html (accessed June 7, 2016).
130. K. Daum, "Why That Other Guy Got the Promotion," *Inc.,* February 9, 2017, https://www.inc.com/kevin-daum/why-that-other-guy-got-the-promotion.html?cid=search; "The Realistic Way to Bounce Back when You're Passed Over for a Promotion," *Forbes,* December 11, 2017, https://www.forbes.com/sites/dailymuse/2017/12/11/the-realistic-way-to-bounce-back-when-youre-passed-over-for-a-promotion/#30055784b23a.
131. "Career Advice," *Monster,* https://www.monster.com/career-advice/ (accessed March 21, 2018); A. Carpenter, "A Millennial's Guide to Asking for a Promotion," *Forbes,* December 5, 2017, https://www.forbes.com/sites/alissacarpenter/2017/12/05/a-millennials-guide-to-asking-for-a-promotion/#5ba365c85697.
132. W. Boston, "Auto Maker Weighs Rotating Executives," *The Wall Street Journal,* December 21, 2015, p. B3.
133. "How Layoffs Hurt Companies," *Knowledge@Wharton,* April 12, 2016, http://knowledge.wharton.upenn.edu/article/how-layoffs-cost-companies (accessed June 7, 2016).
134. T. Lee, "Fired CEOs 'Pursue Other Opportunities,'" *San Francisco Chronicle,* May 30, 2016, pp. A1, A6.
135. M. Conlin, "When the Laid-Off Are Better Off," *BusinessWeek,* November 2, 2009, p. 65.
136. D. Mattioli, "Layoff Sign: Boss's Cold Shoulder," *The Wall Street Journal,* October 23, 2008, p. D6.
137. D. Lyons, "Congratulations! You've Been Fired," *The New York Times,* April 10, 2016, p. SR-7.
138. S. Gleason and R. Feintzeig, "Startups Are Quick to Fire," *The Wall Street Journal,* December 12, 2013, www.wsj.com/articles/SB10001424052702304202204579254540454121188 (accessed June 6, 2016).
139. L. Ryan, "Ten Ways Employment at Will Is Bad for Business," *Forbes,* October 3, 2016, https://www.forbes.com/sites/lizryan/2016/10/03/ten-ways-employment-at-will-is-bad-for-business/#8757545157bd.
140. U.S. Equal Employment Opportunity Commission, "Federal Laws Prohibiting Job Discrimination Questions and Answers," November 21, 2009, https://www.eeoc.gov/facts/qanda.html (accessed March 17, 2018).
141. J. Schleckser, "The 1 Question You Must Ask before You Fire Someone," *Inc.,* February 20, 2018, https://www.inc.com/jim-schleckser/the-1-question-you-must-ask-before-you-fire-someone.html?cid=search.
142. R. Knight, "The Right Way to Fire Someone," *Harvard Business Review,* February 5, 2016, https://hbr.org/2016/02/the-right-way-to-fire-someone.
143. D. Brown, "'You're Fired.' Making the Hard Decision to Let People Go and How to Be Human About It," *Inc.,* November 1, 2017, https://www.inc.com/david-brown/the-best-approach-to-worst-situation-how-to-fire-an-employee.html?cid=search.
144. S. Sudakow, "The Best Advice I Ever Got about Firing Bad Employees," *Inc.,* May 17, 2017, https://www.inc.com/james-sudakow/the-best-advice-i-ever-got-about-firing-bad-employees.html?cid=search.
145. W. Lee, "Best Time to Drop the Hatchet at Work," *San Francisco Chronicle,* April 6, 2016, pp. C1, C3.
146. C. Dessi, "Why You Need to Be Prepared to Get Fired," *Inc.,* July 25, 2017, https://www.inc.com/chris-dessi/why-you-need-to-be-prepared-to-get-fired.html?cid=search.
147. E. Spain and B. Groysberg, "Making Exit Interviews Count," *Harvard Business Review,* April 2016, pp. 88–95.
148. S. Shellenbarger, "Bye, Boss, Let's Stay Friends Forever," *The Wall Street Journal,* August 19, 2015, pp. D1, D3.
149. J. Preston, "Laid-Off Americans, Required to Zip Lips on Way Out, Are Growing Bolder," *The New York Times,* June 12, 2016, pp. News-11, News-19.
150. S. Belskie, "The Progressive Case For and Against a $15 Minimum Wage," *Medium,* June 1, 2017, https://medium.com/@stevebelskie/15-dollar-minimum-wage-possible-4fffc280412c.
151. For more about legislation updating the Toxic Substances Control Act of 1976, see C. Davenport and E. Huetteman, "Deal Is Reached to Expand Rules on Toxic Chemicals," *The New York Times,* May 20, 2016, p. A3; F. Krupp, "When Red and Blue in Congress Makes Green," *The Wall Street Journal,* June 10, 2016, p. A13.
152. C. Martin, "In the Health Law, an Open Door for Entrepreneurs," *The New York Times,* November 24, 2013, p. BU-3; H. Knight, "Health Efforts Work—Experts," *San Francisco Chronicle,* November 30, 2013, pp. A1, A9; Associated Press, "Uninsured Rate Decreases as Law Takes Effect," *San Francisco Chronicle,* January 24, 2014, p. A13.
153. "Affordable Care Act Tracking Survey February–April 2016," *Commonwealth Fund,* May 26, 2016, www.commonwealthfund.org/interactives-and-data/surveys/2016/aca-tracking-feb-apr-2016 (accessed June 6, 2016).
154. "Women's Median Earnings as a Percent of Men's Median Earnings, 1960-2016 (Full-time, Year-round Workers) with Projection for Pay Equity in 2059," *Institute for Women's Policy Research,* https://iwpr.org/publications/women-men-earnings-ratio-1960-2016-pay-equity-2059/ (accessed March 21, 2018).
155. "If Current Trends Continue, Hispanic Women Will Wait 232 Years for Equal Pay; Black Women Will Wait 108 Years," *Institute for Women's Policy Research,* https://iwpr.org/publications/if-current-trends-continue-hispanic-women-will-wait-232-years-for-equal-pay-black-women-will-wait-108-years/ (accessed March 21, 2018).
156. "Latinas Will Wait 216 Years for Equal Pay at Current Rate," *Institute for Women's Policy Research,* https://iwpr.org/latinas-will-wait-216-years-equal-pay-current-rate/ (accessed March 21, 2018).
157. "Pay Equity and Discrimination," *Institute for Women's Policy Research,* https://iwpr.org/issue/employment-education-economic-change/pay-equity-discrimination/ (accessed March 21, 2018).
158. S. Milligan, "Are Salary Histories History?" *HRMagazine,* March 2018, p. 56.
159. "EEOC Releases Fiscal Year 2017 Enforcement and Litigation Data," U.S. Equal Employment Opportunity Commission, https://www.eeoc.gov/eeoc/newsroom/release/1-25-18.cfm (accessed March 21, 2018).
160. J. Platt, S. Prins, and K. Keyes, "Unequal Depression for Equal Work? How the Wage Gap Explains Gendered Disparities in Mood Disorders," *Social Science & Medicine* 149 (2016), pp. 1–8.
161. For a discussion of how to implement affirmative action, see J. Mendez, "The Four Key Components of a Successful Affirmative Action Plan," *PeopleFluent,* January 21, 2016, www.peoplefluent.com/blog/the-four-key-components-of-a-successful-affirmative-action-program (accessed June 6, 2016).

162. J. A. Kovacs, D. M. Truxillo, T. N. Bauer, and T. Bodner, "Perceptions of Affirmative Action Based on Socioeconomic Status: A Comparison with Traditional Affirmative Action," *Employee Responsibilities Rights Journal* 26 (2014), pp. 35–57.
163. E. H. James, A. P. Brief, J. Dietz, and R. R. Cohen, "Prejudice Matters: Understanding the Reactions of Whites to Affirmative Action Programs Targeted to Benefit Blacks," *Journal of Applied Psychology,* December 2001, pp. 1120–1128.
164. L. M. Leslie, D. M. Mayer, and D. A. Kravitz, "The Stigma of Affirmative Action: A Stereotyping-Based Theory and Meta-Analytic Test of the Consequences for Performance," *Academy of Management Journal,* August 2014, pp. 964–989.
165. M. Rotundo, D.-H. Nguyen, and P. R. Sackett, "A Meta-Analytic Review of Gender Differences in Perceptions of Sexual Harassment," *Journal of Applied Psychology,* October 2001, pp. 914–922.
166. C. A. Pierce and H. Aguinis, "Legal Standards, Ethical Standards, and Responses to Social–Sexual Conduct at Work," *Journal of Organizational Behavior* 26 (2005), pp. 727–732; L. A. Baar, "Harassment Case Proceeds Despite Failure to Report," *HR Magazine,* June 2005, p. 159; S. Shellenbarger, "Supreme Court Takes on How Employers Handle Worker Harassment Complaints," *The Wall Street Journal,* April 13, 2006, p. D1.
167. A. Almukhtar, M. Gold, and L. Buchanan, "After Weinstein: 71 Men Accused of Sexual Misconduct and Their Fall from Power," *The New York Times,* February 8, 2018, https://www.nytimes.com/interactive/2017/11/10/us/men-accused-sexual-misconduct-weinstein.html.
168. E. Bernstein, "The Role Power Plays in Sexual Harassment," *The Wall Street Journal,* February 6, 2018, p. A 13.
169. B. M. Galvin, D. A. Waldman, and P. Balthazard, "Visionary Communication Qualities as Mediators of the Relationship between Narcissism and Attributions of Leader Charisma," *Personnel Psychology,* Autumn 2010, p. 510.
170. E. Grijalva, P. D. Harms, D. A. Newman, B. H. Gaddis, and R. C, Fraley, "Narcissism and Leadership: A Meta-Analytic Review of Linear and Non-linear Relationships," *Personnel Psychology,* Spring 2015, pp. 1–47.
171. E. Bernstein, "The Role Power Plays in Sexual Harassment," *The Wall Street Journal,* February 6, 2018, p. A 13.
172. J. Macur, "On Social Media, Misogyny Runs Amok," *The New York Times,* April 29, 2016, pp. B9, B13.
173. Anti-harassment policies are discussed by J. A. Segal, "Upgrade Your Anti-Harassment Policy," *HRMagazine,* March 2018, pp. 64–65.
174. G. Namie, "2017 Workplace Bullying Institute U.S. Workplace Bullying Survey," Workplace Bullying Institute, http://workplacebullying.org/multi/pdf/2017/2017-WBI-US-Survey.pdf (accessed March 21, 2018).
175. D. T. Eesley and P. A. Meglich, "Empirical Evidence of Abusive Supervision in Entrepreneurial and Small Firms," *Journal of Ethics and Entrepreneurship,* Spring 2013, pp. 39–60.
176. G. Namie, "2017 Workplace Bullying Institute U.S. Workplace Bullying Survey," *Workplace Bullying Institute,* http://workplacebullying.org/multi/pdf/2017/2017-WBI-US-Survey.pdf (accessed March 21, 2018).
177. S. M. Heathfield, "How to Deal with a Bully at Work," *The Balance,* September 30, 2017, https://www.thebalance.com/how-to-deal-with-a-bully-at-work-1917901.
178. Society for Human Resource Management, "SHRM Survey Findings: Workplace Bullying." See also E. Bernstein, "Lessons for Shutting Down a Grownup Cyberbully," *The Wall Street Journal,* May 17, 2016, p. D2.
179. D. C. Treadway, B. A. Shaughnessy, J. W. Breland, J. Yang, and M. Reeves, "Political Skill and the Job Performance of Bullies," *Journal of Managerial Psychology* 28, no. 3 (2013), pp. 273–289.
180. Darren C. Treadway, quoted in R. E. Silverman, "Bullies Don't Finish Last, Study Indicates," *The Wall Street Journal,* July 3, 2013, p. B6.
181. R. Feintzeig, "When Co-Workers Don't Play Nice," *The Wall Street Journal,* August 28, 2013, p. B6. Also see interview with psychiatrist J. Foster, head of the Professionalism Program at Penn Medicine at Pennsylvania Hospital, Philadelphia, in "How Disruptive Behavior by Employees Can Devastate a Workplace," *Knowledge@Wharton,* March 27, 2013, http://knowledge.wharton.upenn.edu/article/how-disruptive-behavior-by-employees-can-devastate-a-workplace (accessed June 6, 2016).
182. G. Namie, "2017 Workplace Bullying Institute U.S. Workplace Bullying Survey," *Workplace Bullying Institute,* http://workplacebullying.org/multi/pdf/2017/2017-WBI-US-Survey.pdf (accessed March 21, 2018).
183. S. M. Heathfield, "How to Deal with a Bully at Work," *The Balance,* September 30, 2017, https://www.thebalance.com/how-to-deal-with-a-bully-at-work-1917901.
184. H. Benson, "Porters Found Road to Success Aboard Nation's 'Rolling Hotels,'" *San Francisco Chronicle,* February 11, 2009, pp. A1, A12.
185. S. Maniam, "Most Americans See Labor Unions, Corporations Favorably," *Pew Research Center,* January 30, 2017, http://www.pewresearch.org/fact-tank/2017/01/30/most-americans-see-labor-unions-corporations-favorably/.
186. M. Maynard, "By Helping Detroit, Did the UAW Lose Its Future?" *Forbes,* February 17, 2014, www.forbes.com/sites/michelinemaynard/2014/02/17/by-helping-detroit-did-the-uaw-lose-its-future/#83a8e7b6e2b9 (accessed June 7, 2016); F. V. Vernuccio and T. Bowman, "Right to Work Buffs Up the Rust Belt," *The Wall Street Journal,* September 17, 2015, p. A15; M. Hiltzik, "Are Those Detested Two-Tiered UAW Contracts Finally on the Way Out?" *Los Angeles Times,* October 13, 2015, www.latimes.com/business/hiltzik/la-fi-mh-is-the-two-tiered-union-contract-20151013-column.html (accessed June 7, 2016).
187. J. L. Brown, P. R. Martin, D. V. Moser, and R. A. Weber, "The Consequences of Hiring Lower-Wage Workers in an Incomplete-Contract Environment," *The Accounting Review*, May 2015, pp. 941–966.
188. J. Silver-Greenberg and M. Corkery, "Bank Customers Likely to Regain Access to Courts," *The New York Times,* May 5, 2016, pp. A1, B3; J. Silver-Greenberg and M. Corkery, "Start-Ups Turn to Arbitration in the Workplace," *The New York Times,* May 15, 2016, pp. News-1, News-4.
189. J. Silver-Greenberg and R. Gebeloff, "Arbitration Everywhere, Stacking Deck of Justice," *The New York Times,* November 1, 2015, pp. News-1, News-22, News-23; J. Silver-Greenberg and M. Corkery, "A 'Privatization of the Justice System,'" *The New York Times,* November 2, 2015, pp. A1, B4, B5.
190. G. Zoroya and C. MacLeod, "A World Apart, Meat Workers Share a Bond," *USA Today,* June 26, 2013, pp. 1B, 2B.
191. M. Trottman, "Ruling Clears Way for Unions," *The Wall Street Journal,* August 28, 2015, pp. A1, A4.
192. S. Greenhouse, "Workers Organize, but Don't Unionize, to Get Protection under Labor Law," *The New York Times,* September 7, 2015, pp. B1, B5.
193. K. Cao and E. Newcomer, "Uber Pledges to Back Drivers Guild in N.Y.," *San Francisco Chronicle,* May 11, 2016, pp. C1, C3; N. Scheiber and M. Isaac, "A Guild, Short of a Union, for New York Uber Drivers," *The New York Times,* May 11, 2016, pp. B1, B6.
194. R. E. Silverman, "Workplace Democracy Catches On," *The Wall Street Journal,* March 28, 2016, p. B5.
195. A.N. Kluger and A. DeNisi, "The Effects of Feedback Interventions on Performance: A Historical Review, a Meta-Analysis, and a Preliminary Feedback Intervention Theory," *Psychological Bulletin,* 1996, pp. 254–284.
196. D. Goleman, *Focus: The Hidden Driver of Excellence* (New York: HarperCollins, 2013); N. Buck, "The Brain's Biology: A Negative Feedback Loop System," *Funderstanding,* January 20, 2012, http://www.funderstanding.com/brain/brain-biology-a-negative-feedback-loop-system.
197. R. Hanson and R. Mendius, *Buddha's Brain* (Oakland, CA: New Harbinger Publications, Inc., 2009), p. 42.
198. Y.-K. Woo, J. Song, Y. Jiang, C. Cho, M. Bong, and S.-I. Kim, "Effects of Informative and Confirmatory Feedback on Brain Activation during Negative Feedback Processing," *Frontiers in Human Neuroscience,* June 2015, pp. 1–9; R. Hanson and R. Mendius, *Buddha's Brain* (Oakland, CA: New Harbinger Publications, Inc., 2009), p. 42.

199. A. Christensen, A. Kinicki, Z. Zhang, and F. Walumbwa, "Responses to Feedback: The Role of Acceptance, Affect, and Creative Behavior," *Journal of Leadership and Organizational Studies*, 2018, pp. 1–14.
200. S. Heen and D. Stone, "Find the Coaching in Criticism," *Harvard Business Review*, January–February 2014, https://hbr.org/2014/01/find-the-coaching-in-criticism.
201. A. Kinicki, G. Prussia, B. Wu, and F. McKee-Ryan, "A Covariance Structure Analysis of Employees' Response to Performance Feedback," *Journal of Applied Psychology*, 2004, pp. 1057–1069.
202. D. Grote, "How to Handle Negative Feedback," *Harvard Business Review*, August 17, 2015, https://hbr.org/2015/08/how-to-handle-negative-feedback.
203. L. L. Holmer, "Understanding and Reducing the Impact of Defensiveness on Management Learning: Some Lessons from Neuroscience," *Journal of Management Education*, October 2013, p. 621.
204. D. Grote, "How to Handle Negative Feedback," *Harvard Business Review*, August 17, 2015, https://hbr.org/2015/08/how-to-handle-negative-feedback.
205. A. Christensen, A. Kinicki, Z. Zhang, and F. Walumbwa, "Responses to Feedback: The Role of Acceptance, Affect, and Creative Behavior," *Journal of Leadership and Organizational Studies*, 2018, pp. 1–14; J. Folkman, "You Can Take It! How to Accept Negative Feedback with Ease," *Forbes*, December 5, 2017, https://www.forbes.com/.../you-can-take-it-how-to-accept-negative-feedback-with-ease.
206. J. Kabat-Zinn, "Mindfulness-Based Interventions in Context: Past, Present, and Future," *Clinical Psychology: Science and Practice*, Summer 2003, p. 145.
207. R. Teper and M. Inzlicht, "Mindful Acceptance Dampens Neuroaffective Reactions to External and Rewarding Performance Feedback," *Emotion*, February 2014, pp. 105–114.
208. A. Abramson, "The 3-Day Workweek & 8 Other Benefits of Being a Nurse," *Rasmussen College Blog*, June 2, 2017, http://www.rasmussen.edu/degrees/nursing/blog/benefits-of-being-a-nurse/.
209. "Nursing Turnover and Retention Strategies," *The Sentinel Watch*, January 23, 2018, www.americansentinel.edu/blog/2018/01/23/nursing-turnover-and-retention-strategies/.
210. J. Kauflin, "The 20 College Majors with the Highest Starting Salaries," *Forbes*, October 17, 2016, www.forbes.com/sites/jeffkauflin/2016/10/17/the-20-college-majors-with-the-highest-starting-salaries/#15d913392d50.
211. B. Tuttle, "New College Grads Could Be Looking at the Highest Starting Salaries Ever," *Time*, May 12, 2017, http://time.com/money/4777074/college-grad-pay-2017-average-salary/.
212. U.S. Census Bureau. "Median Household Income in the United States," September 14, 2017, https://www.census.gov/library/visualizations/2017/comm/income-map.html.
213. R. Hess, "We Work Hard for the Money: My Perspective on Nurse Salaries," *Nurse.com*, April 21, 2017, www.nurse.com/blog/2017/04/21/we-work-hard-for-the-money-my-perspective-on-nurse-salaries/.
214. A. Abramson, "The 3-Day Workweek & 8 Other Benefits of Being a Nurse," *Rasmussen College Blog*, June 2, 2017, http://www.rasmussen.edu/degrees/nursing/blog/benefits-of-being-a-nurse/.
215. R. Hess, "We Work Hard for the Money: My Perspective on Nurse Salaries," *Nurse.com*, April 21, 2017, www.nurse.com/blog/2017/04/21/we-work-hard-for-the-money-my-perspective-on-nurse-salaries/.
216. E. Kurnat-Thoma, M. Ganger, K. Peterson, & L. Channell, "Reducing Annual Hospital and Registered Nurse Staff Turnover—A 10-Element Onboarding Program Intervention," *SAGE Open Nursing*, 3 (2017), pp. 1–13.
217. R. Hess, "We Work Hard for the Money: My Perspective on Nurse Salaries," *Nurse.com*, April 21, 2017, www.nurse.com/blog/2017/04/21/we-work-hard-for-the-money-my-perspective-on-nurse-salaries/.
218. M. Kalensky, "More Than 'Minions': Nurses Deserve More Respect from Doctors," *STAT News*, November 3, 2017, www.statnews.com/2017/11/03/gender-gap-health-care-nurses/.
219. B. Wilson, M. Butler, R. Butler, and W. Johnson, "Nursing Gender Pay Differentials in the New Millennium," *Journal of Nursing Scholarship*, 50 (2018) pp. 102–108.
220. M. Kalensky, "More Than 'Minions': Nurses Deserve More Respect from Doctors," *STAT News*, November 3, 2017, www.statnews.com/2017/11/03/gender-gap-health-care-nurses/.
221. M. Kalensky, "More Than 'Minions': Nurses Deserve More Respect from Doctors," *STAT News*, November 3, 2017, www.statnews.com/2017/11/03/gender-gap-health-care-nurses/.
222. A. Robbins, "Doctors Throwing Fits: One of the Hardest Parts of Being a Nurse Is Dealing with Bullying Doctors," *Slate*, April 29, 2015, www.slate.com/articles/health_and_science/medical_examiner/2015/04/doctors_bully_nurses_hospital_mistreatment_is_a_danger_to_patient_health.html.
223. K. Schmidt, "How to Recognize and Prevent Bullying in Nursing," *Nurse.com*, August 23, 2017, www.nurse.com/blog/2017/08/23/how-to-recognize-and-prevent-bullying-in-nursing/.
224. K. Schmidt, "How to Recognize and Prevent Bullying in Nursing," *Nurse.com*, August 23, 2017, www.nurse.com/blog/2017/08/23/how-to-recognize-and-prevent-bullying-in-nursing/.
225. Staff Writer, "Sexual Harassment In Nursing—It's More Common Thank You Think," *Nurse.org*, https://nurse.org/articles/harvey-weinstein-and-harassment-against-nurses/.
226. A. Almendrala, "Nurses Endure a Shocking Amount of Violence on the Job," *Huffington Post*, September 1, 2017, www.huffingtonpost.com/entry/nurses-violence-police_us_59a9c2f9e4b0dfaafcf07093.
227. A. Almendrala, "Nurses Endure a Shocking Amount of Violence on the Job," *Huffington Post*, September 1, 2017, www.huffingtonpost.com/entry/nurses-violence-police_us_59a9c2f9e4b0dfaafcf07093.
228. D. Zwerdling, "Hospitals Fail to Protect Nursing Staff from Becoming Patients," *NPR*, February 14, 2015, www.npr.org/2015/02/04/382639199/hospitals-fail-to-protect-nursing-staff-from-becoming-patients.
229. D. Zwerdling, "Hospitals Fail to Protect Nursing Staff from Becoming Patients," *NPR*, February 14, 2015, www.npr.org/2015/02/04/382639199/hospitals-fail-to-protect-nursing-staff-from-becoming-patients.
230. D. Zwederling, "Hospital to Nurses: Your Injuries Are Not Our Problem," *NPR*, February 18, 2015, www.npr.org/2015/02/18/385786650/injured-nurses-case-is-a-symptom-of-industry-problems.
231. D. Zwerdling, "Hospitals Fail to Protect Nursing Staff from Becoming Patients," NPR, February 14, 2015, www.npr.org/2015/02/04/382639199/hospitals-fail-to-protect-nursing-staff-from-becoming-patients.
232. J. Silvestre, B. Ulrich, T. Johnson, N. Spector, and M. Blegen, "A Multisite Study on a New Graduate Registered Nurse Transition to Practice Program: Return on Investment," *Nursing Economics*, 35, no. 3 (May-June 2017).
233. D. Zwederling, "Hospital to Nurses: Your Injuries Are Not Our Problem," *NPR*, February 18, 2015, www.npr.org/2015/02/18/385786650/injured-nurses-case-is-a-symptom-of-industry-problems.
234. California Nurses Association, "18,000 Kaiser RNs Vote to Authorize Possible Strike at Kaiser Medical Facilities throughout California," *National Nurses United*, March 5, 2018, www.nationalnursesunited.org/press/18000-rns-vote-authorize-possible-strike-at-kaiser-medical-facilities-throughout-california.
235. "Non-Compete Clause," *Wikipedia*, March 19, 2016, https://en.wikipedia.org/wiki/Non-compete_clause.
236. G. Bensinger, "Amazon Sues New Target Executive," *The Wall Street Journal*, March 23, 2016, p. B1.
237. L. Ohnesorge, "Citrix Sues Former Raleigh Employees over Non-compete Clause," *Triangle Business Journal*, October 20, 2017, www.bizjournals.com/triangle/news/2017/10/20/citrix-sues-former-raleigh-employees-over.html.

CHAPTER NOTES

238. C. Dougherty, "How Noncompete Clauses Keep Workers Locked In," *New York Times,* https://www.nytimes.com/2017/05/13/business/noncompete-clauses.html.

239. N. Collamer, "Could a Noncompete Keep You from Getting Work?" *Forbes,* November 13, 2017, www.forbes.com/sites/nextavenue/2017/11/13/could-a-noncompete-keep-you-from-getting-work/#189c321967c.

CHAPTER 10

1. M. McQuaid, "3 Ways to Improve Your Creativity at Work," *Psychology Today,* October 6, 2016, https://www.psychologytoday.com/us/blog/functioning-flourishing/201610/3-ways-improve-your-creativity-work.

2. M. Batey, "Is Creativity the Number 1 Skill for the 21st Century?" *Psychology Today,* https://www.psychologytoday.com/us/blog/working-creativity/201102/is-creativity-the-number-1-skill-the-21st-century.

3. Y. W. Rhee and J. N. Choi, "Knowledge Management Behavior and Individual Creativity: Goal Orientations as Antecedents and In-Group Social Status as Moderating Contingency," *Journal of Organizational Behavior,* 2017, pp. 813–832.

4. M. McQuaid, "3 Ways to Improve Your Creativity at Work," *Psychology Today,* October 6, 2016, https://www.psychologytoday.com/us/blog/functioning-flourishing/201610/3-ways-improve-your-creativity-work.

5. M. McQuaid, "3 Ways to Improve Your Creativity at Work," *Psychology Today,* October 6, 2016, https://www.psychologytoday.com/us/blog/functioning-flourishing/201610/3-ways-improve-your-creativity-work; "Hopelab," *The Omidyar Group,* https://www.omidyargroup.com/pov/organizations/hopelab/ (accessed April 3, 2018).

6. M. McQuaid, "3 Ways to Improve Your Creativity at Work," *Psychology Today,* October 6, 2016, https://www.psychologytoday.com/us/blog/functioning-flourishing/201610/3-ways-improve-your-creativity-work.

7. D. Patel, "6 Proven Ways to Increase Your Creativity," *Forbes,* July 30, 2017, https://www.forbes.com/sites/deeppatel/2017/07/30/6-proven-ways-to-increase-your-creativity/#502576ce4295; Mayo Clinic Staff, "Depression and Anxiety: Exercise Eases Symptoms," Mayo Clinic, https://www.mayoclinic.org/diseases-conditions/depression/in-depth/depression-and-exercise/art-20046495 (accessed April 3, 2018).

8. M McQuaid, "3 Ways to Improve Your Creativity at Work," *Psychology Today,* October 6, 2016, https://www.psychologytoday.com/us/blog/functioning-flourishing/201610/3-ways-improve-your-creativity-work.

9. D. Patel, "6 Proven Ways to Increase Your Creativity," *Forbes,* July 30, 2017, https://www.forbes.com/sites/deeppatel/2017/07/30/6-proven-ways-to-increase-your-creativity/#502576ce4295.

10. Y. Gong, J. Wu, L. J. Song, and Z. Zhang, "Dual Tuning in Creative Processes: Joint Contributions of Intrinsic and Extrinsic Motivational Orientations," *Journal of Applied Psychology,* May 2017, p. 830.

11. "Jake Gyllenhaal Quotes and Sayings," *inspiringquotes.us,* www.inspiringquotes.us/author/4741-jake-gyllenhaal (accessed June 16, 2016).

12. AT&T CEO Randall Stephenson, quoted in Q. Hardy, "AT&T's New Line: Adapt, or Else," *The New York Times,* February 14, 2016, pp. BU-1, BU-5.

13. P. Drucker, "The Future That Has Already Happened," *The Futurist,* November 1998, pp. 16–18.

14. "Intuit 2020 Report: Twenty Trends That Will Shape the Next Decade," *Intuit,* October 2010, http://http-download.intuit.com/http.intuit/CMO/intuit/futureofsmallbusiness/ intuit_2020_report.pdf (accessed June 15, 2016).

15. K. Albrecht, "Eight Supertrends Shaping the Future of Business," *The Futurist,* September–October 2006, pp. 25–29; J. C. Glenn, "Scanning the Global Situation and Prospects for the Future," *The Futurist,* January–February 2008, pp. 41–46; "The Future Issue," *Fortune,* January 13, 2014; "The Future of Everything," *The Wall Street Journal,* July 8, 2014, pp. R1–R24.

16. J. Herrick, "This Marketing Strategy Is a Game Changer for Resource-Strapped Startups," *Entrepreneur,* March 25, 2018, https://www.entrepreneur.com/article/310762.

17. A. Ismael, "This Startup Used a Few Key Measurements to Make Me Perfect-Fitting Custom Clothes—Here's How They Did It," *Business Insider,* August 15, 2017, http://www.businessinsider.com/woodies-clothing-men-custom-shirt-chinos-review; "Create Your Custom Clothing Size Profile Now," *Woodies,* https://woodiesclothing.com/?utm_source=pepperjam&publisherId=133628&clickId=2276041286 (accessed April 9, 2018).

18. R. O. Bagley, "Speed to Market: An Entrepreneur's View," *Forbes,* May 1, 2013, www.forbes.com/sites/rebeccabagley/2013/05/01/speed-to-market-an-entrepreneurs- view/#6ea412712b3c (accessed June 17, 2016).

19. C. M. Christensen, *The Innovator's Dilemma: When New Technologies Cause Great Firms to Fail* (Boston: Harvard Business School Press, 1997). See also J. Howe, "The Disruptor," *Wired,* March 2013, pp. 74–78; J. Lepore, "The Disruption Machine," *The New Yorker,* June 23, 2014, pp. 30–36.

20. C. Mims, "Why Companies Are Being Disrupted," *The Wall Street Journal,* January 25, 2016, p. B4.

21. J. Albanese, "The Death of a Toy Retailer: How a Lack of Digital Transformation Helped Destroy Toys 'R' Us," *Inc.,* November 9, 2017, https://www.inc.com/jason-albanese/the-death-of-a-toy-retailer-how-a-lack-of-digital-transformation-helped-destroy-toys-r-us.html?cid=search.

22. P. Gasca, "Amazon Did Not Kill Toys 'R' Us—It Was a Giraffe," *Inc.,* March 17, 2018, https://www.inc.com/peter-gasca/the-surprising-overlooked-reason-why-toys-r-us-failed.html?cid=search.

23. J. Albanese, "The Death of a Toy Retailer: How a Lack of Digital Transformation Helped Destroy Toys 'R' Us," *Inc.,* November 9, 2017, https://www.inc.com/jason-albanese/the-death-of-a-toy-retailer-how-a-lack-of-digital-transformation-helped-destroy-toys-r-us.html?cid=search.

24. P. Gasca, "Amazon Did Not Kill Toys 'R' Us—It Was a Giraffe," *Inc.,* March 17, 2018, https://www.inc.com/peter-gasca/the-surprising-overlooked-reason-why-toys-r-us-failed.html?cid=search; N. Stern, "Toys 'R' Us Prepares for Its Final Curtain," *Forbes,* March 15, 2018, https://www.forbes.com/sites/neilstern/2018/03/15/toys-r-us-prepares-for-its-final-curtain/#1ddcb7cb2a0b.

25. Bloomberg, "Who Killed Geoffrey the Giraffe? Inside the Last Days of Toys 'R' Us," *Fortune,* March 16, 2018, http://fortune.com/2018/03/16/inside-toys-r-us-closure/?iid=sr-link3.

26. K. Korosec, "Toys 'R' Us Has 15% of the Toy Market and It's Still Going Under. Here's Why," *Fortune,* March 9, 2018, http://fortune.com/2018/03/09/toys-r-us-bankruptcy-why/?iid=sr-link9.

27. T. Johnson, "Mexico Takes Flight as Hub for Aerospace Industry," *McClatchy Newspapers,* July 18, 2012, www.mcclatchydc.com/2012/07/18/156657/mexico-takes-flight-as-hub-for.html (accessed June 17, 2016).

28. "Rolls-Royce in the US," *Rolls-Royce,* https://www.rolls-royce.com/country-sites/northamerica/rolls-royce-in-the-us.aspx (accessed April 4, 2018).

29. "Advanced Manufacturing," *Siemens,* http://www.usa.siemens.com/advanced-manufacturing/ (accessed April 4, 2018).

30. M. B. Sauter and S. Stebbins, "Manufacturers Bringing the Most Jobs Back to America," *USA Today,* April 23, 2016, https://www.usatoday.com/story/money/business/2016/04/23/24-7-wallst-economy-manufacturers-jobs-outsourcing/83406518/.

31. K. Albrecht, "Eight Supertrends Shaping the Future of Business," *The Futurist,* September–October 2006, pp. 25–29.

32. Analysis by J. Zumbrun, "The Rise of Knowledge Workers Is Accelerating Despite the Threat of Automation," *The Wall Street Journal,* May 4, 2016, http://blogs.wsj.com/economics/2016/05/04/the-rise-of-knowledge-workers-is-accelerating-despite-the-threat-of-automation (accessed June 17, 2016).

33. D. Autor, reported in T. Aeppel, "Be Calm, Robots Aren't About to Take Your Job, MIT Economist Says," *The Wall Street Journal,* February 25, 2015, http://blogs.wsj.com/economics/2015/02/25/be-calm-robots-arent-about-to-take-your-job-mit-economist-says (accessed June 17, 2016).
34. S. Waite, "How Emerging Technology Is Empowering Knowledge Workers," *Forbes,* February 28, 2018, https://www.forbes.com/sites/forbescommunicationscouncil/2018/02/28/how-emerging-technology-is-empowering-knowledge-workers/#33a5c4b295f2.
35. *Capitalizing on Complexity: Insights from the Global Chief Executive Officer Study,* International Business Machines, Somers, New York, 2010, www-01.ibm.com/common/ssi/cgi-bin/ssialias?htmlfid=GBE03301USEN&appname=wwwsearch; *Leading Through Connections: Insights from the IBM Global CEO Study,* International Business Machines, Somers, New York, 2012, www-935.ibm.com/services/us/en/c-suite/ceostudy2012; and *PwC's Annual Global CEO Survey,* PricewaterhouseCoopers, 2016, www.pwc.com/gx/en/ceo-agenda/ceosurvey/2016.html (all accessed June 17, 2016).
36. G. Donnelly, "Kroger, Walmart, and Dick's Changed How They Sell Guns, But Here's Why It May Not Make a Difference," *Fortune,* March 1, 2018, http://fortune.com/2018/03/01/kroger-gun-sales-walmart-dicks-cabelas/?iid=sr-link5.
37. J. Fortin, "A List of the Companies Cutting Ties with the N.R.A.," *The New York Times,* February 24, 2018, https://www.nytimes.com/2018/02/24/business/nra-companies-boycott.html.
38. R. Gold, B. Casselman, and G. Chazan, "Oil Well Lacked Safeguard Device," *The Wall Street Journal,* April 29, 2010, pp. A1, A8; S. Power and J. R. Emshwiller, "Investigators Focus on Failed Device," *The Wall Street Journal,* May 6, 2010, p. A5; D. Vergano, "New Equipment Headed to Battle Oil Spill," *USA Today,* May 6, 2010, p. 5A.
39. J. Scheck and S. Williams, "BP: The Makeover," *The Wall Street Journal,* October 25, 2013, pp. B1, B2.
40. C. Robertson and J. Schwartz, "How a Gulf Settlement That BP Once Hailed Became Its Target," *The New York Times,* April 27, 2014, News-1, News-20.
41. A. Neuhauser, "Judge Approves $20B Settlement in 2010 BP Oil Spill," *U.S. News & World Report,* April 4, 2016, www.usnews.com/news/articles/2016-04-04/judge-approves-20b-settlement-in-2010-bp-deepwater-horizon-oil-spill (accessed June 30, 2016).
42. "Seven Years Later: What's Ahead for the Gulf?" *Environmental Defense Fund,* https://www.edf.org/ecosystems/whats-ahead-gulf (accessed April 5, 2018).
43. A. Vaughan, "BP's Deepwater Horizon Bill Tops $65bn," *The Guardian,* January 6, 2018, https://www.theguardian.com/business/2018/jan/16/bps-deepwater-horizon-bill-tops-65bn.
44. P. Robertson, D. Roberts, and J. Porras, "Dynamics of Planned Organizational Change: Assessing Empirical Support for a Theoretical Model," *Academy of Management Journal* 36, no. 3 (1993), pp. 619–634.
45. S. Mautz, "Amazon Is Killing Shopping Malls—Right? Not So Fast Says This Mall Developer CEO," *Inc.,* September 5, 2017, https://www.inc.com/scott-mautz/amazon-is-killing-shopping-malls-right-no-so-fast.html?cid=search.
46. A. Kiersz, "Here's How Many Millennials Live with Their Parents in Each US state," *Business Insider,* May 3, 2017, http://www.businessinsider.com/millennials-living-at-home-state-map-2017-5.
47. K. Schwab, "The Fourth Industrial Revolution: What It Means, How to Respond," *World Economic Forum,* January 14, 2016, https://www.weforum.org/agenda/ 2016/01/the-fourth-industrial-revolution-what-it-means-and-how-to-respond (accessed June 17, 2016).
48. S. Terlep, "For CEO's, Strong Growth—and Turmoil," *The Wall Street Journal,* January 23, 2018, p. R4.
49. M. Isaac, "G.M., Expecting Rapid Change, Invests $500 Million in Lyft," *The New York Times*, January 5, 2016, p. B1.
50. R. Browne, "Uber Makes Changes to Boost Safety in the UK as Appeal to Overturn London Ban Continues," *CNBC,* February 16, 2018, https://www.cnbc.com/2018/02/16/uber-aims-to-boost-safety-in-the-uk-as-london-ban-appeal-continues.html.
51. B. Libert, M. Beck, and J. Wind, "How Automakers Can Think Like a Disruptor," *Knowledge@Wharton,* June 17, 2016, http://knowledge.wharton.upenn.edu/article/headline-automakers-can-think-like-disruptor (accessed June 22, 2016); M. Vella, "Automakers Want to Sell You Much More Than Just a Car," *Time,* January 25, 2016, p. 14.
52. D. Wakabayashi, "Uber's Self-Driving Cars Were Struggling before Arizona Crash," *The New York Times,* March 23, 2018, https://www.nytimes.com/2018/03/23/technology/uber-self-driving-cars-arizona.html.
53. M. Daniels, "Arizona Governor Suspends Uber from Autonomous Testing," *ABC News,* March 26, 2018, https://abcnews.go.com/Technology/wireStory/arizona-governor-suspends-uber-autonomous-testing-54029367.
54. M. Broussard, "Self-Driving Cars Still Don't Know How to See," *The Atlantic,* March 20, 2018, https://www.theatlantic.com/technology/archive/2018/03/uber-self-driving-fatality-arizona/556001/.
55. A. Tomer, "What Uber's Autonomous Vehicle Fatality Tells Us about the Future of Place," *Brookings,* March 20, 2018, https://www.brookings.edu/blog/the-avenue/2018/03/20/what-ubers-autonomous-vehicle-fatality-tells-us-about-the-future-of-place/.
56. A. Marshall, "Uber's Self-Driving Car Just Killed Somebody. Now What?" *Wired,* March 19, 2018, https://www.wired.com/story/uber-self-driving-car-crash-arizona-pedestrian/.
57. M. Mazzoni, "3p Weekend: 12 B Corps Leading Their Industries," *Triple Pundit,* December 9, 2016, https://www.triplepundit.com/2016/12/b-corps-leading-their-industries/.
58. D. Dahlhoff and A. Mantis of research group NPD, interviewed in "How Millennials, Gen Xers, and Baby Boomers Shop Differently," *Knowledge@Wharton,* May 31, 2016, http://knowledge.wharton.upenn.edu/article/new-tools-answer-age-old- question-of-what-do-customers-want (accessed June 18, 2016).
59. E. Fragouli and B. Ibidapo, "Leading in Crisis: Leading Organizational Change & Business Development," *International Journal of Information, Business and Management* 7, no. 3 (2015), pp. 71–90.
60. J. Onyang-Omara and K. Hjelmgaard, "'Brexit' Is Here: What Happens Next," *Reno Gazette-Journal,* June 25, 2016, p. 2B, reprinted from *USA Today*; S. Fidler, V. Pop, and J. Gross, "U.K. Vote Sets Off Shockwaves," *The Wall Street Journal,* June 25–26, 2016, pp. A1, A6.
61. "Obesity Rates & Trends," *The State of Obesity,* https://stateofobesity.org/rates/ (accessed April 5, 2018).
62. R. Hinton and A. Svachula, "Soda Taxes Popping Up around the U.S.," *Chicago Sun Times,* July 23, 2017, https://chicago.suntimes.com/news/soda-taxes-popping-up-around-the-u-s/.
63. C. Dewey, "Why the British Soda Tax Might Work Better than Any of the Soda Taxes That Came Before," *The Washington Post,* March 21, 2018, https://www.washingtonpost.com/news/wonk/wp/2018/03/21/why-the-british-soda-tax-might-work-better-than-any-of-the-soda-taxes-that-came-before-it/?utm_term=.84d7d0f540b1.
64. S. Oster, "Inside One of the World's Most Secretive iPhone Factories," *Bloomberg,* April 25, 2016, http://www.bloomberg.com/news/features/2016-04-24/inside-one-of-the-world-s-most-secretive-iphone-factories (accessed June 15, 2016).
65. D. Seetharaman and N. Andrews, "Facebook to Train against Bias," *The Wall Street Journal,* June 24, 2016, p. B3.
66. This three-way typology of change was adapted from discussion in P. C. Nutt, "Tactics of Implementation," *Academy of Management Journal,* June 1986, pp. 230–261.
67. Radical organizational change is discussed by T. E. Vollmann, *The Transformational Imperative* (Boston: Harvard Business School Press, 1996).
68. J. Vanian, "Amazon's Drone Testing Takes Flight in Yet Another Country," *Fortune,* February 1, 2016, http://fortune.com/2016/02/01/amazon-testing-drones-netherlands (accessed June 27, 2016); "Amazon Prime

Air," Amazon website, https://www.amazon.com/b?node=8037720011 (accessed June 27, 2016); J. Vincent, "Watch Amazon's Prime Air Drone Make Its First Demo Delivery in the US," *The Verge,* March 24, 2017, https://www.theverge.com/2017/3/24/15047424/amazon-prime-air-drone-delivery-public-us-test-mars.

69. K. Lewin, *Field Theory in Social Science* (New York: Harper & Row, 1951).

70. T. T. Lee, "Adopting a Personal Digital Assistant System: Application of Lewin's Change Theory," *Journal of Advanced Nursing,* August 2006, pp. 487–496; P. Guo, K. Watts, and H. Wharrad, "An Integrative Review of the Impact of Mobile Technologies Used by Healthcare Professionals to Support Education and Practice," *Nursing Open,* April 2016, pp. 66–78.

71. M. A. Wolfson, S. I. Tannenbaum, J. E. Mathieu, and M. T. Maynard, "A Cross-Level Investigation of Informal Field-Based Learning and Performance Improvements," *Journal of Applied Psychology,* January 2018, pp. 14–36.

72. L. R. Hearld and J. A. Alexander, "Governance Processes and Change within Organizational Participants of Multi-Sectoral Community Health Care Alliances: The Mediating Role of Vision, Mission, Strategy Agreement, and Perceived Alliance Value," *American Journal of Community Psychology,* March 2014, pp. 185–197.

73. A. E. Rafferty, N. L. Jimmieson, and A. A. Armenakis, "Change Readiness: A Multilevel Review," *Journal of Management,* January 2013, pp. 110–135.

74. S. Ng and C. Dulaney, "P&G's Sales Shrink as It Remakes Itself," *The Wall Street Journal,* October 24–25, 2015, p. B3; S. Terlep, "P&G Posts Higher Profit, but Sales Volume Declines across Most Businesses," *The Wall Street Journal,* April 26, 2016, hwww.wsj.com/articles/p-g-earnings-top-expectations-but-volumes-fall- 1461670557 (accessed June 19, 2016).

75. N. Anand and J-L. Barsoux, "What Everyone Gets Wrong about Change Management," *Harvard Business Review,* November–December 2017, pp. 3–9.

76. B. Shimoni, "A Sociological Perspective to Organization Development," *Organizational Dynamics,* July–September 2017, pp. 165–170; J. R. Austin and J. M. Bartunek, "Organization Change and Development: In Practice and in Theory," in N. W. Schmitt and S. Highhouse (eds.), *Handbook of Psychology* (vol. 12) (Hoboken, NJ: John Wiley & Sons, 2013), pp. 390–411.

77. C. Spreitzer, reported in P. Korkki, "Thwarting the Jerk at Work," *The New York Times,* November 22, 2015, p. BU-4. See also A. Gerbasi, C. L. Porath, A. Parker, G. Spreitzer, and R. Cross, "Destructive De-energizing Relationships: How Thriving Buffers Their Effect on Performance," *Journal of Applied Psychology* 100, no. 5 (2015), pp. 1423–1433.

78. Steve Lohr, "Setting Free the Squares," *The New York Times,* November 15, 2015, pp. BU-1, BU-5. See also T. Brown and R. Martin, "Design for Action," *Harvard Business Review,* September 2015, pp. 56–64.

79. D. Meinert, "United We Stand," *HRMagazine,* June/July 2017, p. 28.

80. J. Valinsky, "5 Ways Amazon Has Already Changed Whole Foods," *CNN Money,* February 9, 2018, http://money.cnn.com/2018/02/09/news/companies/amazon-whole-foods-changes/index.html.

81. M. Weinstein, "Determining Coaching ROI," *Training,* July/August 2017, pp. 38–41.

82. J. Mangan, "Welcome Team Copilot!" *OpenTable,* August 1, 2014, https://blog.opentable.com/2014/welcome-team-copilot/.

83. E. Chait, "Daily Deals vs. Happy Hours: The Impact of Internal Marketing Promos," *Street Fight,* November 16, 2012, http://streetfightmag.com/2012/11/16/daily-deals-vs-happy-hours-the-impact-of-internal-marketing-promos (accessed July 8, 2016).

84. "The Feedback Loop: More Data Doesn't Always Mean Better Customer Service," *Knowledge@Wharton,* April 23, 2014, http://knowledge.wharton.upenn.edu/article/feedback-loop-data-doesnt-always-mean-better-customer-service (accessed July 8, 2016).

85. E. Chait, "The Best and Worst Days of 2012 for Restaurant Business," *Inside Scoop SF,* December 18, 2014, http://insidescoopsf.sfgate.com/blog/2012/12/18/the-best-and-worst-days-of-2012-for-restaurant-business (accessed July 8, 2016).

86. "Change Management: The HR Strategic Imperative as a Business Partner," *Research Quarterly,* Fourth Quarter 2007, pp. 1–9; D. A. Garvin, A. C. Edmondson, and F. Gino, "Is Yours a Learning Organization?" *Harvard Business Review,* March 2008, pp. 109–116.

87. W. G. Dyer, *Team Building: Current Issues and New Alternatives,* 3rd ed. (Reading, MA: Addison-Wesley, 1995).

88. M. Bennett, "The Role of OD," *Training Journal,* March 2014, www.trainingjournal.com (accessed June 30, 2016).

89. P. Atkinson, "OD Strategies: Installing a Lean and Continuous Improvement Culture," *Management Services,* Winter 2014, pp. 12–17.

90. P. J. Robertson, D. R. Roberts, and J. I. Porras, "Dynamics of Planned Organizational Change: Assess Empirical Support for a Theoretical Model," *Academy of Management Journal,* June 1993, pp. 619–634.

91. C.-M. Lau and H.-Y. Ngo, "Organization Development and Firm Performance: A Comparison of Multinational and Local Firms," *Journal of International Business Studies,* First Quarter 2001, pp. 95–114.

92. L. Rupp, "Resuscitating Gap," *Bloomberg Businessweek,* April 25–May 1, 2016, pp. 23–24.

93. D. Meinert, "Leaders Can Drive Innovation—Or Block It," *HR Magazine,* May 2015, p. 18.

94. A. Fisher, "America's Most Admired Companies," *Fortune,* March 17, 2008, p. 66.

95. "Global Apple iPhone Sales from 3rd Quarter 2007 to 1st Quarter 2018 (in million units)," *Statista,* https://www.statista.com/statistics/263401/global-apple-iphone-sales-since-3rd-quarter-2007/ (accessed April 9, 2018).

96. A. Ignatius, "How Indra Nooyi Turned Design Thinking into Strategy," *Harvard Business Review,* September 2015, pp. 83–84.

97. B. Geier, "Using 3-D Printing to Make Jet Engines," *Fortune,* December 1, 2014, p. 76.

98. D. Bochove, "A More Automated Gold Mine," *Bloomberg Businessweek,* October 30, 2017, pp. 26–27.

99. D. Gelles, "Floating Cities Begin to Take Shape," *The New York Times,* November 11, 2017, https://www.nytimes.com/2017/11/13/business/dealbook/seasteading-floating-cities.html.

100. "Benefits of Panelized Homes," *topsiderhomes.com,* http://www.topsiderhomes.com/blog/index.php/building-systems/benefits-of-panelized-homes/ (accessed May 16, 2016).

101. K. Hamey, "Panelized Homes: Factory-Built Components Assembed on Site," *newhomesource.com,* http://www.newhomesource.com/resourcecenter/articles/panelized-homes-factory-built-components-assembled-on-site (accessed May 16, 2016).

102. G. P. Pisano, "You Need an Innovation Strategy," *Harvard Business Review,* June 2015, p. 46.

103. N. Anderson, K. Potocnik, and J. Zhou, "Innovation and Creativity in Organizations: A State-of-the-Science Review, Prospective Commentary, and Guiding Framework," *Journal of Management,* July 2014, pp. 1297–1333.

104. G. P. Pisano, "You Need an Innovation Strategy," *Harvard Business Review,* June 2015, pp. 44–54.

105. G. P. Pisano, "You Need an Innovation Strategy," *Harvard Business Review,* June 2015, p. 46.

106. Y. Dong, K. M. Bartol, Z-X Zhang, and C. Li, "Enhancing Employee Creativity via Individual Skill Development and Team Knowledge Sharing: Influences of Dual-Focused Transformational Leadership," *Journal of Organizational Behavior,* 2017, pp. 439–458.

107. A. Ignatius, "How Indra Nooyi Turned Design Thinking into Strategy," *Harvard Business Review,* September 2015, pp. 81–85.

108. J. Birkinshaw and M. Haas, "Increase Your Return on Failure," *Harvard Business Review,* May 2016, pp. 88–93.

109. A. S-Y. Chen and Y-H. Hou, "The Effects of Ethical Leadership, Voice Behavior and Climates for Innovation on Creativity: A Moderated Mediation Examination," *The Leadership Quarterly,* 2016, pp. 1–13; A. Oh, C. A. Hartnell, A. J. Kinicki, and D. Choi, "Culture in Context:

A Meta-Analysis of the Nomological Network of Organizational Culture," paper presented at the 2016 National Academy of Management Meeting, Anaheim, California.

110. R. Bledow, B Carette, J. Kühnel, and D. Bister, "Learning from Others' Failures: The Effectiveness of Failure Stories for Managerial Learning," *Academy of Management Learning & Education,* 2017, pp. 39–53.

111. J. Birkinshaw and M. Haas, "Increase Your Return on Failure," *Harvard Business Review,* May 2016, p. 90.

112. R. Cross, C. Ernst, D. Assimakopoulos, and D. Ranta, "Investing in Boundary-Spanning Collaboration to Drive Efficiency and Innovation," *Organizational Dynamics,* July–September 2015, pp. 206–207.

113. Christian Kreutz, "36 Great Examples of Crowdsourcing," *wthing.com,* January 19, 2016, http://www.wthing.com/en/blog/2014/08/12/39-Great-Crowdsourcing-Examples.html.

114. J. Goldman, "How This $200 Million Beauty Company Turned Product Development on Its Head," *Inc.,* May 15, 2017, https://www.inc.com/jeremy-goldman/the-200m-beauty-company-that-embraced-a-crowdsourcing-mentality.html?cid=search.

115. Y. Xu, D. E. Ribeiro-Soriano, J. Gonzalez-Garcia, "Crowdsourcing, Innovation and Firm Performance," *Management Decision,* July 2015, pp. 1158–1169.

116. T. Brown, "Design Thinking," https://designthinking.ideo.com/?page_id=1542 (accessed April 9, 2018).

117. "Preparing New Yorkers for Future Flooding," *IDEO,* https://www.ideo.com/case-study/preparing-new-yorkers-for-future-flooding (accessed April 9, 2018).

118. "The Future of Car Servicing," *IDEO,* https://www.ideo.com/case-study/the-future-of-car-servicing (accessed April 9, 2018)

119. "About IDEO," *IDEO,* https://www.ideo.com/about (accessed April 9, 2018).

120. Frank Dobbin, "High Commitment Practices," lecture, Harvard University, October 10, 2012, as referenced in *Wikipedia* article, "IDEO."

121. These suggestions are based on D. K. Rigby, J. Sutherland, and H. Takeuchi, "Embracing Agility," *Harvard Business Review,* May 2016, pp. 41–50.

122. D. Leonard and R. Clough, "Move Fast and Break Things," *Bloomberg Businessweek,* March 21–27, 2016, pp. 58–59.

123. A. Ignatius, "How Indra Nooyi Turned Design Thinking Into Strategy," *Harvard Business Review,* September 2015, pp. 81–85.

124. Techniques for building agility are also discussed by S. Winby and C. G. Worley, "Management Processes for Agility, Speed, and Innovation," *Organizational Dynamics,* July–September 2014, pp. 225–234.

125. X-H. Wang, Y. Fang, I. Qureshi, and O. Janssen, "Understanding Employee Innovative Behavior: Integrating the Social Network and Leader-Member Exchange Perspectives," *Journal of Organizational Behavior,* April 2015, pp. 403–420; F. C. Godart, W. W. Maddux, A. V. Shipilov, and A. D. Galinsky, "Fashion with a Foreign Flair: Professional Experiences Abroad Facilitate the Creative Innovations of Organizations," *Academy of Management Journal,* February 2015, pp. 195–220.

126. D. Leonard and R. Clough, "Move Fast and Break Things," *Bloomberg Businessweek,* March 21–27, 2016, pp. 58–59.

127. G. Nagesh and J. S. Lublin, "Investors Yet to Value GM Changes," *The Wall Street Journal,* February 2, 2016, p. B7.

128. J. Chowhan, "Unpacking the Black Box: Understanding the Relationship between Strategy, HRM Practices, Innovation and Organizational Performance," *Human Resource Management Journal,* April 2016, pp. 112–133.

129. G. Dutton, "A Eureka! Moment," *Training,* January/February 2016, pp. 114–115.

130. D. Leonard and R. Clough, "Move Fast and Break Things," *Bloomberg Businessweek,* March 21–27, 2016, pp. 58–59.

131. B. Gerhar and M. Fang, "Pay, Intrinsic Motivation, Extrinsic Motivation, Performance, and Creativity in the Workplace: Revisiting Long-Held Beliefs," *Annual Review of Organizational Psychology,* 2015, pp. 489–521.

132. D. Meinert, "Wings of Change," *HRMagazine,* November 2012, pp. 30–36.

133. S. Oreg, J. M. Bartunek, G. Lee, and B. Do, "An Affect-Based Model of Recipients' Responses to Organizational Change Events," *Academy of Management Review,* January 2018, pp. 65–86; B. Shimoni, "What Is Resistance to Change? A Habitus-Oriented Approach," *Academy of Management Perspectives,* November 2017, pp. 257–270.

134. L. Brimm, "Managing Yourself: How to Embrace Complex Change," *Harvard Business Review,* September 2015, pp. 108–112.

135. D. A. Tucker, J. Hendy, and J. Barlow, "The Importance of Role Sending in the Sensemaking of Change Agent Roles," *Journal of Health Organization and Management* 29 (2015), pp. 1047–1064.

136. S. H. Appelbaum, M. C. Degbe, O. MacDonald, and T.-S. Nguyen-Quang, "Organizational Outcomes of Leadership Style and Resistance to Change (Part One)," *Industrial and Commercial Times* 47 (2015), pp. 73–80.

137. Adapted in part from J. D. Ford, L. W. Ford, and A. D'Amelio, "Resistance to Change: The Rest of the Story," *Academy of Management Review,* April 2008, pp. 362–377.

138. S. Oreg, M. Bayazit, M. Vakola, L. Arciniega, et al., "Dispositional Resistance to Change: Measurement Equivalence and the Link to Personal Values across 17 Nations," *Journal of Applied Psychology* 23 (2008), pp. 935–944.

139. J. B. Riley, "What to Do When Employees Are Gaming the System: Overcoming Resistance to Change," *Global Business and Organizational Excellence,* January/February 2016, pp. 31–37.

140. J. Georgalis, R. Samaratunge, and N. Kimberley, "Change Process Characteristics and Resistance to Organisational Change: The Role of Employee Perceptions of Justice," *Australian Journal of Management* 40 (2015), pp. 89–113.

141. B. Schlender, "Inside the Shakeup at Sony," *Fortune,* April 4, 2005, pp. 94–104.

142. M. Fugate, A. J. Kinicki, and B. E. Ashforth, "Employability: A Psycho-Social Construct, Its Dimensions, and Applications," *Journal of Vocational Behavior,* 2004, pp. 14–38.

143. S. Gilbert, "The Movement of #MeToo," *The Atlantic,* October 16, 2017, https://www.theatlantic.com/entertainment/archive/2017/10/the-movement-of-metoo/542979; K. Amadeo, "How Does Immigration Affect the Economy and You?" *The Balance,* October 31, 2017, https://www.thebalance.com/how-immigration-impacts-the-economy-4125413.

144. G. L. Cohen and D. K. Sherman, "Self-Affirmation Theory," in R. F. Baumeister and K. D. Vohns (eds.), *Encyclopedia of Social Psychology,* 2007, http://webcache.googleusercontent.com/search?q=cache:_dXcwuoXD80J:people.psych.ucsb.edu/sherman/david/cohernshermanency2007.pdf+&cd=14&hl=en&ct=clnk&gl=us, p. 787.

145. D.K. Sherman and G. L. Cohen, "The Psychology of Self-Defense: Self-Affirmation Theory," *Advances in Experimental Social Psychology,* 2006, pp. 183–242.

146. Z. Hereford, "Examples of Positive Affirmations," *EssentialLifeSkills,* https://www.essentiallifeskills.net/positiveaffirmations.html (accessed April 4, 2018).

147. P. Onderko, "3 Tips to Open Your Heart, Mind and Life to Change," *Success,* August 6, 2015, https://www.success.com/article/3-tips-to-open-your-heart-mind-and-life-to-changeApply.

148. P. Onderko, "3 Tips to Open Your Heart, Mind and Life to Change," *Success,* August 6, 2015, https://www.success.com/article/3-tips-to-open-your-heart-mind-and-life-to-changeApply.

149. A. Abrams, "How to Cultivate More Self-Compassion," *Psychology Today,* March 3, 2017, https://www.psychologytoday.com/us/blog/nurturing-self-compassion/201703/how-cultivate-more-self-compassion.

150. K. Wong, "Why Self-Compassion Beats Self-Confidence," *The New York Times,* December 28, 2017, https://www.nytimes.com/2017/12/28/smarter-living/why-self-compassion-beats-self-confidence.html.

151. A. Abrams, "How to Cultivate More Self-Compassion," *Psychology Today,* March 3, 2017, https://www.psychologytoday.com/us/blog/nurturing-self-compassion/201703/how-cultivate-more-self-compassion.

152. These suggestions were based on A. Abrams, "How to Cultivate More Self-Compassion," *Psychology Today,* March 3, 2017, https://www.psychologytoday.com/us/blog/nurturing-self-compassion/201703/how-cultivate-more-self-compassion; P. Onderko, "3 Tips to Open Your Heart, Mind and Life to Change," *Success,* August 6, 2015, https://www.success.com/article/3-tips-to-open-your-heart-mind-and-life-to-changeApply.

153. "#62 Chipotle Mexican Grill," *Forbes,* August 8, 2017, https://www.forbes.com/companies/chipotle-mexican-grill/.

154. Chipotle, "Chipotle Names Brian Niccol Chief Executive Officer," News release, February 13, 2018, Investor Relations, http://ir.chipotle.com/phoenix.zhtml?c=194775&p=irol-newsArticle&ID=2332262.

155. S. Czarnecki, "Timeline of a Crisis: When Chipotle's New Crisis Met Its Old One," *PR Week,* January 5, 2017, https://www.prweek.com/article/1419873/timeline-crisis-when-chipotles-new-crisis-met-its-old-one.

156. L. Baertlein,"Chipotle Investors See Low-Hanging Fruit for New CEO," *Reuters,* March 1, 2018, https://www.reuters.com/article/us-chipotle-turnaround-ceo/chipotle-investors-see-low-hanging-fruit-for-new-ceo-idUSKCN1GE03E.

157. A. Bhattarai, "4 Ways Taco Bell's CEO Could Improve Chipotle," *Chicago Tribune,* February 16, 2018, http://www.chicagotribune.com/business/ct-biz-new-chipotle-ceo-predictions-20180215-story.html.

158. H. Peterson, "'We Should Expect to See Another Outbreak': Chipotle Is Replacing Its CEO amid Soaring Reports of Illnesses at Its Restaurants," *Business Insider,* November 29, 2017, http://www.businessinsider.com/chipotles-food-safety-problems-are-persisting-2017-11.

159. A. Bhattarai, "4 Ways Taco Bell's CEO Could Improve Chipotle," *Chicago Tribune,* February 16, 2018, http://www.chicagotribune.com/business/ct-biz-new-chipotle-ceo-predictions-20180215-story.html.

160. K. Taylor, "People Are Slamming Chipotle's Queso—but the Cheesy Dip Is Actually Good Now if You Order It Correctly," *Business Insider,* December 3, 2017, http://www.businessinsider.com/chipotle-new-queso-recipe-better-2017-12.

161. N. Meyersohn, "How Taco Bell's Ex-CEO Can Clean Up Chipotle's Mess," *CNNMoney,* February 15, 2018, http://money.cnn.com/2018/02/15/news/companies/chipotle-taco-bell/index.html.

162. J. Jargon, "Chipotle Picks Taco Bell CEO Brian Niccol to Be Its New Chief," *The Wall Street Journal,* February 13, 2018, https://www.wsj.com/articles/chipotle-picks-taco-bell-ceo-brian-niccol-to-be-its-new-chief-1518557401.

163. N. Meyersohn, "How Taco Bell's Ex-CEO Can Clean Up Chipotle's Mess" *CNNMoney,* February 15, 2018, http://money.cnn.com/2018/02/15/news/companies/chipotle-taco-bell/index.html.

164. J. Jargon, "Chipotle Picks Taco Bell CEO Brian Niccol to Be Its New Chief," *The Wall Street Journal,* February 13, 2018, https://www.wsj.com/articles/chipotle-picks-taco-bell-ceo-brian-niccol-to-be-its-new-chief-1518557401.

165. N. Meyersohn, "How Taco Bell's Ex-CEO Can Clean Up Chipotle's Mess," *CNNMoney,* February 15, 2018, http://money.cnn.com/2018/02/15/news/companies/chipotle-taco-bell/index.html.

166. A. Bhattarai, "4 Ways Taco Bell's CEO Could Improve Chipotle," *Chicago Tribune,* February 16, 2018, http://www.chicagotribune.com/business/ct-biz-new-chipotle-ceo-predictions-20180215-story.html.

167. J. Jargon, "Chipotle Picks Taco Bell CEO Brian Niccol to Be Its New Chief," *The Wall Street Journal,* February 13, 2018, https://www.wsj.com/articles/chipotle-picks-taco-bell-ceo-brian-niccol-to-be-its-new-chief-1518557401.

168. R. Abrams, "He Led a Turnaround at Taco Bell. Can He Do It at Chipotle," *The New York Times,* February 15, 2018, https://www.nytimes.com/2018/02/15/business/chipotle-chief.html.

169. R. Abrams, "He Led a Turnaround at Taco Bell. Can He Do It at Chipotle," *The New York Times,* February 15, 2018, https://www.nytimes.com/2018/02/15/business/chipotle-chief.html.

170. A. Oyedele, "Chipotle's Biggest Competitor Is a Soup-and-Sandwich Chain," *Business Insider,* March 29, 2017, http://www.businessinsider.com/chipotle-competition-panera-bread-2017-3.

171. A. Bhattarai, "4 Ways Taco Bell''s CEO Could Improve Chipotle," *Chicago Tribune,* February 16, 2018, http://www.chicagotribune.com/business/ct-biz-new-chipotle-ceo-predictions-20180215-story.html.

172. A. Bhattarai, "4 Ways Taco Bell's CEO Could Improve Chipotle," *Chicago Tribune,* February 16, 2018, http://www.chicagotribune.com/business/ct-biz-new-chipotle-ceo-predictions-20180215-story.html.

173. K.Taylor, "Chipotle's Founder Could Be the Biggest Problem the Struggling Chain's New CEO Has to Tackle," *Business Insider,* February 18, 2018, http://www.businessinsider.com/chipotles-ceos-brian-niccol-vs-founder-steve-ells-2018-2.

174. "Top 300 Patent Owners," *Intellectual Property Owners Association,* June 5, 2017, https://www.ipo.org/index.php/publications/top-300-patent-owners/.

175. "U.S. Patent Activity Calendar Years 1790 to the Present," *U.S. Patent and Trademark Office,* https://www.uspto.gov/web/offices/ac/ido/oeip/taf/h_counts.htm (accessed March 16, 2018).

176. S. Decker and D. Voreaos, "Fired L'Oreal Lawyer Says Patent Push Was Only Cosmetic," *Bloomberg,* April 21, 2015, http://www.bloomberg.com/news/articles/2015-04-21/fired-l-oreal-lawyer-says-company-patent-push-was-only-cosmetic.

177. S. Decker and D. Voreaos, "Fired L'Oreal Lawyer Says Patent Push Was Only Cosmetic," *Bloomberg,* April 21, 2015, http://www.bloomberg.com/news/articles/2015-04-21/fired-l-oreal-lawyer-says-company-patent-push-was-only-cosmetic.

CHAPTER 11

1. S. Shellenbarger, "The Next Step after a Bad First Impression at Work," *The Wall Street Journal,* August 22, 2017, https://www.wsj.com/articles/the-next-step-after-a-bad-first-impression-at-work-1503416463.

2. S. Shellenbarger, "The Mistakes You Make in a Meeting's First Milliseconds," *The Wall Street Journal,* January 31, 2018, p. A9.

3. K. Noel, "8 Body Language Tricks to Instantly Appear More Confident," *Business Insider,* March 31, 2016, http://www.businessinsider.com/body-language-tricks-appear-more-confident-2016-3.

4. R. Knight, "How to Make a Great First Impression," *Harvard Business Review,* September 12, 2016, https://hbr.org/2016/09/how-to-make-a-great-first-impression.

5. C. Brooks, "Starting a New Job? Don't Wait to Make a Good Impression," *Business News Daily,* March 28, 2016, https://www.businessnewsdaily.com/5831-new-hire-good-impression.html.

6. S. Shellenbarger, "The Next Step after a Bad First Impression at Work," *The Wall Street Journal,* August 22, 2017, https://www.wsj.com/articles/the-next-step-after-a-bad-first-impression-at-work-1503416463; D. Clark, "4 Ways to Overcome a Bad First Impression," *Harvard Business Review,* May, 13, 2016, https://hbr.org/2016/05/4-ways-to-overcome-a-bad-first-impression.

7. For a thorough discussion of personality psychology, see P. R. Sackett, F Lievens, C. H. Van Iddekinge, and N. R. Kuncel, "Individual Differences and Their Measurement: A Review of 100 Years of Research," *Journal of Applied Psychology,* March 2017, pp. 254–273.

8. S. A. Woods, F. Lievens, F. De Fruyt, and B. Wille, "Personality Across Working Life: The Longitudinal and Reciprocal Influences of Personality on Work," *Journal of Organizational Behavior,* Vol. 34, No. S1 (2013), pp. S7–S25.

9. J. M. Digman, "Personality Structure: Emergence of the Five-Factor Model," *Annual Review of Psychology,* Vol. 41 (1990), pp. 417–440.

10. R. O'Donnell, "In the Hunt for Soft Skills, Employers Look to Personality Tests," *HR Dive,* January 11, 2018, https://www.hrdive.com/news/in-the-hunt-for-soft-skills-employers-look-to-personality-tests/514572/.

11. D. Zielinski, "Predictive Assessments Give Companies Insight into Candidates' Potential," *Society for Human Resource Management,* January 22, 2018, https://www.shrm.org/resourcesandtools/hr-topics/

talent-acquisition/pages/predictive-assessments-insight-candidates-potential.aspx.

12. J. L. Huang, R. Cropanzaano, A. Li, P. Shao, X-A. Zhang, and Y. Li, "Employee Conscientiousness, Agreebleness, and Supervisor Justice Rule Compliance: A Three-Study Investigation," *Journal of Applied Psychology,* November 2017, pp. 1564–1589; A. Oshio, K. Taku, M. Hirano, and G. Saeed," Resilience and Big Five Personality Traits: A Meta-Analysis," *Personality and Individual Differences,* June 2018, pp. 54–60; M. Egan, M. Daly, L. Delaney, C. J. Boyce, and A. M. Wood, "Adolescent Conscientiousness Predicts Lower Lifetime Unemployment," *Journal of Applied Pyschology,* April 2017, pp. 700–709.

13. T. A. Judge, H. M. Weiss, J. D. Kammeyer-Mueller, and C. L. Hulin, "Job Attitudes, Job Satisfaction, and Job Affect: A Century of Continuity and of Change," *Journal of Applied Psychology,* March 2017, pp. 356–374.

14. T. A. Judge, A. Earez, and J. A. Bono, "The Power of Being Positive: The Relation Between Positive Self-Concept and Job Performance," *Human Performance,* p. 170.

15. A. Byars-Winston, J. Diestelmann, J. N. Savoy, and W. T. Hoyt, "Unique Effects and Moderators of Effects of Sources on Self-Efficacy: A Model-Based Meta-Analysis," *Journal of Counseling Psychology,* November 2017, pp. 645–658; K. Shoji, R. Cieslak, E. Smoktunowicz, A. Rogala, and C. C. Benight, "Associations between Job Burnout and Self-Efficacy: A Meta-Analysis," *Anxiety, Stress, and Coping,* July 2016, pp. 367–386; F. Cetin, D. Askun, "The Effect of Occupational Self-Efficacy on Work Performance through Intrinsic Work Motivation," *Management Research Review,* 2018, pp. 186–201.

16. J. Barling and R. Beattie, "Self-Efficacy Beliefs and Sales Performance," *Journal of Organizational Behavior Management,* Spring 1983, pp. 41–51.

17. A. D. Stajkovic and F. Luthans, "Self-Efficacy and Work-Related Performance: A Meta-Analysis," *Psychological Bulletin,* September 1998, pp. 240–261.

18. W. S. Silver, T. R. Mitchell, and M. E. Gist, "Response to Successful and Unsuccessful Performance: The Moderating Effect of Self-Efficacy on the Relationship between Training and Newcomer Adjustment," *Journal of Applied Psychology,* April 1995, pp. 211–225.

19. J. V. Vancouver, K. M. More, and R. J. Yoder, "Self-Efficacy and Resource Allocation: Support for a Nonmonotonic, Discontinuous Model," *Journal of Applied Psychology,* January 2008, pp. 35–47.

20. V. Mattias, L. Bjørn, and R. Torleif, "Predictors of Return to Work 6 Months after the End of Treatment in Patients with Common Mental Disorders: A Cohort Study," *Journal of Occupational Rehabilitation,* December 2017, pp. 1–11.

21. M. J. Martinko and W. L. Gardner, "Learned Helplessness: An Alternative Explanation for Performance Deficits," *Academy of Management Review,* April 1982, pp. 195–204; C. R. Campbell and M. J. Martinko, "An Integrative Attributional Perspective of Employment and Learned Helplessness: A Multimethod Field Study," *Journal of Management* 2 (1998), pp. 173–200.

22. P. R. Sackett, F. Lievens, C. H. Van Iddekinge, and N. R. Kuncel, "Individual Differences and Their Measurement: A Review of 100 Years of Research," *Journal of Applied Psychology,* March 2017, pp. 254–273.

23. V. K. Jaensch, A. Hirschi, and P. A. Freund, "Persistent Career Indecision over Time: Links with Personality, Barriers, Self-Efficacy, and Life Satisfaction," *Journal of Vocational Behavior,* December 2015, pp. 122–133.

24. V. Gecas, "The Self-Concept," in R. H. Turner and J. F. Short Jr. (Eds.), *Annual Review of Sociology*, vol. 8 (Palo Alto, CA: Annual Reviews, 1982).

25. C. E. Whelpley and M. A. McDaniel, "Self-Esteem and Counterproductive Work Behaviors: A Systematic Review," *Journal of Managerial Psychology,* 2016, pp. 850–863; K. Matzler, F. A. Bauer, and T. A. Mooradian, "Self-Esteem and Transformational Leadership," *Journal of Managerial Psychology,* 2015, pp. 815–831; U. Orth, R. W. Robins, L. L. Meier, and R. D. Conger, "Refining the Vulnerability of Low Self-Esteem and Depression: Disentangling the Effects of Genuine Self-Esteem and Narcissism," *Journal of Personality and Social Psychology,* January 2016, pp. 133–149.

26. B. R. Schlenker, M. F. Weigold, and J. R. Hallam, "Self-Serving Attributions in Social Context: Effects of Self-Esteem and Social Pressure," *Journal of Personality and Social Psychology,* May 1990, pp. 855–863; P. Sellers, "Get Over Yourself," *Fortune,* April 2001, pp. 76–88.

27. D. A. Stinson, C. Logel, M. P. Zanna, J. G. Holmes, J. V. Wood, and S. J. Spencer, "The Cost of Lower Self-Esteem: Testing a Self- and Social-Bonds Model of Health," *Journal of Personality and Social Psychology,* March 2008, pp. 412–428.

28. J. W. McGuire and C. V. McGuire, "Enhancing Self-Esteem by Directed-Thinking Tasks: Cognitive and Affective Positivity Asymmetries," *Journal of Personality and Social Psychology,* June 1996, p. 1124.

29. For an overall view of research on locus of control, see B. M. Galvin, A. E. Randel, B. J. Collins, and R. E. Johnson, "Changing the Focus of Locus (of Control): A Targeted Review of the Locus of Control Literature and Agenda for Future Research," *Journal of Organizational Behavior,* March 2018, pp. 1–14.

30. C. Wu, M. Griffin, and S. Parker, "Developing Agency Through Good Work: Longitudinal Effects of Job Autonomy and Skill Utilization on Locus of Control," *Journal of Vocational Behavior* 89 (2015), pp. 102–108.

31. J. D. Mayer, R. D. Roberts, and S. G. Barsade, "Human Abilities: Emotional Intelligence," *Annual Review of Psychology,* January 2008, http://papers.ssrn.com/sol3/papers.cfm?abstract_id=1082096 (accessed July 1, 2016).

32. Results are based on C. Miao, R. H. Humphrey, and S. Qian, "A Meta-Analysis of Emotional Intelligence and Work Attitudes," *Journal of Occupational and Organizational Psychology,* June 2017, pp. 177–202; C. Miao, R. H. Humphrey, and S. Qian, "Are the Emotionally Intelligent Good Citizens or Counterproductive? A Meta-Analysis of Emotional Intelligence and Its Relationships with Organizational Citizenship and Counterproductive Work Behavior," *Personality and Individual Differences,* October 2017, pp. 144–156.

33. D. Goleman, "What Makes a Leader," *Harvard Business Review,* November–December 1998, pp. 93–102.

34. S. Côté, "Enhancing Managerial Effectiveness via Four Core Facets of Emotional Intelligence: Self-Awareness, Social Perception, Emotion Understanding, and Emotion Regulation," *Organizational Dynamics,* July–September 2017, pp. 140–147.

35. A. Chapman, "Empathy, Trust, Diffusing Conflict and Handling Complaints," *Businessballs.com,* www.businessballs.com/empathy.htm (accessed July 19, 2016).

36. V. Zarya, "Can VR Help Your Coworkers Be More Empathetic?" *Fortune,* April 25, 2017, www.fortune.com/2017/04/25/workplace-empathy-translator-app/?iid=sr-link10.

37. M. Schwantes, "5 Masterful Ways That People with Emotional Intelligence Avoid Drama and Conflict," *Inc.,* December 12, 2017, www.inc.com/marcel-schwantes/5-masterful-ways-that-people-with-emotional-intelligence-will-avoid-drama-conflict.html?cid=search.

38. M. Thakrar, "How (and Why) to Develop Your Emotional Intelligence," *Forbes,* March 22, 2018, www.forbes.com/sites/forbescoachescouncil/2018/03/22/how-and-why-to-develop-your-emotional-intelligence/2/#3695cf4921b3; V. Zarya, "Can VR Help Your Coworkers Be More Empathetic?" *Fortune,* April 25, 2017, www.fortune.com/2017/04/25/workplace-empathy-translator-app/?iid=sr-link10.

39. "Empathy," *Wikipedia,* https://en.wikipedia.org/wiki/Empathy (accessed March 28, 2018).

40. M. Schwantes, "5 Masterful Ways That People with Emotional Intelligence Avoid Drama and Conflict," *Inc.,* December 12, 2017, www.inc.com/marcel-schwantes/5-masterful-ways-that-people-with-emotional-intelligence-will-avoid-drama-conflict.html?cid=search; V. Zarya, "Can VR Help Your Coworkers Be More Empathetic?" *Fortune,* April 25, 2017, www.fortune.com/2017/04/25/workplace-empathy-translator-app/?iid=sr-link10.

41. M. Thakrar, "How (and Why) to Develop Your Emotional Intelligence," *Forbes,* March 22, 2018, www.forbes.com/sites/forbescoachescouncil/2018/03/22/how-and-why-to-develop-your-emotional-intelligence/2/#3695cf4921b3.

42. G. Tredgold, "How to Improve your Emotional Intelligence and Be a Better Leader," *Huffington Post,* December 6, 2017, www.huffingtonpost.com/gordon-tredgold/how-to-improve-your-emotional-intelligence_b_9119398.html.

43. I. Moise, "New Tools Tell Bosses How You're Feeling," *The Wall Street Journal*, March 29, 2018, p. B6.

44. V. Zarya, "Can VR Help Your Coworkers Be More Empathetic?" *Fortune,* April 25, 2017, www.fortune.com/2017/04/25/workplace-empathy-translator-app/?iid=sr-link10.

45. S. Konrath, "Empathy: There's an App for That!" *Psychology Today,* March 14, 2017, www.psychologytoday.com/us/blog/the-empathy-gap/201703/empathy-there-s-app.

46. M. Rokeach, *Beliefs, Attitudes, and Values* (San Francisco: Jossey-Bass, 1968), p. 168.

47. S. H. Schwartz, "An Overview of the Schwartz Theory of Basic Values," *Online Readings in Psychology and Culture*, December 1, 2012, http://dx.doi.org/10.9707/2307-0919.1116.

48. D. Iliescu, D. Ispas, C. Sulea, and A. Ilie, "Vocational Fit and Counterproductive Work Behaviors: A Self-Regulation Perspective," *Journal of Applied Psychology,* January 2015, pp. 21–39.

49. M. Fishbein and I. Ajzen, *Belief, Attitude, Intention and Behavior: An Introduction to Theory and Research* (Reading, MA: Addison-Wesley Publishing, 1975), p. 6.

50. M. Reid and A. Wood, "An Investigation into Blood Donation Intentions among Non-Donors," *International Journal of Nonprofit and Voluntary Sector Marketing,* February 2008, pp. 31–43; J. Ramsey, B. J. Punnett, and D. Greenidge, "A Social Psychological Account of Absenteeism in Barbados," *Human Resource Management Journal,* April 2008, pp. 97–117.

51. T. A. Judge, C. J. Thoresen, J. E. Bono, and G. K. Patton, "The Job Satisfaction–Job Performance Relationship: A Qualitative and Quantitative Review," *Psychological Bulletin,* May 2001, pp. 376–407.

52. S. Landrum, "The Connection between Happiness and Performance for Millennials," *Forbes,* September 29, 2017, https://www.forbes.com/sites/sarahlandrum/2017/09/29/the-connection-between-happiness-and-performance-for-millennials/#379e0edc449b.

53. S. Landrum, "The Connection between Happiness and Performance for Millennials," *Forbes*, September 29, 2017, https://www.forbes.com/sites/sarahlandrum/2017/09/29/the-connection-between-happiness-and-performance-for-millennials/#379e0edc449b.

54. J. S. Becker, "Empirical Validation of Affect, Behavior, and Cognition as Distinct Components of Attitude," *Journal of Personality and Social Psychology,* May 1984, pp. 1191–1205; A. P. Brief, *Attitudes in and around Organizations* (Thousand Oaks, CA: Sage, 1998), pp. 49–84.

55. K. Lowden, S. Hall, D. Elliot, and J. Lewin, "Employers' Perceptions of the Employability Skills of New Graduates," 2011, www.gla.ac.uk/faculties/education/scre.

56. L. Festinger, *A Theory of Cognitive Dissonance* (Stanford, CA: Stanford University Press, 1957).

57. M. Cicerchia, "Learning Disabilities and Self-Esteem," *Touch-type Read and Spell,* December 18, 2017, www.readandspell.com/us/learning-disabilities-and-self-esteem.

58. M. Alvord, "For Teens Knee-Deep in Negativity, Reframing Thoughts Can Help," *NPR,* September 9, 2017, www.npr.org/sections/health-shots/2017/09/09/549133027/for-teens-knee-deep-in-negativity-reframing-thoughts-can-help.

59. C. Ackerman, "CBT's Cognitive Restructuring (CR) for Tackling Cognitive Distortions," *Positive Psychology Program,* February 12, 2018, www.positivepsychologyprogram.com/cbt-cognitive-restructuring-cognitive-distortions/.

60. M. Alvord, "For Teens Knee-Deep in Negativity, Reframing Thoughts Can Help," *NPR,* September 9, 2017, www.npr.org/sections/health-shots/2017/09/09/549133027/for-teens-knee-deep-in-negativity-reframing-thoughts-can-help.

61. C. Gallo, "How Richard Branson Uses a Simple, Psychologically-Proven Brain Trick to Turn a 'Disorder' into a Strength," *Inc.,* January 25, 2018, www.inc.com/carmine-gallo/richard-bransons-letter-to-his-dyslexic-self-reveals-a-powerful-psychological-trait-of-ultra-successful-leaders.html?cid=search.

62. C. Gallo, "How Richard Branson Uses a Simple, Psychologically-Proven Brain Trick to Turn a 'Disorder' into a Strength," *Inc.*, January 25, 2018, www.inc.com/carmine-gallo/richard-bransons-letter-to-his-dyslexic-self-reveals-a-powerful-psychological-trait-of-ultra-successful-leaders.html?cid=search.

63. A. Kinicki and M. Fugate, *Organizational Behavior: A Practical, Problem-Solving Approach,* 2nd ed. (New York: McGraw-Hill, 2018).

64. A. H. Tangari, J. Kees, J. C. Andrews, and S. Burton, "Can Corrective Ad Statements Based on *U.S. v. Philip Morris USA Inc.* Impact Consumer Beliefs about Smoking?" *Journal of Public Policy & Marketing* 29, no. 2 (2010), pp. 153–169.

65. Adapted from R. Kreitner and A. Kinicki, *Organizational Behavior,* 10th ed. (New York: McGraw-Hill/Irwin, 2013), Figure 7–1, p. 181.

66. Definition adapted from C. M. Judd and B. Park, "Definition and Assessment of Accuracy in Social Stereotypes," *Psychological Review,* January 1993, p. 110.

67. R. Riffkin, "Americans Still Prefer a Male Boss to a Female Boss," *Gallup.com,* October 14, 2014, www.gallup.com/poll/178484/americans-prefer-male-boss- female-boss.aspx; "Women and Leadership," *Pew Research Center,* January 14, 2015, www.pewsocialtrends.org/2015/01/14/women-and-leadership; S. C. Paustian-Underdahl, L. S. Walker, and D. J. Woehr, "Gender and Perceptions of Leadership Effectiveness: A Meta-Analysis of Contextual Moderators," *Journal of Applied Behavior* 99, no. 6 (2014), pp. 1129–1145.

68. J. A. Segal, "How Gender Bias Hurts Men," *HR Magazine,* October 2015, pp. 74–75.

69. "How Venture Capitalists Really Assess a Pitch," *Harvard Business Review*, May–June 2017, https://hbr.org/2017/05/how-venture-capitalists-really-assess-a-pitch.

70. M. A. McCord, D. L. Joseph, L. Y. Dhanani, and J. M. Beus, "A Meta-Analysis of Sex and Race Differences in Perceived Workplace Mistreatment," *Journal of Applied Psychology,* February 2018, pp. 137–163.

71. A. J. Koch, S. D. D'Mello, and P. R. Sackett, "A Meta-Analysis of Gender Stereotypes and Bias in Experimental Simulations of Employment Decision Making," *Journal of Applied Psychology,* January 2015, pp. 128–161; J. V. Sanchez-Hucles and D. D. Davis, "Women and Women of Color in Leadership," *American Psychologist,* April 2010, pp. 171–181.

72. G. Huang, "New Data Shows Americans Think Women and Men Are Good at Different Things at Work," *Forbes,* January 16, 2018, https://www.forbes.com/sites/georgenehuang/2018/01/16/new-data-shows-many-americans-still-think-women-and-men-are-good-at-different-things-at-work/#21d480b579eb.

73. T. W. H. Ng and D. C. Feldman, "Evaluating Six Common Stereotypes about Older Workers with Meta-Analytical Data," *Personnel Psychology* 65, no. 4 (2012), pp. 821–858.

74. K. Hannon, "Reaping the Benefits of an Aging Work Force," *The New York Times,* March 2, 2018, https://www.nytimes.com/2018/03/02/business/retirement/aging-workers-opportunity.html.

75. K. Hannon, "Reaping the Benefits of an Aging Work Force," *The New York Times,* March 2, 2018, https://www.nytimes.com/2018/03/02/business/retirement/aging-workers-opportunity.html.

76. D. Reddy, "How Doctors Deal with Racist Patients," *The Wall Street Journal,* January 23, 2018, p. A11.

77. T. DeAngelis, "Unmasking 'Racial Micro Aggressions,'" *Harvard Business Review,* February 2009, pp. 42–46.

78. M. D. C. Triana, M. Jayasinghe, and J. R. Pieper, "Perceived Workplace Racial Discrimination and Its Correlates: A Meta-Analysis," *Journal of Organizational Behavior,* May 2015, pp. 491–513.

79. T. Essig, "13 Things White Men with Black Bosses Should Know," *Forbes,* March 7, 2016, https://www.forbes.com/sites/toddessig/

2016/03/07/13-things-white-men-with-black-bosses-should-know/#340ed11f1ebe.

80. H. R. Roberts, "Implicit Bias and Social Justice," *Open Society Foundations,* December 18, 2011, https://www.opensocietyfoundations.org/voices/implicit-bias-and-social-justice (accessed July 13, 2016).

81. "Helping Courts Address Implicit Bias: Frequently Asked Questions," *National Center for State Courts,* www.ncsc.org/~/media/Files/PDF/Topics/Gender%20and%20Racial%20Fairness/Implicit%20Bias%20FAQs%20rev.ashx (accessed July 13, 2016).

82. J. C. Lee and H. Park, "In 15 High-Profile Cases Involving Deaths of Blacks, One Officer Faces Prison Time," *The New York Times,* December 7, 2017, https://www.nytimes.com/interactive/2017/05/17/us/black-deaths-police.html.

83. K. P. Jones, I. E. Sabat, E. B. King, A. Ahmad, T. C. Mccausland, and T. Chen, "Isms and Schisms: A Meta-Analysis of the Prejudice-Discrimination Relationship across Racism, Sexism, and Ageism," *Journal of Organizational Behavior,* 2017, pp. 1076–1110.

84. R. D. Godsil, "Breaking the Cycle: Implicit Bias, Racial Anxiety, and Stereotype Threat," *Poverty & Race,* January/February 2015, www.prrac.org/newsletters/janfeb2015.pdf (accessed July 13, 2016).

85. C. N. Macrae and S. Quadflieg, "Perceiving People," in S. T. Fiske, D. T. Gilbert, and G. Lindzey (Eds.), *Handbook of Social Psychology* (New York: John Wiley & Sons, 2010), pp. 428–463; M. Snyder and A. A. Stukas Jr., "Interpersonal Processes: The Interplay of Cognitive, Motivational, and Behavioral Activities in Social Interaction," in J. T. Spence, J. M. Darley, and D. J. Foss (Eds.), *Annual Review of Psychology* (Palo Alto, CA: Annual Review, 1999), pp. 273–303.

86. I. Waismel-Manor and Y. Tsfati, "Do Attractive Congresspersons Get More Media Coverage?" *Political Communication* 28 (2011), pp. 440–463; A. E. White, D. T. Kenrick, and S. L. Neuberg, "Beauty at the Ballot Box: Disease Threats Predict Preference for Physically Attractive Leaders," *Psychological Science,* December 2013, pp. 2429–2436.

87. M. M. Clifford and E. H. Walster, "The Effect of Physical Attractiveness on Teacher Expectation," *Sociology of Education* 46 (1973), pp. 248–258; P. Kenealy, N. Frude, and W. Shaw, "Influence of Children's Physical Attractiveness on Teacher Expectation," *The Journal of Social Psychology* 128, no. 3 (2001), pp. 373–383.

88. M. M. Mobius and T. S. Rosenblat, "Why Beauty Matters," *American Economic Review* 96, no. 1 (2006), pp. 222–235; J. T. Halford and S. H. C. Hsu, "Beauty Is Wealth: CEO Appearance and Shareholder Value," *Social Science Research Network,* December 19, 2014, http://papers.ssrn.com/sol3/papers.cfm?abstract_id=2357756 (accessed June 27, 2016). See also A. R. Sorkin, "Never Mind the Résumé: How Hot Is the CEO?" *The New York Times,* January 7, 2014, pp. B1, B4.

89. R. Adams, M. Keloharju, and S. Knüpfer, "Are CEOs Born Leaders? Lesson from Traits of a Million Individuals," *Social Science Research Network,* June 24, 2016, http://papers.ssrn.com/sol3/papers.cfm?abstract_id=2436765.

90. "Lulu Hunt Peters," *Wikipedia,* March 30, 2018, https://en.wikipedia.org/wiki/Lulu_Hunt_Peters.

91. C. Sandvick and A. Gutierrez-Romine, "When Did Americans Begin to Get Obsessed with Weight Loss?" *DailyHistory.org,* www.dailyhistory.org/When_did_Americans_begin_to_get_obsessed_with_weight_loss%3F (accessed March 30, 2018).

92. "Lulu Hunt Peters," *Wikipedia,* March 30, 2018, https://en.wikipedia.org/wiki/Lulu_Hunt_Peters.

93. Obesity Society, "Facts about Obesity," www.obesity.org/obesity/resources/facts-about-obesity/bias-stigmatization (accessed March 30, 2018); R. Alexander, "Only 15% of Hiring Managers Would Consider Hiring an Overweight Woman," *Moneyish,* December 9, 2017, www.moneyish.com/ish/only-15-of-hiring-managers-would-consider-hiring-an-overweight-woman/.

94. S. Lebowitz, "Science Says People Determine Your Competence, Intelligence, and Salary Based on Your Weight," *Business Insider,* September 9, 2015, www.businessinsider.com/science-overweight-people-less-successful-2015-9.

95. D. Paquette, "Even an Extra Five Pounds Can Hurt Your Job Chances," *Washington Post,* September 21, 2016, www.washingtonpost.com/news/wonk/wp/2016/09/21/even-an-extra-five-pounds-can-hurt-your-job-chances/?utm_term=.e78a59f6f62f.

96. S. Flint, M. Čadek, S. Codreanu, V. Ivić, C. Zomer, and A. Gomoiu, "Obesity Discrimination in the Recruitment Process: 'You're Not Hired!'" *Frontiers in Psychology* 7 (May 3, 2016), p. 647, www.ncbi.nlm.nih.gov/pmc/articles/PMC4853419/; B. Nowrouzi, A. McDougall, B. Gohar, B. Nowrouz-Kia, J. Casole, and A. Fizza, "Weight Bias in the Workplace: A Literature Review," *Occupational Medicine & Health Affairs* 3, no. 3 (2015).

97. Obesity Society, "Facts about Obesity," retrieved from www.obesity.org/obesity/resources/facts-about-obesity/bias-stigmatization (accessed March 30, 2018).

98. C. Ross, "I See Fat People," *Psychology Today,* August 7, 2013, www.psychologytoday.com/us/blog/real-healing/201308/i-see-fat-people.

99. T. Odean and B. M. Barber, "All That Glitters: The Effect of Attention and News on the Buying Behavior of Individual and Institutional Investors," *The Review of Financial Studies* 21, no. 2 (2008), pp. 785–818; P. Sullivan, "Want an Active Investment Manager? Here's What to Look For," *The New York Times,* March 30, 2012, p. B8.

100. S. J. Linton and L. E. Warg, "Attributions (Beliefs) and Job Satisfaction Associated with Back Pain in an Industrial Setting," *Perceptual and Motor Skills,* February 1993, pp. 51–62.

101. K. Cherry, "How the Self-Serving Bias Protects Self-Esteem," *Verywellmind,* February 12, 2018, https://www.verywellmind.com/what-is-the-self-serving-bias-2795032.

102. J. Weaver, J. F. Moses, and M. Snyder, "Self-Fulfilling Prophecies in Ability Settings," *Journal of Social Psychology* 156, no 2 (2016), pp. 179–189.

103. D. B. McNatt, "Ancient Pygmalion Joins Contemporary Management: A Meta-Analysis of the Result," *Journal of Applied Psychology,* April 2000, pp. 314–322; D. Nolkemper, H. Aydin, and M. Knigge, "Teachers' Stereotypes about Secondary School Students: The Case of Germany," *Quality and Quantity,* March 2018, pp. 1–21.

104. These recommendations were adapted from J. Keller, "Have Faith—in You," *Selling Power,* June 1996, pp. 84, 86; R. W. Goddard, "The Pygmalion Effect," *Personnel Journal,* June 1985, p. 10; J. S. Livingston, "Pygmalion in Management," *Harvard Business Review,* January 2003, https://hbr.org/2003/01/pygmalion-in-management; R. E. Riggio, "Pygmalion Leadership: The Power of Positive Expectations," *Psychology Today,* April 18, 2009, https://www.psychologytoday.com/blog/cutting-edge-leadership/200904/pygmalion-leadership-the-power-positive-expectations; G. Swanson, "The Pygmalion Effect: How It Drives Employee Performance," *LinkedIn,* September 24, 2014, https://www.linkedin.com/pulse/20140924142003-9878138-the-pygmalion-effect-how-it-drives-employees-performance.

105. N. Angley, "All of Us in a Way Are Climbing Blind," *CNN,* May 11, 2016, www.cnn.com/2016/05/11/health/turning-points-erik-weihenmayer/index.html.

106. *No Barriers,* accessed April 11, 2018, https://www.nobarriersusa.org/?gclid=EAIaIQobChMIgvGlhNWU2gIVVpN-Ch2G2Q4vEAAYASAAEgLtMvD_BwE.

107. "Erik Weihenmayer," *Wikipedia,* March 27, 2018, https://en.wikipedia.org/wiki/Erik_Weihenmayer.

108. C. Marshall, "How the First Blind Man to Summit Mount Everest Changed My Perspective on Fear," *Huffington Post,* May 25, 2017, www.huffingtonpost.com/entry/how-the-first-blind-man-to-summit-mount-everest-changed_us_59161939e4b02d6199b2ef04.

109. *No Barriers,* accessed April 11, 2018, https://www.nobarriersusa.org/?gclid=EAIaIQobChMIgvGlhNWU2gIVVpN-Ch2G2Q4vEAAYASAAEgLtMvD_BwE.

110. M. Dabney, "At No Barriers Summit: Aira Is Showcased as the Novel Technology Service That Helps the Blind Become Even More 'Adventurous,'" *Medium,* July 6, 2016, https://medium.com/aira-io/at-no-barriers-summit-aira-is-showcased-as-the-novel-technology-service-that-helps-the-blind-become-5a98845242ce.

111. *No Barriers,* accessed April 11, 2018, https://www.nobarriersusa.org/?gclid=EAIaIQobChMIgvGIhNWU2gIVVpN-Ch2G2Q4vEAAYASAAEgLtMvD_BwE (accessed April 11, 2018); "Seven Summits," *Wikipedia,* March 19, 2018, https://en.wikipedia.org/wiki/Seven_Summits.

112. "About Erik," *Touch the Top*, www.touchthetop.com/about-erik (accessed March 29, 2018).

113. C. Marshall, "How the First Blind Man to Summit Mount Everest Changed My Perspective on Fear," *Huffington Post,* May 25, 2017, www.huffingtonpost.com/entry/how-the-first-blind-man-to-summit-mount-everest-changed_us_59161939e4b02d6199b2ef04.

114. E. Weihenmayer, interview with the American Foundation for the Blind, www.afb.org/info/for-mentors/interviews-with-careerconnect-mentors/mountain-climber-interview/345 (accessed March 30, 2018).

115. A. B. Bakker, "Strategic and Proactive Approaches to Work Engagement," *Organizational Dynamics,* April–June 2017, p. 67.

116. A. M. Saks, "Translating Employee Engagement Research Into Practice," *Organizational Dynamics,* April–June 2017, pp. 76–86; J. P. Meyer, "Has Engagement Had Its Day: What's Next and Does It Matter," *Organizational Dynamics,* April–June 2017, pp. 87–95.

117. Aon Hewitt, "2012 Engagement Distribution," *2013 Trends in Global Engagement,* p. 8.

118. See M. Christian, A. Garza, and J. Slaughter, "Work Engagement: A Quantitative Review and Test of Its Relations with Task and Contextual Performance," *Personnel Psychology,* 2011, pp. 89–136.

119. See M. Christian, A. Garza, and J. Slaughter, "Work Engagement: A Quantitative Review and Test of Its Relations with Task and Contextual Performance," *Personnel Psychology,* 2011, pp. 89–136.

120. See S. Sonnentag, E. Mojza, E. Demerouti, and A. Bakker, "Reciprocal Relations between Recovery and Work Engagement: The Moderating Role of Job Stressors," *Journal of Applied Psychology,* July 2012, pp. 842–853.

121. See J. Robison, "Building Engagement in This Economic Crisis," *Gallup Management Journal,* February 19, 2009, http://gmj.gallup.com/content/115213/Building-Engagement-Economic-Crisis.aspx.

122. See M. Christian, A. Garza, and J. Slaughter, "Work Engagement: A Quantitative Review and Test of Its Relations with Task and Contextual Performance," *Personnel Psychology,* 2011, pp. 89–136.

123. See C. Knight, M. Patterson, and J. Dawson, "Building Work Engagement: A Systematic Review and Meta-Analysis Investigating the Effectiveness of Work Engagement Interventions," *Journal of Organizational Behavior,* July 2017, pp. 792–812.

124. These definitions were taken from C. Knight, M. Patterson, and J. Dawson, "Building Work Engagement: A Systematic Review and Meta-Analysis Investigating the Effectiveness of Work Engagement Interventions," *Journal of Organizational Behavior,* July 2017, pp. 794–795.

125. These five job dimensions are developed by researchers at Cornell University as part of the Job Descriptive Index. For a review of the development of the JDI, see P. C. Smith, L. M. Kendall, and C. L. Hulin, *The Measurement of Satisfaction in Work and Retirement* (Skokie, IL: Rand McNally, 1969).

126. A. J. Kinicki, F. M. McKee-Ryan, C. A. Schriesheim, and K. P. Carson, "Assessing the Construct Validity of the Job Descriptive Index: A Review and Meta-Analysis," *Journal of Applied Psychology,* February 2002, pp. 14–32.

127. "2017 Employee Job Satisfaction and Engagement: The Doors of Opportunity Are Open," Society for Human Resource Management, April 24, 2017, https://www.shrm.org/hr-today/trends-and-forecasting/research-and-surveys/pages/2017-job-satisfaction-and-engagement-doors-of-opportunity-are-open.aspx.

128. T. A. Judge, C. J. Thoresen, J. E. Bono, and G. K. Patton, "The Job Satisfaction–Job Performance Relationship: A Qualitative and Quantitative Review," *Psychological Bulletin,* May 2001, pp. 376–407; R. Kreitner and A. Kinicki, *Organizational Behavior,* 10th ed. (New York: McGraw-Hill/Irwin, 2013), pp. 168–170.

129. T. A. Judge, H. M. Weiss, J. D. Kammeyer-Mueller, and C. L. Hulin, "Job Attitudes, Job Satisfaction, and Job Affect: A Century of Continuity and of Change," *Journal of Applied Psychology,* March 2017, pp. 356–374.

130. S. Samee Ali, "'Motherhood Penalty' Can Affect Women Who Never Even Have a Child," *NBC News,* April 11, 2016, https://www.nbcnews.com/better/careers/motherhood-penalty-can-affect-women-who-never-even-have-child-n548511.

131. A. H. Kabins, X. Xu, M. E. Bergman, C. M. Berry, and V. L Wilson, "A Profile of Profiles: A Meta-Analysis of the Nomological Net of Commitment Profiles," *Journal of Applied Psychology,* June 2016, pp. 881–904.

132. For a review of commitment research, see the entire May 2016 issue of *Journal of Organizational Behavior*, May 2016, pp. 489–632.

133. M. C. Kocakulah, A. G. Kelley, K. M. Mitchell, and M. P. Ruggieri, "Absenteeism Problems and Costs: Causes, Effects, and Cures," *International Business & Economics Research Journal,* May/June 2016, pp. 81–88.

134. M. R. Barrick and R. D. Zimmerman, "Reducing Voluntary Turnover through Selection," *Journal of Applied Psychology,* January 2005, pp. 159–166.

135. "Average Cost-per-Hire for Companies Is $4,129, SHRM Survey Finds," Society for Human Resource Management, August 3, 2016, https://www.shrm.org/about-shrm/press-room/press-releases/pages/human-capital-benchmarking-report.aspx.

136. J. Altman, "How Much Does Employee Turnover Really Cost?" *Huffington Post,* January 19, 2017, https://www.huffingtonpost.com/entry/how-much-does-employee-turnover-really-cost_us_587fbaf9e4b0474ad4874fb7.

137. T. Arnold, "Ramping Up Onboarding," *HR Magazine,* May 2010, pp. 75–76; D. Robb, "New-Hire Onboarding Portals Provide a Warmer Welcome," *HR Magazine,* December 2015/January 2016, pp. 58–60.

138. P. W. Hom, T. W. Lee, J. D. Shaw, and J. P. Hausknecht, "One Hundred Years of Employee Turnover Theory and Research," *Journal of Applied Psychology,* March 2017, pp. 530–545.

139. D. W. Organ, "The Motivational Basis of Organizational Citizenship Behavior," in B. M. Staw and L. L. Cummings (Eds.), *Research in Organizational Behavior* (Greenwich, CT: JAI Press, 1990), p. 46.

140. N. P. Podsakoff, S. W. Whiting, P. M. Podsakoff, and B. D. Blume, "Individual- and Organizational-Level Consequences of Organizational Citizenship Behaviors: A Meta-Analysis," *Journal of Applied Psychology,* January 2009, pp. 122–141; D. S. Whitman, D. L. Van Rooy, and C. Viswesvaran, "Satisfaction, Citizenship Behaviors, and Performance in Work Units: A Meta-Analysis of Collective Relations," *Personnel Psychology,* Spring 2010, pp. 41–81; J. P. Trougakos, D.J. Beal. B. H. Cheng, I. Hideg, and D. Zweig, "Too Drained to Help: A Resource Depletion Perspective on Daily Interpersonal Citizenship Behaviors," *Journal of Applied Psychology* 100, no. 1 (2015), pp. 227–236.

141. P. E. Spector and S. Fox, "Theorizing about the Deviant Citizen: An Attributional Explanation of the Interplay of Organizational Citizenship and Counterproductive Work Behavior," *Human Resource Management Review,* June 2010, pp. 132–143; K. Tyler, "Helping Employees Cool It," *HR Magazine,* April 2010, pp. 53–55; M. S. Hershcovis, "'Incivility, Social Undermining, Bullying . . . Oh My!': A Call to Reconcile Constructs within Workplace Aggression Research," *Journal of Organizational Behavior* 32 (2010), pp. 499–519; J. Wu and J. M. Lebreton, "Reconsidering the Dispositional Basis of Counterproductive Work Behavior: The Role of Aberrant Personality," *Personnel Psychology* 64 (2011), pp. 593–626; L. L. Meier and P. E. Spector, "Reciprocal Effects of Work Stressors and Counterproductive Work Behavior: A Five-Wave Longitudinal Study," *Journal of Applied Psychology,* May 2013, pp. 529–539.

142. Study by Georgetown University and Thunderbird School of Global Management, cited in R. Feintzeig, "When Co-workers Don't Play Nice," *The Wall Street Journal,* August 28, 2013, p. B6.

143. N. C. Carpenter, B. Rangel, G. Jeon, and J. Cottrell, "Are Supervisors and Coworkers Likely to Witness Employee Counterproductive Work Behavior? An Investigation of Observability and Self-Observer Convergence," *Personnel Psychology,* Winter 2017, pp. 843–889.

144. S. Dilchert, D. S. Ones, R. D. Davis, and C. D. Rostow, "Cognitive Ability Predicts Objectively Measured Counterproductive Work Behaviors," *Journal of Applied Psychology*, May 2007, pp. 616–627; B. Iliescu, D. Ispas, C. Sulea, and A. Ilie, "Vocational Fit and Counterproductive Work Behaviors: A Self-Regulation Perspective," *Journal of Applied Psychology* 100, no. 1 (2015), pp. 21–39.
145. J. R. Detert, L. K. Treviño, E. R. Burris, and M. Andiappan, "Managerial Modes of Influence and Counterproductivity in Organizations: A Longitudinal Business-Unit-Level Investigation," *Journal of Applied Psychology*, July 2007, pp. 993–1005.
146. C. Porath, "How to Avoid Hiring a Toxic Employee," *Harvard Business Review*, February 3, 2016, https://hbr.org/2016/02/how-to-avoid-hiring-a-toxic-employee.
147. T. Foulk, quoted in R. E. Silverman, "Workplace Rudeness Is as Contagious as a Cold," *The Wall Street Journal*, August 12, 2015, p. B7; T. Foulk, A. Woolum, and A. Erez, "Catching Rudeness Is Like Catching a Cold: The Contagion Effects of Low-Intensity Negative Behaviors," *Journal of Applied Psychology* 101, no. 1 (2016), pp. 50–67.
148. G. Spreizer, quoted in B. Hyslop, "Bad Attitudes Can Sap Workers' Energy and Productivity," *Providence Journal*, July 4, 2015; P. Korkki, "Thwarting the Jerk at Work," *The New York Times*, November 22, 2015, p. BU-4; C. L. Porath and A. Erez, "Does Rudeness Really Matter? The Effects of Rudeness on Task Performance and Helpfulness," *Academy of Management Journal* 50, no. 5 (2007), pp. 1181–1197; A. Gerbasi, C. L. Porath, A. Parker, G. Spreitzer, and R. Cross, "Destructive De-energizing Relationships: How Thriving Buffers Their Effect on Performance," *Journal of Applied Psychology* 100, no. 5 (2015), pp. 1423–1433; C. L. Porath, A. Gerbasi, and S. L. Schorch, "The Effects of Civility on Advice, Leadership, and Performance," *Journal of Applied Psychology* 100, no. 5 (2015), pp. 1527–1541.
149. C. Rosen, J. Koopman, A. Gabriel, and R. Johnson, "Who Strikes Back? A Daily Investigation of When and Why Incivility Begets Incivility," *Journal of Applied Psychology* 101, no. 11 (2016), pp. 1620–1634.
150. D. Walker, D. van Jaarsveld, and D. Skarlicki, "Sticks and Stones Can Break My Bones but Words Can Also Hurt Me: The Relationship between Customer Verbal Aggression and Employee Incivility," *Journal of Applied Psychology* 102, no. 2 (2017), pp. 163–179.
151. C. Porath, "No Time to Be Nice," *The New York Times*, June 21, 2015, p. SR-1.
152. M. Housman and D. Minor, "Toxic Workers," *Harvard Business School, Working Paper 16-057*, November 2015, www.hbs.edu/faculty/Publication%20Files/16-057_d45c0b4f-fa19-49de-8f1b-4b12fe054fea.pdf.
153. N. Torres, "It's Better to Avoid a Toxic Employee Than Hire a Superstar," *Harvard Business Review*, December 9, 2015, https://hbr.org/2015/12/its-better-to-avoid-a-toxic-employee-than-hire-a-superstar.
154. C. Porath and C. Pearson, "The Price of Incivility," *Harvard Business Review*, January–February 2013, https://hbr.org/2013/01/the-price-of-incivility.
155. M. Hershcovis, B. Ogunfowora, T. Reich, and A. Christie, "Targeted Workplace Incivility: The Roles of Belongingness, Embarrassment, and Power," *Journal of Organizational Behavior* 38 (2017), pp. 1057–1075.
156. M. Schwantes, "5 Sure Signs That You Work in a Toxic Office," *Inc.*, February 18, 2016, www.inc.com/marcel-schwantes/5-sure-signs-that-you-work-in-a-toxic-office.html.
157. "Immigrants in the United States," American Immigration Council, https://www.americanimmigrationcouncil.org/research/immigrants-in-the-united-states (accessed April 11, 2018).
158. D. R. Hekman, K. Aquino, B. P. Owens, T. R. Mitchell, P. Schilpzand, and K. Leavitt, "An Examination of Whether and How Racial and Gender Biases Influence Customer Satisfaction," *Academy of Management Journal* 55 (2010), pp. 643–666.
159. T. Kroeger and E. Gould, "The Class of 2017," Economic Policy Institute, May 4, 2017, https://www.epi.org/publication/the-class-of-2017/.
160. D. Cohn and A. Caumont, "10 Demographic Trends That Are Shaping the U.S. and the World," Pew Research Center, March 31, 2016, http://www.pewresearch.org/fact-tank/2016/03/31/10-demographic-trends-that-are-shaping-the-u-s-and-the-world/.
161. M. Loden, *Implementing Diversity* (Chicago: Irwin, 1996), pp. 14–15.
162. L. Boyle, "'Even WE'VE Been the Victims of Racism': Obamas Reveal How President Was Mistaken for a Valet and Michelle Was Confused for a Target Worker—When She Was Already First Lady," *Daily Mail*, December 17, 2014, www.dailymail.co.uk/news/article-2877456/The-Obamas-open-racism-President-mistaken-valet-secret-White-House-dance-parties.html (accessed June 27, 2016).
163. S. Ghumman and A. M. Ryan, "Not Welcome Here: Discrimination towards Women Who Wear the Muslim Headscarf," *Human Relations*, May 2013, pp. 671–698.
164. D. Cohn and A. Caumont, "10 Demographic Trends That Are Shaping the U.S. and the World," Pew Research Center, March 31, 2016, http://www.pewresearch.org/fact-tank/2016/03/31/10-demographic-trends-that-are-shaping-the-u-s-and-the-world/.
165. D. Desilver, "More Older Americans Are Working, and Working More, than They Used to," Pew Research Center, June 20, 2016, http://www.pewresearch.org/fact-tank/2016/06/20/more-older-americans-are-working-and-working-more-than-they-used-to/.
166. P. Span, "Many Americans Try Retirement, Then Change Their Minds," *The New York Times*, March 30, 2018, https://www.nytimes.com/2018/03/30/health/unretirement-work-seniors.html; D. Desilver, "More Older Americans Are Working, and Working More, than They Used to," Pew Research Center, June 20, 2016, http://www.pewresearch.org/fact-tank/2016/06/20/more-older-americans-are-working-and-working-more-than-they-used-to/.
167. P. Span, "Many Americans Try Retirement, Then Change Their Minds," *The New York Times*, March 30, 2018, https://www.nytimes.com/2018/03/30/health/unretirement-work-seniors.html.
168. P. Span, "Many Americans Try Retirement, Then Change Their Minds," *The New York Times*, March 30, 2018, https://www.nytimes.com/2018/03/30/health/unretirement-work-seniors.html.
169. "Labor Force Projections to 2024: The Labor Force Is Growing, but Slowly."
170. M. DeWolf, "12 Stats about Working Women," *U.S. Department of Labor Blog*, March 1, 2017, https://blog.dol.gov/2017/03/01/12-stats-about-working-women.
171. M. DeWolf, "12 Stats about Working Women," *U.S. Department of Labor Blog*, March 1, 2017, https://blog.dol.gov/2017/03/01/12-stats-about-working-women.
172. "Women CEOs of the S&P 500," *Catalyst*, http://www.catalyst.org/knowledge/women-ceos-sp-500 (accessed April 12, 2018).
173. L. DePillis, "Moms Still Earn Less than Childless Women—and the Gap Isn't Closing," *CNN Money*, March 13, 2018, http://money.cnn.com/2018/03/13/news/economy/motherhood-penalty/index.html; N. Graff, A. Brown, and E. Patten, "The Narrowing, but Persistent, Gender Gap in Pay," *Pew Research Center*, April 9, 2018, http://www.pewresearch.org/fact-tank/2018/04/09/gender-pay-gap-facts/.
174. M. DeWolf, "12 Stats about Working Women," *U.S. Department of Labor Blog*, March 1, 2017, https://blog.dol.gov/2017/03/01/12-stats-about-working-women.
175. N. Graff, A. Brown, and E. Patten, "The Narrowing, but Persistent, Gender Gap in Pay," *Pew Research Center*, April 9, 2018, http://www.pewresearch.org/fact-tank/2018/04/09/gender-pay-gap-facts/.
176. L. DePillis, "Moms Still Earn Less than Childless Women—and the Gap Isn't Closing," *CNN Money*, March 13, 2018, http://money.cnn.com/2018/03/13/news/economy/motherhood-penalty/index.html.
177. L. Alderman, "Britain Aims to Close Gender Pay Gap with Transparency and Shame," *The New York Times*, April 4, 2018, https://www.nytimes.com/2018/04/04/business/britain-gender-pay-gap.html.
178. M. DeWolf, "12 Stats about Working Women," *U.S. Department of Labor Blog*, March 1, 2017, https://blog.dol.gov/2017/03/01/12-stats-about-working-women.
179. Q. Roberson, A. M. Ryan, and B. R. Ragins, "The Evolution and Future of Diversity at Work," *Journal of Applied Psychology*, March 2017,

pp. 483–499; J. E. Bono, P. W. Braddy, Y. Kiu, E. K. Gilbert, J. W. Fleenor, L. N. Quast, and B. A. Center, "Dropped on the Way to the Top: Gender and Managerial Derailment," *Personnel Psychology*, 2017, pp. 729–768.

180. R. Thomas and S. Brown-Philpot, "Don't Avoid Women, Mentor Them," *The Wall Street Journal*, February 5, 2018, p. A15; J. S. Lublin, "Women Struggle for First Board Seat," *The Wall Street Journal*, February 8, 2018, p. B6; J. O'Leary and J. Sandberg, "Managers' Practice of Managing Diversity Revealed: A Practice-Theoretical Account," *Personnel Psychology*, 2017, pp. 512–536.

181. S. C. Paustain-Underdahl, L. S. Walker, and D. J. Woehr, "Gender and Perceptions of Leadership Effectiveness: A Meta-Analysis of Contextual Moderators," *Journal of Applied Psychology*, November 2014, pp. 1129–1145.

182. J. Burns, "The Results Are In: Women Are Great for Business, But Still Getting Pushed Out," *Forbes*, September 22, 2017, https://www.forbes.com/sites/janetwburns/2017/09/22/2016-proved-women-are-great-for-business-yet-still-being-pushed-out/#962c55e188b6.

183. S. L. Colby and J. M. Ortman, "Projections of the Size and Composition of the U.S. Population: 2014 to 2060," *Current Population Reports*, March 2015, U.S. Census Bureau, https://www.census.gov/content/dam/Census/library/publications/2015/demo/p25-1143.pdf (accessed April 3, 2018).

184. "Real Median Household Income by Race and Hispanic Origin: 1967 to 2016," *Census.gov*, https://www.census.gov/content/dam/Census/library/visualizations/2017/demo/p60-259/figure1.pdf. (accessed April 12, 2018).

185. U.S. Equal Employment Opportunity Commission, "Race-Based Charges FY 1997–FY 2015," www.eeoc.gov/eeoc/statistics/enforcement/race.cfm (accessed June 27, 2016); B. Leonard, "Web, Call Center Fuel Rise in EEOC Claims," *HR Magazine*, June 2008, p. 30; M. Luo, "In Job Hunt, Even a College Degree Can't Close the Racial Gap," *The New York Times*, December 1, 2009, pp. A1, A4.

186. J. Greve, "LGBT America: By the Numbers," *PBS*, June 15, 2016, http://www.pbs.org/weta/washingtonweek/blog-post/lgbt-america-numbers.

187. A. Brown, "5 Key Findings about LGBT Americans," *Pew Research Center*, June 13, 2017, http://www.pewresearch.org/fact-tank/2017/06/13/5-key-findings-about-lgbt-americans/.

188. A. Brown, "5 Key Findings about LGBT Americans," *Pew Research Center*, June 13, 2017, http://www.pewresearch.org/fact-tank/2017/06/13/5-key-findings-about-lgbt-americans/.

189. N. Gutierrez-Morfin, "GLAAD Officially Adds the 'Q' to LGBTQ," *NBC News*, October 26, 2016, https://www.nbcnews.com/feature/nbc-out/glaad-officially-adds-q-lgbtq-n673196.

190. M. Huston, "None of the Above," *Psychology Today*, March/April, 2015, pp. 28–30.

191. G. J. Gates, "UCLA Study Estimates Approximately 700,000 Transgender People in the U.S.A.," June 4, 2011, Williams Institute, UCLA School of Law, https://helenhill.wordpress.com/2011/06/04/ucla-study-estimates-approximate-700000-transgender-people-in-the-usa (accessed July 9, 2016).

192. A. Brown, "5 Key Findings about LGBT Americans," *Pew Research Center*, June 13, 2017, http://www.pewresearch.org/fact-tank/2017/06/13/5-key-findings-about-lgbt-americans/.

193. Kennedy, quoted in W. Richey, "Supreme Court Declares Same-Sex Couples' 'Fundamental Right' to Marry," *The Christian Science Monitor*, June 26, 2015, www.csmonitor.com/USA/Justice/2015/0626/Supreme-Court-declares-same-sex-couples-fundamental-right-to-marry (accessed June 27, 2016).

194. P. Varathan, "Gay Men Now Earn More than Straight Men in the US," *Quartz at Work*, December 6, 2017, https://work.qz.com/1147659/gay-men-now-earn-more-than-straight-men-in-the-us-according-to-a-vanderbilt-study/.

195. N. Thirani Bagri, "New Research Confirms the 'Sexuality Pay Gap' Is Real," *Quartz*, January 12, 2017, https://qz.com/881303/eight-million-americans-are-affected-by-a-pay-gap-that-no-one-talks-about/.

196. S. Singh and L. E. Durso, "Widespread Discrimination Continues to Shape LGBT People's Lives in Both Subtle and Significant Ways," *Center for American Progress*, May 2, 2017, https://www.americanprogress.org/issues/lgbt/news/2017/05/02/429529/widespread-discrimination-continues-shape-lgbt-peoples-lives-subtle-significant-ways/.

197. S. Singh and L. E. Durso, "Widespread Discrimination Continues to Shape LGBT People's Lives in Both Subtle and Significant Ways," *Center for American Progress*, May 2, 2017, https://www.americanprogress.org/issues/lgbt/news/2017/05/02/429529/widespread-discrimination-continues-shape-lgbt-peoples-lives-subtle-significant-ways/.

198. S. Singh and L. E. Durso, "Widespread Discrimination Continues to Shape LGBT People's Lives in Both Subtle and Significant Ways," *Center for American Progress*, May 2, 2017, https://www.americanprogress.org/issues/lgbt/news/2017/05/02/429529/widespread-discrimination-continues-shape-lgbt-peoples-lives-subtle-significant-ways/.

199. "Nearly 1 in 5 People Have a Disability in the U.S., Census Bureau Reports," *U.S. Census Bureau*, July 25, 2012, https://www.census.gov/newsroom/releases/archives/miscellaneous/cb12-134.html.

200. "Nearly 1 in 5 People Have a Disability in the U.S., Census Bureau Reports," *U.S. Census Bureau*, July 25, 2012, https://www.census.gov/newsroom/releases/archives/miscellaneous/cb12-134.html.

201. D. C. Baldridge and M. L. Swift, "Withholding Requests for Disability Accommodation: The Role of Individual Differences and Disability Attributes," *Journal of Management*, March 2013, pp. 743–762.

202. H. Ramer, "Survey: Only 28 Percent of Companies Have Disability Hiring Goals," *Inc.*, October 10, 2017, https://www.inc.com/associated-press/missed-employment-opportunities-workers-with-disabilities-2017.html?cid=search.

203. Z. Henry, "Why More Tech Companies Should Hire People with Disabilities," *Inc.*, August 23, 2017, https://www.inc.com/zoe-henry/aapd-disability-equality-index-2017.html?cid=search.

204. K. Mulhere, "One Quarter of College Grads Are Overqualified for Their Jobs," *Money*, February 2, 2017, http://time.com/money/4658059/college-grads-workers-overqualified-jobs/.

205. "High School Dropout Rates: Indicators on Children and Youth," *Child Trends Databank*, November 2015, www.childtrends.org/wp-content/uploads/2014/10/01_Dropout_Rates.pdf (accessed July 1, 2016).

206. A. Bernstein, "The Time Bomb in the Workforce: Illiteracy," *BusinessWeek*, February 25, 2002, p. 122; M. Kutner, M. Greenberg, and J. Baer, *National Assessment of Adult Literacy (NAAL): A First Look at the Literacy of America's Adults in the 21st Century* (Washington, DC: National Center for Educational Statistics, 2005); D. F. Mellard, E. Fall, and K. L. Woods, "A Path Analysis of Reading Comprehension for Adults with Low Literacy," *Journal of Learning Disabilities*, March–April 2010, pp. 154–165.

207. M. Loden, *Implementing Diversity* (Chicago: Irwin, 1996); E. E. Spragins, "Benchmark: The Diverse Work Force," *Inc.*, January 1993, p. 33; A. M. Morrison, *The New Leaders: Guidelines on Leadership Diversity in America* (San Francisco: Jossey-Bass, 1992).

208. E. Chuck, "James Damore, Google Engineer Fired for Writing Manifesto on Women's 'Neuroticism,' Sues Company," *NBC News*, January 8, 2018, https://www.nbcnews.com/news/us-news/google-engineer-fired-writing-manifesto-women-s-neuroticism-sues-company-n835836.

209. L. Weber, "Diversity Efforts Challenged," *The Wall Street Journal*, March 15, 2018, p. B5.

210. P. Zho and D. D. Park, "Which Organizations Are Best in Class in Managing Diversity and Inclusion, and What Does Their Path of Success Look Like?" Cornell University, ILR School, April 1, 2013, http://digitalcommons.ilr.cornell.edu/cgi/viewcontent.cgi?article=1045&context=student (accessed July 19, 2016).

211. J. A. Gonzalez and A. DeNisi, "Cross-Level Effects of Demography and Diversity Climate on Organizational Attachment and Firm Effectiveness," *Journal of Organizational Behavior*, January 2009, p. 24.

212. Y. Chung, H. Liao, S. E. Jackson, M. Subramony, S. Colakoglu, and Y. Jiang, "Cracking but Not Breaking: Joint Effects of Faultline Strength and Diversity Climate on Loyal Behavior," *Academy of Management Journal*, October 2015, pp. 1495–1515; S. A. Boehm, F. Kunze, and H. Bruch, "Spotlight on Age-Diversity Climate: The Impact of

CHAPTER NOTES

Age-Inclusive HR Practices on Firm-Level Outcomes," *Personnel Psychology,* 2014, pp. 667–704.
213. Y. Chung, H. Liao, S. E. Jackson, M. Subramony, S. Colakoglu, and Y. Jiang, "Cracking but Not Breaking: Joint Effects of Faultine Strength and Diversity Climate on Loyal Behavior," *Academy of Management Journal,* October 2015, pp. 1495–1515; S. A. Boehm, F. Kunze, and H. Bruch, "Spotlight on Age-Diversity Climate: The Impact of Age-Inclusive HR Practices on Firm-Level Outcomes," *Personnel Psychology,* 2014, pp. 667–704.
214. "The Majority of Children Live with Two Parents, Census Bureau Reports," U.S. Census Bureau, November 17, 2016, https://www.census.gov/newsroom/press-releases/2016/cb16-192.html.
215. Bureau of Labor Statistics, "Table 4, Families with Own Children: Employment Status of Parents by Age of Youngest Child and Family Type, 2014–2015 Annual Averages," *Economic News Release,* April 22, 2016, www.bls.gov/news.release/famee.t04.htm (accessed July 19, 2016).
216. C. Cain Miller, "Walmart and Now Starbucks: Why More Big Companies Are Offering Paid Family Leave," *The New York Times,* January 24, 2018, https://www.nytimes.com/2018/01/24/upshot/parental-leave-company-policy-salaried-hourly-gap.html.
217. See L. Peppard, "Hostile Environment for Female Firefighter Upheld," *HR Magazine,* March 2015, p. 70.
218. "Charges Alleging Sex-Based Harassment (Charges filed with EEOC) FY 2010–FY 2017," U.S. Equal Employment Opportunity Commission, https://www.eeoc.gov/eeoc/statistics/enforcement/sexual_harassment_new.cfm (accessed April 12, 2018).
219. "Ultimate Software Ranked #15 Best Company to Work For by *Fortune*, Marking Fifth Consecutive Year on List," *Business Wire,* March 3, 2016, www.businesswire.com/news/home/20160303006160/en/Ultimate-Software-Ranked-15-Company-Work-Fortune.
220. "About Us," *Ultimate Software,* www.ultimatesoftware.com/About-Us (accessed April 2, 2018); "Ultimate Software Ranked #3 on Fortune's Best Workplaces for Diversity List for 2017," December 5, 2017, www.ultimatesoftware.com/PR/Press-Release/Ultimate-Software-Ranked-3-on-Fortunes-Best-Workplaces-for-Diversity-List-for-2017.
221. "The 10 Best Workplaces for Hispanics and Latinos," *Fortune,* www.fortune.com/best-workplaces-for-hispanics-and-latinos/ (accessed March 30, 2018).
222. V. Maza, "How to Create a More Inclusive Workplace," *Entrepreneur,* June 30, 2017, www.entrepreneur.com/article/296635; D. Marcroft, "Ultimate Software Ranked #2 Best Workplace for Women by Fortune [Press Release]," September 15, 2017, www.ultimatesoftware.com/PR/Press-Release/Ultimate-Software-Ranked-2-Best-Workplace-for-Women-by-Fortune.
223. "Ultimate Software," *Great Place to Work,* http://reviews.greatplacetowork.com/ultimate-software (accessed April 2, 2018); D. Marcroft, "Ultimate Software Named #3 Best Company to Work for by Fortune [Press Release]," February 20, 2018, www.ultimatesoftware.com/PR/Press-Release/Ultimate-Software-Named-3-Best-Company-to-Work-For-by-Fortune; V. Maza, "How to Create a More Inclusive Workplace," *Entrepreneur,* June 30, 2017, www.entrepreneur.com/article/296635.
224. "HEAT to Host Second Annual Loud and Proud Dance Party Presented by Ultimate Software," *NBA,* March 4, 2018, www.nba.com/heat/heat-host-second-annual-loud-and-proud-dance-party-presented-ultimate-software.
225. D. Marcroft. "Ultimate Software Ranked #2 Best Workplace for Women by Fortune [Press Release]," September 15, 2017, www.ultimatesoftware.com/PR/Press-Release/Ultimate-Software-Ranked-2-Best-Workplace-for-Women-by-Fortune.
226. "Ultipro Reviews," *Trust Radius,* www.trustradius.com/products/ultipro/reviews/pros-and-cons?f=175 (accessed March 30, 2018); D. Marcroft, "Ultimate Software's UltiPro Helps Diverse Businesses Put Their People First with Unified Human Capital Management [Press Release]," June 10, 2014, www.ultimatesoftware.com/PR/Press-Release/Ultimate-Softwares-UltiPro-Helps-Diverse-Businesses-Put-Their-People-First-with-Unified-Human-Capital-Management.
227. D. Marcroft, "Ultimate Software Extends Talent Management with Career Development and Succession Management in UltiPro Fall 2011 Release [Press Release]," January 12, 2012, www.ultimatesoftware.com/PR/Ultimate-Software-Extends-Talent-Management-with-Career-Development-and-Succession-Management-in-UltiPro-Fall-2011-Release.
228. "Reporting, Workforce Analytics, and Business Intelligence Tools," *Ultimate Software,* www.ultimatesoftware.com/UltiPro-Solution-Features-Reporting-Workforce-Analytics-Business-Intelligence-Tools (accessed March 30, 2018).
229. "Solution Features," *Ultimate Software,* www.ultimatesoftware.com/UltiPro-Solution-Features (accessed March 30, 2018).
230. "Financial Services Company Uses UltiPro Perception to Give Managers Faster, Better Employee Insight," *Business Wire,* January 12, 2018, www.businesswire.com/news/home/20180112005424/en/Financial-Services-Company-UltiPro-Perception-Give-Managers.
231. R. S. Lazarus, *Psychological Stress and Coping Processes* (New York: McGraw-Hill, 1966); R. S. Schuler, "Definition and Conceptualization of Stress in Organizations," *Organizational Behavior and Human Performance,* April 1980, p. 1980.
232. "Work Related Stress on Employees Health," *EKU Online,* https://safetymanagement.eku.edu/resources/infographics/work-related-stress-on-employees-health/ (accessed April 12, 2018).
233. "Stress at Work," Centers for Disease Control and Prevention, https://www.cdc.gov/healthcommunication/toolstemplates/entertainmented/tips/StressWork.html (accessed April 12, 2018).
234. C. Pazzanese, "The High Price of Workplace Stress," *Harvard Gazette,* July 12, 2016, https://news.harvard.edu/gazette/story/2016/07/the-high-price-of-workplace-stress/.
235. "Work Related Stress on Employees Health," *EKU Online,* https://safetymanagement.eku.edu/resources/infographics/work-related-stress-on-employees-health/ (accessed April 12, 2018).
236. "Work Related Stress on Employees Health," *EKU Online,* https://safetymanagement.eku.edu/resources/infographics/work-related-stress-on-employees-health/ (accessed April 12, 2018).
237. "Stress at Work," Centers for Disease Control and Prevention, https://www.cdc.gov/healthcommunication/toolstemplates/entertainmented/tips/StressWork.html (accessed April 12, 2018).
238. C. Pazzanese, "The High Price of Workplace Stress," *Harvard Gazette,* July 12, 2016, https://news.harvard.edu/gazette/story/2016/07/the-high-price-of-workplace-stress/.
239. P. D. Bliese, J. R. Edwards, and S. Sonnentag, "Stress and Well-Being at Work: A Century of Empirical Trends Reflecting Theoretical and Societal Influences," *Journal of Applied Psychology,* March 2017, pp. 380–402.
240. "A Little Stress Is Good for Cellular Health and Longevity," *Science Daily,* November 7, 2017, https://www.sciencedaily.com/releases/2017/11/171107122920.htm.
241. P. D. Bliese, J. R. Edwards, and S. Sonnentag, "Stress and Well-Being at Work: A Century of Empirical Trends Reflecting Theoretical and Societal Influences," *Journal of Applied Psychology,* March 2017, pp. 380–402.
242. K. R. Rosen, "How to Recognize Burnout Before You're Burned Out," *The New York Times,* September 5, 2017, https://www.nytimes.com/2017/09/05/smarter-living/workplace-burnout-symptoms.html.
243. H. Selye, *Stress without Distress* (New York: Lippincott, 1974), p.27.
244. R. S. Lazarus and S. Folkman, "Coping and Adaptation," in W. D. Gentry (Ed.), *Handbook of Behavioral Medicine* (New York: Guilford, 1982).
245. L. Zhou, M. Wang, C-H. Chang, S. Liu, Y Zhan, and J. Shi, "Commuting Stress Process and Self-Regulation at Work: Moderating Roles of Daily Task Significance, Family Interferance with Work, and Commuting Means Efficacy," *Personnel Psychology,* 2017, pp. 891–922.
246. H. Selye, *Stress without Distress* (New York: Lippincott, 1974), pp. 28–29.

247. M. B. Hargrove, D. L. Nelson, and C. L. Cooper, "Generating Eustress by Challenging Employees: Helping People Savor Their Work," *Organizational Dynamics* 42 (2013), pp. 61–69.

248. M. Beck, "When Fretting Is in Your DNA: Overcoming the Worry Gene," *The Wall Street Journal,* January 15, 2008, p. D1; W-D. Li, Z. Zhang, Z. Song, and R. D. Arvey, "It Is Also In Our Nature: Genetic Influences on Work Characteristics and in Explaining Their Relationships with Well-Being," *Journal of Organizational Behavior,* August 2016, pp. 868–888.

249. M. Friedman and R. H. Rosenman, *Type A Behavior and Your Heart* (Greenwich, CT: Fawcett Publications, 1974), p. 84.

250. M. S. Taylor, E. A. Locke, C. Lee, and M. E. Gist, "Type A Behavior and Faculty Research Productivity: What Are the Mechanisms?" *Organizational Behavior and Human Performance,* December 1984, pp. 402–418; S. D. Bluen, J. Barling, and W. Burns, "Predicting Sales Performance, Job Satisfaction, and Depression by Using the Achievement Strivings and Impatience–Irritability Dimensions of Type A Behavior," *Journal of Applied Psychology,* April 1990, pp. 212–216.

251. S. Booth-Kewley and H. S. Friedman, "Psychological Predictors of Heart Disease: A Quantitative Review," *Psychological Bulletin,* May 1987, pp. 343–362; S. A. Lyness, "Predictors of Differences between Type A and B Individuals in Heart Rate and Blood Pressure Reactivity," *Psychological Bulletin,* September 1993, pp. 266–295; T. Q. Miller, T. W. Smith, C. W. Turner, M. L. Guijarro, and A. J. Hallet, "A Meta-Analytic Review of Research on Hostility and Physical Health," *Psychological Bulletin,* March 1996, pp. 322–348.

252. 2016 study by CareerCast, reported in C. Brooks, "Most (and Least) Stressful Jobs for 2016," *Business News Daily,* January 7, 2016, www.businessnewsdaily.com/1875-stressful-careers.html (accessed July 11, 2016).

253. J. O'Donnell, "Wanted: Retail Managers," *USA Today,* December 24, 2007, pp. 1B, 3B; A. Salario, "Retail Manager Stressed by 'Never Enough' Sales Strategy," *Womensenews,* July 15, 2013, http://womensenews.org/2013/07/retail-manager-stressed-never-enough-sales-strategy/ (accessed July 1, 2016).

254. M. Richtel, "In Web World of 24/7 Stress, Writers Blog Till They Drop," *The New York Times,* April 6, 2008, news section, pp. 1, 23.

255. S. Diestel, W. Rivkin, and K.-H. Schmidt, "Sleep Quality and Self-Control Capacity as Protective Resources in the Daily Emotional Labor Process: Results from Two Diary Studies," *Journal of Applied Psychology* 100, no. 3 (2015), pp. 809–827.

256. "Stressful Jobs That Pay Badly," *CNN Money,* March 7, 2014, http://money.cnn.com/gallery/pf/jobs/2013/03/07/jobs-stress-pay (accessed July 19, 2016).

257. E. Gonzalex-Mulé and B. Cockburn, "Worked to Death: The Relationships of Job Demands and Job Control with Mortality," *Personnel Psychology,* 2017, pp. 73–112.

258. W. B. Schaufeli, "Applying the Job Demands-Resources Model: A 'How to' Guide to Measuring and Tackling Work Engagement and Burnout," *Organizational Dynamics,* April–June 2017, pp. 120–132; E. Gonzalex-Mulé and B. Cockburn, "Worked to Death: The Relationships of Job Demands and Job Control with Mortality," *Personnel Psychology,* 2017, p. 73.

259. E. Reid and L. Ramarajan, "Managing the High Intensity Workplace," *Harvard Business Review,* June 2016, pp. 85–90.

260. J. H. Wayne, M. M. Butts, W. J. Casper, and T. D. Allen, "In Search of Balance: A Conceptual and Empirical Integration of Multiple Meanings of Work-Family Balance," *Personnel Psychology,* 2017, pp. 167–210; S. J. Wayne, G. Lemmon, J. M. Hoobler, G. W. Cheung, and M. S. Wilson, "The Ripple Effect: A Spillover Model of the Detrimental Impact of Work-Family Conflict on Job Success," *Journal of Organizational Behavior,* July 2017, pp. 876–894.

261. R. Ilies, X-Y. Liu, Y. Liu, and X. Zheng, "Why Do Employees Have Better Family Lives When They Are Highly Engaged at Work?" *Journal of Applied Psychology,* June 2017, pp. 956–970; J. I. Menges, D. V. Tussing, A. Wihler, and A. M. Grant, "When Job Performance Is All Relative: How Family Motivation Energizes Effort and Compensates for Intrinsic Motvation," *Academy of Management Journal,* April 2017, pp. 695–719.

262. L. Weber, "For New Parents, Equal Footing," *The Wall Street Journal,* February 22, 2018, p. B6.

263. J. Alpert, "Yes, Secondhand Stress Is a Thing. Here's How to Protect Yourself—And Others," *Inc.,* March 31, 2017, https://www.inc.com/jonathan-alper/what-you-need-to-know-about-secondhand-stress.html.

264. J. Kim, " 8 Traits of Toxic Leadership to Avoid," *Psychology Today,* July 6, 2016, https://www.psychologytoday.com/us/blog/culture-shrink/201607/8-traits-toxic-leadership-avoid.

265. C. Pazzanese, "The High Price of Workplace Stress," *Harvard Gazette,* July 12, 2016, https://news.harvard.edu/gazette/story/2016/07/the-high-price-of-workplace-stress/.

266. A. Peters, "One Trick to Make Employees Happy: Ban Emails on Nights and Weekends," *Fast Company,* June 1, 2016, https://www.fastcompany.com/3060349/one-trick-to-make-employees-happy-ban-emails-on-nights-and-weekends.

267. D. Z. Morris, "New French Law Bars Work Email after Hours," *Fortune,* January 1, 2017, http://fortune.com/2017/01/01/french-right-to-disconnect-law/.

268. S. Christie, "Porsche Could Ban Out-of-Hour Emails—but What Other Companies Already Have These Policies in Place?" *The Telegraph,* December 20, 2017, https://www.telegraph.co.uk/business/2017/12/20/porsche-could-ban-out-of-hour-emails-companies-already-have/.

269. D. Z. Morris, "New French Law Bars Work Email after Hours," *Fortune,* January 1, 2017, http://fortune.com/2017/01/01/french-right-to-disconnect-law/.

270. S. Milligan, "Wellness Blows Up," *HRMagazine,* September 2017, pp. 61–67.

271. I. T. Roberson, C. L. Cooper, M. Sarkar, and T. Curran, "Resilience Training in the Workplace from 2003 to 2014: A Systematic Review," *Journal of Occupational and Organizational Psychology,* September 2015, pp. 533–562.

272. "James Dyson," *Forbes,* https://www.forbes.com/profile/james-dyson/ (accessed April 20, 2018).

273. E. Dane, "Where Is My Mind? Theorizing Mind Wandering and Its Performance-Related Consequences in Organizations," *Academy of Management Review,* April 2018, pp. 179–197; K. M. Kiburz, T. D. Allen, and K. A. French, "Work-Family Conflict and Mindfulness: Investigating the effectiveness of a Brief Training Intervention," *Journal of Organizational Behavior,* September 2017, pp. 1016–1037; E. Bernstein, "A Daily Workout for the Brain," *The Wall Street Journal,* December 5, 2017, p. A13.

274. T. Parker-Pope, "How to Build Resilience in Midlife," *The New York Times,* July 25, 2017, https://www.nytimes.com/2017/07/25/well/mind/how-to-boost-resilience-in-midlife.html; P. R. Pietromonaco and N. L. Collins, "Interpersonal Mechanisms Linking Close Relationships to Health," *American Psychologist,* September 2017, pp. 531–542; B. Litwiller, L. A. Snyder, W. D. Taylor, and L. M. Steele, "The Relationship Between Sleep and Work: A Meta-Analysis," *Journal of Applied Psychology,* April 2017, pp. 682–699.

275. K. Pho, "Do Corporate Wellness Programs Really Work?" *USA Today,* September 12, 2013, p. 10A; S. Hananel, "A Workout during Work," *Reno Gazette-Journal,* September 12, 2013, p. 7F; N. Hellmich, "Healthy, Wellness, and Wise about Costs," *USA Today,* December 13, 2013, p. 8B; A. Lukits, "Take Your Bike to Your Desk to Improve Health," *The Wall Street Journal,* May 27, 2014, p. D2; A. Bruzzese, "Mindful Eating, Exercise Boost Work Performance," *Reno Gazette-Journal,* January 18, 2014, p. 9A.

276. "10 Companies with Amazing Workplace Wellness Programs," *Rise,* March 30. 2017, www.risepeople.com/blog/10-companies-with-amazing-workplace-wellness-programs/.

277. L. Martis,"7 Companies with Great Wellness Programs," *Fortune,* August 17, 2017, http://fortune.com/2017/08/17/companies-great-wellness-programs/.

278. L. Bradford, "13 Tech Companies That Offer Cool Work Perks," *Forbes,* July 27, 2016, www.forbes.com/sites/laurencebradford/2016/07/27/13-tech-companies-that-offer-insanely-cool-perks/#723db7d979d1.

279. S. Thieroff, "Wellness Case Study: Google," *Healthyworks,* October 6, 2015, www.healthyworksofpa.com/wellness-case-study-google/.

280. L. Bradford, "13 Tech Companies That Offer Cool Work Perks," *Forbes,* July 27, 2016, www.forbes.com/sites/laurencebradford/2016/07/27/13-tech-companies-that-offer-insanely-cool-perks/#723db7d979d1.

281. L. Martis,"7 Companies with Great Wellness Programs," *Fortune,* August 17, 2017, http://fortune.com/2017/08/17/companies-great-wellness-programs/.

282 J. D'Onfro & K. Smith, "Google Employees Reveal Their Favorite Perks about Working for the Company," *Business Insider,* July 1, 2014, www.businessinsider.com/google-employees-favorite-perks-2014-7#.

283. "10 Companies with Amazing Workplace Wellness Programs," *Rise*, March 30. 2017, www.risepeople.com/blog/10-companies-with-amazing-workplace-wellness-programs/.

284. L. Martis,"7 Companies with Great Wellness Programs," *Fortune,* August 17, 2017, http://fortune.com/2017/08/17/companies-great-wellness-programs/.

285. "10 Companies with Amazing Workplace Wellness Programs," *Rise*, March 30. 2017, www.risepeople.com/blog/10-companies-with-amazing-workplace-wellness-programs/; L. Bradford, "13 Tech Companies That Offer Cool Work Perks," *Forbes,* July 27, 2016, www.forbes.com/sites/laurencebradford/2016/07/27/13-tech-companies-that-offer-insanely-cool-perks/#723db7d979d1.

286. L. Bradford, "13 Tech Companies That Offer Cool Work Perks," *Forbes,* July 27, 2016, www.forbes.com/sites/laurencebradford/2016/07/27/13-tech-companies-that-offer-insanely-cool-perks/#723db7d979d1.

287. L. Martis,"7 Companies with Great Wellness Programs," *Fortune,* August 17, 2017, http://fortune.com/2017/08/17/companies-great-wellness-programs/.

288. A. Kohll, "Why More Employees Don't Embrace Wellness Programs, and How to Fix It," *Forbes,* June 22, 2017, https://www.forbes.com/sites/alankohll/2017/06/22/why-more-employees-dont-embrace-wellness-programs-and-how-to-fix-it/2/#4b4a6f6977c6.

289. M. Hollauf, "5 Companies Where You Can Exercise while Working," *Entrepreneur,* May 12, 2016, www.entrepreneur.com/article/274207.

290. S. Thieroff, "Wellness Case Study: Google," *Healthyworks,* October 6, 2015, www.healthyworksofpa.com/wellness-case-study-google/.

291. "Mentors Help Reduce Stress, Burnout," *San Francisco Chronicle,* February 26, 2016, p. C2, reprinted from *Pittsburgh Post-Gazette.*

292. S. Lucas, "Companies Are Reducing Employee Stress by Doing This 1 Simple Thing," *Inc.,* February 22, 2018, https://www.inc.com/suzanne-lucas/companies-are-reducing-employee-stress-by-doing-this-one-simple-thing.html?cid=search.

293. These questions were adapted from B. Tulgan, *Bridging the Soft Skills Gap* (Hoboken, NJ: John Wiley & Sons, 2015).

294. These steps were based on material in B. Tulgan, *Bridging the Soft Skills Gap* (Hoboken, NJ: John Wiley & Sons, 2015).

295. D. Meinert, "Are You An Emotional Genius?" *HRMagazine,* March 2018, pp. 17–19.

296. S. Côte, "Enhancing Mangerial Effectiveness via Four Core Facets of Emotional Intelligence: Self-Awareness, Social Perception, Emotion Understanding, and Emotional Regulation," *Organizational Dynamics,* July–September 2017, pp. 140–147; R. Hanson and R. Mendius, *Buddha's Brain* (Oakland, CA: Harbinger Publications, 2009).

297. "Financial Services Industry: Trends in Management Representation of Minorities and Women and Diversity Practices, 2007–2015," U.S. Government Accountability Office, November 8, 2017, www.gao.gov/mobile/products/GAO-18-64.

298. J. Davidson, "Federal Report Finds Regression for Black Managers in Financial Services Industry," *Washington Post,* December 12, 2017, www.washingtonpost.com/news/powerpost/wp/2017/12/12/federal-report-finds-regression-for-black-managers-in-financial-services-industry/?utm_term=.14cd27c187ee.

299. J. Davidson, "Federal Report Finds Regression for Black Managers in Financial Services Industry," *Washington Post,* December 12, 2017, www.washingtonpost.com/news/powerpost/wp/2017/12/12/federal-report-finds-regression-for-black-managers-in-financial-services-industry/?utm_term=.14cd27c187ee.

300. S. Singh-Kurtz, "The Bias against Women in Finance Even Extends to Men with Feminine Names," *Quartz at Work,* November 21, 2017, http://work.qz.com/1130108/the-bias-against-women-in-finance-even-extends-to-men-with-feminine-names/.

301. T. Walk-Morris, "Where Are the Women and Minorities in Financial Planning?" *Pacific Standard,* July 18, 2017, https://psmag.com/economics/where-are-the-women-and-minorities-in-financial-planning.

302. T. Marzigliano, "The Financial Services Sector's Not-so-Secret Gender Discrimination and Harassment Problem," *Employment Law Blog,* October 25, 2017, www.employmentlawblog.info/2017/10/the-financial-services-sectors-not-so-secret-gender-discrimination-and-harassment-problem.shtml.

303. E. Pettersson, "Pimco Accused of Discrimination, Retaliation by Female Executive," *Bloomberg,* April 12, 2018, www.bloomberg.com/news/articles/2018-04-12/pimco-accused-of-discrimination-retaliation-by-female-executive.

304. L. Brown, "Wells Fargo Advisors Paying $35.5 Million to Settle Discrimination Case," *St. Louis Post-Dispatch,* January 6, 2017, www.stltoday.com/business/local/wells-fargo-advisors-paying-million-to-settle-racial-discrimination-case/article_bbcda3b9-a820-5401-a7cc-b45a08a087f2.html.

305. Insurance Business, "Judge Approves MetLife's $32.5 Million Race Bias Class Action Settlement," *Insurance Business America,* July 12, 2017, www.insurancebusinessmag.com/us/news/breaking-news/judge-approves-metlifes-32-5-million-race-bias-class-action-settlement-72878.aspx.

306. L. Brown, "Wells Fargo Advisors Paying $35.5 Million to Settle Discrimination Case," *St. Louis Post-Dispatch,* January 6, 2017, www.stltoday.com/business/local/wells-fargo-advisors-paying-million-to-settle-racial-discrimination-case/article_bbcda3b9-a820-5401-a7cc-b45a08a087f2.html.

307. A. Kurtz, "Wells Fargo 25% More Likely to Punish Women Employees than Men, Study Says," *Fortune,* March 13, 2017, http://fortune.com/2017/03/13/wells-fargo-financial-advisers-gender-discrimination/.

308. M. Abelson and J. Holman, "Black Executives Are Losing Ground at Some Big Banks," *Bloomberg,* July 27, 2017, www.bloomberg.com/graphics/2017-black-executives-are-disappearing-from-biggest-wall-street-banks/.

309. G. Donnelly, "Only 3% of Fortune 500 Companies Share Full Diversity Data," *Fortune,* June 7, 2017, http://fortune.com/2017/06/07/fortune-500-diversity/.

310. J. Davidson, "Federal Report Finds Regression for Black Managers in Financial Services Industry," *Washington Post,* December 12, 2017, www.washingtonpost.com/news/powerpost/wp/2017/12/12/federal-report-finds-regression-for-black-managers-in-financial-services-industry/?utm_term=.14cd27c187ee.

311. "Financial Services Industry: Trends in Management Representation of Minorities and Women and Diversity Practices, 2007–2015," *U.S. Government Accountability Office,* November 8, 2017, www.gao.gov/mobile/products/GAO-18-64.

312. G. Donnelly, "Only 3% of Fortune 500 Companies Share Full Diversity Data," *Fortune,* June 7, 2017, http://fortune.com/2017/06/07/fortune-500-diversity/.

313. S. Antilla, "How Wall Street Silences Women," *The Intercept,* December 13, 2017, https://theintercept.com/2017/12/13/wall-street-women-gender-financial-sector/.

314. S. Antilla, "How Wall Street Silences Women," *The Intercept,* December 13, 2017, https://theintercept.com/2017/12/13/wall-street-women-gender-financial-sector/.

315. T. Walk-Morris, "Where Are the Women and Minorities in Financial Planning?" *Pacific Standard,* July 18, 2017, https://psmag.com/economics/where-are-the-women-and-minorities-in-financial-planning.
316. L. Haverty, "Diversity Is Imperative for Financial Services Industry, Business Leaders Say," *Fannie Mae,* October 11, 2016, www.fanniemae.com/portal/media/business/diversity-101116.html
317. L. Haverty, "Diversity Is Imperative for Financial Services Industry, Business Leaders Say," *Fannie Mae,* October 11, 2016, www.fanniemae.com/portal/media/business/diversity-101116.html
318. J. Davidson, "Federal Report Finds Regression For Black Managers in Financial Services Industry," *Washington Post,* December 12, 2017, www.washingtonpost.com/news/powerpost/wp/2017/12/12/federal-report-finds-regression-for-black-managers-in-financial-services-industry/?utm_term=.14cd27c187ee.
319. J. Wattles, "Judges Order FAA to Review Airplane Seat Sizes," *CNN Money,* July 29, 2017, http://money.cnn.com/2017/07/29/news/companies/faa-airline-seat-sizes/index.html.
320. Excerpted from K. Mayo, "Economy Plus Size," *Bloomberg Businessweek,* May 6–May 12, 2013, p. 81.
321. C. Morris, "The FAA May Put an End to Shrinking Airline Seats and Cramped Leg Room," *Fortune,* February 26, 2018, http://fortune.com/2018/02/26/faa-airline-seats-regulation-safety-comfort/.
322. J. Wattles, "Judges Order FAA to Review Airplane Seat Sizes," *CNN Money,* July 29, 2017, http://money.cnn.com/2017/07/29/news/companies/faa-airline-seat-sizes/index.html.
323. C. Morris, "The FAA May Put an End to Shrinking Airline Seats and Cramped Leg Room," *Fortune,* February 26, 2018, http://fortune.com/2018/02/26/faa-airline-seats-regulation-safety-comfort/.
324. A. Schmertz, "Senator Schumer's Silly Idea about Airline Seat Sizes," *Huffington Post,* March 7, 2016, http://www.huffingtonpost.com/andrew-schmertz/senator-schumers-silly- d_b_9400796.html.
325. A. Spaeth, "Swiss Flies First Passenger Flight with New Bombardier Jetliner," June 7, 2016, www.cnn.com/2016/06/06/aviation/bombardier-cseries-cs100-swiss-first-passenger-flight/index.html.

CHAPTER 12

1. R. Kanfer, M. Frese, and R. E. Johnson, "Motivation Related to Work: A Century of Progress," *Journal of Applied Psychology,* March 2017, pp. 338–355.
2. B. Galile, "19 Employee Motivation Statistics and Trends," May 20, 2017, https://brandongaille.com/17-employee-motivation-statistics-and-trends.
3. E. Kaplan, "How to Stay Insanely Self-Motivated, According to Science," *Medium.com,* September, 15, 2017, https://medium.com/the-mission/how-to-create-insane-change-in-your-life-according-to-science-bb3cddd1022; J. D. Meier, "15 Ways to Motivate Yourself and Others," *Time,* March 18, 2016, http://time.com/4262774/motivation-ways/; G. Matthews, "Study Focuses on Strategies for Achieving Goals, Resolutions," Dominican University of California, https://www.dominican.edu/dominicannews/study-highlights-strategies-for-achieving-goals (accessed April 23, 2018); S. Lebowitz, "11 Ways to Trick Yourself into Working Hard, Even When You're Not in the Mood," *Business Insider,* January 9, 2017, http://www.businessinsider.com/tricks-to-self-motivate-2017-1.
4. J. D. Meier, "15 Ways to Motivate Yourself and Others," *Time,* March 18, 2016, http://time.com/4262774/motivation-ways/.
5. E. Kaplan, "How to Stay Insanely Self-Motivated, According to Science," *Medium.com,* September, 15, 2017, https://medium.com/the-mission/how-to-create-insane-change-in-your-life-according-to-science-bb3cddd1022.
6. G. Matthews, "Study Focuses on Strategies for Achieving Goals, Resolutions," Dominican University of California, https://www.dominican.edu/dominicannews/study-highlights-strategies-for-achieving-goals (accessed April 23, 2018).
7. S. Shellenbarger, "Women Try New Strategies to Boost Career Confidence," *The Wall Street Journal,* March 20, 2018, p A13.
8. "Survey: 3 in 4 Employers Planning to Roll Out Student Loan Repayment Benefits," *Tuition.io,* https://www.tuition.io/2017/06/survey-3-4-employers-planning-roll-student-loan-repayment-benefits/ (accessed April 23, 2018).
9. R. Feintzeig, "Getting Paid to Live Near Your Job," *The Wall Street Journal,* February 24, 2016, pp. B1, B7; and "Where Do Silicon Valley's Tech Workers Really Live?" *Marcotte Properties,* November 21, 2017, https://www.marcotteproperties.com/silicon-valleys-workers-live/.
10. Adapted from definition in T. R. Mitchell, "Motivation: New Directions for Theory, Research, and Practice," *Academy of Management Review,* January 1982, p. 81.
11. R. M. Ryan and E. L. Deci, "Intrinsic and Extrinsic Motivations: Classic Definitions and New Directions," *Contemporary Educational Psychology,* January 2000, pp. 54–67.
12. M. S. Patel, D. A. Asch, R. Rosin, D. S. Small, et al. "Framing Financial Incentives to Increase Physical Activity among Overweight and Obese Adults," *Annals of Internal Medicine,* March 15, 2016, pp. 385–394. See also M. S. Patel, D. A. Asch, and K. G. Volpp, "Paying Employees to Lose Weight," *The New York Times,* March 6, 2016, p. SR-10.
13. M. S. Patel, D. A. Asch, R. Rosin, D. S. Small, et al. "Framing Financial Incentives to Increase Physical Activity among Overweight and Obese Adults," *Annals of Internal Medicine,* March 15, 2016, pp. 385–394.
14. K. Gee, "Apps Give Workers Early Access to Pay," *The Wall Street Journal,* November 25-26, 2017, pp A1, A7.
15. S. Vozza, "Why Every Company Should Pay Employees to Volunteer," *Fast Company,* March 11, 2014, www.fastcompany.com/3027465/dialed/why-every-company-should-pay-employees-to-volunteer.
16. M. C. Kocakulah, A. G. Kelley, K. M. Mitchell, and M. P. Ruggieri, "Absenteeism Problems and Costs: Causes, Effects and Cures," *International Business & Economics Research Journal,* May/June 2016, pp. 81–88; C. White, "The Impact of Motivation on Customer Satisfaction Formation: A Self-Determination Perspective," *European Journal of Marketing* 49 (2015), pp. 1923–1940.
17. A. Maslow, "A Theory of Human Motivation," *Psychological Review,* July 1943, pp. 370–396.
18. "Chip Conley," *Huffington Post,* www.huffingtonpost.com/author/chip-conley (accessed April 23, 2018).
19. C. Conley, *Peak: How Great Companies Get Their Mojo from Maslow* (San Francisco: Jossey-Bass, 2007).
20. C. Conley, interviewed by D. Schawbel, "How Emotional Equations Can Change Your Life," *Forbes,* January 12, 2012, www.forbes.com/sites/danschawbel/%202012/01/12/how-emotional-equations-can-change-your-life/#7cc3b8b92e19.
21. C. Conley, interviewed in E. Schurenberg, "Chip Conley: The 5 Things Everyone Wants from You," *Inc.,* December 12, 2011, www.inc.com/eric-schurenberg/Chip-Conley-5-Things-Everyone-Wants.html; C. Webb, interviewed in "How to Have a Good Day at Work," *Knowledge@Wharton,* July 7, 2016, http://knowledge.wharton.upenn.edu/article/160523b_kwradio_webb-caroline-webb.
22. Chip Conley, interviewed by M. Hofman, "The Idea That Saved My Company," *Inc.,* October 11, 2007, www.inc.com/magazine/20071001/the-idea-that-saved-my-company.html.
23. C. Conley, interviewed in K. Pattison, "Chip Conley Took the Maslow Pyramid, Made It an Employee Pyramid, and Saved His Company," *Fast Company,* August 26, 2010, www.fastcompany.com/1685009/chip-conley-wants-your-employees-to-hit-their-peak.
24. C. Conley, interviewed in E. Schurenberg, "Chip Conley: The 5 Things Everyone Wants from You," *Inc.,* December 12, 2011, www.inc.com/eric-schurenberg/Chip-Conley-5-Things-Everyone-Wants.html.
25. "Hotel Rex," review by *Tablet Hotels,* July 9, 2016, www.tablethotels.com/en/san-francisco-bay-area-hotels/hotel-rex?arrDate=2016-07-09&depDate=2016-07-10&nA=1&nC=0&nR=1&hotelId=72&pid=392&language=en.
26. C. Conley, interviewed in E. Schurenberg, "Chip Conley: The 5 Things Everyone Wants from You," *Inc.,* December 12, 2011, www.inc.com/eric-schurenberg/Chip-Conley-5-Things-Everyone-Wants.html.

27. M. Hofman, "The Idea That Saved My Company," *Inc.,* October 1, 2007, www.inc.com/magazine/20071001/the-idea-that-saved-my-company.html.

28. D. Kenrick, quoted in W. Kremer and C. Hammond, "Abraham Maslow and the Pyramid That Beguiled Business," *BBC World Service,* September 1, 2013, www.bbc.com/news/magazine-23902918.

29. R. Kanfer, M. Frese, and R. E. Johnson, "Motivation Related to Work: A Century of Progress," *Journal of Applied Psychology,* March 2017, pp. 338–355.

30. D. C. McClelland, *Human Motivation* (Glenview, IL: Scott, Foresman, 1985).

31. D. McClelland and H. Burnham, "Power Is the Great Motivator," *Harvard Business Review,* March–April 1976, pp. 100–110.

32. Some of these recommendations are based on "McClelland's Human Motivation Theory," *Mind Tools,* www.mindtools.com/pages/article/human-motivation-theory.htm (accessed May 22, 2013).

33. R. M. Ryan and E. L. Deci, "Self-Determination Theory and the Facilitation of Intrinsic Motivation, Social Development, and Well-Being," *American Psychologist,* January 2000, pp. 68–78.

34. R. Kanfer, M. Frese, and R. E. Johnson, "Motivation Related to Work: A Century of Progress," *Journal of Applied Psychology,* March 2017, pp. 338–355.

35. K. W. Rockmann and G. A. Ballinger, "Intrinsic Motivation and Organizational Identification Among On-Demand Workers," *Journal of Applied Psychology,* September 2017, pp. 1305–1316.

36. M. Davis, "A Manager's Guide to Developing Competencies in HR Staff," *Society for Human Resource Management,* October 4, 2017, https://www.shrm.org/hr-today/news/hr-magazine/1017/pages/a-managers-guide-to-developing-competencies-in-hr-staff-.aspx.

37. A. Pignatelli, "The Rise of the Results-Only Work Environment," *E3 Solutions,* February 5, 2017, https://www.e3.solutions/blogs/articles/the-rise-of-the-results-only-work-environment.

38. "The World's Best Workplaces," *Fortune,* October 26, 2017, http://fortune.com/2017/10/26/worlds-best-workplaces/.

39. F. Herzberg, B. Mausner, and B. B. Snyderman, *The Motivation to Work* (New York: Wiley, 1959); F. Herzberg, "One More Time: How Do You Motivate Employees?" *Harvard Business Review,* January–February 1968, pp. 53–62. For a modern look at the application of Herzberg's theory, see C. Christensen, "Clayton Christensen on How to Find Work That You Love," *Fast Company,* May 14, 2012, www.fastcompany.com/1836982/clayton-christensen-how-find-work-you-love (accessed July 9, 2016).

40. "The Container Store," *Fortune,* http://fortune.com/best-companies/the-container-store/ (accessed April 23, 2018).

41. Anecdote recounted by Chip Conley of Joie de Vivre Hotels, reported in C. Conley, interviewed in E. Schurenberg, "Chip Conley: The 5 Things Everyone Wants from You," *Inc.,* December 12, 2011, www.inc.com/eric-schurenberg/Chip-Conley-5-Things-Everyone-Wants.html.

42. Survey by the Conference Board, reported in P. Korkki, "With Jobs Few, Most Workers Aren't Satisfied," *The New York Times,* January 10, 2009, Business section, p. 2. See also P. Coy, "Are Your Employees Just Biding Their Time?" *BusinessWeek,* November 16, 2009, p. 27.

43. "2017 Employee Job Satisfaction and Engagement: The Doors of Opportunity Are Open," Society for Human Resource Management, April 24, 2017, https://www.shrm.org/hr-today/trends-and-forecasting/research-and-surveys/pages/2017-job-satisfaction-and-engagement-doors-of-opportunity-are-open.aspx.

44. "How Is Global Uncertainty Impacting Employee Engagement Levels?' *AON,* http://www.aon.com/engagement17/ (accessed April 23, 2018).

45. J. Flint, "How to Be a Player," *Bloomberg Businessweek,* January 24–January 30, 2011, pp. 108–109.

46. A. Cain, "8 Unbelievable Perks That Come with Working for Google," *Business Insider,* November 17, 2017, http://www.businessinsider.com/google-employee-best-perks-benefits-2017-11.

47. J. S. Adams, "Toward an Understanding of Inequity," *Journal of Abnormal and Social Psychology,* November 1963, pp. 422–436; J. S. Adams, "Injustice in Social Exchange," in L. Berkowitz (Ed.), *Advances in Experimental Social Psychology,* 2nd ed. (New York: Academic Press, 1965), pp. 267–300.

48. D. F. Larcker, N. E. Donatiello, and B. Tavan, "Americans and CEO Pay: 2016 Public Perception Survey on CEO Compensation," *CGRI Survey Series, Corporate Governance Research Initiative, Stanford Rock Center for Corporate Governance,* February 2016, https://www.gsb.stanford.edu/faculty-research/publications/americans-ceo-pay-2016-public-perception-survey-ceo-compensation; D. Choe, "CEO Pay in 2015: When a $468,449 Raise is Typical," *Associated Press,* May 25, 2016, http://bigstory.ap.org/article/3ecc98d4f30b41818d8e8ae032095f42/ceo-pay-climbs-again-even-their-stock-prices-dont (both accessed July 5, 2016).

49. V. Fuhrmans and T. Francis, "Adding Numbers to Compensation Debate," *The Wall Street Journal,* February 2, 2018, p. B5.

50. "Thievery in Workplaces—Trillion-Dollar Industry: Honesty in Deep Decline—Business Theft Becoming Epidemic," *BizShifts—Trends,* July 25, 2015, http://bizshifts-trends.com/2015/07/29/thievery-in-workplaces-trillion-dollar-industry-honesty-in-deep-decline-business-theft-becoming-epidemic.

51. Perceptions of fairness are discussed by L. J. Barclay, M. R. Bashshur, and M. Fortin, "Motivated Cognition and Fairness: Insights, Integration, and Creating a Path Forward," *Journal of Applied Psychology,* June 2017, pp. 867–889.

52. R. Cropanzano, D. E. Rupp, C. J. Mohler, and M. Schminke, "Three Roads to Organizational Justice," in G. R. Ferris (Ed.), *Research in Personnel and Human Resources Management,* vol. 20 (New York: JAI Press, 2001), pp. 269–329.

53. J. A. Colquitt, D. E. Conlon, M. J. Wesson, C. O. L. H. Porter, and K. Y. Ng, "Justice at the Millennium: A Meta-Analytic Review of 25 Years of Organizational Justice Research," *Journal of Applied Psychology,* June 2001, p. 426.

54. D. Jacobe, "Half of Americans Say They Are Underpaid," *Gallup Organization,* August 18, 2008, www.gallup.com/poll/109618/half-americans-say-they-underpaid.aspx.

55. Z. Elinson and D. MacMillan, "YouTube Shooter Expressed Anger over Video Site's Policies," *The Wall Street Journal,* April 4, 2018, https://www.wsj.com/articles/police-scrutinize-youtube-shooters-social-media-for-motive-1522850926.

56. M. Chamberlin, D. W. Newton, and J. A. Lepine, "A Meta-Analysis of Voice and Its Promotive and Prohibitive Forms: Identification of Key Associations, Distinctions, and Future Research Directions," *Personnel Psychology,* 2017, pp. 11–71.

57. S. Tangirala and R. Ramanujam, "Ask and You Shall Hear (but Not Always): Examining the Relationship between Manager Consultation and Employee Voice," *Personnel Psychology* 65, no. 2 (2012), pp. 251–252.

58. J. M. Dorio, "Employee Voice: Listen, Analyze, and Act," *Training,* September/October 2016, pp. 38–41.

59. K. Taylor, "Starbucks Is Spending $120 Million to Address Baristas' Complaints and Raise Wages in a Move 'Accelerated' by the New Tax Law," *Business Insider,* January 24, 2018, http://www.businessinsider.com/starbucks-raises-wages-adds-benefits-for-in-store-workers-2018-1.

60. M. van Dijke, D. D. Cremer, G. Langendijk, and C. Anderson, "Ranking Low, Feeling High: How Hierarchical Position and Experienced Power Promote Prosocial Behavior in Response to Procedural Justice," *Journal of Applied Psychology.* February 2018, pp. 164–181; C. A. Fulmer and C. Ostroff, "Trust in Direct Leaders and Top Leaders: A Trickle-Up Model," *Journal of Applied Psychology,* April 2017, pp. 648–657.

61. R. Levering, "This Year's Best Employers Have Focused on Fairness," *Fortune,* March 3, 2016, http://fortune.com/2016/03/03/best-companies-2016-intro/.

62. D. S. Whitman, S. Caleo, N. C. Carpenter, M. T. Horner, and J. B. Bernerth, "Fairness at the Collective Level: A Meta-Analytic Examination of the Consequences and Boundary Conditions of Organizational Justice Climate," *Journal of Applied Psychology,* July 2012, pp. 776–791.

63. T. Loudenback, "More Tech Companies Have Stopped Keeping Employee Salaries Secret—And They're Seeing Results," *Business*

Insider, May 3, 2017, www.businessinsider.com/why-companies-have-open-salaries-and-pay-transparency-2017-4.
64. L. Ridley, "Meet the Companies That Make Their Salaries Public—And Say They Are Happier for It," *Huffington Post,* June 3, 2016, www.huffingtonpost.co.uk/2016/03/06/transparent-salaries-public-buffer_n_9377452.html.
65. L. Ridley, "Meet the Companies That Make Their Salaries Public—And Say They Are Happier for It," *Huffington Post,* June 3, 2016, www.huffingtonpost.co.uk/2016/03/06/transparent-salaries-public-buffer_n_9377452.html.
66. L. Ridley, "Meet the Companies That Make Their Salaries Public—And Say They Are Happier for It," *Huffington Post,* June 3, 2016, www.huffingtonpost.co.uk/2016/03/06/transparent-salaries-public-buffer_n_9377452.html.
67. E. Volkman,"Buffer Reaffirms Salary Transparency, Benchmarks Cost of Living," *TechCo,* December 7, 2017, https://tech.co/buffer-reaffirms-salary-transparency-cost-living-2017-12; L. Ridley, "Meet the Companies That Make Their Salaries Public—And Say They Are Happier for It," *Huffington Post,* June 3, 2016, www.huffingtonpost.co.uk/2016/03/06/transparent-salaries-public-buffer_n_9377452.html.
68. E. Volkman,"Buffer Reaffirms Salary Transparency, Benchmarks Cost of Living," *TechCo,* December 7, 2017, https://tech.co/buffer-reaffirms-salary-transparency-cost-living-2017-12.
69. "Transparent Salary Calculator," *Buffer,* https://buffer.com/salary/software-engineer-mobile/average/ (accessed April 6, 2018).
70. C. Cawley, "The Good, the Bad, and the Ugly of Transparency in Tech," *TechCo,* January 8, 2018, https://tech.co/examples-transparency-lack-tech-2018-01.
71. L. Ridley, "Meet the Companies That Make Their Salaries Public—And Say They Are Happier for It," *Huffington Post,* June 3, 2016, www.huffingtonpost.co.uk/2016/03/06/transparent-salaries-public-buffer_n_9377452.html.
72. L. Ridley, "Meet the Companies That Make Their Salaries Public—And Say They Are Happier for It," *Huffington Post,* June 3, 2016, www.huffingtonpost.co.uk/2016/03/06/transparent-salaries-public-buffer_n_9377452.html.
73. T. Loudenback, "More Tech Companies Have Stopped Keeping Employee Salaries Secret—And They're Seeing Results," *Business Insider,* May 3, 2017, www.businessinsider.com/why-companies-have-open-salaries-and-pay-transparency-2017-4.
74. See Loudenback, "More Tech Companies Have Stopped Keeping Employee Salaries Secret—And They're Seeing Results," *Business Insider,* May 3, 2017, www.businessinsider.com/why-companies-have-open-salaries-and-pay-transparency-2017-4; L. Ridley, "Meet the Companies That Make Their Salaries Public—And Say They Are Happier for It," *Huffington Post,* June 3, 2016, www.huffingtonpost.co.uk/2016/03/06/transparent-salaries-public-buffer_n_9377452.html.
75. C. Cawley, "The Good, the Bad, and the Ugly of Transparency in Tech," *TechCo,* January 8, 2018, https://tech.co/examples-transparency-lack-tech-2018-01.
76. V. H. Vroom, *Work and Motivation* (New York: Wiley, 1964).
77. T. Higgins, "Tesla Primes Musk's Pay for Blastoff," *The Wall Street Journal,* January 24, 2018, p. B2.
78. A. Ain, "The CEO of Kronos on Launching an Unlimited Vacation Policy," *Harvard Business Review,* November–December 2017, p. 38.
79. M. A. Maltarich, A. J. Nyberg, G. Reilly, D. D. Abdulsalam, and M. Martin, "Pay-for Performance, Sometimes: An Interdisciplinary Approach to Integrating Economic Rationality with Psychological Emotion to Predict Individual Performance," *Academy of Management Journal,* December 2017, pp. 2155–2174.
80. M. J. Pearsall, M. S. Christian, and A. P. J. Ellis, "Motivating Interdependent Teams: Individual Rewards, Shared Rewards, or Something in Between?" *Journal of Applied Psychology,* January 2010, pp. 183–191.
81. B. Silverman, "CEOs and the Pay-for-Performance Puzzle," *Bloomberg Businessweek,* September 23, 2009, www.bloomberg.com/news/articles/2009-09-23/ceos-and-the-pay-for-performance-puzzle.
82. C. Isidore, "Bankrupt Toys 'R' Us Wins OK to Pay $16 Million in Executive Bonuses," *CNN Money,* December 6, 2017, http://money.cnn.com/2017/12/06/news/companies/toys-r-us-executive-bonuses/index.html.
83. For more about the problem of linking executive compensation to performance, see; "CEO Compensation: Do Performance Incentives Pay Off?" *Knowwpcarey,* June 27, 2013, http://knowwpcarey.com/article.cfm?cid=10&aid=1420; A. R. Sorkin, "A Question of What's a Reasonable Reward," *The New York Times,* March 25, 2014, pp. B1, B5; P. Eavis, "Invasion of the Supersalaries," *The New York Times,* April 13, 2014, pp. BU-1, BU4; J. Nocera, "CEO Pay Goes Up, Up, and Away," *The New York Times,* April 15, 2014, p. A2.
84. M. Cowling, "'Celebration Time' at San Tan Foothills Helps Student Grades Go Up," *Florence Reminder & Blade-Tribune,* October 27, 2016, www.pinalcentral.com/florence_reminder_blade_tribune/news/celebration-time-at-san-tan-foothills-helps-student-grades-go/article_2b8b27a4-9bcc-11e6-a9d4-2fcc50345e1b.html.
85. Tim Richard, quoted in D. Dullum, "Principal Nominated for Rodel Honor," *Florence Reminder Blade-Tribune,* October 31, 2013, www.trivalleycentral.com/florence_reminder_blade_tribune/education/principal-nominated-for-rodel-honor/article_00078a42-41a6-11e3-a29b-0019bb2963f4.html.
86. M. Cowling, "'Celebration Time' at San Tan Foothills Helps Student Grades Go Up," *Florence Reminder & Blade-Tribune,* October 27, 2016, www.pinalcentral.com/florence_reminder_blade_tribune/news/celebration-time-at-san-tan-foothills-helps-student-grades-go/article_2b8b27a4-9bcc-11e6-a9d4-2fcc50345e1b.html; Tim Richard, quoted in C. Creno, "Program Helps Students Succeed," *Arizona Republic,* November 27, 2012, p. B2.
87. M. Cowling, "'Celebration Time' at San Tan Foothills Helps Student Grades Go Up," *Florence Reminder & Blade-Tribune,* October 27, 2016, www.pinalcentral.com/florence_reminder_blade_tribune/news/celebration-time-at-san-tan-foothills-helps-student-grades-go/article_2b8b27a4-9bcc-11e6-a9d4-2fcc50345e1b.html.
88. Tim Richard, quoted in C. Creno, "Program Helps Students Succeed," *Arizona Republic,* November 27, 2012, p. B2.
89. N. Green, "4 Ways 'Stretch Goals' Can Bring Your Company Greater Gains," *Business Journals,* September 8, 2017, https://www.bizjournals.com/bizjournals/how-to/growth-strategies/2017/09/4-ways-stretch-goals-can-bring-your-company.html.
90. S. B. Sitkin, C. C. Miller and K. E. See, "The Stretch Goal Paradox," *Harvard Business Review,* January–February 2017, https://hbr.org/2017/01/the-stretch-goal-paradox.
91. M. Egan, "Wells Fargo Uncovers Up to 1.4 Million More Fake Accounts," *CNN Money,* August 31, 2017, http://money.cnn.com/2017/08/31/investing/wells-fargo-fake-accounts/index.html?iid=EL; J. Wattles, B. Geier, and M. Egan, "Wells Fargo's 17-Month Nightmare," *CNN Money,* February 5, 2018, http://money.cnn.com/2018/02/05/news/companies/wells-fargo-timeline/index.html.
92. W. Boston, M. Spector, and A. Harder, "VW Scandal Threatens to Upend CEO," *The Wall Street Journal,* September 23, 2015, pp. A1, A2.
93. M. S. Gary, M. M. Yang, P. W. Yetton, and J. D. Sterman, "Stretch Goals and the Distribution of Organizational Performance," *Organization Science,* May 24, 2017, pp. 395–410.
94. D. Vandewalle, "Goal Orientation: Why Wanting to Look Successful Doesn't Always Lead to Success," *Organizational Dynamics,* November 2001, pp. 162–171; P. R. Sackett, C. H. Van Iddekinge, F. Lievens, and N. R. Kuncel, "Individual Differences and Their Measurement: A Review of 100 Years of Research," *Journal of Applied Psychology,* March 2017, pp. 254–273.
95. J. Lindzon, "10 Wildly Successful People on How They View Failure," *Fortune,* March 25, 2016, http://fortune.com/2016/03/25/successful-people-failure/.
96. J. Schroeder and A. Fishbach, "How to Motivate Yourself and Others? Intended and Unintended Consequences," *Research in Organizational Behavior* 35 (2015), pp. 123–141; E. A. Locke and G. P. Latham,

"Building a Practically Useful Theory of Goal Setting and Task Motivation," *American Psychologist,* September 2002, pp. 705–717.
97. G. P. Latham and E. A. Locke, "Enhancing the Benefits and Overcoming the Pitfalls of Goal Setting," *Organizational Dynamics,* November 2006, pp. 332–340.
98. M. Weinstein, "Race to the Finish," *Training,* November/December 2017, p. 48.
99. D. Morisano, J. B. Hirsh, J. B. Peterson, R. O. Phil, and B. M. Shore, "Setting, Elaborating, and Reflecting on Personal Goals Improves Academic Performance," *Journal of Applied Psychology,* March 2010, pp. 255–264.
100. A. Fox, "Put Plans into Action," *HRMagazine,* April 2013, pp. 27–31.
101. D. Meinert, "An Open Book," *HR Magazine,* April 2013, p. 46.
102. DDI Pulse of the Workforce Survey of 1,000 employees, reported in "Stagnating on the Job," *USA Today,* September 21, 2009, p. 1B.
103. G. R. Oldham and J. R. Hackman, "Not What It Was and Not What It Will Be: The Future of Job Design," *Journal of Organizational Behavior,* February 2010, pp. 463–479.
104. See the related discussion in S. Wagner-Tsukamoto, "An Institutional Economic Reconstruction of Scientific Management: On the Lost Theoretical Logic of Taylorism," *Academy of Management Review,* January 2007, pp. 105–117; P. R. Lawrence, "The Key Job Design Problem Is Still Taylorism," *Journal of Organizational Behavior,* February 2010, pp. 412–421.
105. M. A. Campion and C. L. McClelland, "Follow-Up and Extension of the Interdisciplinary Costs and Benefits of Enlarged Jobs," *Journal of Applied Psychology,* June 1993, pp. 339–351.
106. F. Herzberg, B. Mausner, and B. B. Snyderman, *The Motivation to Work* (New York: Wiley, 1959).
107. R. Levering, "The 100 Best Companies to Work For 2016," *Fortune,* March 15, 2016, p. 152.
108. J. R. Hackman and G. R. Oldham, *Work Redesign* (Reading, MA: Addison-Wesley, 1980).
109. S. K, Parker, F. P. Morgeson, and G. Johns, "One Hundred Years of Work Design Research: Looking Back and Looking Forward," *Journal of Applied Psychology,* March 2017, pp. 403–420.
110. Raytheon," *The Future of Talent: Advertising Supplement to The Wall Street Journal,* 2017, p. 31.
111. R. Kanfer, M. Frese, and R. E. Johnson, "Motivation Related to Work: A Century of Progress," *Journal of Applied Psychology,* March 2017, pp. 338–355; S. K. Parker, F. P. Morgeson, and G. Johns, "One Hundred Years of Work Design Research: Looking Back and Looking Forward," *Journal of Applied Psychology,* March 2017, pp. 403–420.
112. R. C. Rabin, "You're on the Clock: Doctors Rush Patients Out the Door," *USA Today,* April 20, 2014, https://www.usatoday.com/story/news/nation/2014/04/20/doctor-visits-time-crunch-health-care/7822161/; M. Tello, "Physicians, Paperwork, and Paying Attention to Patients," *Harvard Health Publishing,* October 31, 2016, https://www.health.harvard.edu/blog/physicians-paperwork-and-paying-attention-to-patients-2016103110558.
113. P. Ubel, "Your Doctor May Spend More Time with a Computer Than with You," *Forbes,* November 24, 2017, https://www.forbes.com/sites/peterubel/2017/11/24/your-doctor-may-spend-more-time-with-a-computer-than-with-you/#cad8f1f1ca5b.
114. S. B. Soumerai and R. Koppel, "Paying Doctors Bonuses for Better Health Outcomes Makes Sense in Theory. But It Doesn't Work," *Vox,* January 25, 2017, https://www.vox.com/the-big-idea/2017/1/25/14375776/pay-for-performance-doctors-bonuses.
115. A. Elejalde-Ruiz, "Employees Want Their Job to Matter, But Meaning at Work Can Be Hard to Find," *Chicago Tribune,* November 10, 2017, www.chicagotribune.com/business/careers/topworkplaces/ct-biz-top-workplaces-2017-main-story-meaningfulness-20170913-story.html.
116. A. Frost, "10 Companies That Make Sure You'll Never Feel Bored at Work," *The Muse,* www.themuse.com/advice/10-companies-that-make-sure-youll-never-feel-bored-at-work (accessed April 8, 2018).
117. Staff, "How to Balance Autonomy and Accountability in a Digital Workplace," *Broadsoft,* February 23, 2017, www.broadsoft.com/work-it/how-to-balance-autonomy-and-accountability-in-a-digital-workplace.
118. J. Gross, "What Motivates Us at Work? More than Money," *TED,* May 21, 2015, https://ideas.ted.com/what-motivates-us-at-work-7-fascinating-studies-that-give-insights/.
119. J. DeMers, "Research Says This Is the Secret to Being Happy at Work," *NBC News,* May 22, 2017, www.nbcnews.com/better/careers/research-says-secret-being-happy-work-n762926.
120. S. Lebowitz, "What It's Like to Work at HubSpot, One of the Best Workplaces of 2018," *Business Insider,* January 31, 2018, www.businessinsider.com/hubspot-best-workplaces-united-states-2018-1.
121. S. Lebowitz, "What It's Like to Work at HubSpot, One of the Best Workplaces of 2018," *Business Insider,* January 31, 2018, www.businessinsider.com/hubspot-best-workplaces-united-states-2018-1.
122. S. Maier, "What Google, Adobe, and Cargill Changed about Their Performance Management Strategies," *HR Daily Advisor,* November 3, 2017, https://hrdailyadvisor.blr.com/2017/11/03/google-adobe-cargill-changed-performance-management-strategies/.
123. E. L. Thorndike, *Educational Psychology: The Psychology of Learning,* Vol. II (New York: Columbia University Teachers College, 1913); B. F. Skinner, *Walden Two* (New York: Macmillan, 1948); B. F. Skinner, *Science and Human Behavior* (New York: Macmillan, 1953); D. Mozingo, "Contingencies of Reinforcement," in F. R. Volker (Ed.), *Encyclopedia of Autism Spectrum Disorders* (New York: Appleton-Century-Crofts, 1969), p. 799.
124. E. L. Thorndike, *Educational Psychology: The Psychology of Learning,* Vol. II (New York: Columbia University Teachers College, 1913).
125. W. Neuman, "Flights at JFK Sit on Tarmac for Hours," *The New York Times,* December 29, 2010, p. A23.
126. H. Martin, "Airlines Push to Roll Back Consumer-Protection Rules," *The Seattle Times,* March 23, 2018, https://www.seattletimes.com/business/boeing-aerospace/airlines-push-to-roll-back-consumer-protection-rules/.
127. *Fidelity Investments®Evaluate a Job Offer Study,* reported in J. Chew, "Why Millennials Would Take a $7,600 Pay Cut for a New Job," *Fortune,* April 8, 2016, http://fortune.com/2016/04/08/fidelity-millennial-study-career (accessed July 7, 2016).
128. J. Hofherr, "Millennials Would Take a $7,600 Pay Cut for a Better Work Life," *Boston.com,* April 8, 2016, https://www.boston.com/jobs/jobs-news/2016/04/08/millennials-work-life-balance-over-salary (accessed July 7, 2016).
129. J. Schramm, "Not Feeling the Love?" *HRMagazine,* February 2017, p. 65; Gallup Organization study, reported in A. Mann and N. Dvorack, "Employee Recognition: Low Cost, High Impact," Gallup, June 28, 2016, www.gallup.com/businessjournal/193238/employee-recognition-low-cost-high-impact.aspx?g_source=ELEMENT_4_RECOGNITION_AND_PRAISE&g_medium=topic&g_campaign= tiles (accessed July 7, 2016).
130. See "USA Snapshots: Lower Pay, Higher Happiness," *USA Today,* July 25, 2017, p. 4B.
131. R. Eisenberg, "What Workers Crave More than Money," *Forbes,* September 27, 2016, https://www.forbes.com/sites/nextavenue/2016/09/27/what-workers-crave-more-than-money/#23ea2a7b3150.
132. T. Francis and J. S. Lublin, "Divide Persists between Pay, Performance," *The Wall Street Journal,* June 3, 2016, pp. B1, B5.
133. "What Employers Need to Know about Paying Piece Rate," *NFIB,* July 18, 2016, https://www.nfib.com/content/legal-compliance/legal/what-employers-need-to-know-about-paying-piece-rate-74647/.
134. "Financial Advisor Compensation Package," *Edward Jones Careers,* http://careers.edwardjones.com/explore-opportunities/new-financial-advisors/compensation/compensation.html (accessed April 24, 2018).
135. "The Employee Ownership 100: America's Largest Majority Employee-Owned Companies," National Center for Employee Ownership, https://www.nceo.org/articles/employee-ownership-100 (accessed April 24, 2018).

136. M. Atih, "Using 'Gainsharing' to Achieve Sustainability Goals," *HDT Truckinginfo,* April 2, 2014, www.truckinginfo.com/blog/market-trends/story/2014/04/using-gainsharing-to-achieve-sustainability-goals.aspx (accessed July 5, 2016).
137. "The Progressive Corporation 2017 Gainsharing Plan," *Law Insider,* March 1, 2017, https://www.lawinsider.com/contracts/7zPD3wYRJ4lcDBuzvn8rhg/progressive-corporation/80661/2017-03-01.
138. M. Addady, "These 10 Companies Are Generous with Stock Options," *Fortune,* March 11, 2016, http://fortune.com/2016/03/11/equity-programs/.
139. J. Whitcomb, "Culture of Learning Supports High Employee Satisfaction," *Training,* July/August 2015, pp. 60–61.
140. J. Kauffman, "Pizza Performance Spun Off a Full-Scale Culinary Empire," *San Francisco Chronicle,* March 22, 2015, pp. A1, A4.
141. "Defining Success: 2013 Global Research Results," Accenture, www.accenture.com/SiteCollectionDocuments/PDF/Accenture-IWD-2013-Research-Deck-022013.pdf (accessed August 8, 2016); C. Brooks, "Career Success Means Work-Life Balance, Study Finds," *Huffington Post,* March 5, 2013, www.huffingtonpost.com/2013/03/05/career-success-means-work-life-balance_n_2812707.html.
142. *The Millennials: Confident. Connected. Open to Change,* Pew Research Center Publications, February 2010, www.pewsocialtrends.org/2010/02/24/millennials-confident-connected-open-to-change.
143. M. C. Bush and S. Lewis-Kulin, "100 Best Companies to Work For 2018," *Fortune,* March 1, 2018, p. 56.
144. Definition from I. E. Tatara, *Work-Life Benefits: Everything You Need to Know to Determine Your Work-Life Program* (Chicago: CCH KnowledgePoint, 2002), p. 2.
145. J. Sahadi, "No. 1 Cause of Bad Work-Life Balance? Bad Bosses," *CNNMoney,* April 21, 2015, http://money.cnn.com/2015/04/21/pf/work-life-balance (accessed August 1, 2016).
146. M. C. Bush and S. Lewis-Kulin, "100 Best Companies to Work For 2018," *Fortune,* March 1, 2018, pp. 55–78.
147. C. C. Miller, "Leaps in Leave, if Only Parents Would Take It," *The New York Times,* September 2, 2015, pp. A1, A3; R. Lieber, "Paid Leave for Fathers. Any Takers?" *The New York Times,* August 8, 2015, pp. B1, B5; R. E. Silverman, "Challenges of the 'Daddy Track,'" *The Wall Street Journal,* September 2, 2015, pp. B1, B5.
148. K. Doerer, "U.S. Has a Lousy Work-Life Balance," *PBS NewsHour,* July 3, 2015, www.pbs.org/newshour/updates/u-s-lousy-work-life-balance (accessed July 7, 2016).
149. "The 2015 Workplace Flexibility Study," *CareerArc,* 2017, http://web.careerarc.com/2015-workplace-flexibility-study.html (accessed May 2018); L. Dishman, "Why Managers and Employees Have Wildly Different Ideas about Work-Life Balance," *Fast Company,* February 5, 2015, www.fastcompany.com/3041908/the-future-of-work/the-surprising-gap-between-work-life-balance-beliefs-and-reality.
150. K. Strauss, "Flexing Their Muscle: 50 Companies Hiring Flex-Time Employees," *Forbes,* October 17, 2017, https://www.forbes.com/sites/karstenstrauss/2017/10/17/50-companies-hiring-armies-of-flexible-schedule-workers/#1a97302b6122.
151. P. Moen, E. L. Kelly, W. Fanc, S.-R.Leea, D. Almeidad, et al., "Does a Flexibility/Support Organizational Initiative Improve High-Tech Employees' Well-Being? Evidence from the Work, Family, and Health Network," *American Sociological Review,* February 2016, pp. 134–164.
152. C. Rexrode, "Citi to Millennials: Take a Year Off," *The Wall Street Journal,* March 17, 2016, pp. C1, C2.
153. L. Shen, "These 19 Great Employers Offer Paid Sabbaticals," *Fortune,* March 7, 2016, http://fortune.com/2016/03/07/best-companies-to-work-for-sabbaticals/.
154. M. Lang, "Unlimited Vacation Can Have Limited Benefits," *San Francisco Chronicle,* July 11, 2016, pp. D1, D2.
155. K. Tyler, "Sabbaticals Pay Off," *HR Magazine,* December 1, 2011, https://www.shrm.org/hr-today/news/hr-magazine/pages/1211tyler.aspx (accessed July 8, 2016).
156. A. Adkins and B. Rigoni, "Millennials Want Jobs to Be Development Opportunities," *Gallup,* June 30, 2016, http://news.gallup.com/businessjournal/193274/millennials-jobs-development-opportunities.aspx.
157. E. E. Gordon, "Training and Talent Development Regain Momentum," *Training Magazine,* https://trainingmag.com/trgmag-article/training-and-talent-development-regain-momentum (accessed April 24, 2018).
158. "2017 Training Industry Report," *Training Magazine,* https://trainingmag.com/trgmag-article/2017-training-industry-report (accessed April 24, 2018).
159. M. E. Seligman, *Flourish* (New York: Free Press, 2011).
160. B. L. Fredrickson and M. F. Losada, "Positive Affect in the Complex Dynamics of Human Flourishing," *American Psychologist,* 2005, pp. 678–686.
161. C. D. Ryff, B. H. Singer, and G. D. Love, "Positive Health: Connecting Well-Being with Biology," *Philosophical Transactions of the Royal Society of London, Biological Sciences,* September 29, 2004, pp. 1383–1394; C. L. M. Keyes and E. J. Simoes, "To Flourish or Not: Positive Mental Health and All-Cause Mortality," *American Journal of Public Health,* November 2012, p. 2164–2172; M. E. Seligman, *Flourish* (New York: Free Press, 2011).
162. D. Wilkie, "Help Keep Employees' Stress in Check," *HR Magazine,* May 2015, p. 16.
163. "Lee Hecht Harrison Poll Finds Most Workers Losing Sleep Due to Work-Related Stress," *Yahoo! Finance,* April 27, 2015, http://finance.yahoo.com/news/lee-hecht-harrison-poll-finds-100000997.html (accessed August 8, 2015); D. Meinert, "A Hidden Epidemic," *HR Magazine,* March 2016, pp. 31–36.
164. S. Barsade and O. A. O'Neill, "Manage Your Emotional Culture," *Harvard Business Review,* January–February 2016, p. 65.
165. J. Vatner, "Changing a Culture by Removing Walls," *The New York Times,* February 10, 2010, p. B7.
166. C. Congdon, D. Flynn, and M. Redman, "Balancing 'We' and 'Me,'" *Harvard Business Review,* October 2014, p. 57.
167. D. Ward, "Beyond the Open Office," *HR Magazine,* April 2015, pp. 31–35.
168. N. M. Ashkanasy, O. B. Ayoko, and K. A. Jehn, "Understanding the Physical Environment of Work and Employee Behavior: An Affective Events Perspective," *Journal of Organizational Behavior,* November 2014, pp. 1169–1184.
169. A. Hedge, quoted in P. Wen, "Drab Cubicles Can Block Workers' Creativity, Productivity," *San Francisco Chronicle,* March 10, 2000, pp. B1, B3; reprinted from *Boston Globe.*
170. A. Johnson, "It's True: A Nicer Office Can Boost Morale," *Arizona Republic,* September 3, 2007, www.azcentral.com/arizonarepublic/business/articles/0903biz-workenvironment0903.html; I. DeBare, "Shared Work Spaces a Sign of the Times," *San Francisco Chronicle,* February 19, 2008, pp. A1, A7.
171. T. Hill, "Tear Down Those Walls?" *Training,* January/February 2016, pp. 118–119.
172. D. Ward, "Beyond the Open Office," *HR Magazine,* April 2015, pp. 31–35.
173. Survey by B2B marketplace Approved Index, reported in K. Higgenbottom, "Bad Bosses at the Heart of Employee Turnover," *Forbes,* September 8, 2015, www.forbes.com/sites/karenhigginbottom/2015/09/08/bad-bosses-at-the-heart-of-employee-turnover/#35cfb2344075.
174. Gallup survey, reported in B. Snyer, "Half of Us Have Quit Our Job Because of a Bad Boss" *Fortune.com,* April 2, 2015, http://fortune.com/2015/04/02/quit-reasons/ (accessed July 6, 2016).
175. K. Sun, "How to Create a Culture of Gratitude in the Workplace," *Forbes,* December 18, 2017, www.forbes.com/sites/karlsun/2017/12/18/how-to-create-a-culture-of-gratitude-in-the-workplace/#7c1bfdb37a18.
176. A. Vetter, "Want to Win the Hearts and Minds of Your Employees? Do This 1 Simple Thing," *Inc,* December 20, 2017, https://www.inc.com/amy-vetter/want-to-win-hearts-minds-of-your-employees-do-this-1-simple-thing.html?cid=search.

177. K. Sun, "How to Create a Culture of Gratitude in the Workplace," *Forbes,* December 18, 2017, www.forbes.com/sites/karlsun/2017/12/18/how-to-create-a-culture-of-gratitude-in-the-workplace/#7c1bfdb37a18.
178. J. Baldoni, "Gratitude: A Lesson in Two Parts," *Forbes,* April 4, 2018, www.forbes.com/sites/johnbaldoni/2018/04/04/gratitude-a-lesson-in-two-parts/#46bfa7724414.
179. M. Biro, "5 Ways Leaders Rock Employee Recognition," *Forbes,* January 13, 2013, ww.forbes.com/sites/meghanbiro/2013/01/13/5-ways-leaders-rock-employee-recognition/#6476c8cd47ca.
180. R. McCammon, "The Power of Praise in Business—And How to Do It Right," *Entrepreneur,* January 27, 2012, www.entrepreneur.com/article/222573.
181. K. Sun, "How to Create a Culture of Gratitude in the Workplace," *Forbes,* December 18, 2017, www.forbes.com/sites/karlsun/2017/12/18/how-to-create-a-culture-of-gratitude-in-the-workplace/#7c1bfdb37a18.
182. J. Steinfeld, "5 Ways to Show Gratitude at Work," *Inc,* June 8, 2017, www.inc.com/jay-steinfeld/5-ways-gratitude-improves-your-bottom-line.html?cid=search.
183. A. Vetter, "Want to Win the Hearts and Minds of Your Employees? Do This 1 Simple Thing," *Inc,* December 20, 2017, https://www.inc.com/amy-vetter/want-to-win-hearts-minds-of-your-employees-do-this-1-simple-thing.html?cid=search.
184. E. Boxer, "Google and Disney Do This for Happier Employees. Here Are 5 Ways You Can Do It Too," *Inc,* November 16, 2017, www.inc.com/elisa-boxer/google-disney-do-this-for-happier-employees-here-are-5-ways-you-can-do-it-too.html?cid=search.
185. J. Bersin, "New Research Unlocks the Secret of Employee Recognition," *Forbes,* June 13, 2012, www.forbes.com/sites/joshbersin/2012/06/13/new-research-unlocks-the-secret-of-employee-recognition/2/#7b3f3bdf5ede.
186. E. Boxer, "Google and Disney Do This for Happier Employees. Here Are 5 Ways You Can Do It Too," *Inc,* November 16, 2017, www.inc.com/elisa-boxer/google-disney-do-this-for-happier-employees-here-are-5-ways-you-can-do-it-too.html?cid=search.
187. K. Sun, "How to Create a Culture of Gratitude in the Workplace," *Forbes,* December 18, 2017, www.forbes.com/sites/karlsun/2017/12/18/how-to-create-a-culture-of-gratitude-in-the-workplace/#7c1bfdb37a18.
188. E. Boxer, "Google and Disney Do This for Happier Employees. Here Are 5 Ways You Can Do It Too," *Inc,* November 16, 2017, www.inc.com/elisa-boxer/google-disney-do-this-for-happier-employees-here-are-5-ways-you-can-do-it-too.html?cid=search.
189. C. Preston, "Why Expressing Gratitude Is Good for Business and People," *Forbes,* November 9, 2017, www.forbes.com/sites/forbescoachescouncil/2017/11/09/why-expressing-gratitude-is-good-for-business-and-people/#3a4b7ac76eca.
190. T. Nordstrom, "3 Lessons in Gratitude Every Great Leader Needs to Know," *Inc,* June 29, 2017, www.inc.com/todd-nordstrom/travis-kalanicks-uber-resignation-teaches-us-a-val.html?cid=search.
191. S. Maier. "5 Companies Getting Employee Engagement Right." *Entrepreneur,* December 28, 2016, www.entrepreneur.com/article/285052.
192. B. Mikel, "Science Finds You'd Take a 32 Percent Pay Cut if Your New Job Offered This Instead," *Inc.,* October 3, 2017, https://www.inc.com/betsy-mikel/1-compelling-reason-why-youd-take-a-job-that-paid-32-percent-less-science-finds.html.
193. "The 25 Most Meaningful Jobs That Pay Well," *Forbes,* accessed April 24, 2018, https://www.forbes.com/pictures/efkk45elhld/the-25-most-meaningful-jobs-that-pay-well-2/#52fb6a264e55.
194. V. E. Frankl, *Man's Search for Meaning* (New York: Pocket Books, 1959).
195. L. Garrad and T. Chamorro-Premuzic, "How to Make Work More Meaningful for Your Team," *Harvard Business Review,* August 9, 2017, https://hbr.org/2017/08/how-to-make-work-more-meaningful-for-your-team.
196. M. E. Seligman, *Flourish* (New York: Free Press, 2011).
197. R. Levering, "The 100 Best Companies to Work for 2016," *Fortune,* March 15, 2016, pp. 143–165.
198. M. E. Seligman, *Flourish* (New York: Free Press, 2011).
199. M. Bush and S. Lewis-Kulin, "100 Best Companies to Work for 2018," *Fortune,* March 1, 2018, p. 55.
200. D. Linman, "Self-Management Skills for Employees, or How to be a Productive Employee," *MyMG,* January 10, 2011, http://www.mymanagementguide.com/self-management-skills-for-employees-or-how-to-be-a-productive-employee/.
201. "Productivity Stop Checking Off Easy To-Dos," *Harvard Business Review,* November-December 2017, p. 24.
202. L. Effron, C. Ng, and L. Pearle, "When Working 2 Fast Food Jobs, 16 Hours a Day Still Isn't Enough," *ABC News,* January 13, 2017, http://abcnews.go.com/US/working-fast-food-jobs-16-hours-day/story?id=44707695; M. Chen, "Five Myths about Fast-Food Work," *The Washington Post,* April 10, 2015, www.washingtonpost.com/opinions/five-myths-about-fast-food-work/2015/04/10/a62e9ab8-dee0-11e4-a500-1c5bb1d8ff6a_story.html?utm_term=.45002d4bd15e.
203. M. Tuma, "Fight for $15 Protests Fast Food Working Conditions," *Austin Chronicle,* October 14, 2016, www.austinchronicle.com/news/2016-10-14/fight-for-15-protests-fast-food-working-conditions/; T. Evans, "Big Mac and Fried: McDonald's Worker Slams 'Unbearable' Working Conditions after Kitchen Temperature Hit 37C," *The Sun,* June 20, 2017, www.thesun.co.uk/money/3836182/mcdonalds-worker-slams-unbearable-working-conditions-after-kitchen-temperature-hit-37c/; Bloomberg, "McDonald's Workers Say the Company Is Breaking Its Minimum Wage Pledge," *Fortune,* April 2, 2018, http://fortune.com/2018/04/02/mcdonalds-local-minimum-wage-pledge/?iid=sr-link1.
204. "Revenue of the Quick Service Restaurant (QSR) Industry in the United States from 2002 to 2020 (in Billion U.S. Dollars)," *Statista,* https://www.statista.com/statistics/196614/revenue-of-the-us-fast-food-restaurant-industry-since-2002/ (accessed April 25, 2018).
205. J. Woodhall-Melnik, "'It Was a Meaningless Job': Exploring Youth Post-Secondary Students' Employment in the Fast Food Industry," *Canadian Journal of Family and Youth* 10, no. 1 (2018), pp 275–298.
206. M. Locker, "The Fast-Food Industry Is Facing Record Turnover, But It's Not Flippy's Fault Yet," *Fast Company,* March 14, 2018, www.fastcompany.com/40544120/the-fast-food-industry-is-facing-record-turnover-but-its-not-flippys-fault-yet.
207. M. Rothschild, "These Are the Fast Food Chains That Treat Their Workers the Best (and Worst)," *Attn:,* June 30, 2017, www.attn.com/stories/18057/these-are-fast-food-chains-treat-their-workers-best-and-worst.
208. M. Chen, "Five Myths about Fast-Food Work," *Washington Post,* April 10, 2015, www.washingtonpost.com/opinions/five-myths-about-fast-food-work/2015/04/10/a62e9ab8-dee0-11e4-a500-1c5bb1d8ff6a_story.html?utm_term=.45002d4bd15e.
209. K. Norquay, "What I Learned from 4 Years Working at McDonald's," *Huffington Post,* December 3, 2016, www.huffingtonpost.com/kate-norquay/what-i-learned-four-years-working-at-mcdonalds_b_8682928.html.
210. M. Chen, "Five Myths about Fast-Food Work," *Washington Post,* April 10, 2015, www.washingtonpost.com/opinions/five-myths-about-fast-food-work/2015/04/10/a62e9ab8-dee0-11e4-a500-1c5bb1d8ff6a_story.html?utm_term=.45002d4bd15e; "Going Nowhere Fast: Limited Occupational Mobility in the Fast Food Industry," *National Employment Law Project,* July 2013, www.nelp.org/content/uploads/2015/03/NELP-Fast-Food-Mobility-Report-Going-Nowhere-Fast.pdf.
211. L. Effron, C. Ng, and L. Pearle, "When Working 2 Fast Food Jobs, 16 Hours a Day Still Isn't Enough," *ABC News,* January 13, 2017, http://abcnews.go.com/US/working-fast-food-jobs-16-hours-day/story?id=44707695.
212. L. Effron, C. Ng, and L. Pearle, "When Working 2 Fast Food Jobs, 16 Hours a Day Still Isn't Enough," *ABC News,* January 13, 2017, http://abcnews.go.com/US/working-fast-food-jobs-16-hours-day/story?id=44707695.

213. A. Traub, "Poverty Pay and CEO Windfalls: Why Fast Food Is the Most Unequal Industry in the US Economy," *Dēmos,* January 11, 2017, www.demos.org/publication/poverty-pay-and-ceo-windfalls-why-fast-food-most-unequal-industry-us-economy.

214. M. Rothschild, "These Are the Fast Food Chains That Treat Their Workers the Best (and Worst)," *Attn:,* June 30, 2017, www.attn.com/stories/18057/these-are-fast-food-chains-treat-their-workers-best-and-worst.

215. K. Norquay, "What I Learned from 4 Years Working at McDonald's," *Huffington Post,* December 3, 2016, www.huffingtonpost.com/kate-norquay/what-i-learned-four-years-working-at-mcdonalds_b_8682928.html.

216. E. Sherman, "Starbucks Baristas Reveal the Reasons They Hate Working There," *Food & Wine,* May 30, 2017, www.foodandwine.com/news/starbucks-baristas-reveal-reasons-they-hate-working-there.

217. D. Galarza, "More Than 1,200 Fast-Food Workers Are Organizing in NYC," *Eater,* January 10, 2018, www.eater.com/2018/1/10/16873540/fast-food-labor-workers-organizing-nyc.

218. K. Little, "McDonald's Conditions Are Hazardous, Workers Claim," *CNBC,* March 16, 2015, www.cnbc.com/2015/03/16/mcdonalds-conditions-are-hazardous-workers-claim.html.

219. M. Bloudoff-Indelicato, "Work Stress Is Bad For Everyone—But It Hurts One Group More than Anyone Else," *Quartz,* March 9, 2016, https://qz.com/643221/work-stress-is-bad-for-everyone-but-it-hurts-one-group-more-than-anyone-else/.

220. R. Muller, "Fast Food Industry Demands 'Emotional Labour' from Employees," *Psychology Today,* October 5, 2016, www.psychologytoday.com/us/blog/talking-about-trauma/201610/fast-food-industry-demands-emotional-labour-employees.

221. Bloomberg, "McDonald's Workers Say the Company Is Breaking Its Minimum Wage Pledge," *Fortune,* April 2, 2018, http://fortune.com/2018/04/02/mcdonalds-local-minimum-wage-pledge/?iid=sr-link1.

222. M. Locker, "The Fast-Food Industry Is Facing Record Turnover, But It's Not Flippy's Fault Yet," *Fast Company,* March 14, 2018, www.fastcompany.com/40544120/the-fast-food-industry-is-facing-record-turnover-but-its-not-flippys-fault-yet.

223. Bloomberg, "McDonald's Workers Say the Company Is Breaking Its Minimum Wage Pledge," *Fortune,* April 2, 2018, http://fortune.com/2018/04/02/mcdonalds-local-minimum-wage-pledge/?iid=sr-link1.

224. D. Galarza, "More than 1,200 Fast-Food Workers Are Organizing in NYC," *Eater,* January 10, 2018, www.eater.com/2018/1/10/16873540/fast-food-labor-workers-organizing-nyc; "New York City Expands Labor Rights for Fast Food Workers," *Fortune,* May 31, 2017, http://fortune.com/2017/05/31/new-york-city-rights-fast-food-workers/.

225. D. Galarza, "More than 1,200 Fast-Food Workers Are Organizing in NYC," *Eater,* January 10, 2018, www.eater.com/2018/1/10/16873540/fast-food-labor-workers-organizing-nyc.

226. "Wellness Programs," *Healthcare.gov,* www.healthcare.gov/glossary/wellness-programs/ (accessed April 23, 2018).

227. I. Ajunwa, "Workplace Wellness Programs Could Be Putting Your Health Data at Risk," *Harvard Business Review,* January 19, 2017, https://hbr.org/2017/01/workplace-wellness-programs-could-be-putting-your-health-data-at-risk.

228. L. Anderson, "Workplace Wellness Programs Are a Sham," *Slate,* September 1, 2016, www.slate.com/articles/health_and_science/the_ladder/2016/09/workplace_wellness_programs_are_a_sham.html.

229. "Workplace Health Glossary," Centers for Disease Control and Prevention, www.cdc.gov/workplacehealthpromotion/tools-resources/glossary/glossary.html (accessed April 23, 2018).

230. I. Ajunwa, "Workplace Wellness Programs Could Be Putting Your Health Data at Risk," *Harvard Business Review,* January 19, 2017, https://hbr.org/2017/01/workplace-wellness-programs-could-be-putting-your-health-data-at-risk.

231. L. Anderson, "Workplace Wellness Programs Are a Sham," *Slate,* September 1, 2016, www.slate.com/articles/health_and_science/the_ladder/2016/09/workplace_wellness_programs_are_a_sham.html.

CHAPTER 13

1. See J. Boss, "3 Practical Team Strategies for Managing the Fear of Conflict," *Forbes,* May 12, 2017, https://www.forbes.com/sites/jeffboss/2017/05/12/3-practical-team-strategies-for-managing-the-fear-of-conflict/#12fffe97569f; Forbes Coaches Council, "11 Ways You Can Better Resolve Conflicts," *Forbes,* November 14, 2017, https://www.forbes.com/sites/forbescoachescouncil/2017/11/14/11-ways-you-can-better-handle-conflict-resolution/#65f142202854; E. Aguilar, " Managing Conflict in School Leadership Teams," *Edutopia,* March 22, 2016, https://www.edutopia.org/blog/managing-conflict-school-leadership-teams-elena-aguilar; T. Bradberry, "6 Ways Nice People Can Master Conflict," *Inc.,* April 20, 2017, https://www.inc.com/travis-bradberry/6-ways-nice-people-can-master-conflict.html?cid=search.

2. P. F. Drucker, "The Coming of the New Organization," *Harvard Business Review,* January–February 1988, pp. 45–53.

3. K. Caprino, "How Companies Like Uber, Facebook and Salesforce Engage in Team-Building (It's Not What You Think)," *Forbes,* January 14, 2016, https://www.forbes.com/sites/kathycaprino/2016/01/14/how-companies-like-uber-facebook-and-salesforce-engage-in-team-building-its-not-what-you-think/#39757b9c3cc1

4. J. Diehl and D. Witt, "Work Team Training and Performance Goals," *Training,* July/August 2017, pp. 20–23.

5. This definition is based in part on one found in D. Horton Smith, "A Parsimonious Definition of 'Group': Toward Conceptual Clarity and Scientific Utility," *Sociological Inquiry,* Spring 1967, pp. 141–167.

6. J. R. Katzenbach and D. K. Smith, *The Wisdom of Teams: Creating the High- Performance Organization* (Boston: Harvard Business School Press, 1993), p. 45.

7. J. R. Katzenbach and D. K. Smith, "The Discipline of Teams," *Harvard Business Review,* March–April 1995, p. 112.

8. "The Untold Story: How Xero Took a Band Name and Changed Accounting for a Million Companies," *Business Insider,* September 12, 2017, http://www.businessinsider.com/the-untold-story-how-xero-took-a-band-name-and-changed-accounting-for-a-million-companies-2017-9.

9. R. Cross, N. Nohria, and A. Parker, "Six Myths about Informal Networks—and How to Overcome Them," *MIT Sloan Management Review,* Spring 2002, pp. 67–75; C. Shriky, "Watching the Patterns Emerge," *Harvard Business Review,* February 2004, pp. 34–35.

10. D. Krackhardt and J. R. Hanson, "Informal Networks: The Company behind the Chart," *Harvard Business Review,* July-August 1993, p. 104; R. Cross and L. Prusack, "The People Who Make Organizations Go—or Stop," *Harvard Business Review,* June 3003, pp. 104–112; R. McDermott and D. Archibald, "Harnessing Your Staff's Informal Networks," *Harvard Business Review,* March 2010, pp. 82–89.

11. R. Vincent, "Companies Recast Office Break Room as Collaborative Workspace," *Los Angeles Times,* December 31, 2014, http://www.latimes.com/business/la-fi-office-kitchens-20150101-story.html.

12. K. Kim, H. M. Collins, J. Williamson, and J. Chapman, *Participation in Adult Education and Lifetime Learning: 2000–01,* NCES 2004-050, U.S. Department of Education, National Center for Education Statistics (Washington, DC: U.S. Government Printing Office, 2008); L. Dublin, "Formalizing Informal Learning," *Chief Learning Officer,* March 2010, www.clomedia.com/features/2010/March/2870/index.php.

13. T. Lytle, "Catering to an Hourly Workforce," *HR Magazine,* April 2016, 49.

14. J. Stillman, "Google Is Giving Away Its Secrets to Low-Cost, High-Impact Training Absolutely Free," *Inc.com,* October 25, 2017, https://www.inc.com/jessica-stillman/googles-latest-free-guide-explains-its-low-cost-high-impact-approach-to-training.html?cid=search.

15. K. K. Spors, "Getting Workers to Share Their Know-How with Peers," *The Wall Street Journal,* April 3, 2008, p. B6.

16. Forrester Research, reported in R. Reitsma, "The Data Digest: How Democratization of Technology Empowers Employees," *Forrester Blogs,* February 11, 2011, http://blogs.forrester.com/reineke_reitsma/11-02-11-the_data_digest_how_democratization_of_technology_empowers_employees.

17. A. Davis, "Instead of Training, Use Storytelling to Build Employee Knowledge (and Address Challenges, Generate Ideas and Boost Teamwork)," *Inc.com,* March 27, 2018, https://www.inc.com/alison-davis/instead-of-training-use-storytelling-to-build-employee-knowledge-and-address-challenges-generate-ideas-boost-teamwork.html?cid=search.

18. R. Shah, "A New Organizational Learning Goal: The Accrual of Awareness," *Forbes,* May 1, 2012, www.forbes.com/sites/rawnshah/2012/05/01/a-new-organizational-learning-goal-the-accrual-of-awareness.

19. K. Pattison, "How Herman Miller Has Designed Employee Loyalty," September 22, 2010, http://www.fastcompany.com/1689839/how-herman-miller-has-designed-employee-loyalty.

20. "Our Living Office—Herman Miller Tokyo," *Herman Miller Research,* http://hermanmillerreach.com/en/Post/Story/48 (accessed April 27, 2018).

21. L. MacDonald, "What Is a Self-Managed Team," *Houston Chronicle,* 2016, http://smallbusiness.chron.com/selfmanaged-team-18236.html (accessed June 29, 2016).

22. D. W. Parker, M. Holesgrove, and R. Pathak, "Improving Productivity with Self-Organized Teams and Agile Leadership," *International Journal of Productivity and Performance Management,* 2015, pp. 112–128; C. Post, "When Is Female Leadership an Advantage? Coordination Requirements, Team Cohesion, and Team Interaction Norms," *Journal of Organizational Behavior,* 2015, pp. 1153–1175.

23. Based on three meta-analyses covering 70 studies. See P. S. Goodman, R. Devadas, and T. L. Griffith Hughson, "Groups and Productivity: Analyzing the Effectiveness of Self-Managed Teams," in J. P. Campbell, R. J. Campbell, and Associates (Eds.), *Productivity in Organizations* (San Francisco: Jossey-Bass, 1998), pp. 295–327; S. Kauffeld, "Self-Directed Work Groups and Team Competence," *Journal of Occupational and Organizational Psychology,* March 2006, pp. 1–21.

24. N. Collins, Y-M. Chou, and M. Warner, "Member Satisfaction, Communication and Role of Leader in Virtual Self-Managed Teamwork: Case Studies in Asia-Pacific Region," *Human Systems Management,* 2014, pp. 155–170.

25. "Trends in Global Virtual Teams," *RW3 Culture Wizard,* http://cdn.culturewizard.com/PDF/Trends_in_VT_Report_4-17-2016.pdf (accessed April 27, 2018).

26. L. Gilson, M. Maynard, N. Young, M. Varianien, and M. Hakonen, "Virtual Teams Research: 10 Years, 10 Themes, and 10 Opportunities," *Journal of Management,* July 2015, pp. 1313–1337.

27. E. E. Makarius and B. Z. Larson, "Changing the Perspective of Virtual Work: Building Virtual Intelligence at the Individual Level," *Academy of Management Review,* 2017, pp. 159–178.

28. J.E. Hoch and S. W. Kozlowski, "Leading Virtual Teams: Hierarchical Leadership, Structural Supports, and Shared Team Leadership," *Journal of Applied Psychology,* 2012, pp. 1–13.

29. "The Challenges of Working in Virtual Teams," *RW3 Culture Wizard,* http://rw-3.com/VTSReportv7.pdf.

30. "Virtual Teams," Society for Human Resource Management, July 13, 2012, https://www.shrm.org/hr-today/trends-and-forecasting/research-and-surveys/pages/virtualteams.aspx.

31. D. Newman, "5 Key Practices of Successful Remote Work Teams," *Forbes,* October 10, 2017, https://www.forbes.com/sites/danielnewman/2017/10/10/5-key-practices-of-successful-remote-work-teams/#65b7276d5168.

32. J. Hanson, "Virtual Is Viable: Making Your Virtual Firm a Real Success," *Forbes,* November 21, 2017, https://www.forbes.com/sites/forbesagencycouncil/2017/10/31/virtual-is-viable-making-your-virtual-firm-a-real-success/2/#45d6f93f218b.

33. See E. E. Makarius and B. Z. Larson, "Changing the Perspective of Virtual Work: Building Virtual Intelligence at the Individual Level," *Academy of Management Review,* 2017, pp. 159–178; C. Tate, "5 Ways to Make Working Remotely Actually Work," *Fast Company,* July 28, 2015, https://www.fastcompany.com/3048953/5-ways-to-make-working-remotely-actually-work.

34. J. Schiefelbein, "Smart Tips for Working with Your Virtual Teams," *Entrepreneur,* May 24, 2017, https://www.entrepreneur.com/article/292734.

35. See A. Bruzzese, "Keep Remote Workers in the Loop," *Arizona Republic,* March 2, 2011.

36. M. Shroy, "Five Tips for Leading a Virtual Team," *Forbes,* October 4, 2017, https://www.forbes.com/sites/forbesagencycouncil/2017/10/04/five-tips-for-leading-a-virtual-team/#ad5b8f625096.

37. J. Hanson, "Virtual Is Viable: Making Your Virtual Firm a Real Success," *Forbes,* November 21, 2017, https://www.forbes.com/sites/forbesagencycouncil/2017/10/31/virtual-is-viable-making-your-virtual-firm-a-real-success/2/#45d6f93f218b.

38. E. E. Makarius and B. Z. Larson, "Changing the Perspective of Virtual Work: Building Virtual Intelligence at the Individual Level," *Academy of Management Review,* 2017, pp. 159–178.

39. E. Martinez-Mareno, A. Zornoza, P. Gonzalez-Navarro, and L. F. Thompson, "Investigating Face-to-Face and Virtual Teamwork over Time: When Does Early Task Conflict Trigger Relationship Conflict?" *Group Dynamics: Theory, Research, and Practice,* 2012, pp. 159–171.

40. E. Meyer, "The Four Keys to Success with Virtual Teams," *Forbes.com,* August 19, 2010, http://www.forbes.com/2010/08/19/virtual-teams-meetings-leadership-managing-cooperation_print.html; R. F. Maruca, "How Do You Manage an Off-Site Team?" *BusinessWeek,* September 30, 2007, http://www.businessweek.com.

41. B. W. Tuckman, "Developmental Sequence in Small Groups," *Psychological Bulletin,* June 1965, pp. 384–399; B. W. Tuckman and M.A.C. Jensen, "Stages of Small-Group Development Revisited," *Group & Organization Studies,* December 1977, pp. 419–427.

42. D. Meinert, "Team Troubles," *HRMagazine,* February 2017, p. 18.

43. J.-L. Farh, C. Lee, and C. I. C. Farh, "Task Conflict and Team Creativity: A Question of How Much and When," *Journal of Applied Psychology* 95, no. 6 (2010), pp. 1173–1180.

44. Y. Zhang, "Functional Diversity and Group Creativity: The Role of Group Longevity," *Journal of Applied Behavioral Science,* March 2016, pp. 97–123.

45. T. Hall, "Does Cohesion Positively Correlate to Performance in All Stages of a Group's Life Cycle," *Journal of Organizational Culture, Communications and Conflict,* January 2015, pp. 58–69.

46. M. S. Cole, H. Bruch, and B. Vogel, "Energy at Work: A Measurement Validation and Linkage to Unit Effectiveness," *Journal of Organizational Behavior,* May, 2012, pp. 445–467.

47. For an application, see S. Kwak, "'Windows of Opportunity,' Revenue Volatility, and Policy Punctuations: Testing a Model of Policy Change in the American States," *Policy Studies Journal,* May 2017, pp. 265–288.

48. A. Hunt and B. Wheeler, "Brexit: All You Need to Know about the UK Leaving the EU," *BBC,* April 12, 2018, http://www.bbc.com/news/uk-politics-32810887.

49. Based on J. E. Mathieu, J. R. Hollenbeck, D van Knippenberg, and D. R. Ilgen, "A Century of Work Teams," *Journal of Applied Psychology,* March 2017, pp. 452-467; D. D. Warrick, "What Leaders Can Learn about Teamwork and Developing High Performance Teams from Organizations Development Practitioners," *Performance Improvement,* March 2016, pp. 13–21; T. Daniel, "Developing and Sustaining High-Performing Work Teams," SHRM, July 23, 2015, https://www.shrm.org/templatestools/toolkits/pages/developingandsustaininghigh-performanceworkteams.aspx.

50. For a review of related research, see J. E. Mathieu, J. R. Hollenbeck, D van Knippenberg, and D. R. Ilgen, "A Century of Work Teams," *Journal of Applied Psychology,* March 2017, pp. 452-467.

51. J. Hildreth and C. Anderson, "Failure at the Top: How Power Undermines Collaborative Performance," *Journal of Personality and Social Psychology,* February 2016, pp. 261–286.

52. J. Hu and R. Liden, "Making a Difference in the Teamwork: Linking Team Prosocial Motivation to Team Processes and Effectiveness," *Academy of Management Journal,* August 2015, pp. 1102–1127.

53. J. Hüffmeier, M. Filusch, J. Mazei, G. Hertel, A. Mojzisch, and S. Krumm, "On the Boundary Conditions of Effort Losses and Effort Gains in Action Teams," *Journal of Applied Psychology,* December 2017, pp. 1673–1685.

54. David Burkus, "Why Whole Foods Builds Its Entire Business on Teams," *Hartford Courant,* June 8, 2016, http://www.courant.com/business/top-workplaces/hc-tw14-whole-foods-20140921-story.html.

55. C. Duhigg, "What Google Learned from Its Quest to Build the Perfect Team," *The New York Times Magazine,* February 25, 2016, http://www.nytimes.com/2016/02/28/magazine/what-google-learned-from-its-quest-to-build-the-perfect-team.html?_r=0.

56. M. Schneider, "Google Spent 2 Years Studying 180 Teams. The Most Successful Ones Shared These 5 Traits," *Inc.,* July 19, 2017, https://www.inc.com/michael-schneider/google-thought-they-knew-how-to-create-the-perfect.html.

57. S. Shellenbarger, "The Invisible Walls at Work," *The Wall Street Journal,* November 29, 2017, p. A11.

58. D. Meinert, "Collaboration or Distraction?" *HRMagazine,* November 2017, p. 71.

59. K. M. Kniffin, J. Yan, B. Wansink, and W. D. Schulze, "The Sound of Cooperation: Musical Influences on Cooperative Behavior," *Journal of Organizational Behavior,* March 2017, pp. 372–390.

60. A. C. Costa, C. A. Fulmer, and N. R. Anderson, "Trust in Work Teams: An Integrative Review, Multilevel Model, and Future Directions," *Journal of Organizational Behavior,* 2018, pp. 169–184; B. A. De Jong, K. T. Dirks, and N. Gillespie, "Trust and Team Performance: A Meta-Analysis of Main Effects, Moderators, and Covariates," *Journal of Applied Psychology,* August 2016, pp. 1134–1150.

61. K. Caprino, "How Companies Like Uber, Facebook and Salesforce Engage in Team-Building (It's Not What You Think)," *Forbes,* January 14, 2016, http://www.forbes.com/sites/kathycaprino/2016/01/14/how-companies-like-uber-facebook-and-salesforce-engage-in-team-building-its-not-what-you-think/#7c9c52316157.

62. C. Clifford, "Uber's New CEO: 'I Have to Tell You, I am Scared,'" *CNBC,* August 30, 2017, https://www.cnbc.com/2017/08/30/new-uber-ceo-dara-khosrowshahi-i-am-scared.html.

63. G. Llopis, "4 Reasons Great Leaders Admit Their Mistakes," *Forbes,* July 23, 2015, https://www.forbes.com/sites/glennllopis/2015/07/23/4-reasons-great-leaders-admit-their-mistakes/2/#54037f8d6038.

64. "Don't Be Afraid to Be Vulnerable: 6 Ways to Build Trust with Your Team," *Inc.com,* January 22, 2018, https://www.inc.com/young-entrepreneur-council/dont-be-afraid-to-be-vulnerable-6-ways-to-build-trust-with-your-team.html?cid=search.

65. "Don't Be Afraid to Be Vulnerable: 6 Ways to Build Trust with Your Team," *Inc.com,* January 22, 2018, https://www.inc.com/young-entrepreneur-council/dont-be-afraid-to-be-vulnerable-6-ways-to-build-trust-with-your-team.html?cid=search.

66. M. Levin, "8 Ways to Build a Culture of Trust Based on Harvard's Neuroscience Research," *Inc.com,* October 5, 2017, https://www.inc.com/marissa-levin/harvard-neuroscience-research-reveals-8-ways-to-build-a-culture-of-trust.html?cid=search.

67. D. Williams, "How to Ask for Help When You're the Boss and You're Supposed to Know Everything," *Forbes,* October 10, 2016, https://www.forbes.com/sites/davidkwilliams/2016/10/10/how-to-ask-for-help-when-youre-the-boss-and-youre-supposed-to-know-everything/#5b66c9001f0a.

68. M. Levin, "8 Ways to Build a Culture of Trust Based on Harvard's Neuroscience Research," *Inc.com,* October 5, 2017, https://www.inc.com/marissa-levin/harvard-neuroscience-research-reveals-8-ways-to-build-a-culture-of-trust.html?cid=search.

69. "The Science of Trust," *Science of People,* December 13, 2017, https://www.scienceofpeople.com/the-science-of- trust/.

70. T. L. Rapp, D. G. Bachrach, A. A. Rapp, and R. Mullins, "The Role of Team Goal Monitoring in the Curvilinear Relationship between Team Efficacy and Team Performance," *Journal of Applied Psychology,* September 2014, pp. 976–987.

71. J. Schaubroeck, S. S. K. Lam, and S. E. Cha, "Embracing Transformational Leadership: Team Values and the Impact of Leader Behavior on Team Performance," *Journal of Applied Psychology,* July 2007, pp. 1020–1030.

72. E. Bernstein, J. Bunch, N. Canner, and M. Lee, "Beyond the Holacracy Hype," *Harvard Business Review,* July–August 2016, p. 43.

73. S. H. Courtright, G. R. Thurgood, G. L. Stewart, and A. J. Pierotti, "Structural Interdependence in Teams: An Integrative Framework and Meta-Analysis," *Journal of Applied Psychology,* November 2015, pp. 1825–1846.

74. S. H. Courtright, G. R. Thurgood, G. L. Stewart, and A. J. Pierotti, "Structural Interdependence in Teams: An Integrative Framework and Meta-Analysis," *Journal of Applied Psychology,* November 2015, pp. 1825–1846.

75. J. Kahnweiler, "Have We Gone Too Far in Promoting Collaboration?" *HRMagazine,* March 2018, pp. 26–27.

76. J. Morgan, "The Chief People Officer of Cisco Shares Her Top Three Tips for Building High-Performing Teams," *Forbes,* June 6, 2016, http://www.forbes.com/sites/jacobmorgan/2016/04/06/the-chief-people-officer-of-cisco-shares-her-top-three-tips-for-building-high-preforming-teams/#3c3d3b1051ce.

77. J. Y. Seong, W-W. Park, D-S. Hong, and Y. Shin, "Person-Group Fit: Diversity Antecedents, Proximal Outcomes, and Performance at the Group Level," *Journal of Management,* May 2015, pp. 1184–1213.

78. L. L. Gilson, M. T. Maynard, N. C. J. Young, M. Vartiainen, and M. Hakonen, "Virtual Team Research: 10 Years, 10 Themes, and 10 Opportunities," *Journal of Management,* July 2015, pp. 1313–1337.

79. "Teams: Another Argument for Cognitive Diversity," *Harvard Business Review,* July–August 2017, p. 32.

80. F. Hattke and S. Blaschke, "Striving for Excellence: The Role of Top Management Team Diversity in Universities," *Team Performance Management,* 2015, pp. 121–138.

81. D. M. Fisher, "Distinguishing between Taskwork and Teamwork Planning in Teams: Relations with Coordination and Interpersonal Processes," *Journal of Applied Psychology* 99, no. 3 (2014), pp. 423–436.

82. D. C. Feldman, "The Development and Enforcement of Group Norms," *Academy of Management Review,* January 1984, pp. 47–53.

83. D. C. Feldman, "The Development and Enforcement of Group Norms," *Academy of Management Review,* January 1984, pp. 47–53.

84. Jacob Morgan, "4 Things You Need to Know to Build a High Performing Team," *Inc.com,* April 7, 2017, https://www.inc.com/jacob-morgan/4-things-you-need-to-know-to-build-a-high-performing-team.html?cid=search.

85. Jacob Morgan, "4 Things You Need to Know to Build a High Performing Team," *Inc.com,* April 7, 2017, https://www.inc.com/jacob-morgan/4-things-you-need-to-know-to-build-a-high-performing-team.html?cid=search.

86. "Collaborative Team Structures: Norms," *Missouri EduSAIL,* http://www.moedu-sail.org/lessons/collaborative-team-structures-norms/ (accessed April 8, 2018).

87. S. Nawaz, "How to Create Executive Team Norms—and Make Them Stick," *Harvard Business Review,* January 15, 2018, https://hbr.org/2018/01/how-to-create-executive-team-norms-and-make-them-stick.

88. Dan Levy, "How to Build a Culture That Embraces Feedback," *Inc.com,* March 27, 2014, https://www.inc.com/dan-levy/feedback-is-crucial-for-any-leader.html.

89. Jeff Boss, "What to Do when Your Team Members Act Like Children," *Forbes,* February 1, 2018, https://www.forbes.com/sites/jeffboss/2018/02/01/what-to-do-when-your-team-members-act-like-children/#15c157e07d85.

90. S. Nawaz, "How to Create Executive Team Norms—and Make Them Stick," *Harvard Business Review,* January 15, 2018, https://hbr.org/2018/01/how-to-create-executive-team-norms-and-make-them-stick.

91. M. A. Marks, J. E. Mathieu, and S. J. Zaccaro, "A Temporally Based Framework and Taxonomy of Team Processes," *Academy of Management Review,* 2001, p. 357.

92. J. E. Mathieu and T. L. Rapp, "Laying the Foundation for Successful Team Performance Trajectories: The Roles of Team Charters and Performance Strategies," *Journal of Applied Psychology,* 2009, p. 92.

93. S. H. Courtright, B. W. McCormick, S. Mistry, and J. Wang, "Quality Charters of Quality Members? A Control Theory Perspective on Team Charters and Team Performance," *Journal of Applied Psychology,* October 2017, pp. 1462–1470; J. E. Mathieu and T. L. Rapp, "Laying the Foundation for Successful Team Performance Trajectories: The Roles of Team Charters and Performance Strategies," *Journal of Applied Psychology,* 2009, pp. 90–103.

94. J. Chen, P. A. Bamberger, Y. Song, and D. R. Vashdi, "The Effects of Team Reflexivity on Psychological Well-Being in Manufacturing Teams," *Journal of Applied Psychology,* April 2018, pp. 443–462.

95. A. N. Li, H. Liao, and B. M. Firth, "The Content of the Message Matters: The Differential Effects of Promotive and Prohibitive Team Voice on Team Productivity and Safety Performance Goals," *Journal of Applied Psychology,* August 2017, p. 1259.

96. S. Woo, "In Search of a Perfect Team," *The Wall Street Journal,* March 13, 2017, p. R6.

97. E. Bernstein, "When a Co-worker Is Stressed Out," *The Wall Street Journal,* August 26, 2008, pp. D1, D2.

98. J. A. Wall Jr. and R. Robert Callister, "Conflict and Its Management," *Journal of Management* 3 (1995), p. 517.

99. E-Y. Jeong, "Head of Korean Air Says Daughters Quit Posts Amid Uproar," *The Wall Street Journal,* April 23, 2018, p. B3.

100. D. Tjosvold, *Learning to Manage Conflict: Getting People to Work Together Productively* (New York: Lexington, 1993); D. Tjosvold and D. W. Johnson, *Productive Conflict Management Perspectives for Organizations* (New York: Irvington, 1983).

101. T. A. O'Neill, G. C. Hoffart, M. M. J. W. Mclarnon, H. J. Woodley, M. Eggermont, W. Rosehart, and R. Brennan, "Constructive Controversy and Reflexivity Training Promotes Effective Conflict Profiles and Team Functioning in Student Learning Teams," *Academy of Management Learning & Education,* 2017, pp. 257–276.

102. K. Yurieff, "Your Facebook Data Scandal Questions Answered," *CNN Tech,* April 11, 2018, http://money.cnn.com/2018/04/11/technology/facebook-questions-data-privacy/index.html; "If Facebook Will Not Fix Itself, Will Congress?" *The Economist,* April 11, 2018, https://www.economist.com/news/united-states/21740387-if-facebook-will-not-fix-itself-will-congress-fit-it-mr-zuckerberg-goes-washington.

103. M.-L. Chang, "On the Relationship between Intragroup Conflict and Social Capital in Teams: A Longitudinal Investigation in Taiwan," *Journal of Organizational Behavior,* January 2017, pp. 3–27; A. M. O'Leary-Kelly, R. W. Griffin, and D. J. Glew, "Organization-Motivated Aggression: A Research Framework," *Academy of Management Review,* January 1996, pp. 225–253.

104. D. Hansen, "7 Tips for Turning Conflict into Creativity," April 14, 2016, http://www.forbes.com/sites/drewhansen/2016/04/14/conflict-and-creativity/2/#2b90160920e6.

105. M. S. Hershcovis, B. Ogunfowora, T. C. Reich, and A. M. Christie, "Targeted Workplace Incivility: The Roles of Belongingness, Embarrassment, and Power," *Journal of Organizational Behavior,* 2017, pp. 1057–1075; D. Walker, D. D. van Jaarsveld, and D. P. Skarlicki, "Sticks and Stones Can Break My Bones but Words Can also Hurt Me: The Relationship between Customer Verbal Aggression and Employee Incivility," *Journal of Applied Psychology,* 2017, pp. 163–179.

106. C. Porath, "The Hidden Toll of Workplace Incivility," *McKinsey Quarterly,* December 2016, https://www.mckinsey.com/business-functions/organization/our-insights/the-hidden-toll-of-workplace-incivility.

107. "Work Related Stress on Employees Health," *EKU Online,* https://safetymanagement.eku.edu/resources/infographics/work-related-stress-on-employees-health/ (accessed April 27, 2018).

108. "Starbucks Policy Is Murky," *The Wall Street Journal,* April 23, 2018, p. B3.

109. K. A. Crowne, "What Leads to Cultural Intelligence?" *Business Horizons,* September–October 2008, pp. 391–399; N. Goodman, "Cultivating Cultural Intelligence," *Training,* March–April 2011, p. 38. On the subject of listening, see Bob Farrell, CEO of Kewill, interviewed by A. Bryant, "Always Take the Time to Listen," *The New York Times,* June 27, 2014, p. B2.

110. S. Bryant, "7 Tips for Managing Conflict in a Multicultural Workplace," *Country Navigator,* September 15, 2017, https://countrynavigator.com/blog/expert-view/managing-conflict-multicultural-team/.

111. S. Patel, "7 Lessons I Learned when I Started Speaking Internationally," *Inc.,* October 21, 2017, https://www.inc.com/sujan-patel/7-lessons-i-learned-when-i-started-speaking-intern.html?cid=search.

112. S. G. Katzenstein, "The Debate on Structured Debate: Toward a Unified Theory," *Organizational Behavior and Human Decision Processes,* June 1996, pp. 316–332.

113. C. Brooks, "Speak Up! Dissension Is Key to Successful Teamwork," *Business News Daily,* November 23, 2015, https://www.businessnewsdaily.com/8594-dissenting-voice-teamwork.html.

114. J. Winter, "How to Play the Devil's Advocate (without Being Evil)," *The Muse,* https://www.themuse.com/advice/how-to-play-the-devils-advocate-without-being-evil (accessed April 8, 2018).

115. J. Winter, "How to Play the Devil's Advocate (without Being Evil)," *The Muse,* https://www.themuse.com/advice/how-to-play-the-devils-advocate-without-being-evil (accessed April 8, 2018).

116. C. Mui, "3 Key Design Factors for an Effective Devil's Advocate," *Forbes,* April 23, 2014, https://www.forbes.com/sites/chunkamui/2014/04/23/3-keys-to-an-effective-devils-advocate/#2ce099fb83d1.

117. C. Brooks, "Speak Up! Dissension Is Key to Successful Teamwork," *Business News Daily,* November 23, 2015, https://www.businessnewsdaily.com/8594-dissenting-voice-teamwork.html.

118. C. Mui, "3 Key Design Factors for an Effective Devil's Advocate," *Forbes,* April 23, 2014, https://www.forbes.com/sites/chunkamui/2014/04/23/3-keys-to-an-effective-devils-advocate/#2ce099fb83d1.

119. C. Brooks, "Speak Up! Dissension Is Key to Successful Teamwork," *Business News Daily,* November 23, 2015, https://www.businessnewsdaily.com/8594-dissenting-voice-teamwork.html.

120. J. Winter, "How to Play the Devil's Advocate (without Being Evil)," *The Muse,* https://www.themuse.com/advice/how-to-play-the-devils-advocate-without-being-evil (accessed April 8, 2018).

121. J. Winter, "How to Play the Devil's Advocate (without Being Evil)," *The Muse,* https://www.themuse.com/advice/how-to-play-the-devils-advocate-without-being-evil (accessed April 8, 2018).

122. Adapted from T. Allessandra and P. Hunsaker, *Communicating at Work* (New York: Fireside, 1993), p. 107. See also the core emotional elements of negotiation (appreciation, affiliation, autonomy, status, and role) in R. Kreitner and A. Kinicki, *Organizational Behavior,* 10th ed. (New York: McGraw-Hill, 2013), p. 389.

123. M. A. Rahim, "A Strategy for Managing Conflict in Complex Organizations," *Human Relations,* January 1985, p. 84; and M. A. Rahim and N. R. Magner, "Confirmatory Factor Analysis of the Styles of Handling Interpersonal Conflict: First-Order Factor Model and Its Invariance across Groups," *Journal of Applied Psychology,* February 1995, pp. 122–132.

124. M. K. Stewart, "How Can You Be a More Effective Team Member," *Meeteor,* August 11, 2016, http://blog.meeteor.com/blog/effective-team-member.

125. K. Cherry, "What Is the Norm of Reciprocity?" *VeryWellMind,* April 21, 2018, https://www.verywellmind.com/what-is-the-rule-of-reciprocity-2795891.

126. A. Knight and N. Eisenkraft, "Positive Is Usually Good, Negative Is Not Always Bad: The Effects of Group Affect on Social Integration and Task Performance," *Journal of Applied Psychology,* 2015, pp. 1214–1227.

127. R. Serban, "The Teamwork Guide: How to Be a Better Team Player (Part 1)," *Hubgets,* May 16, 2017, https://www.hubgets.com/blog/teamwork-guide-better-team-player-part-1.

128. M. K. Stewart, "How Can You Be a More Effective Team Member," *Meeteor,* August 11, 2016, http://blog.meeteor.com/blog/effective-team-member.

129. J. Keyser, "Active Listening Leads to Business Success," *T+D*, July 2013, pp. 26–28.
130. J. Faulkner, "Beyond the Brainstorm: How to Be a Better Collaborator," *Proposify*, May 10, 2016, https://www.proposify.com/blog/collaborative-workplace.
131. "IBM," *Wikipedia*, https://en.wikipedia.org/wiki/IBM (accessed March 29, 2018).
132. A. Madrigal, "IBMs First 100 Years: A Heavily Illustrated Timeline," *The Atlantic*, June 16, 2011, https://www.theatlantic.com/technology/archive/2011/06/ibms-first-100-years-a-heavily-illustrated-timeline/240502/.
133. S. Lohr, "Even a Giant Can Learn to Run" *The New York Times*, December 31, 2011, https://www.nytimes.com/2012/01/01/business/how-samuel-palmisano-of-ibm-stayed-a-step-ahead-unboxed.html.
134. "IBM," *Wikipedia*, https://en.wikipedia.org/wiki/IBM (accessed March 29, 2018).
135. M. White, "IBM Is Telling Employees Who Work from Home to Come Back to the Office," *NBC News*, May 23, 2017, https://www.nbcnews.com/business/business-news/ibm-tells-its-remote-employees-get-back-office-n763441.
136. "International Business Machines Corporation (IBM) Stock Chart," NASDAQ, https://www.nasdaq.com/symbol/ibm/stock-chart?intraday=off&timeframe=5y&charttype=line&splits=on&earnings=off&movingaverage=None&lowerstudy=volume&comparison=off&index=&drilldown=off&sDefault=true (accessed March 30, 2018).
137. A. Ignatius, "Don't Try to Protect the Past," *Harvard Business Review*, July–August 2017, p. 128.
138. A. Ignatius, "Don't Try to Protect the Past," *Harvard Business Review*, July–August 2017, p. 128.
139. M. White, "IBM Is Telling Employees Who Work from Home to Come Back to the Office," *NBC News*, May 23, 2017, https://www.nbcnews.com/business/business-news/ibm-tells-its-remote-employees-get-back-office-n763441.
140. R. Waters, "IBM Is in a Fight to Keep Up with Big Spending Rivals in the Cloud," *Financial Times*, May 24, 2017, https://www.ft.com/content/290e2936-4054-11e7-9d56-25f963e998b2.
141. M. White, "IBM Is Telling Employees Who Work from Home to Come Back to the Office," *NBC News*, May 23, 2017, https://www.nbcnews.com/business/business-news/ibm-tells-its-remote-employees-get-back-office-n763441
142. J. Simons, "IBM, a Pioneer of Remote Work, Calls Workers Back to the Office," *The Wall Street Journal*, May 18, 2017, https://www.wsj.com/articles/ibm-a-pioneer-of-remote-work-calls-workers-back-to-the-office-1495108802?mg=prod/accounts-wsj.
143. C. Goman, "Why IBM Brought Remote Workers Back to the Office—and Why Your Company Might Be Next," *Forbes*, October 12, 2017, https://www.forbes.com/sites/carolkinseygoman/2017/10/12/why-ibm-brought-remote-workers-back-to-the-office-and-why-your-company-might-be-next/#69a36d4a16d.
144. S. Kasriel, "IBM's Remote Work Reversal Is a Losing Battle against the New Normal," *Fast Company*, July 18, 2017, https://www.fastcompany.com/40423083/ibms-remote-work-reversal-is-a-losing-battle-against-the-new-normal.
145. J. Simons, "IBM, a Pioneer of Remote Work, Calls Workers Back to the Office," *The Wall Street Journal*, May 18, 2017, https://www.wsj.com/articles/ibm-a-pioneer-of-remote-work-calls-workers-back-to-the-office-1495108802?mg=prod/accounts-wsj.
146. J. Simons, "IBM, a Pioneer of Remote Work, Calls Workers Back to the Office," *The Wall Street Journal*, May 18, 2017, https://www.wsj.com/articles/ibm-a-pioneer-of-remote-work-calls-workers-back-to-the-office-1495108802?mg=prod/accounts-wsj.
147. C. Isidore, "IBM Tells Employees Working at Home to Get Back to the Office," *CNN Tech*, May 19, 2017, http://money.cnn.com/2017/05/19/technology/ibm-work-at-home/index.html.
148. J. Useem, "When Working from Home Doesn't Work," *The Atlantic*, October 3, 2017, https://www.theatlantic.com/magazine/archive/2017/11/when-working-from-home-doesnt-work/540660/.
149. D. Madden, "IBM Forces Workers to Colocate and Here's Why," *Huffington Post*, September 21, 2017, https://www.huffingtonpost.com/entry/ibm-forces-workers-to-colocate-and-heres-why_us_59c27fb2e4b082fd4205bb57.
150. Y. Solomon, "Why IBM Move to Eliminate Remote Work Was the Right Thing to Do," *Inc.*, March 28, 2017, https://www.inc.com/yoram-solomon/ibms-move-to-eliminate-remote-work-was-right-even-if-it-wasnt-popular.html.
151. J. Boss, "Why IBM's Move to Rein in Remote Workers Isn't the Answer," *Forbes*, May 19, 2017, https://www.forbes.com/sites/jeffboss/2017/05/19/why-ibms-move-to-rein-in-remote-workers-isnt-the-answer/#4ebaef293de0.
152. M. Zent, "5 Ways to Effectively Lead Remote Teams," *Entrepreneur*, August 20, 2015, https://www.entrepreneur.com/article/249651.
153. S. Kasriel, "IBM's Remote Work Reversal Is a Losing Battle against the New Normal," *Fast Company*, July 18, 2017, https://www.fastcompany.com/40423083/ibms-remote-work-reversal-is-a-losing-battle-against-the-new-normal.
154. J. Simons, "IBM, a Pioneer of Remote Work, Calls Workers Back to the Office," *Fox Business*, May 19, 2017, https://www.foxbusiness.com/features/ibm-a-pioneer-of-remote-work-calls-workers-back-to-the-office.
155. S. Kasriel, "IBM's Remote Work Reversal Is a Losing Battle against the New Normal," *Fast Company*, July 18, 2017, https://www.fastcompany.com/40423083/ibms-remote-work-reversal-is-a-losing-battle-against-the-new-normal.
156. C. Isidore, "IBM Tells Employees Working at Home to Get Back to the Office," *CNN Tech*, May 19, 2017, http://money.cnn.com/2017/05/19/technology/ibm-work-at-home/index.html.
157. M. White, "IBM Is Telling Employees Who Work from Home to Come Back to the Office," *NBC News*, May 23, 2017, https://www.nbcnews.com/business/business-news/ibm-tells-its-remote-employees-get-back-office-n763441.
158. Z. Mejia, "Why Marissa Mayer Is the 'Least Likable' CEO in Tech," *CNBC*, June 1, 2017, https://www.cnbc.com/2017/05/31/why-yahoo-ceo-marissa-mayer-is-the-least-likable-ceo-in-tech.html.
159. M. Berke, J. Berke, and S. Gould, "This Map Shows Every State That Has Legalized Marijuana," *Business Insider*, January 23, 2018, http://www.businessinsider.com/legal-marijuana-states-2018-1.
160. J. Berr, "Should Employers Keep Testing Workers for Pot?" *CBS News*, February 16, 2018, https://www.cbsnews.com/news/should-employers-keep-testing-workers-for-pot/.

CHAPTER 14

1. J. Galvin, "Why You Should Focus on Developing Yourself as a Leader —and 5 Ways to Start," *Inc.*, April 13, 2018, https://www.inc.com/joe-galvin/5-tough-questions-to-ask-yourself-to-become-a-better-leader.html?cid=search.
2. R. G. Lord, D. V. Day, S. J. Zaccaro, B. J. Avolio, and A. H. Eagly, "Leadership in Applied Psychology: Three Ways of Theory and Research," *Journal of Applied Psychology*, March 2017, pp. 434–451.
3. S. Stein Smith, " 4 Tips to Help Improve Your Leadership Skills," *Inc.*, August 7, 2017, https://www.inc.com/sean-stein-smith/leadership-traits-every-entrepreneur-needs-to-have.html?cid=search.
4. S. Stein Smith, " 4 Tips to Help Improve Your Leadership Skills," *Inc.*, August 7, 2017, https://www.inc.com/sean-stein-smith/leadership-traits-every-entrepreneur-needs-to-have.html?cid=search.
5. B. Green, "This Is How Elon Musk Handles Bad Situations. Every Business Leader Should Take Note," *Inc.*, January 23, 2018, https://www.inc.com/bill-green/elon-musk-other-leaders-should-handle-all-situations-good-bad-like-this.html?cid=search.
6. B. Green, "This Is How Elon Musk Handles Bad Situations. Every Business Leader Should Take Note," *Inc.*, January 23, 2018, https://www.inc.com/bill-green/elon-musk-other-leaders-should-handle-all-situations-good-bad-like-this.html?cid=search.

7. R. Power, "Acing Leadership: How to Make Your Employees Feel Valued," *Inc.*, January 9, 2018, https://www.inc.com/rhett-power/acing-leadership-how-to-make-your-employees-feel-valued.html?cid=search.
8. M. Schwantes, "7 Harsh Truths That Will Improve Your Leadership Skills Overnight," *Inc.*, March 27, 2018, https://www.inc.com/marcel-schwantes/7-brutal-truths-every-smart-leader-needs-to-constantly-revisit.html?cid=search.
9. J. Ehrlich, "Mindful Leadership: Focusing Leaders and Organizations," *Organizational Dynamics*, October–December 2017, pp. 233–243.
10. J. Scheltgen, "This 10 Minute Daily Exercise Can Make You a Surprisingly Better Leader," *Inc.*, March 13, 2018, https://www.inc.com/jordan-scheltgen/this-10-minute-daily-exercise-can-make-you-a-surprisingly-better-leader.html?cid=search.
11. L. Garnett, "5 Leadership Rules From the Past That Don't Work Now (If You're Doing Any of These, Stop)," *Inc.*, April 2, 2018, https://www.inc.com/laura-garnett/5-leadership-rules-from-past-that-dont-work-now-if-youre-doing-any-of-these-stop-now.html?cid=search.
12. P. G. Northouse, *Leadership: Theory and Practice*, 6th ed. (Thousand Oaks, CA: Sage, 2012), p. 3.
13. C. N. Lacerenza, D. L. Reyes, S. L. Marlow, D. L. Joseph, and E. Salas, "Leadership Training Design, Delivery, and Implementation: A Meta-Analysis," *Journal of Applied Psychology*, December 2017, pp. 1686–1718; M. Leimbach, "Developing Tomorrow's Leaders Today," *Training*, May/June 2017, pp. 38–43.
14. "What Is Leadership Coaching (And How to Use It for Career Development)?" *Cleverism*, February 21, 2017, https://www.cleverism.com/leadership-coaching-and-career-development.
15. "What Is Leadership Coaching (And How to Use It for Career Development)?" *Cleverism*, February 21, 2017, https://www.cleverism.com/leadership-coaching-and-career-development.
16. T. J. Quigley and D. C. Hambrick, "Has the 'CEO Effect' Increased in Recent Decades? A New Explanation for the Great Rise in America's Attention to Corporate Leaders," *Strategic Management Journal*, 2015, pp. 21–830.
17. B. M. Bass and R. Bass, *The Bass Handbook of Leadership: Theory, Research, and Managerial Applications*, 4th ed. (New York: Free Press, 2008), p. 654.
18. R. Cross, N. Nohria, and A. Parker, "Six Myths about Informal Networks—and How to Overcome Them," *MIT Sloan Management Review*, Spring 2002, pp. 67–75; C. Shriky, "Watching the Patterns Emerge," *Harvard Business Review*, February 2004, pp. 34–35.
19. D. Krackhardt and J. R. Hanson, "Informal Networks: The Company behind the Chart," *Harvard Business Review*, July–August 1993, p. 104; R. Cross and L. Prusack, "The People Who Make Organizations Go—or Stop," *Harvard Business Review*, June 3003, pp. 104–112; R. McDermott and D. Archibald, "Harnessing Your Staff's Informal Networks," *Harvard Business Review*, March 2010, pp. 82–89.
20. M. Uhl-Bien and M. Arena, "Complexity Leadership: Enabling People and Organizations for Adaptability," *Organizational Dynamics*, January–March 2017, pp. 9–20.
21. G. A. Yukl, *Leadership in Organizations*, 7th ed. (Upper Saddle River, NJ: Prentice Hall, 2008), p. 8.
22. J. P. Kotter, "What Leaders Really Do," *Harvard Business Review*, December 2001, pp. 85–96; the role of leadership within organizational change is discussed in J. P. Kotter, *Leading Change* (Boston: Harvard Business School Press, 1996).
23. Managing in the world of complexity is discussed in G. Sargut and R. G. McGrath, "Learning to Live with Complexity," *Harvard Business Review*, September 2011, pp. 68–76; M. J. Mauboussin, "Embracing Complexity," *Harvard Business Review*, September 2011, pp. 88–92.
24. A review of power research can be found in K. Weir, "Power Play," *Monitor on Psychology*, April 2017, pp. 40-44; and R. E. Sturm and J. Antonakis, "Interpersonal Power: A Review, Critique, and Research Agenda," *Journal of Management*, January 2015, pp. 136–163.
25. T. McGhee, "Top Small Workplace 2018: Zoom Video Communications Prioritizes Employee Career Opportunities," *The Denver Post*, April 20, 2018, https://www.denverpost.com/2018/04/20/top-small-workplace-zoom-video-communications/.
26. B. George, "The Massive Difference between Negative and Positive Leadership," March 21, 2016, http://fortune.com/2016/03/21/negative-positive-leadership-politics-ford-alan-mulally/?iid=sr-link2 (accessed July 2016.)
27. L. Reston, "Jeb Bush's Leadership Style: Tough, Methodical, Sometimes Rigid," *Forbes*, June 16, 2015, http://www.forbes.com/sites/laurareston/2015/06/16/jeb-bushs-leadership-style-tough-methodical-sometimes-rigid/#238ad7ffbf8a (accessed July 2016).
28. C. Gallo, "40 Years Later, Steve Jobs' Success Secrets Still Apply to Aspiring Leaders," *Forbes*, March 21, 2016, http://www.forbes.com/sites/carminegallo/2016/03/31/40-years-later-steve-jobs-success-secrets-still-apply-to-aspiring-leaders/#57fc24319b75 (accessed July 2016).
29. K. Blazek, "A Participatory Leadership Style: Nike's CEO Mark Parker," January 19, 2016, http://www.boothco.com/360-feedback-resources/leadership-style-nikes-ceo-mark-parker/ (accessed July 2016).
30. J. Henderson, "5 Ways to Exert Your Influence at Work—without Making Office Enemies," *Forbes*, February 27, 2015, http://www.forbes.com/sites/learnvest/ 2015/02/27/5-ways-to-exert-your-influence-at-work-without-making-office-enemies/ #480f3f176e9b (accessed July 2016).
31. "Tips for Writing Effective Personal Fundraising Emails," February 1, 2016, http://support.causevox.com/article/123-tips-for-writing-effective-personal-fundraising- appeals (accessed July 2016).
32. C. Da Silva, "No Border Wall, No DACA, Trump Warns Democrats as Schumer Withdraws Funding Offer," *Newsweek*, January 24, 2018, http://www.newsweek.com/trump-vows-not-help-dreamers-unless-democrats-agree-support-border-wall-after-789166.
33. A. Goldman, "Lust, Favors and Nepotism: Leadership Promotions Turn Toxic," *Psychology Today*, January 2, 2015, https://www.psychologytoday.com/blog/transforming-toxic- leaders/201501/lust-favors-and-nepotism-leadership-promotions-turn-toxic (accessed July 2016).
34. D. Schawbel, "Cory Booker: Leading through Uniting People and Communities," *Forbes*, February 16, 2016, http://www.forbes.com/sites/danschawbel/2016/02/16/cory-booker-leading-through-uniting-people-and-communities/#5fb2f4c9444b (accessed July 2016).
35. C. Myers, "Why Bullies Make Bad Leaders," *Forbes*, April 2, 2016, http://www.forbes.com/sites/chrismyers/2016/04/01/why-bullies-make-bad-leaders/2/ #4184b2d03b49 (accessed July 2016).
36. J. Calfas, "This Is the Moment Sen. Tammy Duckworth and Her Baby Made History on the Senate Floor," *Time*, April 19, 2018, http://time.com/5247060/tammy-duckworth-vote-baby-senate-floor/.
37. J. Bach, "Phebe Novakovic Hardly Ever Speaks in Public. In a Rare Appearance, the General Dynamics CEO Says Why," *Washington Business Journal*, May 19, 2016, https://www.bizjournals.com/washington/blog/fedbiz_daily/2016/05/phebe-novakovic-hardly-ever-speaks-in-public-in-a.html; C. A. Robbins, "The Spy in General Dynamics' Corner Office," *Fortune*, September 11, 2015, http://fortune.com/2015/09/11/phebe-novakovic-general-dynamics/.
38. R. M. Stogdill, *Handbook of Leadership* (New York: Free Press, 1974); B. M. Bass and R. Bass, *The Bass Handbook of Leadership: Theory, Research, and Managerial Applications*, 4th ed. (New York: Free Press, 2008). An udpate on the role of intelligence can be found in M. Daly, M. Egan, and F. O'Reilly, "Childhood General Cognitive Ability Predicts Leadership Role Occupancy across Life: Evidence from 17,000 Cohort Study Participants," *The Leadership Quarterly*, 2015, pp. 323–341.
39. B. M. Bass and R. Bass, *The Bass Handbook of Leadership: Theory, Research, and Managerial Applications*, 4th ed. (New York: Free Press, 2008).
40. D. S. DeRue, J. D. Nahrgang, N. Wellman, and S. E. Humphrey, "Trait and Behavioral Theories of Leadership: An Integration and Meta-Analytic Test of Their Relative Validity," *Personnel Psychology* 64 (2011), pp. 7–52.
41. These results are based on D. S. DeRue, J. D. Nahrgang, N. Wellman, S. E. Humphrey, "Trait and Behavioral Theories of

Leadership: An Integration and Meta-Analytic Test of Their Relative Validity," *Personnel Psychology* 64 (2011), pp. 7–52; D. L. Joseph, L Y. Dhanani, W. Shen, B. C. McHugh, and M. A. McCord, "Is a Happy Leader a Good Leader? A Meta-Analytic Investigation of Leader Trait Affect and Leadership," *The Leadership Quarterly,* 2015, pp. 558–577; E. H. O'Boyle Jr., D. F. Forsyth, G. C. Banks, and M. A. McDaniel, "A Meta-Analysis of the Dark Triad and Work Behavior: A Social Exchange Perspective," *Journal of Applied Psychology,* May 2012, pp. 557–579.

42. S. M. Spain, P. Harms, and J. M. Lebreton, "The Dark Side of Personality at Work," *Journal of Organizational Behavior,* February 2014, pp. S41–S60.

43. D. Montano, A. Reeske, F. Franke, and J. Hüffmeier, "Leadership. Followers' Mental Health and Job Performance in Organizations: A Comprehensive Meta-Analysis from an Occupational Health Perspective," *Journal of Organizational Behavior,* March 2017, pp. 327–350.

44. D. Montano, A. Reeske, F. Franke, and J. Hüffmeier, "Leadership. Followers' Mental Health and Job Performance in Organizations: A Comprehensive Meta-Analysis from an Occupational Health Perspective," *Journal of Organizational Behavior,* March 2017, pp. 509–537; and O'Boyle et al., "A Meta-Analysis of the Dark Triad and Work Behavior," *Journal of Applied Psychology* 97, no. 3 (May 2012), pp. 557–579.

45. J. Hogan, R. Hogan, and R. B. Kaiser, "Management Derailment," in S. Zedeck (Ed.), *APA Handbook of Industrial and Organizational Psychology* (Washington, DC: American Psychological Association, 2011), pp. 555–575; M F. R. Kets de Vries, "Coaching the Toxic Leader," *Harvard Business Review,* April 2014, pp. 101–109.

46. H. Liu, J. T-J. Chiang, R. Fehr, M. Xu, and S. Wang, "How Do Leaders React When Treated Unfairly? Leader Narcissism and Self-Interested Behavior in Response to Unfair Treatment," *Journal of Applied Psychology,* November 2017, pp. 1590–1599.

47. T. Charmrro-Premuzic, "Could Your Personality Derail Your Career?" *Harvard Business Review,* September–October 2017, pp. 138–141; D. Meinert, "Why Leaders Fail," *HRMagazine,* October 2017, p. 18.

48. J. Marcus, "Why Men Are the New College Minority," *The Atlantic,* August 8, 2017, https://www.theatlantic.com/education/archive/2017/08/why-men-are-the-new-college-minority/536103/; M. DeWolf, "12 Stats about Working Women," *U.S. Department of Labor Blog,* March 1, 2017, https://blog.dol.gov/2017/03/01/12-stats-about-working-women.

49. V. Zarya, "The 2017 Fortune 500 Includes a Record Number of Women CEOs," *Fortune,* June 7, 2017, http://fortune.com/2017/06/07/fortune-women-ceos/?iid=sr-link1.

50. Bloomberg, "You May Want to Buy Stock in Companies Run by Female CEOs. Here's Why," *Fortune,* August 1, 2017, http://fortune.com/2017/08/01/female-ceo-stock-returns/?iid=sr-link2.

51. S-H. Jeong and D. A. Harrison, "Glass Breaking, Strategy Making, and Value Creating: Meta-Analytic Outcomes of Women as CEOs and TMT Members," *Academy of Management Journal,* August 2017, pp. 1219–1252.

52. A. H. Eagly and S. J. Karau, "Gender and the Emergence of Leaders: A Meta-Analysis," *Journal of Personality and Social Psychology,* May 1991, pp. 685–710; R. Ayman and K. Korabik, "Leadership: Why Gender and Culture Matter," *American Psychologist,* April 2010, pp.157–170.

53. A. H. Eagly, S. J. Karau, and B. T. Johnson, "Gender and Leadership Style among School Principals: A Meta-Analysis," *Educational Administration Quarterly,* February 1992, pp. 76–102.

54. R. Hosie, "Women Are Better Leaders than Men, Study of 3,000 Managers Concludes," *Independent,* March 30, 2017, https://www.independent.co.uk/life-style/women-better-leaders-men-study-a7658781.html.

55. S. C. Paustian-Underdahl, L. S. Walker, and D. J. Woehr, "Gender and Perceptions of Leadership Effectiveness: A Meta-Analysis of Contextual Moderators," *Journal of Applied Psychology,* November 2014, pp. 1129–1145.

56. A. Selko, "Confidence Is Top Leadership Difference between Women and Men," *Industry Week,* March 8, 2016, http://www.industryweek.com/leadership/confidence-top-leadership-difference-between-women-and-men.

57. A. Selko, "Confidence Is Top Leadership Difference between Women and Men," *Industry Week,* March 8, 2016, http://www.industryweek.com/leadership/confidence-top-leadership-difference-between-women-and-men.

58. A. Selko, "Confidence Is Top Leadership Difference between Women and Men," *Industry Week,* March 8, 2016, http://www.industryweek.com/leadership/confidence-top-leadership-difference-between-women-and-men.

59. A. Selko, "Confidence Is Top Leadership Difference between Women and Men," *Industry Week,* March 8, 2016, http://www.industryweek.com/leadership/confidence-top-leadership-difference-between-women-and-men.

60. B. Marcus, "New Research Reveals Society's Attitude about Gender Differences," *Forbes,* December 5, 2017, https://www.forbes.com/sites/bonniemarcus/2017/12/05/new-research-reveals-societys-attitude-about-gender-differences/#5f46b24467c5.

61. B. Marcus, "New Research Reveals Society's Attitude about Gender Differences," *Forbes,* December 5, 2017, https://www.forbes.com/sites/bonniemarcus/2017/12/05/new-research-reveals-societys-attitude-about-gender-differences/#5f46b24467c5.

62. E. Bono, P. W. Braddy, Y. Liu, E. K. Gilbert, J. W. Fleenor, L. N. Quast, and B. A. Center, "Dropped on the Way to the Top: Gender and Managerial Derailment," *Personnel Psychology,* 2017, pp. 729–768.

63. V. K. Gupta, S. Han, S. C. Mortal, S. Silveri, and D. B. Turban, "Do Women CEOs Face Greater Threat of Shareholder Activism Compared to Male CEOs? A Role Congruity Perspective," *Journal of Applied Psychology,* February 2018, p. 232.

64. S. Rodrick, "Justin Trudeau: The North Star," *Rolling Stone,* July 26, 2017, www.rollingstone.com/politics/features/justin-trudeau-canadian-prime-minister-free-worlds-best-hope-w494098.

65. S. Reva, "5 Leadership Lessons from Canadian Prime Minister Justin Trudeau," *Fast Company,* June 29, 2016, www.fastcompany.com/3061046/5-leadership-lessons-from-canadian-prime-minister-justin-trudeau.

66. "The Three Pillars of Merkelism," *The Economist,* September 9, 2017, www.economist.com/blogs/kaffeeklatsch/2017/09/how-understand-angela-merkel.

67. J. Chase, "Angela Merkel Defends Germany Accepting 10,000 UN Refugees," *DW,* April 23, 2018, www.dw.com/en/angela-merkel-defends-germany-accepting-10000-un-refugees/a-43499515.

68. K. Vick, "Person of the Year 2015: Chancellor of the Free World," *Time,* http://time.com/time-person-of-the-year-2015-angela-merkel/ (accessed April 23, 2018).

69. R. Reiss, "Leaders Share How the Cognitive Era Is Transforming Business," *Forbes,* January 6, 2016, http://www.forbes.com/sites/robertreiss/2016/01/06/ leaders-share-how-the-cognitive-era-is-transforming-business/#701183b125f7 (accessed July 2016).

70. A. Colberg, "Fortune 500 CEO: The One Quality Every Leader Must Have," *Fortune,* May 9, 2016, http://fortune.com/2016/05/09/fortune-500-assurant-ceo-success-quality/, accessed July 2016.

71. L. Shaw, "Top Three Leadership Skills Often Overlooked," *Forbes,* November 7, 2015, http://www.forbes.com/sites/lyndashaw/2015/11/07/top-three-leadership-skills-often-overlooked/#177653f6775f (accessed July 2016).

72. S. Krupp, "Growing Your Business: Strategic Leadership Skills for the Long Game," *Entrepreneur,* April 23, 2015, https://www.entrepreneur.com/article/245354 (accessed July 2016).

73. R. G. Lord, D. V. Day, S. J. Zaccaro, B. J. Avolio, and A. H. Eagly, "Leadership in Applied Psychology: Three Ways of Theory and Research," *Journal of Applied Psychology,* March 2017, pp. 434–451.

74. A. and J. Bornstein, March 22, 2016, "22 Qualities That Make a Great Leader," *Entrepreneur,* https://www.entrepreneur.com/article/270486 (accessed July 2016).
75. M. Weinstein, "BNSF Railway Is on Board with Topnotch Training," *Training,* January/February 2018, pp. 38-40.
76. C. Boyd, "6 Successful Celebrity Micro and Macro Managers," *Institute of Managers and Leaders,* March 27, 2016, https://managersandleaders.com.au/beta/6-successful-celebrity-micro-and-macro-managers/.
77. T. Shingal, "10 Companies Who Use Psychometric Testing," *Mettl,* accessed April 30, 2018, https://blog.mettl.com/talent-hub/10-companies-using-psychometric-testing.
78. M. Javidan, A. Bullough, and R. Dibble, "Mind the Gap: Gender Differences in Global Leadership Self-Efficacies," *Academy of Management Perspectives,* February 2016, pp. 59–73.
79. G. Yukl, "Effective Leadership Behavior: What We Know and What Questions Need More Attention," *Academy of Management Perspectives,* November 2012, p. 69.
80. D. S. DeRue, J. D. Nahrgang, N. Wellman, S. E. Humphrey, "Trait and Behavioral Theories of Leadership: An Integration and Meta-Analytic Test of Their Relative Validity," *Personnel Psychology* 64 (2011), pp. 7–52.
81. J. Wieczner, "In Boxed," *Fortune.com,* October 1, 2017, p. 90.
82. Fast Company Staff, "32 Leadership Lessons from Peloton, Beautycounter, Omnicom, and More," *Fast Company,* January 10, 2018, https://www.fastcompany.com/40509021/32-leadership-lessons-from-peloton-beautycounter-omnicom-and-more.
83. A definition and description of transactional leadership is provided by B. M. Bass and R. Bass, *The Bass Handbook of Leadership: Theory, Research, and Managerial Applications,* 4th ed. (New York: Free Press), 2008), pp. 618–648.
84. B. O'Keefe, "How Nick Saban Keeps Alabama Football Rolling," *Fortune,* April 23, 2018, http://fortune.com/2018/04/23/nick-saban-coach-university-of-alabama-football/.
85. T. A. Judge, R. F. Piccolo, and R. Ilies, "The Forgotten Ones? The Validity of Consideration and Initiating Structure in Leadership Research," *Journal of Applied Psychology,* February 2004, pp. 36–51.
86. D. S. DeRue, J. D. Nahrgang, N. Wellman, S. E. Humphrey, "Trait and Behavioral Theories of Leadership," *Personnel Psychology* 64 (2011), pp. 7–52.
87. G. Yukl, "Effective Leadership Behavior: What We Know and What Questions Need More Attention," *Academy of Management Perspectives,* November 2012, pp. 66–85.
88. N. V. Quaquebeke and W. Felps, "Respectual Iquiry: A Motivational Account of Leading through Asking Questions and Listening," *Academy of Management Review,* January 2018, pp. 5–27.
89. T. A. Judge, R. F. Piccolo, and R. Ilies, "The Forgotten Ones? The Validity of Consideration and Initiating Structure in Leadership Research," *Journal of Applied Psychology,* February 2004, pp. 36–51.
90. A. Lee, S. Willis, and A. W. Tian, "Empowering Leadership: A Meta-Analytic Examination of Incremental Contribution, Mediation, and Moderation," *Journal of Organizational Behavior,* March 2018, pp. 306–325.
91. M. Schwantes, "20 Leadership Quotes by Successful Women You Should Pay Attention to," *Inc.,* January 27, 2017, https://www.inc.com/marcel-schwantes/20-leadership-quotes-by-successful-female-entrepreneurs-that-will-make-you-jealo.html.
92. M. Smith, "Effective Delegation," *The Achievement Center,* November 1, 2017, https://www.tacresults.com/article/effective-delegation/.
93. S. Doyle, "What Every Boss Can Learn about Leadership from Sheryl Sandberg at Facebook," *Inc.,* September 17, 2017, https://www.inc.com/shawn-doyle/what-every-boss-can-learn-about-leadership-from-sh.html.
94. L. MacLellan, "Sheryl Sandberg Has Inspired More Humane Policies for Grieving Workers at Facebook and Beyond," *Quartz at Work,* October 24, 2017, https://work.qz.com/1106619/sheryl-sandberg-has-inspired-more-humane-policies-for-grieving-workers-at-facebook-and-beyond/.
95. T. W. H. Ng and D. C. Feldman, "Ethical Leadership: Meta-Analytic Evidence of Criterion-Related and Incremental Validity," *Journal of Applied Psychology,* May 2015, pp. 948–965.
96. J. E. Hoch, W. H. Bommer, J. H. Dulebohn, and D. Wu, "Do Ethical, Authentic, and Servant Leadership Explain Variance above and beyond Transformational Leadership? A Meta-Analysis," *Journal of Management,* February 2018, pp. 501–529; W. Zhu, H. He, L. K. Trevino, M. M. Chao, and W. Wang, "Ethical Leadership and Follower Voice and Performance: The Role of Follower Identifications and Entity Morality Beliefs," *The Leadership Quarterly,* 2015, pp. 702–718.
97. T. W. H. Ng and D. C. Feldman, "Ethical Leadership: Meta-Analytic Evidence of Criterion-Related and Incremental Validity," *Journal of Applied Psychology,* May 2015, pp. 948–965.
98. L. Dunn, "Women in Business Q&A: Lauren Bush Lauren, Founder and CEO, FEED," *Huffington Post,* October 24, 2017, www.huffingtonpost.com/entry/women-in-business-qa-lauren-bush-lauren-founder_us_59ef70bee4b04809c0501185.
99. D. Fenn, "Lauren Bush Lauren: Social Enterprise Is Her Bag," *Inc,* August 21, 2013, www.inc.com/donna-fenn/feed-lauren-bush-lauren-social-enterprise.html.
100. K. Schmookler, "Lauren Bush Lauren of Feed Shares Her Motivations and Advice for Social Ventures," *Conscious Magazine,* http://consciousmagazine.co/lauren-bush-lauren-feed-world-hunger/ (accessed April 24, 2018).
101. L. Dunn, "Women in Business Q&A: Lauren Bush Lauren, Founder and CEO, FEED," *Huffington Post,* October 24, 2017, www.huffingtonpost.com/entry/women-in-business-qa-lauren-bush-lauren-founder_us_59ef70bee4b04809c0501185.
102. D. Fenn, "Lauren Bush Lauren: Social Enterprise Is Her Bag," *Inc,* August 21, 2013, www.inc.com/donna-fenn/feed-lauren-bush-lauren-social-enterprise.html.
103. C. Howard, "Lauren Bush Lauren Is Building a Brand by Making a Difference," *Forbes,* September 23, 2014, www.forbes.com/sites/carolinehoward/2014/09/23/lauren-bush-lauren-is-building-a-brand-by-making-a-difference/#d53111a7e22a.
104. "About Feed," *FEED,* www.feedprojects.com/about-feed (accessed April 24, 2018).
105. K. Schmookler, "Lauren Bush Lauren of Feed Shares Her Motivations and Advice for Social Ventures," *Conscious Magazine,* http://consciousmagazine.co/lauren-bush-lauren-feed-world-hunger/ (accessed April 24, 2018).
106. "About Feed," *FEED,* www.feedprojects.com/about-feed (accessed April 24, 2018).
107. K. Schmookler, "Lauren Bush Lauren of Feed Shares Her Motivations and Advice for Social Ventures," accessed April 24, 2018, *Conscious Magazine,* http://consciousmagazine.co/lauren-bush-lauren-feed-world-hunger/ (accessed April 24, 2018).
108. D. Fenn, "Lauren Bush Lauren: Social Enterprise Is Her Bag," *Inc,* August 21, 2013, www.inc.com/donna-fenn/feed-lauren-bush-lauren-social-enterprise.html.
109. L. Dunn, "Women In Business Q&A: Lauren Bush Lauren, Founder and CEO, FEED," *Huffington Post,* October 24, 2017, www.huffingtonpost.com/entry/women-in-business-qa-lauren-bush-lauren-founder_us_59ef70bee4b04809c0501185.
110. A summary of servant leadership is provided by L. C. Spears, *Reflections on Leadership: How Robert K. Greenleaf's Theory of Servant-Leadership Influenced Today's Top Management thinkers* (New York: Wiley, 1995).
111. V. Giang, "The Pros and Cons of New Unconventional Leadership Styles," *Fast Company,* June 3, 2016, www.fastcompany.com/3060371/how-to-be-a-success-at-everything/the-pros-and-cons-of-new-unconventional-leadership-styles.
112. "Salesforce Leadership," *Salesforce,* www.salesforce.com/eu/company/leadership/bios/bio-benioff/ (accessed April 25, 2018).
113. R. Safian, "Salesforce's Marc Benioff on the Power of Values," *Fast Company,* April 17, 2017, www.fastcompany.com/40397514/salesforces-marc-benioff-on-the-power-of-values.

114. J. E. Hoch, W. H. Bommer, J. H. Dulebohn, and D. Wu, "Do Ethical, Authentic, and Servant Leadership Explain Variance Above and Beyond Transformational Leadership? A Meta-Analysis," *Journal of Management,* February 2018, pp. 501–529; A. Newman, G. Schwarz, B. Cooper, and S. Sendjaya, "How Servant Leadership Influences Organizational Citizenship Behavior: The Roles of LMX, Empowerment, and Proactive Personality," *Journal of Business Ethics,* September 2017, pp. 49–62.

115. B. M. Bass, "From Transactional to Transformational Leadership: Learning to Share the Vision," *Organizational Dynamics* 18 (1990), pp. 19–31.

116. A. H. Eagly, M. C. Johannesen-Schmidt, and M. L. van Engen, "Transformational, Transactional, and Laissez-Faire Leadership Styles: A Meta-Analysis Comparing Women and Men," *Psychological Bulletin,* June 2003, pp. 569–591.

117. D. S. DeRue, J. D. Nahrgang, N. Wellman, S. E. Humphrey, "Trait and Behavioral Theories of Leadership," *Personnel Psychology* 64 (2011), pp. 7–52.

118. F. E. Fiedler, "Assumed Similarity Measures as Predictors of Team Effectiveness," *Journal of Abnormal and Social Psychology* 49 (1954), pp. 381–388; F. E. Fiedler, *Leader Attitudes and Group Effectiveness* (Urbana, IL: University of Illinois Press, 1958); F. E. Fiedler, *A Theory of Leadership Effectiveness* (New York: McGraw-Hill, 1967).

119. M. V. Vugt, R. Hogan, and R. B. Kaiser, "Leadership, Followership, and Evolution," *American Psychologist,* April 2008, pp. 182–196.

120. R. J. House, "A Path-Goal Theory of Leader Effectiveness," *Administrative Science Quarterly,* September 1971, pp. 321–338.

121. P. M. Podsakoff, S. B. MacKenzie, M. Ahearne, and W. H. Bommer, "Searching for a Needle in a Haystack: Trying to Identify the Illusive Moderators of Leadership Behaviors," *Journal of Management,* 1995, pp. 422–470; J. Domingues, V. V. Afonso, and R. Agnihotri, "The Interactive Effects of Goal Orientation and Leadership Style on Sales Performance," *Marketing Letters,* December 2017, pp. 637–649.

122. J. R. Turner, R. Baker, and F. Kellner, "Theoretical Literature Review: Tracing the Life Cycle of a Theory and Its Verified and Falsified Statements," *Human Resource Development Review,* 2018, pp. 34–61.

123. G. Wang, I-S. Oh, S. H. Courtright, and A. E. Colbert, "Transformational Leadership and Performance Across Criteria and Levels: A Meta-Analytic Review of 25 Years of Research," *Group & Organization Management* 36, no. 2 (2011), pp. 223–270.

124. P. M. Podsakoff, S. B. MacKenzie, M. Ahearne, and W. H. Bommer, "Searching for a Needle in a Haystack: Trying to Identify the Illusive Moderators of Leadership Behaviors," *Journal of Management* 21, no. 3 (1995), pp. 423–470.

125. J. J. Dahling, S. R. Taylor, S. L. Chau, and S. A Dwight, "Does Coaching Matter? A Multilevel Model Linking Managerial Coaching Skills and Frequency to Sales Goal Attainment," *Personnel Psychology,* 2016, pp. 863–894.

126. The steps were developed by H. P. Sims Jr., S. Faraj, and S. Yun, "When Should a Leader Be Directive or Empowering? How to Develop Your Own Situational Theory of Leadership," *Business Horizons,* March–April 2009, pp. 149–158.

127. For a complete description of the full-range leadership theory, see B. J. Bass and B. J. Avolio, *Revised Manual for the Multi-Factor Leadership Questionnaire* (Palo Alto, CA: Mindgarden, 1997).

128. R. G. Lord, D. V. Day, S. J. Zaccaro, B. J. Avolio, and A. H. Eagly, "Leadership in Applied Psychology: Three Ways of Theory and Research," *Journal of Applied Psychology,* March 2017, pp. 434–451.

129. U. R. Dundum, K. B. Lowe, and B. J. Avolio, "A Meta-Analysis of Transformational and Transactional Leadership Correlates of Effectiveness and Satisfaction: An Update and Extension," in B. J. Avolio and F. J. Yammarino (Eds.), *Transformational and Charismatic Leadership: The Road Ahead* (New York: JAI Press, 2002), p. 38.

130. Supportive results can be found in T. A. Judge and J. E. Bono, "Five-Factor Model of Personality and Transformational Leadership," *Journal of Applied Psychology,* October 2000, pp. 751–765; S. Oreg and Y. Berson, "Leadership and Employees' Reactions to Change: The Role of Leaders' Personal Attributes and Transformational Leadership," *Personnel Psychology* 64 (2011), pp. 627–659.

131. Supportive research is summarized by Antonakis and House, "The Full-Range Leadership Theory: The Way Forward"; W. Zhu, R. E. Riggio, B. J. Avolio, and J. J. Sosik, "The Effect of Leadership on Follower Moral Identity: Does Transformational/Transactional Style Make a Difference?" *Journal of Leadership & Organizational Studies* 18 (2011), pp. 150–163.

132. "Most Powerful Women: 2017," *Fortune*, http://fortune.com/most-powerful-women/ (accessed April 25, 2018).

133. R. Feloni, "Pepsi CEO Indra Nooyi Explains How an Unusual Daily Ritual Her Mom Made Her Practice as a Child Changed Her Life," *Business Insider,* September 9, 2015, www.businessinsider.com/pepsico-indra-nooyi-life-changing-habit- 2015-9.

134. "Can a Positive Impact Be Profitable?" *Yale Insights,* January 18, 2017, https://insights.som.yale.edu/insights/can-positive-impact-be-profitable.

135. H. Schultz, "Indra Nooyi," *Time,* April 30, 2008, www.time.com/time/specials/2007/article/0,28804,1733748_1733758,00.html; D. Brady, "Keeping Cool in Hot Water," *BusinessWeek*, June 11, 2007, p. 49.

136. "Can a Positive Impact Be Profitable?" *Yale Insights,* January 18, 2017, https://insights.som.yale.edu/insights/can-positive-impact-be-profitable.

137. R. Feloni, "PepsiCo CEO Indra Nooyi's Long-Term Strategy Put Her Job in Jeopardy—But Now the Numbers Are in, and the Analysts Who Doubted Her Will Have to Eat Their Words," *Business Insider,* February 1, 2018, www.businessinsider.com/indra-nooyi-pepsico-push-for-long-term-value-2018-1.

138. These definitions are derived from R. Kark, B. Shamir, and C. Chen, "The Two Faces of Transformational Leadership: Empowerment and Dependency," *Journal of Applied Psychology,* April 2003, pp. 246–255; A. E. Colbert, A. L. Kristof-Brown, B. H. Bradley, and M. R. Barrick, "CEO Transformational Leadership: The Role of Goal Importance Congruence in Top Management Teams," *Academy of Management Journal,* February 2008, pp. 81–96.

139. A historical review of transformational leadership is provided by D. V. Knippenberg and S. B. Sitkin, "A Critical Assessment of Charismatic–Transformational Leadership Research: Back to the Drawing Board?" *The Academy of Management Annals,* 2013, pp. 1–60.

140. Charisma is defined and discussed by K. O. Tskhay, R. Zhu, C. Zou, and N. O. Rule, "Charisma in Everyday Life: Conceptualization and Validation of the General Charisma Inventory," *Journal of Personality and Social Psychology,* 2018, pp. 131–152.

141. B. Nanus, *Visionary Leadership* (San Francisco: Jossey-Bass, 1992), p. 8.

142. M. S. Malone, "The Secret to Midcareer Success," *The Wall Street Journal,* February 12, 2018, p. A17.

143. D. Hoffeld, "7 Scientifically Proven Habits of Charismatic Leaders," *Fast Company,* February 3, 2016, http://www.fastcompany.com/3056232/how-to-be-a-success-at-everything/7-scientifically-proven-habits-of-charismatic-leaders (accessed July 2016).

144. "The World's 50 Greatest Leaders," *Fortune,* April 19, 2018, http://fortune.com/longform/worlds-greatest-leaders-2018/#scott.

145. J. Wieczner, "In Boxed," *Fortune.com,* October 1, 2017, p. 89.

146. "Board of Directors," *Conscious Capitalism,* https://www.consciouscapitalism.org/about/boardofdirectors (accessed April 30, 2018).

147. B. Kowitt, "John Mackey, The Conscious Capitalist," *Fortune,* August 20, 2015, http://fortune.com/2015/08/20/whole-foods-john-mackey/ (accessed July 2016).

148. R. G. Lord, D. V. Day, S. J. Zaccaro, B. J. Avolio, and A. H. Eagly, "Leadership in Applied Psychology: Three Ways of Theory and Research," *Journal of Applied Psychology,* March 2017, pp. 434–451; J. Duan, C. Li, Y. Xu, and C.-H. Wu, "Transformational Leadership and Employee Voice Behavior: A Pygmalion Mechanism," *Journal of Organizational Behavior,* 2017, pp. 650–670; S. J. Ashford, N. Wellman, M. S. de Luque, K. E. M. De Stobbeleir, "Two Roads to Effectiveness: CEO Feedback Seeking, Vision Articulation,

and Firm Performance," *Journal of Organizational Behavior,* 2018, pp. 82–95.

149. B. J. Avolio, R. J. Reichard, S. T. Hannah, F. O Walumbwa, and A. Chan, "A Meta-Analytic Review of Leadership Impact Research: Experimental and Quasi-Experimental Studies," *Leadership Quarterly.* 20 (2009), pp. 764–784; J. Kanengieter and A. Rajagopal-Durbin, "Wilderness Leadership—On the Job," *Harvard Business Review,* April 2012, pp. 127–131.

150. S. E. Seibert, L. D. Sargent, M. L. Kraimer, and K. Kiazad, "Linking Developmental Experiences to Leader Effectiveness and Promotability: The Mediating Role of Leadership Self-Efficacy and Mentor Network," *Personnel Psychology,* 2017, pp. 357–397.

151. G. Graen and J. F. Cashman, "A Role-Making Model of Leadership in Formal Organizations: A Developmental Approach," in J. G. Hunt and L. L. Larson (Eds.), *Leadership Frontiers* (Kent, OH: Kent State University Press, 1975), pp. 143–165; F. Dansereau Jr., G. Graen, and W. J. Haga, "A Vertical Dyad Linkage Approach to Leadership within Formal Organizations: A Longitudinal Investigation of the Role-Making Process," *Organizational Behavior and Human Performance,* February 1975, pp. 46–78; K. S. Wilson, H.-P. Sin, and D. E. Conlon, "What about the Leader in Leader–Member Exchange? The Impact of Resource Exchanges and Substitutability in the Leader," *Academy of Management Review,* July 2010, pp. 358–372.

152. D. Duchon, S. G. Green, and T. D. Taber, "Vertical Dyad Linkage: A Longitudinal Assessment of Antecedents, Measures, and Consequences," *Journal of Applied Psychology,* February 1986, pp. 56–60.

153. R. G. Lord, D. V. Day, S. J. Zaccaro, B. J. Avolio, and A. H. Eagly, "Leadership in Applied Psychology: Three Ways of Theory and Research," *Journal of Applied Psychology,* March 2017, pp. 434–451; R. Martin, G. Thomas, A. Legood, and S. D. Russo, "Leader-Member Exchange (LMX) Differentiation and Work Outcomes: Conceptual Clarification and Critical Review," *Journal of Organizational Behavior,* February 2018, pp. 151–168.

154. R. K. Gottfredson and H. Aguinis, "Leadership Behaviors and Follower Performance: Deductive and Inductive Examination of Theoretical Rationales and Underlying Mechanisms," *Journal of Organizational Behavior,* 2017, p. 584.

155. R. K. Gottfredson and H. Aguinis, "Leadership Behaviors and Follower Performance: Deductive and Inductive Examination of Theoretical Rationales and Underlying Mechanisms," *Journal of Organizational Behavior,* 2017, p. 584.

156. S. Shellenbarger, "The Right and Wrong Ways to Manage Up," *The Wall Street Journal,* April 11, 2018, p. A9.

157. A. Y. Ou, A. S. Tsui, A. J. Kinicki, D. A. Waldman, Z. Xiao, and L. J. Song, "Humble Chief Executive Officers' Connections to Top Management Team Integration and Middle Managers' Responses," *Administrative Science Quarterly,* March 2014, pp. 34–72.

158. M. Mayo, "If Humble People Make the Best Leaders, Why Do We Fall for Charismatic Narcissists?" *Harvard Business Review*, April 7, 2017, https://hbr.org/2017/04/if-humble-people-make-the-best-leaders-why-do-we-fall-for-charismatic-narcissists.

159. L. Merrill, "Study: Humble Bosses Are Best," *Arizona Republic,* July 30, 2014, pp. A14, A18; A. Y. Ou, A. S. Tsui, A. J. Kinicki, D. A. Waldman, Z. Xiao, and L. J. Song, "Humble Chief Executive Officers' Connections to Top Management Team Integration and Middle Managers' Responses," *Administrative Science Quarterly,* 2014, pp. 34–72.

160. J. Prime and E. Salib, "The Best Leaders Are Humble Leaders," *Harvard Business Review,* May 12, 2014, https://hbr.org/2014/05/the-best-leaders-are-humble-leaders (accessed April 25, 2016).

161. M. Mayo, "If Humble People Make the Best Leaders, Why Do We Fall for Charismatic Narcissists?" *Harvard Business Review*, April 7, 2017, https://hbr.org/2017/04/if-humble-people-make-the-best-leaders-why-do-we-fall-for-charismatic-narcissists.

162. J. Hu, B. Erdogan, K. Jiang, and T. N. Bauer, "Leader Humility and Team Creativity: The Role of Team Information Sharing, Psychological Safety, and Power Distance, *Journal of Applied Psychology,* March 2018, pp. 313–323; J. Hu, B. Erdogan, K. Jiang, and T. N. Bauer, "Research: When Being a Humble Leader Backfires," *Harvard Business Review,* April 4, 2018, https://hbr.org/2018/04/research-when-being-a-humble-leader-backfires.

163. H. Leroy, F. Anseel, W. L. Gardner, and L. Sels, "Authentic Leadership, Authentic Followership, Basic Need Satisfaction, and Work Role Performance: A Cross-Level Study," *Journal of Management,* September 2015, pp. 1677–1697.

164. N. V. Quaquebeke and W. Felps, "Respectful Inquiry: A Motivational Account of Leading through Asking Questions and Listening," *Academy of Management Review,* January 2018, pp. 5–27; H. Gregersen, "Bursting the CEO Bubble," *Harvard Business Review,* March–April 2017, pp. 76–83.

165. R. Levering, "The 100 Best Companies to Work For 2016," *Fortune,* March 15, 2016, p. 160.

166. D. S. DeRue and S. J. Ashford, "Who Will Lead and Who Will Follow? A Social Process of Leadership Identity Construction in Organizations," *Academy of Management Review,* October 2010, pp. 627–647.

167. T. O'Driscoll, "5 Foundational Elements of Followership," *Training,* May/June 2017, p. 56.

168. B. M. Bass and R. Bass, *The Bass Handbook of Leadership: Theory, Research, and Managerial Applications,* 4th ed. (New York: Free Press, 2008).

169. L. Bossidy, "What Your Leader Expects of You and What You Should Expect in Return," *Harvard Business Review,* April 2007, pp. 58–65.

170. G. Moran, "5 Ways Being a Good Follower Makes You a Better Leader," *Fast Company,* April 30, 2014, http://www.fastcompany.com/3029840/bottom-line/5-ways-being-a-good-follower-makes-you-a-better-leader; L. Mcleod, "7 Ways to Become Your Boss' Dream Employee," *The Muse,* https://www.themuse.com/advice/7-ways-to-become-your-boss-dream-employee (accessed July 2016).

171. A. K. Tjan, "5 Ways to Become More Self-Aware," *Harvard Business Review,* February 11, 2015, https://hbr.org/2015/02/5-ways-to-become-more-self-aware.

172. B. Gardner, "Become a Better Leader with Disciplined Reflection," *Forbes,* December 28, 2015, https://www.forbes.com/sites/forbescoachescouncil/2015/12/28/become-a-better-leader-with-disciplined-reflection/#f60ae9f65c39.

173. These questions were taken from B. Gardner, "Become a Better Leader with Disciplined Reflection," *Forbes,* December 28, 2015, https://www.forbes.com/sites/forbescoachescouncil/2015/12/28/become-a-better-leader-with-disciplined-reflection/#f60ae9f65c39.

174. S. Bahmani, "Improved Critical Thinking in Students Using Current Events Journaling," *International Journal of Sociology and Social Policy,* 2016, pp. 190–202; H. Messenger, "Drawing Out Ideas: Visual Journaling as a Knowledge Creating Medium during Doctoral Research," *Creative Approaches to Research,* 2016, pp. 129–149.

175. H. M. Kraemer, "How Self-Reflection Can Make You a Better Leader," *KelloggInsight,* December 2, 2016, https://insight.kellogg.northwestern.edu/article/how-self-reflection-can-make-you-a-better-leader.

176. T. Herrera, "How to Spot and Overcome Your Hidden Weaknesses," *The New York Times,* April 23, 2018, https://www.nytimes.com/2018/04/23/smarter-living/how-to-spot-and-overcome-your-hidden-weaknesses.html.

177. M. D. Cava, "Nadella Counts on Culture Shock to Drive Microsoft Growth," *USA Today,* February 20, 2017, p. 4B.

178. K. Zezima, "Everything You Need To Know about the VA—And the Scandals Engulfing It," *Washington Post,* May 30, 2014, www.washingtonpost.com/news/the-fix/wp/2014/05/21/a-guide-to-the-va-and-the-scandals-engulfing-it/?utm_term=.d9df15cde916.

179. CNN Library, "Department of Veterans Affairs Fast Facts," *CNN,* May 2, 2018, www.cnn.com/2014/05/30/us/department-of-veterans-affairs-fast-facts/index.html.

180. K. Zezima, "Everything You Need to Know about the VA—And the Scandals Engulfing It," *Washington Post,* May 30, 2014, www.washingtonpost.com/news/the-fix/wp/2014/05/21/a-guide-to-the-va-and-the-scandals-engulfing-it/?utm_term=.d9df15cde916.
181. K. Zezima, "Everything You Need to Know about the VA—And the Scandals Engulfing It," *Washington Post,* May 30, 2014, www.washingtonpost.com/news/the-fix/wp/2014/05/21/a-guide-to-the-va-and-the-scandals-engulfing-it/?utm_term=.d9df15cde916.
182. S. Walsh, P. Murphy, S. Bisaha, and Q. Lawrence, "VA Hospitals Still Struggling with Adding Staff Despite Billions from Choice Act," *NPR,* January 31, 2017, www.npr.org/2017/01/31/512052311/va-hospitals-still-struggling-with-adding-staff-despite-billions-from-choice-act.
183. N. Wentling, "Bob McDonald's Legacy: Trying to Fix the VA amid Constant Conflict," *Stars and Stripes,* January 18, 2017, www.stripes.com/bob-mcdonald-s-legacy-trying-to-fix-the-va-amid-constant-conflict-1.449490.
184. N. Wentling, "Bob McDonald's Legacy: Trying to Fix the VA amid Constant Conflict," *Stars and Stripes,* January 18, 2017, www.stripes.com/bob-mcdonald-s-legacy-trying-to-fix-the-va-amid-constant-conflict-1.449490.
185. N. Wentling, "Bob McDonald's Legacy: Trying to Fix the VA amid Constant Conflict," *Stars and Stripes,* January 18, 2017, www.stripes.com/bob-mcdonald-s-legacy-trying-to-fix-the-va-amid-constant-conflict-1.449490.
186. E. Bell, "Memo: Bob McDonald's Failed VA Legacy," *Concerned Veterans for America,* December 15, 2016, https://cv4a.org/press-release/memo-bob-mcdonalds-failed-va-legacy/.
187. C. Devine and D. Griffin, "Billions Spent to Fix VA Didn't Solve Problems, Made Some Issues Worse," *CNN,* July 6, 2016, www.cnn.com/2016/07/05/politics/veterans-administration-va/index.html.
188. S. Walsh, P. Murphy, S. Bisaha, and Q. Lawrence, "VA Hospitals Still Struggling with Adding Staff Despite Billions from Choice Act," *NPR,* January 31, 2017, www.npr.org/2017/01/31/512052311/va-hospitals-still-struggling-with-adding-staff-despite-billions-from-choice-act.
189. S. Walsh, P. Murphy, S. Bisaha, and Q. Lawrence, "VA Hospitals Still Struggling with Adding Staff Despite Billions from Choice Act," *NPR,* January 31, 2017, www.npr.org/2017/01/31/512052311/va-hospitals-still-struggling-with-adding-staff-despite-billions-from-choice-act.
190. E. Bell, "Memo: Bob McDonald's Failed VA Legacy," *Concerned Veterans for America,* December 15, 2016, https://cv4a.org/press-release/memo-bob-mcdonalds-failed-va-legacy/.
191. E. Bell, "Memo: Bob McDonald's Failed VA Legacy," *Concerned Veterans for America,* December 15, 2016, https://cv4a.org/press-release/memo-bob-mcdonalds-failed-va-legacy/.
192. S. Walsh, P. Murphy, S. Bisaha, and Q. Lawrence, "VA Hospitals Still Struggling with Adding Staff Despite Billions from Choice Act," *NPR,* January 31, 2017, www.npr.org/2017/01/31/512052311/va-hospitals-still-struggling-with-adding-staff-despite-billions-from-choice-act.
193. D. Slack, "VA Knew for Years about Dangerous Conditions at Washington, D.C. Hospital," *USA Today,* March 7, 2018, www.usatoday.com/story/news/politics/2018/03/07/va-veterans-affairs-failures-left-patients-danger-washington-dc-hospital-years-investigation/396914002/.
194. J. Summers, "Systemic Failures Plague DC Veterans Hospital, Inspector General Finds," *CNN,* March 7, 2018, www.cnn.com/2018/03/07/politics/washington-dc-va-hospital-inspector-general/index.html.
195. J. Summers, "Systemic Failures Plague DC Veterans Hospital, Inspector General Finds," *CNN,* March 7, 2018, www.cnn.com/2018/03/07/politics/washington-dc-va-hospital-inspector-general/index.html.
196. H. Yen, "Watchdog Report: Leadership Put Patients at Risk," *US News,* March 7, 2018, www.usnews.com/news/news/articles/2018-03-07/watchdog-report-failed-va-leadership-put-patients-at-risk.
197. H. Yen, "Watchdog Report: Leadership Put Patients at Risk," *US News,* March 7, 2018, www.usnews.com/news/news/articles/2018-03-07/watchdog-report-failed-va-leadership-put-patients-at-risk.
198. H. Yen, "Watchdog Report: Leadership Put Patients at Risk," *US News,* March 7, 2018, www.usnews.com/news/news/articles/2018-03-07/watchdog-report-failed-va-leadership-put-patients-at-risk.
199. D. Slack, "VA Knew for Years about Dangerous Conditions at Washington, D.C. Hospital," *USA Today,* March 7, 2018, www.usatoday.com/story/news/politics/2018/03/07/va-veterans-affairs-failures-left-patients-danger-washington-dc-hospital-years-investigation/396914002/.
200. D. Weigel, "Shulkin Says He Did Not Leave Office Willingly, Setting Up Fight over His Successor," *The Washington Post,* April 1, 2018, www.washingtonpost.com/news/powerpost/wp/2018/04/01/shulkin-says-he-did-not-leave-office-willingly-setting-up-fight-over-his-successor/?utm_term=.bc43747c5a03.
201. N. Fandos, "New Allegations Emerge against Ronny Jackson as White House Digs in," *The New York Times,* April 25, 2018, www.nytimes.com/2018/04/25/us/politics/ronny-jackson-veterans-affairs-nomination.html.
202. J. Cassidy, "The Real Ronny Jackson Scandal Is That Trump Nominated Him at All," *The New Yorker,* April 25, 2018, www.newyorker.com/news/our-columnists/the-real-ronny-jackson-scandal-is-that-trump-nominated-him-at-all.
203. C. Foran, J. Summers, and J. Diamond, "Ronny Jackson Withdraws as VA Secretary Nominee," *CNN,* April 26, 2018, www.cnn.com/2018/04/26/politics/ronny-jackson-va-nominee/index.html.
204. N. Fandos, "New Allegations Emerge against Ronny Jackson as White House Digs in," *The New York Times,* April 25, 2018, www.nytimes.com/2018/04/25/us/politics/ronny-jackson-veterans-affairs-nomination.html; C. Foran, J. Summers, and J. Diamond, "Ronny Jackson Withdraws as VA Secretary Nominee," *CNN,* April 26, 2018, www.cnn.com/2018/04/26/politics/ronny-jackson-va-nominee/index.html; M. Kendall, "I've Seen What a Mess Veterans Affairs Is. Ronny L. Jackson Can't Fix It," *Washington Post,* April 2, 2018, www.washingtonpost.com/news/posteverything/wp/2018/04/02/ive-seen-what-a-mess-veterans-affairs-is-ronny-jackson-cant-fix-it/?utm_term=.f622e7565573.
205. C. Devine and D. Griffin, "Billions Spent to Fix VA Didn't' Solve Problems, Made Some Issues Worse," *CNN,* July 6, 2016, www.cnn.com/2016/07/05/politics/veterans-administration-va/index.html.
206. J. Summers, "Systemic Failures Plague DC Veterans Hospital, Inspector General Finds," *CNN,* March 7, 2018, www.cnn.com/2018/03/07/politics/washington-dc-va-hospital-inspector-general/index.html.
207. K. Zezima, "Everything You Need to Know about the VA—And the Scandals Engulfing It," *Washington Post,* May 30, 2014, www.washingtonpost.com/news/the-fix/wp/2014/05/21/a-guide-to-the-va-and-the-scandals-engulfing-it/?utm_term=.d9df15cde916.
208. A. Swick, "Choose Carefully, Mr. President," *Slate,* April 29, 2018, https://slate.com/news-and-politics/2018/04/who-will-trump-nominate-next-for-next-va-secretary-hed-better-choose-carefully.html.
209. A. Swick, "Choose Carefully, Mr. President," *Slate,* April 29, 2018, https://slate.com/news-and-politics/2018/04/who-will-trump-nominate-next-for-next-va-secretary-hed-better-choose-carefully.html.
210. A. González, "New Starbucks Campaign Touts Role as Global Hangout," *Seattle Times,* September 29, 2014, www.seattletimes.com/business/new-starbucks-campaign-touts-role-as-global-hangout/.
211. M. Gajanan, "Want to Use the Starbucks Bathroom? These Are Your Rights," *Time,* April 16, 2018, http://time.com/5241671/starbucks-philadelphia-bathroom-rights/.
212. B. Hutchinson and M. Stone, "Starbucks Manager Who Made Call Resulting in Black Men's Arrests No Longer Works for Company," *ABC News,* April 16, 2018, https://abcnews.go.com/Business/starbucks-ceo-kevin-johnson-orders-unconscious-bias-training/story?id=54496139.
213. B. Hutchinson and M. Stone, "Starbucks Manager Who Made Call Resulting in Black Men's Arrests No Longer Works for Company," *ABC News,* April 16, 2018, https://abcnews.go.com/Business/starbucks-ceo-kevin-johnson-orders-unconscious-bias-training/story?id=54496139.
214. E. Whack, "Black Men Arrested at Starbucks Settle for $1 and $200K Youth Program," *ABC News,* May 2, 2018, https://abcnews.go.com/US/wireStory/black-men-arrested-starbucks-settle-200k-program-54882092.

215. B. Hutchinson and M. Stone, "Starbucks Manager Who Made Call Resulting in Black Men's Arrests No Longer Works for Company," *ABC News,* April 16, 2018, https://abcnews.go.com/Business/starbucks-ceo-kevin-johnson-orders-unconscious-bias-training/story?id=54496139.

216. B. Hutchinson and M. Stone, "Starbucks Manager Who Made Call Resulting in Black Men's Arrests No Longer Works for Company," *ABC News,* April 16, 2018, https://abcnews.go.com/Business/starbucks-ceo-kevin-johnson-orders-unconscious-bias-training/story?id=54496139.

217. E. Whack, "Black Men Arrested at Starbucks Settle for $1 and $200K Youth Program," *ABC News,* May 2, 2018, https://abcnews.go.com/US/wireStory/black-men-arrested-starbucks-settle-200k-program-54882092.

CHAPTER 15

1. A. Loehr, "7 Practical Tips for Increasing Empathy," *Huffington Post,* May 6, 2016, https://www.huffingtonpost.com/anne-loehr/seven-practical-tips-for-_b_9854350.html.

2. A. Loehr, "7 Practical Tips for Increasing Empathy," *Huffington Post,* May 6, 2016, https://www.huffingtonpost.com/anne-loehr/seven-practical-tips-for-_b_9854350.html; Y. Solomon, "Why Empathy Is the Most Important Skill You'll Ever Need to Succeed," *Inc.,* October 4, 2017, https://www.inc.com/yoram-solomon/10-reasons-empathy-is-most-important-business-skill-you-will-ever-need.html?cid=search.

3. Y. Solomon, "Why Empathy Is the Most Important Skill You'll Ever Need to Succeed," *Inc.,* October 4, 2017, https://www.inc.com/yoram-solomon/10-reasons-empathy-is-most-important-business-skill-you-will-ever-need.html?cid=search.

4. A. Loehr, "7 Practical Tips for Increasing Empathy," *Huffington Post,* May 6, 2016, https://www.huffingtonpost.com/anne-loehr/seven-practical-tips-for-_b_9854350.html; J. Bariso, "Got Empathy? These 7 Tips Will Immediately Make You Better at What You Do," *Inc.,* October 26, 2016, https://www.inc.com/justin-bariso/7-practical-ways-empathy-makes-you-a-better-leader.html?cid=search; T. Citterman, "Three Ways Leaders Can Increase Empathy," *Forbes,* April 20, 2017, https://www.forbes.com/sites/forbescoachescouncil/2017/04/20/three-ways-leaders-can-increase-empathy/#3ccca3df749f.

5. J. Bauer-Wolf, "Overconfident Students, Dubious Employers," *Inside Higher Ed,* February 23, 2018, https://www.insidehighered.com/news/2018/02/23/study-students-believe-they-are-prepared-workplace-employers-disagree.

6. R. S. Wyer Jr. and L. J. Shrum, "The Role of Comprehension Processes in Communication and Persuasion," *Media Psychology,* April 2015, pp. 163–195.

7. J. Kotter, "Power, Dependence, and Effective Management," *Harvard Business Review* 55 (1977), pp. 125–136.

8. S. Dynarski, "Laptops Are Great. But Not during a Lecture or a Meeting," *The New York Times,* November 22, 2017, https://www.nytimes.com/2017/11/22/business/laptops-not-during-lecture-or-meeting.html.

9. T. Musbach, "The Most Annoying, Overused Words in the Workplace," *San Francisco Chronicle,* October 11, 2009, p. A1.

10. R. Bogosian "Volkswagen's New CEO Must Tackle This Other Problem," *Fortune,* September 26, 2015, http://fortune.com/2015/09/26/volkswagen-scandal-matthias-mueller/?iid=sr-link8.

11. A. Cremer, "CEO Says Changing VW Culture Proving Tougher than Expected," *Reuters,* May 23, 2017, https://www.reuters.com/article/us-volkswagen-emissions-culture/ceo-says-changing-vw-culture-proving-tougher-than-expected-idUSKBN18I2V3.

12. "Learn about Volkswagen Violations," U.S. Environmental Protection Agency, August 11, 2017, https://www.epa.gov/vw/learn-about-volkswagen-violations.

13. "Learn about Volkswagen Violations," U.S. Environmental Protection Agency, August 11, 2017, https://www.epa.gov/vw/learn-about-volkswagen-violations.

14. J. Carreyrou, "Under Fire, Theranos CEO Stifled Bad News," *The Wall Street Journal,* July 10, 2016, http://www.wsj.com/articles/under-fire-theranos-ceo-stifled-bad-news-1468195377; R Winkler, "Tech Investors Look for Lessons in Theranos," *The Wall Street Journal,* July 14, 2016, pp. B1, B4.

15. M. Herper, "The SEC Says Elizabeth Holmes' Fraud Was Worse than Anyone Thought," *Forbes,* March 15, 2018, https://www.forbes.com/sites/matthewherper/2018/03/14/sec-elizabeth-holmes-theranos-fraud/#65e0645b18f3.

16. J. Rosenblatt, "Theranos Investors May Vie with SEC to Scavenge Remains," *Chicago Tribune,* March 29, 2018, http://www.chicagotribune.com/business/ct-biz-theranos-investors-fraud-20180329-story.html.

17. J. Demers, "Communication in 2015: Text, Voice, Video or In-Person?" *Inc,* January 29, 2015, http://www.inc.com/jayson-demers/communication-in-2015-text-voice-video-or-in-person.html (accessed July 2016); P. Simon, "When Email and Texting Are Insufficient: An Interview with the Phone Lady," *Huffington Post,* August 24, 2015, http://www.huffingtonpost.com/phil-simon/when-email-and-texting-is_b_8034216. html (accessed July 2016).

18. V. Peltokorpi, "Corporate Language Proficiency and Reverse Knowledge Transfer in Multinational Corporations: Interactive Effects of Communication Media Richness and Commitment to Headquarters," *Journal of International Management,* 2015, pp. 49–62.

19. R. L. Daft and R. H. Lengel, "Information Richness: A New Approach to Managerial Behavior and Organizational Design," in B. M. Staw and L. L. Cummings (Eds.), *Research in Organizational Behavior* (Greenwich, CT: JAI Press, 1984), p. 196; R. H. Lengel and R. L. Daft, "The Selection of Communication Media as an Executive Skill," *Academy of Management Executive,* August 1988, pp. 225–232.

20. M. Lipowski and I. Bondos, "The Influence of Perceived Media Richness of Marketing Channels on Online Channel Use," *Baltic Journal of Management,* 2018, pp. 169–190.

21. D. R. Dunaetz, T. C. Lisk, and M. M. Shin, "Personality, Gender, and Age as Predictors of Media Richness Preference," *Advantages in Multimedia,* 2015, pp. 1–9.

22. B. Barry and I. S. Fulmer, "The Medium and the Message: The Adaptive Use of Communication Media in Dyadic Influence," *Academy of Management Review,* April 2004, pp. 272–292; A. F. Simon, "Computer-Mediated Communication: Task Performance and Satisfaction," *Journal of Social Psychology,* June 2006, pp. 349–379.

23. T. Neeley, "What Managers Need to Know about Social Tools," *Harvard Business Review,* November–December 2017, pp. 118–126; T. Harbert, "Let's Chat," *HRMagazine,* November 2017, pp. 46–51.

24. M. Weinstein, "Leveraging Crowd Power," *Training,* November/December 2017, pp. 42–43.

25. K. Kuhn, T. Galloway, and M. Collins-/Williams, "Near, Far, and Online: Small Business Owners' Advice-Seeking from Peers," *Journal of Small Business and Enterprise Development,* 2016, pp. 189–206.

26. See the related discussion in D. L. Brady, D. J. Brown, and L. H. Liang, "Moving beyond Assumptions of Deviance: The Reconceptualization and Measurement of Workplace Gossip," *Journal of Applied Psychology,* January 2017, pp. 1–25.

27. C. K. Goman, "What Leaders Don't Know about the Rumor Mill," *Forbes,* November 30, 2013, http://www.forbes.com/sites/carolkinseygoman/2013/11/30/what-leaders-dont-know-about-the-rumor-mill/#3dea041b3165; L. Ryan, "The Truth about the Company Grapevine," *Forbes,* December 30, 2014, http://www.forbes.com/sites/lizryan/2014/12/30/the-truth-about-the-company-grapevine/#5339d0f42632.

28. S. Luthi, "Congress Moving on VA Choice Reforms as White House Steps Up Pressure," *Modern Healthcare,* April 13, 2018, http://www.modernhealthcare.com/article/20180413/NEWS/180419961.

29. J. Humphrey "Why You Need to Master In-Person Conversations in Your Slack-Driven Office," *Fast Company,* July 1, 2016, http://www.fastcompany.com/3061470/how-to-be-a-success-at-everything/why-you-need-to-master-in-person-conversations-in-your-sla.

30. A. Davis, "Leaders: 6 Reasons Face-to-Face Communication Is Best," *Inc.,* November 30, 2015, http://www.inc.com/alison-davis/leaders-6-reasons-face-to-face-communication-is-best.html.

31. "How to Improve Face to Face Communication Skills," *ezTalks,* August 25, 2017, https://www.eztalks.com/unified-communications/how-to-improve-face-to-face-communication-skills.html; R. Jenkins, "How Millennials Can Best Communicate Face-to-Face, *Inc.,* August 19, 2016, https://www.inc.com/ryan-jenkins/how-millennials-can-best-communicate-face-to-face.html.

32. See W. Minozzi, M. A. Neblo, K. M. Esterling, and D. M. J. Lazer, "Field Experiment Evidence of Substantive, Attributional, and Behavioral Persuasion by Member of Congress in Online Town Halls," March 31, 2015, http:www.pnas.org/cgi/doi/10.1073/pnas.1418188112.

33. M. Weinstein, "Leveraging Crowd Power," *Training,* November/December 2017, pp. 42–43.

34. L. Perlow, C. Hadley, and E. Eun, "Stop the Meeting Madness," *Harvard Business Review,* June 26, 2017, https://hbr.org/2017/07/stop-the-meeting-madness.

35. P. Economy, "5 Hacks for Running a Remarkably Effective Meeting," *Inc.com,* June 28, 2017, https://www.inc.com/peter-economy/5-hacks-for-running-a-remarkably-effective-meeting.html.

36. N. Hartman, "Seven Steps to Running the Most Effective Meeting Possible," *Forbes,* February 5, 2014, http://www.forbes.com/sites/forbesleadershipforum/2014/02/05/seven-steps-to-running-the-most-effective-meeting-possible/#2db4326c1054; E. McKelvey, "Why Daily Meetings Aren't a Complete Waste of Time," *Fortune,* June 15, 2015, http://fortune.com/2015/06/15/erin-mckelvey-productivity-at-work/.

37. P. Economy, "5 Hacks for Running a Remarkably Effective Meeting," *Inc.com,* June 28, 2017, https://www.inc.com/peter-economy/5-hacks-for-running-a-remarkably-effective-meeting.html.

38. N. Lehmann-Willenbrock, S. G. Rogelberg, J. A. Allen, and J. E. Kello, "The Critical Importance of Meetings to Leader and Organizational Success: Evidence-Based Insights and Implications for Key Stakeholders," *Organizational Dynamics,* January–March 2018, pp. 32–36.

39. O. Keogh, "How Long Should a Work Meeting Last?" *Irish Times,* October 7, 2016, https://www.irishtimes.com/business/work/how-long-should-a-work-meeting-last-1.2816444.

40. S. Shellenbarger, "New Meeting Rules: Five Minutes, Max," *The Wall Street Journal,* November 8, 2017, p. A11.

41. C. McGoff, "How to Run an Efficient Meeting—Without Being Bossy or Taking Over," *Inc.com,* December 21, 2017, https://www.inc.com/chris-mcgoff/how-to-run-an-efficient-meeting-without-being-bossy-or-taking-over.html.

42. K. Hedges, "Why Great Leaders Do These 5 Things in Every Meeting," *Inc.com,* December 19, 2017, https://www.inc.com/the-muse/how-to-stand-out-crowded-meeting-great-leaders-run-meetings-like-this.html.

43. K. Hedges, "Why Great Leaders Do These 5 Things in Every Meeting," *Inc.com,* December 19, 2017, https://www.inc.com/the-muse/how-to-stand-out-crowded-meeting-great-leaders-run-meetings-like-this.html.

44. C. Williams, "Do the Woes of Open-Plan Office Design Outweigh the Benefits?" *Forbes,* February 10, 2017, https://www.forbes.com/sites/bisnow/2017/02/10/do-the-woes-of-open-plan-office-design-outweigh-the-benefits/2/#210fdb6937ca.

45. M. Drake, "Turns Out Open-Plan Isn't Always a Good Thing," *BISNOW,* June 15, 2016, https://www.bisnow.com/national/news/office/is-your-open-plan-office-killing-workplace-productivity-61375.

46. S. Lastoe, "This Is Nuts: It Takes Nearly 30 Minutes to Refocus after You Get Distracted," *The Muse,* https://www.themuse.com/advice/this-is-nuts-it-takes-nearly-30-minutes-to-refocus-after-you-get-distracted (accessed May 14, 2018).

47. N. Wingfield, "Forget Beanbag Chairs. Amazon Is Giving Its Workers Treehouses," *The New York Times,* July 10, 2016, http://www.nytimes.com/2016/07/11/technology/forget-beanbag-chairs-amazon-is-giving-its-workers-treehouses.html.

48. B. Gleeson, "How to Overcome the Barriers That Destroy Communication," *Inc.,* June 29, 2017, https://www.inc.com/brent-gleeson/how-to-overcome-the-barriers-that-destroy-communic.html?cid=search.

49. J. Katz, M. DuBois, and S. Wigderson, "Learning by Helping? Undergraduate Communication Outcomes Associated with Training or Service-Learning Experiences," *Teaching of Psychology,* 2014, pp. 251–255.

50. Quora, " How Technology Is Both Helping and Hurting the Way We Interact," *Inc.,* November 7, 2017, https://www.inc.com/quora/how-technology-is-both-helping-hurting-way-we-interact.html?cid=search.

51. M. Levin, "The 1 Thing That Will Make You a Great Communicator," *Inc.,* June 24, 2016, http://www.inc.com/marissa-levin/the-1-thing-that-will-get-people-to-listen-to-you-instantly.html (accessed July 2016).

52. O. Temby, J. Sandall, R. Cooksey, and G. M. Hickey, "Examining the Role of Trust and Informal Communication on Mutual Learning in Government: The Case of Climate Change Policy in New York," *Organization and Environment,* 2016, pp. 1–27; K. Boies, J. Fiset, and H. Gill, "Communication and Trust Are Key: Unlocking the Relationship between Leadership and Team Performance and Creativity," *The Leadership Quarterly,* 2015, pp. 1080–1094.

53. M. Zwilling, "Entrepreneurs Face Serious Communication Barriers," *Forbes,* July 7, 2013, http://www.forbes.com/sites/martinzwilling/2013/07/07/entrepreneurs-face-serious-communication-barriers/#177b3d385398 (accessed July 2016).

54. R. Riggio, "Are All Leaders Narcissists?" *Psychology Today,* December 13, 2012, https://www.psychologytoday.com/blog/cutting-edge-leadership/201212/are-all-leaders-narcissists?collection=62261 (accessed July 2016).

55. S. Young Wang, "You Don't Need 'Thick Skin'; Try This Instead," *Forbes,* April 17, 2018, https://www.forbes.com/sites/sarayoungwang/2018/04/17/you-dont-need-thick-skin-you-need-these-effective-communication-tools/2/#659d99e77f0c.

56. S. Moore, "Why It's Not about You (and Why That's Awesome)," *Huffington Post,* September 6, 2014, http://www.huffingtonpost.com/susie-moore/why-its-not-about-you-and_b_5744522.html.

57. "'The Daily' Transcript: Interview with James Comey," *The New York Times,* April 20, 2018, https://www.nytimes.com/2018/04/20/us/politics/comey-interview-daily-transcript.html.

58. E J. Langer, "Minding Matters: The Consequences of Mindlessness-Mindfulness," *Advances in Experimental Social Psychology,* 1989, p. 138.

59. "Neuroscience: The Next Competitive Advantage," *360 Magazine*, June 14, 2015, http://www.steelcase.com/insights/articles/think-better/.

60. I. Pozin, "Think You're a Good Communicator? Better Think Again," *Inc.,* April 28, 2016, http://www.inc.com/ilya-pozin/think-youre-a-good-communicator-better-think-again.html.

61. C. R. Rogers and F. J. Roethlisberger, "Barriers and Gateways to Communication," *Harvard Business Review,* July–August 1952, pp. 46–52.

62. Bernie Sanders, https://twitter.com/SenSanders. (accessed May 14, 2018).

63. L. Alton, "Phone Calls, Texts or Email? Here's How Millennials Prefer to Communicate," *Forbes,* May 11, 2017, https://www.forbes.com/sites/larryalton/2017/05/11/how-do-millennials-prefer-to-communicate/#4404f3b66d6f.

64. L. Alton, "Phone Calls, Texts or Email? Here's How Millennials Prefer to Communicate," *Forbes,* May 11, 2017, https://www.forbes.com/sites/larryalton/2017/05/11/how-do-millennials-prefer-to-communicate/#4404f3b66d6f.

65. A. Hofschneider, "That Thing with the Buttons and Receiver? Pick It Up," *The Wall Street Journal*, August 28, 2013, pp. D1, D2.

66. I. Pozin, "Think You're a Good Communicator? Better Think Again," *Inc.,* April 28, 2016, http://www.inc.com/ilya-pozin/think-youre-a-good-communicator-better-think-again.html.

67. A. Davis, "7 Foolproof Ways to Communicate with Millennials (and, Surprisingly, Everyone Else)," *Inc.,* September 16, 2017, https://www.inc.com/alison-davis/7-foolproof-ways-to-communicate-with-millennials-a.html.

68. George Ritzer, *Introduction to Sociology* (Thousand Oaks, CA: SAGE Publications, 2013), p. 116.

69. C. Béal and K. Mullan, "Issues in Conversational Humour from a Cross-Cultural Perspective: Comparing French and Australian Corpora," in B. Peeters, K. Mullan, and C. Béal (Eds.), *Cross-Cultural Speaking, Speaking Cross-Culturally* (Cambridge, UK: Cambridge Scholars Publishing, 2013), pp. 107–140.
70. Businesstopia, "Cultural Barriers to Communication," https://www.businesstopia.net/communication/cultural-barriers-communication (accessed July 2016).
71. B. Patel, "Communicating across Cultures: Proceedings of a Workshop to Assess Health Literacy and Cross-Cultural Communication Skills," *Journal of Pharmacy Practice and Research,* 2015, pp. 49–56.
72. S. Maslin, "A Brooklyn Ambulance Service Speaks Chinese, Like Its Patients," *The New York Times,* May 23, 2016, http://www.nytimes.com/2016/05/24/nyregion/ a-brooklyn-ambulance-service-speaks-chinese-like-its-patients.html?_r=2.
73. M. Carteret, "Cross-Cultural Communication for EMS," *American Ambulance Association,* June 25, 2015, https://the-aaa.org/2015/06/25/cross-cultural-communication-for-ems/.
74. "The Value of Cultural Training for Expatriates," *GLOBAL LT,* https://global-lt.com/wp-content/uploads/2017/07/Value-of-Cultural-Training.pdf?2e5101.
75. N. Slawson, "Dove Apologises for Ad Showing Black Woman Turning into White One," *The Guardian,* October 8, 2017, https://www.theguardian.com/world/2017/oct/08/dove-apologises-for-ad-showing-black-woman-turning-into-white-one.
76. J. Silverstein, "Wendy's Twitter Account Posts Pepe the Frog Meme, a Designated Hate Symbol," *NY Daily News,* January 4, 2017, http://beta.nydailynews.com/news/national/wendy-twitter-account-posts-pepe-frog-meme-article-1.2934477.
77. David Millward, "Tesco under Attack for Offering Bacon Flavoured Pringles as Part of Ramadan Promotion," *The Telegraph,* June 25, 2015, https://www.telegraph.co.uk/news/uknews/11697716/Tesco-under-attack-for-offering-bacon-flavoured-Pringles-as-part-of-Ramadan-promotion.html.
78. "Ramadan," *History.com,* https://www.history.com/topics/holidays/ramadan (accessed April 24, 2018).
79. David Millward, "Tesco under Attack for Offering Bacon Flavoured Pringles as Part of Ramadan Promotion," *The Telegraph,* June 25, 2015, https://www.telegraph.co.uk/news/uknews/11697716/Tesco-under-attack-for-offering-bacon-flavoured-Pringles-as-part-of-Ramadan-promotion.html.
80. M. Nesic and V. Nesic, "Neuroscience of Nonverbal Communication," in A. Kostic and D. Chadee (Eds.), *The Social Psychology of Nonverbal Communication* (New York: Palgrave Macmillan, 2015), pp. 30–64.
81. C. Bank, "Barriers to Nonverbal Communication," October 6, 2015, http://www.livestrong.com/article/189396-barriers-to-nonverbal-communication/.
82. Y. Sato, "Retrospective Verbal Reports as a Way to Investigate Cross-Cultural Pragmatic Problems in Oral Interaction," in B. Peeters, K. Mullan, and C. Béal (Eds.), *Cross-Cultural Speaking, Speaking Cross-Culturally* (Cambridge, UK: Cambridge Scholars Publishing, 2013), pp. 11–46.
83. C. Banks, "Barriers to Nonverbal Communication," October 6, 2015, http://www.livestrong.com/article/189396-barriers-to-nonverbal-communication/ (accessed July 2016).
84. R. Buck and M. Miller, "Beyond Facial Expression: Spatial Distance as a Factor in the Communication of Discrete Emotions," in A. Kostic and D. Chadee (Eds.), *The Social Psychology of Nonverbal Communication* (New York, Palgrave Macmillan, 2015), pp. 172–196.
85. O. Khazan, "Why Some Cultures Frown on Smiling," *The Atlantic,* May 27, 2016, https://www.theatlantic.com/science/archive/2016/05/culture-and-smiling/483827/.
86. L. Ko, "An American Woman Quits Smiling," *The New York Times,* April 21, 2018, https://www.nytimes.com/2018/04/21/opinion/sunday/an-american-woman-quits-smiling.html.
87. P. Economy, "9 Body Language Habits That Make You Look Really Unprofessional," *Inc.,* May 13, 2016, http://www.inc.com/peter-economy/9-body-language-habits-that-make-you-look-really-unprofessional.html (accessed July 2016).
88. L. Talley and S. Temple, "How Leaders Influence Followers through the Use of Nonverbal Communication," *Leadership & Organization Development Journal,* 2015, pp. 69–80; A. Mcconnon, "To Be a Leader, Watch Your Body Language," *The Wall Street Journal,* October 3, 2016, p. R8.
89. C. Blank, "Barriers to Nonverbal Communication," October 6, 2015, http://www.livestrong.com/article/189396-barriers-to-nonverbal-communication/.
90. D. Marsh, *Doing Business in the Middle East* (London: Little, Brown Book Group, 2015); A. Stoy, "Project Communication Tips: Nonverbal Communication in Different Cultures," Bright Hub Project Management, 2012, http://www.brighthubpm.com/monitoring-projects/85141-project-communication-tips-nonverbal-communication-in-different-cultures.
91. D. Carnes, "Do Men & Women Use Nonverbal Communication Differently?" *livestrong.com,* May 17, 2015, http://www.livestrong.com/article/172581-do-men-women-use-nonverbal-communication-differently/.
92. "Non-verbal Communication in Different Cultures," *Businesstopia,* https://www.businesstopia.net/communication/non-verbal-communication-different-cultures (accessed May 14, 2018).
93. S. Johnson, "How a Woman Can Improve Gender Workplace Communication," *The Houston Chronicle,* http://work.chron.com/woman-can-improve-gender-workplace-communication-6587.html (accessed July 2016).
94. S. Shellenbarger, "Women Try New Strategies to Boost Career Confidence," *The Wall Street Journal,* March 20, 2018, p. A 13; L. Evans, "Are We Speaking a Different Language? Men and Women's Communication Blind Spots," *Fast Company,* June, 11, 2014, http://www.fastcompany.com/3031631/strong-female-lead/are-we-speaking-a-different-language-men-and-womens-communication-blind-s.
95. L. Evans, "Are We Speaking a Different Language? Men and Women's Communication Blind Spots," *Fast Company,* June 11, 2014, http://www.fastcompany.com/3031631/strong-female-lead/are-we-speaking-a-different-language-men-and-womens-communication-blind-s.
96. L. Evans, "Are We Speaking A Different Language? Men And Women's Communication Blind Spots," *Fast Company,* June 11, 2014, http://www.fastcompany.com/3031631/strong-female-lead/are-we-speaking-a-different-language-men-and-womens-communication-blind-s.
97. D. Tannen, "The Power of Talk: Who Gets Heard and Why," in R. J. Lewicki and D. M. Saunders (Eds.), *Negotiation: Readings, Exercises, and Cases,* 3rd ed. (Burr Ridge, IL: Irwin/McGraw-Hill, 1999), pp. 147–148.
98. A. Sanow, "21 Eye-Opening Ways Men and Women Communicate Differently," *Sanow Professional Development LLC,* June 4, 2015, https://www.linkedin.com/pulse/21-eye-opening-ways-men-women-communicate-differently-arnold-sanow.
99. D. Manciagli, "5 Ways to Bridge the Gender Communications Gap in the Workplace," *The Business Journals,* October 14, 2015, https://www.bizjournals.com/bizjournals/how-to/human-resources/2015/10/5-ways-to-bridge-the-gender-communications-gap.html.
100. D. Manciagli, "5 Ways to Bridge the Gender Communications Gap in the Workplace," *The Business Journals,* October 14, 2015, https://www.bizjournals.com/bizjournals/how-to/human-resources/2015/10/5-ways-to-bridge-the-gender-communications-gap.html.
101. "6 Ways Men & Women Communicate Differently," *World of Psychology,* July 22, 2017, https://psychcentral.com/blog/6-ways-men-and-women-communicate-differently/.
102. D. Manciagli, "5 Ways to Bridge the Gender Communications Gap in the Workplace," *The Business Journals,* October 14, 2015, https://www.bizjournals.com/bizjournas/how-to/human-resources/2015/10/5-ways-to-bridge-the-gender-communications-gap.html.
103. C. Goman, "Is Your Communication Style Dictated by Your Gender?" *Forbes,* March 31, 2016, https://www.forbes.com/sites/

carolkinseygoman/2016/03/31/is-your-communication-style-dictated-by-your-gender/#45e33bd2eb9d.

104. "Me or the Device?" *USA Today,* July 15, 2016, p. B1; C. Elliot, "Screen Addiction Is Destroying Travel," *USA Today,* February 5, 2018, p. 3B.

105. A. Pilon, "Business Users Trial New Facebook Live Streaming Video—We Have Examples," *Small Business Trends,* February 1, 2016, http://smallbiztrends.com/2016/ 02/facebook-live-examples-streaming-video.html.

106. B. Nguyen, X. Yu, T. C. Melewar, and J. Chen, "Brand Innovation and Social Media: Knowledge Acquisition from Social Media, Market Orientation, and the Moderating Role of Social Media Strategic Capability," *Industrial Marketing Management,* 2015, pp. 11–25; N. Jones, R. Borgma, and E. Ulusoy, "Impact of Social Media on Small Businesses," *Journal of Small Business and Enterprise Development,* 2015, pp. 611–632.

107. D. M. Herszenhorn and E. Huetteman, "House Democrats' Gun-Control Sit-In Turns into Chaotic Showdown with Republicans," *The New York Times,* June 22, 2016, http://www.nytimes.com/2016/06/23/us/politics/house-democrats-stage-sit-in-to-push-for-action-on-gun-control.html.

108. C.K. Johnson and S. Karnowski, "Stopped 52 Times by Police: Was It Racial Profiling?" *Washington Post,* July 9, 2016, https://www.washingtonpost.com/national/stopped-52-times-by-police-was-it-racial-profiling/2016/07/09/81fe882a-4595-11e6-a76d-3550dba926ac_story.html; B. Stelter, "Philando Castile and the Power of Facebook Live," July 7, 2016, http://money.cnn.com/ 2016/07/07/media/facebook-live-streaming-police-shooting/ (accessed July 2016); R. Iyenger, "Read Mark Zuckerberg's Response to the Video of Philando Castile's Shooting," *Time,* July 7, 2016, http://time.com/4397677/philando-castile-shooting-facebook-live-zuckerberg-statement/.

109. K. Ashford, "Employees Feel Guilty for Texting at Work (Do You?)," *Forbes,* April 27, 2015, http://www.forbes.com/sites/kateashford/2015/04/27/guilty-for-texting/#1b4494318397.

110. S. Olenski, "How FlightHub Infiltrates Emerging Markets Using Social Media," *Forbes,* November 7, 2015, http://www.forbes.com/sites/steveolenski/2015/11/07/how-flighthub-infiltrates-emerging-markets-using-social-media/#572658d1535e.

111. G. Hill, "Companies' Social Media Strategies Should Be: Data-Led, Human, and Purposeful," *The Future of Talent: Advertising Supplement to The Wall Street Journal,* 2017, universumglobal.com.

112. "8 Social Media Recruitment Statistics You Need to Know if You're in Recruitment-Infographic," *Talent Works,* 2017, https://www.talent-works.com/2017/09/27/social-media-recruitment.

113. M. Deutsch, "Are Recruiters Texting Candidates and Hiring Managers?" *Top Echelon,* February 7, 2016, https://www.topechelon.com/blog/recruiter-training/do-you-send-text-messages-to-candidates-or-hiring-managers/.

114. K. Gee, "Texting Might Help Land You a Job," *The Wall Street Journal,* June 21, 2017, p. B7.

115. R. Maurer, "Survey: Employers Using Social Media to Find Passive Candidates," Society for Human Resource Management, January 7, 2016, https://www.shrm.org/ResourcesAndTools/hr-topics/talent-acquisition/Pages/Using-Social-Media-Find- Passive-Candidates.aspx.

116. "8 Social Media Recruitment Statistics You Need to Know if You're in Recruitment-Infographic," *Talent Works,* 2017, https://www.talent-works.com/2017/09/27/social-media-recruitment.

117. J. Budzienski, "3 Ways to Be Constantly Recruiting Star Talent through Social Media," *Entrepreneur,* April 23, 2015, https://www.entrepreneur.com/article/245295.

118. J. Budzienski, "3 Ways to Be Constantly Recruiting Star Talent through Social Media," *Entrepreneur,* April 23, 2015, https://www.entrepreneur.com/article/245295.

119. S. Kumar, "Why Monitoring Employees' Social Media Is a Bad Idea," *Time,* May 22, 2015, http://time.com/3894276/social-media-monitoring-work/.

120. L. Salm, "70% of Employers Are Snooping Candidates' Social Media Profiles," *CareerBuilder.com,* June 15, 2017, https://www.careerbuilder.com/advice/social-media-survey-2017.

121. C. Kulkarni, "7 Easy LinkedIn Tweaks That Boost Your Web Presence," *Inc.com,* February 22, 2016, https://www.inc.com/chirag-kulkarni/7-easy-linkedin-tweaks-that-boost-your-web-presence.html.

122. J. T. O'Donnell, "3 Tips to Make Employers Come to You," *Inc.,* April 11, 2016, http://www.inc.com/jt-odonnell/3-tips-to-make-for-making-employers-come-to-you.html.

123. G. Huang, "4 Easy Ways to Improve Your Social Media Profile for Your Job Search," *Forbes,* January 30, 2017, https://www.forbes.com/sites/georgenehuang/2017/01/17/4-easy-ways-to-improve-your-social-media-profile-for-your-job-search/#7622c1277f34.

124. R. Maurer, "Survey: Employers Using Social Media to Find Passive Candidates," *Society for Human Resource Management,* January 7, 2016, https://www.shrm.org/ResourcesAndTools/hr-topics/talent-acquisition/Pages/Using-Social-Media-Find- Passive-Candidates.aspx.

125. S. Vozza, "What Happened When I Gave Up Social Media for a Month," *Fast Company,* July 6, 2016, http://www.fastcompany.com/3061454/your-most-productive-self/what-happened-when-i-gave-up-social-media-for-a-month.

126. B. A. Lautsch and E. E. Kossek, "Managing a Blended Workforce: Telecommuters and Non-Telecommuters," *Organizational Dynamics,* 2011, pp. 10–17; J. Meister, "Want to Be a More Productive Employee? Get on Social Networks," *Forbes,* April 18, 2013, http://www.forbes.com/sites/jeannemeister/2013/04/18/want-to-be-a-more-productive-employee-get-on-social-networks/.

127. S. Patel, "How to Boost Productivity as a Remote Employee," *Forbes,* March 2, 2016, http://www.forbes.com/sites/sujanpatel/2016/03/02/how-to-boost-productivity-as-a-remote-employee/5/#1adc908752d9.

128. N. Burton, "14 Habits of the Most Productive Remote Workers," *Fast Company,* June 8, 2015, http://www.fastcompany.com/3060650/your-most-productive-self/14-habits-of-the-most-productive-remote-workers; D. Aamoth, *Fast Company,* June 15, 2016, http://www.fastcompany.com/3060764/app-economy/25-free-chrome-extensions-to-make-you-an-incredibly-productive-person.

129. D. Brown, Video, *Inc.,* http://www.inc.com/damon-brown/why-every-entrepreneur-should-take-a-social-media-break.html (accessed July 2016).

130. A. Peters, "One Trick to Make Employees Happy: Ban Emails on Nights and Weekends," *Fast Company,* June 1, 2016, http://www.fastcoexist.com/3060349/one-trick-to-make-employees-happy-ban-emails-on-nights-and-weekends.

131. S. Baer, "Social Media Proves to Boost Employee Engagement," *Forbes,* February 13, 2018, https://www.forbes.com/sites/forbesagencycouncil/2018/02/13/social-media-proves-to-boost-employee-engagement/#5a4da4d54db5.

132. R.E. Ployhart, "Social Media in the Workplace: Issues and Strategic Questions," *SHRM Executive Briefing,* November 2011, www.shrm.org/about/foundation/products/documents/social%20media%20briefing-%20final.pdf. See also "Should Companies Monitor Their Employees' Social Media?" *The Wall Street Journal,* May 12, 2014, pp. R1, R2.

133. A. Schneider, "Fantasy Football Expected to Cost $8 Billion in Lost Work Time This NFL Season," *KUHF Public Radio,* September 3, 2013, http://app1.kuhf.org/articles/1377884091-Fantasy-Football-Expected-To-Cost-$8-Billion-In-Lost-Work-Time-This-NFL-Season.html.

134. B. Darrow, "Employers Pay the Real Cost of Fantasy Football," *Fortune,* August 30, 2016, http://fortune.com/2016/08/30/why-fantasy-football-costs-money.

135. "Rethinking Crowdsourcing," *Harvard Business Review,* November–December 2017, pp. 20–22.

136. S. Maslin Nir, "Longer Trains, High-Tech Signals and Robots: Subway 'Genius' Ideas Announced," *The New York Times,* March 9, 2018, https://www.nytimes.com/2018/03/09/nyregion/mta-announces-subway-genius-grants.html.

137. C. Desmarais, "Need Help? Crowdsource Your Work," *Inc.*, July 27, 2015, http://www.inc.com/christina-desmarais/need-help-crowdsource-your-work.html.

138. J. Degraff, "Why Crowdsourcing Has Ruined the Art of Innovation," *Inc.*, December 21, 2015, http://www.inc.com/jeff-degraff/why-crowdsourcing-has-ruined-the-art-of-innovation.html.

139. L. Dahlander and H. Piezunka, "Why Some Crowdsourcing Efforts Work and Others Don't," *Harvard Business Review*, February 21, 2017, https://hbr.org/2017/02/why-some-crowdsourcing-efforts-work-and-others-dont.

140. D. L. Roberts and F. T. Piller, "Finding the Right Role for Social Media in Innovation," *MIT Sloan Management Review*, Spring 2016, pp. 41–42.

141. These four conclusions were based on N. Jones, R. Borgman, and E. Ulusoy, "Impact of Social Media on Small Businesses," *Journal of Small Business and Enterprise Development* 22 (2015), pp. 611–632.

142. Y. Liu and R. A. Lopez, "The Impact of Social Media Conversations on Consumer Brand Choices," *Marketing Letters*, 2016, pp. 1–13.

143. R. Guesalaga, "The Use of Social Media in Sales: Individual and Organizational Antecedents, and the Role of Customer Engagement in Social Media," *Industrial Marketing Management*, 2016, pp. 71–79; L. Collier, "Should You Let Your Employees Shop Online at Work?" *Office-Depot Solutions Center*, October 26, 2015, http://solutions.officedepot.com/leadership/article/should-you-let-your-employees-shop-online-at-work.

144. D. Baasiri, "How to Boost Your Brand through an Effective Social Media Strategy," *Forbes*, December 15, 2016, https://www.forbes.com/sites/forbescommunicationscouncil/2016/12/15/how-to-boost-your-brand-through-an-effective-social-media-strategy/#1dd3be8b7334.

145. J. Martin, "12 Standout Social Media Success Stories," March 25, 2015, *CIO*, http://www.cio.com/article/2901047/social-media/12-standout-social-media-success-stories.html#slide12.

146. J. Martin, "11 Most Memorable Social Media Marketing Successes of 2015," *CIO*, October 1, 2015, http://www.cio.com/article/2988313/social-networking/11-most-memorable-social-media-marketing-successes-of-2015.

147. Guest, "10 Brands Doing an Amazing Job on Social Media," *Ad Week*, July 30, 2015, http://www.adweek.com/socialtimes/michael-patterson-10-brands-amazing-social-media/624169.

148. "TD Bank, N.A.," *Wikipedia*, https://en.wikipedia.org/wiki/TD_Bank,_N.A (accessed April 26, 2018).

149. D. Roberts, "BofA, Wells Fargo Don't Perform the Best on Social Media," *Charlotte Observer*, April 16, 2015, http://www.charlotteobserver.com/news/business/banking/bank-watch-blog/article18646995.html.

150. "Engagement Labs," *Wikipedia*, https://en.wikipedia.org/wiki/Engagement_Labs (accessed April 26, 2018).

151. R. Harris, "TD Goes on Another 'Thank You' Mission," *Marketing Magazine*, August 23, 2016, http://marketingmag.ca/brands/td-goes-on-another-thank-you-mission-181836/.

152. "All You Need Is Love," *Social Media for Business Performance*, February 12, 2018, https://smbp.uwaterloo.ca/2018/02/all-you-need-is-love/.

153. P. Crosman, "Five Things TD Bank Does Right in Social Media," *American Banker*, April 24, 2015, https://www.americanbanker.com/news/five-things-td-bank-does-right-in-social-media.

154. "Financial Literacy and Education," TD Bank, https://www.tdbank.com/community/financial_literacy.html# (accessed April 26, 2018).

155. D. Roberts, "BofA, Wells Fargo Don't Perform the Best on Social Media," *Charlotte Observer*, April 16, 2015, http://www.charlotteobserver.com/news/business/banking/bank-watch-blog/article18646995.html.

156. V. Dutot, E. L. Galvez, and D. W. Versailles, "CSR Communications Strategies through Social Media and Influence on E-Reputation," *Management Decision*, 2016, pp. 363–389; C. Dijkmans, P. Kerkhof, and C. J. Beukeboom, "A Stage to Engage: Social Media Use and Corporate Reputation," *Tourism Management*, 2015, pp. 58–67.

157. S. E. Bohr, "The Link between Social Media Activity and Corporate Reputation," *Forbes*, July 14, 2014, http://www.forbes.com/sites/onmarketing/2014/07/14/the-link-between-social-media-activity-and-corporate-reputation/#2fe7397e6d45.

158. J. LeBret, "Company Reputation Management with Social Media," *Forbes*, November 4, 2014, http://www.forbes.com/sites/jabezlebret/2014/11/04/company-reputation-management-with-social-media/2/#76682d1d125a; P. Cohen, "4 Ways Social Media Can Ruin Your Reputation," *Social Media Today*, February 14, 2014, http://www.socialmediatoday.com/content/4-ways-social-media-can-ruin-your-reputation.

159. J. LeBret, "Company Reputation Management with Social Media," *Forbes*, November 4, 2014, http://www.forbes.com/sites/jabezlebret/2014/11/04/company-reputation-management-with-social-media/2/#a336992125ac.

160. S. Lucas, "Social Media Means Everything You Do Is Public," *Inc.*, June 30, 2016, http://www.inc.com/suzanne-lucas/social-media-means-everything-you-do-is-public.html.

161. J. Budzienski, "3 Ways to Be Constantly Recruiting Star Talent through Social Media," *Entrepreneur*, April 23, 2015, https://www.entrepreneur.com/article/245295.

162. C. Zakrzewski, "The Key to Getting Workers to Stop Wasting Time Online," *The Wall Street Journal*, March 13, 2016, https://www.wsj.com/articles/the-key-to-getting-workers-to-stop-wasting-time-online-1457921545.

163. C. Conner, "Wasting Time at Work: The Epidemic Continues," *Forbes*, July 31, 2015, http://www.forbes.com/sites/cherylsnappconner/2015/07/31/wasting-time-at-work-the-epidemic-continues/#4050cab03ac1.

164. M. Wade, "The Economics of Cyberloafing at Work," *Sydney Morning Herald*, January 30, 2016, https://www.smh.com.au/opinion/the-economics-of-cyberloafing-at-work-20160129-gmhehu.html.

165. L. Collier, "Should You Let Your Employees Shop Online at Work?" *OfficeDepot Solutions Center*, October 26, 2015, http://solutions.officedepot.com/leadership/article/should-you-let-your-employees-shop-online-at-work; C. Zakrzewski, "The Key to Getting Workers to Stop Wasting Time Online," *The Wall Street Journal*, March 13, 2016, http://www.wsj.com/articles/the-key-to-getting-workers-to-stop-wasting-time-online-1457921545.

166. C. Zakrzewski, "The Key to Getting Workers to Stop Wasting Time Online," *The Wall Street Journal*, March 13, 2016, http://www.wsj.com/articles/the-key-to-getting-workers-to-stop-wasting-time-online-1457921545.

167. D. Lavenda, "Loafing Online Can Be a Valuable Part of a Productive Workday," *Fast Company*, April 10, 2013, http://www.fastcompany.com/3008031/loafing-online-can-be-valuable-part-productive-work-day.

168. N. Goodman, "Micro-Aggressions and Phubbing in the Age of FoMO," *Training*, https://trainingmag.com/trgmag-article/micro-aggressions-and-phubbing-age-fomo (accessed May 14, 2018).

169. J. Ducharme, "'Phubbing' Is Hurting Your Relationships. Here's What It Is," *Time*, March 29, 2018, http://time.com/5216853/what-is-phubbing/.

170. N. Goodman, "Micro-Aggressions and Phubbing in the Age of FoMO," *Training*, https://trainingmag.com/trgmag-article/micro-aggressions-and-phubbing-age-fomo (accessed May 14, 2018).

171. N. Goodman, "Micro-Aggressions and Phubbing in the Age of FoMO," *Training*, https://trainingmag.com/trgmag-article/micro-aggressions-and-phubbing-age-fomo (accessed May 14, 2018); J. Ducharme, "'Phubbing' Is Hurting Your Relationships. Here's What It Is," *Time*, March 29, 2018, http://time.com/5216853/what-is-phubbing/.

172. J. Ducharme, "'Phubbing' Is Hurting Your Relationships. Here's What It Is," *Time*, March 29, 2018, http://time.com/5216853/what-is-phubbing/.

173. N. Goodman, "Micro-Aggressions and Phubbing in the Age of FoMO," *Training,* https://trainingmag.com/trgmag-article/micro-aggressions-and-phubbing-age-fomo (accessed May 14, 2018); J. Ducharme, "'Phubbing' Is Hurting Your Relationships. Here's What It Is," *Time,* March 29, 2018, http://time.com/5216853/what-is-phubbing/.
174. K. Weir, "(Dis)connected," *Monitor on Psychology,* March 2017, pp. 42–48.
175. K. Weir, "(Dis)connected," *Monitor on Psychology,* March 2017, pp. 42–48.
176. S. Reid, "5 Questions for Adam Alter," *Monitor on Psychology,* July/August 2017, p. 32.
177. J. L. Ledbord, "Could a Cyber Attack Knock Out Your Computer?" *Lifewire,* February 8, 2018, https://www.lifewire.com/cyber-attacks-4147067; J. Belbey, "How to Avoid Cyber Attacks: 5 Best Practices from SEC and FINRA," *Forbes,* June 30, 2017, https://www.forbes.com/sites/joannabelbey/2017/06/30/how-to-avoid-cyberattacks-5-best-practices-from-sec-and-finra/#71e32e0a1a16.
178. *Norton Cyber Security Insights Report 2017 Global Results,* Norton, https://www.symantec.com/content/dam/symantec/docs/about/2017-ncsir-global-results-en.pdf (accessed May 14, 2018).
179. A. Levin, "Why Your Smartphone Is a Massive Threat to Your Company's Security," *Inc.,* September 26, 2018, https://www.inc.com/adam-levin/why-your-smartphone-is-a-massive-threat-to-your-companys-security.html?cid=search.
180. A. Blau, "Better Cybersecurity Starts with Fixing Your Employees' Bad Habits," *Harvard Business Review,* December 11, 2017, https://hbr.org/2017/12/better-cybersecurity-starts-with-fixing-your-employees-bad-habits.
181. M. Fleckner, "How to Avoid Cybercrime in the Workplace," *Platinum Group,* November 9, 2017, https://www.platinum-grp.com/blog/cybercrime-in-the-workplace.
182. *Norton Cyber Security Insights Report 2017 Global Results,* Norton, https://www.symantec.com/content/dam/symantec/docs/about/2017-ncsir-global-results-en.pdf (accessed May 14, 2018).
183. A. Blau, "Better Cybersecurity Starts with Fixing Your Employees' Bad Habits," *Harvard Business Review,* December 11, 2017, https://hbr.org/2017/12/better-cybersecurity-starts-with-fixing-your-employees-bad-habits.
184. *Federal Communications Commission,* "Cyber Security Planning Guide," https://transition.fcc.gov/cyber/cyberplanner.pdf (accessed May 1, 2018).
185. L. Handley, "Facebook Runs Ad Campaign That Sort of Says Sorry for Data Misuse Scandal," *CNBC,* April 26, 2018, https://www.cnbc.com/2018/04/26/facebook-runs-ad-campaign-somewhat-apologizing-for-data-misuse-scandal.html.
186. S. Lucas, "Social Media Means Everything You Do Is Public," *Inc.,* June 30, 2016, http://www.inc.com/suzanne-lucas/social-media-means-everything-you-do-is-public.html.
187. R. Reed, "Workplace Monitoring Gets Personal, and Employees Fear It's Too Close for Comfort. They're Right," *Chicago Tribune,* March 2, 2018, http://www.chicagotribune.com/business/columnists/reed/ct-biz-amazon-workplace-privacy-dilemma-robert-reed-0304-story.html.
188. K. Ashford, "Employees Feel Guilty for Texting at Work (Do You?)," *Forbes,* April 27, 2015, http://www.forbes.com/sites/kateashford/2015/04/27/guilty-for-texting/2/#7e64f28b6e99.
189. K. Ashford, "Employees Feel Guilty for Texting at Work (Do You?)," *Forbes,* April 27, 2015, http://www.forbes.com/sites/kateashford/2015/04/27/guilty-for-texting/2/#1594aa326e99.
190. "Workplace Privacy and Employee Monitoring," *Privacy Rights Clearinghouse,* April 1, 2016, https://www.privacyrights.org/workplace-privacy-and-employee-monitoring.
191. S. Kumar, "Why Monitoring Employees' Social Media Is a Bad Idea," *Time,* May 22, 2015, http://time.com/3894276/social-media-monitoring-work/.
192. R. Reed, "Workplace Monitoring Gets Personal, and Employees Fear It's Too Close for Comfort. They're Right." *Chicago Tribune,* March 2, 2018, http://www.chicagotribune.com/business/columnists/reed/ct-biz-amazon-workplace-privacy-dilemma-robert-reed-0304-story.html.
193. "Email Statistics Report, 2017–2021," Radicati Group Inc., https://www.radicati.com/wp/wp-content/uploads/2017/01/Email-Statistics-Report-2017-2021-Executive-Summary.pdf (accessed May 14, 2018).
194. R. Mazin, "It's Time to Tame Workplace Texting," https://www.allbusiness.com/its-time-to-tame-workplace-texting-16706751-1.html (accessed July 2016).
195. K. Ashford, "Employees Feel Guilty for Texting at Work (Do You?)," *Forbes,* April 27, 2015, http://www.forbes.com/sites/kateashford/2015/04/27/guilty-for-texting/2/#172ce0a96e99.
196. R. Weborg, "Why Texting Needs to be a Part of Your Workforce Optimization Strategy," *ICMI,* March 30, 2016, http://www.icmi.com/Resources/Workforce-Management/2016/03/Why-Texting-Needs-to-be-a-Part-of-Your-Workforce-Optimization-Strategy.
197. M. Lepore, "Should You Text Your Boss? 5 Tips for Texting Professionally," *skillcrush,* July 10, 2014, http://skillcrush.com/2014/07/10/5-tips-texting-professionally/; H. Crawford, "6 Rules for Texting at Work," *U.S. News & World Report,* February 26, 2015, http://money.usnews.com/money/blogs/outside-voices-careers/2015/02/26/6-rules-for-texting-at-work.
198. K. Ashford, "Employees Feel Guilty for Texting at Work (Do You?)," *Forbes,* April 27, 2015, http://www.forbes.com/sites/kateashford/2015/04/27/guilty-for-texting/ #72616c678397.
199. D. Kline, "Here's What People Are Using Social Media for at Work," *The Motley Fool,* June 27, 2016, http://www.fool.com/investing/2016/06/27/heres-what-people-are-using-social-media-for-at-wo.aspx.
200. "Intel Social Media Guidelines," *Intel,* http://www.intel.com/content/www/us/en/legal/intel-social-media-guidelines.html (accessed July 2016).
201. "IBM Social Computing Guidelines," *IBM,* https://www.ibm.com/blogs/zz/en/guidelines.html (accessed April 26, 2018).
202. "Best Buy Social Media Policy," *Best Buy Support,* July 21, 2016, http://forums.bestbuy.com/t5/Welcome-News/Best-Buy-Social-Media-Policy/td-p/20492.
203. *Standards of Business Conduct. McDonald's,* March 2017.
204. "Walmart Policies and Guidelines," *Walmart,* https://corporate.walmart.com/policies (accessed April 27, 2018).
205. "Walmart," *Wikipedia,* April 26, 2018, https://en.wikipedia.org/wiki/Walmart.
206. "Walmart Policies and Guidelines," *Walmart,* https://corporate.walmart.com/policies (accessed April 27, 2018).
207. "Policies and Standards," *Washington Post,* January 1, 2016, https://www.washingtonpost.com/policies-and-standards/?utm_term=.a4df65b9fdf8.
208. A. Beaujon, "The Washington Post's New Social Media Policy Forbids Disparaging Advertisers," *Washingtonian,* July 11, 2017, https://www.washingtonian.com/2017/06/27/the-washington-post-social-media-policy/.
209. "Intel Social Media Guidelines," *Intel,* https://www.intel.com/content/www/us/en/legal/intel-social-media-guidelines.html (accessed April 26, 2018).
210. W. Vanderbloemen, "How to Safeguard Your Business against a Social Media Nightmare," *Forbes,* June 17, 2016, http://www.forbes.com/sites/williamvanderbloemen/2016/06/17/how-to-safeguard-your-business-against-a-social-media-nightmare/#352271b448ac.
211. P. Economy, "10 Secret Communication Skills of the Best Leaders," *Inc.,* November 5, 2015, http://www.inc.com/peter-economy/10-secret-communication-skills-of-top-leaders.html.
212. "Employers Rate Career Competencies, New Hire Proficiency," *NACE,* December 11, 2017, http://www.naceweb.org/career-readiness/competencies/employers-rate-career-competencies-new-hire-proficiency.
213. J. S. Lublin, "Talkaholics Hurt Their Careers, Firms Say," *The Wall Street Journal,* December 14, 2017, p. B6.

214. N. Van Quaquebeke and W. Felps, "Respectful Inquiry: A Motivational Account of Leading through Asking Questions and Listening," *Academy of Management Review,* January 2018, pp. 5–27; E. Bernstein, "This Conversation Doesn't . . . Have to Be So Hard," *The Wall Street Journal,* July 18, 2017, p. A10.
215. M. Zwilling, "Entrepreneurs Face Serious Communication Barriers," *Forbes,* July 7, 2013, http://www.forbes.com/sites/martinzwilling/2013/07/07/entrepreneurs-face-serious-communication-barriers/#15cde9605398.
216. J. Linkner, "Empathy Is the New Killer App," *Inc.,* June 7, 2016, http://www.inc.com/josh-linkner/empathy-is-the-new-killer-app.html.
217. These definitions were taken from "Nice Guys Finish First," *Mindful,* October 2017, p. 32.
218. J. Kabat-Zinn, "Mindfulness-Based Interventions in Context: Past, Present, and Future," *Clinical Psychology: Science and Practice,* Summer 2003, p. 145.
219. "One Mindful Act," *Mindful,* June 2018, pp. 18–19; C. Bradley, "Winter Got You Down? Move Around," *Mindful,* February 2018, pp. 68–74.
220. "Nice Guys Finish First," *Mindful,* October 2017, pp. 30–33.
221. S. F. Young, E. M. Richard, R. G. Moukarzel, L. A. Steelman, and W. A. Gentry, "How Emphathic Concern Helps Leaders in Providing Negative Feedback: A Two-Study Examination," *Journal of Occupational and Organizational Psychology,* December 2017, pp. 535–558.
222. S.G. Boodman, "How to Teach Doctors Empathy," *The Atlantic,* March 15, 2015, http://www.theatlantic.com/health/archive/2015/03/how-to-teach-doctors-empathy/387784/.
223. S. Lebowitz, "A CEO Says This Is the Single Most Important and Underrated Skill in Business—and in Life," *Business Insider,* February 24, 2016, http://www.businessinsider.com/ceo-listening-is-the-key-to-success-in-business-2016-2.
224. LinkedIn "Virgin Founder Richard Branson: Why You Should Listen More than You Talk," *Fortune,* February 3, 2015, http://fortune.com/2015/02/03/virgin-founder-richard-branson-why-you-should-listen-more-than-you-talk/?iid=sr-link4.
225. K. J. Lloyd, D. Boer, J. W. Keller, and S. Voelpel, "Is My Boss Really Listening to Me? The Impact of Perceived Supervisor Listening on Emotional Exhaustion, Turnover Intention, and Organizational Citizenship Behavior," *Journal of Business Ethics,* 2015, pp. 509–524.
226. J. Keyser, "Active Listening Leads to Business Success," *T+D,* July 2013, pp. 26–28.
227. This discussion is based on C. G. Pearce, I. W. Johnson, and R. T. Barker, "Assessment of the Listening Styles Inventory: Progress in Establishing Reliability and Validity," *Journal of Business and Technical Communication,* January 2003, pp. 84–113.
228. T. Bradberry, "7 Most Common Habits of the Best Listeners," *Inc.,* April 13, 2016, http://www.inc.com/travis-bradberry/7-things-great-listeners-do-differently.html.
229. J. Haden, "6 Ways to Write Irresistibly Effective Emails," *Inc.,* November 9, 2015, http://www.inc.com/jeff-haden/6-ways-to-write-irresistibly-effective-emails.html.
230. J. Samton, "How to Speak—and Listen—Like an Executive," *Inc.,* July 5, 2016, http://www.inc.com/julia-samton/learn-to-speakem-and-/emlisten-like-an-executive-.html.
231. W. Taylor, "The Role of Public Speaking in Career Growth," April 6, 2016, http://www.hrcsuite.com/public-speaking-career-growth/.
232. T. Smedley, "Your Fear of Public Speaking May Be Holding You Back at Work. Here's What You Can Do about It," *BBC,* March 22, 2017, http://www.bbc.com/capital/story/20170321-is-public-speaking-fear-limiting-your-career.
233. F. Fasbinder, "TED Tackles Stage Fright: How 3 Notable Speakers Overcame Their Fear of Public Speaking," *Inc.,* March 6, 2017, https://www.inc.com/fla-fasbinder/the-important-truth-monica-lewisnsky-teaches-us-about-stage-fright.html.
234. F. Fasbinder, "TED Tackles Stage Fright: How 3 Notable Speakers Overcame Their Fear of Public Speaking," *Inc.,* March 6, 2017, https://www.inc.com/fla-fasbinder/the-important-truth-monica-lewisnsky-teaches-us-about-stage-fright.html.
235. T. Hixon, "What Entrepreneurs Can Learn about Public Speaking from TED Talks," *Forbes,* March 1, 2016, http://www.forbes.com/sites/toddhixon/2016/03/01/entrepreneurs-time-to-tune-up-your-public-speaking/#6f0d49172e69.
236. G. Genard, "How to Open a Presentation: Tell 'Em What You're Going to Say," November 22, 2015, http://www.genardmethod.com/blog/bid/192061/How-to-Open-a-Presentation-Tell-Em-What-You-re-Going-to-Say.
237. IESE Business School, "12 Tips For Public Speaking," *Forbes,* April 18, 2016, http://www.forbes.com/sites/iese/2016/04/18/12-tips-for-public-speaking/ #3fae354d5af3.
238. L. Adler, "New Survey Reveals 85% of All Jobs Are Filled via Networking," LinkedIn, February 28, 2016, https://www.linkedin.com/pulse/new-survey-reveals-85-all-jobs-filled-via-networking-lou-adler.
239. D. Burkus, "Networking for Actual Human Beings," *The Wall Street Journal,* April 21–22, 2018, p. C3.
240. "5 Steps to Seriously Improve Your Networking Skills," *Entrepreneur,* May 14, 2015, https://www.entrepreneur.com/article/245995.
241. "5 Steps to Seriously Improve Your Networking Skills," *Entrepreneur,* May 14, 2015, https://www.entrepreneur.com/article/245995.
242. "5 Steps to Seriously Improve Your Networking Skills," *Entrepreneur,* May 14, 2015, https://www.entrepreneur.com/article/245995.
243. P. Stone, "6 Tips to Improve Your Face-to-Face Networking," *Lifehack,* April 27, 2018, https://www.lifehack.org/articles/work/six-tips-improve-your-face-face-networking.html
244. D. Burkus, "Networking for Actual Human Beings," *The Wall Street Journal,* April 21–22, 2018, p. C3.
245. S. Shellenbarger, "Save Yourself from Tedious Small Talk," *The Wall Street Journal,* May 24, 2017, p. A13.
246. S. Shellenbarger, "Save Yourself from Tedious Small Talk," *The Wall Street Journal,* May 24, 2017, pp. A13, A15.
247. I. J. Wright, "4 Exercises to Improve Your Networking Skills," *The SocialShake-Up,* May 1, 2017, http://www.socialshakeupshow.com/4-exercises-improve-networking-skills.
248. M. Castillo, "Festival-Goers Paid Up to $49,000 for Ja Rule's Bash in the Bahamas, and Got Chaos Instead," *CNBC,* April 28, 2017, www.cnbc.com/2017/04/28/fyre-festival-debacle-in-the-bahamas.html.
249. B. Burrough, "Fyre Festival: Anatomy of a Millennial Marketing Fiasco Waiting to Happen," *Vanity Fair,* August 2017, www.vanityfair.com/news/2017/06/fyre-festival-billy-mcfarland-millennial-marketing-fiasco.
250. B. Burrough, "Fyre Festival: Anatomy of a Millennial Marketing Fiasco Waiting to Happen," *Vanity Fair,* August 2017, www.vanityfair.com/news/2017/06/fyre-festival-billy-mcfarland-millennial-marketing-fiasco.
251. L. Wamsley, "Paradise Lost: Luxury Music Festival Turns out to Be Half-Built Scene of Chaos," *NPR,* April 28, 2017, www.npr.org/sections/thetwo-way/2017/04/28/526019457/paradise-lost-luxury-music-festival-turns-out-to-be-half-built-scene-of-chaos.
252. G. Tolentino, "The Fyre Festival Was a Luxury Nightmare," *The New Yorker,* April 28, 2017, *www*.newyorker.com/culture/jia-tolentino/the-fyre-festival-was-a-luxury-nightmare.
253. G. Bluestone, "Let's Just Do It and Be Legends, Man: Fyre Festival Organizers Blew All Their Money Early on Models, Plans, and Yachts," *Vice News,* May 3, 2017 https://news.vice.com/en_ca/article/7xwabq/fyre-fest-organizers-blew-all-their-money-months-early-on-models-planes-and-yachts.
254. B. Burrough, "Fyre Festival: Anatomy of a Millennial Marketing Fiasco Waiting to Happen," *Vanity Fair,* August, 2017, www.vanityfair.com/news/2017/06/fyre-festival-billy-mcfarland-millennial-marketing-fiasco.
255. L. Wamsley, "Paradise Lost: Luxury Music Festival Turns out to Be Half-Built Scene of Chaos," *NPR,* April 28, 2017, www.npr.org/sections/thetwo-way/2017/04/28/526019457/paradise-lost-luxury-music-festival-turns-out-to-be-half-built-scene-of-chaos.
256. T. Murray, "It Was Designed for Terrible Things to Happen: We Spoke to Someone Who Said She Was 'Locked Indoors' with 'No Food or Water' at the Chaotic Fyre Festival," *Business Insider,* April 28, 2017,

www.businessinsider.com/we-spoke-to-someone-with-no-food-or-water-at-the-chaotic-fyre-festival-2017-4.

257. G. Tolentino, "The Fyre Festival Was a Luxury Nightmare," *The New Yorker*, April 28, 2017, *www*.newyorker.com/culture/jia-tolentino/the-fyre-festival-was-a-luxury-nightmare.

258. G. Kaufman, "Fyre Festival Fiasco: Timeline of a Disaster," *Billboard*, May 2, 2017, www.billboard.com/articles/columns/music-festivals/7777047/fyre-festival-timeline-fiasco.

259. A. Greenblatt, "Eight Things You Need to Know before You Start a Music Festival," *NPR*, April 27, 2010, www.npr.org/sections/therecord/2010/08/26/129449645/starting-a-music-festival-eight-things-you-need-to-know; M. Woodward, "Outdoor Music Festival Planning Tips," *The Balance*, October 16, 2017, www.thebalancesmb.com/planning-an-outdoor-music-festival-1223340; Conferences and Events, "Logistical Planning," *Yale University*, https://conferencesandevents.yale.edu/services/logistical-planning (accessed May 11, 2018).

260. B. Burrough, "Fyre Festival: Anatomy of a Millennial Marketing Fiasco Waiting to Happen," *Vanity Fair*, August 2017, www.vanityfair.com/news/2017/06/fyre-festival-billy-mcfarland-millennial-marketing-fiasco.

261. C. Gordon, "I Worked at Fyre Festival. It Was Always Going to Be a Disaster," *The Cut*, April 28, 2017, www.thecut.com/2017/04/fyre-festival-exumas-bahamas-disaster.html.

262. G. Kaufman, "Fyre Festival Fiasco: Timeline of a Disaster," *Billboard*, May 2, 2017, www.billboard.com/articles/columns/music-festivals/7777047/fyre-festival-timeline-fiasco.

263. G. Tolentino, "The Fyre Festival Was a Luxury Nightmare," *The New Yorker*, April 28, 2017, *www*.newyorker.com/culture/jia-tolentino/the-fyre-festival-was-a-luxury-nightmare.

264. C. Moynihan, "Organizer of Failed Fyre Festival Pleads Guilty to Fraud," *New York Times*, March 6, 2018, www.nytimes.com/2018/03/06/arts/organizer-of-failed-fyre-festival-pleads-guilty-to-fraud.html.

265. G. Kaufman, "Fyre Festival Fiasco: Timeline of a Disaster," *Billboard*, May 2, 2017, www.billboard.com/articles/columns/music-festivals/7777047/fyre-festival-timeline-fiasco.

266. A. Reimer, "After His ESPN Firing, Curt Schilling Is Now a Martyr for the Right-Wing," *Forbes*, May 17, 2016, www.forbes.com/sites/alexreimer/2016/05/17/after-his-espn-firing-curt-schilling-is-now-a-martyr-for-the-right-wing/#64c3dcfa3821.

267. C. Gaines, "The Simple Explanation for Why ESPN Did Not Fire Jemele Hill but Did Fire Curt Schilling," *Business Insider*, September 13, 2017, www.businessinsider.com/espn-jemele-hill-curt-schilling-perceived-liberal-bias-2017-9.

268. R. Sandomir, "Curt Schilling, ESPN Analyst, Is Fired over Offensive Social Media Post," *The New York Times*, April 20, 2016, www.nytimes.com/2016/04/21/sports/baseball/curt-schilling-is-fired-by-espn.html?_r=0.

269. A. Grautski, "Curt Schilling Goes on Social Media Bender after Firing," *New York Daily News*, April 22, 2016, www.nydailynews.com/sports/baseball/curt-schilling-social-media-bender-espn-firing-article-1.2611099.

270. R. Sandomir, "Curt Schilling, ESPN Analyst, Is Fired over Offensive Social Media Post," *The New York Times*, April 20, 2016, www.nytimes.com/2016/04/21/sports/baseball/curt-schilling-is-fired-by-espn.html?_r=0.

271. A. Grautski, "Curt Schilling Goes on Social Media Bender after Firing," *New York Daily News*, April 22, 2016, www.nydailynews.com/sports/baseball/curt-schilling-social-media-bender-espn-firing-article-1.2611099.

272. R. Sandomir, "Curt Schilling, ESPN Analyst, Is Fired over Offensive Social Media Post," *The New York Times*, April 20, 2016, www.nytimes.com/2016/04/21/sports/baseball/curt-schilling-is-fired-by-espn.html?_r=0.

CHAPTER 16

1. This definition is based on M. Higgins and K. Kram, "Reconceptualizing Mentoring at Work: A Developmental Network Perspective," *Academy of Management Review*, April 2001, pp. 264–288.

2. A. Prossack, "How to Be a Great Mentee," *Forbes*, April 27, 2018, https://www.forbes.com/sites/ashiraprossack1/2018/04/27/how-to-be-a-great-mentee/#6dc49feb512b; L. Bradford, "8 Tips for an Amazing Mentor Relationship," *Forbes*, January 31, 2018, https://www.forbes.com/sites/laurencebradford/2018/01/31/8-tips-for-an-amazing-mentor-relationship/#584602c221e2; S. Mautz, "12 Keys to Being a SuperMentee (the Kind of Mentee Every Mentor Loves)," *Inc.*, May 17, 2017, https://www.inc.com/scott-mautz/12-keys-to-being-a-supermentee-the-kind-of-mentee-every-mentor-loves.html; B. P. Hardy, "How to Get Mentors (and How to Know If Your Mentors Are Any Good)," *Inc.*, February 26, 2018, https://www.inc.com/benjamin-p-hardy/how-to-get-mentors-and-how-to-know-if-your-mentor-is-any-good.html?cid=search; M. Levin, "Chasing Down a Mentor to Help You Grow? Be Ready to Answer These 4 Questions," *Inc.*, March 19, 2018, https://www.inc.com/marissa-levin/4-questions-to-answer-before-you-ask-someone-to-be-your-mentor.html?cid=search.

3. H. Ueno, "Japan Recalls 7 Million More Cars with Takata Airbags," *The New York Times*, May 28, 2016, http://www.nytimes.com/2016/05/28/business/international/japan-takata-airbag-recall.html; The Editorial Board, *The New York Times*, June 3, 2016, "Why Are Cars with Killer Airbags Still Being Sold?" http://www.nytimes.com/2016/06/03/opinion/why-are-they-still-selling-cars-with-killer-airbags.html.

4. "Takata Airbag Recall: Everything You Need to Know," *Consumer Reports*, April 5, 2018, https://www.consumerreports.org/car-recalls-defects/takata-airbag-recall-everything-you-need-to-know/.

5. P. Ziobro, "Crunch Time for Deliveries," *The Wall Street Journal*, December 18, 2017, p. B3.

6. P. Ziobro, "Crunch Time for Deliveries," *The Wall Street Journal*, December 18, 2017, p. B3.

7. D. Wayabayashi, "Uber's Self-Driving Cars Were Struggling before Arizona Crash," *The New York Times*, March 23, 2018, https://www.nytimes.com/2018/03/23/technology/uber-self-driving-cars-arizona.html.

8. N. M. Ashkanasy, O. B. Ayoko, and K. A. Jehn, "Understanding the Physical Environment of Work and Employee Behavior: An Affective Events Perspective," *Journal of Organizational Behavior*, November 2014, pp. 1169–1184.

9. A. Johnson, "6 Small Office Changes That Create Big Productivity Increases," *Inc.*, March 24, 2016, http://www.inc.com/anna-johansson/6-simple-office-improvements-that-actually-increase-productivity.html.

10. N. Vitezic, and V. Vitezic, "A Conceptual Model of Linkage between Innovation Management and Controlling in the Sustainable Environment," *Journal of Applied Business Research*, January/February 2015, pp. 175–184.

11. L. Miller, "Uniqlo Faces Margin Squeeze from Zara, New-Store Costs: Chart," *Bloomberg*, July 2016, http://www.bloomberg.com/news/articles/2016-07-12/uniqlo-faces-margin-squeeze-from-zara-new-store-costs-chart.

12. M. Schröder, S. Schmitt, and R. Schmitt, "Design and Implementation of Quality Control Loops," *TQM Journal*, 2015, pp. 294–302.

13. Pepsico, "What We Believe," http://www.pepsico.com/Purpose/Performance-with-Purpose/policies (accessed May 4, 2018).

14. A. Christensen, A. Kinicki, Z. Zhang, and F. Walumbwa, "Responses to Feedback: The Role of Acceptance, Affect, and Creative Behavior," *Journal of Leadership and Organizational Studies*, 2018, pp. 1–14.

15. L. Silverman, "The Cure for a Doctor Shortage: Primary Care and Teamwork," *Marketplace*, January 20, 2016, http://www.marketplace.org/2016/01/20/education/cure-doctor-shortage-primary-care-and-teamwork.

16. L. Katz, "Monitoring Employee Productivity: Proceed with Caution," *SHRM*, June 1, 2015, https://www.shrm.org/publications/hrmagazine/editorialcontent/ 2015/0615/pages/0615-employee-monitoring.aspx.

17. C. McWhirter, "Congrats, You Finished the Race! Sorry, We Measured It Wrong!" *The Wall Street Journal,* December 23–24, 2017, p. A1.

18. C. Berardinelli, "A Guide to Control Charts," *i Six Sigma,* https://www.isixsigma.com/tools-templates/control-charts/a-guide-to-control-charts/ (accessed May 15, 2018); A. Foley, "Control Charts: Everything You Need to Know," *Clear Point Strategy,* July 18, 2016, https://www.clearpointstrategy.com/control-charts-everything-you-need-to-know/.

19. R. M. Walter, M. M. Higgins, and H. P. Roth, "Our Greatest Hits: Applications of Control Charts," *CPA Journal,* November 2017, https://www.cpajournal.com/2017/12/08/greatest-hits-applications-control-charts/; "Control Chart," ASQ, http://asq.org/learn-about-quality/data-collection-analysis-tools/overview/control-chart.html.

20. "UPS Integrad Fact Sheet," *UPS Pressroom,* May 2017, https://www.pressroom.ups.com/pressroom/ContentDetailsViewer.page?ConceptType=FactSheets&id=1460489309501-709.

21. D. McMackin, "UPS Driver Training Center Opens in Lake Mary, Florida," *GlobeNewswire,* October 5, 2017, https://globenewswire.com/news-release/2017/10/05/1141510/0/en/UPS-Driver-Training-Center-Opens-In-Lake-Mary-Florida.html.

22. "UPS Integrad Fact Sheet," *UPS Pressroom,* May 2017, https://www.pressroom.ups.com/pressroom/ContentDetailsViewer.page?ConceptType=FactSheets&id=1460489309501-709.

23. "UPS Sets Efficiency Standards by Monitoring Drivers' Every Move," *WDRB,* March 24, 2015, http://www.wdrb.com/story/28604605/ups-sets-efficiency- standards-by-monitoring-drivers-every-move.

24. "UPS Sets Efficiency Standards by Monitoring Drivers' Every Move," *WDRB,* March 24, 2015, http://www.wdrb.com/story/28604605/ups-sets-efficiency- standards-by-monitoring-drivers-every-move.

25. T. Yates, "What UPS Can Teach Fleets About Driver Safety," *Work Truck,* http://www.worktruckonline.com/channel/safety-accident-management/article/story/2007/09/what-ups-can-teach-fleets-about-driver-safety.aspx (accessed April 30, 2018).

26. P. Kozodoy, "The New Trick Brilliant Managers Use to Provide Effective Feedback," *Inc.,* September 26, 2017, https://www.inc.com/peter-kozodoy/the-new-trick-brilliant-managers-use-to-provide-ef.html.

27. C. Dyer, "Fail Well: How to Handle Business Mistakes," *Management Today,* April 16, 2018, https://www.managementtoday.co.uk/fail-well-handle-business-mistakes/reputation-matters/article/1462189.

28. E. Dontigney, "Examples of Concurrent Control in Management," *Houston Chronicle,* 2016, http://smallbusiness.chron.com/examples-concurrent-control-management-80471.html.

29. C. Zillman, "IBM Is Blowing Up Its Annual Performance Review," *Fortune,* February 1, 2016, http://fortune.com/2016/02/01/ibm-employee-performance-reviews.

30. J. Kerr, "Welcome to Strategic Planning 2.0," *Inc.,* June 13, 2016, http://www.inc.com/james-kerr/welcome-to-strategic-planning-2-0.html.

31. M. Davis, "Management Strategies from a Top CEO," *Investopedia,* December 5, 2017, https://www.investopedia.com/articles/financial-theory/10/manage-business-like-jack-welch.asp.

32. J. Markoff, "Artificial Intelligence Swarms Silicon Valley on Wings and Wheels," *The New York Times,* July 18, 2016, http://www.nytimes.com/2016/07/18/technology/on-wheels-and-wings-artificial-intelligence-swarms-silicon-valley.html.

33. "Adidas," *Wikipedia,* https://en.wikipedia.org/wiki/Adidas, (accessed May 1, 201).

34. "Fair Labor Association Announces Accreditation of Three Social Compliance Programs," *PR Newswire,* October 19, 2017, https://www.prnewswire.com/news-releases/fair-labor-association-announces-accreditation-of-three-social-compliance-programs-300539982.html.

35. "Mission & Charter," *Fair Labor Association,* http://www.fairlabor.org/our-work/mission-charter (accessed May 1, 2018).

36. "Fair Labor Association Announces Accreditation of Three Social Compliance Programs," *PR Newswire,* October 19, 2017, https://www.prnewswire.com/news-releases/fair-labor-association-announces-accreditation-of-three-social-compliance-programs-300539982.html.

37. "Adidas Group: Assessment for Reaccreditation," *Fair Labor Association,* October 2017, http://www.fairlabor.org/sites/default/files/documents/reports/adidas_reaccredidation_assessment_october_2017.pdf.

38. "Supply Chain Approach," *Adidas,* https://www.adidas-group.com/en/sustainability/compliance/supply-chain-approach/#/supply-chain-structure/ (accessed May 2, 2018).

39. "Supply Chain Approach," *Adidas,* https://www.adidas-group.com/en/sustainability/compliance/supply-chain-approach/#/supply-chain-structure/ (accessed May 2, 2018).

40. "Sustainability Team," *Adidas,* https://www.adidas-group.com/en/sustainability/compliance/sustainability-team/ (accessed May 2, 2018).

41. "Supply Chain Approach," *Adidas,* https://www.adidas-group.com/en/sustainability/compliance/supply-chain-approach/#/supply-chain-structure/ (accessed May 2, 2018).

42. D. Dietz, "Oregon Rail Officials Look to Push High-Speed Passenger Rail Service into Distant Future," *The Register Guard,* July 17, 2016, http://registerguard.com/rg/news/local/34570094-75/oregon-rail-officials-look-to-push-high-speed-passenger-rail-service-into-distant-future.html.csp.

43. D. Dietz, "Oregon Rail Officials Look to Push High-Speed Passenger Rail Service into Distant Future," *The Register Guard,* July 17, 2016, http://registerguard.com/rg/news/local/34570094-75/oregon-rail-officials-look-to-push-high-speed-passenger-rail-service-into-distant-future.html.csp.

44. K. de Freytas-Tamura and A. Tsang, "KFC Has a Problem in Britain: Not Enough Chicken," *The New York Times,* February 20, 2018, https://www.nytimes.com/2018/02/20/world/europe/kfc-chicken-uk-shortage.html; K. O'Marah, "3 Supply Chain Lessons from the KFC Fowl-Up," *Forbes,* March 1, 2018, https://www.forbes.com/sites/kevinomarah/2018/03/01/three-supply-chain-lessons-from-the-kfc-fowl-up/#2573776d1cb1.

45. M. Wolgelenter, "From KFC, a 3-Letter Apology for Its U.K. Chicken Crisis," *The New York Times,* February 23, 2018, https://www.nytimes.com/2018/02/23/world/europe/uk-kfc-chicken.html.

46. K. de Freytas-Tamura and A. Tsang, "KFC Has a Problem in Britain: Not Enough Chicken," *The New York Times,* February 20, 2018, https://www.nytimes.com/2018/02/20/world/europe/kfc-chicken-uk-shortage.html.

47. "Annual Finanicals for Target Corp.," *Marketwatch,* 2016, http://www.marketwatch. com/investing/stock/tgt/financials (accessed July 2016).

48. P. High, "Target CIO Mike McNamara's Priorities: Digital and Supply Chain Innovation," *Forbes,* July 5, 2016, http://www.forbes.com/sites/peterhigh/2016/07/05/target-cio-mike-mcnamaras-priorities-digital-and-supply-chain-innovation/3/ #3fb5b78872d1.

49. L. Eadicicco, "Amazon Reveals New Details about Drone Deliveries," *Time,* January 19, 2016, http://time.com/4185117/amazon-prime-air-drone-delivery/.

50. I. Linton, "Five Differences between Service and Manufacturing Organizations," *Houston Chronicle,* updated June 28, 2018, http://smallbusiness.chron.com/five-differences-between-service-manufacturing-organizations-19073.html.

51. "Employment by Major Industry Sector," Bureau of Labor Statistics, December 2015, http://www.bls.gov/emp/ep_table_201.htm; D. Short, "The Epic Rise of America's Services Industry [CHARTS]," *Business Insider,* September 1, 2014, http://www.businessinsider.com/growth-of-us-services-economy-2014-9.

52. "6 Benefits to Building Your Dashboard Today," *Guiding Metrics,* http://guidingmetrics.com/benefits-of-metrics/6-benefits-to-building-your-dashboard-today/ (accessed May 14, 2016).

53. R. S. Kaplan and D. P. Norton, "The Balanced Scorecard—Measures That Drive Performance," *Harvard Business Review,* January–February 1992, pp. 71–79.

54. N. Hamid, "Use Balanced Scorecard for Measuring Competitive Advantage of Infrastructure Assets of State-Owned Ports in Indonesia: Case in Pelindo IV, Indonesia," *Journal of Management Development,* 2018, pp. 114–126; A. Kshatriya, V. Dharmadhikari, D. Srivastave, and P. C. Basak, "Strategic Performance Measurement Using Balanced

CHAPTER NOTES

Scorecard: A Case of Machine Tool Industry," *Foundations of Management,* 2017, pp. 75–86.

55. M. Lev-Ram, "John Deere, Modern Farmer," *Fortune,* December 1, 2015, pp. 67–70.

56. A. Hufford, "Bob Evans to Close Some Locations," *The Wall Street Journal,* April 26, 2016, p. B3.

57. "Strategic Balanced Scorecard," *Sunnybrook Hospital,* June 2016, http://sunnybrook. ca/scorecard/.

58. R. S. Kaplan and D. P. Norton, "Having Trouble with Your Strategy? Then Map It," *Harvard Business Review,* September–October 2000, pp. 167–176.

59. "The Balanced Scorecard—Who's Doing It?" *Balanced Scorecard Institute,* http://www.balancedscorecard.org/BSC-Basics/Examples-Success-Stories (accessed May 15, 2018); "National Marrow Donor Program (NMDP) Case Study," *Balanced Scorecard Institute,* http://www.theinstitutepress.com/uploads/7/0/0/1/7001740/nmdp_case_study_cr7_october_2013.pdf (accessed May 15, 2018).

60. See "The Balanced Scorecard—Who's Doing It?" *Balanced Scorecard Institute,* http://www.balancedscorecard.org/BSC-Basics/Examples-Success-Stories (accessed May 15, 2018); "Tolko Industries Ltd. Case Study," *Balanced Scorecard Institute,* http://www.theinstitutepress.com/uploads/7/0/0/1/7001740/tolko_case_study_gp7_august_2013.pdf (accessed May 15, 2018).

61. A sample map for a university can be found in S. Han and Z. Zhong, "Strategy Maps in University Management: A Comparative Study," *Educational Management Administration & Leadership,* 2015, pp. 939–953.

62. An example of creating scorecards for projects is illustrated in M. Scheiblich, M. Maftei, V. Just, and M. Studeny, "Developing a Project Scorecard to Measure the Performance of Project Management in Relation to EFQM Excellence Model," *Total Quality Management,* November 2017, pp. 966–980.

63. R. McGuire, "Ultimate Guide to Gig Economy Data: A Summary of Every Freelance Survey We Can Find," *Nation 1099,* January 29, 2018, http://nation1099.com/gig-economy-data-freelancer-study/.

64. "The Gig Economy by The Numbers," *Time,* June 7, 2016, http://time.com/money/ 4358945/gig-economy-numbers-statistics/.

65. T. Barrabi, "Best Budgeting Apps for Millennials: 3 Money-Saving Options for Young Adults," *International Business Times,* October 1, 2015, http://www.ibtimes.com/best-budgeting-apps-millennials-3-money-saving-options-young-adults- 2118739.

66. A history of budgeting is provided by M. M. Ibrahim, "A Budget for All Seasons," *International Review of Management and Business Research,* December 2015, pp. 963–972.

67. J. Soileau, L. Soileau, and G. Sumners, "The Evolution of Analytics and Internal Audit," *EDP Audit, Control, and Security Newsletter,* 2015, p. 13.

68. R. Kral, "Ensuring a High Quality Audit: Who Is Responsible? Five Ideas for Audit Committees to Maximize Value from the External Audit Process," *EDP Audit, Control, and Security Newsletter,* 2016, pp. 5–12.

69. E. Flitter, "Citi to Refund $330 Million to Credit Card Customers It Overcharged," *The New York Times,* February 23, 2018, https://www.nytimes.com/2018/02/23/business/citigroup-credit-card-refunds.html.

70. M. Statman, "A Different Kind of Financial-Literacy Test," *The Wall Street Journal,* October 23, 2017, p. R6.

71. A. Shell, "Having Right Mind-Set Can Boost Your Finances," *USA Today,* April 22, 2018, p. 3B.

72. A. Tergesen, "Workers Schooled in Money," *The Wall Street Journal,* February 21, 2018, p. B12.

73. "Bristol Tennessee Essential Services, Malcolm Baldrige National Quality Award 2017 Award Recipient, Small Business," *NIST,* https://www.nist.gov/baldrige/bristol-tennessee-essential-services (accessed May 15, 2018).

74. The Foundation for the Malcolm Baldrige National Quality Award, *baldrige.org,* http://www.baldrigepe.org/ (accessed May 4, 2018).

75. "Bristol Tennessee Essential Services, Malcolm Baldrige National Quality Award 2017 Award Recipient, Small Business," *NIST,* https://www.nist.gov/baldrige/bristol-tennessee-essential-services (accessed May 15, 2018).

76. "Bristol Tennessee Essential Services, Malcolm Baldrige National Quality Award 2017 Award Recipient, Small Business," *NIST,* https://www.nist.gov/baldrige/bristol-tennessee-essential-services.

77. W. E. Deming, *Out of the Crisis* (Cambridge, MA: MIT Press, 1986), p. 5.

78. R. N. Lussier, *Management: Concepts, Applications, Skill Development* (Cincinnati, OH: South-Western College Publishing, 1997), p. 260.

79. "About TMMK," *Toyota Kentucky,* http://toyotaky.com/boutdex.asp (accessed May 15, 2018).

80. J. Muller, "Toyota Workers in Kentucky Elevate Their Senses to Properly Build a Lexus," *Forbes,* April 19, 2016, http://www.forbes.com/sites/joannmuller/2016/04/19/toyota-workers-in-kentucky-elevate-their-senses-to-properly-build-a-lexus/ #38ec09167554.

81. M. Jaeger and D. Adair, "Perception of TQM Benefits, Practices and Obstacles," *TQM Journal,* 2016, pp. 317–336.

82. J. Charniga, "Genesis Supplants Audi atop Consumer Reports' Latest Brand Rankings," *Automotive News,* February 22, 2018, http://www.autonews.com/article/20180222/RETAIL03/180229924/genesis-supplants-audi-consumer-reports-brand-rankings.

83. G. Coppola, "Luxury-Car Ranks Upended as Genesis Tops Germany's Stalwarts," *Bloomberg.com,* February 22, 2018, https://www.bloomberg.com/news/articles/2018-02-22/korean-cars-pull-ahead-of-german-brands-consumer-reports-says.

84. A. Honeyman, "How Did Hyundai Do It with Genesis?—Quality, The Only Game in Town," *Torque News,* June 28, 2017, https://www.torquenews.com/3793/hyundai-genesis-quality-game-town.

85. D. Levin, "How Korean Car Makers Beat Out the Japanese," *Fortune,* June 29, 2015, http://fortune.com/2015/06/29/korean-japanese-cars-quality/.

86. A. Honeyman, "How Did Hyundai Do It with Genesis?—Quality, The Only Game in Town," *Torque News,* June 28, 2017, https://www.torquenews.com/3793/hyundai-genesis-quality-game-town.

87. A. Honeyman, "How Did Hyundai Do It with Genesis?—Quality, The Only Game in Town," *Torque News,* June 28, 2017, https://www.torquenews.com/3793/hyundai-genesis-quality-game-town.

88. D. Levin, "How Korean Car Makers Beat Out the Japanese," *Fortune,* June 29, 2015, http://fortune.com/2015/06/29/korean-japanese-cars-quality/.

89. S. Tulp, "Kia Tops J.D. Power Initial Quality Survey. See How Other Cars Rank," *USA Today,* June 22, 2017, https://www.usatoday.com/story/money/cars/2017/06/21/kia-genesis-porsche-top-jd-power-car-quality-study/103050990/.

90. S. Richmond, "How KIA Motors Is Reinventing Itself," *Investopedia,* https://www.investopedia.com/articles/personal-finance/062315/how-kia-motors-reinventing-itself.asp (accessed May 15, 2018).

91. J. Garcia-Bernal and M. Ramirez-Aleson, "Why and How TQM Leads to Performance Improvements," *Quality Management Journal,* 2015, pp. 23–37.

92. S. Banker, "Drones and Robots in the Warehouse," *Forbes,* June 24, 2016, http://www.forbes.com/sites/stevebanker/2016/06/24/drones-and-robots-in-the-warehouse/#4a1e692d6ed7.

93. A. Choudhury, "Kaizen with Six Sigma Ensures Continuous Improvement," *isixsigma.com,* https://www.isixsigma.com/methodology/kaizen/kaizen-six-sigma-ensures-continuous-improvement/ (accessed July 2016).

94. L. Flory, "How 5 Companies Used Kaizen Effectively," *Effex Management Solutions,* October 7, 2014, http://blog.effexms.com/how-5-companies-used-kaizen-effectively.

95. N. Wagner, "The Advantages of the Kaizen Philosophy," *Houston Chronicle,* http://smallbusiness.chron.com/advantages-kaizen-philosophy-61502.html (accessed July 2016).

96. R. Preston, "Trendy Restaurant Wagamama Puts Cloud on the Menu," *Forbes,* June 2, 2016, http://www.forbes.com/sites/oracle/2016/06/02/trendy-restaurant-wagamama-puts-cloud-on-the-menu/#3eb3805254b0.

97. Jack Stewart, "How Boeing Builds a 737 in Just 9 Days," *Wired,* September 27, 2016, https://www.wired.com/2016/09/boeing-builds-737-just-nine-days/.
98. S. Wilhelm, "Boeing to Meet 2017 Goal to Stop Growth of Greenhouse Gas Emissions," *Business Journals,* May 28, 2016, https://www.bizjournals.com/seattle/news/2016/03/28/boeing-to-meet-2017-goal-to-stop-growth-of.html.
99. D. Gates, "How Fast Can Boeing Build 737s?" *Seattle Times,* July 5, 2012, https://www.seattletimes.com/business/how-fast-can-boeing-build-737s/.
100. A. Choudhury, "Kaizen with Six Sigma Ensures Continuous Improvement," *isixsigma.com,* https://www.isixsigma.com/methodology/kaizen/kaizen-six-sigma-ensures-continuous- improvement/ (accessed July 2016).
101. M. Solomon, "Secrets of Consistent Customer Service: How to Be Great Again and Again," *Forbes,* March 31, 2014, http://www.forbes.com/sites/micahsolomon/ 2014/03/31/customer-service-experience-standards-lessons-from-four-seasons-hotels-and-elsewhere/#7b2564e93f9a.
102. J. Garcia-Bernal and M. Ramirez-Aleson, "Why and How TQM Leads to Performance Improvements," *Quality Management Journal,* 2015, pp. 23–37.
103. "NICE inContact Customer Experience Transformation Benchmark Study 2017," *InContact,* https://www.niceincontact.com/call-center-resource-finder/incontact-customer-experience-transformation-benchmark-study-2017 (accessed May 6, 2018).
104. "About Nordstrom," *Nordstrom,* https://shop.nordstrom.com/c/about-us (accessed May 6, 2018).
105. N. Sinclair, "Why Nordstrom Is Beating All of Its Department Store Competitors," *Yahoo! Finance,* August 12, 2017, https://finance.yahoo.com/news/nordstrom-beating-department-store-competitors-125704786.html.
106. H. Khan, "How Nordstrom Made Its Brand Synonymous with Customer Service (and How You Can Too)," *Shopify,* May 2, 2016, https://www.shopify.com/retail/119531651-how-nordstrom-made-its-brand-synonymous-with-customer-service-and-how-you-can-too.
107. M. Solomon, "What Any Business Can Learn from Nordstrom Customer Service," *Forbes,* January 26, 2016, https://www.forbes.com/sites/micahsolomon/2016/01/26/what-any-business-can-learn-from-the-way-nordstrom-handles-customer-service/#54066aeb5b9e.
108. H. Khan, "How Nordstrom Made Its Brand Synonymous with Customer Service (and How You Can Too)," *Shopify,* May 2, 2016, https://www.shopify.com/retail/119531651-how-nordstrom-made-its-brand-synonymous-with-customer-service-and-how-you-can-too.
109. A. Zaczkiewicz, "Nordstrom Makes 'Best Place to Work' List for 20 Consecutive Years," *WWD,* March 09, 2017, http://wwd.com/business-news/business-features/nordstrom-best-place-to-work-list-10840440/.
110. M. Solomon, "What Any Business Can Learn from Nordstrom Customer Service," *Forbes,* January 26, 2016, https://www.forbes.com/sites/micahsolomon/2016/01/26/what-any-business-can-learn-from-the-way-nordstrom-handles-customer-service/#54066aeb5b9e.
111. S. Gleiter, "Trader Joe's Is Tops among Supermarkets in Customer Satisfaction," *PennLive.com,* March 20, 2017, http://www.pennlive.com/food/index.ssf/2017/03/trader_joes_customer_satisfact.html.
112. R. Turcsik, "Publix, Trader Joe's Lead in Customer Satisfaction, Survey Reports," *Supermarket News,* February 27, 2018, http://www.supermarketnews.com/consumer-trends/publix-trader-joe-s-lead-customer-satisfaction-survey-reports.
113. S. Whitten, "Trader Joe's Dethroned as America's Favorite Grocer," *CNBC,* April 14, 2016, https://www.cnbc.com/2016/04/13/trader-joes-dethroned-as-americas-favorite-grocery-store.html.
114. "Trader Joe's," *Wikipedia,* https://en.wikipedia.org/wiki/Trader_Joe's (accessed May 6, 2018).
115. E. Peck, "What Trader Joe's Can Teach Us about Treating Workers Well," *Huffington Post,* January 20, 2016, https://www.huffingtonpost.com/entry/trader-joes-treating-workers-well_us_566b438de4b0e292150df3d6.
116. V. Jaiswal, "How Trader Joe's Provides EXCELLENT Customer Experience CONSISTENTLY—4 Key Takeaways," *CustomerThink,* September 27, 2017, https://customerthink.com/how-trader-joes-provides-excellent-customer-experience-consistently-4-key-takeaways/.
117. V. Jaiswal, "How Trader Joe's Provides EXCELLENT Customer Experience CONSISTENTLY—4 Key Takeaways," *CustomerThink,* September 27, 2017, https://customerthink.com/how-trader-joes-provides-excellent-customer-experience-consistently-4-key-takeaways/.
118. S. Bakhtiari, "Productivity, Outsourcing and Exit: The Case of Australian Manufacturing," *Small Business Economics,* 2015, pp. 425–447.
119. "Job Overseas Outsourcing Statistics," *Statistic Brain Research Institute,* https://www.statisticbrain.com/outsourcing-statistics-by-country/ (accessed May 15, 2018).
120. Trefis Team, "What Are The Challenges Facing Ralph Lauren?" *Forbes,* June 14, 2016, http://www.forbes.com/sites/greatspeculations/2016/06/14/what-are-the-challenges-facing-ralph-lauren/#5c567c2c3214.
121. L. Chao, "Bar-Code Scanners Pick Up Speed," *The Wall Street Journal,* January 8, 2016, p. B6.
122. B. Burnseed and E. Thornton, "Six Sigma Makes a Comeback," *Bloomberg Businessweek,* September 10, 2009, www.businessweek.com/magazine/ content/09_38/b4147064137002.htm.
123. B. W. Jacobs, M. Swink, and K. Linderman, "Performance Effects of Early and Late Six Sigma Adoptions," *Journal of Operations Management,* 2015, pp. 244–257.
124. M. Poppendieck, "Why the Lean in Lean Six Sigma?" *The Project Management Best Practices Report,* June 2004, www.poppendieck.com/pdfs/Lean_Six_Sigma.pdf.
125. Trefis Team, "Why Has 3M's Stock Risen over 20% since the Beginning of the Year?" *Forbes,* July 18, 2016, http://www.forbes.com/sites/greatspeculations/2016/ 07/18/why-has-3ms-stock-risen-over-20-since-the-beginning-of-the-year/ #6c0aea29436a.
126. A. Rongala, "Top 10 Reasons Why Organizations Do Not Use Lean Six Sigma," *Invensis,* November 19, 2015, http://www.invensislearning.com/blog/top-10-reasons-why-organizations-do-not-use-lean-six-sigma/.
127. "ISO 9000 & ISO 9001 DIFFERENCES," *The British Assessment Bureau,* May 8, 2011, http://www.british-assessment.co.uk/guides/whats-the-difference-between-iso-9000-9001/.
128. B. Kumar, "What's the Differences between ISO 9000 & ISO 9001?" *Quora,* May 25, 2015, https://www.quora.com/What%E2%80%99s-the-difference-between-ISO-9000-9001.
129. "About ISO," *International Organization for Standardization,* https://www.iso.org/about-us.html (accessed May 15, 2018).
130. L. L. Bernardino, F. Teixeira, A. R. de Jesus, A. Barbosa, M. Lordelo, and H. A. Lepikson, "After 20 Years, What Has Remained of TQM?" *International Journal of Productivity and Performance,* 2016, pp. 378–400.
131. L. L. Bernardino, F. Teixeira, A. R. de Jesus, A. Barbosa, M. Lordelo, and H. A. Lepikson, "After 20 Years, What Has Remained of TQM?" *International Journal of Productivity and Performance,* 2016, pp. 378–400.
132. K. R. Thompson and M. L. Blazey, "What We Can Learn from the Baldridge Criteria: An Integrated Management Model to Guide Organizations," *Organizational Dynamics,* January–March 2017, pp. 21–29.
133. J. Thomson, "Why CFOs Should Embrace Sustainability for Strategic Growth," *Forbes,* December 3, 2015, http://www.forbes.com/sites/jeffthomson/2015/12/03/why-cfos-should-embrace-sustainability-for-strategic-growth/#1fed30ed5047.
134. S. Su, K. Baird, and H. Schoch, "Management Control System Effectiveness," *Pacific Accounting Review,* 2015, pp. 28–50.
135. L. Daskal, "17 Signs You're Actually a Micromanager," *Inc.,* May 27, 2016, http://www.inc.com/lolly-daskal/17-signs-you-re-actually-a-micromanager.html.

136. K. Boogaard, "4 Ways to Stop Yourself from Micromanaging," *Inc.*, March 14, 2016, http://www.inc.com/the-muse/how-to-stop-micromanaging.html.

137. M. Erb, "How to Stop Micromanaging Your Team," *Entrepreneur*, https://www.entrepreneur.com/article/218028 (accessed May 16, 2018).

138. A. K. Srivastava, "Modeling Organizational and Information Systems for Effective Strategy Execution," *Journal of Enterprise Information Management*, 2015, pp. 556–578.

139. When labor costs rise, productivity slows down, unless other variables are changed. When companies are able to get more output from fewer workers, productivity rises. See C. Dougherty, "Workforce Productivity Falls," *The Wall Street Journal*, May 4, 2012, p. A5.

140. M. Hajli, J. M. Sims, and V. Ibragimov, "Information Technology (IT) Productivity Paradox in the 21st Century," *International Journal of Productivity and Performance Management*, 2015, pp. 457–478.

141. Office of Macroeconomic Analysis, U.S. Treasury, "Profile of the Economy," February 16, 2012, www.docstoc.com/docs/117787321/Profile-of-the-Economy.

142. D. Gross, "Listen, the U.S. Is Better, Stronger, and Faster Than Anywhere Else in the World," *Newsweek*, May 7, 2012, pp. 22–30.

143. B. Eichengreen, D. Park, and K. Shin, "The Global Productivity Lump: Common and Country-Specific Factors," *VOX*, September 17, 2015, http://voxeu.org/article/global-productivity-slump; Total Economy Database: Key Findings, 2016, https://www.conference-board.org/data/economydatabase/ (accessed July 2016).

144. D. Kopf, "US Productivity Growth Is Negative and Economists Aren't Sure Why," *Quartz*, March 31, 2017, https://qz.com/946675/us-productivity-growth-was-negative-in-2016-and-economists-arent-sure-why/.

145. B. Hays, "Effects of Warmer Weather on Productivity Being Felt Worldwide, Scientists Say," *UPI*, June 10, 2016, http://www.upi.com/Science_News/2016/06/10/ Effects-of-warmer-weather-on-productivity-being-felt-worldwide-scientists-say/2061465584525/.

146. V. Golle, and G. Quinn, "Global Jobs Abound But Wage Gains Stay Soft," *Bloomberg*, January 29, 2018, https://www.bloomberg.com/news/articles/2018-01-30/across-g-7-economies-jobs-abound-while-wage-gains-stay-elusive.

147. T. Worstall, "As Delong Says, Brookings Is Wrong on the Productivity Slowdown," *Forbes*, March 5, 2016, http://www.forbes.com/sites/timworstall/2016/03/05/as-delong-says-brookings-is-wrong-on-the-productivity-slowdown/#69d4e7716c82.

148. J. DeLayne Stroud, "Understanding the Purpose and Use of Benchmarking," *iSixSigma*, https://www.isixsigma.com/methodology/benchmarking/understanding-purpose-and-use-benchmarking/ (accessed May 16, 2018).

149. "Best Practices," *Investopedia*, https://www.investopedia.com/terms/b/best_practices.asp (accessed May 16, 2018).

150. H. Stringer, "Boosting Productivity," *Monitor on Psychology*, September 2017, pp. 54–58.

151. R. Fujioka, "3 Ways Cloud Technology Is Boosting Productivity," *Inc.*, July 12, 2016, http://www.inc.com/russ-fujioka/3-ways-cloud-technology-is-boosting-productivity.html.

152. M. Mankins, "Is Technology Really Helping Us Get More Done?" *Harvard Business Review*, January 25, 2016, https://hbr.org/2016/02/is-technology-really-helping-us-get-more-done.

153. K. Granville, "How to Manage Your Career," *The New York Times*, https://www.nytimes.com/guides/business/manage-your-career (accessed May 8, 2018).

154. S. B. McKinney, "How to Manage Your Career in 8 Steps," *BlueSteps*, March 31, 2017, https://www.bluesteps.com/blog/how-manage-your-career-8-steps.

155. B. Aeon and H. Aguinis, "It's about Time: New Perspectives and Insights on Time Management," *Academy of Management Perspectives*, November 2017, pp. 309–330; A. Rastogi, "10 Essential Time Management Strategies," *GreyCampus*, December 19, 2017, https://www.greycampus.com/blog/project-management/ten-essential-time-management-strategies.

156. "Productivity Stop Checking Off Easy To-Dos," *Harvard Business Review*, November–December 2017, p. 24.

157. K. Granville, "How to Manage Your Career," *The New York Times*, https://www.nytimes.com/guides/business/manage-your-career (accessed May 8, 2018).

158. These suggestions were derived from J. Garfinkle, "The Keys to Effective Self-Promotion," https://garfinkleexecutivecoaching.com/articles/self-promotion-spread-the-word-about-you/the-keys-to-effective-self-promotion (accessed May 8, 2018).

159. A. Doyle, "How Often Do People Change Jobs?" *Careers*, January 24, 2018, https://www.thebalancecareers.com/how-often-do-people-change-jobs-2060467.

160. M. Wang and C. Wanberg, "100 Years of Applied Psychology Research on Individual Careers: From Career Management to Retirement," *Journal of Applied Psychology*, March 2017, pp. 546–563.

161. "2017 Recruiter Nation Report," *Jobvite*, September 21, 2017, http://web.jobvite.com/FY17_Website_2017RecruiterNation_LP.html?utm_source=website&utm_medium=blog&utm_content=2017recruiternation.

162. S. Sharf, "What's Your Passion? How Following Your Gut Can Lead to Huge Success," *Forbes*, http://www.forbes.com/sites/samanthasharf/2016/05/12/whats-your-passion-how-following-your-gut-can-lead-to-huge-success/#af88b5d4935d (accessed July 2016).

163. B. Scott, "Diane Von Furstenberg on Self-Discovery, Acceptance, and the American Dream," *Inc.*, http://www.inc.com/bartie-scott/diane-von-furstenberg-and-seth-meyers- on-becoming-the-woman-you-want-to-be.html (accessed July 2016).

164. V. Lipman, "The Hardest Thing for New Managers," *Forbes*, http://www.forbes.com/sites/victorlipman/2016/06/01/the-hardest-thing-for-new-managers/#2d3a7bca218f (accessed July 2016).

165. S. Vozza, "12 Lessons from Business Leaders' Moms," *Fast Company*, http://www.fastcompany.com/3045952/hit-the-ground-running/12-lessons-from-business-leaders-moms (accessed July 2016).

166. J. Hall, "10 Simple Ways to Improve Your People Skills and Build Relationships," *Forbes*, http://www.forbes.com/sites/johnhall/2016/03/20/10-simple-ways-to-improve-your-people-skills-and-build-relationships/#20bc20e62174 (accessed July 2016).

167. C. Liu, "4 Easy Ways to Become a Better Leader at Work," *Inc.*, http://www.inc.com/the-muse/develop-leadership-skills-4-easy-steps.html (accessed July 2016).

168. J. Benjamin, "For Bryce Drew, People Matter More Than Results," *Forbes*, http://www.forbes.com/sites/joshbenjamin/2016/03/29/for-bryce-drew-people-matter-more-than-results/#1eddcba07648 (accessed July 2016).

169. J. Benjamin, "For Bryce Drew, People Matter More Than Results," *Forbes*, http://www.forbes.com/sites/joshbenjamin/2016/03/29/for-bryce-drew-people-matter-more-than-results/#1eddcba07648 (accessed July 2016).

170. D. Overbye, "Stephen Hawking Dies at 76; His Mind Roamed the Cosmos," *The New York Times*, March 14, 2018, https://www.nytimes.com/2018/03/14/obituaries/stephen-hawking-dead.html.

171. M. P. Seligman, *Flourish* (New York: Free Press, 2011).

172. "Tesla, Inc," *Wikipedia*, https://en.wikipedia.org/wiki/Tesla,_Inc. (accessed April 11, 2018).

173. D. Sherman, "2015 Tesla Model S 70D Instrumented Test: Review," *Car and Driver*, May 2015, https://www.caranddriver.com/reviews/2015-tesla-model-s-70d-instrumented-test-review.

174. "2018 Tesla Model S," *U.S. News & World Report*, https://cars.usnews.com/cars-trucks/tesla/model-s (accessed April 11, 2018).

175. J. Bhuiyan, "Elon Musk's Launch of His First Mass-Market Electric Car Could Be Teslas IPhone Moment," *Recode*, July 28, 2017, https://www.recode.net/2017/7/28/16051942/elon-musk-tesla-model-3-handover-event-mass-market-electric-cars.

176. Z. Estrada, "Tesla Burns through $2 Billion in 2017," *The Verge*, February 7, 2018, https://www.theverge.com/2018/2/7/16986396/tesla-2017-full-year-earnings-model-3-production.

177. N. Boudette, "Tesla Looked Like the Future. Now Some Ask If It Has One," *The New York Times*, March 29, 2018, https://www.nytimes.com/2018/03/29/business/tesla-elon-musk.html.

178. N. Boudette, "Tesla Looked Like the Future. Now Some Ask If It Has One," *The New York Times*, March 29, 2018, https://www.nytimes.com/2018/03/29/business/tesla-elon-musk.html.

179. B. Saporito, "Tesla's Manufacturing 'Hell' Won't Slow Down Electric Cars," *The New York Times*, April 3, 2018, https://www.nytimes.com/2018/04/03/opinion/tesla-model3-elon-musk.html.

180. L. Lopez, "Tesla Model 3 Production Is Being Killed by Robots, Say Bernstein & Co Analysts," *Business Insider Australia*, March 29, 2018, https://www.businessinsider.com.au/tesla-robots-are-killing-it-2018-3.

181. A. Hawkins, "Tesla Relied on Too Many Robots to Build the Model 3, Elon Musk Says," *The Verge*, April 13, 2018, https://www.theverge.com/2018/4/13/17234296/tesla-model-3-robots-production-hell-elon-musk.

182. L. Lopez, "Tesla Model 3 Production Is Being Killed by Robots, Say Bernstein & Co Analysts," *Business Insider Australia*, March 29, 2018, https://www.businessinsider.com.au/tesla-robots-are-killing-it-2018-3.

183. L. Lopez, "Tesla Model 3 Production Is Being Killed by Robots, Say Bernstein & Co Analysts," *Business Insider Australia*, March 29, 2018, https://www.businessinsider.com.au/tesla-robots-are-killing-it-2018-3.

184. L. Lopez, "Tesla Model 3 Production Is Being Killed by Robots, Say Bernstein & Co analysts," *Business Insider Australia*, March 29, 2018, https://www.businessinsider.com.au/tesla-robots-are-killing-it-2018-3.

185. R. Mitchell, "Some Early Owners of Tesla's Model 3 Are Reporting Quality Problems. Do Buyers Care?" *Los Angeles Times*, February, 18, 2018, http://www.latimes.com/business/autos/la-fi-hy-tesla-model3-quality-20180218-story.html.

186. A. Nabila and S. Bakewell, "Tesla's Burning through Nearly Half a Million Dollars Every Hour," *Bloomberg.com*, November 21, 2017, https://www.bloomberg.com/news/articles/2017-11-21/tesla-is-blowing-through-8-000-every-minute-amid-model-3-woes.

187. C. Isidore, "Elon Musk's Brash Promise: Tesla Will Soon Make Money," *CNNMoney*. April 13, 2018, http://money.cnn.com/2018/04/13/technology/elon-musk-tesla-profit/index.html.

188. S. Gibbs, "Elon Musk Drafts in Humans after Robots Slow Down Tesla Model 3 Production," *The Guardian*, April 16, 2018, https://www.theguardian.com/technology/2018/apr/16/elon-musk-humans-robots-slow-down-tesla-model-3-production.

189. A. Hawkins, "Tesla Relied on Too Many Robots to Build the Model 3, Elon Musk Says," *The Verge*, April 13, 2018, https://www.theverge.com/2018/4/13/17234296/tesla-model-3-robots-production-hell-elon-musk.

190. D. Baer, "Elon Musk on Being a Product-Obsessed 'Nano-Manager': 'It's Not a Recipe for Happiness,'" *Business Insider*, January 12, 2015, http://www.businessinsider.com/elon-musk-calls-himself-a-nano-manager-2015-1.

191. S. Gibbs, "Elon Musk Drafts in Humans after Robots Slow Down Tesla Model 3 Production," *The Guardian*, April 16, 2018, https://www.theguardian.com/technology/2018/apr/16/elon-musk-humans-robots-slow-down-tesla-model-3-production.

192. C. Isidore, "Tesla Model 3 Will Start 24/7 Production to Meet Target," *CNNMoney*, April 18, 2018, http://money.cnn.com/2018/04/18/news/companies/elon-musk-tesla-model-3-production/index.html.

193. R. Mitchell "Musk Has Second Thoughts on Aggressive Automation for Tesla Model 3," *Baltimoresun.com*, April 18, 2018, http://www.baltimoresun.com/la-fi-hy-tesla-model-3-20180417-story.html.

194. C. Woodyard, "Tesla's Elon Musk Vows '24/7' Model 3 Production, Lots of New Jobs," *USA Today*, April 17, 2018, https://usat.ly/2qFpuWK.

195. C. Isidore, "Tesla Model 3 Will Start 24/7 Production to Meet Target," *CNNMoney*, April 18, 2018, http://money.cnn.com/2018/04/18/news/companies/elon-musk-tesla-model-3-production/index.html.

196. C. Woodyard, "Tesla's Elon Musk Vows '24/7' Model 3 Production, Lots of New Jobs," *USA Today*, April 17, 2018, https://usat.ly/2qFpuWK.

197. C. Isidore, "Tesla Model 3 Will Start 24/7 Production to Meet Target," *CNNMoney*, April 18, 2018, http://money.cnn.com/2018/04/18/news/companies/elon-musk-tesla-model-3-production/index.html.

198. D. Hull, "Tesla Moves to 24/7 Model 3 Production to Hit Goal," *Detroit News*, April 17, 2018, https://www.detroitnews.com/story/business/autos/mobility/2018/04/17/tesla-model-three-suspension-production-elon-musk/33909927/.

199. K. Waddell, "Why Bosses Can Track Their Employees 24/7," *The Atlantic*, January 6, 2017, https://www.theatlantic.com/technology/archive/2017/01/employer-gps-tracking/512294/.

200. J. Scott, "Park Hills to Begin Tracking City Vehicles," *Daily Journal News*, April 8, 2018, https://dailyjournalonline.com/news/local/park-hills-to-begin-tracking-city-vehicles/article_b9a36c68-2a04-502b-9287-6fbaa4ee0d71.html.

201. K. Waddell, "Why Bosses Can Track Their Employees 24/7," *The Atlantic*, January 6, 2017, https://www.theatlantic.com/technology/archive/2017/01/employer-gps-tracking/512294/.

202. "What Do Workers Really Think about GPS Monitoring?" *TSheets*, https://www.tsheets.com/gps-survey (accessed April 23, 2018).

203. H. Kelly, "Amazon's Idea for Employee-Tracking Wearables Raises Concerns," *CNNMoney*, February 2, 2018, http://money.cnn.com/2018/02/02/technology/amazon-employee-tracker/index.html.

204. K. Waddell, "Why Bosses Can Track Their Employees 24/7," *The Atlantic*, January 6, 2017, https://www.theatlantic.com/technology/archive/2017/01/employer-gps-tracking/512294/.

NAME INDEX

Q

R

S

T

U

V

W

ORGANIZATION INDEX

GLOSSARY/SUBJECT INDEX

GLOSSARY/SUBJECT INDEX

J

K

N

GLOSSARY/SUBJECT INDEX

P

Q

R

GLOSSARY/SUBJECT INDEX

S

T

U

V

W

Z

.redits

Online Supplements

connect®

Connect Online Access for Management, Ninth Edition

McGraw-Hill Connect is a digital teaching and learning environment that improves performance over a variety of critical outcomes. With Connect, instructors can deliver assignments, quizzes and tests easily online. Students can practice important skills at their own pace and on their own schedule.

HOW TO REGISTER

Using a Print Book?

To register and activate your Connect account, simply follow these easy steps:

1. **Go to the Connect course web address provided by your instructor or visit the Connect link set up on your instructor's course within your campus learning management system.**
2. **Click on the link to register.**
3. **When prompted, enter the Connect code found on the inside back cover of your book and click Submit. Complete the brief registration form that follows to begin using Connect.**

Using an eBook?

To register and activate your Connect account, simply follow these easy steps:

1. **Upon purchase of your eBook, you will be granted automatic access to Connect.**
2. **Go to the Connect course web address provided by your instructor or visit the Connect link set up on your instructor's course within your campus learning management system.**
3. **Sign in using the same email address and password you used to register on the eBookstore. Complete your registration and begin using Connect.**

**Note: Access Code is for one use only. If you did not purchase this book new, the access code included in this book is no longer valid.*

Need help? Visit mhhe.com/support